Lecture Notes in Computer Science 2869

Edited by G. Goos, J. Hartmanis, and J. van Leeuwen

Springer
Berlin
Heidelberg
New York
Hong Kong
London
Milan
Paris
Tokyo

Adnan Yazici   Cevat Şener (Eds.)

Computer and Information Sciences – ISCIS 2003

18th International Symposium
Antalya, Turkey, November 3-5, 2003
Proceedings

Springer

Volume Editors

Adnan Yazici
Cevat Şener
Middle East Technical University
Department of Computer Engineering
06531 Ankara, Turkey
E-mail: {yazici/sener}@ceng.metu.edu.tr

Cataloging-in-Publication Data applied for

A catalog record for this book is available from the Library of Congress.

Bibliographic information published by Die Deutsche Bibliothek
Die Deutsche Bibliothek lists this publication in the Deutsche Nationalbibliografie; detailed bibliographic data is available in the Internet at <http://dnb.ddb.de>.

CR Subject Classification (1998): H, C, B, D, F, I

ISSN 0302-9743
ISBN 3-540-20409-1 Springer-Verlag Berlin Heidelberg New York

Springer-Verlag Berlin Heidelberg New York
a member of BertelsmannSpringer Science+Business Media GmbH

http://www.springeronline.com

Typesetting: Camera-ready by author, data conversion by PTP-Berlin GmbH
Printed on acid-free paper SPIN: 10963555 06/3142 5 4 3 2 1 0

Preface

The International Symposium on Computer and Information Sciences (ISCIS) brought together researchers and practitioners from all over the world to exchange ideas and experiences on their recent research in all areas of the computer and information sciences. This year, the 18th ISCIS was organized by the Department of Computer Engineering at the Middle East Technical University, and was held in Antalya, Turkey.

This year was the first in which the proceedings of ISCIS were published in the LNCS series by Springer-Verlag. The proceedings include 135 papers that were selected by the program committee from over 360 contributions submitted from 25 different countries.

The symposium this year covered the following topics in the computer and information sciences: architectures and systems, computer science theory, databases and information retrieval, e-business, graphics and computer vision, intelligent systems and robotics, multimedia, networks and security, parallel and distributed computing, soft computing, and software engineering.

The support from the following institutions is deeply appreciated:

- METU (Middle East Technical University)
- TÜBİTAK (Scientific and Technical Research Council of Turkey)
- IEEE, Turkey Section
- IFIP (International Federation for Information Processing)

I must also express my sincere thanks to all the people who contributed their time and great effort to make the symposium possible. My very special thanks go to the organizing committee, namely Semra Doğandağ, Sertan Girgin, İsmail Öztürk, Ahmet Saçan and Cevat Şener, who did very active and endless work and put tremendous effort into the symposium. I also thank many other colleagues for their special contributions to the symposium. Some of them are Neşe Yalabık, Göktürk Üçoluk, Ayşe Kiper, Halit Oğuztüzün, Panagiotis Chountas, Lee Dong Chun, Yo-Sung Ho, Alper Üngör, Alfred Hofmann and Anna Kramer. In addition, I would also like to thank all of this year's invited speakers and the members of the program committee of ISCIS 2003, whose reviews were very important for the quality of the symposium.

November 2003 Adnan Yazıcı

Organization

ISCIS 2003 was organized by the Department of Computer Engineering, Middle East Technical University.

Executive Committee

Honorary Chair	Erol Gelenbe (University of Central Florida, USA)
Conference and PC Chair	Adnan Yazıcı (Middle East Technical University, Turkey)

Program Committee

Sibel Adalı
Levent Akın
Ergun Akleman
Varol Akman
Demet Aksoy
Reda Alhajj
Ferda Nur Alpaslan
Ethem Alpaydın
Mehmet Altınel
Makoto Amamiya
Troels Andreasen
Peter Arbenz
Volkan Atalay
Işık Aybay
Cevdet Aykanat
Fevzi Belli
Semih Bilgen
Arndt Bode
Müslim Bozyiğit
Bob Brazile
Selçuk Candan
Panagiotis Chountas
Maurice Clint
İlyas Çiçekli
Nihan Çiçekli
Hasan Davulcu
Kudret Demirli
Asuman Doğaç
Jack Dongarra
Iain Duff
Bob Duin
Kemal Ebcioğlu
Jean-Michel Fourneau
Roy George
Muhittin Gökmen
Ratan Guha
Uğur Güdükbay
Marifi Güler
Atilla Gürsoy
Dilek Hakkani-Tur
Emre Harmancı
Pete Harrison
Sven Helmer
Alain Jean-Marie
Janusz Kacprzyk
Laszlo T. Koczy
Çetin Kaya Koç
Uzay Kaymak
Ayşe Kiper
Taşkın Koçak
Selahattin Kuru
Jonathan Lee
Dan Marinescu
Sinan Neftçi
Halit Oğuztüzün
Sema Oktuğ
Gültekin Özsoyoglu
Fatma Özcan
Tamer Özsu
Ilias Petrounias
Fred Petry
Faruk Polat
Ramon Puigjaner
Guy Pujolle
Yücel Saygın
Roberto Scopigno
Marek Sergot
Pavlos Spirakis
Andreas Stafylopatis
George Stamon
Erol Şahin
Abdullah Uz Tansel
Hakkı Toroslu
Özgür Ulusoy
Alper Üngör
Fatos (Yarman) Vural
Roman Wyrzykowsky
Tatyana Yakhno
Berrin Yanıkoğlu
Kokou Yetongnon
Slawomir Zadroznz
Emilio Zapata

Organizing Committee

Semra Doğandağ
Sertan Girgin
İsmail Öztürk
Ahmet Saçan
Cevat Şener

Sponsoring Institutions

Middle East Technical University
Scientific and Technical Research Council of Turkey
IEEE, Turkey Section
International Federation for Information Processing

Table of Contents

Invited Talk

Architectures and Systems

Computer Science Theory

Database and Information Retrieval

E-Business

Graphics & Computer Vision

Intelligent Systems and Robotics

Multimedia

Networks and Security

Soft Computing

Software Engineering

Review of Experiments in Self-Aware Networks*

Erol Gelenbe

Dennis Gabor Chair
Department of Electrical and Electronic Engineering
Imperial College
London SW7 1BT
e.gelenbe@imperial.ac.uk

Abstract. We show how "self-awareness", through on-line self-monitoring and measurement, coupled with intelligent adaptive behaviour in response to observed data, can be used to offer quality of service to network users based on the "Cognitive Packet Network" (CPN) design.

1 Introduction

At the periphery of the Internet novel networked systems are emerging to offer user oriented flexible services, using the Internet and LANs to reach different parts of the same systems, and to access other networks, users and services. Examples include Enterprise Networks, Home Networks (Domotics), Networks for Military Units and for Emergency Services. The example of home networks is significant in that a family may be interconnected as a unit with PDAs for the parents and children, health monitoring devices for the grand-parents, video cameras connected to the network in the infants' bedroom, connections to smart home appliances, the home education server, the entertainment center, the security system, etc.. As an example, the home network will simultaneously use different wired and wireless communication modalities including WLAN, 3G, wired Ethernet and will tunnel packets through IP in the Internet. Such systems must allow for diverse Quality of Service (QoS) requirements, and they raise interesting issues of intelligence and adaptation to user needs and to the networking environment, including routing, self healing, security and robustness. the "Cognitive Packet Network (CPN)" [7,8,10,6]. CPN has the ability to address "QoS" in a significantly broader sense than typically employed in networking. Examples of QoS Goals that a user can request of a CPN include: "Get me the data object *Ob* via the path(s) of highest bandwidth which you can find", where *Ob* is the handle of some data object [2], or "Find the paths with least power consumption to the mobile user *Mn*", "Get the video output *Vi* to my PDA as quickly as possible". The CPN *Accepts Direction*, by inputing Goals prescribed by users. It exploits *Self-Observation* with the help of *smart*

* This research is supported by U.S. Army PEOSTRI via NAWC under Contract No. N61339-02-C0117, and NSF under Grants No. EIA0086251 and EIA0203446.

A. Yazici and C. Şener (Eds.): ISCIS 2003, LNCS 2869, pp. 1–8, 2003.

packets (SPs) so as to be aware of its state including connectivity of fixed or mobile nodes, power levels at mobile nodes, topology, paths and path QoS. It performs *Self-Improvement*, and *Learns from the experience of smart packets* using neural networks and genetic algorithms to determine routing schemes with better QoS. It will *Deduce* hitherto unknown routes by combining or modifying paths which have been previously learned so as to improve QoS and robustness. CPN makes use of four types of packets: smart packets (SP) for discovery, source routed dumb packets (DP) to carry payload, source routed probe packets (P) to test paths, acknowledgments (ACK) to bring back information that has been discovered by SPs and Ps. Conventional IP packets tunnel through CPN to seamlessly operate mixed IP and CPN networks. SPs are be generated by a user (1) requesting that a path having some QoS value be created to some CPN node, or (2) requesting to discover parts of network state, including location of certain fixed or mobile nodes, power levels at nodes, topology, paths and their QoS. SPs *exploit the experience of other packets* using random neural network (RNN) based Reinforcement Learning (RL) [3,7]. RL will be carried out using a Goal which is specified by the user who generated a request for a connection. The decisional weights of a RNN will be increased or decreased based on the observed success or failure of subsequent SPs to achieve the Goal. Thus RL will tend to prefer better routing schemes, more reliable access paths to data objects, and better QoS. (2) Secondly, the system can **deduce** new paths to users, nodes and data objects by combining previously discovered paths, and using the estimated or measured QoS values of new paths select the best new paths. This is similar conceptually to a genetic algorithm which generates new entities by combination or mutation of existing entities, and then selects the best among them using a fitness function. These new paths will then be tested by forwarding Ps so that the actual QoS or success can be evaluated. When a SP or P arrives to its destination, an ACK is generated and heads back to the source of the request. It updates *mailboxes* (MBs) in the CPN nodes it visits with information which has been discovered, and provides the source node with the successful path to the node. All packets have a life-time constraint based on the number of nodes visited, to avoid overburdening the system with unsuccessful requests. A node in the CPN acts as a storage area for packets and mailboxes (MBs). It also stores and executes the code used to route smart packets. It has an input buffer for packets arriving from the input links, a set of mailboxes, and a set of output buffers which are associated with output links. CPN software is integrated into the Linux kernel 2.2.x, providing a single application program interface (API) for the programmer to access CPN. CPN routing algorithms also run seamlessly on ad-hoc wireless and wired connections [9], without specific dependence on the nature (wired or wireless) of the links, using QoS awareness to optimize behavior across different connection technologies and wireless protocols.

Smart packet routing outlined above is carried out by code stored in each router whose parameters are updated at the router. For each successive smart packet, the router computes the appropriate outgoing link based on the outcome of this computation. A recurrent RNN with as many "neurons" as there are possible outgoing links, is used in the computation. The weights of the RNN are updated so that decision outcomes are reinforced or weakened depending on how they have contributed to the success of the QoS goal. In the RNN [1] the state q_i of the $i-th$ neuron in the network is the probability that the $i-th$ neuron is excited. Each neuron i is associated with a distinct outgoing link at a node. The q_i satisfy the system of non-linear equations:

$$q_i = \lambda^+(i)/[r(i) + \lambda^-(i)], \tag{1}$$

where

$$\lambda^+(i) = \sum_j q_j w_{ji}^+ + \Lambda_i, \quad \lambda^-(i) = \sum_j q_j w_{ji}^- + \lambda_i, \tag{2}$$

w_{ji}^+ is the rate at which neuron j sends "excitation spikes" to neuron i when j is excited, w_{ji}^- is the rate at which neuron j sends "inhibition spikes" to neuron i when j is excited, and $r(i)$ is the total firing rate from the neuron i. For an n neuron network, the network parameters are these n by n "weight matrices" $\mathbf{W}^+ = \{w^+(i,j)\}$ and $\mathbf{W}^- = \{w^-(i,j)\}$ which need to be "learned" from input data. RL is used in CPN as follows. Each node stores a specific RNN for each active source-destination pair, and each QoS class. The number of nodes of the RNN are specific to the router, since (as indicated earlier) each RNN node will represent the decision to choose a given output link for a smart packet. Decisions are taken by selecting the output link j for which the corresponding neuron is the most excited, i.e. $q_i \leq q_j$ for all $i = 1, .. , n$. Each QoS class for each source-destination pair has a QoS Goal G, which expresses a function to be minimized, e.g., Transit Delay or Probability of Loss, or Jitter, or a weighted combination, and so on. The reward R which is used in the RL algorithm is simply the inverse of the goal: $R = G^{-1}$. Successive measured values of R are denoted by R_l, $l = 1, 2, ..$; These are first used to compute the current value of the decision threshold:

$$T_l = aT_{l-1} + (1-a)R_l, \tag{3}$$

where $0 < a < 1$, typically close to 1. Suppose we have now taken the $l-th$ decision which corresponds to neuron j, and that we have measured the $l-th$ reward R_l. We first determine whether the most recent value of the reward is larger than the previous value of the threshold T_{l-1}. If that is the case, then we increase very significantly the excitatory weights going into the neuron that was the previous winner (in order to reward it for its new success), and make a small increase of the inhibitory weights leading to other neurons. If the new reward is not greater than the previous threshold), then we simply increase moderately all excitatory weights leading to all neurons, except for the previous winner, and increase significantly the inhibitory weights leading to the previous winning neuron (in order to punish it for not being very successful this time). Let us denote by r_i the firing rates of the neurons before the update takes place:

$$r_i = \sum_1^n [w^+(i,m) + w^-(i,m)], \tag{4}$$

We first compute T_{l-1} and then update the network weights as follows for all neurons $i \neq j$:

- If $T_{l-1} \leq R_l$
  - $w^+(i,j) \leftarrow w^+(i,j) + R_l$,
  - $w^-(i,k) \leftarrow w^-(i,k) + \frac{R_l}{n-2}$, $if\ k \neq j$.
- Else
  - $w^+(i,k) \leftarrow w^+(i,k) + \frac{R_l}{n-2}, k \neq j$,
  - $w^-(i,j) \leftarrow w^-(i,j) + R_l$.

Since the relative size of the weights of the RNN, rather than the actual values, determine the state of the neural network, we then re-normalize all the weights by carrying out the following operations. First for each i we compute:

$$r_i^* = \sum_1^n [w^+(i,m) + w^-(i,m)], \tag{5}$$

and then re-normalize the weights with:

$$w^+(i,j) \leftarrow w^+(i,j) * \frac{r_i}{r_i^*},$$
$$w^-(i,j) \leftarrow w^-(i,j) * \frac{r_i}{r_i^*}.$$

Finally, the probabilities q_i are computed using the non-linear iterations (1), (2). The largest of the q_i's is again chosen to select the new output link used to send the smart packet forward. This procedure is repeated for each smart packet for each QoS class and each source-destination pair.

2 Review of Some Experiments

Cold Start Set-Up Time Measurements. One of the major requirements of a CPN is that it should be able to start itself with no initial information, by first randomly searching, and then progressively improving its behaviour through experience. Since the major function of a network is to transfer packets from some source S to some destination D, it is vital that the CPN be able to establish a path from S to D even when there is no prior information available in the network. The network topology we have used in these experiments is shown at the top of Figure 1, with the source and destinations nodes marked at the left and right ends of the diagram. The network contains 24 nodes, and each node is connected to 4 neighbours. Because of the possibility of repeatedly visiting the same node on a path, the network contains an unlimited number of paths from S to D. However, the fact that SPs are destroyed after they visit 30 nodes, does limit this number though it still leaves a huge number of possible paths. In this set of experiments, the network is always started with empty mailboxes, i.e. with no prior information about which output link is to be used from a node, and with neural network weights set at identical values, so that the neural network descison algorithm at nodes initially will produce a random choice. Each point

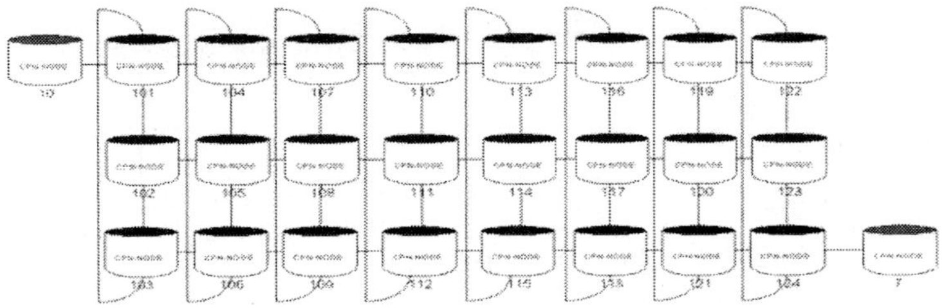

Fig. 1. CPN Network Topology for Cold Start Experiments

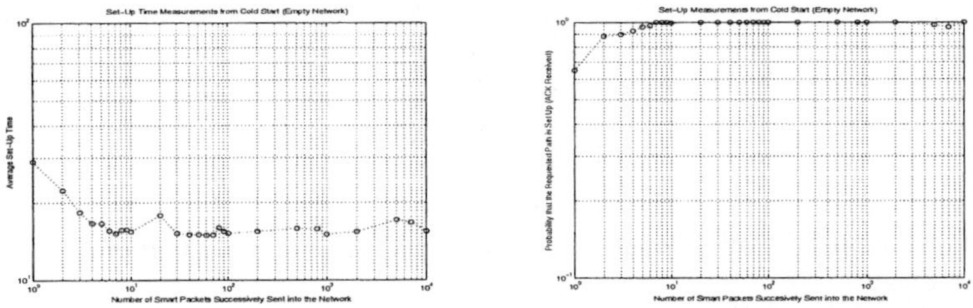

Fig. 2. Average Network Set-Up Time (Left) and Probability of Successful Connection (Right) from Cold Start, as a Function of the Initial Number of Smart Packets

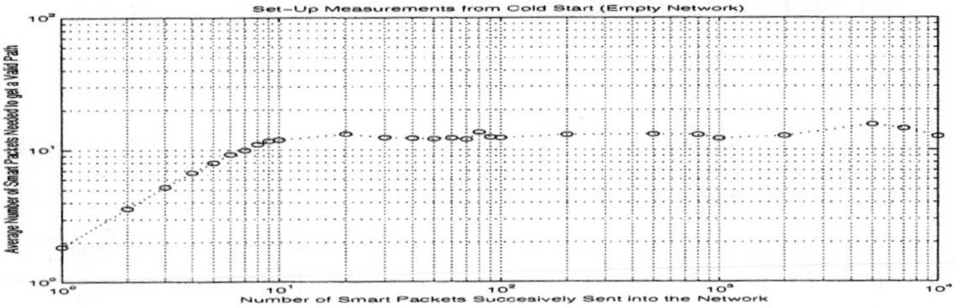

Fig. 3.

shown on the curves of Figure 1 is a result of 100 repetitions of the experiment under identical starting conditions. Let us first comment on the left-hand topmost curve. An absissa value of 10 indicates that the number of SPs used was 10, and – assuming that the experiment resulted in an ACK packet coming back to the source – the ordinate gives the average time (over the 100 experiments) that it elapse between the instant that the first SP was sent out, and the first ACK comes back. Note that the first ACK will be coming back from the correct destination node, and that it will br bringing back a valid forward path that can be used by the subsequent useful traffic. We notice that the average set-up time decreases significantly when we go from a few SPs to about 10, and after that, the average set-up time does not improve appreciably. Its value somewhere between 10 and 20 milliseconds actually corresponds to the round-trip transit time through the hops. This does not mean that it suffices to have a small number

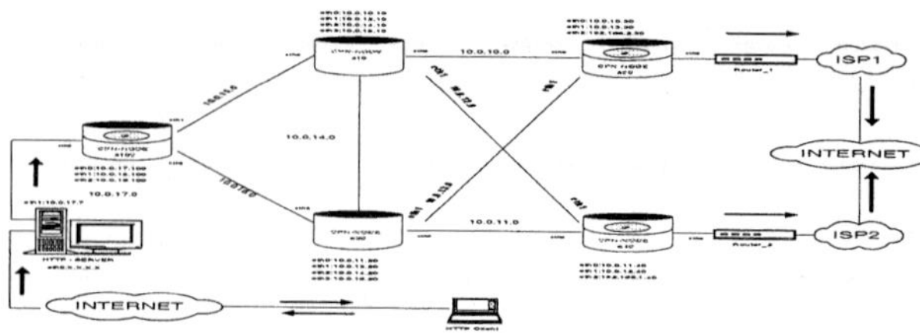

Fig. 4. Experimental Set-Up for Dynamic QoS Control

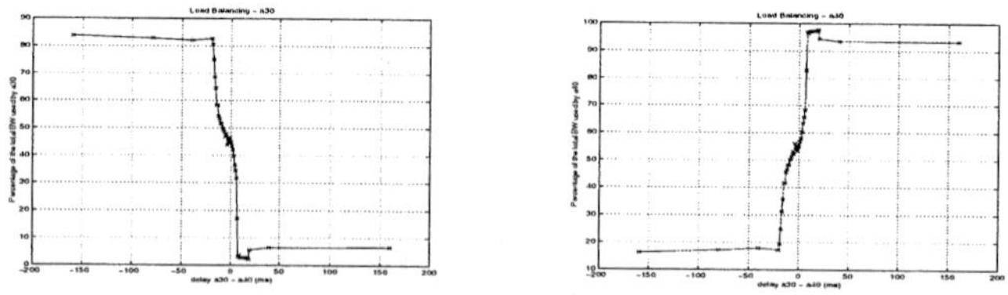

Fig. 5. Percentage of traffic flow through ports A30 (L) and A40 (R) function of difference in delay

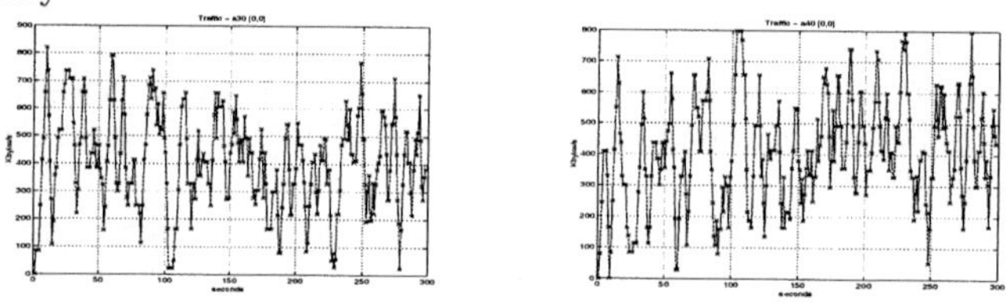

Fig. 6. Instantaneous traffic flow through ports A30 (L) and A40 (R) when delays are identical

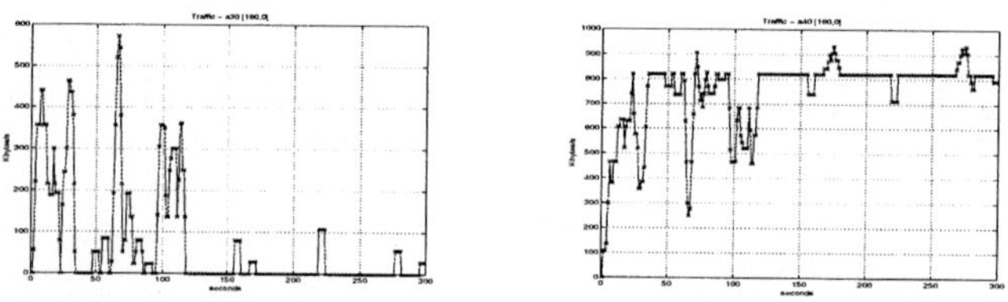

Fig. 7. Instantaneous traffic flow through ports A30 (L) and A40 (R) when DA30-DA40 = 160ms

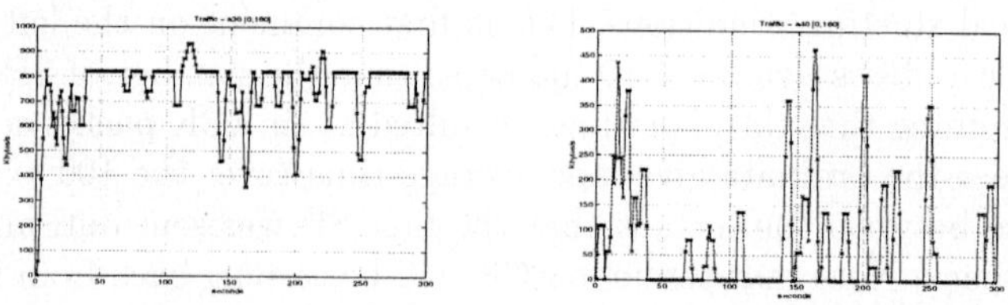

Fig. 8. Instantaneous traffic flow through ports A30 (L) and A40 (R) when DA30-DA40 = -160ms

of SPs at the beginning, simply because the average set-up time is only being measured for the SPs which are *successful*; unsuccessful SPs are destroyed after 30 hops. Thus the top-most curve on the righ-hand-side of Figure 1 is needed to obtain a more complete understanding of what is happening. Again for an x-axis value of over 10 packets, we see that the probability of successfully setting up a path is 1, while with a very small number of packets this figure drops down to about 0.65. These probabilities must of course be understood as the empirically observed fraction of the 100 tests which result in a successful connection. The conclusion from these two sets of data is that to be safe, starting with an empty system, a fairly small number of SPs, in the range of 20 to 100, will provide almost guaranteed set-up of the connection, and the minimum average set-up time. The third curve that we show as a result of these experiments provides some insight into the dynamics of the path set-up. Inserting SPs into the network is not instantaneous, and they are fed into the network sequentially by the source. The rate at which they are fed in is determined by the processing time per packet at the source, and also by the link speeds. Since the link speed is $100Mb/s$ and because SPs are only some $200Bytes$ long at most, we think that the limiting factor here is the source node's processing time. Since, on the other hand, the previous curves show that connections are almost always established with as few as 10 SPs, and because the average round-trip connection establishment time is quite short, we would expect to see that the connection is generally established before all the SPs are sent out by the source. This is exactly what we observe on this third curve. The x axis shows the number of SPs sent into the network, while the y axis shows the average number sent in (over the 100 experiments) before the first ACK is received. For small numbers of SPs, until the value 10 or so, the relationship is linear. However as the number of SPs being inserted into the network increases, we see that after (on the average) 13 packets or so have been sent out, the connection is already established (i.e. the first ACK has returned to the source). This again indicates that a fairly small number of SPs suffice to establish a connection.

Dynamic QoS Control over the Internet. The Internet uses the Internet Protocol (IP) is a *de facto* standard. Thus any new system will have to inter-operate seamlessly with this existing world-wide system. We demonstrate experimentally the seamless operation of a CPN together with the Internet, and show how a CPN can be used to *control QoS in the Internet* according to requests formulate by a user. In order to provide this practical demonstration, we set up the experimental environment described at the top of Figure 1. The Workstation (W) shown at the bottom of the figure is used to generate requests to the web server (WS) shown at the left-hand side of the figure. The WS responds to these requests by generating standard Internet IP packets which enter into the CPN CPN set-up at the top of the figure, so that the WS creates connections back to W which tunnel through the CPN. These packets then are dynamically directed back into the Internet via two distinct Internet Service Providers (ISP) ports A30 and A40 shown at the right-hand-side of the figure. From there they merge into the Internet, and return to the W as shown on the figure. Thus the experimental set-up demonstrates that we are able to seamlessly transmit IP packets into a CPN, and that the CPN can forward them back into the Internet again seamlessly. In the experiments we have run using this set-up, user QoS requested by the W as it makes requests to the WS has been selected to be to minimize delay. Thus we have artificially introduced different delay values at A430 and A40 so that the *difference in delay between the two* can be varied. The second top-most set of curves show the fraction of traffic taking A30 (L) and A40 (R) as this delay is varied, and demonstrates that the CPN is indeed dynamically directing traffic quite sharply in response to the user's QoS goal. Figure 6 shows that when the delay through either port is identical, the instantaneous traffic is very similar. On the other hand, Figures 7 and 8 clearly show that the instantaneous traffic strongly differs depending on which port has a higher measured delay.

Acknowledgements. Special thanks go to my former and current PhD students who have contributed to and participated to this research, including Dr. Zhiguan Xu, Dr. Ricardo Lent, and Juan Arturo Nunez, Peixiang Liu, Pu Su, Michael Gellman.

References

1. E. Gelenbe. "Learning in the recurrent random neural network", *Neural Comp.* 5(1), 154–164, 1993.
2. R. E. Kahn, R. Wilensky "A framework for digital object services", *c.nri.dlib/tn95-01.*
3. U. Halici, "Reinforcement learning with internal expectation for the random neural network" *Eur. J. Opns. Res.*, 126 (2) 2, 288–307, 2000.
4. E. Gelenbe, E. Şeref, Z. Xu. "Simulation with learning agents", *Proc. IEEE*, Vol. 89 (2), 148–157, 2001.
5. E. Gelenbe, R. Lent, Z. Xu, "Towards networks with cognitive packets", Opening Invited Paper, *International Conference on Performance and QoS of Next Generation Networking*, Nagoya, Japan, November 2000, in K. Goto, T. Hasegawa, H. Takagi and Y. Takahashi (eds), "Performance and QoS of next Generation Networking", Springer Verlag, London, 2001.
6. E. Gelenbe, R. Lent, Z. Xu, "Design and performance of cognitive packet networks", *Performance Evaluation*, 46, pp. 155–176, 2001.
7. E. Gelenbe, R. Lent, Z. Xu "Measurement and performance of Cognitive Packet Networks", *J. Comp. Nets.*, 37, 691–701, 2001.
8. E. Gelenbe, R. Lent, Z. Xu "Networking with Cognitive Packets", *Proc. ICANN.*, Madrid, August 2002.
9. E. Gelenbe, R. Lent "Mobile Ad-Hoc Cognitive Packet Networks", *Proc. IEEE ASWN*, Paris, July 2–4, 2002.
10. E. Gelenbe et al. "Cognitive packet petworks: QoS and performance", Keynote Paper, *IEEE MASCOTS Conference*, San Antonio, TX, Oct. 14–16, 2002.
11. E. Gelenbe, K. Hussain "Learning in the multiple class random neural network", *IEEE Trans. on Neural Networks* 13 (6), 1257–1267, 2002.

Web Information Resource Discovery: Past, Present, and Future

Gultekin Ozsoyoglu and Abdullah Al-Hamdani

Dept of Electrical Engineering and Computer Science
Case Western Reserve University, Cleveland, Ohio 44106
{tekin,abd}@eecs.cwru.edu

1 Introduction

In a time span of twelve years, the World Wide Web--only a computer and an internet connection away from anybody anywhere, and with abundant, diverse and sometimes incorrect, redundant, spam, and bad information--has become *the* major information repository for the masses and the world. The web is becoming all things to all people, totally oblivious to nation/country/continent boundaries, promising mostly free information to all, and quickly growing into a repository in all languages and all cultures. With large digital libraries and increasingly significant educational resources, the web is becoming an equalizer, a balancing force, and an opportunity for all, especially for underdeveloped/developing countries. The web is both exciting and overwhelming, changing the way the world communicates, from the way businesses are conducted to the way masses are educated, from the way research is performed to the way research results are disseminated. It is fair to say that the web will only get more diverse, larger and more chaotic in the near future.

As it is, the web is a repository of text, multimedia, and hypertext documents, which are mostly display-only (HTML) documents, or information-exchange (XML) documents created for the consumption of web-based applications.

The web continually grows and changes, with an estimated size of 5B(illion) to 8B pages (largest web index, OpenFind (www.openfind.com.tw) is 3.5B pages; not including hidden web, intranets, and database-enabled pages). Two strengths of the web are: it grows incrementally (and thus scalable), and each individual in each nation, with a connection to the internet, can contribute to content generation on the web, leading to the dissemination of facts (and propaganda), and (sometimes, incorrect) ideas and opinions, in an independent and very democratic manner.

As valuable and rich as the web is, presently, there are few ways to search and locate information on the web: one can use (i) the existing search engines to reach to a select set of ranked sites, (ii) meta search engines that in turn employ multiple search engines, and aggregate and rank search results, (iii) question-answering systems (e.g., AskJeeves (www.ask.com) that allow users to pose questions, and return their answers; or, one can (iv) follow links and browse web pages. In this paper, we review the underlying technologies for collecting information (metadata) about the web, and employing these technologies for searching and querying the web. Full paper with larger references is at art.cwru.edu/WebSearchQuerying.pdf.

In section 2, we summarize the history and capabilities of web search engines. Sections 3 and 4 are devoted to the automated and manual ways of adding semantics to the web, to help understand and, thus, search the web better. Section 5 offers our predictions on what the near future holds for improving web search and querying.

A. Yazici and C. Şener (Eds.): ISCIS 2003, LNCS 2869, pp. 9–18, 2003.

2 Web Search Engines

First, a brief note on the history of web: in 1980, Tim Berners-Lee at CERN (European Nuclear Research Organization) wrote a program that used bidirectional links to browse documents in different directories. By 1990, Berners-Lee designed a graphical user interface to hypertext, named the "world wide web". By 1993, CERN had developed the three pillars of the present web: HTML markup language, http (the hypertext transport protocol), and the very first http server. Mosaic, created by Mark Anderson as the first web browser, was launched in February 1993, and later became Netscape. And, the rest is history. See www.archive.org for an archive of the web (10Billion pages)

2.1 History

Earliest forms of search engines, launched in 1990, were for searching ftp and gopher directories. 1994 was a busy year for the launch of a number of significant search engines. In January 1994, MCC Research introduced EINet Galaxy (www.galaxy.com), with a hand-organized directory of submitted URLs and search features for Telnet and Gopher, and limited web search features. In April 1994, Yahoo! directory was created by David Filo and Jerry Yang, two Stanford PhD students to help Stanford students locate useful web pages. Yahoo manually created and maintained hierarchically organized topic directories—until October 2002, which is when it started to incorporate Google's crawler-based listings, "enhanced by" Yahoo directories. Yahoo (www.yahoo.com) became a company in 1995. Also in early 1994, WebCrawler (bought, in order, by Excite, AOL, InfoSpace) from the University of Washington was released. The distinctive feature of the Web Crawler was its full text-indexing feature (of the first 200 words in each document). In June 1994, Lycos from Carnegie Mellon University was released; Lycos search engine is powered by HotBot since 1999.

In late 1995, AltaVista search engine (now 1B pages), running on clusters of Alpha workstations and with main memory indexing, was launched by the Digital Equipment Corporation. Inktomi (now 2B pages), which powers HotBot (bought by Lycos, then Yahoo)), was released in 1996. Another major search engine, Google (www.google.com) (now 2.4B pages) was launched in September 1998 by Sergey Brin and Larry Page, two PhD students at Stanford. By 2000, Google's coverage reached to about %50 of the web, with crawl refreshment rates of once every month. Each of Google and Yahoo now handles about 30% of web search requests.

In the last five years, thousands of web search engines, some powered by the above-listed search providers and others using their own directories or crawler-based indexes, were launched. Search Engine Watch lists [37], in nine categories, more than a thousand search engines. Search Engine Colossus [34] lists search engines from 195 countries and 39 territories (with 18 search providers from/about Turkey). Search Engine Watch lists as "major" (well-known or well-used) search engines [35] Google, Yahoo, AllTheWeb.com (powered by a crawler-based search engine; now 2.1 billion pages), and MSN Search (powered by its own directory, LookSmart Directory, and Inktomi's crawler-generated URLs). As search engines in the "strongly consider" category, Search Engine Watch lists AOL search (powered by Google), AskJeeves (a question-answering system powered by crawling-based Teoma search provider), Hotbot (owned by Yahoo; powered by search providers Google, Inktomi, Teoma, and AllTheWeb.com), Lycos, and Teoma.

Since 1996, three years after the launch of web search engines, it occurred to people that, perhaps, employing a large number of search engines for a query and then aggregating their results somehow would provide more useful information; hence the notion of metasearch engines or metacrawlers came about. Presently, there are about 50 metacrawlers. See www.searchenginewatch.com/links/article.php/2156241 for a review and evaluation of metasearch engines.

There are also a large number of specialized search engines, such as those that find people (www.whowhere.com), universitics (www.campusregistry.com), publications (CiteSeer), etc. See http://cui.unige.ch/1 for a list.

2.2 Techniques and Capabilities

The requirements for web search engines are to (a) locate and rank web documents effectively and efficiently, (b) provide unbiased and up-to-date access to the web, with expressive and useful web search results, and (c) adapt to user queries.

Search engines can be classified according to how they index the web: (1) those that use web crawling, and automatically create web listings such as Google, (2) those that manually maintain directories, such as Yahoo (until recently) by dividing manually-submitted information about web sites into categories, and (3) those that use both: hybrid search engines that maintain manually generated association directories and crawler-generated indexes.

A search engine is composed of three main parts: a crawler (spider), an indexing software, and a search and ranking software. Crawler scans web documents and collects information about them. Indexing software is used to construct a data structure that can be quickly searched. Search and ranking software is used to analyze a given query, and compare it to the existing indexes to find relevant items and URLs.

2.2.1 Crawling

Crawlers crawl the web by starting from a given set of URLs, and iteratively fetch and scan for new URLs, caching them as "URLs to be evaluated". Building a basic crawler is easy; building an industrial-strength crawler is not. Crawlers built for research purposes fetch up to hundreds of pages a second; commercial crawlers are much more scalable and fetch hundreds of thousands of pages a second. Understandably, crawler details of commercial search engines are not available. However, basic design issues involve concurrent page fetches, design of a powerful storage manager, concurrent address resolution, avoiding spider traps/spams, and detecting duplicate pages/URLs, which we very briefly review next. For more details, read chapter 2 of Chakrabarti's excellent book [14].

Links extracted from web pages need to be processed, and normalized so that pages will not be fetched multiple times—a difficult task due to *virtual hosting* (i.e., proxy pass) and multiple hostnames mapping to multiple IP addresses, mostly due to load balancing. Extracted URLs may be absolute or relative; regardless, a canonical URL needs to be formed by the crawler.

Crawlers must control the number of service requests to any one http server at a time since commercial servers have safeguards against denial of service attacks, and limit the service to any given client at a time.

The crawler repository, managed by a storage manager, contains HTML pages, and quickly becomes very large. For research purposes, single-disk-based storage managers are freely available (www.sleepycat.com); commercial-strength storage managers manage disk farms over a fast local area network, and are much more complex to build.

Refreshing crawled pages is another issue with large crawlers. See Cho et al [13] for the design of an incremental crawler.

2.2.2 Document Model and Query Language

Web search engines preprocess (usually the first 100 to 200 words of) documents by removing/replacing stopwords (e.g., *the, a, in, of,* etc.), stemming the text (i.e., reducing the words to the root forms such as changing *walking* to *walk*), and replacing documents and words with identifiers. Then, various indexing structures and/or index compression techniques are built on preprocessed documents.

As for modeling documents themselves (in order to compare them), the commonly accepted model is the vector-space model from Information Retrieval (IR). By using a vocabulary (terms that appear in all documents), a document is represented as a vector of real numbers where each vector element contains the weight of a term, usually computed using the Term Frequency-Inverse Document Frequency (TF-IDF) weighting scheme [33].

Most web search engines allow "Boolean Queries" (from IR) that are conjunctions and/or disjunctions of words and phrases. Such a language, compared to the existing database query languages, is very limited in expressive power, and not employed by users—average web search requests are 1.3 words long.

2.2.3 Retrieval Relevance

To judge the relevance (in terms of precision and recall, two basic measures from IR) of a web page to a given query (i.e., a set of terms), the query and all existing documents (already retrieved by the crawler) are represented as document vectors by using the TF-IDF scheme. Then, the issue of the similarity of a query and a web page becomes the issue of the similarity between the associated vectors (always in the L_1 or L_2 Euclidean metric). The most commonly used similarity measure for this purpose is the cosine similarity, which computes the cosine of the angle between the two vectors.

In the case where users are not satisfied with the response of a search engine and are willing to provide feedback to the search engine to refine the search, relevance feedback models are developed, which include the Rocchio's method and pseudo-relevance feedback [14]. More advanced models include probabilistic relevance feedback models or bayesian inference networks. As it turns out, users rarely provide feedback, and most search engines do not incorporate relevance feedback features.

2.2.4 Hyperlink Analysis

In web retrieval, the linkage information among web pages is found to be more informative than the IR-based document similarities. To employ linkage information, concepts from *Bibliometrics,* a field that studies the citation patterns of scientific papers, are employed: (i) *prestige* of an article: a real, normalized number representing the number of citations to it, and, iteratively, to those that refer to it and so on, and (ii) *co-citation* between two documents (the number of documents that co-cite the two documents, normalized by the total number of documents.

PageRank and HITS (hyperlink induced topic search) are two very influential algorithms for ranking pages, developed in early 1996, respectively, by Sergey Brin and Larry Page at Stanford [17, 32], and Jon Kleinberg at IBM Almaden [24]. PageRank of a page is a normalized sum of the prestiges of pages linking to it. In essence, PageRank definition is based on the intuition that a page has high rank (i.e., important) if the sum of the ranks of its incoming links, recursively, is high [32]. PageRank computation converges rapidly for the web.

In HITS, first, a set of documents are selected from the web by using the user's query and, perhaps, IR techniques. One can view the selected documents as nodes and the hyperlinks among them as edges, resulting in a "subgraph" of the web. In this subgraph, *authoritative pages* are nodes/pages to which many pages have links (directed edges), and *hub pages* are nodes with many links (outgoing edges) to authoritative pages, and the system reports the highest-ranking authorities and hubs in the selected set of documents. Intuitively, in Bibliometrics, authorities are articles with definitive, high-quality information, and hubs are high-quality survey articles.

PageRank and HITS are similar in that they are both recursive, and involve computing the eigenvalues of the adjacency matrix of a subgraph of the web (using power iterations). It is known that the utilization of such linkage information in retrieval leads to higher retrieval effectiveness, as exemplified by Google [9]. Note however that Google is more than the PageRank mechanism; it employs phrase matches, anchor text information, and match proximity. The basic criticism of PageRank [14] is that the prestige scores are query-independent, leading to a disconnect between the ranking and a given query.

Several stochastic variants of PageRank and HITS are researched in the literature, e.g., stochastic link structure analysis (SALSA) [26], more stable HITS algorithm [31], eliminating the effects of two-way self referencing (nepotistic links) [5], eliminating the effects of self-created cliques [14], outlier elimination [5], mixed hubs [14], eliminating the effects of topic contamination and topic drift [14], and exploiting anchor text [11].

2.2.5 Focused Crawlers

General-purpose crawlers do not make an attempt to crawl only pages satisfying a certain criteria. It does make sense however to crawl pages that are likely to have high "importance", where importance may be defined in terms of PageRank values, or high indegree/outdegree link values of pages, or any other user-defined function. Cho et al [13] studies various URL prioritization and keyword-sensitive web search strategies. It is also found that [30] breath-first crawl quickly locates pages with higher PageRank. Others proposed IR-based heuristics (e.g., pages containing specific words, or containing phrases that match a given regular expression) such as the FishSearch [8] and its followup SharkSearch [22].

Focused crawlers are systems with a crawler and a classifier system, where the crawler bases its crawling strategies on the judgments of the classifier system, possibly a supervised classifier trained a priori and updated as documents are found.

Thus, focused crawlers search only a subset of the web (not necessarily only a specific web resource) that pertains to a specific relevant topic. A number of focused crawlers are proposed in the literature [12, 13, 15, 29], which differ by the properties of the employed classifiers, the heuristics used to judge the importance of pages to be fetched or to identify and exploit the hubs, and learning the structure of paths relevant for and leading to important pages [15].

3 Automated Metadata Extraction from Web

If it were possible to extract entities and relationships about entities from web documents, such metadata could then be used to define more powerful queries over the set of web documents. Thus, the field of data extraction is important to web querying. In this section, we briefly list a number of recent works in the field of data extraction, with an interest to using the metadata for web search and querying.

DIPRE [10] employs a handful of training tuples of a structured relation R (that represents a specific meta-relationship among entities in the data) to extract all the tuples of R, from a set of HTML documents. Consider the relation R(Organization, Location) with the tuple <Microsoft, Redmond>. Assume that DIPRE encounters the text "Microsoft's headquarters in Redmond", which it changes into the pattern p: "<STRING1>'s headquarters in <STRING2>". DIPRE then searches the html documents for phrases matching p. Assume that it encounters the string "Boeing's headquarters in Seattle", which results in the new tuple <Boeing, Seattle> being added into R. That is, DIPRE uses the new tuples to generate more patterns, and uses the newly generated patterns to extract more tuples, and so on.

Snowball [1, 2], an extension to DIPRE, improves the quality of the extracted data by including automatic patterns and tuple evaluation. QXtract [3] uses automated query-based techniques to retrieve documents that are useful for extracting a target relation from large collection text documents. The Proteus information extraction system [20, 21] uses finite-state patterns to recognize {names, nouns, verbs, and other special forms}, scenario pattern matching to extract events and relationships for a given relation, and an inference process to locate implicit information and to make it explicit. Then, Proteus combines all the information about a single event using event emerging rules.

The field of (meta)data extraction from the web has a long way to go at this stage. However, we believe that it provides an alternative to manual content-generator-dependent ways of adding semantics to the web, which is discussed next.

4 Adding Manually-Supplied Semantics to Web

Next we briefly summarize the leading web information representation models with extensive research and standardization efforts, namely, the Resource Description Framework (RDF), the semantic web, and ontologies.

4.1 Resource Description Framework

Resource Description Framework (RDF) [27] is designed to describe web information sources by attaching metadata specified in XML. RDF identifies resources using

Uniform Resource Identifiers (URI), and describes them in terms of properties and their values [28]. RDF is a graph-based information model, and consists of a set of statements, represented as triples. A triple denotes an edge between two nodes, and has a property name (edge), a resource (node), and a value (a node). A resource can be anything from a web document to an abstract notion. A value can be a resource or a literal (an atomic type). RDF Schema [4] defines a type system for RDF, similar to the type systems of object-oriented programming languages such as Java.

RDF Schema allows the definition of *classes* for resources and property types. The resource *Class* is used to type resources, and the resource *Type* is used to type properties. Various properties such as *SubClassOf, SubPropertyOf, isDefinedBy, seeAlso, type* are available. Various constraints on resources and on properties are defined.

It remains to be seen how widely RDF will be adapted by web content generators. Initial results are not encouraging. Eberhart [16] investigated the amount and the type of RDF data on the web. The RDF data were gathered from the web in 2001-2002. The results indicate that (i) RDF is not widely used on the web, (ii) RDF data on the web is not easily reachable, and (iii) it is not very sophisticated.

4.2 Semantic Web

Semantic Web [7, 36] is an RDF schema-based effort to define an architecture for the web, with a schema layer, logical layer, and a query language. The overall goal of the semantic web is to support richer information discovery, data integration, task automation, and navigation--by providing standards and techniques for web content generators to add more semantics to their web data [25].

A complex set of layers of web technologies and standards are defined to implement the semantic web [25]. *The Unicode and URI layers* are used to identify objects in the semantic web, and to make sure that international character sets are used. *The XML layer* is used to integrate the semantic web definitions with other XML-based standards. *The RDF* and *RDF Schema layer* are used to define statements about objects and vocabularies that can be referred using URIs. *The Ontology layer* is used to evaluate vocabularies, and to define relationships between different concepts. *The Digital Signature layer* detects alterations to documents. *The Logic layer* is used to write rules that are executed by *the Proof layer*, while *the Trust layer* is used to decide whether to trust a given proof or not.

It remains to be seen whether the concepts and standards defined by the semantic web effort will be adapted. One major problem is the complexity of the semantic web, as defined now. The Semantic Web is an active, industry-led research area.

4.2.1 Ontologies

An ontology is a specification of a conceptualization (i.e., meta information) [18]. It is used to describe the semantics of the data, with a role similar to the database schema [23]. Ontologies establish a joint terminology between members of a community of interest. An example is the Gene Ontology (www.geneontology.org), for geneticists and biologists. To represent a conceptualization, a representation language can be (and, usually, are not) used, and there are several representation languages [19], RDF and RDF Schema being among them.

Horrocks et al. [23] proposed the *Ontology Inference Layer* (OIL), which is a standard for a web-based representation and inference layer to express ontologies based on RDF and XML schemas. OIL provides rich modeling primitives from frame-based languages, a well-defined semantics based on Description Logic, and automated reasoning support. Ontologies are describes in OIL using three different layers: the *object level*, the *first meta-level* (ontology definition), and the *second meta-level* (ontology container). The object level used to describe concrete instances for a given ontology. The first metal level provides structured vocabulary and well-defined semantics by defining terminology that can be used in the object level. The second meta-level describes the features of a given ontology such as author, name, subject, etc. OIL is compatible with RDF schema; [6] uses RDF modeling primitives to map OIL specifications to their corresponding RDF serializations.

Ontologies form another effort to add community-supported and manually-generated semantics to the web; it remains to be seen how broadly they will be adapted.

5 What Next?

Major search engines have come a long way in recent years in crawler coverage of the web, fast search over very large indexed data, and providing users with very good responses for one- or two-word queries. The research on general-purpose web search technology has also started to mature with well-developed techniques; surely, in the near future, effective keyword-based web search using most languages will be provided by the major search engines.

However, the next natural step of providing more informative accesses to web information resources (not to the whole web) is yet to come. Consider the query: "*Find from ACM SIGMOD Anthology five most important prerequisite papers of the paper "Predicate Migration" by Hellerstein and Stonebraker*". Presently, no tools exist to answer such a query.

The next enabling step for effective web search and querying will come when metadata about the web becomes widely available. It is not clear that the RDF and the semantic web efforts will succeed in adding semantics to a significant portion of the web due to (a) the complexity of the semantic web architecture with its numerous layers, and (b) the additional manual effort needed to define and add semantics to web data. The alternative direction of automated metadata extraction from the web is yet premature. We think that when it matures, automated metadata extraction will co-exist with, if not take over, the manually generated metadata.

Regardless, in the future, web information resources, but not the whole web, will have metadata available, allowing users to search and query web information resources using highly powerful, 1st or higher order logic-based query languages. Such languages will be unique and different than database query languages.

References

1. E. Agichtein, E. Eskin, L. Gravano, "Combining Strategies for Extracting Relations from Text Collections", ACM SIGMOD, 2000.
2. Agichtein, E., Gravano, L., "Snowball: Extracting relations from large plain-text collections", The 5th ACM International Conference on Digital Libraries, June 2000.
3. Agichtein, E., Gravano, L., "Querying Text Databases for Efficient Information Extraction", Proce. of the 19th IEEE Intl Conference on Data Engineering (ICDE), 2003.
4. Brickley, D., Guha, R.V., "Resource Description Framework Schema (RDFS)", W3C Proposed Recommendation, 1999, available at http://www.w3.org/TR/PR-rdf-schema.
5. K. Bharat, M.R. Henzinger, "Improved algorithms for topic distillation in a hyperlinked environment", ACM SIGIR Conf., 1998.
6. J. Broekstra, M. Klein, D. Fensel, and I. Horrocks, "Adding formal semantics to the Web: building on top of RDF Schema", In Proc. of the ECDL, 2000.
7. Berners-Lee, T., "Semantic Web Roadmap", W3C draft, Jan 2000, available at http://www.w3.org/DesignIssues/Semantic.html
8. P.M.E. De Bra, R.D.J. Post, "Searching for arbitrary information in the WWW: Making Client-based searching feasible", WWW Conf., 1994.
9. Sergey Brin, Lawrence Page, "The anatomy of a large-scale hypertextual Web search engine", Computer Networks and ISDN Systems, Brisbane, Australia, 1998.
10. Sergey Brin, "Extracting patterns and relations from the world wide web", In WebDB Workshop at EDBT, 1998. http://citeseer.nj.nec.com/brin98extracting.html.
11. S. Chakrabarti et al, "Mining the web's link structure", IEEE Computer, Aug. 1999.
12. S. Chakrabarti, M. van den Berg, B. Dom, "Focused crawling: A new approach to topic-specific web resource Discovery", In Proceedings of WWW 8 Conf., 1999.
13. J. Cho, H. Garcia-Molina, L. Page, "Efficient crawling through URL ordering", In Proceedings of the Seventh International World-Wide Web Conference, 1998.
14. Mining the Web: Discovering knowledge from hypertext data, Chakrabarti, S., Morgan-Kaufmann Publishers, 2003.
15. M. Diligenti, F. Coetzee, S. Lawrence, C. L. Giles, M. Gori, "Focused Crawling using Context Graphs", VLDB 2000.
16. Eberhart, A., "Survey of RDF data on the web", In Proc. of the 6th World Multi-conference on Systemics, Cybernetics and Informatics (SCI), 2002.
17. Google History, at http://www.google.com/corporate/history.html.
18. Gruber, T., "A translation approach to portable ontologies", Knowledge Acquisition, 1993.
19. Guarino, N., "Formal Ontology and Information Systems", In N. Guarino (ed.), Formal Ontology in Information Systems, Proc. of the 1st International Conference, 1998.
20. R. Grishman, S. Huttunen, R. Yangarber, "Real-Time Event Extraction for Infectious Disease Outbreaks", In Proceedings of Human Language Technology Conference, 2002.
21. Ralph Grishman, "Information extraction: Techniques and challenges", In Maria Teresa Pazienza, editor, Information Extraction, Springer-Verlag, LNAI, 1997.
22. M. Hersovici et al, "The sharksearch algorithm—an application: Tailored web site mapping", WWW 7 Conf., 1998.
23. Horrocks et al, "The Ontology Inference Layer OIL", Technical report, Free University of Amsterdam, 2000. http://www.ontoknowledge.org/oil/.
24. Kleinberg, J., "Authoritative Sources in hyperlinked environments", In the 9th ACM-SIAM Symposium on Discrete Mathematics, 1998.
25. M. Koivunen and E. Miller, "W3C Semantic Web Activity", In the proceedings of the Semantic Web Kick-off Seminar in Finland Nov 2, 2001.
26. R. Lempel, S. Moran, "SALSA: The stochastic approach for link-structure analysis", ACM TOIS, April 2001.
27. Lassila, O., Swick, R., "Resource Description Framework (RDF) Model and Syntax Specification", W3C Recommendation 22 February 1999.
28. Frank Manola, Eric Miller, "RDF Primer", W3C Working Draft, 23 January 2003

29. F. Menczer, G. Pant, M. Ruiz, P. Srinivasan, "Evaluating topic-driven Web crawlers", In Proc. 24th Intl. ACM SIGIR Conf., 2001
30. M. Najork, J. Weiner,"Breadth-First search crawling yields high-quality pages", WWW'98.
31. Ng, A. Zheng, M. Jordan, "Stable algorithms for link analysis", ACM SIGIR, 2001.
32. L. Page, S. Brin, R. Motwani, T. Winograd, "The PageRank citation ranking: Bringing order to the web", Stanford Digital Libraries Working Paper, 1998.
33. G. Salton, Automatic Text Processing, Addison-Wesley, 1989.
34. International Directory of Search Engines, Search Engine Colossus, 2003, available at http://www.searchenginecolossus.com.
35. The Major Search Engines and Directories, Search Engine Watch Report, Danny Sullivan, 2003, available at searchenginewatch.com/links/article.php/2156221.
36. The Semantic Web Community Portal, at http://www.semanticweb.org
37. Search Links, available at http://searchenginewatch.com/links/index.php.

Courses Modeling in E-learning Context

Vincenza Carchiolo, Alessandro Longheu, Michele Malgeri, and Giuseppe Mangioni

Dipartimento di Ingegneria Informatica e delle Telecomunicazioni
Universita' di Catania - Viale Andrea Doria, 6 - I95125 Catania (Italy)
{car,alongheu,mm,gmangioni}@diit.unict.it

Abstract. The computer-based sharing and dissemination of knowledge and learning activities are known as "E-learning". In this paper we propose an E-learning model, focusing in particular on courses modeling, which aims at promoting the sharing and reuse of courses contents and teaching materials, allowing the construction of personalized learning paths.

1 Introduction

Many services today benefit significantly from the stressed use of computer-based technologies, thus leading to the "E-anything" paradigma. Among these, the set of services ranging from the sharing and dissemination of knowledge to learning activities, is nowadays known as "E-learning" ([1,2,3]).

Whenever computer-based technologies are adopted in an existing context, it is important to re-consider features and purposes of the desired service in order to assure its real enhancement, avoiding to simply automatize its functions.

Considering the learning process, its aims can be summarized as follows:

- to share courses contents among teachers, in order to provide students with a single and (possibly) uniform set of concepts to be learned;
- to share teaching materials (lessons), in order to exploit as far as possible existing material developed by teachers; to provide this modularity, material is actually separated from contents (set of concepts);
- to promote active learning, allowing the construction of courses which are personalized in terms of both contents and teaching materials, selected according to each student's needs and capabilities, also taking teacher guidelines into account;
- to provide students with an adaptive environment which dynamically adjusts the personalized course during the learning process;
- to provide both teachers and students with a simple, flexible, open, modular learning environment.

To satisfy such goals, an E-learning system must be characterized with a complete management (storing, creation and retrieval) of courses and teaching materials (as well as of student capabilities and teachers guidelines), and a proper

A. Yazici and C. Şener (Eds.): ISCIS 2003, LNCS 2869, pp. 19–26, 2003.

model for course contents and teaching materials, in terms of both data they should include and the structure such data should be organized into, in order to guarantee concepts/lessons sharing and reuse. Moreover the E-learning system must provide an open and modular interface (e.g., web-based) for end-users (both students and teachers), and a generator of on-demand customized courses, to create and propose to the student all the (customized) paths starting from his previous knowledge towards the desired knowledge (topic of interest)

This paper deals with these aspects, introducing a model for an E-learning environment. We first show the architecture of the model, then we consider in detail how courses contents and teaching materials are modeled.

2 Learning System Architecture

In order to build a complete learning system, various tasks must be performed [4,5,6,7]. Figure 1 shows our model for a learning system consisting of Courses, Engine, Profiles and E-Learning Interface module.

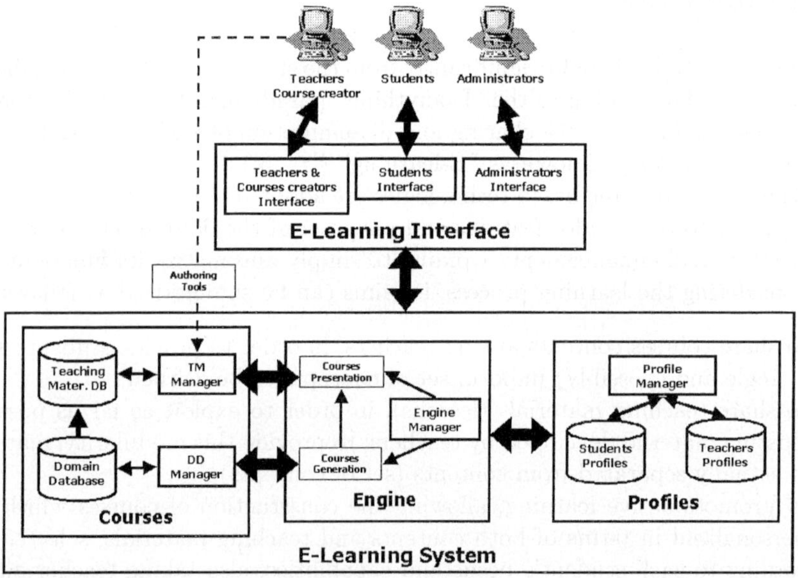

Fig. 1. Learning system architecture

Courses module consists of two sub-modules, called Domain Database (DDB) and Teaching Materials Database (TMDB), each with its manager sub-module.

DDB contains all lessons, each intended as an atomic set of concepts to be learned separated from its teaching materials, and all courses, each intended as a set of lessons properly grouped together. Lessons (and courses) are connected together through precedence-succession relations. The DDB manager interacts with the Engine module by providing all lessons and courses. For each lesson, the DDB also contains a link to the related teaching materials (e.g. slides), placed in the TMDB, separated from its related lesson(s). Teaching materials are extracted by the TMDB manager and properly arranged by the Engine module.

Engine module contains the course generation and course presentation sub-modules, together with their management sub-module. The course generation sub-module is devoted to building courses and learning paths, based on lessons (courses) contained in the domain database, as well as on information in the profile databases. Once courses/learning paths are built by the course generation sub-module, the course presentation sub-module retrieves all the related teaching materials and organizes the way courses are made available, e.g. depending on the media actually available or desired, for instance a PC or a palmtop, or based on the available bandwidth, always considering profile information, so that the proper teaching material can be provided.

After preparation, courses are finally attended by students and/or consulted by teachers through the E-learning Interface module as shown in Figure 1; the virtual learning environment can be simply a web site, or it may also integrate different media (e.g. a PC to attend lessons or cell phone text messages for news about courses).

Profiles module contains all relevant information about teachers and students, stored in proper databases, together with their management sub-module. Profile Databases are used by the course generation and course presentation sub-modules when courses/learning paths are generated to tailor their contents (and the related teaching materials). Access to the Profile databases is actually granted through the Profile manager, similarly to DDB/TMDB managers.

The last module is the E-learning Interface, through which students attend courses (perform exercises and tests, view/modify their profile), teachers/course creators view and manage their courses, and administrators manage the whole system.

3 Courses Module

The databases in the Course module have been designed on the basis of two important requisites: modularity and reusability. Meeting the first requirement made it possible to design easily extensible databases (by adding new topics to an existing domain or inserting new domains). The aim of the second requisite was to make it possible to reuse or share part or all of the teaching material. For these reasons databases have been developed with a clear separation between the contents and descriptions of the various topics. From the logical viewpoint, the information contained in the databases is structured on three levels: *course level*, *unit level* and *teaching level* (see Figure 2).

From the physical point of view, Courses Module contains the DDB and the TMDB. The DDB contains implementation of the *course* and *unit level*, while the TMDB contains all the information for the *teaching material level*.

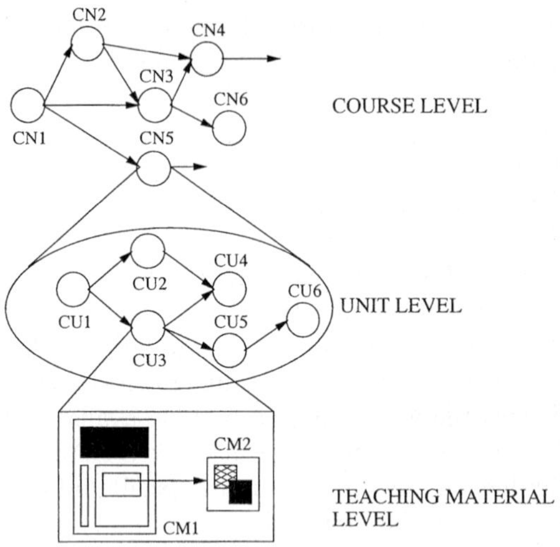

Fig. 2. Databases logical view

Typical database reading operations are performed during the generation and presentation of courses, while writing operations are performed when new courses, lessons or teaching material are inserted. New information can be inserted into the database while creating a new course/lesson or while creating a new learning path meeting the specific requirements of a student.

Those involved in the first case are teachers (or course creators) who can use various authoring tools to insert a new course (*course level*), lesson (*unit level*) or teaching material (*teaching material level*). The operations are supervised by the engine, which ensures correct and efficient use of the Course Database (for more details see [8]). The second case is when a student expresses the need to learn a given topic (not included in the courses at the *course level*) and the engine generates a new learning path for the student's specifications (adaptive), combining the lessons and teaching material already in the database. The general learning path will become part of the information in the *course level* and can be reused in future on request.

3.1 Domain Database

The DDB contains information about the courses and lessons available to students, according to their particular domain of interests. It has two levels: *course level* and *unit level*. The *course level* contains a representation of the relations linking the various courses, using an oriented graph of the `and/or` type. The nodes of the graph, called Course Nodes (CN), contain information about the structure of each course. The arcs between the various nodes indicate whether one course has to be completed before another can be taken.

The sequence of lessons making up a course is stored in each CN as a graph of Course Units (CU) contained in the *unit level*. In reality a CN does not directly contain the single CU but a pointer to them, as they can be used in different courses. For this reason, all the CU, irrespective of the courses they belong to, are in turn organized in an `and/or` graph with the various nodes connected by arcs representing whether one is preliminary to another. In this way the CU have an independent existence from the courses using them, and this increases the possibility of reusing them in different courses.

The orientation of the arcs between both courses (CN) and units (CU) is defined as follows: *an arc oriented from X to Y means that node X depends on node Y*; in the case of CN (or CU), that is, if X depends on Y, it means that all concepts included in CN (or CU) X must be learned before concepts of CN (or CU) Y can be understood.

This precedence-succession is the only type of relation considered since it appears to be the most unbiased, i.e. when X is connected to Y this should depend on the concepts of both X and Y, even different arcs may connect X and Y (e.g. a direct one and a second $X \to Z \to Y$). Moreover, the criteria according to which courses are connected can be refined or even re-defined by teachers - course creators.

Two or more arcs involving the same node, for example the two arcs $X \to Z$ and $Y \to Z$ can represent alternative paths (`or` arcs, whereby either X or Y must be known in order to understand the concepts in Z), or they may represent paths that are both necessary to understand the concepts in the node Z to which they refer. The two situations are modelled as `or` and `and` arcs.

Arcs are not weighted in the context of the DDB, but weights are evaluated when considering personal profile information, in order to provide learning paths in the best order for a given student (in other words, weights for arcs are not absolute but depend on each student profile).

Precedence-succession relationships are provided when courses are created and stored in the DDB in a semi-automatic fashion, i.e. based on course concepts and mediated by teachers-course creators.

Description of CN and CU. Courses can be built by the system if simple precedence-succession relationships are considered, or a teacher may build his own course based on personal educational guidelines, or again a group of teachers may provide predefined courses within a specific study context, or finally a student may require the system to build a course for his specific needs. In all these cases, courses are built considering the personal profile information stored in the Profile Database as shown in Figure 1. Moreover, not all lessons belonging to the same course need to be explicitly related by a precedence-succession relation; this occurs, for instance, when a course includes several different topics. Moreover, teachers can also explicitly indicate lesson relationships, as when suggesting specific paths to students; such relationships, however, should always be subject to precedence-succession relationships.

The DDB contains both predefined courses as well as all personalized courses created on students requests; in this way, even personalized courses can be shared and reused.

Each CN in the graph in Figure 2 features a series of information which allow the dynamic construction of adaptive learning paths: More specifically:

1. Prerequisites. The previous knowledge required.
2. Objectives. The knowledge that will be acquired.
3. Title. A title describing the course.
4. Timing (e.g. duration of the course, total time required for learning).
5. Level of abstraction of the course (e.g. highly theoretical, mostly practical)
6. Level at which topics are dealt with (e.g. introductory course, in-depth treatment, for specialists).
7. Level of detail with which contents are dealt with (general overview of problem, details of specific problems). It should be noted that the level of detail and the general level at which topics are dealt with may overlap, although there may be courses on specialist topics with a low level of detail (e.g. a survey of a specialist problem).
8. Graph of lessons making up the course.

The prerequisites indicate the knowledge the student needs to have to be able to learn the course, while the objectives indicate the knowledge that will have been acquired by the end of the course and will be included in the profile of students passing the end-of-course test. Both the prerequisites and the objectives comprise a list of keywords from the vocabulary of the domain of interest (to which the Domain Database refers).

The descriptive information associated with each CU is essentially the same as that used for the CN. This time, instead of the graph of lessons in CN, at the CU level we find information about the teaching material (called *course material* or CM) used in CU.

General remarks. It is important to establish the size (i.e. the extent in terms of contents) of each CU. From an exclusively qualitative point of view, it can be stated that too large a size (i.e. too many concepts) may make a difficult to combine CU with others when constructing a course, while too small a size may boil down to a single statement, thus becoming too fragmentary and making the CU graph very complex, with negative repercussions on the course creation algorithms as well. However, as neither of these two extreme situations is a technically insurmountable problem, it is only teaching requirements (and therefore teachers and course creators) that can establish the optimal size for each lesson.

In the case of CN size is not a problem, as the minimum is a coinciding with a CU, whereas the maximum size can only be established on the basis of teaching requirements.

Each teacher-course creator can insert new CN and/or CU into the Domain Database. To ensure the maximum teaching flexibility, it was decided not to have any control in terms of either size or overlapping of contents. In accordance with this principle, the Domain Database may contain courses that partially share the same contents but differ in the level of overall detail, for example, or the time required, or may simply reflect the different teaching methods used by several teachers.

3.2 Teaching Material Database

The TMDB contains all the teaching material (CM) used in the various stages of a course/lesson (e.g. presentation, testing), and generally comprises multimedia and/or hypertext material (e.g. HTML pages, animated graphics). It is possible to associate each CU with the flow of associated CM, where each CM is a self-contained unit of teaching material. This flow models the sequence in which the CM have to be followed. It is also possible to provide different templates for paths in which the CU can be arranged when they are associated with a given CU. For example, a typical template (as illustrated in Figure 3) could have a presentation I, followed by one or more sequences of pairs (detailed study D_i and relative test T_i), ending with an overall test T; other criteria for the creation of templates could consider the type of media, the length of the CM, the type of contents (theoretical, practical) and so on.

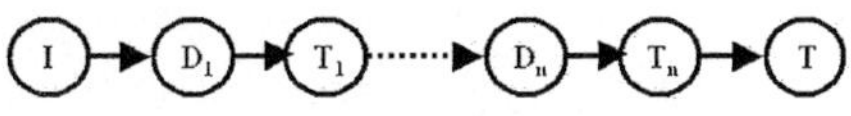

Fig. 3. A typical template for a lesson presentation path

Some remarks should be made about the relation between CU and CM. First of all, the separation between a lesson and the corresponding teaching material makes it possible to create CU without corresponding CM and vice versa, although a CU can clearly only be used if there is at least one CM connected with it, and vice versa although a inserted CM into the TMDB increases the set of available, it will only be used if there exists at least one CU in which it is inserted. Again, besides the fact that a CU can be associated with various CM, a CM can be used at the same time in different CU. This situation is not only possible but advisable to promote the reuse of teaching material.

The principle of separating lessons and teaching material also requires appropriate choice of the granularity of a CM (size in terms of contents) and its relation with the granularity of the CU, so as to:

- have an acceptable size for the CM, on the basis of considerations similar to those made for CU, that is, excessively small sizes lead to fragmentation, while excessively large sizes make them difficult to combine with other CM;
- avoid situations in which a CU cannot be associated with the teaching material because there are no CM small enough to contain only the concepts of that CU.

It is beyond the scope of this work to consider all aspects relating to the insertion of CM in the TMDB, e.g. classification criteria according to the media involved, choice of storage format, media adaptation.

4 Conclusions and Future Work

In this paper we introduced a model for an e-learning system aiming at promoting active learning, allowing the construction of courses which are personalized in terms of both contents and teaching materials, thus providing students with an adaptive environment. In particular, we focused on lessons and courses modeling, introducing a representation based on a hierarchical graph. It permits to express precedence-succession relationships among concepts as well as courses. We validated the model above presented by a prototype, it allows a student to attend on-line courses: each user logs into the system, possibly specifying his membership in a given user class (with specific characteristics), then he chooses a course (or searches for a specific topic), and consequently all the related learning paths are built, also based on that student's needs; finally, the student selects one of these paths and attends the course, which also includes exercises and tests (for details see [8]).

References

1. Soine, R.: Instructional design in a technological world: Fitting learning activities into the larger picture. (In Proc. of ICALT 2001)
2. Luchini et al., K.: An engineering process for constructing scaffolded work environments to support student inquiry: A case study in history. (In Proc. of ICALT 2001)
3. Heinrich et al., E.: Teaching cognitively complex concepts: Content representation for audiograph lectures. (In Proc. of Ed-Media 2001)
4. Vassileva, J.: Dynamic courseware generation: at the cross point of cal, its and authoring. (In Proc. of ICCE'95)
5. Anido et al., L.: A standards-driven open architecture for learning systems. (In Proc. of ICALT 2001)
6. Hampel, T., Keil-Slawik, R.: steam - designing an integrative infrastructure for web-based computer-supported cooperative learning. in Proc. of WWW10 (2001)
7. Gehne et al., R.: Technology integrated learning environment - a web-based distance learning system. (In Proc. of IASTED 2001)
8. Carchiolo, V., Longheu, A., Malgeri, M.: A model for a web-based learning system. Technical report, Dip. di Ingegneria Informatica e delle Telecomunicazioni (2002)

Fast Hardware of Booth-Barrett's Modular Multiplication for Efficient Cryptosystems

Nadia Nedjah and Luiza de Macedo Mourelle

Department of Systems Engineering and Computation,
Faculty of Engineering, State University of Rio de Janeiro, Brazil
{nadia, ldmm}@eng.uerj.br

Abstract. Modular multiplication is fundamental to several public-key cryptography systems such as the RSA encryption system. It is also the most dominant part of the computation performed in such systems. The operation is time consuming for large operands. This paper examines the characteristics of yet another architecture to implement modular multiplication. An experimental modular multiplier prototype is described in VHDL and simulated. The simulation results are presented.

1 Introduction

The modular exponentiation is a common operation for scrambling and is used by several public-key cryptosystems, such as the RSA encryption scheme [1]. It consists of a repetition of modular multiplications: $C = T^e \bmod M$, where T is the plain text such that $0 \leq T < M$ and C is the cipher text or vice-versa, e is either the public or the private key depending on whether T is the plain or the cipher text, and M is called the modulus. The decryption and encryption operations are performed using the same procedure, i.e. using the modular exponentiation [2], [3], [4]. The performance of such cryptosystems is primarily determined by the implementation efficiency of the modular multiplication and exponentiation. As the operands (the plain text of a message or the cipher or possibly a partially ciphered) text are usually large (i.e. 1024 bits or more), and in order to improve time requirements of the encryption/decryption operations, it is essential to attempt to minimise the number of modular multiplications performed and to reduce the time requirement of a single modular multiplication.

In the rest of this paper, we start off by describing the algorithms used to implement the modular operation. Then we present the architecture of the hardware modular multiplier and explain in details how it executes a single multiplication. Then we comment the simulation results obtained for such architecture.

2 Multiplication Algorithm

Algorithms that formalise the operation of multiplication generally consist of two steps: one generates a partial product and the other accumulates it with the previous partial products. The most basic algorithm for multiplication is based

A. Yazici and C. Şener (Eds.): ISCIS 2003, LNCS 2869, pp. 27–34, 2003.

on the add-and-shift method: the shift operation generates the partial products while the add step sums them up [5]. The straightforward way to implement a multiplication is based on an iterative adder-accumulator for the generated partial products. However, this solution is quite slow as the final result is only available after n clock cycles, n is the size of the operands. A faster version of the iterative multiplier should add several partial product at once. This could be achieved by unfolding the iterative multiplier and yielding a combinatorial circuit that consists of several partial product generators together with several adders that operate in parallel. In this paper, we use such a parallel multiplier as described in Fig. 1. Now, we detail the algorithms used to compute the partial products and to sum them up.

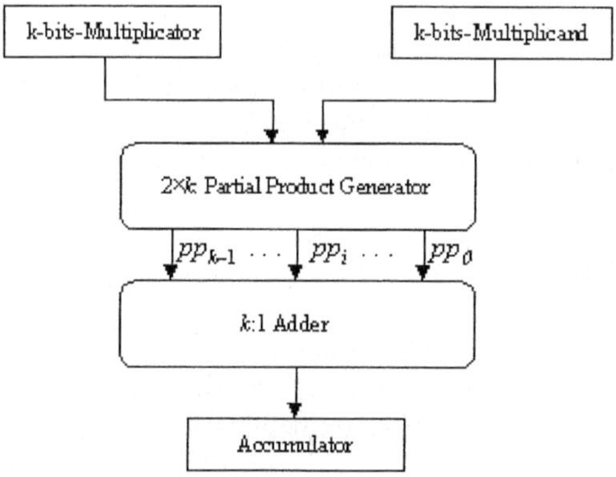

Fig. 1. Parallel multiplier architecture

Now, we concentrate on the algorithm used to compute partial products as well as reducing the corresponding number without deteriorating the space and time requirement of the multiplier. Let X and Y be the multiplicand and multiplicator respectively and let n be their size. So, we can denote X, Y and the product $X \times Y$ as follows:

$$X = \sum_{i=0}^{n-1} x_i \times 2^i,\ Y = \sum_{i=0}^{n-1} b_i \times 2^i,\ X \times Y = \sum_{i=0}^{n-1} x_i \times Y \times 2^i \tag{1}$$

Inspired by the above notation of X, Y and that of $X \times Y$, the add-and-shift method [5] generates n partial products: $x_i \times Y, 0 \leq i < n$. Each partial product obtained is shifted left or right depending on whether the starting bit was the less or the most significant and added up. The number of partial products generated is bound above by the size (i.e. number of bits) of the multiplier operand. In cryptosystems, operands are quite large as they represent blocks of text (i.e. $\geq$ 1024 bits). Another notation of X and Y allows to halve the number of partial products without much increase in space requirements. Consider the following notation of X and $X \times$Y:

$$X = \sum_{i=0}^{\lceil (n+1)/2 \rceil + 1} \tilde{x}_i \times 2^{2\times i}, \quad (2)$$

$$\tilde{x}_i = x_{2\times i-1} + x_{2\times i} - 2 \times x_{2\times i+1}, \tilde{x}_{-1} = \tilde{x}_n = \tilde{x}_{n+1} = 0 \quad (3)$$

$$X = \sum_{i=0}^{\lceil (n+1)/2 \rceil + 1} \tilde{x}_i \times Y \times 2^{2\times i}, \quad (4)$$

The possible values of with the respective values of $\tilde{x}_{2\times i+1}, x_{2\times i}$, and $x_{2\times i-1}$ are -2 (100), -1 (101, 110), 0 (000, 111), 1 (001, 010) and 2(011). Using this recoding will generates $\lceil (n+1)/2 \rceil$ partial products.

Inspired by the above notation, the modified Booth algorithm [6], [7] generates the partial products $\tilde{x} \times Y$. These partial products can be computed very efficiently due to the digits of the new representation $\tilde{x}_i$. The hardware implementation will be detailed in Section 3.

In Algorithm 1, the terms $4 \times 2^{n+1}$ and $3 \times 2^{n+1}$ are supplied to avoid working with negative numbers. The sum of these additional terms is congruent to zero modulo $2^{n+\lceil (n+1)/2 \rceil - 1}$. So, once the sum of the partial products is obtained, the rest of this sum in the division by $2^{n+\lceil (n+1)/2 \rceil - 1}$ is finally the result of the multiplication $X \times Y$.

Algorithm 1. ModMulti($x_{2\times i-1}, x_{2\times i}, x_{2\times i+1}, Y$)
  int product = 0; int[] pp[$\lceil (n+1)/2 \rceil - 1$];pp[0]= $(\tilde{x}_i \times Y + 4 \times 2^{n+1}) \times 2^{2\times i}$;
  for i=0 to $\lceil (n+1)/2 \rceil - 1$
    pp[i] = $(\tilde{x}_i \times Y + 3 \times 2^{n+1}) \times 2^{2\times i}$;product = product + pp[i];
  return product mod $2^{n+\lceil (n+1)/2 \rceil - 1}$;
end.

3 Reduction Algorithm

A modular reduction is simply the computation of the remainder of an integer division. It can be denoted by:

$$X mod M = X - \left\lfloor \frac{X}{M} \right\rfloor \times M \quad (5)$$

However, a division is very expensive even compared with a multiplication. Using Barrett's method [8], we can estimate the remainder using two simple multiplications. The approximation of the quotient is calculated as follows:

$$\left\lfloor \frac{X}{M} \right\rfloor = \left\lfloor \frac{\left\lfloor \frac{X}{2^{n-1}} \right\rfloor \times \left\lfloor \frac{2^{n-1} \times 2^{n+1}}{M} \right\rfloor}{2^{n+1}} \right\rfloor \approx \left\lfloor \frac{\left\lfloor \frac{X}{2^{n-1}} \right\rfloor \times \left\lfloor \frac{2^{2\times n}}{M} \right\rfloor}{2^{n+1}} \right\rfloor \quad (6)$$

The equation above can be calculated very efficiently as division by a power of two 2^x are simply a truncation of x-least significant digits of the operand. The term $\lfloor 2^{2\times n}/M \rfloor$ depends only on the modulus M and is constant for a given modulus. Hence, can be pre-computed and saved in an extra register. Hence the approximation of the remainder using Barrett's method [8] is a positive integer smaller than $2 \times (M - 1)$. So, one or two subtractions of M might be required to yield the exact remainder.

4 Modular Multiplier Architecture

In this section, we outline the architecture of the multiplier, which is depicted in Fig. 2. Later on in this section and for each of the main parts of this architecture, we give the detailed circuitry, i.e. that of the partial product generator, adder and reducer. The multiplier of Fig. 2 performs the modular multiplication $X \times Y$ mod M in four main steps:

1. Computing the product $P = X \times Y$;
2. Computing the estimate quotient $Q = P/M \Rightarrow Q \approx P/2^{n-1} \times \lceil 2^{2\times n}/M \rceil$;
3. Computing the product $Q \times M$;
4. Computing the final result $P - Q \times M$.

During the first step, the modular multiplier first loads $register_1$ and $register_2$ with X and Y respectively; then waits for PPG to yield the partial products and finally waits for the $ADDER$ to sum all of them. During the second step, the modular multiplier loads $register_1, register_2$ and $register_3$ with the obtained product P, the pre-computed constant $\lceil 2^{2\times n}/M \rceil$ and P respectively; then waits for PPG to yield the partial products and finally waits for the $ADDER$ to sum all of them. During the third step, the modular multiplier first loads $register_1$ and $register_2$ with the obtained product Q and the modulus M respectively; then awaits for PPG to generate the partial products, then waits for the $ADDER$ to provide the sum of these partial products and finally waits for the $REDUCER$ to calculate the final result $P - Q \times M$, which is subsequently loaded in the accumulator ACC.

4.1 The Multiplier

The multiplier interface is composed of the multiplicand and multiplicator as input signals and the partial products $PP_i, 0 \leq i < k$, each one of $n + 3$ bits, as output signals. It is composed of a partial product generator and an adder. The partial product generator is in turn composed of k *Booth recoders* [6], [7] that communicate directly with k partial product selectors. The interface of the Booth decoder is composed of three bits, $lsb, midle$ and msb, as input signals and it outputs the signals $SelectY, Select2Y$ and $Sign$.

The Booth selection logic circuitry used is very simple. The inputs are the three bits forming the Booth digit and outputs are three bits: the first one

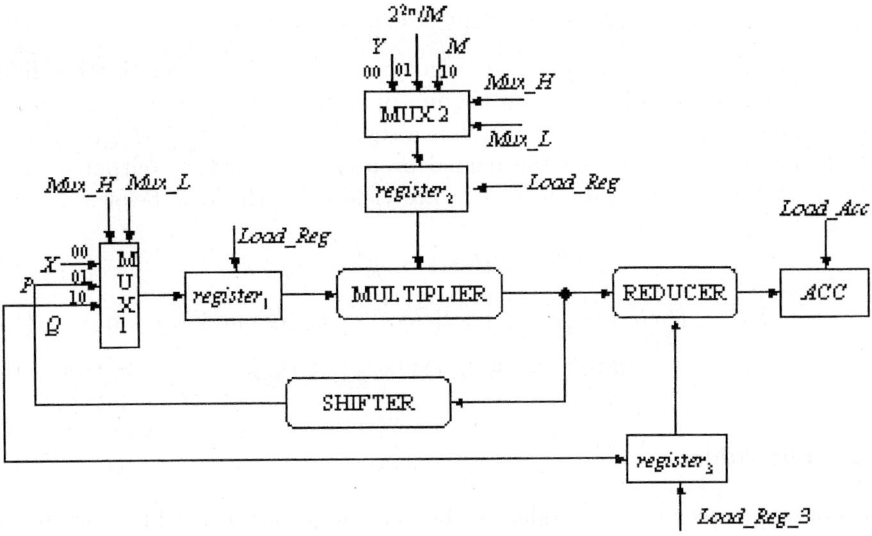

Fig. 2. Architecture of the modular multiplier

SelectY is set when the partial product to be generated is Y or $-Y$, the second one *Select*$2Y$ is set when the partial product to be generated is $2 \times Y$ or $-2 \times Y$ and the last bit is simply the last bit of the Booth digit given as input. It allows us to complement the bits of the partial products when a negative multiple is needed. The output signals are yielded from the input ones as follows:

$$SelectY = lsb \oplus midle; \; Sign = msb \tag{7}$$

$$Select2Y = \neg(\neg(middle \oplus msb) + (lsb \oplus midle)) \tag{8}$$

The required partial products, i.e. $\tilde{x} \times Y$ are easy multiples. They can be obtained by a simple shift. The negative multiples in 2's complement form, can be obtained form the positive corresponding number using a bit by bit complement with a 1 added at the least significant bit of the partial product. The additional terms introduced in the previous section can be included into the partial product generated as three/two/one most significant bits computed as follows, whereby, $++$ is the bits concatenation operation, $\langle A \rangle$ is the binary notation of integer A, 0^i is a run of i zeros and $B_{[n:0]}$ is the selection of the n less significant bits of the binary representation B.

$$\langle pp_0 \rangle = \overline{s_0} s_0 s_0 + + \langle |\tilde{x_0} \times Y \oplus s_0 \rangle + s_0 \tag{9}$$

$$\langle pp_{2\times j} \rangle = (1\overline{s_{2\times j}} + + \langle |\tilde{x}_{2\times j}| \times Y \oplus s_{2\times j} \rangle + s_{2\times j}) + + 0^{2\times j} \tag{10}$$

For $1 \leq j < k-1$ and $j = k-1 = k\prime$, we have:

$$\langle pp_{2\times k\prime} \rangle = (1\overline{s_{2\times k\prime}} + + \langle |\tilde{x}_{2\times k\prime}| \times Y \oplus s_{2\times k\prime} \rangle + s_{2\times k\prime}) + + 0^{2\times k\prime} \tag{11}$$

$$\langle pp_{2\times k}\rangle = \langle|\tilde{x}_{2\times k} \times Y\rangle_{[n:0]} + +0^{2\times k} \tag{12}$$

The interface of the partial product generator is consists of the Booth's digit, which is constituted of 3 bits and the multiplicand, which has n bits, as input signals and the partial product, which is a signal of $n+1$ bits, and an extra bit which represents the sign of the partial product generated, as output signals. The $n+1$ bits of partial products PP_i are yield using the logic below:

$$PP_i^0 = (SelectY \times y_0) \oplus Sign \tag{13}$$

$$PP_i^i = (Select2Y \times y_{i-1}) + SelectY \times y_i \oplus Sign, 1 \leq i \leq n \tag{14}$$

$$PP_i^{n+1} = (Select2Y \times y_n) \oplus Sign \tag{15}$$

4.2 The Adder

In order to implement the adder of the generated partial products, we use a hybrid new kind of adder. It consists of an initial stage of carry save adders followed by a cascade of stages of delayed carry adders [7] and a final stage of full adder. The carry save adder CSA is simply a parallel ensemble of f full adders without any horizontal connection. Its function is to add three f-bit integers a, b and c to yield two new integers *carry* and *sum* such that $carry + sum = a + b + c$. The pair $(carry, sum)$ will be called a delayed carry integer. The delayed carry adder DCA is a parallel ensemble of f half adders. Its function is to add two delayed carry integers (a_1, b_1) and (a_2, b_2) together with an integer c to produce a delayed carry integer $(sum, carry)$ such that $sum + carry = a_1 + b_1 + a_2 + b_2 + c$. The general architecture of the proposed adder is depicted in Fig. 3, where the partial products $PP_i, 0 \leq i \leq 15$ are the input operands.

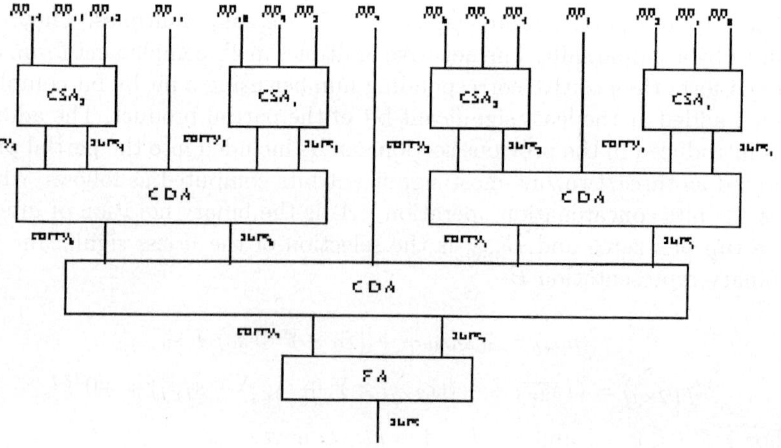

Fig. 3. The main cell of the proposed adder

Using the carry save adder, the ith bit of $carry$ and sum are defined as $sum_i = a_i \oplus b_i \oplus c_i$ and $carry_i = a_i \times b_i + a_i \times c_i + b_i \times c_i$ respectively. The architecture of the delayed carry adder uses $5 \times n$ half adders as in Fig. 4.

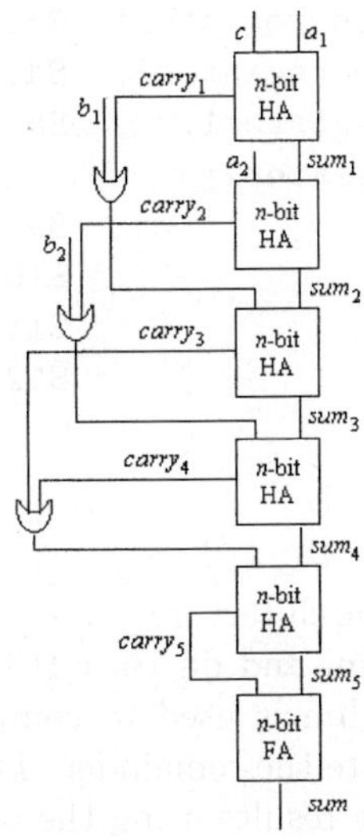

Fig. 4. The structure of the delayed carry adder

4.3 The Reducer

The main task of the reducer consists of subtracting $Q \times M$, i.e. the product obtained in the third step of the modular multiplier from P, i.e. the product computed in the first step of the modular multiplier. A subtraction of an p-bit integer K is equivalent to the addition of $2^p - x$. Hence the reducer simply performs the addition $P + (2^{n+m} - Q \times M)$. The latter value is simply the two's complement of $Q \times M$.

The addition is performed using a carry look-ahead adder. It is based on computing the carry bits C_i prior to the actual summation. The adder takes advantage of a relationship between carry bits C_i and input bits A_i and B_i, wherein $G_i = A_i \times B_i$ and $P_i = A_i + B_i$.

$$C_i = G_{i-1} + (G_{i-2} + \ldots + (G_1 + (G_0 + C_0 P_0) \times P_1 \ldots) \times P_{i-1}) \qquad (16)$$

4.4 The Controller

In order to synchronise the work of the *MULTIPLIER*, *ADDER* and *REDUCER*, we designed a module called the *CONTROLLER* that consists of a simple state machine, that has 13 states defined as follows: where $next(S_i) = S_{i+1}$ and $next(S_{12}) = S_0$.

```
S0: Initialise state machine;
S1: Load multiplicator into register1;
    Load multiplicand into register2;
S2: Wait for MULTIPLIER;
S3: Wait for ADDER;
S4: Wait for the SHIFTER;
S5: Load product P into register1;
    Load constant into register2;
    Load P into register3;
S6: Wait for MULTIPLIER;
S7: Wait for ADDER;
S8: Load Q into register1;
    Load M into register2;
S9: Wait for MULTIPLIER;
S10: Wait for ADDER;
S11: Wait for REDUCER;
S12: Load ACC with result.
```

5 Conclusion

In this paper, an alternative architecture for computing modular multiplication based on Booth's algorithm and on Barrett's relaxed residium method is described. The Booth's algorithm is used to compute the product while Barrett's method is used to calculate the remainder. The architecture was validated through behavioural simulation results using the 0.6mm CMOS-AMS standard cell library. The total execution time is 3570 nanoseconds for 1024-bit operands. One of the advantages of this modular multiplication implementation resides in the fact that it is easily scalable with respect to the multiplier and modulus lengths.

References

1. R. Rivest, A. Shamir and L. Adleman, A method for obtaining digital signature and public-key cryptosystems, Communications of the ACM 21, (1978) 120–126
2. E. F. Brickell, A survey of hardware implementation of RSA, Proc. of CRYPTO'98, Lecture Notes in Computer Science 435, Springer-Verlag, (1989) 368–370
3. C. D. Walter, Systolic modular multiplication, IEEE Transactions on Computers 42(3), (1993) 376–378
4. S. E. Eldridge and C. D. Walter, Hardware implementation of Montgomery's Modular Multiplication Algorithm, IEEE Transactions on Computers 42(6), (1993) 619–624
5. J. Rabaey, Digital integrated circuits: A design perspective, Prentice-Hall, (1995)
6. A. Booth, A signed binary multiplication technique, Journal of Mechanics and Applied Mathematics, (1951) 236–240
7. O. MacSorley, High-speed arithmetic in binary computers, Proc. of the IRE, (1961) 67–91
8. P. Barrett, Implementating the Rivest, Shamir and Aldham public-key encryption algorithm on standard digital signal processor, Proc. of CRYPTO'86, Lecture Notes in Computer Science 263, Springer-Verlag, (1986) 311–323

Classification of a Large Web Page Collection Applying a GRNN Architecture

Ioannis Anagnostopoulos, Christos Anagnostopoulos, Vergados Dimitrios, Vassili Loumos, and Eleftherios Kayafas

School of Electrical and Computer Engineering,
Heroon Polytechneiou 9, Zographou, 15773, Athens, GREECE
janag@telecom.ece.ntua.gr

Abstract. This paper proposes an information system that classifies web pages according a taxonomy, which is mainly used from seven search engines/ directories. The proposed classifier is a four-layer Generalised Regression Neural Network (GRNN) that aims to perform the information segmentation according to web page features. Many types of web pages were used in order to evaluate the robustness of the method, since no restrictions were imposed except for the language of the content, which is English. The system can be used as an assistant and consultative tool in order to help the work of human editors.

1 Introduction

The techniques most usually employed in the classification of web pages use concepts from the field of information filtering and retrieval [1], [2]. Such techniques usually analyse a corpus of already classified web page contents, extract from them words and phrases with the use of specific algorithms, process the terms and then form thesauri and indices. A second large group of techniques are neural networks. Neural networks are chosen mainly for computational reasons, since once trained, they operate very fast and the creation of thesauri and indices is avoided [3], [4]. Nevertheless, basic concepts from information filtering and retrieval are still used in the computations in order to achieve the best possible results. In addition, the use of evolution-based genetic algorithms, and the utilization of fuzzy function approximation have also been presented as possible solutions for the classification problem [5], [6]. Finally, many experimental investigations on the use of neural networks for implementing relevance feedback in an interactive information retrieval system have been proposed [7].

2 Collection of Web Pages

Based on both information filtering techniques and artificial neural networks this paper describes a Generalised Regression Neural Network that distinguishes web

A. Yazici and C. Şener (Eds.): ISCIS 2003, LNCS 2869, pp. 35–42, 2003.

pages under a common taxonomy used by seven search engines/directories. The classification is performed by estimating the likelihood of an input feature vector according to computations of Parzen window estimations. Moreover, the information filtering technique is based on a multi-dimensional descriptor vector (Web Page Delineator - WPD), which when applied in a proper way, it assigns a unique profile to every processed web page. The composed initial material consists of 4000 randomly collected web pages (8 classes x 500 web pages per class) with the help of a meta-search tool described in [8]. This large set was used in order to find the terms that are capable of describing each one of the eight information clusters. An information cluster is represented as a separate class in the proposed classifier and it is equivalent to the classified web page class. Furthermore, the same large amount of web pages was used for training purposes. It must be noted that only web pages with English content were finally used in this work. The content of each web page was distinguished to the meta-tags, to some special tags and finally to the disseminated plain text. Table 1 presents the search engines used, the eight distinct classes as well as the contributed information clusters per search engine/directory respectively.

Table 1. Distinct classes and contributed information categories per search engine/directory

	Arts Humanities	**Computers Internet**	**Health**	**News Media**	**Recreation Sports**	**Reference Libraries**	**Science**	**Business Economy**
Directory \ Class	z_1	z_2	z_3	z_4	z_5	z_6	z_7	z_8
AltaVista		√			√	√		√
DMOZ	√	√	√	√		√	√	
Excite		√	√	√	√			
Lycos		√	√	√				√
MSN Search		√			√	√		√
Netscape Search	√	√	√	√	√	√	√	√
Yahoo!	√	√	√	√	√	√	√	√

3 Feature Selection

The WPD holds a large amount of terms and scopes to assign a unique profile in each tested web page, as it will be described during the next sections. It consists of eight term groups, which correspond to the eight candidate information clusters. This section describes how the required terms were collected in order to construct the term group "Business – Economy", while the rest term groups were created similarly.

In order to extract the semantic terms, which represent in a sufficient way the pages that provide Business or Economy information to the web users, 500 web pages were collected from the used search engine directories, except DMOZ and Excite as depicted in Table 1. These pages are considered as the sample set for the respective information cluster. After this process, all the indexed terms were collected and a specific value-weight is assigned to them. In addition this procedure used a stop list in order to remove common function words [9]. In parallel, a character filter excluded numbers, punctuation symbols, accented letters and other worthless text marks. The frequency of each term was calculated in respect to how many times the specific term appeared in the disseminated content of the tested web page. In the literature this weight is called normalised frequency of term *k* (tf_k) [2]. After applying the stop list, a suffix-stripping method generated word stems for the remaining entries according to Porter's Algorithm and all terms were transformed to their corresponding word-stem [10]. Then in each stem, the cumulative normalised frequency of all the collected words produced by this stem was assigned. In order to finally determine the terms (word-stems) that best describe the specific information cluster, the distribution of the normalised frequency tf_k in respect to the rank order of each term, was examined. At the left of Figure 1 is presented the distribution of the extracted word-stems according to their re-weighted frequencies versus their rank order for the "Business – Economy" information cluster. The threshold for this information cluster in terms of tf_k was equal to 0.0035 and stems with higher values, which exist in area A was considered as candidate terms.

However, 35 from 43 stems were finally collected, since the rest terms were not considered as suitable for the respective information cluster according to the knowledge of expert editors. Hence, they were excluded from the respective term group. After applying the above procedure in order to create the term groups for all the information clusters, an additional information filtering technique was followed. Nevertheless, this time the inverse document frequency was taken under consideration [2]. This indicator distinguishes the terms, which have a large discriminative power to characterise a document over a massive document collection. Thus, having the URLs for the 4000 web pages, which were randomly selected as described in section 2, the source codes were downloaded and all words were transformed to their corresponding stems along with their re-weighted inverse document frequencies. Using this kind of frequency, terms that best distinguish each information clusters and potentially were not collected in the previous procedure were eventually included in the 'Business – Economy' term group. The inverse document frequency corresponds to the logarithmic ratio of the number of web pages that contain the term *k* in the total indexed web pages per information cluster, as expressed in Equation 1, where idf_k, n_k and N is the inverse document frequency of term k, the number of web pages that contain term k and the total indexed web pages per information cluster. In addition f_k^m, NW_m and tf_k^m correspond to the frequency of term *k*, the total number of terms as well as the normalised frequency of term *k* in web page *m*, respectively. At the right, Figure 1 also presents the correlation between the average values of inverse document frequencies for each word-stem, according to their rank order for all information clusters. The above correlation was modelled with a Normal distribution, according to the inverse document frequencies of the indexed terms. The mean value $(\bar{x})$ was equal to 0,088194 and the variance (σ) equal to 0,011305.

It was finally decided to use as a representative term set the ranking region, which its inverse document frequency value is above $(\bar{x})+5\sigma$. The highlighted area above this value (threshold *T*), hold the terms, which presents the 53 higher values in terms of discriminative power. However, 44 terms were added in the WPD term index, since 9 of them had been already collected during the previous information filtering procedure

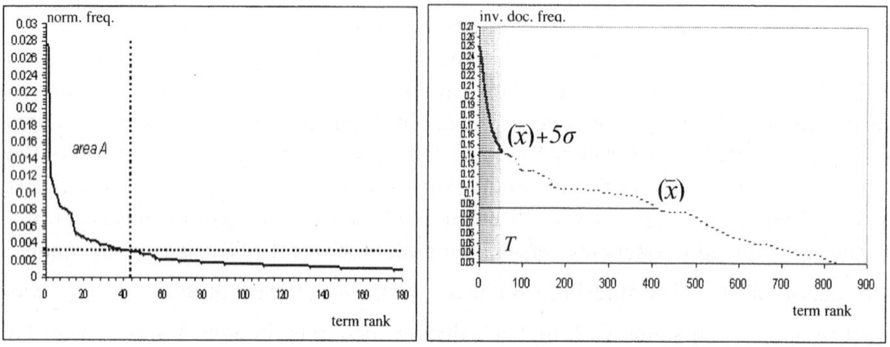

Fig. 1. Norm. frequencies and inv. doc. freq. according to stem rank order

$$w_k^m = tf_k^m \cdot idf_k = \left(\frac{f_k^m}{NW_m}\right) \cdot \left|\log\left(\frac{n_k}{N}\right)\right| \tag{1}$$

Finally, having completed the aforementioned procedure for all information clusters, the extracted word-stems from the eight term groups were merged and the duplicate fields were eliminated creating by this the final term set of the WPD. The amount of the collected terms according the normalised frequency for all the information clusters was 267 word-stems, while in respect to the inverse document frequency 44 word stems. Thus, the total amount of the unique terms used in the descriptor vector was 311. This number is quite important since it is related to the number of the neural network nodes in the input layer.

4 The Proposed Neural Network Classifier

Generalised Regression Neural Networks (GRNNs) have the special ability to deal with sparse and non-stationary data whose statistical properties change over time. Due to their generality, they can be also used in various problems where non-linear relationships exist among inputs and outputs. The addressed problem can be considered to belong in this category since it is a document-mapping problem. A GRNN is designed to perform a non-linear regression analysis. Thus, if $f(x,z)$ is the probability density function of the vector random variable x and its scalar random variable z, then the GRNN calculates the conditional mean $E(z \setminus x)$ of the output vector. The joint probability density function (pdf) $f(x,z)$ is required to compute the above conditional mean. GRNN approximates the pdf from the training vectors using Parzen windows estimation, which is a non-parametric technique approximating a function by constructing it out of many simple parametric probability density functions. Parzen windows are considered as Gaussian functions with a constant diagonal covariance matrix according to Equation 2.

$$E(z \setminus x) = \frac{\int_{-\infty}^{\infty} z \cdot f(x,z)dz}{\int_{-\infty}^{\infty} f(x,z)dz} \text{, where} \tag{2}$$

$$f_p(x \setminus z) = \frac{1}{(2\pi\sigma^2)^{(N+1)/2}} \cdot \frac{1}{P} \sum_{i=1}^{P} \left(e^{\frac{-D_i^2}{2\sigma^2}} \cdot e^{\frac{-(z-x_i)^2}{2\sigma^2}} \right)$$

In the above equation P equals to the number of sample points x_i, N is the dimension of the vector of sample points, D_i is the Euclidean distance between x and x_i calculated by $D_i = \|x - x_i\| = \sqrt{\sum_{i=1}^{N} (x - x_i)^2}$, where N is the amount of the input units to the network. Additionally, σ is a width parameter, which satisfies the asymptotic behaviour as the number of Parzen windows becomes large according to Equation 3 where S is the scale. When an estimated pdf is included in $E(z \setminus x)$, the substitution process defines Equation 4 in order to compute each component z_j.

$$\lim_{P\to\infty}(P\sigma^N(P)) = \infty \text{ and}$$

$$\lim_{P\to\infty} \sigma(P) = 0 \text{, when } \sigma = \frac{S}{P^{E/N}},\ 0 \le E < 1 \tag{3}$$

$$z_j(x) = \frac{\sum_{i=1}^{P} z_j^i c_i}{\sum_{i=1}^{P} c_i} \text{, where } c_i = e^{\frac{-D_i^2}{2\sigma^2}} \tag{4}$$

However, due to the fact that the computation of Parzen estimation is a time consuming procedure when the sample is large, a clustering procedure is often incorporated in GRNN, where for any given sample x_i, instead of computing the new Gaussian kernel k_i at centre x each time, the distance of that sample to the closest centre of a previously established kernel is found, and the old closest kernel $(k\text{-}1)_i$ is used again. Taking into account this approach, Equation 4 is transformed to Equation 5.

$$z_j(x) = \frac{\sum_{i=1}^{P} A_i(k)c_i}{\sum_{i=1}^{P} B_i(k)c_i},\ 1 \le j \le M,\ A_i(k) = A_i(k-1) + z_j,\ B_i(k) = B_i(k-1) + 1 \tag{5}$$

The topology of the proposed neural network is 311-80-8-8 and it is presented in Figure 2. The input layer consists of 311 nodes, which correspond to the number of the WPD terms. The second layer is the pattern layer, which organises the training set in such a way, that 50 training exemplars from the same information cluster are represented by an individual element that averages their term weights. Therefore, 8 nodes represent each information cluster (400 training exemplars per cluster / 50 averaged training exemplars), while the total number of nodes in the pattern layer is 80 (8 nodes per cluster x 10 clusters). It follows the summation/division layer, which consists of 8 nodes that feed a same amount of processing elements in the output layer representing the 8 web page classes to be recognised. The total number of synapses between the input and the pattern layer is *311x80*, while between the pattern and the summation layer is *80x8.*

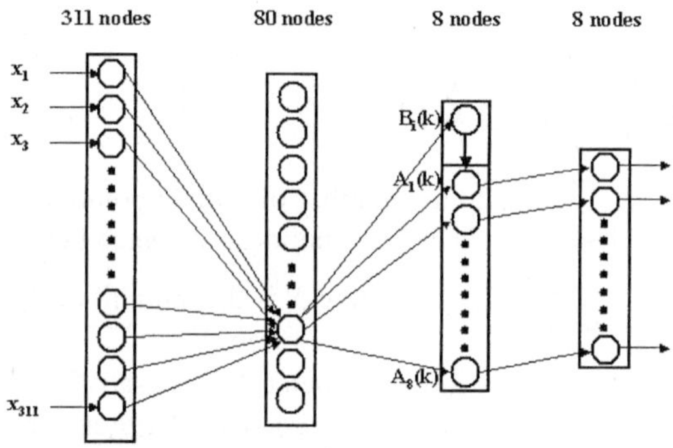

Fig. 2. The topology of the proposed GRNN

From the input to the pattern layer a training/test vector X is distributed, while the connection weights from the input layer to the kth unit in the pattern layer store the centre X_i of the kth Gaussian kernel. In the pattern layer the summation function for the kth pattern unit computes the Euclidean distance D_k between the input vector and the stored centre X_i and transforms it through the previously described exponential function c_i. Afterwards, the B coefficients are set as weights values to the remaining units in the next layer. In the summation/division layer the summation function computes the denominator of Equation 4 for the first unit j and then the numerator for the next unit $(j+1)$. Thus, in order to compute the output of the respective function, the summation of the numerator is divided by the summation of denominator and such output is forwarded to the output layer. Finally, the output layer receives inputs from the summation/division layer and outputs are estimated conditional means, computing the error on the basis of the desired output.

4.1 Training/Testing the Classifier

The GRNN was implemented in C++ and trained in a Pentium IV, 1.5 GHz, 1024 MB RAM. The time needed for the completion of the training epoch, was approximately 4 minutes. During the training period, the 'beta' coefficient for all the local approximators of the pattern layer, which was used to smooth the data being monitored, was set to 100 $(\beta = 1/2\sigma^2=100)$. In addition, the mean and the variance values of the randomised biases were equal to 0 and 0.5 respectively. The values inside the parentheses in Table 2 correspond to the confusion matrix of the training epoch in percentage values. This matrix is defined by labelling the desired classification on the rows and the predicted classifications on the columns. Since the predicted classification has to be the same as the desired classification, the ideal situation was to have all the exemplars end up on the diagonal cells of the matrix. This implies that in the diagonal cells the ideal percentage has to be 100. However, this was not attained, verifying the complexity of the problem addressed. Therefore, the training confusion matrix displays values, where each one corresponds to the percentage effect that a particular input has on a particular output. As it is obvious, higher values in the non-diagonal cells imply more uncertainty, which would eventually lead to higher probabilities of misclassification between the involved classes.

Table 2. Confusion Matrices: training (percentage values) / testing (absolute values)

		Class Assigned by the GRNN								P (%)
		z_1	z_2	z_3	z_4	z_5	z_6	z_7	z_8	
Actual Page Type	z_1	(100) 829	(0) 28	(0) 31	(0) 29	(0) 22	(0) 16	(0) 24	(0) 21	**82.9**
	z_2	(0) 26	(99.2) 798	(0.2) 38	(0.4) 44	(0) 25	(0.1) 29	(0.1) 22	(0) 18	**79.8**
	z_3	(0.2) 48	(0.2) 36	(98.4) 742	(0.8) 44	(0) 32	(0.3) 27	(0.1) 28	(0) 43	**74.2**
	z_4	(0.1) 42	(0) 29	(0.7) 48	(98.4) 734	(0) 57	(0.5) 39	(0.2) 27	(0.1) 24	**73.4**
	z_5	(0) 21	(0) 26	(0) 25	(0) 38	(100) 822	(0) 23	(0) 19	(0) 26	**82.2**
	z_6	(0) 19	(0) 21	(0) 10	(0) 24	(0) 22	(100) 868	(0) 19	(0) 17	**86.8**
	z_7	(0) 25	(0) 27	(0) 23	(0) 25	(0) 19	(0) 28	(100) 835	(0) 18	**83.5**
	z_8	(0) 12	(0) 14	(0) 19	(0) 14	(0) 22	(0) 18	(0) 24	(100) 877	**87.7**
							Overall Performance			**81.31**

The proposed information system was tested with 8000 web pages of different size in Kbytes (1000 web pages per tested class). Values not included in parentheses in Table 2 form the testing confusion matrix between the tested classes. The diagonal cells correspond to the correctly classified web pages for each class respectively (absolute values), while the other cells show the misclassified pages. In every row, the system's ability in terms of correct classification over an 'a priori' known type of web pages is tested. The overall performance of the system outlines the ability to correctly classify the tested web pages in respect to the sample set for all the tested classes. Therefore, it is derived from the total amount of the correctly classified web pages residing in the diagonal cells, versus the total amount of the sample set (*overall performance* $= 6505/8000 \approx 81.3\%$). Generally, the implemented GRNN presents a high level of accuracy in testing most of the classes. Lower discrimination performance has been measured for classes z_3, z_4. However, this was expected, since in the training period there was an important amount of not properly 'learned' training elements between these classes, as highlighted in the respective percentage values in Table 2.

5 Conclusions

This paper proposes a four layer Generalised Regression Neural Network with biases and radial basis neurons in the middle layer and competitive neurons in the output layer in order to classify a massive collection of several types of web pages. The classification is based on a taxonomy followed by seven popular search engines and directories. The neural network was trained with 4000 randomly collected web pages with equivalent amount for every trained class. The testing set consists of 8000 web pages, measuring the overall performance as well as the performance of the classifier in respect to each distinct class. Serious limitations in terms of large memory requirements and execution speed did not appear, establishing this proposal as an innovative and sufficient solution for the 1-of-K class classification problem. An interesting aspect, which is left for future work is to expand the system ability in order to relative classify the tested web pages in the respective 10 categories.

References

1. C.J. van Rijsbergen, Information Retrieval, Butterworths, London, Second Edition, 1979.
2. G. Salton, Automatic Text Processing, Addison-Wesley Publishing Company Inc, 1989.
3. Kohonen T., Kaski S., Lagus K., Salojarvi J., Honkela J., Paatero V. and Saarela A., 'Self organization of a massive document collection', IEEE Transactions on Neural Networks, 11(3):574–585, Special Issue on Neural Networks for Data Mining and Knowledge Discovery, May 2000.
4. Chung-Hsin Lin, Hsinchun Chen, 'An automatic indexing and neural network approach to concept retrieval and classification of multilingual (Chinese-English) documents', IEEE Transactions on Systems, Man and Cybernetics, Part B, pp. 75–88 Feb. 1996.
5. Rialle V., Meunier J., Oussedik S., Nault G., 'Semiotic and Modeling Computer Classification of Text with Genetic Algorithm: Analysis and first Results', Proceedings ISAS'97, pp. 325–30, 1997.
6. Petridis, V., Kaburlasos, V.G, 'Clustering and classification in structured data domains using Fuzzy Lattice Neurocomputing (FLN)', IEEE Transactions on Knowledge and Data Engineering, Volume: 13 Issue: 2 , March-April 2001, pp. 245–260.
7. Anagnostopoulos I., Anagnostopoulos C., Papaleonidopoulos I., Loumos V. and Kayafas E., 'A proposed system for segmentation of information sources in portals and search engines repositories', 5th IEEE International Conference of Information Fusion 2000, IF2002, pp. 1450–1456, vol.2, 7–11 July 2002, Annapolis, Maryland, USA.
8. Anagnostopoulos I., Psoroulas I., Loumos V. and Kayafas E., Implementing a customised meta-search interface for user query personalisation, IEEE 24th International Conference on Information Technology Interfaces, ITI 2002 pp. 79–84, June 24–27, 2002, Cavtat/Dubrovnik, CROATIA.
9. Fox C., A stop list for general text,. ACM Special Interest Group on Information Retrieval, 24 (1–2), pp. 19–35.
10. Ricardo B., Berthier R., Modern Information Retrieval, Addison-Wesley Longman Publishing Co. Inc., 1999, Appendix: Porter's Algorithm.

Fast Less Recursive Hardware for Large Number Multiplication Using Karatsuba-Ofman's Algorithm

Nadia Nedjah and Luiza de Macedo Mourelle

Department of Systems Engineering and Computation,
Faculty of Engineering, State University of Rio de Janeiro, Brazil
{nadia, ldmm}@eng.uerj.br

Abstract. Multiplication of long integers is a cornerstone primitive in most cryptosystems. Multiplication for big numbers can be performed best using Karatsuba-Ofman's divide-and-conquer approach. Multiplying long integers using Karatsuba-Ofman's algorithm is fast but the algorithm is highly recursive. We propose a less recursive and efficient hardware architecture for this algorithm. We compare the proposed multiplier to other existing ones.

1 Introduction

Modular exponentiation is nonlinear scrambling operation used in most cryptosystems [1]. It consists of performing modular multiplication repeatedly. Modular multiplication can be performed by first multiplying then reducing or by interleaving the multiplication and reduction steps [2]. The former way is preferred as there are very fast multiplication on-the-shelf algorithms [3] while the latter is used when there is only a limited storage as it is the case of smart cards [4]. Here, we concentrate on specifying a novel recursive hardware that is most adequate to the recursive multiplication algorithm proposed by Karatsuba and Ofman [3].

Karatsuba-Ofman's algorithm is based on a divide-and-conquer strategy. A multiplication of a $2n$-digit integer is reduced to two n-digits multiplications, one $(n+1)$-digits multplication, two n-digits subtractions, two left-shift operations, two n-digits additions and two $2n$-digits additions. However, the algorithm is highly recursive. Here, we engineer a less recursive architecture [5] and thus more compact but not less efficient.

This paper is organised as follows: In Section 2, we describe the Karatsuba-Ofman's algorithm and sketch its complexity. In Section 3, we adapt the algorithm so that it can be implemented efficiently. In Section 4, we propose a less recursive and efficient architecture of the hardware multiplier for Karatsuba-Ofman's algorithm. In Section 5, we engineer a novel architecture for 4-bit multiplier. In Section 6, we present some figures concerning time and space requirements of the obtained multiplier. We then compare our hardware with two other multipliers that implement Booth's multiplication algorithm.

A. Yazici and C. Şener (Eds.): ISCIS 2003, LNCS 2869, pp. 43–50, 2003.

2 Karatsuba-Ofman's Algorithm

We now describe the details of Karatsuba-Ofman's multiplication algorithm [3]. Let X and Y be the binary representation of two long integers:

$$X = \sum_{i=0}^{n-1} x_i \times 2^i,\ Y = \sum_{i=0}^{n-1} b_i \times 2^i \tag{1}$$

We wish to compute efficiently the product XY. The operands X and Y can be decomposed into to equal-size parts X_H and X_L, Y_H and Y_L respectively, which represent the n higher order bits and lower order bits of X and Y. Let $k = 2n$. If k is odd, it can be right-padded with a zero. The product $P = XY$ can be computed as indicated in Equation (4) and Equation (5):

$$X = 2^n \left(\sum_{i=0}^{n-1} x_{i+n} 2^i\right) + \sum_{i=0}^{n-1} x_i 2^i = X_H 2^n + X_L, \tag{2}$$

$$Y = 2^n \left(\sum_{i=0}^{n-1} y_{i+n} 2^i\right) + \sum_{i=0}^{n-1} y_i 2^i = Y_H 2^n + Y_L, \tag{3}$$

$$P = XY = (X_H 2^n + X_L)(Y_H 2^n + Y_L) \tag{4}$$

$$P = 2^{2n}(X_H Y_H) + 2^n (X_H Y_L + X_L Y_H) + X_L Y_L \tag{5}$$

Using the equation above, it needs 4 n-bits multiplications to compute the product P. The standard multiplication algorithm is based on that equation. So assuming that a multiplication of k-bits operands is performed using $T(k)$ one-bit operations, we can formulate $T(k)$ as in Equation (6), wherein δk is a number of one-bit operations to compute all the additions and shift operations. Considering that $T(1) = 1$, we find that the standard multiplication algorithm has the complexity stipulated in Equation (7). However, The computation of P can be improved by noticing Equation (8):

$$T(k) = 4T(n) + \delta k \tag{6}$$

$$T(k) = \theta\left(k^{log_2 4}\right) = \theta\left(k^2\right) \tag{7}$$

$$X_H Y_L + X_L Y_H = (X_H + X_L)(Y_H + Y_L) - X_H Y_H - X_L Y_L \tag{8}$$

The Karatsuba-Ofman's algorithm is based on the above observation and so the $2n$-bits multiplication can be reduced to three n-bits multiplications, namely $X_H Y_H$, $X_L Y_L$ and $(X_H + X_L)(Y_H + Y_L)$. The Karatsuba-Ofman's multiplication method can then be expressed as in Algorithm 1, wherein function $|X|$ represents the number of bits of X, function $High(X)$ returns the higher half part of X, function $Low(X)$ returns the lower half of X, $RShift(X, n)$ returns $X2^n$ and $OneBitMultiplier(X, Y)$ returns XY when both X and Y are of size 1. If $|X|$ is odd, then we right-pad X with a zero before extracting the high and the low half respectively.

```
Algorithm 1. KO(X, Y)
  if |X| = 1 then KO := OneBitMultiplier(X, Y)
  else P1 := KO(High(X), High(Y));
       P2 := KO(Low(X), Low(Y));
       P3 := KO(High(X) + Low(X), High(Y) + Low(Y));
       KO := RShift(P1,|X|) + RShift(P3 - P1- P2, |X|/2) + P2;
end.
```

The algorithm above requires 3 n-bits multiplications to compute the product P as shown in Equation (9), wherein $\delta' n$ is a number of one-bit operations to compute all the additions, subtractions and shift operations. Considering that $T(1) = 1$, we find that the Karatsuba-Ofman's algorithm has the complexity stipulated in Equation (10), and so is asymptotically faster than the standard multiplication algorithm.

$$T(k) = 2T(n) + T(n+1) + \delta' k \approx 3T(n) + \delta\prime k, \tag{9}$$

$$T(k) \approx \theta\left(k^{log_2 3}\right) = \theta\left(k^{1.58}\right) \tag{10}$$

3 Adapted and Less Recursive Algorithm

We now modify Algorithm 1 so that the third multiplication is performed efficiently. For this, consider the arguments of the third recursive call, which computes P_3. They have $|X|/2+1$ bits. Let Z and U be these arguments left-padded with $|X|/2 - 1$ zeros. Now Z and U have $|X|$ bits. So we can write the third product P_3 as follows, wherein $|X| = 2n$, Z_H and U_H are the high parts of Z and U respectively and Z_L and U_L are the low parts of Z and U respectively. Note that Z_H and U_H are equal to 0 or 1.

$$P_3 = ZU = (Z_H 2^n + Z_L)(U_H 2^n + U_L) \tag{11}$$

$$P_3 = 2^{2n}(Z_H U_H) + 2^n(Z_H U_L + Z_L U_H) + Z_L U_L \tag{12}$$

Depending on the value of Z_H and U_H, the above expression can be obtained using one of the alternatives of Table 1. As it is clear from Table 1, computing the third product requires one multiplication of size n and some extra adding, shifting and multiplexing operations.

Table 1. Computing the third product

Z_H	U_H	$Product_3$
0	0	$Z_L Y_L$
0	1	$2^n Z_L + Z_L Y_L$
1	0	$2^n U_L + Z_L Y_L$
1	1	$2^{2n} + 2^n(U_L + Z_L) + Z_L Y_L$

So we adapt Algorithm 1 to this modification as shown in Algorithm 2. On the other hand, the adapted Karatsuba-Ofman's algorithm is less recursive as it stops at operand size 4, and so uses instead of *OneBitMultiplier* component a *FourBitMultiplier* component. In Algorithm 2, *ALKO* stands for Adapted Less Recursive Karatsuba-Ofman's algorithm.

```
Algorithm 2. ALKO(X, Y)
  A := 0; B := 0;
  if |X| = 4 then ALKO := FourBitsMultiplier(X, Y)
  else P1 := ALKO(High(X), High(Y)); P2 := ALKO(Low(X), Low(Y));
       P  := ALKO(Low(High(X)+Low(X)), Low(High(Y)+Low(Y)));
       if Msb(High(X)+Low(X))=1 then A :=  Low(High(Y)+Low(Y))
       if Msb(High(Y)+Low(Y))=1 then B :=  Low(High(X)+Low(X))
       P3:= LShift(Msb(High(X)+Low(X)).Msb(High(X)+Low(X)),|X|)
                                           + LShift(A+B, |X|/2) + P;
       ALKO := LShift(P1, |X|) + LShift(P3-P1-P2, |X|/2) + P2;
end.
```

4 Less Recursive Hardware Architecture

In this section, we concentrate on explaining the proposed architecture of the hardware. The component *KaratsubaOfman* implements the computation of Algorithm 2. The input ports are the multiplier X and the multiplicand Y and the single output port is the product XY. It is clear that the multiplication of 2 n-bit operands yields a product of $2n$-bits product.

The detailed architecture of component *KaratsubaOfman* is depicted in Fig. 1. In this figure, the signals SX_L and SY_L are the two n-bits results of the additions $X_H + X_L$ and $Y_H + Y_L$ respectively. The two one-bit carryout of these additions are represented in by CX and CY respectively.

The architecture of 4-bit Karatsuba-Ofman multiplier is shown in Fig. 2. It uses three 4-bit multipliers identified by *FourBitMultiplier*. The architecture of the latter will be described in details in Section 5.

The component *ShiftnAdd* (in Fig. 2) first computes the sum S as $SX_L + SY_L, SX_L, SY_L$, or 0 depending on the values of CX and CY (see also Table 1), then computes $P3$ as depicted in Fig. 3(a), wherein T represents $CX.CY$. The computation implemented by component *ShiftSubnAdd* (in Fig. 2) i.e. the computation specified in the last line of Algorithm 1 and Algorithm 2 can be performed efficiently if the execution order of the operations constituting it is chosen carefully. This is shown in the architecture of Fig. 4.

Component *ShiftSubnAdd* proceeds as follows: first computes $R = P_1 + P_2$; then obtains $2CR$, which is the two's complement of R; subsequently, computes $U = P_3 + 2CR$; finally, as the bits of P_1 and U must be shifted to the left $2n$ times and n times respectively, the component reduces the first and last additions as well as the shift operations in the last line computation of Karatsuba-Ofman's algorithm to a unique addition that is depicted in Fig. 3(b).

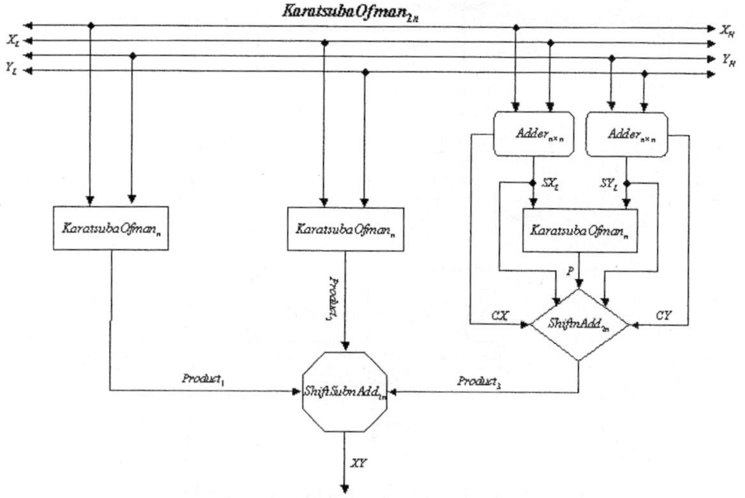

Fig. 1. Architecture of $KaratsubaOfman_{2n}$ for size $2n$ with $n > 4$

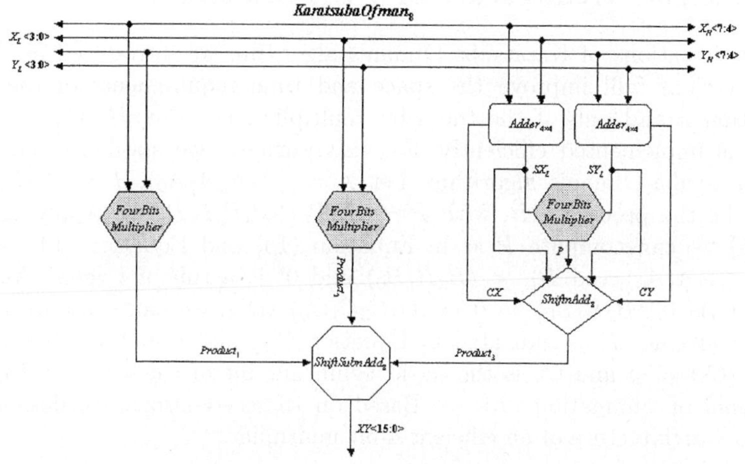

Fig. 2. Architecture of $KaratsubaOfman_8$

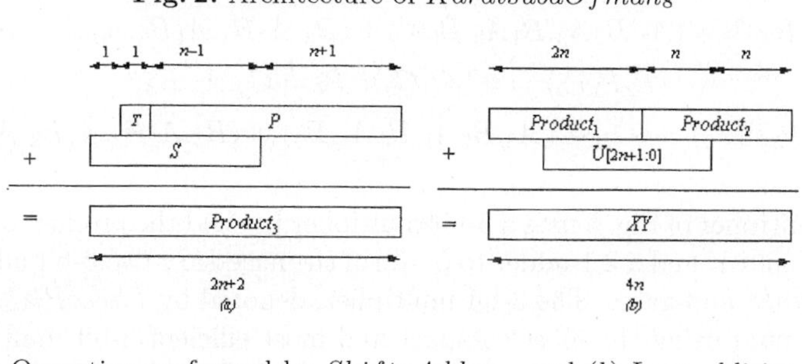

Fig. 3. (a) Operation performed by $ShiftnAdder_{2n}$ and (b) Last addition performed by the $ShiftSubnAdder_2$

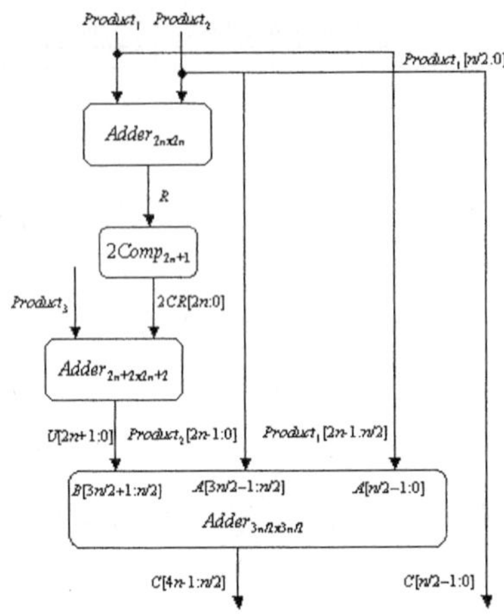

Fig. 4. Architecture of $ShiftSubnAdder_{2n}$

5 Efficient Architecture of 4-Bit Multiplier

The modifications of Karatsuba-Ofman's algorithm we introduced in the previous sections will improve the space and time requirements of the implementation if and only if the the 4-bit multiplier, i.e. *FourBitsMultiplier* in Fig. 2 is implemented efficiently. For this purpose, we specialise once again the Karatsuba-Ofman's algorithm. Let $A = \langle A_3A_2A_1A_0\rangle, B = \langle B_3B_2B_1B_0\rangle$ and P be the product AB, with $P = \langle P_7P_6P_5P_4P_3P_2P_1P_0\rangle$. Applying Equation (5) we can compute P as in Equation (13) and Equation (14), wherein $A_L = \langle A_2A_1A_0\rangle$ and $B_L = \langle B_2B_1B_0\rangle$ and 0^i is a run of i zeros. Assuming that $\langle A_3A_2A_0\rangle\langle B_2B_1B_0\rangle = \langle C_5C_4C_3C_2C_1C_0\rangle$ then, we can compute the bits forming product P as indicated in Equation (15) and Equation (16), wherein $C_H = \langle C_5C_4C_3\rangle$ and C_y is the most significant bit of the sum, i.e. the carry out signal of summation process. Based on these eqautions, we designed the hardware architecture of an efficient 4-bit multiplier.

$$P = 2^6\langle 0^2A_3\rangle\langle 0^2B_3\rangle + 2^3\left(\langle 0^2A_3\rangle B_L + \langle 0^2B_3\rangle A_L\right) + A_LB_L \tag{13}$$

$$P = \langle A_3.B_30^6\rangle + \langle A_3.B_2A_3.B_1A_3.B_00^3\rangle + \langle B_3.A_2B_3.A_1B_3.A_00^3\rangle + A_LB_L \tag{14}$$

$$\langle P_2P_1P_0\rangle = \langle C_2C_1C_0\rangle,\ P_7 = C_y.A_3.B_3, \tag{15}$$

$$\langle C_yP_6P_5P_4P_3\rangle = \langle C_H + \langle A_3.B_2A_3.B_1A_3.B_0\rangle + \langle B_3.A_2B_3.A_1B_3.A_0\rangle \tag{16}$$

The multiplier of Fig. 5 uses a 3-bit multiplier to yield the product of the lower 3 bits of X and Y and a 3:1-adder to perform the necessary two 3-bit additions. It also employs 8 and-gates. The 3-bit multiplier, denoted by *ThreeBitMultiplier*, is implemented using the most compact and most efficient 3-bit multiplier that was obtained through an evolutionary process [6]. It uses 24 gates and is the 8-levels circuit shown in Fig. 6.

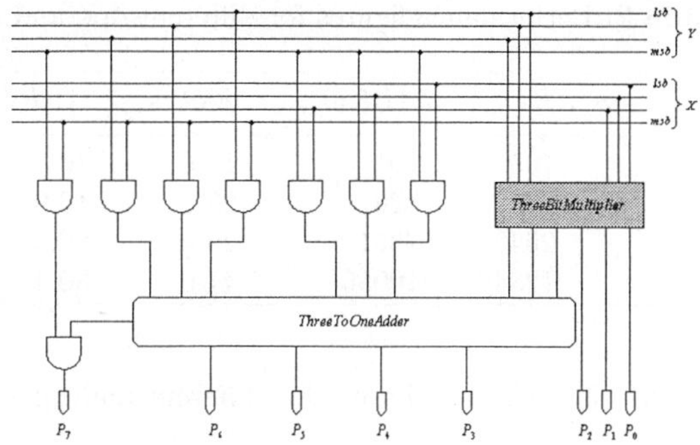

Fig. 5. Architecture of *FourBitMultiplier* using the evolved *ThreeBitMultiplier*

6 Area and Time Requirements

The design of the fully recursive as well as the less recursive were engineered using the Xilinx Project Manager (version Build 6.00.09) [7]. The design was elaborated using VHDL and implemented into logic blocks using SPARTAN S05PC84-4.

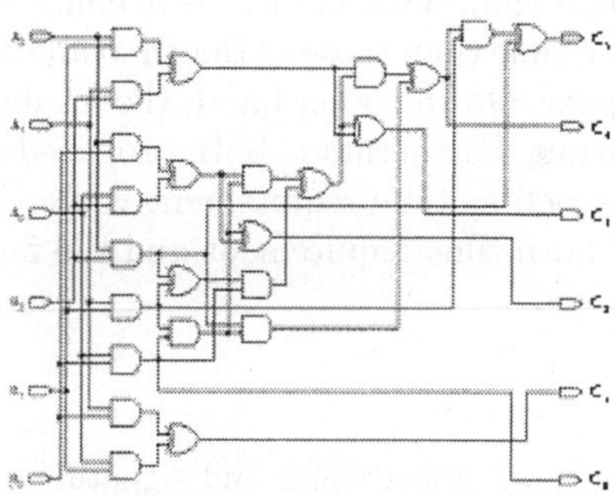

Fig. 6. Architecture of *FourBitMultiplier* using the evolved *ThreeBitMultiplier*

Table 2 shows the time and area in terms of required CLBs obtained from the Xilinx project manager for the fully recursive (KO) versus the adapted and less recursive ($ALKO$) Karatsuba-Ofman's multiplication algorithm. Table 3 shows the delay and area required by the hardware implementation of the modified Booth multiplier which uses a Wallace tree for adding up the partial products (BW) and another hardware implementation of Booth's algorithm that uses a redundant binary Booth encoding (PRB) [8]. The engineered Karatsuba-Ofman multiplier works faster than the other three multipliers. However, it consumes more hardware area. Nevertheless, it also improves also the the area× time factor. Moreover, we strongly think that for larger operands, the proposed Karatsuba-Ofman multipliers will yield much better characteristics.

Table 2. Performance figures for different operand size

operand size	KO_{area}	$ALKO_{area}$	KO_{delay}	$ALKO_{delay}$
8	108	101	12.6	10.7
16	525	428	22.8	16.9
32	2645	2351	29.1	22.4
64	12348	10056	41.0	30.4

Table 3. Delays and areas for different multipliers

operand size	BW_{delay}	BW_{area}	PRB_{delay}	PRB_{area}
8	44.6	1092	31.8	862
16	93.9	5093	46.6	3955
32	121.5	20097	64.9	17151

7 Conclusion

In this paper, we designed a hardware for big number multiplication using Karatsuba-Ofman's algorithm. This hardware is efficient and less recursive. It provides better response time than those of Booth-Wallace and redundant binary encoding Booth multiplier. On the other hand, the hardware consumes less area than the fully recursive one. Furthermore, both proposed multipliers improve the area$\times$ time product as well as time requirement while the other three improve area at the expense of both time requirement and the factor area$\times$ time.

References

1. T. ElGamal, A public-key cryptosystems and signature scheme based on discrete logarithms, IEEE Transactions on Information Theory 31,(1985) 469–472
2. Ç. K. Koç, High speed RSA implementation, Technical report, RSA Laboratories, RSA Data Security Inc. CA, version 2, (1994)
3. D.E. Knuth, The art of computer programming: seminumerical algorithms, vol 2, 2nd Edition, Addison-Wesley, (1981)
4. J.F. Dhem, Design of an efficient public-key cryptographic library for RISC-based smart cards, Ph.D. Thesis, Catholic University of Louvain, (1998)
5. N. Nedjah,L. Mourelle, A reconfigurable recursive and efficient hardware for Karatsuba-Ofman's multiplication algorithm, Proc. of IEEE Conference on Control Applications, (2003)
6. J.F. Miller, D. Job and V.K. Vassilev, Principles in the evolutionary design of digital circuits, Journal of Genetic Programming and Evolvable Machines 1, (2000) 259–288
7. Xilinx, Inc. Foundation Series Software, http://www.xilinx.com.
8. J.H. Kim, J. H. Ryu, A high speed and low power VLSI multiplier using a redundant binary Booth encoding, Proc. of Korean Semiconductor Conference, PA-30, (1999)

Topological and Communication Aspects of Hyper-Star Graphs

Jong-Seok Kim[1], Eunseuk Oh[2], Hyeong-Ok Lee[3], and Yeong-Nam Heo[1]

[1] Department of Computer Science, Sunchon National University, Sunchon, Chonnam, 540-742, KOREA,
{rockhee,hyn}@sunchon.ac.kr

[2] Department of Computer Science, Texas A&M University, College Station, TX 77843-3112, USA,
eunseuko@cs.tamu.edu

[3] Department of Computer Education, Sunchon National University, 315, Maegok-dong, Sunchon, Chonnam, 540-742, KOREA,
oklee@sunchon.ac.kr

Abstract. A hyper-star graph $HS(m,k)$ has been introduced as a class of lower cost interconnection networks. Hyper-star graph has more merit than hypercube when degree $\times$ diameter is used as a cost measure. In other words, they have smaller degree and diameter than hypercubes. In this paper, we consider some of the important properties of hyper-star graphs such as symmetry, w-diameter, and fault diameter. We show that $HS(2n,n)$ is node-symmetric. We also show that the w-diameter of $HS(2n,n)$ is bounded by the shortest path length plus 4, and fault diameter of $HS(2n,n)$ is bounded by its diameter plus 2. In addition, we introduce an efficient broadcasting scheme in hyper-star graphs based on a spanning tree with minimum height.

1 Introduction

Graph theory has provided powerful mathematical tools for designing interconnection networks, where vertices represent processing nodes and edges correspond to communication links. The performance of a particular parallel computer is heavily dependent on the graph topology chosen for it. Many graph topologies have been proposed in literature, ranging from simple graphs such as trees to more sophisticated graphs such as hypercubes and de Bruijn graphs. They possess various degrees and diameters. These graphical parameters not only have their importance in graph theory and combinatorics but also have relevance to applications in commercial networks. The graph model having a smaller degree and diameter is considered more desirable because this implies a lower hardware implementation cost and shorter transmission time of messages[8]. Several new topologies have been proposed as alternatives to hypercube, which is one of the most popular graph topologies, to further improve the degree and diameter of the hypercube[2,6,9]. A hyper-star graph is one of such new topologies.

A hyper-star graph $HS(m,k)$ where $1 \leq k \leq \frac{m}{2}$, possesses many desirable properties as an interconnection network topology. It has been shown that it

A. Yazici and C. Şener (Eds.): ISCIS 2003, LNCS 2869, pp. 51–58, 2003.

has better scalability, a simple routing algorithm, maximum fault-tolerance, and lower cost of degree × diameter than hypercube and its variations[7]. In this paper, we further investigate its desirable properties as an interconnection network topology and its communication aspects based on fault diameter and broadcasting. Specifically, a hyper-star graph $HS(m,k)$ is a regular graph only when $m=2k$. Thus, we focus on a regular hyper-star graph $HS(2n,n)$.

The first graphical parameter we consider is symmetry. Symmetry is an important feature for most graph models for interconnection networks. In a symmetric interconnection network, the load can be evenly distributed through all nodes, reducing congestion problems. Moreover, symmetry makes the design of routing algorithms easier because it allows routing between any two nodes to be mapped to routing between an arbitrary node and a specific node. With regard to the reliability and communication efficiency of $HS(2n,n)$ in the presence of failures, we study w-diameter and fault diameter. The w-diameter of a graph is a natural generalization of the diameter of the graph. The concept of w-diameter is also closely related to the concept of fault diameter. A hyper-star graph $HS(2n,n)$ is n-connected [7]. For any copy of HS_f of $HS(2n,n)$ with at most $n-1$ faults, the fault diameter of $HS(2n,n)$ is the maximum diameter of HS_f. If the fault diameter of $HS(2n,n)$ is bounded by its diameter plus a small additional constant, then the communication delay of $HS(2n,n)$ would not increase dramatically. In this paper, we show that the fault diameter of $HS(2n,n)$ possesses the feature of having a small constant increase in the diameter.

Finally, we address a one-to-all broadcasting scheme in $HS(2n,n)$. One-to-all broadcasting is a mechanism for disseminating information from a designated node in a graph to all other nodes in the graph. It is not difficult to see that broadcasting is central to many applications on interconnection networks. These applications include a variety of linear algebra algorithms such as matrix-vector multiplication, LU-factorization, and Householder-transformations [4]. For single source broadcasting, we consider the spanning tree as a one-to-all communication graph. The graph of minimum height is desirable because it provides a minimum propagation time of messages. Our scheme takes time equal to the diameter of $HS(2n,n)$, which is optimal.

2 Preliminaries

A *hyper-star graph* $HS(m,k)$ is an undirected graph consisting of $\binom{m}{k}$ nodes, where a node is represented by the string of m bits $b_1b_2\ldots b_i\ldots b_m$ such that the cardinality of the set $\{i|1\le i\le m, |b_i=\text{“1”}|\}=k$. Let σ_i be an operation that exchanges b_1 and b_i, $2\le i\le m$, where b_i is a complement of b_1. Then, two nodes $u=b_1b_2\ldots b_i\ldots b_m$ and $v=b_ib_2\ldots b_1\ldots b_m$ are connected when v is obtained from the operation $\sigma_i(u)$. The edge (u,v) is called an *i-edge*.

For a node u, we denote by $[k_1,k_2,\ldots,k_t]$ a path obtained by applying operations $\sigma_{k_1},\sigma_{k_2},\ldots,\sigma_{k_t}$ to u. For example, there is a path $[3,2,4]$ or $[4,2,3]$ from 0011 to 1100. In this paper, we will concentrate on a hyper-star graph $HS(2n,n)$, which is regular and node-symmetric. Its node-symmetric properties will be discussed below. We write a node $\overbrace{0\ldots0}^{n}\overbrace{1\ldots1}^{n}$ in $HS(2n, n)$ as 0^n1^n. Fig. 1 shows a hyper-star graph $HS(6, 3)$. Let $dist(u, v)$ be the distance from

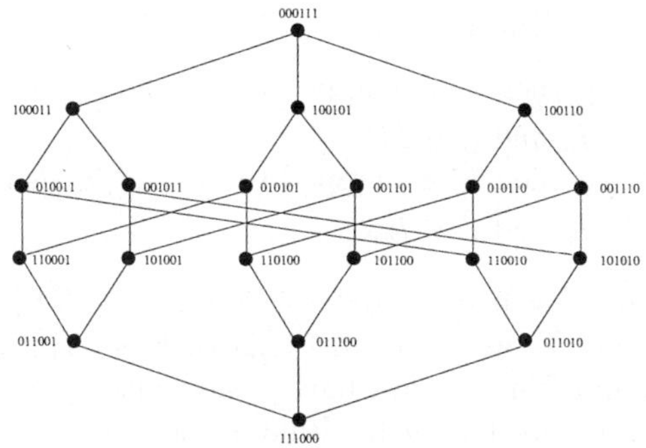

Fig. 1. $HS(6, 3)$ graph

$u = u_1u_2\ldots u_{2n}$ to $v = v_1v_2\ldots v_{2n}$. If a bit string R is obtained by applying the bitwise Exclusive-OR operation to them such as $r_1r_2\ldots r_{2n}$ where $r_i = u_i \oplus v_i$, then $dist(u, v) = \sum_{i=2}^{2n} r_i$. Let R^- be the set of bit positions i such that $r_i = 1$.

Property 1. For a node w in a path $\mathcal{P}$ from u to v, consider an i-edge connecting w and its neighbor w'. If $i \in R^-$ and an edge (w, w') is on $\mathcal{P}$, then the edge (w, w') leads to a shortest path from u to v.

Definition 1. *For two nodes u and v in $HS(2n, n)$, a node w on a path from u to v is said to* be in the level L_m *if $dist(u, w)$ is m.*

Property 2. For a node u in $HS(2n, n)$, any two paths $\mathcal{P} = [k_1, \ldots, k_t]$ and $\mathcal{Q} = [h_1, \ldots, h_t]$ from u lead to the same node if the sets of numbers with even indices in $\mathcal{P}$ and $\mathcal{Q}$ are the same, and the sets of numbers with odd indices in $\mathcal{P}$ and $\mathcal{Q}$ are also the same.

3 Symmetry Properties

A graph $G = (V, E)$ is said to be *node-symmetric* if, for any two nodes u and v, there exists an automorphism of the graph G that maps u into v. In other words, G has the same shape from any node. For two given nodes $u = u_1\ldots u_{2n}$ and $v = v_1\ldots v_{2n}$, we first provide a mapping scheme.

Definition 2. *For a node u in $H(2n, n)$, a* mapping tree *T_u rooted at u consists of n children of u, $c_1, \ldots, c_n$ and $n-1$ children of c_1, $g_1, \ldots, g_{n-1}$.*

Let $I_u = (i_1, \ldots, i_{2n-1})$ be a sequence of i-edges on a mapping tree T_u such that u and c_j are connected by an i_j-edge, and c_1 and g_k are connected by an i_{n+k}-edge. Similarly, consider a sequence $I_v = (i'_1, \ldots, i'_{2n-1})$ for a node v. A mapping node u to node v can be constructed using the following rules:

Mapping Rules(briefly **m-rules**)

Rule 1. If $u_1 = v_1$, then u_1 is mapped to v_1, and u_{i_j} is mapped to $v_{i'_j}$ for $i_j \in I_u$ and $i'_j \in I_v$.

Rule 2. If $\overline{u_1} = v_1$, then $\overline{u_1}$ is mapped to v_1, and $\overline{u_{i_j}}$ is mapped to $v_{i'_j}$ for $i_j \in I_u$ and $i'_j \in I_v$.

Let two nodes be $u = 010110$ and $v = 000111$ in $HS(6,3)$, then we have mapping trees, T_u and T_v as shown in Fig.2(a). From T_u, we have a sequence $I_u = (2,4,5,3,6)$, and from T_v, we have a sequence $I_v = (4,5,6,2,3)$. Since $u_1 = v_1$, u can be mapped to v by Rule 1. Let two nodes be $u = 110001$ and $v = 001011$, then we have mapping trees, T_u and T_v as shown in Fig.2(b). Similarly, we have a sequence $I_u = (3,4,5,2,6)$ and a sequence $I_v = (3,5,6,2,4)$. Since $\overline{u_1} = v_1$, u can be mapped to v by Rule 2.

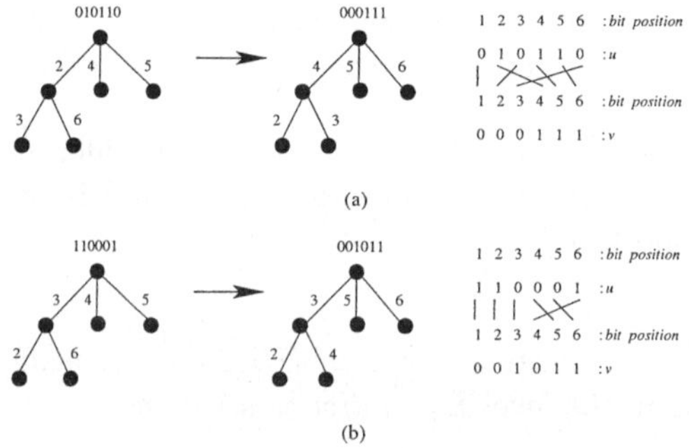

Fig. 2. Mapping from a node u into a node v in $HS(6,3)$ by corresponding mapping trees: (a) Mapping from $u = 010110$ into $v = 000111$ by Rule 1 (b) Mapping from $u = 110001$ into $v = 001011$ by Rule 2

It is easy to verify that there is an automorphism of the graph that maps u into v by the m-rules. Thus:

Theorem 1. *A hyper-star graph $HS(2n,n)$ is node-symmetric.*

Similarly, we can reduce routing between two arbitrary nodes u' and v' to routing from an arbitrary node u to a special node v, say 0^n1^n. If we find a path $\mathcal{P} = [p_1, p_2, \ldots, p_t]$ from u' to v', then we can reduce the path P to a path $\mathcal{Q} = [q_1, q_2, \ldots, q_t]$ from u to v such that p_i is mapped to q_i by m-rules applied to two nodes v' and v. Consider a path $\mathcal{P} = [6,4,3,2]$ between 001011 and 010110 in $HS(6,3)$ whose mapping trees for 010110 and 000111 are as shown in

Fig.2(a). Then the path $\mathcal{P}$ is reduced to a path $\mathcal{Q} = [3, 5, 2, 4]$ between 011001 and 000111.

Lemma 1. *From a node $u = 0^n 1^n$ in $HS(2n, n)$, a subgraph consisting of nodes in L_i, $0 \le i \le n-1$, and a subgraph consisting of nodes in L_j, $n \le j \le 2n-1$, are symmetric.*

Proof. The number of nodes of $HS(2n, n)$ is $\binom{2n}{n}$. To construct a shortest path, we apply operations σ_i, $n+1 \le i \le 2n$, and σ_j, $2 \le j \le n$, alternately. Thus, there is no edge between nodes in the same level or between nodes in levels L_i and L_j such that $|L_i - L_j| \ge 2$. A node $v = 1^n 0^n$ is in L_{2n-1} and u can be connected to it by a path $\mathcal{P} = [n+1, 2, n+2, 3, \ldots, n, 2n]$. Since a shortest path from u can be constructed by applying unique operations σ_i, $n+1 \le i \le 2n$, and σ_j, $2 \le j \le n$, alternately, any shortest path $[k_1, \ldots, k_t]$ from u to a node has the same sets of numbers with even and odd indices as $\mathcal{P}$. Thus, by Property 2, the node v is a unique node in L_{2n-1}. Nodes in L_1 are connected to u by operations σ_i, $n+1 \le i \le 2n$, and nodes in L_{2n-2} are connected to v by the same operations. For a node u' in L_1, some nodes $u'', \ldots, u'''$ in L_2 are connected to u' by operations σ_j, $2 \le j \le n$, and some nodes $v''(=\overline{u''}), \ldots, v'''(=\overline{u'''})$ in L_{2n-3} are connected to a node $v'(=\overline{u'})$ by the same operations, and so on. In other words, nodes in L_i and nodes in L_{2n-i-1}, $0 \le i \le n-1$, are complements, and the number of nodes and corresponding edges in these levels are also the same. □

4 w-Diameter and Fault Diameter

Following the conventions introduced in [3], let $C(u, v)$ be a *container*, which is a set of node-disjoint paths between u and v in a graph G. The *width* of $C(u, v)$ is the number of paths in $C(u, v)$, and the *length* of $C(u, v)$ is the length of the longest path in $C(u, v)$. The *w-distance* is the minimum length over all containers $C(u, v)$ of width w. The *w-diameter* $D_w(G)$ of G is the maximum w-distance between any pair of nodes in G. If G is k-connected, then for any copy G_f of G with at most $k-1$ faults, the *fault-diameter* $D^f_{k-1}(G)$ of G is the maximum diameter of G_f.

The concept of w-diameter is closely related to the concept of *fault diameter*. It is well-known that $D(G) \le D^f_{k-1}(G) \le D_k(G)$, where $D(G)$ is the diameter of G [1]. If the fault diameter is bounded by the diameter of G plus a small additional constant, then the communication delay of G will not increase dramatically. $HS(2n, n)$ is n-connected and its diameter is $2n-1$ [7]. In this section, we discuss w-diameter and fault diameter of $HS(2n, n)$.

Consider the cyclic permutation of two sequences $S_1 = (a_1, a_2, \ldots, a_p)$ and $S_2 = (b_1, b_2, \ldots, b_q)$ denoted by $S_1 \odot S_2$. $S_1 \odot S_2$ is the set of sequences obtained by merging symbols in S_1 and S_2 alternately. If only one sequence is permuted, say S_2, then we write $S_1 \odot S_2^-$. For example, if $S_1 = (5, 6, 7)$ and $S_2 = (2, 3, 4)$, then $S_1 \odot S_2 = \{(5,2,6,3,7,4),(6,3,7,4,5,2),(7,4,5,2,6,3)\}$. Also, $S_1 = (5, 6, 7)$ and $S_2 = (2, 3)$, then $S_1 \odot S_2^- = \{(5,2,6,3,7),\ (6,2,7,3,5),\ (7,2,5,3,6)\}$. Paths obtained by applying operations corresponding to sequences of $S_1 \odot S_2$ are node-disjoint because the number of symbols in the set sharing an internal node is $p+q$. Similarly, paths obtained by applying operations corresponding to sequences of $S_1 \odot S_2^-$ are also node-disjoint. For simplicity, we regard a symbol i in a sequence as an operation σ_i. other. In addition, $|S_1 \odot S_2| = max\{p,q\}$ and $|S_1 \odot S_2^-| = p$. Let $\phi = dist(u,v)$.

Lemma 2. *For two nodes $u = 0^n1^n$ and v in $HS(2n,n)$, there is a length ϕ container of width $\lceil\frac{\phi}{2}\rceil$.*

Proof. Suppose $\phi = dist(u,v)$ is even. Consider the set of paths constructed by $S_1 \odot S_2$, where $S_1 = (n+1, n+2, \ldots, n+\frac{\phi}{2})$ and $S_2 = (2,3,\ldots,\frac{\phi}{2}+1)$. They are node-disjoint, and the number of paths constructed by $S_1 \odot S_2$ is $\frac{\phi}{2}$. Let us assume that u is in L_0. Then, for any pair of adjacent nodes (p_i,p_j) in $\mathcal{P}$, $dist(u,p_j) = dist(u,p_i)+1$. In other words, each node in $\mathcal{P}$ is in a unique level. Suppose $\phi = dist(u,v)$ is odd. Consider the set of paths constructed by $S_1 \odot S_2^-$, where $S_1 = (n+1, n+2, \ldots, n+\lceil\frac{\phi}{2}\rceil)$ and $S_2^- = (2,3,\ldots,\lceil\frac{\phi}{2}\rceil)$. Paths constructed by $S_1 \odot S_2^-$ are node-disjoint, and the number of such paths is $\lceil\frac{\phi}{2}\rceil$. Therefore, the lemma holds. □

Theorem 2. *For any two nodes u and v in $HS(2n,n)$, $D_n(HS(2n,n)) \leq dist(u,\ v)+4$.*

Proof. Since $HS(2n,n)$ is node-symmetric, we assume that a node u is 0^n1^n. Suppose there is a shortest path $\mathcal{P}$=$[n+1,2,n+2,3,\ldots,n+\frac{\phi}{2},\frac{\phi}{2}+1]$ from u to v. From lemma 2, we know that ϕ is even, and there are $\frac{\phi}{2}$ node-disjoint paths of length $dist(u,v)$ from u to v. They are constructed by $S_1 \odot S_2$ where $S_1 = (n+1,n+2,\ldots,n+\frac{\phi}{2})$ and $S_2 = (2,3,\ldots,\frac{\phi}{2}+1)$. Also, there are $n-\frac{\phi}{2}$ symbols between $n+\frac{\phi}{2}+1$ and $2n$ which are unused in paths constructed by $S_1 \odot S_2$. We construct $n-\frac{\phi}{2}$ paths of the form $[j,\mathcal{P}',j]$ for all j, $n+\frac{\phi}{2} \leq j \leq 2n$ from u to v where $\mathcal{P}'$ is a sequence that transposes adjacent symbols (p_i,p_j) in $\mathcal{P}$. That is, $\mathcal{P}'$=$(2,n+1,3,n+2,\ldots,\frac{\phi}{2}+1,n+\frac{\phi}{2})$. Paths constructed by $S_1 \odot S_2$ and paths of the form $[j,\mathcal{P}',j]$ are node-disjoint because j is a unique symbol. Thus, if ϕ is even, then we can construct n node-disjoint paths that consist of $\frac{\phi}{2}$ paths of length $dist(u,v)$ and $n-\frac{\phi}{2}$ of length $dist(u,v)+2$.

Suppose there is a shortest path $\mathcal{P}$=$[n+1,2,n+2,3,\ldots,\lceil\frac{\phi}{2}\rceil,n+\lceil\frac{\phi}{2}\rceil]$ from u to v. Similarly, from lemma 2, ϕ is odd, and there are $\lceil\frac{\phi}{2}\rceil$ node-disjoint paths of length $dist(u,v)$ from u to v. They are constructed by $S_1 \odot S_2^-$ where $S_1 = (n+1,n+2,\ldots,n+\lceil\frac{\phi}{2}\rceil)$ and $S_2^- = (2,3,\ldots,\lceil\frac{\phi}{2}\rceil)$. Also, there are $n-\lceil\frac{\phi}{2}\rceil$ pairs of symbols (j,k) where $n+\lceil\frac{\phi}{2}\rceil+1 \leq j \leq 2n$ and $\lceil\frac{\phi}{2}+1\rceil \leq k \leq n$. These are unused in paths constructed by $S_1 \odot S_2^-$. We construct $n-\lceil\frac{\phi}{2}\rceil$ paths of the form $[j,k,\mathcal{P},j,k]$, for all j, $n+\lceil\frac{\phi}{2}\rceil \leq j \leq 2n$, and for all k, $\lceil\frac{\phi}{2}+1\rceil \leq k \leq n$, from u to v where $j = k+n$. Paths constructed by $S_1 \odot S_2^-$ and paths of the form $[j,k,\mathcal{P},j,k]$ are node-disjoint because a pair (j,k) is unique. Let v' be a node obtained by σ_k, σ_j from v, and $\mathcal{Q}$ be a path of the form $[j, k, \mathcal{P}, j, k]$. Thus, if ϕ is odd, then we can construct n node-disjoint paths that consist of $\lceil \frac{\phi}{2} \rceil$ paths of length $dist(u, v)$ and $n - \lceil \frac{\phi}{2} \rceil$ of length $dist(u, v) + 4$. □

Theorem 3. $D^f_{n-1}(HS(2n, n)) = D(HS(2n, n)) + 2 = 2n + 1$.

5 Broadcasting Scheme

For broadcasting from a source node, we define a spanning tree rooted at the source node of $HS(2n, n)$. We assume that a source node u is $0^n 1^n$, but our construction can be easily generalized for trees rooted at arbitrary nodes. Let Parent(v) be a function that represents the parent of v, and Children(v) be a function that represents the children of v. Then for a node v and its grandparent g, Parent(Parent(v)), let $\mathcal{I} = \{i | r_i = g_i \oplus v_i = 1\}$, and define $i^0 \in \mathcal{I}$ and $i^1 \in \mathcal{I}$ with $1 \leq i^0 \leq n$ and $n+1 \leq i^1 \leq 2n$ when v is in an even level and $1 \leq i^1 \leq n$ and $n+1 \leq i^0 \leq 2n$ when v is in an odd level. Also, let $r_h = 0$ for all $h \in \Psi$ where $\Psi = \{i^1+1, i^1+2, \ldots, 2n\}$ or $\Psi = \{i^1+1, i^1+2, \ldots, n\}$, in the first instance and second instance, respectively. That is, Ψ is the set of trailing zeros in R from the i^1th position.

Definition 3. *Let a source node u be $0^n 1^n$. Then a spanning tree $ST(u)$ rooted at u is defined by the functions Parent(v) and Children(v) as follows:*
Children(v) $= \sigma_h(v)$, for all h in Ψ,
Parent(v) $= \sigma_{i^0}(v)$.

Specifically, for the source node $u = v$, let $i^1 = n$ and Parent(v) $= \phi$, and for children of u, let $i^1 = 1$ and $\mathcal{I} = \{i | r_i = u_i \oplus v_i = 1\}$. It is easy to see that children of v are nodes connected by h-edges for all h in Ψ, and the parent of v is the node connected by an i^0-edge.

Theorem 4. *For the source node $u = 0^n 1^n$, the spanning tree $ST(u)$ has optimum height equal to $2n - 1$.*

Proof. For any node w in $ST(u)$, consider a bit string $R = r_1 \ldots r_{2n}$ obtained by applying the bitwise Exclusive-OR operation to w and u, and the set of bit position i, R^- such that $r_i = v_i \oplus u_i$. Then the function Parent(w) finds a parent $\sigma_{i^0}(w)$ such that $i^0 \in R^-$. Thus, by Property 1, the edge (w, Parent(w)) leads to a shortest path to u. Since the hyper-star graph is node-symmetric, the height of $ST(u)$ is equal to the diameter of the hyper-star graph. Specifically, if $w = 1^n 0^n$, then edges connecting w and u in $ST(u)$ construct a shortest path between w and u of length $2n - 1$. □

In our broadcasting scheme, we restrict communication to a single-port at a time. We briefly mention our broadcasting scheme: First, the source node u sends a message M to the left-most child u_1, with the result that u and u_1 hold M. Then u sends M to the next left-most child u_2, and u_1 sends M to its left-most child. We continue this operation until all nodes in $ST(u)$ receive the message M. This scheme takes $2n - 1$ time, which is optimal.

6 Concluding Remarks

We have shown that $HS(2n, n)$ is node-symmetric. Further study on other properties of $HS(2n, n)$ such as Hamiltonicity would be interesting. We also showed that the fault diameter of $HS(2n, n)$ is its diameter plus 2. Our result is optimal because some node-disjoint path must lead to that bound. Latifi[5] has suggested investigating whether the whole family of Cayley graphs have the feature that their fault diameters are one greater than their diameters. We suspect that $HS(2n, n)$ is a member of the Cayley graph family. Further investigation would be interesting. Finally, we developed a broadcasting algorithm of $HS(2n, n)$ based on a spanning tree with optimal height. We restricted communication to a single-port at a time. Developing a communication graph with other capabilities such as multi-port or all-port for concurrent communication would also be interesting.

References

1. C.-P. Chang, T.-Y. Sung, and L.-H. Hsu, "Edge Congestion and Topological Properties of Crossed Cubes," *IEEE Trans. Parallel and Distributed Systems*, Vol. 11, No. 1, pp. 64–80, 2000.
2. K. Efe, "A Variation on the Hypercube with Lower Diameter," *IEEE Trans. Computers*, vol. 40, no. 11, pp. 1312–1316, 1991.
3. D. F. Hsu, "On Container Width and Length in Graphs, Groups, and Networks," *IEICE Trans. Fundamentals E77-A*, pp. 668–680, 1994.
4. S. L. Johnsson, "Communication Efficient Basic Linear Algebra Computations on Hypercube Architectures," *J. Parallel Distrib. Comput.*, vol. 4, pp. 133–172, 1987.
5. S. Latifi, "Combinatorial Analysis of the Fault-Diameter of the n-cube," *IEEE Trans. Computers*, vol. 42, no.1, pp. 27–33, 1993.
6. C.-N. Lai, G.-H. Chen, and D.-R. Duh, "Constructing One-to-Many Disjoint Paths in Folded Hypercubes," *IEEE Trans. Computers*, vol. 51, no. 1, pp. 33–34, 2002.
7. H.-O. Lee, J.-S. Kim, E. Oh, and H.-S. Lim, "Hyper-Star Graph: A New Interconnection Network Improving the Network Cost of Hypercube," *Proc. EurAsia ICT: Information and Communication Technology*, LNCS 2510, pp. 858–865, 2002.
8. B. Parhami and D.-M. Kwai, "Unified Formulation of Honeycomb and Diamond Networks," *IEEE Trans. Parallel and Distributed Systems*, vol.12, no.1, pp. 74–80, 2001.
9. S.-K. Yun and K.-H.Park, "Comments on Hierarchical Cubic Networks," *IEEE Trans. Parallel and Distributed Systems*, vol.9, no.4, pp. 410–414, 1998.

An E-tutoring Service Architecture Based on Overlay Networks

Nikolaos Minogiannis, Charalampos Patrikakis, Andreas Rompotis, and Frankiskos Ninos

Telecommunications Laboratory
National Technical University of Athens,
Heroon Politechniou 9, Zographou Campus, Greece 15773,
tel: +30 210 7721513, fax: +30 210 7722534
{minogian,bpatr,arobot,ninosf}@telecom.ntua.gr

Abstract. In this paper, a comprehensive e-tutoring service framework is presented. It compromises a set of individual applications implemented based on the use of existing open source tools. The significant point here is the flexibility of the implementation proposed, that allows it to use a combination of unicast and multicast without posing any requirements for the supporting network infrastructure. This is achieved through the use of an overlay network architecture that allows for dynamic configuration of the media transmission and relay points.

1 Introduction

Recently, there is a remarkable increase in research around online tutoring and learning and their respective use in educational technology. There are many academic journals in research community study this area, while IEEE has appointed a relative committee, Computer Society Learning Technology Task Force (LTTF) to work on the topic. There is a focus on collaborative discourse [1], [2] and the individual development of meaning through construction and sharing of texts, image, video streaming and other social artifacts. From these perspectives, learners are apprenticed into "communities of practice" which embody certain interests and educational behaviors. An e-tutoring service imposes a great burden to the underlying network in terms of bandwidth resources and packet traffic administration. In order to fulfill such requirements, many technologies have been utilized, such as Multi-agent systems [3], multicasting [4] and adaptive network mechanisms for controlling and adjusting the generated traffic.

This paper proposes an implementation of an e-tutoring service based on standard IP and using overlay networks. The rest of the paper is organized as follows: First a definition of the service framework for an e-tutoring application is provided in which the requirements for such a service, together with a presentation of the supporting technology for implementing such a service are presented. In the next section, and after having set the framework for the e-tutoring service to be presented, the actual implementation scheme is provided in details covering both architectural issues and specific implementation details. Closing the paper, a section about future (and in fact ongoing work) for providing a more dynamic model of the presented idea is provided.

A. Yazici and C. Şener (Eds.): ISCIS 2003, LNCS 2869, pp. 59–66, 2003.

2 Definition of the Service Framework for E-tutoring

The methodology for the definition of the required application components for an e-tutoring service arises by answering the following questions: what is the functionality provided by a real classroom, which applications can support it and what are the features of these applications. The criterion for the success is to efficiently provide all the necessary tools available in a real school environment.

2.1 The E-classroom Framework

This service framework is presented in Figure 1, in which the outside circle entities represent the actual needs of a real life classroom, covering the whole process of lectures, while the inner "grey" circle gives the equivalent applications offered by this platform to cover these needs, respectively [6].

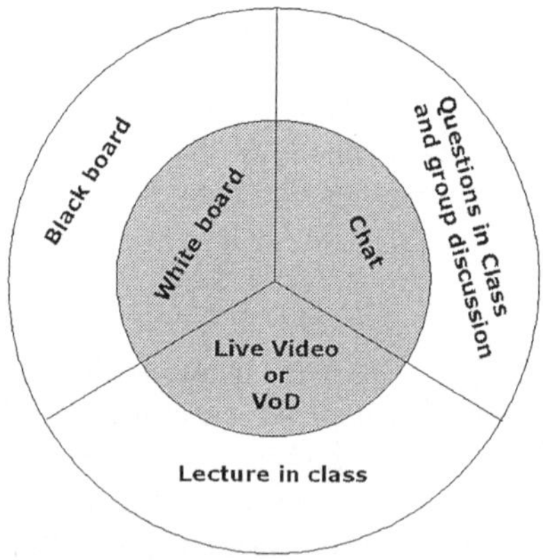

Fig. 1. E-classroom framework in relation to real classroom needs

Lecture in class. This is the lesson itself delivered through the presentation provided by the tutor. It is covered by a Live Video or Video on Demand application that is used to send the video of the class presentation to the students.

Questions in class and group discussion. This covers the process of interaction between the teacher and the students during the presentation. To cover this need in the most efficient and cost effective way, a chat application can be used.

Blackboard. This represents the means for communicating with the students through written or image projected information. In the blackboard, not only the teacher, but also the students (having the consent of the teacher) may have access. The related application is a whiteboard, access to which is administered by the teacher.

Taking into account the above presentation and trying to balance the need for a comprehensive e-tutoring service with the need for supporting it through a cost effective, easy to install service platform, we will proceed in the following sections of the paper by presenting such a platform for covering the lecturing phase of the lesson.

Before we proceed in the design and implementation details of the e-tutoring service, we have to stress the requirements that drove us to the selection of overlay networks as the supporting infrastructure. For this, a presentation of the requirements of an e-learning (and especially e-tutoring) service follows, together with the existing state of the art for supporting them in real implementations.

2.2 Requirements for Collaborative Applications

There is a diverse range of applications that inherently require group communication and collaboration: video conferencing, distance tutoring, distance learning, distributed databases, data replication, multi-party games and distributed simulation, network broadcast services and many others. The diversity of these applications demands versatile support from the underlying system in many dimensions. Examples of these dimensions include bandwidth, latency, reliability, multi-source, scalability and dynamics requirements.

The main interest of this paper is focused on distance learning, and specifically in e-tutoring. Supporting these applications has imposed a serious challenge to the current communication systems. Due to the prevalence of underlying point-to-point connections, communication systems are quickly reaching their limit. A typical example is that requests to a popular web server usually experience long response time due to server overload since it has to establish individual connections for each incoming data request, even for requests for the same objects. The inadequacy of unicast-only systems is more significant for these forward-looking applications, especially in distributed systems where data needs to be constantly updated and synchronized.

2.3 The Native IP Multicast Deployement and Torsion to Overlay Architectures

The IP Multicast service was proposed as an extension to the Internet architecture to support efficient multi-point packet delivery at the network level. In a multicast network, the connections of the routers that form a multicast tree are maintained by a multicast routing protocol. Many protocols have been proposed and are in use today on the Internet. In spite of the rigorous efforts of a generation of researchers, there remains many unresolved issues in the IP multicast model that hinder its development and deployment of multicast applications.

To overcome the fundamental problems related to IP multicasting "global" deployment, research effort has been turned to other solutions based on application layer data forwarding. As a consequence overlay network architectures have been proposed for supporting data distribution and in some cases used for serving streaming applications. The primary advantage of an overlay network architecture is that it does not require universal network support (which has become increasingly hard to achieve) to be useful. This enables faster deployment of desired network functions and adds flexibility to the service infrastructure, as it allows the co-existence of multiple overlay networks each supporting a different set of service functions. An Overlay Multicast Network is one type of overlay network that provides multicast services to end users on top of the general Internet unicast infrastructure [7]. For this, the present model focuses on the deployment of an overlay network incorporating and exploiting the application-layer multicasting capabilities.

3 Presentation of the Implementation

In the following paragraphs, an implementation of an e-tutoring service based on the above ideas will be presented with specific implementation details on the modules developed and the open source tools used.

3.1 Description of the Architecture

The proposed platform provides a solution for media distribution through peripheral reflector points. The whole architecture incorporates multicasting techniques deployed at a local level while the further communication with users don't reside at the same network neighbourhood can be accomplished through unicast streams.

The group of students participate in the e-tutoring framework accessing the lecture information through different serving points. A dedicated Video Server -VS is used in order to transmit and manage the streams produced by the camera located near the teacher's site. These streams before entering the VS should be encoded in appropriate formats. In our architecture the MPEG-4 encoding technique is selected. The main components of the distribution chain are the Video Streaming Server used for sending the video and the Video Relay Nodes - VRNs (both based on a QTSS implementation), used for retransmitting the video to neighbouring nodes in the overlay architecture. The VRN is also responsible for transforming a unicast stream coming from the VS to multicast for supporting the clients within its vicinity (e.g. a LAN). Another significant part of the architecture is the Web Server. Web Server is used as staring point to which students are addressing their requests for participating in an e-tutoring session. The Web-Server (Content Management Element) is the key component for the provisioning of a user-friendly interface for Chat and Whiteboard applications and also for the redirection of user requests for Streaming Video access to the VS or the closest VRN. The students terminals, make use of the Chat and Whiteboard applications through separate software modules.

Live Video Application/Streaming Service. In Live Video Application, digitally compressed video and audio streams are sent to the end-user upon demand and can be retrieved on an individual basis. The Live Video System supports the MPEG family of protocols, namely MPEG-2 and MPEG-4. For the implementation, MPEG4 standard was adopted due to its inherent ability to support video transmission even to very low rates. Figure 2 depicts the stages that the overlay architecture encompasses in order to provide real-time services (live video) as well as e-tutoring applications.

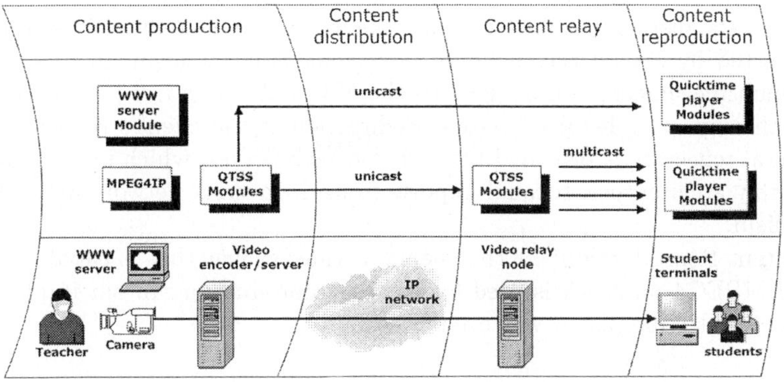

Fig. 2. Stages followed in live video distribution procedure

The top row represents the content production procedure, while the bottom row provides the description of the distribution mechanism in terms of network elements. Apart from the camera located at the teacher's site, the main components of the content production stage are the VS and the encoder.

Content Preparation: The MPEG4IP encoder [10] used for this purpose, provides a tool that incorporates the necessary functionality for MPEG-4 real-time encoding. The package includes many existing open source packages and the "glue" to integrate them together. This is a tool for streaming video and audio that is standards-oriented and free from proprietary protocols and extensions. Input to the MPEG4IP was provided through a camera connected to a PC running LINUX.

Content Management: The Web Server initiates the communication between the teacher and the students group. Once the e-tutoring session starts, the students follow a URL in order to open the corresponding Web page hosted by the Server (in our case an Apache web server). Through the HTTP protocol, the students have intermediate access to the video content. The Web Server is responsible for the user's redirection to a Video Streaming Server (this being the VS itself or a VRN according the process described later in the paper) which is streaming the teacher's lecture video to the students.

Content Distribution: The QTSS server [9] is the key component in the distribution chain. It is responsible for the manipulation and transmission of the video content to the rest network infrastructure, with ulterior scope the video delivery to student's group. The distribution of the video content may be accomplished through two different methods: Unicast transmission used in cases where the student does not reside in the same cluster as the origin VS is located and Unicast/Multicast transmission in cases the overlay procedure is activated. In this approach QTSSs are placed at the edges of the network or other cooperating networks exploiting application data forwarding capabilities. This architecture appeals to peer-to-peer collaboration activities.

Content Relaying: A QTSS is also used for this purpose. Each client instead of using a direct connection to the VS, as it would in normal data distribution; it receives the distributed data through the use of the nearest relay server. This is supported by the overlay network management mechanism. In this way, we avoid multiple unicast connections to the VS, and instead, we serve these requests through peripheral reflectors. Redirection of the client's requests to the peripheral reflectors is provided through the Web Server, which is kept aware of the overlay architecture, through reports from the overlay network management mechanism.

Content Reproduction: At the clients, a video player that is capable of supporting MPEG4 playback is used for content reproduction. In our implementation the QuickTime player was used.

Overlay Network Implementation and Management. Proceeding to our analysis, we will introduce the basic notions of the applied overlay structure implemented for supporting the e-tutoring service. As it is depicted in Figure 3, the overlay architecture is based on four modules: the Overlay Architecture Server (OAS), the Overlay Architecture Relay (OAR), the Overlay Architecture Client (OAC) and the Overlay Architecture Manager (OAM). These three modules are responsible for the manipulation of the video access requests of the clients, the connection of each client to the most suitable point (this being either a VRN or a VS) for video access.

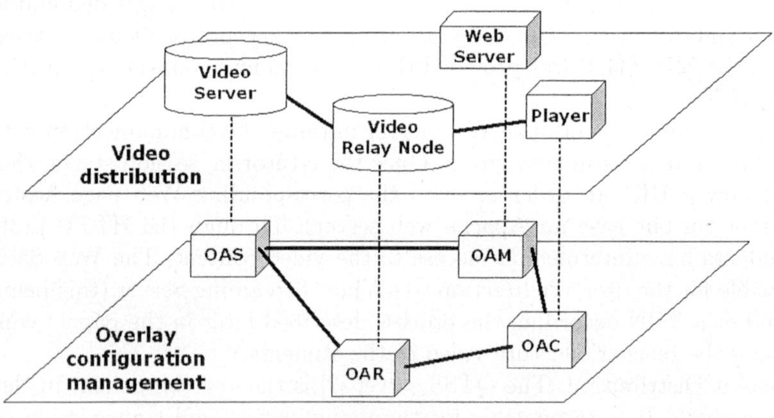

Fig. 3. Overlay network architecture

The way this architecture works is the following: Prior to the connection of a student's terminal to the VS serving the live transmission of the e-lecture stream, the student connects to the web server in order to request access to the e-tutoring service. Once access is granted, the OAC (located at the student's terminal) is activated and by communicating with the OAM (located on the Web server), it receives the address of the OAS, (located on the same node as the VS), and of all the available OARs for the specific e-lecture class (located at the VRNs). Following, the OAC initiates an inquiry mechanism for determining the closest node for video transmission (or video relaying). This mechanism is based on the sending ping like messages to all the nodes reported by the OAM as possible video serving nodes. Upon receipt of all the answers to this ping, the OCM selects the closest one and reports this selection to the OAM. This in turn, provides the address of the selected video serving node to the web server, which presents it to the student. Now the student can be directed to this node for accessing the video of the lecture. The OAM keeps a list of all connections to a VS or VRN during an e-lecture session for monitoring and administrative purposes (i.e indication of a problematic relay node as we will present later).

The above procedure covers the discovery of the closest video serving point. But what happens when we need to deploy multicasting for a number of clients in the same LAN, and how is the student's player notified about this possibility of receiving video over multicast? The answer is the ping like message used for closest server discovery. This message, instead of transporting only information about the distance between a server/relay node and the requesting client, it also transfers information about the availability of multicast transmission, the local domain of the video serving node and the clients it can serve. The last is needed in cases where a relay node is serving clients through unicast, where a limited number of clients is supported in order to avoid degradation in the QoS of relayed video due to insufficient processing power. Based on this information, the client may perform a comprehensive selection over the available solutions, and report this selection to the web server through OAC to OAM communication. The overlay modules are independent from these responsible for video distribution. In this way, they introduce a dynamic video distribution configuration through the use of an administrating web server acting as the intermediate link.

Completing the Service Framework with Chat and Whiteboard Applications. As it has been presented earlier, to support the e-tutoring process the service framework needs to be completed by some additional applications that assist the tutor - students' communication. These are the chat and whiteboard applications that may operate individual and autonomously in relation to the live video application.

Chat Application. The most significant part is the creation of a multi-channel environment, where students participating in a working group could be able to talk with each other in virtual rooms managed by their teacher. The teacher's role in this case is to create and manage the channels according to the existing working groups. In order to achieve this, the e-lecturing chat application consists of three IRC sub-components: a typical IRC server application and two versions of the chat client, each providing student and teacher functionality respectively.

Whiteboard Application. The Whiteboard application allows the user (a teacher or student) to draw an arbitrary number of elements on a single surface and share that surface with other participants of an e-learning session. The application also allows a surface to be persisted between sessions by use of the 'Save' command. All these commands are easily accessible through a typical Windows GUI. At last, a custom protocol was designed to guarantee that all participants share the same Whiteboard surface.

4 Future Work

The implementation presented here, though it makes use of an overlay architecture for providing dynamic configuration of the e-tutoring service in terms of media distribution, is still depending on some decisions taken from the student regarding the connection to the video serving node. This is due to the fact that the web server is treated as the link point between the open source components used for serving video transport and the developed modules for overlay network architecture management. An alternative implementation in which these modules are integrated within a compact application deployed at the relay points and the users' terminals would offer the ability for providing a dynamically self-configured e-tutoring service, transparently to the user.

References

1. D. Keegan: Theoretical Principles of Distance Education. Routledge (1993)
2. C. J. Bonk, & K. S. King (eds.): Electronic collaborators: Learner-centered technologies for literacy, apprenticeship, and discourse. Erlbaum (1998)
3. A. Garro: An XML Multi-Agent System for e-Learning and Skill Management. Third International Symposium on Multi-Agent Systems, Large Complex Systems, and E-Businesses (MALCEB'2002), Erfurt, Thuringia Germany, (2002)
4. Sirgio Deusdado, Paulo Carvalho: An Adaptive e-learning System based on IP Multicast Technology. International Conference on Information and Communication Technologies in Education (ICTE2002), Badajoz, Espanha, Nov 20-23 (2002)
5. Ch. Patrikakis, K. Karapetsas, N. Minogiannis, S. Vrontis, N. Igoumenidis, G. Diakonikolaou: A QoS aware e-learning service framework: The MOICANE case. International Conference on Cross-Media Service Delivery, Santorini, May (2003)
6. Y. S. Shi: Design of Overlay Networks for Internet Multicast. Washington University Severe Institute of Technology, Dept of Computer Science, Phd Thesis, August 2002
7. QuickTime Streaming Server:
http://developer.apple.com/darwin/projects/streaming
8. MPEG4IP Project: http://www.mpeg4ip.net

A Simple Scheme for Local Failure Recovery of Multi-directional Multicast Trees

Vladimír Dynda

Department of Computer Science and Engineering
Faculty of Electrical Engineering, Czech Technical University in Prague
Karlovo náměstí 13, 121 35 Prague 2, Czech Republic
xdynda@fel.cvut.cz

Abstract. When a node in a multicast tree fails, the tree is divided into several fragments. To achieve a fault-tolerant communication, failure recovery schemes are necessary to restore the tree. We present a simple recovery scheme for overlay multicast trees that involves only failure-neighboring nodes into the restoration and keeps the original structure of the rest of the tree. The scheme is based on virtual bypass rings providing alternative paths to eliminate the faulty node and reroute the traffic. Our scheme is scalable, independent of message source and traffic direction in the tree, restores the multicast tree in real time without a significant delay penalty and our experiments show that it is efficient even under a heavy traffic in the tree.

1 Introduction

Recently, many distributed applications, particularly peer-to-peer internet-based systems, have become increasingly popular. As these systems need to provide reliable multiple-point communicating service, an efficient and fault-tolerant multicast is critical for their success.

As some failures occur, a multicast tree, which is usually used to connect all participating nodes, may be partitioned into two or more sub-trees not connected with one another, which are called fragments thereafter. There are two approaches for a distributed tree restoration. Dynamic restoration does not care about partitioning before it occurs, and only when partitioning is detected does the system attempt to rejoin the fragments into a connected graph using a capacity search algorithm. This on-demand recovery usually forces affected group members to abandon the existing connections and rejoin the tree ([1], [7]). The shortcoming is the long restoration latency, which could be undesirable for many real-time applications, and it is not acceptable for some other time-critical applications which require guaranteed non-interrupted communications. The alternative is the preplanned approach where backup routes are set beforehand in addition to the primary (core) routes, and they are activated when a failure on the primary route is detected ([4], [5]). Although dynamic restoration schemes are more capacity efficient, it is usually profitable to deploy a simple preplanned method first, before a more time consuming dynamic restoration is possibly used, especially in the case of single or small-scale failures.

A. Yazici and C. Şener (Eds.): ISCIS 2003, LNCS 2869, pp. 67–74, 2003.

We present a preplanned fault recovery scheme based on virtual cyclic backup paths, called *bypass rings*, used to bypass the faulty node and restore the tree without traffic interruption, keeping the original tree structure, instead of starting from scratch. Since our protocol ensures that all fragments are reconnected and that no cycle is formed during restoration, no matter at how many nodes the fault is detected, it can be used as a platform for various methods of tree reconnection that influence the resulting tree topology in the local area of the failure. The scheme can be used universally in applications using overlay tree-topology networks for message propagation (unicasting, routing, object location, replica management, etc.).

The rest of paper is structured as follows. In section 2 the related work is summarized. Section 3 presents the model and the notations used further in the text. In section 4 we introduce the fault recovery scheme, describe the failure recovery mechanism and deal with methods for tree reconnection. Section 5 discusses the properties of our protocol and section 6 contains conclusion and sets some future directions.

2 Related Work

Several fault recovery schemes for multicast trees have been previously reported based on preplanned failure recovery. Path restoration or link restoration schemes maintain pre-computed backup virtual paths that either protect an entire individual end-to-end virtual path or are used to reroute the traffic originally carried by a single failed link. In schemes [6] and [9], a vertex-disjoint backup path from the multicast source to each destination is setup. The restoration process is fast, but the schemes are suitable only for single-source multicast trees. Link restoration scheme [10] protects against a single link failure; a backup path for each link is maintained. This scheme is scalable and preserves locality of the restoration, however, it can not be easily extended to recover the tree from a multiple failure of adjacent nodes.

In the Dual-Tree Scheme [4], a secondary tree providing alternative delivery paths is built and it is activated when node or link failure is detected in the primary tree. The scheme assumes that the underlying network is a bi-connected graph where a secondary tree disjoint from the primary tree can be constructed. In the Efficient Fault-Tolerant Multicast Routing Protocol [5], bypass paths connect nodes and their grandparents in the tree and are used to reconnect fragments when the parent node of these nodes fails. This solution is not designed for multi-source multicast trees, where the message direction often alters.

A different approach is used in Bayeux architecture [12]. The messages are routed in a tree determined by a common prefix of addresses with small salt values enabling delivery even in the case that a particular intermediate address is not available. Bayeux architecture requires Tapestry [11] as its underlying infrastructure.

3 Model and Notations

The underlying network substrate that we consider in this paper is a network providing a routing service (e.g., IP network, Tapestry [11], Pastry [8], or just a set of virtual inter-process connections with routing capability) modeled as a graph $SN = (V, E)$ where V is a finite set of vertices representing nodes; E is a finite set of edges, representing links between nodes in the network.

A multicast group MG (i.e. a set of nodes receiving multicast messages) is an arbitrary subset of nodes from V; $MG = \{n_i; i = 1, \ldots, k; n_i \in V\}$ where n_i are nodes from SN that are to exchange information and $k = |MG|$ is the multicast group size. Members of a given multicast group are connected by an overlay multicast tree, which is used as a source-independent structure for message propagation to the group members. The multicast tree is modeled as a graph $MT = (MG, CE)$ where CE is a set of *core tree edges* - virtual links (built on top of SN) connecting nodes in MG. An arbitrary set of nodes from MG is the set of multicast source nodes disseminating messages to other nodes in the tree. Thus, messages are transmitted along each virtual link in both directions (as opposed to a single source multicast tree).

We assume that nodes in MT may fail and that their faulty state can be detected by neighboring nodes. Note that we do not have to deal with physical link failures, since the multicast tree is an overlay structure. Thus, message delivery across a virtual link connecting two MT-neighbors n_1 and n_2 depends on routing in the underlying network fabric, and we expect it to deliver the message if there is a path from node n_1 to node n_2 in SN. Further, we consider each node $n \in V$ to be assigned with an SN-unique identifier ID_n from a totally ordered set of identifiers (e.g., IP address or its hash).

4 Fault Recovery Scheme

Multiple-point communication using a multicast tree is vulnerable to even a single node failure. We introduce a protocol based on virtual bypass rings constructed around each node in a multicast group and used to bypass the node in the case of failure and to reconnect the tree fragments avoiding cycles.

4.1 Basic Definitions

Let $MT = (MG, CE)$ be the tree-topology communication network. Bypass ring, further denoted $BR_c(1)$, centered at node $c \in MG$ is a circuit consisting of an ordered sequence of nodes $n_1, n_2, \ldots, n_{t+1} \in MG$, $n_1 = n_{t+1}$ such that:

1.1 For all n_i, $i = 1, \ldots, t$, distance in the tree $dist_{MT}(n_i, c) = 1$ and
1.2 $ID_{n_i} < ID_{n_{i+1}}$ for $i = 1, \ldots, t$-1.

The bypass ring $BR_c(1)$ shown in Fig. 1 consists of the ordered sequence of nodes 18, 20, 8B, A0, C3, 18 having property 1.2. The distance of each of these nodes from the center node c is 1 hop (property 1.1).

A directed *bypass edge* $be_i = (n_i, n_{i+1})$ (for all $i = 1, \ldots, t$) is a virtual link from node n_i to node n_{i+1}, where n_i is the initial node and n_{i+1} the terminal node of be_i.

Integration of all bypass rings and an MT graph creates an *extended multicast tree* $EMT = (MG, CE \cup BE)$ where CE is the set of core tree edges of original MT and BE is the set of all bypass edges. MT is then a spanning tree of EMT.

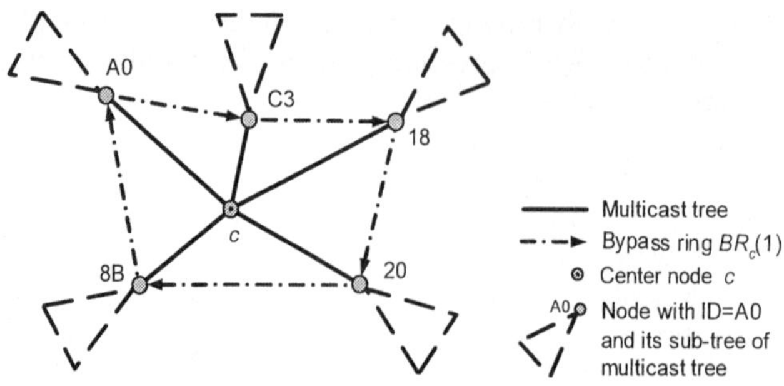

Fig. 1. Example of a bypass ring

4.2 Failure Recovery

The goal of the failure recovery is multicast tree restoration after failure of a single tree node. The restoration process creates new core tree edges using a bypass ring to connect tree fragments and restore the multicast tree *MT* to the connected and consistent state. It has to be assured that the restoration process operates properly no matter where and at how many nodes the tree restoration is simultaneously initiated.

Let node c be the faulty node in $EMT = (MG, CE \cup BE)$ and $BR_c(1)$ its bypass ring consisting of nodes $n_1, \ldots, n_t$. Define function $\mathrm{R}(n_i)$ for all n_i, $i = 1, \ldots, t$ as follows:

2.1 $\mathrm{R}(n_i) = ID_{n_f}$, if node n_i has been first notified about node c failure by node $n_f \in BR_c(1)$. If n_i detects the failure itself then $n_f = n_i$.
2.2 $\mathrm{R}(n_i)$ is undefined if n_i has not yet been involved in node c failure recovery.

Define relation $\rightarrow$: $n_i \rightarrow n_j$ if and only if:

3.1 (n_i, n_j) is the bypass edge of $BR_c(1)$ and
3.2 $\mathrm{R}(n_i)$ is defined and
3.3 $\mathrm{R}(n_i) < \mathrm{R}(n_j)$ or $\mathrm{R}(n_j)$ is not defined.

The basic idea behind the restoration process is that each neighbor $n_f = n_i$ of faulty node c detecting the failure consecutively iterates along the ring $BR_c(1)$ in the direction of the bypass edges through the nodes $n_{i_1}, n_{i_2}, \ldots \in BR_c(1)$ (n_{i_1} is the ring-neighbor of $n_i = n_{i_0}$, n_{i_2} is the ring-neighbor of n_{i_1}, etc.) until it reaches a node n_{i_p} that has already been notified about failure (i.e., $\mathrm{R}(n_{i_p})$ is defined). At each hop n_{i_q}, $1 \le q \le p$, it is determined if $n_{i_{q-1}} \rightarrow n_{i_q}$ and n_{i_q} is notified about failure of node c such that $\mathrm{R}(n_{i_q}) = ID_{n_i}$. Termination of this process is guaranteed, since $BR(1)$ consists of a finite number of nodes (each node has a finite set of neighbors in *MT*).

After node n_{i_q} has been notified and if $n_{i_{q-1}} \rightarrow n_{i_q}$ then a new core tree edge $ce_{i_q} = (n_{i_q}, n_{i_r})$ is constructed with the following properties:

4.1 $r < q$ and
4.2 $n_{i_{q-1}} \rightarrow n_{i_q}$ and
4.3 There is a path $n_{i_q}, n_{i_r}, \ldots, n_i$ in the restored *MT*.

Several methods can be deployed for selection of node n_{i_r} (see Sect. 4.3).

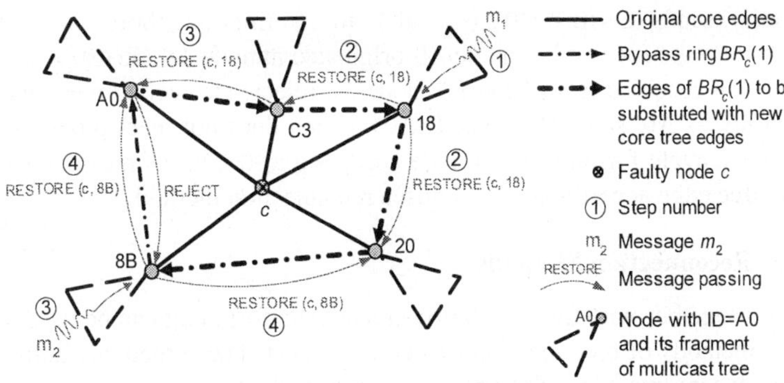

Fig. 2. Example of single failure recovery using a two-way restoration algorithm

After all nodes $n_1, \ldots, n_t \in BR_c(1)$ have been notified, the relation $\rightarrow$ between the incident nodes of all bypass edges be_i is known. With the definition of the bypass ring and $\rightarrow$ relation, it can be proven that relation $\rightarrow$ is not cyclic on the bypass ring and that there is only one edge $be_i = (n_u, n_v) \in BR_c(1)$ such that $n_u \rightarrow n_v$ is not true. Together with properties 4.1 – 4.3 of newly constructed core tree edges, we can get the following:

5.1 The restored *MT* consists of all fragments induced by a node failure.

5.2 The restored *MT* is a tree graph.

Moreover, the described technique is independent of the restoration initiating node and also prevents collisions in cases when multiple nodes initiate restoration simultaneously (which can easily happen in a distributed system).

A practical tree restoration algorithm may incorporate several performance improvements:

- The iteration along the ring from the failure detecting node n_i is performed in both directions (further referred to as a *two-way algorithm*).
- The iteration is not performed by n_i, it is rather delegated by the ring members.
- The new core tree edges are constructed on the fly, immediately after node n_{i_q} is notified and relation $n_{i_{q-1}} \rightarrow n_{i_q}$ determined.

The two-way algorithm works as follows:

Each node n_i that during message routing through the multicast tree realizes that one of its neighbors, say, node c, is down, excludes node c from its bypass ring $BR_{n_i}(1)$ and sends `RESTORE` (ID_c, ID_{n_i}) messages to the both its ring-neighbors on the ring $BR_c(1)$. Upon receiving a `RESTORE` message from its ring-neighbor, each node n_{i_q} determines relation $n_{i_{q-1}} \rightarrow n_{i_q}$ and forwards the `RESTORE` message along the ring. If there is relation $n_{i_{q-1}} \rightarrow n_{i_q}$, node n_{i_q} selects n_{i_r} according to the chosen reconnection method and creates a new core tree edge $ce_{i_q} = (n_{i_q}, n_{i_r})$.

An example of the distributed construction of relation $\rightarrow$ on BR(1) is shown in Fig. 2. In the first step, upon routing of multicast message m_1, node `18` finds that node c is not available so it sends `RESTORE(c, 18)` messages to its ring-neighbors (step 2) to determine the $\rightarrow$ relation. In step 4, another node (`8B`) initiates the tree restoration and similarly sends a `RESTORE(c, 8B)` to its ring-neighbors. Since the first `RESTORE` message received by node `A0` originated at node `18` (R(`A0`) = `18`) and the second one was received from node `8B`, node `A0` rejects the second message (there is no relation 8B $\rightarrow$ A0, since R(`8B`) $\nless$ R(`A0`), which does not meet property 3.3) and thus prevents a cycle forming. Each node accepting a `RESTORE` message establishes a new core tree edge according to the chosen reconnection method.

4.3 Tree Reconnection Methods

Bypass rings together with the $\rightarrow$ relation create a platform that can be used as a basis for various methods of reconnection of tree fragments. These methods define how to construct new core tree edges through selection of node n_{i_r} .

For convenience, SMT_c further denotes the sub-graph of a multicast tree that consists of all member-nodes of $BR_c(1)$ and the set of new core tree edges constructed during the restoration after node c failure. Based on optimization requirements, one of the following approaches to creation of new core tree edges can be chosen:

- *LRM method.* When creating a new core tree edge, node $n_{i_{q-1}}$ is chosen as node n_{i_r} ; the sub-graph *SMT* forms a linear tree. This approach is preferable if optimization priority is not to increase the degree of nodes in *MT*
- *TRM method.* Node R(n_i) is chosen as n_{i_r} . Thus, all nodes n_i on the ring are connected to R(n_i) and also to R(n_j) if there is a node n_j such that $n_i \rightarrow n_j$ and R(n_j) $\neq$ R(n_i). This method is preferable if optimization priority is to retain the mutual distance of nodes n_i and thus not to increase the *MT* diameter.
- *HRM method.* This method is a combination of both LRM and TRM methods. Specifically, it is similar to TRM except that the path from R(n_i) to n_i may contain one or more intermediate nodes n_j with R(n_j) = R(n_i).

LRM and TRM methods behave extremely in terms of the node degree increase and *SMT* diameter after restoration; HRM method represents a compromise between these two methods. For an illustration, Fig. 3a shows the maximum degree increase of nodes in *SMT* sub-graph relative to the average degree of these nodes before the failure. LRM method produces the lowest maximum node degree increase since it forms *SMT* as a linear tree. The highest degree increase is caused by TRM method.

5 Discussion

Bypass rings *BR*(1) are capable of the recovery from failure of a multicast tree member node, which normally causes the tree to be partitioned into several fragments. The scheme uses only neighboring nodes to reroute the traffic and does not influence the rest of the tree. For any tree restoration to be successful, there has to be a path not containing faulty nodes in the underlying routing infrastructure between each two neighboring nodes on the bypass ring.

The asymptotical memory overhead of a bypass ring *BR*(1) is $O(d)$, where d is the average node degree in *MT*. Tree restoration can be done in the worst case in $O(d)$ steps. However, the time to perform a recovery is inversely proportional to the num-

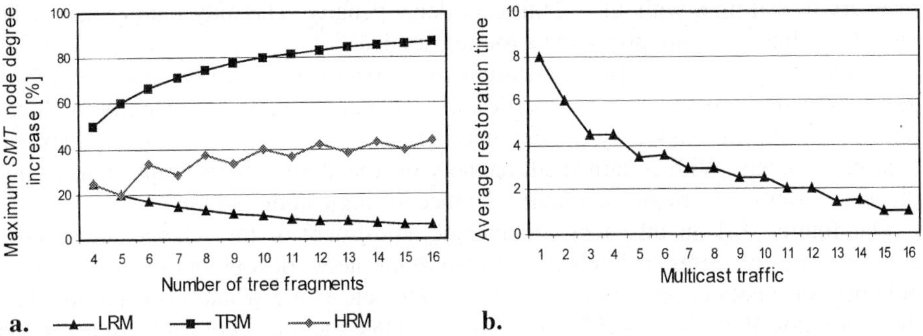

Fig. 3. a. Maximum degree increase of nodes in *SMT* sub-graph after restoration, **b.** Average restoration time

ber of nodes simultaneously initiating the restoration, and it is further reduced if the `RESTORE` message is routed in both directions in a bypass ring (two-way algorithm).

Fig. 3b shows the average restoration time vs. multicast traffic in the multicast tree provided that the message sources are located evenly in all tree fragments. The measure for the restoration time is the highest number of nodes of the bypass ring that a single `RESTORE` message has to go through; the multicast traffic is expressed as the number of the $BR(1)$ member nodes initiating the tree restoration simultaneously. The diagram in Fig. 3b shows the average restoration time of failure recovery using a two-way algorithm for reconnection of 16 tree fragments.

The important property of the bypass ring scheme is the fact that the tree restoration (as well as the other operations with bypass rings) is independent of the size of multicast group. The restoration affects only the closest neighbors of the failed node, the failure recovery is performed locally and it does not influence nor alter the rest of the tree. Thus the scheme is scalable and it allows more restorations ($\lfloor \frac{k}{2} \rfloor$ in the best case) to be performed simultaneously in a single multicast tree (i.e. more simultaneous nonadjacent failures are recoverable by the scheme).

The scheme can be extended to be able to recover the tree from even a cluster of adjacent failed nodes. The idea is to create bypass rings of higher radii in addition to rings $BR(1)$. A bypass ring of radius r centered at node c, denoted $BR_c(r)$, consists of multicast group members in the distance r from center node c. By suitable `RESTORE` message routing, which can combine more bypass rings of different radii centered at different nodes, it is possible to recover from a failure of clusters with the diameter less or equal to $2(r_{max}\text{-}1)$ where r_{max} is the greatest radius of deployed bypass rings.

6 Conclusion

We have proposed a novel failure recovery scheme for tree-topology communication networks based on virtual bypass rings that are used to restore the tree when a member node fails. The important properties of the scheme are scalability, locality, independence of the direction of multicast traffic in the tree and capability to perform the recovery in real time without a significant delay penalty. The only requirement is an underlying infrastructure providing a routing service.

Multicasting is not the only application where our scheme can be successfully deployed. Owing to its favorable properties, the scheme can be used generally in all applications using tree-topology overlay networks to connect or communicate between their components. With certain small memory overhead, the scheme represents a simple and versatile way to provide fault-tolerance to single node failures.

Our future work in this area will include adjustment of the scheme for specific characteristics of different kinds of the underlying network topologies, including topologies for parallel computing (grid, hypercube, etc.). We would also like to adapt the restoration algorithm for *BR*(*r*) rings and evaluate the impact of ring radius *r* to the fault-tolerance level provided in typical scenarios.

Acknowledgement. This work was elaborated as a part of the Gaston project at the Czech Technical University in Prague. Gaston [3] is a peer-to-peer large-scale file system designed to provide a fault-tolerant and highly available file service.

References

1. Ballardie, A., Francis, P., Crowcroft, J.: Core Based Trees (CBT). In Proc. of ACM SIGCOMM '93 (1993)
2. Chang, E.G., Roberts, R.: An Improved Algorithm for Decentralized Extrema-Finding in Circular Configuration of Processors. In Comm. of the ACM, vol. 22, no. 5 (1979)
3. Dynda, V., Rydlo, P.: Large-scale Distributed File System Design and Architecture. In Acta Polytechnica, vol. 42, no. 1, (2002)
4. Fei, A., Cui, J., Gerla, M., Cavendish, D.: A Dual-Tree Scheme for Fault-Tolerant Multicast. In Proc. of ICC 2001, Helsinki, Finland (2001)
5. Jia, W., Zhao, W., Xuan, D., Xu, G.: An Efficient Fault-Tolerant Multicast Routing Protocol with Core-Based Tree Techniques. In Proc. of IEEE ICPP, Wakamatsu, Japan (1999)
6. Kawamura, R., Sato, K., Tokizawa, I.: Self-Healing ATM Networks Based on Virtual Path Concept. In IEEE J. Selected Areas In Comm. (1997)
7. Mehra, P., Chatterjee, S.: Efficient Data Dissemination in OceanStore. http://www-video.eecs.berkeley.edu/~pmehra/classes/cs262/paper.pdf (2001)
8. Rowstron, A. et al.: Pastry: Scalable, Distributed Object Location and Routing for Large-Scale Peer-To-Peer Systems. In Proc. of ACM DSP (Middleware '01) (2001)
9. Wu, C., Lee, W., Hou, Y.: Back-Up VP Preplanning Strategies for Survivable Multicast ATM Networks. In Proc. of IEEE ICC '97 (1997)
10. Wu, C., Lee, W., Hou, Y., Chu, W.: A New Preplanned Self-Healing Scheme for Multicast ATM Network. In Proc. of IEEE ICC '97 (1997)
11. Zhao, B.Y et al.: Tapestry: An Infrastructure for Fault-Tolerant Wide-Area Location and Routing. U. C. Berkeley Technical Report UCB/CSD-01-1141 (2001)
12. Zhuang, S. et. al.: Bayeux: An Architecture for Scalable and Fault-Tolerant Wide-Area Data Dissemination. In Proc. of NOSSDAV '01 (2001)

Modelling Multi-disciplinary Scientific Experiments and Information

Ersin Cem Kaletas, Hamideh Afsarmanesh, and L.O. (Bob) Hertzberger

University of Amsterdam, Informatics Institute
Kruislaan 403, 1098 SJ Amsterdam, The Netherlands
{kaletas, hamideh, bob}@science.uva.nl

Abstract. Emergence of advanced complex experiments in applied sciences resulted in a change in the way of experimentation. Information management plays an important role in supporting such scientific experiments. In this paper, we address the modelling requirements of scientific experiments and information. We describe a novel experiment model as the base for a support environment, and data models developed for the representation of different components of the experiment model.

1 Introduction

Advances in the laboratory instruments and techniques have caused the automation of many steps in scientific experiments, which in turn resulted in a change in the way of experimentation. Such changes to experimentation have naturally affected scientists. The following can be mentioned among the characteristics of emerging experiments, which created a burden on the shoulders of scientists: Increasing complexity of laboratory instruments; longer and more complex experimental procedures (e.g. clone preparation phase of a micro-array experiment contains up to 51 steps [1]); large amounts of data generated during experiments; heterogeneity of experiments and their results (e.g. 281 biological database resources in 18 different categories were listed in 2001 [2]); and need for collaboration to share resources and experience.

Information management plays an important role in supporting scientific experiments, in the sense that it is involved in all types of scientific experiments, and at any and all stages of the experimental procedures. For scientific experiments, not only the proper management of results are important, but also the management of information related to the followed experimental procedures, and utilized instruments and tools are important. Information management related problems that a scientist faces during experiments can be summarized as follows:

- Increasing number and complexity of instruments and procedures used in a lab requires significant effort to perform an experiment while avoiding mistakes. Expertise is very important here, however, it is generally not well documented and its transfer depends on the availability of the expert.
- Heterogeneity causes difficulties in modelling and storage of experimental information, often resulting in unorganized collections of large data sets.

A. Yazici and C. Şener (Eds.): ISCIS 2003, LNCS 2869, pp. 75–82, 2003.

– Lack of standards for modelling and representation of information causes wasted efforts for developing *specific solutions* to overcome *common problems* and difficulties in comparing the results obtained in multiple experiments.

In this paper, we address the modelling requirements of scientific experiments. In specific, we will focus on modelling experimental designs (i.e. procedures), activities (i.e. history of events), experimental data / information (i.e. results), and metadata (i.e. annotations and conclusions). The adopted *experiment model* has a direct influence on modelling different aspects of scientific experiments, making the experiment model the main topic of this paper. We first describe the approach taken to model experimental information in Section 2. Section 3 presents the proposed experiment model. Section 4 describes the data models developed for representing the different components of the experiment model. Section 5 gives an overview of the related work. Finally, Section 6 concludes by briefly describing the implementation of the experiment model in the VLAM-G virtual laboratory environment.

2 Approach for Modelling Experimental Information

In this section, the approach taken for systematic modelling of experimental information is described, in the form of steps involved in the approach.

2.1 Process-Data Flows

The first step in the approach is to perform a detailed analysis of the experimental procedures of experiments from a certain domain. The resulting conceptual model includes a comprehensive step-by-step definition of the experiments, which is referred to as the Process-Data Flow (PDF). In a PDF, every step involved in an experiment, the attributes of each step, and the relationships among the steps are defined. Three different types of steps (elements) are defined in a PDF: Activity steps; data steps; and related data elements whose instances are common to all experiments (e.g. organism information in micro-array experiments).

2.2 Common Characteristics of Scientific Experiments

In order to provide *generic* solutions to support experiments from different applied science domains, common characteristics of these experiments need to be identified. Personal experiences of the authors with micro-array, confocal microscopy, material analysis, and traffic simulation experiments, and an extensive study of several other experiments and applications from the literature allowed the identification of the most common characteristics of scientific experiments:

– *Scientist* performing the experiment (owner of the experiment)
– *Input data* (e.g. acquired from a device)
– A set of *processes*, applied on the input data

- *Output data* (e.g. obtained by applying a process on an input data)
- Devices (*hardware*) (e.g. to acquire data, or to perform a process)
- *Software* (e.g. to control a specific device, or to perform a specific process)
- *Conditions* and *parameters* for the processes, devices, and software
- A ***recursive flow of processes and data*** where a specific order is followed during an experiment

2.3 General Structure of Scientific Experiments

Before describing the proposed experiment model in details, it is necessary to describe scientific experiments in general terms. The extensive study, as described in the previous subsection, has lead to the definition of the general structure of scientific experiments: Scientific experiments consist of a number of steps, where a step may correspond to an entity (e.g. a sample), a data element (e.g. an image of the sample), or an activity (e.g. treating the sample, analyzing the image). Steps in an experiment follows the order corresponding to the experiment logic. A project is a grouping of related experiments. Experiments in a project may follow an order (e.g. time course experiments), or may be unordered (e.g. comparison experiments). The proposed experiment model builds on the general structure of scientific experiments as described here.

3 The Proposed Experiment Model

What characterizes a support environment for scientific experiments is its underlying experiment model. Among others, the experiment model defines how the functionality of the support environment is presented to the users, how scientists interact with the environment, and how experiments as well as experimental data / information are stored and managed. Furthermore, it allows a methodological definition and modelling of complex experiments in a problem domain.

The three main components of the proposed experiment model are the *procedure*, the *context*, and the *processing*. A graphical illustration of the experiment model is shown in Fig. 1, using parts from micro-array experiments as example.

3.1 Procedure

A *procedure* is a formalized abstraction of common data and processing steps that are typically involved in a certain type of scientific experiment. Many of these steps are identical and follow the same order in successive instantiations of the experiment, thus a procedure can be seen as a template for that type of experiments. However, in the proposed experiment model, a procedure means more than a template. Since it is defined by an expert, a procedure captures the expertise and knowledge of the expert in his/her domain. Hence, a procedure serves as a facilitator for modelling complex experiments in a scientific domain and for preventing the loss of expertise and knowledge by transferring them to the users of the procedure. Furthermore, procedures are used to provide context-sensitive assistance to novice users for complex studies; helping them to avoid making mistakes and to increase the efficiency and accuracy of their experiments.

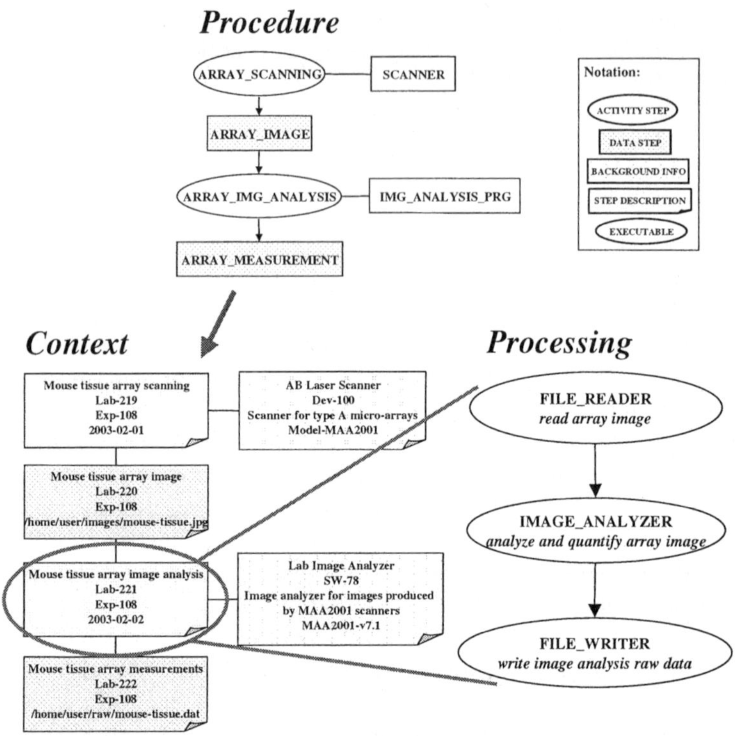

Fig. 1. Graphical illustration of the proposed experiment model

3.2 Context

A *context* is the instantiation of a procedure, consisting of the descriptions of steps involved in the procedure. A context is about the meaning and the processing of data. It is defined by a series of steps, that are formalized as a procedure, intended to solve a particular problem in a particular domain. It includes descriptions of both data steps (i.e. metadata) and process steps for handling the data (i.e. history of activities). Process steps may correspond to raw data generation from instruments, data processing, retrieval and storage of raw or processed data, or visualization steps. Data elements, in turn, correspond to both raw data generated by instruments and used as input to processes, and to processed data and/or information generated by processes. Data steps may also correspond to generic data elements that are not directly used in experiments but provide for background for the experiment being performed, such as information about organisms or genes, or description of the scanner used in a micro-array experiment.

3.3 Processing

The process steps in a context correspond to the actual data flow in an experiment; usually from an instrument, through analysis software, to data storage facilities. Consequently, the process steps are represented by a data flow graph, called *processing*. A processing usually consists of self-contained software entities, each of which may be performing an experiment specific task or a generic task. An example of experiment specific tasks is instrument control, while file manipulation is an example of generic tasks. A processing for analyzing a data set may be defined by a scientist by connecting a number of software entities to each other to represent the analysis as a flow of data through the processes. When defined, a processing is executed on one or more computers.

4 Representing the Proposed Experiment Model

In this section, the data models designed for representing the three components of the proposed experiment model are described.

4.1 Modelling Procedures: Procedure Data Model

A procedure is composed of the data types defined in an application database (e.g. micro-array DB). In other words, every procedure element has a corresponding data type in the application database schema. The *Procedure Data Model* (Fig. 2) facilitates the representation and storage of experimental procedures.

A `Procedure` object contains the generic information about a procedure. Multiple versions of the same procedure can exist. Every `Procedure` consists of a set of `ProcedureElements`. The corresponding data type for an element is represented by the `className` attribute. `isProcessing` indicates whether the element actually corresponds to a *processing*, i.e. a computational activity. The `reusePolicy` attribute is used to define what to do in case of a query on the type represented by this element. `ProcedureConnections` correspond to the relationships between classes, indicated by the `relName` attribute. `ProcedureGUI` objects keep information about the graphical properties of the procedure.

4.2 Modelling Contexts: Experimentation Environment Data Model

A context is an instance of a procedure, and the procedure elements correspond to data types in an application database. This means, a context actually consists of a number of objects in the application database, hence, modelling the

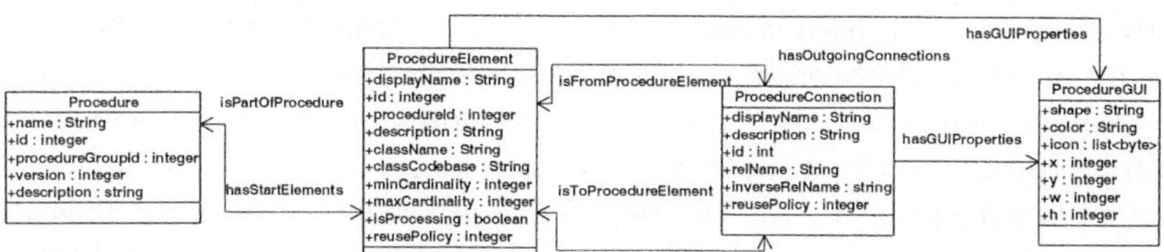

Fig. 2. The Procedure Data Model

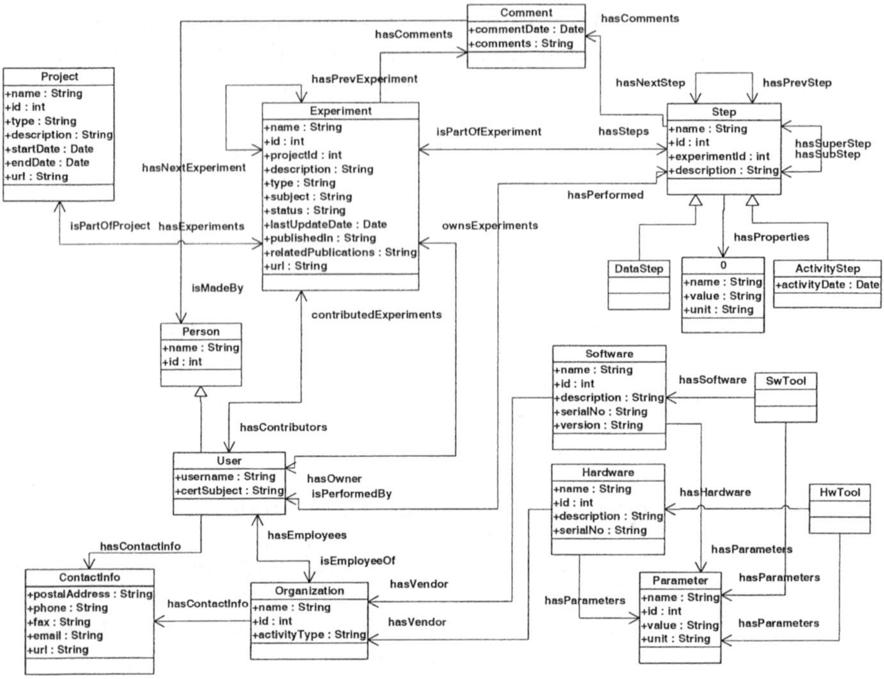

Fig. 3. Experimentation Environment Data Model (EEDM)

application database schema for the domain of an experiment is sufficient for modelling the contexts of that experiment.

Using the general structure of scientific experiments, a base data model for experimental information called *Experimentation Environment Data Model* (EEDM) is designed (see Fig. 3). EEDM aims at the storage and retrieval of *generic definition of the steps and information* involved in a scientific experiment, for the purpose of *investigation and reproducibility*. EEDM covers the general aspects of an experiment while maintaining its recursive nature. It includes elements from existing standards, such as Dublin Core [3].

The most important aspect of the EEDM is that it allows any ordering of activity and data steps, which enables the model to represent any process-data flow in an experiment. The key to this aspect is the application of recursion as described in Sec. 2.3, used within the experiment step definition. The order is given by using recursive *next* and *previous* pointers from one step to another. The same method is used for experiments, to represent the order of experiments within a project. An experiment step can also be represented as an aggregation of a number of steps, using the *sub-step* and *super-step* relationships. This allows the abstraction of experiment steps at any desired level. Experimental information (e.g. conditions and results) are modelled by sub-typing the activity or data steps. Conditions can also be modelled as *properties* attached to a step.

The `Project` class is the root of the EEDM hierarchy. It keeps information about a project, and groups together the (logically) related experiments. The `Experiment` class lies in the center of the EEDM. It defines the experiment being performed, covering only the high-level information such as the type, subject, and a brief textual description. *Multi-disciplinary experiments* are represented by attaching experiments from different domains under the same project.

A detailed description of EEDM constructs can be found in [4].

4.3 Modelling Processings: Software Entity and Processing Data Models

A context provides descriptions of processing steps involved in an experiment, while a processing provides both descriptions of the actual executables used (i.e. software entities) and run-time information for the processing. Data models are described below; however, UML diagrams are omitted due to space limitations.

Modelling information about software entities. Software entities are self-contained executable programs. They are mainly characterized by the tasks that they perform, their input and output data types, parameters, and run-time requirements. A software entity can be atomic or aggregate (consisting of a number of other software entities). Every atomic software entity corresponds to an executable, for which, its developer specifies the run-time requirements to help the users to decide which software entities to use in his/her processing.

Modelling processing designs. A user designs a *processing* by attaching a number of software entities to each other through their input and output ports. This design must be stored for future references and for possible re-runs. For each process executed as part of the processing, run-time information associated with the process is saved, such as the actual host that the process was scheduled for execution, and the actual values of the parameters and environment variables. A processing is executable and every process in the processing has different information for each execution of the processing. Hence, processes executed as part of a processing are considered as *instances* of the software entity descriptions.

5 Related Work

There are two main approaches to modelling scientific experiment and information. The first approach considers *experiments* as the base for modelling. In *Moose* [5], similar to the experiment model presented here, experiments are modelled as schemas that are instances of a meta-model. However, experimentation is achieved through the derived relationship mechanism, where output of an experiment is described as derived relationships based on the input. The *Object Protocol Model* (OPM) [6] provides a protocol class for modelling experiments, with input and output attributes. Protocols are modelled as recursive expansions of alternative sub-protocols, sequences of sub-protocols, and optional sub-protocols. OPM does not include any constructs for actual processings.

The second approach, on the other hand, is more computation oriented, and considers experiments as *jobs*. Among the examples of the second approach, *Ecce* [7] stores experimental designs in XML, data as binary files, and metadata as name-value pairs. *UNICORE* [8] defines a protocol for job descriptions called *Abstract Job Object* (AJO), which contains other AJOs and/or atomic tasks, their dependencies, information about the destination site, and site-specific security.

6 Conclusions

In this paper, we presented a novel experiment model that covers all aspects of a scientific experiment in applied sciences. Furthermore, data models that are developed for the representation of the experiment model were described. The experiment model and the data models presented here, to our knowledge, are novel and unique in the sense that no such other models exist that *uniformly* cover all aspects of an experiment.

The models described here are implemented by the **VLAM-G** virtual laboratory environment [9] and its information management platform **VIMCO**. Both **Expressive DB** for micro-array [1] and **MACS DB** for material analysis [10] studies implement the procedure data model and extend the EEDM for modelling domain specific information. Another VIMCO database (**RTS DB**) implements the software entity and processing design data models. The processings are executed by VLAM-G using the distributed resources on the Grid.

References

1. E.C. Kaletas et.al: EXPRESSIVE: A Database for MicroArray Gene Expression Studies. University of Amsterdam, Informatics Intitute. Tech.Rep. CS-2001-02
2. A.D. Baxevanis: The Molecular Biology Database Collection: An Updated Compilation of Biological Database Resources. Nucleic Acids Research. **29** 2001 1–10
3. Dublin Core Metadata Initiative - Web page. `http://dublincore.org/` 2003
4. E.C. Kaletas et.al: Virtual Laboratory Experimentation Environment Data Model. University of Amsterdam, Informatics Intitute. Tech.Rep. CS-2001-01
5. Y.E. Ioannidis et.al: ZOO: A Desktop Experiment Management Environment. In Proceedings of the 22nd International Conference on Very Large Data Bases (VLDB 1996) 1996 274–285
6. I.A. Chen, V.M. Markowitz: An Overview of the Object Protocol Model (OPM) and the OPM Data Management Tools. Information Systems. **20–5** 1995
7. K.L. Schuchardt et.al: A Web-Based Data Architecture for Problem Solving Environments: Application of Distributed Authoring and Versioning to the Extensible Computational Chemistry Environment. Cluster Computing. **5** 2002 287–296
8. D.W. Erwin: UNICORE - A Grid Compuing Environment. Concurrency and Computation: Practice and Experience. **14** 2002 1395–1410
9. H. Afsarmanesh et.al: VLAM-G: A Grid-based Virtual Laboratory. Scientific Programming. **10** 2002 173–181
10. A. Frenkel et.al: Information Management for Material Science Applications in a Virtual Laboratory. In Proceedings of the 12th International Conference on Database and Expert Systems Applications (DEXA 2001) 2001 165–174

KinCA: An InfiniBand Host Channel Adapter Based on Dual Processor Cores

Sangman Moh[1], Kyoung Park[2], and Sungnam Kim[2]

[1]School of Internet Eng., Chosun University
375 Seoseok-dong, Dong-gu, Gwangju, 501-759 Korea
smmoh@chosun.ac.kr

[2]Computer System Dept., ETRI
161 Gajeong-dong, Yuseong-gu, Daejeon, 305-350 Korea
{kyoung, ksn}@etri.re.kr

Abstract. InfiniBand technology is being accepted as the future system interconnect to serve as the high-end enterprise fabric for cluster computing. This paper presents the design and implementation of an InfiniBand host channel adapter (HCA) based on dual ARM9 processor cores. The HCA is an SoC called KinCA which connects a host node onto the InfiniBand network both in hardware and in software. Since the ARM9 processor core does not provide necessary features for multiprocessor configuration, novel inter-processor communication and interrupt mechanisms between the two processors were designed and embedded within the KinCA chip. KinCA was fabricated as a 564-pin enhanced BGA (Ball Grid Array) device using 0.18μm CMOS technology. Mounted on host nodes, it provides 10 Gbps outbound and inbound channels for transmit and receive, respectively, enabling a high-performance cluster system.

1 Introduction

Since the first computer called ENIAC was developed in 1946, computers have been evolved and sometimes revolved. InfiniBand is a new system interconnection technology that improves the way servers interconnect with input/output devices and with each other. It is a point-to-point, switched fabric architecture [1]. InfiniBand architecture is a well-defined technology with a specification that was initially announced by the InfiniBand Trade Association (IBTA) in October 2000 [2]. InfiniBand was initially come from a play on the words "infinite bandwidth" [1].

Initially, the InfiniBand technology is a PCI (Peripheral Component Interconnect) replacement, promoting faster and more powerful adapters [3]. However, InfiniBand is much more than a PCI replacement. It provides many advanced capabilities necessary for server clustering. Two primary goals of InfiniBand are overcoming PCI limitations (performance bottlenecks, expandability, scalability, etc.) and improving the proprietary technologies emerging in the clustering space as a standard [4-8].

The InfiniBand technology is being widely accepted as the future system interconnect to serve as the universal enterprise fabric for cluster computing [9]. The scope of InfiniBand covers a large range and spans many market segments (storage, communi

A. Yazici and C. Şener (Eds.): ISCIS 2003, LNCS 2869, pp. 83–90, 2003.

cations, networking, server platforms, etc.) from standard high-volume server products to high-end server solutions [4]. In other words, InfiniBand is a rich and complex technology designed to overcome existing barriers and, at the same time, to provide the framework for new and enhanced features and capabilities.

In this paper, we present the design and implementation of an InfiniBand host channel adapter (HCA) based on dual ARM9 processor cores. The HCA is an SoC called KinCA which connects a host node onto the InfiniBand network both in hardware and in software. Since the ARM9 processor core does not provide necessary features for multiprocessor configuration, new inter-processor communication and interrupt mechanisms between the two processors were designed and embedded within the KinCA chip. Many DFT (Design For Testability) features are included in KinCA for design verification and testability. KinCA was fabricated as a 564-pin enhanced BGA (Ball Grid Array) device using 0.18μm CMOS technology. Mounted on host nodes, it provides 10 Gbps outbound and inbound channels for transmit and receive, respectively, resulting in a high-performance cluster system.

The rest of the paper is organized as follows: The architecture of the InfiniBand technology are described briefly in the following section. Section 3 presents and discusses the design of KinCA including layered architecture, multiprocessor issues, and verification. The implementation results and performance are presented in Section 4. Finally, conclusion is discussed in Section 5.

2 InfiniBand Architecture

There are four primary components for an InfiniBand fabric. An HCA, an interface within a server, communicates directly with the server's memory, processor, and the IBA (InfiniBand Architecture) fabric. A TCA (Target Channel Adapter) is categorized mainly into two adapters of a storage adapter and a network adapter. It can be regarded as a bridge between a host computer and some I/O devices. A switch allows HCAs and TCAs to connect to it and controls network traffic within the corresponding subnet. A router is a kind of bridge between a local network (called subnet) and other external subnets [1, 4-5]. Fig. 1 shows an InfiniBand-based system area network.

The end nodes interconnected via the InfiniBand network communicate each other [7-8]. An application program issues message send/receive requests and gets completion information of the requests from a kind of programming interface called Verb. An HCA or a TCA retrieves a request queue, reads the corresponding message from the host memory, and then packetizes and sends it to the network. Received packets are assembled again into a message and stored in a work queue. The node recognizes the completion status of the requested message by retrieving the corresponding completion queue element.

There are four layers in IBA; *i.e.*, physical layer, link layer, network layer, and transport layer [4-8]. The InfiniBand physical layer defines the electrical and mechanical characteristics of IBA, including cables, connectors, and hot-swap characteristics. The link layer is central to IBA and includes packet layout, point-to-point link instructions, switching within a subnet and data integrity. The network layer is responsible for routing packets from one subnet to another. The transport layer processes various kinds of messages and the delivery sequence of packets as well as partitioning, multiplexing and transport services requiring reliable connections and datagrams [1, 4-5].

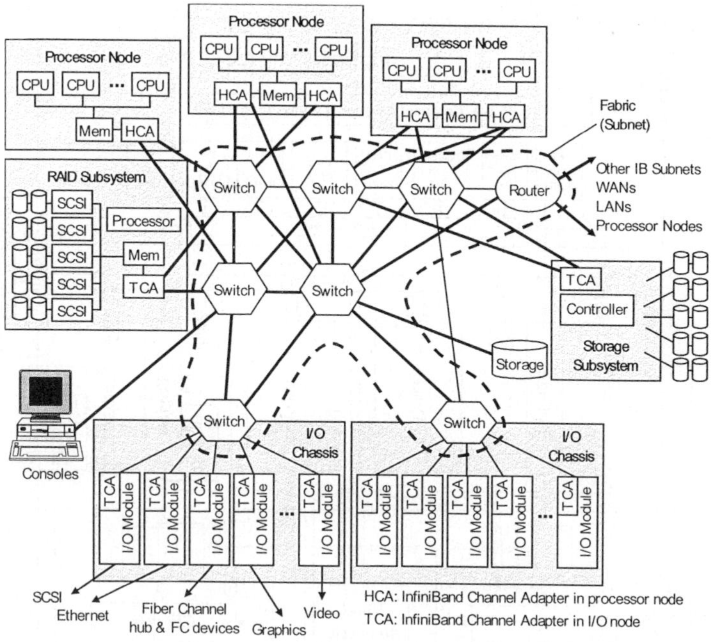

Fig. 1. System area network of InfiniBand.

3 Design of KinCA

The InfiniBand HCA, KinCA, is an IBA device which produces and consumes packets between a host node and the InfiniBand network. In this section, the design and verification issues of KinCA are presented, focusing on layered architecture, multiprocessor issues, and verification.

3.1 Layered Architecture

KinCA has a layered architecture as shown in Fig. 2 where host interface, transport, network/link, and physical layers are explicitly depicted. KinCA transmits and receives messages simultaneously, and the transmit and receive flows are separate from each other along with all the protocol stacks (layers).

The host interface contains not only a protocol engine that processes commands and messages but also DMA engines that read and write message data from/to the host main memory. In our design, the host bus is the industry standard PCI-X bus, so the host interface can be regarded as a bridge between the PCI-X bus and the Infini-

Band transport layer. Hardware doorbells, a set of registers, provide the communication interface between the host processor and the transport layer of KinCA.

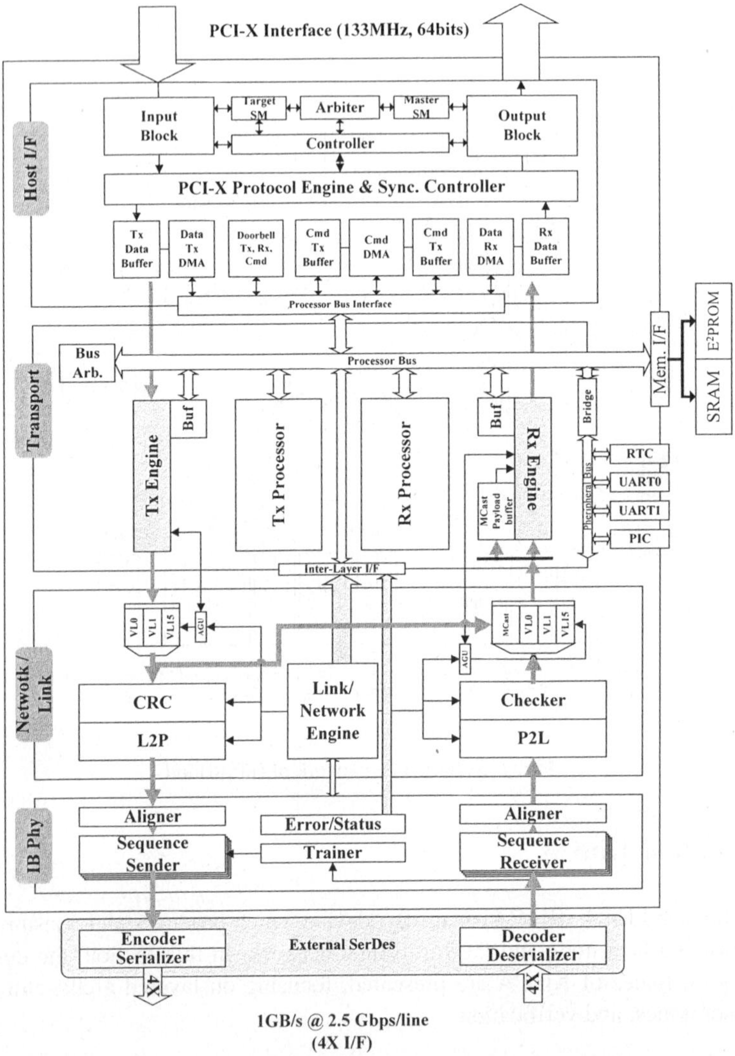

Fig. 2. Architectural organization of KinCA.

The transport layer processes the InfiniBand transport protocol both in hardware and in software. For software processing, two ARM9 processors are embedded in KinCA, each of which handles transmit and receive protocols, respectively. The transmit processor and transmit engine receive message send requests from the host interface via doorbell and packetize them in accordance with the InfiniBand transport protocol using DMA interface, and then forward the packets down to the network/link layer. On the other hand, the receive processor and receive engine depacketize and validate the packets come up from the network/link layer and store the received data onto the host main memory using DMA interface, and then finally notify the fact of a message receive to the host interface via doorbell. Note here that a message consists of one or more packets. Even though the two processors have to communicate and cooperate each other in KinCA for initial setup and message transfer operations, the ARM9 processor does not have any features for multiprocessing. This fact makes us design new inter-processor communication and interrupt mechanisms which are discussed in detail in the following subsection.

The network/link layer handles the network and link layers of the InfiniBand protocol, controlling data packets as well as link packets. For deadlock avoidance, buffering, and flow control, three virtual lanes (two for data and one for management) are provided for each direction. The CRC generator and checker are also designed for error control at hardware level. FSM-style design of the network/link engine makes the protocol processing very fast.

The physical layer transmits and receives bit stream to/from the InfiniBand network. The link trainer, 8b/10b conversion logic, bit aligners, packet sequence sender and receiver, and error and status controllers carry out the role of the physical layer together in conjunction with external serializer/deserializer. The transmit and receive channels transfer the InfiniBand packets at the peak rate of 10 Gbps, respectively.

3.2 Multiprocessor Issues

When packets of 2 Kbytes in MTU are transferred through 10 Gbps channels with 8b/10b coding, KinCA has to process approximately 500K packets a second on peak; i.e., 10 Gbps / (2 Kbytes/packet × 8 bits/byte × 10b/8b) ≈ 500K packets/sec.

Moreover, since KinCA processes the transmit and receive flows simultaneously, both 500K transmit packets and 500K receive packets should be processed at the same time in KinCA. When a single processor core of ARM9 provides the performance of 200 MIPS, about 200 IPS (Instructions Per Second) can be assigned to each packet. According to implementation constraints, however, the performance budget per packet is decreased considerably.

Instead of a single processor, therefore, dual ARM9 processor cores are used for transmit and receive processing, respectively. This has the performance budget per packet increase to at least 250 IPS. Such a design of dual processor cores gives two advantages that software design becomes simpler due to separate handling of transmit and receive flows and a real-time operating system is not required. On the other hand, in order to perform two independent tasks of transmit and receive flows using a single processor core, a small real-time operating system is highly required to manage processes between the two tasks. Such an operating system, however, leads to system overhead. By running the transmit and receive routines in separate processor cores in firmware level, the operating system is not required and, thus, the overhead due to OS interference is removed.

The embedded dual ARM9 processor cores [11] share memory and peripherals through the internal buses, resulting in a multiprocessor system. The two ARM9 processor cores are connected to high-performance peripherals [12-13] including memories though the processor bus [14]. Notice here that the 32-bit processor bus consists of separate address and data lines and has a bus arbitration feature to allow multiple bus masters. Low-performance peripherals [15-16] are connected to the peripheral bus. The processor and peripheral buses are interconnected transparently to software through the bridge.

The following devices are connected to the internal buses: two ARM922T processors, host interface block, vector interrupt controller, static memory controller, IPC (Inter-Processor Communication) controller, local interface to transmit and receive engines, bridge, two RTCs, and two UARTs.

For performance and programmability, memories and all peripherals are shared by the two ARM9 processors, resulting in a kind of symmetric multiprocessors. For a multiprocessor system, specific processor identifiers, inter-processor communication, and inter-processor interrupt are necessarily required. However, the ARM9 processor does provide nothing suitable for those features. Therefore, we had to and did design the following features:

- Processor identifier assignment: After system initialization, a specific processor identifier is assigned to each processor in accordance with the randomly selected booting sequence of two processors.
- Inter-processor communication: A mail box mechanism, which contains communication request commands and messages, is provided between the processors for delivering inter-processor communication messages.
- Asynchronous inter-processor interrupt: Asynchronous programmable interrupt hardware is provided for handling asynchronous inter-processor interrupts between the processors.
- Interrupt redirection: For the load balancing of vectored interrupts, new interrupt redirection mechanism is provided. A processor can redirect an interrupt to be processed to the other processor, along with this mechanism.

3.3 Verification

KinCA is a high-density SoC that integrates more than 4 million gates, making the design verification complex. In order to reduce verification time and minimize computing resource, we developed a macro engine simulating the ARM9 processor. This can be regarded as a simplified version of the ARM9 processor specialized for the functional verification of our KinCA design. Some other simulation models including memory models were developed as well.

For DFT features, ARM-provided logic of ARM9 and peripherals, memory BIST, internal full scan associated with ATPG, and JTAG boundary scan were included in the KinCA design. In particular, for the verification of the ARM9 processor itself and peripherals connected to the internal buses, the vendor-specific TIC vectors [14], which were provided by ARM, were used. The environment of design verification was also used in part for netlist verification and timing analysis, and many of them became test patterns of the KinCA chip.

4 Implementation Results

After design and verification phases, KinCA was fabricated with 0.18μm 4-layer metal CMOS standard cell technology. Fig. 3 shows the layout result of KinCA implemented on a 10 mm × 10 mm die. The major implementation specifications of KinCA also include 4.4 million gates, 250 MHz, and 3.5 Watts in total.

Fig. 3. Layout result of KinCA.

Fig. 4. KinCA chip.

KinCA was manufactured with a 564-pin enhanced BGA package, which is shown in Fig. 4. It was mounted on the PCI card (board) with a PCI-X slot. With the KinCA cards, multiple hosts can be interconnected each other via the InfiniBand fabric to configure a high-end cluster system of multiple nodes. Fig. 5 shows the testbed in which two nodes with the KinCA cards are interconnected through the InfiniBand fabric, resulting in a high-performance cluster system.

Fig. 5. Testbed of a KinCA based cluster system.

5 Conclusion

In this paper, the design and implementation of an InfiniBand HCA, called KinCA, based on dual ARM9 processor cores has been presented and discussed. Since the ARM9 processor core does not provide necessary features for multiprocessor configuration, new inter-processor communication and interrupt mechanisms were designed and embedded within the chip. In-depth design verification associated with many DFT features considerably improves the function and performance of KinCA. The fabricated KinCA is a 564-pin enhanced BGA device where 0.18μm 4-layer metal CMOS standard cell technology was used. Mounted on host nodes, KinCA provides 10 Gbps outbound and inbound channels for transmit and receive, respectively, resulting in a high-performance cluster system. The effective bandwidth varies with the communication characteristics of applications.

References

1. JNI Corporation, An Introduction to InfiniBand: Bridging I/O up to Speed. White Paper, http://www.jni.com/Products/ib.cfm (2001)
2. InfiniBand Trade Association (IBTA) Official Homepage. http://www.infinibandta.org/ (2003)
3. Pendery, D., Eunice, J.: InfiniBand Architecture: Bridge over Troubled Waters. Research Note, http://www.infinibandta.org/newsroom/whitepapers/ (2000)
4. Futral, W. T.: InfiniBand Architecture Development and Deployment: A Strategic Guide to Server I/O Solution. Intel Press (2001)
5. Shanley, T.: InfiniBand Network Architecture. Edited by Winkles J., Addison-Wesley (2002)
6. Moh, S.: Trend and Perspective of the InfiniBand Technology. Electronic Times, Mar. 6 (2001)
7. Park, K., Moh, S.: InfiniBand: Next-Generation System Interconnect. Communications of the KISS, Vol. 19, No. 3 (2001) 43–51
8. Moh, S., Kim, Y. Y.: Technology Evolution of High-Performance Computers and Development Trend of Next-Generation Cluster Interconnects. Weekly IT Trend, Vol. 1000 (2001) 93–107
9. Hartmann, A.: InfiniBand Architecture: Evolution/Revolution – InfiniBand Adoption in the Enterprise Datacenter. White Paper, http://www.vieo.com/vieo_whit.html (2001)
10. Russell, Steczkowski, J.: Introduction to the InfiniBand Architecture. White Paper, http://www.crossroads.com/govt/whitepapers.asp (2000)
11. ARM922T Technical Reference Manual. ARM Ltd. (2000)
12. ARM PrimeCell Vector Interrupt Controller(PL190) Techincal Reference Manual. ARM Ltd. (2000)
13. ARM PrimeCell Static Memory Controller(PL092) Techincal Reference Manual. ARM Ltd. (2000)
14. AHB Example AMBA System Techinca Reference Manual, ARM Ltd. (1999)
15. ARM PrimeCell RTC(PL031) Techincal Reference Manual, ARM Ltd. (2000)
16. ARM PrimeCell UART(PL011) Techincal Reference Manual, ARM Ltd. (2000)

Ontological Cognitive Map for Sharing Knowledge between Heterogeneous Businesses

Jason J. Jung[1], Kyung-Yong Jung[2], and Geun-Sik Jo[1]

[1] Intelligent E-Commerce Systems Laboratory, School of Computer Engineering, Inha University, 253 Yonghyun-dong, Incheon, Korea 402-751
j2jung@intelligent.pe.kr, gsjo@inha.ac.kr

[2] HCI Laboratory, School of Computer Engineering, Inha University, 253 Yonghyun-dong, Incheon, Korea 402-751
kyjung@gcgc.ac.kr

Abstract. We consider that a cognitive map is one of the most efficient ways to solve problems such as the lack and uncertainty of knowledge on e-commerce. In this paper, we have designed knowledge management systems based on a cognitive map and ontology and have proposed an OntoCM (Ontological Cognitive Map) framework to collaboratively share knowledge between businesses by using an OntoCM Repository. Thereby, we have defined OntoCM operations to manipulate them such as expansion, contradiction, augmentation, and screener. Simulating synthesis patterns on OntoCM, we have extracted potential relationships between the existing concepts.

1 Introduction

Since web technology and environments have been developing rapidly and network infrastructures are spreading widely, on-line information exchange has emerged as the main concern in electronic commerce (e-commerce). While most e-commerce commpanies have been trying to integrate their systems with each other, the heterogeneous business environment has made sharing knowledge with others more difficult.

In order to solve these problems we propose supporting decision makers with Cognitive Maps (CM), a kind of graphical knowledge representations [1]. CM is a well-known approach to model a virtual environment through simulating and testing phenomena happening inside [3]. Even if the understandability of the nonlinear dynamics in a real world is low, CM is an appropriate way to learn and adapt to it based on several learning algorithms [2]. With respect to semantic interoperability, we have exploited ontology to conceptualize the CM's. Many concepts, however, are impossible to be included in only one CM because of the limited understandability of users. Moreover, a concept has to be specified and generalized on the concept hierarchy, according to the user queries.

This paper assumes that CM can be extended to OntoCM based on ontology and that it can be superposed upon the others. This means that knowledge represented as OntoCM can be shared. As an instance of applicable domains,

A. Yazici and C. Şener (Eds.): ISCIS 2003, LNCS 2869, pp. 91–98, 2003.

we have been focusing on customer relationship management (CRM) faced with several problems in e-commerce such as the lack of initial information about customers and the uncertainty of information while interacting with them.

2 Related Work

Ontology has been developed and investigated to facilitate knowledge sharing and reuse this knowledge in order to deal with semantic interoperability between business partners [10], [11]. On2Broker [13], On-To-Knowledge and IBROW can be regarded as the most representative research to support this [12]. Nowadays, especially, as concerns about semantic web, ontology infrastructure has become a more significant and focused research topic. Using already established ontologies, knowledge networking can present knowledge integration, reuse and revalidation, including knowledge management systems (KMS) [10]. The difficulty in inferring and extracting logical rule is still problems and also the knowledge visualization for high unstandability requires graphical knolwedge representation method.

3 Ontological Cognitive Maps on E-commerce

Cognitive map (CM) is a knowledge representing and reasoning method that offers a more powerful and flexible framework than any other semantic network [1], [2], [7]. Traditionally, this has been regarded as an appropriate tool to model virtual worlds and predict the effect of certain stimuli. It shows how causal concepts affect one another as illustrated graphically in a signed fuzzy graph with feedback [4], [5]. CM consists of three fundamental elements: the cause (or concept, $C = \{c_1, c_2, ..., c_n\}$); the causal relationship (or arc); and the effect (or weight, $W = [w_{i,j}]$) where $w_{i,j}$ is the weight value of the arc from concept j to concept i. Generally, arcs are oriented and represent causal links between concepts, and weights of arcs are associated with a causal link value matrix. Therefore, a CM can be composed of a number of concepts causally related and directly concerned with each other, and also send feedback to themselves.

CM has the ability to quickly converge. This means that CM can be trained while it is approaching the stable state space [3], [6]. Once the CM is trained, it can be utilized to extract knowledge by analyzing its responses to particular stimuli. Hence, the periodical repetitions of a set of states or the concentration of causal flow into a particular concept are "hidden" knowledge that we must recognize and make note of. Secondly, with CM it is easy to represent not only knowledge, such as strategies and know-how used in a company, but also cases classified to strategically important facts. Furthermore, CM can be augmented to create a new CM when it is combined with the others [3].

3.1 Extending CM to OntoCM

This paper proposes Ontological CM (OntoCM), which is provided with semantic information by ontology. Basically, ontology is defined as a specification of a conceptualization [9] and is organized on a tree-like hierarchical structure. Decision makers, therefore, understand what each concept on an OntoCM is exactly meaning and which ones are related to it. Indeed, they can represent their business policies and experiences as OntoCM, keeping the uncertainties of OntoCM low. An OntoCM is organized by semantic analysis of every concept on a CM, more practically, the combination of CM with the concept hierarchy, as shown in Fig. 1.

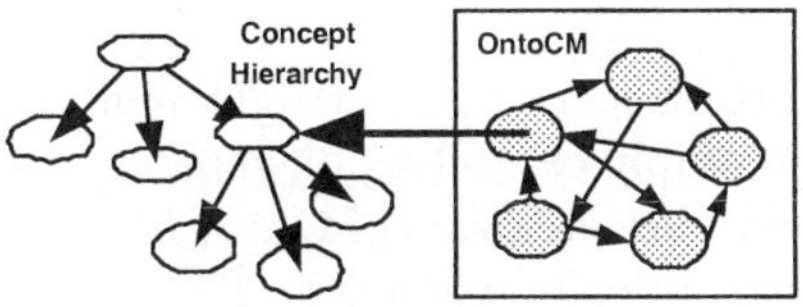

Fig. 1. OntoCM with concept hierarchy

We can, thereby, perform two important tasks which are horizontal and vertical operations. Semantic bridging for OntoCM's from a heterogeneous knowledge source is the horizontal task used for sharing information. Comparison between arbitrary OntoCM's retrieves common concepts, which are semantically equivalent, to both of them, even though their labels are differnent. This means that OntoCM's established by different businesses can be integrated for OntoCM augumention by finding common concepts. Secondly, specifying and generalizing a concept also makes it possible not only to increase understandability but also to execute integration processes, because these tasks can, vertically, level a concept with the others on the concept hierarchy. Concept memberships have to be considered to specify to children or generalize to parent concepts. Depending on the data type of a concept, the membership function is separatively defined. The membership function for a continuous concept is

$$\mu_{c_{cont}}(v) = \frac{1}{1 + \exp[-\alpha(v + bias)]} \tag{1}$$

where the v on concept c_{cont} is continuous value and the α is the slope parameter. In a case with enumerative data, the membership function is simply defined as

$$\mu_{c_{enum}}(v) = \frac{1}{n} \times v \tag{2}$$

where the n is the number of sibling concepts. This means that a particular concept on OntoCM has identical influence on its sibling enumarative concepts inherit relationships to from its parent concept.

We have to mention the weight matrix and its manipulation for OntoCM. Semantic expansion (and contradiction) and semantic bridging between OntoCM are regarded as vertical and horizontal operations, respectively. First, the vertical operation is a weight matrix transformation substituting matrix elements in a matrix with other matrices. Hierarchically related concepts in OntoCM consist of a complex influence transferring structure. We assume that the degree of membership for a concept determines how causal influence is distributed to the sibling concepts. If t-th concept c_t on an OntoCM `A` is semantically expanded to OntoCM `B`, the weight matrix transformation is given as

$$w_{i,j}^{A\leftarrow(B)} = \begin{cases} W^B & \text{if } i = j = t; \\ w_{i,j}^{A} \times \mu_B \times Diag(W^B) & \text{if } i = t \text{ or } j = t; \\ w_{i,j}^{A} & \text{otherwise;} \end{cases} \quad (3)$$

where $w_{i,j}^{A}$ is the (i,j)-th element of the weight matrix of the OntoCM `A` and the function *Diag* is for simply extracting diagonal elements of a weight matrix. Because of the geometric characteristics of OntoCM, only the diagonal elements in the matrix can be semantically expanded. Thereby, at every expansion, not only the weight value of the concept but also those of arcs from and to that concept are replaced with new weight matrices.

Next, the horizontal operation is a matrix transformation to partially superimpose knowledge used in different worlds. The matrix transformation of semantic bridging is derived as

$$w_{i,j}^{A+B} = \begin{cases} w_{i,j}^{A}, w_{i-m+k,j-m+k}^{B} \\ \text{if } i = \{m-k+1,...,m\} \text{ and } j = \{m-k+1,...,m\}; \\ w_{m-k+1+u,j}^{A} \times w_{i-m+k,1+u}^{B} \\ \text{if } i = \{m+1,...,m+n-k\} \text{ and } j = \{1,...,m-k\}; \\ w_{i,m-k+1+u}^{A} \times w_{i+m-k+u,j}^{B} \\ \text{if } i = \{1,...,m-k\} \text{ and } j = \{m+1,...,m+n-k\}; \end{cases} \quad (4)$$

where the variables m and n are the numbers of concepts on OntoCM `A` and `B`, respectively. The variable k is the number of common concepts on both. A matrix pivoting operation is additionally necessary to rearrange the order of the concepts. If OntoCM `A` is integrated with OntoCM `B`, the common concepts on both OntoCM `A` and `B` are moved to the rightmost and the leftmost columns, respectively. Thus, the size of the integrated matrix is equal to $(m+n-k)$ by $(m+n-k)$. As a result, the amount of information generated by the matrix augmentation is $2\times(m-k)\times(n-k)$. This means that concepts and knowledge in different circumstances become accessible to be affected or be simulated. When more than one concept is commonly shared, a set of weight values is assigned to each element of the weight matrix.

3.2 OntoCM Operations

We have already introduced two kinds of weight matrix transformation, a vertical and a horizontal operation. In order to represent these operations formally, we have to establish OntoCM operators that can describe the operation between OntoCM's, as shown in Table 1. In vertical operations, the level of the left-side operands in O-Repository is higher than that of the right-side operands. The horizontal operation is minutely classified as not only augmentation but also union, and screening operations are added. Union is the operation finding the set of common concepts before the augmentation operation, and screening is the operation which retrieves the relationship information between the specific set of concepts after the augmentation operation.

Table 1. Definition of OntoCM operators between OntoCM `A` and `B`. The a and b are concepts on both OntoCM, respectively.

Class	Operator	Notation	Example
Vertical Operation	Expander	$\leftarrow ()$	$A \leftarrow (B)$
	Contractor	$() \rightarrow$	$(A) \rightarrow B$
Horizontal Operation	Union	$\cap$	$A \cap B$
	Augmentor	$+$	$A + B$
	Screener	$R(\rightarrow)$	$R(a \rightarrow b)$

The operations expansion and contraction can assign a concept more specified concepts in the lower level of an OntoCM and more generalized concepts in the upper level of an OntoCM, respectively. This is similar to the specialization and generalization in version space [8]. Actually, this is so important that decision makers want complex causal flows to be analyzed. In other words, such vertical operations can tell them which concepts are related to each other as well as the degree of the relationships between them. Moreover, this means that we can retrieve relational information between concepts on the difference levels of concept hierarchy.

Augmentation of OntoCM is semantic bridging between the heterogeneous worlds. According to the environment of the system or its experts, there can be many different kinds of OntoCM's. However, in order to infer relationships between OntoCM's or between specific concepts on them, these OntoCM's are augmented while sharing the similarities between each other. Thus, the common concepts, which separately belong to each OntoCM, must be found. OntoCM `A` and `B` are combined by sharing one common concept in both of them. The augmentation of an OntoCM can recognize unpredictable patterns in different virtual worlds. As they are connected with each other, new relationships between concepts in separated worlds can be expected and inferable. This means that decision makers are able to not only manage the existing knowledge but also derive new emerging knowldge by sharing OntoCM's between heterogeneous businesses.

3.3 OntoCM Repository

Basically, the OntoCM Repository (O-Repository) contains background knowledge for OntoCM's. It is organized as a hierarchical tree structure for a semantic dictionary. This is the main index server for OntoCM's of businesses and the brokerage between them. Additionally, this plays a role of semantic caching for efficient OntoCM operations. By referring to this O-Repository, the set of common concepts is able to be easily searched. In order to do so, all concepts on OntoCM's have to be registered in the O-Repository. For example, the concept HUMIDITY is used on the set of OntoCM's {OntoCM_PERSONALITY, OntoCM_WEATHER}.

4 Managing Customer Relationships Based on Ontological Cognitive Maps

Decision makers in e-commerce have their own cognition states for strategic management. Customers leave transactional information depending on their own preferences. Companies try to collect this information in order to efficiently manage these customers. Every company has independently established their own strategic business processes. It is, however, difficult to expect instantaneous responses for many dynamic and complex changes of environment such as business processes, financial conditions, relationships with other companies and even natural phenomena. As an example, food companies, in order to manage their stocks and inventories, can strategically cooperate with logistics companies that have already applied weather information to their shipping scheduling process.

4.1 Generating Look-up Table by Simulation

As previously mentioned, one of the most important advantages of OntoCM is predictability by simulation. After each transformation operation of the weight matrix, responses for the set of particular patterns artificially synthesized by experts are used for simulation about testing. Thereby, sensitivity measurements are applied to filter the most remarkable relationships between concepts and synthesis patterns. This is a simple partial deviation based on flux analysis. There are two kinds of flux emitting out of and absorbing into the surface of a concept, called *out_flux* and *in_flux*, respectively. They are given as

$$\begin{cases} in\_flux = \sum_{j=1}^{n}(w_{i,j} \times \theta_j) \\ out\_flux = \sum_{j=1}^{n}(w_{j,i} \times \theta_i) \end{cases} \tag{5}$$

Next, the most sensitive concept for a particular concept can be acquired by sensitivity measurement based on

$$\begin{cases} DEPENDENT = \max\left(\frac{\partial(in\_flux)}{\partial w_{i,j}}|_{w_{kj}=0,k\neq i}\right) \\ DOMINANT = \max\left(\frac{\partial(out\_flux)}{\partial w_{i,j}}|_{w_{kj}=0,k\neq i}\right) \end{cases} \tag{6}$$

The i-th concept meeting these equations is the most dependent or dominant for a certain concept. This means that we must constantly observe these concepts because they are playing a critical role in the whole OntoCM.

4.2 Example

CRM is the challenge of managing customers for the profit of a company or organization. With respect to marketing, it can be a strategy for personal advertising, selling or even pricing policy. Assume that the companies A and B have their own Onto-CM's, as shown in the Fig. 2.

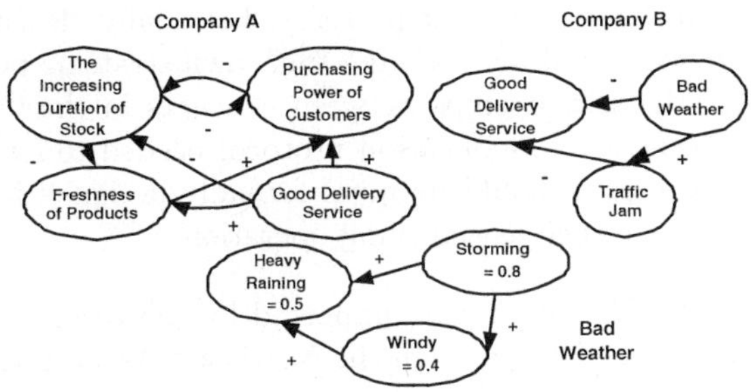

Fig. 2. OntoCM's of company A and B; The children concepts of the concept "bad-weather"

If Companies A and B are cooperatively related with each other, Company A can augment the factors affecting delivery problems by supports from Company B since "bad weather" and "traffic jam" are in the OntoCM of Company B. Indeed, the set of children concepts can be considered even further by expanding the concept "bad-weather." With the OntoCM operators, we can describe the manipulation of OntoCM's in the following equation.

$$[OntoCM\_CompanyA + OntoCM\_CompanyB] \leftarrow OntoCM\_bad{-}weather \quad (7)$$

We considered two cases as the particular stimuli. In the first case, we activated the concept "Storming" five times, in order to evaluate knowledge about weather from company B. In the second case, we simultaneously activated the concepts "Freshness" and "Duration of Stock." This was to investigate the complex stimulation.

Table 2. The result of simulation

Concept	Freshness	Duration of stock
in_flux	Traffic jam (0.514)	Bad weather (0.624)
out_flux	Purchasing power (0.67)	Purchasing power (0.482)

We discriminated the top ranked concepts for the concepts "Freshness" and "Duration of Stock." After 14 iterations, this O-CM converged to be stable (the tolerance e = 0.001). Finally, we retrieved which concept is the most influential to the concepts "Freshness" and "Duration of Stock," respectively.

5 Conclusions and Future Work

In this paper, a framework for sharing knowledge represented as OntoCM has been designed. Additionally, by referring to ontology, a semantic interoperability between heterogeneous businesses has been shown. In conclusion, we have been attempting to reduce the number of interaction with customers by predicting and referring to the look-up table generated by OntoCM. It was possible to simulate and predict the results for particular patterns. Especially, decision makers can be instantaneously supported for planning their own strategic policies.

In future work, the relationships between concepts in the OntoCM will be visualized. Also, business communication protocol needed to exchange the OntoCM's between businesses should be more formally designed in order to reinforce the query language such as screening operation.

Acknowledgement. This work was supported by the Korea Science and Engineering Foundation(KOSEF) through the Northeast Asia e-Logistics Research Center at University of Incheon.

References

1. Axelrod, R.: Structure of Decision: The Cognitive Maps of Political Elites. Princeton University press, New Jersey (1976)
2. Kosko, B.: Fuzzy Cognitive Maps. Int. J. Man-Machine Studies, Vol. 24. (1986) 65–75
3. Dickerson, J.A., Kosko, B.: Virtual Worlds as Fuzzy Cognitive Maps. Presence, **3**(2) (1994) 173–189
4. Kosko, B.: Bidirectional Association Memories. IEEE Tran. Systems, Man, and Cybernetics, Vol. 18. (1988) 49–60
5. Kosko, B.: Fuzzy Systems as Universal Approximators. Proc. of the First IEEE Int. Conf. on Fuzzy Systems, (1992) 1153–1162
6. Miao, Y., Liu, Z.-Q.: On Causal Inference in Fuzzy Cognitive Maps. IEEE Tran. on Fuzzy Systems, **8**(1) (2000) 107–119
7. Miao, Y., Liu, Z.-Q., Siew, C.K., Miao, C.Y.: Dynamic Cognitive Network – an Extension of Fuzzy Cognitive Map. IEEE Tran. on Fuzzy Systems, **9**(5) (2001) 760–770
8. Mitchell, T.M.: Generalization as Search. Artificial Intelligence, Vol. 18 (1982) 203–226
9. http://www-ksl.stanford.edu/kst/what-is-an-ontology.html
10. Tiwana, A., Ramesh, B.: Integrating Knowledge on the Web. IEEE Internet Computing, **5**(3) (2001) 32–39
11. Decker, S., Melnik, S., van Harmelen, F., Fensel, D., Klein, M., Broekstra, J., Erdmann, M., Horrocks, I.: The Semantic Web: the roles of XML and RDF. IEEE Internet Computing, **4**(5) (2000) 63–74
12. Fensel, D.: Ontologies: A Silver Bullet for Knowledge Management and Electronic Commerce. Springer-Verlag (2001)
13. Fensel, D., Angele, J., Decker, S., Erdmann, M., Schnurr, H.-P., Staab, S., Studer, R., Witt, A.: On2broker: Semantic-Based Access to Information Sources at the WWW. Proc. of the World Conf. on the WWW and Internet (1999) 25–30

Template-Based E-mail Summarization for Wireless Devices

Jason J. Jung[1] and Geun-Sik Jo[2]

[1] Intelligent E-Commerce Systems Laboratory,
School of Computer Engineering, Inha University,
253 Yonghyun-dong, Incheon, Korea 402-751
j2jung@intelligent.pe.kr
http://www.intelligent.pe.kr

[2] School of Computer Engineering, Inha University,
253 Yonghyun-dong, Incheon, Korea 402-751
gsjo@inha.ac.kr

Abstract. Mobile users have been suffering from low hardware capacity, poor interface, and high communication cost of their wireless devices. In this paper, we propose a wireless e-mail framework extracting user-relevant pieces of information from each e-mail text, instead of sending the full text e-mails themselves. Not only user-defined templates but also automatically generated templates based on semantic tagging are applied to be ruleset in order to discriminate which parts of the text should be extracted. E-mails that users are anticipating are especially suited to wireless notifying applications than any other kind of information. In experiments, we have verified that this system has shown an average removal of 74% redundant textual information and a maximum accurate filling of 93% of the template slots by collecting e-mails from DBWorld.

1 Introduction

Recently the demands on wireless devices such as mobile phones and PDAs (Personal Digital Assistant) have been ever increasing. By the end of 2001, there were over 850 million mobile phone users worldwide. Other devices such as PDAs and pagers will also contribute to the growth of mobile communication [1]. Many kinds of wireless messaging services, including e-mail, fax, voice, and video data have been introduced. High mobility, so-called "anytime, anywhere," is one of the most beneficial reasons why users have been interested in these mobile services.

There are, however, several drawbacks to wireless devices such as low hardware capacity, poor interface, and high communication costs. Because of expensive usage fees, especially, when requesting data on the web, mobile users often hesitate. Not only the number of accessing times but also the amount of transmitted packets is the main factor determining the total subscription. Therefore, we decided to study a template-based information extraction system as a way to send summarized information instead of a full-text document to a wireless device. In order to analyze the free or semi-structured text document, such as an

A. Yazici and C. Şener (Eds.): ISCIS 2003, LNCS 2869, pp. 99–106, 2003.

e-mail, there have been many information extraction studies such as the Naive Bayes sliding window model [2], the hidden markov model [3], and the template filling model [4], [5]. Also, with respect to a user's intervention, while most studies needed user involvement [11], wapper induction [7] was best able to perform automatic information extraction without user supervision.

In this paper, we are focusing on wireless e-mail access, one of the most basic and essential services of mobile devices. We have tried to summarize e-mails by extracting relevant parts of them by using not only user-defined templates but also automatically generated templates. Therefore, in the following section, notations for semantic tagging will be introduced to represent templates and, more importantly, template induction will be described to automatically generate templates.

2 Template-Based Information Extraction

Basically, IE (Information Extraction) identifies specific pieces of information (data) in unstructured or semi-structured text documents and transforms this unstructured information from a corpus of documents or web pages into a structured database. For example, in a financial transaction, an information extraction system could extract the transaction type, date, customer, principal, currency, and interest rate, which would usually be formatted as a database record suitable for subsequent processings such as data trend analyses, summaries, and report generations [6].

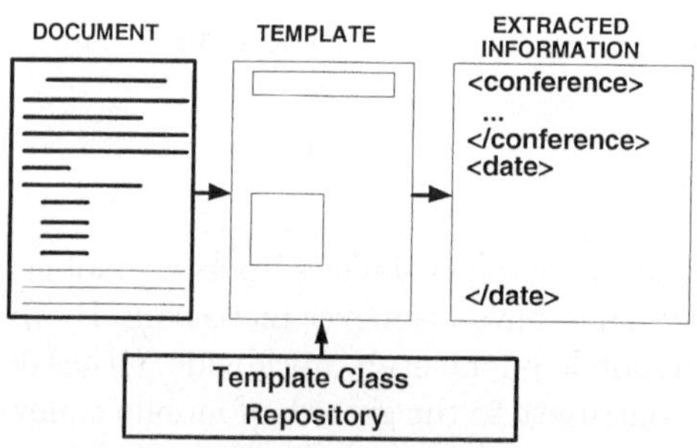

Fig. 1. Template-based Information Extraction

For the lightweight use of NLP (Natural Language Processing), we have focused on how to represent the template class and generate template instances and then, how to select templates in order to extract information from a particular text, as shown in Fig. 1. A particular class of documents whose structures are similar is defined as a prototype of a document template. Therefore, a collection of template instances generated from a prototype can extract information by filling slots on these templates.

2.1 Template Representation and Generation

A template class is composed of slots, which contain relevant pieces of information, and two kinds of tags. Tags on the left-hand side and on the right-hand side are the indicators of the beginning and ending of the corresponding slots. Each template class is represented as semantic tagging, which is the process whereby keyphrases (or keywords) in a document are matched with predefined tags. During training by user's supervision, these keyphrases have, in advance, been classified, according to the semantically identical tags. Therefore, a template class $template_i$ is defined as

$$template_i = \{slot_1, slot_2, ..., slot_n\} \tag{1}$$

and a slot $slot_i$ in a template instance is represented as

$$slot_i = [\{ltag_1, ltag_2, ..., ltag_m\}, \{rtag_1, rtag_2, ..., rtag_n\}] \tag{2}$$

where $ltag$ and $rtag$ are a set of candidate tags located in left and right side of $slot_i$, respectively.

There are two approaches to automatically generate template classes, which are frequency measure and lexical entry extraction via dictionary exploration [9]. Similar to CRYSTAL [10], which is a well-known IE system from free text by inducing a conceptual dictionary, we have organized template classes using a bottom-up covering algorithm that begins with the most specific rule to cover a seed instance and generalizes the rule by merging it with similar rules.

2.2 Template Matching

A text classifier can most efficiently find out which kinds of information are included in a certain document and what features are extractable from that document. The exact template, therefore, can be instantiated and also easily applied to extract relevent information. On the other hand, when a document fails to be classified, this document should be semantically tagged, in other words, structurized, by referring to a set of predefined tags. The template slot on the document can be expected by matched tag pairs. Then, the similarity between a tagged document doc and each template class in a template class repository, as shown in Fig. 1, can be measured by using the following equation

$$Similaity(doc, template_i) = \frac{a}{(1+\alpha^2)(d-a)+(1+\beta^2)(t-a)} \tag{3}$$

where the d and t are the number of slots in a tagged document doc and a template class, respectively. The variable a is the number of common slots in both documents and the coefficients α and β are the factors for weighting. As a result, a template instance is derived from a template class whose similarity with the tagged document is maximum.

3 Template-Based E-mail Summarization for Wireless Devices

Due to the domain specific properties of e-mail, certain features must first be extracted from an e-mail. According to SMTP (Simple Mail Transfer Protocol), an e-mail consists of two main parts, the headers and the body [8]. While the body of the e-mail is usually unstructured text that needs semantic tagging, the headers already provide tagged information such as sender, subject, and message type. Therefore, e-mails can be classified based on extracted features in order to select a proper template class.

3.1 Template Generation and Matching

There are two ways to generate templates, both of which are based on manual coding and, as previously mentioned, inducing a conceptual dictionary. Manual coding, which is the explicit construction of template classes by users, is much more effective for an e-mail that a user has already been waiting for such as "notification of acceptance." This is also effective for private e-mails as well. In this case, all extracted features must be definitely matched with user-defined conditions, for example, "ISCIS committee will notify the acceptance of our paper on May 1, 2003."

An inductive conceptual dictionary based on e-mail classification is the other way to generate a template class. Features can be extracted by learning the user's categorization patterns. Therefore, e-mails in the same category are lexically analyzed in order to enrich the conceptual dictionaty and semantic tagging. For example, by analyzing e-mails posted from a particular mailing-list in a folder, we can recognize sender, subject pattern, and more importantly, the appended user-defined header information.

A template class repository manages these two types of template classes, separately. For template matching, a new e-mail should be semantically tagged and structured, by searching the proper slots. Then, according to the type of features extracted from this e-mail, it is decided which part of the template class repository should be searched and the most suitable template class is obtained by measuring the similarity among template classes in the selected part of the repository.

As an example, a template class "call for papers" and a semantic tag <date> are generated as follows.:

```
(template_class call_for_papers
  <conference>              ; Title of Conference
  <date>                    ; Schedule of the conference
  <location>                ; Place in which the conference will be held
  <submission>
    <submission:deadline>     ; Submission Dealine
    <submission:notification> ; Notification of Acceptance
    <submission:camera_ready> ; Camera-ready papers
```

```
    <URL>                  ; Website of the conference
    <topics>               ; Topics of interest for the conference
    <publication>          ; Publisher
    <committee>            ; Peoples in conference committee
    <contact>              ; Contact information
  )
  (semantic_tag call_for_papers:date
     { "important dates * conference *", "\crlf" }
     { "workshop dates *", "\crlf" }
     { "conference dates *", "\crlf" }
     { "submission deadline * conference *", "\crlf" }
  )
```

3.2 Template Instance Derivation and Information Extraction for Wireless Devices

A template instance can be derived from the matched template class. The detail configuration of this template instance depends on the number of slots and thier positions as obtained by semantic tagging. Relevant information, therefore, can be extracted by overlapping this template instance on the tagged e-mail. Another important focus is to refine these piececs of extracted relavant information by reorganizing them and removing redandunt words and stop words. More seriously, with respect to communication cost, the limited size of data for one transmission is the maximum length of a fragment for reorganization of the the extracted texts. This refinement is shown in the following algorithm

Algorithm *Refinement*

Input:

Set of Extracted Texts, $T = \{t_1, t_2, ..., t_a\}$;
Maximum Length of a Fragment, L;
Set of Refined Texts $RT = \{\}$;

Procedure:

for each $t_i \in T$ **do**
  if (**not** $IsStopwords(t_i)$)
  then if (**not** $IsRedundant(RT, t_i)$)
    switch $(L - length(t_i))$
      case > 0: $merge(t_i)$
      case < 0: $fragment(t_i)$
      case 0: $RT := RT + \{t_i\}$
return RT

where the functions *merge* and *fragment* are used to combine residues and then generate residues in order to save null space.

4 System Architecture

This system consists of three main components, which are e-mail client, template generator, and template matcher, as shown in Fig. 2.

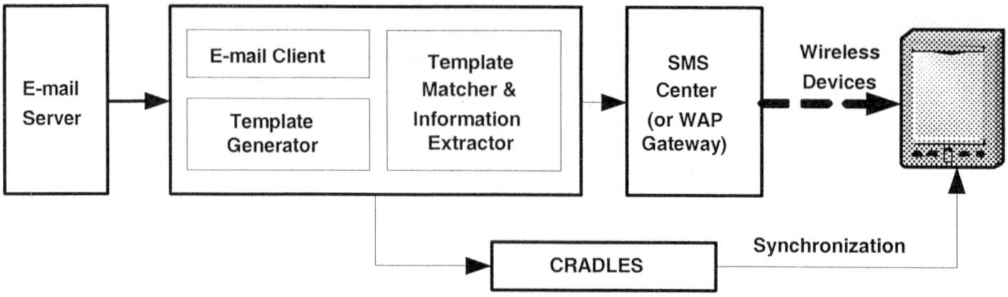

Fig. 2. System Architecture

The e-mail client has to be able to classify e-mails based on extracting features such as the headers of each e-mail. The Template Generator establishes the conceptual dictionary and provide GUI for users' manual coding, then stores them in the template class repository. Template Matcher and Information Extractor can look up the most appropriate template in a template class repository and organize the set of extracted texts in the final message format.

Mobile devices have to be "wirely synchronized," in advance, with the template class repository of Template Generator. Thereby, a template instance can be effectively derived by receiving messages from the SMS center [14] or the WAP gateway [12], [13].

5 Experiments

In our experiments, we considered e-mails from DBWorld [15], which posts job/conference announcement messages and shares this information via e-mails that has been reveived. Based on the extracted features, we placed these e-mails into four categories, "job announcements," "call for papers," "call for participation," and "other." DBWorld e-mails additionally contain particularly well-organized headers which support to effective classification such as *X-DBWorld-Message-Type*, *X-DBWorld-Call-For*, *X-DBWorld-Deadline*, and so on. Overall, we collected 250 messages from DBWorld and split them into two groups, 80% of them as training and the rest of them as testing data. During training for inducing conceptual dictionary, each template class of the corresponding categories was generated.

By testing data, we attained the results, as shown in Table 1. We verified that the system was able to remove, an average, 74% of the redundant textual information and that 93% of the template slots were accurately filled. Furthermore, we were able to implement this system by using a SMTP-based e-mail client and a PalmOS simulator [16].

Table 1. Results of information summarization based on template instance derivation

	Ratio of Summarization $= \frac{size(extraced)}{size(raw)}$	*Accuracy of Template Filling* $= \frac{number(relavant)}{number(total)}$
job announcement	0.796	0.775
call for papers	0.83	0.926
call for participation	0.812	0.875
others	0.52	0.795

6 Conclusion and Future Work

Not only hardware limitations of wireless devices but also high communication costs are a serious obstacle to instant accessing of wireless e-mail service. We have attempted to summarize e-mails by using template filling. We have thereby proposed the way to generate and match template classes and also derive template instance that is the most suitable for a certain e-mail. Some template class can be manually constructed by user intervention in order to customize adaptive information extraction. The heterogeneous screen specifications of mobile devices and the various communication policies of service providers have also been considered.

We are now developing a GUI system to support users so they can more easily construct template classes based on manual coding. Moreover, we are studying ontologies as background knowledge for semantic analysis of texts.

Acknowledgement. This work was supported by INHA UNIVERSITY Research Grant. (INHA-30305)

References

1. Sadeh, N.: M-Commerce: Technologies, Services, and Business Models. Wiley computer publishing (2002)
2. Freitag, D.: Using grammatical inference to improve precision in information extraction. ICML-97 Workshop on Automata Induction, Grammatical Inference, and Language Acquisition (1997)
3. Freitag, D., McCallum, A.: Information extraction using HMMs and shrinkage. Proceedings of the AAAI-99 Workshop on Machine Learning for Information Extraction (1999)
4. Doorenbos, R.B., Etzioni, O., Weld, D.S.: A Scalable Comparison-Shopping Agent for the World Wide Web. Proceedings of Autonomous Agent '97 (1997)
5. Sumita, K., Miike, S., Chino, T.: Automatic Abstract Generation Based on Document Structure Analysis and Its Evaluation as a Document Retreival Presentation Function. Systems and Computers **26**(13) (1995) 32–43
6. Wee, L.K.A., Tong, L.C., Tan, C.L.: A generic information extraction architecture for financial applications. Expert Systems with Applications **16**(4) (1999) 343–356

7. Kushmerick, N., Weld, D.S., Doorenbos, R.: Wrapper Induction for Information Extraction. Intl. Joint Conference on Artificial Intelligence (1997) 729–737
8. Crocker, D.H.: Standard For The Format Of ARPA Internet Text Messages. ftp://ftp.rfc-editor.org/in-notes/rfc822.txt (1982)
9. Maedche, A.: Ontology Learning for the Semantic Web. Kluwer Academic Publishers (2002)
10. Soderland, S., Fisher, D., Aseltine, J., Lehnert, W.: CRYSTAL: Inducing a Conceptual Dictionary. Proceedings of the Fourteenth International Joint Conference on Artificial Intelligence (1995) 1314–1319
11. Ciravegna, F., Petrelli, D.: User involvement in customizing adaptive Information Extraction. Proceedings of the IJCAI-2001 Workshop on Adaptive Text Extraction and Mining (2001)
12. Open Mobile Alliance Ltd. http://www.openmobilealliance.org (2002)
13. WAP 2.0 Specifications. http://www.wapforum.org (2002)
14. Wireless Short Message Service (SMS). http://www.iec.org (2002)
15. DBWorld, http://www.cs.wisc.edu/dbworld
16. PalmOS Simulator, http://www.palm.com

Some Intrinsic Properties of Interacting Deterministic Finite Automata

Hürevren Kılıç

Department of Computer Engineering, Atilim University,
Kızılcaşar Köyü, 06836, Incek Gölbasi, Ankara, Turkey
hurevren@atilim.edu.tr

Abstract. The agent controllability of the environment is investigated using simple deterministic interacting automata pair model. For this purpose, a general extended design approach for such couple is developed. In the experiments, we focused on simple binary state case and generated stability/cycle behavior characteristics map for the couple. Examinations on the map showed that the behavior of the couple shows some initial value sensitivity. Also, we observed some non-controllable agent/environment couple definition which may imply an inherent communication border between agent and the environment.

1 Introduction

Complex behavior can be generated from simple primitive elements if they are interconnected and in interaction. Automata networks are such models in which locally interconnected set of cells evolve at discrete time steps through mutual interactions. The first appearance of automata networks in literature is due to John Von Neumann [1] in order to model various phenomena in physics and biology. Even though its simplicity, pair of automata can be used to model the interaction between "system under design" and the "environment" it resides. "Reactive system design" in [2] and "situated agent design" in [3] are based on such model. In both approaches, one automaton defines the system under design (or agent) and the other one defines the environment it resides. One important question that tried to be answered is, "Using the information about the environment how can we design a system (or an agent) such that we can ensure correct joint operation of the system and the environment". Some related works on the notions of compatibility of agents and environments represented by interacting automata pair can be found in, [4]. It should be obvious that such simple pair of automata model is not sufficient to describe the interactions of real systems that perform complicated transformations of data. However, it is shown that the technique and methodology proposed in [2], [3] respectively, can be used to design the control (or perceptual) part of such systems (or agents) which is responsible for the interaction with the environment. Interacting pair of automata can also be used as a model for processor representation [5]. An analysis of interacting automata with some limited nondeterministic properties can be found in [6]. In this paper we consider the deterministic case.

A. Yazici and C. Şener (Eds.): ISCIS 2003, LNCS 2869, pp. 107–114, 2003.

Our purpose is to investigate the controllability of discrete, deterministic environment by agent. We define the agent control over the environment simply as whether it can "stabilize" its environment and itself or not. However, the agent automaton has no direct control over environment. It can communicate with the environment or switch itself to another automaton. Agent automaton (but not the environment) switch-property results in asymmetry in agent/environment couple definition.

For our purpose, we extend the "interacting pair of automata" model representing the agent/environment couple definition by adding a "stability detection" unit and an "agent automaton switch" unit to the agent. The functions of the new units are goal-test and agent automaton change, respectively. In the experiments, we worked on simple two-state (binary) case. We observed that there exists such environment automaton definition which cannot be stabilized by any independent agent automaton definition. The existence of such inherently "non-controllable" (or "non-writable") environments even in such simple interacting automata pair may imply the existence of an inherent communication border between the situated agent and its environment. Another result is the couple's "initial value sensitivity". Existence of such property points to an interesting criterion that must be considered in agent designs.

In section 2, we define the automata networks in general and interacting automata pair model we used. In section 3, a formal description of our extended interacting automata design for the agent/environment controllability check is given. In section 4, the obtained experimental results are given. The last section is the conclusion.

2 The Model

In automata networks model space, time and cells (i.e. automata) are discrete. An automata network can be described as mapping F from S^n into S^n, where S is usually a finite state space and n is the number of inter-connected cells. The cell connection structure is determined by F. If the ith component of mapping F depends on the jth component, cell i receives an input connection from cell j. Interacting pair of automata model is a fully connected instance of the automata network model where n=2. Each automaton considers the state of itself and take inputs from the other (see Fig. 1).

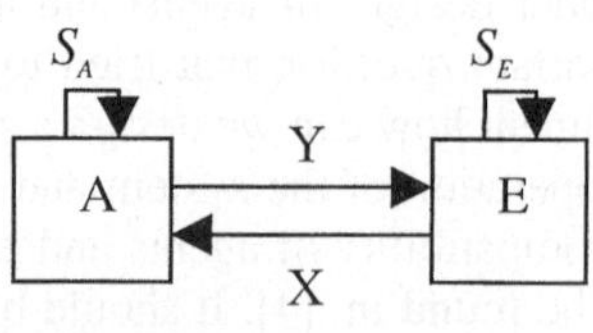

Fig. 1. Interacting pair of automata

Definition 1. A *deterministic finite (X-Y) automaton component A* of an interacting pair of automata is defined by a *quintuple* (X, Y, S_A, δ_A, η_A) where

X is a finite input alphabet;
Y is a finite output alphabet;
S_A is a finite set of states;
δ_A is a transition function $S_A \times X \to S_A$;
η_A is an output function $S_A \to Y$.

A *deterministic finite (X-Y) automaton* is called *partially defined* if there exist some $x \in X$ and $s \in S_A$ such that $\delta_A(s, x) = \emptyset$. Also, if $|X| = 1$ the automaton A is called *autonomous Y-automaton* [4]. In this paper, both agent and the environment automata are *everywhere (or fully) defined, deterministic, non-autonomous* and constitute an interacting pair. An important property of the above *deterministic finite (X-Y) automaton* is its "cyclicity". In other words, automaton operation never terminates since there exist no final state. Also, from Fig. 1, we can say that Y_A=X_E and similarly X_A=Y_E. We assumed that the output function η_A to be the "identity function" (i.e. $\eta_A(S_A)$=S_A). Then, the global state of the agent/environment automaton pair is determined by the values of the state variables (S_A and S_E). As a result, *X*, *Y* and S_A are defined in the same domain. The automata evolve in discrete time steps, with the value of the variable at one site (at time *t*) being affected by the value of itself and the other variable at the previous time step (at time *t*-1). The state values at each site are updated synchronously and determined by the state transition rules δ_A and δ_E. For the agent automaton, the number of different δ_A transition functions is equal to $|S_A|^{|S_A||S_E|}$. Similarly, it is $|S_E|^{|S_E||S_A|}$ for the environment automaton. Then, for our interacting agent/environment automata, the number of possible automata transition function configurations is equal to $(|S_A|^{|S_A||S_E|})(|S_E|^{|S_E||S_A|})$. When we look at the long term behavior of the interaction defined by δ_A and δ_E, the agent/environment state space is either freezing at some particular state or cycling around two or more states. In fact, freezing at some state is a special case for cycling where cycle length is one. In our design, the goal of the agent is to find the rule that freezes (or stabilizes) its environment and itself at some state.

3 The Design

The goal of the agent leads us to answer an important question: Is there an environment that cannot be controlled by its agent counterpart? For our answer, the agent/environment couple defined above has necessary but not sufficient capabilities. Basically, we need two additional functions: to detect whether the agent/environment pair reached some stability or not (i.e. goal test) and if not, to be able to change the current agent automaton definition to another. Fig. 2 shows our extended agent definition including "stability detection" (automaton C) and "agent automaton switch" (automaton R) units. Both units can be defined as deterministic automata. "Stability Detection" unit C is a *deterministic finite (X-Y) automaton* with some slight differences. It reads from both the agent *A* and the environment *E* tapes simultaneously. Unit C directs its decision Y_C, neither to automaton A nor to the automaton E but to the "Agent Automaton Switch" unit R. Note that, $S_E = Y_E = X_A = X_C^E$ and $S_A = Y_A = X_E = X_C^A$ where all values are defined for the same state domain. However, the decision value $Y_C = \{0, 1\}$ where "1" means *A* and *E* are stabilized and "0" otherwise.

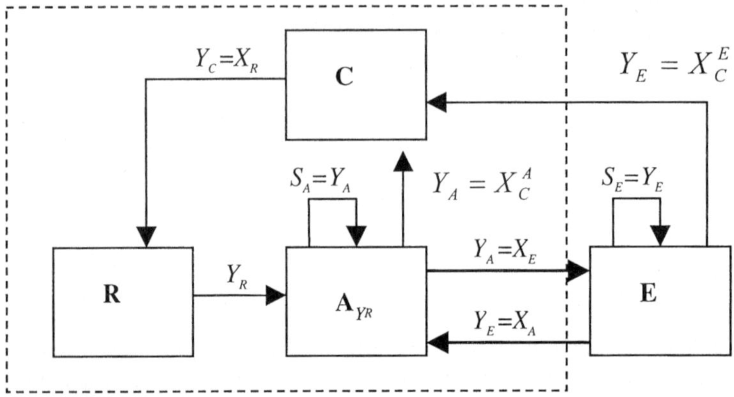

Fig. 2. Extended agent automaton design for environment stabilization test

Lemma 1. Given *deterministic finite (X-Y) automata couple A* and *E where* $k=|S_A|$, the environment E is guaranteed to be stabilized on a particular state if it generates $(k+1)$ number of the same consecutive $p \in Y_E$ output values.

Proof. Since E is deterministic, generation of k number of consecutive output values by E implies at most k different state values of the agent to be used by the transition function $\delta_E : S_E \times X \rightarrow S_E$ where Y_E=S_E by definition and $p_i \in Y_E$ is repeated state value and also X=Y_A=S_A. Then, if $(k+1)^{\text{th}}$ output has the same p_i value then one of the previously applied transition rules is guaranteed to be reapplied which means p_i output value to be generated, continuously.

Lemma 2. Any *deterministic finite (X-Y) automaton couple A-E* is guaranteed to either be stabilized at some global state or enter into a cycle of two or more global states at the end of execution of at least $|S_A||S_E|$ transition steps.

Proof. The number of possible configurations (i.e. the global states) for the A-E couple is m=$|S_A||S_E|$. Then, for any completed i^{th} execution step where i>m, the couple will still be in one of the m different previous global states. Since, both A and E are deterministic their joint behavior either be converging to some fixed global state or cycling around two or more global states. When $i \leq m$, one cannot decide on whether the couple is stabilized or cycling around two or more states. While considering the above lemma we can define unit C as;

Definition 2. Given *deterministic finite (X-Y) automata couple A-E* where $k=|S_A|$ and l=$|S_E|$, the stability detection automaton C can be defined as a *deterministic finite (X-Y) automaton* where

X= $\{x_iy_j \mid x_i \in S_A , y_j \in S_E, 1 \leq i \leq k$ and $1 \leq j \leq l\}$

Y = {0, 1} where "1" means *A-E* couple is stabilized and "0" otherwise

S_C = $\{p_0, p_1, p_2, \ldots\ldots, p_m , q_1, q_2, \ldots\ldots, q_m, r_1, r_2\}$ where p_0 is a distinguished start state and m=kl.

δ_C : For the following δ_C definitions assume $1 \leq i \leq k$ and $1 \leq j \leq l$ and m=kl

δ_C $(p_s, *)$=p_{s+1} where s = 0 to m-1 and * means any input

$\delta_C(p_m, x_iy_j)=q_{(i-1)l+j}$

$$\delta_C(q_s, x_iy_j) = \begin{cases} r_1 & \text{when } (i-1)l+j \text{ is equal to } s, \\ r_2 & \text{otherwise} \end{cases}$$

where s may take any value from 1 to m

$\delta_C(r_s, *)=p_0$ where s = 1, 2 and * means any input.

$\eta_C(r_1) = 1$ and for any other state $z\in S_C$, $\eta_C(z)=0$.

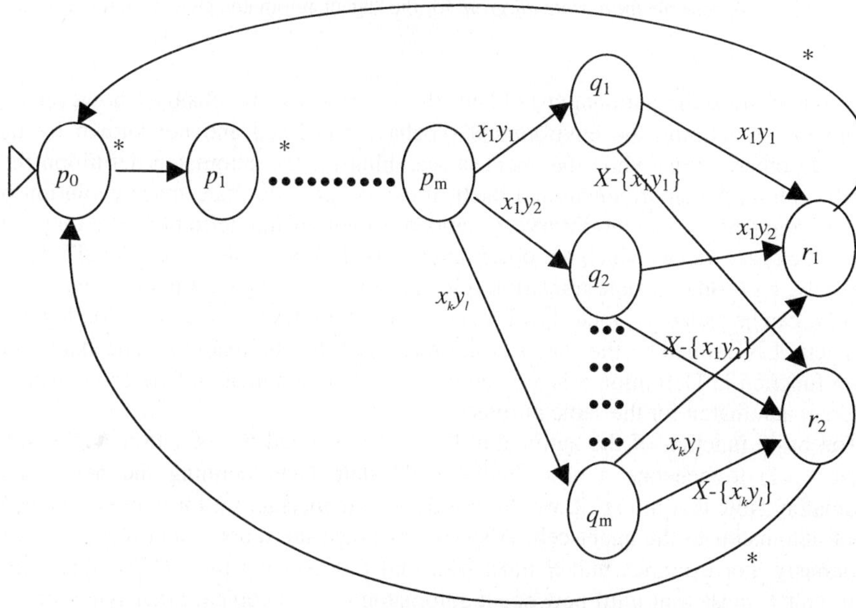

Fig. 3. Generic *finite state diagram* for the "stability detection" automaton C

In Fig. 3, * shows any input x_iy_j in the set X and X-$\{x_iy_j\}$ means any input alphabet element other than x_iy_j. For the automaton C, being in state r_1 means the couple is stabilized and r_2 means it is cycling. Note that, during q and r type states of automaton C decides on whether the *A-E* couple is stabilized or not. In that period, the *A-E* couple may continue their communication.

Definition 3. Given *deterministic finite (X-Y) automata couple A* and *E* where $k=|S_A|$ and $l=|S_E|$, the "agent automaton switch" automaton R can be defined as a deterministic finite *(X-Y)* automaton where

$X = \{0, 1\}$ Y = $\{a_1, a_2, \ldots\ldots, a_m\}$ $S_R = \{p_1, p_2, \ldots\ldots, p_m\}$

$\delta_R : \delta_R(p_i, 1)=p_i$

$\delta_R(p_i, 0)=p_{(i \bmod m)+1}$

$\eta_R(p_i) = a_i$, where $m = k^{kl}$ and $1 \le i \le m$.

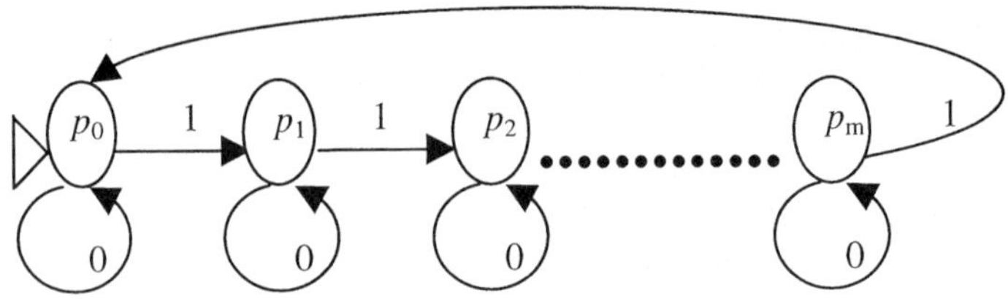

Fig. 4. A possible *finite state diagram* for the "agent automaton switch" automaton R

In our design, the automaton hold by the agent A can be changed however the automaton E defining the environment's behavior is fixed and not known by the agent. In other words, while the agent is searching for the automaton definition that stabilizes both the environment and itself, it can observe the state space evolution of the environment but cannot observe its embedded automaton definition. We may call such state space values which are observable by both A and E as "object-level" states. Similarly, each other's state transition rule space values which are not observable by A and E can be called as "meta-level" states. The "meta-level" state transition logic of the agent A is defined by the state transition rules of the automaton R. The state transition function in Definition 3 is an example switching automaton. One can construct different automaton for the same purpose.

The basic function of the automaton R is: once excited by the automaton C (i.e. when X_R=1) to generate a new "meta-level" state label defining the new agent automaton. Note that in Fig. 2, we did not define the mechanism for copying the new agent automaton to the agent cell. Also, we assumed the units C and R work asynchronously. For example, unit R must wait unit C's decision for (kl+2) steps. Similarly, unit C must wait until new agent automaton (A_{YR}) is copied. Such synchronization can be achieved by introducing time delay mechanism.

It should be clear that the interacting automata pair defined is not a "pure perception" agent/environment couple. In other words, both the outputs of the agent and the environment automaton influence each other. The agent is not a passive observer, it sees and seen by the environment. The agent's actions in "meta-level" state space result in some responses of the environment in "object-level" state space.

4 Experimental Results

The above abstract design can be implemented in hardware, software or any other. For our experiments, we developed a simple software program realizing the interacting agent/environment couple. We worked on simple binary-state case where S_A=S_E={0,1} (i.e. k=l=2). Note that, both space and time complexity of unit C are O(kl) (i.e. linear) (see Defn. 2). However, the space requirement for unit R design grows exponentially; O(k^{kl}) (see Defn. 3). The number of different agent automata for the binary case is 2^{2*2}=16. Similarly, since k=l, it is 16 for environment also. Therefore, the number of possible automata transition function configurations for such simple agent/environment couple is 256.

Also, it is assumed that the agent/environment couple works synchronously. Otherwise, if, for example, the agent's "object-level" state perception speed is less than the environment's "object-level" state generation speed, one cannot guarantee the deterministic behavior of the *A-E* couple. Then, the "stability detection" unit cannot decide on whether the couple is stabilized or entered into a cycle.

Enumeration and corresponding logical connectives for 16 possible automata definitions for simple binary case can be seen in Table 1. Values P and Q show "object-level" state values generated by the agent and the environment automata, respectively.

Table 2 is the stability/cycle characteristic map for all possible pairs of the simple binary-case *A-E* couple. Rows of the table show the numbered agent automaton and similarly, the columns show the environment automata. The map can also be interpreted as the characteristic map for the interaction dynamics of Boolean logical connectives. Automata pair interaction can be thought as a higher-level operator defined over logical operator domain. For example, when the logical $\wedge$ operator (i.e. #3) defining the agent interacts with the logical $\vee$ operator (i.e. #8) defining the environment whatever the initial values (i.e. 00, 01, 10, 11) they both reach stability (see S value in Table 2). On the other hand, if the logic defining the environment is $\neg$Q, one cannot find any left-side positioned agent automaton which stabilizes both agent and the environment (see C values in Table 2). The existence of such inherently "non-controllable" (or "non-writable") environment even in such simple interacting automata pair may imply the existence of an inherent communication border between the situated agent and its environment.

Another important behavior characteristic that can be drawn from the map is; the sensitivity to the initial "object-level" states. For example, when we look at the interaction between $\neg$(P$\Rightarrow$Q) and P$\Leftrightarrow$Q, if the initial "object-level" state values for the agent and the environment automata are 1 and 0, respectively then both agent and the environment are stabilized, for any other 3 possible cases, on the other hand, they show cycling behavior. In Table 2, we denote such cases by letter I. The stability/cycle relation between the interacting agent and environment automaton is not symmetric. For example, the interaction between agent automaton #2 and environment automaton #11 does not show in the same behavior like the configuration agent automaton #11 and environment automaton #2. The first configuration shows "cycling" behavior however, the second one shows "stable" behavior. Such an asymmetry justifies the existence of another property that must be considered in our agent/environment couple definitions.

5 Conclusion

In this work, we checked the agent controllability of the environment using simple deterministic interacting automata model. For this purpose, we proposed a general extended design approach for such couple. Our agent extended with C (stability detection) and R (agent automaton switch) units can be classified as a reflex-agent.

In the experiments, we focused on simple binary case and generated the interaction characteristics map for the couple. From the map, we observed that the behavior of the couple shows some initial value sensitivity. Also, there exists *non-controllable in any case* environments for some given agent/environment positions. Then, one can conclude that at least for the defined automata-based *A-E* interaction framework, because of some inherent environment characteristics, only an "object-level" communication between agent and environment may not always be sufficient to achieve some goals of the agent.

As a result, examination of automata pair (or networks in general) dynamics may contribute to our understanding about the interaction characteristics and/or possible limitations (if exists) of different agent/environment definitions.

Table 1. Enumeration and logical connective meanings for binary-case

#1	#2	#3	#4	#5	#6	#7	#8
0	$P \wedge Q$	$\neg(P \Rightarrow Q)$	P	$\neg P \wedge Q$	Q	$\neg(P \Leftrightarrow Q)$	$P \vee Q$

#9	#10	#11	#12	#13	#14	#15	#16
$\neg(P \vee Q)$	$P \Leftrightarrow Q$	$\neg Q$	$P \vee \neg Q$	$\neg P$	$P \Rightarrow Q$	$\neg(P \wedge Q)$	1

Table 2. The stability/cycle characteristic map for all pairs of binary-case *A*-*E* couple

	Environment Automata																
Agent Automata	**#**	**1**	**2**	**3**	**4**	**5**	**6**	**7**	**8**	**9**	**10**	**11**	**12**	**13**	**14**	**15**	**16**
	1	S	S	S	S	S	S	S	S	C	C	C	C	S	S	S	S
	2	S	S	S	S	S	S	S	S	C	I	C	I	S	S	S	S
	3	S	S	S	S	S	S	S	S	I	I	C	C	S	S	S	S
	4	S	S	I	S	S	S	I	S	I	I	C	I	S	S	S	S
	5	S	S	I	I	S	I	S	I	C	C	C	C	C	C	C	C
	6	S	S	I	I	S	S	I	S	C	I	C	I	C	S	C	S
	7	S	S	S	I	S	I	S	I	S	S	C	C	I	I	C	C
	8	S	S	I	S	S	S	I	S	S	S	C	S	S	S	C	S
	9	C	C	C	C	I	I	S	S	C	C	C	C	I	S	I	S
	10	C	I	C	I	I	I	S	S	C	S	C	S	I	S	S	S
	11	S	S	C	C	S	S	I	S	I	I	C	C	I	S	I	S
	12	S	S	C	S	S	S	I	S	S	S	C	S	S	S	I	S
	13	C	C	C	C	C	C	C	C	C	C	C	C	C	C	C	C
	14	C	I	C	I	C	I	C	S	C	S	C	I	C	S	C	S
	15	S	S	C	C	S	I	C	C	I	S	C	C	I	I	C	C
	16	S	S	C	S	S	S	C	S	S	S	C	S	S	S	C	S

References

1. Aspray, W., Burks, A.W.: Papers of John Von Neumann on Computing and Computer Theory, MIT Press, Cambridge Mass. (1987)
2. Chebotarev, A.N., Morokhovets, M.K.: Resolution-based Approach to Compatibility Analysis of Interacting Automata, Theoretical Computer Science, Vol. 194 (1–2) (1998) 183–205
3. Rosenschein, S.J., Kaelbling, L.P.: A Situated View of Representation and Control, Artificial Intelligence, Vol. 73 (1995) 149–173
4. Kurganski, A.N.: Indistinguishability of Finite-State Automata with respect to Some Environments, Cybernetics abd Systems Analysis, Vol. 37 (1) (2001) 33–41
5. Kurgaev A.F., Petrenko N.G.: Processor Structure Design, Cybernetics abd Systems Analysis, Vol. 31 (4) (1995) 618–625
6. Buchholz, T., Klein, A., Kutrib, M.: On Interacting Automata with Limited Nondeterminism, Fund Inform, Vol. 52 (1-3) (2002) 15–38

Design and Evaluation of a Source Routed Ad Hoc Network

Faysal Basci, Hakan Terzioglu, and Taskin Kocak

School of Electrical Engineering and Computer Science
University of Central Florida
Orlando, Florida 32816-2450
{fbasci, hakan, tkocak}@cs.ucf.edu

Abstract. Effects of network parameters on the performance of mobile ad hoc networks (MANETs) have been widely investigated. However, there are certain issues related to the hardware implementation and internal parameters of the nodes present in the network that effect performance dramatically. In this work a source routed wireless network is implemented in VHDL. Basic modules in the design are mobile ad hoc nodes and a switch that emulates the wireless channel and controls the connectivity between nodes. By varying hardware parameters of the nodes under different network conditions performance of the overall system is measured and simulation results are presented.

1 Introduction

Source routing is one of the most popular approaches in Manets [7]. Among them most widely accepted one is Dynamic Source Routing (DSR) protocol [1, 6,5]. DSR allows the network to be completely self organizing and self configuring. The protocol is composed of two mechanisms: Route discovery and Route Maintenance. The use of source routing allows packet routing to be trivially loop free, avoids the need for up-to-date routing information in the intermediate nodes through which packets are forwarded, and allows nodes that are forwarding or overhearing packets to cache the routing information in them for their own future use. Route discovery is used when a node 'A' tries to send a packet to node 'B' and does not have a routing information in its table for that destination. A discovery packet is then sent and the route is stored when an acknowledgement packet is received as a response of that discovery packet. When a route is no longer exists, an intermediate node (which is now not in that route) finds out that the next hop is not its neighbor anymore and sends that information to the source node. Source node then invalidates that route and sends another discovery packet for that destination if the node needs that route. This procedure is called Route Maintenance. In this work, we have implemented a simplified version of DSR. One of the main simplifications is in the route maintenance part. Instead of using route validation through the nodes it is assumed that the route is correct at the time of packet delivery to next hops, and every entry in the routing table of nodes are invalidated after a time period.

A. Yazici and C. Şener (Eds.): ISCIS 2003, LNCS 2869, pp. 115–122, 2003.

When a routing entry is invalidated a route discovery packet is generated for the corresponding destination. As it is explained in section /refnode architecture of routing table ensures the freshness of routing entry. One may expect that sending frequent route discovery packets would increase the traffic in the network. To minimize the traffic a packet validation scheme is introduced. Each packet carries information about the nodes it has traversed and has a unique ID. This way double passes are prevented. Another important issue is the multiple replies to discovery packets. A node will generate acknowledgements for every discovery packet it receives. However, when a node receives an acknowledgement packet, which is not destined to it, it will check if it received the same acknowledgement before. If so it will drop the packet. This way there will be only one reply to each discovery packet and that reply will carry the shortest route information between the source and the destination.

2 Implementation

In our design, there are three different types of packets: Discovery packets, acknowledgement packets and payload packets. Discovery packets are flooded through the network to find out a route between two nodes. Acknowledgement packets are replies to the incoming discovery packets that contain the routing information. Payload packets are information carrying packets and they have their routes in their header.

2.1 Packet Format

The packet used in the design has the format shown in Fig. 1. As can be seen packet header contains not only the route but also the history of the visited nodes. When any packet leaves a node, the ID of the node is added to visited nodes. This history allows nodes that receive the packet extract routing information and validate the packets. One of the crucial fields in the packet header is the packet identifier part. It is unique to the packet, and is especially very useful in packet validation. An acknowledgement packet in reply to a discovery packet carries the same identity. Each node has a cache that keeps the identity of previous acknowledgement packets received. This way multiple-acknowledgement problem is overcome. TTL (Time To Live) is decremented by one each time a node is traversed. When it becomes zero, the packet is dropped.

2.2 The Node

The implemented node has 6 different modules: fragmentation-scheduling and accounting block, header buffer, dynamic routing table, table update algorithm, microprocessor interface and output queue. Fig. 3 shows the overall architecture of the node.

The fragmentation-scheduling and accounting block acts like the main controller. Packet validation, internal control signaling, and the orchestration of

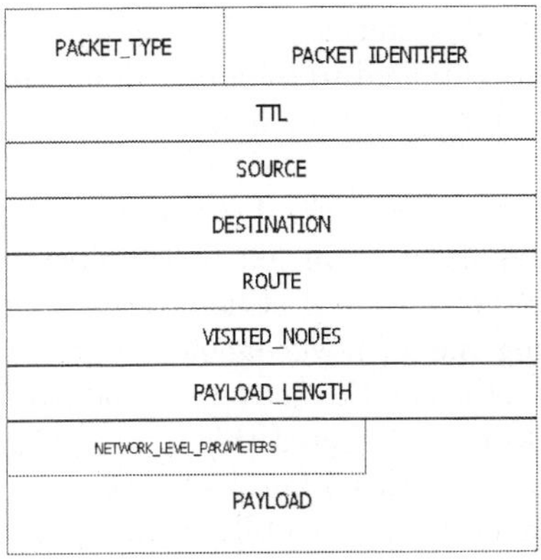

Fig. 1. Packet format

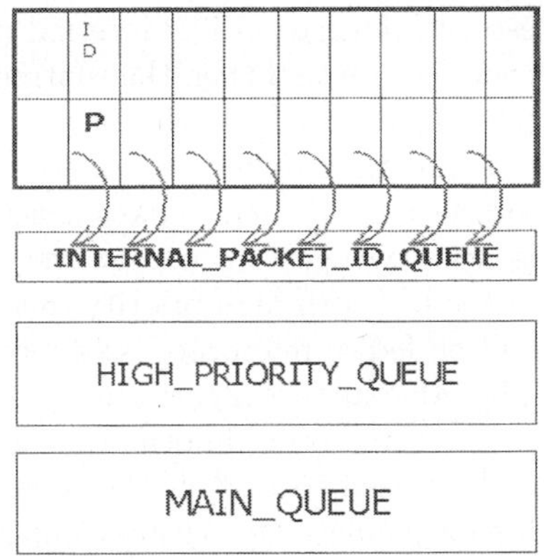

Fig. 2. Architecture of the output queue

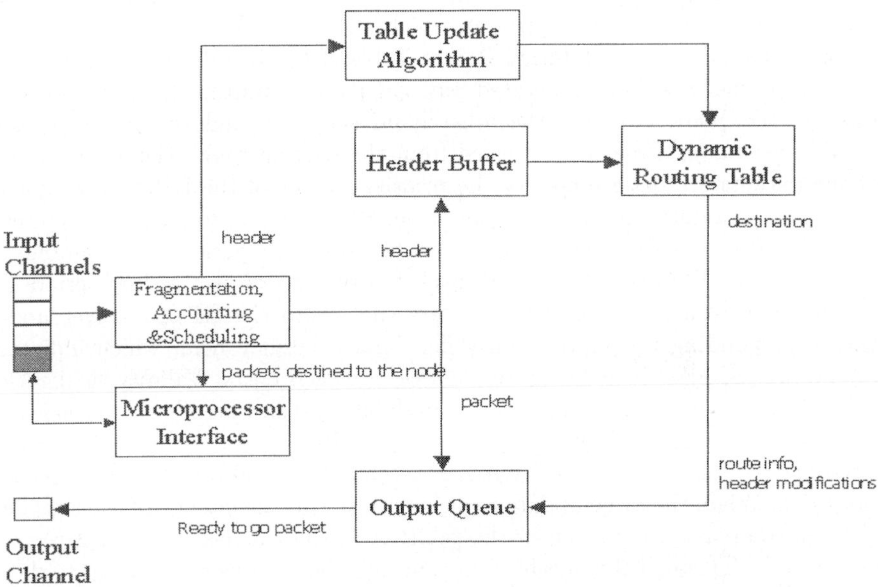

Fig. 3. Node Architecture

the blocks are done by this component. A node has a number of input channels, which is re-configurable and related to the maximum number of immediate neighbors allowed, and one output channel. Besides that, there is one more input channel that is dedicated to the packets generated internally. When a packet is validated and if the destination of the packet is different than the node itself, then the packet will be fed to output queue. If the packet is an internal packet that means there is a need for route lookup and packet header is fed to header buffer. Header buffer signals dynamic routing table for lookup supplying necessary information like internal packet tags and destination of the packet. If a route is returned then the routing information is supplied to the queue and output queue schedules the packet for departure. On the other hand if no route is found then queue is signaled to issue a route discovery, and microprocessor interface is signaled to pause packet generation for some time. If the packet type is acknowledgement or discovery, and validated, it is again fed to the output queue but with high priority this time. Any received packet destined to the node will be fed to microprocessor interface, including the acknowledgement packets. The table update algorithm block, meanwhile, listens all the activity in the node to extract routing information. If any information is extracted this information will be used to update the routing table. Microprocessor interface is responsible for connecting routing components of the node to higher OSI layers. In this implementation it is responsible for creating packets and keeping experimental performance measures. Output queue internally has three queues and one table (Fig. /refqueuefig). Main Queue (MQ) is the place where payload packets which are received from other nodes and which traverse the node are placed. The high priority queue (HPQ) is the queue in which all the discovery and acknowledgement packets are stored. Internal Packet Table (IPT) is a direct mapped cache that keeps the internally generated payload packets waiting for route lookup. Internal ID Queue (IIQ) on the other hand keeps the indexes of the packets in IPT, for whom a route is returned from the routing table. Departure orders of the packets are determined by the priority weight of the HPQ. A weight of one means amount of packet departing from HPQ is equal to amount of packets departing from other queues in total over the same time period. For example, 10 packets from HPQ and a total of 10 packets from others over a time period T.

Dynamic Routing Table has registers that store the ID of receiver nodes and corresponding routes, a validity field and a latency field, which indicates the latency of a route between two nodes, for each entry. Validity field is set to maximum when a routing entry is updated and decreased with each clock tick. When a validity of an entry is dropped below a certain threshold a route discovery request will be done. Moreover, latency field is also increased with each clock tick. When the table update request is received, the latency of the supplied route is compared to the one in the table. And the smallest value will remain in the table. Through this mechanism routing table entries are kept up to date. This module has two interfaces, one with table updater algorithm and one with header buffer. The table update algorithm module updates the entries in the dynamic routing table. When the table is being updated, lookup operation is frozen until update is over.

2.3 Wireless Channel Emulation

Emulation of wireless channel is achieved by a central switch like component which schedules packets and keeps link states between the nodes. This component is also responsible for updating the nodes positions.

2.4 Simulations

To measure the effect of the hardware and network parameter several simulations listed below are done. Nodes are uniformly distributed over a 100m by 100m area. Simulations are done by varying parameters of a base configuration and then comparing the results with the base configurations simulation results. Table 1 shows the base configuration parameters. In each transmission period, position of the nodes are updated by the following formula

$$P(x, y) = P(x, y) + MF * r_m * TR \tag{1}$$

where P(x,y) is the position of the node, TR is the transmission range, MF is mobility factor and r_m is the mobility probability which is a real random number uniformly distributed between -1 and 1. Network traffic is produced randomly and each time with the same pattern. Each node opens a session to a randomly chosen node and the amount of traffic to the destination node is also chosen randomly. If a node is not transmitting at any moment in time, it may start a session with a certain probability, which is listed in Table 1. Throughout the results presented in this section of the paper all the parameters are same as the ones in Table 1, unless otherwise stated. It should be noted that, at any time not all of the nodes are involved in a transmission session and there might be isolated nodes.

Performance measure is based on average throughput, which is in packets per node per transmission period, The throughput is measured by dividing the total number of packets received by all nodes, including acknowledgement packets, by the number of transmission periods elapsed and number of nodes in the network.

As the number of nodes increased in MANETs expected lengths of the routes will increase. Therefore, we expect to have less average throughput. Moreover, when the mobility of the nodes is increased the average throughput will also decrease due to broken links. Indeed when we compare the throughputs in Fig. 4 and Fig. 5 which are throughputs for 20 and 40 nodes we can see that for the base configuration throughput is higher for 20-node case. Fig. 6 shows the 40 node configuration when the mobility is high. Comparing this to Fig. 5, for the base configurations we see that higher mobility results in performance degradation. Similar results are presented in [4,2,3]. Fig. 4 shows that throughput can be increased by increasing the size of the MQ and/or IPT. In Fig. 5 throughput performance of a 40-node configuration for different parameters is shown. As seen increasing TTL of the packets or increasing IPT and MQ sizes increases performance for this case too. On the other hand effect of routing table size has negligible effect on the performance. Fig. 6 shows the throughput performance of the 40-node configuration under mobility factor 0.3. It is seen that even under high mobility increasing IPT size and MQ has a positive effect. Moreover, increasing priority weight of HPQ reduces the performance. An interesting observation is reducing the size of the HPQ increases performance.

Table 1. Base Configuration Parameters

Parameter	Value
Transmission range	30m
Number of nodes	21
TTL	10
Mobility Factor	0.01
Routing Table Size	10
Main Output Packet Queue (MQ) size	10
Internal Packet Table (IPT) Size (and IIQ)	10
High Priority Queue (HPQ) Size	30
High Priority Queue (HPQ) Priority Weight	1 (2 packets from HPQ and 1 from MQ and 1 from IPT)
Maximum no of packets in a session	50
Probability of starting a session	50

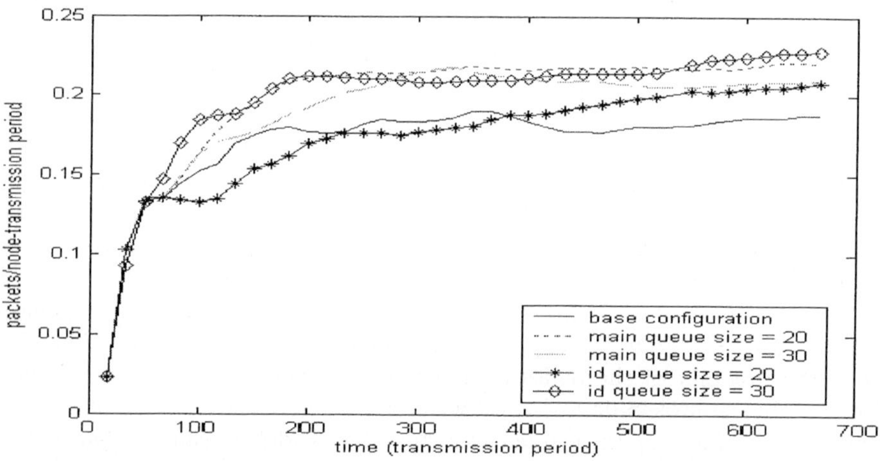

Fig. 4. Throughput with different hardware parameters

3 Conclusion

VHDL implementation of a source routed wireless ad hoc node and a wireless channel emulator switch is completed. Simulations are performed to observe the performance of the network with different hardware parameters under different network conditions. It is observed that increasing size of MQ and IPT, performance improvement is achieved. This is also true when the number of nodes or mobility increased. This is something expected because these will reduce the amount of packet drops in a congested node. Simulations results indicate that if we increase the priority weight of HPQ, the throughput significantly decreases. Furthermore, under high mobility reducing the size of HPQ also increases the

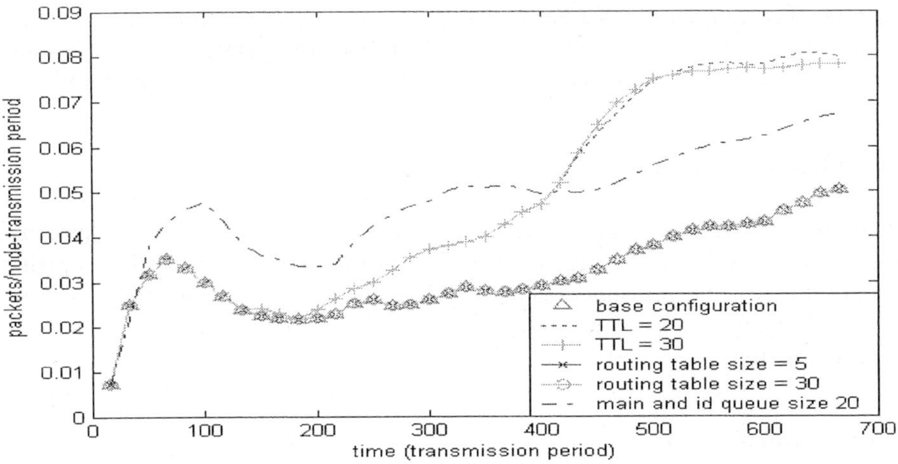

Fig. 5. Throughput with different hardware and network parameters when the number of nodes is 40

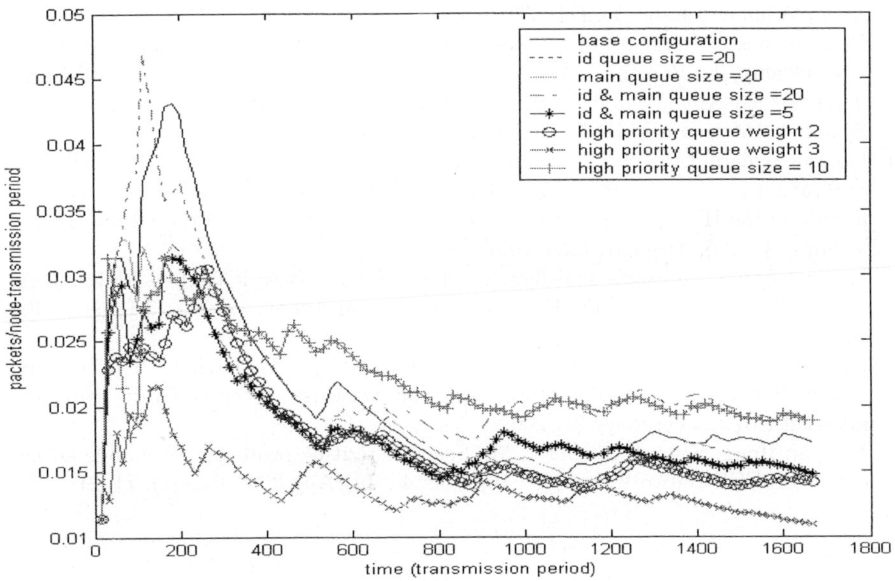

Fig. 6. Throughput with different hardware and network parameters when the number of nodes is 40 and mobility factor is 0.3

performance. Although it is not the aim of this work to measure the impact of network parameters alone it is worth mentioning that in big networks probability of longer routes increases and with a low TTL value, this routes will be invalid. Based on that observation we also simulated the system with a higher TTL values and observed that increasing TTL increases performance up to some point and from that point on further increase in TTL reduces the performance.

4 Future Work

The architecture of the node allows the usage of other approaches like Cluster Gateway Source Routing: In near future this and other possible routing approaches will be implemented. The effect of hardware parameters on these approaches will also be investigated. Non perfect channel conditions should also be investigated.

References

1. Maltz, D.A.; Broch, J.; Jetcheva, J.; Johnson, D.B.; The effects of on-demand behavior in routing protocols for multihop wireless ad hoc networks.; Selected Areas in Communications, IEEE Journal on , Volume: 17 Issue: 8 , Aug 1999
2. Perkins, C.E.; Royer, E.M.; Das, S.R.; Marina, M.K.;IEEE Personal Communications, Volume: 8 Issue: 1 , Feb 2001 Page(s): 16–28
3. Performance comparison of two location based routing protocols for ad hoc networks Camp, T.; Boleng, J.; Williams, B.; Wilcox, L.; Navidi, W.; INFOCOM 2002. Twenty-First Annual Joint Conference of the IEEE Computer and Communications Societies. Proceedings. IEEE , Volume: 3, 2002 Page(s): 1678–1687 vol.3
4. On the scalability of ad hoc routing protocols Santivanez, C.A.; McDonald, B.; Stavrakakis, I.; Ramanathan, R.; INFOCOM 2002. Twenty First Annual Joint Conference of the IEEE Computer and Communications Societies. Proceedings. IEEE , Volume: 3 , 2002 Page(s): 1688–1697 vol.3
5. Lessons from a full-scale multihop wireless ad hoc network testbed Maltz, D.A.; Broch, J.; Johnson, D.B.;IEEE Personal Communications, Volume: 8 Issue: 1, Feb 2001 Page(s): 8–15
6. David B. Johnson; David A. Maltz; Yih-Chun Hu; Jorjeta G. Jetcheva; The Dynamic Source Routing Protocol for Mobile Ad Hoc Networks. Internet Draft, draft-ietf-manet-dsr-07.txt February 21, 2002.
7. Xiaoyan Hong; Kaixin Xu; Gerla, M.; Scalable routing protocols for mobile ad hoc networks;IEEE Network, Volume: 16 Issue: 4 , Jul/Aug 2002 Page(s): 11–21

Temporal Modelling in Flexible Workflows

Panagiotis Chountas[1], Ilias Petrounias[2], and Vassilis Kodogiannis[1]

[1] School of Computer Science, Univ. of Westminster, London, HA1 3TP, UK
[2]Department of Computation UMIST, Manchester PO BOX 88, M60 1QD, UK
chountp@wmin.ac.uk

Abstract. The need for explicit time representation in workflow environments has been recently identified. Although the concept of time is an intrinsic part of a workflow application, time management has been treated as an issue of ordering the constructs of the workflow specification. This traditional approach aids mainly in the monitoring of activity deadlines. There is limited support for modelling and representation of time constraints associated with the processes and their activities or cases. This paper presents a temporal formalism for representing indeterminacy to workflow specifications. We further argue that integrating workflows with temporal databases can further enhance the workflow specification.

1 Introduction

The purpose of a workflow is to support the specification and execution of business processes. A workflow specification describes the tasks of a business process, their dependencies and the executors of each task. The combination of workflow specification and temporal databases significantly facilitates the specification of reliable and complex business processes [1].

Existing workflow management systems offer limited support for management and representation of activities with constrained or infinite duration [2]. Furthermore the addition of time dimension to workflow specifications will provide mechanisms for encoding and querying the history of all processes. Therefore a workflow specification should provide information about an activity, its calendric restrictions, and the time requirements about the activity. A temporal formalism proposed in [3] to describe simple workflow specifications where one activity follows another in a sequential manner. In this paper we investigate the ways in which time formalisms can be used as the basis for more complicated workflow specifications where parallel and concurrent activities can be modelled. The rest of the paper is organised as follows. Section 2 defines a reference model for workflow specification. Section 3 defines the basic elements of temporal workflow representation. Section 4 defines process dimension of a workflow. Section 5 captures and queries activities and their paths as part of a post-relational environment. Section 6 concludes and suggests ways for enhancing the current framework.

A. Yazici and C. Şener (Eds.): ISCIS 2003, LNCS 2869, pp. 123–130, 2003.

2 The Workflow Specification

The Workflow Management Coalition calls a workflow specification [4] a process definition. A business process is an ordered set of business activities. The main components of an activity are: cases and case-items 'Figure 1'. The goal of a business process is to deliver a certain requested service or product. A business activity is an amount of effort that is uninterruptible and is performed in a span of time. For example "Check Credit", "Authorise loan" are possible activities. An instance of a workflow specification is called a case. An example of a case is the process that handles the "Loan claim" of John Smith. An example of a case-item is the fact-claim for John Smith. Case-items are stored in a database. At any moment in time case-items may be allocated to agents.

With reference to the process dimension the WMC [4] defines a reference model, which describes the major components of the workflow architecture. According to this reference model four major elements can be identified in describing the paths between activities participating in a workflow schema:

Sequence: Activities are executed in sequence (e.g. one activity is executed after another).

Parallel: Two or more activities are executed in parallel. Two different blocks can be identified: AND-Split, AND-Join. Here synchronisation is required.

a) The AND-Split enables parallel execution of two or more activities after successful completion of the parent-activity.

b) The AND-Join enables synchronisation of two or more parallel activities into an inheritor activity after successful completion of the ancestor activities.

Condition: one of the selected activities is executed. Modelling a choice amongst two or more selections two blocks may be utilised: a) XOR-split and b) XOR-join. Here no synchronisation is required.

Iteration: sometimes it is crucial to execute a single activity or a set of activities repeatedly over time. The novelty in our approach is the capture and representation of the iteration feature as an intrinsic part of a time model.

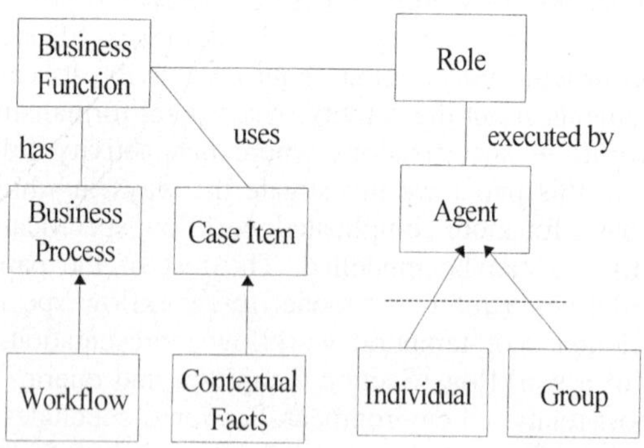

Fig. 1. Resource & Process Definition of a Workflow Specification

For the rest of the paper we discuss how the process dimension can be modelled with the aid of time formalism and a temporal post-relational database environment.

3 Time and Workflow Specification

Time is involved in the ordering of the different workflow constructs as well as in the capturing and representation of case-items. Hence constrained or iterative cases must be expressed as an intrinsic part of the time formalism for a workflow specification. Therefore time formalisms for a workflow specification must capture these constraints if they are to be enforced in the business process.

Temporal inequalities-constraints [2, 5] can be used for encoding rules that regulate the time component of a business and can be modelled as part of the main workflow constructs (sequence, parallel, condition, iteration). Furthermore temporal inequalities can be used to express temporal uncertainty [6].

In our representation time has a standard geometric metaphor. In this metaphor, time itself is a line; a point on the time-line is called a *time point*; the time between two *time points* is known as a time interval. We assume that the representation is both discrete and bounded, that is, we presuppose that we are limited to representing a constrained number of different times, or "collections" of times With reference to the temporal bibliography there are three main types of temporal processes or cases Definite, Indefinite, Infinite) that can be defined. We provide the definition for each type of process with the aid of the basic temporal concepts, equation (**a**)

$$KX + B \text{ where } (K, B, X) \in \mathrm{N} \wedge \mathrm{C} \leq \mathrm{B} \leq C', (\mathrm{C}, C') \in \mathrm{N} \quad (\mathbf{a})$$

Definition 3.1-Definite Temporal Case: is defined over the interval $T_1=[G_L, G_R]$ when the time points G_L, G_R are defined with precision over the time line. To put it differently the absolute distance $K=0 \wedge D = | G_L - G_R | \in \mathrm{N}$ is constant.

Definition 3.2-Indefinite Temporal Case: is defined over the interval $T_1=[G_L, G_R]$ when the time points G_L, G_R are not defined with precision over the time line but are bounded. To put it differently the absolute distance or duration between the time points G_L, G_R is tight bounded between two values $D_L \leq D \leq D_R$. In this case G_L, G_R are expressed by local inequalities, while $K=0$.

Definition 3.3-Infinite Temporal Case: is defined over a sequence of time intervals $< T_1, T_2, \ldots, T_V >$ with either constant or bounded frequency, $K_L \leq K \leq K_R$ of reoccurrence and either constant or bounded duration $D_L \leq D \leq D_R$.

Applying the proposed time formalism on a sample activity-cases we can define three distinct types of situation with reference to activity-case (e.g.(a_1)).

Strict situation **(a_1)*:*** $G_1 \leq \Delta T(a_1) \leq G_2$ (1) where G_1 G_2 are defined with precision on top of a linear time hierarchy, in that sense a calendar may be arbitrary [2,5]. A strict situation simply declares that time constraints implied to a specific activity must be met with precision. With reference to the proposed time model this refers to definite temporal-cases.

Reluctant situation **(a_1):** $G_1 \leq \Delta T(a_1) \leq G_2$, (2) and G_1 ,G_2 are further constrained with the aid of local inequalities $C_L \leq G_1 \leq C_R$, $C_{L1} \leq G_2 \leq C_{R1}$, where G_1, G_2, are defined with imprecision on top of an arbitrary calendar. C_L, C_R, C_{L1}, C_{R1} are defined with precision of a linear time hierarchy. A reluctant situation simply declares that the duration of an activity cannot be specified exactly. Using the best case approach it is expected that an activity will start at the earliest time point C_L and it will finish at earliest time point C_{L1}. Using the worst case approach it is expected that an activity will start at the latest time point C_R and it will finish at latest time point C_{R1}. Reluctant situation implies temporal uncertainty. With reference to the proposed time model this refers to indefinite temporal-cases.

Repetitive situation **(a_1):** An activity is executed more than once in a sequential manner. With reference to the proposed time model this refers to infinite temporal-cases.

We will use the proposed time model for modelling workflow constructs, thus the workflow process dimension as part of post relational workflow specification.

4 Representing and Querying the Workflow Process Dimension

In representing a workflow schema W, 'Figure 2' as a relational structure R, hierarchical structures are used instead of flat relations [8], [9]. If $\{A_1, \ldots, A_n\} \subset U$ and $A_1 \ldots An$ are atomic valued or zero order attributes then $R=\{A_1,\ldots, A_n\}$ is a relation schema. If $\{A_1, \ldots, A_n\} \subset U$ and $A_1 \ldots A_n$ are atomic valued attributes and $R_1,\ldots,R_n$ are relation schemas or high order attributes then $R=(A_1,\ldots,A_n,R_1 \ldots R_n)$ is a relation schema. With reference to workflow process two types of relations are defined. Activity relation is defined for modelling the ordering constructs of a workflow schema thus the routes-paths between activities-cases. The other is identified as a state relation, and it is defined for modelling temporal case items as part of a temporal database formalism.

Definition 4.1: An activity relation R_A: is a relational schema of high and atomic order attributes, in which a high order attribute corresponds to a path between activities, (*sequence, parallel, condition*), thus constituting the workflow schema W (a_1, a_2, a_3, a_4) in its entirety 'Figure 2'.

Definition 4.2: A state relation R_S in turn shows the different temporal case-items (or activity instances) consisting of an individual activity (a_1) which participates in an activity relation R_A [7,10]. The activity identifier indicates a link between a state and activity relation. Formally a state relation is defined as follows:

Definition 4.3- State Relation: Let T a set of time intervals $T=\{G_L, G_R\}$ where $G_L=C+K \times X$, $G_R=C'+K \times X \wedge a_1 \leq X \leq a_v\}$ and D a set of non temporal values. A generalised tuple of temporal arity x and data arity l is an element of $T^x \times D^l$ together with constraints on the temporal elements. In that sense a tuple can be viewed as defining a potentially infinite set of tuples.

Considering that activity relations refer to state relations there is a need to define the relationship in terms of time between the two different types of relations. Case-items *(activity relations)* are defined separately over the time dimension (Valid time) but are always executed between the time limits specified in either *Strict situation (*a_1*)* or *Reluctant situation (*a_1*)* or *Repetitive situation* (a_1) formally noted as state relations: .In that sense if a reluctant or strict situation are not predetermined, we can still derive a temporal inequality for a specific activity (e.g. a_1), which occurs in the interval of time points $G_L = [G_1, G_1']$ defining thus the earliest time for an activity to be executed.

Earliest time: G_L $[G_1= t_{Best\text{-}Earliest}(a_{1\iota} \ldots a_{1\nu}), G_1' = t_{Worst\text{-}Earliest}(a_{1\iota} \ldots a_{1\nu})]$ (1) and the interval of time points $[G_2, G_2']$ for defining the latest time for an activity to be completed, $G_R = [G_2= t_{Best\text{-}Latest}(a_{1\iota} \ldots a_{1\nu}), G_2' = t_{Worst\text{-}Latest}(a_{1\iota} \ldots a_{1\nu})]$ (2) noted as follows

$$G_L \leq \Delta T(a_{1\iota} \ldots a_{1v}) \leq G_R \tag{3}$$

$$t_L a_{1\iota} \leq \Delta T a_{1\iota} \leq t_R a_{1\iota}$$

$$\ldots$$

$$t_L a_{1v} \leq \Delta T a_{1v} \leq t_R a_{1v}$$

$$G_1 = t_{Best\text{-}Earliest}(a_{1\iota} \ldots a_{1v}) = \min(t_L a_{1\iota} \ldots t_L a_{1v}) \tag{4}$$

$$G_1' = t_{Worst\text{-}Earliest}(a_{1\iota} \ldots a_{1v}) = \max(t_L a_{1\iota} \ldots t_L a_{1v}) \tag{5}$$

$$G_2 = t_{Best\text{-}Latest}(a_{1\iota} \ldots a_{1v}) = \min(t_R a_{1\iota} \ldots t_R a_{1v}) \tag{6}$$

$$G_2' = t_{Worst\text{-}Latest}(a_{1\iota} \ldots a_{1v}) = \max(t_R a_{1\iota} \ldots t_R a_{1v}) \tag{7}$$

where $a_{1\iota}$ is the first activity instance a_{1v} is the latest activity instance (case-item). $(a_{1\iota} \ldots a_{1v})$ is the set of the case-items (states). Therefore (4), (5), (6), (7) are defining the best and worst earliest or latest times that a state relation R_S is defined over time.

In the general case (4), (5), (6), (7) are used to define the best and worst earliest or latest times for a state relation R_A to be defined over the dimension of time. However in the case of parallel execution synchronisation is required. Additional or spare time t_s is needed for synchronising parallel activities. Synchronisation is required only in the case of the AND-Join. Synchronisation will occur between the latest time points between activities under AND-Join.

In 'Figure 2', (a_2, a_3) are executed in parallel. Assuming that a_2, finishes before a_3 then a_2 has to wait until a_3 is completed. Thus (6), (7) are modified as follows;

$$G_2 = t_{Best\text{-}Latest}(a_{1\iota} \ldots a_{1v}) = \min(t_R a_{1\iota} \ldots t_R a_{1v}) + t_s \tag{8}$$

$$G_2' = t_{Worst\text{-}Latest}(a_{1\iota} \ldots a_{1v}) = \max(t_R a_{1\iota} \ldots t_R a_{1v}) + t_s \tag{9}$$

In summarising, it can be said that the distinction between activity and state relation, permits the separable expression of paths between activities in a workflow schema, with the aid of an activity relation, while a state relation allows the independent evolution of a case-item through its states over the time. In section-5 the workflow schema presented in 'Figure 2' is translated to a temporal relational representation.

5 Defining the Workflow Process

We translate the process dimension to a relational representation. The activity relations for the AND-Split, AND-join, XOR-Split, XOR-Join constructs are defined. Furthermore with the aid of an extended relational algebra a way for querying the process dimension of a workflow schema 'Figure 2' is presented.

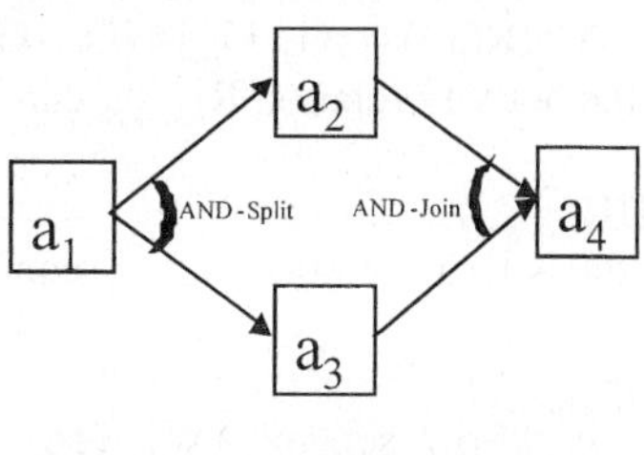

Fig. 2. W, Sample Workflow Schema with Paths

With reference to 'Figure 2' the following activity relations $R_{AND\text{-}Split}$ and $R_{AND\text{-}Join}$ are defined. For each activity relation a new time dimension is introduced named as path time **PT(R$_A$)**. The purpose of the path time dimension is to enable the sychronisation of concurrent activities. G_{L1} , $G_{L2,}$ G_{L3} are defined individually by (4) and (5). Similarly G_{R1} , $G_{R2,}$ G_{R3} are defined by (6) and (7), thus expressing the best and worst earliest or latest times. The semantics of the AND-Split are determined that G_{R1}=$G_{L2,}$ and G_{R1}=G_{L3}. The $R_{AND\text{-}Split}$ activity relation is defined as follows.

$R_{AND\text{-}Split}$	Act-1	Act-2	PT($R_{AND\text{-}Split}$)
X_1	a_1	A_2	$G_{L1} \leq \Delta T(a_{1t}\ldots a_{1v}) \leq G_{R1}$ $\cap$ $G_{L2} \leq \Delta T(a_{2t}\ldots a_{2v}) \leq G_{R2}$
X_2	a_1	A_3	$G_{L1} \leq \Delta T(a_{1t}\ldots a_{1v}) \leq G_{R1}$ $\cap$ $G_{L3} \leq \Delta T(a_{3t}\ldots a_{3v}) \leq G_{R3}$

A path time **PT(R$_A$)** is determined using the intersection semantics and is defined as follows: PT($R_{AND\text{-}Split}$) = VT(R(a_1)) $\cap$ …$\cap$ VT(R(a_V)) where VT(R(a_1)) the time that a_1 is defined through its executed case items presented by a state relation. Therefore

$$PT(R_{AND\text{-}Split}) = VT(R(a_1)) \cap VT(R(a_2)) = [G_{R1},G_{L2}] = [G_{R1}, G_{R1,}] \tag{10}$$

$$PT(R_{AND\text{-}Split}) = VT(R(a_1)) \cap VT(R(a_3)) = [G_{R1},G_{L3}] = [G_{R1}, G_{R1}], \tag{11}$$

(11) is a dummy temporal interval since the upper and lower ends are equal. In the same way the $R_{AND\text{-}Join}$ activity relation can be defined.

$R_{AND\text{-}Join}$	Act-2	Act-3	PT($R_{AND\text{-}Join}$)
X_1	A_2	A_4	$[G_{L2} \leq \Delta T(a_{2t}\ldots a_{2v}) \leq G_{R2} + t_s]$ $\cap$ $[G_{L4} \leq \Delta T(a_{4t}\ldots a_{4v}) \leq G_{R4}]$
X_2	a_3	a_4	$[G_{L3} \leq \Delta T(a_{3t}\ldots a_{3v}) \leq G_{R3}]$ $\cap$ $[G_{L4} \leq \Delta T(a_{4t}\ldots a_{4v}) \leq G_{R4}]$

G_{L2} , $G_{L3,}$ G_{L4} are defined individually by (4) and (5). G_{R4} is defined by either (6) or (7). Similarly G_{R2}, $G_{R3,}$ are defined by (8) and (9). Equations (8) and (9) are achieving synchronisation between activities a_2 and a_3.

The semantics of the AND-Join are determined as $G_{R2} + t_s = G_{L4,}$ and G_{R3}=G_{L4} where t_s is the time needed in achieving synchronisation between a_2 and a_3. Assuming for example that a_2, finishes before a_3 then a_2 have to wait until a_3 is completed. Therefore

$$PT(R_{AND\text{-}Join}) = VT(R(a_2)) \cap VT(R(a_4)) = [G_{R2}+t_s,G_{L4}] = [G_{L4}, G_{L4}] \tag{12}$$

$$PT(R_{AND\text{-}Join}) = VT(R(a_3)) \cap VT(R(a_4)) = [G_{R3},G_{L4}] = [G_{L4}, G_{L4}] \tag{13}$$

Considering (10), (11) then the activity relation $R_{AND\text{-}Split}$ can be restructured as follows (14), presented in 'Figure 3'

$$R_{AND\text{-}Split} = \{a_1\{ a_2, a_3\})\ PT(R_{AND\text{-}Split}) \tag{14}$$

Considering (12), (13) then the activity relation $R_{AND\text{-}Join}$ can be restructured as follows (15), presented in 'Figure 4'

$$R_{AND\text{-}Join} = \{\{ a_2, a_3\}\ a_4\}\ PT(R_{AND\text{-}Split}) \tag{15}$$

Joining (14), (15) then the workflow schema (W), (16) is derived and presented respectively in Figure 3 and Figure 5.

$$R_W = \{ a_1\{ a_2, a_3\}\ a_4\}\ PT(R_W) \tag{16}$$

where $PT(R_W) = \min [PT(R_{AND\text{-}Split}), PT(R_{AND\text{-}Join})]$ & $\max [PT(R_{AND\text{-}Split}), PT(R_{AND\text{-}Join})] = [G_{R1}, G_{L4}]$. We define the semantics of the AND- operator will be defined with the aid of the Path Join and Selection post relational operators.

Selection (σ): For all nodes $\in$ node S where $S_a \neq S_b$, if node S_a is a child of an ancestor of a node S_b, then S_a, S_b are called selection comparable nodes ($S_a \,{}^{\sigma}\!\!\rightarrow S_b$). For example, in 'Figure 4' ($PT=[G_{R1}, G_{L4,}]^{\sigma}\rightarrow$Act-1) are selection comparable nodes. Since there is a path between $PT=[G_{R1}, G_{L4,}]$ and Act-1.$PT=[G_{R1}, G_{L4,}]\rightarrow$Act-2 are not selection comparable nodes. However $PT=[G_{R1}, G_{L4,}]\rightarrow$(Act-2 instances) are selection comparable nodes. The same applies to $PT=[G_{R1}, G_{L4,}]\rightarrow$(Act-3).

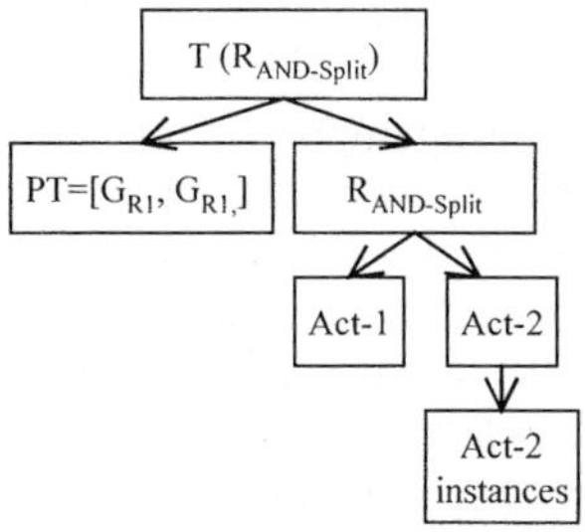

Fig. 3. $R_{AND\text{-}Split}$

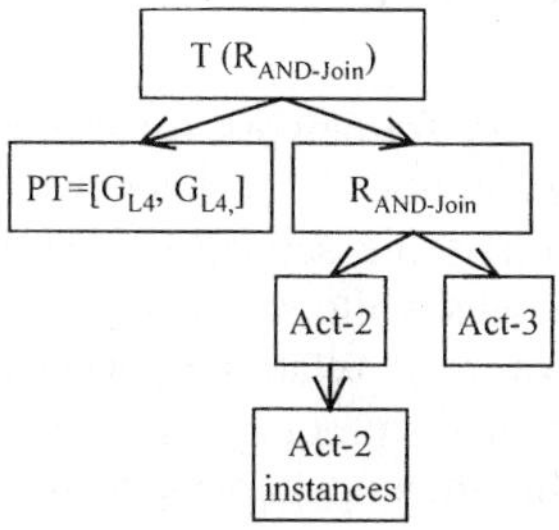

Fig. 4. $R_{AND\text{-}Split}$

P Join ($^{P}\times$): The idea behind the extended Join is to combine relations with common high order attributes not only at the top level but also at the subschema level. Let R be the relational relation schema and S be the schema tree of R, the path $P_r = (M_1 ... M_k)$ is a join-path of R if M_1 is a child of root (S) and M_k is a non-leaf node of S. The idea is to combine to high order relational attributes not only at the top level but also at the sub-schema level. Considering 'Figure 3' and 'Figure 4' there is a path between $R_{AND\text{-}Split}$, (14), and $R_{AND\text{-}Join}$ (15), noted as (Act-2. Act-2 instances) which is the joint point of the two relations. The result of the Join operation between is defined by (16) and presented in 'Figure 5', which in turns represents our sample workflow schema presented in 'Figure 2'.

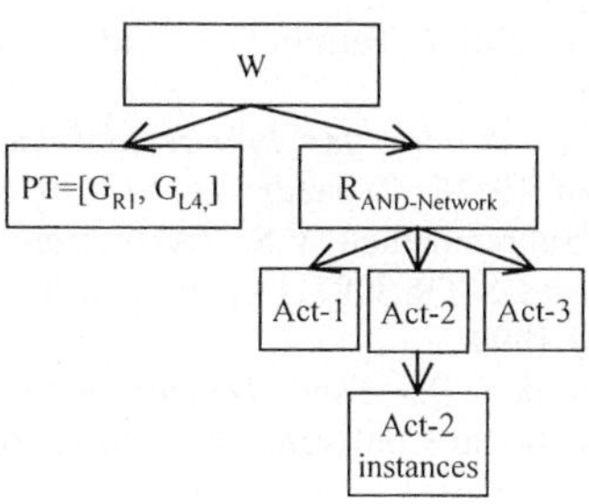

Fig. 5. Workflow schema W, through activity relation R_W

The definition of the activity relations and algebraic operators requires the satisfaction of the transitive closure. The transitive closure of a workflow schema W^* is a workflow schema that has the same vertex as W but whose edges consists of all paths in W. The sequence of steps to derive the transitive closure requires two join operations. This is because the longest path in the schema W passes through two intermediate notes. If this information was not available then no relational algebra operation could decide when the transitive closure is achieved. Generally for a given schema W the transitive closure W^* is the least fixed point solution of the recursive equation: $W^* = W^* \cup (W \bowtie W^*)$. In SQL3 a recursion operation 'RECURSIVE' has been proposed to handle the transitive closure operation.

6 Conclusions

An initiatory framework for representing and querying a temporal workflow schema and the evolution of its states over the time has been presented. The innovation in our framework is the separable representation of a temporal workflow schema and its activity states while paths between activities are also encoded and can be queried with the aid of post relational operators. The framework is currently extended in the direction of developing a complete and sound post relational query mechanism that will enable the engagement of state and activity relations, showing thus the evolution of case-items over the time while following a fixed but arbitrary path policy defined over a model workflow-schema. The functionality of such an environment is to express case-items the information element of a process considering that case-items may be expressed with the aid moving hierarchies.

References

1. Panagos E. and Rabinovich M., *Reducing escalation-related costs in WFMSs*, NATO Advanced Study Institue on Workflow Management Systems and Interoperability, Springer Verlag, 1997.
2. Chountas, P, Petrounias, I., *Representation of Definite, Indefinite and Infinite Temporal Information,* Proc. of (IDEAS'2000), *IEEE Computer Society*, pp 167–178.
3. Cicekli-Kesim, N., *A Temporal Reasoning Approach to Model Workflow Activities,* LNCS, Springer-Verlag, NGITS'99.
4. Workflow Management Coalition, Terminology and Glossary: A Workflow Management Coalition, Brussels, 1996.
5. Koubarakis, M., *Database Models for Infinite and Indefinite Temporal Information*, Information Systems, Vol. 19, No. 2, pages 141–173, 1994.
6. Dekhtyar, A., Ross, R., Subrahmanian, V.S., *TATA Probabilistic Temporal Databases, I: Algebra*, Technical Report CS-TR-3987, Department of Computer Science, University of Maryland, USA, pp 1–81 1999
7. Petrounias, I., Loucopoulos P., *Time Dimension in Fact-Based Model Systems*, Proceedings of 1st International Conference on Object Role Modeling, Australia, 1994, pp.1–17
8. Liu, H., Ramamohanarao, K., *Algebraic Equivalences Among Nested Relational Expressions*, Proceedings of ACM International Conference on Information and Knowledge Management (CIKM), pp 234–243, 1994
9. Kifer, M., Kim, W., Sagiv,Y., *Querying Object Oriented Databases*, Proceedings of ACM Symposium on Principles of Database Systems (PODS), pp 393–402, 1992.

Low Cost and Trusted Electronic Purse System Design

Mehmet Ercan Kuruoglu[1] and Ibrahim Sogukpinar[2]

[1]National Research Institute of Electronic & Cryptology, 41470 Gebze, Kocaeli TURKEY
kmehmet@uekae.tubitak.gov.tr
[2]Gebze Institute of Technology, 41400,Gebze KOCAELI, TURKEY
ispinar@bilmuh.gyte.edu.tr

Abstract. Electronic purse systems are more trusted than magnetic credit card payment systems. However, electronic purse technology is difficult and expensive to realize. Security is a major problem in payment systems, but off-line electronic payments have security gaps. Public Key Infrastructure (PKI) solutions, which are applicable with third parties included to the system, have some risks. Smart cards are not fully trusted. In this study, a low cost and easily applicable electronic purse system is proposed. The proposed solution is as trusted as its global world samples. Applying a simple user authentication method, memory protected smart cards is used without requiring microprocessor smart card security.

1 Introduction

The rapid growth of computer networks had made the Electronic Commerce (EC) an integral part of our life. Therefore any person wants to use virtual money for their payments over the computer networks. EMV (Europay-Master-Visa) cards are used in conventional payment systems. Due to the security and processing requirements, payment with magnetic cards forces to study on electronic purse payments with smart cards. As an electronic payment system, smart card technology offers numerous advantages, including shorter transaction time and greater convenience for consumers, lower cash handling cost and fewer transaction errors for merchants, and greater earned float and less assumed risk for financial institutions [1]. While these and other advantages exist, electronic purse technology is difficult and expensive related to the infrastructure and application. Therefore, to obtain an easy and low cost solution is a meaningful work.

In this study, a new electronic purse system is proposed and implemented. The proposed solution is cheaper, simpler and faster, while still being as secure as electronic purse systems that are available in some regions of world. In this method, by using a simple user authentication scheme, security is increased on protected memory smart cards which are cheaper but less secure than smart cards with microprocessor. At the scheme, password or verification tables are not held in database and no user password is sent to the central server computer. As another feature, by the timestamp method, security breaks are prevented [2]. With the mutual authentication central server is also authenticated [3].

A. Yazici and C. Şener (Eds.): ISCIS 2003, LNCS 2869, pp. 131–138, 2003.

The rest of the papers is organized as follows: In the second section smart cards and electronic purse is presented. To propose the system, an application is realized in the university campus. In the third section the application and related topics such as authentication scheme is explained. In the fourth section over all application and security is analyzed. Last section is conclusion.

2 Smart Cards and Electronic Purse

The traditional smart card is a credit-card sized piece of plastic housing a small microchip. The microchip contains elements for data transmission, storage and processing. Data transfer can take place either via electrical contacts or without contact through electromagnetic fields. While identification data or operating system is stored in ROM, application data is stored in EEPROM. Smart cards can be divided into two portions: memory cards and microprocessor cards. Memory cards are also divided into two: free or protected memory cards. While memory cards contain address and security logic as a processing unit, microprocessor cards contain a CPU and a working memory called as RAM. Older smart cards use an 8-bit processor but today 32- bit processors are routinely available, especially in java cards. Since memory cards are ten or more times cheaper than microprocessor cards, we can distinguish smart cards as cheap or expensive. In figure 1, some smart card applications with required memory and computing power are summarized [4].

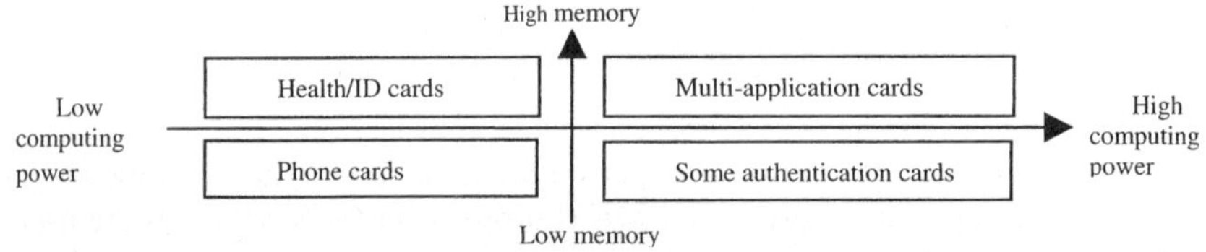

Fig. 1. Some type of smart cards and their required memory and computing power.

Although microprocessor smart cards known to be secure, they have security gaps. The contents of memory cells might be read or modified, probes can be used to read the contents of data buses, wires can be cut and alternative circuits added [6]. But such physical attacks are difficult, expensive and the card may be destroyed. It is possible to measure minute fluctuations in the time required to perform a cryptographic operation [7] or to measure fluctuations in the power consumed by the smart card [8]. This can provide important information on the computation-taking place. Besides the identification of computation, the value of the operands (such as private keys) in the computation can even be read from the screen of an oscilloscope. This side-channel cryptanalysis is not destructive as physical attacks but still is difficult to accomplish. By forcing the processor to make errors or by forcing the smart card to react in an unusual way, sensitive information might be obtained by the attacker [9]. Such manipulative attacks can be very harmful to the system.

Electronic purse (e-purse) systems deal with the electronic payments using smart cards. The money must previously be paid to purse providers, such as banks. Purse providers then load the electronic money (account information) onto the card. During payment process, customer (card user) inserts the smart card to the merchant's card accepting device. After entering the card PIN, unidirectional or mutual authentication process starts. If authentication succeeds, the balance in the user's card is reduced and in parallel that merchant's electronic purse is increased. The electronic amount received is then passed on to the purse provider against corresponding funds. E-purse systems can be divided into there according to transactions or authentications take place: 1) Off-line systems, 2) Both off-line and on-line systems, 3) On-line systems.

Off-line systems are generally closed systems where cards and terminals are issued by only one firm (provider). As has been applied to public phones, prepaid memory cards are used in advance to magnetic stripe ones. Although slowly being replaced with microprocessor cards, memory cards are widely used because of their low cost. Functionally, they only need a logic unit and an irreversible decrementing counter. In addition, recent versions allow a unidirectional authentication of the card by a terminal. Theoretically, no unauthorized terminals or cards can be used in the system.

Real world e-purse systems mostly work both off-line and online. Authentication process generally goes on off-line between the terminal and smart card. So the smart card must contain a microprocessor. When the customer is suspected by a manipulative card, it should be possible for the terminal to interact with the central server (provider) on-line. In non-busy hours, especially after midnights, daily transaction information is sent to the server to gain overall system control.

To prevent security gaps of off-line transactions, fully on-line systems are provided. These systems are different from magnetic credit card payment systems in the case of prepayment, smart cards, authentication processes and security concepts. On-line e-purse systems can be adapted to magnetic credit card infrastructure easily.

PKI (Public Key Infrastructure) and digital certificates are used to improve the security in fully online e-purse systems [10] in the light of papers [11] and [12]. The purse provider applies to the Certification Authority (a third party in the system) to get a certificate. A certificate is just a public key digitally signed with the certificate issuer's private key. By signed with the Certification Authority's private key, the card's digital ID is ready. The smart card can be deployed after writing the digital ID and private key onto it [13]. However, trusting and paying a lot of money to a third party is another problem to overcome in e-purse systems. To overcome this problem, new but expensive smart cards are deployed with embedded functions that generate public and private keys inside the card which means the private key is not exported to anywhere. Besides all, PKI has a lot risks according to C. Ellison and B. Schneier [14]. Such as: Who do we trust and for what? Who is using my key? Is the Certification Authority a real authority? And etc.

In short, today's e-purse systems have a lot problems to overcome: Smart cards are not exactly secure. More trusted microprocessor cards are very expensive compared to magnetic stripe cards even to memory smart cards. So it is a trade of to change low cost but insecure credit card payments to high cost but secure e-purse payments. Besides its high cost, off-line payments are always open to frauds, therefore global systems sometimes need on-line communication. On-line systems using PKI and digital certificates need a third party as an authority, yet it is expensive and has questions to be answered. Requirements for trusted but low cost e-purse system which is proposed with this study are presented in this article.

3 More Trusted Electronic Purse System Design with Memory Cards

Since smart cards do not offer exact security and highly secure microprocessor cards' cost is very high in price, protected memory cards are used in this work. Security does not depend fully on smart card here, instead depends on the authentication scheme used.

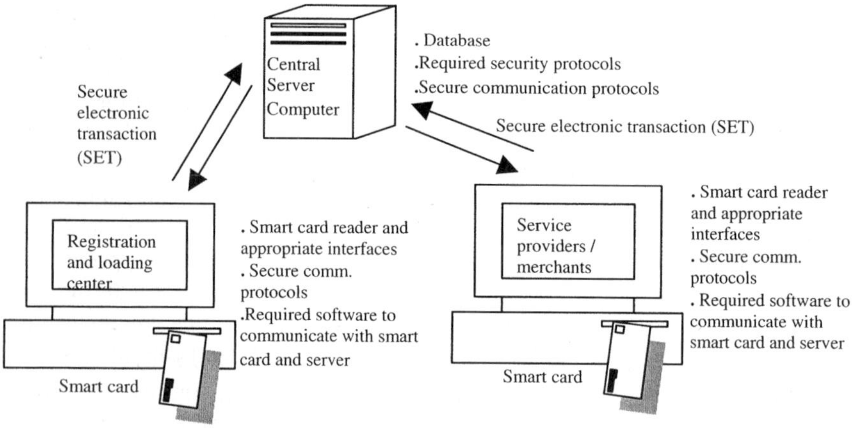

Fig. 2. Block diagram of the implemented electronic purse system.

Because of security gaps and in order to control overall system, off-line payment is not taken into account. The proposed system stands on magnetic stripe credit card payments' on-line infrastructure. This infrastructure is low in cost and trusted in communication; therefore it is used all over the world. Only appropriate card reader terminals are needed.

Based on the authentication scheme, no certification authorities and no third parties are needed to obtain digital certificates. This makes the system simple and not to face with the problems of PKI.

University campus is chosen as an application area. Since it is not commercial yet, no POS terminals or huge servers are used. Instead, a simple server for controlling transactions and personal computers with appropriate smart card readers for loading and payments are used (See figure 2). In the system partners have five types of jobs: 1) Electronic purse provider: administration of university. Allows the system, prepares the required devices, places and staff. 2) Central server computer: stores customer identification and account information in a trusted database. Authenticates smart card (identify customer) and terminal. Controls account transactions. Transfers the money from customer accounts to merchant accounts. 3) Registration and loading center: loads and deploys the electronic purse smart card to the customers. Reloads or terminates the card. Real money transactions take place here. 4) Service providers / merchants: cafe, restaurant, library, computer labs etc. The places where goods and services are bought. 5) Customers; card users: Academic staff, students and other personal.

The authentication scheme used in the study depends on one way hash function and timestamp [2], [3]. While similar scheme is proposed in both papers, [3] further offers mutual authentication. Instead, alternative authentication schemes can be used, which are proposed in [15], [16] and [17] with different but more difficult calculations. We have two main phases to consider: registration, login&authentication phases that are shown in Fig 3. and 4.

Registration: Customer C_i gives his/her identity (name, surname, birthday, place of birth, national ID, tax no, addresses, telephone numbers and etc.) and account (A_i - money to be balanced at first time) information to the registration office. Then the customer chooses a two or three byte long password (PW_i). Password will also be used as card PIN, therefore its length depends on the smart card. The office terminal sends A_i, customer identity information and unique card number (ID_i) to the central server computer. After receiving all, the server stores the customer information into the database. Then the secret information SI_i is computed.

$$SI_i = h(ID_i \oplus A_i \oplus K_s). \tag{1}$$

Where K_s is the server's secret key and $\oplus$ denotes the bitwise exclusive OR operation. Then the server sends SI_i back to the registration center. The registration terminal first computes $h(PW_i)$, where h is a one-way standard hash function called as SHA1 [5] then computes card secret information CSI_i using equation (2).

$$CSI_i = SI_i \oplus h(PW_i). \tag{2}$$

After all, registration center stores some customer information (name, surname, and etc. but not A_i) and CSI_i into the card. Then the card is released to the customer.

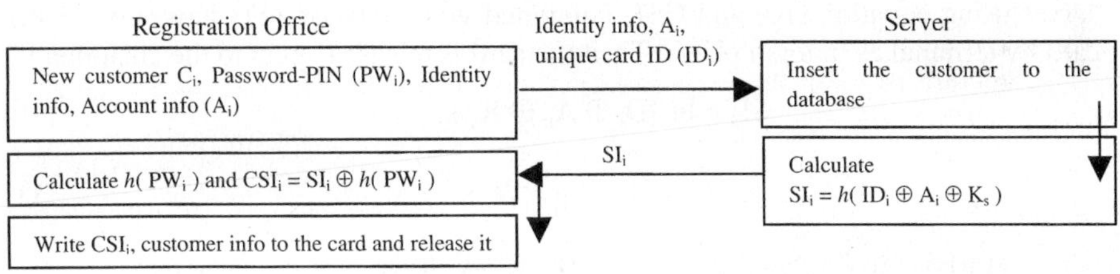

Fig. 3. Registration Phase

Login&Authentication: When card user C_i goes either to the registration center or to the service provider/merchant he/she first inserts his/her card to the terminal, then enters the password (PW_i) via a client device. If needed, C_i clarifies his/her identity. Terminal reads the card secret information CSI_i from the card and computes equations (3) and (4):

$$SI_i = CSI_i \oplus h(PW_i), \{ = h(ID_i \oplus A_i \oplus K_s) \}. \tag{3}$$

$$TTF = h(SI_i \oplus T_i) . \tag{4}$$

Here TTF represents **T**erminal **T**ime **F**unction where T_i is the terminal current transaction **T**imestamp. Then terminal sends customer information, TTF and T_i to the central server.

At the server the following procedures take place in order to verify customer C_i:

- Check if any customer C_i exists, if not C_i is rejected.
- Check if the time interval between the time T_i' when the server receives message and T_i exceeds a predetermined legal time interval ΔT of transmission delay. That is if equation (5) holds, then C_i is rejected.

$$T_i' - T_i > \Delta T . \tag{5}$$

- If equation (6) holds:

$$TTF = h(\, h(\, ID_i \oplus A_i \oplus K_s\,) \oplus T_i\,) . \tag{6}$$

Then customer C_i is authenticated and access to the server is granted. But also for mutual authentication, server computes its own server time function with eqn. (7):

$$STF = h(\, h(\, ID_i \oplus A_i \oplus K_s\,) \oplus T_s\,) . \tag{7}$$

Then server sends A_i, STF and T_s back to the terminal. Here T_s is the timestamp of server action. At the terminal, if equation (8) and (9) holds:

$$T_s' - T_s < \Delta T . \tag{8}$$

$$STF = h(\, SI_i \oplus T_s\,) . \tag{9}$$

Then the server is authenticated. Here T_s' is the timestamp of terminal received message. From now on, transactions can begin with A_i. The terminal and server might accept any account information changes.

With new account information A_n, new secret information is computed by server using equation (10) and CSI_n computed with equation (11) is written to the card by terminal as in login phase. Then the card is released again to the customer.

$$SI_n = h(\, ID_i \oplus A_n \oplus K_s\,). \tag{10}$$

$$CSI_n = SI_n \oplus h(\, PW_i\,). \tag{11}$$

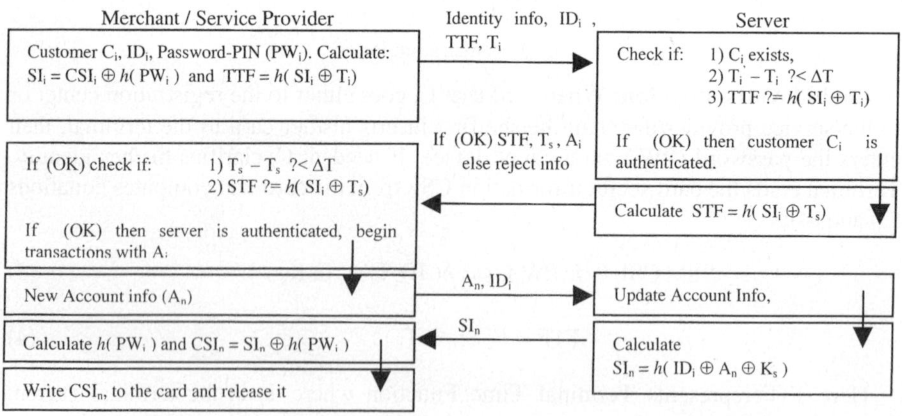

Fig. 4. Login&Authentication Phase

4 Application Results and Security Analysis

The proposed electronic purse system deals with protected memory smart cards. Therefore with an appropriate reader, data can be read from the card, but can not be written on easily. In order to write on the card, one must pass the PIN protection. Any wrong attempts more than 8, locks the card to be written. This is a primitive protection for unskilled frauds. Counters as in prepaid memory cards can not be used in this system. Because card will be credited in the proposed system as it is debited. Of course using a tamper resistant microprocessor smart card improves the security. But as explained in section 2, smart card security can be broken. Therefore the importance of authentication method used in the proposed system increases the card security. Yet, using a microprocessor card increases the system cost.

Server secret key K_s is protected by one way hash function $h(.)$. In theory it is infeasible to access the key. One possible enhancement of key considerations is to generate keys for every user by means of key generators. So breaking down or knowing a key for one card does not affect other cards. However, this time consuming process for the server enlarges database tables.

The timestamp T prevents the replay attack. With the timestamp, the server or the terminal is able to pinpoint an intruder who replays a message. To pass the authentication phase, the intruder must change T in order to satisfy $(T' - T) < \Delta T$. However, if T is changed, the authentication phase cannot be passed unless TTF is also changed.

In case the user loses his/her smart card, the thief can not obtain the password PW_i, and also can not compute SI_i. Then the thief will fail in the authentication phase. Even if the fraud be the card owner, he/she can not pass the secure communication between terminal and server.

5 Conclusions

In this study, a low cost but trusted and easily applicable electronic purse system is proposed. The proposed system is then tested in a closed area. According to authors of [2] and [3], the used authentication scheme is time-saving and has simple computations. The security analysis shows that it is also trusted against frauds. Since used smart cards cost low and no third parties are needed, the proposed system cost gets lower. Also using the magnetic card payment infrastructure and only by changing the POS terminals an easily applicable system can be obtained. If microprocessor smart card is used instead of protected memory cards, the terminals operate with less computation and the system gets more secure. However, proposed method can be a very good alternative solution for EMV low cost magnetic stripe credit cards in electronic payments.

References

1. Gregory E. Truman, Kent Sandoe, Tasha Rifkin: An empirical study of smart card technology. Elsevier Science B.V. Information & Management 2004, 1–15, (2002)
2. Min-Shiang Hwang, Cheng-Chi Lee, Yuan-Liang Tang: A Simple Remote User Authentication Scheme. Mathematical and Computer Modeling 36, 103–107, (2002)
3. Hung-Yu Chien, Jin-Ke Jan, Yuh-Min Tseng: An Efficient and Practical Solution to Remote Authentication: Smart Card. Computers & Security Vol 21, No 4, 372–375, (2002)
4. W. Rankl, W. Effing: Smart Card Handbook. John Wiley & Sons (1997)
5. U. S. NIST, Computer Systems Lab, Secure Hash Standard, FIBS PUB 180, May (1993).
6. R. Anderson: Security Engineering. John Wiley (2001)
7. P. Kocher: Timing Attacks on Implementations of Diffie-Hellman, RSA, DSS, and Other Systems. In: N. Koblitz, editor, Proceedings of Crypto'96. Lecture Notes in Computer Science, 104–113, 1109, Springer Verlag (1996)
8. P. Kocher, J. Jaffe, B. Jun: Differential Power Analysis. In: M. Wiener, editor, Proceedings of Crypto'99. Lecture Notes in Computer Science, 388–397, 1666, Springer Verlag (1999)
9. D. Boneh, R. DeMillo and R. Lipton: The Importance of Checking Cryptographic Protocols for Faults. In: W. Fumy, editor, Proceedings of Eurocrypt'97. Lecture Notes in Computer Science, 37–51, 1233, Springer Verlag (1997)
10. David Corcoran, David Sims and Bob Hillhouse: Smart Cards and Biometrics: Your Key to PKI. URL: http://www.linuxjournal.com/article.php?sid=3013. Issue 59: March 01, (1999)
11. W. Diffle, M. E. Hellman: New Directions in Cryptography. IEEE Trans. Inform. Theory, IT, Vol. 22, No. 6, 644–654, November (1976)
12. R. L. Rivest, A. Shamir, L. Adleman: A Method for Obtaining Digital Signatures and Public Key Cryptosystem. Communication of the ACM, Vol. 21, No. 2, 120–126, (1978)
13. T.K•l•çl•, Smart Cards in PKI. URL: http://deepnight.org/publications/smartcard-howto/smartpki.html., (2002)
14. Carl Ellison, Bruce Schneier: Ten Risks of PKI: What You're not Being Told about Public Key Infrastructure. Computer Security Journal, Volume XVI, No. 1, (2001)
15. Hung-Yu Chien, Jinn-Ke Jan, Yuh-Min Tseng: A modified remote login authentication scheme based on geometric approach. The Journal of Sys. and Software 55, 287–290, (2001)
16. Lei Fan, Jian-Hua Li and Hong-Wen Zhu: An Enhancement of TimeStamp-based Authentication Scheme. Computers & Security Vol 21, No 7, 665–667, (2002)
17. K. Tan, H. Zhu: Remote password authentication scheme based on cross-product. Computer Communications 22, 390–393, (1999)

Uncorrelating PageRank and In-Degree in a Synthetic Web Model

Mieczysław A. Kłopotek[1] and Marcin Sydow[2]

[1] Institute of Computer Science, Polish Academy of Sciences, Warsaw, Poland also Institute of Computer Science, University of Podlasie, Siedlce, Poland,
klopotek@ipipan.waw.pl

[2] Polish-Japanese Institute of Information Technology, Warsaw, Poland
msyd@pjwstk.edu.pl

Abstract. An important part of the Web research nowadays concentrates on developing increasingly sophisticated models of the Web graph. Properties of these graphs are measured and compared with the properties of the real Web. This paper briefly summarizes the most important measures and models of the Web and suggests a new model wich is an improved version of a few existing models.

1 Introduction

During last few years there have been proposed many Web graph models. There have been also made many experiments aiming in measuring various properties of the Web graph. The quality of each artificial Web graph model can be evaluated by comparing its properties with the properties of the real Web. One of the recent models, *hybrid* model proposed by Pandurangan, Raghavan et al.[20] is the first one, up to the authors' knowledge, claimed to simulate three important measures of the real Web: in-degree, out-degree and PageRank distributions. Some problem with this model is, as authors report, high correlation between in-degree and PageRank in this model while such a correlation, as stated in [20], is much lower in the real Web. This paper presents an overview of existing models and experimental results of the Web. Due to space limitations the overview is brief and restricted to selected topics. In addition there is presented a new model, $multi - hybrid$ model which may overcome a correlation problem.

Section 2 briefly lists the most important experimental results of the Web measurements. Section 3 is an overview of the graph models related to the Web graph research with brief quality evaluation. In Section 4 the authors suggest some improvements to the existing models in order to achieve higher similarity to the real Web graph.

2 Real Web Measurements

A good model of the Web graph should exhibit some statistical and structural properties which are typical for the real Web graph. Because of the space limitations we list only these, which are essential to evaluate a new Web graph model proposed in this paper, the $multi - hybrid$ model.

A. Yazici and C. Şener (Eds.): ISCIS 2003, LNCS 2869, pp. 139–146, 2003.

Degree Distributions. Despite the fact that individual Web pages are created in very different way, there is a striking regularity in global degree distributions. All known experiments report that in-degree and out-degree distributions in the Web follow the power law [14,17]. It means that the fraction of the pages having the degree k is proportional to $1/k^g$, where g is called exponent of the distribution. This exponent seems to be very stable and equal 2.1 for in-degree and 2.7 for out-degree, independently on scale or choice of subset of Web pages being measured [14]. Most sources report that average degree in the Web graph is close to 7 e.g. [14] while the measurements reported in [21] result in much higher average degree being about 17. There is a possibility that these experiments use different preprocessing rules for Web pages.

PageRank Distribution and Correlation. The experiment described in recent paper by Pandurangan et al. [20] shows that PageRank [19] distribution also follows power law, moreover with exactly the same value of exponent (2.1) as in-degree distribution. This result raised a question whether PageRank and in-degree are highly correlated in the real Web. Because of the fact that both measures can be potentialy used as ranking measures for Web pages in search engines, such a correlation would be very important for practical reasons. Computation of PageRank is much harder than in-degree so using in-degree instead of PageRank would be economical. The same paper [20] says however that such a correlation is very low in the real Web. In addition in-degree as a local property is much easier to be manipulated by individual page creators than global PageRank.

Fractal Structure. Recent experimental results presented in paper by Dill, Kumar et al. [12] reveal self-similar structure in the Web. In this experiment various portions of the Web were measured with regard to in-degree and out-degree distributions, weakly and strongly connected components and bipartite cliques sizes. Each of the examined portions of the Web formed *thematically unified cluster* (TUC) with regard to: containing some key words, having the same host or geographical location etc. The main result is that each of such a TUCs has very similar structural and statistical properties as others and the whole Web. For example the in-degree distribution is the same in each TUC (power law with exponent 2.1). Other result is that SCC's of all TUC's are tightly connected to each other forming a kind of the "backbone" of the Web. The fractal-like nature of the Web structure may be explained in the way that evolution of the Web is the composition of many independent evolution processes rather than single global process.

Other Measures. We refer the reader to the literature on the topics we had to omit here: Broder, Kumar et al.[11] - very interesting report on connectivity structure of the Web graph, [13,14,15] - bipartite cliques and distance issues.

3 Artificial Web Models

During the last two decades there have been proposed many random graph models. Here we briefly list the most known ones but we remind the details only of the most recent models in Web research. The quality of each model is evaluated mainly by comparison of measurements made on the model with analogue measurements made on the real Web (see prev. section for examples).

"Classic" Erdös-Renyi Models. The first well known random graph models in literature are: $G(n, M)$ and $G(n, p)$ where n, M are natural numbers, $M \leq n(n-1)/2$ and $0 < p < 1$ is real number. The former one corresponds to a graph which is drawn from all the undirected graphs of n vertices with exactly M edges (without loops and multiple edges) with uniform distribution. The latter model considers undirected graphs without loops and multiple edges with n vertices, where each of possible $n(n-1)/2$ edges exists with probability p, independently of other edges. Both models were subjects of deep theoretical studies (e.g. [7]). Despite the important role of these models as a foundation of random graph theory, they are not suitable for Web modeling for at least two important reasons: (1) number of vertices is fixed, which is not true in the Web; (2) the properties of these models are very different than observed properties of the real Web. For instance degree distribution is Poisson rather than power law [7]. The number of bipartite cliques even in the more "realistic" $G(n, p)$ model is very low in comparison with the real Web [16].

ACL Model. Aiello Chung and Lu analyzed the graph of telephone calls [1]. They proposed the simple method of constructing a random directed graph with a given degree distribution. After fixing some degree sequence of vertices (which follows the power law), the graph is constructed as follows: each vertex n forms a group of $d(n)$ copies, where $d(n)$ is its degree. Then random matching between all the groups is chosen. After this, each group "collapses" to one vertex. The resulting graph has obviously power law distribution with desired exponent. Multiple edges are possible in this model. Theoretical investigation [16] showed that the expected value of the number of bipartite cliques in this model is much too low in comparison with the real Web. Also recent experiments [17] on slightly modified version of this model showed that clustering coefficient value corresponding to this model is much lower than real Web analogue.

Degree-Based Model. In this random graph process [5] there is a new vertex added in each time step and directed edge between this new vertex and a vertex chosen randomly among "old" vertices. The probability of choosing a destination vertex is proportional to its in-degree. A random graph constructed in such a way follows a power law for in-degree distribution. The exponent, however is always tending to the value of 2 rather than 2.1 - the value being observed in the real Web. It exhibits fractal properties [4,6,8].

Evolving Copying Models. Kumar et al. have presented interesting random graph models called *evolving copying* models [16]. These models were especially designed for modeling the Web. Besides following power law distribution with exponent similar to the real, these models simulate the creation of new pages (vertices) and hyperlinks (directed edges) over time. In addition the authors tried to model the concept of page content category. A graph corresponding to such a model can be treated as a stochastic process $G(t) = (V(t), E(t))$, where $V(t)$ and $E(t)$ denote the sets of vertices and edges in time t respectively. At each time step t there are added some vertices and edges according to some general random functions $v(V(t), t)$ and $e(v, G(t), t)$ respectively. In linear growth copying model, which is parameterized by constant out-degree d and real copy factor $0 < a < 1$, there is 1 vertex v added in each time step and d edges. The edges are attached to the new vertex as follows: there is a prototype vertex chosen at random uniformly from "old" vertices. For each of d new edges of v its destination is either with probability a copied from the corresponding edge of the prototype or with probability $1-a$ uniformly picked from all the vertices. In exponential growth variant, there are three other real parameters: $growth$ factor $p > 0$, $self-loop$ factor $s > 0$ and $tail$ factor $t > 0$. In each time step t there is added some number of new vertices according to the standard binomial distribution $B(V(t), p)$. Each new vertex has s $self-loop$ edges. The remaining edges are created as follows: for each "old" vertex v and each edge u pointing to it a new edge pointing to it is created with probability $d \cdot p/(d+s)$. The "starting" vertex of this edge is chosen either with probability t from the "old" vertices or, with probability $1-t$ from the "new" edges. It is easy to check that the expected number of "$non-loop$" edges added in each step is d. The $self-loops$ in this model seem to be added because of the desired mathematical properties of the model. In-degree distributions of both the evolving models follow the power law with exponents depending on the models' parameters: $(2-a)/(1-a)$ for linear variant and $log_b(1+p)$, where $b = 1 + p \cdot d/(d+s)$. Thus it is easy to check that properly chosen values for parameters of these models may result in the desired 2.1 value of the exponent. The same paper [16] contains profound mathematical analysis of the above models. Besides modeling in-degree distribution observed in the Web, copying models contain many more large bipartite cliques than any previously introduced model. Many large cliques are also present in the real Web. There has been also proposed [14] some model with deletion of vertices and edges. The estimates of degree and cliques were promising but no further analysis were done in this paper. Mathematical analysis of such a model seems to be hard.

Preferential Attachment Models. Bollobas et al. have recently proposed very interesting family of parameterized graph models [9]. There are 5 real, non-negative parameters a, b, c, d, e, with $a + b + c$ being equal to 1. The graph process starts with some initial graph. Lets denote by $G(t)$ the graph at the time step t, and by $n(t)$ the number of vertices in $G(t)$. We will say that a vertex v is chosen according to the $in-rule$ iff probability of choosing it is equal to $(in(v)+d)/(t+d \cdot n(t))$, where $in(v)$ denotes in-degree of v. Analogously we say that v is chosen according to the $out-rule$ iff the probability of choosing it is equal to: $(out(v)+e)/(t+e \cdot n(t))$, where $out(v)$ denotes the out-degree of v. $G(t+1)$ is obtained from $G(t)$ according to the following rules:

A) with probability a a new vertex v is added and an edge between v and some vertex w picked randomly from "old" vertices according to the $in-rule$.

B) with probability b there is a new edge added between "old" vertices v and w according to the $out-rule$ and $in-rule$ respectively.

C) with probability c a new vertex w is added with a new edge between v and w, where w is chosen according to the $out-rule$. This model is obviously a very wide generalization of the degree based selection model. The authors' objective [9] was to propose a general random graph process that is on the one hand suitable for modeling various random graphs interesting from the scientific point of view, and on the other hand which is still quite simple. The same paper contains mathematical analysis of the model which results in the observation that both in-degree and out-degree distributions follow a power law with exponents being functions of the models' parameters. Thus there is possibility to obtain the desired values of exponents by manipulation of parameters.

Multi-layer Model. In order to explain the fractal-like structure [12] of the Web, Laura et al. proposed a $multi-layer$ model of the Web graph [17]. According to this model a random graph is viewed as a union of L non-disjunctive subgraphs called layers. The concept of layer corresponds to a notion of topic community in the Web. At each time step t a new vertex x is added. The vertex x is assigned to a constant number l of layers, which are picked randomly with probability proportional to their sizes. Let $L(x)$ denote the set of layers x belongs to. After this we add d edges pointing from x to vertices in $L(x)$, always c or $c+1$ vertices per each layer in $L(x)$, where $c = \lfloor d/l \rfloor$. For each layer from $L(x)$ destination vertices are chosen as follows: we choose a prototype vertex p from the layer randomly and then with probability a we copy the destination vertex from p or with the probability $1-a$ we choose a destination vertex according to its in-degree inside this layer. Computer simulations reported in the same paper [17] showed that multi-layer model follows the power law distribution for in-degree with exponent value 2.1 and undirected coefficient factor value being very close to the value observed in the experiment done by the authors on the real Web.

PageRank-Based and Hybrid Models. In order to model the PageRank distribution, Pandurangan, Raghavan and Upfal [20] have recently proposed a variant of the *degree based* model. In this model the destination of a new edge is chosen according to the PageRank distribution instead of the in-degree distribution. More precisely, with probability b destination is chosen uniformly and with probability $1-b$ chance of choosing any vertex is proportional to its PageRank. Analysis contained in this paper shows that PageRank distribution in this model follows power law with exponent being a function of b. The problem is that for $b = 0$ the value of exponent is 3 and even increases with b. The authors proposed also another variant with 2 real parameters a, b, where $0 < a$, $b < 1$ and $a + b = 1$, called *hybrid* model. In this model probability of choosing the destination of new edge is proportional to its in-degree with probability a, or with probability b proportional to its PageRank, or with remaining probability $1 - a - b$ the destination is chosen uniformly. The authors report that computer simulations showed that for $a = b$ being close to 0.33, in-degree, out-degree and even PageRank distributions were power law. Moreover all the exponents were identical to these observed in the real Web. Even more interestingly, still in the same paper [20] the authors report that capturing all the three exponents was also successful for some other model in their experiments. Modeling all the three exponents in a single model is an important achievement. On the other hand, there was very high in-degree and PageRank correlation (0.99) in both reported models, while up to [20] such a correlation in the real Web is rather low.

4 A Concept of In-Degree-PageRank Uncorrelation. A Multi-hybrid Model

Now we suggest a new graph model having 3 propeties: 1) in-degree, out-degree, PageRank distributions are power law, with correct parameters; 2) in-degree and PageRank correlation is lower than in *hybrid* model; 3) structure is multi-level.

For this purpose let us consider a graph consisting of many disconnected subgraphs, each of them having property 1). First of all we can observe that such a graph has all the properties - assuming that sizes of subgraphs are non-uniformly distributed for the sake of property 2). Property 1) of the union is obvious for in-degree and out-degree distributions as for the sample being created by just merging together samples from the same distribution. Now let us see how to derive global PageRank of the union from local PageRanks of subgraphs. Let G_1 and G_2 be two subgraphs without any common edges. Let us calculate their respective PageRanks from the standard formulas:

$$r_i = (1-d) \cdot M_i + d \cdot A_i \cdot r_i \tag{1}$$

with d being a *continuation* factor, M_i a column vector of size $m_i = |G_i|$, $M_{i_j} = 1/m_i$ and A_i the transposed adjacency matrix of G_i modified in this way that each zero-column of it is filled uniformly to sum up to 1. Now let us compute the PageRank for the graph G being union of G_1 and G_2 (without adding any new nodes). Of course

$$r = (1-d) \cdot M + d \cdot A \cdot r, \tag{2}$$

$$\textit{where} \quad M = 1/m, \quad m = |G|, \quad A^T = (A_1^T, A_2^T)\,(\textit{block diagonal}).$$

It is not difficult to observe that the global PageRank of G is a composition of rescaled local PageRank vectors, due to their sizes:

$$r^T = ((m_1/m) \cdot r_1^T, (m_2/m) \cdot r_2^T) \tag{3}$$

By means of the mathematical induction this "rescaling" effect can be easily generalized for the case of union of any natural number k of disjoint subgraphs. More precisely the corresponding i-th fragment of the global PageRank vector is $(m_i/m) \cdot r_i$. This "rescaling" effect of PageRank was also confirmed by our computer simulations. Due to this the union should exhibit property 2), assuming that sizes of subgraphs are non-uniformly distributed. The last thing to check is that the union preserves the power law distribution of PageRank. For simplicity let us focus on the case with 2 subgraphs what can be easily generalised by mathematical induction for higher number of subgraphs. Let us keep the denotations from equations (1,2), and let $f(x), f_i(x)$ denote the total number of nodes with PageRank value being x in the union and subgraph G_i respectively. Because of the power law distribution inside each subgraph, we have: $f_i(x) = c_i/x^g$, where c_i is some proportionality coefficient and $g = 2.1$. So due to (3) we have:

$$f(x) = f_1(x/(m_1/m)) + f_2(x/(m_2/m)) = (c_1(m_1/(x \cdot m))^g + c_2(m_2/(x \cdot m))^g) =$$

$$= (c_1(m_1/m)^g + c_2(m_2/m)^g)/x^g \tag{4}$$

This means that the global PageRank distribution of G is power law with the same exponent g.

Up to now our graph consisted of many disjoint components. If we want the subgraphs to play the role of "Web communities" we have to make our "ideal" model a bit more realistic allowing for some connectivity between them. An analysis of connectivity in the Web made by Broder et al. [11] and Bayeza et al. [3] suggest that even if there are some islands, most of the Web - about 90 percent - is connected. The overall distribution of PageRank should not change significantly as far as we do not add links from high PageRank nodes to low PageRank nodes. For PageRank stability analysis we refer the reader to [18].

Implementation. Here we suggest how to implement the above ideas. Let $G(0)$ be some small initial graph. At each time step t we add some number of new nodes to a graph acording to some constant growth fraction p, like in the *evolving exponential* model. For each new node we do the following: with very small probability the new node forms a new community. Otherwise we choose a community it will belong to by preferential attachement, with regard to the sizes of existing communities. Due to this, distribution of communities' sizes should be non-uniform, for the sake of property 2). To make possible that communities overlap we can choose another communities the node belongs to. Chance of belonging to each additional community should be initially small and strongly decrease after choosing each subsequent community. After this we link each new node inside each of its communities like in the *hybrid* model. With respect to results in [20] this should guarantee keeping desired distributions inside communities. We can call this new concept a $multi-hybrid$ model for the names of previous ideas it extends.

5 Conclusions and Further Work

We presented in this paper the most important models of the Web graph and their properties. We also suggested a new, $multi-hybrid$ model that may help to overcome a problem with too high correlation between in-degree and PageRank [20]. Despite the fact that intuitions and some theoretical considerations presented here seem to confirm our hypothesis, more work and experiments are needed to obtain solid evidence.

References

1. W. Aiello, F. Chung, L.Lu. A random graph model for massive graphs. Proc ACM Symp. On Theory of computing, pp.171–180, 2000.
2. A. Arasu, J. Cho, H. Garcia-Molina, A. Paepcke, S. Raghavan. Searching the Web. ACM Transactions on Internet Technology, 1(1), 2001, 2–43.
3. R. Baeza-Yates, F. Saint-Jean and C. Castillo Web Structure, Age, and Page Quality, 2nd International Workshop on Web Dynamics, Honolulu, Hawaii, 7th May 2002,http://www.dcs.bbk.ac.uk/webDyn2/onlineProceedings.html
4. A. Barabasi and R. Albert. Emergence of Scaling in Random Networks. Science , 286(509), 1999.
5. A. Barabasi, R. Albert, and H. Jeong. Scale-free characteristics of random networks: The topology of the World Wide Web. Physica A, 281, 2000, 69–77.
6. A. Barabasi, R.Albert and H. Jeong. Mean-field theory for scale-free random graphs. Physica A, 272, 1999, 173–187.
7. B. Bollobas. Random Graphs. Academic Press, 1990.
8. B. Bollobas, O. Riordan, J. Spencer, and G. Tusnady. The degree sequence of a scale-free random graph process. Random Structures & Algs, 18(3), 2001, 279–290.
9. B. Bollobas, C. Borgs, J. Chayes and O. Riordan Directed scale-free graphs Proc. of the 14th ACM-SIAM Symposium on Discrete Algorithms 2003, 132–139.
10. S. Brin and L. Page. The anatomy of a large-scale hypertexual Web search engine. In Proceedings of the 7th WWW conference, 1998.
11. A. Broder, R. Kumar, F. Maghoul, P. Raghavan, S. Rajagopalan, R. Stata, Andrew Tomkins, J. Weiner. Graph Structure in the Web. Proceedings of the 9th WWW Conference, 2000.
12. S. Dill, R. Kumar, K. McCurley, S. Rajagopalan, D. Sivakumar, and A. Tomkins. Self-Similarity in the Web. In Proceedings of the 27th International Conference on Very Large Databases (VLDB), 2001.
13. D. Gibson, J.M. Kleinberg and P. Raghavan. Inferring Web communities from link topology. Proc. of the ACM Symposium on Hypertext and Hypermedia, 1998.
14. J.M. Kleinberg, S. Ravi Kumar, P. Raghavan, S. Rajagopalan and A. Tomkins. The Web as a graph: measurements, models and methods. In Proceedings of the 5th Annual International Computing and Combinatorics Conference, 1999.
15. R. Kumar, P. Raghavan, S. Rajagopalan, and A. Tomkins. Trawling the Web for Emerging Cyber-Communities. Proc. of the 8th WWW Conference, 1999, 403–416.
16. R. Kumar, P. Raghavan, S. Rajagopalan, D. Sivakumar, A. Tomkins, and E. Upfal. Stochastic Models for the Web. In Proceedings of the 41st Annual Symposium on the Foundations of Computer Science, 2000.
17. L. Laura, S. Leonardi, G. Caldarelli, P. De Los Rios. A Multi-Layer Model for the Web Graph. 2nd International Workshop on Web Dynamics, Honolulu, Hawaii, 7th May 2002.
18. A.Y. Ng, A. X. Zheng, M. I. Jordan Stable Algorithms for Link Analysis. In Proc. 24th Annual Intl. ACM SIGIR Conference. ACM, (2001)
19. L. Page, S. Brin, R. Motwani, and T. Winograd. The PageRank Citation Ranking. Bringing order to the Web, Technical Report, Computer Science Department, Stanford University, 1998.
20. G. Pandurangan, P. Raghavan, E. Upfal. Using PageRank to Characterize Web Structure Computer Science Department, Brown University, Box 1910, Providence, RI 02912–1910, USA, 2002.
21. K. H. Randall , R. Stata, R.G.Wickremesinghe, J.L Wiener. The Link Database Fast Access to Graphs of the Web, 2000

Integration of Static and Active Data Sources

Gilles Nachouki

IRIN, Faculté des Sciences et des Techniques,2, rue de la Houssinière - BP 44322
Nantes Cedex 03, France
nachouki@irin.univ-nantes.fr

Abstract. This paper describes the design of a system, which facilitates Accessing and Interconnecting heterogeneous data sources. Data sources can be static or active: static data sources include structured or semistructured data like databases, XML and HTML documents; active data sources include services which are localised on one or several servers including web services. The main originality of this work is to make interoperability between actives and/or static data sources based on XQuery language.

1 Introduction

The problem of interconnecting and accessing heterogeneous data sources is an old problem known under the name of Interoperability. As organisations evolve over time interoperability was and is still an important field of current research in both academic and industry. With the advent of the World Wide Web (WWW) data management has branched out from traditional framework to deal with the variety of information available on the WWW [2]. In the literature many project and systems are developed in order to connect structured and semistructured data sources; among them we cite Tsimmis [5], Information Mainfold [10], Momix [9], Agora [6], [7]. In such systems (except the Agora system), integration of heterogeneous data sources follows static approach called Global as View (GAV) where query treatment is centric: it chooses a set of queries, and for each such query it provides a procedure to answer the query using the available sources. Given a new query, the approach used in this system consists to try to relate this query to existing ones. AGORA unlike the systems follows another approach called Local As View (LAV). It starts from a global view of data sources expressed with XML data model. Recent projects like C-Web [1] and Verso projects [8] provide new approaches for data integration. C-Web proposes an ontology-based integration approach of XML web resources. Like Agora, C-Web start from a global virtual schema (data resides in some external sources) expressed with a given model. The virtual schema allows users to formulate queries (without aware of the source specific structure). The query language is similar to OQL language. Each query can be rewritten to the XQuery expression that the local source can answer. Verso project proposes an extension of XML called Active XML (AXML). AXML is a XML document that may include some

A. Yazici and C. Şener (Eds.): ISCIS 2003, LNCS 2869, pp. 147–154, 2003.

special elements carrying the tag <sc> (for service call). These elements embed calls to (web) services

Section 2 gives an overview of our contribution in the domain of interoperability between heterogeneous data sources. Section 3 describes our system based on XQuery language, Corba and Web technologies (XML framework, web services). Section 4 summarises XQuery language and its extension in order to call services. We show in this section some possible scenarios expressed with EXQL. Section 5 gives a concrete example.

2 Overview of Our Approach

Our approach unlike previous approaches proposed in the literature follows a loosely coupled approach where the data sources are under the responsibility of the user. This approach permits the integration of services with static data sources. This integration permits to build a unique view of the integrated sources and facilitates the task to users in their interrogation of data sources using services like existing services web at the WWW.Our approach is different of the approach proposed in [8]: the authors in [8] integrate services in an XML documents and the results of the execution of these services are returned in this document; in our approach services, are considered like static data sources and, are integrated together (with eventually static data sources) in a single XQuery query. Data Sources (static and active) exchange data between them via the query in order to run a specific task. In [3] we show how resolve some conflicts between distinct data sources. In [4] we show how create dynamically a web data warehouse in order to help the user to understand the usage of the web. In this work, we propose several senarios. A scenario is an EXQL (Extended XQuery Langage) that integrates services in its body. Services including in a single query are executing sequentially and can be inter-operate with others static data sources necessarily for the realisation of this scenario (fig. 1).

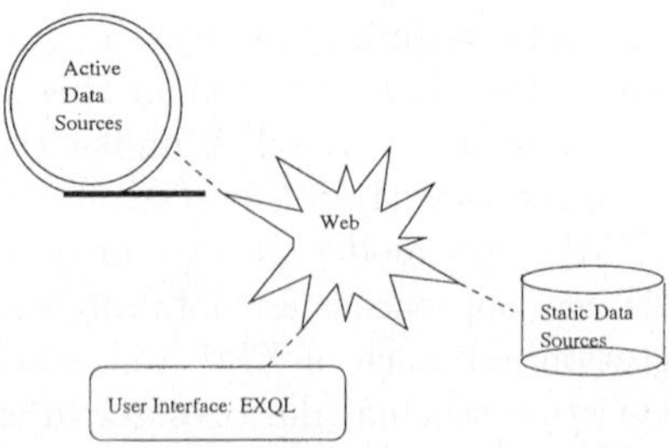

Fig. 1. Accessing heterogeneous Data Sources based on EXQL

3 System Architecture

This section describes briefly the design of our system (see [3] for more detail). This system is composed of three components T-Wrappers, Mediators and Interfaces (figure 2).

1. T-Wrappers: this component is a wrapper for data sources of type T. For static data sources we have developed two wrappers denoted SQL-Wrapper and XML-Wrapper that correspond to the most important sources of information existing over the web (e.g. SQL databases, XML and ((X)HTML). For active data sources we have developed a wrapper denoted Service-Wrapper that permits to run services. The role of T-Wrappers is to extract automatically DTD from data sources and registers it beside the mediator, then executes queries on data sources and returns results to the mediator.

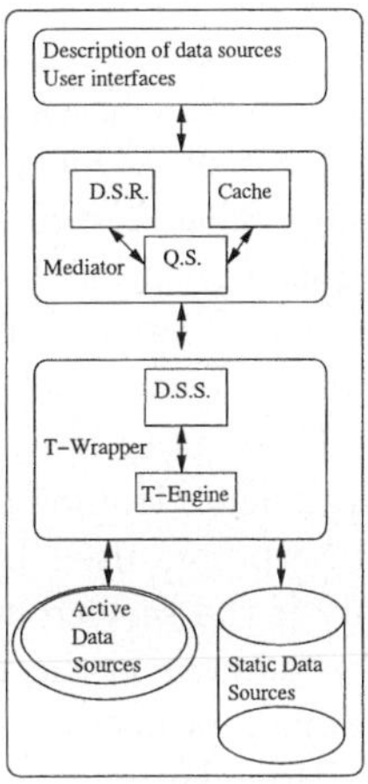

Fig. 2. Design of the system

   Data Source Server (DSS): A DSS is designated as responsible of a data source (static or active). It represents the interface of data sources of any type. There's no way to reach data sources directly in this model, all the communications toward data sources have to go through the DSS.
   T-Engine: T-Engine is an engine dedicated to a type T of data source (static or active). It is composed of all the pieces necessarily to extract DTDs, retrieve data from data sources or running services.
2. Mediator: This component offers to users views of data sources expressed with their DTDs. A mediator receives queries from users interfaces, processes queries and returns results to users as XML documents. The mediator has the knowledge necessary to forward a specific query to the concerned server DSS.

Data Source Repository (DSR): the goal of a DSR is to collect information about the Data Sources (references, addresses, names, descriptions and most importantly the DTD of the associate data source).
Query Server (QS): A Query Server receives complex (Extended) XQuery queries from the client, and processes them. The QS communicates with the DSR in order to obtain more information about data sources and with T-Wrappers in order to execute specific sub-queries.

3. Interfaces: User interface offers to users a list of DTD of data sources. The system provides distinct interfaces:user interface and administrator interface. The first one permits to user non familair with EXQL to generate queries. The second interface is able to activate (or stopped)data sources dynamically.

4 Extended XQuery Language and Scenarios

We propose in this section an extension of the XQuery language, called EXQL, in order to call services and we show some scenarios that show the integration of services with (or without) static data sources in a single query expressed with EXQL. In this paper, the extension of XQuery consists to define only a new function in the core of the language called 'Service'. This function is incorporated into the library of functions and is defined like the function 'Document' existing in the library function of the XQuery language. This new function defined in the XQuery language permits to call services, which are localised on one or several servers including Web services. The syntax of this function is given as follows:

service(Interpreter,Name,Arguments,HomeDirectory,Display).

The first argument is the interpreter used by the service at run time. It's optionally and it's specified only if the service needs some interpreter software in order to run it. The second argument is the name of the service. The third argument provides a list of parameters necessary for the execution of the service. The next argument is the 'HomeDirectory' argument. It's the path to the directory homework of the user. 'Display' argument is optionally. It consists to return the result of the execution of the service at the screen of the user. We show three possible scenarios in this paper. Other scenarios are possible and can be deduced from the three ones given below.In [4] we show a scenario where the system help users to understand the usage of the web.

- The first scenario (A) integrates two services. The result of the first service is used as input in the second service;

- The second scenario (B) is composed of a static data source and a service. This service takes, as input, data from the static data source and produces the final result;

- The third scenario (C) is similar to the scenario (A) but the result of the execution of the service is send toward a static data source.

These scenarios are expressed with EXQL in figure 3 as follows:

AS1, AS2 are the names of two active data sources. These data sources are described in two XML documents having unique DTD (Data Type Document)called service.dtd given in figure 4.

```
<Scenario-A>
  Let $a := document(AS1)/description
  Let $b := document (AS2)/description
Return
  <sc1>service($a/interpreter /text()/, $a/name/text(),$a/parameter/text(),$a/ HomeDirectory/text())</sc1>,
  <sc2>service($b/interpreter/text(),sb/name/text(),R1,$b/parameter/text(),
  $b/HomeDirectory/text(),Display)</sc2>
</Scenario-A>
 ----------------------------------------------------------
 <Scenario-B>
  Let $a := document(SS1)/path
  Let $b := document (AS2)/description
Return
  <sc1>service($b/interpreter/text(),$b/name/text(),$b/parameter/text(),
  $a/path/text(),$b/HomeDirectory/text())</sc1>
 </Scenario-B>
 ----------------------------------------------------------
 <Scenario-C>
  Let $a := document(AS1)/description
  Let $b := document (AS2)/description
 Return
 <sc1>service($a/interpreter/text(),$a/name/text(),$a/parameter/text(),$a/HomeDirectory/text())</sc1>,
 <sc2>service($b/interpreter/text(),sb/name/text(),R1,$b/parameter/text(), R1,DSLocation,
  $b/HomeDirectory/text())</sc2>
 </Scenario-C>
```

Fig. 3. Scenarios

```
<!ELEMENT description (interpreter,name,parameter,HomeDirectory)>
<!ELEMENT parameter(para*)>
<!ELEMENT interpreter (#PCDATA)>
<!ELEMENT HomeDirectory (#PCDATA)>
<!ELEMENT name (#PCDATA)>
<!ELEMENT para (#PCDATA)>
```

Fig. 4. Data Type Document of active data sources

SS1 is a static data source from which we extract its DTD automatically. R1 is the name of a file containing the result of a service and DSLocation describes how to connect to the Data source in update mode. In the following section we show a concrete example that integrate active data source or services with static data sources in order to realise a specific scenario.

5 Concrete Example

In this section, we present a concrete scenario using three data sources: (1) a static data source (an XML document) describing researchers; (2) a Web service (Google Service) that permits to search information on the WWW (URLs, title,...) about a topic and (3) a local Service called FilterURL that works on the results returned by Google Service in order to select the URLs of the web sites (reuturned by the Google Search Service).

The administrator interface DSManager makes the three data sources accessible by the user (figure 7a). The user interface called SwingClient (figure 7b) connects to the DSManager in order to obtain the structure of these data sources. Users not familiar with EXQL language can use the generator interface in order to formulate their querie (not showing in this paper). Otherwise, users can put directly their queries into the interface and obtain the result from it (figure 7b).

The scenario we suggest is the following: "Find URLs from the WWW about each existing researcher in the static data source Researchers"

The structure of data sources (static and active) are described in figure 5 :

```
<?xml version="1.0" encoding="ISO-8859-1"?>
<!DOCTYPE researchers SYSTEM "researcher.dtd">
<researchers>
<person>
  <num>4</num>
  <name>Agrawal</name>
  <address>2 street Gold London</adress>
  <salary> ...</salary>
</person>
 ...
</researchers>
```

(a) :"Researchers" data source

```
<?xml version="1.0" encoding="ISO-8859-1"?>
<!DOCTYPE description SYSTEM service.dtd">
<description>
<interpreter>java</interpreter>
<name>googleAPIDemo/name>
<parameter>
<para>search</para>
</parametrer>
</description>
```

(b) : "Google service" data source

```
<xml version="1.0" encoding="ISO-8859-1"?>
<!DOCTYPE description SYSTEM service.dtd">
<description>
<interpreter>java</interpreter>
<name>Synthese</name>
<parameter>
  <para>URL</para>
</parameter>
<HomeDirectory>c:/project</HomeDirectory>
</description>
```

(c) : "Synthese" data source

Fig. 5. Structure of the active and static data sources

The query given in figure 6 represents our scenario expressed with the EXQL language. (figure7).

```
<results>
For $a in document("researchers")/researchers/person/name
Let $b := document(("GoogleService")/description
return
 <google>
<service($b/interpreter/text(),$b/name/text(),$b/parameter/para[0]/text(),$b/paramater/para[1]/text(),"F",$a/text())
</google>
Let $c := document("FilterURLService")/description
return <Local>
service($c/interpreter/text(),$c/name/text(),$c/parameter/para[0]/text(),"F",$c/HomeDirectory/text(),"Display")
</Local>
</results>
```

Fig. 6. EXQL : Find, from the web, URLs where researchers are published

The execution of this query follows the following algorithm:

begin
For each researcher in the "Researchers" DataSource do
Read the name of one researcher
Use GoogleService DataSource in order to find web sites that concerns the name of this person and write the result in the file F
enddo
Call FilterURLService in order to filter from the file "F" only the interresting URLs
endbegin

Figure 7(a) gives the DSManager interface. In this figure, we see the three data sources activated by the administrator:"Researchers", "GoogleService" and "FilterURLService" correspond respectively to data sources given in fig5(a),fig5(b) and fig5(c).

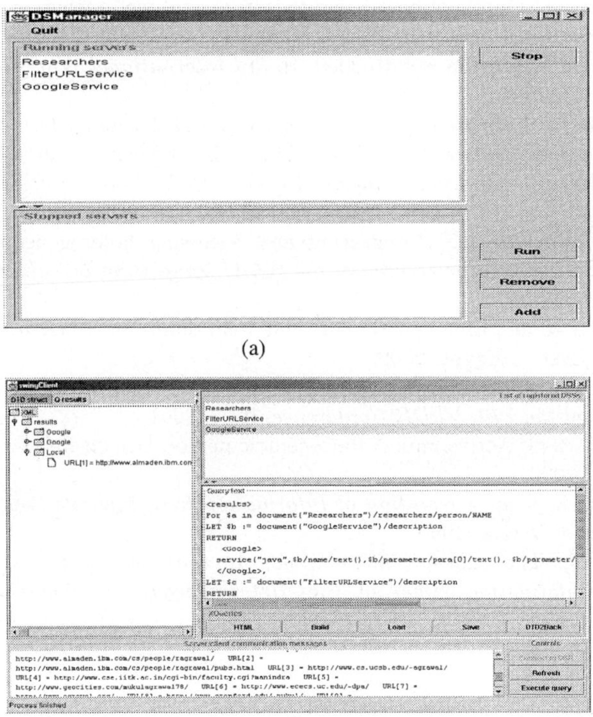

(a)

(b)

Fig. 7. DSManager and SwingClient interfaces

Figure 7(b) shows the SwingClient Interface. In this interface, we show the three activated data sources by the administrator, the extended XQuery of the user and the result of this query.

6 Conclusion

Our approach is based on the EXQL language in order to extract, interconnect and access heterogeneous data sources. This approach follows loosely coupled approach where the data sources are of the responsibility of users. We have proposed the design of a system that accepts static and active data sources. We have implemented XQuery language and we have extended this language in order to put services. Services permit to resolve conflicts existing between heterogeneous data sources and realise specific scenarios. In this work services given in a query are executed sequentially. In the future, we plan to study queries where more complex scenarios are possible and queries optimisation.

References

1. B.Amman & al. Ontology-based integration of xml web resources. In *proceeding of the International Semantic Web Conference*, pages 117–131, 2002.
2. D. Suciu & al. Report on webdb 2000. In *3rd International Workshop on the Web and databases*, 2000.
3. G. Nachouki & al. *Extracting, Interconnecting and Accessing Heterogeneous Data Sources: An XML Query Based Approach.* Springer-Verlag, Iran, 2002.
4. G. Nachouki & al. *On Line Analysis of a Web Data Warehouse.* Springer-Verlag, Japan, 2003.
5. H. Garcia-Molina & al. Integrating and accessing heterogeneous information sources in tsimmis. In *proceeding of the AAAI symposium on information gathering*, California, 1995.
6. I. Manolescu & al. Living with xml and relational. In *proceedings of the 26th VLDB Conference*, Egypt, 2000.
7. I. Manolescu & al. Answering xml queries over heterogeneous data sources. In *in proceedings of the 27th VLDB Conference*, Italy, 2001.
8. S. Abiteboul & al. Active xml: A data-centric perspective on web services. In *BDA 2002*, Paris, 2002.
9. S. Bergamaschi & al. *Integration of Information from Multiple Sources of Textual Data.* Springer-Verlag, 1999.
10. T. Kirk & al. The information manifold. In *working Notes of the AAAI symposium on information gathering from Heterogeneous Distributed Environments*, California, 1995.

Conditional Access Module Systems for Digital Contents Protection Based on Hybrid/Fiber/Coax CATV Networks

Won Jay Song[1], Won Hee Kim[2], Bo Gwan Kim[2],
Byung Ha Ahn[3], Munkee Choi[1], and Minho Kang[1]

[1] Optical Internet Research Center and Grid Middleware Research Center,
Information and Communications University, 305-732, Republic of Korea
songwonjay@ieee.org {mkchoi,mhkang}@icu.ac.kr
[2] VLSI and CAD Labs, Department of Electronics Engineering,
Chungnam National University, 305-764, Republic of Korea
kimwonhee@ieee.org & bgkim@cnu.ac.kr
[3] Systems Control and Management Labs, Department of Mechatronics,
KwangJu Institute of Science and Technology, 500-712, Republic of Korea
bayhay@kjist.ac.kr

Abstract. In this paper, we have proposed the merging of the OpenCable reference model with the smart card interface defined by ISO/IEC 7816-3 and have implemented a new Conditional Access System (CAS) using this interface along with a Personal Computer Memory Card International Association (PCMCIA) interface. In addition, we have also designed the hardware architecture of the Point-of-Deployment (POD) security module, designed with the Verilog HDL, using the above two interfaces. The designed POD security module has an embedded 32-bit Reduced Instruction Set Computer (RISC) microprocessor that manages applications, such as an MPEG-2 filter, descrambler, and Data Encryption Standard (DES). We have tested this modeled and designed system using a prototype and show satisfactory simulation results.

1 Introduction

In the digital multimedia world, effective industrial standards should be required to provide a common compatibility or inter-connection between the digital Cable Television (CATV) system and the other consumer electronic devices. The OpenCable system seeks to specify a common set of requirements for the Set-Top Box (STB) in the digital CATV system, so that new suppliers from the consumer electronics and computer industries develop new electronic equipment with a common compatibility for the well-defined digital CATV system.

The OpenCable architecture is designed to take advantage of the real-time and two-way operation capabilities of digital CATV systems. The OpenCable reference diagram defines and has a set of headend interfaces (OCI-H1, OCI-2, and OCI-3), the network interface (OCI-N), the consumer interface (OCI-C1), and the security module interface (OCI-C2), as shown in Figure 1 [Adams99]. The importance of the OpenCable reference diagram is that it specifies a number of standard interfaces among a variety of components

A. Yazici and C. Şener (Eds.): ISCIS 2003, LNCS 2869, pp. 155–162, 2003.

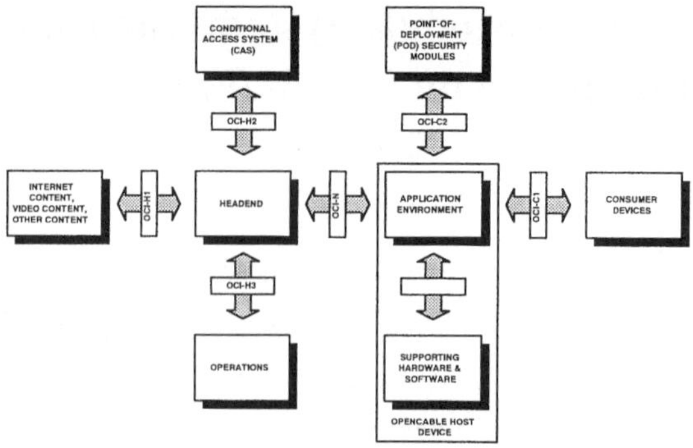

Fig. 1. The OpenCable reference model and architecture.

within the cable system. By specifying these interfaces, it is possible to replace certain components with others without redesigning the entire system [Adams99].

2 Conditional Access Module System Design

2.1 POD Security Module Architecture

The design of the Point-of-Deployment (POD) security module varies from a general implementation to the proposed implementation in this paper. Figure 2(a) and 2(b) show the proposed POD security module design in this paper. Although the POD security module separates the security functions into a replaceable module, the system operation is identical to the integrated Set-Top Box (STB).

After the payload is decrypted, it is fed into the copy protection engine, which encrypts the protected content. As shown in Figure 2(a) and 2(b), the same secure and replaceable microprocessor that supports conditional access functions generates the encryption keys for content encryption. The final payload is re-multiplexed into an MPEG-2 multi-program transport stream and leaves the POD security module via the PCMCIA connector.

2.2 Content Protection System

The Point-of-Deployment (POD) security module interface support a sophisticated Content Protection System (CPS) that encrypts the MPEG-2 payload. The CPS authenticates the host device and allows revocation of service to fraudulent hosts. The POD security module interface is one link in the content distribution chain from the content provider to the consumer. Figure 3 illustrates the path of the MPEG-2 payload from the headend via the cable network to the host.

The CPS prevents unauthorized copying of the MPEG payload when it is exposed at any interface in the content distribution chain. In all exposed interfaces (i.e., OCI-N, OCI-C2, and OCI-C1), the digital payload is encrypted to prevent unauthorized copying, but is present in a clear text form within devices. The POD CPS is very similar in operation to a Conditional Access System (CAS).

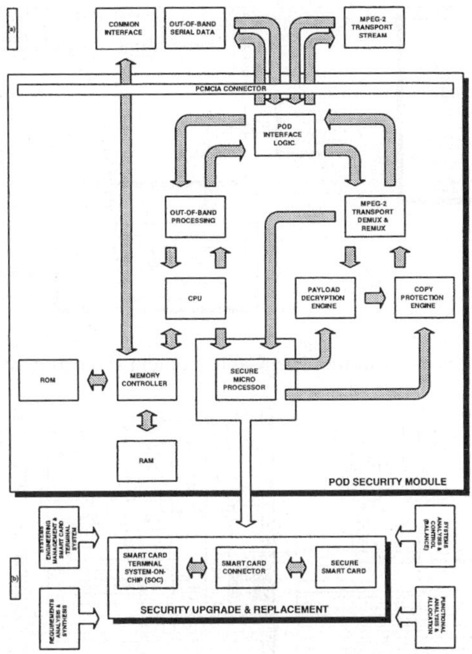

Fig. 2. The Point-of-Deployment (POD) security module using smart card in connection with the host.

3 Conditional Access Module System Development

3.1 POD Security Module with PCMCIA and ISO/IEC 7816-3 Interfaces

In general, the most common method of updating security information for the Set-Top Box (STB) is achieved by inserting a smart card into a slot of the STB. When the smart card is inserted into a slot in the STB, the card co-operates with the embedded secure microprocessor of the Conditional Access System (CAS). The function of security co-operation with the STB should also support flexible and portability, whose ability is related to move the STB from one system to another.

However, the smart card does not allow complete co-operation with the security system, since the actual decryption of the signal still resides in the digital STB. Therefore, we adopted the Type II PC Card format defined by the Personal Computer Memory Card International Association (PCMCIA) [PCMCIA01]. The interface of the PCMCIA is more robust and flexible than that of smart card defined by ISO/IEC 7816-3 [Mori+99]. In addition, the PCMCIA connector has 68-pin and its module is shielded to prevent damage from the external attacks [Mori+99].

In our proposed system, the POD security module has been designed to accept a smart card, which will allow for security information upgrades, with complete co-operation with the module, as shown in Figure 2. Subscribers need to insert their smart cards into the designed POD security module system for conditional access services, for both commercial and copyrighted contents.

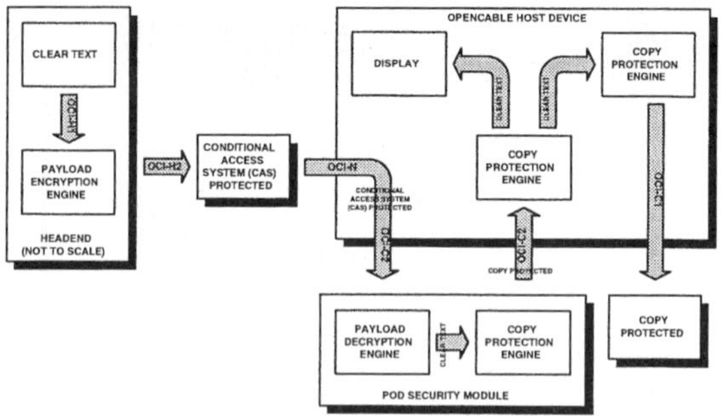

Fig. 3. The overview of the OpenCable Content Protection System (CPS).

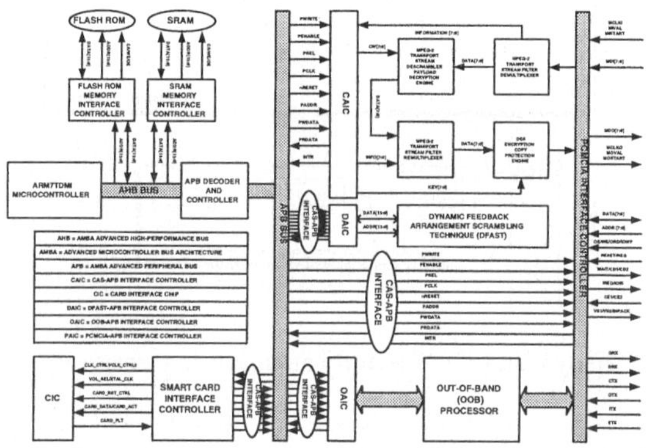

Fig. 4. The designed and developed Point-of-Deployment (POD) security module chip architecture for conditional access system (CAS).

3.2 In-Band Processor for the POD Security Module

The same secure microprocessor that supports conditional access functions generates the encryption keys for content encryption. The final MPEG-2 payload is re-multiplexed into an MPEG-2 multi-program Transport Stream (TS) and leaves the POD security module via the Personal Computer Memory Card International Association (PCMCIA) connector.

As shown in Figure 4, the Central Processing Unit (CPU) controls and coordinates all POD security module functions by executing applications stored in FLASH memory. The command interface allows messages to be exchanged between the host and the POD security module by reading and writing locations in Random-Access Memory (RAM) [DVB96,DVB97a].

3.3 Out-of-Band Processor for the POD Security Module

DVB Common Scrambling Algorithm. Digital encryption is used to scramble the MPEG-2 Transport Stream (TS) in a general digital Set-Top Box (STB). The MPEG-2 payload decryption is responsible for deciphering the scrambled MPEG-2 TS. The

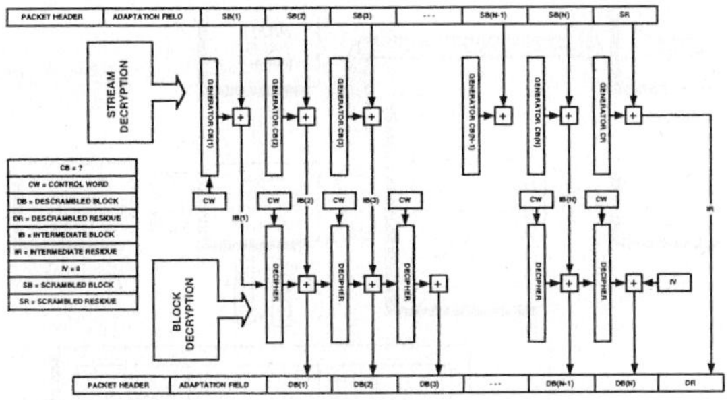

Fig. 5. The implementation of super descrambling operation at Conditional Access System (CAS).

scrambling mechanism of the DVB involves two ciphers, a block cipher and a stream cipher. The block cipher works in a reverse cipher block changing mode with block units and the stream cipher works like a pseudo-random byte generator [DVB97b,DVB98]. Both are designed so as to not be independently operated.

The stream cipher protects the block cipher from attack. The entire mechanism is much more firm than when each ciphers works independently. According to these characteristics, the super descrambling operation is constructed in the hardware as shown in Figure 5 [Song+02c,Song+02e,Song+02f,Song+02g].

DES Electronic Code Book. We have analyzed the 'OpenCable HOST-POD Interface Specification' and 'OpenCable POD Copy Protection System' for copy protection. In accordance with the analyses results, we have designed an encryption module in DES Electronic Code Book (ECB) mode with HDL [OC02j]. We then constructed a smart card interface according to ISO/IEC 7816-3 and the interface for Out-of-Band (OOB) communication has been verified [Song+02c,Song+02e,Song+02f,Song+02g]. Finally the MPEG-2 filter was designed for the ISO/IEC 13818-1 in HDL [ISO96b].

4 Conditional Access Module System Verification

4.1 Construction of the Integrated Test Environments

In this study, we have constructed an integrated test environment to verify our developed system, which consists of a Conditional Access System (CAS) processor and an Out-of-Band (OOB) processor, belonging to the Point-of-Deployment (POD) security module for the OpenCable specification. According to integrated test environment of the POD security module, the MPEG-2 Transport Stream (TS) bit stream is transferred from the MPEG-2 TS generator to host emulator, as shown in Figure 6.

The host emulator is a Set-Top Box (STB) emulator, which then sends the MPEG-2 data to the POD security module through a Personal Computer Memory Card International Association (PCMCIA) interface using both an In-Band (IB) and OOB channel. The POD security module then processes the MPEG-2 data by descrambling it and providing copy protection.

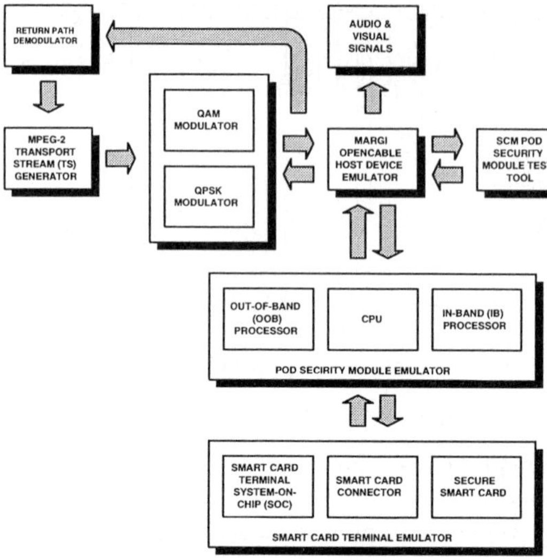

Fig. 6. The developed OpenCable integrated test environments.

The processed MPEG-2 TS bit stream is then transferred from the POD security module to the host emulator though PCMCIA connector. Finally the video and audio data decoded by STB (host emulator) is transmitted to the users (subscribers) through a TV (screen and speaker) [Song+02c,Song+02e,Song+02f,Song+02g].

4.2 Operation Procedures of the POD Security Module

As shown in Figure 7, the flow chart shows data parsing or filtering for the MPEG-2 TS packet header. Firstly, after the TS packet enters the MPEG-2 system, the system finds the packets with a PID of 0 and analyzes the packets. The PID=0 packets, called PAT, provide the PID information of Program Management Message (PMM), Receiver Command Message (RCM), and PMT sessions. The system assigns a PN of 0 and 1 to the PMM and RCM, respectively. All TSs should include a completely valid PAT, because the PAT connects the PN and the PMT_PID, which is the PID of TS packet defining each valid program.

After the MPEG-2 filter analyzes the PAT, the filter can get the PN and its PID from the PAT. In this process, PN=0 is assigned to the network PID. And a value of PN=1 is also assigned to RCM_PID in typical digital broadcasting systems. Operators at the headend can use other numbers except 0 and 1 (i.e., all numbers except 0 and 1).

In this case, the PN used in the MPEG-2 system is assigned to the program map PID. Therefore we can obtain the PMT, PN=X, and PID=PX. If the MPEG-2 filter is analyzing the PMT using the above procedure, we can obtain the PIDs of the video, audio, and private data at the ECM. As well, each header is filtered. The filtered video and audio payloads are then transmitted to descrambler and the ECM makes a working key using the session key from EMM that is processed in the OOB processor, and this working key is transferred to the descrambler [ISO96b].

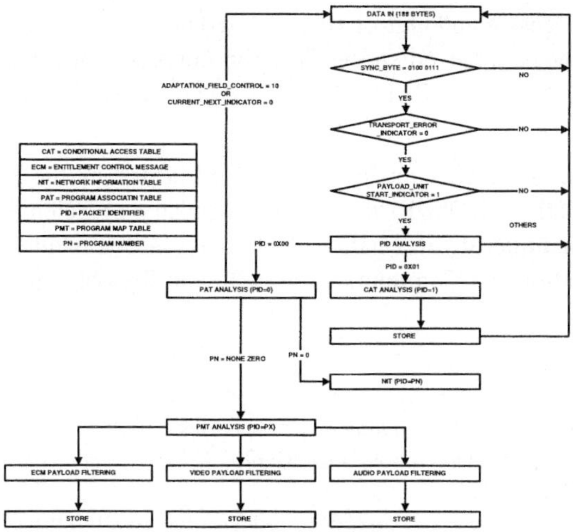

Fig. 7. The flow chart of the MPEG-2 Transport Stream (TS) packet header parsing or filtering algorithm.

4.3 Copy Protection and Authentication

The specification of the 'OpenCable POD Copy Protection System' defines the measures to protect the highly valued contents and the connection between the Point-of-Deployment (POD) security module and the host device [OC02j]. The program provider demands a guarantee of a stable system from the headend to the home of the end-user. The cable Set-Top Box (STB) use copy protection technology to secure the digital/analog output of the customers [SCTE97].

Depending upon the use of the POD security module, it is needed to block any unauthorized search for communication at the HOST-POD. Basically, the POD security module has to decipher an encryption of service as a control of the headend, and encrypt useful data to protect information from pirating [OC02j].

5 Concluding Remarks

This study proposes conditional access flow using a subscriber smart card. This conditional access mechanism can be used as a reference of the digital Cable Television (CATV) system or other digital services system, while defining additional messages between the Set-Top Box (STB), with the Point-of-Deployment (POD) security module, and the subscriber smart card, can easily extend this algorithm.

The OpenCable system has adopted an MPEG-2 payload descrambling process, for the MPEG-2 Transport Stream (TS), and data encryption, using a DES algorithm, for content protection. This study presents a new design and implementation of the POD security module that is based on the OpenCable specifications.

We have also constructed an integrated test environment to verify our developed system. Using this test environment, we should be able to check all the operations of the In-Band (IB) processor and Out-of-Band (OOB) processor, as well as the STB. The correct operations were achieved successfully on our test board, which also included some peripheral devices (i.e., ARM7, FPGA, FLASH, and RAM).

Acknowledgement. This work has been supported in part by the Korea Science and Engineering Foundation (KOSEF) through the Ministry of Science and Technology (MOST) and the Institute of Information Technology Assessment (IITA) through the Ministry of Information and Communication (MIC), in Republic of Korea.

References

[Adams99] M.Adams, *OpenCable Architecture*, Cisco Press, 1999.

[Adams+01] M.Adams and D.Dulchinos, "OpenCable," *IEEE Communication Magazine*, vol.39, no.6, pp.98–105, June 2001.

[DVB96] DVB Blue Book A011, *Digital Video Broadcasting (DVB) – DVB Common Scrambling Distribution Agreements*, Digital Video Broadcasting Project (DVB), June 1996.

[DVB97a] DVB Blue Book A007, *Digital Video Broadcasting (DVB) – Support for Use of Scrambling and Conditional Access (CA) within Digital Broadcasting Systems*, Digital Video Broadcasting Project (DVB), February 1997.

[DVB97b] DVB Blue Book A028, *Digital Video Broadcasting (DVB) – DVB SimulCrypt – Part 1: Head-End Architecture and Synchronization*, Digital Video Broadcasting Project (DVB), May 1997.

[DVB98] DVB Blue Book A045, *Digital Video Broadcasting (DVB) – Head-End lmplementation of SimulCrypt*, Digital Video Broadcasting Project (DVB), November 1998.

[ISO96b] ISO/IEC 13818–2, *MPEG-2 Video*, International Organization for Standardization, 1996.

[Mori+99] M.T.Mori and W.D.Welder, *The PCMCIA Developer's Guide*, 3rd Edition, Sycard Technology, December 1999.

[OC02j] OC-SP-PODCP-IF-I08-021126, *OpenCable POD Copy Protection System*, Cable Television Laboratories, November, 2002.

[PCMCIA01] PCMCIA, *PC Card Standard Release 8.0*, Personal Computer Memory Card International Association (PCMCIA), April 2001.

[SCTE97] SCTE/DVS 064, *National Replaceable Security Standard (IS-679 Part B)*, Society of Cable Telecommunications Engineers (SCTE), January 1997.

[Song+02c] W.H.Kim, W.J.Song, B.G.Kim, and B.H.Ahn, "Design and Development of a New POD Module Chip-Set Based on the OpenCable Specification," *Proceedings in the 2002 IEEE International Conference on Consumer Electronics*, pp.208–209, June 2002.

[Song+02e] W.H.Kim, W.J.Song, B.G.Kim, and B.H.Ahn, "Conditional Access System Using Smart Card Interface for Digital CATV Contents Protection Based on the OpenCable Specification," *Proceedings in the 2002 IEEE International Conference on Telecommunications*, vol.3, pp.286–290, June 2002.

[Song+02f] W.H.Kim, W.J.Song, B.G.Kim, and B.H.Ahn, "Design and Development of a New POD Security Module Chip-Set Based on the OpenCable Specification," *IEEE Transactions on Consumer Electronics*, vol.48, no.3, pp.770–775, August 2002.

[Song+02g] W.H.Kim, W.J.Song, B.G.Kim, and B.H.Ahn, "Conditional Access System Using Smart Card Interface for Contents Protection of Digital CATV Based on the OpenCable Specification," *Proceedings in the 2002 IEEE International Symposium on Consumer Electronics*, pp.C29–C32, September 2002.

Approximation Algorithms for Degree-Constrained Bipartite Network Flow

Elif Akçalı[1] and Alper Üngör[2]

[1] Department of Industrial & Systems Engineering
University of Florida, Gainesville, FL 32611, USA
akcali@ise.ufl.edu

[2] Department of Computer Science
Duke University, Durham, NC 27708, USA
ungor@cs.duke.edu

Abstract. We consider a tool- and setup-constrained short-term capacity allocation problem that arises in operational level planning at a semiconductor wafer fabrication facility. We formulate this problem as a degree-constrained network flow problem on a bipartite graph. We show that the problem is NP-hard and propose the first constant factor (1/2) approximation algorithms. Experimental study demonstrates that, in practice, our algorithms give solutions that are on the average less than 1.5% away from the optimal solution in less than a second.

Keywords: Approximation algorithms, network flows, scheduling, capacity allocation

1 Introduction

The application that motivates this work is a capacity allocation problem encountered at the photolithography work centers in semiconductor wafer fabrication facilities. A photolithography work center is a parallel machine environment with assignment restrictions, where an operation can be performed by only a subset of the machines. A tool setup is required on the machine to change processing from one operation to another. Both the number of tools available for an operation and the number of setups that can be performed on a machine (throughout a specified time horizon) are limited. Therefore, we refer to this problem as the *dual-constrained capacity allocation* (DCA) problem. The objective is to maximize the total throughput of the work center over a time horizon.

We, next, give a formulation for this problem, illustrate how it can be interpreted as a degree-constrained network flow problem and discuss related work. Then, we review the computational complexity of the problem, resolving the status of open cases. The remainder of the paper presents constant factor approximation algorithms, some heuristics, and results from computational experiments.

A. Yazici and C. Şener (Eds.): ISCIS 2003, LNCS 2869, pp. 163–170, 2003.

Problem Formulation. We are given a set of operations $S = \{s_1, ..., s_n\}$ and a set of machines $T = \{t_1, ..., t_m\}$. Each operation $s \in S$ has an available work-in-process (WIP) inventory of $f(s)$ measured in minutes and each machine $t \in T$ has a capacity of $f(t)$ minutes, where $f : S \cup T \to \mathbb{R}$. An operation-machine assignment matrix M specifies the assignment restrictions for the operations. If operation s can be processed by machine t, then the element $M(s,t) = 1$, and 0 otherwise. Let A be the set all possible operation-machine assignments, i.e. $A = \{(s,t)|M(s,t) = 1; s \in S; t \in T\}$. Moreover, each operation $s \in S$ has a limitation $g(s)$ on the number of machines it can be assigned to and each machine $t \in T$ can be assigned at most $g(s)$ operations, where $g : S \cup T \to \mathbb{N}$. Let x_{st} denote the amount of WIP inventory of operation s allocated to machine t, y_{st} be 1 if any WIP inventory of operation s is assigned to machine t and 0 otherwise, where $s \in S$ and $t \in T$. Then DCA can be formulated as follows [10]:

$$\text{maximize} \sum_{(s,t)\in A} x_{st} \qquad \text{subject to}$$

$$\sum_{\forall t \in T} x_{st} \leq f(s), \forall s \in S \qquad \sum_{\forall s \in S} x_{st} \leq f(t), \forall t \in T \quad (1)$$

$$\sum_{\forall t \in T} y_{st} \leq g(s), \forall s \in S \qquad \sum_{\forall s \in S} y_{st} \leq g(t), \forall t \in T \quad (2)$$

$$0 \leq x_{st} \leq y_{st} \min\{f(s), f(t)\}, \qquad \forall (s,t) \in S \times T \quad (3)$$

$$y_{st} \in \{0,1\} \leq M(s,t), \qquad \forall (s,t) \in S \times T \quad (4)$$

The objective function of this formulation maximizes the total WIP inventory allocated. Constraints (1) enforce the available WIP inventory and machine capacity limits. Constraints (2) respectively restrict the number of machines that can simultaneously process a given operation and the number of operations that can be assigned to a given machine. Constraint (3) ensures that unless the required tool is assigned to a machine, an operation is not allocated to that machine.

Degree-Constrained Network Flow Formulation. The set of operations S, the set of machines T and the set of all possible operation-machine assignments A naturally constitutes a directed bipartite graph where the sets S and T correspond to the graph nodes and A corresponds the arcs between them. For each arc $(s,t) \in A$ we allocate a capacity of $\min\{f(s), f(t)\}$. We also introduce s_0 and t_0 as the superficial sink and supply nodes respectively. For each $s \in S$ we introduce an arc from s_0 to s with capacity $f(s)$. Similarly, for each $t \in T$ we build an arc from t to t_0 with capacity $f(t)$. Let A' be the set of these arcs from s_0 and to t_0. The resulting graph $G = (S \cup T \cup \{s_0, t_0\}, A \cup A')$ is depicted in Figure 1 (a). To solve the $DCA(G, f, g)$ problem a maximum flow is sought on this graph from s_0 to t_0 such that the number of arcs with positive flow from a node $s \in S$ is at most $g(s)$ and the number of arcs with positive flow to a node $t \in T$ is at most $g(t)$.

Related Work. DCA consists of two interconnected sub-problems. The capacity constraints on their own specify a *network flow problem* whereas the indegree and

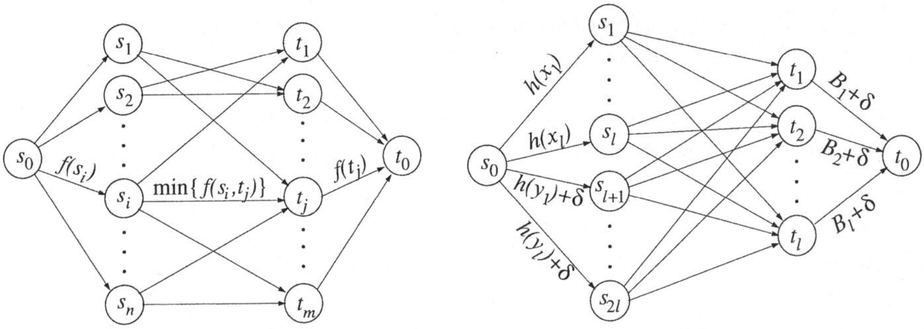

Fig. 1. (a) Bipartite graph representation of *DCA*; (b) Reduction from *NMWTS*

outdegree constraints specify a *degree problem.* A subset of the arc set that does not violate the degree constraints constitutes a solution to the degree problem. The maximum network flow problem is well-studied and has polynomial-time solutions [5]. Various versions of the degree problem, e.g. computing maximum cardinality/weighted degree-constrained subgraph, have polynomial-time solutions [7]. However, we show in the next section that even the simplest combination of these two polynomially solvable problems is computationally hard. The *DCA* problem also resembles other recently studied bicriteria optimization problems, such as the knapsack problem with cardinality constraints [3], variable bin packing with color constraints [6]. However, the structure of the *DCA* problem is considerably different and hence the solutions proposed for these problems do not apply. We refer the reader to [1] for a detailed discussion of these and relations to some other well-known combinatorial optimization problems.

2 Computational Complexity

For the complexity analysis, we classify the instances of *DCA* according to the largest values of the degree constraint function g. $DCA[g(S) \le k_1, g(T) \le k_2]$ represents the class of problems where $\forall s \in S\ g(s) \le k_1$ and $\forall t \in T\ g(t) \le k_2$. With this notation we can use other relational operators, e.g., $DCA[g(S) = k_1, g(T) = k_2]$. Notice that due to symmetry the complexity of the problem remains same when k_1 and k_2 are switched. So without loss of generality we only consider the cases where $k_1 \le k_2$.

Toktay and Uzsoy [10] show that $DCA[g(S) \le 1, g(T) \le 3]$ is strongly $\mathcal{NP}$-hard by a reduction from 3-PARTITION. In our notation this also implies that $DCA[g(S) \le 1, g(T) \le k]$ is strongly $\mathcal{NP}$-hard for any $k \ge 3$. On the other hand, $DCA[g(S)=1, g(T)=1]$ reduces to the classical assignment problem and $DCA[g(S)=|T|, g(T)=|S|]$ reduces to the network flow problem and hence both have polynomial time solutions. However, the complexity of the other interesting cases such as $DCA[g(S) \le 1, g(T) \le 2]$ was left open. We next prove that $DCA[g(S) \le 1, g(T) \le 2]$ is strongly $\mathcal{NP}$-hard by constructing a reduction from NUMERICAL MATCHING WITH TARGET SUMS (NMWTS) problem [8]:

NMWTS(X, Y, h, B): Two disjoint sets $X = \{x_1, \ldots, x_l\}$ and $Y = \{y_1, \ldots, y_l\}$ each containing l elements, a size $h(a) \in Z^+$ for each $a \in X \cup Y$, and a target vector $(B_1, \ldots, B_l)$ with positive integer entries are given. Can the set $X \cup Y$ be partitioned into l disjoint sets $A_1, \ldots, A_l$ each containing one element from each of X and Y, such that $\sum_{a \in A_i} h(a) = B_i$ for $i = 1, \ldots, l$?

Theorem 1. *$DCA[g(S) \leq 1,\ g(T) \leq 2]$ is strongly $\mathcal{NP}$-hard.*

Proof. We reduce a given instance of $NMWTS(X, Y, h, B)$ to an instance of $DCA(G, f, g)$ where the underlying bipartite graph G, the capacity constraint function f, and the degree constraint function g are defined as follows. $G = (S \cup T \cup \{s_0, t_0\}, A)$ where $S = \{s_1, \ldots, s_{2l}\}$, $T = \{t_1, \ldots, t_l\}$, and $A = \{(s,t) | s \in S, t \in T\} \cup \{(s_0, s) | s \in S\} \cup \{(t, t_0) | t \in T\}$. Let $\delta = \sum_{i=1}^{l} h(x_i) + h(y_i)$. Then,

$$\begin{aligned} f(s_i) &= h(x_i) & s_i \in S,\ x_i \in X,\ i &= 1, \ldots, l \\ f(s_i) &= h(y_i) + \delta & s_i \in S,\ y_i \in Y,\ i &= l+1, \ldots, 2l \\ f(t_i) &= B_i + \delta & t_i \in T,\ i &= 1, \ldots, l \end{aligned}$$

In addition, $g(s) = 1, \forall s \in S$ and $g(t) = 2, \forall t \in T$.

Clearly, this is an instance of $DCA[g(S)=1, g(T)=2]$ for which the maximum possible flow is at most $(l+1)\delta$. The resulting bipartite graph is depicted in Figure 1 (b). We now show that the solution for $DCA(G, f, g)$ is equal to $(l+1)\delta$ if and only if $NMWTS(X, Y, h, B)$ has a satisfying partition.

($\rightarrow$) Suppose $(l+1)\delta$ is the optimum solution to $DCA(G, f, g)$. This means that all the arcs from s_0 and to t_0 utilize flow of their maximum capacity. Note that flow from no two among the first l nodes of S can satisfy the demand of a node in T, and flow from no two among the last l nodes of S can fit in a single node in T. Only two operation nodes in S such that one is among the first l nodes in S and the other among the last l in S, i.e., one corresponds to an element in X and the other to an element Y, can combine to meet the demand at a sink node in T without exceeding it. Thus, a solution to *NMWTS* has been found.

($\leftarrow$) Suppose that a satisfying solution for the *NMWTS* exists, that is we can partition the elements in $X \cup Y$ into l sets, $A_1, \ldots, A_l$, each containing exactly two elements, one from each of X and Y such that $\sum_{a \in A_k} h(a) = B_k$ for $1 \leq k \leq l$. Consider a flow on G where for $k = 1, \ldots, l$, $A_k = \{x_i, y_j\}$, the arcs (s_0, s_i), (s_0, s_{l+j}), (s_i, t_k), (s_{l+j}, t_k), and (t_k, t_0) are assigned flow values of $h(x_i)$, $h(y_j) + \delta$, $h(x_i)$, $h(y_j) + \delta$, and $B_k + \delta$ respectively. This flow assignment on G satisfies the degree constraints imposed by the degree function g also resulting in a total flow of $(l+1)\delta$. □

We remark that if the demands of all sink nodes in T are same, i.e., $f(t) = C$, $\forall t \in T$ for some constant C and the underlying bipartite graph is fully-connected, then $DCA[g(S)=1, g(T)=2]$ is equivalent to the 2-PARTITION problem which is polynomially solvable by the *folding algorithm* [2].

3 $\frac{1}{2}$-Approximation Algorithms for *DCA*

In this section we present the first approximation algorithms for the *DCA* problem. There is no limitation on the values of f and g. Notice that a solution to our degree-constrained network flow problem, a.k.a. the *DCA* problem, can be described by the flow assignments on the S to T arcs. The flow values from s_0 and to t_0 are implicit and it just needs to be verified if they satisfy the edge capacity constraints. Hence, in describing our algorithms we focus on the flow values between S and T nodes.

The following algorithm greedily picks the arc with maximum flow from an operation to a machine node, and repeats this until no more arcs can be added to the solution without violating the degree and flow feasibility.

`Algorithm Greedy Arc (GA)`

0. $k \leftarrow 0, \quad G_0 \leftarrow G, \quad f_0 \leftarrow f, \quad g_0 \leftarrow g.$
1. Let $z_k = \max_{(s,t)\in A_k}\{\min\{f_k(s), f_k(t)\}\}$ such that $g_k(s), g_k(t) \geq 1$. Find an arc $a_k = (s,t)$ with flow z_k.
2. $G_{k+1} \leftarrow (V, A_k - a_k)$,
   $g_{k+1} \leftarrow g_k, \quad g_{k+1}(s) \leftarrow g_k(s) - 1, \quad g_{k+1}(t) \leftarrow g_k(t) - 1,$
   $f_{k+1} \leftarrow f_k, \quad f_{k+1}(s) \leftarrow f_k(s) - z_k, \quad f_{k+1}(t) \leftarrow f_k(t) - z_k.$
3. If $z_k > 0$ then $k \leftarrow k+1$ go to Step 1. Otherwise go to Step 4.
4. Output $\sum_{m=1}^{k} z_m$ as the total flow value.

The algorithm executes at most mn iterations which is upper bound on the number of arcs. On each iteration we spend at most mn time to find the maximum flow arc giving a straightforward $O(m^2n^2)$ time complexity. This could be improved to $O(mn\log(mn))$ using a priority queue. We next define a relation between two instances of a *DCA* problem and then present some observations that we use to prove that `Algorithm GA` provides (1/2)-approximation for *DCA*.

Definition 1. *Let $DCA(G,f,g)$ and $DCA(G',f',g')$ be two instances of DCA problem. We say the former is* more constrained *than the latter, denoted by $DCA(G,f,g) \leq DCA(G',f',g')$, if $G \subseteq G'$, $f \leq f'$, and $g \leq g'$.*

Let $\overline{DCA}(G,f,g)$ denote the optimum flow value for $DCA(G,f,g)$. We make the following observation which is crucial in proving the next theorem.

Observation 1 *$DCA(G,f,g) \leq DCA(G',f',g')$ implies that $\overline{DCA}(G,f,g) \leq \overline{DCA}(G',f',g')$, since any feasible solution for $DCA(G,f,g)$ is also feasible for $DCA(G',f',g')$. Moreover, arc with max feasible flow in $DCA(G',f',g')$ carries no less flow than the arc with max feasible flow in $DCA(G,f,g)$.*

Theorem 2. *The flow computed by* `Algorithm GA` *is at least $\overline{DCA}(G,f,g)/2$.*

Proof. Let $x^* = \overline{DCA}(G,f,g)$ and H^* be a subgraph of G defined by the set of arcs carrying positive flow in an optimum solution. Then, $DCA(H^*,f,g) \leq DCA(G,f,g)$. Moreover, $\overline{DCA}(G,f,g) = \overline{DCA}(H^*,f,g) = x^*$. Our proof relies on an accounting of the flow x^* on H^* as we iterate `Algorithm GA` on G.

Let z be the total flow found by `Algorithm GA` and z_k the flow in the kth iteration of `Algorithm GA` on G_k. Suppose that the greedy algorithm terminates after p iterations. Let $H_0^* = H^*$. On each iteration there are two possible cases for the arc (s,t) chosen by `Algorithm GA`: (i) $(s,t) \in H_k^*$, or (ii) $(s,t) \notin H_k^*$. Whenever (i) is the case, let $H_{k+1}^* = H_k^* - \{(s,t)\}$. Otherwise, let $H_{k+1}^* = H_k^*$. This ensures that the relation $DCA(H_k^*, f_k, g_k) \leq DCA(G_k, f_k, g_k)$ is maintained for all k. Note that if (i) is the case then

$$\overline{DCA}(H_{k+1}^*, f_{k+1}, g_{k+1}) \geq \overline{DCA}(H_k^*, f_k, g_k) - z_k.$$

On the other hand, if (ii) is the case then

$$\overline{DCA}(H_{k+1}^*, f_{k+1}, g_{k+1}) \geq \overline{DCA}(H_k^*, f_k, g_k) - 2z_k.$$

In both cases, the second inequality holds, which when summed for $k = 1, \ldots, p-1$, gives

$$\overline{DCA}(H_p^*, f_p, g_p) \geq \overline{DCA}(H_0^*, f_0, g_0) - 2\sum_{k=1}^{p} z_k.$$

Since $DCA(H_p^*, f_p, g_p) \leq DCA(G_p, f_p, g_p)$, and the algorithm terminated at the pth iteration $\overline{DCA}(H_p^*, f_p, g_p) = 0$. Hence, $\sum_{k=1}^{p-1} z_k \geq \overline{DCA}(H_0^*, f_0, g_0)/2$, i.e., $z \geq x^*/2$. □

We also developed another algorithm called `Algorithm Greedy Matching (GM)`, which also has a 1/2 approximation bound. On each iteration a maximum matching is computed and the solution is built incrementally. The proof of the approximation bound is similar to that of `Algorithm (GA)`. Due to space limitation, we omit the details and refer to [1]. Performances of `Algorithms GM` and `GA` are presented in Section 5.

4 Heuristics

We next propose additional (heuristic) algorithms taking into account the assignment flexibility and available capacities. Following two rules replace Step 1 of `Algorithm GA` each to give a new algorithm:

- *Highest Flow Density* (`HFD`). For a node $s \in S$, let $\alpha_k(s) = |\{t|(s,t) \in A_k\}|$ denote its flexibility at iteration k. Then, the flow density of s is defined by the ratio $f_k(s)/\alpha_k(s)$. At each iteration we pick an arc with the largest flow from a largest flow density operation node. Ties are broken in favor of the operations with higher WIP inventory.
- *Most Penalized* (`MP`). For every operation, we find the two machines with the highest possible flow assignments. We select the operation for which the difference between the highest and next highest flows is the largest. Ties are broken in favor of the operations with higher WIP inventory.

5 Computational Experimentation

In order to test the practical performance of our algorithms we have conducted experiments using randomly generated test instances. In generating these, the parameters considered are the number of operations and machines, the operation-machine matrix density, and the shop load. The number of operations and machines dictate the shop size, and we consider levels of 10, 30, and 50. The operation-machine matrix density is a measure of the flexibility of the work center, and we consider levels of 0.3, 0.6, and 0.9. Finally, the shop load is a measure of the traffic in the work center, which is the ratio of the total WIP inventory available to the available total machine capacity, and we consider levels of 0.4, 0.8, and 1.2. Our experimental design yields 729 total settings, and we generate 20 instances for each of the settings. We consider the tool constraints to be 1, 2, 3, or 4 and the setup constraints to be 2, 4, or 6. Our random test instances are representative of the problems that are encountered in practice.

We have implemented our algorithms in C on a Unix operating platform, and performed the experiments on SUN Ultra 10 Workstations with SPARC 300MHz processor and 128MB RAM. In order to evaluate the quality of the solutions obtained, we find the optimum solutions for the test instances using CPLEX Mixed Integer Optimizer 7.5. About 5% of the instances cannot be solved by CPLEX within the specified time limit of 20 minutes, and for such cases we use the objective function value of the best linear programming relaxation bound found by CPLEX instead of the optimum flow value. Thus, the ratios we present are conservative estimates. Moreover, as CPLEX cannot solve all the test instances within reasonable computation times, it is not viable to use CPLEX to obtain the optimum solution to the problem in the practical setting, as the problem may have to be solved 15-20 times within a 5-10 minute window.

In Table 1, we report the average percent deviation of the total flow values (found by our algorithms) from the best upper bound (which, in most cases, is the optimum flow value) as well as the average CPU requirement of our algorithms. Our algorithms have very good practical performance, as they yield solutions that are on the average less than 1.5% away from the optimal solution in less than a second.

Table 1. Summarized results from the computational experiments

	Solution Algorithm			
Performance Metric	GM	GA	HFD	MP
Average Deviation (%)	1.39	1.37	1.13	1.19
Average CPU Time (secs.)	0.120	0.004	0.001	0.012

6 Conclusions

We presented the first constant factor approximation algorithms for the degree-constrained maximum network flow problem on a bipartite graph. We also proposed some heuristics, which perform slightly better than our approximation algorithms. Establishing approximation bounds for these heuristics requires further investigation. More importantly, it would be interesting to find a bound on the best possible constant-factor approximation.

From a broader perspective, the degree-constrained network flow problem has a rich combinatorial structure, which generalizes several other well-known problems. On bipartite graphs, it models a set of matching and assignment type problems with a variety of applications, such as capacity allocation, portfolio optimization, and machine scheduling. On general graphs, it models numerous applications in communication and transportation network design. Perhaps due to the difficulty of this problem, weaker models such as degree-constrained minimum spanning trees [9] has been studied in an attempt to provide solutions for these applications. Extending our results to general graphs is important future research due all such applications.

Acknowledgements. The authors thank Reha Uzsoy for introducing the tool- and setup-constrained capacity allocation problem.

References

1. E. Akçalı. On Tool- and Setup-Constrained Short-Term Capacity Allocation Problem. Ph.D. Dissertation, Purdue University, West Lafayette, Indianapolis, 2001.
2. L. Babel, H. Kellerer, and V. Kotov. The k-partitioning problem, *Mathematical Methods of Operations Research*, 47, 59–82, 1998.
3. A. Caprara, H. Kellerer, U. Pferschy, and D. Pisinger. Approximation algorithms for knapsack problems with cardinality constraints, *European Journal of Operational Research*. 123, 333–345, 2000.
4. E.G. Coffman, Jr., M.R. Garey, and D.S. Johnson. Approximation algorithms for bin packing – an updated survey. In *Algorithm Design for Computer System Design*. G. Ausiello, M. Lucertini, and P. Serfini, Eds., Springer-Verlag, 1984.
5. T.H. Cormen, C.E. Leiserson, R.L. Rivest, and C. Stein. *Introduction to Algorithms*, MIT Press, 2001.
6. M. Dawande, J. Kalagnanam, and J. Sethuraman. Variable sized bin packing with color constraints, Technical Report RC 21350, I.B.M. Research Division, T.J. Watson Research Center, 1998.
7. H.N. Gabow. An efficient reduction technique for degree-constrained subgraph and bidirected network flow problems. *Proc. of the ACM Symp. on Theory of Computing*, 448–456, 1983.
8. M.R. Garey and D.S. Johnson. *Computers and Intractability: A Guide to the Theory of NP-Completeness.* W. H. Freeman and Co., 1979.
9. J. Könemann and R. Ravi. Primal-dual meets local search: approximating MST's with nonuniform degree bounds. *Proc. of the ACM Symp. on Theory of Computing*, 389–395, 2003.
10. L.B. Toktay and R. Uzsoy. A capacity allocation problem with integer side constraints, *European Journal of Operational Research*, 109, 170–182, 1998.

Demonic I/O of Compound Diagrams Monotype/Residual Style

Fairouz Tchier

Mathematics Department, King Saud University
P.O.Box 22452, Riyadh 11495, Saudi Arabia
ftchier@hotmail.com

Abstract. We show how the notion of **relational diagram**, introduced by Schmidt, can be used to give a single demonic definition for a wide range of programming constructs. Our main result is Theorem 1, where we show that the **input-output**(I/O) relation of a **compound** diagram is equal to that of the diagram in which each sub-diagram has been replaced by its input-output relation. This process is repeated until we obtain elementary diagrams to which we apply the results given in previous work. This is achieved by using monotypes and residuals.

Keywords: Relational diagrams, compound diagrams, demonic semantics, operational semantics, monotypes, residuals.

1 Relation Algebras

Definition 1. *A* relation algebra $\mathfrak{A}$ *is a structure* $(\mathcal{A}, \vee, \wedge, \circ, -\ , \breve{\ })$ *over a non-empty set* $\mathcal{A}$ *of elements, called* relations. *The unary operations* $-\ ,\ \breve{\ }$ *are total whereas the binary operations* $\vee, \wedge, \circ$ *are partial. We denote by* $A_{\vee R}$ *the set of those elements* $Q \in \mathcal{A}$ *for which the union* $R \vee Q$ *is defined. If* $Q \in A_{\vee R}$*, we say that* Q *has the same type as* R*. The following conditions are satisfied.*

- $(A_{\vee R}, \vee, \wedge, \bar{\ })$ *is a Boolean algebra, with* zero *element* $\emptyset_R$ *and* universal *element* 1_R*. The elements of* $A_{\vee R}$ *are ordered by* inclusion, *denoted by* $\subseteq$.
- *If the products* $P \circ R$ *and* $Q \circ R$ *are defined, so is* $P \circ Q^{\smile}$*. If the products* $P \circ Q$ *and* $P \circ R$ *are defined, so is* $Q^{\smile} \circ R$*. If* $Q \circ R$ *is defined, so does* $Q \circ P$ *for every* $P \in A_{\vee R}$.
- *Composition is associative:* $P \circ (Q \circ R) = (P \circ Q) \circ R$.
- *The Schröder rule* $P \circ Q \leq R \Leftrightarrow P^{\smile} \circ \overline{R} \leq \overline{Q} \Leftrightarrow \overline{R} \circ Q^{\smile} \leq \overline{P}$ *holds whenever one of the three expressions is defined.*
- $1 \circ R \circ 1 = 1$ *holds for every* $R \neq \emptyset$ *(provided* $1 \circ R \circ 1$ *is defined) (Tarski rule).*

In the calculus of relations, there are two ways for viewing sets as relations; each of them has its own advantages. The first is via vectors: a relation x is a *vector* [15] iff $x = x \circ 1$. The second way is via *monotypes* [1]: a relation a is a monotype iff $a \leq id$.

A. Yazici and C. Şener (Eds.): ISCIS 2003, LNCS 2869, pp. 171–178, 2003.

The set of monotypes $\{a \mid a \in A_{\vee R}\}$, for a given R, is a complete Boolean lattice. We denote by $a^{\sim}$ the *monotype complement* of a. Monotypes have very simple and convenient properties. We present the following property; we will often use it without mention. It shows that for monotypes, composition and meet have the same effect. Let a and b be monotypes. We have $a \circ b = a \wedge b = b \circ a$. We now present some operations which are closely related to composition and Galois connections the *residuals* [1], defined as follows:

$$R \leq T/S \Leftrightarrow R \circ S \leq T, \text{ and } R \leq S\backslash T \Leftrightarrow S \circ R \leq T$$

where R, S and T are relations. The operators $/, \backslash$ have been given a variety of names in the literature, *left and right factor operators* [9]. We prefer terminology viz.*left and right residual operators* [12].

For simplicity, the universal, zero, and identity elements are all denoted by $1, 0, I$, respectively. One can use subscripts to make the typing explicit, but this will not be necessary here. $R^{\smile}$ is called the *converse* of R.

We need to define also the *reflexive transitive closure*[14,15] (*) is defined as follows :

$$R^* = \bowtie_{i \geq 0} R^i \quad \text{and} \quad R^* = I \vee R \circ R^* = I \vee R^* \circ R,$$

where $R0 = I$ and $R^{i+1} = R \circ R^i$.

The precedence of the relational operators, from highest to lowest, is the following: $^-$ and $^{\smile}$ bind equally, followed by $\circ$, followed by $\wedge$ and finally by $\vee$. The scope of $\bowtie_i$ and $\bigwedge_i$ goes to the right as far as possible. The domain and codomain of a relation R can be characterized by the vectors $R \circ 1$ and $R^{\smile} \circ 1$, respectively [15]. They can also be characterized by the corresponding monotypes. In this paper, we take the last approach. The *domain* and *codomain* operators of a relation R, denoted respectively by : $R^<$ and $R^>$, are the monotypes defined by the equations

(1) $R^< = I \wedge R \circ 1$, and $R^> = I \wedge 1 \circ R$.

1.1 Monotype Residuals

Definition 2. *Let R be a relation and a be a monotype. The monotype right residual and monotype left residual of a by R (called factors in [2]) are defined respectively by*

$$\text{(a) } a \mathbin{/\!\!\cdot} R := ((1 \circ a)/R)^>, \qquad \text{(b) } R \mathbin{\cdot\!\!\backslash} a := (R\backslash(a \circ 1))^<.$$

An alternative characterization of residuals can also be given by means of a Galois connection as follows [3]:

(2) $b \leq a \mathbin{/\!\!\cdot} R \Leftrightarrow (b \circ R)^> \leq a$, *and* $b \leq R \mathbin{\cdot\!\!\backslash} a \Leftrightarrow (R \circ b)^< \leq a$.

We now define the refinement ordering (*demonic inclusion*) we will be using in the sequel. This ordering induces a complete join semilattice, called a *demonic semilattice*. The associated operation is demonic composition ($\square$). For more details on relational demonic semantics and demonic operators, see [2,4,5,6,11].

Definition 3. *(a) We say that a relation Q refines a relation R [13], denoted by*
$Q \sqsubseteq R, \quad \Leftrightarrow \quad R^{<} \circ Q \leq R$ and $R^{<} \leq Q^{<}$.
(b) The demonic composition of relations Q and R [2] is $Q \mathbin{\square} R = (R^{<} \not/ Q) \circ Q \circ R$.

A monotype matrix is a diagonal matrix such that each entry of the diagonal is included in the identity relation. We can define the operators $^{<}, ^{>}, \not/, ^{\sim}$, and $^{\prec}$ applied to matrices.

2 Relational Diagrams

In the following, we will give the formal definition of a *diagram* and different types of diagrams. We define a *diagram* as being a quadruple constructed of a relation, a set of monotypes mutually disjoint; they have a role identical to the vertices of a graph and also of two particular monotypes characterizing the input and the output of the diagram. The word *diagram* is well justified by the use of matrices and graphs.

Even though we don't use matrices and graphs in our formal treatment (already used in our anterior work [16,17]), we use them in our informal and intuitive explications.

Definition 4. *Let $\mathcal{A}$ be a homogeneous relational algebra.*

(a) A quadruple $\mathcal{P} = (P, C, e, s)$ is a diagram *on $\mathcal{A}$ iff,*
- *P is a relation of $\mathcal{A}$, called the associated relation of diagram $\mathcal{P}$,*
- *C is a set of monotypes disjoint from each other, verifying the condition :*
  $(\bowtie C) \circ P \circ (\bowtie C) = P$,
- *e (entry) and s (sortie, which means exit in french) are monotypes ($e \circ s \in C$) called respectively the* input relation *and the* output relation *of the diagram $\mathcal{P}$.*

(b) A diagram $\mathcal{P}_1 = (P_1, C, e_1, s_1)$ is a sub-diagram *of diagram $\mathcal{P} = (P, C, e, s)$ iff : $P_1 \leq P$ and $e_1^{\sim} \circ s_1^{\sim} \circ (\bowtie C) \circ P = P \circ e_1^{\sim} \circ s_1^{\sim} \circ (\bowtie C) = 0$. In other words, a sub-diagram is a diagram such that its associated relation is included in the associated relation of the principal diagram. When the principal diagram is executed, the sub-diagram is also executed. The control begins by the input node e_1 to $\mathcal{P}_1$ and terminates by the output node s_1. The diagram $\mathcal{P}_1$ communicates no information to the diagram $\mathcal{P}$ through the internal nodes of the diagram $\mathcal{P}_1$. We distinguish two types of diagrams :* elementary *and* compound *diagrams.*

(c) A diagram $\mathcal{P} = (P, C, e, s)$ is atomic *iff $C = \{e, s\}$ and $P = e \circ P \circ s$. The graph and the matrix associated with this diagram are :*

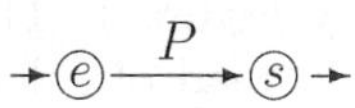

and

$$P = \begin{matrix} & e & s \\ e & 0 & P \\ s & 0 & 0 \end{matrix}.$$

An atomic diagram consists of a unique atomic step i.e. the transition between the input node and the output node is formed in exactly one step (there is only one input which is different from 0 in the matrix).

(d) *A diagram is compound if it is not elementary.*

3 Demonic Input-Output Relation of Compound Diagrams

During the execution of a program in an input state, by considering a demonic point of view (if there is a possibility for the program not to terminate normally then it will not terminate normally), three cases may happen : normal termination, abnormal termination and infinite loops. As our goal is to define formally the input-output relation of a diagram by supposing its worst execution, we have to consider these three cases together at the same time. For more details see [17]. In the following, the expression "input-output relation" means the demonic input-output relation. The input-output relation of a diagram $\mathcal{P}$ is given by a relation $\mathcal{E}(\mathcal{P})$ where $\mathcal{E}$ is a function from the set of diagrams to a relational algebra, which associates to each diagram $\mathcal{P}$ the relation $\mathcal{E}(\mathcal{P})$ given by :

(3) $\mathcal{E}(\mathcal{P}) = e \,\Box\, (T \wedge \mathcal{I}(P)) \,\Box\, s, \quad \text{with } T := P^* \circ P^{\prec}.$

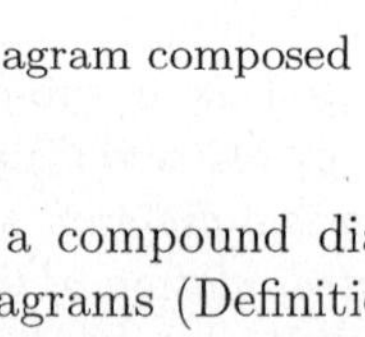

Fig. 1. Diagram composed of two sub-diagrams

Suppose that we have a compound diagram $\mathcal{P} = (\bowtie_{i=1}^{n} P_i, C, e, s)$ composed of elementary sub-diagrams (Definition 4) $\mathcal{P}_i = (P_i, C_i, e_i, s_i)$. Instead of calculating the input-output relation $\mathcal{E}(\mathcal{P})$ of diagram $\mathcal{P}$ directly by applying Equation 3, which is a laborious task, we will prove that the relation $\mathcal{E}(\mathcal{P})$ is equal to the input-output relation of the diagram obtained from diagram $\mathcal{P}$ by replacing each sub-diagram $\mathcal{P}_i$ by its input-output relation $\mathcal{E}(\mathcal{P}_i)$. The process continues until we obtain elementary diagrams for which we apply the results given in [17]. Let us give an example:

Example 1. Let $\mathcal{P} = (P, C, e, s)$ be a diagram constructed of two sub-diagrams $\mathcal{P}_1 = (P_1, C, e, c)$ and $\mathcal{P}_2 = (P_2, C, c, s)$, as illustrated by Figure 1. The sub-diagrams $\mathcal{P}_1$ and $\mathcal{P}_2$ may even be compound diagrams. Instead of calculating directly the input-output relation $\mathcal{E}(\mathcal{P})$ of diagram $\mathcal{P}$ by applying Equation 3, we want to show that $\mathcal{E}(\mathcal{P}) = \mathcal{E}(\mathcal{P}')$, with

$$\mathcal{P}' = (\mathcal{E}(\mathcal{P}_1) \vee \mathcal{E}(\mathcal{P}_2), C, e, s), \quad C = \{e, c, s\}, \quad \mathcal{E}(\mathcal{P}_1) = e \circ \mathcal{E}(\mathcal{P}_1) \circ c,$$
$$\mathcal{E}(\mathcal{P}_2) = c \circ \mathcal{E}(\mathcal{P}_2) \circ s \quad .$$

We remark that $\mathcal{P}'$ is a sequence diagram (see the graph of Figure 2). By applying Equation the results in previous work [17,18] to diagram $\mathcal{P}'$, we obtain $\mathcal{E}(\mathcal{P}') = \mathcal{E}(\mathcal{P}_1) \,\square\, \mathcal{E}(\mathcal{P}_2)$, whence we deduce $\mathcal{E}(\mathcal{P}) = \mathcal{E}(\mathcal{P}_1) \,\square\, \mathcal{E}(\mathcal{P}_2)$.

It is clear that behind this result a whole preliminary formal treatment is hidden. We also have to consider the other types of diagrams, *i.e.* the branching diagram and the loop diagram. Instead of treating each case separately, we will give a general result which regroups all the cases. We will restrict ourselves to the following constraints that we explain below:

Hypothesis 1. *Let $\mathcal{R} = (R, C, e, s)$, be a diagram in which we identify a sub-diagram $\mathcal{P} = (P, C_P, a, c)$ (Figure 3) such that:*

(a) $R = P \vee Q$,
(b) $C = \{a, b, c, d\}$,
(c) $P = (a \vee b) \circ P \circ (a \vee b \vee c)$,
(d) $Q = (c \vee d) \circ Q \circ (a \vee c \vee d)$,
(e) $C_P = \{a, b, c\}$,
(f) $e \leq a \vee c \vee d$,
(g) $s \leq c \vee d$.

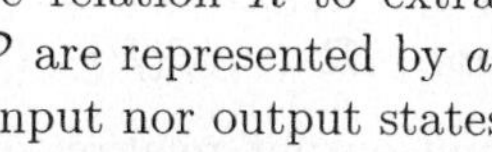

Fig. 2. A sequence diagram $\mathcal{P}'$

Our goal is to decompose the relation R to extract a sub-diagram $\mathcal{P}$ of diagram $\mathcal{R}$. The input states of $\mathcal{P}$ are represented by a, the output states by c and the states which are neither input nor output states, which we call internal states, are represented by b. These three elements are mutually disjoint, in other words $a \wedge b = c \wedge a = c \wedge b = 0$, also $c \circ P^{\smile} = 0$ (*i.e.* $c \circ P = 0$) which means that c is terminal. The monotype d represents all the states of $\mathcal{R}$ except those of a, b, c. Therefore, $d \circ P = 0$, $P \circ d = 0$ and $d \wedge a = d \wedge b = d \wedge c = 0$. By considering these conditions and the fact that P is the associated relation of the sub-diagram $\mathcal{P}$, we have $P = (a \vee b) \circ P \circ (a \vee b \vee c)$. We suppose that the internal states of $\mathcal{P}$ cannot be used to transmit the control from P to Q or from Q to P, which gives $b \circ Q = Q \circ b = 0$. We suppose also that the states of a are used as entries to P only, then $a \circ Q = 0$. We obtain : $Q = (c \vee d) \circ Q \circ (a \vee c \vee d)$. In the same way, the input in $\mathcal{R}$ cannot be done by b, then $e \leq a \vee c \vee d$. Finally, the output states of the principal diagram $\mathcal{R}$ have to be output states of sub-diagrams, thus $s \wedge a = s \wedge b = 0$, which implies $s \leq c \vee d$. The relation Q represents the union of associated relations of sub-diagrams of $\mathcal{R}$ other than $\mathcal{P}$. From these hypotheses, the matrices R and P associated respectively with diagrams $\mathcal{R}$ and $\mathcal{P}$ can be represented as follows :

$$R = \begin{array}{c} \\ a \\ b \\ c \\ d \end{array} \begin{array}{c} \begin{array}{cccc} a & b & c & d \end{array} \\ \begin{pmatrix} P_1 & P_2 & P_3 & 0 \\ P_4 & P_5 & P_6 & 0 \\ Q_1 & 0 & Q_2 & Q_3 \\ Q_4 & 0 & Q_5 & Q_6 \end{pmatrix} \end{array}, \qquad P = \begin{array}{c} \\ a \\ b \\ c \\ d \end{array} \begin{array}{c} \begin{array}{cccc} a & b & c & d \end{array} \\ \begin{pmatrix} P_1 & P_2 & P_3 & 0 \\ P_4 & P_5 & P_6 & 0 \\ 0 & 0 & 0 & 0 \\ 0 & 0 & 0 & 0 \end{pmatrix} \end{array}.$$

Remark 1. Each compound diagram $\mathcal{R} = (\bowtie_{i=1}^{n} P_i, C, e, s)$ composed of sub-diagrams $\mathcal{P}_i = (P_i, C, e_i, s_i)$ can be brought back to Hypotheses 1 by identifying a sub-diagram $\mathcal{P}_k = (P_k, C_k, e_k, s_k)$, where $1 \leq k \leq n$, and by taking

a) $P := P_k$,
b) $Q := \bowtie_{i=1}^{n} P_i,\ i \neq k$,
c) $a := e_k$,
d) $b := (e_k \vee s_k)^{\sim} \circ (\bowtie C_k)$,
e) $c := s_k$,
f) $d := (\bowtie C_k)^{\sim} \circ (\bowtie_{i=1}^{n} C_i)$,
g) $e := e$.

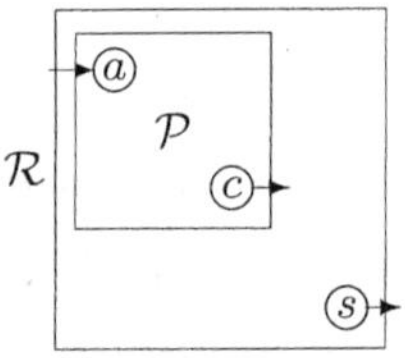

Fig. 3. A compound diagram

In the following, we will present the main result of this paper. It is sufficient to give an explication of this theorem and also its application in Section 4.

Theorem 1. *Let* $\mathcal{R} := (R, C, e, s)$ *and* $\mathcal{P} := (P, C, a, c)$ *verify Hypotheses 1. We have* $\mathcal{E}(\mathcal{R}) = \mathcal{E}(\mathcal{R}')$, *where* $\mathcal{R}' := (\mathcal{E}(\mathcal{P}) \vee Q, C, e, s)$.

This means that the input-output relation of diagram $\mathcal{R} = (P \vee Q, C, e, s)$ is equal to the input-output relation of diagram $(\mathcal{E}(\mathcal{P}) \vee Q, C, e, s)$; the associated relation of diagram $\mathcal{P}$ has been replaced by the input-output relation of the last one (see the matrix below). We note that the diagram $(\mathcal{E}(\mathcal{P}), \{a, c\}, a, c)$ is an atomic diagram (Definition 4(c)).

$$R' = \begin{array}{c} \\ a \\ b \\ c \\ d \end{array} \begin{array}{c} \begin{array}{cccc} a & b & c & d \end{array} \\ \begin{pmatrix} 0 & 0 & \mathcal{E}(\mathcal{P}) & 0 \\ 0 & 0 & 0 & 0 \\ Q_1 & 0 & Q_2 & Q_3 \\ Q_4 & 0 & Q_5 & Q_6 \end{pmatrix} \end{array}$$

The same reasoning may be applied to the rest of diagram $\mathcal{R}$; it is enough to identify in the diagram $\mathcal{R}'$ a sub-diagram which verifies Hypotheses 1 and we apply this until we obtain elementary diagrams for which we apply the results of the second chapter of the Thesis [17,18] and also in [7].

In the following section, we will show how to apply Theorem 1 to certain types of diagrams.

4 Applications

In this section, we will illustrate the application of Theorem 1 calculating the input-output relation of compound diagrams which may be reduced to sequence diagrams.

Let the diagrams $\mathcal{P}$, $\mathcal{P}_1$ and $\mathcal{P}_2$ be such that

$$\mathcal{P} = (P_1 \vee P_2, C, e_1, s_2),\ \ \mathcal{P}_1 = (P_1, C_1, e_1, s_1) \ \text{ and } \ \mathcal{P}_2 = (P_2, C_2, s_1, s_2),$$

where $C = C_1 \vee C_2$, $\quad (\bowtie C_1) \wedge (\bowtie C_2) = s_1 \quad$ and $\quad s_1 \circ P_1^{\prec} = 0$.

Suppose that diagrams $\mathcal{P}_1$ and $\mathcal{P}_2$ are not atomic. Our aim is to calculate the input-output relation $\mathcal{E}(\mathcal{P})$ of diagram $\mathcal{P}$ by applying Theorem 1 and the results from [17]. To do that, we reduce P_1 and P_2 to obtain a sequence diagram (Definition 4).

Substitution 1. *Consider the following substitutions where the variables on the left side are those of Theorem 1 :*

a) $a := e_1$,
b) $b := e_1 \vee s_1^{\sim} \circ (\bowtie C_1)$,
c) $c := s_1$,
d) $d := s_1^{\sim} \circ (\bowtie C_2)$,
e) $P := P_1$,
f) $Q := P_2$,
g) $e := e_1$,
h) $s := s_2$.

The relation $(e_1 \vee s_1)^{\sim} \circ (\bowtie C_1)$ represents the states of the diagram $\mathcal{P}_1$ which are different from input and output states (the internal states). By using $c \circ P = 0$ and also the properties verified by a, b (Substitution 1 and Hypothesis 1), we obtain

$$(a \vee b) \circ P \circ (a \vee b \vee c) = (\bowtie C_1) \circ P \circ (\bowtie C_1) = P.$$

It is not difficult to verify that Hypotheses 1 are satisfied. By Theorem 1, we have then

$$\mathcal{E}(\mathcal{P}) = \mathcal{E}(\mathcal{E}(\mathcal{P}_1) \vee P_2, C', e, s), \ \text{ where } \ C' = C_2 \vee \{e_1\}.$$

By hypotheses, $\mathcal{P}_2 = (P_2, C_2, s_1, s_2)$ is a diagram; we will proceed in the same way and apply once more Theorem 1 to the new diagram $(\mathcal{E}(\mathcal{P}_1) \vee P_2, C, e, s)$ to obtain $\mathcal{E}(\mathcal{P}) = \mathcal{E}(\mathcal{P}')$, where $\mathcal{P}' = (\mathcal{E}(\mathcal{P}_1) \vee \mathcal{E}(\mathcal{P}_2), C'', e_1, s_2)$, where $C'' = \{e_1, s_1, s_2\}$. By the definitions of $\mathcal{E}$, $\mathcal{P}_1$ and $\mathcal{P}_2$, we have $\mathcal{E}(\mathcal{P}_1) = e_1 \circ \mathcal{E}(\mathcal{P}_1) \circ s_1$ and $\mathcal{E}(\mathcal{P}_2) = s_1 \circ \mathcal{E}(\mathcal{P}_2) \circ s_2$. So, $\mathcal{P}'$ is a sequence diagram (Definition 4). By applying previous results, we obtain :

$$\mathcal{E}(\mathcal{P}) = \mathcal{E}(\mathcal{P}_1) \,\square\, \mathcal{E}(\mathcal{P}_2).$$

References

1. Backhouse, R. C., Hoogendijk, P., Voermans, E. and van der Woude, J. A Relational Theory of Datatypes. Research report, Department of Mathematics and Computer Science, Eindhoven University of Technology, The Netherlands, 1992.
2. R. C. Backhouse and J. van der Woude. Demonic operators and monotype factors. *Mathematical Structures in Computer Science*, 3(4):417–433, December 1993. Also: Computing Science Note 92/11, Dept. of Mathematics and Computer Science, Eindhoven University of Technology, The Netherlands, 1992.
3. R. C. Backhouse and H. Doornbos. Mathematical induction made calculational. Computing Science Note 94/16, Dept. of Mathematics and Computer Science, Eindhoven University of Technology, The Netherlands, 1994.
4. R. Berghammer. Relational specification of data types and programs. Technical report 9109, Fakultät für Informatik, Universität der Bundeswehr München, Germany, September 1991.
5. R. Berghammer and G. Schmidt. Relational specifications. In C. Rauszer (ed.), *Algebraic Logic, Banach Center Publications*, 28, Polish Academy of Sciences, 1993.
6. R. Berghammer and H. Zierer. Relational algebraic semantics of deterministic and nondeterministic programs. *Theoretical Computer Science*, 43:123–147, 1986.
7. C. Brink, W. Kahl, and G. Schmidt, editors. *Relational Methods in Computer Science*. Springer, 1997.
8. L. H. Chin and A. Tarski. Distributive and modular laws in the arithmetic of relation algebras. *University of California Publications*, 1:341–384, 1951.
9. Conway, J. H.*Regular Algebra and Finite Machines*.In Chapman and Hall, London, 1971.
10. J. Desharnais, B. Möller, and F. Tchier. Kleene under a demonic star. *8th International Conference on Algebraic Methodology And Software Technology (AMAST 2000)*, May 2000, Iowa City, Iowa, USA, *Lecture Notes in Computer Science*, Vol. 1816, pages 355–370, Springer-Verlag, 2000.
11. J. Desharnais, N. Belkhiter, S. B. M. Sghaier, F. Tchier, A. Jaoua, A. Mili and N. Zaguia. Embedding a demonic semilattice in a relation algebra. *Theoretical Computer Science*, 149(2):333–360, 1995.
12. Dilworth, R. P. Non-commutative Residuated Lattices. *Trans. Amer. Math. Sci.*, **46**, 426–444 (1939).
13. A. Mili, J. Desharnais and F. Mili. Relational heuristics for the design of deterministic programs. *Acta Informatica*, 24(3):239–276, 1987.
14. G. Schmidt. Programs as partial graphs I: Flow equivalence and correctness. *Theoretical Computer Science*, 15:1–25, 1981.
15. G. Schmidt and T. Ströhlein. *Relations and Graphs*. EATCS Monographs in Computer Science, Springer-Verlag, Berlin, 1993.
16. F. Tchier and J. Desharnais. A generalisation of a theorem of Mills. *Proceedings of the Tenth International Symposium on Computer and Information Sciences, ISCIS X*, pages 27–34, October 1995, Turkey.
17. F. Tchier. Sémantiques relationnelles démoniaques et vérification de boucles non déterministes. Ph. D. thesis, Département de mathématiques et de statistique, Université Laval, Canada, 1996. *http://auguste.ift.ulaval.ca/ desharn/Theses/index.html.*
18. F. Tchier and J. Desharnais. Applying a generalization of a theorem of Mills to generalized looping structures. In *Science and Engineering in Software Development. A recognition of Harlan D. Mills' Legacy*, Los Angeles, CA, May 1999, pages 31–38, IEEE Computer Society Press, 1999.

Fuzzy Logic and Neural Network Applications on the Gas Sensor Data: Concentration Estimation

Fevzullah Temurtas[1], Cihat Tasaltin[2], Hasan Temurtas[3], Nejat Yumusak[1], and Zafer Ziya Ozturk[2]

[1] Sakarya University, Department of Computer Engineering, Adapazari, Turkey
[2] Tubitak Marmara Research Center, Material and Chem. Tec. Res. Inst., Gebze, Turkey
[3] Dumlupınar University, Department of Electric - Electronic Engineering, Kutahya, Turkey

Abstract. In this study, a fuzzy logic based algorithm is presented for the concentration estimation of the CCl_4 and $CHCl_3$ gases by using the steady state sensor response and an artificial neural network (ANN) structure is proposed for the concentration estimation of the same gases inside the sensor response time by using the transient sensor response. The Quartz Crystal Microbalance (QCM) type sensors were used as gas sensors. A computer controlled measurement and automation system with IEEE 488 card was used to control the gas concentration values and to collect the sensor responses. Acceptable performance was obtained for the concentration estimation with fuzzy inference. The appropriateness of the artificial neural network for the gas concentration determination inside the sensor response time is observed.

1 Introduction

The volatile organic vapours in ambient air are known to be reactive photochemically, and can have harmful effects upon long-term exposure at moderate levels. These type organic compounds are widely used as a solvent in a large number of the chemical industry and in the printing plants [1]. Developing and designing sensors for the specific detection of hazardous components in the mixture of many others is important [2]. In recent years, a variety of sensitive and selective coating materials have been investigated for chemical sensors. The molecules to be detected interact with the sensitive coating. They may be identified quantitatively by changes of physical or chemical parameters of adsorbate/analyte systems such as the refracting index, capacitance, conductivity, total mass, etc. The total mass changes can be monitored by means of quartz crystal microbalance (QCM) sensors, which are widely used as thickness monitors [3,4]. One of the most important problems which is related to the sensor parameters encountered in the high sensitive sensor research is slow response times [5].

In this study, fuzzy inference is employed as a concentration estimation method with a QCM gas sensor, which shows good performance regardless of the ambient temperature- humidity variations as well as the concentration changes and the performance for the CCl_4 and $CHCl_3$ gases and the suitability of this method are discussed based on the experimental results. In this method, the steady state responses

A. Yazici and C. Şener (Eds.): ISCIS 2003, LNCS 2869, pp. 179–186, 2003.

of the sensors were used. Steady state response means no signals varying in time. So, it's easy to apply fuzzy inference mechanism. For realizing the determination of the concentrations before the response times and decreasing the estimation time, the transient responses of the sensors must be used. Transient response means varying signals in time. And it's difficult to handle this type signals with fuzzy inference for concentration estimation. For decreasing the estimation time, an artificial neural network (ANN) structure with tapped time delays is proposed. The performance and the suitability of the proposed method are discussed based on the experimental results.

2 Sensors and Measurement System

The Quartz Crystal Microbalances (QCM) is useful acoustic sensor devices. The principle of the QCM sensors is based on changes Δf in the fundamental oscillation frequency to upon ad/absorption of molecules from the gas phase. To a first approximation the frequency change Δf results from increase in the oscillating mass Δm [6].

$$\Delta f = -\frac{C_f f_0^2}{A} \Delta m \tag{1}$$

where, A is the area of the sensitive layers, C_f the mass sensitivity constant (2.26 10-10 $m^2 s\ g^{-1}$) of the quartz crystal, f_o fundamental resonance of the quartz crystals, Δm mass changes.

The piezoelectric crystals used were AT-Cut, 10 *MHz* quartz crystal (ICM International Crystal Manufacturers Co., Oklahoma, USA) with gold plated electrodes (diameter $\phi = 3\ mm$) on both sides mounted in a HC6/U holder. The both faces of two piezoelectric crystals were coated with the phthalocyanine [4]. The instrumentation utilized consist of a Standard Laboratory Oscillator Circuit (ICM Co Oklahoma, USA), power supply and frequency counter (Keithley programmable counter, model 776). The frequency changes of vibrating crystals were monitored directly by frequency counter.

A Calibrated Mass Flow Controller (MFC) (MKS Instruments Inc. USA) was used to control the flow rates of carrier gas and sample gas streams. Sensors were tested by isothermal gas exposure experiments at a constant operating temperature. The gas streams were generated from the cooled bubblers (saturation vapour pressures were calculated using Antoine Equation [7]) with synthetic air as carrier gas and passed through stainless steel tubing in a water bath to adjust the gas temperature. The gas streams were diluted with pure synthetic air to adjust the desired analyte concentration with computer driven MFCs. Typical experiments consisted of repeated exposure to analyte gas and subsequent purging with pure air to reset the baseline. The sensor data were recorded every 3-4 *s* at a constant of 200 *ml/min*.

In this study, the frequency shifts (*Hz*) versus concentrations (*ppm*) characteristics were measured by using QCM sensor for the CCl_4 and $CHCl_3$ gases as shown in Figure 1. At the beginning of each measurement gas sensor is cleaned by pure synthetic air. Each measurement is composed of six periods. Each period consists of 10 minutes cleaning phase and 10 minutes measuring phase. During the periods of the measurements, at the first period 500 *ppm*, and at the following periods 1000, 3000, 5000, 10000, and 12000 *ppm* gases are given.

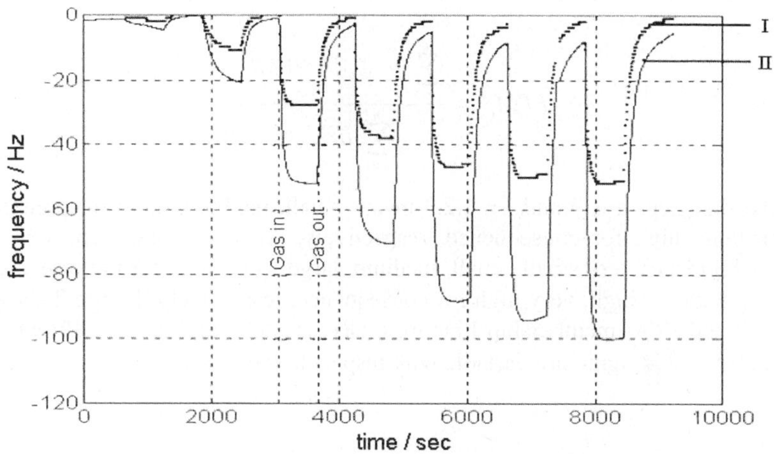

Fig. 1. For CCl_4 and $CHCl_3$ characteristic QCM sensor response: I-sensor response of QCM for CCl_4 gas, II-sensor response of QCM for $CHCl_3$ gas

3 Fuzzy Logic Based Concentration Estimation

Fuzzy logic is widely used in the field of intelligent control, classification, pattern matching, image processing, etc. In such applications, it describes the imprecise, vague, qualitative, linguistic, nonlinear relationship between input and output states of a system with a set of rules generally. Such rules are called fuzzy, and can be expressed as follows in general form [8]:

$$\text{IF } x_1 \text{ is } A_1^i \text{ AND} \cdots \text{AND } x_n \text{ is } A_n^i \text{ THEN } y \text{ is } B^j \tag{2}$$

where x is input, y is output, A_k^i , $k = 1, \ldots, n$ and B^j are linguistic variables which represent vague terms such as small, medium or large defined on the input and output variables, respectively.

For determination of the concentrations of the CCl_4 and $CHCl_3$ gases within steady state sensor response, a fuzzy logic based algorithm which includes Mamdani's [9] fuzzy inference method was used. In this system, one input, frequency change of the sensor Δf and one output, concentration of the introduced gas *PPM* are used. From the relations of the input and output, that is, the frequency change of the sensor is large, when the concentration of the introduced gas is high and small when the concentration is low, we can extract n fuzzy rules and corresponding defuzzification equation as follows:

Rule i: IF Δf is A_i THEN PPM is B_i $(i = 1,2,\ldots,n)$ (3)

$$\mu_{\Delta fi} = A_i(\Delta f), \ \mu_{PPMi} = B_i(PPM) \tag{4}$$

$$PPM = \frac{\sum_{i=1}^{n} \mu_{PPMi} * PPMi}{\sum_{i=1}^{n} \mu_{PPMi}} \tag{5}$$

At the first step, n is 3 and i = 1,2,3 means small, medium, large for premise and low, medium, high for consequence, respectively. At the second step, n is 5 and i = 1,2,3,4,5 means very small, small, medium, large, very large for premise and very low, low, medium, high, very high for consequence, respectively. Figure 2 shows the sample Δf and PPM membership functions. $\Delta f1,\ldots, \Delta f4$ and $PPM1,\ldots,PPM4$ values which given in this figure are variable with respect to the gases.

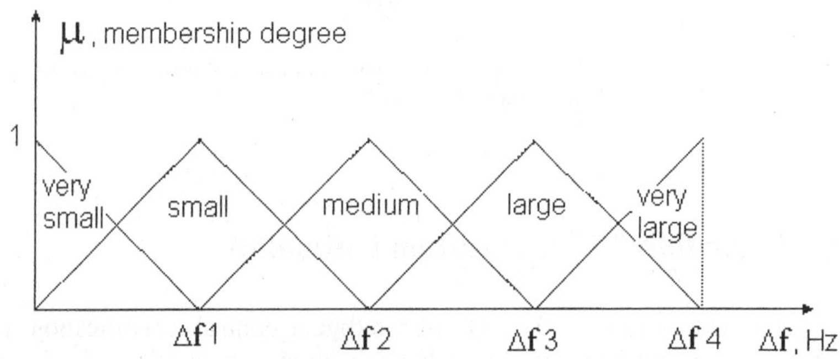

(a)

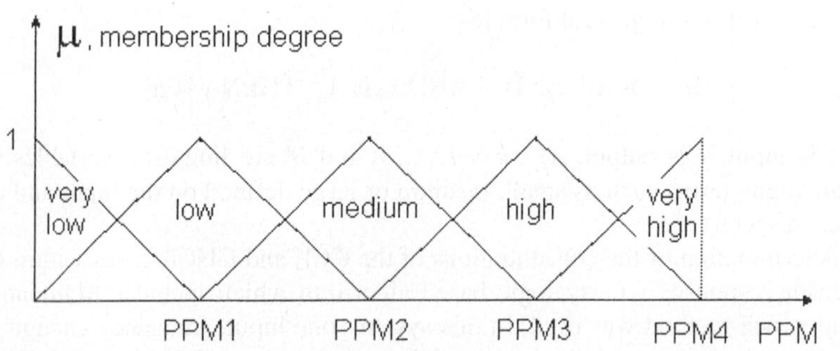

(b)

Fig. 2. Δf (a) and PPM (b) membership functions for n=5.

Figure 3 illustrates an example of the fuzzy inference, aggregation and defuzzification for the concentration estimation.

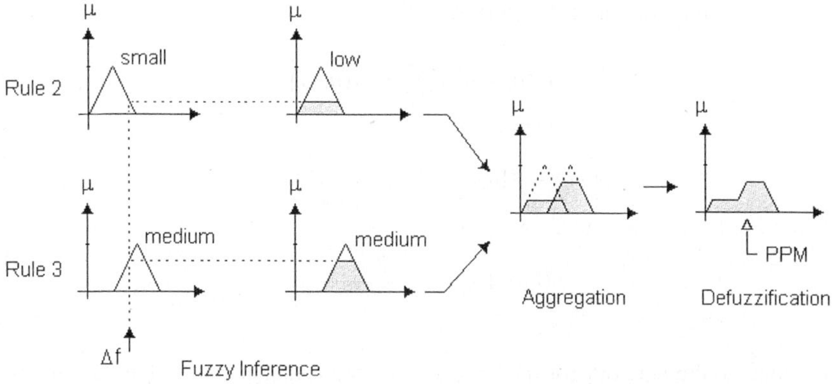

Fig. 3. An example of the fuzzy inference, aggregation and defuzzification.

4 Decreased Estimation Time by Using Artificial Neural Network

A multi-layer feed-forward ANN with tapped time delays is proposed for determination of the concentrations of the CCl_4 and $CHCl_3$ gases inside the sensor response time. The network structure is shown in Figure 4. The input, *u*, is the sensor frequency shift value and the output, *y*, is the estimated concentration. The inputs to the network are the frequency shift and the past values of the frequency shift. The network has a single hidden layer with 10 hidden layer nodes and a single output node.

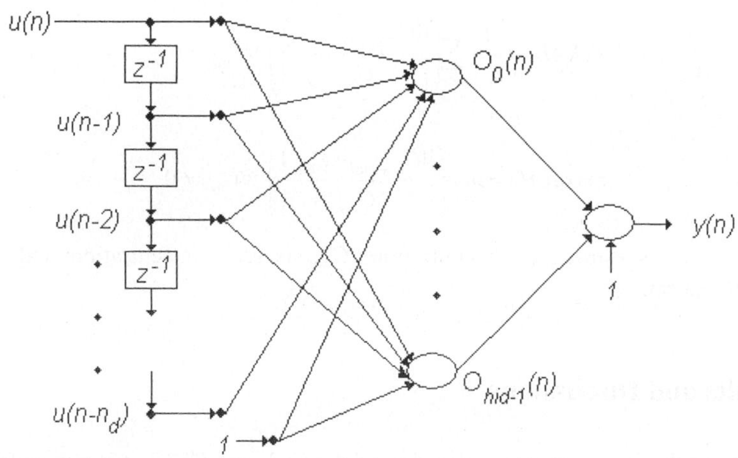

Fig. 4. Multi-layer feed-forward neural network model with a time delayed structure

Equations which used in the neural network model are shown in (6), (7), and (8). As seen from equations, the activation functions for the hidden layer nodes and the output node are tangent-sigmoid transfer function. The back propagation algorithm was used for training of neural network model [10].

$$net_j(n) = b_j + \sum_{i=0}^{n_d} w_{j,i} u(n-i) \tag{6}$$

$$O_j(n) = f\left(net_j(n)\right) = 1 - \frac{2}{1 + e^{2 \cdot net_j(n)}} \tag{7}$$

$$y(n) = 1 - \frac{2}{1 + e^{\left(b + \sum_{j=0}^{hid-1} w_j O_j(n)\right)}} \tag{8}$$

The inputs to the network for the CCl_4 gas are the frequency shift and the nine past values of the frequency shift (ten input). For the $CHCl_3$ gas, five different numbers of inputs to the networks are used. These are,

- the frequency shift (one input),
- the frequency shift and the two past values of the frequency shift (three input),
- the frequency shift and the four past values of the frequency shift (five input),
- the frequency shift and the seven past values of the frequency shift (eight input),
- the frequency shift and the nine past values of the frequency shift (ten input).

5 Performance Evaluation

For the performance evaluation, we have used the mean relative absolute error, $E(RAE)$, and the corresponding maximum error, $\max(RAE)$ [2]:

$$E(RAE) = \frac{1}{n_{test}} \sum_{tetset} \left(\left| \frac{\left(C_{prdicted} - C_{true}\right)}{C_{true}} \right| \right) \quad \forall C_{\text{true}} \neq 0 \tag{9}$$

$$\max(RAE) = \max_{testset} \left(\left| \frac{\left(C_{predicted} - C_{true}\right)}{C_{true}} \right| \right) \quad \forall C_{\text{true}} \neq 0 \tag{10}$$

where, $C_{predicted}$ is estimated concentration, C_{true} is real concentration and n_{test} is number of test set.

6 Results and Discussions

The ability of the fuzzy logic to estimation of the CCl_4 and $CHCl_3$ gas concentrations related to the number of memberships functions are given in table 1. As seen in the table, accuracy of the estimation can be improved by increasing the number of membership functions. This result supports the expectations of the B.Yea at all [8]. When the number of memberships functions is 5, fuzzy estimation results in an acceptable error [8,11]. In fuzzy inference, the estimation times are equal to or greater than the sensor response times, because it uses steady state responses of sensors.

Table 1. Fuzzy logic concentration estimation results for CCl_4 and $CHCl_3$ gases

Gas	Number of memberships functions (n)	Sensor response time (sec)	Fuzzy estimation time (sec)	E(RAE) (%)	Max(REA) (%)
CCl4	3	~250	≥ 250	19.04	5.57
	5	~250	≥ 250	5.13	15
CHCl3	3	~250	≥ 250	19.64	41
	5	~250	≥ 250	7.4	15.62

The ability of the ANN to estimation of the CCl_4 and $CHCl_3$ gas concentrations related to number of ANN inputs are given in table 2. As seen in this table, ANN estimation times are generally at the level of seconds while sensor response times are at the level of minutes. This means that the determination of the concentrations of the CCl_4 and $CHCl_3$ gases inside the sensor response by using ANN with tapped time delays is achieved. But, when the numbers of the ANN inputs are small, i.e. 1 or 3, the results are not acceptable.

Table 2. ANN estimation results for CCl_4 and $CHCl_3$ gases

Gas	Numbers of ANN inputs	Sensor response time (sec)	ANN estimation time (sec)	E(RAE) (%)	Max(REA) (%)
CCl4	1	~250	2	138.5	483.4
	3	~250	6	34.6	83.6
	5	~250	10	7.4	30.6
	8	~250	16	6.6	29.6
	10	~250	20	5.5	21.4
CHCl3	10	~250	20	2.5	14.4

For easy understanding of the effect of the numbers of the ANN inputs, error (%) versus numbers of ANN inputs graph for CCl_4 is given in Figure 5. From these figure and table, it's shown that the increasing number of ANN inputs results improving accuracy at the concentration estimations.

In this study we saw that fuzzy logic structures are simple applicable and acceptable errors can be achieved. Because of the simplicity of the fuzzy structure, fuzzy logic can be easily adapted to the handle systems for detection of gas concentration. Another important result is that the proposed ANN structure with tapped time delays is useful for realizing the determination of the concentrations inside the response times and optimum estimation results can be achieved by using enough number of ANN inputs.

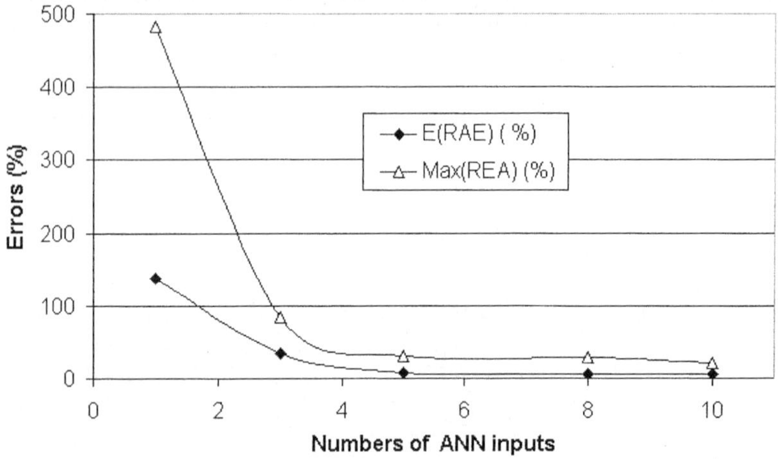

Fig. 5. Error (%) versus numbers of ANN inputs graph for CCl_4

References

1. Ho, M.H., Gullbault, G.G., Rietz, B.: Continuos Detection of Toluene in Ambient Air with a Coated Piezoelectric Crystal, Anal. Chem., 52(9), (1980)
2. Vaihinger, S., Gopel, W.: Multi - Component Analysis in Chemical Sensing in Sensors: A Comprehensive Survery Ed. W. Gopel, S. Hense, S.N. Zemel, VCH. Weinhe, New York, 2(1) (1991) 192
3. Ozturk, Z.Z., Zhou, R., Wiemar, U., Ahsen, V., Bekaroglu, O., Gopel, W.: Soluble Phthalocyanines For the Detection of Organic Solvents Thin Film Structure With Quartz Microbalance and Capacitance Transducers , Sensors And Actuators B, 26–27 (1995) 208–212
4. Zhou, R., Josse, F., Gopel, W., Ozturk, Z. Z., Bekaroglu, A.: Phthalocyanines As Sensitive Materyals For Chemical Sensors, Applied Organometallic Chemistry, 10 (1996) 557–577
5. Gopel, W., Schierbaum, K.D., Sensors A Comprehensive Survey Ed., chap 1, 18–27, VCH Weinheim, New York, (1991)
6. King, H. W.: Piezoelectric Sorption Detector, Anal. Chem., 36 (1964) 1735–1739.
7. Riddick, J., Bunger, A., in Weissberger, A., (ed.): Organic Solvents' in Techniques of Chemistry, Volume 2, Wiley Interscience, (1970)
8. Yea, B., Osaki, T., Sugahara, K., Konishi, R.: The concentration estimation of inflammable gases with a semiconductor gas sensor utilizing neural networks and fuzzy inference, Sensors and Actuators-B, 41 (1997) 121–129
9. Mamdani, E.H., and Assilian, S.: An experiment in linguistic synthesis with a fuzzy logic controller, International Journal of Man-Machine Studies, 7 (1), (1975) 1–13
10. Haykin, S.: Neural Networks, A Comprehensive Foundation, Macmillan Publishing Company, Englewood Cliffs, N.J. (1994)
11. Huyberechts, G., Szecowka, P., Roggen, J., Licznerski, B.W.: Sensors & Actuators B, 41 (1997) 123–130

A Security Embedded Text Compression Algorithm

Ebru Celikel and Mehmet Emin Dalkılıç

Ege University, International Computer Institute, 35100 Bornova-Izmir, Turkey
{celikel, dalkilic}@ube.ege.edu.tr

Abstract. Although conventional compression tools achieve good compression rates, they ignore the security issue. This study presents the design and implementation of a lossless compression algorithm with embedded security to fill that gap. The scheme introduced is a system with *encoding* and *decoding* and is oriented for text type of data. It is implemented on sample text files from standard English *Calgary Corpus*. Two ideas, one hiding the *encryption key* by using a *PRNG* and the other employing *multiple iterations* to dissipate language statistics, are suggested to strengthen the security of the system. Both ideas are implemented and promising results have been obtained.

1 Introduction

Compression is a practical way of providing efficient channel and storage utilization during data communication and archiving. It is the type of data being transmitted or saved that determines whether the compression is to be performed in a lossy or lossless manner. If the data of concern is of type text then original data recovery is necessary. Hence, compression must be lossless. A good text compression algorithm is required to provide a reasonable level of compression and be fast enough to be used for storage and transmission of text. Many off the shelf lossless compression algorithms offer performances to varying levels in terms of compressibility (measured in *bits per character –bpc*) and execution speed. Some of these algorithms are *Huffman Coding* which is based on the idea of using longer codewords for rarely occurring symbols [1], *Lempel-Ziv* methods using dictionary-based compression [2], *Arithmetic Coding* that represents symbol sequences as floating point numbers [3], *Prediction by Partial Matching (PPM)* which is based on predicting the upcoming symbols depending on a context of predetermined length [4] and *Burrows-Wheeler Transform* which transposes the position of symbols throughout text to compress them better [5].

What is common for all these algorithms is that, they intend to provide compression, not security. We introduce a new text compression algorithm to make up for that lack: A novel scheme to provide not only compression, but also security.

2 Text Compression with Embedded Security

The proposed scheme is called security embedded text compression (Figure 1). For *encoding* and *decoding* it employs the same *key*, which is an *n*-dimensional *matrix* (called *Encryption matrix E*). Thus, it is *symmetrical*. The *Encoder* (*Enc*) first divides

A. Yazici and C. Şener (Eds.): ISCIS 2003, LNCS 2869, pp. 187–195, 2003.

plaintext (*P*) into *n* parts to generate $|P|/n$ *n-grams*, where $|P|$ denotes the length of *P*. This division yields an *initial compression ratio* of $100\times(n-1)/n$ percent (Eq.1).

$$100 \times \left(1 - \frac{(|P|/n)}{|P|}\right) = 100 \times \left(\frac{n-1}{n}\right)\% \qquad \textbf{(1)}$$

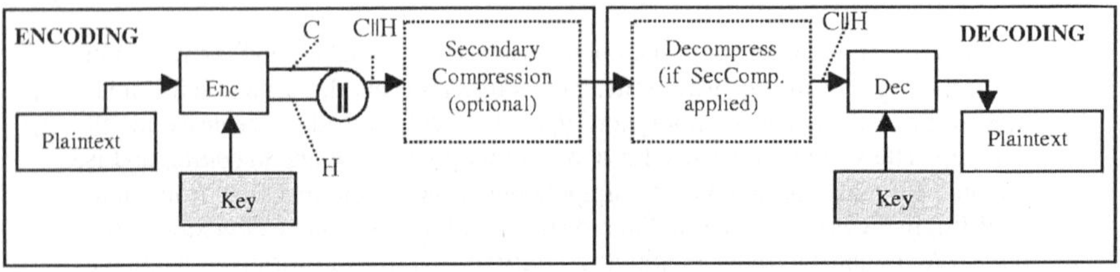

Fig. 1. Text Compression with Embedded Security

Both *encoding* and *decoding* are performed in a symbolwise manner with simple table lookup: At each *encoding* step, the *encoder* takes the ith *n-gram*, finds its *encryption matrix* counterpart and generates the ith *cipher symbol* (C_i). Meanwhile, a varying length special bitstream, called the ith *help string* (H_i), is created. At the end of $|P|/n$ *encoding* steps, C_is and H_is are combined to form $(C||H)$. Although using *help string* degrades the *initial compression ratio* (Eq.1), it makes *ciphertext* uniquely decodable. A *secondary compression algorithm*, which can be any efficient conventional lossless compression algorithm, can be used to compress $(C||H)$ further. The final output, whether compressed or uncompressed $(C||H)$, is then sent to the *decoder* (*Dec*).

While implementing the scheme, *cipher symbols* are chosen out of a *symbol space* (*S*) and the set of all distinct *plaintext symbols* is called the *alphabet A*. If the source language is English, *A* would contain 26 English alphabet symbols plus the space character, giving 27 symbols. The *symbol space* can be as large as the number of distinct elements in the *Encryption matrix,* so it may contain up to $|A|^n$ entries.

2.1 Using FSM Model to Recover Plaintext

Decoder first decompresses the final output sent by *Enc,* if secondary compression was applied. Upon obtaining $(C||H)$, if the *key* is unknown, predictions to determine probable *plaintexts* need to be employed. There exist mechanisms like exploiting language rules to make better probability estimations during recovery. A *Finite State Machine (FSM) Model*, which uses *Markov models* of *degree m* (*m* being the *context* length) to determine the next symbol is one of them [6]. In this *model*, *cipher symbols* are assigned to predetermined *states* and transition probabilities are assigned *probability values* reflecting the usage statistics of the source language. As the *degree* of the *model* increases, the success of determining the right symbol increases.

Assume that we are given a *ciphertext* '∈αβγ∈' without *key* over an *alphabet* *A*={α, β, γ, ∈} with *n*=2, and *transition probabilities matrix T* of *degree m*=1, representing the probability that one symbol follows another, as follows:

$$T = \begin{array}{c} \\ \alpha \\ \beta \\ \gamma \\ \in \end{array} \begin{array}{c} \begin{array}{cccc} \alpha & \beta & \gamma & \in \end{array} \\ \left[\begin{array}{cccc} 0.1 & 0.4 & 0.2 & 0.3 \\ 0.7 & 0.0 & 0.1 & 0.2 \\ 0.3 & 0.5 & 0.1 & 0.1 \\ 0.5 & 0.2 & 0.0 & 0.3 \end{array}\right] \end{array}$$

For decoding *C*, it is possible to draw an *FSM model* of the language for the alphabet *A* as in Figure 2, where *states* are symbols of *A* and *arcs* represent the *transition probabilities*. According to this *FSM*, if *P* begins with ∈, then it is highly probable for *P* to be "∈αβα∈βγβ∈α" but impossible for it to be "∈αββ∈γγβ∈α".

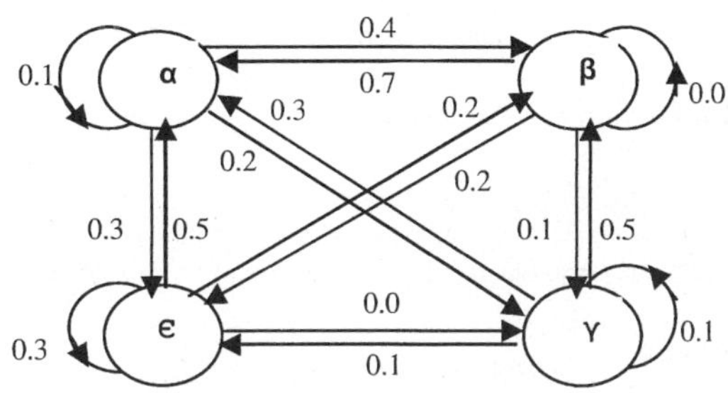

Fig. 2. *FSM Model* of *degree* 1 for the sample *alphabet A*={α, β, γ, ∈}

2.2 A Dynamic Length Encoding Scheme for Help String

Although *FSM* helps much in determining the most probable *plaintext* alternatives, it might be misleading. On the other hand, if an *auxiliary message* (called the *help string*) is constructed during *encoding C*, then recovering the original *plaintext* would be guaranteed. Employing *help string* imposes an extra load to the system, but it can be compensated to some degree by representing it with as few bits as possible. For that, a *dynamic length encoding scheme* is used to encode it.

During the encoding of the ith *n-gram*, the ith *help string* (H_i) bits are encoded based on a length-*m context*. *Context* together with the ith *n-gram* forms a *q-gram,* where *q*=*m*+*n*. (C_i) being the *cipher symbol* counterpart of the ith *n-gram* is first searched within the ith *context* list. Given the *context*, the number of *n-grams*, say *d*, that are mapped into the same *cipher symbol* as C_i determines H_i's length. If the ith *n-gram* is found in the ith *context* list, then its index is encoded as H_i with $\lceil \log_2(d) \rceil$ bits. If not found, then first H_{esc}, called *escape sequence*, is issued. Second, the *Encryption matrix* index of the not found *n-gram* is emitted as H_i with $\lceil \log_2(r) \rceil$ bits, where *r* is the number of times C_i occurs in *E* minus the number of C_i-encoded *n-grams* following the ith *context*. Finally, the not found *n-gram* is added to the end of the ith *context* list. In this manner, next time the same *n-gram* follows the same *context*, no *escape se-*

quence would be needed, which means fewer bits for the *help string*. This is why *help string* encoding is called *dynamic*.

If m=n=2 then, we need to use *fourgram* statistics of English. The full English *fourgram* list contains 27^4=531.441 entries. Since not every *fourgram* occurs in English texts, we only keep a list of the most frequent *fourgrams* (e.g. 24.688 *fourgrams* for the current implementation) [7].

Below, the *encoding* and *decoding* algorithms of the scheme are given:

```
procedure Encode(P,E,n)

repeat
  i=1;  read(nGram_i);                         // nGram_i=P[(2*i-1),(2*i)]
  C_i=E[nGram_i[1],nGram_i[2], ...,nGram_i[n]];    // Issue C_i
  ListIndex=0;  FlagFound=0;  Context='';
  repeat
    if ((Context||nGram_i)=qGramList[ListIndex]) then FlagFound=1;
    else ListIndex++;
  until (FlagFound=1 or EndOfList)
  // D=number of n-grams mapped into the same cipher symbol as C_i
  if (FlagFound=1) then H_i=EncodeWithLogDBits(ListIndex);
  else H_esc=000...0;              // Issue H_esc (escape seq.) of log2⌈D⌉ bits
  ┌   HoldIndex=1;                 // HoldIndex = number of C_is in E
Θ │   for j=1 to |A|^(n-1)         // rows in E
  │       for k=1 to |A|           // columns in E
  └             if E[j,k]=C_i then HoldIndex++; break;
      // R=HoldIndex - number of C_i encoded n-grams following Context
      H_i=EncodeWithLogRBits(HoldIndex);          // Issue H_i
      AppendToList((Context||nGram_i), qGramList);
  Context=nGram_i;  i++;
until EOF
```

```
procedure Decode(C,H,E,n)
repeat
 i=1;  C0='';  Context=C i-1;
 read(Ci);  Hi=read(LogDBitsFromH);
 if (Hi≠0...0) then nGrami=qGramList[Hi]; // within current Context
 else Θ;                              // See procedure Encode()
      Hi=read(LogRBitsFromH);         // Processing escape seq.
      nGrami=E[(Hi + number of Ci encoded n-grams following Context),k];
                                      //where k is the column Ci resides
      AppendToList((Context||nGrami), qGramList);
 i++;
// Issue nGrami to construct P=[nGram1 || nGram2 || ... || nGram|P|/n]
until EOF
```

Decoding needs to be performed *in order*, i.e. to decode the $(i+1)^{th}$ *cipher symbol*, all *cipher symbols* from 1 to *i* must already have been decoded.

The system introduced has been implemented with *n=2* on English text files *bib* and *book1* of the *Calgary Corpus* [8]. For compression performance tests 5 lossless compression algorithms, namely *ARTH*, *HUFF*, *LZ77*, *PPM** and *BWMN* have been used. In section 3, experimental results are presented.

3 Text Compression with Embedded Security Implementation

We first describe and compare various *encryption matrix* (*E*) alternatives. Our algorithm is flexible enough to let any *encryption matrix* to be employed. Different *matrix* layout schemes directly affect the system performance, i.e. the compressibility. *Vigenère Matrix* is one of the layouts that is based on the alphabetical ordering of *cipher symbols* with circular shift on each *E* row. *Encoding* and *decoding formulae* for the *Vigenère* scheme are given below:

$$C_i = (P_i + k_i) \bmod |A| \qquad \text{and} \qquad P_i = (C_i - k_i) \bmod |A|$$

The next *encryption matrix* layout randomly distributes *cipher symbols* throughout the *matrix* with the rule that each *cipher symbol* occurs only once in each row. This is called the *Random* layout. The last scheme (*DiFreq*) exploits the *digram* frequencies of English and assigns '*a*' to the most frequent *n-gram*, '*b*' to the next most frequent *n-gram*, and so on at each row.

Randomly organized *Encryption matrix* is hard-to-break because, it is not easy to determine to which *n-gram* each *cipher symbol* corresponds. On the other hand, *DiFreq* layout highly reflects the source language statistics. Hence, it is considerably easier to recover *DiFreq matrix* than *Random*.

In Table 1, compressibility values (measured in *bpc*) for 5 compression algorithms on pure *plaintext (P)* and *(C||H)* outputs, which are obtained by implementing the new scheme over each of the 3 *Encryption matrix* (*E*) layouts, are compared:

Table 1. Performances of Various *E* Layouts for *n*=2 on sample English Text Files

ENGLISH	ARTH		HUFF		LZ77		PPM*		BWMN	
	bib	book1	bib	book1	bib	book1	bib	book1	bib	book1
P_{bpc}	4,15	4,09	4,15	4,12	3,19	3,73	1,91	2,16	2,16	2,59
Vigenère $(C\|\|H)_{bpc}$	3,77	3,69	4,37	4,30	5,17	5,48	4,05	4,30	3,74	3,97
Random $(C\|\|H)_{bpc}$	3,79	3,69	4,40	4,32	5,21	5,49	4,08	4,32	3,77	3,99
DiFreq $(C\|\|H)_{bpc}$	3,59	3,45	4,27	4,20	5,30	5,60	4,24	4,57	3,88	4,09

According to Table 1, implementing *secondary compression* together with the new scheme yields different performance levels (rows *Vigenère*, *Random*, *DiFreq*) than that of applying the *secondary compression* on pure *plaintext* (row P_{bpc}). The Table indicates that for *ARTH* and *HUFF*, the best *matrix* layout in terms of compressibility is *DiFreq* because it has the lowest *bpc* rates compared to the *Vigenère* and *Random* cases. Only for *ARTH*, our scheme outperforms P_{bpc} under each *E* layouts. To analyze the degree of performance increase, we have plotted the chart on Figure 3:

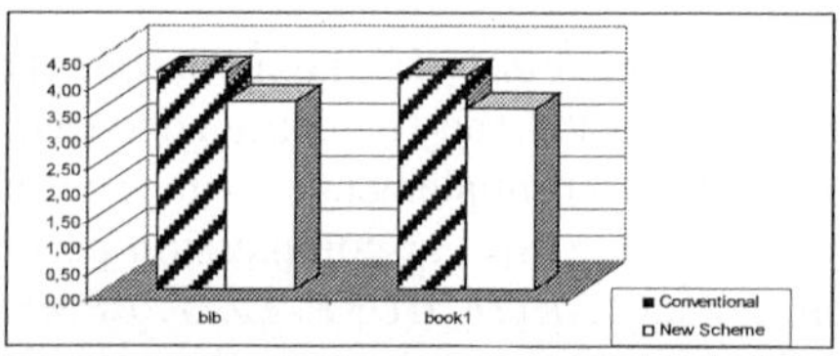

Fig. 3. Comparison of Performances in *bpc*: *Conventional* vs. *New Scheme* (*n*=2, *E*=*DiFreq*)

When we use *ARTH* as the *secondary compression algorithm* in our novel scheme for *E=DiFreq*, then we get better performance (lower *bpc*) than conventionally compressing the pure *plaintext* (*P*) with *ARTH*. The performance improvements obtained for *bib* and *book1* are 13.49% and 15.65%, respectively (Figure 3). This is fairly promising in that, combining the new scheme with some conventional lossless compression algorithms (eg. *ARTH*) may improve their performances.

To decode (*C||H*) properly, *decoder* needs to have the same *q-gram* list as *encoder*. We know that when we start with empty initial *q-gram* statistics, the scheme suffers from intensive "early" *escape* costs. To decide whether empty initial statistics cause performance loss in terms of *bpc* compression quality, we also run the tests for 24.688 *fourgrams*. The effect of statistics list size on *help string* cost can be seen on Table 2:

Table 2. *Help String* Cost Variation with and without Language Statistics

Filename	H_{bpc} non-empty initial stats	H_{bpc} empty initial stats	difference %
bib	3.26	2.79	-14.42%
book1	3.12	2.81	-9.94%

For *Vigenère Matrix* and n=2, when the system begins encoding with empty initial statistics, *help string* cost is lower for both *bib* and *book1* than that of non-empty initial statistics containing 24.688 *fourgrams*. The *help string* cost gains are 14.42% and 9.94% for *bib* and *book1*, respectively. It is encouraging to see that, using empty initial statistics not only removes the burden for extra storage, but also decreases H cost.

3.1 Secret Encoding Matrices

If security is of main concern for the scheme, then it is extremely important to hide the *key*, i.e. *encryption matrix E*, from the third parties who may easily obtain it during transfer. For that, instead of sending the whole *matrix* overtly to the receiver, only a *key* to regenerate it can be transmitted. This can be accomplished by using a *Pseudo Random Number Generator* (*PRNG*), which takes a predetermined *key* as the seed and generates the whole *Encryption matrix.*

A secure *Encryption matrix* has been generated with a *Blum Blum Shub (BBS) PRNG*, which is a *cryptographically secure pseudorandom bit generator* (*CSPRBG*) [9]. Random bit sequences (B_i) are generated by *BBS* according to this algorithm [6]:

```
procedure BBS

n = p × q             //p and q are large primes with p ≡ q ≡ 3 (mod 4)

X0 = s^2 mod n        //gcd(n,s) = 1

for i = 1 to ∞

      Xi = (Xi-1)^2 mod n

      Bi = Xi mod 2
```

Using *Groups, Algorithms and Programming (GAP)* tool [10], we have generated the following large (each having 95-digits) p, q and s values yielding the *Encryption matrix* shown in Table 3, where '~' symbol denotes the space character.

p= 22788303839461363407749945475449823944032500694962619493285588653648957344119657385217197601999
q= 24485798954787150931313025957424808698643887356129012774631994731939390496157936492998354406443
s= 28659613151185466611595221202499928045858311695013368858596111792766033656898923852594183133919

The *Encryption matrix* generated with *BBS* scheme is *cryptographically secure*. Therefore, it is extremely hard to predict the *matrix* without the *key*, i.e. the *BBS* seed.

3.2 Multiple Iterations

Text compression with embedded security scheme is expected to provide stronger security if multiple rounds of encryption is employed. Each round of encryption makes the frequency of *ciphertext* characters more nearly equal than in *plaintext*. Thus, *multiple iterations* cause *plaintext* language characteristics (redundancy) to dissipate better, yielding hard-to-decode *ciphertexts*.

Table 3. Encryption Matrix generated with BBS Pseudo Random Number Generator (PRNG)

	~	a	b	c	d	e	f	g	h	i	j	k	l	m	n	o	p	q	r	s	t	u	v	w	x	y	z
~	c	i	d	k	h	j	g	e	z	v	r	q	n	~	o	u	f	p	s	m	t	w	b	l	a	y	x
a	y	c	i	l	o	g	f	v	j	q	w	s	r	k	t	~	d	m	z	x	e	a	b	u	h	p	n
b	k	y	p	~	e	m	l	x	u	j	b	d	v	s	g	z	h	i	a	c	f	o	n	r	w	t	q
c	x	z	b	f	u	o	i	l	m	w	a	v	y	d	~	e	c	h	k	s	t	r	g	j	p	n	q
d	q	z	f	i	h	y	o	m	t	n	p	l	r	x	d	a	e	s	g	c	u	k	j	w	v	b	~
e	e	f	d	n	j	m	w	i	v	s	p	b	y	a	r	t	l	k	h	q	~	o	c	g	x	u	z
f	p	j	v	k	h	r	n	z	f	w	s	u	x	m	a	d	l	g	t	b	~	o	y	q	c	e	i
g	k	x	u	d	z	i	q	l	o	e	s	j	y	t	h	~	a	c	m	n	v	f	w	g	p	b	r
h	g	v	m	f	z	q	i	w	~	j	b	p	c	u	y	d	l	n	k	h	r	t	a	x	s	o	e
i	i	f	~	b	z	v	d	k	r	l	e	p	h	t	j	g	m	a	o	u	c	w	n	y	q	x	s
j	g	b	u	w	k	o	x	s	r	m	n	f	q	v	y	t	h	~	z	c	a	e	p	j	i	d	l
k	j	q	k	c	b	i	m	o	r	y	e	d	v	w	x	s	h	t	u	g	a	l	f	p	~	z	n
l	c	z	y	f	h	o	n	w	u	~	s	j	e	v	m	a	d	i	p	g	x	t	k	q	l	b	r
m	p	o	h	r	y	k	z	m	i	b	f	d	x	w	j	l	v	~	q	e	n	u	s	g	a	c	t
n	~	s	v	e	m	l	u	w	t	z	a	j	k	p	d	c	g	x	r	h	b	y	o	f	n	i	q
o	m	o	i	k	d	r	w	y	u	v	t	a	l	~	z	p	f	s	n	g	c	h	e	b	q	j	x
p	e	y	r	j	~	a	l	d	b	c	g	t	u	f	q	n	w	o	p	x	m	i	k	s	z	v	h
q	b	h	q	s	f	p	k	r	n	g	a	d	~	v	y	z	u	i	l	w	o	m	x	e	j	c	t
r	q	l	g	h	o	p	t	k	a	z	v	b	d	s	c	j	u	i	f	y	n	r	x	m	~	e	w
s	i	u	k	d	b	j	v	m	y	a	e	r	~	s	x	c	g	w	l	n	p	f	q	o	t	h	z
t	q	o	b	j	i	p	s	l	z	d	x	c	n	m	t	~	g	v	h	a	f	r	w	e	k	y	u
u	c	a	i	z	x	h	m	n	w	v	o	b	f	k	p	~	y	j	s	q	r	u	l	g	d	t	e
v	r	~	p	c	x	j	h	n	v	f	q	w	y	b	t	z	g	i	u	k	a	d	m	l	o	e	s
w	q	u	i	~	x	o	f	p	k	n	g	m	w	z	c	a	h	l	t	y	b	v	r	e	s	j	d
x	a	t	i	k	l	~	y	o	x	m	j	n	s	w	q	h	r	f	p	z	g	d	e	c	v	u	b
y	i	c	f	t	x	w	m	o	s	r	p	b	q	u	g	a	k	n	e	d	h	v	~	j	l	z	y
z	p	d	j	y	r	b	m	n	t	s	u	v	o	i	c	k	a	w	h	e	z	x	f	g	q	l	~

If iteration refers to the number of times the *plaintext* is passed through the *encryption matrix*, and C_i is the *ciphertext* and H_i is the *help string* for iteration i then:

Iteration #1: $P_1=C_1+H_1$

Iteration #2: $C_1=C_2+H_2 \Rightarrow$ $P_1=C_2+H_2+H_1$ ....

Iteration #8: $C_7=C_8+H_8 \Rightarrow$ $P_1=C_8+H_8+H_7+H_6+H_5+H_4+H_3+H_2+H_1$

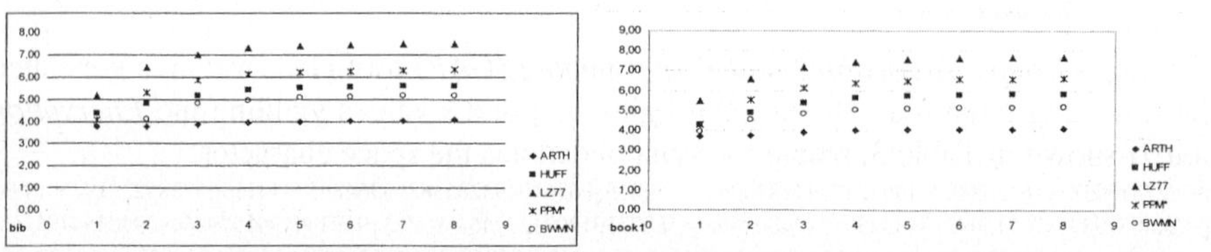

Fig. 4. Multiple iteration *bpc* values for *Vigenère Encryption Matrix* with n=2 on sample text files (with empty initial statistics)

Figure 4 displays the *bpc* rates for *(C||H)* on each of the 8 iteration steps. *Bpc* values here reveal that passing *plaintext* through *Encryption Matrix* (*E*) iteratively causes overall *bpc* values to rise. It means that, multiple iterations do improve the security of our scheme. In Figure 4, *bpc* levels of 5 lossless compression algorithms are ordered, although with slight variations, as *ARTH*, *BWMN*, *HUFF*, *PPM** and *LZ77* from lowest to the highest for each iteration.

Multiple iteration method behaves similarly on *Random* and *DiFreq* layouts: *bpc* increases at each iteration step, although *bpc* levels are different. Because various *matrix* layouts yield different *ciphertexts* that are compressible to varying degrees.

4 Conclusion

We have presented a novel security embedded lossless text compression algorithm to meet the fundamental needs of communication environments today: security and better utilization of the transmission channel. The idea is explained in detail and experimental results are presented. While implementing the algorithm, various *key*, i.e. *matrix* layouts have been employed.

Further work is ongoing in two directions: One is to apply the introduced scheme for $n>2$ values and the other is to implement the algorithm on different source languages. A preliminary work is already being carried out for Turkish texts.

References

1. Witten I., Moffat A., Bell T.C.: Managing Gigabytes, San Fransisco (1999)
2. Nelson M.: The Data Compression Book, M&T Publishing, NewYork (1996)
3. Nelson M.:Arith. Coding+Stat. Modeling=Data Comp., Dr. Dobb's Journal (1991)
4. Teahan W. J.: Modelling English Text, PhD Thesis, Univ. of Waikato, NZ (1998)
5. Burrows M.,Wheeler D.J.:A Block-Sorting Lossless Comp. Alg., SRC, USA(1994)
6. Stallings W.: Cryptography and Network Security, Prentice Hall, NJ (1999)
7. Dalkilic, G.: Statistical Properties of Contemporary Turkish and a Text Compression Application., MSc.Thesis. (In Turkish), Ege Univ., Turkey (2001)
8. Calgary Corpus URL: ftp.cpcs.ucalgary.ca/pub/projects/text.compression.corpus
9. Menezes A., van Oorschot P., Vanstone S.:Handbook of Crypto. CRC Press (1997)
10. GAP Manual, http://www.gap-system.org

An Alternative Compressed Storage Format for Sparse Matrices

Anand Ekambaram and Eurípides Montagne

School of Electrical Engineering and Computer Science
University of Central Florida
Orlando, FL 32816
{ekambara,eurip}@cs.ucf.edu

Abstract. The handling of the sparse matrix vector product(SMVP) is a common kernel in many scientific applications. This kernel is an irregular problem, which has led to the development of several compressed storage formats such as CRS, CCS, and JDS among others. We propose an alternative storage format, the Transpose Jagged Diagonal Storage(TJDS), which is inspired from the Jagged Diagonal Storage format and makes no assumptions about the sparsity pattern of the matrix. We present a selection of sparse matrices and compare the storage requirements needed using JDS and TJDS formats, and we show that the TDJS format needs less storage space than the JDS format because the permutation array is not required. Another advantage of the proposed format is that although TJDS also suffers the drawback of indirect addressing, it does not need the permutation step after the computation of the SMVP.

1 Introduction

The irregular nature of sparse matrix-vector multiplication, $Ax = y$, has led to the development of a variety of compressed storage formats, which are widely used because although these formats suffer the drawback of indirect addressing, they have the advantage that they do not store any unnecessary elements [1], [4], [5]. The main idea considered in compressed storage formats is to avoid the handling and storage of zero values. This is accomplished by means of the storage of the non-zero elements of the sparse matrix in a contiguous way using a linear array. However, some additional arrays are needed for knowing where the non-zero elements fit into the sparse matrix. The number of subsidiary arrays varies depending on the storage format used. Research into sparse matrix reorganization has dealt with developing various static storage reduction schemes such as Compressed Row Storage(CRS), Compressed Column Storage(CCS), and Jagged Diagonal Storage(JDS). One of these methods, the Jagged Diagonal Storage format(JDS) is, in addition, considered very convenient for the implementation of iterative methods on parallel and vector processors [3], [5]. In this work we present the Transpose Jagged Diagonal Storage format(TJDS), which is inspired from the Jagged Diagonal Storage format. The performance of both

A. Yazici and C. Şener (Eds.): ISCIS 2003, LNCS 2869, pp. 196–203, 2003.

algorithms is similar in terms of the memory access pattern, four load operations and one store operation to compute each partial result. However, TJDS does not need a permutation array nor does it need a permutation step to compute the matrix vector product, $Ax = y$.

In Sect. 2 we describe how departing from the CRS and CCS formats we obtain the compressed matrices, A_{jds} and A_{tjds}, using the JDS format and the TJDS format respectively. In Sect. 3 we show a comparison of the memory space required for a set of matrices using each storage format. Also we give the execution times for the matrix-vector product using the JDS and TJDS algorithms. Finally, in Sect. 4 we present our conclusions.

2 Storage Requirements for the JDS and TJDS Formats

When a sparse matrix A is compressed using the Jagged Diagonal Storage format, all the non-zero elements(nze) in each row are shifted to the left and this way we obtain the matrix A_{crs}, a compressed row version of matrix A. Then we reorder the rows of the matrix A_{crs} in decreasing number of non-zero elements from top to bottom, in order to create a A_{jds} matrix, which is the jagged diagonal version of A_{crs}. As follows, we present the three steps required to transform a matrix A into is JDS version A_{jds}.

Step 1: The matrix vector product $Ax = y$ is expressed in matrix form as follows:

$$\begin{bmatrix} a_{11} & a_{12} & 0 & a_{14} & 0 & 0 \\ 0 & a_{22} & a_{23} & 0 & a_{25} & 0 \\ a_{31} & 0 & a_{33} & a_{34} & 0 & 0 \\ 0 & a_{42} & 0 & a_{44} & a_{45} & a_{46} \\ 0 & 0 & 0 & 0 & a_{55} & a_{56} \\ 0 & 0 & 0 & 0 & a_{65} & a_{66} \end{bmatrix} \begin{bmatrix} x_1 \\ x_2 \\ x_3 \\ x_4 \\ x_5 \\ x_6 \end{bmatrix} = \begin{bmatrix} y_1 \\ y_2 \\ y_3 \\ y_4 \\ y_5 \\ y_6 \end{bmatrix}$$

Step 2: By applying the CRS scheme to the sparse matrix A we obtain the matrix A_{crs}, while the vectors x and y remain the same.

$$A_{crs} = \begin{bmatrix} a_{11} & a_{12} & a_{14} & 0 & 0 & 0 \\ a_{22} & a_{23} & a_{25} & 0 & 0 & 0 \\ a_{31} & a_{33} & a_{34} & 0 & 0 & 0 \\ a_{42} & a_{44} & a_{45} & a_{46} & 0 & 0 \\ a_{55} & a_{56} & 0 & 0 & 0 & 0 \\ a_{65} & a_{66} & 0 & 0 & 0 & 0 \end{bmatrix} \quad x = \begin{bmatrix} x_1 \\ x_2 \\ x_3 \\ x_4 \\ x_5 \\ x_6 \end{bmatrix} \quad y = \begin{bmatrix} y_1 \\ y_2 \\ y_3 \\ y_4 \\ y_5 \\ y_6 \end{bmatrix}$$

Step 3: We obtain A_{jds} a Jagged Diagonal Storage version from A_{crs} by reordering the rows of A_{crs} in decreasing order from top to bottom according to the number of nonzero elements per row. It can be seen that the rows one and four of the matrix A_{crs} were permuted as shown below.

$$A_{jds} = \begin{bmatrix} a_{42} & a_{44} & a_{45} & a_{46} & 0 & 0 \\ a_{11} & a_{12} & a_{14} & 0 & 0 & 0 \\ a_{22} & a_{23} & a_{25} & 0 & 0 & 0 \\ a_{31} & a_{33} & a_{34} & 0 & 0 & 0 \\ a_{55} & a_{56} & 0 & 0 & 0 & 0 \\ a_{65} & a_{66} & 0 & 0 & 0 & 0 \end{bmatrix} \quad x = \begin{bmatrix} x_1 \\ x_2 \\ x_3 \\ x_4 \\ x_5 \\ x_6 \end{bmatrix} \quad y = \begin{bmatrix} y_1 \\ y_2 \\ y_3 \\ y_4 \\ y_5 \\ y_6 \end{bmatrix}$$

We now store the A_{jds} as a single dimension array. The nonzero elements of the A_{jds} matrix are stored in a floating-point linear array *value_list*, one column after another. Each one of these columns is called a jagged diagonal and we use a semi-colon(;) in the array *value_list* to separate them. The length of the array *value_list* is equal to the number of non-zeros elements in A_{jds}. We also need another array *column_indexes* to store the column indices of the non-zero elements. Since the rows have been permuted to obtain a different matrix, A_{jds}, from the original matrix A, we need an array *perm_vector* to permute the resulting vector back to the original ordering. Obviously the size of this array is n for an n-dimensional matrix. A fourth array is also needed, *start_positions*, which stores the starting position of the jagged diagonals in the array *value_list*. The length of this array is the number of elements in the row of A having the maximum number of non-zero elements plus one. The last element of this array is used to control the inner *for* loop of the algorithm shown below. The data structures required to compute $Ax = y$ using JDS are shown below:

value_list	a_{42}	a_{11}	a_{22}	a_{31}	a_{55}	$a_{65};$	a_{44}	a_{12}	a_{23}	a_{33}	a_{56}	$a_{66};$	a_{45}	a_{14}	a_{25}	$a_{34};$	a_{46}

column_indexes	2	1	2	1	5	5;	4	2	3	3	6	6;	5	4	5	4;	6

start_positions	1	7	13	17	18

perm_vector	4	2	3	1	5	6

X	x_1	x_2	x_3	x_4	x_5	x_6

Y	y_1	y_2	y_3	y_4	y_5	y_6

The sequential algorithm to perform the matrix-vector product $Ax = y$ using the JDS format is shown below. In this algorithm, *num_jdiag* stands for the number of jagged diagonals:

```
disp := 0
for i ← 1 to num_jdiag
    for j ← 1 to (start_position[i+1] - start_position[i] - 1)
        Y[j] := Y[j] + value_list[disp] × X[column_indexes[disp]]
        disp := disp + 1
    endfor
endfor
```

The performance of this algorithm is clearly determined by the number of memory accesses which are four load operations and one store operation to compute each partial result. In addition, we need to perform the permutation of the resulting vector back to the original ordering using an algorithm similar to the one shown below:

for $i \leftarrow 1$ to N
  $Temp[perm\_vector[i]] := Y[i]$
for $i \leftarrow 1$ to N
  $Y[i] := Temp[i]$

Another popular format for storing sparse matrices is the Compressed Column Storage(CCS) format or Harwell-Boeing sparse matrix format. In this storage format a matrix A is compressed along the columns by shifting all the non-zero elements(nze) upwards. By applying the CCS to the sparse matrix A we obtain the A_{ccs} matrix, while the vectors x and y remain the same, as shown below:

$$A_{ccs} = \begin{bmatrix} a_{11} & a_{12} & a_{23} & a_{14} & a_{25} & a_{46} \\ a_{31} & a_{22} & a_{33} & a_{34} & a_{45} & a_{56} \\ 0 & a_{42} & 0 & a_{44} & a_{55} & a_{66} \\ 0 & 0 & 0 & 0 & a_{65} & 0 \\ 0 & 0 & 0 & 0 & 0 & 0 \\ 0 & 0 & 0 & 0 & 0 & 0 \end{bmatrix} \quad x = \begin{bmatrix} x_1 \\ x_2 \\ x_3 \\ x_4 \\ x_5 \\ x_6 \end{bmatrix} \quad y = \begin{bmatrix} y_1 \\ y_2 \\ y_3 \\ y_4 \\ y_5 \\ y_6 \end{bmatrix}$$

The Transpose Jagged Diagonal Storage(TJDS) scheme is obtained from the CCS format by reordering the columns of A_{ccs}, from left to right, in decreasing order of the number of non-zero elements per column and reordering the elements of the vector x accordingly as if it were an additional row of A. This new arrangement, A_{tjds}, is presented as follows:

$$A_{tjds} = \begin{bmatrix} a_{25} & a_{12} & a_{14} & a_{46} & a_{11} & a_{23} \\ a_{45} & a_{22} & a_{34} & a_{56} & a_{31} & a_{33} \\ a_{55} & a_{42} & a_{44} & a_{66} & 0 & 0 \\ a_{65} & 0 & 0 & 0 & 0 & 0 \\ 0 & 0 & 0 & 0 & 0 & 0 \\ 0 & 0 & 0 & 0 & 0 & 0 \end{bmatrix} \quad x = \begin{bmatrix} x_5 \\ x_2 \\ x_4 \\ x_6 \\ x_1 \\ x_3 \end{bmatrix} \quad y = \begin{bmatrix} y_1 \\ y_2 \\ y_3 \\ y_4 \\ y_5 \\ y_6 \end{bmatrix}$$

To obtain the corresponding arrays, $value\_list$, $row\_indexes$, and $start\_position$ we proceed as follows. The nonzero elements of the compressed ordered matrix A_{tjds} are stored in a floating point linear array $value\_list$, one row after another. Each of these rows is called a transpose jagged diagonal(tjd). Another array of the same length of $value\_list$ is used to store the row indexes of the non-zero elements in the original matrix A. This new array that we denote, $row\_indexes$, is of type integer. Finally, a third array called $start\_position$ stores the starting position of each tjd stored in the array $value\_list$. These arrays are shown below:

value_list	a_{25}	a_{12}	a_{14}	a_{46}	a_{11}	$a_{23};$	a_{45}	a_{22}	a_{34}	a_{56}	a_{31}	$a_{33};$	a_{55}	a_{42}	a_{44}	$a_{66};$	a_{65}

row_indexes	2	1	1	4	1	2;	4	2	3	5	3	3;	5	4	4	6;	6

start_position	1	7	13	17	18

X	x_5	x_2	x_4	x_6	x_1	x_3

Y	y_1	y_2	y_3	y_4	y_5	y_6

In the above data structures, each transpose jagged diagonal is separated by a semi-colon(;) in the array *value_list*. The sequential algorithm to perform the matrix-vector product $Ax = y$ using the TJDS format is shown below. In this algorithm, *num_tjdiag* stands for the number of transpose jagged diagonals:

```
for i ← 1 to num_tjdiag
    k := 1
    for j ← start_position[i] to start_position[i + 1] − 1
        p := row_indexes[k]
        Y[p] := Y[p] + value_list[j] × X[k]
        k := k + 1
    endfor
endfor
```

3 Evaluation of Memory Requirements and Execution Times

We present a selection of sparse matrices from the Matrix-Market collection [2] to evaluate the storage requirements of TJDS compared to JDS. For each matrix we present its name, dimension, N_{nze}, the longest N_{nze} per column and the longest N_{nze} per row as shown in Table. 1 and Table. 2.

We see that, to store the non-zero elements that constitutes the actual data, we also need subsidiary data, which varies for each storage scheme. This subsidiary data includes storing of row/column indices(JDS, TJDS), the permutation vector(JDS), and the number of jagged diagonals(JDS, TJDS). As you can see in the case of JDS, we need an array of size N to store the original permutation. However, TJDS eliminates the need for this array of size N. The subsidiary storage requirements for the JDS, and TJDS formats are calculated using the following equations respectively:

$$STORAGE_{jds} = (N_{nze} \times 1) + N + N_{jd}. \quad (1)$$

$$STORAGE_{tjds} = (N_{nze} \times 1) + N_{tjd}. \quad (2)$$

Where,
N_{nze} denotes the number of non-zero elements of matrix A.

Table 1. Selection of small sparse matrices from Matrix Market.

	Matrix	Dimension	N_{nze}	Longest N_{nzec}	Longest N_{nzer}
1	CRY2500	2500 x 2500	12349	6	5
2	GEMAT11	4929 x 4929	33185	28	27
3	LNS3937	3937 x 3937	25407	13	11
4	SHERMAN5	3312 x 3312	20793	17	21
5	BCSPWR10	5300 x 5300	13571	14	14
6	DW8192	8192 x 8192	41746	8	8
7	DWT_2680	2680 x 2680	13853	19	19
8	LSHP3466	3466 x 3466	13681	7	7
9	BCSSTM25	15439 x 15439	15439	1	1

Table 2. Selection of large sparse matrices from Matrix Market.

	Matrix	Dimension	N_{nze}	Longest N_{nzec}	Longest N_{nzer}
1	CRY10000	10000 x 10000	49699	6	5
2	BCSSTK18	11948 x 11948	80519	49	49
3	BCSSTK25	15439 x 15439	133840	59	59
4	MEMPLUS	17758 x 17758	126150	353	353

$(N_{nze} \times 1)$ gives the storage required to store the array indices of the non-zero elements.
N denotes the number of rows and M denotes the number of columns. Since we are considering square matrices, $N = M$. In the case of JDS, N stands for the length of the *perm_vector*.
N_{jd} denotes the number of jagged diagonals.
N_{tjd} denotes the number of transpose jagged diagonals.

In Fig. 1 we show the subsidiary storage required for the selected matrices using the two storage formats. On the other hand, it is worthwhile mentioning that the number of jagged diagonals in any sparse matrix is equal to the maximum number of non-zero elements per row. Likewise, in the case of the TJDS format the number of transpose jagged diagonals is equal to the maximum number of non-zero elements per column. Hence, for symmetric matrices we have $N_{jd} = N_{tjd} = longest\_N_{nzpr} \leq N$.

When we compare TJDS with other widely used storage formats such as Compressed Row Storage(CRS) and Compressed Column Storage(CCS)[6], we still have a substantial subsidiary storage that is saved. These two storage formats need to store the starting positions of either the rows or the columns which is of size N or M. For square matrices, we will have that N equals M and N_{tjd} is generally much smaller than N or M. For example, in the case of the matrix MEMPLUS in Table. 2, $N = M = 17,758$ and $N_{tjd} = 353$.

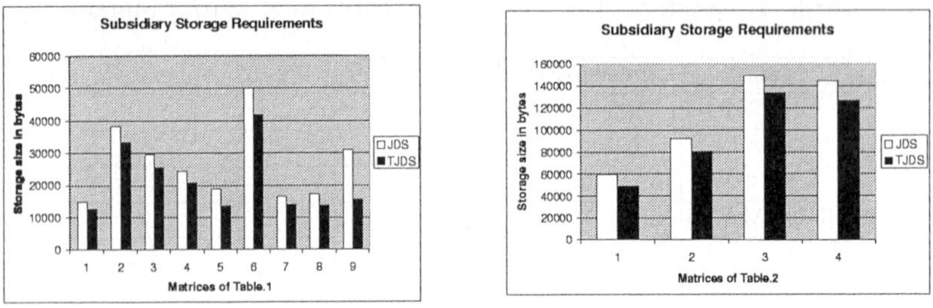

Fig. 1. Subsidiary storage requirements using the JDS and TJDS formats.

The matrix-vector product algorithm for JDS and TJDS are similar in the sense that they both have four load operations and one store operation to compute each partial result. But we see that TJDS outperforms JDS because the permutation step needed in the JDS algorithm is not required for the TJDS algorithm. Fig. 2 gives the execution time for the matrix-vector product using the JDS and TJDS algorithms. The JDS algorithm and TJDS algorithm have been executed sequentially on a AMD T-Bird 900MHz processor with 256MB RAM. The matrix-vector product was executed 1000 times to obtain the timing results.

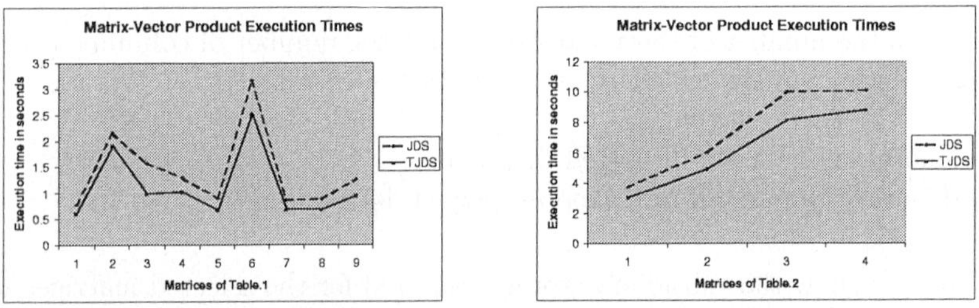

Fig. 2. Matrix-Vector product execution time using the JDS and TJDS algorithms.

4 Conclusions

We have presented a solution to the sparse matrix vector product problem using TJDS, an alternative storage format that requires less storage space than the JDS format. We have also shown that TJDS does not need the permutation vector required by JDS to permute the resulting vector back to the original ordering nor does it need the permutation step to compute the sparse matrix vector product. This new format is suitable for parallel and distributed processing because the data partition scheme inherent to the data structures keeps the locality of reference on the non-zero values of the matrix and the elements of the x array. Currently a parallel implementation of the SMVP using the TJDS format is under way.

Acknowledgements. We would like to thank the anonymous referees for their valuable comments and suggestions to improve the presentation of this paper.

References

1. J. Dongarra, *Sparse Matrix Storage Formats*, In Zhaojun Bai et al, Eds., Templates for the Solution of Algebraic Eigenvalue Problems: A Practical Guide, SIAM, Philadelphia, 2000. Electronic version available at: http://www.cs.utk.edu/˜dongarra/etemplates/node372.html.
2. Matrix Market, the electronic version is available at the following URL: http://math.nist.gov/MatrixMarket/.
3. Y. Saad,*Krylov Subspace methods on Supercomputers*, Siam J. Sci. Stat. Comp., vol 10(6), pp. 1200–1232, 1989.
4. Y. Saad, *SPARSKIT : A basic tool kit for sparse matrix computations Report RIACS-90-20*, Research Institute for Advanced Computer Science, NASA Ames Research Center, Moffet Field, CA, 1990.
5. Y. Saad, *Iterative Methods for Sparse Linear Systems*, PWS publishing company, ITP, Boston, MA, 1996.
6. E. Montagne and A. Ekambaram, *An Optimal Storage Format for Sparse Matrices*, Dec. 2002(submitted for publication).

Ranking the Possible Alternatives in Flexible Querying: An Extended Possibilistic Approach

Guy de Tré, Tom Matthé, Koen Tourné, and Bert Callens

Computer Science Laboratory, Department of Telecommunications and Information Processing, Ghent University, Sint-Pietersnieuwstraat 41, B-9000 Gent, Belgium
Guy.DeTre@telin.ugent.be

Abstract. An important facet of flexible querying and information retrieval is the ranking of the possible alternatives in the result. Adequate ranking information simplifies decision making and helps the user in finding faster the requested information. This paper deals with the construction of ranking methods, which are based on the use of extended possibilistic truth values. Extended possibilistic truth values are a flexible means to model query satisfaction, which additionally allow to deal with cases where some of the imposed query criteria are not applicable. Three alternative ranking approaches are presented and compared with each other based on their applicability in flexible database querying.

Keywords: Flexible database querying, extended possibilistic truth values, ranking functions.

1 Introduction

With the incorporation of more flexibility in database querying and information retrieval, query satisfaction is no longer a matter of bivalence, but becomes a matter of degree. The 'degrees' to which a record in the database satisfies the criteria imposed by a given query, determine to which extent the instance belongs to the result of the query. Providing an adequate ranking method for the possible alternatives in the result of a query is important, since it simplifies and fastens the retrieval by associating an indication of relative importance. An adequate ranking method is also necessary for a satisfactory representation of the results of a flexible database query.

The current state of the art in the modelling of flexible query satisfaction can be summarized in three approaches. The first approach is to associate a fuzzy grade of membership with each record in the result. This grade may be interpreted as a degree of satisfaction or as a degree of confidence [1]. Such an approach is taken, for instance, by Baldwin and Zhou [2]. The second approach is to associate a so-called possibilistic truth value with each record. This approach is taken, for instance, by de Tré et al. [3] and has been extended by using so-called extended possibilistic truth values, which additionally allow to deal with cases where some of the imposed query criteria are not applicable [4]. The third approach is based on the use of a $[0,1]$-valued possibility measure (and an

A. Yazici and C. Şener (Eds.): ISCIS 2003, LNCS 2869, pp. 204–211, 2003.

associated necessity measure) [5,6] in order to represent (un)certainty about the satisfaction of the querying criteria for a given record. This approach is taken, e.g., by Prade and Testemale [7], by Bosc et al. [8], by Yazici et al. [9,10], and by Bordogna et al. [11].

In this paper the ranking problem in the approach with extended possibilistic truth values is discussed and handled. In Section 2, the basic definitions and properties of extended possibilistic truth values (EPTV's) are summarized. In general an EPTV has three components, which respectively denote the possibility that an instance belongs to the result of a query, the possibility that an instance does not belong to the result of a query and the possibility that (some of) the query criteria do not apply for the instance. It is the third component which makes the ranking problem of EPTV's non-trivial. This problem and the impossibility to define a natural ordering on the universe of EPTV's are described in Section 3. In Section 4, three approximate ranking alternatives for EPTV's are introduced: in the first alternative the ranking function is approximated by a 'weighted sum' of Eucledian distances. In the second alternative a more simple analytical ranking function is used, whereas the idea behind the third alternative is to minimize the impact of the third component of an EPTV on the ranking. The presented ranking approaches are summarized and compared with each other on the basis of their practical applicability in flexible database querying in Section 5. Finally, some conclusions are given in Section 6.

2 Extended Possibilistic Truth Values

The concept 'extended possibilistic truth value' (EPTV) is defined as an extension of the concept 'possibilistic truth value' (PTV) which was originally introduced by Prade in [12]. Possibilistic truth values provide an epistemological representation of the truth of a proposition, which allows to reflect our knowledge about the actual truth. Their semantics is defined in terms of a possibility distribution.

Definition 1 (Possibilistic Truth Value). *With the understanding that P represents the universe of all propositions and $\tilde{\wp}(I)$ denotes the set of all ordinary fuzzy sets that can be defined over the Boolean set $I = \{T, F\}$ of truth values (where T represents 'True' and F represents 'False'), the so-called possibilistic truth value $\tilde{t}(p)$ of a proposition $p \in P$ is formally defined by means of a mapping*

$$\tilde{t} : P \rightarrow \tilde{\wp}(I)$$

which associates with each $p \in P$ a fuzzy set $\tilde{t}(p)$. The semantics of the associated fuzzy set $\tilde{t}(p)$ is defined in terms of a possibility distribution. With the understanding that

$$t : P \rightarrow I$$

is the mapping function which associates the value T with p if p is true and associates the value F with p otherwise, this means that

$$(\forall\, x \in I)(\Pi_{t(p)}(x) = \mu_{\tilde{t}(p)}(x)), \text{ i.e. } (\forall\, p \in P)(\Pi_{t(p)} = \tilde{t}(p))$$

where $\Pi_{t(p)}(x)$ *denotes the possibility that the value of* $t(p)$ *conforms to* x *and* $\mu_{\tilde{t}(p)}(x)$ *is the membership grade of* x *within the fuzzy set* $\tilde{t}(p)$.

The truth value of a proposition can be unknown. This is the case if some data in the proposition exist but are not available. For example, the truth value of the proposition "*the price of car A is 20.000*" is unknown if car A is for sale, but no information about its price is given. An unknown truth value is modelled by the possibility distribution $\{(T,1),(F,1)\}$, which denotes that it is completely possible that the proposition is true (T), but it is also completely possible that the proposition is false (F).

For the definition of an extended possibilistic truth value, an extra element $\bot$, which represents an undefined truth value, is added to the Boolean set I [13]. The addition of the element $\bot$ is inspired by the assumption that the truth value of a proposition can be undefined. This is for example the case if the proposition can not be evaluated due to the non-applicability of (some of) its elements. For example, the truth value of the same proposition "*the price of car B is 20.000*" is considered to be undefined if it is known for sure that car B is not for sale, in which case it does not make sense to ask for its price (in the supposition that price information is not applicable to cars that are not for sale).

Definition 2 (Extended Possibilistic Truth Value). *With the understanding that* P *represents the universe of all propositions and* $\tilde{\wp}(I^*)$ *denotes the set of all ordinary fuzzy sets that can be defined over the universal set* $I^* = \{T, F, \bot\}$, *the so-called extended possibilistic truth value* $\tilde{t}^*(p)$ *of a proposition* $p \in P$ *is formally defined by means of a mapping*

$$\tilde{t}^* : P \to \tilde{\wp}(I^*)$$

which associates with each $p \in P$ *a fuzzy set* $\tilde{t}^*(p)$. *The semantics of the associated fuzzy set* $\tilde{t}^*(p)$ *is defined in terms of a possibility distribution. With the understanding that*

$$t^* : P \to I^*$$

is the mapping function which associates the value T *with* p *if* p *is true, associates the value* F *with* p *if* p *is false and associates the value* $\bot$ *with* p *if (some of) the elements of* p *are not applicable, undefined or not supplied, this means that*

$$(\forall\, x \in I^*)(\Pi_{t^*(p)}(x) = \mu_{\tilde{t}^*(p)}(x)),\ i.e.\ (\forall\, p \in P)(\Pi_{t^*(p)} = \tilde{t}^*(p))$$

where $\Pi_{t^*(p)}(x)$ *denotes the possibility that the value of* $t^*(p)$ *conforms to* x *and* $\mu_{\tilde{t}^*(p)}(x)$ *is the membership grade of* x *within the fuzzy set* $\tilde{t}^*(p)$.

EPTV's are not necessarily assumed to be normalized. For practical applications putting a normalization restriction on EPTV's makes sense. This however excludes the existence of other truth values than T, F and $\bot$, which is rather a philosophical matter.

Special cases are:

$\tilde{t}^*(p)$	interpretation
$\{(T,1)\}$	p is true
$\{(F,1)\}$	p is false
$\{(T,1),(F,1)\}$	p is unknown
$\{(\bot,1)\}$	p is undefined
$\{(T,1),(F,1),(\bot,1)\}$	p is unknown or undefined

New propositions can be constructed from existing propositions, using so-called logical operators. An unary operator '$\tilde{\neg}$' is provided for the negation of a proposition and binary operators '$\tilde{\wedge}$', '$\tilde{\vee}$', '$\tilde{\Rightarrow}$' and '$\tilde{\Leftrightarrow}$' are respectively provided for the conjunction, disjunction, implication and equivalence of propositions. The arithmetic rules to calculate the EPTV of a composite proposition and the algebraic properties of extended possibilistic truth values are presented in [13].

As illustrated in [4], EPTV's can be used to express query satisfaction in flexible database querying: the EPTV representing the extent to which a given record satisfies a flexible query can be obtained by aggregating the calculated EPTV's that denote the extents to which the instance satisfies the different criteria imposed by the query [14].

3 The Problem of Ranking EPTV's

It turns out that the algebraic structure $(\tilde{\wp}(I^*), \tilde{\wedge}, \tilde{\vee}, \tilde{\neg})$ is not a lattice [13]. This is due to the semantics of the extra truth value $\bot$, which has been interpreted as representing the "undefined" cases. As a consequence, there does not exist a natural ordering relation for this structure. Nevertheless, an adequate ordering function is needed, in order to obtain an efficient representation of the results of a flexible query.

With the understanding that $\tilde{t}_1 = \{(T, \mu_{\tilde{t}_1}(T)), (F, \mu_{\tilde{t}_1}(F)), (\bot, \mu_{\tilde{t}_1}(\bot))\}$ and $\tilde{t}_2 = \{(T, \mu_{\tilde{t}_2}(T)), (F, \mu_{\tilde{t}_2}(F)), (\bot, \mu_{\tilde{t}_2}(\bot))\}$ are two EPTV's, a partial ordering '$\geq$' can e.g. be defined by

$$\tilde{t}_1 \geq \tilde{t}_2 \Leftrightarrow (\mu_{\tilde{t}_1}(T) \geq \mu_{\tilde{t}_2}(T)) \wedge (\mu_{\tilde{t}_1}(F) \leq \mu_{\tilde{t}_2}(F)) \wedge (\mu_{\tilde{t}_1}(\bot) \leq \mu_{\tilde{t}_2}(\bot))$$

However, such a partial ordering function is less adequate for practical purposes since only a limited number of EPTV-pairs can be compared.

4 Three Alternative Ranking Methods for EPTV's

In this section three approximate ranking alternatives for EPTV's are presented. In the first alternative, the ranking function is approximated by a 'weighted sum' of Eucledian distances (Subsection 4.1). In the second alternative, an extension of the analytical ranking function for PTV's [15] is used (Subsection 4.2). The third alternative is based on the minimization of the impact of the $\bot$-component of an EPTV on the ranking (Subsection 4.3).

4.1 'Weighted Sum' Approach

In order to have an idea of the relative importance of EPTV's, the ranking function

$$r_w : \tilde{\wp}(I^*) \to [0,1]$$

has been introduced and obtained by considering the 3D-universe of EPTV's and by associating a 'weight' w_i, $i = 1, 2, \ldots, 7$ with the relevant angular points $\tilde{t}_1 = \{(T,1)\}$, $\tilde{t}_2 = \{(T,1),(\perp,1)\}$, $\tilde{t}_3 = \{(T,1),(F,1)\}$, $\tilde{t}_4 = \{(T,1),(F,1),(\perp,1)\}$, $\tilde{t}_5 = \{(\perp,1)\}$, $\tilde{t}_6 = \{(F,1),(\perp,1)\}$ and $\tilde{t}_7 = \{(F,1)\}$ of the cube (the origin is excluded since it does not represent a valid truth value) [14].

For a given EPTV $\tilde{t} = \{(T,\mu_T),(F,\mu_F),(\perp,\mu_\perp)\}$, the ranking value $r_w(\tilde{t})$ is defined as the 'weighted' sum of the Euclidian distances $d(\tilde{t},\tilde{t}_i)$, $i = 1, 2, \ldots, 7$, i.e.

$$r_w(\tilde{t}) = \sum_{i=1}^{7} w_i \, d(\tilde{t},\tilde{t}_i)$$

In order to calculate the 'weights' w_i, $i = 1, 2, \ldots, 7$ the following ordering is considered:

$$\{(T,1)\} > \{(T,1),(\perp,1)\} > \{(T,1),(F,1)\} > \{(T,1),(F,1),(\perp,1)\} > \{(\perp,1)\} > \{(F,1),(\perp,1)\} > \{(F,1)\}$$

i.e.

$$\tilde{t}_1 > \tilde{t}_2 > \tilde{t}_3 > \tilde{t}_4 > \tilde{t}_5 > \tilde{t}_6 > \tilde{t}_7$$

This ordering can be justified with the initial ordering

$$\{(T,1)\} > \{(\perp,1)\} > \{(F,1)\}$$

The respective weights are then obtained by solving the linear system of equations $r(t_1) = 1$ (the 'best' truth value), $r(t_2) = 5/6$, $r(t_3) = 4/6$, $r(t_4) = 3/6$, $r(t_5) = 2/6$, $r(t_6) = 1/6$ and $r(t_7) = 0$ (the 'worst' truth value), i.e.

$$\begin{cases} w_2 + w_3 + \sqrt{2}w_4 + \sqrt{2}w_5 + \sqrt{3}w_6 + \sqrt{2}w_7 = 1 \\ w_1 + \sqrt{2}w_3 + w_4 + w_5 + \sqrt{2}w_6 + \sqrt{3}w_7 = 5/6 \\ w_1 + \sqrt{2}w_2 + w_4 + \sqrt{3}w_5 + \sqrt{2}w_6 + w_7 = 4/6 \\ \sqrt{2}w_1 + w_2 + w_3 + \sqrt{2}w_5 + w_6 + \sqrt{2}w_7 = 3/6 \\ \sqrt{2}w_1 + w_2 + \sqrt{3}w_3 + \sqrt{2}w_4 + w_6 + \sqrt{2}w_7 = 2/6 \\ \sqrt{3}w_1 + \sqrt{2}w_2 + \sqrt{2}w_3 + w_4 + w_5 + w_7 = 1/6 \\ \sqrt{2}w_1 + \sqrt{3}w_2 + w_3 + \sqrt{2}w_4 + \sqrt{2}w_5 + w_6 = 0 \end{cases}$$

which yields $w_1 = -0.199$, $w_2 = -0.082$, $w_3 = -0.088$, $w_4 = 0.123$, $w_5 = 0.195$, $w_6 = 0.062$ and $w_7 = 0.434$.

4.2 Extended Analytical Approach

The 'weighted sum' approach involves a lot of calculations, that can introduce a lot of overhead when comparing a large number of EPTV's. Therefore, a simpler analytical ranking function[1] has been defined by

$$r_a : \tilde{\wp}(I^*) \to [0,1]$$

$$\{(T,\mu_T),(F,\mu_F),(\bot,\mu_\bot)\} \mapsto \frac{1+(\mu_T-\mu_F)(1-\frac{\mu_\bot}{2})}{2}$$

With this ranking function, the ordering of the relevant angular points of the cube of EPTV's becomes

$$\{(T,1)\} > \{(T,1),(\bot,1)\} > \{(T,1),(F,1)\} = \{(T,1),(F,1),(\bot,1)\} = \{(\bot,1)\} > \{(F,1),(\bot,1)\} > \{(F,1)\}$$

Since no distinction can be made between the EPTV's $\{(T,1),(F,1)\}$, $\{(\bot,1)\}$ and $\{(T,1),(F,1),(\bot,1)\}$, this ranking is more crude than the one obtained by function r_w.

4.3 Minimization of the Impact of the ⊥-Component

For both the 'weighted sum' and the extended analytical approaches, it has been assumed that the initial ordering of the 'basic' truth values is the following

$$\{(T,1)\} > \{(\bot,1)\} > \{(F,1)\}$$

Furthermore, the impact (on the ranking process) of the (F)alse component is considered to be more negative than the impact of the ⊥-component.

As an alternative, the impact of the ⊥-component on the ranking process could be minimized. This can be done by ranking the EPTV's as if there were PTV's —using ranking the function r (cf. footnote [1])— and by subsequently using a threshold value α for the ⊥-component. The EPTV's are then ranked with a decreasing possibility of being true (i.e. μ_T) and the additional restriction that their respective possibilities of being inapplicable (i.e. $\mu_\bot$) must not be greater than α.

The resulting ranking function is then defined by

$$r_\alpha : \tilde{\wp}(I) \times [0,1] \to [0,1]$$

$$(\{(T,\mu_T),(F,\mu_F),(\bot,\mu_\bot)\},\alpha) \mapsto \begin{cases} \dfrac{\mu_T+(1-\mu_F)}{2} & \text{if } \mu_\bot \leq \alpha, \\ 0 & \text{if } \mu_\bot > \alpha \end{cases}$$

[1] The ranking function r_a is in fact an extension of the ranking function

$$r : \tilde{\wp}(I) \to [0,1] : \{(T,\mu_T),(F,\mu_F)\} \mapsto \frac{\mu_T+(1-\mu_F)}{2}$$

for PTV's as presented in [15].

5 Applicability in Flexible Database Querying

The presented ranking functions r_w, r_a and r_α are in fact mappings from the three dimensional space $[0,1]^3$ onto the unit interval $[0,1]$. For each of these functions, there exist subsets of EPTV's which all have the same ranking value and therefore are indistinguishable. So the presented ranking functions are still not perfect. (As an illustration, the subsets corresponding with the ranking values 0.25, 0.5 and 0.75 of both functions r_w (left cube) and r_a (right cube) have been presented in Figure 1.)

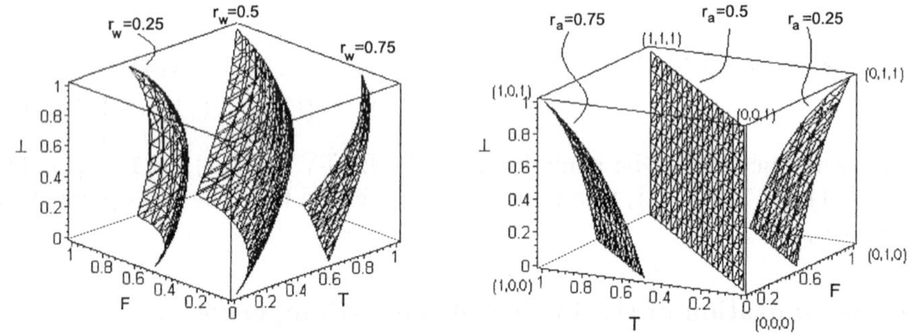

Fig. 1. Subsets of indistinguishable EPTV's w.r.t. the ranking functions r_w and r_a.

Each of the presented ranking functions can be used in flexible database querying. Which function is best suited, depends on the application and is mainly determined by performance requirements and the expectations of the user about the impact of non-applicability of (some of) the query criteria on the query results:

- Ranking function r_w involves most calculations, but the resulting ranking is less crude than with ranking functions r_a and r_α.
- Ranking function r_a is a useful alternative, which can more easily be calculated.
- Ranking function r_α is preferable in those cases where the existence of non-applicability of (some of) the query criteria in only allowed to a given extent (α). All EPTV's $\{(T,\mu_T),(F,\mu_F),(\perp,\mu_\perp)\}$ where $\mu_\perp > \alpha$ will be ignored in the ranking. Database instances with such an associated EPTV will be omitted from the query result.

6 Conclusions

An adequate method to rank the possible alternatives in the result of a flexible database query is essential, since adequate ranking information simplifies decision making and helps the user to find quickly the requested information. This paper deals with the ranking of EPTV's. EPTV's can be used to model query satisfaction and explicitly allow to model the impact of the non-applicability of some of the querying criteria. Three alternative ranking functions are presented and compared with each other based on their applicability in flexible database querying. The first function r_w is obtained as a 'weighted sum' of Eucledian distances, the second function r_a is an extension of the analytical ranking function for PTV's, whereas the third function r_α uses a threshold value α to minimize the impact of non-applicable querying criteria. Which function to use in flexible querying, depends on the performance requirements and the expectations of the user about the impact of non-applicability of query criteria on the query results.

References

1. Dubois, D., Prade, H.: Certainty and Uncertainty of (Vague) Knowledge and Generalised Dependencies in Fuzzy Databases. In: Proc. of Int. Fuzzy Engineering Symposium '91, Yokahoma, Japan (1991) 239–249
2. Baldwin, J.F., Zhou, S.Q.: A Fuzzy Relational Inference Language. Fuzzy Sets and Systems **14** (1984) 155–174
3. De Tré, G., De Caluwe, R., Van der Cruyssen, B.: A Generalised Object-Oriented Database Model. In: Recent Issues on Fuzzy Databases, Bordogna, G., Pasi, G. (eds.) Physica-Verlag, Heidelberg, Germany (2000) 155–182
4. De Tré, G., De Caluwe, R.: Modelling Uncertainty in Multimedia Database Systems: An Extended Possibilistic Approach. Int. Journal of Uncertainty, Fuzziness and Knowledge-Based Systems **11** 1 (2003) 5–22
5. Zadeh, L.A.: Fuzzy sets as a basis for a theory of possibility. Fuzzy Sets and Systems **1** 1 (1978) 3–28
6. Dubois, D., Prade, H.: Possibility Theory. Plenum Press, New York, USA (1988)
7. Prade, H., Testemale, C.: Generalizing Database Relational Algebra for the Treatment of Incomplete or Uncertain Information and Vague Queries. Information Sciences **34** (1984) 115–143
8. Bosc, P., Pivert, O.: Some Approaches for Relational Databases Flexible Querying. Journal of Intelligent Information Systems (JIIS) **1** 3–4 (1992) 323–354
9. Yazici, A., George, R., Aksoy, D.: Design and Implementation Issues in the Fuzzy Object-Oriented Data Model. Information Sciences **108** 1–4 (1998) 241–260.
10. Yazici, A., Buckles, B.P., Petry, F.E.: Handling Complex and Uncertain Information in the ExIFO and NF^2 Data Models. IEEE Trans. on Fuzzy Systems **7** 6 (1999) 659–676.
11. Bordogna, G., Pasi,G., Lucarella, D.: A Fuzzy Object-Oriented Data Model for Managing Vague and Uncertain Information. Int. Journal of Intelligent Systems **14** 7 (1999) 623–651
12. Prade, H.: Possibility sets, fuzzy sets and their relation to Lukasiewicz logic. In: Proc. of the 12th Int. Symp. on Multiple-Valued Logic, Paris, France (1982) 223–227
13. De Tré, G.: Extended Possibilistic Truth Values. Int. Journal of Intelligent Systems **17** (2002) 427–446
14. De Tré, G., De Caluwe, R. , Verstraete, J., Hallez, A.: Conjunctive Aggregation of Extended Possibilistic Truth Values and Flexible Database Querying. Lecture Notes in Artificial Intelligence **2522** (2002) 344–355
15. Dubois, D., Prade, H.: Degree of Truth and Truth-Functionality. In: Proc. of the 2nd conf. on mathematics at the service of man, Las Palmas, Spain (1982) 262–265

Global Index for Multi Channel Data Dissemination in Mobile Databases

Agustinus Borgy Waluyo[1], Bala Srinivasan[1], and David Taniar[2]

[1] School of Computer Science and Software Engineering, Monash University, Australia
{Agustinus.Borgy.Waluyo, Bala.Srinivasan}@infotech.monash.edu.au

[2] School of Business Systems, Monash University, Australia
David.Taniar@infotech.monash.edu.au

Abstract. Data broadcasting strategy is known as a scalable way to disseminate information to mobile users. However, with a very large number of broadcast items, the access time of mobile clients increase accordingly, due to high waiting time for mobile clients to find their data of interest. One possible solution is to split the database information into several broadcast channels. In this paper, we introduce global indexing technique for multi broadcast channels. A simulation model is developed to find out the performance of the technique.

1 Introduction

Nowadays, people are no longer attached to a stationary machine to do their work, with wireless application they are enabled to conduct their business anywhere and anytime using portable size wireless computer powered by battery. These portable computers communicate with central stationary server via wireless channel. The technology is known as *mobile computing* [1, 3]. Mobile computing has its own database management system (DBMS) that provides the same function as in traditional databases called *mobile databases*. Mobile databases face a number of limitations particularly power, storage and bandwidth capacity. In regard to power capacity, it has been investigated that the life expectancy of a battery is anticipated to increase only 20% in every 10 years [7]. Consequently, the need to use power *efficiently* and *effectively* are crucial issues.

Data dissemination strategy or known as broadcast strategy refers to periodically broadcast database items to clients through one or more broadcast channels. Mobile clients filter their desired data on the fly. This strategy is an effective way to disseminate database information to a large set of mobile clients. However, the challenge in broadcast strategy is to maintain the query performance of the client to obtain information from the channel.

In general, each mobile user communicates with a Mobile Base Station (MBS) to carry out any activities such as transaction and information retrieval. MBS has a wireless interface to establish communication with mobile client and it serves a large number of mobile users in a specific region called *cell*. Mobile units or mobile clients

A. Yazici and C. Şener (Eds.): ISCIS 2003, LNCS 2869, pp. 212–219, 2003.

in each cell can either connect to the network via wireless radio or wireless Local Area Network (LAN).

With the increase number of mobile users in a cell, the required number of data items to be broadcast also increases accordingly. This situation may cause some mobile clients to wait for a substantial amount of time before receiving desired data item. Consequently, the advantages of broadcast strategy will be eliminated. Thus, in order to maintain the query access time over a vast amount of broadcast data items, we can split the broadcast cycle into several broadcast channels. Mobile clients can pick the desired data in the right channel without having to wait too long. Consequently, energy consumption and time can be reduced. Number of broadcast channels in a cell that can be simultaneously utilized is up to 200 channels [5].

Having known the number of broadcast channels for given data items, it is necessary to broadcast index structure in order to reduce the tuning time of the mobile client. Tuning time is the time clients listen to the channel, which indicates their power consumption. Broadcast indexing enables mobile clients to determine when the desired data arrives in the broadcast cycle. Thus, it allows them to switch into "doze mode"[1] while waiting for the data. On the other hand, it is also important to maintain the amount of time or waiting time needed from the time a request is initiated until all data item of interest are received, or defined as the access time.

In order to maintain the performance of accessing data from the broadcast channel, we introduce Global indexing that sustains the average access time for accessing data items over multiple broadcast channels considerably low. In our previous work, we have applied global indexing model in the context of parallel database systems [8] and now we extend the application of global index to mobile database query optimization.

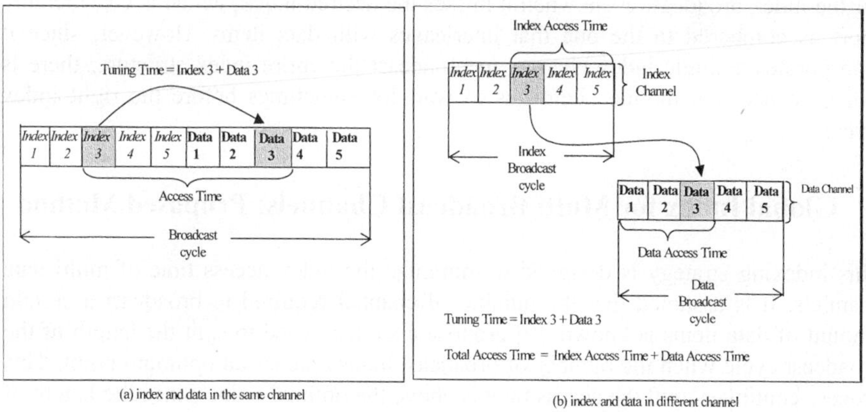

Fig. 1. Integrated and Separated Index Channel

Figure 1 illustrates integrated and separated index channel. Global index relates to the context of separated index channel that involve multi broadcast channels. The term mobile client, mobile user and client are used interchangeably.

[1] Doze mode is when mobile clients are inactive or not listening into the channel

The next section of this paper contains the related work of the proposed technique. It is then followed by the description of the Global index, and its application in section 3. The simulation model to measure the performance of our proposed technique, as compared to other technique is given in section 4. Finally, section 5 concludes the paper.

2 Related Work

[4] have proposed clustering index, non-clustering index, and multiple index methods. In this scheme, some form of directory is broadcast along with the data, the clients obtain the index directory from the broadcast and use it in subsequent reading. The information also contains the exact time of the data to be broadcast. However, these techniques combines index and data segment in a single channel. When the index and data segments stay in the same channel, the length of broadcast cycle increases. Consequently, the average access time improves. This situation is even worse when client misses the appropriate index, and has to wait for the whole broadcast cycle that includes data and index segment, before receiving the desired data item. Even though clients can switch into a doze mode during the process, but the response time or access time becomes very large.

Another indexing technique is used by [5]. This technique is based on B^{+}-tree structure, and it incorporates a separate index channel to locate the data segment in multi data channel. The physical pointer not only indicates the time value but also the channel in which the indexed item will be broadcast. Using this mechanism, client first tunes into the index channel, find the indexed time value, switch to data channel and wait for the data item to arrive. The advantage is mobile client only needs to wait for the index broadcast cycle when it misses the desired index, which is considerably short as compared to the one that interleaves with data items. However, since it incorporates a single index channel to broadcast the entire index structure, there is still a chance that mobile client has to wait for sometimes before the right index arrives.

3 Global Index for Multi Broadcast Channels: Proposed Method

This indexing strategy is designed to minimize the index access time of multi data channels. It is assumed that the number of channel required to broadcast a certain amount of data items is known. [9] propose a strategy used to split the length of the broadcast cycle when the number of broadcast items reaches an optimum point. This process continues until the access time is above the optimal point. Since the length of the broadcast cycle is optimal, the waiting time will be considerably short.

Global index is designed based on B^{+}-tree structure. It consists of non-leaf nodes, and leaf node. Leaf node is the bottom most index that consists of up to k keys, where each key point to actual data items and each node has one node pointer to a right-side neighbouring leaf node. Unlike leaf node, non-leaf node may consist of up to k keys and k+1 pointers to the nodes on the next level on the tree hierarchy (i.e. child nodes). All child nodes, which are on the left-hand side of the parent node, have the key values less than or equal to the key of their parent node. On the other hand, keys of child nodes on the right-hand side of the parent node are greater than the key of their parent node.

Having all data pointers stored on the leaf nodes is considered better than storing data pointers in the non-leaf nodes like the original *B* trees [2]. Moreover, by having node pointers in the leaf level, it becomes possible to trace all leaf nodes from the left most to the right most nodes producing a sorted list of keys. When being broadcast, each physical pointer to the neighbouring leaf node as well as actual data item are replaced by a time value, which indicates when the leaf node or data item will be broadcast.

Our simple scenario is to broadcast weather condition for all cities in Australia. There are 30 cities altogether to be broadcast, and we assume the optimum number of cities in a data channel is 10. Subsequently, we end up with 3 data channels, each channel contains 10 cities. In this case, we use a table consisting of records of IDs, city, weather condition, and temperature. The index is inserted based on the order of the data item in the table. Similarly, to construct our data channels, the data item is placed based on the order of the table, and once it reaches optimum number of cities, a new data channel is created. Assume that in the index tree, the maximum number of node pointers from any non-leaf node is 4, and the maximum number of data pointers from any leaf node is 3.

Global index exhibited in Figure 2 uses the ID attribute as the index-partitioning attribute, which is different from the table partitioning. We assume the range partitioning rules used are that index channel 1 holds data IDs between 1 to 30, index channel 2 holds data IDs between 31 to 60, and the rest go to index channel 3. Notice from Figure 4 that the fifth leaf node (28, 33, 37) is replicated to channel 1 and 2 because key 28 belongs to index channel 1, while keys 33 and 37 belong to index channel 2. Also notice that some non-leaf nodes are replicated whereas others are not. For example, the non-leaf node 15 is not replicated and located only in index channel 1, whereas non-leaf node 18 is replicated to index channel 1 and 2. It is also clear that the root node is fully replicated.

We must stress that the location of each leaf node is the not same as where the actual data is broadcast. Our index is broadcast separately with the data, and each index key points to the relevant data channel. Thus, once the right index is found in a specific index channel, mobile client switch to the right data channel and wait for the data of interest to arrive.

The data structure for our Global index employs single node pointers model. In the single node pointer model, each node pointer has only one outgoing node pointer.

If a child node exists locally, the node pointer points to this local node only, even when this child node also replicated to other index channels. For example, from node 37 at index channel 1, there is only one node pointer to the local node 18. The child node 18 at index channel 2 will not receive an incoming node pointer from the root node 37 at index channel 1; instead it will receive one node pointer from the local root node 37 only.

If a child node does not exist locally, the node pointer will choose one node pointer pointing to the nearest child node (in case if multiple child nodes exist somewhere else). For example, from the root node 37 at index channel 1, there is only one outgoing right node pointer to child node (48,60) at index channel 2. In this case, we assume that index channel 2 is the nearest neighbour of index channel 3. The child node (48,60), which also exists at index channel 3, will not receive a node pointer from root node 37 at index channel 1.

Table (ID, City, Weather Condition, Temperature):

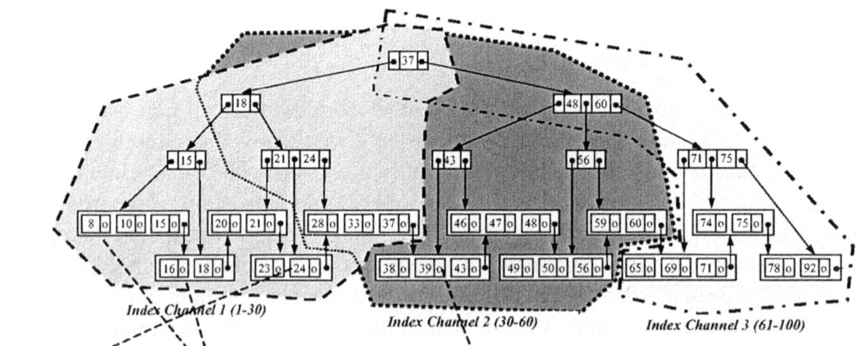

Data Channel 1			
23	Adelaide	Mostly Sunny	24°C
65	Albany	Local Shower	15°C
37	Ballarat	A few showers	12°C
60	Barton	Mostly Fine	19°C
46	Beechworth	Shower or Two	14°C
92	Belmont	Partly Cloudy	10°C
48	Brisbane	Fine	17°C
71	Broome	Shower or two	15°C
56	Bunbury	Mostly sunny	20°C
59	Busselton	Shower	21°C

Data Channel 2			
18	Cairns	Shower	16°C
21	Canberra	Partly Cloudy	23°C
10	Cervantes	Fine	26°C
34	Darwin	A few shower	21°C
78	Gosford	Mostly fine	23°C
15	Grafton	Thunderstorm	21°C
16	Kingscote	Possible Hail	13°C
20	Kingston	Fine	15°C
24	Lismore	Partly cloudy	17°C
28	Maitland	Shower	15°C

Data Channel 3			
39	Melbourne	Mostly fine	25°C
43	Miranda	Thunderstorms and Hail	12°C
47	Newcastle	A few shower or two	15°C
50	Northbridge	Fine	25°C
69	Philip	Cloudy	26°C
75	Queensland	Fine	30°C
8	Queenstown	Mostly sunny	28°C
49	Surfers Paradise	Shower	22°C
33	Sydney	Cloudy	21°C
38	Torguay	Fine	23°C

Fig. 2. Global Index Model

Using this single node pointer model, it is always possible to trace a node from any parent node. For example, it is possible to trace to node (71,75) from the root node 37 at index channel 1, although there is no direct link from root node 37 at index channel 1 to its direct child node (48,60) at index channel 3. Tracing to node (71,75) can still be done through node (48,60) at index channel 2. A more formal proof for the single node pointer model is as follows. First, given a parent node is replicated when its child nodes are scattered at multiple locations, there is always a direct link from whichever copy of this parent node to any of its child nodes. Second, using the same methodology as the first statement above, given a replicated grandparent node, there is always a direct link from whichever copy of this grandparent node to any of the parent nodes. Considering the first and the second statements above, we can conclude that there is always a direct link from whichever copy of the grandparent node to any of its child nodes.

Figure 3 shows an example of a single node pointer model. It only shows the top three levels of the index tree exhibited previously in Figure 2.

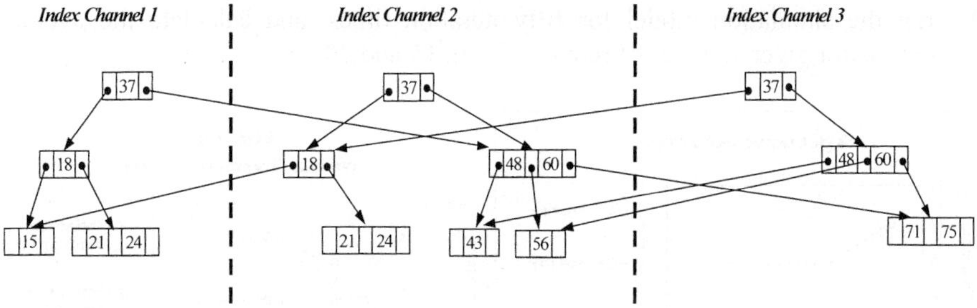

Fig. 3. Single Node Pointers Model

Data retrieval mechanism in this scheme can be described as follows:

- Mobile client tunes in one of the index channel (i.e. can be any index channel).
- Mobile client follow the index pointer to the right index key. The pointer may lead to another index channel that contains the relevant index. While waiting for the index to arrive, mobile clients can switch to doze mode.
- Mobile client tunes back on at the right index key, which point to the data channel that contains the desired data item. It indicates a time value of the data to arrive in the data channel.
- Mobile client tunes into the relevant data channel, and switch back to doze mode while waiting for the data item to come.
- Mobile client switches back to active mode just before the desired data item arrives, and retrieve the information.

4 Performance Evaluation

In this section, we analyze the performance of our Global index model. The simulation is carried out using a simulation package *Planimate,* animated planning platforms [6]. As for the simulation case, we use the weather scenario as illustrated in Figure 3, using the same set of data items. We incorporate our Global index in three index channels, and compare the access time performance with single index channel that contains the entire index structure. The performance evaluation in this paper relates to single index retrieval. Table 1 shows the parameters of concern.

Table 1. Parameters of Concern

Parameters	Value
Number of Index node in Global Index (Channel 1)	17
Number of Index node in Global Index (Channel 2)	22
Number of Index node in Global Index (Channel 3)	12
Number of Index node in Non-Global Index	41
Node Pointer Size	5 bytes
Data Pointer Size	5 bytes
Indexed Attribute Size	2 bytes
Bandwidth	19200 bytes
Index Arrival Rate	2 per sec

We run the simulation model for fifty iteration times, and calculate the average access time for given number of request: 5, 10, 15 and 20.

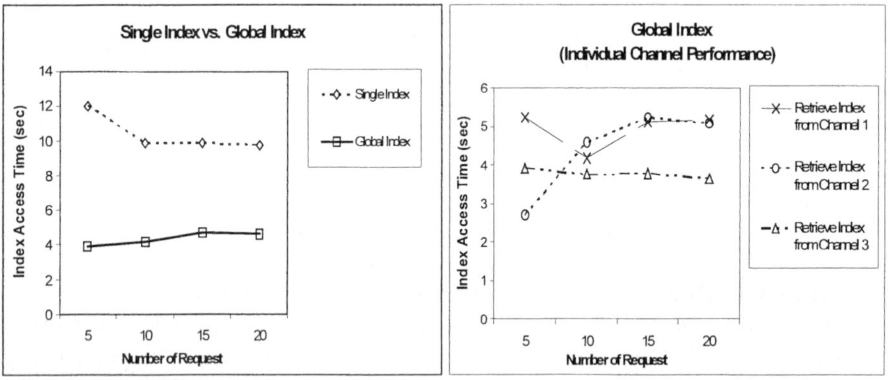

(a) Access Time of Single Index vs. Global Index

(b) Global Index – Individual Channel Performance

Fig. 4. Single Index Channel vs. Global Index Access Time

As shown in Figure 4 (a), we can see that our Global Index outperforms the Single Index with more or less two to three times lower average access time. Furthermore, among three channel within Global Index, we found from Figure 4 (b) that index channel 3 provides a better average access time as compared to others channel. It indicates that more requests with index key located in channel 3, the better average access time is. This is due to the short index broadcast cycle that exists in index channel 3, so that mobile clients do not wait too long to find the right index key. Consequently, it reduces substantial amount of power consumption.

5 Conclusions and Future Work

Data dissemination or known as data broadcasting strategy is an effective way to keep up with number of clients in a cell and their frequency of requests. To maintain the performance of broadcast strategy over a large set of data items, we introduce an indexing technique called Global index to keep the average access time low. Our Global index model incorporates multiple index channels, and the data items are broadcast separately in multiple data channels. Mobile clients only need to tune in one of the index channel, and the Global index guides the client to the right node that may be located in different index channel.

We compare the performance of our Global index to Single index channel. It is found that Global index provides about three times better access time than Single index model. Consequently, it utilizes power more efficiently.

For future work, we will consider multi index attributes in the global index structure. Thus, it will support mobile clients to find the data item efficiently using alternative search key or combination thereof. Moreover, we plan to extend the global index to involve joint attributes from two or more different tables.

References

1. Barbara D., "Mobile Computing and Databases-A Survey", *IEEE Trans. on Knowledge and Data Engineering*, 11(1): 108–117, 1999.
2. Elmasri R. and Navathe S. B., *Fundamentals of Database Systems,* Third Edition, Addison Wesley, U.S.A., 2000.
3. Imielinski T. and Viswanathan S., "Adaptive Wireless Information Systems", *Proc.of SIGDBS (Special Interest Group in Database Systems) Conference*, October, 1994.
4. Imielinski T., Viswanathan S. and Badrinath B. R., "Data on Air: Organisation and Access", *IEEE Trans. on Knowledge and Data Engineering,* 9(3): 353–371, 1997.
5. Leong H. V. and Si A., "Data Broadcasting Strategies Over Multiple Unreliable Wireless Channels", *Proc. of the 4th International Conference on Information and Knowledge Management*, pp.96–104, December, 1995.
6. Seeley D. et al, *Planimate^{tm}-Animated Planning Platforms*, InterDynamics Pty Ltd, 1997.
7. Sheng S., Chandrasekaran A. and Broderson R. W., "A Portable Multimedia Terminal for Personal Communication", *IEEE Communications*, pp.64–75, December, 1992.
8. Taniar, D., Rahayu J.W., "A Taxonomy of Indexing Schemes for Parallel Database Systems", *Distributed and Parallel Databases*, 12: 73–106, 2002.
9. Waluyo, A.B., Srinivasan B., Taniar D., "Optimal Broadcast Channel for Data Dissemination in Mobile Database Environment", *Advanced Parallel Processing Technologies*, LNCS, Springer-Verlag, 2003 (in press).

A Robust Scheme for Multilevel Extendible Hashing

Sven Helmer, Thomas Neumann, and Guido Moerkotte

University of Mannheim, Mannheim, Germany

Abstract. Dynamic hashing, while surpassing other access methods for uniformly distributed data, usually performs badly for non-uniformly distributed data. We propose a robust scheme for multi-level extendible hashing, allowing efficient processing of skewed data as well as uniformly distributed data. In order to test our access method, we implemented it and compared it to several existing hashing schemes. The results of the experimental evaluation demonstrate the superiority of our approach in both index size and performance.

1 Introduction

Skewed data is ubiquitous, and the ways in which it is skewed are typically unpredictable. Thus, while it is possible to choose a well-behaved hash function if the data is known beforehand, this is rarely helpful in practice. We propose a robust extendible hashing scheme that performs well on both uniformly distributed and skewed hash keys. The main idea is dividing the directory of our hash table hierarchically into several subdirectories, such that the subdirectories on lower levels share pages in an elegant way. This allows us to save space without introducing a large overhead or compromising retrieval performance. We show the effectiveness of our approach by presenting results from our extensive experiments.

What are the reasons for skewed hash keys? The dominant opinion is that by using appropriate hash functions hashing skewed data will result in a reasonably uniform distribution of the hash keys [1,8]. We do not share this point of view. Obviously good hash functions can be chosen when the data that is to be indexed is known beforehand. In practice, this is very rarely the case. Here, one has to expect bursts of data that are heavily skewed in not always anticipated ways. Furthermore, multiple identical data values also induce skew in hash keys as do specialized hash functions, e.g. those allowing order preserving hashing. One of the unresolved issues with respect to the distribution of the hash keys is the lack of hashing schemes whose performance does not deteriorate when faced with non-uniformly distributed hash keys. This has prevented the large-scale use of indexes based on hashing in practice. Vendors of commercial databases are reluctant to integrate these access methods into their database management systems and rely on the more robust B-trees instead. We try to remedy this situation by proposing a robust hashing index.

A. Yazici and C. Şener (Eds.): ISCIS 2003, LNCS 2869, pp. 220–227, 2003.

The paper is organized as follows. In the next section we describe the problems associated with dynamic hashing. Section 3 covers our new approach. In Section 4 we describe the results of our experimental evaluation. Section 5 contains a brief comparison with other approaches. Section 6 concludes our paper.

2 Problems with Extendible Hashing

An extendible hashing index is divided into two parts, a directory and buckets (for details see also [4]). In the buckets we store the full hash keys of and pointers to the indexed data items. We determine the bucket into which a data item is inserted by looking at a prefix h_d of d bits of the hash key h. For each possible bit combination of the prefix, we find an entry in the directory pointing to the corresponding bucket. The directory has 2^d entries, where d is called *global depth* (see Figure 1). When a bucket overflows, it is split and all its entries are divided among the two resulting buckets. In order to determine the new home of a data item, the length of the inspected hash key prefix has to be increased until at least two data items have different hash key prefixes. The size of the current prefix d' of a bucket is called *local depth.* If we notice after a split that the local depth d' of a bucket is larger than the global depth d, we have to increase the size of the directory. This is done by doubling the directory as often as needed to have a new global depth d equal to the local depth d'. For the bucket that was split, the new pointers are put into the directory. For the other buckets, the directory entries are copied.

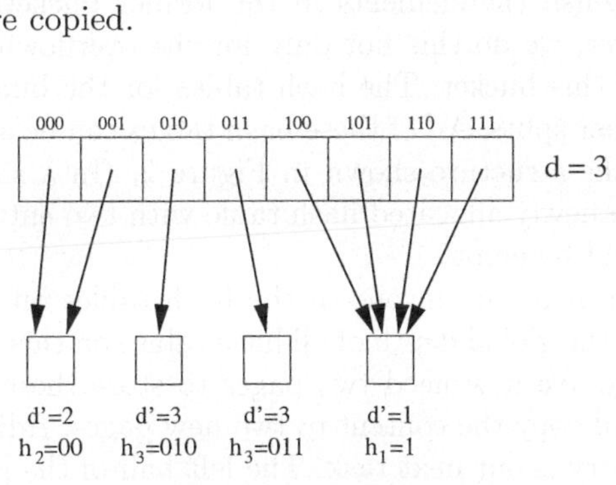

Fig. 1. Extendible hashing

Inserting skewed data into an extendible hash table makes the directory grow exponentially, as some buckets split rapidly while other parts of the table stay almost empty. The physical limit of the directory growth is reached quite fast.

When the limit is reached, we have two alternatives. We can introduce overflow buckets or use a hierarchical directory. Overflow buckets are contrary to the basic idea of extendible hashing [9], because long chains of overflow buckets lead to severe performance losses. Simply organizing the extendible hash directory hierarchically as a hash tree (as suggested in [4] and [14]) does not get the job done either. Although superior to an ordinary extendible hashing scheme for skewed data, extendible hash trees waste a lot of space for uniformly distributed data. When a bucket overflows, we have to allocate another hash table beneath the current one and insert the elements of the split bucket into this table. Inserting uniformly distributed data leads to "waves of expansions": many buckets split at roughly the same time, so many new tables are created at once. However, most of these tables hold only a few overflow records, which results in a waste of space.

3 Our Approach

Due to space constraints, we can only give a brief description, for details see [6]. We propose a multi-level extendible hash tree in which hash tables share pages according to a buddy scheme. In this buddy scheme, z-*buddies* are hash tables that reside on the same page and their stored hash keys share a prefix of z bits. Consequently, buddy hash tables have the same global depth, namely z.

Let us illustrate our index with an example. We assume that a page can hold 2^n entries of a hash table directory. Furthermore, we assume that the top level hash table directory (also called the root) is already filled, contains 2^n different entries at the moment, and that another overflow occurs (w.l.o.g. in the first bucket). In this case, we allocate a new hash table of global depth 1 (beneath the root) to distinguish the elements in the former bucket according to their $n+1$th bit. However, we do this not only for the overflowing bucket, but also for all 1-buddies of this bucket. The hash tables for the buddies are created in anticipation of further splits. All of these hash tables can be allocated on a single page, resulting in the structure shown in Figure 2. (In a simple hash tree, we would have just one newly allocated hash table with two entries. The rest of the table directory would be empty.)

If another overflow occurs in one of the hash tables on level 2, causing its growth, we increase the global depth of all hash tables on this page by 1, doubling their directory sizes. We now need two pages to store these tables, so we split the original page and copy the content to two new pages. Adjusting the pointers in the parent directory is our next task. The left half of the pointers referencing the original page now point to one of the new pages, the right half to the other new page (see Figure 3).

The space utilization of our index can be improved by eliminating pages with unnecessary hash tables. The page on the right-hand side of the second level in Figure 3 is superfluous, as the entries in the directories of all hash tables point to a single bucket, i.e. all buckets have local depth 0. In this case, the page is discarded and all buckets are connected directly to the hash table on the next higher level.

Due to our buddy scheme, we have a very regular structure we can exploit. Indeed, we can compute the global depths of all hash tables (except the root) by looking at the pointers in the corresponding parent table. Finding 2^{n-i} identical pointers there means that the referenced page contains 2^{n-i} i-buddies of global

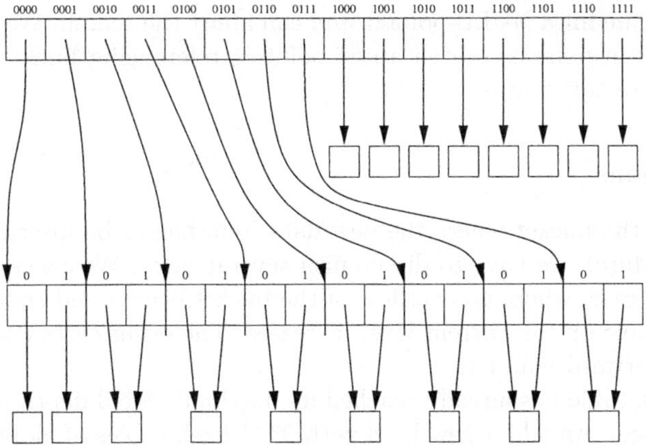

Fig. 2. Overflow in our multi-level hash tree

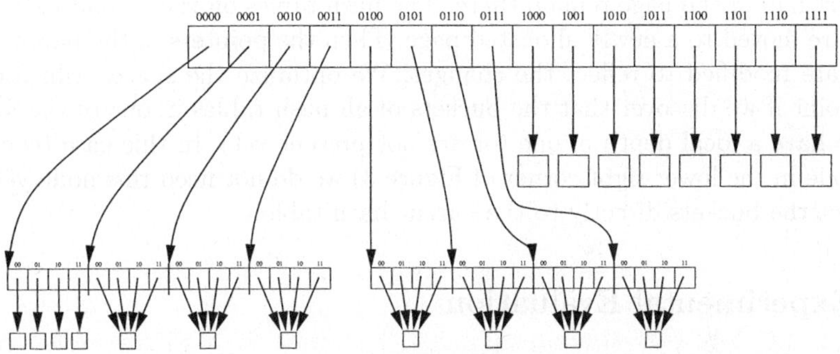

Fig. 3. Overflow on the second level

depth i. Consequently, we can utilize the whole page for storing pointers, as no additional information has to be kept.

3.1 Lookups

Lookups are easily implemented. We have to traverse inner nodes until we reach a bucket. On each level we determine the currently relevant part of the hash key. This gives us the correct slot in the current hash table. As more than one hash table can reside on a page, we may have to add an offset to access the right hash table. Due to the regular structure, this offset can be easily calculated. We just multiply the last $n-i$ bits of the relevant pointer in the parent table by the size of a hash table on the shared page. If $n-i=0$, we do not need an offset, as only one hash table resides on this page. If we reach a bucket, we search there for the data item. If the bucket does not exist (no data item is present there at the moment), we hit a NULL-pointer and can abort the search. We use the most significant bit in pointers to tell apart pointers referencing buckets from those referencing directory pages.

3.2 Insertions

After finding the bucket where the new data item has to be inserted (using the lookup procedure), we have to distinguish several cases. We concentrate on the most difficult case, where an overflow of the bucket occurs and the global depth of the hash table on the current level increases. The other cases can be handled in a straightforward manner.

If the hash table has already reached its maximal global depth (i.e. it resides alone on a page), we add a new level with 2^{n-1} hash tables of global depth 1 to the existing index structure (comparable to Figure 2). If we have not reached the maximal global depth yet (the hash table shares a page with its buddies), the global depth of all hash tables on this page is increased by 1. The hash tables on the first half of the page remain there. The hash tables on the second half of the page are moved to a newly allocated page. Then the pointers in the parent hash table are modified to reflect the changes. We optimize the space utilization at this point if we discover that the buckets of all hash tables in one of the former halves have a local depth of one (or are not present yet). In this case (compare the node in the lower right corner of Figure 3) we do not need this node yet and connect the buckets directly to the parent hash table.

4 Experimental Evaluation

We used different sets of data to compare our index structure to extendible hashing and a simple extendible hashing tree. First, we generated synthetic hash keys with varying degrees of skew by creating bit vectors with a length of 64 bits. The state of each bit (0 or 1) was determined randomly with different distributions (uniform, 40% probability and 30% probability that the bit is set to 1). Second, we indexed a list of URLs generated by a Web crawler. The strings of the URLs were hashed using a shift-XOR scheme.

4.1 Comparing the Size of the Directories

In Figure 4 we plotted the growing directory sizes depending on the number of inserted hash keys. (Note that we used double-logarithmic scales.) While the extendible hashing scheme (Figure 4(a)) performs poorly for skewed data (we limited the directory size to 4096 pages, reverting to overflow buckets), the simple hash tree (Figure 4(b)) has severe problems with uniformly distributed data. The smallest directories are found in our multi-level hashing scheme (Figure 4(c)). Neither skewed nor uniformly distributed data pose any problems.

When comparing the results for real data in Figure 4(d) with those for synthetic data, we clearly see that real data is far from uniformly distributed. (Note

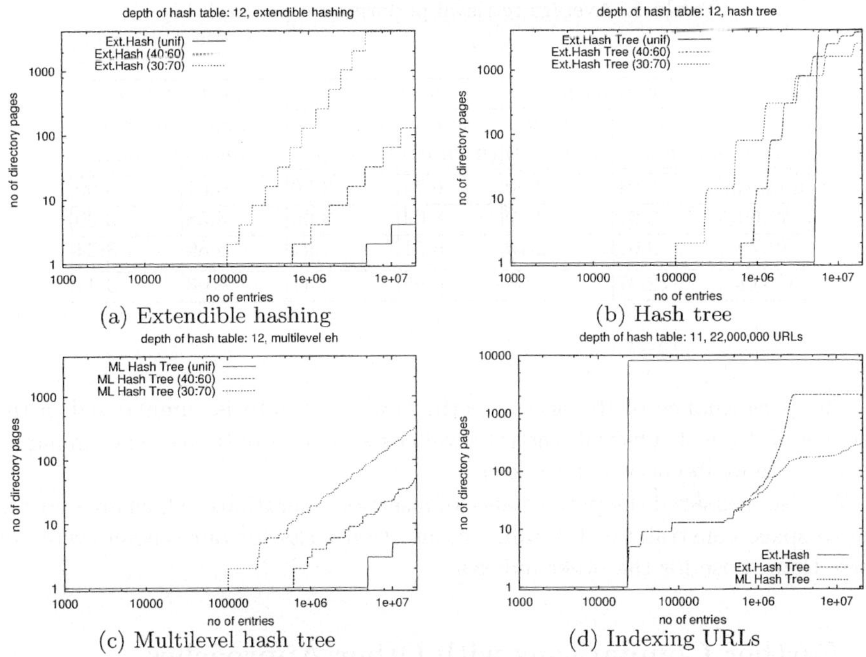

Fig. 4. Size of directory in pages for varying data skew

that the depth of the hash tables is 11, as we increased the pointer size from 32 to 64 bits.) The directory of extendible hashing reaches the limit (set to 8192 pages this time) almost instantaneously. Indexing this kind of data with extendible hashing is out of the question. The extendible hash tree starts out strong, but deteriorates as more hash keys are inserted.

4.2 Comparing the Retrieval Costs

Table 1 shows the retrieval performance of the different hashing schemes. The left column for each index structure contains the average running time in milliseconds for a lookup in a completely filled index (20,000,000 inserted hash keys). In each right column, the average number of page accesses is displayed. We determined the numbers by averaging 20,000,000 random accesses to the hash tables.

Several observations are worth mentioning. The increase in page accesses for extendible hashing for heavily skewed data is due to the increased use of overflow buckets in this case. As fewer pages of the index can be held in main memory with increasing skewedness of the hash keys, we have more page faults during access, which results in a higher running time. Although our hashing scheme has the highest number of page accesses, its performance measured in run time is, on average, still better than that of the other schemes. This emphasizes the importance of a small directory, as it directly influences the retrieval performance.

Table 1. Average retrieval performance per hash key

	ext. hash		hash tree		ml hash tree	
skew	time (in msec)	page acc. (in pages)	time (in msec)	page acc. (in pages)	time (in msec)	page acc. (in pages)
uniform	5.91	2.00	6.74	3.00	6.01	3.00
40:60	5.91	2.00	8.04	3.00	5.58	3.00
30:70	9.01	2.10	6.51	3.01	5.86	3.24
URLs	12.37	2.38	6.95	3.41	6.08	3.41

The performance of the access methods for real data is summarized in the last row of Table 1. Overall, the retrieval costs for real data are very similar to those for skewed synthetic hash keys.

We also measured the performance of insertion operations (which are omitted due to space constraints). Overall, the insertion costs for our scheme were not worse than those for the other indexes.

5 Further Comparisons with Other Approaches

Since the initial work by Larson [7], there have been many proposals for improving dynamic hashing (for an overview see [3]). Most of these schemes, e.g. [8,12, 13], assume that the hash values are distributed in a reasonable way, i.e. close to uniform distribution, so that any skew in the original keys is eliminated for the most part by an adequate hash function. Theoretical analyses [5,10] also have not considered heavily skewed hash keys.

The papers published on non-uniform distributions of hash keys are few and far between. Otoo proposes a balanced extendible hash tree in [11], which grows from the leaves to the root, similar to a B-tree. Although this solves the problem of wasted space, the lookup costs increase. In a balanced extendible hash tree all lookups will cost as much as the most expensive lookup. For example, if we can store tables up to a depth of 10 on a page and we need 30 bits to distinguish the most skewed data items, the tree will have (at least) three levels. Due to the balancing, all queries have to traverse them. In our scheme, only the most frequent hash keys are found on the lowest level of the tree.

Finally, Du and Tong suggest a multi-level extendible hash tree in [2], which is also based on page sharing. They try to reduce the space expenditure further by compressing the entries. This, however, backfires as their scheme is very complicated, due to the fact that compression destroys the regular structure of extendible hashing. Consequently, more organizational data has to be stored, which cancels out the effect of compression. We give a more detailed comparison with the approaches by Otoo and Du/Tong in [6]

6 Conclusion and Outlook

We developed an extendible hashing index able to efficiently handle skewed data. We implemented the hashing scheme and tested it thoroughly, comparing it to several other existing access methods. Our approach proved to be superior in view of directory size as well as retrieval performance, especially for real data. Moreover, our index also performs excellently for uniformly distributed data, making it a very robust scheme. The size of our directory does not grow exponentially. Consequently, our index is also faster, because a larger fraction of the directory can be held in main memory.

The results obtained from our experiments encourage us to extend the scheme to allow processing of multi-attribute queries and partial-match retrieval. Another important subject is the creation time of the index. The current version of creating the index is not efficient enough. So a next step would be to devise efficient bulk-loading procedures to reduce the creation time significantly.

References

1. J.L. Carter and M. Wegman. Universal classes of hash functions. *J. Comput. Syst. Sci.*, 18(2):143–154, 1979.
2. D.H.C. Du and S.-R. Tong. Multilevel extendible hashing: A file structure for very large databases. *IEEE Trans. on Knowledge and Data Engineering*, 3(3):357–370, 1991.
3. R.J. Enbody and H.C. Du. Dynamic hashing schemes. *ACM Computing Surveys*, 20(2):85–113, June 1988.
4. R. Fagin, J. Nievergelt, N. Pippenger, and H.R. Strong. Extendible hashing – a fast access method for dynamic files. *ACM Transactions on Database Systems*, 4(3):315–344, September 1979.
5. P. Flajolet. On the performance evaluation of extendible hashing and trie searching. *Acta Informatica*, 20(4):345–369, 1983.
6. S. Helmer, T. Neumann, and G. Moerkotte. A robust scheme for multilevel extendible hashing. Technical Report 19/01, Universität Mannheim, 2001. http://pi3.informatik.uni-mannheim.de.
7. P.A. Larson. Dynamic hashing. *BIT*, 18:184–201, 1978.
8. D.B. Lomet. Bounded index exponential hashing. *ACM Transactions on Database Systems*, 8(1):136–165, March 1983.
9. Y. Manolopoulos, Y.Theodoridis, and V.J. Tsotras. *Advanced Database Indexing.* Kluwer Academic Publishers, Dordrecht, 1999.
10. H. Mendelson. Analysis of extendible hashing. *IEEE Trans. Software Eng.*, 8(6):611–619, November 1982.
11. E.J. Otoo. Linearizing the directory growth in order preserving extendible hashing. In *Int. Conf. on Data Engineering*, pages 580–588, 1988.
12. M.V. Ramakrishna and P.A. Larson. File organization using composite perfect hashing. *ACM Transactions on Database Systems*, 14(2):231–263, June 1989.
13. K. Ramamohanarao and J.W. Lloyd. Dynamic hashing schemes. *The Computer Journal*, 25(4):478–485, 1982.
14. M. Tamminen. Order preserving extendible hashing and bucket tries. *BIT*, 21:419–435, 1981.

A Cooperative Paradigm for Fighting Information Overload

Daniel Gayo-Avello, Darío Álvarez-Gutiérrez, and José Gayo-Avello

Department of Informatics, University of Oviedo, Calvo Sotelo s/n 33007 Oviedo (SPAIN)
{dani, darioa}@lsi.uniovi.es

Abstract. The Web is mainly processed by humans. The role of the machines is just to transmit and display the contents of the documents, barely being able to do something else. Nowadays there are lots of initiatives trying to change this situation; many of them are related to fields like the Semantic Web [1] or Web Intelligence. In this paper we describe the Cooperative Web [2] that can be seen as a new proposal towards Web Intelligence. The Cooperative Web would allow us to extract semantics from the Web in an automatic way, without the need of ontological artifacts, with language independence and, besides of this, allowing the usage of browsing experience from individual users to serve the whole community of users.

1 Introduction

Although the Web provides access to a huge amount of information it is not a perfect information retrieval mechanism. Search engines perform a really useful task but we can say that they are toping out since they provide a view of the Web quite poor to get a more powerful use. This claim can seem exaggerated but if we take into account two latest initiatives from the main search engine –Google Answers[1] and the First Annual Google Programming Contest[2]– it is clear that, implicitly, Google admits that state of the art techniques have reached their limit and "something more" is needed.

However, and for the moment, users continue using search engines that provide only a lexical view of the Web and force them to browse hundreds of documents for an increasing time until they find the piece of information they are looking for.

Besides of this, the current Web shows a problem as serious as its lack of semantics: each time a user browses the Web, he opens a path which could be useful for others and, in the same way, other users can have yet followed such path and have found its worth or its uselessness. However, all that experimental knowledge is lost.

Such situation is flawed and something is required to provide intelligence and semantics to the Web. We think that this is possible in an automatic way, transparent to the user, and language independent by using software agents and computational biology algorithms. Through this paper we will show in which way we think this task could be accomplished.

---

[1] http://answers.google.com/answers/faq.html#whatis
[2] http://www.google.com/programming-contest/

A. Yazici and C. Şener (Eds.): ISCIS 2003, LNCS 2869, pp. 228–235, 2003.

2 The Web as an Information Retrieval System

2.1 Traditional Information Retrieval Systems

The pair Web + search engines can be considered as a text retrieval system. So it is suitable for being assessed in terms of two measures, recall and precision. Both measures should ideally tend to 100% but in real systems the task of balancing them falls on the user at the moment of making his queries with more or less detail.

Likely, the main problem remains in the use of keyword-based queries. It is well known that the probability of two users employing the same keyword to refer a unique concept is below 20% [3]. So, if the query keywords are only looked for in the HTML META tags or in the document title the results are quite poor and if the search is performed using free text from the documents the recall is larger but at the expense of a serious lack of precision [4].

Such lack of precision lies, mainly, in the ambiguity of the words, even in well defined domains [5]. It is the meaning given to a word, more than the word itself, what allows us to distinguish relevant from irrelevant documents and what would permit to resolve queries that should return documents which do not include all the keywords but synonymous or semantically close words.

2.2 First Search Engines

The first main goal of the Web was to avoid the loss of information intrinsic to a large organization as well as making easier the access to available information. The initial proposal [6] suggested to develop the Web starting from a semantic ground by using concept nodes, which would be linked from the documents, and shows the drawbacks of using keyword-based information retrieval systems.

However, the Web was finally developed in a much simpler way, very similar to traditional hypertext, thus, making it an artifact designed to grow very quickly but with no document retrieval mechanisms.

In 1994 the first search engines appear: ALIWEB [7], WebCrawler [4] and Lycos [8]. These search engines showed clearly that links directories were not enough to find information but they raised new problems. On one hand, each search engine used a different Web exploring technique so the created databases were also different forcing the users to try their queries with several search engines. On the other hand, most of the returned documents had little relevance.

2.3 Modern Search Engines

Kleinberg [9] stated that documents' relevance requires human assessment. But, could this understanding of relevance be algorithmically computed? To perform this task, Kleinberg defined the concepts of "authority" and "hub".

An "authority" is a heavily linked document. If each link to a document is considered a vote for that document then such a link would indicate the relevance of the document from a human point of view since it was established by a person. By analyzing the text employed in the links to the target document and in the document itself it can be set for which topics the document is an authority. On the other hand, a hub is a document that links to many authorities.

Later, Page et al introduce the PageRank algorithm [10], based on the Kleinberg algorithm but with some new ideas to assess the relevance of documents and which turned out to be the kernel of the Google search engine. With this algorithm each document receives a score that shows the document's relevance. To compute this score the different links have different weights and the PageRank flows from one document to documents linked from this one. Thus, very linked documents would get top PageRanks and, this is the novelty, not very linked documents but from authoritative ones would inherit top PageRanks. Doing this, the search engine gets higher recall although only knowing something about their contents and the user interests could reject many of the return documents for a query.

2.4 Fighting against Information Overload

Thus, more than lack of precision the problem of the Web is information overload. A problem almost as old as the Internet since the users have suffered it with e-mail and especially with USENET posts.

For the last decade there have been many proposals to alleviate such a situation – [11], [12], [13], [14], or [15] to only quote some of them– Several ones were proposed specifically for some of the previously mentioned services while others wanted to filter any kind of information from the Internet. The technologies employed in this task were mainly three, combined or on its own: software agents, collaborative filtering and content-based recommendation.

Such initiatives did not have great success; this is not very shocking since most of them forced the user to evaluate the obtained results in order to improve the system performance. In fact, the users rarely are willing to do this extra work [14] since they consider it bothersome, so, it is imperative to use only implicit feedback [15]. On the other hand, the approaches that took into account the contents only processed automatically extracted keywords something that provides poor solutions.

3 The Semantic Web

Part of the problem can be attributed to the continuous attempts of adapting techniques to perform text retrieval in local systems to an ever-growing worldwide system. Such attempts do not perform in the expected way and, although the exploitation of hyperlinks has allowed better search engines, the increasing number of documents hinders the precision of the results and keeps the users under a flood of information.

In 1998 Tim Berners-Lee started to outline the Semantic Web. The main idea is to mark up the documents on the Web with "semantic tags" that would provide metainformation about the tagged text.

In a sense, this idea is quite similar to the use of "concept nodes" described in the original Web proposal [6] and now again the crux of the matter is the way to provide such semantic tags and state the relationships between them. To perform this task ontologies and ontological languages are being used.

Other approaches were proposed before the Semantic Web itself and have contributed greatly to it. Some of the most relevant have been: SHOE and Exposé [16], WebKB [17] and Ontobroker [18]. All of them showed similar characteristics to the ones that the Semantic Web, according to Berners-Lee, would need: a system to state asserts (RDF), a model to define new properties and relationships (RDF Schema) and a logic layer (inference and queries).

Later, a more elaborated version [1] of the Semantic Web was introduced; in this one ontologies take a leading role similar to the one played in above proposals.

3.1 Information Retrieval and Limitations of the Semantic Web

The Semantic Web is not widespread enough as to provide search engines comparable to those from traditional Web. However, some solutions have been proposed, such as Metalog [19], SquishQL [20] or SiLRI [21] that allow queries on RDF data and RQL/Sesame [22] that allows queries on RDF and RDF(S) data by means of a functional language.

Projects such as DAML, SHOE or OIL rely on some kind of query language that, in turn, relies on one or more ontologies. Because of that, in spite of differences on syntax or architecture, the Semantic Web "search engines" can be seen as a kind of inference engines which accept queries expressed in terms of one or more ontologies and return as results objects belonging to such ontologies.

Thus, the Semantic Web depends heavily on ontologies, because of that many efforts are being made to provide semi-automatic generation of ontologies [23] and automatic semantic markup of documents [24].

This dependence is also the cause of the two main limitations of the Semantic Web. On one hand the creation of huge ontologies with large numbers of classes and relationships between them will require, at least in the short time, human supervision [23]. On the other hand, the ontologies developed up to now and the queries for which the Semantic Web best performs are more metasemantics than semantics (e.g. it is possible to build an ontology to allow finding papers from a specific author but quite difficult to model an ontology to fit all the topics which could appear in the papers).

In short, the Semantic Web will make the access to information much easier in well-defined environments such as corporate intranets [25] but it would be really difficult to apply the same techniques to the Web as a whole.

4 The Cooperative Web

As we can see, approaches to fight against information overload are not suitable to help the user in his information searches on the Web. Some of them require explicit feedback from the user to evaluate the retrieved information. On the other hand, most of the proposals cannot process documents with language independence. As for the Semantic Web, it will play a vital role in well-defined domains but it is difficult to apply it to the whole Web in an automatic way.

Thus, we propose a possible, and complementary, solution in order to contribute towards the Web Intelligence, the so-called Cooperative Web:

"The Cooperative Web is a layer on top of the current Web to give it semantics in an automatic, global, transparent and language independent way. It does not require explicit user participation but implicit feedback that would be acquired by software agents. The Cooperative Web relies on the use of concepts and document taxonomies, both of them can be obtained with no human supervision from free text."

Many researchers involved in the Web Intelligence field share similar views and proposals. Nishida introduces the concept of "virtualized ego" [26], a kind of software agents quite similar to the ones proposed for the Cooperative Web. Han and Chang also explain the need for automatic building of documents taxonomies [27]. Cercone et al state the future relevance of recommender systems and software agents in the Intelligent Web [28].

4.1 Concepts vs. Keywords

The retrieval of information using keywords has many drawbacks. The use of ontologies can improve precision in some cases. However, developing ontologies to support any conceivable query on the Web would be insurmountably hard.

There is a middle point: the use of concepts. A concept would be a more abstract entity (and with more semantics) than a keyword. It would not require complex artifacts such as ontology languages or inference systems. A concept can be seen as a cluster of words with similar meaning in a given scope, ignoring tense, gender, and number. For instance, `(actor, actress, artist, celebrity, star)`.

Concepts would be useful if they could be automatically generated and processed as keywords. We think that techniques such as Latent Semantic Indexing [29] or concept indexing [30] could serve this task.

4.2 Documents Taxonomies

The Cooperative Web would use the whole text of the document without using any markup as the source for semantic meaning. How could this be done without the need to "understand" the text? A document can be seen as an individual from a population. Among living beings an individual is defined by its genome, which is composed of chromosomes, divided into genes constructed upon genetic bases. Alike, documents are composed of passages (groups of sentences related to just one subject), which are divided into sentences built upon concepts.

Using this analogy, it seems clear that two documents are semantically related if their "genome" is alike. Big differences between genomes mean that the semantic relationship between documents is weak.

We think that it is possible to adapt some algorithms used in computational biology to the field of document classification. Similar individuals or species have similarities in their genetic codes so it is possible to classify individuals and species into taxonomies or dendrograms without the need to know what every gene "does".

Such dendrograms cluster different species in "categories" which provide useful information to understand species evolution and confirm (or rebut) the Linnaean classification system.

This system establishes the taxonomic groups basing on noticeable attributes in the living beings, that is the phenotype. Dendrograms, however, build the groups from the genotype, which in turn influences the phenotype. Because of this, categories obtained in an automatic way from the species DNA can be very similar to other categories built by a human.

In the same way, documents could be classified into taxonomic trees depending on the similitude found in their "conceptual genome". The important thing about such a classification is that it would provide semantics (similitude at the conceptual level between documents or between documents and user queries) without requiring the classification process to use any semantics. In fact, it should be able to cluster documents in categories similar to the ones that a person would build.

4.3 Collaboration between User Agents

The Cooperative Web intends to employ user browsing experience, extracting useful semantics from it. Each user in the Cooperative Web would have an agent with two main goals: to learn from its master (developing a user profile without explicit feedbak), and to retrieve information for him.

Thus, having each user attached to a profile, it is possible to assign to each pair `(profile, document)` a utility level. Having an agent for each user it would be responsible for deciding that utility level. In order for this utility valuation to be really practical, the utility level should be determined in an implicit way (just by observing users' behavior, without querying them). The utility level should also be assigned to individual passages within a document, and not to the document as a whole.

4.4 Information Retrieval

The agent would have two different ways to perform information retrieval: to find information satisfying a query formulated by the user, or to explore in the background on his behalf to recommend him unknown documents.

To perform both tasks we want to employ two well-known techniques: Collaborative Filtering (CF) and Content-Based Recommendation (CBR). If the agent uses CF it would recommend the user documents that have obtained a high utility level from users with his same (or similar) profile. On the other hand, if the agent uses CBR it would retrieve documents that would be conceptually related with the user profile, with a query or with an initial document, without priorizing the utility level.

The first system would allow "queries" similar to the following ones: (1) "Find documents related to `star`". Because of the ambiguity of the term, the agent should not provide results but more terms related to the initial one depending on the different topics to help the user to refine the query. (2) "Find documents related to this sentence/paragraph/document". The user would select a piece of text and the agent would find conceptually related information.

The recommender system would work in a different way. It would be, mainly, a personal assistant that would help the user by performing tasks such as information retrieval on behalf of the user or unsolicited recommendation of interesting not previously visited documents.

5 Conclusion

We have described a proposal to provide Web Intelligence: the Cooperative Web. We have compared it with the Semantic Web and older proposals to avoid information overload in the Internet.

In more detail we have describe the information retrieval techniques that the Cooperative Web could provide. If they are compared with modern search engines we think it is clear that our proposal would obtain less but more relevant results since it would employ conceptual taxonomies.

References

1. Berners-Lee, T., Hendler, J., Lassila, O.: The Semantic Web. Scientific American, 284 (5) (2001) 34–43
2. Gayo-Avello, D., Álvarez-Gutiérrez, D.: The Cooperative Web: A Complement to the Semantic Web. Proc. of 26th Annual International Computer Software and Applications Conference. Oxford, England (2002) 179–183
3. Furnas, G.W., Landauer, T.K., Gómez, L.M., Dumais, S.T.: The vocabulary problem in human-system communication. CACM, Vol. 30, No. 11 (1987) 964–971
4. Pinkerton, B.: Finding what people want: Experiences with the WebCrawler. Proc. of the Second International World Wide Web Conference. Chicago, IL, USA (1994)
5. Krovetz, R., Croft, W.B.: Lexical Ambiguity and Information Retrieval. ACM Transactions on Information Systems, Vol. 10, No. 2 (1992) 115–141
6. Berners-Lee, T.: Information Management: A Proposal `http://www.w3.org/History/1989/proposal.html` (1989)
7. Koster, M.: ALIWEB: Archie-Like indexing in the Web. Computer Networks and ISDN Systems, Vol. 27, No. 2 (1994) 175–182
8. Mauldin, M.L, Leavitt, J.R.R.: Web agent related research at the Center for Machine Translation. Proc. of the ACM Special Interest Group on Networked Information Discovery and Retrieval (ACM-SIGNIDR-V). McLean, VA, USA (1994)
9. Kleinberg, J.M.: Authoritative Sources in a Hyperlinked Environment. Proc. of the 9th Annual ACM-SIAM Symposium on Discrete Algorithms. San Francisco, CA, USA (1998)
10. Page, L, Brin, S. Motwani, R., Winograd, T.: The PageRank Citation Ranking: Bringing Order to the Web. Stanford Digital Libraries Working Paper (1998)
11. Morita, M., Shinoda, Y.: Information filtering based on user behavior analysis and best match text retrieval. Proc. of the 17th Annual International Retrieval. Dublin, Ireland (1994)
12. Maes, P.: Agents that Reduce Work and Information Overload. CACM Vol. 37, No. 7 (1994) 811–821
13. Lieberman, H.: Letizia: An Agent That Assists Web Browsing. Proc. of the 14th International Joint Conference on Artificial Intelligence. Montreal, QC, Canada (1995)
14. Starr, B., Ackerman, M.S., Pazzani, M.: Do-I-Care: A Collaborative Web Agent. Proc. of the ACM on Human Factors in Computing Systems. Vancouver, Canada (1996) 273–274

15. Balabanovic, M.: An interface for learning multi-topic user profiles from implicit feedback. Proc. of AAAI Workshop on Recommender Systems. Madison, WI, USA (1998)
16. Luke, S., Spector, L., Rager, D.: Ontology-Based Knowledge Discovery on the World-Wide Web. Working Notes of the Workshop on Internet-Based Information Systems at the 13th National Conference on Artificial Intelligence (AAAI96) (1996)
17. Craven, M., DiPasquo, D., Freitag, D., McCallum, A., Mitchell, T., Nigam, K., Slattery, S.: Learning to Extract Symbolic Knowledge from the World Wide Web. Proc. of the 15th National Conference on Artificial Intelligence (AAAI98), Madison, WI, USA (1998)
18. Fensel, D., Decker, S., Erdmann, M., Studer, R.: Ontobroker: Or How to Enable Intelligent Access to the WWW. Proc. of the 11th Workshop on Knowledge Acquisition, Modeling, and Management. Banff, Canada (1998)
19. Marchiori, M., Saarela, J.: Query + Metadata + Logic = Metalog. Proc. of Query Languages Workshop. Boston, MA, USA (1998)
20. Brickley, D., Miller, L.: RDF: Extending and Querying RSS channels. ILRT discussion document. http://ilrt.org/discovery/2000/11/rss-query/ (2000)
21. Decker, S., Brickley, D., Saarela, J., Angele, J.: A Query and Inference Service for RDF. Proc. of Query Languages Workshop. Boston, MA, USA (1998)
22. Karvounarakis, G, Christophides, V., Plexousakis, D., Alexaki, S.: Querying RDF Descriptions for Community Web Portals. The French National Conference on Databases. Agadir, Maroc (2001)
23. Maedche, A., Staab, S.: Discovering Conceptual Relations from Text. Technical Report 399". Institute AIFB, Karlsruhe University (2000)
24. Erdmann, M., Maedche, A., Scnurr, H.P., Staab, S.: From Manual to Semi-automatic Semantic Annotation: About Ontology-based Text Annotation Tools. ETAI Journal - Section on Semantic Web (Linköping Electronic Articles in Computer and Information Science), 6 (2001)
25. Fensel, D.: Ontology-Based Knowledge Management. IEEE Computer, IEEE Computer Society, Washington, D.C., 35(11) (2002) 56–59
26. Nishida, T.: Social Intelligence Design for the Web. IEEE Computer, IEEE Computer Society, Washington, D.C., 35(11) (2002) 37–41
27. Han, J., Chang, K.C.-C.: Data Mining for Web Intelligence. IEEE Computer, IEEE Computer Society, Washington, D.C., 35(11) (2002) 64–70
28. Cercone, N., Hou, L., Keselj, V., An, A., Naruedomkul, K., Hu, X.: From Computational Intelligence to Web Intelligence. IEEE Computer, IEEE Computer Society, Washington, D.C., 35(11) (2002) 72–76
29. Foltz, P.W.: Using Latent Semantic Indexing for Information Filtering. Proc. of the ACM Conference on Office Information Systems. Boston, USA (1990) 40–47
30. Karypis, G., Han, E.: Concept indexing: A fast dimensionality reduction algorithm with applications to document retrieval and categorization. Technical Report TR-00-0016. University of Minnesota (2000)

Comparison of New Simple Weighting Functions for Web Documents against Existing Methods

Byurhan Hyusein, Ahmed Patel, and Ferad Zyulkyarov

Computer Networks and Distributed Systems Research Group,
Department of Computer Science,
University College Dublin,
Belfield, Dublin 4,
Ireland
{bhyusein, apatel, feradz}@cnds.ucd.ie

Abstract. Term weighting is one of the most important aspects of modern Web retrieval systems. The weight associated with a given term in a document shows the importance of the term for the document, i.e. its usefulness for distinguishing documents in a document collection. In search engines operating in a dynamic environment such as the Internet, where many documents are deleted from and added to the database, the usual formula involving the inverse document frequency is too costly to be computed each time the document collection is updated. This paper proposes two new simple and effective weighting functions. These weighting functions have been tested and compared with results obtained for the PIVOT, SMART and INQUERY methods using the WT10g collection of documents.

1 Introduction

An important question in text retrieval is how to assign weights to the terms either in the documents or in the queries. Weighting is usually an automatic process. Manual weighting or indexing of documents would be more precise, but it requires a huge amount of human resources. The most successful and widely used function for automatic generation of weights for static databases are so-called $tf \cdot idf$ (or *TF-IDF*) weighting functions [1], where the abbreviations *tf* and *idf* denote term frequency and inverse document frequency.

The term frequency *tf* is the number of occurrences of the given term t within the given document D. It is a document-specific statistic and can vary from one document to another. Document frequency for a term t in the collection of documents C is the number of documents in that collection which contain the term t. Inverse document frequency *idf* is usually defined as a natural logarithmic function $ln\frac{N}{df}$ where N is the number of documents in the entire collection and *df* is the document frequency for the given term t.

A vector T is used to represent the set of unique terms t_j in the collection C, i.e. $T = (t_1, t_2, \ldots, t_{N_C})$ (dictionary vector), where N_C is the number of unique terms in C. Then each document D_i in the collection C is represented by set of terms t_j and/or their frequency tf_{ij} (or associated weight w_{ij} of the term) i.e.

A. Yazici and C. Şener (Eds.): ISCIS 2003, LNCS 2869, pp. 236–243, 2003.

$$D_i = \{(t_1, tf_{i1}), (t_2, tf_{i2}), \ldots, (t_{N_C}, tf_{iN_C})\}$$
$$(\text{or } D_i = (tf_{i1}, tf_{i2}, \ldots, tf_{iN_C}))$$

or

$$D_i = \{(t_1, w_{i1}), (t_2, w_{i2}), \ldots, (t_{N_C}, w_{iN_C})\}$$
$$(\text{or } D_i = (w_{i1}, w_{i2}, \ldots, w_{iN_C}))$$

The terms with frequency zero are usually omitted and the document is represented only by the terms which occur in the document with associated term frequency or weight. (We use this assumption throughout the rest of the paper.)

Two main problems arise from using *TF-IDF* weighting functions. The first problem is if a document D_i is represented by a set of terms t_j and/or their frequency tf_{ij} then the weighting has to be done at search time. If a document is represented by the terms and associated weights, then when new documents are added to or deleted from the collection the weights of the terms in the documents will change because *df* for the collection will be changed.

The second problem arises when a collection contains documents from several different topics in which case the document frequency factor may be large for the *topic specific terms*, decreasing the average contribution of these terms towards the query-document similarity. This problem has been found to be the case in the *Adaptive Distributed Search & Advertising* (*ADSA*) search engine (SE) which is a topic specific SE [2].

Typically the search process consists of checking the similarity between the query and documents in order to find the relevant documents. We assume that a document is represented as a weight vector $D_i = (w_{i1}, w_{i2}, \ldots, w_{iN_c})$, and a user's query $Q = (q_1, q_2, \ldots, q_{N_C})$, where q_i is a real number (usually $q_i \in [0, 1]$) which shows the importance of the term t_j for the query. Then the similarity between the query and the document is usually checked using the *inner product* function between the query vector and the given document vector:

$$sim(Q, D_i) = \sum_{j=1}^{N_c} q_j w_{ij}$$

When the similarity between the query and the documents in the collection is checked, the top documents (with the highest similarity to the query) are returned to the user.

2 Weighting

Three main components that affect the importance of a term in a text [3] are:

- the term frequency factor;
- the inverse document frequency factor; and
- document length normalization.

In SEs operating in a dynamic environment such as the Internet where many documents are deleted from and added to the SEs' databases in real time. In such instances if the weights of the terms in the documents depend on the *idf* then existing indexed documents need to be re-indexed everytime a new document (that has even just one term in common) is indexed simply because the *idf* of those terms has changed.

Document length normalization of term weights is used to remove the advantage that the long documents have in retrieval over the short documents. However many recent experiments show that document length normalization has little or no effect on Web document retrieval [4]. One of the main reasons that document length normalization is not successful for the Web is that such documents contain significantly less terms than ordinary text documents.

Having tested by experiments, we observed that weighting functions involving maximum term frequency normalization give very good results. The SMART and INQUERY systems define the weights by applying augmented maximum term frequency normalization [5,6]. However this may also cause problems when documents contain terms with unusually high frequency. In order to reduce the impact of the terms with unusually high frequency, the PIVOT function[7] applies logarithmic scale to term frequencies.

Based on the observation of the results of SMART, INQUERY and PIVOT and their shortcomings, we created the following weighting functions:

$$(W1) \qquad c_1 + \frac{1 + \ln(tf)}{1 + \ln(tf_{max})}$$

$$(W2) \qquad c_2 - \frac{1}{1 + \ln(tf)}$$

where $tf \geq 1$, $tf_{max} \geq 1$, $c_1 \geq 0$ and $c_2 > 1$ are constants (belief coefficients). The belief coefficients ensure that documents containing more keywords from the query will be considered to be more relevant than documents containing less keywords even though these terms appear more frequently.

The proposed new functions W1 and W2 are simple and do not depend on document requency. The purpose is that the weight (the importance) of a term in a given document should depend on its absolute frequency of occurrence but at the same time the terms with high frequency of occurrence should not drag the weights of other terms with less frequencies way down the scale. This is achieved by using the combination of *ln* function and belief coefficients that restricts the weights to a maximum values of $(c_1, c_1 + 1]$ for W1 and $[c_2 - 1, c_2)$ for W2.

The main advantages of the proposed weighting functions W1 and W2 are that they are suitable for use in dynamic document databases. Adding or deleting documents from a collection does not affect the terms' weights because the functions do not involve *idf.* W1 is similar to the function used for the calculation of the term frequency factor in PIVOT [7]. However, W1 can be used without *idf*. The second proposed weighting function W2 is simpler than W1 and does not depend on the term frequency of other terms belonging to the document.

From all our experiments for SMART, INQUERY, PIVOT, W1 and W2, we show in the next section how the proposed weighting functions achieve better results when querying documents.

3 Experiments and Results

In our experiments, we use the 10 gigabyte collection of documents (WT10g) [8] available for participants of Web track main task in the TREC-9 [9] experiments. This collection is a subset of the 100 gigabyte VLC2 collection created by Internet Archive in 1997 [10].

Queries are created using only the title part of Web track topics 451-500. The full text of all the documents was indexed. Stop word's lists of 595 English, 172 German and 352 Spanish words were used. Porter's stemming algorithm [11] was applied to both documents and queries. Average index size per document was 132.54 words. All terms in the query were equally weighted by one. Inner product is used as the similarity function in the experiments.

Many variations of PIVOT, SMART and INQUERY weighting functions have been used with different document collections by other researchers. In our experiments we used the functions shown below to calculate the term frequency factor for a term t within a document D. From each of the three families of weighting functions, the following gave the best results for the WT10g collection of documents:

$$(PIVOT) \qquad 0.4 + 0.6\frac{1+\ln(tf)}{1+\ln(tf_{max})}$$

$$(SMART) \qquad 0.5 + 0.5\frac{tf}{tf_{max}}$$

$$(INQUERY) \qquad 0.4 + 0.6\frac{tf}{tf_{max}}$$

Table 1. Summary statistics

	W1	W2	PIVOT	SMART	INQUERY
Retrieved	50000	50000	50000	50000	50000
Relevant ret.	1260	1223	1268	1220	1137
Relevant	2617				
Num. of queries	50				

The results obtained for W1, W2, PIVOT, SMART and INQUERY weighting functions are given in Tables 1, 2 and 3. The explanation of the results in the tables are as follows:

Table 2. Recall level precision averages

Recall	Precision				
	W1	W2	PIVOT	SMART	INQUERY
0.00	0.4260	0.4593	0.4260	0.4086	0.3696
0.10	0.3199	0.3068	0.3199	0.2893	0.2460
0.20	0.2593	0.2644	0.2592	0.2298	0.1897
0.30	0.2323	0.2234	0.2325	0.2004	0.1626
0.40	0.1837	0.1859	0.1830	0.1542	0.1289
0.50	0.1647	0.1705	0.1640	0.1363	0.1080
0.60	0.1236	0.1321	0.1228	0.0950	0.0846
0.70	0.1033	0.0970	0.1036	0.0830	0.0562
0.80	0.0664	0.0769	0.0675	0.0509	0.0288
0.90	0.0591	0.0689	0.0588	0.0413	0.0240
1.00	0.0362	0.0473	0.0360	0.0237	0.0175
Average precision over all relevant documents					
	W1	W2	PIVOT	SMART	INQUERY
non-interpolated	0.1592	0.1673	0.1591	0.1368	0.1126

- *Summary statistics*:
  - Retrieved - number of documents retrieved.
  - Relevant ret. - total number of relevant documents returned for all queries.
  - Relevant - total possible relevant documents within a given task.
  - Num. of queries - the number of queries used in the search runs.
- *Recall Level Precision Averages*:
  - Precision at eleven standard recall levels.
    The precision averages at eleven standard recall levels are used to compare the performance of the weighting functions and as the input for plotting the recall-precision graph (see Figure 1).
  - Average precision over all relevant documents, non-interpolated.
    This is a single-valued measure that reflects the performance over all relevant documents. The measure is not an average of the precision at standard recall levels. Rather, it is the average of the precision value obtained after each relevant document is retrieved.
- *Document Level Averages*:
  - Precision at nine document cut-off values.
    Each document precision average is computed by summing the precisions at the specified document cut-off value and dividing by the number of queries (50).
  - R-Precision - precision after R documents have been retrieved, where R is the number of relevant documents for the queries. The average R-Precision is computed by taking the mean of the R-Precisions of the individual queries.

The results are evaluated using the trec_eval package written by Chris Buckley of Sabir Research (available at ftp://ftp.cs.cornell.edu/pub/smart/).

Table 3. Document level averages

	Precision				
	W1	W2	PIVOT	SMART	INQUERY
At 5	0.2400	0.2480	0.2360	0.2000	0.1840
At 10	0.2060	0.2000	0.2060	0.1800	0.1720
At 15	0.1813	0.1640	0.1840	0.1587	0.1520
At 20	0.1660	0.1490	0.1660	0.1480	0.1390
At 30	0.1527	0.1387	0.1540	0.1367	0.1300
At 100	0.1034	0.0912	0.1030	0.0928	0.0802
At 200	0.0739	0.0707	0.0740	0.0691	0.0578
At 500	0.0419	0.0400	0.0418	0.0398	0.0366
At 1000	0.0252	0.0245	0.0254	0.0244	0.0227
R-Precision					
	W1	W2	PIVOT	SMART	INQUERY
Exact:	0.1909	0.1895	0.1934	0.1678	0.1380

4 Discussion of Results

To soften the influence of the terms with a high frequency of occurrence, the natural logarithm function was used in W1 and W2 weighting functions. Independence of document frequency ensures that adding or deleting documents from a collection does not affect the term's weights. Varying the weights of the indexed terms in the range of $(c_1, c_1+1]$ for W1 and in $[c_2-1, c_2)$ for W2 and using inner product similarity function, the documents containing more keywords from the query are considered to be more relevant than documents containing less keywords even if these terms appears more frequently.

We also found that the W1 and W2 proposed weighting functions are not sensitive to the belief coefficients c_1 and c_2. We achieved approximately the same precision and recall varying c_1 in the interval of *(0, 0.9]* and c_2 in the interval of *(1, 2.5]*. The best results are achieved using constant $c_1 = 0.9$ and $c_2 = 2.5$. We obtained 1260 *relevant* documents with W1 (48.14%), 1223 with W2 (46.73%), 1268 with PIVOT (48.45%), 1220 with SMART (46.61%) and 1137 with INQUERY (43.44%) weighting function of the total possible 2617 relevant documents (Table 1).

The recall-precision graph in Figure 1 compares the results obtained by newly proposed weighting functions W1 and W2 against the results obtained for PIVOT, SMART and INQUERY weighting functions. This graph is created using the eleven recall levels from the recall level precision averages (Table 2).

Figure 1 also shows that W1 and W2 give significantly better precision than SMART and INQUERY weighting functions in all of the eleven standard recall levels. For most of the recall levels W1 and W2 give better precision than PIVOT as well. In two recall levels W1 has the same precision as PIVOT and in six recall levels W1 is superior. W2 is superior in eight of possible eleven recall levels.

W1 and W2 weighting functions also give better results than PIVOT, SMART and INQUERY with respect to average precision over all relevant doc-

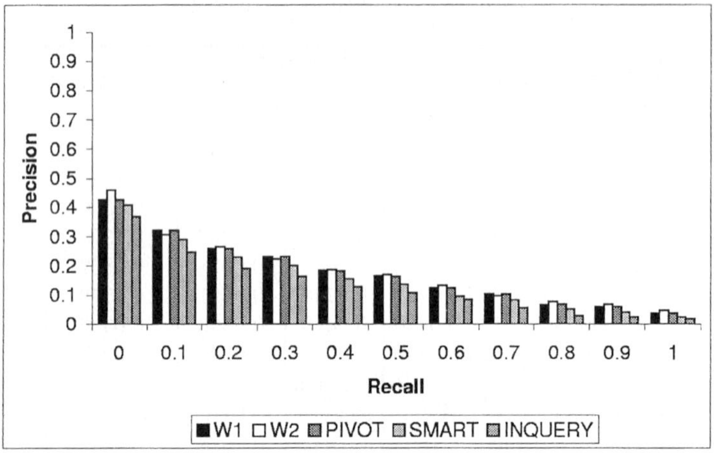

Fig. 1. Recall-precision graphs

uments (Table 2), significantly better R-Precision and precision at the nine document cut-off values than SMART and INQUERY (Table 3). Because of the greater number of retrieved documents for PIVOT it gives better R-Precision and better precision in the most of the document cut-off values.

5 Conclusions and Future Work

In this paper we proposed two new simple and effective weighting functions for Web document retrieval. The weighting schemes are tested and compared with results obtained for the PIVOT, SMART and INQUERY methods on the WT10g collection of documents.

Experiments showed that our weighting functions perform better than SMART, INQUERY and PIVOT weighting functions with respect to average precision and recall. The proposed weighting functions are computationally fast and suitable for use in SEs. Weighting function W2 is currently in use in the ADSA search engine because it gives better precision than W1 (which was used in the previous version of the ADSA search engine).

From the experimental results, our current research work is concentrating on the development of a more complex indexer which will allow any attribute of Web documents to be indexed. This will permit us to investigate in detail how the different parts of the documents contribute to the average precision in the process of search in a much more comprehensive manner.

Acknowledgement. The research was funded by Enterprise Ireland as part of the Enterprise Ireland Informatics Research Initiative.

References

1. G. Salton and C. Buckley. Term Weighting Approaches in Automatic Text Retrieval. *Information Processing and Management*, 24(5):513–523, 1988.
2. R. Khoussainov, T. O'Meara, and A. Patel. Independent Proprietorship and Competition in Distributed Web Search Architectures. In *Proceeding of the Seventh IEEE International Conference on Engineering of Complex Computer Systems (ICECCS 2001)*, pages 191–199. IEEE Computer Society Press, 2001.
3. G. Salton and M. McGill. *Introduction to Modern Information Retrieval.* McGraw-Hill, New York, NY, 1983.
4. C. Buckley and J. Walz. SabIR Research at TREC 9. In *Proceeding of the 9th Text REtrieval Conference (TREC-9)*, pages 475–477. The National Institute of Standards and Technology, 2000.
5. R. Larson. Term Weighting in Smart, October 1998 Available from: http://www.sims.berkeley.edu/courses/is202/f98/Lecture18/sld021.htm [Accessed July 14th, 2003].
6. J. Broglio, J. P. Callan, W. B. Croft, and D. W. Nachbar. Document Retrieval and Routing Using the Inquery System. In *Proceeding of the Third Text REtrieval Conference (TREC-3)*, pages 29–38. The National Institute of Standards and Technology, 1995.
7. A. Singhal, C. Buckley, and M. Mitra. Pivoted Document Length Normalization. In Hans-Peter Frei, Donna Harman, Peter Schäuble, and Ross Wilkinson, editors, *Proceedings of the Nineteenth Annual International ACM SIGIR Conference on Research and Development in Information Retrieval*, pages 21–29, New York, 1996. ACM Press.
8. P. Bailey, N. Craswell, and D. Hawking. Engineering a Multi-Purpose Test Collection for Web Retrieval Experiments. *Information Processing and Management*, 2002.
9. D. Hawking, CSIRO Mathematical, and Information Sciences. Overview of the TREC-9 Web Track. In *Proceeding of the 9th Text REtrieval Conference (TREC-9)*, pages 87–102. The National Institute of Standards and Technology, 2000.
10. Internet Archive: Building an Internet Library, http://www.archive.org.
11. M. F. Porter. An algorithm for suffix stripping. *Program*, 14(3):130–137, July 1980.

Stemming in Agglutinative Languages: A Probabilistic Stemmer for Turkish

B. Taner Dinçer and Bahar Karaoğlan

Ege Üniversitesi, Uluslararası Bilgisayar Enstitüsü, 35100 Bornova, İzmir, Türkiye
{dtaner, bahar}@ube.ege.edu.tr

Abstract. In this paper, we introduce a new lexicon free, probabilistic stemmer to be used in a developing Turkish Information Retrieval system. It has a linear computational complexity and its test success ratio is 95.8%. The main contribution of this paper is to give a thorough description of a probabilistic perspective for stemming which can also be generalized to apply to other agglutinative languages like Finnish, Hungarian, Estonian and Czech.

1 Introduction

In analytic languages like English, stemming is relatively unsophisticated, because morphological variations of words forms are limited. On the other hand, in the agglutinative languages like Turkish, stemming is still a hard problem, since they have the capacity to generate theoretically an infinite number of possible word forms [1, 2]. The morphology analyzers are the only precise tools as stemmers for Information Retrieval (IR) systems in agglutinative languages [1, 3, and 4]. But in this way, stemming for IR Systems in agglutinative languages results in a paradox that can be defined by a conflicted pair of requirements: low storage and increased performance[1]. Stemming is demanded from IR systems for agglutinative languages to overcome storage complexity and to enhance precision/recall metrics [5, 6]. In fact, IR systems' overall performance decrease, because of a high level of computational complexity that is raised from using morphology analyzers as stemmers [7]. The probabilistic stemming that we proposed here can be used to overcome this challenge, effectively.

In this paper, we present a probabilistic stemming model based on the proposed statistical framework for Turkish IR systems. Additionally, we also validate the proposed model by the analyses of the results of an experiment. The results reveal that, the new stemmer overcomes the mentioned obstacles by having a computational complexity of O(n) (i.e., linear) and a compression level of 69% (i.e., storage complexity).

[1] In information Retrieval, performance is measured by Precision and Recall [2]. In fact, response time of the overall system is also a performance measure, but in this study it is referred by computational complexity, unless otherwise mentioned.

A. Yazici and C. Şener (Eds.): ISCIS 2003, LNCS 2869, pp. 244–251, 2003.

The paper is organized as follows: In section 2, we give brief definitions and clarify the need for stemming in IR systems for agglutinative languages. In section 3, we overview related previous work, in addition, we present basic notations and we explain the statistical framework and the probabilistic stemming model. In Section 4, we assert the probabilistic stemming model and the method. In section 5, we summarize the analyses and results of our experiment. The conclusions are given in section 6.

2 Stemming and Information Retrieval

IR systems are used to handle information gathered from large amounts of electronic documents. Information in a document is basically composed of words' semantics. Hence, IR systems actually deal with those words which are the representatives of semantics that are truly the building blocks of intended information. A word in a document may have different morphological forms according to its grammatical usage in the text sequence, but the semantic that is represented by its stem remains unchanged. Therefore, IR systems generally use the stems instead of word forms both to overcome storage problems and to increase performance [8].

The definition of stemming is given by Lovins [9] as "a procedure to reduce all words with the same stem to a common form, usually by stripping each word of its derivational and inflectional suffixes". Stemming for IR in analytic languages like English is rather effortless than in agglutinative languages. As an example, Porter's algorithm [10] for English is based on a series of a limited number of cascaded rewrite rules, and can accept nearly all word forms by only exhausting about 1200 morphological variations [1]. But in Turkish as an agglutinative language, even there are approximately 23,000 stems; theoretically an infinite number of different word forms can be generated [1, 2]. With this level of morphological complexity, the morphology analyzers which are transducer models from a lexicon plus embedded rules are the merely accepted standard for morphological parsing [1]. But these morphology analyzers are based on two-level language model [3, 11] which is theoretically NP-Hard [7]. As a consequence, there are two challenges for IR systems: 1) With morphology analyzer as a stemmer computational complexity arises 2) without a stemmer, storage complexity arises from indexing each different form of a word which has the same semantic, but a different morphology. Therefore, stemming is demanded from IR systems for agglutinative languages to reach a manageable storage size and a satisfactory level of performance [5, 6]. But in turn, linear computational complexity is important for stemming algorithms to be efficiently used for IR purposes [8].

To highlight the necessity of stemming in agglutinative languages, the degree of compression achieved by Porter's [10] stemmer applied to a newswire database containing 567,564 English words and Oflazer's [4] morphology analyzer used as a stemmer applied to political news database that contained 376,187 Turkish words are tabulated in Table 1.

Table 1. Level of compression for Turkish and English text corpora with stemming[5].

Corpus	Word Tokens	Distinct terms	Distinct stems	Compression (%)
Turkish	376,187	41,370	6,363	84.6
English	567,574	18,384	11,671	36.4

As seen in Table-1, despite the fact that English database has many more word tokens than Turkish database; the number of distinct Turkish terms are greater than the number of distinct English terms. This indicates the diversity of Turkish word derivations which is also verified by the compression ratio results. The compression level of 36.4% is far smaller than 84.6% which clearly indicates the lower degree of morphological variations of words in English. The compression ratio of 84.6% observed for Turkish database emphasizes the need for stemming.

3 Stemming and Related Work

The stemming algorithms used for IR purposes can be grouped in four: 1) Table Lookup algorithms, 2) Successor Variety algorithms, 3) n-gram algorithms 4) Affix Removal algorithms. All of these four groups of stemmers are developed for either analytic languages like English or some indo-European languages like French and German. But, these algorithms can not cope with high level of morphological richness in languages having inflection paradigm like south-western or Oghuz group Turkic agglutinative languages which also include Turkish, Turkmen, Azerbaijani or Azeri, Ghasghai and Gagauz [12, 13].

There are also a number of stemming algorithms developed for Turkish which are based on the effort of fitting the morphology analyzer into an IR system by decreasing the strictness of some methods such as the tagging and identification of morphemes down to an acceptable level of accuracy. Examples of these stemmers are of Duran's [14], Alpkoçak et al [15]. These algorithms search a pre-constructed electronic lexicon to find a probable stem. Then, they verify that it is correct by matching the rest of the word form with a recognizable suffix sequence by looking up possible combinations of suffixes according to morphotactics of Turkish. Degree of comparison of this later verification phase affects both the accuracy and the computational complexity; in a high level of verification, accuracy will be high, but the computational complexity will be closed to NP-hard, and vice versa. Therefore, for these stemmers, the level of computational complexity increases over again from a point close to linear, to a point close to NP-Hard as much as the level of morphological knowledge use is increased.

One of the first attacks to the stemming problem in Turkish is done by Köksal [16]. It is completely a different effort from the others by its non-linguistics perspective. He has developed a stemmer that simply takes a fixed length part of a word form from the start as the stem of that word form. Originally, Köksal claimed that a stem length of 5 gives the best result in tests. But in practice, there is no common fixed length for all document sets. A value that works well with a particular document set under a particular topic may decrease the performance of IR system dealing with a document set under a different topic. Despite its inefficiencies, this approach is our reference concept, since it proves that even at worst case (i.e., without any morphological knowledge), the IR performance for Turkish can be increased by just taking fixed length substrings from the start of the word forms as of their stems. Therefore, it is reasonable to expect that the performance could further be increased by enhancing this simple concept with pragmatics of the morphological knowledge. In our proposed model, we use the statistics of generalized morphological knowledge gathered from a previously analyzed text database as the pragmatics, to enhance this prior reference model. By the use of pre-computed statistics, we also have guaranteed to stay around a linear computational complexity.

3.1 Notation

We denote a word form in any agglutinative language by a string that is represented by $s_n = h_1 h_2 \cdots h_n$, where each h_i ($i = 1,2,\ldots,n$) is a member of the corresponding alphabet A and n is the number of letters (i.e., length of the string). In our study, we used the Turkish alphabet which has 29 letters and the underscore '_' for blank character as follows:

$$A = \{a, b, c, ç, d, e, f, g, ğ, h, ı, i, j, k, l, m, n, o, ö, p, r, s, ş, t, u, ü, v, y, z, '\_'\}$$

and, we adapted the following notations to denote substrings of any string s_n for $1 \le i \le j \le n$,

$$s_n[i:j] = h_i h_{i+1} \cdots h_j$$

$$s_n[:j] = h_1 h_2 \cdots h_j \quad \text{and} \quad s_n[i:] = h_{i+1} \cdots h_n$$

Based on our notation, the special substring $s_n[i:i+1] = h_i h_{i+1}$ is denoted by the ordered pair of letters $(h_1, h_2)_i$ where sub-index, i ($i = 1,2,\ldots,n-1$), indicates the starting position of the ordered pair in that string and $h_1 = h_i, h_2 = h_{i+1} \in A$. For $i = n$, the ordered pair is formed by an added blank as $(h_n, '\_')_{i=n}$. Thus any string $s_n = h_1 h_2 \cdots h_n$ has n ordered pairs in our study.

For a given ordered pair of letters $(h_1, h_2)_j$ that can appear at a position $1 \le j \le n_{\max}$ in any Turkish word form (where $n_{\max}$ is the maximum number of letters that a Turkish word form can have, in our database $n_{\max} = 23$), and a given particular word form denoted by $s_n = h_1 h_2 \cdots h_n$ where $n \ge j$, the notation $(h_1, h_2)_j \in s_n$ refers that there exists an ordered pair $(h_1, h_2)_i$ at position i ($1 \le i \le n$) in s_n provided that $(h_1, h_2)_i = (h_1, h_2)_j$ for $i = j$. Finally, we define two more symbols namely $g_m = s_n[:m]$ and $e_m = s_n[m:]$ in order to represent any word form as an ordered pair of two substrings by $s_n^m = (g_m, e_m)$ for all m where $1 \le m \le n$.

3.2 The Sample Space and the Ordered Pair Probabilities

If we let L be the set of all possible ordered pairs of letters $(h_1, h_2)_i$ that can appear in any Turkish word form at positions $i = 1,2,\ldots,n_{\max}$, then, L will be the sample space and can be defined as follows:

$$L = \{(h_1, h_2)_i \mid h_1, h_2 \in A \text{ and } 1 \le i \le n_{\max}\}$$

And further suppose that the sets G_k, E_k and T_k where $G_k, E_k, T_k \subset L$ and $1 \le k \le n_{\max}$ represent the events defined below:

$$G_k = \{(h_1, h_2)_i \mid i = k \text{ and } (h_1, h_2)_i \in g_m \text{ and } 1 \le \mathrm{m} \le n_{\max}\}$$

$$E_k = \{(h_1, h_2)_i \mid i = k \text{ and } (h_1, h_2)_i \in e_m \text{ and } 1 \le \mathrm{m} \le n_{\max}\}$$

$$T_k = \{(h_1, h_2)_i \mid i = k,\ h_1 = s_n[k:k],\ h_2 = s_n[k+1, k+1],\ 1 \le i \le n_{\max}\}$$

Thus, for each ordered pair $(h_1, h_2)_i$ at positions $i = 1,2,\ldots,n$ of any given word form denoted by $s_n = h_1 h_2 \cdots h_n$, one can define probabilities of being in the above three sets as follows,

$$\Pr(s_n[i:i+1] \in G_i) = \Pr((h_1, h_2)_i \in G_i) = \mathrm{P_G}((h_1, h_2)_i) \tag{1}$$

$$\Pr(s_n[i:i+1] \in E_i) = \Pr((h_1, h_2)_i \in E_i) = \mathrm{P_E}((h_1, h_2)_i) \tag{2}$$

$$\Pr(s_n[i:i+1] \in T_i) = \Pr((h_1, h_2)_i \in T_i) = \mathrm{P_T}((h_1, h_2)_i) \tag{3}$$

Where, equation (1) refers to the probability of the ordered pair $(h_1, h_2)_i$ being in the stem part of the given word form. Similarly, equation (2) refers to the probability of the ordered pair $(h_1, h_2)_i$ being in the suffix part of the given word form and finally, equation (3) refers to the probability of the ordered pair $(h_1, h_2)_i$ being in between the stem part and the suffix part of the given word form (i.e., h_1 is the last letter of the stem part and h_2 is the first letter of suffix part).

4 Probabilistic Stemming Assertion

The probabilistic framework in this study is formalized in the Model 1 and the probabilistic stemming algorithm is based on the Method 1. The validity of the model and the method is examined by an experiment described as follows.

Model 1: If there exists an integer m, where $1 \le m \le n$ that satisfies

$$[P_E((h_1, h_2)_m) > P_G((h_1, h_2)_m)] \text{ and } P_T((h_1, h_2)_{m-1}) \ge \alpha,$$

for a word form $s_n^m = (g_m, e_m)$ and a constant $0 \le \alpha \le 1$, then g_{m-1} is said to be the probable stem of that word form.

Method 1: The probabilistic stemming of any word form denoted by $s_n = h_1 h_2 \cdots h_n$ ($1 \le n \le n_{\max}$) is done by stripping off substring e_{m-1} and taking substring g_{m-1} as the stem of that word form at the position m that satisfies the conditions of the Model for a particular $0 \le \alpha \le 1$.

In fact, the stemmer finds different stems for a particular word form for different values of α. In our test, we used 10 different values of α that steps the interval by equal standardized percentiles. Then, the resultant stems of each 10 trials are merged into a single collection. Thus, we have the collection which has the possible stems that can be produced by our proposed method. The fact that the selection of a particular value for α affects the overall IR system performance; it will be observed empirically when the intended IR system is completed. Because, the α value is subject to change dynamically with respect to IR system's performance needs. At this time, it is sufficient to validate that one can determine the intended stems by a probabilistic method over all possible α values as we proposed.

5 Experiment and the Results

Both experimentation and test databases are selected from a Turkish text database which is a collection of Turkish news texts having 1M words forms which are morphologically analyzed and disambiguated by Hakkani-Tür et al. [17]. Properties of the selected databases and the results are given in Table 2.

Table 2. Properties of Experimentation and Test databases

Databases	Term Count	Distict Terms	Distinct Stems	Unknown Stems	Produced (Correct)	Pair Count	Success level (%)
Experimental	149,189	36,902	10,568	0	0	5,648	0
Test	148,486	36,563	10,253	4,102	9828	-	95.8

Terms in both databases have been preprocessed to identify stem and suffix parts according to their tagged morphological analyses results. The databases are not processed any further such as elimination of stop words, determination of mis-spelled words etc. It has to be noted that if a morphology analyzer is used as a stemmer for the test database, the absolute upper bound of the compression ratio is 71%, (i.e., when all of the 36,563 distinct terms are reduced completely into their 10,253 actual stems), and the proposed stemmer can reach a compression ratio of 69% (i.e., 10,982 stems of which the 9,828 stems are correctly found and 1,154 terms are missed, out of 36,563 distinct terms).

The probabilities given in equations (1), (2) and (3) are calculated by the following formulas.

$$P_G((h_1,h_2)_i) = f_{g,i} * w_{g,i} / N \quad ; \; P_E((h_1,h_2)_i) = f_{e,i} * w_{e,i} / N \quad ;$$
$$P_T((h_1,h_2)_i) = f_{t,i} * w_{t,i} / N$$

where, $f_{g,i}$, $f_{e,i}$, and $f_{t,i}$ are the frequencies observed from the experimentation database for the events that the ordered pairs of letters have appeared in a stem part, suffix part, and transition between a stem part and suffix part of a word form, respectively. The correction factors $w_{g,i}$, $w_{e,i}$, and $w_{t,i}$ are previously calculated positive real values for the corresponding frequencies $f_{g,i}$, $f_{e,i}$, and $f_{t,i}$. N is the total number of ordered pairs in the experimentation database.

After the processing of the experimentation database, the total number of 5,648 unique ordered pairs of letters are observed for the sample space L, of which 2,845 pairs only belong to the event set G_k, 1084 pairs only belong to the event set E_k and 322 pairs only belong to the event T_k. In the intersection of the event sets G_k and E_k, there are 1,397 unique ordered pairs. Indeed, these observations are very encouraging, since they indicate that 50% of all ordered pairs of letters appear only in the stem part, 19% of them appear only in suffix part and 24% of them are shared by stem and suffix parts. This statistics clearly explains why our proposed model has succeeded. Our test database has 10,253 distinct stems of which 4,102 stems are not in the experimental database. This ratio is fairly large, and amounts to about 40% of unknown stems. The stemmer produced 72,967 possible stems for 36,563 distinct test terms for 10 predetermined α values. Thus, for each term approximately 2 stems have been produced. In fact, most of these 72,967 produced possible stems are recognized Turkish word forms, but either, they are understemmed to a root which has a diffent semantic than the target stem, or overstemmed to a derivational or inflectional form which is morphologically different from the target stem. In calculations, we accepted the exact match with the target stem as correct. As a result, our proposed stemmer achieved to produce correct stems for the 95.8% of the test terms (i.e., 9,828/10,253). Our stemmer couldn't stem 1,154 distinct terms, which were the variations of 425 distinct stems, out of 36,561. But, most of the missed terms are found to be foreign words, abbreviations, acronyms, or pronouns that are possibly eliminated by any text preprocessors used in an ordinary IR system.

6 Conclusions

We have presented here a new stemming model based on a probabilistic framework for agglutinative languages. Our model has a linear computational complexity and is capable of achieving a success of 95.8%. This result suggests that the proposed model of stemming can be generalized to apply to other agglutinative languages like Hungarian, Finnish, Estonian and Czech which have production and inflection paradigms.

Acknowledgements. We thank K. Oflazer for providing us with morphologically analyzed Turkish database, and A. Öztürk for very helpful insights and comments about statistical aspects and Ö. Berk and K. Demir of Muğla University and A. C. Koroğlu for very helpful discussions on linguistics background in this study.

References

1. Jurafsky D., Martin J. M.: Speech and Language Processing. Prentice-Hall, New Jersey USA (2000)
2. Hankamer, J.: Turkish generative morphology and morphological parsing. In: Second International Conference on Turkish Linguistics. Istanbul, Turkey (1984)
3. Koskenniemi, K.: Two-level Morphology: A General Computational Model for Word-Form Recognition and Production. In: Publications of the Department of General Linguistics, Vol.11. University of Helsinki, Helsinki (1983)
4. Oflazer, K.: Two Level Description of Turkish Morphology. In: Proceedings of EACL'98. Utrecht, the Netherlands (1993)
5. Ekmekçioglu, F. Çuna, L., Michael F., Willett, P.: Stemming and N-gram matching for term conflation in Turkish texts. In: Information Research, **1**(1) Available at: http://informationr.net/ir/2-2/paper13.html (1996)
6. Solak, A., Can. F.: Effects of Stemming on Turkish Text Retrieval. Technical Report BU-CEIS-94-20. Department of Computer Engineering and Information Science, Bilkent University, Ankara (1994)
7. Barton, G. Edward.: Computational Complexity in Two-Level morphology. In: ACL Proceedings, 24th Annual Meeting. (1986)
8. R. Baeza-Yates, B. Ribeiro-Neto.: Modern Information Retrieval. 1st ed. Addison-Wesley, England (1999)
9. Lovins, J.B.: Developing of a Stemming Algorithm. In: Mechanical Translation and Computational Linguistics, Vol. 11 (1968) 22–31
10. Porter, M. F.: An Algorithm for Suffix Stripping. In: Program, Vol.14, No.3 (1980) 130–137
11. Öztaner, S. M.: A Word Grammar of Turkish with Morphophonemic Rules. M. Sc. Thesis. Department of Computer Engineering, METU, Ankara, Turkey (1996)
12. Crystal, D.: The Cambridge Encyclopedia of Language. Cambridge University Press , Cambridge, UK (1987)
13. Lewis, G.L.: Turkish Grammar. Oxford University Press, UK (1991)
14. Duran, G.: Turkish Stemming Algorithm. M. Sc. Thesis. Department of Computer Engineering, Hacettepe University, Ankara (1997)
15. Alpkoçak A., Kut A., Özkarahan E.: Bilgi Bulma Sistemleri için Otomatik Türkçe Dizinleme Yöntemi. In: Bilişim Bildirileri. Dokuz Eylül Üniversitesi, İzmir, Türkiye (1995) 247–253
16. Köksal, A.: Bilgi Erişim Sorunu ve Bir Belge Dizinleme ve Erişim Dizgesi Tasarım ve Gerçekleştirimi. Doçentlik Tezi. Fen Bilimleri Enstitüsü, Bilgisayar Bilimleri Mühendisliği Anabilim Dalı, Hacettepe Üniversitesi, Ankara (1979)
17. Hakkani-Tür D.Z., Oflazer K., Tür G.: Statistical Morphological Disambiguation for Agglutinative Languages. In: COLLING (2000)

A Multi-relational Rule Discovery System

Mahmut Uludağ[1], Mehmet R. Tolun[2], and Thure Etzold[1]

[1] LION Bioscience Ltd., Compass House, 80-82, Newmarket Road, Cambridge, CB5 8DZ, United Kingdom
{mahmut.uludag, thure.etzold}@uk.lionbioscience.com
[2] Atilim University, Dept. of Computer Engineering, 06836 Incek, Ankara, Turkey
tolun@atilim.edu.tr
http://cmpe.emu.edu.tr/rila/

Abstract. This paper describes a rule discovery system that has been developed as part of an ongoing research project. The system allows discovery of multi-relational rules using data from relational databases. The basic assumption of the system is that objects to be analyzed are stored in a set of tables. Multi-relational rules discovered would either be used in predicting an unknown object attribute value, or they can be used to see the hidden relationship between the objects' attribute values. The rule discovery system, developed, was designed to use data available from any possible 'connected' schema where tables concerned are connected by foreign keys. In order to have a reasonable performance, the 'hypotheses search' algorithm was implemented to allow construction of new hypotheses by refining previously constructed hypotheses, thereby avoiding the work of re-computing.

1 Introduction

Most of the current data mining algorithms are designed to use data from a single table. They require each object to be described by a fixed set of attributes. Compared to a single table of data, a relational database containing multiple tables makes it possible to represent more complex and structured data. In addition, today, a significant amount of scientific data is stored in relational databases. For these reasons, it is important to have discovery algorithms running for relational data in its natural form without requiring the data to be viewed in a single table.

A relational data model consisting of multiple tables may represent several object classes, i.e. within a schema while one set of tables represents a class of object, a different set of tables may represent another class. Before starting discovery processes, users should analyze the schema and select the list of tables that represents the kind of objects they are interested in. One of the selected tables will be central for the objects and each row in the table should correspond to a single object in the database. In the previous multi-relational data mining publications, this central table is named as 'target table' in [1] and [2], 'primary table' in [3], 'master relation' in [4], and 'hub table' in [5].

A. Yazici and C. Şener (Eds.): ISCIS 2003, LNCS 2869, pp. 252–259, 2003.

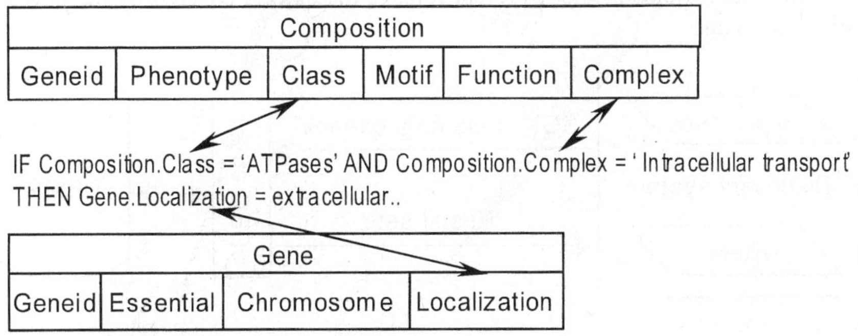

Fig. 1. An example multi-relational rule that refers to the composition table in its conditions and refers to the gene table in its right hand side

For a multi-relational rule, attribute names in its conditions are annotated using the name of the relational table to which the attribute is related. Figure 1 shows an example of such a multi-relational rule.

The concepts suggested in the multi-relational data-mining framework described in [1]; selection graphs, target table and target attribute, all helped during the initial stages of the process of building the present multi-relational rule discovery system.

2 Architecture

The architecture of the rule discovery system developed can be depicted as shown in Figure 2. The discovery system uses the JDBC API to communicate with the database management systems (DBMS). When a data mining session is started the system sends meta-data queries to the DBMS connected. After the user selects a set of tables, the target table and the target attribute, the data mining process starts, during which the system sends a number of SQL queries to the DBMS. SQL queries sent to the database management system are generally for building valid hypotheses about the data.

In order to reduce the complexity of communication between the rule discovery system and the DBMS, the information about covered objects and the discretized columns are both stored in temporary tables in the DBMS rather than in the internal data structures in the rule discovery system side. It was also decided to use these temporary tables for performance reasons.

The temporary table 'covered' has two columns named 'id' and 'mark'. Each time the rule discovery system starts processing a new class, inserting a new row for each object belonging to the current class reinitializes this table. The 'id' field is given the value of the primary key and the 'mark' field is set to zero. When a new rule is generated, the 'mark' fields of the rows that refer to the objects covered by the new rule are changed to one.

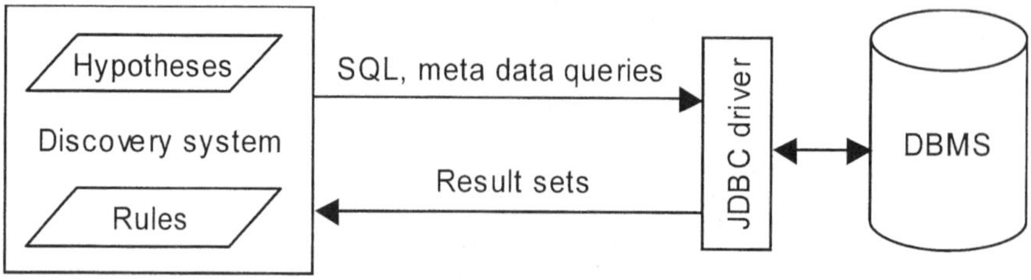

Fig. 2. The basic architecture of the system

The rule discovery system discretizes the numeric attribute values during the pre-processing stage of a data mining session, and initializes the table 'disc' by inserting one row per discretization interval. The following columns represent an interval.

- table_name: name of the table the numeric attribute is from
- column_name: name of the column the numeric attribute is associated with
- interval_name: name of the interval between two successive cut points
- min_val: minimum value of the interval
- max_val: maximum value of the interval

There is a concurrency problem with using the temporary tables if more than one user wants to use the rule discovery system simultaneously on the same data. Therefore we want to improve the solution taking into account the concurrency issues.

3 The Algorithm

The multi-relational rule discovery algorithm of the system that has been developed was adapted from ILA (Inductive Learning Algorithm) [6]. ILA is a 'covering' type learning algorithm that takes each class in turn and seeks a way of covering all instances, at the same time excluding instances which are not in the class. There is also an improved version of the ILA algorithm named ILA-2 that uses a penalty factor that helps to produce better results for noisy data [7]. In this paper, the adapted version of the ILA-2 algorithm is named Relational-ILA.

ILA requires a particular feature of the object under consideration to be used as a dependent attribute for classification. In Relational-ILA, however, the dependent attribute corresponds to the target attribute of the target table. It is assumed that the target table is connected to other tables through foreign key relations. Relational-ILA is composed of initial hypotheses generation, hypotheses evaluation, hypotheses refinement and rule selection steps. The relationship between these steps is summarized in Figure 3 for processing examples of a single class.

The database schema is treated as a graph where nodes represent relations (tables) and edges represent foreign keys. The schema graph is searched in a breadth-first search manner starting from the target table. While searching the schema graph, the algorithm keeps track of the path followed; no table is processed for the second time.

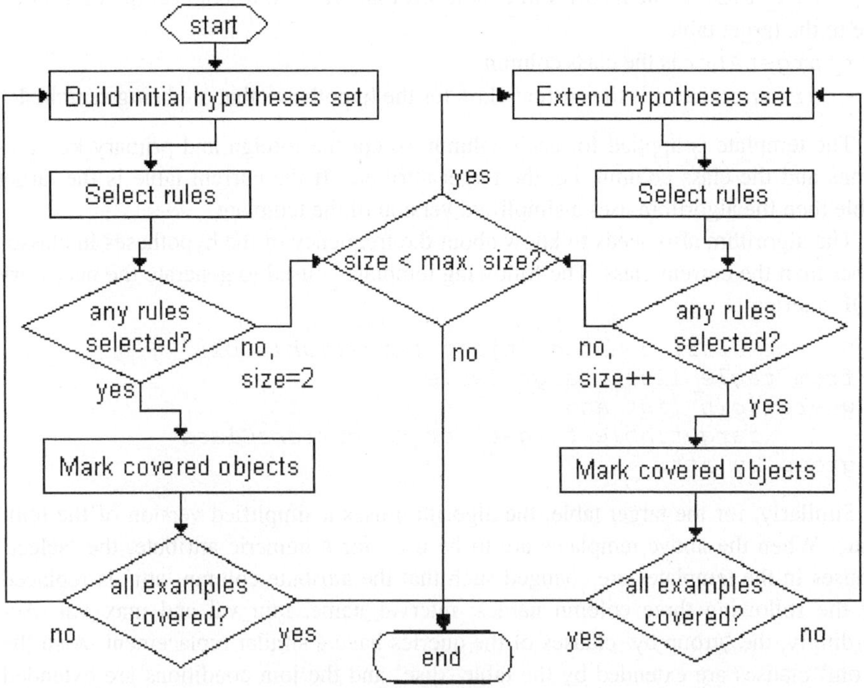

Fig. 3. The simplified Relational-ILA algorithm for processing examples of a single class

Initial hypotheses are composed of only one condition. During the building of the initial hypotheses set, the following template is used to generate SQL queries for finding hypotheses together with their frequency values, each time a table in the schema graph is visited.

```
Select attr, count(distinct targetTable.pk)
from table, covered, table_list
where join_list and
      targetTable.targetAttr = currentClass and
      covered.id = targetTable.pk and
      covered.mark=0
group by attr
```

In the template,

- `attr` is the column name for which hypotheses are being searched
- `targetTable` is the table that has one row for each object being analyzed

- `pk` is the name of the primary key column in the target table
- `table` refers to the current table where the hypotheses are being searched
- `table_list` is the list of the tables that are used to connect the current table to the target table
- `join_list` is the list of join conditions that are used to connect the current table to the target table
- `targetAttr` is the class column
- `currentClass` is the current class for the hypotheses that are being searched

The template is applied for each column except the foreign and primary key columns and the class column, i.e. the target attribute. If the current table is the target table then the algorithm uses a simplified version of the template.

The algorithm also needs to know about the frequency of the hypotheses in classes other than the current class. The following template is used to generate the necessary SQL queries.

```
Select attr, count(distinct targetTable.pk)
from table_list, targetTable
where join_list and
      targetTable.targetAttr <> currentClass
group by attr
```

Similarly, for the target table, the algorithm uses a simplified version of the template. When the above templates are to be used for a numeric attribute, the 'select' clauses in the templates are changed such that the attribute column 'attr' is replaced by the following three column names; interval_name, min_val and max_val. Accordingly, the 'group by' clauses of the queries have a similar replacement. Also the 'from' clauses are extended by the table 'disc' and the join conditions are extended using the following two conditions.

```
disc.attribute_name = 'attr' and
attr > disc.min_val and
attr < disc.max_val
```

After the initial hypotheses are generated they are sorted based on the output of the ILA hypothesis evaluation function, which shows how a hypothesis satisfies the conditions for being a valid rule. If any of the hypotheses can be used for generating a new rule then the one with the maximum score is converted to a new rule and the objects covered by the new rule are marked in the temporary table 'covered'. After the rule selection processes if some rules were selected but there are still objects not yet covered, then the initial hypotheses are rebuilt using only the objects that are not covered by the rules already generated. If no new rule can be generated then the hypotheses refinement step is started.

Refinement of a multi-relational hypothesis means extending the description of the hypothesis. It results in a new selection of objects that is a subset of the selection associated with the original hypothesis.

Similar to the initial hypotheses build case, to extend a hypothesis, the schema graph is searched, starting from the target table, by following the foreign key relations between tables. When a table in the schema graph is reached the following template is used to generate SQL queries for refining the hypothesis.

```
Select attr, count(distinct targetTable.pk)
from covered, table_list, hypothesis.table_list()
where targetAttr = currentClass and
      join_list and
      hypothesis.join_list()
      covered.id = targetTable.pk and
      covered.mark=0
group by attr;
```

Here the hypothesis is the hypothesis object being refined. The object has two methods to help SQL construction processes. The `table_list` method returns the list of the tables to which the features in the hypothesis refer, plus the tables that connect each feature to the target table. The `join_list` method returns the list of join conditions for the features in the hypothesis plus the list of join conditions to connect each feature to the target attribute.

In order to know the frequency of the extended hypotheses in the classes other than the current class the following SQL template is used.

```
Select attr, count(distinct targetTable.pk)
from targetTable, table_list, hypothesis.table_list()
where targetAttr <> currentClass and
      join_list and
      hypothesis.join_list()
group by attr;
```

4 Experiments

A set of experiments was conducted using the *genes* dataset of KDD Cup 2001 [8]. There are two tables in the original *genes* dataset. One table (*interaction*) specifies which genes interact with which other genes. The other table (*gene*) specifies a variety of properties of individual genes. The *gene* table has information about 862 different genes. There could be more than one row for each gene. The attribute *gene_id* identifies a gene uniquely. Tests have been conducted to generate rules for the localization attribute. Because the discovery system requires the target table to have a primary key, the schema has been normalized as shown in Figure 4.

The dataset has one numeric attribute and several attributes with missing values. The numeric attribute, 'expr', in the interaction table was divided into 20 bins using the class-blind binning method. Missing attribute values were ignored. In the experiments, the ILA-2 penalty factor was selected as 1, and the maximum hypothesis size limited to 4.

The results of the experiments are presented in Table 1 and Table 2. In both of the two tables, the first column shows the selected minimum support pruning parameter. In Table 1, the second column shows the amount of time the learning process required on a 1.8 MHz Atlahon processor machine. The third column shows the percentage of the training objects covered and the last column shows the number of rules generated.

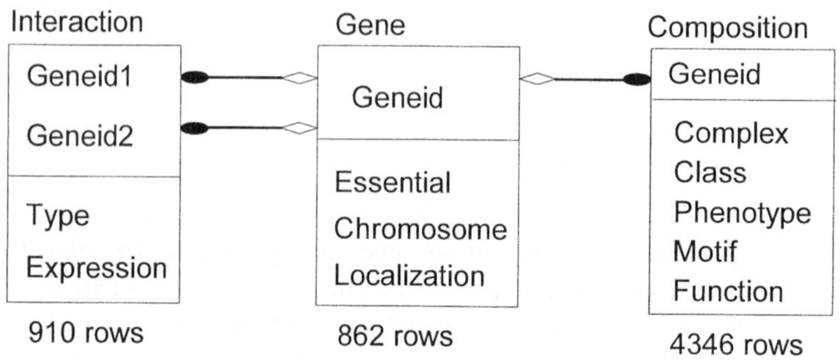

Fig. 4. Schema of the KDD Cup 2001 genes data after normalization

Table 1. The results of the training process

Minimum support pruning percentage	time (sec.)	% covered	# of rules
0%	1536	74.71	218
2%	883	58.93	87
5%	354	44.78	37

In Table 2, the second column shows the percentage of the test objects covered by the rules and the third column shows the accuracy of the rules on the objects covered. The last column shows the accuracy of the rules if a default rule is used for objects not covered by any rule. The default rule was selected as the majority class value.

Table 2. The results on the test data

Minimum support pruning percentage	% covered	% accuracy	%accuracy using a default rule
0%	64.57	79.67	62.20
2%	55.90	84.50	61.94
5%	46.50	87.00	60.60

The results in the last column of Table 2 indicate that the discovered rules have about 10% less prediction accuracy then the cup the winner's test set accuracy which was 72% [8]. The poor performance is because of the present system's inability to read the relational information between genes defined by the interaction table.

5 Conclusions and Future Work

A multi relational rule discovery system, Relational-ILA, has been implemented which extracts rules from relational database management systems where the tables concerned are directly or indirectly connected to each other using foreign key relations. The system requires a primary key in the target table to identify individual objects.

One of the important issues we would like to address during the next stage of this study is to make the hypotheses search algorithm more aware of the path followed to reach a table and to allow tables to be visited for a second time if they previously were reached via a different route. It will then be possible to mine schemas having related objects that are recursively defined. For example, the present system discovers rules that can help to understand properties of individual genes but the next version will discover rules that can help to understand the relations between genes.

References

1. Knobbe, A.J., Blockeel, H., Siebes, A., Van der Wallen, D.M.G.: Multi-Relational Data Mining, In Proceedings of Benelearn'99, (1999)
2. Leiva, H., and Honavar, V.: Experiments with MRDTL—A Multi-Relational Decision Tree Learning Algorithm. In Dzeroski, S., Raedt, L.D., and Wrobel, S. (editors): Proceedings of the Workshop on Multi-Relational Data Mining (MRDM-2002), University of Alberta, Edmonton, Canada, (2002) 97–112
3. Crestana-Jensen, V. and Soparkar, N.: Frequent Item-set Counting across Multiple Tables. PAKDD 2000, (2000) 49–61
4. Wrobel, S.: An Algorithm for Multi-Relational Discovery of Subgroups, Proceedings of PKDD'97, Springer-Verlag, Berlin, New York, (1997)
5. SRS-Relational White Paper, Working with relational databases using SRS, LION Bioscience Ltd. http://www.lionbioscience.com/solutions/products/srs
6. Tolun, M.R. and Abu-Soud, S.M.: ILA: An Inductive Learning Algorithm for Rule Extraction, Expert Systems with Applications, 14(3), (1998) 361–370
7. Tolun, M.R., Sever, H., Uludağ, M. and Abu-Soud, S.M.: ILA-2: An Inductive Learning Algorithm for Knowledge Discovery, Cybernetics and Systems: An International Journal, Vol. 30, (1999) 609–628
8. Cheng, J., Krogel, M., Sese, J., Hatsiz, C., Morishita, S., Hayashi, H. and Page, D.: KDD Cup 2001 Report, ACM Special Interest Group on Knowledge Discovery and Data Mining (SIGKDD) Explorations, Vol. 3, issue 2, (2002)

A Flexible Querying Framework (FQF): Some Implementation Issues

Bert Callens, Guy de Tré, Jörg Verstraete, and Axel Hallez

Computer Science Laboratory, Department of Telecommunications and Information Processing, Ghent University, Sint-Pietersnieuwstraat 41, B-9000 Gent, Belgium
Bert.Callens@ugent.be

Abstract. Fuzzy data are a common concept in today's information society. Some data can be unknown, other data may be inaccurate or uncertain. Still, this fuzzy data must be accounted for in modern businesses and therefore must be stored. Fuzzy relational databases have been studied extensively over time, which resulted in numerous models and representation techniques, some of which have been implemented as software layers on top of database systems. Different query languages and end-user interfaces have been extended to perform flexible queries on both regular and fuzzy databases. In this paper, a framework is presented that not only enables flexible querying on the relational model, but on other database models as well, of which the most important are object-oriented database models. This framework, called FQF or *Flexible Querying Framework*, is built on the recently developed Java Data Objects (JDO) standard.

1 Introduction

In today's information society, not all data that are considered are completely determined, accurate and certain [1]. Sometimes pieces of data can be missing or unknown, other data can be inaccurate or uncertain. At first sight, this kind of data may seem useless in modern businesses, but in their information processing activities such information must often be accounted for. This unknown or inaccurate data models uncertainty in our knowledge about the actual facts, and is called fuzzy data. As an example that storage of fuzzy data can be necessary, a database of people with their date of birth stored is considered. The age of a certain person might be known, but the exact birthday might be unknown. So the date of birth can't be precisely determined, although there is some incomplete information about it, which is desired to be stored in the database. Consider the same database for an example on data retrieval. Say one wants a list of al *young* people in the database, a relation between the linguistic term *young* and the date of birth must be modelled. In traditional database systems, fuzzy data is often represented in a simple way, as null or default values.

Many efforts have been made to modify and extend existing database models, query languages and database applications in order to apply them to fuzzy data. Fuzzy relational databases, as well as other systems, have been studied

A. Yazici and C. Şener (Eds.): ISCIS 2003, LNCS 2869, pp. 260–267, 2003.

extensively, resulting in several models and representation techniques of fuzzy database systems, e. g. [2]. Some of these models have been implemented as software layers on top of existing database systems, e. g. [3]. In this way, query languages, such as the popular SQL, have been extended and end-user interfaces have been modified and can now be used for retrieval and visualization of fuzzy data.

This paper presents an extension of the programming interface *Java Data Objects* (JDO), resulting in a new framework that allows flexible querying on different database models like relational and object-oriented ones. It is called the *Flexible Querying Framework* or FQF.

In the course of this paper, the potentials of FQF are illustrated by means of examples. A database consisting of instances of two Java classes will be used for these examples: a class *Address* with fields *street* and *city*, and a class *Person* with *name*, *address* and *dateOfBirth* fields. Both classes contain the necessary methods.

The next section will clarify some concepts that appear in FQF. In section 3 the Flexible Querying Framework itself and its facilities will be described. Section 4 concludes this paper, and some directives on what might be needed more for easy usage and interpretation of fuzzy data in database systems are presented, and some planned expansions of FQF are proposed.

2 Concepts

2.1 Java Data Objects (JDO)

Java Data Objects (JDO) is a recently developed standard that allows the handling of persistent data in Java applications. Java offers other, more established persistence mechanisms, but these each have some flaws which JDO does not have, as mentioned in the following overview.

- Serialization is the most basic technique for persistence in Java. Objects are easily persisted, but the paradigm lacks basic database capabilities such as transactions and querying.
- JDBC (*Java DataBase Connectivity*) is an interface between Java programs and SQL and provides capabilities like querying and transaction management. Two languages, Java and SQL need to be known to write applications. SQL is the standard language for dealing with relational databases and can only be used with the relational data model of tables, rows and columns which makes Java objects harder to persist. Most database vendors have their own version of the SQL-language which are compliant to the SQL standard, but often offer additional functionalities. When using any of these additional things, not defined in the SQL standard, there is a loss of portability of the application.
- *Enterprise JavaBeans Container Managed Persistence* (EJB-CMP) allows objects to be easily persisted, but because EJB assumes a distributed model of computation, a complex domain model results in poor performance.

JDO provides a unified approach to access data from an external source, making use of a *business object persistence manager*. The mapping between persistent Java objects and the actual data in the external data source is automated, an enhancer modifies classes into *Persistence Capable* classes, and this without any effort from the programmer. As prescribed by the ODMG standard, all the application programmer gets to see are objects and nothing but objects, in this case Java objects. Whether these instances are persistent or transient is of no importance to the application programmer, both are handled in the same way, because the persistence manager deals with the differences. As a result of this approach, an application programmer is not responsible to provide a mapping between the persistent objects and the way the data is stored in the database. This means that the application programmer doesn't need to know the specific structure of the external database to write an application for it, because a *PersistenceManager* instance takes care of all the mapping issues. From these properties, a very strong point of JDO is elucidated: Because an application is totaly unaware of how mapping is done and which database system is used, the same application can be used on different database systems, even different database models, as long as there is a JDO implementation that supports that database. This property is called *logical data independency* and is highly recommended when working with persistent data.

Another advantage that comes with the use of JDO is that an application is written in Java and Java alone, meaning that only one language has to be learned, unlike JDBC, where SQL is also required in the developing process. This results in a reduced build-time for applications.

JDO provides a query interface called *JDO Query Language*. JDOQL guarantees a high insulation from the underlying database architecture, which may for example support a relational query language like SQL or an object query language like OQL. Queries constructed with JDOQL consist of Boolean filters. The filter's condition, actually a regular Boolean expression, is constructed in Java syntax and is then applied to a collection of candidate instances of which the class name must be specified, from the external data source.

2.2 Extended Possibilistic Truth Values

An important factor in the process of handling fuzzy data, is the development of an epistemological model that is used to represent such uncertain, inaccurate and unknown data. When a query is executed on fuzzy data, a proposition is no longer either true or false, but can be something in between, a certain truth value. In FQF, a model based on truth measure is used, namely *Extended Possibilistic Truth Values* [4]. This paradigm will be briefly explained here.

Possibilistic Truth Values. By using the classic two-valued propositional logic, where the truth values are in the set $I = \{True, False\}$, propositions on data are either true or false. In reality however, one cannot always undoubtedly determine whether a proposition is completely true or false. Prade introduced the *Possibilistic Truth Value*, where a possibility measure to generalize the classic concept of a truth value is used.

The *Principle of Bivalence*:

Every proposition is either true or false

is replaced by the more general *Principle of Valence*:

Every proposition has a (possibilistic) truth value.

Fuzzy set theory and the related possibility theory provide adequate means to model the 'degree' to which an instance satisfies a certain proposition. For some formal definitions of *possibilistic truth values*, see [1,4,5].

Extended Possibilistic Truth Values. For the definition of an extended possibilistic truth value, an extra element $\perp$ is added to the universal set I [4], representing an undefined truth value to model the cases where a truth value of a proposition cannot be (completely) determined. This can be the case if (some of) the elements of the proposition are not applicable, undefined or not supplied. This resulted in the *Principle of Trivalence*:

Every proposition is either true, false, or undefined.

Following the same reasoning as for *possibilistic truth values*, *extended possibilistic truth values* are defined in [4].

2.3 Aggregated and Weighted Propositions

A proposition used as query condition can be composed out of several other propositions, which in turn can be composed themselves. By evaluating every simple proposition and then aggregating their result, the result of the composed proposition is achieved. Several definitions of aggregation-operators can be found, some widely used are defined in [6]. E. g. The *logical conjunction aggregation operator* $\tilde{\wedge}_l$, and the *algebraic conjunction operator* $\tilde{\wedge}_a$.

A simple proposition can be weighted, where a weight signifies the importance of its proposition in the overall condition. When a simple proposition is attached to a weight, its evaluation is influenced by this weight. This will also affect the result of the composed proposition. Some important conditions on a weight definition are described in [7]. Let $w_i \in [0,1]$ be the weight attached to constraint C_i. $w_i = 0$ means that the constraint can be forgotten. The satisfaction degree of such a weighted proposition should be 1, because it is of no importance whether this constraint is satisfied or not. $max_{i=1..n} w_i = 1$ is assumed to have an appropriate scaling of the levels of importance. When $w_i = 1$ and $u_i = \mu_{C_i}(S_u) = 0$, i. e. if the constraint C_i is not satisfied at all, but has the highest importance, then the satisfaction degree should be 0. If $u_i = 1$, so the constraint is completely satisfied, the satisfaction degree should be 1. More generally we should have

$$\forall w_i, w_i \perp u_i = 1 \text{ if } u_i = 1,$$

and

$$\forall u_i, w_i \perp u_i = 1 \text{ if } w_i = 0,$$

where $w_i \perp u_i$ represents the weighted constraint. From these properties, the following property is derived:

$$(\forall i, w_i > 0 \implies \mu_{C_i}(S_u) = 1) \implies \mu_C(S_u) = 1,$$

where C is the weighted version of C_i.

3 Framework Description

This section gives an overview of the design and capabilities of the Flexible Querying Framework.

3.1 Implementation and Design Issues

FQF is a framework that allows flexible querying on traditional database systems. FQF was initially developed as an environment for evaluating new theories on flexible data-retrieval from existing database systems. However, due to the increasing performance of JDO implementations, FQF could as well be used as a query engine in practical applications.

The main design goal of FQF is to keep it as general as possible, and therefore make it useful and usable for a wide range of users. The application programmer who makes use of FQF therefore has a lot of facilities at her disposal:

- The underlying database model is free to choose, as long as there is a JDO implementation that supports it. If an application has to be written for an existing database system, FQF can be used in the majority of cases. The javax.jdo API and the API offered by the JDO vendor are used.
- Different aggregation operators and weight interpretations are implemented and can be used, according to the data administrator's preference. More than one set of aggregation operators and weight interpretations can be supported by the same application.
- End-user interfaces for an FQF application are virtually without limitations. They can vary from command-line interfaces, to form-based and graphical interfaces. These interfaces must only specify the filter condition and candidate class, and deliver these to the framework.

Additional functionalities that are to be implemented in FQF are described in section 4.

3.2 The FastObjects JDO Implementation

As stated before, JDO is a new technology and is therefore not widely spread to this day. Because JDO is just a specification, its success will largely depend on the implementations that are available. In FQF, the *FastObjects j1 Community Edition* is used. It implements the obliged functionalities of JDO. In the future, several optional features will be available too. Some JDO implementations have extra features, to aid in the ease of use of JDO, but these are better left aside, for portability's sake, because other implementations probably don't offer these.

3.3 Querying Methods

To perform a query with FQF, conditions that are passed to an interface must be transformed in a JDOQL filter, and the class of the candidate instances must be declared in some way. The latter will be called *resultclass* form here on.

When a simple proposition is constructed, a weight can be attached to it. As previously mentioned, different weight interpretations are available and can be chosen from. These propositions can be combined into composed propositions, using one of the aggregation operators *AND*, *OR* and *NOT*. Again, for these, several definitions are available.

Following is an overview of the different kinds of single propositions that can be constructed with FQF. For clarity, the possible operators, the possible left operands and right operands are considered separately.

For the left operand, the following kinds of propositions are possible, each of which will be clarified with a concrete example:

- Any attribute of the resultclass can be in the left operand of the proposition, whether it's a Java primitive type, a Java standard library type or a user-defined type, as long as the FastObjects implementation supports it. E. g. with resultclass '*Person*' following queries are possible: '*getName== "Bert Callens"*' for the *name* attribute, '*getAddress== myAddress*' for the *address* attribute.
- Queries aren't limited to an attribute depth of one when going down the attribute hierarchy starting from the resultclass. E. g. with resultclass '*Person*': '*getAddress.getStreet== "streetx"*' is valid.

For the operator facilities, there is a distinction between *traditional* operators and *flexible* operators. Traditional operators are used in this way:

- When comparing primitive data types, operators like ==, <=, etc. are possible.
- When comparing user-defined data types, only == can be used.

For flexible operators:

- The operator *FEQ* means '*fuzzy equality*'. When a query uses this operator, the result is no longer necessarily *true* or *false*, but can be something in between, as explained in 2.2, for example when left and right operands are almost, but not exactly, equal. The actual result of the query evaluation in this case depends on the definition of '*almost equal*' for these instance types. Other flexible operators are *FNE* or '*fuzzy non-equality*', *FLT* or '*fuzzy less than*', and so on. E. g. with resultclass '*Person*': the query '*getAge~FEQ~23*' searches for Person-instances with age close to 23.
- In the future, FQF will also be able to deal certain linguistic terms like '*almost*', '*around*', which would make the construction of a flexible query more natural.

The possibilities of the right part of the proposition are of course dependent on the left operand and the operator specified in the query. The types of the left and right operand must correspond, but when working with flexible operators it is slightly different. Say a query '*getAge∼FEQ∼23*', searching for all people aged close to 23. The left operand is a normal integer, and the right operand seems like one too, but in fact the latter represents a fuzzy set.

3.4 Query Results

In a traditional query engine, the result of a query is an enumeration of instances from the external data store, and whether they evaluated true or false to the query. In most cases, only instances that evaluated true are displayed to the user. But when working with flexible systems, FQF in particular, there's often no such thing as true or false for a persistent instance. In stead, an enumeration of the instances with their corresponding truth value is given. Because not all instances satisfy the query to the same degree, some order in the result is desired. For example, an instance can have an extended truth value

$$\{(true, 0.7), (false, 0.5), (\bot, 0.0)\}$$

and another can have

$$\{(true, 0.8), (false, 0.7), (\bot, 0.0)\}.$$

Because a natural partial ordering relation does not exist for these elements [4], a ranking function

$$r : \tilde{\wp}(I^*) \rightarrow [0, 1]$$

is introduced [6].

4 Conclusions and Future Work

Fuzzy data and querying is a very important research domain, but it is quite complicated for inexperienced people to understand and to use. Therefore specialized interfaces are necessary, to offer an easy to use and interpret querying mechanism to users of all levels of experience. New querying techniques and data visualization are required, because a list of which data instances evaluate *true* to a proposition are not sufficient anymore.

The Flexible Querying Framework offers application programmers an easy to use framework for writing information retrieval applications which involve fuzzy data and flexible querying. Researchers who work on theories for fuzzy data processing can use FQF as a platform for performing tests. Application programmers often lack the knowledge of flexible database technologies and flexible information retrieval techniques, but this is taken care of by using FQF, who encapsulates the major part of techniques specific to flexible data processing used in FQF. If however, one is eager to learn about several aspects of flexible data processing, FQF can give an initial insight of how things work in this research domain.

FQF can now handle a variety of flexible queries on crisp data, but in the near future it should also be able to handle the same queries on fuzzy data. The difficulties to do this are not caused by FQF itself, but in the way that fuzzy data is stored in databases. The final step for FQF is that it allows queries to be expressed in natural language. Although posing any question in natural language to a querying system is still far off, FQF can be used to experiment with elements of natural language, such as context-dependent words and user-dependent questions.

References

1. Bosc, P., Prade, H.: An Introduction to Fuzzy Set and Possibility Theory Based Approaches to the Treatment of Uncertainty and Imprecision in Database Management Systems. In: Proc. of the 2nd Workshop on Uncertainty Management in Information Systems: From Needs to Solutions, Catalina, California (1993).
2. De Caluwe, R.: Fuzzy and Uncertain Object-oriented Databases: Concepts and Models, World Scientific, Singapore (1997).
3. Sicilia, M.-A., García, E., Díaz, P., Aedo, I.: Extending Relational Data Access Programming Libraries for Fuzziness: The fJDBC Framework. In: Proc. of the 5th International Conference on Flexible Query Answering Systems (FQAS2002), Copenhagen, Denmark (2002) 314–328, .
4. De Tré, G.: Extended Possibilistic Truth Values. In: International Journal of Intelligent Systems **17** 4 (2002) 427–446.
5. Zadeh, L.A.: Fuzzy sets as a basis for a theory of possibility. In: Fuzzy Sets and Systems**1** 1 (1978) 3–28.
6. De Tré, G., De Caluwe, R., Verstraete, J., Hallez, A.: Conjunctive Aggregation of Extended Possibilistic Truth Values and Flexible Database Querying. In: Proc. of the FQAS 2002 Conference, Copenhagen, Denmark (2002) 344–355.
7. Dubois, D., Fargier, H., Prade, H.: Beyond min aggregation in multicriteria decision: (ordered) weighted min, discri-min, leximin. In: The ordered weighted averaging operators, Yager, R., Kacprzyk, J. (eds.), Kluwer Academic Publishers (1997) 181–192.

Similarity for Conceptual Querying

Troels Andreasen, Henrik Bulskov, and Rasmus Knappe

Department of Computer Science,
Roskilde University,
P.O. Box 260, DK-4000 Roskilde, Denmark
{troels,bulskov,knappe}@ruc.dk

Abstract. The focus of this paper is approaches to measuring similarity for application in content-based query evaluation. Rather than only comparing at the level of words, the issue here is conceptual resemblance. The basis is a knowledge base defining major concepts of the domain and may include taxonomic and ontological domain knowledge. The challenge for support of queries in this context is an evaluation principle that on the one hand respects the formation rules for concepts in the concept language and on the other is sufficiently efficient to candidate as a realistic principle for query evaluation. We present and discuss principles where efficiency is obtained by reducing the matching problem - which basically is a matter of conceptual reasoning - to numerical similarity computation.

1 Introduction

The goal for concept-based querying, in text retrieval systems, is to include semantics, looking for improvements that can enhance the systems ability to generate ideal answers. In this context, one of the major problems is to determine the similarity between the semantic elements. It is no longer only simple match of keywords in the text objects, but also the meaning of them, we have to take into consideration when we calculate the similarity between queries and objects in our database.

The foundation of this paper is our previous work[1] and our affiliation to the interdisciplinary research project OntoQuery[1] (Ontology-based Querying)[3, 4].

We assume that text objects are described by compound concepts in a description language and that queries are expressed in the language or can be transformed into this, and that these descriptions refer to a knowledge base clarifying the domain of the database. The environment for this type of querying may be a system that automatically can produce conceptual descriptions (conceptual indexing) of text objects and support textual/word list queries by initial transformation into descriptions.

[1] The project has the following participating institutions: Centre for Language Technology, The Technical University of Denmark, Copenhagen Business School, Roskilde University and the University of Southern Denmark.

A. Yazici and C. Şener (Eds.): ISCIS 2003, LNCS 2869, pp. 268–275, 2003.

2 Concepts and Concept Language

The first thing is therefore to describe the basis of this environment, what concepts are in this context, and the expressiveness of the languages used.

The concept language ONTOLOG[5] is based on a set of atomic concepts which can be combined with semantic relations to form compound concepts. Expressions in ONTOLOG are descriptions of concepts situated in an ontology formed by an algebraic lattice with concept inclusion as the ordering relation.

Attribution of concepts, i.e. combining atomic concepts into compound concepts, can be written as feature structures. Simple attribution of a concept c_1 with relation r and a concept c_2 is denoted $c_1[r\colon c_2]$.

We assume a set of atomic concepts $\mathbf{A}$ and a set of semantic relations $\mathbf{R}$. Then the set of well-formed terms $\mathbf{L}$ of the ONTOLOG language is recursively defined as follows.

- if $x \in \mathbf{A}$ then $x \in \mathbf{L}$
- if $x \in \mathbf{L}$, $r_i \in \mathbf{R}$ and $y_i \in \mathbf{L}, i = 1, \ldots, n$
  then $x[r_1\colon y_1, \ldots, r_n\colon y_n] \in \mathbf{L}$

It appears that compound terms can be built from nesting, for instance $c_1[r_1\colon c_2[r_2\colon c_3]]$ and from multiple attribution as in $c_1[r_1\colon c_2, r_2\colon c_3]$. The attributes of a multiple attributed term $T = x[r_1\colon y_1, \ldots, r_n\colon y_n]$ is considered as a set, thus we can rewrite T with any permutation of $r_1\colon y_1, \ldots, r_n\colon y_n$.

The basis for the ontology is a simple taxonomic concept inclusion relation ISA_{KB}, which is atomic in the sense that it defines the hyponymy lattice over the set of atomic concepts $\mathbf{A}$. It is considered as domain or world knowledge and may for instance express the view of a domain expert.

Based on ISA, the transitive closure of ISA_{KB}, we can generalize into a relation over all well-formed terms of the language $\mathbf{L}$ by the following.

- if x ISA y then $x \leq y$
- if $x[\ldots] \leq y[\ldots]$ then also
  $x[\ldots, r\colon z] \leq y[\ldots]$, and
  $x[\ldots, r\colon z] \leq y[\ldots, r\colon z]$,
- if $x \leq y$ then also
  $z[\ldots, r\colon x] \leq z[\ldots, r\colon y]$

where repeated ... in each inequality denotes identical lists of zero or more attributes of the form $r_i\colon w_i$.

The purpose of the language introduced above is to describe fragments of meaning in text at a more thoroughly way than what can by obtained from simple keywords, while still refraining from full meaning representations which is obviously not realistic in general search applications (with a huge database).

Take as an example the noun phrase: "*the dark grey cat*" which can be translated into this semantic expression *cat[CHR: grey[CHR: dark]]*. Descriptions of text expressed in this language goes beyond simple keyword descriptions partly due to formation of compound terms and to the reference to the ontology. A key question in the framework of querying is of course the definitions of similarity or nearness of terms, now that we no longer can rely on simple matching of keywords.

3 From Ontology to Similarity

In building a query evaluation principle that draws on an ontology, a key issue is of course how the different relations of the ontology may contribute to similarity.

We have to decide for each relation to what extent related values are similar and we must build similarity functions, mapping values into similarities, that reflect these decisions.

We discuss firstly below how to introduce similarity based on the key ordering relation in the ontology, ISA, as applied on atomic concepts (concepts explicitly represented in the ontology). Secondly we discuss how to extend the notion of similarity to cover – not only atomic but – general compound concepts as expressions in the language ONTOLOG. Finally we introduce a refinement that uses all possible relations, in the calculation of similarity.

3.1 Similarity on Atomic Concepts

As discussed in [1] the hyponymy relation imply a strong similarity in the opposite direction of the inclusion (specialization), but also the direction of the inclusion (generalization) must contribute with some degree of similarity.

Take as an example the small fraction of an ontology shown in figure 1a. With reference to this ontology the atomic concept *dog* can be directly expanded to cover also *poodle* and *alsatian*. The intuition is that to a query on *dog* an

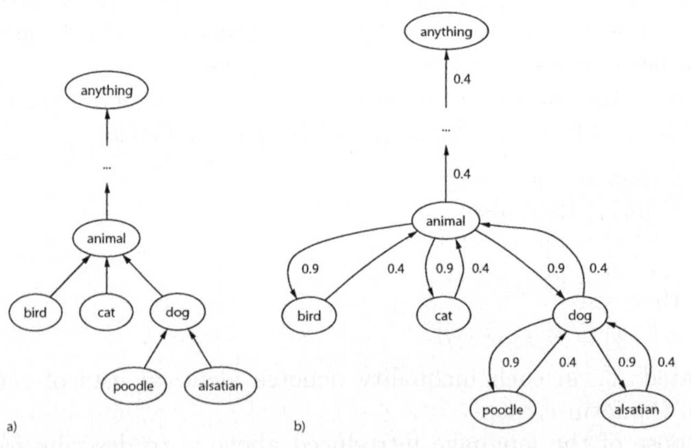

Fig. 1. Inclusion relation (*ISA*) with upwards reading, e.g. dog *ISA* animal, and the ontology transformed into a directed weighted graph, with the immediate specialization and generalization similarity being $\delta = 0.9$ and $\gamma = 0.4$ respectively as weights. Similarity is derived as maximal (multiplicative) weighted path length, thus $sim(poodle, alsatian) = 0.4 * 0.9 = 0.36$.

answer including instances *poodle* is satisfactory (a specific answer to a general query). Since the hyponymy relation obviously is transitive we can by the same argument expand to further specializations e.g. to include *poodle* in the extension of *animal*. However similarity exploiting the lattice should also reflect 'distance' in the relation. Intuitively greater distance (longer path in the relation graph) corresponds to smaller similarity.

Further also generalization should contribute to similarity. Of course it is not strictly correct in an ontological sense to expand the extension of *dog* with instances of *animal*, but because all *dogs* are *animals*, *animals* are to some degree similar to *dogs*. This substantiates that also a property of generalization similarity should be exploited and, for similar reasons as in the case of specializations, that also transitive generalizations should contribute with decreasing degree of similarity.

To make "distance" influence similarity we need either to be able to distinguish explicitly stated, original references, from derived or to establish a transitive reduction ISA$_{\text{REDUC}}$ of the ISA relation. Similarity reflecting distance can then be measured from path-length in the ISA$_{\text{REDUC}}$ lattice. A similarity function *sim* based on distance in ISA$_{\text{REDUC}}$ $dist(x,y)$ should have the properties:

1. sim: $U \times U \rightarrow [0,1]$, where U is the universe of concepts
2. $sim(x,y) = 1$ only if $x = y$
3. $sim(x,y) < sim(x,z)$ if $dist(x,y) < dist(x,z)$

By parameterizing with two factors δ and γ expressing similarity of immediate specialization and generalization respectively, we can define a simple similarity function: If there is a path from nodes (concepts) x and y in the hyponymy relation then it has the form

$$P = (p_1, \cdots, p_n) \text{ where } p_i \text{ISA}_{\text{REDUC}}\, p_{i+1} \text{ or } p_{i+1} \text{ISA}_{\text{REDUC}}\, p_i \text{ for each } i \tag{1}$$

with $x = p_1$ and $y = p_n$.

Given a path $P = (p_1, \cdots, p_n)$, set $s(P)$ and $g(P)$ to the numbers of specializations and generalizations respectively along the path P thus:

$$s(P) = \left|\{\, i |\; p_i \text{ ISA}_{\text{REDUC}}\; p_{i+1} \,\}\right| \text{ and } g(P) = \left|\{\, i |\; p_{i+1} \text{ ISA}_{\text{REDUC}}\; p_i \,\}\right| \tag{2}$$

If $P_1, \cdots, P_m$ are all paths connecting x and y then the degree to which y is similar to x can be defined as

$$sim(x,y) = \max_{j=1,\ldots,m} \left\{ \delta^{s(P_j)} \gamma^{g(P_j)} \right\} \tag{3}$$

and therefore denotes the shortest path between concepts x and y in the hyponymy lattice.

This similarity can be considered as derived from the ontology by transforming the ontology into a directional weighted graph, with δ as downwards and γ as upwards weights and with similarity derived as the product of the weights on the paths.

An atomic concept c can then be expanded to a fuzzy set, including x and similar values $x_1, x_2, \ldots, x_n$ as in:

$$x+ = 1/x + sim(x,x_1)/x_1 + sim(x,x_2)/x_2 + \cdots sim(x,x_n)/x_n \tag{4}$$

Thus for instance with $\delta = 0.9$ and $\gamma = 0.4$ the expansion of the concepts *dog*, *animal* and *poodle* into sets of similar values would be:

$$dog+ = 1/dog + 0.9/poodle + 0.9/alsatian + 0.4/animal$$
$$poodle+ = 1/poodle + 0.4/dog + 0.36/alsatian + 0.16/animal + 0.144/cat$$
$$animal+ = 1/animal + 0.9/cat + 0.9/dog + 0.81/poodle + 0.81/alsatian$$

3.2 General Concept-Similarity

The semantic relations, used in forming concepts in the ontology, indirectly contribute to similarity through subsumption. For instance *cat[CHR: grey[CHR: dark]]* is subsumed by - and thus extensionally included in - each of the more general concepts *cat[CHR: grey[CHR: dark]], cat[CHR: grey]* and *cat*. Thus with a definition of similarity covering atomic concepts, and in some sense reflecting the ordering concept inclusion relation, we can extend to similarity on compound concepts by a relaxation, which takes subsumed concepts into account when comparing descriptions.

The principle can be considered to be a matter of subsumption expansion of a concept c, denoted $\epsilon(c)$. Any compound concept is expanded (or relaxed) into the set of subsuming concepts, thus $\epsilon(cat[CHR\colon grey[CHR\colon dark]])$ is expanded to the set:

$$\{cat[CHR\colon grey[CHR\colon dark]], cat[CHR\colon grey], cat\}$$

Corresponding to the fuzzy set

$$\{1/cat[CHR\colon grey[CHR\colon dark]] + 1/cat[CHR\colon grey] + 1/cat\}$$

The similarity between compound concepts x and y can be expressed as the degree to which the intersection of $\epsilon(x)$ and $\epsilon(y)$ is included in $\epsilon(x)$.

One approach to query-answering in this direction is to expand the description of the query along the ontology and the potential answer objects along subsumption.

For instance a query on *dog* could be expanded to a query on similar values like:

$$dog+ = \{1/dog + \ldots + 0.4/animal + \ldots\}$$

and a potential answer object like $cat[CHR\colon grey[CHR\colon dark]]$ would then be subsumption expanded as exemplified above.

While not the key issue here, we should point out the importance of applying an appropriate averaging aggregation when comparing descriptions. It is essential that similarity based on subsumption expansion, exploits that for instance the degree to which $c_1[r_1\colon c_2]$ is matching $c_1[r_1\colon c_2[r_2\colon c_3]]$ is higher than the degree for c with no attributes is matching $c_1[r_1\colon c_2[r_2\colon c_3]]$. Approaches to aggregation that can be tailored to obtain these properties, based on order weighted averaging[6] and capturing nested structuring[7], are described in [2].

3.3 Possible Paths and Shared Nodes

We have indicated above that the shortest path (3) between concepts in an ontology can be used as a measure for similarity.

The intuition is that the similarity between $cat[CHR : grey]$ and $dog[CHR : grey]$ is larger than the similarity between either of these and $bird[CHR : yellow]$, because both cat and dog are characterized by being grey, whereas the bird is yellow. But we are not able to capture this if the basis for the similarity measure is subsumption expansion of the objects in the database and expansion of the query by means of the ontology.

A possible solution to this problem is to introduce all relations in the calculation of similarity and thereby letting the attribution of concepts influence the similarity measure. This gives rise to at least the following considerations. Firstly we have to create the theoretical foundations for such a similarity measure and secondly the approach has the be scalable.

Figure 2 shows the introduction of compound concepts and semantic relations, visualized as dotted edges. The general idea now is a similarity measure

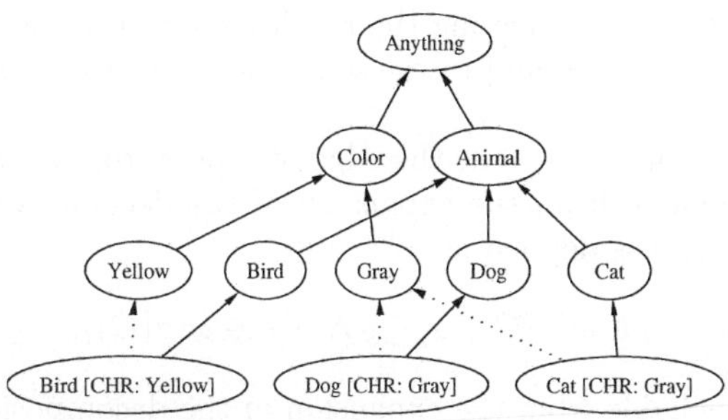

Fig. 2. An example ontology covering colored animals

between concepts c_1 and c_2 based upon the set of all nodes reachable from both concepts in the graph, representing the part of the ontology covering c_1 and c_2. These shared node reflect the similarity between concepts, both in terms of similar attribution and subsuming concepts.

The inclusion of both the hyponymy relation and the attribution of concepts in the calculation of similarity increases the complexity. We therefore devise a similarity measure that utilizes a well-defined subset of the ontology for measuring similarity.

To this end we define first the term-decomposition $\tau(c)$ and the upwards expansion $\omega(C)$ of a set of terms C. The term-decomposition is defined as the set of all subterms of c, which thus includes all concepts subsuming c and all attributes of subsuming concepts for c. The term-decomposition is defined as follows:

$$\tau(c) = \{x | c \leq x \vee c \leq y[r : x], x \in \mathbf{L}, y \in \mathbf{L}, r \in \mathbf{R}\}$$

Consider as an example the decomposition of the term

$$\tau(disorder[CBY\colon lack[WRT\colon vitaminC]]) =$$

$$\begin{aligned}\{\ & disorder[CBY\colon lack[WRT\colon vitaminC]],\\ & disorder[CBY\colon lack]],\\ & disorder,\\ & lack[WRT\colon vitaminC],\\ & lack,\\ & vitaminC\}\end{aligned}$$

The upwards expansion $\omega(C)$ of a set of terms C is the closure of C with respect to ISA.

$$\omega(C) = \{x|x \in C \vee y \in C, y\ ISA\ x\}$$

This expansion thus only adds atoms to C.

We define further the upwards spanning subgraph (subontology) $\theta(C)$ for a set of concepts $C = \{c_1, \dots, c_n\}$ as the graph that appears when expanding the decomposition of C and connecting the resulting set of terms with edges corresponding to the ISA relation and to the semantic relations used in attribution of elements in C.

We define the triple (x, y, r) as the edge of type r from concept x to concept y. The nodes reachable from the expansion of the decomposition of a concept via the ISA relation, α is defined as

$$\{(x, y, \text{ISA})|x, y \in \omega(\tau(C)), x \leq y \wedge \neg\exists z \in \omega(\tau(C)), z \leq y, x \leq z\}$$

And the nodes reachable from the expansion of the decomposition of a concept via the semantic relations, β is defined as

$$\{(x, y, r)|x, y \in \omega(\tau(C)), r \in \mathbf{R}, x[r\colon y] \in \tau(C)\}$$

We can then define the subontology $\theta(C)$ as the union of α and β.

$$\theta(C) = \alpha \cup \beta$$

Figure 2 is an example of such an subontology spanned by three terms.

We can now define the set of shared nodes σ for two concepts c_1 and c_2 as the intersection of the expansion of the decomposition of the two terms.

$$\sigma(c_1, c_2) = \omega(\tau(c_1)) \cap \omega(\tau(c_2))$$

4 Conclusion

We have described different principles for measuring similarity between both atomic and compound concepts, all of which incorporate meta knowledge. 1) Similarity between atomic concepts based on distance in the ordering relation of the ontology, concept inclusion (ISA), 2) Similarity between general compound concepts based on subsumption expansion, and 3) Similarity between both atomic and general compound concepts based on shared nodes.

The notion of measuring similarity as distance, either in the ordering relation or in combination with the semantic relations, seems to indicate a usable theoretical foundation for design of similarity measures. The inclusion of the attribution of concepts, by means of shared nodes, in the calculation of similarity, gives a possible approach for a measure that captures more details and at the same time scale to large systems.

The purpose of similarity measures in connection with querying is of course to look for similar rather than for exactly matching values, that is, to introduce soft rather than crisp evaluation. As indicated through examples above one approach to introduce similar values is to expand crisp values into fuzzy sets including also similar values. Expansion of this kind, applying similarity based on knowledge in the knowledge base, is a simplification replacing direct reasoning over the knowledge base during query evaluation. The graded similarity is the obvious means to make expansion a useful - by using simple threshold values for similarity the size of the answer can be fully controlled.

References

[1] Bulskov, H., Knappe, R. and Andreasen, T.: On Measuring Similarity for Conceptual Querying, LNAI 2522, pp. 100–111 in T. Andreasen, A. Motro, H. Christiansen, H.L. Larsen (Eds.): Flexible Query Answering Systems 5th International Conference, FQAS 2002. Copenhagen, Denmark, October 27–29, 2002. Proceedings

[2] Andreasen, T.: Query evaluation based on domain-specific ontologies. In *NAFIPS'2001, 20th IFSA / NAFIPS International Conference Fuzziness and Soft Computing*, pp. 1844–1849, Vancouver, Canada, 2001.

[3] Andreasen, T., Nilsson, J. Fischer & Thomsen, H. Erdman: Ontology-based Querying, in Larsen, H.L. *et al.* (eds.) Flexible Query Answering Systems, *Flexible Query Answering Systems, Recent Advances*, Physica-Verlag, Springer, 2000. pp. 15–26.

[4] Andreasen, T., Jensen, P. Anker, Nilsson, J. Fischer, Paggio, P., Pedersen, B. Sandford & Thomsen, H. Erdman: Ontological Extraction of Content for Text Querying, to appear in NLDB 2002, Stockholm, Sweden, 2002.

[5] Nilsson, J. Fischer: A Logico-algebraic Framework for Ontologies ONTOLOG, in Jensen, P. Anker & Skadhauge, P. (eds.): Proceedings of the First International OntoQuery Workshop *Ontology-based interpretation of NP's*. Department of Business Communication and Information Science, University of Southern Denmark, Kolding, 2001.

[6] Yager, R.R.: On ordered weighted averaging aggregation operators in multicriteria decision making, in IEEE Transactions on Systems, Man and Cybernetics, vol 18, 1988.

[7] Yager, R.R.: A hierarchical document retrieval language, in Information Retrieval vol 3, Issue 4, Kluwer Academic Publishers pp. 357–377, 2000.

Virtual Interval Caching Scheme for Interactive Multimedia Streaming Workload

Kyungwoon Cho[1], Yeonseung Ryu[2*], Youjip Won[3**], and Kern Koh[1]

[1] School of Computer Science and Engineering, Seoul National University, Korea
[2] Department of Computer Software, Myongji University, Korea
[3] Division of Electrical and Computer Engineering, Hanyang University, Korea

Abstract. We carefully believe that server workload for interactive multimedia service exhibits different characteristics from legacy application, e.g. ftp server, web server, ASP server and etc., and that there are greater chance of improvement with better understanding of streaming workload. In this work, we present a novel buffer management algorithm for interactive multimedia streaming workload. We carefully examine the workload traces obtained from several streaming servers in service. The analysis results show that most users exhibit non-sequential access pattern using VCR-like operations such as jump backward and jump forward. We exploit the workload characteristics of the VCR-like operation and develop a buffer caching algorithm called *Virtual Interval Caching* scheme. Simulation based experiment shows that the proposed buffer management scheme yields better performance than the legacy schemes.

1 Introduction

Buffer cache management scheme for multimedia workload has been the subjects of numerous works during past several years. Most of these works assume that the streaming workload exhibits sequential access characteristics with bandwidth guarantee. There have been widely proposed interval-based buffer caching schemes for multimedia servers [6,2,4]. Interval-based buffer caching schemes take advantage of sequential access characteristics of continuous media data. They cache data blocks in the *intervals* of consecutive streams accessing the same file. In order to maximize the number of playbacks accessing data from buffer cache, interval based schemes sort intervals with increasing order and cache data blocks from the shortest intervals.

A few studies recently examine the user access logs obtained from streaming servers in service and show that there are non trivial amount of VCR-like operations, e.g. jump forward, jump backward, or etc [13,1,3,12,7]. These works also deliver insightful information on the usage of the multimedia server and the user behavior, e.g. access frequency distribution, file popularity, aging of file

* Corresponding author

** Work of this author is in part funded by Hanyang Faculty Research Initiative Grant 2002.

A. Yazici and C. Şener (Eds.): ISCIS 2003, LNCS 2869, pp. 276–283, 2003.

access popularity, etc. From these works we can easily see that the data access pattern is more than sequential. For example, [1] showed that for short media files, interactive requests like jump backward are common.

In this work, we analyze the user access behavior on three different types of contents: (i) educational contents, (ii) game contents, and (iii) movie. Typical user accesses the content via broadband Internet access, e.g. ADSL, cable modem. User access patterns for these contents are extracted from the commercial streaming service site: *Hanmir Education Center*[8], *Ongamenet*[10] and *Myung Films*[9], respectively. There is no geographical limitation on accessing these contents since these are accessed via public network. Examining the access pattern on this site enables us to understand the access behavior in broadband Internet access. We find that non-sequential accesses constitutes significant fraction of multimedia file accesses. There are relatively large number of VCR-like operations, e.g. jump forward, jump backward, etc. The fraction of VCR-like operations varies dependent upon the type of contents.

We aim at developing the buffer cache management algorithm which is optimized for *real* streaming workload. In order to manages the buffer space effectively exploiting the streaming workload which is mixture of sequential and bidirectional skip operation, we develop buffer management scheme, *Virtual Interval Caching (VIC)*. The proposed VIC scheme maintains past intervals as virtual intervals and increases buffer cache hit ratio. Experimental results show that the proposed buffer management scheme yields better performance than the legacy schemes such as interval-based schemes, LRU, etc.

The remainder of this paper is organized as follows. In section 2, we show the access activity to media files by analyzing trace data obtained from three streaming servers in service. In section 3, we presents proposed buffer caching scheme called virtual interval caching. Section 4 presents performance results and finally section 5 summarizes our works.

2 Analysis of Multimedia Streaming Workload

To characterize the user access pattern over video contents, we analyze the access logs[5] from three different streaming service site each of which services different types of contents: (i) education, (ii) game and (iii) movie. They are *Hanmir Education Center* [8], *Ongamenet* [10] and *Myung Films* [9]. Table 1 illustrates the summary of the analysis. It is worth noting that there are the significant number of VCR-like operations such as *jump forward* or *jump backward.* In case of educational contents in *www.hanmir.co.kr*, the number of jump operations per each session is 1.62 on the average. Fig. 1 illustrates the distribution of the number of jump operations for each site.

We define *Jump distance* as a distance between the playback positions before and after the jump operation. As is shown in Fig. 2, we find the this distance is short in most cases. However, there are small number of jump operations which skips most of the contents. This phenomenon can be clearly observed in Fig. 2(c). We carefully believe that intolerable nature of human behavior significantly contributes to this phenomena.

Table 1. Analyzed results of 3 Windows Media Servers

	Hanmir	Ongamenet	Myung Films
Log Duration	10 days	3 days	43 days
Number of log entries	192457	98640	69330
Number of file	3432	953	468
File Length	1009 secs	809 secs	141 secs
Number of sessions	73655	55423	42119
jump operations	1.62	0.78	0.64
backward distance	281.28 secs	254.32 secs	77.93 secs
forward distance	311.68 secs	153.63 secs	26.31 secs
Concurrent sessions	38.78	166.28	1.1

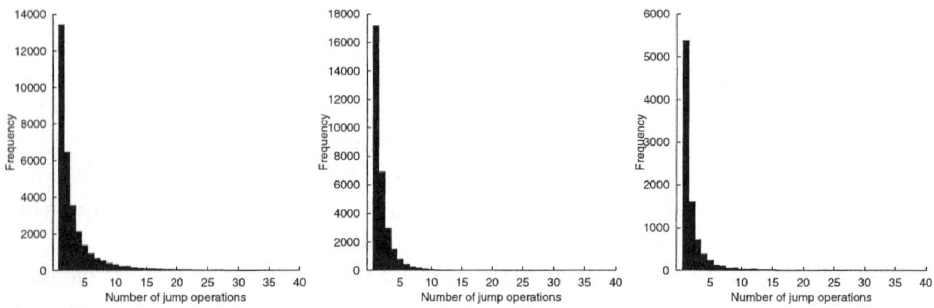

(a) *Hanmir* (b) *Ongamenet* (c) *Myung Films*

Fig. 1. The distribution of jump operations

3 Virtual Interval Caching

3.1 Concept of Interval

We first introduce the concept of *interval* and briefly explain the existing interval-based buffer caching algorithms[6].

In Fig. 3, S_i denotes the stream accessing the file i and the small arrows marked by stream S_i denote the current playback position. Interval is the distance between two session, e.g. S_i and S_j. It is denoted by I_{ij}. For example, I_{21} and I_{32} are intervals formed by two consecutive streams. The two streams of an interval are referred to as the preceding and the following streams.

The basic idea of interval-based caching algorithms is that by caching the blocks brought in by the preceding stream, it is possible to serve the following stream from the cache. The cache requirement of an interval is defined to be the number of blocks needed to store the interval and is a function of the time-interval between the two streams and the compression method used. When the

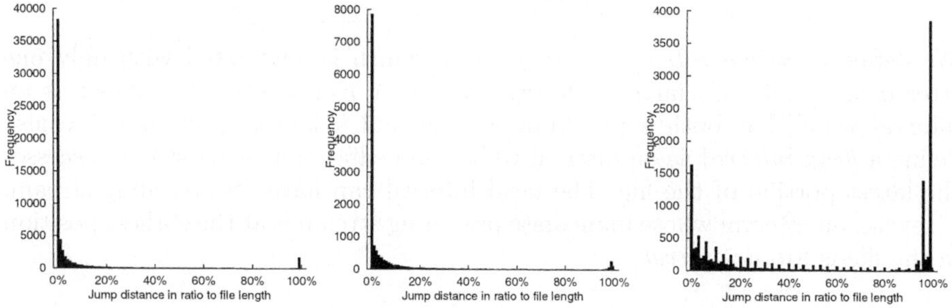

(a) *Hanmir* (b) *Ongamenet* (c) *Myung Films*

Fig. 2. Jump distance distribution

server services multiple number of streams, it is possible that more than one stream accesses the same video contents and thus a number of interval is created. The objective of the interval caching scheme is to select the intervals to be cached so as to maximize the number of streams served from cache. If all the streaming session have the same playback rates and all accesses are sequential, caching the shortest interval first will yield the best performance.

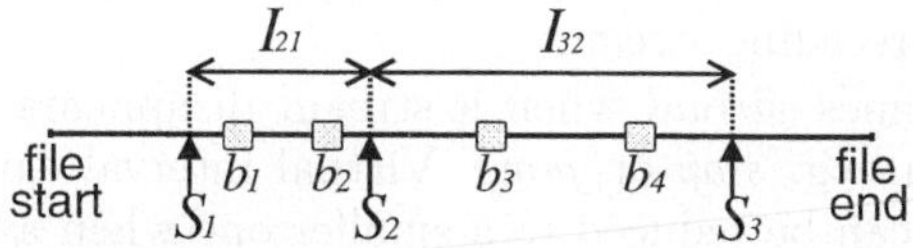

Fig. 3. Interval between two consecutive streams

When all streaming sessions are sequential playback only, the interval length does not change unless either preceding or following session finishes. Start of new streaming session creates new interval when there has been ongoing streaming session for the same file. When the successor stream finishes earlier than the predecessor stream, the respective interval is removed. Cache management module releases the space used by the interval and examines the next shortest interval for possible caching. If there exist VCR operations, intervals changes dynamically. The intervals can be merged, split, created and/or removed when VCR request is issued. The relative access position may be switched. For example, the successor can be predecessor and the predecessor can be successor as a result of jump backward operation.

3.2 Virtual Interval Caching

We define a *virtual interval* as an interval which is associated with only one stream or is not associated with any stream. A *real interval* is defined as an interval which has both a preceding stream and a following stream. We also define a *head interval* as an interval whose immediate following stream accesses the latest portion of the file. The head interval can have no preceding stream. Likewise, an interval whose immediate preceding stream is at the earliest position in the file is a *tail interval.*

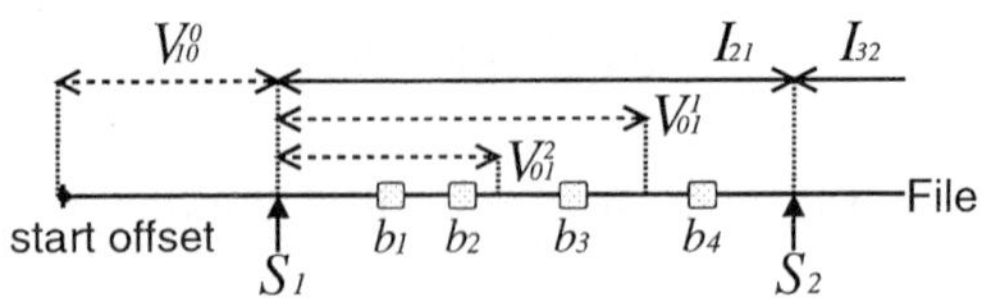

Fig. 4. Virtual Interval

Fig. 4 shows relationship between real interval and virtual interval. I_{21} represents a real interval which is generated by two streams S_2 and S_1. In contrary, V^1_{01}, V^2_{01} and V^0_{10} are virtual intervals which have only a following stream or neither of streams. We can see that I_{21}, V^1_{01}, V^2_{01} have the same following stream but only I_{21} has a preceding stream.

An interval becomes *virtual* when a stream disappears due to the change in playback position, e.g. *stop* or *jump*. Virtual interval can also be split into two smaller ones or can be reduced to a smaller one when a new stream arrives or an existing stream resumes playing from a new position. Fig. 5 shows that new virtual interval is created. In this figure, as the preceding stream of I_{ji} disappears, the respective interval becomes virtual and we denote the respective interval as V^1_{0i}. Its interval length does not change. However, the interval size of V^0_{0j} becomes longer because its immediate following stream becomes I_{ih}. Fig. 6 illustrates that a virtual interval becomes smaller due to the advent of new stream. As a result of the advent of the stream S_j, I_{ki} is split into I_{ji} and I_{kj}. At the same time V^1_{0i} in Fig. 6(a) also get split but is regarded as being reduced into V^1_{0j} because its immediate following stream becomes S_j.

The objective of buffer cache management policy is to minimize buffer cache miss rate. Our buffer cache management algorithm compute the access probability of individual intervals and caches the interval with largest *normalized* access probability. As an approximation to access probability of each interval, *virtual interval caching* conducts replacement policy based upon access probabilities of each interval which is linearly proportional to interval length. In the case of a tail interval, interval size should be estimated from a average number of streams within a file as $max\{interval\ size\ , \frac{file\ length}{average\ number\ of\ streams}\}$. By treating the virtual intervals as same as regular interval, access probabilities of intervals can

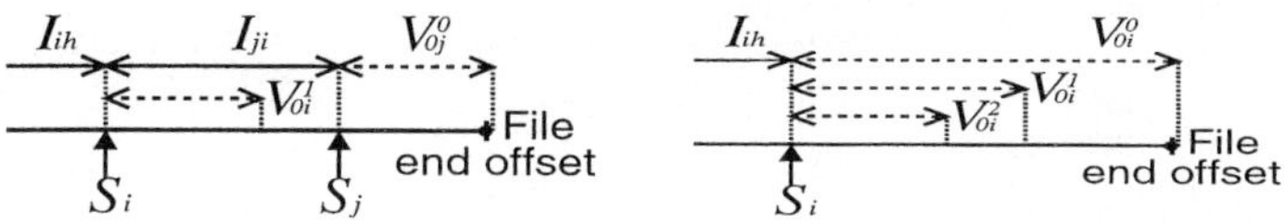

(a) Before S_j disappears (b) After S_j disappears

Fig. 5. A real interval is converted into a virtual interval due to the disappearance of an existing stream

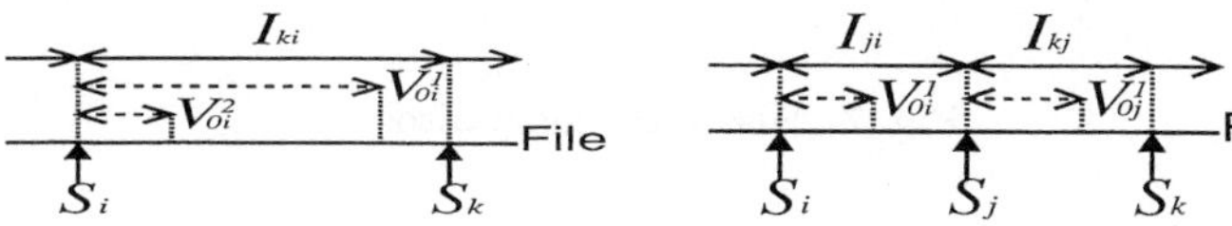

(a) Before S_j appears (b) After S_j appears

Fig. 6. A virtual interval is reduced to a smaller one due to the advent of a new stream

be computed using the uniform method. As such, *VIC* selects a buffer in the interval with largest virtual size as a victim at replacement time.

4 Simulation

In this section, we examine the performance of VIC based replacement algorithm via simulation based experiment. We compare the performance of VIC based buffer replacement algorithm with legacy algorithms: Interval Caching(IC), LRU, LRU-k[11][1], MRU and Optimal algorithm(OPT). The performance metric we use is cache miss ratio.

Fig. 7 illustrates buffer cache miss ratio under different cache management policy. The system is fed with two different workloads: (i) access trace from online game site(Fig. 7(a)) and (ii) access trace from movie-on-demand site(Fig. 7(c)). The size of the buffer cache varies from 2000 to 16000 (in terms of the number of buffer blocks). According to our simulation study, VIC exhibits superior buffer cache miss ratio to other algorithms. VIC is average 6% better than IC or LRU-k.

Figure 7(a) shows results using game trace(*Ongamenet*). In this server, there are relatively larger number of concurrent streams. This implies that there exist relatively larger number of intervals. This leads to good performance of interval caching and virtual interval caching, which is very close to OPT. With small buffer size (i.e., less than 8000), difference of miss ratio between IC and VIC

[1] Throughout experiments LRU-k takes into account knowledge of the last two references.

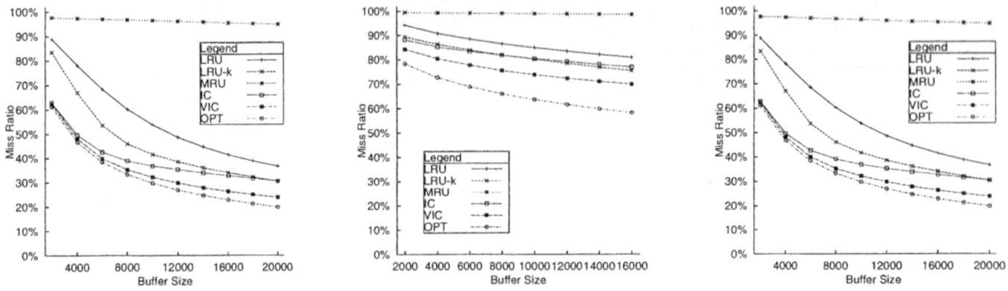

(a) *Ongamenet* trace (b) *Hamir* trace (c) *Myung Films* trace

Fig. 7. Miss ratio comparison

is not significant. However, VIC still exhibits better miss ratio as buffer size increases. The miss ratio of the VIC is 6.7% lower than IC or LRU-k and 12.9% lower than LRU with buffer size 20000.

Results with Movie-On-Demand trace(*Myung Films*) is shown in Fig. 7(c). When buffer size is 500, VIC is 2.8% and 8.6% better than LRU-k and IC, respectively. However, we can see that VIC does not provide a lower miss ratio any more as the buffer size increases. This is because there are too few concurrent streams and thus the number of intervals is not so sufficient that VIC runs effectively.

It is worth noting that there are significant amount VCR operations, e.g. *backward jump* and *forward jump* in real world trace data. In media servers with such workload, proposed VIC scheme can deliver better performance than legacy schemes.

5 Conclusion

In this work, we show that there exist a significant number of non-sequential access in real multimedia workload through analysis of real-world media server's log. Most of the non-sequential file accesses are jump forward or backward operations, which are triggered by VCR control capable client player. Moreover, the distance of skip(or jump) operations are in most cases very short. We need new buffer caching algorithms that exploit various file access workload in multimedia streaming servers.

Our buffer replacement algorithm, *Virtual Interval Caching (VIC)*, handles buffer cache effectively under such a real workload that a non-sequential access pattern exists. Unlike the existing interval caching scheme, VIC keeps intervals that were removed by VCR operations as virtual intervals. By keeping data blocks in the buffer cache that frequently accessed by VCR operations, VIC significantly improves the cache hit probability. We showed through trace-driven simulations that VIC algorithm can perform over 5% better than well-known legacy algorithms.

Acknowledgement. Authors would like to thank Sun-Nyoung Kim for collecting access traces from various streaming service sites.

References

1. Jussara M. Aimeida, Jeffrey Krueger, Derek L. Eager, and Mary K. Vernon. Analysis of educational media server workloads. In *Proceedings of International Workshop on Network and Operating System Support for Digital Audio and Video*, June 2001.
2. Matthew Andrews and Kameshwar Munagala. Online algorithms for caching multimedia streams. In *European Symposium on Algorithms*, pages 64–75, 2000.
3. M. Chesire, A. Wolman, G. Voelker, and H. Levy. Measurement and analysis of a streaming media workload. In *Proceedings of 3rd USENIX Symp. on Internet Technologies and Systems*, San Francisco, CA, USA, March 2001.
4. K. Cho, Y. Ryu, Y. Won, and K. Koh. A hybrid buffer cache management scheme for vod server. In *Proceeding of IEEE International Conference on Multimedia and Expo*, August 2002.
5. Microsoft Corporation. Windows media service sdk, version 4.1.
6. A. Dan, Y. Heights, and D. Sitaram. Generalized interval caching policy for mixed interactive and long video workloads. In Proc. of SPIE's Conf. on Multimedia Computing and Networking, 1996.
7. N. Harel, V. Vellanki, A. Chervenak, G. Abowd, and U. Ramachandran. Workload of a media-enhanced classroom server. In *Proceedings of IEEE Workshop on Workload Characterization*, Oct. 1999.
8. Hanmir education center. `http://edu.hanmir.com`.
9. Myung films. `http://www.myungfilm.co.kr`.
10. Ongamenet. `http://www.ongamenet.com`.
11. E. O'Neil, P. O'Neil, and G. Weikum. Page replacement algorithm for database disk buffering. SIGMOD Conf., 1993.
12. J. Padhye and J. Kurose. An empirical study of client interactions with a continuous-media courseware server. In *Proceedings of International Workshop on Network and Operating System Support for Digital Audio and Video*, July 1998.
13. Lawrence A. Rowe, Diane Harley, and Peter Pletcher. Bibs: A lecture webcasting system. Technical report, Berkeley Multimedia Research Center, UC Berkeley, June 2001.

RUBDES: A Rule Based Distributed Event System

Ozgur Koray Sahingoz[1] and Nadia Erdogan[2]

[1] Air Force Academy, Computer Engineering Department, Yesilyurt, Istanbul, TURKEY,
o.sahingoz@hho.edu.tr

[2] Istanbul Technical University, Electrical-Electronics Faculty,
Computer Engineering Department, Ayazaga, 80626, Istanbul, TURKEY
erdogan@cs.itu.edu.tr

Abstract. In the last years, event-based communication paradigm has been largely studied and considered as a promising approach to develop the communication infrastructure of distributed systems. RUBDES (Rule Based Distributed Event System) is a distributed event system that allows the use of composite events in publish/subscribe computational model. In this system, an event is represented as an object and a rule is represented as an expression or a function that is evaluated or executed depending on the occurrence of events. This paper presents the design details of RUBDES and usage of Rule Definition Language (RDL) to describe composite events and event filters.

1 Introduction

In the traditional client/server computing model, which is used in RPC and RMI, communication is typically synchronous, tightly coupled and point-to-point. As shown in Figure 1.a, clients invoke a method on the remote server and wait for the response to return. This type of communication requires clients and servers to have some prior knowledge of each other.

With the use of mobile or large-scale systems, the need for asynchronous, loosely coupled and point to multipoint communication pattern arises. Event models are application independent infrastructures that satisfy communication requirements of such systems. Event-based communication generally implements what is commonly known as the publish/subscribe protocol. As shown in Figure 1.b, an *event supplier (publisher)* asynchronously communicates event data to a group of *event consumers (subscribers)*, ideally without knowledge of their number and location.

To receive event data, subscribers register to an event service with the definitions of the particular interested events. A definition can include a simple subscription message, a subscription message with filtering on events or a subscription message for composite events. In this paper, we present RUBDES which is a distributed event-based system that uses Rule Definition Language (RDL) to define subscription criteria in the form of a rule and relies on dynamic queries for filtering operations. RUBDES uses a content-based subscription policy, thus enhancing the efficiency of the two main processes of publish/subscribe systems, namely, the publishing and delivering processes.

A. Yazici and C. Şener (Eds.): ISCIS 2003, LNCS 2869, pp. 284–291, 2003.

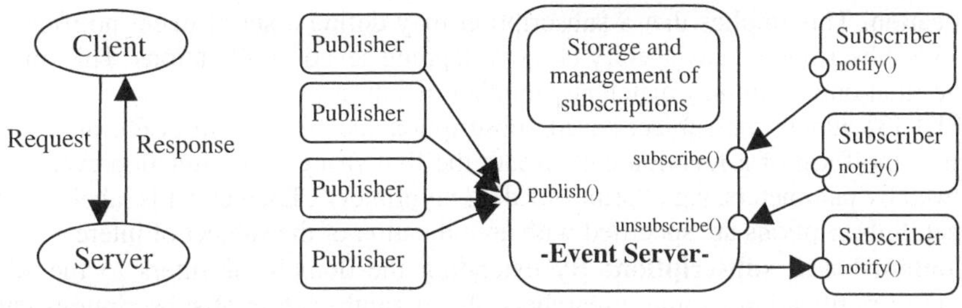

a. Client/Server b. Event-based

Fig. 1. Client/Server and Event-based Computing Models

The rest of this paper is organized as follows. In the next section, we present a classification of publish/subscribe systems with references to related work. Section 3 introduces the computational model of RUBDES. Section 4 focuses on event types and how Rule Definition Language (RDL) is used. Section 5 presents an evaluation of the performance of the system. Our conclusions and plans for future work are presented in Section 6.

2 Publish/Subscribe Systems

Publish/subscribe programming paradigm is characterized by the complete decoupling of producers (publishers) and consumers (subscribers). The event service that provides message transfers between publishers and subscribers can be decomposed along three dimensions, time decoupling, space decoupling, flow decoupling. Publish/subscribe systems can be classified into four groups according to their subscription mechanism. Each one is discussed in detail below, with references to representative work.

Channel-based subscriptions: The simplest subscription mechanism is what is commonly referred to as a *channel*. Subscribers subscribe or listen to a channel. Applications explicitly notify the occurrence of events by posting notification to one or more channels. The part of an event that is visible to the event service is the identifier of the channel to which the event has been sent. Every notification posted to a channel is delivered by the event service to all the subscribers that are listening to that channel. The abstraction of the channel resembles to the one given by a mailing list. A user sends an e-mail to an address, and the message is forwarded to those who have registered to that mailing list. CORBA Event Service [1] adopts a channel-based architecture. Another widely used channel based model is the Java Delegation Event Model [2], which encapsulates events from the platform's Graphical User Interface.

Subject-based subscription: Some systems extend the concept of a channel with a more flexible addressing mechanism that is often referred to as *subject-based* addressing. In this case, an event notification consists of two different parts: a well-known attribute, *the subject,* that determines the address, which is followed by *the remaining information* of the event data. The main difference with respect to a channel is that subscriptions can express interest in many subjects/channels by specifying some form of expression to be evaluated against the subject of a notification. This implies that a subscription may define a set of event notifications, and two subscriptions may specify two overlapping sets of notifications. This, in turn, implies that one event may match any number of subscriptions.

JEDI [3] adopts the subject-based subscription mechanism. In JEDI, an event is given in the form of a function call, where the first string is the function/event name followed by parameters, e.g., "print (tez.doc, myprinter)". Each event is labeled with a subject. Subscriptions are specified with an indication of the subject of interest

Content-based subscription: By extending the domain of filters to the whole content of notifications, some researchers obtain another class of subscriptions called content-based [5]. Content-based subscriptions are conceptually very similar to subject-based ones. However, since they can access the whole structured content of notifications, an event server gets more freedom in encoding the data upon which filters can be applied and that the event service can use for setting up routing information. Examples of event systems that provide this kind of subscription are Yeast [4] (uses a centralized structure) and SIENA[5]. In SIENA, an event notification is a set of attributes in which each attribute is a triple, as in "attribute = (name; type; value)". Attributes are uniquely identified by their names. An event filter defines a class of event notifications by specifying a set of attribute names and types and some constraints on their values, e.g., "attr filter = (name; type; operator; value)".

Object-based subscription: Type based publish/subscribe model [6], proposed by Eugster, is a new model of subscription that has been developed to access event data in a more structured manner. Events are often viewed as low-level messages, and a predefined set of such message types are offered by most systems, providing very little flexibility. To overcome this deficiency, type-based publish/subscribe mechanism manipulates events as objects, called *obvents*. The core idea underlying this integration consists in viewing events as first class citizens, and subscribing to these events by explicitly specifying their type. So an application-defined event data can be used in the event system.

3 RUBDES Computational Model

RUBDES is an event-based publish/subscribe system that uses rules for subscribing to an event service. Many of the event systems described in literature, as referenced in the previous section, use predefined events. RUBDES implements a content-based subscription mechanism, similar to that proposed by Carzaniga [5], which enables handling of application-defined events.

RUBDES, being implemented in Java, makes use of Java RMI facility extensively to access remote objects. To create a uniform structure, the components of the system are designed to be accessed over well-defined interfaces and, naturally, they are expected to implement the methods included in those interfaces. Fig. 2 depicts the general architecture of RUBDES. The system consists of three main components: Subscribers, Publishers and Event Servers.

SUBSCRIBER: Subscribers of events determine what types of information they are interested in and describe them in a rule form usable by the Event Service. A subscriber has to know the address of the Event Server to which it should register. Subscribers have to implement the *Subscriber* interface, which consists of a single method, *"notify"*. An event server issues a remote call to the notify method of the subscriber to deliver an event. The subscriber is expected to process the event in the context of this method.

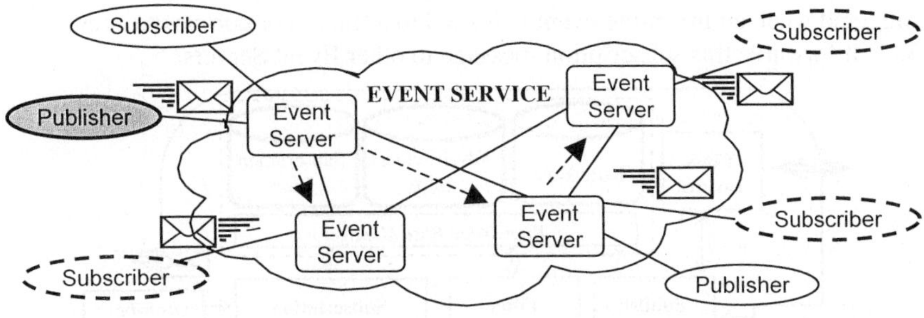

Fig. 2. RUBDES Architecture

PUBLISHER: Publishers of information decide on what events are observable, how to name or describe those events, how to actually observe the event, and then how to represent the event as a discrete entity. A publisher process is not required to implement a particular interface. The Event Server's address has to be known by the publisher so that it can issue a remote call to its *"publish"* method.

EVENT SERVER: The main function of the Event Server is to dispatch incoming event notifications from publishers to (possibly multiple) subscribers. The event server implements the *EventServer* interface, which consists of the following three methods:

`subscribe:` A client (a subscriber or an event server) registers interest in a particular event by invoking the subscribe method of the event server. It supplies its RMI contact address and a rule that describes the events it is interested in as parameters to the call.

`unsubscribe:` A client can cancel its registration by calling the unsubscribe method, supplying parameters needed to identify the subscription previously made.

`publish:` A dispatcher (a publisher or an event server) calls the *`publish`* method to announce an event.

The Event Server consists of manager modules that handle the basic functionalities of the system and several structures to hold various data. The internal architecture of the Event Server and message flow between its components are shown in Fig. 3. In the following, we describe the execution flow of registration and dispatching operations.

Execution Flow of Registration: A client can register (or unregister) to an event server by invoking it's *subscribe* (or *unsubscribe*) method. When a client subscribes to an event server, it sends certain parameters (its address and rule) to register on. The *Subscription Manager* adds these parameters into the Subscription Base. The Subscription Manager follows the following algorithm to process a subscription:

1. It checks subjects of interest in the *Advertisement Base.* To prevent subscription on an unpublished event, we use an Advertisement Base which keeps a list of events published previously.

2. It adds the incoming subscription to the *Subscription Base*, which consists of subscriptions formerly received. Its entries consist of the fields (Event_type, Triggering_SQL, owner_address, send_address). *Triggering_SQL* is a set of SQL commands, which are generated according to a subscription rule, and is to be triggered when an incoming event is related to a filtered or composite event.
3. It forwards this subscription message to other Event Servers.

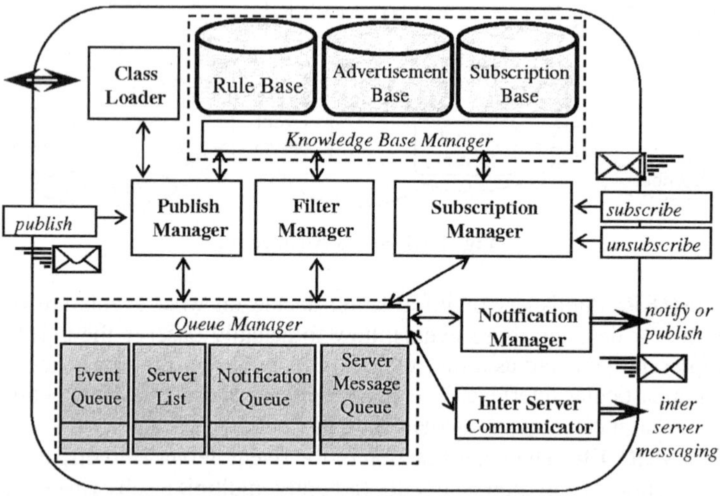

Fig. 3. The Architecture of the Event Server

Execution Flow of Dispatching: A dispatcher sends an event message by invoking the *publish* method of the event server with the required parameters (published event data). The *Publish Manager* creates a *Class Loader* thread to download the classes the published object belongs to from the publisher site and adds this incoming notification to the *Event Queue.* Messages in the Event Queue are processed by the *Filter Manager* later. When a new event (for example, event_x) arrives, the Filter Manager follows the following algorithm to process it:

1. It examines the Subscription Base to find out if there is a subscription on event_x and adds the published event type to the Advertisement Base.
2. For each subscription on event_x, it generates a notification according to the subscription rule and puts it into the *Notification Queue*. All incoming events are not stored in the same event table. For different types of events, different tables are created in the RuleBase. To generate notifications, the Filter Manager runs a query on the subscription record and the event data in the corresponding RuleBase table. Therefore, selections of filtered and composite subscriptions are performed faster when compared to other event-based systems previously mentioned.

Notification Manager is an autonomous thread that sends the notification requests that are placed into the Notification Queue to target clients (subscribers or event servers). *Inter Server Communicator* is used for messaging between Event Servers.

4 Event Types and Rules

`Event` class is the base class of all event classes and defines common attributes for all types of events. The class definition of the event extends the base class `Event` and may contain additional structures. A subscriber specifies the type of the event it wishes to be notified of. Fig. 4 shows the specification of a sample event type class named HeatEvent. In addition to the attributes inherited from the `Event` class, this class defines a new attribute `loc` to identify the location of the event produced and `value` to represent a measure of some kind, for example, a temperature reading of a thermometer.

```
public class HeatEvent extends Event implements
                                        Serializable
{   int loc;          // location of the event
    double value;    // measurement of the temperature}
```

Fig. 4. A User Defined Event Type

A rule is an expression or function that is evaluated or executed depending on the occurrence of events. Rule Definition Language (RDL) is used to state rules to aid the specification of a single or a pattern of events in distributed systems. The grammar of the Rule Definition Language (RDL) and various programming examples are given in RUBCES [7], which is a centralized (with a single Event Server) version of RUBDES. A subscription rule can be created by the Graphical User Interface (GUI) at the subscriber site. This GUI can be specific to subscription event type and specific types of rules can be produced. Otherwise, a rule can be written manually in a text area component of a general GUI. Of course, this rule must conform to the RDL's grammar.

rule rule_1 onEvent HeatEvent h1 getData h1.value	rule rule_2 onEvent HeatEvent h1 getData h1.value where (h1.value > 25 and h1.value < 37)	rule rule_3 onEvent Temperature t1, Humidity h1 getData h1.value,t1.value where (t1.value < 27 and h1.value < 70)
a. Simple Event	b. Filtered Event	c. Composite Event

Fig. 5. Filtered Events in RDL

A rule definition is composed of four parts, each introduced by the keywords *rule, onEvent, getData* and *where*, respectively, as shown in Fig. 5. The first part sets a unique identifier for the rule, the second part specifies the type of the target event, the third part specifies the specific information data about the event that subscriber wants to be notified with, and the last part describes the conditions on which a filtered or a composite event should be caught. In RUBDES, it is possible to define rules for three different event types: *simple events, events with filtering* and *composite events*. Simple events, shown in Fig. 5.a, are used when subscribers are interested in only one event type. An event-based system may include a multiple number of publishers. Thus, the number of events propagated in an event-based system may be quite large. However, a particular consumer is usually interested in only a subset of the events propagated in the system. Event filters are a means to control the propagation of events. Filters enable a particular consumer to subscribe to the exact range of events it is interested in receiving. An event that is delivered uses network bandwidth and CPU processing power on the consumer side. It is therefore desirable to prevent the delivery of unwanted events. RUBDES allows for event filtering as shown in Fig. 5.b.

Clients may require to be notified on events from multiple sources and may want to detect a specific pattern of event occurrences from these different publishers. Such a combination of event occurrences, where a client is interested in a sequence of event occurrences but not in any of the events alone, is called an *event composition*. Intuitively, while a filter selects one event notification at a time, a pattern can select several notifications that together match an algebraic combination of filters. An advanced feature of RUBDES is that it allows subscribers to specify composite events, as shown in Fig. 5.c.

5 System Performance

We've selected average message distribution time as an appropriate benchmark for evaluating performance of a communication framework. We define *event distribution time* as the elapsed time from the generation of an event to its reception by all subscribers that are interested in that event. In our analysis, event generation is the submission of an event to the Event Server by a publisher. In our preliminary analysis, we established an objective of determining the efficiency of the Event Server delivery without incurring concurrency into the system. Our goal was to examine the performance and scalability of the system.

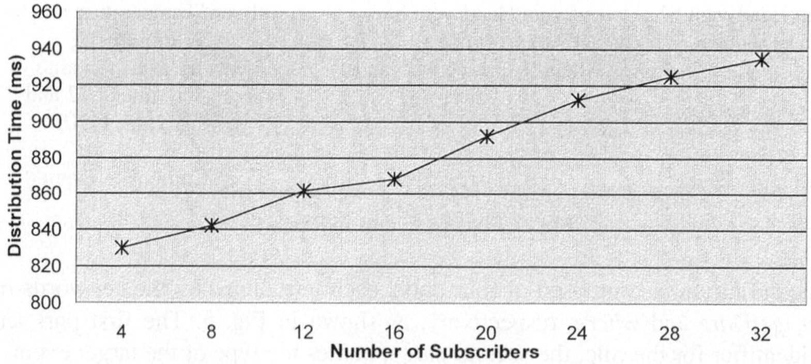

Fig. 6. Average Distribution Time with Respect to Number of Subscribers

We ran a simple benchmark with a single publisher, strongly connected to four event servers and a multiple number of subscribers, which were distributed evenly on these event servers. The number of subscribers was varied from 4 to 32 on successive trials. The experiment used a single event source whose event generation rate was slow enough to allow all the listeners to complete processing a given event before the next one was generated. As we were sure that there was no concurrent event delivery, we could compute the theoretical best average delivery time. Fig. 6 shows event distribution times we have measured for increasing number of subscribers. Although, RUBDES has not been tested with very large numbers of subscribers and publishers, the results we have obtained suggest that RUBDES is scalable.

6 Conclusion and Future Work

In this paper, we have presented RUBDES, an event-based publish/subscribe system that uses rules to specify subscription on events. RUBDES uses a content-based subscription mechanism that allows users to subscribe on different event types. A new Rule Definition Language (RDL) is used to enable specification of different types of subscription (simple subscription, subscription with filtering and subscription for composite events). Implementation of a prototype system in Java is completed. As future work, we plan to apply the system in different application domains and focus on new design decisions to improve its performance and scalability. We want to add features for mobile subscribers that can connect from different locations to different Event Servers and test the entire system in a large scale platform.

References

1. Object Management Group, "CORBAservices: Common Object Service Specification", Technical Report, Object Management Group, July (1998).
2. "Java AWT: Delegation Event Model". Available online at http://java.sun.com/j2se/1.4.1/docs/guide/awt/1.3/designspec/events.html (2003)
3. G. Cugola, E. Di Nitto, and A. Fuggetta, "The JEDI event-based infrastructure and its application to the development of the OPSS WFMS", Technical Report, CEFRIEL – Politecnico di Milano, Italy, August (1998).
4. B. Krishnamurthy and D. S. Rosenblum, "Yeast: A General Purpose Event-Action System", IEEE Transactions on Software Engineering, 21(10):845–857, Oct. (1995).
5. A. Carzaniga, "Architectures for an Event Notification Service Scalable to Wide-area Networks", PhD Thesis, Politecnico di Milano, Italy, December (1998).
6. P.T.Eusgter, "TypeBased Publish/Subscribe", PhD Thesis. Ecole Polytechnique Federale De Lausanne, France, (2001)
7. O. K. Sahingoz, N. Erdogan, "RUBCES: Rule Based Composite Event System", accepted for publication in XII. Turkish Artificial Intelligence and Neural Network Symposium (TAINN), Turkey, July (2003)

A Statistical μ-Partitioning Method for Clustering Data Streams

Nam Hun Park and Won Suk Lee

Department of Computer Science, Yonsei University
134 Shinchon-dong Seodaemun-gu Seoul, 120-749, Korea
{zyonix, leewo}@amadeus.yonsei.ac.kr

Abstract. A data stream is a massive unbounded sequence of data elements continuously generated at a rapid rate. Due to this reason, most algorithms for data streams sacrifice the correctness of their results for fast processing time. This paper proposes a clustering method over a data stream based on statistical μ-partition. The multi-dimensional space of a data domain is divided into a set of mutually exclusive equal-size *initial cells*. A cell maintains the distribution statistics of data elements in its range. Based on the distribution statistics of a cell, a dense cell is dynamically split into two mutually exclusive smaller cells called *intermediate cells*. Eventually, the dense sub-range of an initial cell is recursively partitioned until it becomes the smallest cell called *a unit cell*. A cluster of a data stream is a group of adjacent dense unit cells. As the size of a unit cell is set to be smaller, the resulting set of clusters is more accurately identified. Through a series of experiments, the performance of the proposed algorithm is comparatively analyzed.

1 Introduction

Clustering is a process of finding groups of similar data elements which are defined by a given similarity measure. Clustering techniques are categorized into several methods: partitioning, hierarchical, density-based and grid-based. The partitioning method such as k-means[1] and k-medoid[2] divides the data space of a data set into k mutually disjoint regions called clusters. The number of clusters should be predefined in advance. The k-medoid algorithm selects k data elements as the centers of k clusters initially, and repeatedly replaces one of the selected centers until it finds the best set of k centers. In this method, noise data elements can substantially influence the generation of a cluster, so that it may be difficult to produce a correct result in some cases. The hierarchical method such as BIRCH[3] and CURE[4] decomposes a data set into a tree-like structure. A typical density-based clustering algorithm[5] which regards a cluster as a region in a data space with a high density of data elements. Its strong points are that it can discover an arbitrarily shaped cluster, and control noise data easily. In the grid-based clustering method, the data space of a problem is divided statistically into a set of equal-size cells. A cluster is generated by merging adjacent cells that have more than a predefined number of data elements. Its time

A. Yazici and C. Şener (Eds.): ISCIS 2003, LNCS 2869, pp. 292–299, 2003.

complexity is very efficient but the accuracy of a cluster is affected by the size of a cell. STING[6] uses a grid-based multi-resolution data structure in which a data space is divided into rectangular cells. There are several levels of such rectangular cells corresponding to the different levels of resolution.

Recently, several data mining methods for a data stream are actively proposed. A data stream is a massive unbounded sequence of data elements continuously generated at a rapid rate. Due to this reason, it is impossible to maintain all elements of a data stream. Consequently, data stream processing should satisfy the following requirements[7]. First, each data element should be examined at most once to analyze a data stream. Second, memory usage for data stream analysis should be restricted finitely although new data elements are continuously generated in a data stream. Third, newly generated data elements should be processed as fast as possible to produce the up-to-date analysis result of a data stream, so that it can be instantly utilized upon request. To satisfy these requirements, data stream processing sacrifices the correctness of its analysis result by allowing some errors.

In [8], a k-median algorithm is proposed to find the clusters of data elements generated in a data stream. It regards a data stream as a sequence of stream chunks. A stream chunk is a set of consecutive data elements generated in a data stream. Whenever a new stream chunk containing a set of newly generated data elements is formed, the LSEARCH routine which is an O(1)-approximate k-medoid algorithm is performed to select k data elements from the data elements of the stream chunk as the local centers of the chunk. The algorithm confines its memory space to holding a fixed number of local centers for previous stream chunks. Therefore, if retaining *ik* centers is impossible at the ith stream chunk, the LSEARCH routine is performed again to cluster the weighted *ik* points to retain *k* centers.

This paper proposes a grid-based clustering method that dynamically partitions the range of a grid-cell based on its distribution statistics of data elements in a data stream. Initially the multi-dimensional space of a data domain is partitioned into a set of mutually exclusive equal-size initial cells. As a new data element is generated continuously, each cell monitors the distribution statistics of data elements within its range. When the support of a cell becomes high enough, the cell is dynamically divided into two mutually exclusive smaller cells, called *intermediate cells*, based on its distribution statistics. Similarly, a dense intermediate cell itself can be partitioned but it is replaced by its two-divided cells. Eventually, the dense sub-range of an initial cell is recursively partitioned until it becomes the smallest cell called a *unit cell*. A cluster of a data stream is a group of adjacent dense unit cells. As the size of a unit cell is set to be smaller, the resulting set of clusters is more accurately identified. In order to minimize the number of cells, a sparse intermediate or unit cell can be pruned if its support becomes much less than a minimum support.

The rest of this paper is organized as follows. Section 2 presents the proposed statistical μ-partition clustering algorithm in detail. In Section 3, several experiment results are comparatively analyzed to illustrate the various characteristics of the proposed method. Finally, Section 4 presents conclusions.

2 μ-Partition Clustering

Given a data stream $\boldsymbol{D}$ of d-dimensional data space $\mathbf{N}=N_1\times N_2\times\ldots\times N_d$, a data element generated at the jth turn is denoted by $\mathbf{e}^j=<e_1^j,e_2^j,\ldots,e_d^j>$, $e_i^j\in N_i$, $1\le i\le d$. When a new data element $\mathbf{e}^t$ is generated at the tth turn in a data stream $\boldsymbol{D}$, the current data stream $\boldsymbol{D}^t$ is composed of all the data elements that have ever generated so far i.e. $\boldsymbol{D}^t=\{\mathbf{e}^1,\mathbf{e}^2,\ldots,\mathbf{e}^t\}$. The total number of data elements generated in the current data stream $\boldsymbol{D}^t$ is denoted by $|\boldsymbol{D}^t|$.

Finding a cluster of similar data elements in the current data stream $\boldsymbol{D}^t$ is identifying a region whose current density of data elements is dense enough. A unit cell whose length in each dimension is less than λ is used to define the similarity between data elements. The current support of a cell is the ratio of the number of those data elements in $\boldsymbol{D}^t$ that are inside the cell over the total number of data elements in $\boldsymbol{D}^t$. Therefore, a cluster at $\boldsymbol{D}^t$ is a group of adjacent dense unit cells whose current supports are greater than or equal to a predefined minimum support S_{min}.

The range of each dimension N_i is initially partitioned by p number of mutually exclusive equal-size intervals $I_i^j=[s_i^j,f_i^j)$ $1\le j\le p$ where s_i^j and f_i^j denote the start and end values in the jth interval of the ith dimension. Consequently, p^d number of initial cells are formed in $\mathbf{N}$ and each initial cell g is defined by a set of d intervals $\{I_1,I_2,\ldots,I_d\}$ $I_i\subseteq N_i$ $1\le i\le d$. The range R(g) of an initial cell g is a rectangular space $\mathbf{rs}=I_1\times\ldots\times I_d$. However, the initial rectangular space of an initial cell becomes a set of rectangular spaces as a series of cell partitioning and pruning operations are performed subsequently. Each cell keeps the current distribution statistics of those data elements in the current data stream $\boldsymbol{D}^t$ that are within its range. For the current data stream $\boldsymbol{D}^t$, a term $g(\mathbf{RS}, c^t, \boldsymbol{\mu}^t, \boldsymbol{\sigma}^t)$ is used to denote the distribution statistics of a cell g which is defined by a set of its rectangular spaces $\mathbf{RS}=\{\mathbf{rs}_1,\mathbf{rs}_2,\ldots,\mathbf{rs}_q\}$. When these rectangular spaces are projected to the ith dimension, the intervals of the ith dimension of a cell g can be found and they are denoted by $IS_i(g)=\{I_i^1,I_i^2,\ldots,I_i^q\}$. The sum of these intervals is defined as the interval size of the ith dimension of the cell g. The range of the cell g is the united spaces of all the rectangular spaces $\mathbf{rs}_1,\ldots,\mathbf{rs}_q$, $R(g)=\bigcup_{i=1}^{q}\mathbf{rs}_i$. Let $\boldsymbol{D}_g^t$ denote those elements in $\boldsymbol{D}^t$ that are in the range of the cell g, i.e., $\boldsymbol{D}_g^t=\{\mathbf{e}\,|\,\mathbf{e}\in\boldsymbol{D}^t$ and $\mathbf{e}\in R(g)\}$. The distribution statistics of the cell g are defined as follows:

i) c^t : the number of data elements in $\boldsymbol{D}_g^t$

ii) $\boldsymbol{\mu}^t=<\mu_1^t,\ldots,\mu_d^t>$: μ_i^t denotes the average of the ith dimensional values of the data elements in $\boldsymbol{D}_g^t$. $\mu_i^t=\sum_{j=1}^{c^t} e_i^j / c^t$, $1\le i\le d$

iii) $\boldsymbol{\sigma}^t=<\sigma_1^t,\ldots,\sigma_d^t>$: σ_i^t denotes the standard deviation of the ith dimensional values of the data elements in $\boldsymbol{D}_g^t$.

$$\sigma_i^t=\sqrt{\sum_{j=i}^{c^t}(e_i^j-\mu_i^t)^2 / c^t}\ ,\ 1\le i\le d$$

When a new data element $\mathbf{e}^t$ is generated in the current data stream $\boldsymbol{D}^t$, its corresponding initial cell among the p^d initial cells is identified based on the initial partitions of the data space **N**. If the data element is in the range of the initial cell g and the distribution statistics of the cell g were updated most recently at the insert of the vth data element ($v \leq t$), its statistics remain the same as g(**RS**, c^v,$\boldsymbol{\mu}^v$,$\boldsymbol{\sigma}^v$) and they are updated to g(**RS**, c^t,$\boldsymbol{\mu}^t$,$\boldsymbol{\sigma}^t$) as follow: for$\forall$i, $1 \leq i \leq d$,

$$c^t = c^v + 1,\ \mu_i^t = \frac{\mu_i^v \times c^v + e_i^t}{c^t},\ \sigma_i^t = \sqrt{\frac{c^v}{c^t} \times (\sigma_i^v)^2 + \frac{(\mu_i^v)^2 + (e_i^t)^2}{c^t} - (\mu_i^t)^2}$$

For the current data stream $\boldsymbol{D}^t$, the current support of an initial cell g(**RS**, c^t, $\boldsymbol{\mu}^t$, $\boldsymbol{\sigma}^t$) is defined by the ratio of its count over the total number of data elements generated so far ,i.e. $c^t/|\boldsymbol{D}^t|$. When the current support of the cell becomes the same as a *predefined split support* S_{split}(S_{split}<S_{min}), two intermediate cells g_1 and g_2 are created as the children of the initial cell. To split the range of the cell g, a dividing dimension is selected based on the distribution deviation of data elements in the cell g. Among the dimensions whose interval sizes for the cell g are larger than λ, the one with the largest standard deviation, say σ_k^t, is chosen as a dividing dimension. In order to split the count of the cell g evenly with respect to the dividing dimension, the rectangular spaces of the cell g are divided into two mutually exclusive sets based on the average value μ_k^t in the dividing dimension. These two sets of the rectangular spaces are assigned to the ranges of the two divided cells g_1 and g_2 respectively. If a rectangular space of the cell g includes μ_k^t, the corresponding interval of the dividing dimension is actually divided. Figure 1 illustrates how to divide the rectangular spaces of a cell g (**RS**,c,$\boldsymbol{\mu}$,$\boldsymbol{\sigma}$) in a two-dimensional data space.

By assuming the distribution of data elements in the original cell g is a normal distribution, the distribution statistics of the two divided cells g_1(**RS1**, $c1^t$, $\boldsymbol{\mu 1}^t$, $\boldsymbol{\sigma 1}^t$) and g_2(**RS2** , $c2^t$, $\boldsymbol{\mu 2}^t$, $\boldsymbol{\sigma 2}^t$) are initialized as follows. The count of the cell g is evenly distributed into the two cells i.e., $c1^t = c2^t = c^t/2$. Let $\varphi(x) = \frac{1}{\sqrt{2\pi}\sigma^t} e^{-\frac{(x-\mu^t)^2}{2(\sigma^t)^2}}$ be the normal distribution function of the data elements in the range of the cell g. The remaining distribution statistics of the two divided cells are estimated as follows.

$$\boldsymbol{\mu 1}^t = \boldsymbol{\mu 2}^t = \boldsymbol{\mu}^t \text{ except } \mu 1_k^t \text{ and } \mu 2_k^t,\ \mu 1_k^t = \int_{s_k(g_1)}^{f_k(g_1)} x\varphi(x)dx\ \ \mu 2_k^t = \int_{s_k(g_2)}^{f_k(g_2)} x\varphi(x)dx$$

$$\boldsymbol{\sigma 1}^t = \boldsymbol{\sigma 2}^t = \boldsymbol{\sigma}^t \text{ except } \sigma 1_k \text{ and } \sigma 2_k,$$

$$\sigma 1_k^t = \sqrt{\int_{s_k(g_1)}^{f_k(g_1)} x^2 \varphi(x)dx - \left(\mu 1_k^t\right)^2}\quad \sigma 2_k^t = \sqrt{\int_{s_k(g_2)}^{f_k(g_2)} x^2 \varphi(x)dx - \left(\mu 2_k^t\right)^2}$$

where $s_k(g_i)$ and $f_k(g_i)$ denote the smallest start and largest end value of the intervals of the kth dividing dimension for the divided cell g_i, i=1,2. At the same times, the distribution statistics of the original cell $g(\mathbf{RS}, c^t, \boldsymbol{\mu}^t, \boldsymbol{\sigma}^t)$ are reset as $c^t=0$ and $\mu_i^t=\sigma_i^t=0$ for $\forall i$, $1\leq i\leq d$ since they are carried to those of g_1 and g_2.

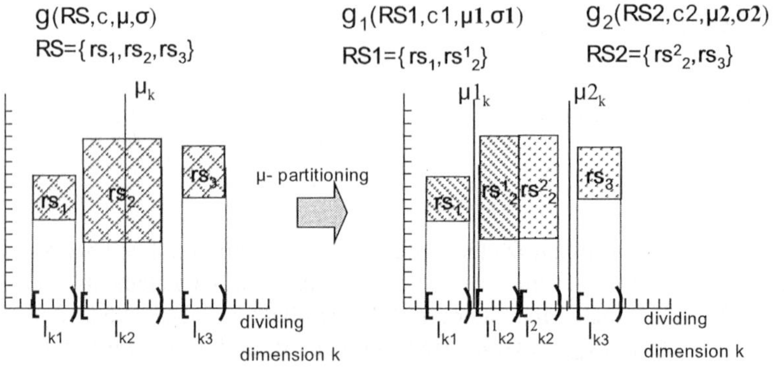

Fig. 1. The μ-partition method

When a newly generated data element is not in the range of its corresponding initial cell, the children of the initial cell are searched to find the one whose range includes the element. After the target intermediate cell *g* is found, its distribution statistics are updated by the same way as in an initial cell. When the updated support of the intermediate cell itself becomes the same as S_{splt} and the range of the cell is larger than that of a unit cell, the intermediate cell g is divided into two smaller intermediate cells by the same way of dividing an initial cell. However, unlike an initial cell, the original intermediate cell is replaced by the two divided cells. Consequently, the parent initial cell of the original cell becomes the parent of each divided cell.

On the other hand, when the current support of an intermediate cell *g* becomes less than a *predefined pruning support* S_{prn} ,i.e., $c^t/|\boldsymbol{D}|^t < S_{prn}$, the probability of finding a cluster in the range of the cell in the near future is very low. Consequently, the cell is removed and its distribution statistics $g(\mathbf{RS}, c^t, \boldsymbol{\mu}^t, \boldsymbol{\sigma}^t)$ are returned back to its parent initial cell g_p. Suppose the distribution statistics of the parent cell g_p were updated lastly at the vth element of the data stream($v\leq t$) and they are denoted by $g_p(\mathbf{RSp}, cp^v, \boldsymbol{\mu p}^v, \boldsymbol{\sigma p}^v)$ where $\boldsymbol{\mu p}^v = <\mu p_1^v, \mu p_1^v, \ldots, \mu p_d^v>$ and $\boldsymbol{\sigma p}^v = <\sigma p_1^v, \sigma p_2^v, \ldots, \sigma p_d^v>$. Its new statistics $g_p(\mathbf{RSp}, cp^t, \boldsymbol{\mu p}^t, \boldsymbol{\sigma p}^t)$ at $\boldsymbol{D}^t$ are updated as follows:

for all dimensions $i(1\leq i\leq d)$, $cp^t = cp^v + c^t$ and $\mu p_i^t = (\mu p_i^v \times c^v + \mu_i^t \times c^t) / cp^t$,

$$\sigma p_i^t = \sqrt{\frac{cp^v \times (\sigma p_i^v)^2 + c^t \times (\sigma_i^t)^2}{cp^t} + \frac{(\mu p_i^v)^2 + (\mu_i^t)^2}{cp^t} - (\mu p_i^t)^2}$$

```
divide N1,…,Nd into p intervals and create p^d initial cells;
 /*  S(g) : the support of cell g , S(g)=c^t / |D^t|  */
for a data stream D^t={ e^1, e^2, ..., e^t } do /* t is enlarging */
   read current data element e^t;
   search the cell g which include e^t;
   update μ^t, σ^t, c^t of a cell g;
   if g is a unit cell or an intermediate cell{
       if S(g) >= S_splt {
           if |f_i(g) – s_i(g)| > λ in any i dimension { /* dividing an intermediate cell g*/
                  find the largest σ_k^t among σ^t where |f_k(g) – s_k(g)| > λ;
                  generate g1 and g2;
                  set the statistics of g1 and g2; eliminate cell g;
           }
       }
       else if S(g) <= S_prn {  /* pruning a cell g */
           find the parent initial cell g_p where g is included to g_p
           update g_p with statistics of g;
           eliminate cell g;
       }
   }
   else if g is an initial cell {
       if S(g) >= S_splt {  /* dividing an initial cell g */
            find the largest σ_k^t among σ^t where |f_k(g) – s_k(g)| > λ;
            generate g1 and g2;    set the statistics of g1 and g2;
           set c^t=0 and μ_i^t=σ_i^t=0 for ∀i dimension;
       }
   }
End
```

Fig. 2. Statistic μ-partition clustering

Figure 2 shows the detail steps of the proposed algorithm. The pruning support S_{prn} should be less than the half of S_{splt} in order to avoid pruning a newly split cell too soon. A unit cell in the current data stream $\boldsymbol{D}^t$ is dense if its current support is greater than or equal to a predefined minimum support S_{min}. A cluster in the current data stream is a set of adjacent dense unit cells. As the size of a unit cell λ is defined to be smaller, the range of a cluster is more precisely identified. On the other hand, a possible dense cell is split earlier as the value of a split support S_{splt} is lower. Due to this reason, a dense unit cell is found earlier, which enables a unit cell to monitor its actual count more accurately. Furthermore, As the gap between S_{prn} and S_{splt} is increased, more number of intermediate cells are maintained while the support of identified clusters are more precisely found.

3 Experimental Results

In order to analyze the performance of the proposed method, a data set containing one million 4-dimensional data elements is generated by the data generator used in ENCLUS[9]. Most of data elements are concentrated on randomly chosen 10 distinct data regions whose sizes in each dimension are also randomly varied from 10 to 20 respectively. The accuracy of the proposed method is measured relatively to that of STING. In other words, it is the ratio of the number of correctly clustered elements by the proposed method over the total number of data elements clustered by STING. The values of a pruning support S_{prn} and a split support S_{splt} are assigned relatively to a predefined minimum support S_{min}. The entire data space of the data set is divided into 4 initial cells. In all experiments, data elements are looked up one by one in sequence to simulate the environment of a data stream.

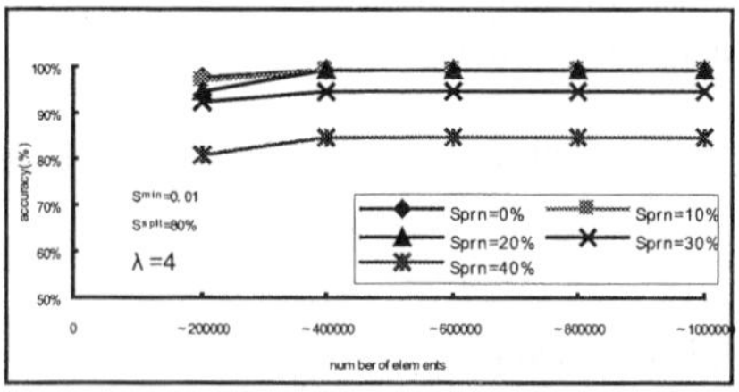

Fig. 3. Accuracy variations to S_{prn}

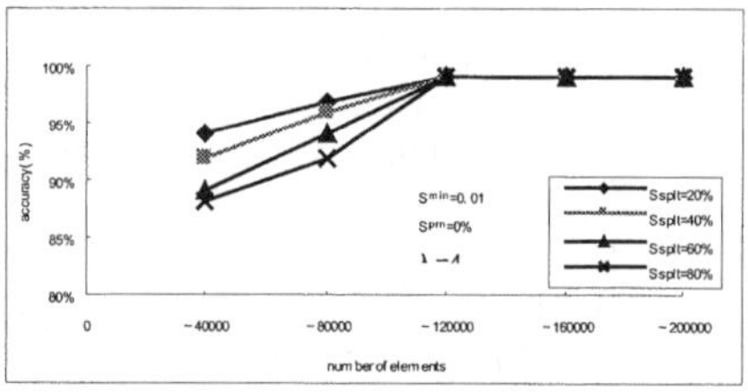

Fig. 4. Accuracy variations to S_{splt}

Figure 3 shows the accuracy of the proposed method by varying the value of S_{prn}. The sequence of generated data elements is divided into 5 intervals each of which consists of 200 thousand elements. The average accuracy in each interval is shown. As noticed in this figure, the accuracy of the first interval is relatively lower than those of the other intervals. This is because the support of an intermediate cell is too sensitively varied in the first interval. As a result, a lot of cell partitioning operations are performed in the first interval to produce a set of meaningful unit cells. However, it becomes stabilized as the total number of data elements is increased. As the value of S_{prn} is increased, the accuracy becomes lower since a considerable number of possible dense intermediate cells are pruned before they become unit cells. Figure 4 shows the effect of S_{splt} on the accuracy in the first interval. As the value of S_{splt} is set to be lower, unit cells are generated more quickly, so that the accuracy is improved. However, regardless of the values of S_{splt}, the stabilized accuracy is the same.

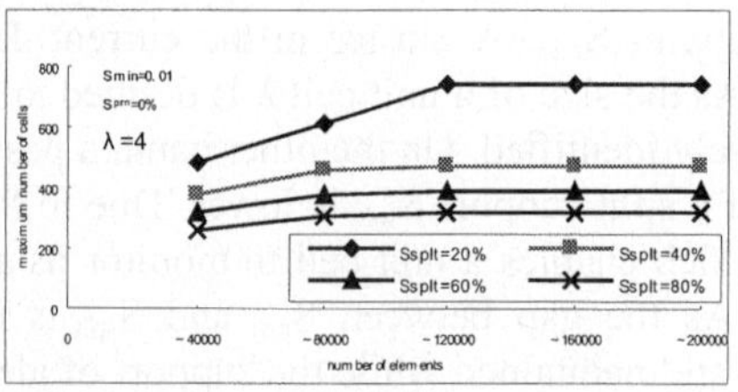

Fig. 5. Memory usage variations to S_{splt}

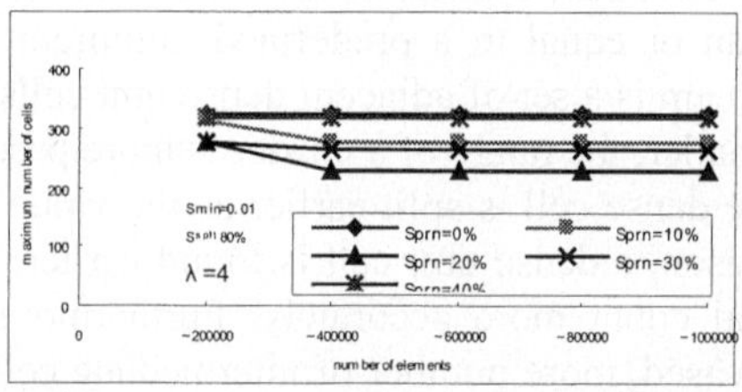

Fig. 6. Memory usage variations to S_{prn}

Figure 5 shows the maximum number of cells in the first interval in Figure 3 when no cell is pruned. The maximum number of cells is stabilized after the second interval. As the value of S_{splt} is set to be low, the maximum number of cells is increased since cell partitioning operations are performed frequently to generate meaningful unit cells. As the number of dense unit cells is increased, the maximum number of cells is stabilized. In Figure 6, the variation of the maximum number of cells is shown when sparse cells are pruned. After most of dense unit cells are generated, the maximum number of cells can be decreased by setting the value of S_{prn} adequately. When S_{prn} is set to the half value of S_{splt}, i.e., 40%, the memory usage is not decreased. The reason is that most of divided intermediate cells are pruned too quickly and their initial cells are repeatedly partitioned again. On the contrary, when the value of S_{prn} is set to 20%, the memory usage is minimized since dense intermediate cells are successfully divided into its dense unit cells while sparse ones are pruned properly.

4 Conclusion

In this paper, a grid-based statistical μ-partition clustering method for a data stream is proposed. The multi-dimensional data space is dynamically divided into a set of cells with different sizes. By maintaining only the distribution statistics of data elements in each cell, its current support is precisely monitored. A dense sub-range of a data space is partitioned repeatedly until it becomes a set of dense unit cells. Two thresholds S_{splt} and S_{prn} are proposed to control the performance of the proposed method in a data stream. A split support S_{splt} is used to determine how fast dense unit cells are identified. A pruning support S_{prn} is used to remove meaningless sparse intermediate or unit cells. Therefore, it can be used to minimize the usage of main memory. However, if it is too high, a less accurate clustering result can be obtained. By controlling these two thresholds properly, the performance of the proposed algorithm can be flexibly controlled.

References

1. R. O. Duda and P. E. Hart. *Pattern Classification and Scene Analysis*. Wiley, 1972.
2. L. Kaufman and P.J. Rousseeuw. *Finding Groups in Data. An Introduction to Cluster Analysis*. Wiley, New York, 1990.
3. T. Zhang, R. Ramakrishnan, and M. Livny. BIRCH: an efficient data clustering method for very large databases. In *Proc. SIGMOD*, pages 103–114, 1996
4. S. Guha, R.Rastogi, and K. Shim. CURE: An efficient clustering algorithm for large databases. In *Proc. SIGMOD*, pages 73–84, 1998
5. M. Ester, H. Kriegel, J. Sander, and X. Xu. A density-based algorithm for discovering clusters in large spatial databases, 1996.
6. W. Wang, J. Yang, and R. Muntz. Sting: A statistical information grid approach to spatial data mining, 1997.
7. M. Garofalakis, J. Gehrke and R. Rastogi. Querying and mining data streams: you only get one look. In *the tutorial notes of the 28th Int'l Conference on Very Large Databases*, Hong Kong, China, Aug. 2002.
8. Liadan O'Callaghan, Nina Mishra, Adam Meyerson, Sudipto Guha, and Rajeev Motwani. STREAM-data algorithms for high-quality clustering. In *Proc. of IEEE International Conference on Data Engineering*, March 2002.
9. Cheng, C., Fu, A., and Zhang, Y. *Entropy-based subspace clustering for mining numerical data*. KDD-99, 84–93, San Diego, August 1999.

Text Categorization with ILA

Hayri Sever[1], Abdulkadir Gorur[2], and Mehmet R. Tolun[3]

[1] Department of Computer Engineering
Baskent University
06530 Baglica, Ankara, Turkey
sever@baskent.edu.tr

[2] Department of Computer Engineering
Eastern Mediterranean University
Famagusta, T.R.N.C. (via Mersin 10, Turkey)
abdulkadir.gorur@emu.edu.tr

[3] Department of Computer Engineering
Atilim University
06836 Incek, Ankara, Turkey
tolun@atilim.edu.tr

Abstract. The sudden expansion of the web and the use of the internet has caused some research fields to regain (or even increase) its old popularity. Of them, text categorization aims at developing a classification system for assigning a number of predefined topic codes to the documents based on the knowledge accumulated in the training process. We propose a framework based on an automatic inductive classifier, called ILA, for text categorization, though this attempt is not a novel approach to the information retrieval community. Our motivation are two folds. One is that there is still much to do for efficient and effective classifiers. The second is of ILA's (Inductive Learning Algorithm) well-known ability in capturing by canonical rules the distinctive features of text categories. Our results with respect to the Reuters 21578 corpus indicate (1) the reduction of features by information gain measurement down to 20 is essentially as good as the case where one would have more features; (2) recall/precision breakeven points of our algorithm without tuning over top 10 categories are comparable to other text categorization methods, namely similarity based matching, naive Bayes, Bayes nets, decision trees, linear support vector machines, steepest descent algorithm.

Keywords: Text Categorization, Inductive Learning, Feature Selection.

1 Introduction

In the last decade, there has been enormous growth in the amount of electronic text documents. At the same time the popularity of information retrieval field, especially on text categorization among others, has grown up considerably [1]. In recent years text categorization has been applied to information services on technical abstracts and newswire articles. Interesting applications of text categorization are to assign subject categories to documents (and/or vice versa) and to aid human indexers in assigning such categories.Until the late '80s, the most effective approach to classifying texts seemed

A. Yazici and C. Şener (Eds.): ISCIS 2003, LNCS 2869, pp. 300–307, 2003.

to be that of manually building automatic classifiers using knowledge engineering techniques [1]. On the other hand, the construction of rule based models engineered by human experts for the assignment of subject labels, while relatively effective, could be considered as very expensive process in terms of time and effort [2]. Machine learning along with statistical models has emerged as a family of successive approaches for text categorization(TC)[1]. This statement should not come for surprise since the lion's share of the research in machine learning goes to the studies on empirical learning (or induction) of classification rules. The goal is here to automatically build classifiers being charged for mapping document vectors to class labels.

In this paper, we propose a framework for the TC problem based on *inductive classifier* with information gain measurement for feature reduction that becomes a critical preprocessing step when documents have potential for being represented by many keywords. Specifically, the ILA(Inductive Learning Algorithm) which produces IF-THEN rules directly from a set of inconclusive training examples in a general-to-specific way (i.e. starting off with the most general rule possible and producing specific rules whenever it is deemed necessary). ILA eliminates all unnecessary and irrelevant conditions from the extracted rules and therefore its rules are more simple and general than those obtained from ID3 and AQ that are well-known members of inductive learning techniques. ILA also produces rules fewer in number than ID3 and AQ most of the time[3]. The generality of rules increases the classification capability of ILA. A rule becomes more general as the number of conditions on its IF-part becomes fewer. A general rule also help in classifying incomplete examples in which one or more features may be unknown. ILA addresses some of the pitfalls in symbolic learning algorithms which use decision trees. For example, most algorithms such as ID3 give poor results on unseen training examples(small junctions problem) because the decision tree produced overfits the training examples which leads to decision trees that are too specific. Thus the algorithm is unable to classify unknown examples. ILA, on the other hand, selects the features after considering all of the examples for a given decision(or class). So, its rules are general and do not contain unnecessary and irrelevant conditions. More importantly, using nonconclusive positive and negative examples, ILA are able to generate distinctive features of a category rather than just characterizing it.

We show that with respect to the Reuters 21578 corpus

- the reduction of features by information gain measurement down to 20 is essentially as good as the case where one would have more features;
- recall/precision breakeven points of our algorithm, without making any further tuning-up, over top 10 categories are comparable to other text categorization methods, namely similarity based matching, naive Bayes, Bayes nets, decision trees, linear support vector machines, steepest descent classifier[4].

This paper is organized as follows. In next section, we introduce prelimenary information for ILA followed by effectiveness measures in Section 3. Details of the experiment is presented in Section 4.

2 Preliminaries

The TC system entertains with given a training set in order to induce a decision rule set (or a decision function/relation) with the hope that expected effectiveness will be applicable to the test set. In information retrieval, it is a usual practice to preprocess documents such as removing punctation marks, numbers, and text words in a stop list and then stemming the remaining words, i.e., application of a conflation procedure for reducing morphological variants of the words derived from the same root to a single form. Before feature selection step that is described in Section 2.2, the relative weights of features in a given document are computed. One common way to do this is as follows. The relative weight of jth document feature, denoted by w_j, is to multiply the feature (is widely known as term in IR community) frequency (tf_j) factor with the inverse document frequency (idf_j) factor, defined as

$$w_j = tf_j * \log(N/n_j), \tag{1}$$

where: N is the number of documents in a collection; n_j is the number of documents containing the jth feature; and tf_j is the number of occurrences of the jth term within given a document. We use a slightly different version of Eq.1 as shown below:

$$w_j = (0.5 + 0.5\frac{tf_j}{\max(tf)} \log(N/n_j), \tag{2}$$

which has been empirically found to be more effective than Eq.1. Note that the tf factor of a feature here is proportional to the frequency of the feature within the document. Upon the feature selection step, the document representation decisions for inductive learning are realized. One such plausible decision would be of switching from spare representation to the dense one by portioning features with respect to some interval values of relative weights, which is called *dense concept learning* [5]. We have converted continuous values of features simply by assigning 1 if feature is present with some value; otherwise 0 to absent features. In this section, we first discuss induction model of our own and then present feature selection measurements.

2.1 Induction Model

Text categorization can be regarded as supervised learning with many relevant features. Let us represent training set by a a quadruple (or decision table, say S) $S = (U, Q = CON \cup DEC, V, \rho)$ where: U is a finite set of documents; Q is union of features (or condition attributes), denoted by CON, and class labels (or decision attributes), denoted by DEC; V is the union of domains of features in Q; and $\rho : UXQ \Rightarrow V$ is a total description function. Thus, one can easily see that there is a close relation between a decision system and a text categorization system.

ILA outputs production rules; that is, conjunction of features constitutes the antecedent part of a rule and a class label is included in consequent part of that rule. Furthermore, in the context of induction from a decision table, we say a rule r_i is more general than r_j, if the antecedent part of r_i is included in that of r_j, i.e., it covers more instances than r_j does, where $i \neq j$. For all $x \in U$ and $a \in Q$, $\rho(x, a) = \rho_x(a)$. For given $P \subseteq Q$, let $|P| = m$. We introduce following notations.

(i) $\overline{\rho_x}(P)$ denotes extended version of total description function, that is, $\overline{\rho_x}(P) =< v_1, v_2, \ldots, v_m >$, where $v_i = \rho_x(Pi)$.

(ii) $\widetilde{P}$ denotes the equivalence relation on U defined by the values of P, that is, $\widetilde{P} = \{(x, y)|x, y \in U \wedge \overline{\rho_x}(P) = \overline{\rho_y}(P)\}$.

(iii) $[x]_{\widetilde{P}} = \{y \mid \overline{\rho_x}(P) = \overline{\rho_y}(P)\}$ denotes a block of $\widetilde{P}$.

(iv) $U/\widetilde{P}$ denotes the set of blocks of $\widetilde{P}$.

A decision algorithm, induced from S, relates the elements of $U/\widetilde{CON}$ to that of $U/\widetilde{DEC}$, which is also main concern of a TC system.

ILA considers the combinations of features whose distinct values clearly distinguishes a class from the others, under the assumption that training set is consistent. On other words, for $P \subseteq CON$, if $[x]_{\widetilde{P}} \subseteq [y]_{\widetilde{DEC}}$, where $x, y \in U$, we say that the description of corresponding feature(s), $\overline{\rho_x}(P)$, functionally determines the class label, $\rho_y(DEC)$. ILA uses stepwise forward technique to search instance space. That is, ILA inspects the partitions of U with respect to individual features, $|P| = 1$. If description of a feature, say $\rho_x(c \in P)$, functionally determines a class label, say $d \in DEC$, then a rule is generated and all instances covered by that rule,i.e. $[x]_{\tilde{c}}$, is marked. This process is continued for $P = 2, 3, ...$ over unmarked instances and ILA stops when all instances of U are marked. It is evident from our discussion that ILA applies stepwise forward technique to select an equivalence block of feature(s) included in that of a class, which provides basis for generating certain rules. It is worth stating that ILA with version of ILA-2[3] operates on incomplete features, where documents are non-exclusively partitioned by class labels. On other words, ILA is able to generate almost true rules when a document is attributed to more than one class label.

2.2 Feature Selection

Feature selection is the problem of choosing a small subset of features that is necessary and sufficient to describe target concepts. We consider in this study two measurements: Information Gain (IG) and χ^2 (CHI). In the following formulas, probabilities are interpreted as usual on an event space of documents (e.g., $P(\bar{t}_k, c_i)$ thus means the probability that, for a random document d, k^{th} feature t_k, does not occur in d and d belongs to category c_i), and are estimated by counting occurrences in the training set[1].

Information Gain (IG). One of the most popular feature selection method that has been applied for TC. It takes into account the *term goodness criterion*, which is basically equivalent to the number of bits of information gained for a category prediction by knowing the presence or absence of a feature in a document [1]. Let $\{c_i\}_{i=1}^m$ denote the set of categories in the target space. The information gain of feature t is defined as:

$$IG(t_k, c_i) = P(t_k, c_i) \cdot \log \frac{P(t_k, c_i)}{P(t_k) \cdot P(c_i)} + P(\bar{t}_k, c_i) \cdot \log \frac{P(\bar{t}_k, c_i)}{P(\bar{t}_k) \cdot P(c_i)} \quad (3)$$

The above formula measures the goodness of a feature globally with respect to all categories on average.

Simplified χ^2 (CHI). χ^2 (Chi-square) is a measure of association. It checks whether there is a certain degree of dependence between feature and category. By selecting the features with highest χ^2-values, one can determine the most distinctive features of given a category. For the feature selection in our experiments we have used equation 4 (see [1] for further discussions).

$$s\chi^2(t_k, c_i) = P(t_k, c_i) \cdot P(\bar{t}_k, \bar{c}_i) - P(t_k, \bar{c}_i) \cdot P(\bar{t}_k, c_i) \tag{4}$$

3 Effectiveness Measures

In order to measure the performance of a text classifier, we use text categorization effectiveness measures. There are a number of effectiveness measures employed in evaluating text categorization algorithms. Most of these measures are based on the *contingency table* model. Consider a system that is required to categorize n documents by a query, the result is an outcome of n binary (or multi-level) decisions from which a 2X2 dichotomous table is generated. In this table, the cell values show the number of documents being predicted as relevant and also truly relevant (say a), relevant and also truly non-relevant (say b), non-relevant and also truly relevant (say c), and non-relevant and also truly non-relevant (say d).

In our experiment, the performance measures are based on *precision* and *recall* whose values are computed as $a/(a+b)$ and $a/(a+c)$. Usually a single composite recall-precision graph is reported reflecting the average performance of all individual queries in the system. Two average effectiveness measures, widely used in the literature, are: *Macro-average* and *Micro-average* [6]. In information retrieval, Macro-average is preferred in evaluating query-driven retrieval, while in text categorization Micro-average is preferred. Consider a system with n documents and q queries. Then there are q dichotomous tables each of which represents the outcomes of two-level decisions (relevant or nonrelevant) by the filtering system (predicted label) and the user/expert (actual label) when a query is evaluated against all n documents. Macro-average computes precision and recall separately from the dichotomous tables for each query, and then computes the mean of these values. Micro-average, on the other hand, adds up the q dichotomous tables all together, and then precision and recall are computed.

For the purpose of plotting a single summary figure for recall versus precision values, an adjustable parameter is used to control assignment of documents to profiles (or categories in text categorization). Furthermore recall and precision values at different parameter settings are computed to show trade-off between recall and precision. This single summary figure is then used to compute what is called *breakeven* point, which is the point at which recall is approximately equal to precision [6]. It is possible to use linear interpolation to compute the breakeven point between recall and precision points.

4 The Experiment

In this section, we describe the experimental set up in detail. First, we describe how the Reuters-21578 dataset is parsed and the vocabulary for indexing is constructed. Upon discussion of our approach to training, the experimental results are presented.

4.1 Reuters-21578 Data Set and Text Representation

To experimentally evaluate the proposed information filtering method, we have used the corpus of Distribution 1.0 of Reuters-21578 text categorization test collection [1]. This collection consists of 21,578 documents selected from Reuters newswire stories. The documents of this collection are divided into training and test sets. Each document has five category tags, namely, *EXCHANGES*, *ORGS*, *PEOPLE*, *PLACES*, and *TOPICS*. Each category consists of a number of topics that are used for document assignment. We restrict our study to only *TOPICS* category. To be more specific, we have used the Modified Apte split of Reuters-21578 corpus that has 9,603 training documents, 3,299 test documents, and 8,676 unused documents.

The training set was reduced to 7,775 documents as a result of screening out training documents with empty value of *TOPICS* category. There are 135 topics in the *TOPICS* category, with 118 of these topics occurring at least once in the training and test documents[2]. Each of the three topics out of 118 ones has been assigned to only one document in the test set. We have chosen to experiment with all of these 118 topics despite the fact that three topic categories with no occurrence of training set automatically degrades system performance.

We have produced a dictionary of single words excluding numbers as a result of pre-processing the corpus including performing parsing and tokenizing the text portion of the title as well as the body of both training and unused documents. We have used a universal list of 343 stop words to eliminate functional words from the dictionary [3]. The Porter stemmer algorithm was employed to reduce each remaining words to word-stems form [4]. Since any word occurring only a few times is statistically unreliable, the words occurring less than five times were eliminated. The remaining words were then sorted in descending order of frequency. Our categorization framework is based on the inductive classifier model in which documents and queries are represented as vectors of binary features as described in previous section. A category is assigned to a test document, if distinctive features of the category is included in the descriptive features of that document with some degree of certainty.

4.2 Training

In contrast to information retrieval systems, in text categorization systems, we have neither a retrieval output nor a user query. Instead, we have a number of topics and for each topic the document collection is partitioned into training and test cases. The training set contains only positive examples of a topic. In this sense, the training set is not a counterpart of the retrieval output due to the fact that we do not have any negative examples. We can, however, construct a training set for a topic that consists of positive

[1] Reuters-21578 collection is available at: http://www.research.att.com/~lewis.

[2] In the description of the Reuters-21578 read-me file it was stated that the number of topics with one or more occurrences in *TOPICS* category is 120, but we have found only 118. The missing two topics were assigned to unused documents.

[3] The stop list is available at: http://www.iiasa.ac.at/docs/R_Library/libsrchs.html.

[4] The source code for the Porter Algorithm is found at: http://ils.unc.edu/keyes/java/porter/index.html.

and negative examples, under the plausible assumption that any document considered as positive example for the other topics and not in the set of positive examples of the topic at hand is a candidate for being a negative example of this topic.

The maximum number of positive examples per topic in the corpus is 2877 and the average is 84. The size and especially the quality of the training set is an important issue in generating an induction rule set. In an information routing study [7], the learning method was not applied to the full training set but rather to the set of documents in the local region for each query. The local region for a query was defined as the 2000 documents nearest to the query, where similarity was measured using the inner product score to the query expansion of the initial query. Also, in [2] the rules for text categorization were obtained by creating local dictionaries for each classification topic. Only single words found in documents on the given topic were entered in the local dictionary.

In our experiment, the training set for each topic consists of all positive examples while the negative data is sampled from other topics. The reason for including the entire set of positive examples is based on the conjecture that larger the number of positive examples are more effective induction rules, if preventive steps are incorporated in the production of rules to avoid from the overfitting problem. Additionally, the result published by Dumais et al. [8] for the Reuters-21578 data shows that with respect to micro-averaged score of the SVM (Support Vector Machine) over multiple random samples of training sets for the top 10 categories with varying sample size, but keeping size of negative data the same, performance of the SVM was degraded from 92% to 72.6% while the size was reduced from whole training set down to 1%. Another important finding reported in that study shows that performance of the SVM becomes somewhat unstable when a category has fewer than 5 positive training examples. In our previous study[4], we have found that the quality of the induction is effectively enhanced best when proportion of negative data is in the range of 50%-80%. Therefore we fixed the size of negative sample to 50% of the positive set.

In this study, we preferred IG over CHI measure for the following reason. We fixed the size of features to 100 and produced production rules with IG and CHI separately. In the result, we have found that precision (or accuracy) of the rules with IG is 3% better than that of rules with CHI, which is not considered as statistically important difference to pick up one over another.

4.3 Results

As a comparative study, Table 1 presents results of ILA and other six inductive algorithms that were experimented on Reuters-21578 dataset [8,4]. *Findsim* method is a variant of Rocchio's method for relevance feedback. The weight of each term is the average (or centroid) of its weight in positive instances of the topic. The SDA is based on utilizing preference relation through Steepest Descent Algorithm [4]. The list of names such as *NBayes, BayesNets, Trees,* and *SVM* in Table 1 stand for Naive Bayes, Bayes Nets, Decision Trees, and Linear Support Vector Machines methods, respectively. For further details of these methods the reader is referred to [8].

ILA rules with 20 features and with penalty factor of 2 ,i.e., a/b, are produced. ILA yields comparable results when compared with others. It represents, however, the categories with the smallest number of features.

Table 1. Comparing results with other five inductive algorithms. Breakeven is computed on top 10 topics and on overall 118 topics.

Topic	Findsim	NBayes	BayesNets	Trees	SDA	SVM	ILA
earn	92.9%	95.9%	95.8%	97.8%	98.5%	98.0%	95.4%
acq	64.7%	87.8%	88.3%	89.7%	95.9%	93.6%	79.2%
money-fx	46.7%	56.6%	58.8%	66.2%	78.4%	74.5%	61.4%
grain	67.5%	78.8%	81.4%	85.0%	90.6%	94.6%	80.1%
crude	70.1%	79.5%	79.6%	85.0%	86.5%	88.9%	86.5%
trade	65.1%	63.9%	69.0%	72.5%	76.06%	75.9%	74.0%
interest	63.4%	64.9%	71.3%	67.1%	77.29%	77.7%	72.4%
wheat	68.9%	69.7%	82.7%	92.5%	82.2%	91.9%	79.4%
ship	49.2%	85.4%	84.4%	74.2%	88.1%	85.6%	69.7%
corn	48.2%	65.3%	76.4%	91.8%	82.36%	90.3%	71.0%
Avg. Top 10	64.6%	81.5%	85.0%	88.4%	87.99%	92.0%	76.9%
Avg All Cat.	61.7%	75.2%	80.0%	N/A	81.28%	87.0%	71.4%

Acknowledgments. This research is partly supported by TUBITAK-EEEAG (The Scientific and Technical Research Council of Turkey) with the grant of 199E003.

References

1. Fabrizio Sebastiani. Machine learning in automated text categorization. *ACM Computing Surveys*, 34(1):1–47, 2002.
2. Chidanand Apte, Fred Damerau, and Sholom M. Weiss. Automated learning of decision rules for text categorization. *Information Systems*, 12(3):233–251, 1994.
3. M.R. Tolun H. Sever M. Uludag and S.M. Abu-Soud. Ila-2: An inductive learning algorithm for knowledge discovery. *Cybernetics and Systems: An International Journal*, 30(7):609–628, Oct-Nov 1999.
4. A.H. Alsaffar, J.S. Deogun, and H. Sever. Optimal queries in information filtering. In Z.W. Ras, editor, *12th International Symposium on Methodologies for Intelligent Systems (ISMIS'00)*, volume 1932 of *Lecture Notes in Artificial Intelligence*, pages 435–443. Springer-Verlag, 2000.
5. Thorsten Joachims. Text categorization with support vector machines: learning with many relevant features. In Claire Nédellec and Céline Rouveirol, editors, *Proceedings of ECML-98, 10th European Conference on Machine Learning*, volume 1398, pages 137–142. Springer Verlag, 1998.
6. D. D. Lewis. Evaluating Text Categorization. In *Proceedings of Speech and Natural Language Workshop*, pages 312–318. Morgan Kaufmann, 1991.
7. Hinrich Schutze, David A. Hull, and Jan O. Pedersen. A comparison of classifiers and document representations for the routing problem. In *Research and Development in Information Retrieval*, pages 229–237, 1995.
8. Susan Dumais, John Platt, David Heckerman, and Mehran Sahami. Inductive learning algorithms and representations for text categorization. In *Proceedings of the seventh international conference on Information and knowledge management*, pages 148–155. ACM Press, 1998.

Online Mining of Weighted Fuzzy Association Rules

Mehmet Kaya[1] and Reda Alhajj[2]

[1]Department of Computer Engineering, Fırat University, Elazığ, TURKEY
kaya@firat.edu.tr
[2]Department of Computer Science, University of Calgary, Calgary, AB, CANADA
alhajj@cpsc.ucalgary.ca

Abstract. Mining useful information and helpful knowledge from data transactions is evolving as an important research area. Current online techniques for mining association rules identify the relationship among transactions using binary values. However, transactions with quantitative values are commonly encountered in real-life applications. In this paper, we address this problem by introducing a fuzzy adjacency lattice, and then integrate the lattice structure with linguistic weights in a way to reflect the importance of items. Experiments conducted using synthetic data show the effectiveness of the proposed method for online generation of weighted fuzzy association rules.

1 Introduction

Data mining is the process of extracting previously unknown and potentially useful hidden predictive information from large amounts of data. Discovering association rules is one of the several data mining techniques described in the literature. Associations allow capturing all possible regularities that explain the presence of some attributes according to the presence of other attributes in the same transaction.

An association rule is defined as an implication $X \Rightarrow Y$, where both X and Y are defined as sets of attributes (interchangeably called items); it is interpreted as follows: "for a specified fraction of the existing transactions, a particular value of an attribute set X determines the value of attribute set Y as another particular value under a certain confidence". For instance, an association rule in a supermarket basket data may be stated as, "in 20% of the transactions, 75% of the people buying butter also buy milk in the same transaction"; 20% and 75% represent the support and the confidence, respectively. The significance of an association rule is measured by its support and confidence. Simply, support is the percentage of transactions that contain both X and Y, while confidence is the ratio of the support of $X \cup Y$ to the support of X. So, the problem can be stated as: *find all association rules that satisfy user-specified minimum support and confidence.*

Early research in the field concentrated on boolean association rules, which are concerned only with whether an item is present in a transaction or not, without considering its quantity [2]. However, quantity is a very useful piece of information. Realizing the importance of quantity, people started to concentrate on quantitative attributes. The main reason for quantitative association rule mining is that numerical

A. Yazici and C. Şener (Eds.): ISCIS 2003, LNCS 2869, pp. 308–315, 2003.

attributes typically contain a number of distinct values. The support for any particular value is likely to be low, while the support for intervals is much higher.

However, while a data mining system is designed for decision making, people intuition has to be considered too. Some sociologists carried out survey on 60 highly successful California enterprise managers. These managers were asked how they make business decisions. The common answer was that they use the combination of their intuition and the data. No single response indicated that decisions are based solely on data.

In a given database, an item which is of interest to one user may be of no interest to another user. For instance, by considering the adult information of United States census in 2000, a pretty girl selecting a boyfriend might be more interested in the attribute "occupation" than the other attributes. However, for the case of an insurance consultant, "age" should be the most important among all items. For this purpose, Cai *et al* [4] proposed weighted mining to reflect different importance into different items. Each item was attached to a numerical weight given by users. Weighted support and weighted confidence values were then defined to determine interesting association rules. Later, Yue *et al* [22] extended their concepts to fuzzy item vectors.

In the studies mentioned above, minimum support and minimum confidence were set as numerical values. However, linguistic minimum support and minimum confidence values are more intuitive; they are more natural and understandable to human beings [13].

However, these algorithms do not satisfy the recent requirements of online association rules mining, where a set of transactions is frequently updated. The basic idea in online mining is that an end user should be able to query the database for association rules for differing support and confidence values, without excessive I/O or computation. For this purpose, Aggarwal and Yu [1] proposed a method based on the adjacency lattice; it works for a special category of quantitative association rules.

In this paper, our aim is to combine the advantages of fuzziness, weighted mining and linguistic minimum support and minimum confidence concepts in order to generate online association rules, according to threshold and weight changes. For this purpose, we propose what we call *weighted fuzzy lattice*, which is considered as one of our main contributions.

The rest of this paper is organized as follows. Fuzzy representation of item importance, minimum support and minimum confidence are given in Section 2. The weighted fuzzy adjacency lattice is defined in Section 3. Our approach of extracting rules from the weighted fuzzy lattice is described in Section 4. Experimental results are presented in Section 5. Section 6 is the conclusions.

2 Fuzzy Representation of Item Importance, Minimum Support, and Minimum Confidence

In general, for a rule to be interesting, it should have enough support and high confidence value, i.e., larger than user specified thresholds. However, as weighted mining is concerned, items are assigned weights to reflect their importance and weighted support and confidence values are employed in deciding on interesting association rules.

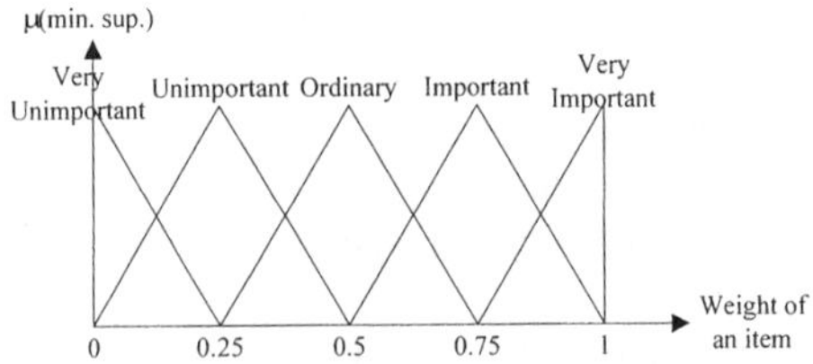

Fig. 1. Membership functions that represent the weights of an item

Most data mining algorithms set weights of items as numerical values, with the weight of an attribute varies between 0 and 1, according to user's experience or intuition; "0" means the attribute will be neglected and "1" identifies the most interesting attribute for the user. Most conventional data mining algorithms set the weights of items at numerical values. However, based on our understanding, the measure showing the importance of an item should be expressed as linguistic term in order to be more flexible and more understandable for humans. For this purpose, we use fuzzy sets to represent the weights of items. The membership functions used to represent the weight of an item are given in Figure 1, which shows that the weight of an item can take 5 different linguistic terms and the membership functions have uniform structure.

The importance of the considered attributes is not only an important measure of interestingness, but also a way to permit users to control the mining results by taking some specific actions.

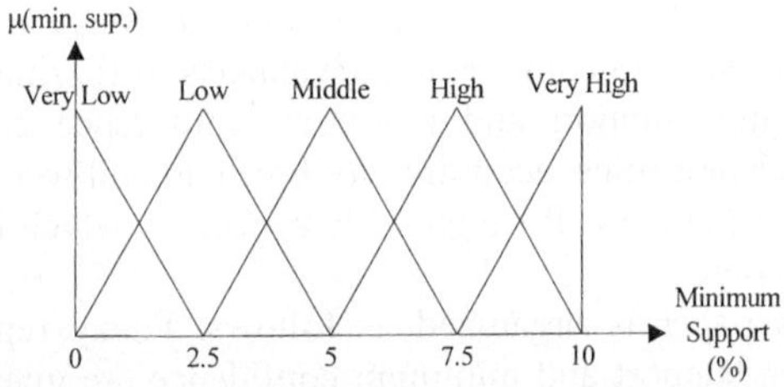

Fig. 2. Membership functions that represent minimum support values

In this study, we also used linguistic minimum support and minimum confidence values in a way similar to item importance. Thus, instead of a sharp boundary, we achieved a boundary with continuous interval of minimum support or confidence. Figure 2 shows the membership functions defined for minimum support.

3 Fuzzy Adjacency Lattice

According to Aggarwal and Yu [1], an itemset *X* is adjacent to an itemset *Y* if one of them can be obtained from the other by adding a single item. In other words, if itemset X is a parent of itemset Y, then Y can be obtained from X by adding a single item to the set X, i.e., Y may be considered as a child of X. Therefore, an itemset may possibly have more than one parent and more than one child. Also, the number of parents for an itemset X is exactly equal to the cardinality of the set X. If there is a directed path from the vertex corresponding to Z to the vertex corresponding to X in the adjacency lattice, then it is denoted $X \supseteq Z$. In such a case, X is a descendant of Z and Z is an ancestor of X. On the other hand, in a fuzzy adjacency lattice, an itemset cannot include different fuzzy sets of the same item. Rather, each vertex denotes a set of item-fuzzy set pairs and has linguistic weight and support values.

So, let $\langle X, A \rangle$ denote an itemset-fuzzy set pair, where X is a set of attributes and A is the set of corresponding fuzzy sets. A weight $0 \leq w_{<x,a>} \leq 1$ is assigned to each instance $<x, a>$ of $\langle X, A \rangle$, to show its importance. And by assigning weights to attributes, we employ weighted fuzzy support and weighted fuzzy confidence in deciding on large weighted <itemset, fuzzy-set> pairs and interesting association rules, respectively.

The weighted fuzzy support of an itemset-fuzzy set pair $\langle X, A \rangle$, is defined based on the weights assigned to the instances $<x_j, a_j>$ of $\langle X, A \rangle$ and the membership function of fuzzy set a_j, which is a mapping from the domain of x_j into the interval [0,1]. This way, an itemset-fuzzy set pair $\langle X, A \rangle$ is called large if its weighted fuzzy support is greater than or equal to the specified minimum support threshold.

Given two vertices S_i and S_j in a weighted fuzzy adjacency lattice, we say that S_i is a descendent of S_j if and only if S_i includes only one additional itemset-fuzzy set pair compared to S_j.

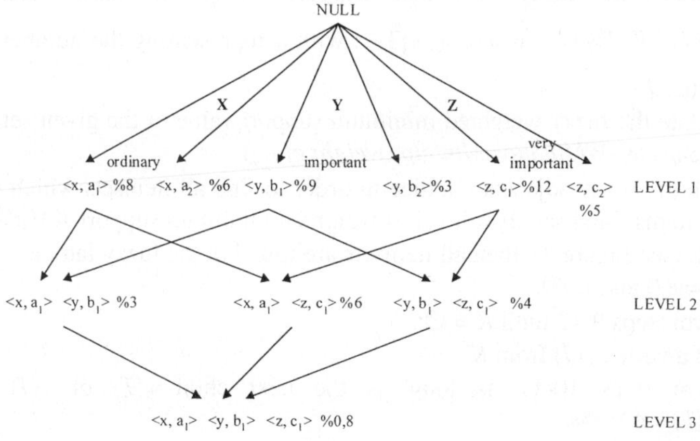

Fig. 3. Weighted Fuzzy Adjacency Lattice

Figure 3 shows a weighted fuzzy adjacency lattice for three items, each has two fuzzy sets. As can be easily seen from Figure 3, as the level increases, the weighted support values of the itemsets decrease.

4 Online Generation of Weighted Fuzzy Association Rules

The main target of this paper is integrating fuzzy set concepts and adjacency lattice to find online interesting fuzzy association rules from quantitative data. As described above, fuzzy concepts are used to represent item importance, item quantities, minimum support and minimum confidence. All of this has been incorporated in the following proposed fuzzy mining algorithm.

Mining Algorithm:

Input: Quantitative transaction data entered online, a set of membership functions, a predefined linguistic minimum support value, a predefined linguistic confidence value and fuzzy weight values given for each item.

Output: A set of weighted fuzzy association rules.

Steps:

1. Transform each linguistic term of importance for item i_j entered online into a fuzzy set w_j of weights, using the given membership functions of item importance.
2. Transform the quantitative value v_j of each item i_j entered into a fuzzy set represented as $(\frac{f_{j1}}{R_{j1}}+\frac{f_{j2}}{R_{j2}}+...\frac{f_{jk}}{R_{jk}})$ by using the given membership functions for item quantities, where k is the number of regions for i_j.
3. Construct the fuzzy adjacency lattice, such that $v(J)$ is reachable from $v(I)$ by a directed path in the lattice.
4. Calculate the fuzzy weighted support $WSup$ of each vertex J as $WSup(J) = W_j.Sup(J)$, where $W_j = \prod_{i=1}^{n} w_i$, with n representing the number of items in vertex J
5. Calculate the fuzzy weighted minimum support value of the given set, denoted $WMinSup$, as: $WMinSup{=}MinSup.(weight\ of f_{ave})$
6. Search the fuzzy adjacency lattice in order to find all itemsets which contain a set of items I and satisfy a level of weighted minimum support $WMinSup$. If I is NULL (see Figure 3), then all itemsets are found in the fuzzy lattice.
7. Let $K{=}v(I)$ and $L{=}\varnothing$.
8. Perform steps 9-12 until $K = \varnothing$:
9. Select a vertex $v(J)$ from K
10. Perform steps 10-11 as long as the next child $v(T)$ of $v(J)$ satisfies $WSup(T) \geq WMinSup$,
11. If $v(T) \notin L$ then $K = K \cup v(T)$; $L = L \cup (v(T), WSup(T))$
12. Delete the vertex $v(J)$ from K
13. Calculate the fuzzy weighted minimum confidence value of the given set, denoted $WMinConf$, as: $WMinConf{=}MinConf.(\ weight\ of f_{ave})$
14. Construct the association rules from each large weighted vertex with items $(i_1, i_2, ..., i_r)$, $r{\geq}2$, by executing the following steps:

    a) Form all possible association rules as follows:

    $i_1 \wedge ... \wedge i_{j-1} \wedge i_{j+1} \wedge ... \wedge i_r \rightarrow i_j$, $j{=}1, r$

b) Calculate the weighted confidence value $WConf_G$ of each possible association rule G as: $WConf_G = \frac{WSup(i)}{WSup(i-i_j)} * W_i$, where $W_j = \prod_{i=1}^{r} w_i$

15. Check whether the weighted confidence $WConf_G$ of association rule G is greater than or equal to the fuzzy weighted minimum confidence *WMinConf* by fuzzy ranking. If $WConf_G$ is greater than or equal to *WMinConf*, keep rule G in the interesting rule set.

5 Experimental Results

We conducted some experiments in order to analyze and demonstrate the efficiency and effectiveness of the proposed method; we mainly run two experiments with synthetic data. All of the experiments have been conducted on a Pentium III 650 MHz CPU with 256 MB of memory and running Windows 2000. As experimental data is concerned, we used a synthetic dataset generated by using DataGen program [25]. The dataset contains 50K transactions with 8 quantitative attributes and three fuzzy sets are defined for each attribute.

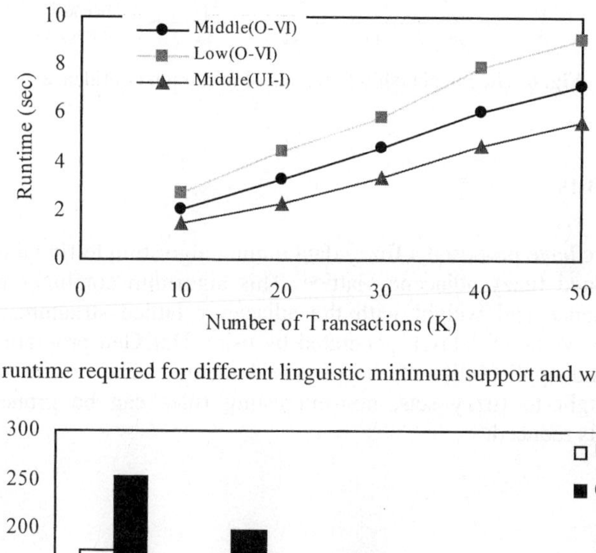

Fig. 4. The runtime required for different linguistic minimum support and weights values

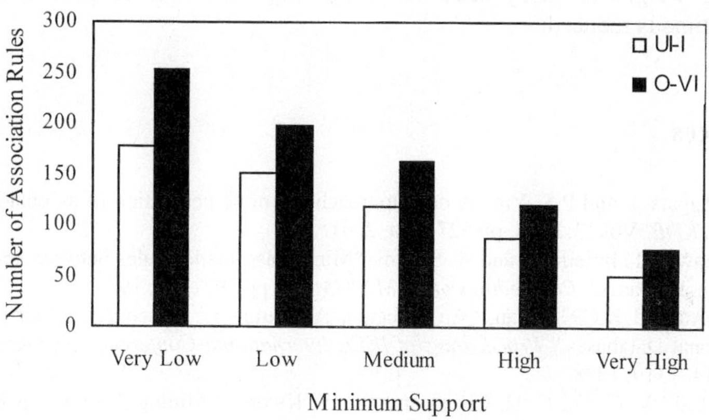

Fig. 5. The relationship between the number of mined rules and linguistic minimum support values

In the first experiment, we examined how the performance varies with the number of transactions. This is confirmed by the curves plotted in Figure 4, which shows the runtime as we increase the number of input records from 10K to 50K, for three different cases. The curves show that the method scales quite linearly for this dataset. Here, we used two linguistic intervals, namely (Ordinary – Very Important) and (Unimportant –Important), denoted (O-VI) and (UI-I), respectively, from which random linguistic weights were generated.

Figure 5 shows the number of generated rules as a function of linguistic minimum support, for two different linguistic weight intervals. In this experiment, the linguistic minimum confidence is "Middle", as shown in Figure 6. The results are as expected; the number of rules for the higher weighted case is larger, but all cases decrease with increase linguistic support threshold.

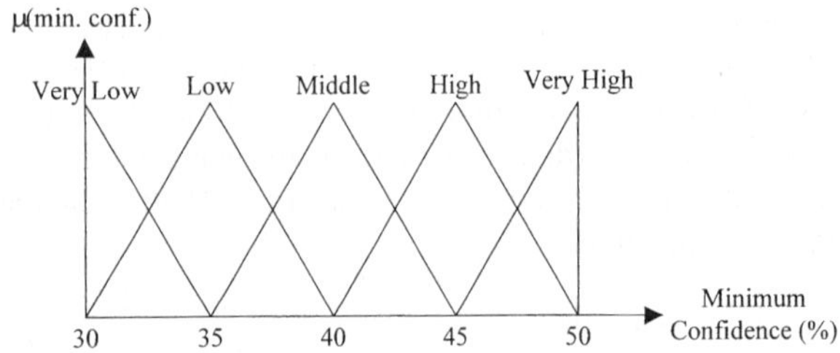

Fig. 6. The membership functions of minimum confidence

6 Conclusions

In this paper, we have proposed a fuzzy data mining algorithm to find the rules online by using weighted fuzzy adjacency lattice. This algorithm combines the linguistic support, confidence and weight with the adjacency lattice structure. Experiments conducted on a synthetic dataset, generated by using DataGen program, showed the effectiveness and applicability of the proposed method. The results show that by associating weight to fuzzy sets, non-interesting rules can be pruned early and execution time is reduced.

References

[1] C.C. Aggarwal and P.S. Yu, "A new approach to online generation of association rules," *IEEE TKDE,* Vol.13, No.4, pp.527–540, 2001.

[2] R. Agrawal, T. Imielinski and A. Swami. "Mining association rules between sets of items in large databases," *Proceedings of ACM SIGMOD,* pp.207–216, 1993.

[3] W.H. Au and K.C.C. Chan, "An Effective Algorithm for Discovering Fuzzy Rules in Relational Databases," *Proceedings of IEEE International Conference on Fuzzy Systems*, pp.1314–1319, 1998.

[4] C. H. Cai, W. C. Fu, C. H. Cheng and W. W. Kwong, "Mining Association Rules with Weighted Items," *Proceedings of IDEAS*, pp.68–77, 1998.

[5] K.C.C. Chan and W.H. Au, "Mining Fuzzy Association Rules," *Proceedings of ACM CIKM,* Las Vegas, pp.209–215, 1997.
[6] B.C. Chien, Z.L. Lin and T.P. Hong, "An Efficient Clustering Algorithm for Mining Fuzzy Quantitative Association Rules," *Proceedings of IFSA World Congress and NAFIPS International Conference*, Vol.3, pp.1306–1311, 2001.
[7] A.W.C. Fu, et al, "Finding Fuzzy Sets for the Mining of Association Rules for Numerical Attributes," *Proceedings of the International Symposium of Intelligent Data Engineering and Learning,* pp.263–268, Oct. 1998.
[8] A. Gyenesei, "A Fuzzy Approach for Mining Quantitative Association Rules," *TUCS Technical Report No.336*, 2000.
[9] K. Hirota and W. Pedrycz, "Linguistic Data Mining and Fuzzy Modelling," *Proceedings of IEEE International Conference on Fuzzy Systems*, Vol.2, pp.1448–1496, 1996.
[10] J.H. Holland, *Adaptation in Natural and Artificial Systems*, The MIT Press, Cambridge, MA, MIT Press edition, 1992. First edition: University of Michigan Press, 1975.
[11] T.P. Hong, C.S. Kuo and S.C. Chi, "A fuzzy data mining algorithm for quantitative values," *Proceedings of the International Conference on Knowledge-Based Intelligent Information Engineering Systems*, pp.480–483, 1999.
[12] T.P. Hong, C.S. Kuo and S.C. Chi, "Mining Association Rules from Quantitative Data," *Intelligent Data Analysis*, Vol.3, pp.363–376, 1999.
[13] T. P. Hong, M. J. Chiang and S. L. Wang, "Mining from Quantitative Data with Linguistic Minimum Supports and Confidences," *Proceedings of IEEE International Conference on Fuzzy Systems*, pp. 494–499, 2002.
[14] H. Ishibuchi, T. Nakashima and T. Yamamoto. "Fuzzy Association Rules for Handling Continuous Attributes," *Proceedings of IEEE International Symposium on Industrial Electronics*, pp.118–121, 2001.
[15] M. Kaya, R. Alhajj, F. Polat and A. Arslan, "Efficient Automated Mining of Fuzzy Association Rules," *Proceedings of DEXA,* 2002.
[16] C.M. Kuok, A.W. Fu and M.H. Wong, "Mining fuzzy association rules in databases," *SIGMOD Record*, Vol.17, No.1, pp.41–46, 1998.
[17] R.J. Miller and Y. Yang, "Association Rules over Interval Data," *Proceedings of ACM SIGMOD*, pp.452–461, 1997.
[18] R. Ng and J. Han, "Efficient and effective clustering methods for spatial data mining," *Proceedings of VLDB*, 1994.
[19] W. Pedrycz, "Fuzzy Sets Technology in Knowledge Discovery," *Fuzzy Sets and Systems*, pp.279–290, 1998.
[20] R. Srikant and R. Agrawal, "Mining quantitative association rules in large relational tables," *Proceedings of ACM SIGMOD,* Montreal, Canada, pp.1–12, 1996.
[21] R.R. Yager, "Fuzzy Summaries in Database Mining," *Proceedings of the International Conference on Artificial Intelligence for Application*, pp.265–269, 1995.
[22] S. Yue. E. Tsang. D. Yeung, and D. Shi, "Mining fuzzy association rules with weighted items," *Proceedings of IEEE-SMC*, pp. 1906–1911, 2000.
[23] L.A. Zadeh, "Fuzzy Sets," *Information and Control*, Vol.8, pp.338–353, 1965.
[24] W. Zhang, "Mining Fuzzy Quantitative Association Rules," *Proceedings of IEEE ICTAI,* Illinois, pp.99–102, 1999.
[25] G. Melli, "Dataset Generation Overview," (http://www.datasetgenerator.com), 2000.

Application of Data Mining Techniques to Protein-Protein Interaction Prediction*

A. Kocatas[1], A. Gursoy[1], and R. Atalay[2]

[1] Computer Engineering Department,
Koç University, 34450 İstanbul, Turkey
[2] Department of Molecular Biology and Genetics
Bilkent University, 06800 Ankara, Turkey

Abstract. Protein-protein interactions are key to understanding biological processes and disease mechanisms in organisms. There is a vast amount of data on proteins waiting to be explored. In this paper, we describe application of data mining techniques, namely association rule mining and ID3 classification, to the problem of predicting protein-protein interactions. We have combined available interaction data and protein domain decomposition data to infer new interactions. Preliminary results show that our approach helps us find plausible rules to understand biological processes.

1 Introduction

With recent advances in modern biology and biotechnology, the amount of biological data keeps accumulating in unprecedented speed. Therefore, it is extremely important to analyze such a vast and diverse collection of data to understand biological processes. Data mining is one of the emerging areas to extract knowledge from large sets of data. In this paper, we will discuss application of rule mining and ID tree learning methods to the prediction of protein-protein interactions.

Protein-protein interactions are key to understanding biological processes and disease mechanisms in organisms. Most protein-protein interactions have been discovered by laboratory techniques such as yeast two-hybrid system that can detect all possible combinations of interactions. However, these findings can be superfluous and do not necessarily explain exact relationship between proteins. It is important to relate certain features of proteins and their functions for both to understand the process and also lead new knowledge based on this understanding.

In this study, we focus on relationship between the sites of proteins that are involved in interactions. Such regions of proteins are called domains. Proteins can be characterized by combination of domains and proteins interact with each other through their domains to carry out biological functions. Using databases

* This work was partially supported by the Turkish Academy of Sciences to RCA (in the framework of young Scientist Award Program-RCA/TUBA-GEBIP/2001-2-3)

A. Yazici and C. Şener (Eds.): ISCIS 2003, LNCS 2869, pp. 316–323, 2003.

of known protein-protein interactions and databases of domain decomposition of proteins, it is possible to draw certain relationships. For example, if we can conclude rules such as proteins having domain x generally interact with proteins having domain y, then this knowledge might help biologists to interpret biological processes better, and predict unknown interactions as well.

This paper is organized as follows: First, we briefly explain association rule mining and its application to protein-protein interaction and domain decomposition data. Then, ID3 classification method and its application is discussed. Specific databases, namely DIP [1], Pfam [3], and Yeast [6] databases, and preprocessing of them to be used in rule mining is explained. Finally, we present preliminary results and some plausible biological explanations for the rules found.

2 Association Rule Mining

Association rule mining is a data mining technique that was proposed in [4]. It has emerged because of the need for extracting rules from the supermarket shopping basket data. With the use of bar code system, experimental data about shopping baskets is very easy to collect. Such databases include a set of transactions. Every transaction represents the shopping basket of a customer, which simply includes a list of different items that she bought.

Below is a sample database of transactions, where $T = \{T_1, T_2, ..., T_M\}$ is the set of transactions and $I = \{i_1, i_2, ..., i_N\}$ are the set of distinct items that can appear in a typical transaction.

$$T_1 = \{i_1, i_2, i_3, i_4\}$$
$$T_2 = \{i_1, i_2, i_3, i_5\}$$
$$T_3 = \{i_2, i_3, i_4\}$$
$$T_4 = \{i_1, i_2, i_5, i_7\}$$
$$T_5 = \{i_1, i_2, i_3\}$$

An example association rule that can be extracted from this database is: $i_1, i_2 \rightarrow i_3$. This rule basically means that if a customer has bought i_1 and i_2, he also bought i_3. There are two variables that measure the dependability of an association rule. First one is the *support* value, which is defined as the number of transactions that contain all the items in the rule. For the rule $i_1, i_2 \rightarrow i_3$, the support value is 3. The second value that characterizes an association rule is its *confidence* value, which is the ratio of the support of the rule to the number of transactions that contain the left side (if part) of the rule. Again for the rule above, the confidence value is $(3 \div 4) * 100 = 75\%$.

Finding association rules over a large database of transactions is a time consuming operation. However, recent methods that use clever algorithms, efficient data structures and parallel algorithms cope well with the problem. Both parallel and sequential efficient algorithms were implemented to face the high computational needs of the problem. However, details of these algorithms are beyond the scope of this paper. For our experiments, we have used an implementation [8] of *Apriori* [2], which is one of the most efficient sequential algorithms.

2.1 Proposed Method

In this section, we present a method that is used to adapt the protein-protein interaction data to be used in association rule mining. Clearly, the nature of the protein-protein interaction data is not the same as the supermarket basket data. However, we have the freedom of modifying the layout of the data to make it to be used in association rule mining.

A database of supermarket basket data simply includes only a list of transactions with the items per shopping basket stored in every record. However, interaction data is not that much plain. Every interaction involves two proteins, say protein A_x and protein B_y. A typical protein interaction database entry is like: $ProteinA_x \iff ProteinB_y$.

Using a second database, which stores the domain decomposition of the proteins, we convert the database of interacting proteins to a format where every protein is substituted with its set of domains. After all of the interacting proteins are decomposed into their set of domains, the final data entry looks like: $\{d_i, d_j, d_k ...\} \iff \{d_l, d_m, d_n, ...\}$. In this data, left hand side (LHS) and right side (RHS) of the $\iff$ declaration corresponds to the set of domains for protein A_x and B_y, respectively.

Further, we should collapse RHS and LHS of the above interactions into a single set in order to make it applicable for association rule mining. However, it would be impossible to interpret the output of the association rule miner if we solely merge two sets into one set. For instance, assuming that we have merged the LHS and RHS of $ProteinA_x$ and $ProteinB_y$ into one set, where $x, y = 0, 1, ...p$ and p is the number of distinct proteins, resulting transactions are like: $T = \{d_i, d_j, d_k, ...d_l, d_n, d_m\}$. If we give interaction data in this form to the association rule miner, output rules will be like $d_i, d_j, ... \rightarrow d_k, d_l....$ The problem is that we cannot identify which domain in such a rule refers to which side of an interaction in the initial interaction data. The LHS and RHS information is eventually lost in such kind of approach, which is not acceptable. The solution is to put tags on the domains, which make us able to differentiate between the LHS and RHS domains. After putting the tags, an interaction looks like: $T_p = \{d_{iL}, d_{jL}, d_{kL} ...d_{lR}, d_{nR}, d_{mR}\}$. Now that we know which domain is a RHS domain and which is a LHS protein by looking at the elements in the resulting rules, a final modification is to add the reverse of every interaction to the set of interactions. This is because an interaction among two proteins is not a directional relation and $ProteinA_x \iff ProteinB_y$ is the same as saying $ProteinB_y \iff ProteinA_x$. What's more, results of association rule miner can be biased in cases such as a set of domains are often seen in LHS of the interactions.

When this final form of data is given as an input to the association rule miner, we expect various kind of rules. Some of the rules will appear with higher support and confidence values, while some will appear with lower dependability parameters.

Let α and β denote the set of domains that appear in the LHS and RHS of an association rule, respectively. Then, we typically expect rules like: $\alpha \rightarrow \beta$.

Rules which have only LHS domains on one side and only RHS domains on the other side and vice versa are the most meaningful ones, because they imply a rule on the opposite sides of an interaction. Finding such rules enables us to make predictions like "if a protein has α domains and another protein has β domains, they will probably interact. We represent these rules as:

$$\alpha \rightarrow \beta : \alpha \in LHS \;\&\; \beta \in RHS \text{ and } \alpha \rightarrow \beta : \alpha \in RHS \;\&\; \beta \in LHS$$

Another rule type can be the following, where LHS and RHS of the interaction is composed of the same kind of domains (i.e all LHS domains):

$$\alpha \rightarrow \beta : \alpha \in LHS \;\&\; \beta \in LHS \text{ and } \alpha \rightarrow \beta : \alpha \in RHS \;\&\; \beta \in RHS$$

The third type is more complex. Namely, at least one side of the rule is composed of different kind of domains (i.e. left side of the rule is composed of LHS and RHS domains.) Following is one possible rule of this type, which we call as *composite rules.*:

$$\alpha \rightarrow \beta : \alpha \in LHS \;\&\; \beta \in LHS \;\&\; \beta \in RHS$$

Machine learning techniques have been used for extraction of knowledge on protein-protein interactions in other studies as well. The work done in [5] uses association rule mining to extract similar rules about proteins like: a protein which has the features α interacts with a protein which has the features β. Their work is similar to our approach however we only concentrate on domains of proteins whereas their work considers many features of proteins such as sequence, location in the cell etc.

3 ID3 Classification

Identification tree learning algorithm is another popular machine learning algorithm. The goal of ID3 is to find an approximate function that maps the a set of predicates to discrete values. ID3 represents this function as a decision tree. Decision trees classify instances by sorting them from the root of the tree down to the leaves. In a decision tree, going down from the root, towards any of the leaves, one can make a certain decision about the current problem instance represented by that leaf.

A set of examples are needed to train an ID3 learning algorithm. Every single record of an example has a set of attributes that classify the example to a distinct set according to the value of an attribute. Decision trees simply ask questions about the attributes to the whole example set at every node in order to classify the examples in consideration. Given this example set, output of an ID3 algorithm is a decision tree, which can be represented by a set of rules. The rules are constructed in such a way that from the root, down to the leaves, every single path in the tree can be represented as a rule.

ID3 algorithm tries to find the optimum decision tree among the set of possible decision trees. In order to build the best decision tree, the algorithm tests which attribute is the best classifier at every node. The measure used for the attributes is the *information gain* of the classification, due to an attribute. In other words, in every node, we measure the information gain of an attribute that classifies the set of examples at that node and select the attribute with highest *information gain* to apply to that node. We cannot mention the full details of the algorithm here, because of the space considerations.

3.1 Proposed Method

In order to create an example set out of a set of protein-protein interactions, we should find a suitable representation. It is important that we decide on what an *attribute* is and what are its *values.* The simplest way of doing this is to represent the existence of every domain as an attribute. Then, every attribute becomes a boolean predicate and can only take values 0 and 1. To complete this representation, we should name the attributes. A simple way of naming the attributes is to give names to the domains as $\{d_1, d_2, ..., d_{2N}\}$ where N is the number of distinct domains. In this representation, d_i is the name of the attribute that tests if the domain indexed by i exists in the interaction. All i's where $i > N$ represents the attributes that test the existence of the domains that appear in RHS of the protein-protein interaction.

We can categorize the types of rules that the ID3 algorithm can produce from such an example set into a few categories:

1. $\forall\ \alpha\ : \alpha \in LHS \rightarrow +$
2. $\forall\ \alpha\ : \alpha \in RHS \rightarrow +$
3. $\forall\alpha\ : (\exists\alpha : \alpha \in LHS\ \&\ \alpha = 1)\ \&\ (\exists\alpha : \alpha \in RHS\ \&\ \alpha = 1) \rightarrow +$
4. $\alpha \in (LHS\ or\ RHS)\ \&\ \alpha = 0 \rightarrow +$
5. $\alpha \in (LHS\ or\ RHS)\ \&\ \alpha \in \{0,1\} \rightarrow -$

Where α is the attributes included in the rule and $\alpha \in LHS$ means that α is an attribute seen on LHS of the interactions, + and − determines the presence of interaction. Among these rules, the most interesting type is the third one. First two types include information about only one side domains, namely left or right hand side. Fourth type has all its attributes set to zero, meaning that if a set of domains does not exists, then interaction occurs. This is very hard to interpret, because it is about rules that depend on the non-existence of some domains. Last type is the negative interaction rules, so they should not be considered as interaction rules.

Negative examples should also be presented to the ID3 learning algorithm. Since there is no database of non-interacting proteins, we have used a method that shuffles the domains and creates artificial proteins while preserving the domain occurrence frequencies within the generated proteins. This provides a better way of creating a negative example set instead of taking the complement of the interaction data, because the resulting proteins are more like natural and a small error rate is expected on classification of these proteins. This is because we don't expect a large number of proteins from a random set to interact with each other. However, the best approach would be to get the results of biological experiments that were carried out to find the protein-protein interactions. Extracting the negative samples from those experiments would give the best results because they are natural data, obtained from biological experiments. Nevertheless, ID3 learning algorithm is known to be robust to errors in the training set. So, we expect that this randomized artificial protein interactions will not contribute to the error too much.

4 Databases Used

DIP [1] database stores information about protein-protein interactions that are confirmed experimentally. Over 17000 interactions are listed in DIP database, which can be used freely for academic purposes. DIP is presented in both html and xml format. Information in the xml file is basically divided into two major sections: nodes and edges. Nodes are presented by their IDs and various other fields like cross-links and features. Edges (which represent the interactions) are listed with two nodes per entry. Number of nodes listed in the database is 6807 and the number of edges listed is 17693.

Yeast Database was created by Uetz et al. [6] and presented in the Curagen's web site in html format. All of the interactions presented here are identified experimentally by high throughput yeast two-hybrid screens on open reading frames of Saccharomyces Cerevisiae genome sequence. Every protein listed in the database is associated with its interacting pairs and also cross-links to other databases, also with a visualization that shows the role of the protein in the whole genetic network.

Pfam is the protein family database [3]. It supports searching by keywords or sequences and retrieves the domains (families) of a given protein. We have used Pfam in order to get the domain decomposition of the proteins, by extracting data from a large text file. This is the swisspfam part of Pfam, which is keyed by the Swiss-Prot [7] names and accession numbers of the proteins.

5 Results and Discussion

23910 interactions were given to the association rule miner and various experiments were carried out with varying support and confidence values. As the support and confidence values get more strict, number of rules found by the algorithm decreases. However, it is important to decide on which support and confidence value pair gives the closest match to a set of rules which consists of logical, valuable rules. For example, number of rules generated given a minimum support of 0.1% and a minimum confidence of 10% is around 130000, which is very high. Indeed, when examined more closely, one can see that most of these rules are trivial, or does not mean much at all, because their dependability measures are very low. In order to find more meaningful rules, one should increase the minimum support and confidence variables. However, then, we face the risk of missing some valuable, but not so frequent rules. Below is a table which shows the change in the number of rules with fixed support and varying confidence and varying support and fixed confidence.

Support	Confidence	Number of Rules
0.5	10	416
0.5	50	398
0.5	90	376
0.1	50	111872
0.5	50	398
0.9	50	4

It is seen from the table above that the number of rules is gradually decreasing as the minimum confidence requirement is increased linearly. The same is true with the minimum support value, but the table proves that the support is a more constraining variable than the confidence value. As the support increases linearly, a rapid decrease in the number of rules is observed.

Still in the search for optimum support and confidence pair for our data, we look for other conclusions. For example, looking at the number of composite rules may give us an idea about the dependability of the resulting rules. Composite rules, by their nature, contain both RHS and LHS domains in either side of the rule. Although we have observed composite rules, it is hard to associate a biologically meaningful explanation for such rules. A careful look at the data, however, leads to an explanation. Assume that the rules $L_1 \rightarrow R_1$ and $L_1 \rightarrow R_1R_2$ have been already produced. Then the algorithm will produce $L_1R_1 \rightarrow R_2$ as well since the following is always true: $support(L_1) \geq support(L_1R_1) \geq support(L_1R_1R_2)$. It was observed that the number of composite rules also gradually decreases with increasing support and confidence requirements. In our experiments, it was observed that beyond 0.2% support and 20% confidence, these rules totally disappeared from the resulting rule sets.

On the other hand, the number of useful rules detected by the ID3 algorithm were far fewer than that of the association rule mining. One of the rules that were detected by the ID3 algorithm was: $PF01423\_L = 1, PF01423\_R = 1 \rightarrow +$. This rule briefly says that if both the right hand side and the left hand side proteins contain PF01423 domain, they will interact. Indeed, this domain is a domain that is specific to *Sm proteins.* In the literature, Sm proteins are known to be involved in mRNA splicing. Seven Sm Proteins form a complex around the Sm site to splice the mRNA. This information verifies that the rule is indeed, correct.

Following are two of the rules that were detected by association rule mining method:

$$PF00227\_L \rightarrow PF00227\_R$$
$$PF00069\_L \rightarrow PF00134\_R$$

PF00227 of rule 1 is the Proteosome A-type and B-type domain annotated in Pfam. It is also claimed that members of this domain form a large ring based complex, which verifies that proteins that contain this domain interact with each other. Rule 2, on the other hand, is related with two distinct domains: PF00134 is the cyclin, N-terminal domain and PF00069 is the protein kinase domain. It is mentioned in Pfam that cyclins regulate the cell division cycle in eukaryotes and protein kinases form a complex with them.

6 Conclusion

In this paper, we have described and used two different methods to find rules about protein-protein interactions in domain decomposition level. It was observed that some of the rules found out by the techniques were indeed true and interactions among these domains were mentioned in the literature. It was also observed that not both techniques produce the same set of rules. In fact, association rule mining outperforms the ID3 method in the number of rules generated. However, it is difficult to find the correct support and confidence values for the association rule mining algorithm.

As a future work, different features can be incorporated along with the domain decomposition of the proteins. We believe, for example, motifs and amino acid patterns, as well as expression profiles and micro-array data would yield to interesting rules about protein-protein interactions. From the biological side, rules that are generated frequently with reasonable support and confidence value pairs can be checked with laboratory experiments. By this way, we can understand if the method can discover novel protein-protein interactions.

References

1. Ioannis Xenarios, Lukasz Salwinski, Xiaoqun Joyce Duan, Patrick Higney, Sul-Min Kim and David Eisenberg: DIP, the Database of Interacting Proteins: a research tool for studying cellular networks of protein interactions. Nucleic Acids Research Vol. 30 No. 1 303–305, 2002
2. Rakesh Agrawal, Ramakrishnan Srikant: Fast Algorithms for Mining Association Rules. Proc. 20th Int. Conf. Very Large Data Bases, VLDB 1994
3. Bateman A, Birney E, Cerruti L, Durbin R, Etwiller L, Eddy SR, Griffiths-Jones S, Howe KL, Marshall M, Sonnhammer EL: The Pfam Protein Families Database. Nucleic Acids Research, Vol. 30 276–280, 2002
4. R. Agrawal, T. Irnielinski, and A. Swami: Mining Association Rules between Sets of Items in Large Databases. Proceedings of A CM SIGMOD, 207–216, May 1993
5. T. Oyama, K. Kitano, K. Satou and T. Ito: Extraction of knowledge on protein-protein interaction by association rule discovery, Bioinformatics. Vol. 18, no. 5 2002
6. Uetz et al: A comprehensive analysis of protein-protein interactions in Saccharomyces cerevisiae. Nature, Vol. 403. Page 623–627, 2000
7. Boeckmann B., Bairoch A., Apweiler R., Blatter M.-C., Estreicher A., Gasteiger E., Martin M.J., Michoud K., O'Donovan C., Phan I., Pilbout S., Schneider M: The SWISS-PROT protein knowledgebase and its supplement TrEMBL in 2003. Nucleic Acids Res, Vol. 31. Page 365–370, 2003
8. Christian Borgelt's Software Page: http://fuzzy.cs.uni-magdeburg.de/~borgelt/

A Heuristic Lotting Method for Electronic Reverse Auctions

Uzay Kaymak, Jean Paul Verkade, and Hubert A.B. te Braake

Erasmus University Rotterdam, Faculty of Economics
P. O. Box 1738, 3000 DR, Rotterdam, The Netherlands
u.kaymak@ieee.org

Abstract. An increasing number of commercial companies are using online reverse auctions for their sourcing activities. In reverse auctions, multiple suppliers bid for a contract from a buyer for selling goods and/or services. Usually, the buyer has to procure multiple items, which are typically divided into lots for auctioning purposes. By steering the composition of the lots, a buyer can increase the attractiveness of its lots for the suppliers, which can then make more competitive offers, leading to larger savings for the procuring party. In this paper, a clustering-based heuristic lotting method is proposed for reverse auctions. Agglomerative clustering is used for determining the items that will be put in the same lot. A suitable metric is defined, which allows the procurer to incorporate various approaches to lotting. The proposed lotting method has been tested for the procurement activities of a consumer packaged goods company. The results indicate that the proposed strategy leads to 2–3% savings, while the procurement experts confirm that the lots determined by the proposed method are acceptable given the procurement goals.

1 Introduction

Electronic auctions are one of the more promising applications of e-business. In addition to the selling of many items through online auction sites (e.g. www.ebay.com), many industries also consider the use of reverse auctions for industrial sourcing and procurement. Nowadays, virtually every major industry has begun to use electronic sourcing (e–sourcing) and adopt online reverse auctions [1]. More than 40 specialized solutions providers such as the FreeMarkets Inc. offer e–sourcing platforms, services and the technology for online reverse auctions [2]. It has been estimated that the annual throughput in online reverse auctions is over $40 billion [1].

Price negotiation is one of the most time–intensive activities in the purchasing process [3]. Online reverse auctions can significantly speed up the pricing process. Apart from the gains in the time spent on purchasing, the popularity of the online reverse auctions stems from the fact that they can help reduce the purchasing costs. It has been reported in the literature that online reverse auctions can produce cost savings from 5% to 40% [4]. Furthermore, online auctions have the potential to restructure the procurer's relation to its suppliers, for example, by allowing contact with more suppliers.

Multiple issues must be considered for a successful online reverse auction, such as the auditing of the suppliers, training of the users, implementation of the technology

A. Yazici and C. Şener (Eds.): ISCIS 2003, LNCS 2869, pp. 324–331, 2003.

and the specification of the auctioned items. One of the important considerations for maximizing the cost savings is the so–called lotting, the grouping of items that will be auctioned as a single entity. On one hand, the lots must be as attractive as possible for the suppliers, so that they will have the incentive to make good offers that will save money for the buyer. On the other hand, the buyer wants to ensure that all the items are bid for, even if some of them are of less interest for the suppliers. Therefore, the optimal lotting should balance the interests of the suppliers and of the buyer. This suggests that the lotting problem should be handled through negotiations between the suppliers and the buyer. There are indeed auctioning systems in development, which allow negotiation between different parties during the auctions [5]. However, many existing online reverse auction systems do not allow negotiations. Furthermore, one of the main advantages of sourcing through reverse auctions is that it saves time through the elimination of negotiations, and hence negotiations should never become a substantial aspect of online auctions. In other words, attention must be paid to the lotting strategy that will lead to the maximal benefits.

In this paper, we investigate automated approaches to lotting that can support the lottig decisions of the procurement experts. We propose a clustering-based approach for lotting in online reverse auctions. Agglomerative clustering is used for determining the items that are put in the same lot. A suitable metric is defined, which allows the procurer to incorporate various approaches to lotting. We have applied the proposed lotting algorithm to a procurement campaign of a consumer packaged goods company. The results are encouraging, indicating that the proposed algorithm leads to 2–3% savings, while the procurement experts confirm that the lots determined by the proposed strategy are acceptable, given the procurement goals.

The outline of the paper is as follows. Reverse auctions and the significance of lotting for reverse auctions are discussed in Section 2. An overview of clustering methods is given in Section 3. A lotting algorithm based on clustering is proposed in Section 4. The algorithm uses hierarchical clustering and a distance metric that allows the procurer to incorporate various approaches to lotting. The application of the proposed method in a procurement campaign of a consumer packaged goods company is discussed in Section 5, where the results from the proposed lotting method are compared to the solution provided by experts. Finally, conclusions are given in Section 6.

2 Reverse Auctions and Lotting

An *auction* is a mechanism to re-allocate goods or services to a set of market participants on the basis of bids and asks [6]. In general, there are two types of participants in an auction: the *auctioneer* and the *bidders*. In reverse auctions, the auctioneer is the buyer of a good or service, while the bidders are the suppliers of the good or service. An integral part of every auction are the *auction rules*, which consist of two parts: the *bidding rules* and the *market clearing rule*. The bidding rules define what the bidders may bid for and when they may place their bids. The market clearing rule defines when and how the allocation of items to bidders is decided, and what the bidders have to pay. The bids in a reverse auction evolve from large amounts to smaller amounts, hence making the bids more and more attractive for the auctioneer (i.e. the buyer). It is possible to design different reverse auction mechanisms, such as *descending* reverse auctions or *sealed-bid* reverse auctions [7]. In all these auctions, the suppliers bid for entities called lots.

A *lot* is an item or a combination of items that the suppliers can bid for in its entirety. *Lotting* is the process of dividing the items into lots. Lotting is needed, because it is not efficient to auction all the items separately. A company may need to procure thousands of different items. It is then simply not time and cost efficient to auction the items separately. Furthermore, if the quantity of an item to be procured is very large, it may be desirable to divide the total amount into multiple lots. It is important to realize that lotting gives the procurer the possibility to influence the attractiveness of the auctioned items for the suppliers, balancing two (possibly conflicting) goals. On one hand, the lots must be as attractive as possible for the suppliers, so that they will have the incentive to make good offers that will save costs for the buyer. On the other hand, the buyer wants to ensure that all the items are bid for, even if some of them are of less interest for the suppliers.

Let the items to be procured be represented by K–dimensional vectors $\boldsymbol{x}_n$, $n = 1, \ldots, N$. Hence, each item is described by a vector of K features. The goal of lotting is to divide the vectors $\boldsymbol{x}_n$ into I lots, so that some criterion (e.g. total procurement costs) is minimized, while the constraints imposed by the auctioneer are satisfied. Mathematically,

$$\begin{aligned} \text{minimize } & \sum_{i=1}^{I} f_i(w_{i1}, \ldots, w_{iN}, \boldsymbol{x}_1, \ldots, \boldsymbol{x}_N) \\ \text{such that } & g_p(w_{i1}, \ldots, w_{iN}, \boldsymbol{x}_1, \ldots, \boldsymbol{x}_N) \leq 0, \qquad p = 1, \ldots P, \\ & \sum_{i=1}^{I} w_{in} = 1, \qquad n = 1, \ldots, N. \end{aligned}$$

In the above formulation, f_i denotes the price for lot i, and g_p are the constraints that may be imposed by the auctioneer. These constraints can be a result of the procurement approach, or they can be the result of boundary conditions. The decision variables are the allocation weights $w_{in} \in \{0, 1\}$, which indicate whether the item n is included in lot i.

Despite the mathematical formulation of the lotting problem, it can not be solved as a mathematical optimization problem, because the functions f_i are in general unknown. Therefore, expertise and heuristic–based approaches are often used for determining the lots. Note that the lotting problem is related to combinatorial reverse auctions, but it is not the same. In combinatorial auctions, all items are auctioned and the bidders can bid for subsets of the items, thereby revealing their preference information during the auction. Lotting is done before the auction, and hence much less information is available regarding the valuation of the items by the bidders.

The auctioneer can use different strategies for lotting. For example, one can group all items with similar characteristics together. In this case, the suppliers may be able to exploit economies of scale, which could be reflected in their bids. However, there may be lots, which consist of rather unattractive items, for which the bids are very high. In that case, the overall procurement costs are not minimized. Alternatively, one may consider putting different types of items in the same lot. However, this may increase the complexity of production for the supplier, which may be reflected in their bids as increased costs. In the following sections, we investigate the use of clustering algorithms as a method for supporting the lotting decisions of procurers.

3 Data Clustering

When the allocation weights w_{in} are determined, the items to be procured are distributed over multiple lots. In this sense, the lotting problem could be interpreted as a segmentation problem. One of the methods that can be used for segmentation is clustering [8]. In clustering, a set of vectors is partitioned into several groups based upon similarity within the group and dissimilarity amongst the groups. There are two general types of clustering algorithms, the hierarchical clustering algorithms, and the objective function based (non-hierarchical) clustering algorithms. Objective function based clustering algorithms solve an optimization problem to partition the data set into a pre-determined number of groups (see e.g. [9]). In contrast, the hierarchical clustering techniques proceed by a series of successive divisions or mergers of data to determine the partitions. Hence, the number of clusters is not pre-determined. This gives the user the possibility to analyze the clustering results at different resolutions, without additional computational burden of re-clustering.

Within the group of hierarchical clustering techniques, the most popular are the linkage algorithms. In linkage algorithms, the distance between all clusters is computed, and at each step the most similar clusters are merged. The linkage algorithms can be summarized as follows [10].

Algorithm 1.
Given N items, place each item in a separate cluster.
do
  Compute the distance between all possible cluster pairs.
  Merge the most similar (minimum distance) clusters.
until all clusters are merged

One obtains different linkage algorithms by modifying the way the distance between the clusters is measured. In the *single linkage* algorithm, the distance between two clusters is defined as the distance between their nearest members. In the *average linkage* algorithm, the distance between two clusters is defined as the average distance between pairs of the members in the two clusters. In the *complete linkage* algorithm, the distance between two clusters is defined as the distance between their farthest members.

The result of hierarchical clustering can be represented graphically in a *dendogram.* A dendrogram is a special kind of tree structure that visualizes clusters as the branches in a tree. It is usual in a dendogram to convert the distance into similarity, which is normalized between 0 and 1. In that case, one can obtain different clusters by thresholding with different values of $\lambda \in [0, 1]$ (see Fig. 2 for an example of a dendogram).

4 Clustering-Based Lotting

In this section, we propose a clustering-based lotting algorithm that can be incorporated in a procedure for reverse auctions. The lotting algorithm is based on hierarchical clustering in order to analyze the clustering results at different resolutions. We have chosen to use a complete linkage algorithm. Complete linkage algorithm has the attractive property that for merging two clusters, all the items in those clusters must be within a certain level of similarity to one another. Consequently, the complete linkage algorithm has a tendency to find relatively compact clusters composed of highly similar items. Furthermore, long chains of clusters are avoided, a disadvantage associated with single linkage and average linkage algorithms.

After having selected a clustering algorithm, the distance metric to be used in the algorithm must be determined. A suitable metric is defined in consultation with procurement experts of a consumer packaged goods company. Procurement experts find it important to have an algorithm that can be tailored in various ways according to the knowledge and the expertise they have developed in many years. The experts have confirmed that, in many cases, they try to put items that look alike in the same lots. This is thought to provide economies of scale for the suppliers, who are then expected to reflect it in their bids. However, in some other cases, the experts want to place the items that are dissimilar in the same lots, for example because of policy reasons. This decision is taken on a feature-by-feature basis. Similarity of items in the same lot is required for some features, but it is not required for other features. Furthermore, some features take nominal or categorical values, while some other features take real values. Keeping these considerations in mind, the following distance metric is proposed for lotting.

$$d_{ij} = \frac{\sum_{k \in F_S} \alpha_k \delta_{ijk} + \sum_{k \notin F_S} \alpha_k (1 - \delta_{ijk})}{\sum_{k=1}^{K} \alpha_k}, \tag{1}$$

where d_{ij} is the distance between item $\boldsymbol{x}_i$ and $\boldsymbol{x}_j$, F_S is the set of features where items are judged on their similarity (the items are judged on their dissimilarity in the complementary set), $\alpha_k \in \{0, 1\}$ indicates whether feature k is of importance for the lotting problem considered and δ_{ijk} indicates the distance between item $\boldsymbol{x}_i$ and $\boldsymbol{x}_j$ measured along feature k. The way δ_{ijk} are computed depends on the type of the feature. For nominal or categorical features, δ_{ijk} is given by

$$\delta_{ijk} = \begin{cases} 0 & \text{if } x_{ik} = x_{jk} \\ 1 & \text{otherwise} \end{cases}, \tag{2}$$

while for continuous valued features it is given by

$$\delta_{ijk} = \frac{|x_{ik} - x_{jk}|}{R_k} \tag{3}$$

with R_k representing the range of feature k.

Note that all distances are normalized in $[0, 1]$, so that their complements indicate the similarity between the items $\boldsymbol{x}_i$ and $\boldsymbol{x}_j$. Complete linkage algorithm is now applied with distance metric (1) after the analyst decides which features should be clustered on similarity and which features on dissimilarity. Once the clustering results are obtained, one need to select a threshold $\lambda \in [0, 1]$, from which the final lot compositions are obtained.

Figure 1 shows the difference between clustering on similarity and clustering on dissimilarity for a data set consisting of three groups described by two features. Note that similarity based clustering finds the three natural groups in the data, while dissimilarity based clustering results ensures that all clusters have members from the three natural groups present in the data. This is the type of behavior expected by procurement experts when the items in a lot should be dissimilar.

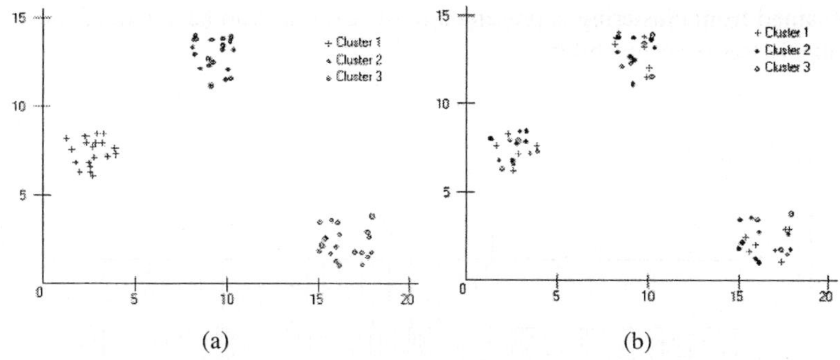

Fig. 1. A clustering example based on (a) similarity, and (b) dissimilarity.

5 Application

We have tested the performance of the clustering-based lotting by using the distance metric (1) applied to data from the online procurement campaigns of a consumer packaged goods company. The data set consists of 913 different items that the company had to procure for packaging purposes. Each item is described by 45 variables regarding the brand characteristics, the geographical region, the quality of the material, the size of the packaging material, type of print, etc. All variables except for the required volume are nominal or categorized. The data set contains missing values, which we have treated as separate categories for each of the features.

Twelve suppliers have taken part in an online reverse auction that was set up by the company. The lots had been defined by the procurement experts of the company, based upon their expertise and expectations from the auction. After the auction, the suppliers have been asked to provide a cost breakdown for the lots that they have bidden for. Hence, the suppliers provided an estimate of their bids for each of the items that they have bidden for. For purposes of testing the proposed clustering-based lotting algorithm, two subsets of data have been selected. The first subset (case 1) consists of the items for which five suppliers made a bid. There are 90 items in this data set, divided into four lots by the experts. The second subset (case 2) consists of five lots for which four suppliers made a bid. There are 142 items in this data set.

For the clustering-based lotting, the experts have indicated which features they consider to be relevant for the study, which ones should be clustered based on similarity and which ones should be clustered based on dissimilarity. Then the algorithm is applied on the data sets. Figure 2 shows the dendogram obtained for case 2. In order to compare the cluster-based lotting to the lotting of experts, the threshold for determining the lots is selected in such a way that the number of lots obtained equals the number of lots that the experts had used in their lotting. It may be the case, as in Fig. 2, that no threshold gives the same number of lots as the experts. In that case, the threshold has been selected so as to obtain a larger number of lots and then some of the obtained lots are combined manually such that the final number of lots equals the number of lots used by the experts. Then, the performance of the final lot composition has been determined and compared to the performance of the lots determined by the experts. Additionally, the lot composition obtained from clustering is presented to the experts who have judged the solution qualitatively for its acceptability.

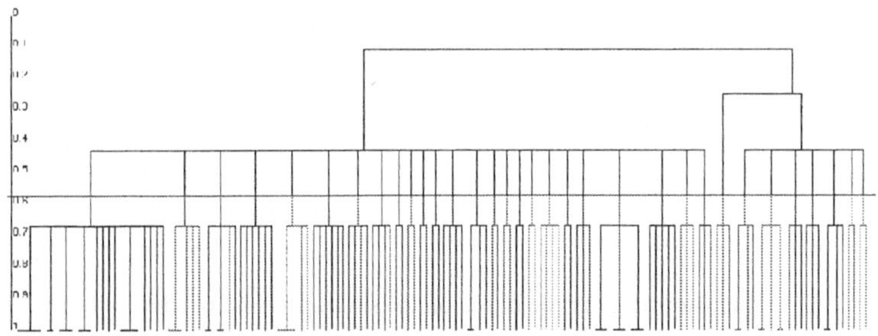

Fig. 2. A dendogram obtained as a result of cluster-based lotting.

The cost breakdown estimates by the suppliers have been used to compare the performance of the clustering-based lotting to the lotting determined by the experts. It is assumed that the cost breakdown estimates correspond to the true valuation of an item by the supplier. In reality, the valuation for an item depends on the lot composition, and hence the "true" valuation is unobserved for different lot compositions. However, a better estimate of an item's valuation is not available, and so we have assumed that the cost breakdown from the suppliers is independent of the lot composition.

The performance of different lotting solutions is depicted in Table 1. In case 1, the clustering-based lotting achieves a cost saving of 1.9%, while it achieves a saving of 2.5% in case 2. The column titled "optimal solution" indicates the optimal solution when one assumes that the cost breakdown estimates provide the true valuations independent of the lot composition. We conclude from these results that the clustering-based lotting leads to about 2–3% savings in costs, which is significant when one considers the total throughput in online reverse auctions. The solutions provided by the clustering-based lotting have also been presented to the procurement experts, who have confirmed that the solutions are acceptable, given the procurement goals.

Table 1. Performance (in M€) of different lotting solutions

	Expert solution	Clustering solution	Optimal solution
Case 1	1.06	1.04	0.85
Case 2	9.73	9.49	9.00

6 Conclusions

Lotting is an important component of electronic reverse auctions. Large savings can be achieved and significant value can be added to the procurement by carefully considering the lotting strategy employed in a reverse auction. In this paper, we have considered a clustering-based heuristic lotting method. The method uses complete linkage hierarchical clustering algorithm. A special distance metric is defined for this problem, which allows the procurement experts to specify which features are relevant for the problem, for which features the items in a lot should resemble one another and for which feature they should not resemble one another. This metric corresponds to the way the procurement experts reason about the lotting problem.

The proposed algorithm has been applied to the procurement activities of a consumer packaged goods company by using online reverse auctions. It has been found that compared to the expert-based lotting, the proposed lotting algorithm leads to 2–3% savings in the procurement costs, while the procurement experts have confirmed that the resulting lotting solution is acceptable, given the procurement goals.

References

1. Jap, S.D.: Online reverse auctions: issues, themes and prospects for the future. Journal of the Academy of Marketing Science **30** (2002) 506–525
2. Minahan, T., Howarth, F., Vigoroso, M.: Making e-sourcing strategic. Research report, Aberdeen Group, Boston (2002)
3. Emiliani, M.L.: Business-to-business online auctions: key issues for purchasing process improvement. Supply Chain Management **5** (2000) 176–186
4. Tully, S.: The B2B tool that really is changing the world. Fortune **141** (2000) 132–145
5. Teich, J.E., Wallenius, H., Wallenius, J., Zaitsev, A.: Designing electronic auctions: an internet-based hybrid procedure combining aspects of negotiations and auctions. Electronic Commerce Research **1** (2001) 301–314
6. Müller, R.: Auctions – the big winner among trading mechanisms for the internet economy. Merit–infonomics research memorandum series, University of Maastricht, MERIT – Maastricht Economic Research Insititute on Innovation and Technology (2001) 2001–016.
7. Klemperer, P.: Auction theory: a guide to the literature. Journal of Economic Surveys **13** (1999) 227–286
8. Wedel, M., Kamakura, W.A.: Market Segmentation: conceptual and methodological foundations. Kluwer, Boston (1998)
9. Bezdek, J.C.: Pattern Recognition with Fuzzy Objective Function. Plenum Press, New York (1981)
10. Johnson, R.A., Wichem, D.W.: Applied Multivariate Statistical Analysis. Prentice Hall, New Jersey (1982)

A Poisson Model for User Accesses to Web Pages

Şule Gündüz[1] and M. Tamer Özsu[2]

[1] Department of Computer Engineering, Istanbul Technical University
Istanbul, Turkey, 34469
gunduz@cs.itu.edu.tr

[2] School of Computer Science, University of Waterloo
Waterloo, Ontario, Canada N2L 3G1
tozsu@db.uwaterloo.ca

Abstract. Predicting the next request of a user as she visits Web pages has gained importance as Web-based activity increases. There are a number of different approaches to prediction. This paper concentrates on the discovery and modelling of the user's aggregate interest in a session. This approach relies on the premise that the visiting time of a page is an indicator of the user's interest in that page. Even the same person may have different desires at different times. Although the approach does not use the sequential patterns of transactions, experimental evaluation shows that the approach is quite effective in capturing a Web user's access pattern. The model has an advantage over previous proposals in terms of speed and memory usage.

1 Introduction

Web mining is defined as the use of data mining techniques to automatically discover and extract information from Web documents and services [5]. With the rapid growth of the World Wide Web, the study of modelling and predicting a user's access on a Web site has become more important. There are three steps in this process [2]. Since the data source is Web server log data for Web usage mining, the first step is to clean the data and prepare for mining the usage patterns. The second step is to extract usage patterns, and the third step is to build a predictive model based on the extracted usage patterns. The prediction step is the real-time processing of the model, which considers the active user session and makes recommendations based on the discovered patterns.

An important feature of the user's navigation path in a *server session*[1] is the time that a user spends on different pages [12]. If we knew the desire of a user every time she visits the Web site, we could use this information for recommending pages. Unfortunately, experience shows that users are rarely willing

[1] The term *server session* is defined as the click stream of page views for a single visit of a user to a Web site [2]. In this paper we will use this term interchangeably with "user session" and "user transaction".

A. Yazici and C. Şener (Eds.): ISCIS 2003, LNCS 2869, pp. 332–339, 2003.

to give explicit feedback. Thus, the time spent on a page is a good measure of the user's interest in that page, providing an implicit rating for that page. If a user is interested in the content of a page, she will likely spend more time there compared to the other pages in her session. However, the representation of page visit time is important. If the representation is not appropriate for the model, the prediction accuracy will decrease.

In [3] we proposed a new model that uses only the visiting time and visiting frequencies of pages without considering the access order of page requests in user sessions. Our experiments showed that Poisson distribution can be used to model user behavior during a single visit to a Web site. In that paper we examine the effect of several representation methods of time that a user spent on each page during her visit. In our previous work we employed a model-based clustering approach and partitioned user sessions according to the similar amount of time spent on similar pages. In this paper, we present a key extension to the representation of user transactions that improves the resulting accuracy for predicting the next request of a Web user. To confirm our findings, the results are compared to the results of two other well known recommendation techniques.

The rest of the paper is organized as follows. Section 2 briefly reviews the work related to model based clustering. Section 3 presents the proposed model. Section 4 provides detailed experimental results. In Section 5, we examine related work. Finally, in Section 6 we conclude our work.

2 Model-Based Cluster Analysis

In this section, we first describe the mixture model for clustering objects and then describe how the parameters of the clusters are derived in the context of the mixture model.

Model-based clustering methods optimize the fit between the given data and some mathematical model. Such methods are often based on the assumption that the data are generated by a mixture of underlying probability distributions, defined by a set of parameters, denoted Θ [6]. An observation $\mathbf{x}_i$ in a data set of K observations, $\mathbf{D} = \{\mathbf{x}_1, ..., \mathbf{x}_K\}$, is generated by a mixture of G components as follows:

$$p(\mathbf{x}_i|\Theta) = \sum_{g=1}^{G} p(c_g|\Theta)p(\mathbf{x}_i|c_g, \Theta_g) = \sum_{g=1}^{G} \tau_g p(\mathbf{x}_i|c_g, \Theta_g) \tag{1}$$

where Θ_g ($g \in [1...G]$) is a vector specifying the probability distribution function (pdf) of the gth component, c_g, and $\sum_{g=1}^{G} p(c_g|\Theta) = \sum_{g=1}^{G} \tau_g = 1$.

Statisticians refer to such a model as *mixture model with G components*. The *maximum likelihood* (*ML estimation*) approach maximizes the *log* likelihood of the training data in order to learn the model parameters:

$$L(\Theta_1, ..., \Theta_G; \tau_1, ..., \tau_G|D) = \sum_{i=1}^{K} \ln \left(\sum_{g=1}^{G} \tau_g p(\mathbf{x}_i|c_g, \Theta_g) \right) \tag{2}$$

3 Web Page Recommendation Model

In this research, we use three sets of server logs. The first one is from the NASA Kennedy Space Center server over the months of July and August 1995 [8]. The second log is from ClarkNet (C.Net)Web server which is a full Internet access provider for the Metro Baltimore-Washington DC area [7]. This server log was collected over the months of August and September, 1995. The last server log is from the Web server at the University of Saskatchewan (UOS) from June to December, 1995 [11]. For each log data set we apply the same pre-processing steps. Since the cleaning procedure is beyond the scope of this paper, the details of this procedure are not given here.

In this work, *visiting page times*[2], which are extracted during pre-processing step, are represented by four different normalization values in order to evaluate the effect of time to the prediction accuracy. The visiting times are normalized across the visiting times of the pages in the same session, such that the minimum value of normalized time is 1. We try 4 different maximum values: 2, 3, 5 and 10. If a page is not in the user session, then the value of corresponding normalized time is set to 0. This normalization captures the relative importance of a page to a user in a transaction. The *aggregate interest* of a user in a transaction is then defined by a vector which consists of the normalized visiting times of that transaction. The details of this step is given in [3].

Our previous work has presented a new model that uses only the visiting time and visiting frequencies of pages. The resulting model has lower run-time computation and memory requirements, while providing predictions that are at least as precise as previous proposals [3]. The key idea behind this work is that user sessions can be clustered according to the similar amount of time that is spent on similar pages within a session without considering the access order of page requests. In particular, we model user sessions in log data as being generated in the following manner: (i) When a user arrives to the Web site, his or her current session is assigned to one of the clusters, (ii) the behavior of that user in this session, in terms of visiting time, is then generated from a Poisson model of visiting times of that cluster. Since we do not have the actual cluster assignments, we use a standard learning algorithm, the Expectation-Maximization (EM) [4], to learn the cluster assignments of transactions as well as the parameters of each Poisson distribution. The resulting clusters consist of transactions in which users have similar interests and each cluster has its own parameters representing these interests. Our objective in this paper is to assess the effectiveness of *non-sequentially ordered* pages and the representation methods of normalized time values in predicting navigation patterns.

In order to obtain a set of pages for recommending and rank these pages in this set, *recommendation scores* are calculated for every page in each cluster using the Poisson parameters of that cluster. The cluster parameters of a cluster c_g are then in the form:

$$pc_g = \{\tau_g; (rs_{g1}, ..., rs_{gn})\}$$

[2] It is defined as the time difference between consecutive page requests.

where τ_g is the probability of selecting the cluster c_g and $rs_{gj}, j = [1...n]$ is the recommendation score of cluster c_g at dimension[3] j. Those are the only parameters that the system needs in order to produce a set of pages for recommendation. We define the number of parameters stored in the memory as *model size*. It is clear that the smaller the model size the faster the online prediction.

We use five different methods for calculating recommendation scores for every page. The recommendation scores are then normalized such that the maximum score has a value of 1. These methods can be briefly summarized as follows: For the first method, we only use the Poisson parameters of the active cluster as recommendation scores. In the second method we use only the popularity of each page, which we define as the ratio of the number of the requests of a page in a cluster to the total number of page requests in that cluster. The intuition behind this is to recommend pages that are most likely visited in a cluster. For the third method, we calculate recommendation scores by multiplying the popularity by the Poisson parameter. For the last two methods we take advantage of a technique used in decision theory called the *entropy*. We calculate the entropy for each page using the relative frequency of each of the ten possible values of normalized times. A low entropy value means that the visiting time of that page mostly has one of the normalized values. High entropy value, on the other hand, indicates wide divergence in page visiting times among transactions. We calculate the recommendation scores of the fourth method by multiplying the inverse of entropy by popularity and Poisson parameters. For the last calculation, the *log* of the popularity is taken in order to decrease the effect of the popularity in recommendation score and is multiplied by the inverse of entropy and Poisson parameters.

The real-time component of the model calculates cluster posterior probability $P(c_g|w)$ for every cluster $c_g \in C = \{c_1, ..., c_G\}$ where w is the portion of a transaction in test set that is used to find the most similar cluster. The active transaction is assigned to the cluster that has the highest probability. We define this cluster as the *active cluster*. A *recommendation set*, which is the set of predicted pages by the model, is then produced ranking the recommendation scores of active cluster in descending order.

4 Experimental Results

In this research we use three different transaction sets prepared for experiments as mentioned in Section 3. We measure the performance of our technique using the proposed methods for calculating recommendation scores. Approximately 30% of these cleaned transactions are randomly selected as the test set, and the remaining part as the training set. The experiments are repeated with different number of clusters and with different initial parameters for EM algorithm.

We define the following metrics to evaluate our method:

Hit-Ratio. Given the visiting time of a page in the current transaction, the model recommends three pages that have the highest recommendation score

[3] Each page in the Web site corresponds a dimension in the model

in the active cluster. A hit is declared if any one of the three recommended pages is the next request of the user. The hit-ratio is the number of hits divided by the total number of recommendations made by the system.

Precision. For each transaction t in the test set we select the first w requests in t. These w requests are used to calculate the active cluster and produce the recommendation set. The recommendation set contains all the pages that have a recommendation score greater than the threshold ξ and that are not in the first w requests. We denote this set as $PS(w, \xi)$ and the number of pages in this set that match with the remaining part of active transaction as m. Then the precision for a transaction is defined as:

$$precision(t) = \frac{m}{|PS(w, \xi)|} \tag{3}$$

In our experiments, we try different values for the threshold, ξ, of recommendation scores ranging from 0.1 to 0.9. If the threshold is high then fewer recommendation are produced. If it is small then irrelevant pages are recommended with a low recommendation score. Our experiments show that setting ξ to 0.5 and w to 2 produces few but highly relevant recommendations. We perform the experiments with different number of clusters changing from 4 to 30. These experiments show that normalizing time between 1 and 2 improves the prediction accuracy. Due to lack of space, we just present the results of the experiments in which the normalized time has a value between 1 and 2. We identify that the values for the number of clusters in Table 1 are best among the other values we consider if page time is normalized between 1 and 2. For these numbers we have a higher *log* likelihood for the training sets as well as a better prediction accuracy for the test sets. The increase of the *log* likelihood means that the model fit better to the data. Figure 1(a) presents the prediction accuracy of the model for different number of clusters where time is normalized between 1 and 2. Figure 1(b) presents the prediction accuracy for different normalization values of time. As can be seen from Figure 1(a), the model is insensitive to the number of clusters in a reasonable range around the best numbers of clusters. The remarkable changes in the number of clusters results in a decrease of the performance of the model.

Table 1. Results (in %) of the model. Visiting time is normalized between 1 and 2.

Data Set	No.Of	Method 1		Method 2		Method 3		Method 4		Method 5	
	Clusters	H-R	Pre.	H-R	Pre.	H-R	Pre.	H-R	Pre.	H-R	Pre.
NASA	30	51.5	34.4	51.3	34.7	52	35	51.1	33.8	47.5	33.8
C.Net	10	48.7	37.9	49.2	37.6	49.6	38.2	48.2	35.4	46.6	32.9
UOS	30	50.8	40.6	50.6	40.7	50.8	40.7	50.5	39.3	50.1	38.7

As mentioned in the previous section, we use 5 different methods for calculating recommendation scores. The application of methods that calculate the recommendation scores using popularity term results in marked improvement of

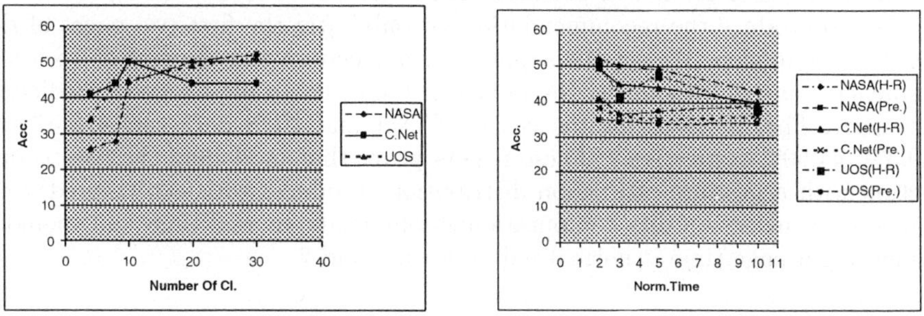

(a) Number of Clusters-Accuracy (b) Normalization values-Accuracy

Fig. 1. Impacts of number of clusters and normalization values on prediction accuracy

the prediction accuracy. This is not surprising, because the popularity represents the common interest among transactions in each cluster. The results show that using entropy during calculation of recommendation score does not improve the accuracy. This is not surprising for the experiments where page time is normalized in a narrow range. However, even for a wide change in normalized time the entropy does not improve the prediction accuracy. This may be due to the fact that the popularity of some pages in most of the clusters are zero due to the sparse and scattered nature of the data. Thus, we can not calculate entropy values for most of the pages in a cluster. All of our experiments show that in general we can use method 3 for calculating recommendation scores discarding the metric we use for evaluation.

Table 2. Comparison of recommendation models.

Data Set	Poisson Model	Model 1	Model 2
NASA	52	4	47.84
C.Net	49.6	15	49.3
UOS	50.8	5	44.59

For evaluating the effect of the Poisson model, we repeated the experiments with the same training and test sets using two other recommendation methods[9, 10]. The recommendation model proposed in [10] (Model 1 in Table 2) is comparable to our model in terms of speed and memory usage. Since the hit-ratio metric has not performed well for the model in [10], we use the precision metric for evaluation. The C.Net data set has a precision of 15%, whereas the NASA data set has 4% and the UOS has 5%. Since the model in [9] is based on association rule discovery, it has obviously a greater model size than our model. We select this model in order to compare our results to the results of a model that uses a different approach. For the method in [9] (Model 2 in Table 2) we use a sliding window with a window size 2. The sliding window is the last portion of the active user session to produce the recommendation set. Thus, the model is able to produce the recommendation set only after the first two pages of the active user session. We set the support for association rule generation to a low value such as 1 % discarding the model size in order to have a good prediction accuracy. The hit ratio for the NASA, C.Net and UOS data sets are 47.8%, 49.3%, 44.50% respectively. These results prove that modelling the user transaction with a mixture of Poisson distributions produces satisfactory prediction rates with an acceptable computational complexity in real-time and memory usage when page time is normalized between 1 and 2.

5 Related Work

The major classes of recommendation services are based on collaborative filtering techniques and the discovery of navigational patterns of users. The main techniques for pattern discovery are sequential patterns, association rules, Markov models, and clustering.

Collaborative filtering techniques predict the utility of items of an active user by matching, in real-time, the active user's preferences against similar records (nearest neighbors) obtained by the system over time from other users [1]. One shortcomings of these approaches is that it becomes hard to maintain the prediction accuracy in a reasonable range while handling the large number of items (dimensions) in order to decrease the on-line prediction cost.

Some authors have used association rules, sequential patterns and Markov models in recommender systems. These techniques work well for Web sites that do not have a complex structure, but experiments on complex, highly interconnected sites show that the storage space and runtime requirements of these techniques increase due to the large number of patterns for sequential pattern and association rules, and the large number of states for Markov models. It may be possible to prune the rule space, enabling faster on-line prediction.

Page recommendations in [10] are based on clusters of pages found from the server log for a site. The system recommends pages from clusters that most closely match the current session. Two crucial differences between our approach and the previous one are that we consider the user interest as a statistical model and we partition user sessions using a model-based approach. As the experiments demonstrate, our model's precision and robustness is superior. Furthermore, our model has the flexibility to represent the user interest with a mixture of binomial distributions (or with different distributions) if one wishes to ignore the visiting time in determining the navigational pattern. We provide some intuitive arguments for why our model has an advantage in terms of speed and memory usage. The online prediction time correlates strongly with the model size. The smaller the model size the faster the online recommendation. Since we only store the cluster parameters for the prediction of the next page request, our model size is very small. The model size only increases with the number of clusters or the number of pages in the Web site when the Web site has a complex structure. However, it is clear that in that case the application of methods such as sequential pattern mining, association rules or Markov models generate more complex models due to the increasing size of rules or states. Thus, all of these models require some pruning steps in order that they be effective. However, our model provides a high prediction accuracy with a simple model structure.

6 Conclusion

We have considered the problem of representing page time in a user session. In this article, the mixture of Poisson model is used for modelling the interest of a user in one transaction. The experiments show that the model can be used on Web sites with different structures. To confirm our finding, we compare our model to two previously proposed recommendation models. Results show that our model improves the efficiency significantly.

References

1. J. S. Breese, D. Heckerman, and C. Kadie. Empirical analysis of predictive algorithms for collaborative filtering. *Proceedings of the Fourteenth Conference on Uncertainty in Artificial Intelligence*, pages 43–52, 1998.
2. R. Cooley, B. Mobasher, and J. Srivastava. Data preparation for mining world wide web browsing patterns. *Journal of Knowledge and Information Systems*, 1(1), 1999.
3. Ş. Gündüz and M. T. Özsu. A user interest model for web page navigation. In *Proc. of Int. Workshop on Data Mining for Actionable Knowledge*, Seoul, Korea, April 2003. to appear.
4. A. P. Dempster, N.M. Laird, and D.B. Rubin. Maximum likelihood from incomplete data via the em algorithm. *Journal of Royal Statistical Society*, 39(1):1–38, 1977.
5. O. Etzioni. The world wide web: Quagmire or gold mine. *Communications of the ACM*, 39(11):65–68, 1996.
6. D. Hand, H. Mannila, and P. Smyth. *Principles of Data Mining*. The MIT Press, 2001.
7. ClarkNet WWW Server Log. http://ita.ee.lbl.gov/html/contrib/ClarkNet-HTTP.html.
8. NASA Kennedy Space Center Log. http://ita.ee.lbl.gov/html/contrib/NASA-HTTP.html.
9. B. Mobasher, H. Dai, T. Luo, and M. Nakagawa. Effective personalization based on association rule discovery from web usage data. In *Proceedings of the 3rd ACM Workhop on Web Information and Data Management*, pages 9–15, November 2001. Atlanta, USA.
10. B. Mobasher, H. Dai, T. Luo, and M. Nakagawa. Improving the effectiveness of collaborative filtering on anonymous web usage data. *Proceedings of the IJCAI 2001 Workshop on Intelligent Techniques for Web Personalization (ITWP01)*, Aug. 2001. Seattle.
11. The University of Saskatchewan Log. http://ita.ee.lbl.gov/html/contrib/Sask-HTTP.html.
12. C. Shahabi, A. Zarkesh, J. Adibi, and V. Shah. Knowledge discovery from users web-page navigation. *Proceeding of the IEEE RIDE97 Workshop, pages 20-29, Birmingham, England*, April 1997.

An Activity Planning and Progress Following Tool for Self-Directed Distance Learning

Nigar Şen and Neşe Yalabik

Informatics Institute, Middle East Technical University, Turkey
{nigar,yalabik}@ii.metu.edu.tr

This paper presents an overview of the design and implementation of an Activity Planning and Progress Following Tool (APT) for e-learning. APT is a software based support tool designed to assist learners with their self directed distance learning (SDDL). A literature survey for the additional components of Learning Management Systems (LMS) that are needed for SDDL is conducted. As a result, the importance of "planning", "feedback" and "resources" properties are revealed. In the continuation of the study, APT was developed by adding "Recommended Study Time Periods", "Resources", "Study Planning", "User Goals" and "Progress Report" modules to the "Content Administration Tool" (CAT), which was developed before in another study.

Keywords: Self-directed learning, self-directed distance learning, self-planning, progress following

1 Introduction

Self-directed learning (SDL) can be defined as any study form in which individuals have primary responsibility for planning, implementing, and even evaluating their learning effort. Today, many learners, especially adults, prefer SDL strategy for aims like improving work performance, gaining new skills and knowledge, participating in a hobby or simply increasing intellectual capacity. The rapidity of creation of new knowledge, and increasing opportunities to access information make such acquisitions necessary in today's world.

Many educational institutions are already offering their courses through the Internet, partially or entirely. These courses need software tools for administering, monitoring and student assessments. These tools are known as Learning Management Systems (LMS). The LMS developed by Informatics Institute of METU, NET-Class, is one of these. However, NET-Class is designed for instructor-assisted distance learning and hence it lacks the modules needed for SDDL [1]. As new modules and features are added to NET-Class, it is also expected to be used for in-company training in Turkey. The companies with large number of employees who are usually distributed in location all over the country show interest in LMS's. However most of the time they do not want to deal with teachers/teaching and desire the employees to be self-learners. So a need for an SDDL version of NET-Class arises.

A. Yazici and C. Şener (Eds.): ISCIS 2003, LNCS 2869, pp. 340–347, 2003.

Activity Planning and Progress Following Tool (APT) is designed as a complementary component for any existing distance learning platform. APT is not a stand-alone LMS like NET-Class, but it can be used as a self-planning module for NET-Class or any other LMS. It is embedded into another simple content administration tool (CAT) as an experimental set up for testing.

2 Definition and Objectives of the Tool

Time management is one of the important concepts and time planning tools are main components of an SDDL. Considering this, it is aimed to supply an online self-planning environment to self-directed distance learners using APT. Almost all self-directed learning systems have feedback tools, but not all have self-planning tools for facilitating self-direction. Among the searched examples it is seen that "TeLLmeMore" language training tool is one of those that has complete feedback and self-planning modules. It was for the purpose of providing a complete language learning solution **[2]**. The tool developed here is inspired of "TeLLmeMore" but it is different in a number of aspects, such as keeping study time intervals, being web based and therefore making it more flexible.

APT aims the learners to gain the habit of making their study program according to their available time, learning style and learning level, by taking into consideration the recommended study time periods and additional resources information given by the instructor.

- *Additional resources module* is designed for supplying an online environment for facilitator to locate all available resources for students. This property of APT is ground on the idea that fostering of SDL requires that many resources be made available to learners and these resources need to be made accessible during an entire learning process because of varied learner needs, pacing requirements, and plans. This also means there are needs to continuous evaluation of resource selections and feedback by the facilitator **[3]**. Types of resources that can be used for SDDL activities may be articles, books, web page addresses, etc.
- Determining their learning needs, making their study programs are responsibility of the learners, but facilitator is also responsible for determining learning path, orientating learning process and giving directions to help learners for self-management activities such as time management, effort management, and motivation. *Recommended study time periods module* is designed to contribute to these purposes in some degree. Using this module the facilitator is required to recommend average study time periods for chapters, exercises, exams etc. of the course.
- The objective of *study plan module* is to supply an online self-scheduling platform to learners. Learning plans are argued to be the most important tool for successful and positive independent study experiences for both students and facilitators. There are many benefits to the use of learning plans. They provide a way to deal with the wide differences among any group of learners, increase student motivation for learning, facilitate the development of mutual respect between the educators and participants, provide for more individualized mode of instruction, and foster the skills of self-directedness **[4]**.

- After a successfully done planning, learner is directed to *user goals* module, which is another module of the system designed for helping to learner to complete his/her study plan. This module gives opportunity to learner of selecting activities (course chapter, resources, exercises etc.) for selected time intervals.

3 Technical Details

This section gives more detailed information about design details of APT; users and users' modules are described in first part and then system architecture such as used software, hardware and database properties are revealed.

3.1 Users of the System

APT is designed for two different types of users, instructor (facilitator) and student (learner). But there is also an administrator of the CAT system (the simple platform that APT is currently embedded in), whose functions are defined by CAT system. This administrator is not authorized to use APT modules, but s/he is responsible for administrative functions of the whole system. Figure 1 shows the summary of the user functions of CAT and APT.

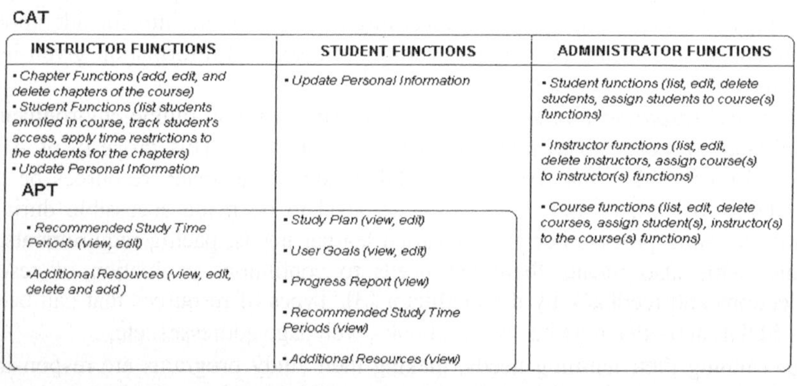

Fig. 1. Functions of CAT and APT According to User Groups **[5]**

3.2 Description of User Modules

The aim of this section is to give detailed information about functions of the APT system. Figure 2 shows the level 1 data flow diagram (DFD) of the system for explaining system's functions-database relation more explicitly.

3.2.1 All User Modules

These modules are used by all users regardless of user type and can be called from all screens. The top bar on screens contains buttons directing users to these functions. Also the message board on screens produces messages according to user's last action. This property of interfaces supplies immediate feedbacks to learners, which are important in learner-centered strategies like SDDL. Figure 3 shows a common view of user screens.

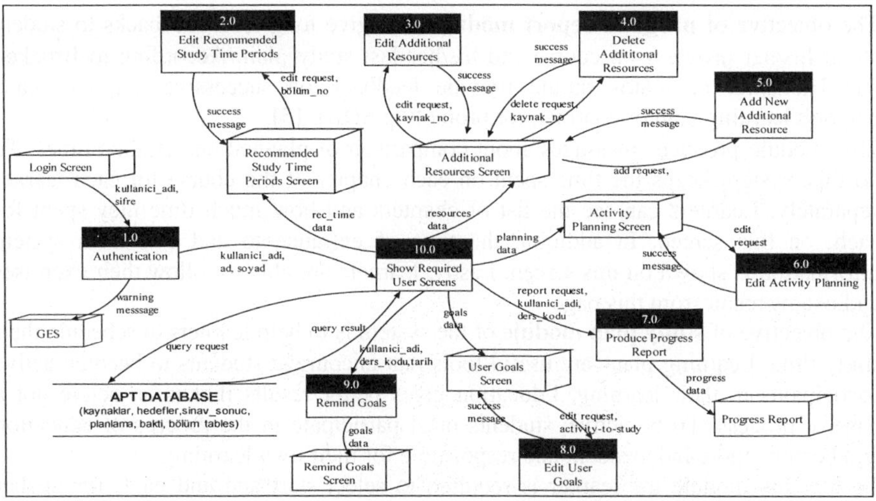

Fig. 2. Level-1 DFD of the APT system

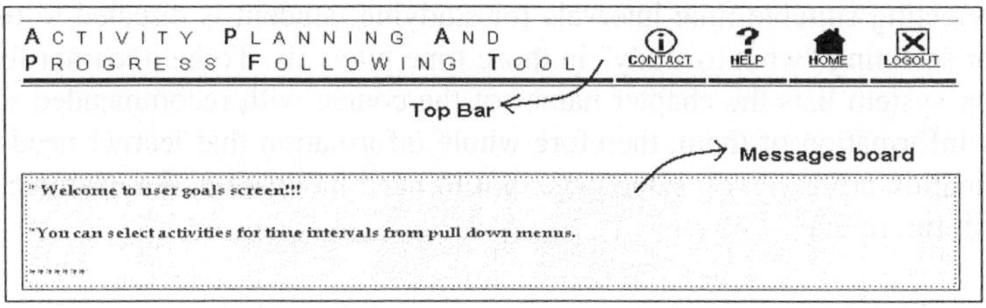

Fig. 3. Common view of all user screens

3.2.2 Instructor Modules

Login function determines the type of user and directs it to the main screen of this user. If user is instructor the instructor main screen is opened for enabling selection of a course from the list of the courses that instructor conducts. Clicking a course in the list directs instructor to course main screen, which enables navigating the selected course.

By using related interfaces instructor adds resources to system with their subject, reference (online or library reference) and explanations information. Another important responsibility of instructor is to enter recommended study time periods for the chapters. System lists the chapter names and instructor selects recommended study time periods from the pull down menus.

3.2.3 Student Modules

Student can view content of a chapter by clicking a chapter button on student course main screen. System keeps the time spent by the student for each chapter of the course. This information is used for comparing studied and planned time, and guiding student for new plans. This comparison information is shown to student in progress report screen.

The objective of **progress report module** is to give long-term feedbacks to student about his/her progress on course and his/her last study plan. According to Brockett and Hiemstra, facilitator should provide feedback on successive drafts of each person's learning plan or contract, for promoting SDDL **[3]**.

This module produces messages about comparison of planned and studied times. To do this, system keeps the time spent on each chapter of the course for each learner separately. Learners can see the list of chapters and how much time they spent for each, on this screen. In addition, the time of entrance to and exit from system information is shown on this screen. Lastly, learners are able to follow their exercises and exams result from this page.

The objective of **study plan module** of the system is to help learners to schedule their study time. Learning plans are useful tools that encourage students to become active participants in their learning. Education gives better results if it is an active not a passive process. To be active, students must participate in the process of education and become more independent and responsible for their own learning.

To use this module the learner is required to select start and end dates for his/her study periods. Then from weekly table s/he should select available time intervals for each day of the week by putting checks on check boxes as shown in figure 4-a.

After selecting suitable time intervals for studying, student is directed to **user goals** page for selecting "what to study" in those time intervals. To help learner for activity selection system lists the chapter names of the course with recommended study time periods information of them, therefore whole information that learner needs for goal determination are given on same page, not to need navigation. An example screen is shown in figure 5-a.

a)

b)

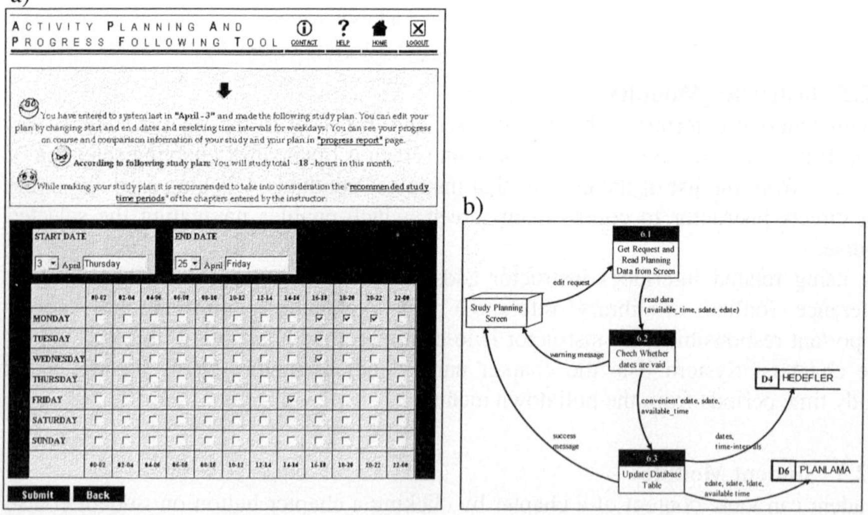

Fig. 4. a) Study plan screen b) Level-2 DFD of study plan function

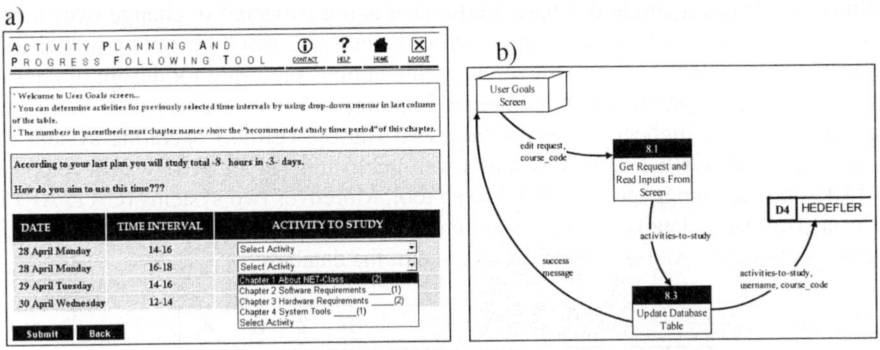

Fig. 5. a) User goals screen b) Level-2 DFD of user goals function

Moreover, there is a sub module of this user goals module, which is used to remind learner his/her daily plan by a pop-up menu just after s/he login to the system. The aim of this sub module is to attract student interest to his/her daily plan and encourage him/her to obey this plan.

Another module to assist learners with their SDDL is "**additional resources module**" whose objective is to give opportunity to the learner for viewing additional resources related to course content, which are entered by the instructor of the course. Figure 6 shows an example screen for this module.

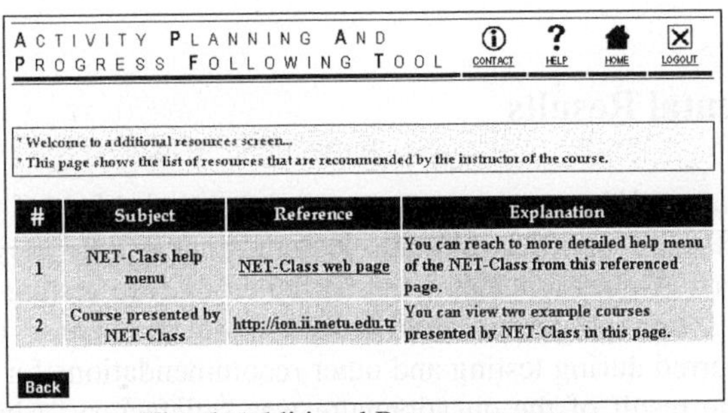

Fig. 6. Additional Resources screen

Lastly, **recommended study time periods module** of the tool was designed to give chance to learners to learn more about the structure of the course, which helps learners for managing their study time. The facilitator is required to recommend average study time periods for chapters, exercises, and exams etc. of the course and student views them by this module. Figure 7 shows an example screen for this module.

3.3 The Architecture of the System

APT is a database application and it handles data storage and retrieval in the database process and manipulation. Therefore, APT provides multiple users with access to same data. Because of meeting these requirements it is built in client/server architecture. It has a single database whose size is not expected to change over time and database server and the application server is the same machine having properties explained below. So two-tier client-server architecture is preferred for design of APT. Users access the system through Internet Explorer (v5.0 or higher) and Netscape Navigator (v4.7 or higher). At server side; Red Hat 6.2 (Linux) operating system is installed and APACHE 1.3.20 is used as a web-publishing server. APT was developed by PHP 4.0 script language and HTML web tool. Moreover two systems (CAT, APT) have a common database, which is created by using MySQL 3.22.32., and PhpMyAdmin 2.1.0 tool is used to reach and edit the database.

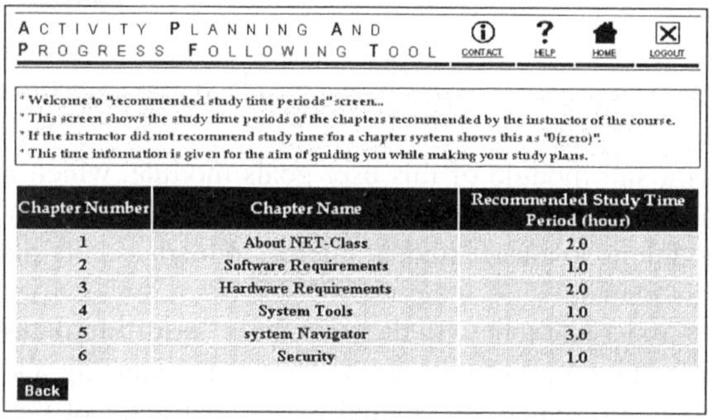

Fig. 7. Recommended Study Time Periods screen

4 Experimental Results

20 different users tested the system in a two weeks period. Most of these users were research assistants experienced in distance learning that is why they are selected as potential customers. A questionnaire was distributed to ease testing for them. Some main requirements and properties were asked in questionnaire. They also wrote system errors occurred during testing and other recommendations for further progress of the system. The result of the questionnaire was satisfactory. Almost %40 of the testers agreed and the remaining %60 strongly agreed that the system met all software requirements. A few problems reported by the users about the system, almost all were related to login process. These problems were corrected immediately and continued to test.

Some main recommendations coming from these users were:

1. A mailing system for informing users about their progress, news etc. can be added
2. An exam and grading module can be added
3. Embedding this system into NETClass can be useful

5 Conclusion and Future Works

Latest trends in developing SDDL platforms are combining artificial intelligence (AI) solutions with learning strategies. One of the long-term goals of METU Informatics

Institute is to improve NET-Class platform with these AI enhanced facilities and APT may be a start point for these projects.
As future work there are two alternatives, one of them being the addition of some new modules to this system to make it a complete stand-alone SDDL platform. Second alternative to use this system more effectively is to modify it to embed in NET-Class. So this will result in an important contribution to the NET-Class since a self-planning module does not exist currently.

References

1. Yilmaz, B.; Yalabik, N.; Karagoz, A..; "NET-Class and a Comparison of the Web Based Course Management Tools", 2001, [Online], Available at http://ecommerce.lebow.drexel.edu/eli/pdf/YilmazEBKNet-C.pdf
2. "TeLL me More The Complete Solution", [Online], Available at http://www.auralog.com/en/tellmemore.html
3. Brockett, R.G.; Hiemstra R.; *Self-Direction in Adult Learning: Perspectives on Theory, Research, and Practice*, Routledge, 1991
4. Knowles, M. S.; *Self-Directed Learning. A guide for learners and teachers*, Englewood Cliffs: Prentice Hall/Cambridge, 1975
5. CAT-Team; "Software Requirements Specification for CAT ",v3.1, Informatics Institute, METU, 2002

MAPSEC: Mobile-Agent Based Publish/Subscribe Platform for Electronic Commerce

Ozgur Koray Sahingoz[1] and Nadia Erdogan[2]

[1] Air Force Academy, Computer Engineering Department, Yesilyurt, Istanbul, TURKEY, o.sahingoz@hho.edu.tr

[2] Istanbul Technical University, Electrical-Electronics Faculty, Computer Engineering Department Ayazaga, 80626, Istanbul, TURKEY
erdogan@cs.itu.edu.tr

Abstract. Electronic commerce technology offers the opportunity to integrate and optimize the global production and distribution on supply chain. Computers of various corporations, located throughout the world, communicate with each other to determine the availability of components, to place and confirm orders, and to negotiate delivery timescales. Software agents help to automate a variety of tasks including those involved in buying and selling products over the Internet. This paper presents MAPSEC, an e-commerce system based on mobile agents, that uses publish/subscribe protocol for registration and transaction processes. In this system, (as in a large-scale and dynamic environment) there can be any number of buyers and suppliers. Any supplier can connect, register or unregister to the system at any time, thus preserving the dynamic structure of the system.

1 Introduction

The number of businesses and individuals throughout the world who are discovering and exploring the Internet is growing dramatically. Through the past decades, we have seen an increasing rate of globalization of the economy and thereby of supply chains. Products are no longer produced and consumed within the same geographical area. Even the different parts of a product may, and often do, come from all over the world. This creates longer and more complex supply chains, and therefore it changes the requirements within supply chain management. The Internet is a cheap, open, distributed, and easy to use environment, which provides an easy way to set up shops and conduct commerce at any place [1].

Computer networks have the ability to rapidly distribute information to all concerned entities of an enterprise. Networks also present an infrastructure for coordination of planning and operational processes, not only within organizations, but also among them. Nowadays, people can shop for products and services online at the Internet and the World Wide Web have made electronic commerce possible. Web

A. Yazici and C. Şener (Eds.): ISCIS 2003, LNCS 2869, pp. 348–355, 2003.

sites that display products and take orders are becoming common for many types of businesses.

To enable the deployment of dynamic e-Commerce environments the European and the US Agentcities initiatives [2], combined with international initiatives in FIPA [3], aim to create a global and open information-exchange environment where dynamic services from geographically distributed organizations can be deployed, tested, interconnected and composed. Examples of such dynamic services are B2B (Business to Business) dynamic value chain creation, dynamic pricing through trading exchange, automatic discovery of business partners, advertising and marketing.

Accompanied by the growth of e-commerce, rapid responses to changes in demand and customer preference, and the ability to exploit new technologies, are becoming critical. As information on the Internet becomes more dynamic and heterogeneous, 'software agents' have been thought of as the new building blocks for a new Internet structure. In this paper, we propose a new architecture for e-commerce systems. We present a platform that uses the publish/subscribe mechanism for dynamic utilization of the system, and mobile agents as mediators between buyers and suppliers.

The rest of the paper is organized as follows. In the next section, we present some significant e-commerce systems. Section 3 introduces the computational model of MAPSEC. Our conclusions and directions for future work are presented in section 4.

2 Electronic Commerce Systems

An electronic commerce system covers any form of computerized buying and selling, both by customers and from company to company. These systems are distinguished by their implementation (or lack thereof) of the six stages of the consumer buying behavior model [4]. These stages are need identification, product brokering, merchant brokering, negotiation, purchase and delivery, and product service and evaluation. We describe several existing electronic commerce systems below.

AuctionBot [5,6] is a well-known experimental Internet auction server developed at the University of Michigan. Its users can create new auctions by choosing from a selection of auction types and specifying its parameters. Buyers and suppliers can then bid according to the auction's multilateral distributive negotiation protocols. The agents are dispatched to, and operate at, the single auction server; they do not move from supplier to supplier.

MIT Media Lab's Kasbah [7] is an online World Wide Web marketplace for buying and selling goods. A user creates a buyer agent, provides it with a set of criteria and dispatches it into the marketplace. The criteria include price, time constraints and quantity of merchandise desired. Users can select one of several price decay functions for goods they are attempting to sell. Supplier agents post their offers on a common blackboard and wait for interested buyer agents to establish contact. A buyer agent filters the available offers according to the user's criteria, and then proceeds to negotiate a deal. Both buyer and supplier agents operate within the single marketplace server and are dispatched by the buyer or supplier to that server; they do not move from server to server.

The Minnesota AGent Marketplace Architecture (MAGMA) [8] is a prototype for a virtual marketplace targeted towards items that can be transferred over the Internet (such as information). It consists of Java-based trader agents (buyer and supplier agents), an advertising server that provides a classified advertisement service, and a bank that provides financing support and payment options. Independent agents can register with a relay server that maintains unique identifiers for the agents and routes inter-agent messages.

MAGNET (Multi AGent NEgotiation Testbed) [9] is an experimental architecture developed at University of Minnesota to provide support for complex agent interactions, such as in automated multi-agent contracting, as well as other types of negotiation protocols. Agents in MAGNET negotiate and monitor the execution of contracts among multiple suppliers. A customer agent issues a Request for Quotes for resources or services it requires. In response, some supplier agents may offer to provide the requested resources or services, for specified prices, over specified periods. Once the customer agent receives bids, it evaluates them based on cost, risk, and time constraints, and selects the optimal set of bids that can satisfy its goals.

eNAs (e-Negotiation Agents) [10] and FeNAs (Fuzzy eNAs) [11] are prototypical intelligent trading agents developed at CSIRO to autonomously negotiate multiple terms of transactions in e-commerce trading. The agents can engage in integrative negotiations in the presence of limited common knowledge about other agents' preferences, constraints and objectives through an iterative exchange of multi-attribute offers and counter-offers. Fuzzy eNAs can also flexibly negotiate with fuzzy constraints and preferences. The F/eNAs environment can consist of many autonomous trading agents representing buyers and suppliers that can engage in concurrent bilateral negotiations according to a number of user-selected negotiation strategies.

3 MAPSEC

MAPSEC is a Mobile-Agent based Publish/Subscribe platform for Electronic Commerce systems. In many of e-commerce systems, a buyer (or the system) has a fixed number of suppliers, which are initialized with the system at start up. In case a new supplier is to be added, it has to be registered manually by supplying its address and the necessary parameters. In a large-scale and dynamic environment, any number of buyers and suppliers may be present at any time. In the dynamically changing electronic marketplace, we have to adopt out our electronic commerce system to this world. Therefore we propose a new architecture for e-commerce systems which uses the publish/subscribe mechanism for registration and transaction operations to increase efficiency and effectiveness of the procurement process, in terms of costs, quality, performance, and time for both buyers and suppliers. We use mobile agents as mediators to automate a variety of tasks including buying and selling of products over the Internet.

Our electronic commerce system (as most of the e-commerce systems) involves three actors. *Buyers* are looking to purchase services from suppliers. *Suppliers* or sellers offer the services and *Dispatch Service* facilitates communication between buyers and suppliers.

MAPSEC has an extensible architecture, as depicted in Fig.1, which provides all the services, which are essential to agent-based commercial activities. This includes a communication infrastructure, a mechanism for storage, transfer of goods, banking and monetary transaction along with an economic mechanism for brokered buyer-supplier transactions.

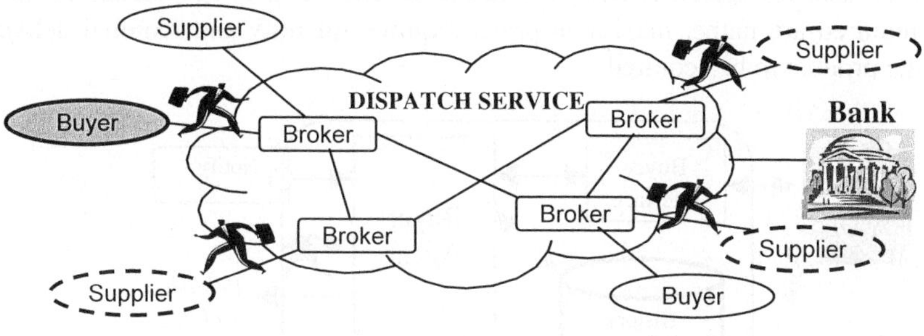

Fig. 1. The Architecture of MAPSEC

A user who wants to buy a product creates an agent, gives it some strategic directions, and sends it off into the logically centralized agent marketplace. MAPSEC mobile agents proactively visit suppliers and negotiate with them on behalf of their owners. Each agent's goal is to complete an acceptable deal, subject to a set of user-specified constraints such as a desired price, limit of an acceptable price, and a date by which to complete the transaction.

Banking: In order for an agent-based marketplace to become anything more than an experimental platform, it has to be able to communicate with existing banking and financial services. When an agent needs to make a payment, it sends a request to its bank to withdraw funds, and receive a secure wrapper, called a check. Before sending out a check, the bank verifies the existence of sufficient funds in the agent's account.

We will now describe the infrastructure details of MAPSEC subsystems (buyer, supplier and dispatch service), explain their functionalities and discuss the major design decisions.

3.1 Buyer Subsystem

An electronic transaction starts with a buyer agent. A user, whom the agent represents, specifies the name of an item(s) he wants to buy. For instance, attributes for describing a CD may be 'type', 'album', 'language', 'artist', etc.

To request a purchase order from the MAPSEC system, a buyer has to initialize a **buyer subsystem** on its machine. The Buyer Subsystem includes interfaces that are used to develop the Buyer Agent, necessary database connections and Buyer Interfaces as depicted in Fig.2.

As several transaction scenarios are possible, allowing users to generate mobile agents with different behavioral characteristics enhances the flexibility of the system. A human user interacts with the Buyer Agent via a *Buyer Interface* module. In the beginning of a transaction, the user supplies the necessary information. The buyer interface allows users to control and monitor the progress of transactions and to query past transactions from the *History DBMS*. Category of goods may include generic names such as 'car', 'CD', 'TV'. With this category information, a buyer agent prompts the user for search criteria to find the specific item to be purchased. Information required are name, maximum price, required quantity and required delivery date of the product to be acquired.

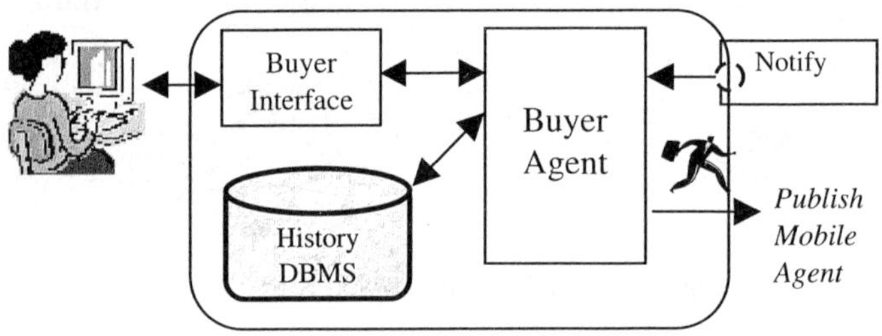

Fig. 2. Buyer Subsystem Architecture

A *Buyer Agent* is created with the basic capability to perform routine and simple tasks. Tasks that are more complicated may involve human instructions but once instructed, the agents cache them for future use. The function of a Buyer Agent is to search for product information and to perform goods or services acquisition. When a buyer agent receives a purchase request from a user, it creates a *Mobile Agent* to search for product information and to perform goods or services acquisition in MAPSEC. The Buyer Agent specifies the criteria for the acquisition of the product, and dispatches the mobile agent to the potential suppliers. The mobile agent visits each supplier site, searches the product catalogs according to the buyer's criteria, and returns to the buyer site with the best deal it finds and adds it to the History DBMS.

3.2 Supplier Subsystem

To subscribe to the system, a supplier has to initialize a **supplier subsystem** on its machine. The supplier subsystem includes interfaces that will be used for developing the Supplier Agent, necessary database connections and Supplier Interfaces as depicted in Fig.3.

The *supplier interface* module facilitates the interaction between a user and supplier agent. For instance, a user may inquire about past and current transactions from the agent. A user may also specify selling strategies through this module. When an agent is created for the first time, information regarding its name and URL is supplied through this interface to the web site maintenance component.

Supplier Agent processes purchase orders from buyer agents and decides how to execute transactions according to selling strategies specified by the user.

Since organizations differ in the products they sell, a supplier agent should be customized before it is placed online. To customize the supplier agent is to let it 'know' the goods it will sell. The *Products Database Management System* is designed for this purpose. It provides product information when requested by a supplier agent. The products database is not an operational database in the organization. As not all operational data is meant for public access, the products database only stores information that the organization has sanctioned for placement on web sites and for supplier agents. Goods will be added to the inventory either by manually adding a resource to the database or by purchasing goods from other agents.

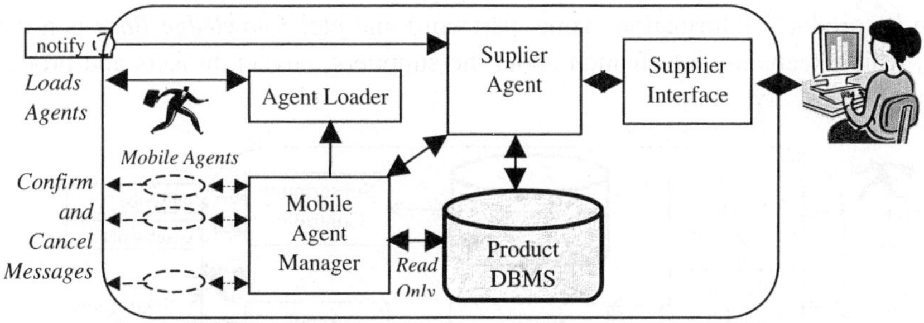

Fig. 3. Supplier Subsystem Architecture

Each *Mobile Agent* on the supplier side searches the supplier database for the product it is interest in. It determines whether the required quantity is already in the inventory and thus available to offer or not. If so, the supplier agent gives an immediate quotation to the buyer's mobile agent.

After a broker takes necessary decisions, there may be some requests to reserve a component, cancel a reservation or confirm a purchase. If a buyer cancels a reservation, the supplier agent may impose a reservation fee for the quantities of reservation reserved and bill to the buyer agent. Cancellation penalties discourage competitors from making malicious reservations that freeze stock. Because the buyer's mobile agents are fast, reservations are typically held for a short time and reservation fees are small.

3.3 Dispatch Service

The Dispatch Service plays an important role in cyberspace. A Dispatch Service is a logically centralized party, which mediates between buyers and suppliers in a marketplace. The main component of the Dispatch Service is the "broker". A Dispatch Service may consist of a single Broker or several brokers connected in a topology as shown in Fig.1. Brokers are useful when a marketplace has a number of buyers and suppliers, when the search cost is relatively high, or when trust services are necessary. The inner structure of a broker is given in Fig.4.

The client-server paradigm is not sufficient to solve satisfactorily all the problems that may arise during the life cycle of an e-commerce system. Often one needs to add a new supplier or a buyer to the system after the design-time. MAPSEC is basically an event-based system and a broker implements the publish/subscribe paradigm in which purchase events are published and made available to the supplier components of the system, through notifications.

Both suppliers and buyers have to know the address (URL) of the broker agent that they will connect, just like the URLs well-known sites, such as Yahoo!, Alta Vista or Excite. When a buyer wants to buy a product, it creates a mobile agent with the necessary information and sends this mobile agent by calling the *publish()* method of the broker. If a supplier wants to register (or unregister) to the broker, it calls broker's *subscribe()* (or *unsubscribe()*) method supplying the necessary parameters that include its products information, name, password and etc. *Knowledge Base* is a database, which keeps the information about the suppliers, buyers, brokers and products in the MAPSEC system

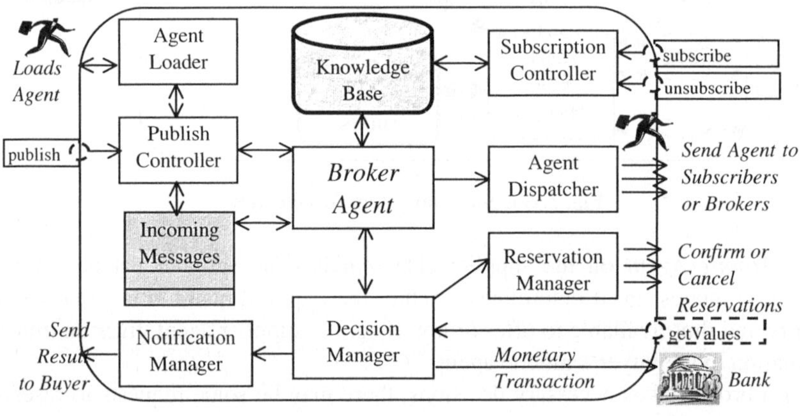

Fig. 4. Inner Structure of a Broker

Incoming agents are downloaded by the *Agent Loader* and then are dispatched to suppliers by the Agent Dispatcher when a request arrives from the Broker Agent. *Publish Controller* manages a queue of incoming messages. The Broker Agent processes these messages. *Broker Agent* is the main component of Broker System. It keeps controls all operations in the system. It evaluates an incoming message and, by using the Knowledge Base, selects a list of target suppliers and brokers to forward the mobile agent. The Broker Agent then sends copies of the mobile agent to the selected brokers and suppliers on the list, through the *Agent Dispatcher*. Suppliers and brokers return their results by calling the *getValue()* method of the Decision Manager. The *Decision Manager* compares the incoming results from the suppliers and selects the one that satisfies the constraints the best and sends a reply message to the brokers and suppliers through *Reservation Manager*. Decision Manager also sends its decision to the Buyer, to be added to its History Database, by means of *Notification Manager*.

4 Conclusions and Directions for Future Work

In this paper we introduced a general framework for a Mobile Agent based Publish/Subscribe platform for Electronic Commerce systems including mechanism for a communication infrastructure based on the publish/subscribe paradigm. The publish/subscribe protocol we have implemented allows for addition of new participants to the system dynamically, thus extending the adaptability of the system to new conditions. Another novel feature of the system is that it enables the utilization of mobile agents as mediators between buyers and suppliers. Currently a prototype of system is being implemented in Java. As future work, we have plans to change the API to conform to a standard Agent Communication Language (ACL) like KQML[12] or FIPA ACL[3].

References

1. Guanghao Yan, Wee-Keong Ng and Ee-Peng Lim. Toolkits for a Distributed, AgentBased Web Commerce System, In Proceedings of the International IFIP Working Conference on Trends in Distributed Systems for Electronic Commerce (TrEC '98), Hamburg, Germany, July 1998.
2. Agentcities Web, http://www.agentcities.org.
3. Foundation for Intelligent Physical Agents, http://www.fipa.org.
4. R. Guttman, A. Moukas and P. Maes, "Agent-mediated electronic commerce: A survey," Knowledge Engineering Review, vol. 13, no. 2 (June 1998) 147–159.
5. AuctionBot URL: http://auction.eecs.umich.edu.
6. P. R. Wurman, M. P. Wellman and W. E. Walsh, "The Michigan Internet AuctionBot: A configurable auction server for human and software agents," Proceedings of the Second International Conference on Autonomous Agents, Minneapolis, MN (May 1998), pp. 01–308.
7. A. Chavez and P. Maes, "Kasbah: An agent marketplace for buying and selling goods," Proceedings of the First International Conference on the Practical Application of Intelligent Agents and Multi-Agent Technology, London, UK (April 1996), pp. 75–90.
8. M. Tsvetovatyy, B. Mobasher, M. Gini and Z. Wieckowski, "MAGMA: An agent-based virtual market for electronic commerce," Applied Artificial Intelligence, vol. 11, no. 6 (September 1997), pp. 501–523.
9. MAGNET: Mobile Agents for Networked Electronic Trading. http://alpha.ece.ucsb.edu/ ~pdg/magnet/
10. Kowalczyk R. and Bui V. "On Constraint-based Reasoning in e-Negotiation Agents". In F. Dignum and U. Cortes (Eds.) Agent Mediated Electronic Commerce III, LNAI (2000), Springer-Verlag, pp. 31–46.
11. Ryszard Kowalczyk, Van Anh Bui (2000). "On Fuzzy e-Negotiation Agents: Autonomous negotiation with incomplete and imprecise information". DEXA Workshop on e-Negotiation, UK, 2000
12. Finn, T., Labrou, Y. and Mayfield, J. "KQML as an agent communication language. In: Software Agents." Bradshaw, J. (Ed.) AAAI Press/MIT Press. ISBN 0-262-52234-9 (1997).

CEVS – A Corporative E-voting System Based on EML

Dessislava Vassileva[1] and Boyan Bontchev[2]

[1] Institute of Mathematics and Informatics,
Bulgarian Academy of Sciences,
"Acad. G. Bontchev" Str., Bl. 8, 1113 Sofia, Bulgaria
www@math.bas.bg

[2] Dep. of Information Technologies,
Faculty of Mathematics and Informatics, Sofia University,
5 J. Bauchier Blvd., 1164 Sofia, Bulgaria
bbontchev@fmi.uni-sofia.bg

Abstract. In recent years, e-voting systems become more and more important as they contribute to the overall democratic process worldwide. CEVS (Corporative E-Voting System) is a new Internet voting application developed by means of EML (Election Markup Language) technologies. The article presents an overview of the EML structure and extensions and, as well, a JAXB (Java Architecture for XML Binding) technology, both used for building the CEVS application. Next, we describe in details the CEVS software architecture and discuss aspects of its system functionality. There are given directions for elaboration of CEVS and future works according to the state-of-the-arts trends in the area.

1 Introduction

During last decades, human societies are involved into steadily accelerating democratic processes worldwide. Voting is one of the most important characters of overall democratic developments. It provides citizens with governing power and responsibilities giving them trust and confidence in state and corporative organizations. In the past, changes in the election process have proceeded deliberately and judiciously, often entailing lengthy debates over every detail. Nowadays, with the progress done in development of electronic voting systems (so called e-voting) elections and inquiries are organized and maintained much more efficiently and at rather lower costs.

Paper-based elections make use of paper ballots, while *electronic elections* make use of some kind of voting software, which automates the voting procedures. In *offline voting* systems the computers running the voting programs may be viewed as a stand-alone computer. On other side, in *online voting* systems the computers used are connected to an intranet and/or to Internet, leading to an essential distinction between clients and servers.

CEVS (Corporative E-Voting System) was developed for the Institute of Mathematics and Informatics at the Bulgarian Academy of Sciences. It may be viewed as a

A. Yazici and C. Şener (Eds.): ISCIS 2003, LNCS 2869, pp. 356–363, 2003.

part of the future Bulgarian *e-Government* system, which is going to form a broad class of systems related to public services targeted at informing citizens on political issues. Such systems may also cater for online discussions between citizens, possibly involving politicians too. These systems may also include mechanisms for *online polls*, which may be used for conducting informal surveys without seeking a high level of accuracy of the result [8]. CEVS as an online voting system is based on EML (Election Markup Language) much more formal than online polling systems [7], because it seeks to accurately reflect the voters' preferences. It is a remote *Internet voting system* and uses unsupervised computer not necessarily owned and operated by election personnel in order to cast a ballot over the Internet. Moreover, it is extendible towards a mobile phone voting system by adding pluggable transformation modules for WML, XHTML, etc.

The paper presents the EML features and, next, the XML and Java technologies used for developing the CEVS. Further, we continue with a description of the CEVS software architecture and explain some of the basic system functionalities. In conclusion, there are given some remarks on our future work.

2 Challenges of E-voting Systems

The major advantages of electronic election systems are cost efficiency, speed, correctness, and privacy. Successful implementations of online voting, according appropriate testing criteria and measures of evaluation, require thoughtful planning and development. Nowadays research in online voting finds at least three groups of challenges in successful implementation and deployment of e-vote systems:

- Correctness: the computed result should correspond to the real votes cast by the voters
- Security: voters should be sure that nobody could change their vote by malicious intervention into the e-voting system
- Validation: only persons that have the right to vote should be able to participate
- Anonymity: for voters, it should be not possible to determine what a person was voted for

In traditional elections there are many physical obstacles that prevent large-scale cheating in most situations. Thanks to the fact, that it is impossible for a voter to prove that he/she voted in a specific way, it is impossible for a buyer of votes to verify that the seller voted the way he/she promised. Such obstacles are not present in the electronic world; if an adversary can mount a successful attack once he can do it many times, with marginal additional effort [1]. Moreover, in traditional voting process the votes are counted always several times by independent authorities in different physical locations. The correctness of e-vote systems should be guaranteed by an well-proven system design and well defined and non-breakable rules of usage.

The security of the e-voting systems is addressed in three main aspects:

- Secure network protocols - over an e-voting protocol strong requirements regarding security and functionality;
- Secure mobile code - an open systems implementation may involve a mobile code usage at the client level;
- Security policy management - a large-scale voting system must be able to address the issue of authorized access in a secure and scalable manner.

To ensure that only valid votes are taken into account, to each voter can be associated a secret key (e.g., on a smart card), and a public key. The voter can use her smart card to digitally sign her encrypted vote, and the candidates can verify that the data was indeed signed by a specific voter. However, usage of digital signatures allows voters to sell their vote, since during the encryption and signing process it is possible to compute a data prove for the candidate they have voted for. The problem is still under intensive research [1, 4].

3 Technology Background

3.1 EML Structure and Usage

As stated above, the CEVS application is strongly based on usage of EML (Election Markup Language). EML specification defines two basic subjects [7]:

- vocabulary (the EML core);
- message syntax (the individual message schemas).

Using EML, most voting-related terms are defined as elements in the core with the message schemas referencing these definitions. The core also contains data type definitions, thus, these types can be reused with different names. For example, there is a common type to allow messages in different channel formats. As well, the data type can be used as bases for deriving new definitions.

There is a third category of schema document within EML - the EML externals. This schema document contains definitions that are expected to be changed on a national basis. Currently this schema comprises the name and address elements, which are based on the OASIS extensible name and address language [7], but may be replaced by national standards for each country worldwide. Such changes can be made by replacing only this single file.

As well as these, several external schemas are used. The W3C has defined standard schemas for XML [3], XLink [5, 10] and XML signature [6]. OASIS has defined schemas for the extensible Name and Address Language (xNAL) [7]. As part of the definition of EML, the E&VSTC of OASIS has defined a schema for the Timestamp used within EML. All these schemas use their appropriate namespaces, and are accessed using *xsd:import* directives.

Each message (or message group) type is specified within a separate a schema document. All messages use the EML element from the election core as their document element. Elements declared in the individual schema documents are as descendents of the EML element. The example instance messages in the scenarios document demonstrate this structure.

XML elements, which contain the names of certain data items, may have an identifier, represented as an ID attribute. This identifier exists purely because of the channel (e.g. Internet voting) being used and is likely to be system generated. Some *ID's* are optional and some are mandatory. Each schema element has an id attribute that relates to the message-numbering scheme in the Process document. Each message also carries this number.

Many e-voting messages are intended for some form of presentation to a user, be it through a browser, a mobile device, a telephone or another mechanism. These messages need to combine highly structured information (such as a list of the names of candidates in an election) with more loosely structured, often channel-dependent information (such as voting instructions). Such messages start with one or more *Display* elements. It follows a XML example of an e-voting message:

```
<?xml version="1.0" encoding="UTF-8"?>
<EML Id="410" SchemaVersion="0.1" xml:lang="en"
xmlns=http://www.math.bas.bg/e-vote/temp
xmlns:xsi=http://www.w3.org/2001/XMLSchema-instance
xsi:schemaLocation=" http://www.math.bas.bg/e-
vote/temp/.../schemas/ballot.xsd">
<Display>
<Stylesheet Ty-
pe="text/xsl">../stylesheets/ballot.xsl</Stylesheet>
<Stylesheet Ty-
pe="text/css">../stylesheets/eml.css</Stylesheet>
</Display>
<Ballots>
...
```

This example shows a *Display* element providing information to the receiving application about an XSL stylesheet, which transforms the message into HTML for displaying the ballot in a Web browser. The *xml:lang* attribute on the EML element indicates that the message content is in English. Other *Display* elements can be added to cover other formats. In the *Display* element in the example, the XSLT stylesheet reference is followed by a CSS stylesheet reference. In this case, the XSLT stylesheet referenced will pick up the reference to the CSS stylesheet as it transforms the message, and generate appropriate output to enable the displaying browser to apply that cascading stylesheet to the resulting HTML.

3.2 Advantages of the Java™ Architecture for XML Binding (JAXB)

JAXB (Java Architecture for XML Binding) provides a fast, convenient way to create a two-way mapping between XML documents and Java objects [9]. Given a schema, which specifies the structure of XML data, the JAXB compiler generates a set of Java classes containing all the code to parse XML documents based on the schema. An application that uses the generated classes can build a Java object tree representing an XML document, manipulate the content of the tree, and regenerate XML documents from the tree, all without requiring the developer to write complex parsing and processing code. Using JAXB for a data-processing application has many benefits because a JAXB application uses Java Technology and XML, guarantees valid data, is fast, easy to use, customizable, extensible, can constrain data.

To start building a JAXB application all you need is an XML schema. JAXB version 1.0 requires that the schema be a DTD, as defined in the XML 1.0 specification, but later versions will likely support other schema languages.

After you obtain your DTD, you build and use a JAXB application with these steps:

- Write the *binding schema*, an XML document containing instructions on how to bind a schema to classes. For example, the binding schema might contain an instruction on what primitive type an attribute value should be bound in the generated class;
- Generate the Java source files using the *schema compiler*, which takes both the DTD and the binding schema as input. After compiling the source code, you can write an application based on the resulting classes. This process is shown in fig. 1;

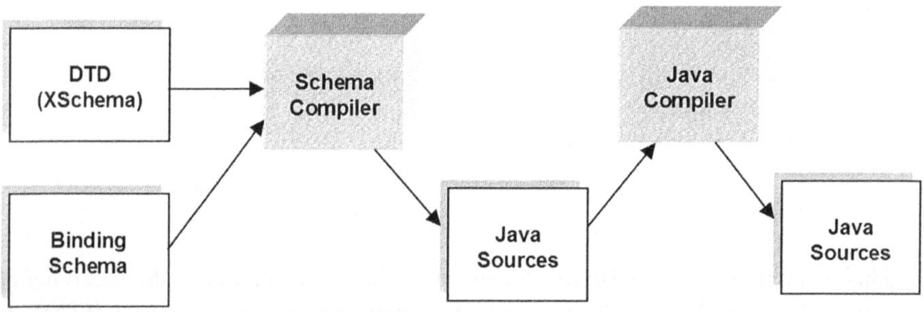

Fig. 1. The process of generating Java classes by means of the schema compiler

- With your application, build a tree of Java objects representing XML data that is valid against the DTD by either - instantiating the generated classes, or invoking the unmarshalling method of a generated class and passing in the document. The unmarshalling method takes a valid XML document and builds an object-tree representation of it. The object tree is called a content tree. This process is presented in fig. 2;
- Use your application to access the data of the content tree and modify the data of the tree;
- Also can generate an XML document from the content tree by invoking the marshal method on the root object of the tree.

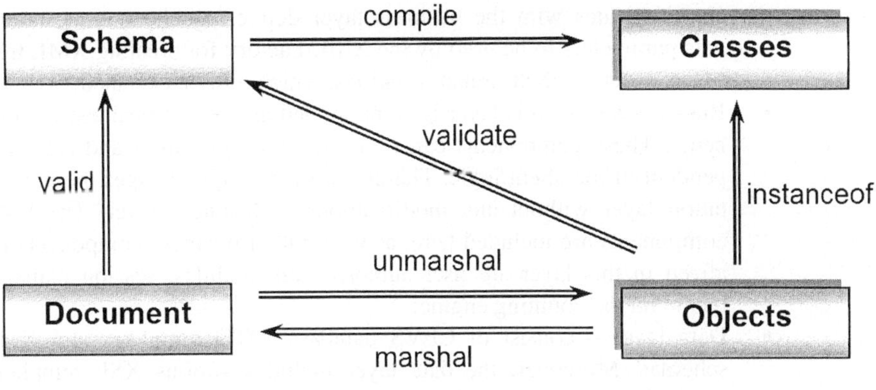

Fig. 2. Workflow diagram of building data representations

4 CEVS Design and Implementation

Following architectural principles of modern Internet applications, CEVS system design aims in separation of presentation from the content [2]. The overall system architecture of CEVS is presented in fig. 3. It consists of four layers:

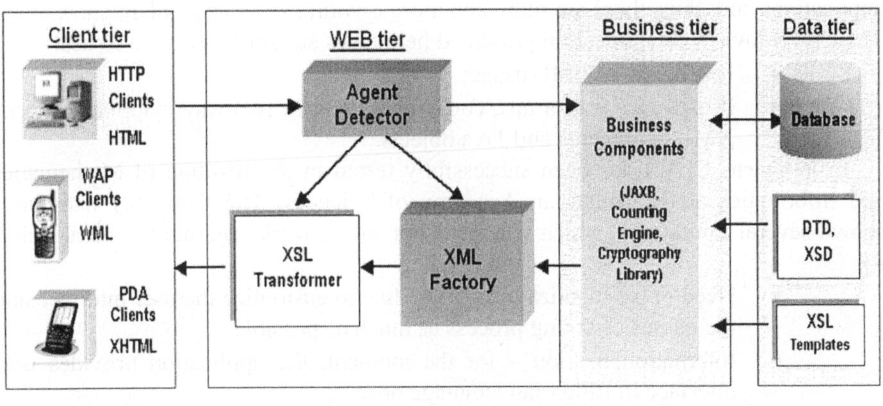

Fig. 3. CEVS system architecture

- Client layer – it is the presentation layer. Here users are asked to insert their authorization data and receive replies from the Web layer. It may realize interaction between the server-side application and different clients (Web browsers, PDA devices and mobile phones) by means of using their markup languages such as HTML, XHTML or WML;
- Web layer – defined which templates must been used and how the presentation must be structured according the user type. It consists of JSP's (Java Server Pages) and XML Transformers. The Web layer

communicates with the business layer delivering client requests and gets parameters to be used by the XML Factory for creating XML tree. More, it defines XSL transformations, which will be executed;

- Business layer – this layer is compounded as a set of business components. These components can be reused multiple times and are independent of the client logic. Thereby we can easily changes the presentation layer without any modifications to business layer. The EML components are included here, as well. Other business components realized in this layer are user authorization modules, session management and the counting engine;
- Data layer – consist of CEVS database, DTD templates and XML schemas. Moreover, the data layer includes various XSL templates needed for building the presentation layer.

The application is running under Apache Tomcat JSP engine. The database used is MySQL but can run under any relational database management servers. For the moment, the presentation layer (HTML only) has been tested with the most popular Web browsers.

5 Conclusions

The need to accelerate democratic processes worldwide pushes the market of Internet applications and, thus, there are more and more e-voting systems available nowadays. The CEVS Java Web application presented here takes advantages of two issues:

- It is based on EML usage;
- It uses JAXB as a fast, convenient way for two-way mapping between XML documents and Java objects.

In last year, CEVS has been successfully tested in the Institute of Mathematics and Informatics at the Bulgarian Academy of Sciences. The feasibility tests have shown several limitations, which will trace our future work regarding system usability:

- Need of personalization – users like to customize the user interface and the passes of voting process as much as possible
- Internationalization – for the moment, the application provides user interface in Bulgarian language only
- Mobile clients – CEVS is an open Java applications and due to its extendible system architecture, it may be elaborated with mobile communication channels for SMS/MMS voting, WML/XHTML interface, etc. Some of them like adding more markup presentations will be implemented by simple adding of new XSL templates [9].

Moreover, we plan to redo the business layer of the CEVS application using the EJB (Enterprise Java Beans) technological advantages. The business layer will be able to run on a separate machine (districts from both the Web and data layer) and thus, the next version of CEVS will provide users with more scalability.

References

1. Bonsor K.: How E-Voting Will Work. HowStuffWorks, http://www.howstuffworks.com/e-voting.htm (2000)
2. Bontchev B. and Ilieva S.: Middleware Service Support for Modern Application Presentations, Proc. of 15-th SAER Conference, St. Constantine, Varna, Bulgaria (2001) 138–142
3. Bray, T., et al: Extensible Markup Language (XML) 1.0. Second Edition, Worldwide Web Consortium, http://www.w3.org/TR/REC-xml (2000)
4. Cowling, D.: Analysis: Does e-voting work? BBC News, http://news.bbc.co.uk/2/hi/uk_news/politics/2122142.stm (2002)
5. De Rose, S., et al: XML Linking Language (XLink). V•rsion 1.0, Worldwide Web Consortium, http://www.w3.org/TR/xlink (2001)
6. Eastlake, D., et al: XML-Signature Syntax and Processing. Worldwide Web Consortium, http://www.w3.org/TR/xmldsig-core (2002)
7. eXtensible Name and Address (XNAL) Specifications and Description Document (v1.0) Customer Information Quality Technical Committee OASIS. http://www.oasis-open.org/committees/ciq/xnal/xnal_spec.zip (2001)
8. Killian, J., Sako, K.: Receipt-Free Mix-Type Voting Scheme - a practical solution to the implementation of a voting booth. Proceedings of EUROCRYPT '95, Lecture Notes in Computer Science, Springer Verlag (1995) 393–403
9. Sun Microsystems Inc.: The Java™ Architecture for XML Binding. Technical Report, Palo Alto, CA 94303, U.S.A. (2001)
10. van der Vlist, E.. XML Schema - The W3C's Object-Oriented Descriptions for XML. O'Reilly (2002)

Smart Card Terminal Systems Using ISO/IEC 7816-3 Interface and 8051 Microprocessor Based on the System-on-Chip

Won Jay Song[1], Won Hee Kim[2], Bo Gwan Kim[2],
Byung Ha Ahn[3], Munkee Choi[1], and Minho Kang[1]

[1] Optical Internet Research Center and Grid Middleware Research Center,
Information and Communications University, 305-732, Republic of Korea
songwonjay@ieee.org & {mkchoi,mhkang}@icu.ac.kr

[2] VLSI and CAD Labs, Department of Electronics Engineering,
Chungnam National University, 305-764, Republic of Korea
kimwonhee@ieee.org & bgkim@cnu.ac.kr

[3] Systems Control and Management Labs, Department of Mechatronics,
KwangJu Institute of Science and Technology, 500-712, Republic of Korea
bayhay@kjist.ac.kr

Abstract. A smart card terminal designed and developed to communicate with smart cards via a single System-on-Chip (SoC) is described in this paper. This proposed and developed SoC-based smart card terminal, designed with the Verilog Hardware Description Language (HDL) and the Simulation Program with Integrated Circuit Emphasis (SPICE), can be achieved and operated by proper connections to a Personal Computer (PC) and by dedicated software drivers that control the communication protocol between the smart card and the card terminal. We have also constructed an integrated test environment to verify the system developed. Through this test environment, we should be able to check all operational functions of the SoC-based developed smart card terminal microprocessor and smart card interface. The results showed that our test board operated successfully.

1 Introduction

In recent years, a need for an efficient method of storing personalized data, while providing security, reliability and portability, has arisen. The current PC-based smart card terminal should not only be designed to interface with smart cards and to control the retrieval or storage of data on the card but should also consist of several hardware components [Rankl+00].

Since the smart card terminal is mainly and deeply related to semiconductor Application-Specific Integrated Circuit (ASIC) technologies, in the view of hardware using a microprocessor to control the communication protocol with the smart card, the advantages of the System-on-Chip (SoC) can reduce the total number of analog and digital hardware components, as well as the total implementation cost for design and development of our proposed SoC-based smart card terminal [Razavi01,Glensner+00], which consists of only one Integrated Circuit (IC) chip, a crystal oscillator, a built-in power supply unit, and a card acceptor, as shown in Figure 1.

A. Yazici and C. Şener (Eds.): ISCIS 2003, LNCS 2869, pp. 364–371, 2003.

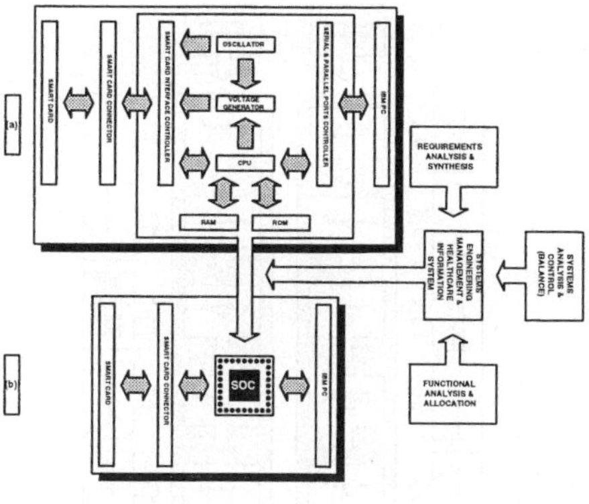

Fig. 1. The system overview of proposed smart card terminal.

We have developed a controller IC for smart card terminals by focusing on the reliability of card operations and the flexibility of the specification upgrade in ISO/IEC 7816-3, as shown in Figure 1 and **??** [ISO98]. The embedded microprocessor has a better throughput than general microprocessors that are not able to support an Answer-to-Reset (ATR) function. As a supporting protocol for the interfacing of the smart card, the developed IC has the advantages of improved reliability and cost reduction.

2 Smart Card Terminal System Design

2.1 Functions of the System-on-Chip

In our proposed terminal, the SoC-based smart card terminal should be able to accept both synchronous and asynchronous cards. These cards are interfaced to a standard Personal Computer (PC) via parallel and serial ports, respectively. The terminal should be designed in order to support both 3V and 5V cards and to provide a bi-directional data line to the card. Many researchers have designed and developed the currently existing smart card system consisting of smart cards, a card terminal, and a computer system to control card application functions [Lim+93].

However, the motivation for this study focused on reducing the total cost of the system implementation by directly encompassing the smart card terminal to a PC and integrating all analog and digital hardware components into one single SoC to integrate all components and circuits. However, another essential module of the SoC-based smart card terminal should be the software driver that controls the communication protocol with the smart card, which is dictated by ISO/IEC 7816-3.

2.2 Functions of Security

Smart cards in the area of security applications should often include a built-in co-processor. In some cases, the co-processor executes multiple-length arithmetic operations, such as module exponentiation. In other cases, the co-processor directly executes

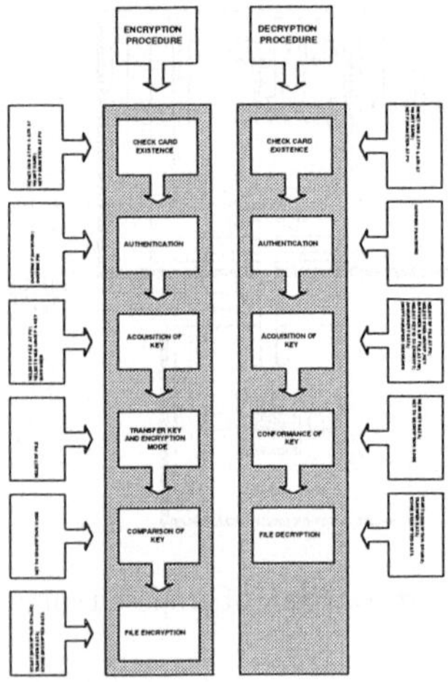

Fig. 2. The encryption and decryption procedures in the developed SoC-based smart card system.

common cryptographic functions, such as a Data Encryption Standard (DES) or RSA signatures [Trichina+01].

In our system's operation between the smart card and the proposed terminal, the secure microprocessor in the chip of the SoC-based smart card terminal generates the encryption keys for content encryption, while the command interface allows messages to be exchanged between the Personal Computer (PC) and the smart card by reading and writing the locations in the secure memory. The procedures of encryption and decryption are shown in Figure 2.

3 Smart Card Terminal System Development

3.1 Microprocessor

Most smart card microprocessor chips have been adopted with a conventional von Neumann architecture. We have also included the same architecture of an 8-bit 8051 microprocessor in the chip, for the SoC-based smart card terminal systems to support compatibility with other smart cards [Schultz99,Stewart+99,Yeralan+95]. The microprocessor, designed with the Verilog Hardware Description Language (HDL), should be optimized for control of various smart card applications.

Byte-processing and numerical operations on small data structures are facilitated by a variety of fast addressing modes for the internal memory [Schultz99,Stewart+99, Yeralan+95]. The core of the microprocessor is composed of a main controller and datapath surrounded by four functional blocks, such as a timer, serial Universal Asynchronous Receiver and Transmitter (UART), parallel Input and Output (I/O) port, and memory, as shown in Figure 3 [Song+02h].

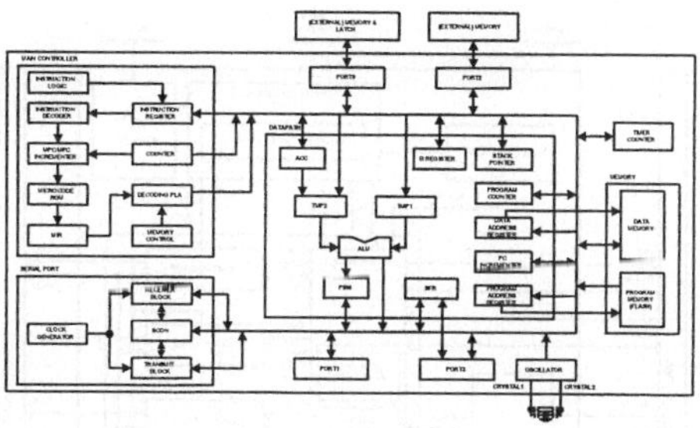

Fig. 3. The block diagram of 8-bit microprocessor.

3.2 Smart Card Interface Controller

There is a need of additional analog circuits, which are related to voltage generators, in order to supply multiple voltages for smart cards, while the circuits are also related to transceivers, to support card interface. Therefore, we have designed and integrated the Smart Card Interface (SCI) controller to include a voltage generator. The SCI controller consists of the digital blocks, designed with the Verilog Hardware Description Language (HDL), based on ISO/IEC 7816-3 and the voltage generator, designed with the Simulation Program with Integrated Circuit Emphasis (SPICE), to feed a stable supply voltage, as shown in Figure 4.

The voltage generator that was developed can be divided into a reference voltage generator, voltage doublers, and a voltage regulator [Favrat+98,Kim01]. In this study, a charge pump circuit for positive high voltage generators is suitable, As well, the proposed heap-pump circuit should provide a high voltage generator functionality, which not only offers a high pumping efficiency through the elimination of a threshold voltage drop of witches but also the simplest control single-phase clock scheme [Favrat+98,Kim01].

The fundamental limitation of conventional charge pump circuits is related to the pumping gain-loss brought on by threshold voltage drops as well as body effects of pass transistors [Favrat+98,Kim01]. This study proposes the use of a heap-pump circuit for the development of a positive high voltage generator with a single-phase clock [Song+02h].

3.3 Serial and Parallel I/O Interfaces

Serial I/O Interface. The serial interface blocks, designed with the Verilog Hardware Description Language (HDL), consist of two independent modules, as shown in Figure 5. One module implements the transmitter, while the other implements the receiver. The transmitter and receiver modules can be combined at the final level of the design for any combination of transmitter and receiver channels that may be required. Data can be written to the transmitter and read out from the receiver, all through a single 8-bit bi-directional microprocessor interface [IEEE01a]. Address mapping for the transmitter and receiver channels can easily be built into the interface, also at the final level of the design. As well, both modules share a common main clock, which, within each module, is divided down into independent baud rate clocks.

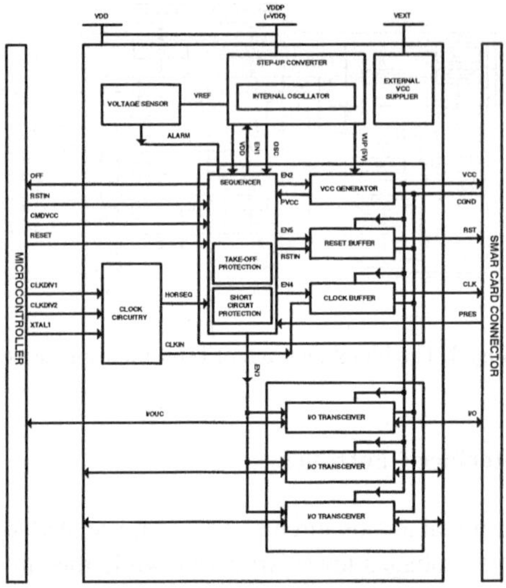

Fig. 4. The block diagram of Smart Card Interface (SCI) controller consisting of digital blocks based on ISO/IEC 7816-3 and the voltage generator.

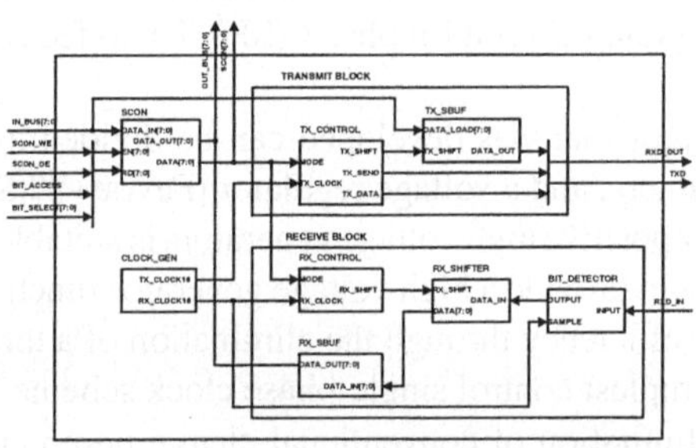

Fig. 5. The block diagram of serial interface with transmitter and receiver modules.

Parallel I/O Interface. The parallel interface block, designed with the Verilog HDL, consist of two independent modules, is an integrated solution that can be used to provide a standard interface for any parallel port peripheral, as shown in Figure 6. In particular, the parallel interface block designed for this study can be used with appropriate firmware to provide a peripheral interface. This interface provides fast, bi-directional data transfer, and control information when connected to a host parallel port [IEEE00a,IEEE00b]. This block is also suitable for providing the peripheral interface for a wide variety of devices [IEEE01b].

The interface to the parallel port supports the standard Input and Output (I/O) signals, plus has an additional support for external transceiver control and the daisy chain interface. This interface may be connected to the parallel port of the host Personal Computer (PC) or to the pass-through port of a peripheral with daisy chain capabilities [IEEE01b]. A data direction pin is also provided to interface to the external transceivers, while the

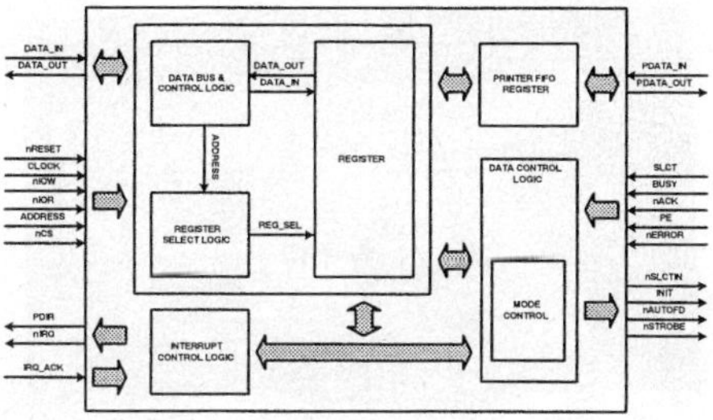

Fig. 6. The block diagram of parallel interface with transmitter and receiver modules.

host port connects to the parallel port of the PC or to the pass-through port of another daisy chain device.

4 Smart Card Terminal System Verification

4.1 Simulation of Analog Blocks

Simulations have been performed on a functional software model of the smart card terminal with this block design. In our smart card interface block, the developed voltage regulator is a very important circuit since it determines the correct operations of the smart card. The voltage regulator is a circuit that generates a stable operational voltage from the smart card using the microprocessor's supply voltage. In addition, we have adopted a series regulator architecture. The voltage regulator used supports two different voltages, such as 3V and 5V. In addition, the regulator can detect an over-current through the smart card and generate an alarm signal to protect all the circuits. The results of the simulation show that satisfactory results have been obtained [Song+02h].

The waveform of the outputs from the voltage doublers and the voltage regulators were also considered. When the supply voltage is 5V, we assumed that the VUP output of the voltage doublers is greater than 8V and the VCC output of the voltage regulator is stable at 5V $\pm 5\%$ [Song+02h]. In addition, there is also the results for the over-current detection function [Song+02h]. The VSEQ signal was generated when an over-current existed, in this case when a 75mA flow in the circuits during 50μsec [Song+02h]. Finally, the waveform after switching the card voltage between 3V and 5V should be considered. The selected signal is defined by the card controls generating the supply to the smart card [Song+02h].

4.2 Simulation of Digital Blocks

The digital block of the Smart Card Interface (SCI) supports automatic activation and deactivation sequences based on ISO/IEC 7816-3. In power-on settings and the internal pulse width delay, the microprocessor checks the presence of the card with this signal. If the smart card is in the smart card terminal, the microprocessor starts a card session [ISO98]. The automatic activation and deactivation sequences follow an input of the

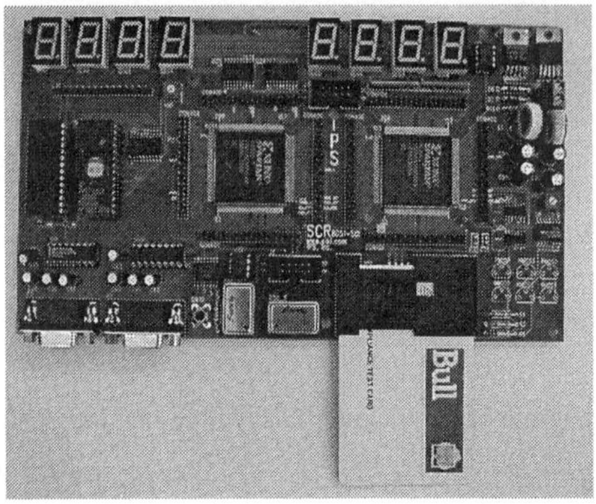

Fig. 7. The integrated test board made in IPS Corporation for development of smart card terminal.

signal from the microprocessor, after which their sequence is enabled. Next the voltage doublers are started, which increases the card voltage from 0V to 3V or 5V [Song+02h].

The supplied voltage also makes the all interface signal (i.e., I/O, AUX1, and AUX2) available. The clock is then applied and the reset enabled. The reset signal is set on HIGH in order to get the Answer-to-Reset (ATR) from the card. Afterwards, the automatic deactivation sequence follows. When a session is completed, the automatic activation sequence input from microprocessor is disabled and the circuit then executes an automatic deactivation sequence by counting the sequencer back and ends in the inactive state.

Next the reset signal is enabled, and the clock is disabled. At this time, all interface signals are output into high-impedance states. Finally the card voltage falls to zero. The deactivation sequence is completed when the card voltage reaches its inactive state [Song+02h]. Tests have shown that the correct operations are achieved successfully on our test board, shown in Figure 7.

5 Concluding Remarks

The main challenge in smart card hardware implementations is minimizing the consumption of area, including all circuits, while achieving a required throughput. Quick developments in Very Large Scale Integration (VLSI) semiconductor technology has enabled all semiconductor chip designers to integrate both completely electronic systems, which were formerly built on several separate chips, onto one single piece of silicon.

These developments have also brought the notion of single System-on-Chip (SoC) solutions. Trends in microelectronic system's design have focused on higher integration levels, smaller form factors, lower power consumption, and cost-effective implementations. This study has presented a new design and implementation of smart card terminals based on the ISO/IEC 7816-3 standard and can be applied to single SoC solutions.

We have also constructed an integrated test environment to verify our developed system. Through this test environment, we should be able to check all operational functions of both the SoC-based developed smart card microprocessor and smart card interface.

Acknowledgement. This work has been supported in part by the Korea Science and Engineering Foundation (KOSEF) through the Ministry of Science and Technology (MOST) and the Institute of Information Technology Assessment (IITA) through the Ministry of Information and Communication (MIC), in Republic of Korea.

References

[Favrat+98] P.Favrat, P.Deval, and M.J.Declercq, "A High-Efficiency CMOS Voltage Doubler," *IEEE Journal of Solid-State Circuits*, vol.33, no.3, pp.410–416, March 1998.

[Glensner+00] M.Glensner, J.Becker, and T.Pionteck, "Future Research, Application and Education Perspectives of Complex Systems-on-Chip (SoC)," *Proceedings of the 2000 Baltic Electronic Conference*, October 2000.

[IEEE00a] IEEE Std 1284–2000, *IEEE Standard Signaling Method for a Bidirectional Parallel Peripheral Interface for Personal Computers*, IEEE Standards Department, 2000.

[IEEE00b] IEEE Std 1284.4–2000, *IEEE Standard for Data Delivery and Logical Channels for IEEE 1284 Interfaces*, IEEE Standards Department, 2000.

[IEEE01a] IEEE Std 1174–2000, *IEEE Standard Serial Interface for Programmable Instrumentation*, IEEE Standards Department, 2001.

[IEEE01b] IEEE Std 1284.3–2000, *IEEE Standard for Interface and Protocol Extensions to IEEE 1284-Compliant Peripherals and Host Adapters*, IEEE Standards Department, 2001.

[ISO98] ISO/IEC 7816–1:1998, *Identification Cards – Integrated Circuit(s) Cards with Contacts – Part 1: Physical Characteristics*, International Organization for Standardization, 1998.

[Kim01] S.Kim, J.Tsouhlarakis, J.V.Houdt, and H.Maes, "A CMOS DC Voltage Doubler with Nonoverlapping Switching Control," *IEICE Transactions on Electronics*, vol.E84-C, no.2, February 2001.

[Lim+93] C.H.Lim, Y.H.Dan, K.T.Lau, and K.Y.Choo, "Smart Card Reader," *IEEE Transactions on Consumer Electronics*, vol.39, no.1, pp.6–12, February 1993.

[Rankl+00] W.Rankl and W.Effing, *Smart Card Handbook*, 2nd Edition, New York, John Wiley & Sons, 2000.

[Razavi01] B.Razavi, *Design of Analog CMOS Integrated Circuits*, McGraw-Hill, 2001.

[Schultz99] T.W.Schultz, *C and the 8051: Building Efficient Applications*, Prentice-Hall, 1999.

[Song+02h] W.H.Kim, W.J.Song, B.G.Kim, and B.H.Ahn, "Design and Development of Systems-on-Chip for Smart Card Reader," *Proceedings in the 2002 IEEE International Symposium on Consumer Electronics*, pp.B43–B46, September 2002.

[Stewart+99] J.W.Stewart and K.X.Miao, *The 8051 Microcontroller: Hardware, Software, and Interfacing*, 2nd Edition, Prentice-Hall, 1999.

[Trichina+01] E.Trichina, M.Bucci, D.D.Seta, and R.Luzzi, "Supplemental Cryptographic Hardware for Smart Cards," *IEEE Micro*, vol.21, no.6, pp.26–35, November/December, 2001.

[Yeralan+95] S.Yeralan and A.Ahluwalia, *Programming and Interfacing the 8051 Microcontroller*, Addison-Wesley, 1995.

Practical Gaze Detection by Auto Pan/Tilt Vision System

Kang Ryoung Park

Division of Media Technology, Sangmyung University, 7 Hongji-dong, Jongro-ku, Seoul, Republic of Korea

Abstract. This paper presents a practical method for detecting the point in the monitor where a user gazes by moving his face and eyes. Previous gaze detection system uses a wide view camera, which can capture the whole face of user. In such case, the image resolution is so low that the fine movements of user's eye cannot be exactly detected and the accurate eye gaze position cannot be located consequently. So, we implement the gaze detection system with a wide view camera and a narrow view camera. Because the narrow view camera captures the eye image with high magnification, the eye position easily escapes from the narrow view camera by user's facial movements. For these reasons, we adopt the functionalities of auto focusing and auto panning/tilting into the narrow view camera and those are performed based on the information of the detected 3D facial feature positions by the wide view camera. As experimental results, our gaze detection system operates in real-time and the gaze detection accuracy between the computed positions and the real ones is about 3.57 cm of RMS error.

Keyword: Gaze detection, Wide View and Narrow View Camera

1 Introduction

In the fields of human computer interaction, the gaze point on a monitor screen is very important information and locating the user's gaze position can provide useful functionalities for numerous applications. They are applicable to the interface of man-machine interaction, such as the view control in three dimensional simulation programs. Furthermore they can help the handicapped to use computers and are also useful for those whose hands are busy doing another job[19]. Most previous researches have been focused on computing 2D/3D facial rotation/translation[1][15][20][21], the gaze detection considering only facial movement[2-8][16][17][19] and the gaze detection only by eye movement[9-14][18]. Due to computational complexities, the gaze detection considering both face and eye movement has been rarely researched. Ohmura and Ballard et al.[4][5]'s methods have the disadvantages that the Z distance between facial feature points and camera must be measured manually in the initial stage. Their method take much time(over 1 minute) to compute the gaze direction vector. Gee et al.[6] and Heinzmann et al.[7]'s methods only compute the gaze direction vector whose origin is located between the eyes in the face coordinate and do not obtain the gaze

A. Yazici and C. Şener (Eds.): ISCIS 2003, LNCS 2869, pp. 372–380, 2003.

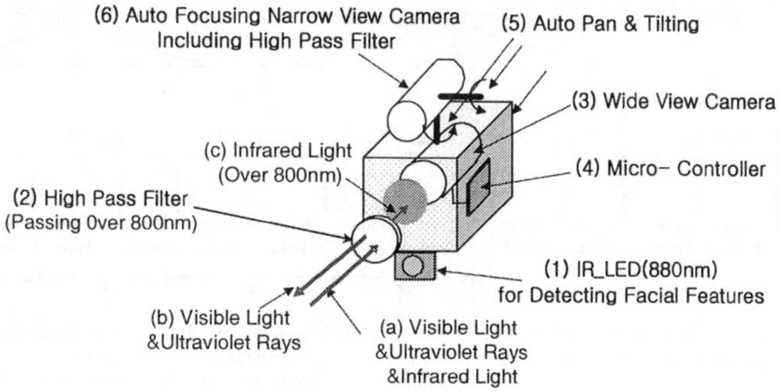

Fig. 1. The gaze detecting camera

position on a monitor. In addition, their methods do not allow the simultaneous motion of the 3D facial rotation and translation due to the increase of complexity of their least-square fitting algorithm, which takes much processing time. Rikert et al.[8]'s method has the intrusive constraints that the Z distance between a face and the monitor must be always kept same for training and testing procedures. In the researches of [10][13][14][16][17], a pair of glasses having marking points is required to detect facial features, which can give inconvenience to a user. The studies of [2][3] propose the gaze detection method only considering facial movements and suppose that the eye movements do not happen. The method of [22] shows the gaze detection by facial and eye movements, but uses only one wide view camera, which can capture the whole face of user. In such case, the image resolution is so low that the fine movements of user's eye cannot be exactly detected and the accurate eye gaze position cannot be located consequently. So, we implement the gaze detection system with two camera systems(a wide view camera and a narrow view camera). Because the narrow view camera captures the eye image with high magnification, the eye position easily escapes from the narrow view camera by user's facial movements. For these reasons, we adopt the functionalities of auto focusing and auto panning/tilting into the narrow view camera and those are performed based on the information of the detected 3D facial feature positions by the wide view camera.

2 Detecting Facial Features by Gaze Detecting Camera

In this paper, the facial features(both eye centers, eye corners, nostrils and lip corners) in input images are used for computing the gaze position on a monitor. There have been so many researches to locate the facial features robustly, but so many factors like environmental illuminations or racial skin color make it difficult to be solved. So, we use the method of detecting specular reflection to detect eyes[22]. It requires a camera system equipped with some hardware as shown in Fig. 1.

In Fig. 1, the IR-LED(InfraRed Light Emitting Diode)(1) is used to make the specular reflections on eyes[22]. The specular reflection is the reflection spot on

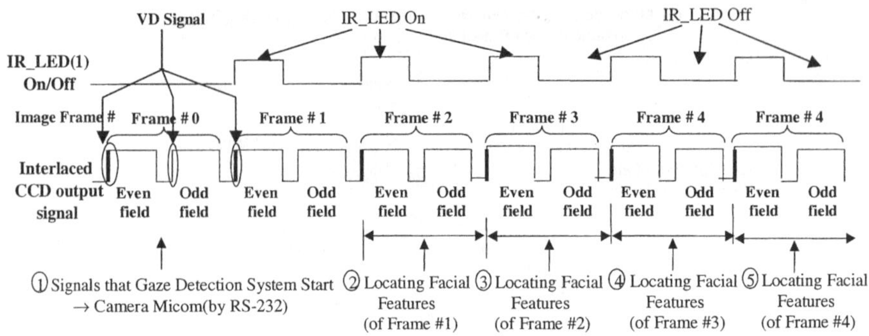

Fig. 2. The IR-LED controls for detecting facial features

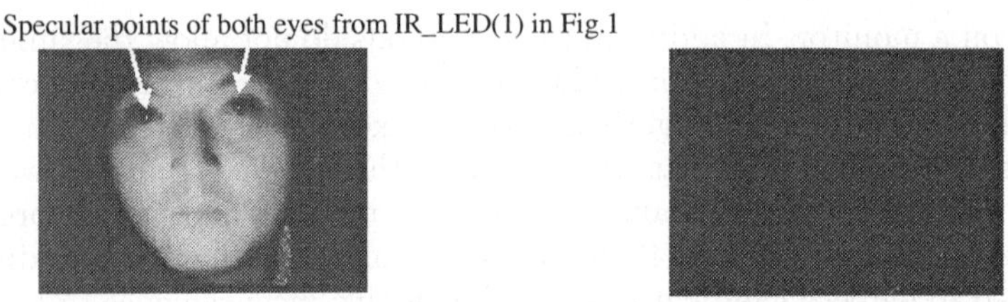

(a) (b)

Fig. 3. The even and odd images of frame #1 (a)Even field image (b)Odd field image

the cornea by the illuminator. The HPF(2)(High Pass Filter) in front of camera lens can only pass the infrared lights(95 percent transmission rate of over 800 nm) and most of the environmental illuminations including visible light cannot pass through. So, we can reduce the effect of the environmental light on our gaze system and it is unnecessary to normalize the illumination of the input image. We use the interlaced CCD camera for wide(3) and narrow view camera(6). A micro-controller(4) is used for detecting the every VD signal (Vertical Drive signal, which is the starting signal of even or odd field as shown in Fig. 2) from CCD and TG(Timing Generator) output signal and controlling the illuminators as shown in Fig. 2. General human eye can perceive the illumination with the wavelength of below 850nm and we use the IR-LED illuminators of 880nm against irritating the user's eye. However, the bigger the wavelength of the illuminators is(from 700nm to 900nm), the smaller the light sensitivity of CCD sensor is and the darker the input image is. So, we use 3 IR-LEDs as one illuminator(1) for making the specular reflection and detecting facial features. In Fig. 2, when a user starts our gaze detection system, the micro-controller successively controls IR-LEDs as shown in Fig. 2. The Fig. 3 shows the Frame #1 of Fig. 2.

From that, we can get a difference image between the even and the odd field image and the specular reflections of eyes can be easily detected because its gray level is higher than any other region(like the reflection of skin, etc)[22]. In addition, even if small amount of environmental light passes through the

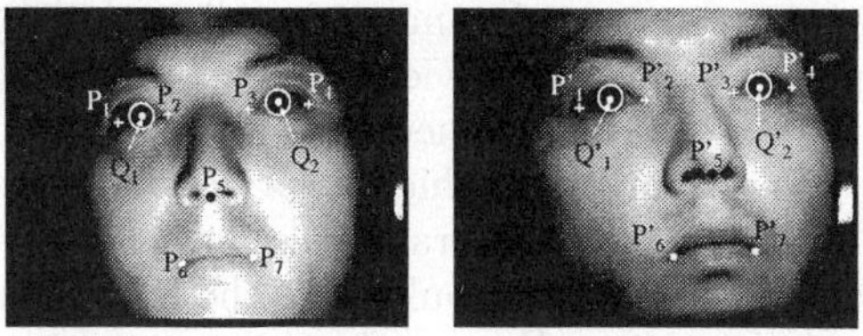

(a) (b)

Fig. 4. The seed points for detecting facial and eye movements (a)Gazing at monitor center (b)Gazing at left up monitor position

HPF, it may be exposed in both even and odd field image and it can be easily excluded by the difference between both field images. When the specular reflections are detected, we can determine the eye searching boundaries around the detected specular points and we locate the accurate eye center by the circular edge matching method[23]. After locating the eye center, we detect the eye corner by using eye corner shape template based on SVM(Support Vector Machine) and the detecting performances can be shown in [22]. After locating eye centers and eye corners, the positions of both nostrils and lip corners can be detected by anthropometric constraints in a face and SVM. Experimental results show that RMS error between the detected feature positions and the real ones(manually detected positions) are 1 pixels(of both eye centers), 2 pixels(of both eye corners), 4 pixels(of both nostrils) and 3 pixels(of both lip corners) in 640×480 pixel image[22]. From the detected feature positions, we select 9 seed points($P_1, P_2, P_3, P_4, P_5, P_6, P_7, Q_1, Q_2$) for facial and eye gaze detection as shown in Fig. 4. When the user gazes at other point on a monitor, the positions of 9 seed points are changed to $P_1', P_2', \sim Q_2'$ as shown in (b) Fig. 4.

3 4 Steps for Computing Gaze Positions on a Monitor

After feature detection, we take 4 steps in order to compute gaze positions on a monitor[2][3][22]. At the 1st step, when a user gazes at 5 known positions(calibration positions) on a monitor, the 3D positions(X, Y, Z) of initial feature points($P_1, P_2, P_3, P_4, P_5, P_6, P_7$) in the monitor and face coordinate are computed automatically. At the 2nd/3rd step, when the user rotates/translates his head in order to gaze at another monitor position like (b) of Fig. 4, the moved 3D feature positions can be computed from 3D motion estimation and affine transformation. At the 4th step, one facial plane is determined from the moved 3D feature positions and the normal vector of the plane represents a gaze vector by facial movements[2][3][22].

4 Auto Panning/Tilting/Focusing of Narrow View Camera

As mentioned in the section 3, if the moved 3D feature positions(especially eye positions) are computed at the 3rd step, they can be converted into the positions in the monitor coordinate and camera coordinate[2][3][22]. With this information, we can pan/tilt the narrow view camera in order to capture the eye image. In general, the narrow view camera has a small viewing angle(large focal length of about 30 - 45mm) with which it can capture eye image with high magnification. So, if the user rotates/translates face, his eyes may escape the narrow camera view and the camera should have the functionalities of auto panning/tilting to track the user's eye. For panning/tilting, we use 2 stepping motors with 420 pps(pulse per seconds). In addition, general narrow view camera has small DOF(Depth of Field) and the input image can be easily defocused(blurred) according to user's Z movement. The DOF is the Z distance range in which the object can be captured clearly in the camera image. The DOF has the characteristics that if the the hole diameter of the frontal camera lens is smaller or the Z position of object to be captured is farther in front of camera or the focal length is smaller, the DOF is bigger. In our case of gaze detection, we cannot make the user's Z distance farther arbitrarily because general users sit in 50 - 70 cm in front of monitor. In addition, making the hole size smaller reduces the penetrated light to camera CCD sensor and the input image is much darker consequently. So, in order to cover the eye's Z positions(50 - 70 cm) and capture the clear eye image, we use the auto focusing lens for our gaze system. These auto panning/tilting/focusing are manipulated by micro-controller(4) in the camera of Fig. 1. For focusing of narrow view eye image, the Z distance information between the eye and the camera is required. As mentioned in the section 3, the moved 3D feature positions are computed at the 3rd step and the Z distance of user's eye can be obtained consequently. However, the Z distance has the computation error(below 1.97 cm) which exceeds in the DOF(about 1 cm) of narrow view camera and accurate auto focusing cannot be achieved only with the Z distance. So, we adopt a simple focus checking algorithm which computes the pixel disparities in the input image. In detail, the auto panning/tilting and the preliminary auto focusing for eye image is completed based on the computed eye's Z distance at the 3rd step. After that, the captured eye image is transferred to PC and our focus checking algorithm calculates the gray level difference between the spacing pixels. That is, if the input image is defocused, then the difference value between the pixels is low. If the image is highly focused and clear, the difference value is high. If the difference value does not exceed in predefined threshold(70), we send the controlling command of focus lens to camera micro-controller(4) in Fig. 1. Here, when the defocused(blurred) eye image is captured, it is difficult to determine the moving direction of focus lens (moving forward or backward) and we use various information/scheme(for example, image brightness and gradient based lens searching, etc). From them, we can get the focused eye image from narrow view camera for computing the eye gaze position.

5 Computing the 3D Facial Rotation and Translation

This section explains the 2nd step shown in the section 3. There have been many 3D motion estimation researches, for example, EKF(Extended Kalman Filter)[1], neural network[21] and affine projection method[6][7], etc. Among them, the EKF is reported as showing the most stable performances[22] and we use the

EKF for 3D motion estimation and the moved 3D positions of those features can be computed from 3D motion estimations by EKF and affine transform[2][22]. Detail explanations can be referred to [1][20][22]. The estimation accuracy of the EKF is compared with 3D position tracker sensor[24]. Our experimental results show that the RMS errors are about 1.4 cm and 2.98° in translation and rotation.

6 Detecting the Gaze Position on the Monitor

6.1 Gaze Detection by Facial Movement

This subsection explains the 3rd and 4th steps shown in section 3. As mentioned in section 5, The moved 3D feature positions can be obtained by EKF and affine transform. and the feature positions can be converted into them in the monitor coordinate[2][22]. From them, one facial plane can be determined and the normal vector of the plane shows a gaze vector. The gaze position on a monitor is the intersection position between the monitor and the gaze vector.

6.2 Gaze Detection by Eye Movement

In the subsection 6.1, the gaze position is determined only by facial movement. As mentioned before, the user has tendency to move both the face and eyes in case of gazing at a monitor position. So, we compute the gaze position by the eye movements based on the detected facial features. The detail methods for capturing the eye image by narrow view camera are already shown in the section 4. When a user rotates his face severely, even the auto panning/tilting of narrow view camera cannot capture both eyes and his one eye may disappear in narrow view camera. So, we detect both eyes in case the user gazes at a monitor center and when the user rotates his face severely and his one eye disappears in the auto panning/tilting narrow camera view, we track only one visible eye. Our experiments show that the eye movements and shape are changed according to a user gaze position. Especially, the distances between the eyeball center and left/right eye corner are also changed according to user's gaze positions. However, there exist the complicated 3D transformations between the distances and the monitor gaze position and we use a neural network(Multi-layer Perceptron) to map the eye movements into gaze positions. Here, the input values for neural network are normalized by the distance between the eye center and the eye corner, which are obtained in case of gazing monitor center. That is why we only use auto focusing lens for narrow view camera without zooming lens and the eye image size can be changed according to user's Z distance. In other words, even if user gazes at the same monitor position, the distance between the eye center and the eye corner can be changed with the user's Z distance. For these reasons, the distance normalizations for neural network are required.

6.3 Gaze Detection by Facial and Eye Movement

From the gaze positions in subsection 6.1 and 6.2, we can locate final gaze position on a monitor by the vector summation of facial and eye gaze position[22].

7 Performance Evaluations and Discussions

The gaze error of this method is compared to our previous researches[2][3][19][22] like table 1, 2. The researches[2][3][19] only consider the facial movements for detecting gaze position. The research[22] considers both facial and eye movements with only one wide view camera for detecting gaze position. The test data are acquired when 10 users gaze at 23 gaze positions(on a 19" monitor) 5 times. Here, the gaze error is the RMS error between the real gaze position and the computed ones. Shown in table 1, the gaze error of the proposed method is the smallest. As mentioned before, the user has tendency to move both the face and eyes in case of gazing at a monitor position. So, we have tested the gaze error including facial and eye movements like table 2.

Table 1. Gaze error about test data including only facial movements (cm)

Method	Linear interpol.[19]	Single neural net[19]	Two neural nets[19]	[2] method	[3] method	[22] method	Proposed method
error	5.1	4.23	4.48	5.35	5.21	3.40	3.1

Table 2. Gaze error about test data including face and eye movements (cm)

Method	Linear interpol.[19]	Single neural net[19]	Two neural nets[19]	[2] method	[3] method	[22] method	Proposed method
error	11.8	11.32	8.87	7.45	6.29	4.8	3.57

Shown in table 2, the gaze error of the proposed method is the smallest. In the second experiment, points of radius 5 pixels are spaced vertically and horizontally at 150 pixel intervals(2.8 cm) on a 19" monitor with 1280×1024 pixels like Rikert's research[8][22]. The RMS gaze error of between the real position and the computed one is 3.61 cm and it is superior to Rikert's method(almost 5.08 cm). In addition, Rikert has the constraints that user's Z distance should not be changed, but we do not. For verification, we tested the gaze errors according to the Z distance(55, 60, 65cm). The RMS errors are like these; 3.45cm at the distance of 55cm, 3.57cm at 60cm, 3.63cm at 65cm. It shows that our method can allow user to change the Z distance. In addition, Rikert's method takes much processing time(1 minute in alphastation 333MHz), compared to our method(about 700ms in Pentium-II 550MHz). The material cost of our system is below 90 dollars and we can mass-produce with below 270 dollars

8 Conclusions

This paper presents a practical method for detecting the point in the monitor where a user gazes by moving his face and eyes. The gaze error is about 3.57 cm. Such gaze error can be compensated by the additional facial movement(like mouse dragging).

Acknowledgment. This work was supported (in part) by Korea Science and Engineering Foundation (KOSEF) through Biometrics Engineering Research Center(BERC) at Yonsei University

References

1. A. Azarbayejani., Visually Controlled Graphics. IEEE Trans. PAMI, Vol. 15, No. 6, (1993) 602–605
2. K. R. Park et al., Gaze Point Detection by Computing the 3D Positions and 3D Motions of Face, IEICE Trans. Inf.&Syst.,Vol. E.83-D, No.4, (2000) 884–894
3. K. R. Park et al., Gaze Detection by Estimating the Depth and 3D Motions of Facial Features in Monocular Images, IEICE Trans. Fundamentals, Vol. E.82-A, No. 10, (1999) 2274–2284
4. K. OHMURA et al., Pointing Operation Using Detection of Face Direction from a Single View. IEICE Trans. Inf.&Syst., Vol. J72-D-II, No.9, (1989) 1441–1447
5. P. Ballard et al., Controlling a Computer via Facial Aspect. IEEE Trans. on SMC, Vol. 25, No. 4, (1995) 669–677
6. A. Gee et al., Fast visual tracking by temporal consensus, Image and Vision Computing. Vol. 14, (1996) 105–114
7. J. Heinzmann et al., 3D Facial Pose and Gaze Point Estimation using a Robust Real-Time Tracking Paradigm. Proceedings of ICAFGR, (1998) 142–147
8. T. Rikert et al., Gaze Estimation using Morphable Models. Proc. of ICAFGR, (1998) 436–441
9. A.Ali-A-L et al., Man-machine interface through eyeball direction of gaze. Proc. of the Southeastern Symposium on System Theory, (1997) 478–482
10. A. TOMONO et al., Eye Tracking Method Using an Image Pickup Apparatus. European Patent Specification-94101635, (1994)
11. Seika-Tenkai-Tokushuu-Go, ATR Journal, (1996)
12. Eyemark Recorder Model EMR-NC, NAC Image Technology Cooperation
13. Porrill-J et al., Robust and optimal use of information in stereo vision. Nature. Vol. 397, No. 6714, (1999) 63–66
14. Varchmin-AC et al., image based recognition of gaze direction using adaptive methods. Gesture and Sign Language in Human-Computer Interaction. Int. Gesture Workshop Proc. Berlin, Germany, (1998) 245–257
15. J. Heinzmann et al., Robust real-time face tracking and gesture recognition. Proc. of the IJCAI, Vol. 2, (1997) 1525–1530
16. Matsumoto-Y, et al., An algorithm for real-time stereo vision implementation of head pose and gaze direction measurement. Proc. the ICAFGR, (2000) 499–504
17. Newman-R et al., Real-time stereo tracking for head pose and gaze estimation. Proceedings the 4th ICAFGR, (2000) 122–128
18. Betke-M et al., Gaze detection via self-organizing gray-scale units. Proc. Int. Workshop on Recog., Analy., and Tracking of Faces and Gestures in Real-Time System, (1999) 70–76
19. K. R. Park et al., Intelligent Process Control via Gaze Detection Technology. EAAI, Vol. 13, No. 5, (2000) 577–587
20. T. BROIDA et al., Recursive 3-D Motion Estimation from a Monocular Image Sequence. IEEE Trans. Aerospace and Electronic Systems, Vol. 26, No. 4, (1990) 639–656

21. T. Fukuhara et al., 3D-motion estimation of human head for model-based image coding. IEE Proc., Vol. 140, No. 1, (1993) 26–35
22. K. R. Park et al., Facial and Eye Gaze detection. LNCS, Vol. 2525, (2002) 368–376
23. John G. Daugman, High confidence visual recognition of personals by a test of statistical independence. IEEE Trans. Pattern Anal. Machine Intell., Vol. 15, No. 11, (1993) 1148–1160
24. http://www.polhemus.com

License Plate Character Segmentation Based on the Gabor Transform and Vector Quantization

Fatih Kahraman[1], Binnur Kurt[2], and Muhittin Gökmen[2]

[1] İstanbul Technical University Institute of Informatics
Maslak 80626, İstanbul
kahraman@be.itu.edu.tr

[2] İstanbul Technical University Computer Engineering Department
Maslak 80626, İstanbul
{kurt,gokmen}@ce.itu.edu.tr

Abstract. This paper presents a novel algorithm for license plate detection and license plate character segmentation problems by using the Gabor transform in detection and local vector quantization in segmentation. As of our knowledge this is the first application of Gabor filters to license plate segmentation problem. Even though much of the research efforts are devoted to the edge or global thresholding-based approaches, it is more practical and efficient to analyze the image in certain directions and scales utilizing the Gabor transform instead of error-prone edge detection or thresholding. Gabor filter response only gives a rough estimate of the plate boundary. Then binary split tree is used for vector quantization in order to extract the exact boundary and segment the plate region into disjoint characters which become ready for the optical character recognition.

1 Introduction

Applications such as traffic measurement and management, traffic surveillance, car park automation require successful license plate recognition (LPR) system. A typical LPR system is comprised of two parts: license plate detection (LPD) and license plate character segmentation (LPS), each targets different aims. LPD aims at detecting the presence of any plate in an image, while LPS aims at extracting the actual boundary and segmenting the license plate into characters which are sent to optical character recognition. There are several factors which have a negative influence on the results of any LPD and LPS system including weather conditions, lightning conditions, physical damages in the license plate.

There have been a number of studies in LPD. Most LPD algorithms are based either on edge detection or on thresholding. Edge detection and thresholding are both used to convert the color or gray-level image into binary image. The binary image is then analyzed by searching the histograms obtained by taking vertical or horizontal

A. Yazici and C. Şener (Eds.): ISCIS 2003, LNCS 2869, pp. 381–388, 2003.

projections along the image. Inherent nature of license plates causes specific transition characteristics on these histograms. In [1], gradient magnitude and their local variance in an image are computed. Then, regions with a high edge magnitude and high edge variance are identified as license plate regions. In another study [2], the straight lines are detected using Hough transform and horizontally parallel lines are grouped as candidate plate regions assuming that the lines in the real scene are preserved also in the captured image. Since the proposed methods are generally color or shape-based, they fail at detecting various license plates with varying colors and shapes. This is due to the fact that license plates are actually textures. The other one detects the license plate "signature" as it is presented in [3].

LPS prepares the license plate to optical character recognition. The aim is to segment the characters that appear in the plate. Proposed methods generally use the same approach as used in LPD. In [4], a relatively new neural network architecture called fuzzy ARTMAP is used together with edge detector filters. In [5], to segment the characters in the number plate image, they search for valleys in the vertical projection of the binary image.

We have developed a computer vision system that detects license plates and segments license plate into characters in an image by using the Gabor transform in detection and vector quantization [6][7] in segmentation. The overall system is depicted in Fig.1.

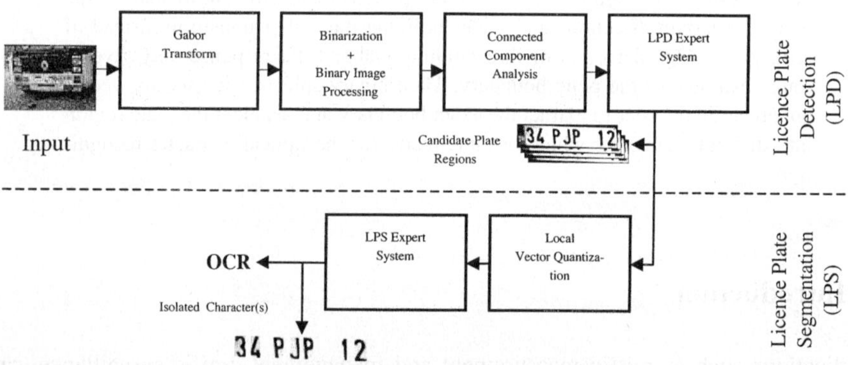

Fig. 1. Overview of the license plate detection and license plate character segmentation.

The output of the system is the bounding box for the license plates detected and their segmented characters. The paper is organized as follows: Section 2 examines Gabor transform and its application to license plate detection. Section 3 presents license plate character segmentation and introduces an expert system to filter out the segmentation results and apply a priori information if there is available any. Results of the methods described in this paper are presented in Section 4. Finally future works and conclusions are given in Section 5.

2 License Plate Detection

Gabor filters have been one of the major tools for texture analysis. This technique has the advantage of analyzing texture in an unlimited number of directions and scales. Physiological studies have found simple cells, in human visual cortex, that are selectively tuned to orientation as well as to spatial frequency. The Gabor filters are local spatial bandpass filters that achieve the theoretical limit for conjoint resolution of information in the 2D spatial and 2D frequency domains.

An input image $I(x,y), x, y \in \Omega$, where Ω is the set of image points, is convolved with a 2D Gabor function $g(x,y), x, y \in \Omega$, to obtain a Gabor feature image $r(x,y)$ as follows:

$$r(x,y) = \iint_{\Omega} I(\xi,\eta) g(x-\xi, y-\eta) d\xi d\eta \tag{1}$$

We use the following family of Gabor functions;

$$g_{\lambda,\theta}(x,y) = e^{-\frac{(x'^2+y'^2)}{\sigma^2}} \cos\left(2\pi \frac{x'}{\lambda}\right) \tag{2}$$

$$x' = x\cos\theta + y\sin\theta$$
$$y' = -x\sin\theta + y\cos\theta$$

The standard deviation σ of the Gaussian factor determines the effective size of the surrounding of a pixel in which weighted summation takes place. The parameter λ is the wavelength and $1/\lambda$ is the spatial frequency of the harmonic factor $\cos(2\pi x'/\lambda)$. The ratio σ/λ determines the spatial frequency bandwidth of the Gabor filters. The angle parameter θ specifies the orientation of the normal to the parallel positive and negative lobes of the Gabor filters.

The filter responses that result from the convolution with Gabor filters are directly used as license plate detector. Three different scales and 4 directions are used, resulting in a 12 Gabor filters. Fig.2. shows an intensity image and its Gabor filter response ($r(x,y)$). High values in the image $r(x,y)$ indicate probable plate regions. In order to segment these regions, first we have utilized thresholding algorithm and obtained a binary image. Then morphological dilation operator is applied to the binary image in order to merge nearby regions. Finally we extract plate regions simply by applying eight-connected blob coloring. The results of the detection by the given method are shown in Fig.3. where each region is painted with different color.

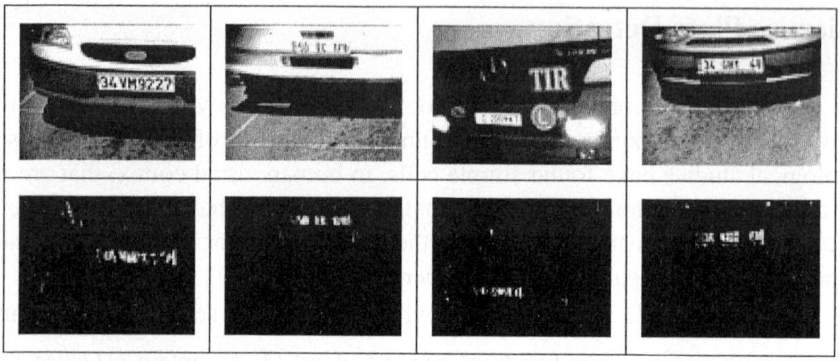

Fig. 2. Original images and normalized the Gabor filter responses.

3 License Plate Character Segmentation

Although Gabor filter performs well at detection, its segmentation performance is poor. We apply nonlinear vector quantization to eliminate the false alarms and segment the license plate characters to its exact boundary. Vector quantization is a process to assign pixel values in one of a finite number of vectors. First step in vector quantization is the decomposition of vector set. In binary split tree approach, these vectors are determined in such a way that the quantization error is minimized.

$$E = \sum_{n \in Q} \sum_{s \in C_n} \| I_s - q_n \|^2 \tag{3}$$

where $\{q_n\}$ is the set of quantization vectors and C_n is the set of pixels assigned to the vector q_n. Initially all pixels belong to the same class whose vector is the average of the image. Then the class is divided into two sub classes denoted by C_{2n} and C_{2n+1}. The vectors associated with these sub classes are chosen based on the second order statistics within the class

$$\begin{aligned} R_n &= \sum_{s \in C_n} I_s I_s^T \\ m_n &= \sum_{s \in C_n} I_s \\ K_n &= |C_n| \end{aligned} \tag{4}$$

Quantization vector (q_n) is assumed to be equal to the class mean:

$$q_n = \frac{m_n}{K_n} \tag{5}$$

(a) (b) (c)

Fig. 3. (a) Original Image, (b) Thresholded (Otsu) filter response, (c) Candidate plate regions each labeled with different color.

Class covariance matrix is given as

$$\tilde{R}_n = R_n - \frac{1}{K_n} m_n m_n^T . \tag{6}$$

When a class (C_n) is decided to divide into two classes, new class vectors (q_{2n}, q_{2n+1}) are computed. This computation requires the calculation of unit vector e_n which minimizes the expression.

$$\sum_{s \in C_n} \left((I_s - q_n)^T e \right)^2 = e^T \tilde{R}_n e \tag{7}$$

This is the largest eigenvalue of $\tilde{R}_n$. Once the unit vectors are obtained, the pixels belonging to the class C_n are assigned to C_{2n} or C_{2n+1} as follows

$$\begin{aligned} C_{2n} &= \left\{ s \in C_n : e_n^T I_s \le e_n^T q_n \right\} \\ C_{2n+1} &= \left\{ s \in C_n : e_n^T I_s > e_n^T q_n \right\} \end{aligned} \tag{8}$$

Splitting classes stops either when maximum vector number is reached or when the class variance is less than a predefined threshold.

Vector quantization explained above is applied only to the regions obtained by LPD system. Quantized image could be treated as n-ary image. Since we use two levels ($n = 2$), the resultant image is binary. Finally connected component analysis is applied to the quantized image to obtain the character segments.

4 Experimental Results

We have performed a series of experiments with real data where we demonstrate the robustness of our system and present the results in this section. The real data are provided by Multimedia Center at Istanbul Technical University. The image database contains vehicle (e.g., car, truck) images captured at daylight or night. We have made no assumption on the source of the plate (e.g., Turkey, Germany, Bulgarian, etc.), on the style, or on the format. We also performed experiments where there is more than one license plate in the image.

In our implementation, we first apply the Gabor filter at three different scales (9, 11, 15 pixels) and in four directions (0°, 45°, 90°, 135°) where large values indicate possible plate locations. We label each candidate plate region by using connected component analysis. Local vector quantization is applied over these regions. After local vector quantization, blob coloring process is applied to the quantized image to segment the characters and the segmented characters are labeled with different color.

Fig. 4. Isolation of touching characters

We assume that each blob represents a single character and is not connected with any other object in the plate image. In practice, it is common to find digits connected to other digits that will appear as one big blob in the system. In the latter case, more complicated segmentation algorithms are needed to separate multiple characters into individual digits. Our expert system separates the connected character to individual characters by using vertical histogram of the blobs and other pre-defined rules. Fig.4. shows this segmentation process and the expert system gives the final decision. The expert system finally resolves any ambiguities associated with the segmented regions by using some local and geometrical rules as well as regular expressions of license plate character sequence.

The expert system compares the blob features with certain expected empirically calculated values. These features and rules are extracted based on experimental studies. Basic features of the blobs are;

- Blob area
- Number of blobs
- Blob height
- Blob width
- Blob position
- Distance between blobs

The expert system reduces the false alarm and output of the expert system is the bounding box for the license plates detected and their segmented characters.

Fig.5. shows four samples from the experimental results on 300 images of which 167 were taken day and the remaining were taken night conditions with various sizes, styles and forms of license plates. The resolution of these images ranged from 512×384 to 768×576 while the sizes of license plate regions in these images ranged from 173×37 to 211×47.

Fig. 5. Experimental results for five test images which include various sizes and forms of license plates.

Total computation time for a 512x384 pixels image was approximately 3.12 seconds on Intel® Pentium® 4, 1.4 GHz. The computation time depended on the image size and number of license plates in input image.

To evaluate the performance of LPD, detection metrics in [8] were used. In order to determine the performance of LPS, numbers of the correct characters were detected by the algorithm divided by the total number of actual characters in the test data set. Our license plate data set has 2198 characters. The actual number of characters was counted manually by visually inspecting all the test images. There are 2154 characters in the correctly detected licence plates. To evalute the performance of LPS we used only correctly detected license plates by the LPD. LPS and LPD performance results are shown in Table 1. These results indicate that the system is quite able to discriminate whether a given image contains a license plate and to produce a rough estimate of the plate.

Table 1. License plate detection and license plate character segmentation performance

	Rate	**Result**
LPD Performance	294/300	98 %
LPS Performance	2029/2154	94.2 %

5 Conclusions and Future Work

The results presented above have shown that our system is very effective in locating and segmenting the plate characters. However, the method is computationally expensive. For a 2D input image of size *NxN*, and a 2D Gabor filter of size *WxW*, the computational complexity of 2D Gabor filtering is in the order of W^2N^2, given that the image orientation is fixed at a specific angle. Future work will consider the way of alleviating the limitations of 2D Gabor filtering.

In conclusion, we presented a novel and robust approach for detecting and locating license plates in images and showed that it was capable of locating plate characters with high accuracy. As of our knowledge this is the first application of Gabor filters to license plate detection and license plate character segmentation problems. Our future work includes integration of this method with an optical character recognition system and analysis of the overall performance of the integrated system. We also seek cues for a fast implementation in order to apply the technique in real time.

Acknowledgements. We would like to thank Abdulkerim Capar for his contributions and suggestions to improve the expert system of this work.

References

1. Gao, D. and Zhou, J.: Car License Plates Detection from Complex Scene, International Conference on Signal Processing (2000) 1409–1414
2. Kamat, V. and Ganesan, S.: An efficient implementation of the Hough transform for detecting vehicle license plates using DSP'S, Real-Time Technology and Applications Symposium, (1995).
3. Barroso, J., Rafael, A., Dagless, E. L., Bulas-Cruz, J.: Number plate reading using computer vision, IEEE – International Symposium on Industrial Electronics ISIE'97. Universidade do Minho, Guimarães, (1997)
4. Siah, Y. K. and Haur, T. Y.: Vehicle license plate recognition by fuzzy Art-map neural network, Centre for Artificial Intelligence and Robotics, Kuala Lumpur.
5. Lu, Y.: Machine printed character segmentation. Pattern Recognition, vol. 28, n. 1 Elsevier Science Ltd, UK, (1995) 67–80
6. Gray, R.: Vector Quantization, IEEE ASSP Magazine, 4–29, Apr., (1984)
7. Rovetta S., Zunino R.: License-plate localization by using Vector Quantization. IEEE Int.Conf. on Acou.,Speech, Sig.Proc.ICASSP'99. Phoenix USA, vol.II, (1999) 1113–1116.
8. Kim, K., Jung K., and Kim, J. H., Color Texture-Based Object Detection: An Application to License Plate Localization,LNCS 2388, p. 293 ff.

Segmentation of Protein Spots in 2D Gel Electrophoresis Images with Watersheds Using Hierarchical Threshold

Youngho Kim[1], JungJa Kim[2,*], Yonggwan Won[1], and Yongho In[3]

[1] Department of Computer Engineering, Chonnam National University 300 Yongbong-Dong Buk-Gu Kwangju, REPUBLIC OF KOREA
melchi@grace.chonnam.ac.kr, ykwon@chonnam.ac.kr
http://grace.chonnam.ac.kr/~melchi

[2] Research Institute of Electronics and Telecommunications Technology, Chonnam National University 300 Yongbong-Dong Buk-Gu Kwangju, REPUBLIC OF KOREA
jjkim@grace.chonnam.ac.kr

[3] BioInfomatix, Inc. eighth floor, Sung Woo bldg., 1424-2, Seocho 1-dong Seocho-gu Seoul 137-864, REPUBLIC OF KOREA
inyh66@bioinfomatix.com

Abstract. 2D Gel Electrophoresis (2DGE) image is the most widely used method for the isolation of the objective protein by comparative analysis of the protein spot pattern in the gel plane. The process of protein analysis is the method, which compares the protein pattern that is spread in the gel plane with the contrast group and finds interesting protein spot by image analysis. Previous 2DGE image analysis is composed of *gaussian fitting*, and segments protein spots by *watersheds*, a morphological segmentation. Watersheds have a benefit that is fast in global threshold, but induces under-segmentation and over-segmentation of spot area when gray level is continuous. The drawback was somewhat solved by marker point institution, but needs the split and merge process. This paper introduces a novel segmentation of protein spots by watersheds using hierarchical threshold, which can resolve the problem of marker-driven watersheds.

1 Introduction

In the post genomic era, as the direction of the genome research progresses to the functional genomics, the research of the proteomics, which is based on, the protein analysis is accelerating. The proteomics is the science that analyzes the qualitative and quantitative status of many proteins in the cell or organ from many species and uniformly understands the physiologic phenomena of the cell by finding the physical and functional relationship between the protein molecules. The proteomic research basically has three steps. The first step is the process that separates proteins. In this step, thousands of proteins are divided by two-dimensional electrophoresis and are

* To whom correspondence should be addressed.

This study was financially supported by Chonnam National University in the program, 1999.

A. Yazici and C. Şener (Eds.): ISCIS 2003, LNCS 2869, pp. 389–396, 2003.

spread in the gel plane. Then, comparison of the protein spot pattern in the gel plane with the contrast protein pattern and discovery of interesting protein spot using computer analysis are made. In the second step, we obtain the information of the protein mass, peptide mass fingerprinting, peptide sequence tag, etc, using the protein microanalysis technique. The final step is the process for finding what protein a spot is by searching various biological databases with information obtained in the previous step.

As a method of the protein analysis, pattern analysis and recognition is helpful to express the protein content in the biological sample and measure the protein content. 2DGE pattern analysis technique has been widely used as a method of finding proteins. The technique is divided into two parts. The first step is the process that takes images with digital camera or scanner, and segments protein spots from background. The second step is the process that compares more than two gels and matches the protein spot pattern [1]. The result of distinct segmentation in quantitative measure of a spot reflects the amount of protein expression, and matching detects the change in protein expression through the samples and identifies unknown proteins [1],[2].

Although the morphological segmentation techniques for 2DGE image distinguish and separate thousands of protein spots from the background image, it has several problems. First, it is difficult to distinguish indistinct spot because various types of noises are mixed in the image. Second, multiple spots exist as one spot by overlapping. Third, it is difficult to provide segmentation criteria between background and weak spots [2]. Furthermore, most spots have the problems mentioned previously and there is nearly no definitely distinguishable spot. Although the watersheds are mostly used for segmentation of the protein spots, the problem of over-segmentation and under-segmentation of spot area occurs, and split and merge process is required as a post-processing step. To resolve this problem, marker-driven watersheds segmentation was proposed [3]. However, selection of makes is difficult and it brings a *priori* knowledge to bear on the segmentation problem.

This paper proposes hierarchical segmentation method based on watersheds to distinguish protein spots without using markers. Thus, our proposed segmentation method can resolve the selection of makers and eliminate split-and-merge process. It first performs usual pre-processing for image enhancement such as noise elimination, contrast enhancement and background subtraction. The image is then reversed. We apply thresholding with a high value, which produces a large region on which watersheds is applied. If watersheds produces more than one segmented blob, a new threshold value only for that large region is selected which separates the blob into more than one region in the next step. More precisely speaking, the new threshold value is selected locally only for the inside of that large region. The process, hierarchical threshold and watersheds, is recursively applied until only one blob is produced as a result of watersheds.

This paper is composed as follows. Chapter 2 briefly introduces 2DGE image and its analysis. Segmentation using watersheds is described in Chapter 3 with its problems. Our proposed method of hierarchical segmentation with watersheds is then explained in Chapter 4, which is followed by the result of the method presented in Chapter 5. Finally, Chapter 6 has conclusion and further works.

2 2D Gel Electrophoresis Image and Its Analysis

2-dimensional gel electrophoresis (2DGE) is a process that enables separation of mixtures of proteins due to differences in their pI (isoelectric point), in the so-called first dimension, and subsequently by the MWt (Molecular weight) in the second dimension. A 2D pattern of spots, each of which represents a protein, is the result of the 2D gel process, and the pattern is captured as an image by digital camera or scanner. The images, shown in the later chapters, include thousands of protein spots.

To find useful biological information, one uses the comparison of several 2D gel images to recognize disease-associated protein expression. However, for the visual comparison, substantial difficulties arise from the fact that images are heavily distorted due to inaccuracies in the electrophoresis process. Therefore, a computer-assisted process is definitely needed. 2DGE image analysis technique is divided into two steps. The first step is the segmentation of the protein spots from the image that was appropriately pre-processed. There are several issues in this procedure such as irregular distribution of spots, overlapped multiple spots, intensity variation of background across the image, etc. The second step is the process that matches the protein spots across the images obtained from different conditions or samples [2]. The reliability of the second step is obviously dependent on the result of the spot segmentation performed in the first step.

3 Watersheds Segmentation

3.1 Watersheds Transform

Watersheds transform is researched in topological study, and is applied in image processing as think the slope of brightness in pixel about simplified image as altitude in topology. It is the algorithm that finds the fields, which are attached to each catchment basin by finding the watersheds which divides catchment basin through regional minima. Until now, many algorithms to find the watersheds have been proposed, but the most efficient method is the one using immersion simulation. It is the process of widening the catchment basin as increasing the height of water from the lowest height and forming the lakes which have regional minima as base point [3]. When it contacts another catchment basin as the height of water is increasing, it builds a supposed watersheds line at the catchment basin and divides it [4].

3.2 Problems of Watersheds Transform

Watersheds transform has the benefit that it easily finds neighboring edge through regional minima and catchment basin, but also has the problem that the location and number of regional minima is not exact because 2D image has continuous gray level.

Therefore, when excessively many regional minima exist in the image, the problem of over-segmentation occurs as shown in Fig. 1 (b). In contrast, when the number of regional minima is so small, under-segmentation occurs as shown in Fig. 1 (c). To solve this problem, watersheds transform generates boundary between spot and background through internal marker and external marker [5]. It requires a controller to find the locations of the suitable markers. Although one finds suitable markers, he or she should execute a split-and-merge process with neighboring segmentation boundary through median gray value of segmented field [6], [7], [8], [9], [10], [11].

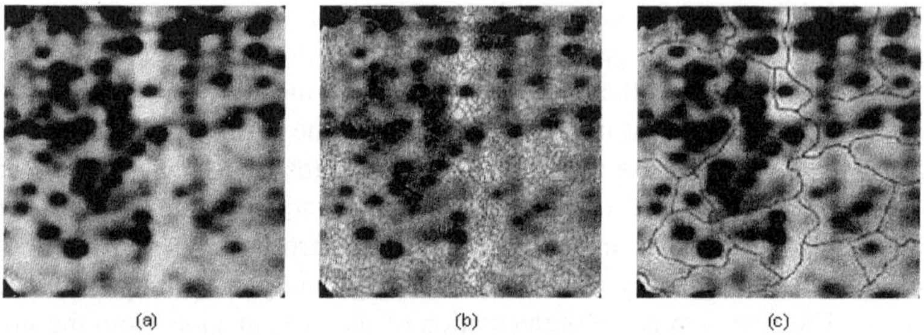

Fig. 1. (a) The original image obtained by a scanner. (b) Over-segmentation due to excessive regional minima (c) Under-segmentation due to insufficient regional minima.

4 Watersheds with Hierarchical Segmentation

This paper proposes a hierarchical segmentation method that uses a step-by-step threshold in a 2DGE image to reduce the problem of watersheds transform. Proposed hierarchical segmentation pays attention to the fact that if spot is strictly distinguishable from background, watersheds transform has a benefit that is faster in reaching to global segmentation.

It first removes background information by an operation given in the Equation 1, and counterbalances the continuous gray level, in some degree, but gray value in spot field is lowered.

$$\mathrm{Output}(x,y)=255-(\mathrm{EI}(x,y) - \mathrm{MFI}(x,y)). \quad (1)$$

Where EI stands for *enhanced image* and MFI does for *median filter image* of EI. As the result of this operation, if the threshold is done for the local region which has regular gray level pixel in the image, we can make background extracted image discontinuous gray level.

Fig. 2 shows the workflow of hierarchical segmentation method. First, in step (a), the distance between maximum value and minimum value of spot gray level is applied to threshold. Threshold image calculates the total boundary number of spot (n) in the boundary through minimum size and maximum size in step (b). In step (c), the number of spots (n) in threshold boundary is calculated. In the steps of (d)-(h)-(i), when n is zero, it means that no spot is in the image as the result of threshold. So, local boundary image of the result of previous threshold is stored. In the steps of (e)-(h)-(i), when n is 1, it means that only one spot exists in the image as the currently threshold result is stored. In the step of (c)-(f)-(g), when n is larger than 1, it means that currently more than two spots exist in the boundary, so repeats threshold process as n value.

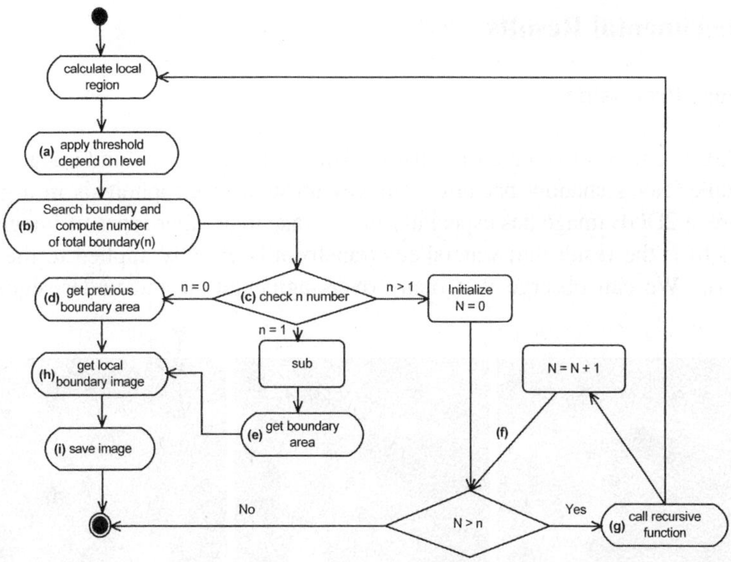

Fig. 2. Hierarchical Segmentation workflow chart using recursive call function

Fig. 3 is an example of hierarchical segmentation. (a) is the background subtracted image, (b) is the image that has many spots in one boundary as a result of watersheds transform for the image in (a). (c) shows the watersheds-transformed image of the image in (b) through first hierarchical segmentation, and the result of the second hierarchical segmentation is presented in (d). By this procedure described in the Fig. 2, we can distinguish spot region without using marker controller.

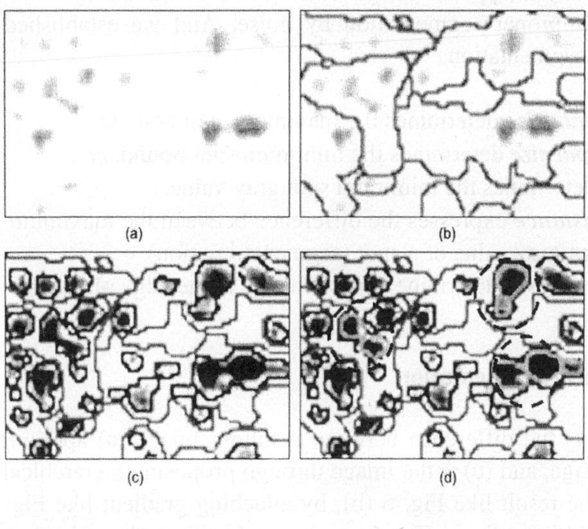

Fig. 3. (a) Background subtracted image. (b) Watersheds image through only background extraction. (c) Watersheds image through first hierarchical segmentation image. (d) Watersheds image through second hierarchical segmentation.

5 Experimental Results

5.1 Image Processing

In a 2DGE image, spot is not easily distinguishable from background image. It means that sample leaves shadow because it moves through electrophoresis in a gel plate. Therefore, a 2DGE image has especially more noise than other types of image.

Fig. 4(b) is the result that watersheds transform is directly applied to the original image (a). We can observe that many over-segmentation and under-segmentation occur.

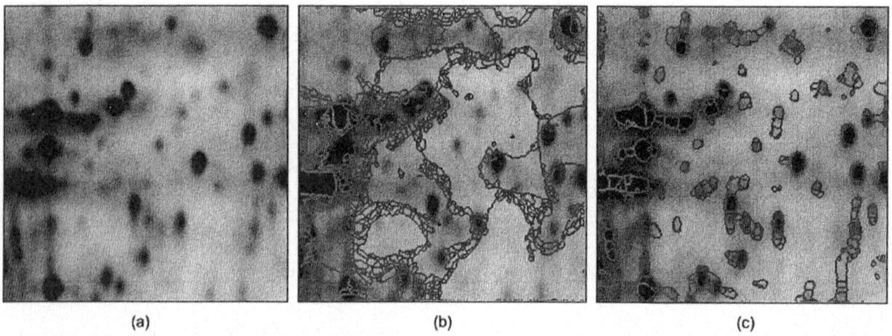

Fig. 4. (a) The original image by scanner. (b) The image over-segmentation and under-segmentation by applying watersheds transform without markers. (c) The image of over-segmentation by applying background subtraction.

Proposed method applied image enhancement and background subtraction to minimize the improper segmentation by noise. And we established the following parameters for segmentation.

- ***Maximum spot size*** determines the maximum spot boundary.
- ***Minimum spot size*** determines the minimum spot boundary.
- ***Faint spot*** determines the minimum spot gray value.
- ***Min-Max distance*** expresses the difference between the maximum gray value and the minimum gray value of a spot (segmented region).
- ***Slopes of gray level*** determine abrupt change at the edge of a spot.

5.2 Hierarchical Segmentation

Fig. 5 (b) shows the difference between resulting image (a) applying median filter and original image, and (c) is the image through proposing hierarchical segmentation. We can have the result like Fig. 6 (b), by attaching gradient like Fig. 6 (a), and applying watersheds transform. Fig. 6 (c) shows the ellipse boundary superimposed on the image to heighten the discriminating power to resulting image.

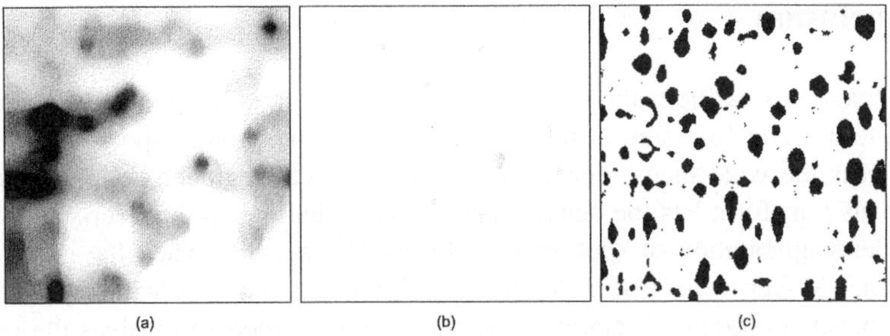

Fig. 5. (a) The median filter image from enhancement image. (b) The background extraction image from enhancement image to median filter image. (c) The hierarchical-threshold image from background extraction image.

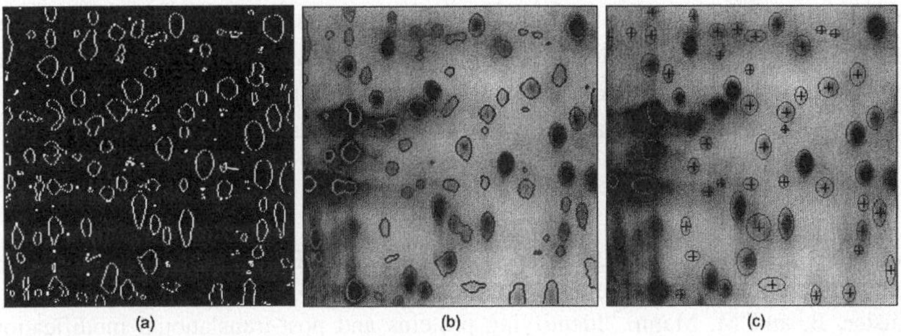

Fig. 6. (a) The image of regional minima and catchments basin attaching gradient to the hierarchical segmentation image. (b) The watersheds lined image. (c) The image taken ellipse boundary of spot.

Table 1 shows the performance measurement for our system. This result shows that our method gives a highly reliable detection capability for the protein spots by producing the specificity 0.9, the confidence 0.99, and high probability of protein spot pre-detection with low true negative value and low false positive value.

Table 1. Result of performance measurement

Total Spot	TP	TN	FP	FN	Specificity	Confidence	PS-PDP
116	106	9	1	0	0.900	0.991	0.914

TP : True Positive, TN : True Negative, FP : False Positive, FN : False Negative
Specificity = TN / (TN + FP), Confidence = TP / (TP + FP)
PS-PDP : Protein Spot Pre-Detection Probability = (TP + FN) / (TP + TN+FP + FN)

6 Conclusion

2DGE image processing is the method to find target protein by the analysis of protein spot patterns. The first step is the segmentation of the protein spots, and this step mostly uses the watersheds transform, a morphological segmentation. Although the watersheds transform has the benefit that fast in global threshold, over-segmentation and under-segmentation of spot area easily occur especially when the gray level is continuous. Maker-controlled methods were introduced to overcome this problem.

This paper proposed a hierarchical segmentation method to resolves the problem of watersheds transform, which can also substitute the selection of markers and remove a merge-and-split process. As a result, the hierarchical threshold does not induce over-segmentation and under-segmentation by changing the image of continuous gray values to the image of discontinuous values. Performance evaluation of our proposed method showed the specificity 0.9 and the confidence 0.99, which proves the highly reliable capability of our method for the protein spot detection.

Now, our research focus is on the 2DGE image matching across multiple images with the result of the spot detection to analyze the change of protein expression. It involves a point matching, spot size analysis, gray values in the spots, etc. We also investigating the sensitivity analysis of the parameters defined for segmentation.

References

1. Wilkins, M.R., Williams, K.L., Appel, R.D. and D.F. Hochstrasser (Ed) "Proteome research : New frontiers in functional genomics", Springer-Verlag, Berlin. (1997)
2. Kuster, B. and M. Mann. "Identifying proteins and post-translational modifications by mass spectrometry" Current Opinions in Structual Biology. (1998) 8:393–400.
3. L. Vincent , P. Soille, "Watershed in Digital Space: An Efficient Algorithm Based on Immersion Simulation" IEEE Transactions on Pattern Analysis and Machine Intelligence, v.13 n.6, p.583–598, June 1991.
4. F. Meyer and S. Beucher, "Morphological segmentation" J. Visual Comm. Image Representation, Vol.1, No. !, Sep. 1990
5. Rafael C. Gonzalez and Richard E. Woods "Digital Image Processing", Second Edition, Prentice Hall, chapter 10, page 617.2001
6. Stanislav L. Stoev and Wolfgang Straßer, "Extracting Regions of Interest Applying a Local Watershed Transformation" To appear in the proceedings of 'IEEE Visualization 2000', 8-13 Oct 2000, Salt Lake City, UT
7. Jos B.T.M. Roerdink and Arnold Meijster, "The Watershed Transform: Definitions, Algorithms and Parallelization Strategies" Fundamentn Informaticae 41 (2000) 187–228
8. Wang, D., Labit, C., and Ronsin, J. "Segmentation-based motion-compensated video coding using morphological filters" IEEE Transactions on Circuits and Systems for Video Technology, 7(3):549–555.
9. Milan Sonka, Vaclav Hlavac and Roger Royle. "Image Processing, Analysis, and Machine Vision" Second Edition, PWS Publishing at Brooks/Cole Publishing Company (1998), page 58–122.
10. Ralph Highnam, Michael Brady: "Model-Based Image Enhancement of Far Infrared Images." IEEE Transactions on Pattern Analysis and Machine Intelligence (1997) 19(4): 410–415.
11. Lars Pedersen "Analysis of Two-dimensional Electrophoresis Gel Images" Information and Mathematical Modeling, Revision 1.36 Exp, February 12, 2002.

Multi-resolution Modeling in Collaborative Design

JungHyun Han[1], Taeseong Kim[1], Christopher D. Cera[2], and William C. Regli[2]

[1] Computer Graphics Laboratory, School of Information and Communications Engineering, Sung Kyun Kwan University, Suwon, 440-746, Korea
`http://graphics.skku.ac.kr`

[2] Geometric and Intelligent Computing Laboratory, Department of Computer Science, Drexel University, Philadelphia, PA 19104, USA
`http://gicl.mcs.drexel.edu`

Abstract. This paper provides a framework for information assurance within collaborative design, based on a technique we call role-based viewing. Such role-based viewing is achieved through integration of multi-resolution geometry and security models. 3D models are geometrically partitioned, and the partitioning is used to create multi-resolution mesh hierarchies. Extracting an appropriately simplified model suitable for access rights for individual designers within a collaborative design environment is driven by an elaborate access control mechanism.

1 Introduction

In collaborative design, *access control* is mission-critical. Suppose a team of designers working collaboratively on a 3D assembly model. In collaboration, designers must interface with others' components, but do so in a way that provides each designer with only the level of information he or she is permitted to have about each of the components.

In the authors' recent work [1], integration of *multi-resolution geometry* and *access control models* has been proposed. Its conceptual architecture can be stated as follows:

- An assembly model consists of a set of component parts, grouped into sub-assemblies.
- Each component part is represented as a NURBS-based boundary model.
- Design is performed collaboratively by a group of designers. A standard client-server architecture is assumed, where the *collaborative CAD server* maintains and synchronizes the master design model.
- The collaborative CAD server tessellates the master model into polygon meshes. Multi-resolution mesh hierarchies are constructed.
- Depending on the accessibility privilege of a designer, an appropriately simplified model is extracted from the multi-resolution hierarchies, and provided to the designer at the collaborative CAD client.
- When a component part or sub-assembly gets modified, the server reconstructs only the corresponding (changed) portion of the hierarchy, and then passes these updates to the other clients according to their accessibility privileges.

This paper proposes a new elaborate scheme for multi-resolution hierarchies and access control mechanism, which has demonstrated a better performance than the previous work of the authors [1].

A. Yazici and C. Şener (Eds.): ISCIS 2003, LNCS 2869, pp. 397–404, 2003.

2 Related Work

Out of the vast body of work on concurrent engineering and collaborative design, some of existing work most relevant to our efforts deals with real-time 3D collaboration and communication, including Distributed Virtual Environments (DVEs) [2,4,5,9,12], immersive environments such as CAVE [3], etc. These systems support real-time interaction, but do not necessarily support collaborative CAD.

In CAD and collaborative design contexts, few research results on access control have been reported. A most relevant work in the domain of collaborative assembly design can be found in Shyamsundar and Gadh [15]. Their work could be taken as a simple implementation of information-hiding techniques, but lacks an elaborate access control mechanism. Further, they do not provide fine-grained levels of detail.

Polygon mesh simplification has been adopted for generating *multi-resolution* models or various *levels of detail* (*LOD*). Rossignac and Borrel [8] proposed *vertex clustering* approach to mesh simplification, where the initial cluster is recursively divided into cells and vertices in a cell are replaced by a representative vertex. Luebke [11] extended the approach to *hierarchical dynamic simplification*(*HDS*) with *vertex tree*. Runtime algorithm computes an *active tree*, which corresponds to an appropriately simplified mesh. Recently, vertex clustering has been adapted to out-of-core simplifications by Lindstrom [10] and Garland [7]. Their algorithms used *quadric error metrics*, which was originally proposed by Garland [6], for generating a representative vertex of each cell.

3 Role-Based Viewing

3.1 Role-Based View

A *role-based view* is a tailored 3D model which is customized for a specific user based on the roles defining the user's access permissions on the model [1]. Consider the component shown in Figure 1-(a). Suppose that the designer of the part wants to hide the design details from other participating designers. Our solution to the problem is to present the component to others in some "lower" resolutions. Figure 1 shows three different resolutions or LODs. Figure 1-(a) is a full-resolution model, which the component's owner sees and may also be presented to, for example, project supervisors.

The holes of the component might be critical features which should be hidden from other designers. Then, all holes are removed from the original model, and the model in Figure 1-(b) is presented. Suppose that the component is to be presented to a supplier from another organization. Then, the model in Figure 1-(b) can be again simplified to generate the crude model in Figure 1-(c), which just presents the outline of the component. Those are examples of role-based views. Our system provides an appropriate resolution to each designer according to the designer's roles.

3.2 Role-Based Access Control Policies

Among various *access control policies* commonly found in contemporary systems [14], we adopt a *Role-based Access Control*(*RBAC*) [13]. In RBAC, system administrators

(a) (b) (c)

Fig. 1. Role-based View Examples (from [1]) : (a) Original model, (b) Genus-reduced model, (c) Simplified model

create *roles* according to the job functions in an organization, grant permissions (access authorizations) to the roles, and then assign users to the roles. The permissions associated with a role tend to change much less frequently than the users who fill the job function that role represents. Users can also be easily reassigned to different roles as needs change. These features have made RBAC attractive, and numerous software products such as Microsoft's Windows NT currently support it.

Roles, $R = \{r_0, r_1, \ldots, r_m\}$, are abstract objects that define both the specific users allowed to access resources and the extent to which the resources are accessed. The engineers (designers, process engineers, project supervisors, etc.) correspond to a set of *actors* $A = \{a_0, a_1, \ldots, a_n\}$, each of which will be assigned to a set of roles.

The entire assembly design is represented as a *solid model* M. Let $b(M)$ represent the boundary of M. We define a set of *security features*, $SF = \{f_0, f_1, \ldots, f_k\}$, where each f_i is a topologically connected point set on $b(M)$ and $\bigcup SF = b(M)$. CAD models are often hierarchically represented, and Figure 2-(a) shows the group and security feature hierarchy of a certain assembly design example.

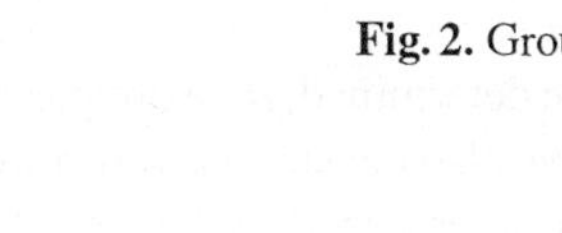

(a) Group Hierarchy

	g_0	g_1	g_2	f_0	f_1	f_2	f_3	f_4	f_5
r_0	w	$r(0.2)$	p	-	-	$r(0.5)$	-	-	$r(1.0)$
r_1	$r(0.2)$	w	p	-	-	$r(1.0)$	-	-	$r(0.5)$
r_2	p	p	w	$r(0.5)$	$r(0.5)$	-	$r(1.0)$	$r(1.0)$	-

(b) Access Matrix

Fig. 2. Group Hierarchy and Access Matrix Example

3.3 Access Matrix

In our security framework, RBAC is implemented as an *access matrix*. Figure 2-(b) is the access matrix for the group and security feature hierarchy of Figure 2-(a). In this matrix, there is a row for each role, and a column for each group and security feature. For simplicity, only three roles, r_0, r_1 and r_2, are created. Suppose that actors $designer_0$, $designer_1$, and $designer_2$ are assigned to roles r_0, r_1, and r_2 respectively.

Each cell of the access matrix is assigned *read* (with weight value in parenthesis), *write*, or *pass* (only for group) permissions. It is reasonable to assume that write permission of a feature is exclusively given to single role. In contrast, read permissions of a feature can be given to multiple roles. The pass permission of a group allows an actor to access its children, and the permissions associated with the children determine their readability/writability.

Let us discuss the read/write permissions of r_0. It has write permission to g_0. Then, write permissions to g_0's children, f_0 and f_3, are automatically set up. In contrast, the role r_0 has 20% Read permission to g_1. Then, r_0 cannot directly access g_1's children, f_1 and f_4, and a low resolution model of g_1 will be presented to r_0. Finally, r_0 has pass permission to g_2, and the permissions associated with f_2 and f_5 should be checked: r_0 has 50% Read permission to f_2, and full read permission to f_5.

Let us then discuss f_0. As explained above, write permission to f_0 is automatically given to r_0, and r_0 will edit NURBS model of f_0. (Of course, f_0 is 100% Readable to r_0.) The role r_1 does not have read permission to f_0, but has 20% Read permission to its parent g_0. Therefore, f_0 itself is not visible to r_1, but a low resolution version of combination of f_0 and f_3 will be presented to r_1. In contrast, r_2 has 50% Read permission to f_0, and will see an appropriately simplified version of f_0.

4 Role-Based View Generation

4.1 Multi-resolution Mesh Hierarchy

It is more storage-efficient to have a single dynamic/continuous hierarchy rather than multiple discrete LODs. A continuous hierarchy guarantees extremely fine granularity in the sense that a distinct LOD can be presented to each actor. Vertex-clustering-based octree structure, *vertex tree*, is a good choice for the continuous hierarchy.

In collaborative design, a security feature is assigned a *design space*, which limits the boundary the feature can reach. In 3D design, the design space is represented as an axis-aligned box. The box is used as the initial cluster of vertex-clustering. The cluster is recursively partitioned into 8 cells until each cell contains a single vertex. For each cell, a *representative* vertex is computed using *fundamental quadric* [7]. In this way, a vertex tree is constructed per a security feature. The leaf nodes provide the finest version of the security feature model, and internal nodes (with representative vertices) constitute simplified versions.

The quality of the coarsest mesh (of a vertex tree) can be determined, for example, by specifying the number of vertices of the coarsest version. We also construct a vertex tree per a group. For each child of the group (whether a sub-group or a security feature), the vertices of the coarsest mesh is collected. A collection of such vertices (from all children) constitutes the finest mesh of the group. The initial cluster of the group is the bounding box of its children's design spaces, and the vertex tree of the group is constructed with the same strategy used for building security features' vertex trees.

4.2 Role-Based Viewing within RBAC

The problem of how much of a security feature/group is made visible to a role is reduced to the task of what subtree of its vertex tree to select, or how to choose a set of *boundary nodes* [11] of the vertex tree.

Note that the minimum quadric error of the vertex tree, e_{min}, is found from the leaf nodes of the vertex tree. Similarly, the maximum error of the vertex tree, e_{max}, is found from the coarsest mesh's vertices of the vertex tree. $[e_{min}, e_{max}]$ is then normalized into [0,1]. Such a normalized error is depicted for each node in Figure 3. (The vertex tree is an octree, but depicted here as a binary tree just for easy illustration. For implementation purpose, the error values of all root nodes are made 1.0.)

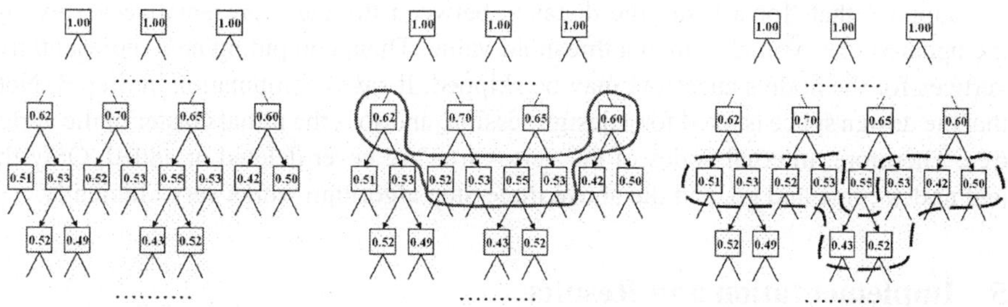

(a) Vertex Tree (b) Boundary Nodes with α=0.36 (c) Boundary Nodes with α=0.46

Fig. 3. Vertex Tree and Boundary Nodes Examples

As shown in Figure 2-(b), the read permission is associated with *weight* value. Let us call it α. We use α to extract an appropriately simplified mesh from the vertex tree. The vertex tree is traversed to select *boundary nodes* which bound a subset of nodes whose error values are greater than or equal to "1-α." The boundary nodes lead to a simplified mesh, and is transmitted to clients. Figure 3-(b) shows the boundary nodes determined by α=0.36(1-α=0.64), and Figure 3-(c) by α=0.46(1-α=0.54). As 0.46 is larger than 0.36, a higher resolution should be presented for the case of α=0.46. Therefore the boundary nodes of α=0.46 lies lower than that of α=0.36.

If α=1.0, the leaf nodes are collected to provide the full resolution version. If α=0.0, the current implementation completely hides the feature, but we could present the coarsest mesh of the security feature or replace the feature with its convex hull or bounding box. It is implementation dependent.

4.3 Design Change Support

We support adding, deleting, and editing NURBS patches. In vertex tree, we preserve links between vertices and NURBS patches, i.e. which patch a vertex is from. Using these links, design change is propagated as follows.

- Step 1: For each NURBS patch being removed or edited, all vertices from the patch are removed from the vertex tree. When a vertex is removed, its parent is marked "to be updated."
- Step 2: Each patch being added or edited is tessellated, and all new vertices from the patch are added to the vertex tree (always expanding the leaf nodes). When a new leaf node is added, its parent is marked "to be updated."
- Step 3: Selecting the nodes marked "to be updated," recursively update representative vertices in a bottom-up fashion.

Suppose that, for a node, the distance between the old representative vertex and the updated one is smaller than a threshold value. Then, computing new representative vertices for the node's ancestors may be skipped. It saves computation in Step 3. Note that the design space is fixed for a design session, and so is the initial cluster of the vertex tree. Therefore, internal nodes of the vertex tree are never deleted or added. Only the leaf nodes come and go, and the above three-step algorithm works very efficiently.

5 Implementation and Results

To test the approach proposed in this paper, a prototype system has been simultaneously developed using OpenGL on Solaris 2.7-2.8 and Windows, and using both Mesa and nVidia's native OpenGL drivers on Linux operating systems.

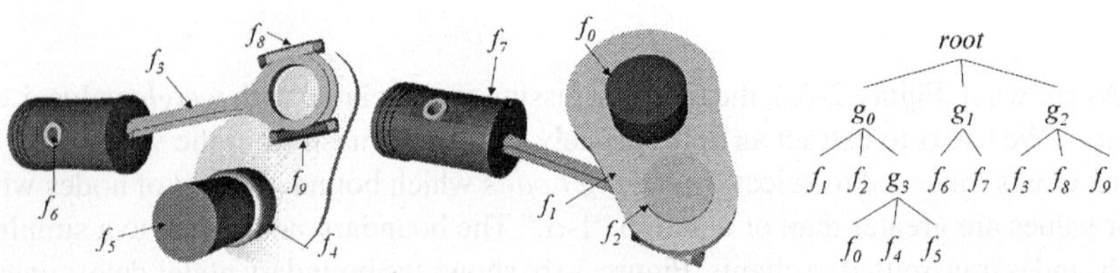

(a) Security Features (b) Group Hierarchy

Fig. 4. Security Features and Group Hierarchy on Piston Assembly

Figure 4-(a) shows a piston assembly model with 10 security features. (The model is illustrated from two viewpoints.) Figure 4-(b) shows its hierarchy. Figure 5 is the access matrix for the assembly.

The role r_0 is in charge of designing piston pin f_6 and piston body f_7, which are grouped under g_1. Write permission to g_1 is assigned to r_0, and therefore r_0 can edit both of f_6 and f_7. (Of course, r_0 sees the full resolution models of f_6 and f_7.) Observe that r_0 has pass permission to g_2 and therefore the permissions associated with its children should be checked. 100% Read permission is associated with the connecting rod f_3, but just 50% Read permission is with f_8 and f_9. As a result, the full resolution model of f_3 and simplified models of f_8 and f_9 will be presented to r_0. In contrast, r_0 has 10% Read permission to g_0 and therefore crude models of g_0 will be presented to r_0. The role-based view rendered for r_0 is illustrated in Figure 6-(a). The other role-based views for r_1 and r_2 are depicted in Figure 6-(b) and -(c) respectively.

	g_0	g_1	g_2	g_3	f_0	f_1	f_2	f_3	f_4	f_5	f_6	f_7	f_8	f_9
r_0	$r(0.1)$	w	p	-	-	-	-	$r(1.0)$	-	-	-	-	$r(0.5)$	$r(0.5)$
r_1	p	$r(0.0)$	$r(0.5)$	p	$r(1.0)$	$r(1.0)$	$r(0.5)$	-	w	$r(1.0)$	-	-	-	-
r_2	p	p	p	$r(0.5)$	-	$r(0.7)$	$r(1.0)$	w	-	-	$r(1.0)$	$r(0.7)$	$r(1.0)$	$r(1.0)$

Fig. 5. Access Matrix for the group hierarchy in Figure 4 : r_0 for Piston Designer, r_1 for Crank Shaft and r_2 for Connecting Rod

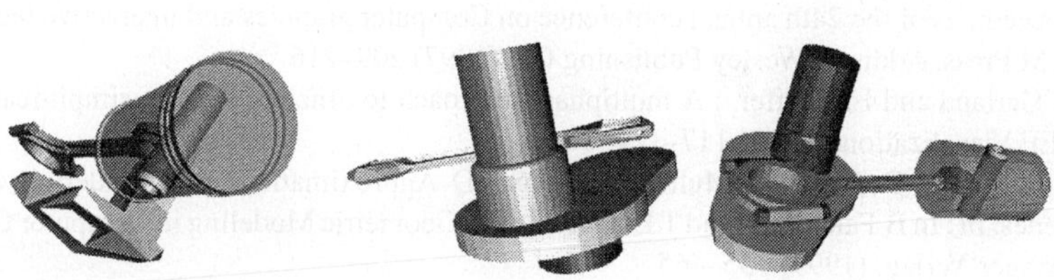

(a) View Generation for r_0

(b) View Generation for r_1

(c) View Generation for r_2

Fig. 6. Role-Based Viewing for Piston Assembly

6 Conclusions

This paper has presented a new technique, *role-based viewing*, for collaborative 3D assembly design. By incorporating security with collaborative design, the costs and risks incurred by multi-organizational collaboration can be reduced. Aside form digital 3D watermarking, research on how to provide security issues to distributed collaborative design is largely non-existent. The authors believe that this work is the first of its kind in the field of collaborative CAD and engineering.

Acknowledgements. This work was supported in part by the grant No. 1999-2-515-001-5 from the Basic Research Program of the Korea Science & Engineering Foundation. Additional support has been provided by US National Science Foundation (NSF) Knowledge and Distributed Intelligence in the Information Age (KDI) Initiative Grant CISE/IIS-9873005; CAREER Award CISE/IIS-9733545 and Office of Naval Research (ONR) Grant N00014-01-1-0618.

References

1. C. Cera, T. Kim, J. Han and W. Regli.: Role-based Viewing Envelopes for Information Protection in Collaborative Modeling. In : Journal of Computer-Aided Design Special Issue on Distributed CAD and Collaborative Design (to appear)
2. J. W. Barrus and R. C. Waters.: Supporting Large Multiuser Virtual Environments. In : IEEE Computer Graphics and Applications Vol. 16(6) (1996) 50–57
3. C. Cruz-Neira, D. J. Sandin, and T. A. DeFanti : Surround-screen projection-based virtual reality : the design and implementation of the cave. In : Proceedings of the 20th annual conference on Computer graphics and interactive techniques. ACM Press (1993) 135–142
4. J. M. S. Dias, R. Galli, A. C. Almeida, C. A. C. Bello, and J. M. Rebordao. : mWorld: A Multiuser 3D Virtual Environment. In : IEEE Computer Graphics and Applications, Vol 17(2). (1997) 55–65
5. H. Eriksson. : MBONE: The Multicast Backbone. In : Communications of the ACM, Vol. 37(8) Augest (1994) 54–60
6. M. Garland and P. S. Heckbert : Surface Simplification Using Quadric Error Metrics. In : Proceedings of the 24th annual conference on Computer graphics and interactive techniques. ACM Press. Addison-Wesley Publishing Co. (1997) 209–216
7. M. Garland and E. Shaffer. : A multiphase approach to efficient surface simplification. In : IEEE Visualization. (2002) 117–124
8. R. Jarek and P. Borrel. : Multi-Resolution 3D Approximations for Rendering Complex Scenes. In : In B.Falcidieno and T.L.Kunii, (eds). Geometric Modeling in Computer Graphics. Springer-Verlag. (1993) 455–465
9. S. Jayaram, U. Jayaram, Y. Wang, H. Tirumali, K. Lyons, and P. Hart. : VADE: a Virtual Assembly Design Environment. In : IEEE Computer Graphics and Applications, Vol. 19(6) (1999)
10. P. Lindstrom. : Out-of-core simplification of large polygonal models. In K. Akeley (eds), Siggraph 2000, Computer Graphics Proceedings.ACM Press / ACM SIGGRAPH / Addison Wesley Longman. (2000) 259–262
11. D. Luebke and C. Erikson. : newblock View-dependent simplification of arbitrary polygonal environments. Computer Graphics Vol. 31, Annual Conference Series (1997) 199–208
12. M. Macedonia, M. Zyda, D. Pratt, P. Barham, and S. Zeswitz. : NPSNET: A Network Software Architecture for Large-Scale Virtual Environments. In : Presence, Vol. 3(4) (1994) 265–287
13. R. S. Sandhu, E. J. Coyne, H. L. Feinstein, and C. E. Youman. : Role-Based Access Control Models. In : IEEE Computer, Vol 29(2) (1996) 38–47
14. R. S. Sandhu and P. Samarati. : Access Control: Principles and Practice. In : IEEE Communications Vol. 32(9). (1994) 40–48
15. N. Shyamsundar and R. Gadh. : Internet-based Collaborative Product Design with Assembly Features and Virtual Design Spaces. In : CAD, Vol. 33. (2001) 637–651

Model-Based Human Motion Capture from Monocular Video Sequences

Jihun Park[1], Sangho Park[2], and J.K. Aggarwal[2]

[1] Department of Computer Engineering
Hongik University
Seoul, Korea
jhpark@hongik.ac.kr

[2] Department of Electrical and Computer Engineering
The University of Texas at Austin
Austin, TX 78712
{sh.park,aggarwaljk}@mail.utexas.edu

Abstract. Generating motion and capturing motion of an articulated body for computer animation is an expensive and time-consuming task. Conventionally, animators manually generate intermediate frames between key frames, but this task is very labor-intensive. This paper presents a model-based singularity-free automatic-initialization approach to capturing human motion from widely-available, static background monocular video sequences. A 3D human body model is built and projected on a 2D projection plane to find the best fit with the foreground image silhouette. We convert the human motion capture problem into two types of parameter optimization problems: static optimization and dynamic optimization. First, we determine each model body configuration using static optimizations for every input image. Then, to obtain better description of motion, the results from all static optimizations are fed into a dynamic optimization process where the entire sequence of motion is considered for the user-specified motion. The user-specified motion is defined by the user and the final form of the motion they want. A cost function for static optimization is used to estimate the degree of overlapping between the foreground input image silhouette and a projected 3D model body silhouette. The overlapping is computed using computational geometry by converting a set of pixels from the image domain to a polygon in the real projection plane domain. A cost function for dynamic optimization is the user-specified motion based on the static optimization results as well as image fitting. Our method is used to capture various human motions: walking, pushing, kicking, and handshaking.

1 Introduction and Previous Work

Generating articulated body motion for computer animation is time consuming and computationally expensive. Because an articulated body has many degree of freedom (DOF), its computation is nonlinear, which makes motion generation

A. Yazici and C. Şener (Eds.): ISCIS 2003, LNCS 2869, pp. 405–412, 2003.

difficult. Probably the simplest form of computer-based animation is *key frame animation*, in which the animator denotes the key positions of the body at both the initial and goal configurations. The animation system then smoothly interpolates the intermediate positions between these key positions. In this paper, we present a cost-effective method of motion capture for computer animation using widely-available monocular video sequences with a static background.

Tracking non-rigid objects such as moving humans presents problems, including segmentation of the human body into meaningful body parts, handling occlusion, and tracking the body parts over the image sequence as well as automatic tracking of the first image frame. Approaches for tracking a human body can be classified into two groups: model-based approaches and view-based approaches[1,2]. (Park et al.[3] combined view-based and model-based techniques by processing color video at both pixel and object level.) We present here a model-based singularity-free automatic-initialization approach to capturing human motion that uses computational geometry for model fitting computation. One of the unique contributions of this paper is the ability to automatically track the initial frame[4].

We define animation to be *motion* with *motion control.* This motion can be either computed via *simulation*[5,6] or captured using a motion capture device. We require *motion control* to satisfy kinematic goals/constraints; usually for animation this involves meeting the configuration goals of a body while satisfying constraints. If we want to do *animation*, we must be able to do *motion control.* Basically we need a tool that will consider the entire motion (from the beginning of a motion until the end) to help us to find the *best* motion that suits our animation purpose. In order to do this, we convert our animation problem into a single nonlinear cost function of *(control) variables* with nonlinear equality and inequality constraints. By finding the best values of these variables, we can find the best motion for the animation. The technique of finding local optimum values for a nonlinear cost function with nonlinear equality and inequality constraints is called *parameter optimization.* Our proposed method processes motion capture twice. At the first level, we get the proper model body configuration for an input image. There is no time concept involved in this process, which is called *static optimization.* The body configuration must be interpolated to get motion for computer animation. But the motion we get from image motion capture is not a suitable character motion that satisfies user (animator) motion specifications. For this purpose, we need to modify the input data such that the resulting motion satisfies the user-specified motion. This second-level process considers the entire motion in animation, and is called *dynamic optimization.* Witkin and Kass[5] and Park and Fussell[6] both take user input of initial motion guessing and find the user-specified motion, but use inverse dynamics or forward dynamics, respectively, to improve the quality of the animated motion. The dynamic optimization approach presented here is quite similar; however our approach takes initial motion input using static optimization, and the quality of the entire motion is supported by the image fitting, whereas the others[5,6] are based on simulation. In order to find the motion that satisfies the user-specific constraint, the degree of image fitting is sacrificed.

All kinematics-based motion tracking methods may be classified into two groups depending the use of inverse kinematics. If no inverse kinematics is used, we call that approach a "forward kinematics-based approach"; otherwise we call it an "inverse kinematics-based approach". Our work is forward kinematics-based, while the paper [7] is inverse kinematics-based. Singularity is inevitable for methods with differential inverse kinematics.

2 Human Body Modeling and Overview of Our System

As shown in figure 1(a), the body is modeled as a configuration of nine cylinders and one sphere. These are projected onto a 2D real projection plane. A sphere represents the head, while the rest of the model body is modeled using cylinders of various radii and lengths. Currently, we use only nine 1-DOF (1 degree-of-freedom) joints plus body displacement DOF, and a vertical rotation to compensate for the camera view. These are our control variables for the cost function. Figure 1(b) shows the initial state of searching for the best overlapping configuration, given the first frame image of video sequence of figure 4. As can be seen in figure 1(b), initial joint angle values of the model body for parameter

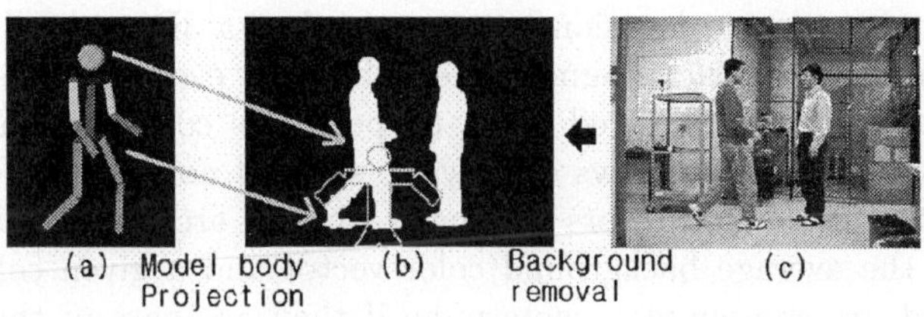

Fig. 1. 3D Model body (a), overlapping between background removed image and projected body (b), and original input image(c).

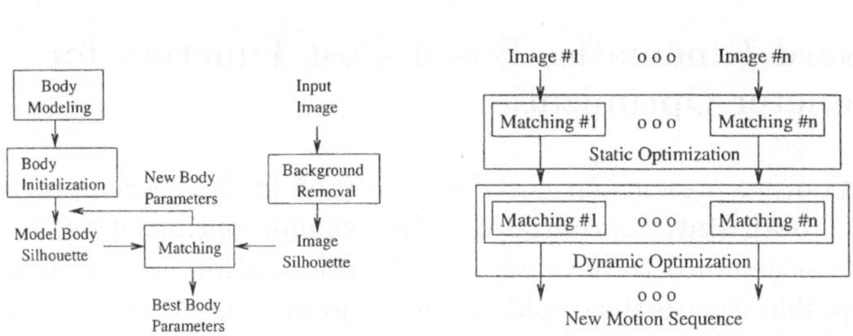

(a) Computation of a single image fitting. (single static optimization.)

(b) Computation considering all image fittings. (dynamic optimization)

Fig. 2. (a) Process of determining the best fitting model body configuration given an image, (b) finding the best motion considering all image fittings.

optimization are arbitrary. This shows that our initial model body configuration detection for the first image frame is automatic, which is a great improvement over other methods[4].

Figure 2(a) shows a fitting (matching) process (i.e. computing the overlapping between the foreground input image and projected model body silhouette) given an input image. A 3D model body is built. Model body joint angles and displacements are determined, and the body is projected on a 2D projection plane. On the 2D projection plane, we get a model body silhouette. The boxes in figure 2 represent computational processes. The *fitting* process uses parameter optimization [8], which modifies the model body parameters and checks the resulting level of fitting between the image silhouette and the model body silhouette. When the best fitting model body configuration is found for a single image, then the process is done for that image; thus for n input images, we run the fitting computation n times. Figure 2(b) shows the sequence of fitting process tasks. When the fitting computation is completed, we have a model body configuration for each image. Then we have a complete motion sequence for the input images. Static optimization determines the best body configuration for a single input image, while dynamic optimization finds the best motion for a sequence of input images.

3 Background Subtraction

A pixel color at an image location is represented as a 3D vector $(R, G, B)^T$ in the RGB color space. A background model is built for every pixel using 30 background images that are captured when no person is contained in the camera view. In order to handle shadows effectively, we used normalized RGB models. Average background color vectors for image location are computed. Vector angles between the average background color vector and a given color vector to be determined are computed to determine if they are part of the foreground or background. A foreground image is obtained by thresholding and applying morphological filters to remove small regions of noise pixels.

4 Forward Kinematics-Based Cost Function for Parameter Optimization

In this section, we present our cost function used in the overlapping area computation for both static optimization and dynamic optimization. A projected model body is assumed to have an affine transformation[7]. This is mathematically acceptable if an orthographic camera model is used and the model body moves parallel to the projection plane. Given a set of joint angles and body displacement values, the forward kinematics function computes points of body segment boundaries. The projection matrix then projects the computed boundary points on a 2D projection plane, which will be compared to a foreground image silhouette. The overlapping area computation in the real number domain makes the derivative-based parameter optimization possible. Refer to the authors' papers [3,9] for more detailed explanation. The differences are that we do not use body part information as well as distance maps. Because the input is a vector of joint DOF values, this computation is purely forward kinematics-based and thus presents no singularity problem[3,9].

We compute the image overlapping area using a computational geometry-based method on each pixel. An image silhouette is one that is converted from the 2D integer pixel domain to a real domain such that the resulting image silhouette becomes a jagged-edge polygon with only horizontal and vertical edges. Projected objects are either polygon-shaped or circular. The resulting polygon(s) may even have holes. We compute the polygon intersection between the image silhouette and the model silhouette. Our computation is a modified version of Weiler-Atherton's polygon intersection/union computation [10]. We found the best overlapping configuration using the GRG2 [8] optimization package with the cost function discussed above.

5 Parameter Optimization

A parameter optimization problem is of the following form: minimize a nonlinear cost function $c(\bar{z})$ subject to $g_i(\cdot) = 0, 1 \leq i \leq l, q_j(\cdot) \leq 0, 1 \leq j \leq m$ where l is the number of equality constraints, m is the number of inequality constraints, and $g(\cdot)$ and $q(\cdot)$ are nonlinear constraint functions, where $\cdot$ is a generic variable(s), The parameter optimization problem solver we used is GRG2[8]. Nonlinear functions usually have many local optima as well as ridges.

5.1 Static Optimization

Given an image, we preprocess to get a foreground image silhouette. Then, to find the best model body configuration for the image silhouette, we solve parameter optimization. In solving the parameter optimization, we define a cost function that computes the degree of the overlapping between the foreground input silhouette and a projected 3D model body silhouette. We call this process static optimization. Figure 3(a) shows the processing flow of a static optimization for the *i-th* image. The input variable vector $\bar{z}_i$ consists of body DOF variables, body displacement as well as joint angles. Because we have n body DOF variables, we have n variables for static optimization. For m input images, we run the static optimization m times. We initialize $\bar{z}_i$ with poor (arbitrary) input values. Figure 1(b) shows the initial search state for the best overlapping configuration, given arbitrary input values. For every control variable, the static optimization perturbs each variable to compute derivatives of constraint functions and the cost function and then checks for the Kuhn-Tucker condition[8], which guarantees a local minimum while satisfying constraints.

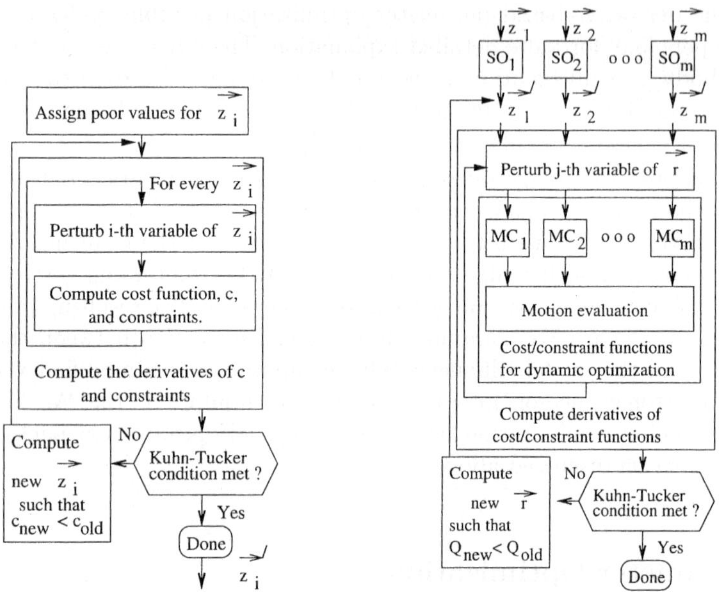

(a) Static optimization. (b) Dynamic optimization.

Fig. 3. Static and dynamic optimization.

5.2 Dynamic Optimization

To find a motion over an entire sequence of input video sequences, we need dynamic (global) optimization. We use the term *dynamic* to mean considering the entire image sequence. Figure 3(b) shows the process of dynamic optimization. SO_i is static optimization process for *i-th* image. Because we have m images, we run static optimization m times. Each static optimization has n variables. For m input images, we have total $n \times m$ variables for dynamic optimization. Static optimization results, $z_i^{'}$, for all image sequences become the initial guessing values for dynamic optimization. Figure 4 shows the subject with the model figure superimposed for a sequence containing a pushing motion. We used overlapping area computation as a cost function for static optimization, shown in figure 5(a-c). The example of a cost function of dynamic optimization presented in figure 5(d-f) includes non-violent motion evaluation as well as the degree of overlapping between image and model silhouettes. (By *violent motion* we mean motion with large absolute velocity/acceleration values.) MC_i is a process of computing the degree of overlapping between the model silhouette and the *i-th* image silhouette. The computation results we get from every MC_i are interpolated using C^2 continuous Natural Cubic Spline. Then, the motion evaluation process evaluates the model figure motion. The optimizer will find the best solution, $\vec{r}^{'}$, a collection of the model body configurations for all image silhouettes.

Fig. 4. The subject with the model figure superimposed, shown over a pushing motion.

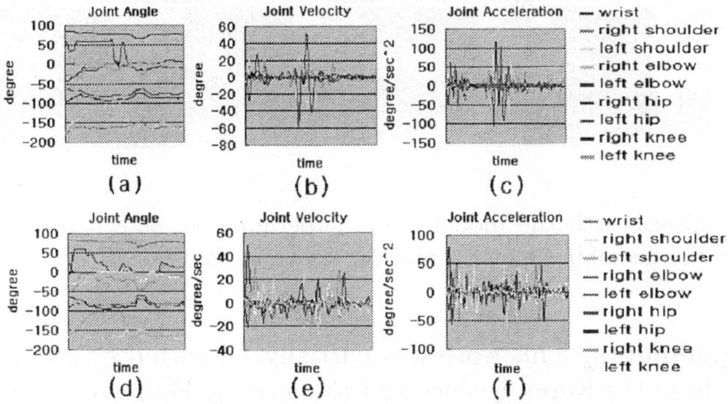

Fig. 5. Joint angles, velocities, and accelerations of the pushing motion. Results from static optimization(a,b,c), and results from dynamic optimization(d,e,f).

6 Experimental Results

The 2D-based human motions we have studieded include pushing, kicking, walking and handshaking. The example shown in figure 4 has a static background with one person (the left) pushing another (right) person away. The white line shows the result of union of every model body part. The holes in the resulting body (the polygon-like object) indicate our geometry union works well. As long as there is no heavy occlusion between the subjects, motion tracking is satisfactory. Using joint angular values from each frame, we perform motion interpolation using the Natural Cubic Spline. These velocity and acceleration values are based on the motion interpolation. Despite the presence of violent motion in the middle of the sequence, as can be seen in the graphs, the tracking is excellent. The violent motion of the left shoulder and left elbow joint can be observed from the velocity and acceleration graphs of Figure 5(b,c). Figure 5(d-f) shows the same motion solved using dynamic optimization. The results of static optimization are used as the input values for dynamic optimization. The part of the cost function is to reduce any violent velocity and acceleration in the static optimization-based motion. As you can see, the violent motion is quite reduced. Figure 6 shows walking (departing), shaking hands, and kicking motions, respectively.

Fig. 6. The subject with the model figure superimposed, shown over (a) a walking motion, (b) a hand-shaking motion, and (c) a kicking motion.

Acknowledgements. This work was partially supported by grant No. 2000-2-30400-011-1 from the Korea Science and Engineering Foundation. We thank Ms. Debi Prather.

References

1. Aggarwal, J., Cai, Q.: Human motion analysis: a review. Computer Vision and Image Understanding **73** (1999) 295–304
2. Gavrila, D.: The visual analysis of human movement: a survey. Computer Vision and Image Understanding **73** (1999) 82–98
3. Park, J., Park, S., Aggarwal, J.K.: Human motion tracking by combining view-based and model-based methods for monocular video sequences. Lecture Notes in Computer Science (2003 International Conference on Computational Science and Its Applications) **2669** (2003)
4. Bregler, C., Malik, J.: Tracking people with twists and exponential maps. In: IEEE Conference on Computer Vision and Pattern Recognition, Santa Barbara, California (1998) 8–15
5. Witkin, A., Kass, M.: Spacetime constraints. Computer Graphics **22** (1988) 159–168
6. Park, J., Fussell, D.: Forward dynamics based realistic animation of rigid bodies. Computers and Graphics **21** (1997)
7. Huang, Y., Huang, T.S.: Model-based human body tracking. In: International Conference on Pattern Recognition. (2002)
8. Lasdon, L., Fox, R., Ratner, M.: Nonlinear Optimization using the Generalized Reduced Gradient Method. Department of Operations Research 325, Case Western Reserve University (1973)
9. Park, S., Park, J., Aggarwal, J.K.: Video retrieval of human interactions using model-based motion tracking and multi-layer finite state automata. Lecture Notes in Computer Science (2003 Intl. Conf. on Image and Video Retrieval) **2728** (2003)
10. Hill, F.: Computer Graphics. Macmillan (1990)

Robust Skin Color Segmentation Using a 2D Plane of RGB Color Space

Juneho Yi, Jiyoung Park, Jongsun Kim, and Jongmoo Choi

School of Information and Communication Engineering
Sungkyunkwan University
Suwon 440-746, Korea
{jhyi, jypark, jskim, jmchoi}@ece.skku.ac.kr

Abstract. This research features a new method for skin color segmentation using a 2D plane in the RGB color space. The RGB color values of the input color image do not need to be converted into HSI or YIQ color coordinates that have popularly been used for color segmentation. We have observed an important fact that skin colors in the RGB color space are approximately distributed in a linear fashion. Based on this fact, we have applied PCA (Principal Component Analysis) techniques to RGB values of skin colors from a set of training images. We detect skin regions by the lookup of skin color histogram computed based on a 2D color plane of which two axes correspond to two directions with smallest spread of skin colors.

The proposed 2D color plane for color histogram lookup has an advantage over HS or IQ color planes. By using this plane, the problem of color constancy is much relieved. A learned color histogram contains most skin colors detected in the input images and at the same time, the distribution of skin colors in the plane is invariant compared to those in the HS or IQ planes. We have evaluated the performance of the proposed method by comparing with the performance of color histogram lookup methods based on HS or IQ color plane. The experimental results show that the performance of our method is robust to illumination changes.

1 Introduction

Face and hand gesture recognition is critical to the realization of natural human-computer interfaces based on computer vision. In order to recognize a face or gesture, skin regions should be first detected in the input image. An efficient way of doing this is color segmentation and a practical method is to employ a 2D lookup table of skin colors based on a learned color histogram [1,2].

Color segmentation based on a RGB color space is known to be sensitive to illumination changes. In most cases, the RGB color space is converted to HSI [7-10] or YIQ [11] color spaces where the luminance and the chrominance components of a color are separated. Two dimensional subspaces such as the HS plane of HSI color space and the IQ plane of YIQ color space that correspond to the chrominance

A. Yazici and C. Şener (Eds.): ISCIS 2003, LNCS 2869, pp. 413–420, 2003.

component (I of HIS or Y of YIQ) have usually been used for building a color histogram because the luminance component is very sensitive to illumination changes.

One of the most desirable properties that a 2D color plane for color histogram must satisfy is as follows. The distribution of skin colors in a learned color histogram should not be much variant. At the same time, the learned color histogram should contain most skin colors detected in the input images. If a 2D color plane that is used for the color histogram provides this property, we rarely need to update the histogram. In the case of illumination changes, the distribution of skin colors in the HS or IQ planes is very variant. Figure 1 shows a color histogram of H (hue) and S (saturation) values of the same skin region under various lighting conditions due to illumination or hand pose changes. The distributions of H and S values of the same skin region are quite different. This makes the use of a color histogram without its update for skin color segmentation very hard [9, 12]. It is quite probable that HS or IQ values of many skin pixels in the input image do not belong to the skin color regions of the learned color histogram and that those pixels are classified as non-skin pixels. In most cases, color histograms based on the HS or IQ plane need to be updated in order to give performance robust to illumination changes.

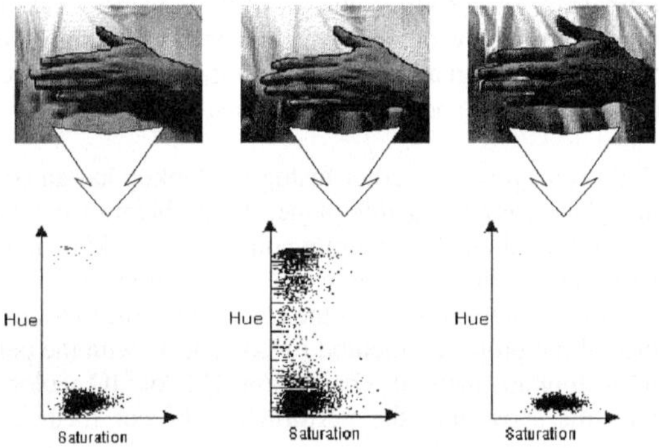

Fig. 1. Histograms of H and S values of the same skin region under various lighting conditions due to illumination or hand pose changes

We propose a 2D color plane of RGB color space that performs better than commonly used HS or IQ color planes for color segmentation. The idea is based on the fact that skin colors in the RGB color space are approximately distributed in a linear fashion [3-6]. We have observed ourselves this fact through experiments as can be seen in Fig 5. We have applied PCA techniques to RGB values of skin colors from a set of training images. We detect skin regions by the lookup of skin color histogram computed based on a 2D color plane of which two axes correspond to two directions with smallest spread of skin colors. In the color histogram based on the proposed 2D plane, the distribution of skin colors form a tight cluster in a small region and is relatively invariant in case of illumination changes. Thus, the problem of color constancy is less severe than when HS or IQ planes are used. This alleviates the need to update the color histogram. In addition, at the time of on-line detection, RGB pixel values do not need to be converted into another color coordinates such as HSI and YIQ, resulting in saving of computation time and space. We have evaluated the performance of the proposed plane by comparing with the performance of color histogram lookup methods based on HS or IQ color plane using images under varying illumination conditions. The Experimental results show that our method gives a good segmentation performance robust to illumination changes.

This paper is organized as follows. The following section briefly reviews related work. Section 3 presents the proposed method. Experimental results are reported in section 4.

2 Related Work

A practical method for skin color segmentation is to employ a lookup table (i. e. 2D color histogram) of skin colors [1,2] where the two axes of the lookup table correspond to the chrominance component of an appropriate 3D color space. Most commonly used color planes for building color histograms are the HS plane of HSI color space and the IQ plane of YIQ color space as displayed in Fig. 2.

Lookup table methods typically process the input image pixel by pixel for segmentation. In off-line, a two-dimensional lookup table of chrominance components is computed from training images by using an appropriate color space. In on-line, a pixel of the input image is simply classified as a skin pixel if it is one of the entries in the lookup table computed off-line.

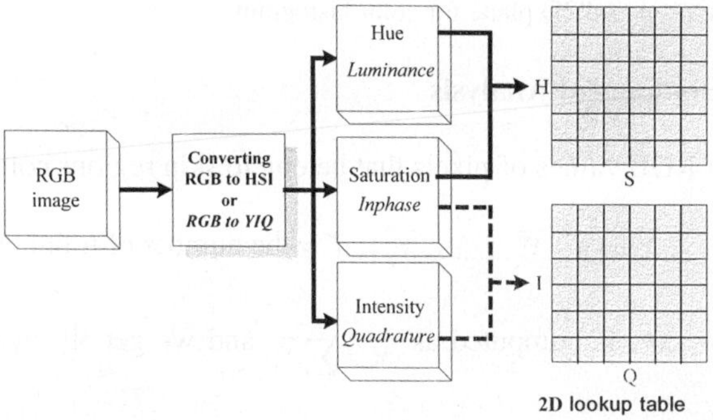

Fig. 2. 2D color planes, HS and IQ, for building a color lookup table (i. e. color histogram)

3 The Algorithm Overview

We have implemented a simple algorithm for skin color segmentation to evaluate the performance of the proposed 2D color plane for color histogram. The algorithm processes the input image pixel by pixel for segmentation. The algorithm is shown in Fig. 3.

In off-line, we apply PCA techniques to RGB values of skin colors from a set of training images and get a linear projection matrix. We build a 2D color histogram based on a plane of which two axes correspond to directions of smallest spread of RGB values of skin pixels. The vectors representing these two directions are the column vectors of a linear projection matrix. In on-line, a pixel of the input image is simply projected using the linear projection matrix computed off-line and simply classified as a skin pixel if it is one of the entries in the lookup table.

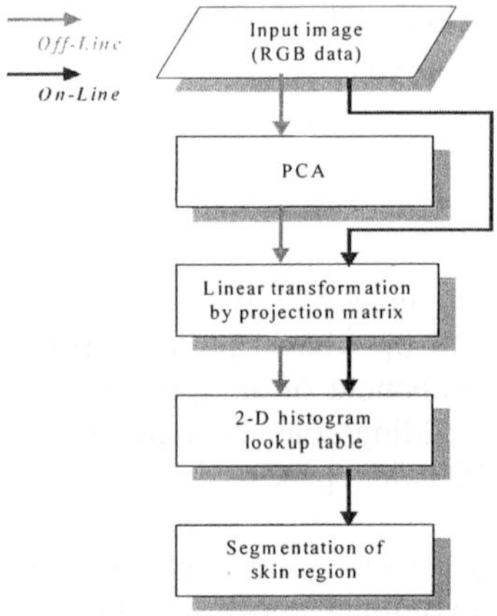

Fig. 3. A simple color histogram lookup algorithm for skin color segmentation to evaluate the performance of the proposed 2D plane for color histogram

3.1 Principal Component Analysis

Let X be a set of RGB values of pixels that belong to skin regions collected off-line.

$$X = [\overrightarrow{X_1}, \overrightarrow{X_2}, ...,\overrightarrow{X_T}],\ T = \text{the number of training images} \tag{1}$$

The mean vector, $\overrightarrow{M}$, is computed as $\overrightarrow{M} = \sum_{i=1}^{T} \overrightarrow{X_i}$ and we get Φ by subtracting $\overrightarrow{M}$ from $\overrightarrow{X_i}$'s:

$$\Phi = [\overrightarrow{\Phi_1}, \overrightarrow{\Phi_2}, ...,\overrightarrow{\Phi_T}] \tag{2}$$

where $\overrightarrow{\Phi_i} = \overrightarrow{X_i} - \overrightarrow{M}$. The covariance matrix, S_T, is computed as:

$$S_T = \sum_{i=1}^{T} \overrightarrow{\Phi_i}\overrightarrow{\Phi_i}^T = \Phi\Phi^T \tag{3}$$

The eigenvalues and eigenvectors of S_T are obtained using equation (4).

$$S_T \Psi = \Psi \Lambda \tag{4}$$

where $\Psi = [\vec{\psi}_1, \vec{\psi}_2, \vec{\psi}_3]$ and $\Lambda = [\lambda_1, \lambda_2, \lambda_3] (\lambda_1 \geq \lambda_2 \geq \lambda_3)$ represent the eigenvectors and eigenvalues, respectively.

Two eigenvectors, $\vec{\psi}_2$ and $\vec{\psi}_3$, that correspond to smallest eigenvalues, λ_2 and λ_3, represent two directions with smallest spread of $\vec{X}_i$'s (i. e. RGB values of skin pixels). A 2D lookup table (i. e. color histogram) is built by projecting all $\vec{X}_i$'s onto the 2D plane defined by the two axes, $\vec{\psi}_2$ and $\vec{\psi}_3$, as in equation (5). This lookup table is loaded for online detection of skin colors. W_{pca} is a linear projection matrix of which two column vectors are $\vec{\psi}_2$ and $\vec{\psi}_3$.

$$\vec{Y}_i = W_{pca}^T \vec{X}_i \tag{5}$$

4 Experimental Results

For the experiment, we have used facial images. Facial images are captured at three meters away in three different lighting directions under varying lighting intensity. Refer to Fig. 4. Images from frontal and side lighting were used for training and images from 45° lighting for test.

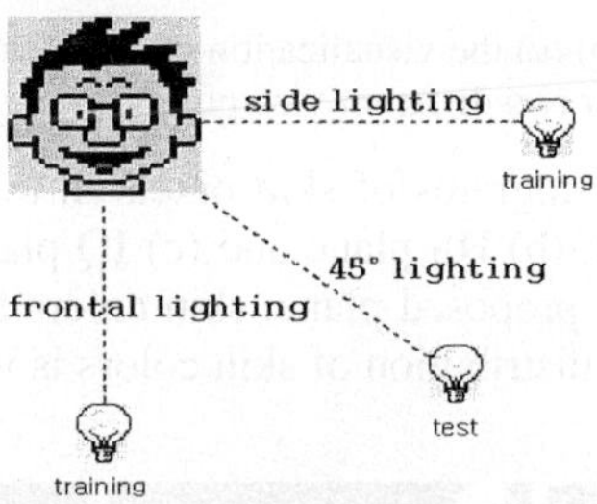

Fig. 4. Facial images are captured in three different lighting directions for the experiment.

Fig. 5 shows a set of example images used in the experiment. Three levels of lighting intensity were used: high, medium and low. Fig. 6 displays the distribution of RGB values of skin pixels in the RGB color space. We can see that the distribution is quite linear and that the first eigenvector from the PCA analysis will be in this direction of the greatest change of RGB values.

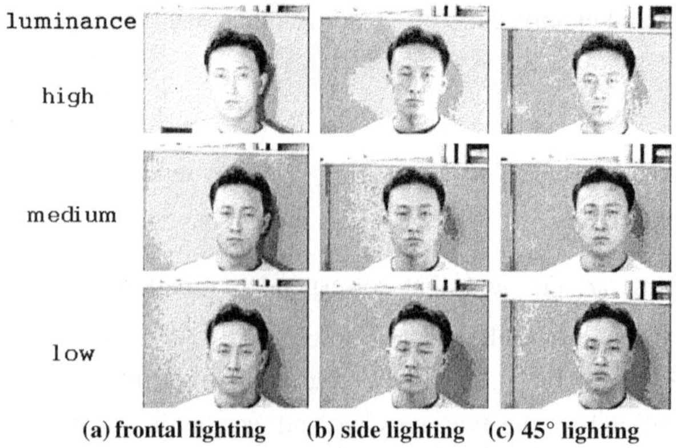

Fig. 5. Examples of images used in the experiment

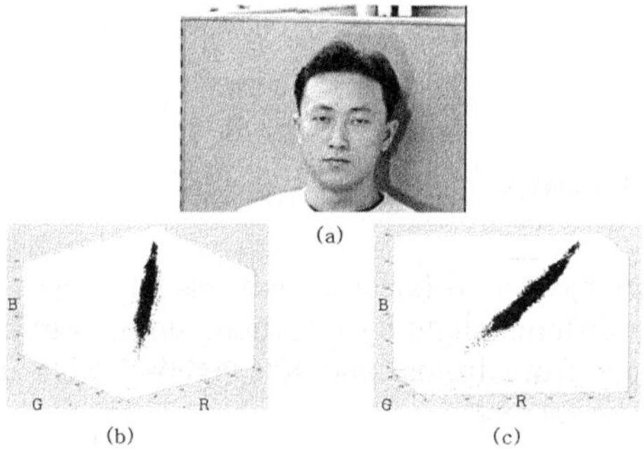

Fig. 6. (a) An example image, (b) (c) the visualization of the distribution of RGB values of skin pixels in the RGB color space for two different viewpoints

Fig. 7 visualizes the color histograms of skin pixels in the training images for three cases: (a) the proposed plane, (b) HS plane and (c) IQ plane. We can see that, in the color histogram based on the proposed plane, skin colors form a much tighter cluster than in HS or IQ planes. The distribution of skin colors is very wide and variant in the HS and IQ planes.

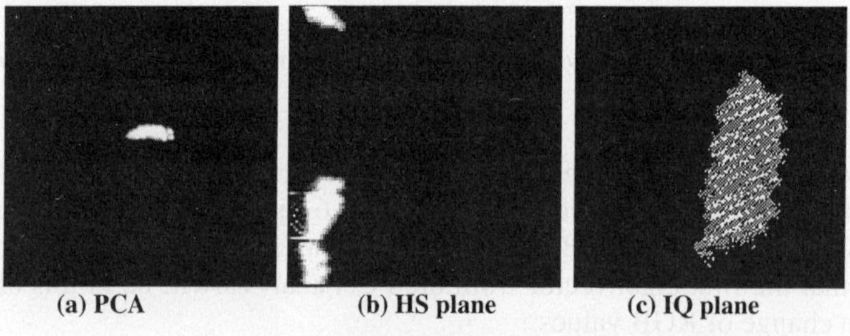

Fig. 7. The visualization of 2D color histograms for three cases: (a) using the proposed plane, (b) HS plane and (c) IQ plane. More frequent values are displayed brighter.

Fig. 8 shows a set of results for skin color segmentation in the cases of the three planes. As can be seen in Fig. 8 (b) and (c), when HS and IQ planes are used for color segmentation, many non-skin pixels are classified as skin pixels under illumination changes. This indicates that they were found in the entries of the color histogram computed offline. The main reason for the errors is because the initial distribution of HS and IQ values of skin pixels is not valid any longer as the illumination changes. In contrast, the segmentation result using the proposed plane experimentally shows that the color histogram based on the proposed plane does not vary as much as HS and IQ planes. Based on the experimental results, we claim that the proposed plane has much less problem of color constancy. These results indicate that color histograms based on the HS or IQ planes need to be updated from time to time while color histogram based on the proposed plane does not.

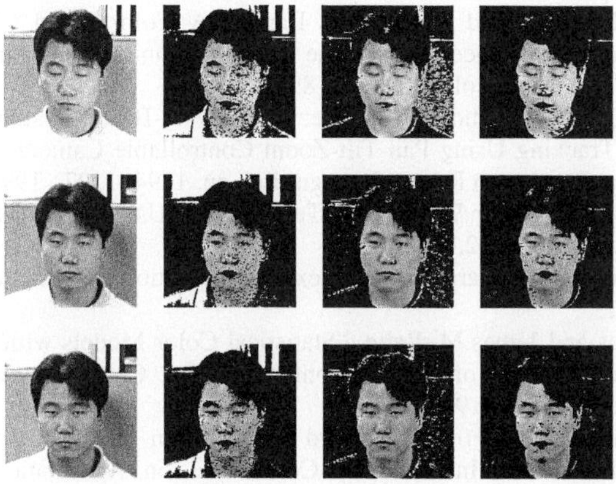

(a) (b) (c) (d)

Fig. 8. Segmentation results: (a) test images (b) for the HS plane (c) for the IQ plane , and (d) for the proposed plane

5 Conclusions

Based on the fact that skin colors in the RGB color space are approximately distributed in a linear fashion, we have proposed a novel but simple 2D plane in the RGB color space for skin color segmentation that employs color histogram lookup. The RGB color values of the input color image do not need to be converted into HSI or YIQ color coordinates that have popularly been used for color segmentation. The proposed 2D color plane is formed by the two axes of an RGB color space that correspond to two directions with smallest spread of RGB values of skin pixels. The experimental results show that the performance of skin color segmentation using the proposed plane is much more robust to illumination changes compared to those using HS or IQ planes.

Acknowledgements. This work was supported by grant number R01-1999-00339 from the Basic Research program of the Korean Science and Engineering Foundation.

References

1. R. Kjeldsen and J. Kender: Finding Skin in Color Images. International Conference on Automatic Face and Gesture Recognition, 1995.
2. F. Quek, T. Mysliwiec, and M. Zhao, FingerMouse: A Freehand Pointing Interface. Proceedings of IEEE International Conference on Automatic Face and Gesture Recognition, pp. 372–376, 1995.
3. Leonid Sigal, Stan Sclaroff, and Vassilis Athitsos: Estimation and Prediction of Evolving Color Distributions for Skin Segmentation Under Varying Illumination. Proceedings of IEEE Conference on omputer Society Conference on Computer Vision and Pattern Recognition, pp. 152–159, 2000.
4. Rogerio Schmidt Feris, Teofilo Emidio de Campos, and Roberto Marcondes Cesar Junior: Detection and Tracking of Facial Features in Video Sequences. Springer-Verlag press MICAI-2000, pp. 197–206, 1793.
5. Richard P. Schumeyer and Kenneth E. Barner: A Color-Based Classifier for Region Identification in Video. Proceedings of the Visual Communications and Image Processing to (VCIP 98) Conference, vol. 3309, pp. 189–200.
6. Gang Xu and Takeo Sugimoto: Rits Eye: A Software-Based System for Realtime Face Detection and Tracking Using Pan-Tilt-Zoom Controllable Camera. Proceedings of 14th International Conference on Pattern Recognition, pp. 1194–1197 , 1998.
7. Gary R. Bradski: Computer Vision Face Tracking For Use in a Perceptual User Interface. Intel Technology Journal Q2, 1998.
8. M. J. Swain and D. H. Ballard: Color Indexing. International Journal of Computer Vision, pp. 11–32, 1991.
9. Michael J. Jones and James M. Rehg, "Statistical Color Models with Application to Skin Detection", Proceedings of IEEE Conference on Computer Vision and Pattern Recognition, pp. 274–280, 1999.
10. David Saxe and Richard Foulds: Toward Robust Skin Identification in Video Images. Proceedings of the 2nd International Conference on Automatic Face and Gesture Recognition, pp. 379–384, 1996.
11. Jung Soh, Ho-Sub Yoon, Min Wang and Byung-Woo Min: Locating Hands in Complex Images Using Color Analysis. IEEE International Conference on Computational Cybernetics and Simulation, pp. 2142–2146, 1997.
12. M. Mottleb and A. Elgammal: Face Detection in Complex Environment from Color Images, International Conference on Pattern Recognition, pp 622–626, 1999.

Background Estimation Based People Detection and Tracking for Video Surveillance

Murat Ekinci and Eyüp Gedikli

Karadeniz Technical University
Department of Computer Engineering
Trabzon 61080, Turkiye,
ekinci@ktu.edu.tr

Abstract. This paper presents a real-time background estimation and maintenance based people tracking technique in an indoor and an outdoor environments for visual surveillance system. In order to detect foreground objects, first, background scene model is statistically learned using the redundancy of the pixel intensity values during learning stage, even the background is not completely stationary. A background maintenance model is also proposed for preventing some kind of falsies, such as, illumination changes, or physical changes. And then for people detection, candidate foreground regions are detected using thresholding, noise cleaning and their boundaries extracted using morphological filters. From these, a body posture is estimated depending on skeleton of the regions. Finally, the trajectory of the people in motion is implemented for analyzing the people actions tracked in the video sequences. Experimental results demonstrate robustness and real-time performance of the algorithm.

1 Introduction

Automated video surveillance has emerged as an important research topic in the computer vision community. The growth in this area is being driven by the increased availability of inexpensive computing power and image sensors, as well as the inefficiency of manual surveillance and monitoring systems [1] [2]. Applications such as event detection, human action recognition, and semantic indexing of video are being developed in order to partially or fully automate the task of surveillance. To be successful, such applications require real time motion detection and tracking algorithms, which provide low-level functionality upon which higher level recognition capabilities can be built.

Background subtraction techniques are mostly used for detection of motion in many real-time tracking applications [1][2] [7]. There has been a large amount of work addressing the background subtraction and adaptation [1][2][5][6] [7]. Often the assumption is made that an initial background model can be obtained by using a short training sequence in which no foreground objects are present. But, at some monitoring areas, such as public area or crowded corridors, this situation is difficult or impossible to control the are being monitored. In such cases there

A. Yazici and C. Şener (Eds.): ISCIS 2003, LNCS 2869, pp. 421–429, 2003.

may be needed to train the model using a sequence which contains foreground objects. An ideal background subtraction could produced good results while foreground regions in motions during training sequence. There is also needed to maintenance background model to adapt all possible changes in the monitoring area.

There are many works on background modeling. They mainly focused on model representation and techniques for adaptation on background modeling. The ability for representing multiple models to have the background values some techniques to model motion which is part of the background [6][10]. Unimodal representations, which store a single mean intensity value per pixel, are more prone to have false detections in the case of moving any background regions. Similar methods estimate background intensity values using temporal smoothing [7][9][10], and choose a single value from the set of past observations [11]. In [2] minimum and maximum intensity values , and maximum temporal derivative for each pixel are stored for initialization background model. The study in [12] proposed an edge-based background representation called the background primal sketch. However, no perfect system exists.

This paper presents a new fast background modeling and maintenance technique for real time visual surveillance system for tracking and implementing people activities in indoor and outdoor environments. The initial stage of the human motion analysis problem is the extraction of moving targets from a video sequence. There are three conventional approaches to moving target detection: temporal differencing (two-frame or three frame) [3][4], optical flow [5], and background estimation [1][2][6][7]. The use of background estimation is popular in real time tracking applications such as surveillance [7], and also in video coding community [8], which focuses on problems such as video compression and content-based functionality for multimedia.

2 Background Model Initialization

The initial background model is obtained even if there are moving foreground objects in the field of view, such as walking people, moving cars, etc. At the beginning of the background model initialization, the redundancy ratios of the intensity values for each pixel at the same position in the frames are calculated to several second of video (typically 10-30seconds) to distinguish moving pixels from stationary pixels, as shown in figure 1. In the training sequence, each values of the pixel at the same position on every frame are compared each other in an history map and then intensity variations of that pixel are stored into the cell string in the history map using following process, as shown in figure 1. In the history map, the first cell in the string (is shown with D) stores the number of different intensity values on the pixel in that sequence. At the following two cells, the first one (1a) stores intensity value, the other (1b) stores the number of the redundancy of the that intensity value during the training sequence. The following every two cells in the cell string are also used to store similar information for other possible intensity values on the pixel and their redundancy numbers.

The size of the history map is dynamic and depending on the number of possible different pixel intensity values at the same position on the frame in the training sequence.

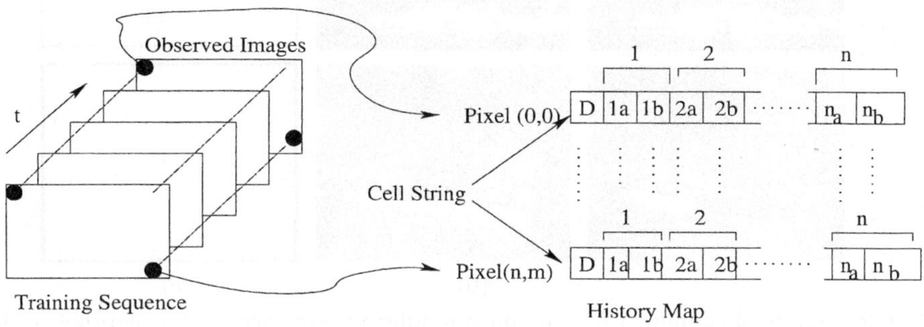

Fig. 1. To obtain initial background model. (Left) Training sequence, (Right) Estimation of the history map during training sequence for each pixel.

As a result, all of the data explained above are stored as becoming a link related to one another in an history map for each pixel. At the end of the learning stage, the biggest redundancy ratio (BRR) is estimated using the history map obtained above. The intensity value linked with the BRR estimated in the history map is assigned as the intensity value of the pixel in the background model. Those all processes are repeated for each pixel in the background model. The output of our algorithm for several example provided in different training sequences is shown in figure 2. At the top in figure 2.a, two people are traveling in a room, at the bottom a crowded traffic includes people and cars is being on the street in the university campus. The results of the BRR algorithm to produce the initial background model on the related scenario are shown in figure 2.b. In figure 2.c, the map of error pixels between ideal background and the estimated background model obtained by the BRR algorithm are shown.

The idea of the BRR algorithm developed is inspired from median filter but it is not same with that. The advantages of the BRR algorithm to the other algorithms depend on the median filter are; **1)** Use of the median relies on an assumption that the background at every pixel will be visible more than fifty percent of the time during the training sequence. But, in the algorithm presented, the assumption for the background visibility at the every pixel is becoming to the biggest redundancy ratio of the intensity values during the training sequence. This is more flexible and applicable for real events than median and also includes all advantages of the algorithms depending on median process. **2)** The requirement memory size for applying the BRR algorithm is more less than the others based on median. **3)** The realization processing time of the BRR algorithm is also rather less because there is no need the sorting of the intensity values taken during training and maintenance sequences after end of that sequences. As ex-

(a) (b) (c)

Fig. 2. Results of running algorithm on two different sequences: (a) a snapshot of the training sequence, (b)the computed background model, (c)map of error pixels (black).

plained three advantages two of which very important for real time maintenance of the background are successfully provided advantages of the BRR algorithm.

3 Maintenance Background Model

The difficult part of background subtraction is not the differencing itself, but the maintenance of a background model -some representation of the background and its associated statistics [6]. Background maintenance is called to this modeling process. Also, real-time background maintenance is important for real surveillance applications. Because, the monitoring area may not be stay the same for long periods of time. There could be illumination changes, such as the sun being blocked by clouds causing changes in brightness, or physical changes, such as a car that comes into the scene and parks should not be considered as a part of the scene background, however it stationary pixels should play the role of background for detecting motion of a person getting out or passing in front of the car.

In these cases, the notion in this study is to use an adaptive background model to accommodate changes to the background while maintaining the ability to detect independently moving targets. To have that background model (maintenance background), two approaches independent each other are performed. The first approach is a mechanism to adapt to slow changes in the environment using a statistical model of the background. This is performed using a temporal filtering. The filter is implemented:

$$\overline{K}_{n+1} = \alpha * K_{n+1} + (1 - \alpha)\overline{K}_n \tag{1}$$

Where K_n is value of each pixel in the n *th* frame, $\overline{K}_n$ is a running average, $\alpha = t * f$, t is a time constant which can be configured to refine the behavior of the system, and f is the frame rate.

The second approach uses a pixel-based update method updates the background model periodically (50-100 frames) using the BRR algorithm in order to adapt to illumination and physical changes in the background scene. A deposited/removed object, or a parked car would be added into the background scene if it does not move for along period of time. Implementation of the BRR algorithm is performed as explained previous section. In other words, the second approach is periodically re-initialization of the background model. This has produced robust results for maintenance background process.

4 Foreground Region Detection

The process of subtracting the current image from the background model is a simple and fast way to obtain foreground region while the background model is successfully upgraded. How the background upgrading process is performed is explained before. Foreground objects are segmented from the background in each frame of the video sequence by a four stage process: thresholding, noise cleaning, morphological filters, and object detection. Each pixel is the first classified as either a background or a foreground pixel using the background model.

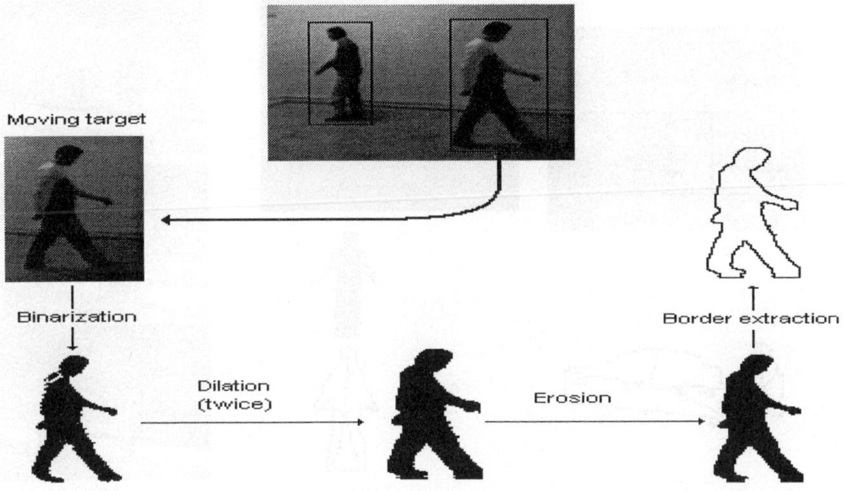

Fig. 3. Foreground region pre-processing. A moving foreground region is morphologically dilated (twice) then eroded. Then its border is extracted.

If a pixel has a value which is more than 2σ from $\overline{K}_n$, then it is considered a foreground pixel. In here, σ is standard deviation of each pixel, and $\overline{K}_n$ is explained in section 3. The standard deviation value for each pixel is temporally upgraded using ;

$$\overline{\sigma}_{n+1} = \alpha(K_{n+1} - \overline{K}_{n+1}) + (1-\alpha)\overline{\sigma}_n \quad (2)$$

where $\overline{\sigma}$ running average of the standard deviation for that pixel.

Thresholding alone is not sufficient to obtain clear foreground regions; it results in a significant level of noise. The algorithm in this study uses region-based noise cleaning to eliminate noise regions. As the final step of foreground region detection, a binary connected component analysis is applied to the foreground pixels to assign a unique label to each foreground object. And then the algorithm generates a set of shape and appearance features for each detected foreground object that are used to distinguish human from other objects.

The shape of a 2D binary silhouettes is represented by its projection histogram. The detection algorithm computes the 1D vertical and horizontal projection histograms of the silhouettes in each frame. Vertical and horizontal projection histograms are computed by projecting the binary foreground region on an axis perpendicular to the major axis and along the major axis, respectively. Using that projection histograms, the position of all foreground regions boundaries are detected as shown in figure 3 (Up-Center).

The first pre-processing step in the foreground region boundary is to clean up anomalies. This is implemented by a morphological filter (dilation followed by an erosion). That is the silhouette region is dilated twice followed by a single erosion. This removes any small holes in the silhouette and smoothies out any interlacing anomalies. And then the outline of the silhouette region is extracted using a border following algorithm as shown in figure 3.

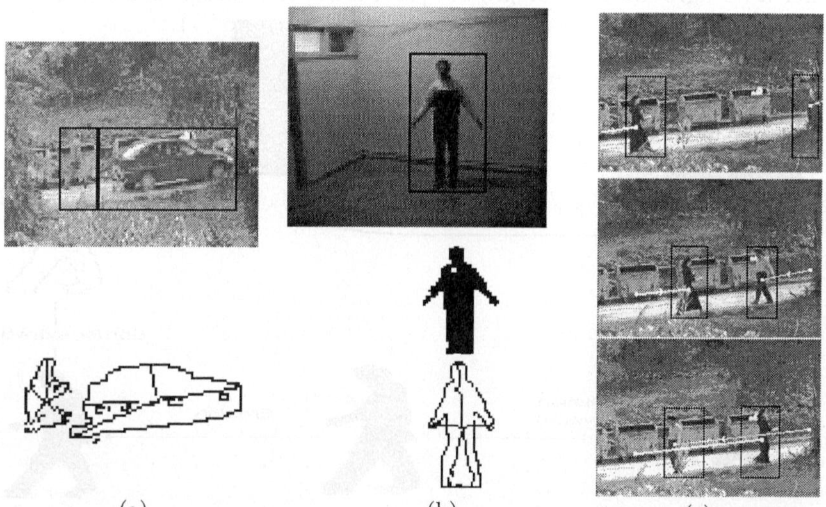

(a) (b) (c)

Fig. 4. a) The skeletonizations of people and a car foreground regions detected, **b)** Detected foreground object, binarizations region, and skeletonization of the object, **c)** Tracking of the foreground regions and obtained trajectory shown as white lines.

Next step is to decide whether the motion region detected is human being or not. The size of the box surrounding the around of the motion region detected before may be implemented to classify the motion regions. To get more robust classification of the motion region (shape) a skeleton process of the motion shape is used. An important cue in determining the internal motion of a moving region is the change in its boundary shape over time and a good way to quantify this is to use skeletanization. The method presented here uses a simple real-time, robust way of detecting extremal points on the boundary of the motion region to produce its skeleton. The steps of this skeleton process are following; the center of the gravity of the foreground region boundary is determined, then the distance from the center of the region to each border point are calculated. Finally local maximal of the filtered signal which is obtained using a low pass filter into 1D distance signals above are detected, and this local maximal of that signal are taken as extremal points, then the skeleton of the motion region is constructed by connecting them to the motion region centroid. Therefore, local maximal of the distances are determined and using human model criteria are decided whether the object detected is human or not as shown in figure 4.a. (human and a car). It is clear that the structure and rigidity of the skeleton are important cue in analyzing different type of motion regions. It also these informations can be used to understand human activities in the scene [1]. Using the skeleonization approach, no such models are required, so the method can be applied to other objects like vehicles and animals (see figure 4.a-b)

5 Tracking and Analysis of the Human Motion

The algorithm developed for tracking of human motion is based on foreground region detection while the CCD camera produced sequences is static. Some experimental results of the foreground regions detections on different sequences are shown in figure 4.b. At the tracking process, the center of the detected foreground region in the sequences is stored in a trajectory map. This is shown in figure 4.c as white points. The stored data in the trajectory map is used to implement each foreground region motions in the scene.

When any foreground object in tracking is hidden to any non-motion area (like passing at the behind of parked car), or temporarily occluded by other foreground object as they pass, the detected data of that object may not be obtained at the low level processing. At that or similar situations, high level implementation procedure is activated to estimate the possible position of that object using the previous tracked data obtained from trajectory. At the following frames, if the low level data about it is not obtained, its confidence is reduced. If the confidence of that object drops below a given threshold, it is considered lost, and is dropped from the tracking list stored in the trajectory map. High confidence objects (ones that have been tracked for a reasonable period of time) will persist for several frames, so if an object is momentarily occluded but then reappears, the foreground object tracker will reacquire it. A sample trajectories resulting from this approach are shown in figure 4.c.

6 Conclusions

This paper has described real-time background scene modeling and maintenance techniques for real visual surveillance system for tracking people in an indoor and outdoor environments. It operates on monocular gray-scale video imagery from a CCD camera. The system learns and models background scene statistically to detect foreground objects, even when the background is not completely stationary (*e.g.* motion of people and/or tree branches) and distinguishes people from other objects (*e.g.* cars) using skeleton based shape and motion cues. The background model presented was updated periodically to eliminate non-motion regions while at the beginning in motion, such as, a vehicle traveling in the scene and then parked. The background model was also upgraded every frame using temporal filtering to adapt small changes in the scene such as illumination changes (the sun being blocked by clouds causing changes in brightness). To classification object detected in motion, a skeleton process was developed in real time applications.

The algorithm has been implemented in C++ and runs under Windows 98 operating systems without using any special hardware. Currently, for 192x149 resolution gray scale images sequences, the algorithm code without optimizing runs at 8-17 fps, on a PC which has 400 MHz Celeron processors depending on the number of people in its field of view. Tests were performed on several sequences (each at least 30 minutes or more) representative of situations which might be commonly encountered in surveillance video.

Acknowledgment. This research work is supported by Karadeniz Technical University Research Foundation grant to (KTU-2002.112.009.1).

References

1. R.T. Collins, A. J. Lipton, H. Fujiyoshi, T. Kanade.: Algorithms for Cooperative Multi sensor Surveillance. Proc. of IEEE Vol. 89. No.10, (2001).
2. I. Haritaoglu, D. Harwood, L.S. Davis.: W4: Real-Time Surveillance of People and Their Activities. IEEE Trans. on PAMI, Vol. 22, No.8, (2000).
3. P.L. Rosin, T. Ellis.: Image Difference Threshold Strategies and Shadow Detection. in Proceeding. British Machine Vision Conference, (1995).
4. M. Ekinci, V. V. Nabiyev.: Vehicle Classifications and Tracking in Traffic Video sequences, SIU2001 9th Signal Proc. and its App., Istanbul, (2001) *(in Turkish)*.
5. D. Gutshess, *et. al.*: A Background Model Initialization Algorithm for Video Surveillance. IEEE Int. Conf. on Computer Vision, (2001).
6. K. Toyama, J. Krumn, B. Brumit, B. Meyers.: Wallflower: Principles and Practice of Background Maintenance. 7th IEEE Inter. Conf. on Computer Vision, Nov., (1999).
7. W. Grimson, *at. al.* .: Using Adaptive Tracking to Classify and Monitor Activities in a Site. in Proc. of IEEE Conf. on Computer Vision and Recognition, (1998).
8. J. Vass, K. Palaniappan, X. Ahuang.: Automatic Spatio-Temporal Video Sequence Segmentation, in Proceeding IEEE Inter. Conf. on Image Processing, (1998).

9. C . Wren, *et. al.* .: Pfinder: Real-Time Tracking of the Human Body. IEEE Trans. on Pattern Analysis and Machine Vision Intelligence, July (1997), Vol. 19, no. 7.
10. A. Elgammal, D. Harwood, and L. Davis.: Non-parametric model for background subtraction. in Proc. 6th Eur. Conf. on Computer Vision, Dublin, Ireland, (2000).
11. W. Long and Y. H. Yang.: Stationary Background Generation : An alternative to the Difference of Two Images. Pattern Recognition, vol. 23, no. 12, (1990).
12. Y. H. Yang and M. D. Levine.: The Background Primal Sketch: An Approach for tracking moving objects. Machine Vision and Applications, vol.5, (1992).

Quaternion-Based Tracking of Multiple Objects in Synchronized Videos*

Quming Zhou[1], Jihun Park[2], and J.K. Aggarwal[1]

[1] Department of Electrical and Computer Engineering
The University of Texas at Austin
Austin, TX 78712
zhou@ece.utexas.edu, aggarwaljk@mail.utexas.edu

[2] Department of Computer Engineering
Hongik University
Seoul, Korea
jhpark@hongik.ac.kr

Abstract. This paper presents a method for tracking multiple objects using multiple cameras that integrates spatial position, shape and color information to track object blobs. Given three known points on the ground, camera calibration is computed by solving a set of quaternion-based nonlinear functions rather than solving approximated linear functions. By using a quaternion-based method, we can avoid the singularity problem. Our method focuses on establishing correspondence between objects and templates as the objects come into view. We fuse the data from individual cameras using an Extended Kalman Filter (EKF) to resolve object occlusion. Results based on calibration via Tsai's method as well as our method are presented. Our results show that integrating simple features makes the tracking effective, and that EKF improves the tracking accuracy when long term or temporary occlusion occurs.

1 Introduction and Previous Work

The efficient tracking of multiple objects is a challenging and important task in computer vision, with applications in surveillance, video communication and human-computer interaction. Many factors such as lighting, weather, unexpected intruders or occlusion may affect the efficiency of tracking in an outdoor environment. One solution is to use multiple cameras [1–3].

In our previous paper [4], we presented a single camera module for tracking moving objects in an outdoor environment and classifying them into three categories: single person, people group or vehicle. Our method integrates motion, spatial position, shape and color information to track object blobs. Although we were encouraged by the results of our single camera tracker, several unresolved problems remain, mainly due to object occlusion.

---

* This work was partially supported by grant No. 2000-2-30400-011-1 from the Korea Science and Engineering Foundation. We thank Ms. Debi Prather for proofreading.

A. Yazici and C. Şener (Eds.): ISCIS 2003, LNCS 2869, pp. 430–438, 2003.

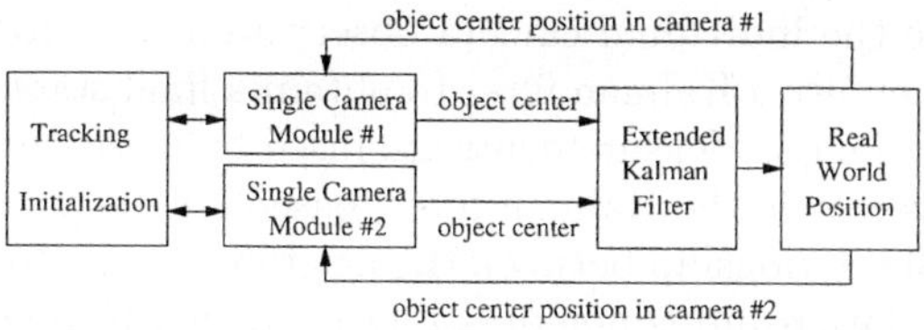

Fig. 1. Architecture of the proposed system using multiple cameras.

In this paper, we address the issue of 3D object trajectory [5]. The contributions of our paper are (1) data fusion from two cameras' observations using a simple Kalman filter(an approach that has not been explored in computer vision) and (2) a three point based camera calibration method that is developed and compared to Tsai's calibration method. Our tracking objective is to establish a correspondence between the image structures of consecutive frames over time to form persistent object trajectories. We focus on developing a methodology for tracking multiple objects in the view of two different fixed cameras, whose transformation matrix and focal length are estimated from coplanar control points. Real-world coordinates are used for multiple camera tracking. (Our single camera system [4] used 2D image coordinates.) We apply an Extended Kalman Filter to fuse the separate observations from the two cameras into a position and velocity in real world coordinates. If the target object becomes occluded from the view of one camera, our tracker switches to the other camera's observation. Tracking is initialized by solving a constrained linear least squares problem. The constraint is that a moving object in the real world always has some height. It helps us to remove the shadow on the ground plane, whose height is zero. The Kalman filter has been used in multi-sensor data fusion [6, 7]. Usually, the Kalman filter is applied to each sensor's data [8] or to combined data with additional logic [9]. We use the Kalman filter to fuse data based on the assumption that there is a mathematical relationship between the target object's image positions in the two synchronized cameras. Measurements from two synchronized cameras provide enough information to estimate the state variables of the system, the position and velocity in real world coordinates. Figure 1 shows the architecture of our proposed multiple camera system.

2 Multiple Camera Tracking

This section focuses on developing a methodology for tracking objects in the view of two fixed cameras. Compared to Tsai's five-point calibration method[10], we use only three planar control points. The theory is based on an image homography, the transformation from one plane to another. We consider the tracking problem as a dynamic target tracked by two cameras, each with different measurement dynamics and noise characteristics. We combine the multiple cameras to obtain a joint tracking that handles occlusion better than single camera-based tracking. We fuse the individual camera observations to obtain combined measurements and then use a Kalman filter to obtain a final state estimate based on the fused measurements. Measurements are fused by increasing the dimension of the observation vector of the Kalman filter, based on the assumption that there is a mathematical relationship between the positions of an object in each camera view. Since the relationship is nonlinear, an Extended Kalman Filter is used to estimate the state vector.

2.1 Quaternion and Its Expansion to Translation

A quaternion needs four variables to represent a single rotation or orientation, which has 3 DOFs(degrees of freedom). Euler angles sometimes create problems such as the Gimbal lock problem, where we lose one degree of freedom and may get an infinite number of solutions, leading to singularity. But we avoid this by using a quaternion. A quaternion is also computationally faster since it does not require the computation of trigonometric equations. Because a quaternion can represent only rotation, we have extended the quaternion by adding a translation step[11]. The quaternion is defined by $q = (\cos\frac{\theta}{2}, \bar{n}\sin\frac{\theta}{2}) = (w, pi + qj + rk)$, where $\bar{n}$ represent axis of rotation, θ rotation angle around $\bar{n}$, and $\cos\frac{\theta}{2} = w$ represents the real part of a quaternion, while $\bar{n}\sin\frac{\theta}{2} = pi + qj + rk$ represents the imaginary part of a quaternion. We denote $\bar{v}$ to be a v vector. Let h be an extension of the quaternion, $h = (w, p, q, r, x, y, z)$. The rotational part, (w, p, q, r) where $w^2 + p^2 + q^2 + r^2 = 1$, is the same as that of a quaternion. The translational part is (x, y, z). Multiplication of two extended-quaternions is defined as follows.

$$\begin{aligned} h_1 * h_2 &= (w_1, v_1, t_1) * (w_2, v_2, t_2) \\ &= (w_1 * w_2 - \bar{v}_1 \cdot \bar{v}_2, w_1 * \bar{v}_2 + w_2 * \bar{v}_1 + \bar{v}_1 \times \bar{v}_2, \\ &\quad (w_1^2 - \bar{v}_1 \cdot \bar{v}_1)\bar{t}_2 + 2\bar{v}_1(\bar{v}_1 \cdot \bar{t}_2) + 2w_1(\bar{v}_1 \times \bar{t}_2) + \bar{t}_1) \qquad (1) \\ \text{where} \quad & \bar{v}_i = (p_i, q_i, r_i),\ \bar{t}_i = (x_i, y_i, z_i),\ |w_i|^2 + |v_i|^2 = 1, i = 1, 2 \end{aligned}$$

2.2 Camera Calibration with Three Known Planar Points

Let us assume we know three planar points $\bar{a}$, $\bar{b}$, and $\bar{u}$, where $\bar{a} = [a_x\ a_y\ a_z]^T$ etc. without any camera distortion. These points are represented in world coordinates and the same notation for these points is ${}^W\bar{a}, {}^W\bar{b}$, and ${}^W\bar{u}$, respectively. Because we need to handle coordinate transformations, we denote W as world coordinate, C_1 and C_2 (for short, C) as coordinates of camera #1 and #2, respectively. ${}^W_C T$ is a homogeneous transformation matrix that transforms data represented in C coordinate to corresponding data in W coordinate. Let the three input points be ${}^W\bar{a}, {}^W\bar{b}$, and ${}^W\bar{u}$, represented in real world coordinate, W. Let I_1 and I_2 (for short, I) denote the 2D image coordinates of camera #1 and #2, respectively. Input points in image coordinates that are projected points of three real world points are ${}^I a_x$, ${}^I a_y$, ${}^I b_x$, ${}^I b_y$, ${}^I u_x$ and ${}^I u_y$. The unknowns are transformation matrices between W and C_i (where i, $i = 1, 2$, is the camera index) coordinates, and focal length, f_i. In order to convert points represented in world coordinates to camera #1 coordinates, we compute the following equations. $h_1 = (w_1, p_1, q_1, r_1, x_1, y_1, z_1)$ is camera #1 coordinate's quaternion-based representation in W. (w_1, p_1, q_1, r_1) is camera orientation representation in quaternion, while (x_1, y_1, z_1) is camera #1 coordinate origin represented in W. We solve these equations for each camera transformation. The following equations are scalar components of the translational vector part of equation 1.

$$
\begin{aligned}
R_1 &= w_1 * w_1 - p_1 * p_1 - q_1 * q_1 - r_1 * r_1, \\
h_1 &= (w_1, p_1, q_1, r_1, x_1, y_1, z_1) \\
{}^{C_1}a_X &= (R_1 * {}^{W}a_x + 2. * (p_1 * {}^{W}a_x + q_1 * {}^{W}a_y + r_1 * {}^{W}a_z) * p_1 \\
&\quad +2. * w_1 * (q_1 * {}^{W}a_z - r_1 * {}^{W}a_y) + x_1) \\
{}^{C_1}a_Y &= (R_1 * {}^{W}a_y + 2. * (p_1 * {}^{W}a_x + q_1 * {}^{W}a_y + r_1 * {}^{W}a_z) * q_1 \\
&\quad +2. * w_1 * (r_1 * {}^{W}a_x - p_1 * {}^{W}a_z) + y_1) \\
{}^{C_1}a_Z &= -(R_1 * {}^{W}a_z + 2. * (p_1 * {}^{W}a_x + q_1 * {}^{W}a_y + r_1 * {}^{W}a_z) * r_1 \\
&\quad +2. * w_1 * (p_1 * {}^{W}a_y - q_1 * {}^{W}a_x) + z_1)
\end{aligned}
\tag{2}
$$

Similarly we can compute for ${}^{C_1}b_X$, ${}^{C_1}b_Y$, ${}^{C_1}b_Z$, ${}^{C_1}u_X$, ${}^{C_1}u_Y$, and ${}^{C_1}u_Z$. Then corresponding points on camera image #1 are computed as ${}^{I_1}a_X = \frac{{}^{C_1}a_X}{-{}^{C_1}a_Z} f_1$, ${}^{I_1}a_Y = \frac{{}^{C_1}a_Y}{-{}^{C_1}a_Z} f_1$, ${}^{I_1}b_X = \frac{{}^{C_1}b_X}{-{}^{C_1}b_Z} f_1$, ${}^{I_1}b_Y = \frac{{}^{C_1}b_Y}{-{}^{C_1}b_Z} f_1$, ${}^{I_1}u_X = \frac{{}^{C_1}u_X}{-{}^{C_1}u_Z} f_1$, and ${}^{I_1}u_Y = \frac{{}^{C_1}u_Y}{-{}^{C_1}u_Z} f_1$ as well as $w_1^2 + p_1^2 + q_1^2 + r_1^2 = 1$. There are seven equations to be solved. Our eight unknowns are w_1, p_1, q_1, r_1, x_1, y_1, z_1, and f_1. While moving the origin of camera coordinate along the gaze vector, we can get an infinite proper combination of x_1, y_1, z_1, f_1, satisfying the projection. For the numerical solution, we fix f_1 values and solve a set of nonlinear equations with seven equations and seven unknowns. Given a fourth known planar point, the final set of solutions was selected among the infinite set of possible solutions such that it gives minimum calibration error.

In order to determine the mathematical relationship between the observations from two different views, we calibrate the two cameras using three coplanar control points as explained above. After the calibration, we know the homogeneous transformation ${}^{W}_{C_1}T^{-1} = T$, ${}^{W}_{C_2}T^{-1} = S$, focal length, $f_1 = f_T$ and $f_2 = f_S$. If a point $(x,\ y,\ z)$ on a plane in the real world is projected on both cameras, a pixel of the *k-th* image from camera #1 is denoted as $(Q_{1x,k}, Q_{1y,k})$, while a pixel of the *k-th* image from camera #2 is denoted as $(Q_{2x,k}, Q_{2y,k})$.

2.3 Extended Kalman Filter (EKF)

Knowing the cameras' calibration, we are able to merge the object's tracking from two different views into a real world coordinate view. The 3D tracking data is the state vector, which cannot be measured directly. The object's positions in two camera views are the measurement . We assume a constant velocity between two consecutive frames.

The dynamic equation related to the state vector X_k is described as follows,

$$X_{k+1} = \Phi_k X_k + W_k \tag{3}$$

where $X_k = [x\ y\ z\ \dot{x}\ \dot{y}\ \dot{z}]^T$ is the spatial position and velocity in real world coordinates; W_k is a white noise with known covariance structure, $E(W_k, W_j) = R_k \delta_{k,j}$, t represents time, and

$$\Phi_k = \begin{bmatrix} 1\,0\,0 & \Delta t & 0 & 0 \\ 0\,1\,0 & 0 & \Delta t & 0 \\ 0\,0\,1 & 0 & 0 & \Delta t \\ 0\,0\,0 & 1 & 0 & 0 \\ 0\,0\,0 & 0 & 1 & 0 \\ 0\,0\,0 & 0 & 0 & 1 \end{bmatrix}$$ is the transition matrix.

We derive the observation equation from the object's positions in two camera views. Let $(Q_{1x,k}, Q_{1y,k})$ and $(Q_{2x,k}, Q_{2y,k})$ be the corresponding image positions of object Q in two camera views. The observation vector

$$Z_k = [Q_{1x,k}, Q_{1y,k}, Q_{2x,k}]^T = h_k(X_k) + V_k \tag{4}$$

where V_k is a white noise with known covariance structure $E(V_k, V_j) = Q_k \delta_{k,j}$ and $E(V_k, V_j) = 0$, $h_k$is a non-linear function relating the state vector X_k to the measurement Z_k.

The dynamic equation is linear but the measurement equation is nonlinear, so the EKF is used to estimate the state vector X_k. Expanding in a Taylor series and neglecting higher order terms,

$$\begin{aligned} Z_k = h_k(X_k) + V_k &= h_k(\hat{X}_{k|k-1}) + H_k^{'}(X_k - \hat{X}_{k|k-1}) + V_k \\ &= H_k^{'} X_k + V_k + h_k(\hat{X}_{k|k-1}) - H_k^{'} \hat{X}_{k|k-1} \end{aligned} \tag{5}$$

where $H_k^{'}$is the Jacobian matrix of partial derivations of $h_k(X_k)$ with respect to X_k, $\hat{X}_{k|k-1}$ means the estimation of X_k from the X_{k-1}.

$$H_k^{'} = \frac{\partial h_k}{\partial X} = \begin{bmatrix} \frac{\partial Q_{1x,k}}{\partial x} & \frac{\partial Q_{1x,k}}{\partial y} & \frac{\partial Q_{1x,k}}{\partial z} & \frac{\partial Q_{1x,k}}{\partial \dot{x}} & \frac{\partial Q_{1x,k}}{\partial \dot{y}} & \frac{\partial Q_{1x,k}}{\partial \dot{z}} \\ \frac{\partial Q_{1y,k}}{\partial x} & \frac{\partial Q_{1y,k}}{\partial y} & \frac{\partial Q_{1y,k}}{\partial z} & \frac{\partial Q_{1y,k}}{\partial \dot{x}} & \frac{\partial Q_{1y,k}}{\partial \dot{y}} & \frac{\partial Q_{1y,k}}{\partial \dot{z}} \\ \frac{\partial Q_{2x,k}}{\partial x} & \frac{\partial Q_{2x,k}}{\partial y} & \frac{\partial Q_{2x,k}}{\partial z} & \frac{\partial Q_{2x,k}}{\partial \dot{x}} & \frac{\partial Q_{2x,k}}{\partial \dot{y}} & \frac{\partial Q_{2x,k}}{\partial \dot{z}} \end{bmatrix} \tag{6}$$

2.4 Tracking Initialization

Tracking initialization is a process of labeling a new object in one camera. If this new object has a correspondence in the other camera, it should be assigned the same tag number. The reason behind tracking initialization is that when we recover 3D coordinates of an object by computing $Q_{1x,k}$, $Q_{1y,k}$ and $Q_{2x,k}$, and project the estimated (x, y, z) using the transformation matrix computed using camera calibration, the estimated $Q_{2y,k}$ should be near the observed $Q_{2y,k}$. We

(a) (b) (c)

Fig. 2. Two input video streams.

initialized tracking by solving a constrained linear least squares problem, which is described as follows:

$$\min_{y} \quad \|GY - D\|_2^2 \quad \text{such that } z > z_0$$

$$\text{where } Y = [x\ y\ z]^T$$

$$G = \begin{bmatrix} T_{11}f_T - Q_{1x}T_{13} & T_{21}f_T - Q_{1x}T_{23} & T_{31}f_T - Q_{1x}T_{33} \\ T_{12}f_T - Q_{1y}T_{13} & T_{22}f_T - Q_{1y}T_{23} & T_{32}f_T - Q_{1y}T_{33} \\ S_{11}f_S - Q_{2x}S_{13} & S_{21}f_S - Q_{2x}S_{23} & S_{31}f_S - Q_{2x}S_{33} \\ S_{12}f_S - Q_{2y}S_{13} & S_{22}f_S - Q_{2y}S_{23} & S_{32}f_S - Q_{2y}S_{33} \end{bmatrix}$$

$$D = \begin{bmatrix} Q_{1x}T_{43} - T_{41}f_T & Q_{1y}T_{43} - T_{42}f_T & Q_{2x}S_{43} - S_{41}f_S & Q_{2y}S_{43} - S_{42}f_S \end{bmatrix}^T .$$

We add the constraint $z > z_0$ since a moving object in the real world always has some height. This helps us to remove the shadow on the ground plane, whose height is zero. We regard the object Q_1 in camera #1 and the object Q_2 in camera #2 as the same object Q if the sum from the above optimization problem is the minimum of all possible combinations.

3 Experiments in Multiple Camera Tracking

We use the data sets provided by the PETS2001 and other videos to evaluate the proposed tracking system. Figs. 2-3 give multiple camera examples. In Fig. 2, the first row frames are from camera #1 and the second row frames are from camera #2. In column (a), the van is still. Column (b) shows a new candidate template is created when the van's movement is detected by camera #2. (The van's motion is not detected by camera #1 because the motion is too small.) The frames in column (c) show the point at which the candidate template becomes a true template and tracking begins for both cameras. The van in Fig. 2(a)

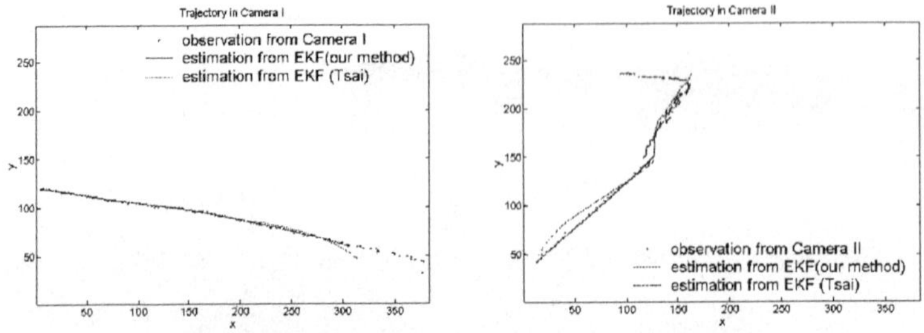

(a)Trajectory of the two people in Fig. 2.

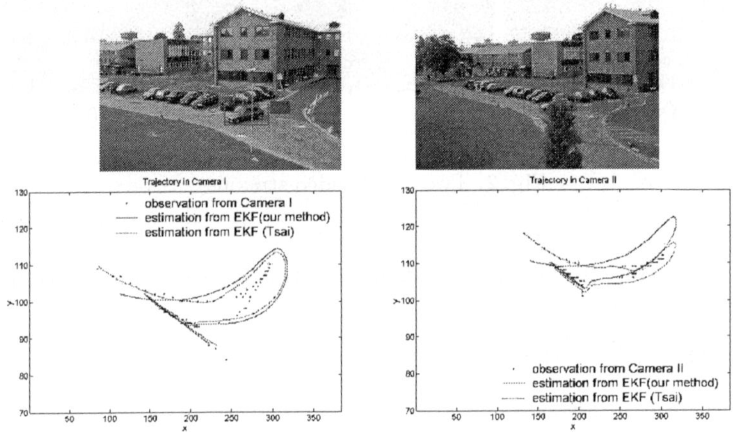

(b)Trajectory of the car.

Fig. 3. Trajectory of the two people and a car.

stays still for a long time; hence, it is merged into the background. It suddenly starts in the next frame. A 15-frame median filter updates the background, and a candidate new template is created, as shown by the rectangular blob in Fig. 2(b). This new candidate lasts more than three successive frames and thus begins to be tracked as a moving object in both camera as is seen in Fig. 2(c). When the object moves out of the overlapping views of cameras #1 and #2, it is tracked by the single camera module.

Fig. 3(a)-(b) shows two trajectory examples. The dots are the observations in each camera and the lines are estimates from the EKF using Tsai's 5-point calibration method and our 3-point method. In Fig. 3(a), the projections from the real world trajectory estimated by EKF fit the observations from the two cameras pretty well. It can be seen that our three point based method is better than Tsai's five point based method. In Fig. 3(b), there is some divergence between the projections and the observations. The divergence comes from the complex trajectory of the car. In this case Tsai's method gives better results than our method.

Our experiments demonstrate that the overall performance of multiple camera tracking is better than that of a single camera, especially when occlusion occurs. The EKF works well with most temporary occlusions, and the tracking initialization process can deal with long-term occlusion of say, more than 100 frames. Using multiple cameras, we can track the bicyclist in data set #2, which is occluded for a long time by the tree in camera #1 and thus would be difficult to track using only that camera. More accurate camera calibration will reduce the tracking error at the cost of having a more complex observation equation in the EKF. Multiple camera tracking relies on the objects remaining in two camera views most of time. When the target object moves out of the field of view of one camera permanently, the tracking returns to the single camera model.

4 Conclusions

In this paper, we have presented a system for tracking using synchronized multiple cameras in an outdoor environment. We combine spatial position, shape and color to achieve good performance in tracking people and vehicles. Our three point based calibration method is comparable to Tsai's five point based method. The Extended Kalman Filter fuses data from multiple cameras and performs quite well with occlusion. However, EKF may not work as well when long-term occlusion happens in both camera views. Based on our success of tracking multiple objects across multiple video streams, the reported research may be extended to recognizing moving object activities in multiple perspectives.

References

1. Cai, Q., Aggarwal, J.: Tracking human motion in structured environments using a distributed-camera system. IEEE Trans. on PAMI **21** (1999) 1241–1247
2. Khan, S., Javed, O., Rasheed, Z., Shah, M.: Human tracking in multiple cameras. In: Proc. of 8th Int. Conf. on Computer Vision. Volume Jan., Vancouver, Canada (2001) 331–336
3. S.L.Dockstsder, Tekalp, A.: Multiple camera tracking of interacting and occluded human motion. Proc. of the IEEE **89** (2001) 1441–1455
4. Zhou, Q., Aggarwal, J.: Tracking and classifying moving objects from video. In: Int. Workshop on Performance Evaluation of Tracking and Surveillance, Kauai, Hawaii (2001)
5. Bradshaw, K., Reid, I., Murray, D.: The active recovery of 3d motion trajectories and their use in prediction. IEEE Trans. on PAMI **19** (1997) 219–234
6. Gan, Q., Harris, C.: Comparison of two measurement fusion method for kalman-filter-based multisensor data fusion. IEEE Trans. on Aerospace and Electronic System **37** (2001) 273–279
7. Sasiadek, J., Hartana, P.: Sensor data fusion using kalman filter. In: Proc. of 3rd Int. Conf. on Information Fusion. Volume 2., Paris, France (2000) 19–25
8. Loffeld, O., Kramer, R.: Phase unwrapping for sar interferometry. a data fusion approach by kalman filtering. In: Proc. of Int. Symposium on Geosciences and Remote Sensing. Volume 3., Hamburg, Germany (1999) 1715–1717

9. Escamilla-Ambrosio, P., Mort, N.: A hybrid kalman filter-fuzzy logic architecture for multisensor data fusion. In: Proc. of Int. Symposium on Intelligent Control, Mexico City, Mexico (2001) 364–369
10. Tsai, R.: A versatile camera calibration technique for high-accuracy 3d machine vision metrology using off-the-shelf tv cameras and lenses. IEEE Journal of Robotics and Automation **RA-3** (1987) 323–344
11. Park, J., Kim, S.: Kinematics and constrained joint design using quaternion. In: The 2002 International Conf. on Imaging Science, Systems, and Technology. (2002)

License Plate Segmentation for Intelligent Transportation Systems[1]

Muhammed Cinsdikici and Turhan Tunalı

International Computer Institute Ege University, Bornova, İzmir, 35100, Turkey
cinsdiki@bornova.ege.edu.tr, tunali@ube.ege.edu.tr

Abstract. *A license plate segmentation system is designed and developed. The system has preprocessing, approximate region finding, plate extraction and character segmentation modules. For each module, alternative available methods are examined and proper sequence of operations is developed. In character segmentation module, a novel method is devised. Finally, overall performance of the system is reported.*

1 Introduction

As Intelligent Transportation Systems (ITS) are developed and constructed on highways and expressways, it has been observed that License Plate Recognition (LPR) has to be a well performing feature of these systems, particularly at the automatic toll-collection stage. Even though, LPR problem is well studied, developing systems yielding high performance for real-life pictures is not an easy task. Due to high commercial value and competition, no document is published for most of the high performance systems developed so far. Consequently, even if one carries out experiments, any performance comparison lacks theoretical reasoning.

LPR problem can basically be divided into two steps: Segmentation of plate area and recognition. These two steps may not necessarily be decoupled from each other. Even if a coupled approach is considered, candidate plate segmentations have to be determined. Hence plate segmentation problem has particular importance independent of the approach used.

Published work on the subject of LPR systems generally focus on recognition phase of the whole system. In many cases, segmentation phase has not caught much attention nor explained in detail. In literature, various techniques of LPR segmentation are reported to be useful. Among these are gap-line projections, color codes, histogram checks, closed objects and knowledge based methods. Many of the experiments we performed with the above-mentioned methods yielded limited performance for the real life pictures we used. The cause for poor performance of these systems can be unsuitable light conditions, noisy patterns connecting characters and poor edge enhancement.

---

[1] This work is supported in part by Aselsan A.Ş., Turkey.

A. Yazici and C. Şener (Eds.): ISCIS 2003, LNCS 2869, pp. 439–446, 2003.

We aimed at developing a system that would operate under all conditions without imposing restrictions on the license plates. For this reason, we have collected a set of 500 pictures that would represent a good sample of various light and weather conditions. We then started developing our system according to this data set. The segmentation system proposed in this paper can be divided into four main modules: Preprocessing, Approximate Region Finder (ARF), Plate Extractor (PE) and Character Segmentation (CS).

The paper is organized as follows: In section 2, related work and some drawbacks are explained. In section 3, an overview of the developed system is given together with its four main modules. Finally in section 4, performance results are reported and concluding remarks are made.

2 Related Work

In this section, we summarize some of the essential techniques. Deferring the discussion on preprocessing for the moment, we will first examine ARF, PE and CS. Table 1 gives alternative methods developed in the literature. Note that ARF, PE and CS are our own classification of functions and some of the techniques of Table 1 can be used for more than one function. The methods and their drawbacks for ARF systems can be summarized as follows: In template matching, the feature extraction step is left out altogether and the character image itself is used as a "feature vector". To identify the similarity between the template and the original picture, a measurement is performed. This suffers from size, rotation, noise and small variations on matched vector [1, 2]. Another method is Counter. It is defined as the closed piecewise linear curve that passes through the centers of all the pixels which are 4-connected to the outside background, and no other pixels. This technique suffers from noisy connected component patterns on the characters [1, 2]. In line projection method, raster line scanning is made to find the line carrying special frequency on projection [3]. Fig.1 shows this frequency as a set of continuous maxima and minima for some predefined characteristics like number, relative distance and amplitude. This process may yield some plate projection patterns that do not exhibit the dynamic nature expected from a plate and hence the method inadvertently concludes that the plate border has been reached [3]. In knowledge based searching method and special pattern searching method, special symbols such as prefix of national flags, Hiragana like icons or basic shapes are observed. Drawback of these methods is that special pattern constraints are too strict and not standard for every case [2, 4]. Closed frame search is the method of finding rectangular frames of connected lines. This fails when the lines of plate are lost due to the lack of edge enhancement [4]. Color code is another method of searching special color area over image. National flag color on plate is a good example for this method. This case is too restrictive since most of the license plates are black and white [1]. Histogram analysis is the method of searching special histogram of the template characters on image. This method does not work on images that have high brightness, like the ones taken at twilight [5].

The methods and their drawbacks for PE systems can be summarized as follows: Corner finding method is the process of searching line overlaps during edge enhancement. This can be missed when edge detection looses the pure characteristics of lines [4, 7]. Character width method is defined as searching template suitable for possible character width sizes like 14 pixels. This method can not be used on plates carrying characters of variable size [5, 6].

The methods and their drawbacks for CS systems can be summarized as follows: Blob Coloring method can be used as a region-growing procedure which labels pixels that form 8-connected contiguous regions ("blobs") that receive a unique label. But this method has weakness of connected character problem [7]. Gap search is another method which is based on finding exact gap between the character patterns. This is not applicable when some portions of characters are overlapping or noisy patterns are connecting the characters [1, 4, 5, 7].

As can be seen from the above discussion, one single method can not fully realize one of the functions of ARF, PE or CS for actual pictures. Therefore developing a sequence of operation that would eliminate these deficiencies is essential for high performance. In this study, we have devised these operation sequences for each function.

3 The Structure of the Developed System

General structure of our segmentation system is given in Fig.2 (a). The input to the system is a triggered car image and output is a set of character images. Fig.2 (b) shows two real triggered images. Following sections give details of segmentation steps and compare them with other alternatives.

3.1 Preprocessing for LPR

Converting color images to gray scale is the first step of preprocessing. This is essential for eliminating color information that is redundant for our purposes. The original images triggered are pressed in the vertical dimension due to the type of CCD camera used. This makes the image difficult to analyze. Resizing can be done by using several methods: *Line cloning* is the simplest method of resizing in which each line from image is added as successor of it. Applying this method causes the image to loose its valuable information like edges and smooth gray level variation. It is reported to be unsuitable for analyzing image [8]. *Linear interpolation* is another way of making resizing with preserving approximate smooth variation on gray levels. Disadvantage is discrete step size of interpolation interval that may negatively affect edge detection performance. *Frequency domain based transformations* such as Bilinear, Hann and Hamming, Blackman and Lanczos methods can also be used [8]. We tried all of them and observed that Lanczos method yielded better results than others [8]. It uses Sinc (x) function as base transformation function (1). This transformation function is windowed and differentiated with convolution functions of (2).

Fig. 1. (a) Three lines are taken .(b) These lines are horizontally projected. Last signal shows high frequency object on this line. This is candidate plate location.

Table 1. Alternative Methods for the segmentation process.

Approximate Region Finding		**Plate Extraction**	**Character Segmentation**
Template matching	Counter	Corner Finding	Template matching
Line projection	Knowledge-based search	Closed frame search	Character width/height
Special pattern	Closed frame search	Line projection	Gap on projection
Color codes		Character w/h	Counter
Histogram analysis			Color codes

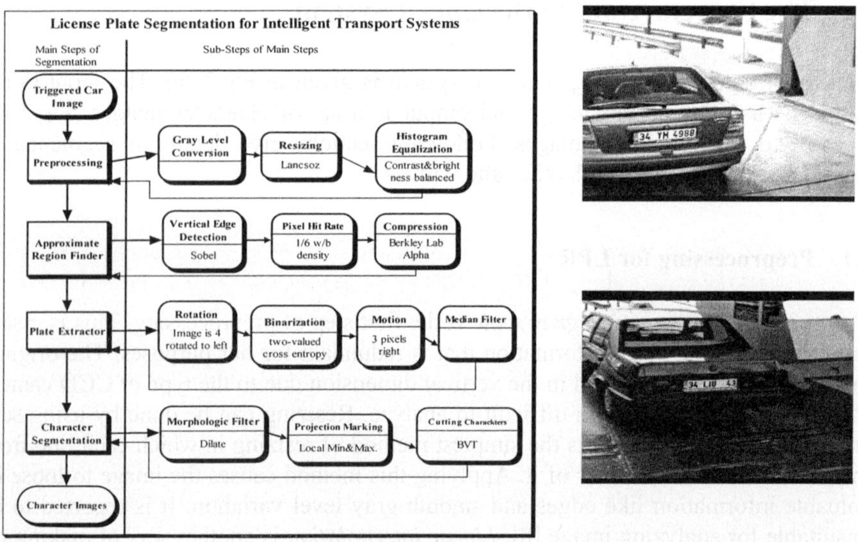

Fig. 2. (a) System flowchart. **(b)** Triggered image

$$\mathrm{Sinc}(x)=\sin(x)/x\,, \qquad L(x,\tau)=\begin{cases}\dfrac{\sin(\pi\frac{\pi}{\tau})}{(\pi\frac{\pi}{\tau})} & |x|<\tau\\ 0 & otherwise\end{cases} \qquad (1,2)$$

Lanczos method reproduces a unique continuous signal that passes through the pixel corners with the correct pixel values and is bandwidth limited to the Nyquist limit for the pixel samples [8]. It gives good balance between preserving sharpness and it does not introduce ringing effects. The disadvantage is its long computational time. Other methods like Hann and Blackman are not as successful as Lanczos method [8]. In Fig.3, a kernel of Lanczos filter is demonstrated in spectral form. In our proposed system, Lancsoz method is used to resize image vertically with 1.5 rate.

After *Lanczos resizing*, the image is taken through the *histogram equalization* process to balance gray level contrast over image [5]. Histogram equalization gives the advantage of taking images under different sunlight conditions. Image taken in the afternoon, evening or at night can be internally balanced with histogram equalization. After histogram equalization the image is ready for approximate region finder module.

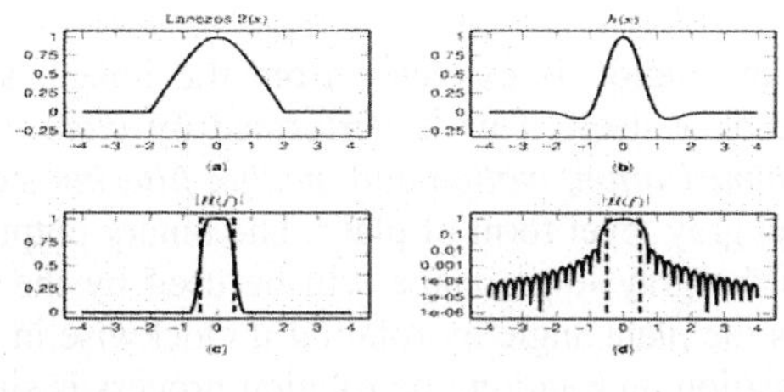

Fig. 3. (a)Lanczos (b)Win.Sinc (c)Spectrum (d)Logaritmic zoom

3.2 Approximate Region Finder Module

Preprocessed image is ready for overall segmentation process. Proposed system divides segmentation into three phases. The first phase is the *approximate region finder* module. This module includes *vertical edge detection*, *pixel hit rate region finding* and *compression* sub-modules.

The plates contain characters that have dense vertical and horizontal information. Therefore search for vertical and horizontal information can lead us to the plate. However, in a car image, horizontal information is also dense in many other regions such as the rear window and the trunk. Therefore, we only concentrate on vertical edge detection. Typical methods for extracting vertical edges are Prewitt, Sobel filters and Canny edge detector. We preferred Sobel filter over Prewitt filter and Canny edge detector [2] due to its simplicity and performance. Fig.4 (a) depicts the output of a Sobel filtering process with tolerance value of 0.2.

In pixel hit rate region finding step, we slide a rectangular window of size 25×150 pixels and compute the matching white pixel density. All candidates are recorded with their coordinates. As depicted in Fig.4 (b), a candidate extracted from the image may not contain plate itself yet.

To extract the plate itself, we need to isolate the foreground (that contains characters) from background. We will use thresholding to perform this isolation. However, the candidate extracted plate contains 256 gray levels that is too high for an input to thresholding process. For this purpose, we apply compression to reduce the number of gray levels by approximately %70. Berkley Labs Alpha compression algorithm is selected as the tool of this latter process.

Fig. 4. (a) Sobel filtered image Fig.2(b) plate region obtained in our case

3.3 Plate Extractor Module

After approximate plate region is extracted from the image, some extra steps are needed to extract the plate itself. This is performed by *plate extractor module* that consists of *rotation, binarization, motion* and *median filtering* steps. Two outputs are obtained as binary and gray level form of plate. The binary output is used for character isolation whereas the gray level image will be used by the recognition module. Rotation step corrects the plate angle by rotating it clockwise in the range of (0°-4°). Because of static distortion on rotation, the rotation process is simple to apply. There are some other alternative methods to rotate the plate dynamically. For instance Hough transform is a popular method, but since it is more complex and it is not used on images carrying detailed information like character patterns. Next is binarization of the plate. There are several methods for binarization like, Niblack [7], two-valued cross entropy thresholding [9], mean and standard deviation thresholding. Niblack method is based on local neighboring thresholding using the equation (3). In this equation, T is new value of pixel and ω is local weight, (σ,μ) are standard deviation and mean value of (5x5) neighboring pixels respectively. Niblack method is valuable for the whole image like in Fig.2 (a). But for small images like plate region, it looses one or two characters on plate while thresholding.

$$T(\chi,\gamma) = \omega * \sigma(\chi,\gamma) + \mu(\chi,\gamma), \qquad \mu_1(t) = \frac{\sum_{fi<t}\sum_{cij<s} f_i}{N_1} \qquad \mu_2(t) = \frac{\sum_{fi>t}\sum_{cij>s} f_i}{N_2} \qquad (3,4)$$

We observed that two-valued cross entropy thresholding [9] as given in (4) is more successful on small images. It is not suitable for bigger images like in Fig.2 (a) because it is slow. Proposed system uses two-valued cross entropy thresholding. In (4), μ_1, μ_2 are two thresholding values over gray level distribution matrix [9]. Third step is artificial motion application to the plate region. The plate is shifted to the right by 3 pixels in proposed system. The choice of right shift is arbitrary. We could as well have shifted left to serve the same purpose. This shifted plate region image is subtracted from the original plate region image. The resultant image shows us the shadows of characters on the plate. This motion clears the unwanted horizontal lines. To clear the salt and pepper noise, the plate binarized form is passed through the median high pass filter and then dilation morphologic filter [1] as depicted in Fig.5 (a). Proposed system uses the corners of shadowed image and extracts original plate itself like in Fig.5 (b).

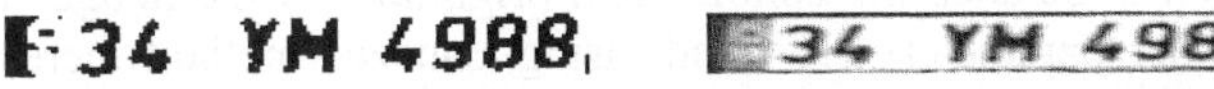

Fig. 5. (a) Extracted plate and (b) its gray level final form.

3.4 Character Segmentation Module

Plate with its binarized form is ready for character isolation. Character segmentation module takes binary extracted plate, passes it through the dilate morphologic filter to overcome of the problem of noisy pattern connections between characters. It then searches local minima and maxima. Then, to find candidate cut points, a new technique called Bidirectional Vertical Thresholding (BVT) is applied. The first step is taking vertical projection of the binarized extracted plate form like in Fig.5 (a). Then all the local minima and maxima are signed by using (5). This signal on Fig.6 is linearly transformed along "y" axis. Then bidirectional standard deviation based thresholding is applied to mark character cut point on the signal as depicted in Fig.7 (a). For real extracted patterns, all cut points are used to obtain Fig.7 (b). The final decision about the cut points is to be made at the recognition stage.

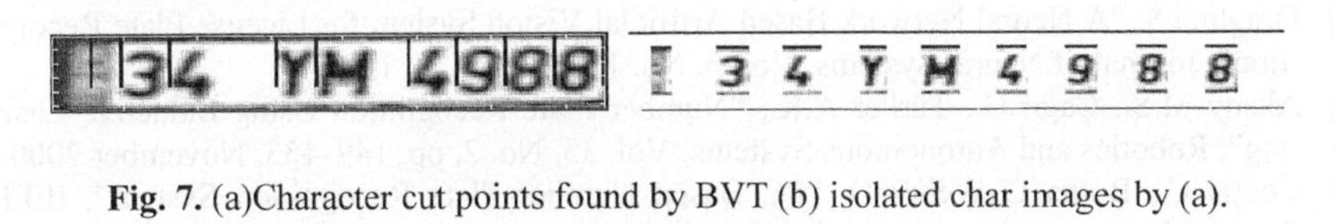

Fig. 6. Horizontal projection of binarized form of the plate on Fig.9.

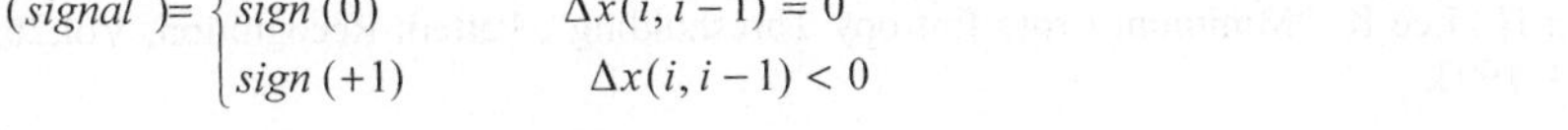

Fig. 7. (a)Character cut points found by BVT (b) isolated char images by (a).

$$Sign\ (signal\ ) = \begin{cases} sign\ (-1) & \Delta x(i, i-1) < 0 \\ sign\ (0) & \Delta x(i, i-1) = 0 \\ sign\ (+1) & \Delta x(i, i-1) < 0 \end{cases} \quad (5)$$

4 Performance and Conclusion

We have tested our system on 500 images captured at the non-stop toll collection gates of the Bosphorus Bridge. These images are triggered in bitmap colored form in the size of 312x640 pixels. All images have some rotation distortion about 4° counterclockwise. The images were captured at different hours of a day. We used Matlab in all of our computations. The preprocessing module performs converting color images to gray scale and then resizes images into 468×640 pixel form and then makes histogram equalization to balance the contrast and brightness of the image. We observed that when all other parameters are fixed, using Lanczos method increases the performance from 40% to 73%, with percentage referring to license plates in which all characters are properly isolated. For approximate region finder, we have compared performance of our system with that of line projection [3]. We have observed that our system (Lanczos method and Vertical Edge Detection) found 80% of all plate regions whereas line projection was at 40%.

We have assessed the overall performance of our system by human eye. In 365 out of 500 images, our system was able to isolate all of the characters properly. On the rest of the plates, the isolation process failed due to mostly single fault of either missing the cut point or adding extra cut point. We expect that, the recognition module that we are in the process of developing will be able to reject those candidates and overall performance of the system will be significantly improved.

References

[1] Oivind D.T., Anil K.J., Torfinn T. "Feature Extraction Methods for Character Recognition – A Survey", Pattern Recognition, Vol.29, No.4, pp. 641–662, 1996.

[2] Takashi N.,Tsukada T.,Yamada K.,Kozuka K., Yamamato S. "Robust License-Plate Recognition Method for Passing Vehicles Under Outside Environment", IEEE Transactions on Vehicular Technology, Vol. 49, No. 6, pp. 2309–2319, July 2000.

[3] Barroso J., Rafeal A. "Number Plate Reading Using Computer Vision", Proceedings of the IEEE International Symposium on Industrial Electronics ISIE'97, University of Minho, Portugal Julho, 1997.

[4] Min Y.J., Choi U.J. "Development of License Plate Extraction Algorithm Using Prior Knowledge", Proceedings of the 5th World Congress on Intelligent Transport Systems, Seul, Korea, October 1998.

[5] Draghici S. "A Neural Network Based Artificial Vision System for License Plate Recognition", Journal of Neural Systems, Vol. 8, No. 1, pp.113–126, 1997.

[6] Aksoy M.S., Çağıl G., Türker A.K., "Number Plate Recognition Using Inductive Learning", Robotics and Autonomous Systems, Vol. 33, No. 2, pp. 149–153, November 2000.

[7] Coetzi C., Botha C.,Weber D. "PC Based Number Plate Recognition System", IEEE., http://cpbotha.net, e-mail: cpbotha@ieee.org.

[8] George W. "Digital Image Warping-Image Manipulation", IEEE Computer Society Press , Los Alamitos, CA, 1990.

[9] Li H., Lee K. "Minimum Cross Entropy Thresholding", Pattern Recognition, Vol.26, No. 4, 1993.

A Turkish Handprint Character Recognition System

Abdulkerim Çapar[1], Kadim Taşdemir[2], Özlem Kılıc[2], and Muhittin Gökmen[1]

[1] İstanbul Technical University Computer Engineering Department
Maslak 34469, İstanbul
capar@itu.edu.tr gokmen@cs.itu.edu.tr

[2] İstanbul Technical University Institute of Informatics
Maslak 34469, İstanbul
{tasdemir,kilicoz}@be.itu.edu.tr

Abstract. This paper presents a study for recognizing isolated Turkish handwritten uppercase letters. In the study, first of all, a Turkish Handprint Character Database has been created from the students in Istanbul Technical University (ITU). There are about 20000 uppercase and 7000 digit samples in this database. Several feature extraction and classification techniques are realized and combined to find the best recognition system for Turkish characters. Features, obtained from Karhunen-Loéve Transform, Zernike Moments, Angular Radial Transform and Geometric Features, are classified with Artificial Neural Networks, K-Nearest Neighbor, Nearest Mean, Bayes, Parzen and Size Dependent Negative Log-Likelihood methods. Geometric moments, which are suitable for Turkish characters, are formed. KLT features are fused with other features since KLT gives the best recognition rate but has no information about the shape of the character where other methods have. The fused features of KLT and ART classified by SDNLL gives the best result for Turkish characters in the experiments.

1 Introduction

Optical Character Recognition (OCR) is one of the most widely researched areas in pattern recognition applications. The works on this topic mainly focus on recognizing high quality printed text documents. On the other hand, computer recognition of handwritten characters has received relatively less attention, when compared to OCR [1]. However, recognition of handprint documents is becoming a very popular pattern recognition problem thanks to the updating of human needs. The process of handprint character recognition is usually named ICR (Intelligent Character Recognition).

The main problems at ICR systems are the big variations of character shapes among people, and the randomness in the written characters even for the same person. The more you get rid of these problems, the more successful you are.

There are two goals to be achieved in order to maximize the performance of handwritten character recognition. The first one is designing a feature extractor which

A. Yazici and C. Şener (Eds.): ISCIS 2003, LNCS 2869, pp. 447–456, 2003.

does not miss meaningful aspects where the second one is designing a classifier, which has good generalization power and minimum substitution error [2]. Recognition of Turkish characters is a harder problem with respect to recognition of characters in English alphabet, because of some additive letters (Fig. 1).

Although there are some commercial works, this paper is the one in the few academic studies on Turkish Handprint Character Recognition, which utilizes the first comprehensive Turkish Handprint Database. In this work, we investigated additive recognition rules that are special for Turkish letters.

2 Handprint Character Recognition System

The history of handwriting recognition systems is not complete without mentioning the Optical Character Recognition (OCR) systems [3]. Optical Character Recognition (OCR) is a problem recognized as being as old as the computer itself. Nowadays, researchers focus on handprint numeral and character recognition. Unfortunately, the success of OCR could not be carried on to Intelligent Character Recognition (ICR), due to the variations in people's handwriting. As for the recognition of isolated handwritten numerals, Suen [4], addresses many researches which have already obtained very promising results using various classification methods. Suen mentions that the key issue reaching high recognition rates is the feature extraction.

The off-line isolated handwritten character recognition systems include three major parts: Preprocessing Part, Feature Extraction Part and Classification Part.

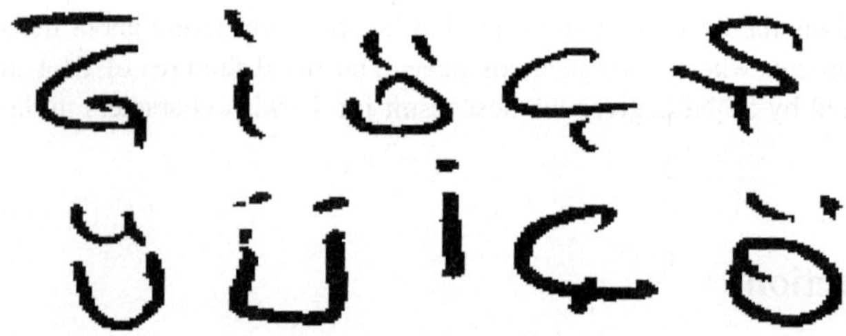

Fig. 1. Sample characters from Turkish Handprint Database

2.1 Preprocessing

Preprocessing algorithms provides the required data suitable for the further processing. In other words, it establishes the link between real world and recognition engine. Preprocessing steps consist of digitization, binarization, blob coloring, segmentation, size normalization and skeletonization (Fig. 2).

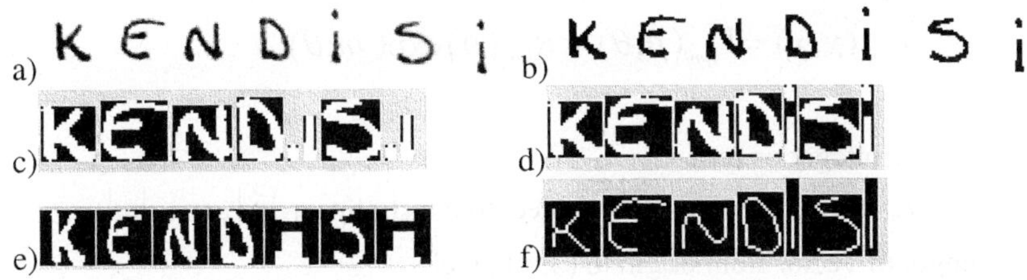

Fig. 2. Output of preprocessing steps. a) Digitization, b)Binarization, c)Blob Coloring, d) Segmentation, e) Size Normalization, f) Skeletonization

2.2 Feature Extraction

Feature extraction problem is that of extracting from the raw data the information which is most relevant for classification purposes, in the sense of minimizing the within-class pattern variance while enhancing the between-class pattern variance.

Feature extraction methods used in this study are Karhunen-Loéve transform (KLT), Angular Radial Transform (ART), Zernike moments and geometric features. KLT features are linear features but do not have any information about the shape of the pattern. On the other hand, ART, Zernike, and geometric features are formed according to the geometric properties of the pattern. Therefore, some geometric moments ,which are suitable for Turkish characters, are formed. In addition, KLT features are combined with other features since KLT gives the best recognition rates but has no information about the shape where other methods have.

The first extractor method, KLT, is a linear transform and corresponds to the projection of images onto the eigenvectors of the covariance matrix, where the covariance matrix is formed by the character images of training set [5]. The covariance matrix is formed from training samples and diagonalized using standard linear algebra routines, producing eigenvalues D_λ and corresponding eigenvectors Φ , that is

$$R\Phi = \Phi D_\lambda . \tag{1}$$

The K-L Transform v of the vector x is the projection of the vector minus the mean vector onto the eigenvector basis Φ ,

$$v = \Phi^T (x - \mu) . \tag{2}$$

The second method, Zernike moments, is introduced by Zernike [6]. He introduced a set of complex polynomials which form a complete set over the interior of the unit circle. If the set of these polynomials is denoted by $\{V_{nm}(x, y)\}$, the form of these polynomials is:

$$V_{nm}(x,y)=V_{nm}(\rho,\theta)=R_{nm}(\rho)\exp(jm\theta)\,. \tag{3}$$

where

n	Positive integer or zero
m	Positive and negative integers subject to constraints n-$\lvert m\rvert$ even , $\lvert m\rvert \le$n
ρ	Length of vector from origin to (x, y) pixel
θ	Angle between vector ρ and x axis in counterclockwise direction

and $R_{nm}(\rho)$, radial polynomial, is defined as

$$R_{nm}(\rho)=\sum_{s=0}^{(n-|m|)/2}(-1)^s\frac{(n-s)!}{s!\left(\frac{n+|m|}{2}-s\right)!\left(\frac{n-|m|}{2}-s\right)!}\rho^{n-2s}\,. \tag{4}$$

Zernike moments are the projection of the image function onto the orthogonal basis functions and the Zernike moment of order n with repetition m for a continuous image function *f(x, y)* that vanish outside the unit circle is

$$A_{nm}=\frac{n+1}{\pi}\iint_{x^2+y^2\le 1}f(x,y)V^*_{nm}(\rho,\theta)dxdy\,. \tag{5}$$

To compute the Zernike moments of a given image, first the image is interpolated with a predetermined constant β [7].

The third method, Angular Radial Transform, is a 2-D complex transform defined on a unit disk in polar coordinates,

$$F_{nm}=\langle V_{nm}(\rho,\theta),f(\rho,\theta)\rangle=\int_0^{2\pi}\int_0^1 V^*_{nm}(\rho,\theta)f(\rho,\theta)\rho d\rho d\theta\,. \tag{6}$$

Here, F_{nm} is an ART coefficient of order *n* and *m*, $f(\rho,\theta)$ is an image function in polar coordinates, and $V_{nm}(\rho,\theta)$ is the ART basis function [8]. The ART basis functions are separable along the angular and radial directions,

$$V_{nm}(\rho,\theta)=A_m(\theta)R_n(\rho), \tag{7}$$

The angular and radial basis functions are defined as follows:

$$A_m(\theta)=\frac{1}{2\pi}\exp(jm\theta), \tag{8}$$

$$R_n(\rho)=\begin{cases}1 & n=0\\ 2\cos(\pi n\rho) & n\neq 0\end{cases}, \tag{9}$$

The imaginary parts have similar shape to the corresponding real parts but with different phases.

The geometric features, the fourth extractor method, are formed since KLT assumes no model of the human perception mechanism, but more directly references statistical information on how handwritten characters are formed [9]. Therefore, some additional rule-based methods need to be used to find features, in order to recognize many variations of the same character.

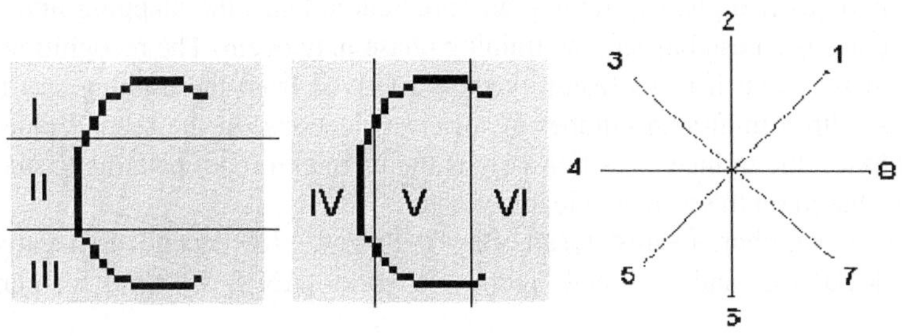

Fig. 3. Special point features a) End/Connection point regions b) End point directions

End points and connection points of a character image carries robust information about the character, especially for Turkish letters ‘Ç’ and ‘Ş’. Direction and location of these special points on the character region are labeled as in Figure 3 to extract features.

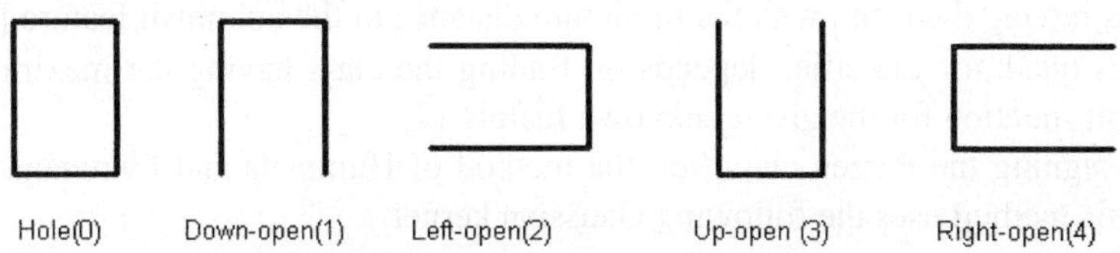

Fig. 4. Background region types and their labels

While most character-recognition systems are concerned with the pixels belonging to the characters themselves, there are good parameters which can be found by analyzing the size, shape and the position of background region surrounding the character image. For example ‘B’ has two holes, one in the upper part and the other in the lower part; ‘O’ has only one hole in the middle; ‘Z’ has a left-facing concave region at the top half and a right-facing concave region at the bottom half. Each background region is found and labeled with the code of region type as in Figure 4. Than we calculated Hu’s second and third order central moment invariants [9] over these background regions. Number of each type of background regions over the character region is used as features too.

The number of connected components (blobs) in a character image also gives reliable features for Turkish characters, such as ‘İ’, ‘Ü’ and ‘Ö’.

In addition to use the four feature extraction methods individually; we have combined KLT features with the other three methods to strength statistical KLT features with the geometric properties of the patterns.

2.3 Classification

The task of pattern classification is to assign an input pattern Z represented a feature vector X to one of the pre-specified classes $C_1, C_2, C_3, \ldots\ldots, C_K$. After the feature set is defined and the feature extraction algorithm is applied, a typical recognition process involves two phases: training and prediction. Once the mapping into the feature space has been established, the training phase may begin. The recognition engine is adjusted such that it maps feature vectors (derived from the training set) into the categories with a minimum number of misclassifications. In the second phase (prediction phase), the trained classifier assigns the unknown input patterns to one of the categories based on the extracted feature vector.

K-nearest neighbor, nearest mean, Bayes, Parzen, size dependent negative log-likelihood(SDNLL) and Artificial Neural Networks (ANN) are used for classification.

K- nearest neighbor (knn) and nearest mean classifiers depend on finding the feature vector of minimum distance to the unknown feature vector. In order to find the nearest feature vector, several distance measures are used. In this paper, the Euclidean distance metric is used [2]. In knn, k is a predetermined value. The k nearest neighbors to the unknown feature vector, are found, and the vote of each class is assigned to the number of neighbors they have. The classification result is the class which has the maximum vote of k nearest neighbors [2]. In nearest mean classifier, the result is the class having the mean with the minimum distance to the unknown feature [2].

Bayes quadratic classifier depends on finding the class having the maximum discriminant function for the given unknown feature [2].

In designing the Parzen classifier, the method of Hummels and Fukunaga is used [10]. This method uses the following Gaussian kernel

$$k(x) = \frac{1}{\sqrt{(2\pi)^n |\Gamma_c| h^n}} e^{\frac{-d^2(x)}{2h^2}} . \quad (10)$$

where d is the Mahalonobis distance. The class conditional probability density at a point is estimated by

$$p(x) = p(x \mid w) = \frac{1}{N_c} \sum_{i=1}^{Nc} k(x - x_i^{(c)}) . \quad (11)$$

Hummels and Fukunaga use a threshold, t, for biases. There are four different options for these biases. The one used in this paper assumes the distributions be nearly Gaussian. The bias for this case is

$$t = \frac{1}{2}(\frac{h^2}{h^2+1}) \ln(\Gamma_c) + \frac{1}{h^2+1} \ln P_c , \quad (12)$$

so the discriminant function becomes

$$gc\ (x) = -\ln p_c(x) - t\ . \tag{13}$$

The class with the maximum discriminant value is the classification result.

The SDNLL classifier is proposed by Hwang and Weng [11]. The idea behind this classifier is to use the available information as efficient as possible. There are three measures in terms of belongingness: likelihood, Mahalonobis distance, and Euclidean distance. In order to estimate the correct covariance matrices, it requires many samples. In the case of Mahalonobis, fewer samples are sufficient and in the case of Euclidean the least number is required. Therefore, a size dependent scatter matrix is proposed [11]. The resulting matrix is

$$W_i = w_e \rho^2 I + w_m S_w + w_c \Gamma_i\ . \tag{14}$$

where ρ is the standard deviation, I is the identity matrix, Sw is the within scatter matrix , Γ is the covariance matrix and w_e, w_m, w_c are weights of distance matrices. Thus, the discriminant function is obtained as follows:

$$g_c(x) = \frac{1}{2}(x-c)^T W_i^{-1}(x-c) + \frac{q-1}{2}\ln(2\pi) + \frac{1}{2}\ln(|W_i|)\cdot \tag{15}$$

where q is the class size. The classification result is the class with the maximum discriminant function.

In this study, we worked on an important class of neural networks, namely, multi-layer feed-forward networks. Typically, the networks consists of a set of sensory units (x_i) (source node) that constitute the input layer, one or more hidden layers of computation nodes (z_j), and an output layer of computation nodes (y_k) [12]. The input signal propagates through the network in a forward direction, on a layer-by-layer basis. These neural networks are commonly referred as multilayer perceptrons (MLPs), which represent a generalization of the single-layer perceptron. We used error back-propagation algorithm as training method for multi-layer feed-forward neural networks, which uses gradient-descent methods. Back-propagation training algorithm involves an iterative procedure for minimizing the specific cost function.

3 Experimental Results

In this section, the results of combining the feature extraction techniques and the classifiers are discussed by using the ITU Handprint Character Database, which includes about 20000 uppercase letters. 12644 of them have been used as training patterns while 6322 of them have been used as test patterns.

The feature extraction methods, examined in the paper, are formed in the following way. Zernike features are calculated up to the 12th order, which provides 47 dimensional features while ART features are calculated with order 3 and repetition 12, which provides 36 dimensional features. For geometric features, we have extracted totally 39 features from the geometric properties of characters. KLT features are extracted from either 64 or 128 eigenvectors. Finally, the fused features are formed by KLT features with 64 eigenvectors.

Table I indicates the percent classification results for statistical and template based classifiers versus individual feature sets. It is observed that SDNLL gives the best recognition rate for all features except ART of order 3 with repetition 12. In that case Parzen gives the best result. The best result for these feature sets is obtained as 93 %.

Table II presents percent classification results for statistical and template based classifiers versus these fused feature sets. Although the results are worse than the results of KLT features with the classifiers k-NN, NMN, and Bayes quadratic classifier, there is improvement for KLT with SDNLL and Parzen. The overall performance increases by using additive Zernike or ART features. The classification rate becomes 93.6 % for KLT with ART and 93.4 % for KLT with Zernike features by using SDNLL classifier.

Table 1. Percent classification results for statistical and template based classifiers versus individual feature sets

	Feature				
Classifier	KLT (64)	KLT(128)	ZERNIKE (47)	ART (36)	ART(64)
k-NN k=1	92,0	91,7	79,8	77,5	80,1
k-NN k=3	91,9	91,6	80,7	78,5	80,9
k-NN k=5	91,9	91,5	80,9	79,0	81,1
NMN	75,3	75,4	58,7	56,0	57,7
Bayes	92,2	90,6	82,0	82,9	83,5
Parzen	92,3	90,9	81,5	**83,2**	84,1
SDNLL	**93,0**	**92,2**	**83,0**	83,1	**84,2**

Table 2. Percent classification results for statistical and template based classifiers versus fused feature sets

	Feature		
Classifier	KLT + ZERNIKE	KLT+ ART	KLT + ART
k-NN k=1	83,8	90,1	90,2
k-NN k=3	84,3	90,0	90,1
k-NN k=5	84,7	90,0	90,1
NMN	63,6	75,4	75,4
Bayes	91,9	92,1	92,1
Parzen	92,5	92,8	92,7
SDNLL	**93,4**	**93,6**	**93,4**

The results for the Artificial Neural Network (ANN) classifier for the feature sets KLT, ART, KLT with ART, and KLT with ART features are shown in Table III. The performance of fused features is also overperformed KLT and ART individually. The best result for ANN is obtained for KLT with the geometric features.

The k-NN classifier has the best performance for the KLT feature of dimension 64 where nearest mean has the best result for KLT with dimension of 128. In addition, the best recognition rate for Bayes quadratic classifier is obtained by KLT features. On the other hand, in the case of Parzen classifier and SDNLL, the fused features of KLT and ART with order three and repetition twelve, give the best result.

Table 3. Percent classification results for artificial neural networks versus feature sets

	Feature					
Classifier	KLT(32)	KLT(64)	ART	KLT+ART	KLT+ART	KLT+Geometric
ANN	85,9	88,3	69,1	89,2	90,4	**91,9**

4 Conclusion

In this paper, we study on the recognition of Turkish uppercase handprint characters. We have formed the first comprehensive Turkish handprint character database, which consists of about 20000 characters.

We have used different feauture extraction methods such as KLT, Zernike, ART. In addition, geometric features are evaluated especially for Turkish characters. Moreover, KLT features are fused with Zernike, ART, or geometric features in order to include the shape information of characters.

In the study, k-nearest neighbor, nearest mean neighbor, Bayes quadratic classifier, Parzen classifier, SDNLL, and ANN are used. The best classification percentage is performed by SDNLL. The fused features give better results than the individual ones for SDNLL, Parzen, and ANN. The best classification result obtained in this paper is 93.6 %.

References

1. J. Hu, "HMM Based On-Line Handwriting Recognition", IEEE Trans. On Pattern Analysis and Machine Intelligence, vol. 18, pp. 1039–1045, 1996.
2. K. Fukunaga, *Introduction to Statistical Pattern Recognition*, 2nd ed., Boston: Academic Press, 1990
3. B. Verma, M. Blumenstein, and S. Kulkarni, "Recent Achievements in Off-Line Handwriting Recognition Systems", School of Information Technology Griffith University – Gold Coast Campus PMB 50,1997.
4. C.Y. Suen, et al., "Building a New Generation of Handwriting Recognition System", Pattern Recognition Letters, vol. 14, pp. 303–315, 1993.
5. P. J. Grother, "Karhunen-Loéve Feature Extraction For Neural Handwritten Character Recognition", Image Recognition Group, National Institute of Standards and Technology, 1709, pp. 155-166, 1992.
6. F. Zernike, *Physica*, vol. 1. p. 689, 1934.

7. A. Khonzad, Y. H. Hong, "Invariant Image Recognition by Zernike Moments", vol 12, No. 5, May 1990.
8. B.D. Ripley, *Pattern Recognition and Neural Networks*, Cambridge University Press, 1996.
9. O. D. Trier, A. K. Jain and T. Taxt, "Feature Extraction Methods For Character Recognition: A survey", Revised July 19, 1995.
10. K. Fukunaga, and R.R. Hummels, "Bayes error estimation using Parzen and k-NN procedures", IEEE Trans. Pattern Analysis and Machine Intelligence, vol.9, no 5, pp. 634–643, Sept. 1987
11. W.S. Hwang, J. Weng, "Hierarchical Discriminant Regression", IEEE Trans. Pattern Analysis and Machine Intelligence, vol.22, no 11, pp. 1–17, Nov. 2000
12. A. K. Jain, J. Mao and K. Mohiuddin, "Artificial Neural Networks: A Tutorial", Accepted to appear in IEEE Computer Special Issues on Neural Computing, March 1996.

Image-Space-Parallel Direct Volume Rendering on a Cluster of PCs*

B. Barla Cambazoglu and Cevdet Aykanat

Bilkent University, Department of Computer Engineering,
06800, Ankara, Turkey
{berkant,aykanat}@cs.bilkent.edu.tr

Abstract. An image-space-parallel, ray-casting-based direct volume rendering algorithm is developed for rendering of unstructured data grids on distributed-memory parallel architectures. For efficiency in screen workload calculations, a graph-partitioning-based tetrahedral cell clustering technique is used. The main contribution of the work is at the proposed model, which formulates the screen partitioning problem as a hypergraph partitioning problem. It is experimentally verified on a PC cluster that, compared to the previously suggested jagged partitioning approach, the proposed approach results in both better load balancing in local rendering and less communication overhead in data migration phases.

1 Introduction

In many scientific simulations, data is located at the vertices (data points) of a 3D grid that represents the physical environment. Unstructured datasets are a special case of grid-based volumetric datasets in which the data points are irregularly distributed and there is no explicit connectivity information. Direct volume rendering (DVR) is a popular volume visualization technique [1] employed in exploration and analysis of such 3D grids used by scientific simulations.

The main aim in DVR is to map a set of data values defined throughout a 3D volumetric grid to some color values over a 2D image on the screen. DVR algorithms are able to produce high-quality images, but due to the excessive amount of sampling and composition operations performed, they suffer from a considerable speed limitation. Furthermore, memory requirements for some recent datasets are beyond the capacities of today's conventional computers.

These facts bring parallelization of DVR algorithms into consideration [9]. Image-space-parallel (IS-parallel) [5,8] or object-space-parallel (OS-parallel) [6,7] methods can be used for distributed-memory parallelization. OS-parallel methods decompose the 3D data into subvolumes and distribute these subvolumes to processors. Each processor works only on its assigned subvolume and produces a partial image using its local data. IS-parallel methods try to decompose the screen and assign subscreens to processors. Each processor computes only

* This work is partially supported by The Scientific and Technical Research Council of Turkey (TÜBİTAK) under project EEEAG-199E013.

A. Yazici and C. Şener (Eds.): ISCIS 2003, LNCS 2869, pp. 457–464, 2003.

a small but complete portion of the whole image on the screen. In IS-parallel DVR, screen decomposition and subscreen-to-processor mapping is important for successful load balancing and minimization of the data migration overhead.

This work investigates IS-parallel DVR of unstructured grids on distributed-memory architectures, and focuses on load balancing and minimization of data migration overhead. In the following section, we start with a brief description of the underlying sequential DVR algorithm. In Section 3, we present the details of our parallel algorithm together with a description of the proposed screen partitioning model. In Section 4, we present some experimental results that verify the validity of the proposed work. We give our conclusions in Section 5.

2 Sequential Algorithm

The underlying sequential algorithm used in our IS-parallel DVR algorithm is based on Koyamada's ray casting algorithm [4]. The algorithm starts with scan-converting all front-facing external faces. From each pixel found, a ray is shot into the volume and is followed until it exits from a back-facing external face, forming a ray segment (Fig. 1). Along a ray segment, some sampling points are determined. The number and location of the sampling points depend on the sampling technique used. In this work, mid-point sampling technique is used.

At each sampling point, new sampling values are computed by interpolating the actual data values on nearby data points. Passing the sampling values from appropriate transfer functions, RGB color triples and opacity values are obtained. The color and opacity values found along a ray segment are composited in visibility order, using a weighting formula that assigns higher weights to values on points closer to the screen. Consequently, for each ray segment, a final color is generated. The generated color is put in the related pixel buffer to which the ray segment contributes. Due to the concavity of the volume, there may be more than one ray segments generated for the same pixel, and hence more than one color values may be stored in the same pixel buffer (two in the example of Fig. 1). After all ray segments are traced, the colors in pixel buffers are composited in visibility order and the final colors over the screen are generated.

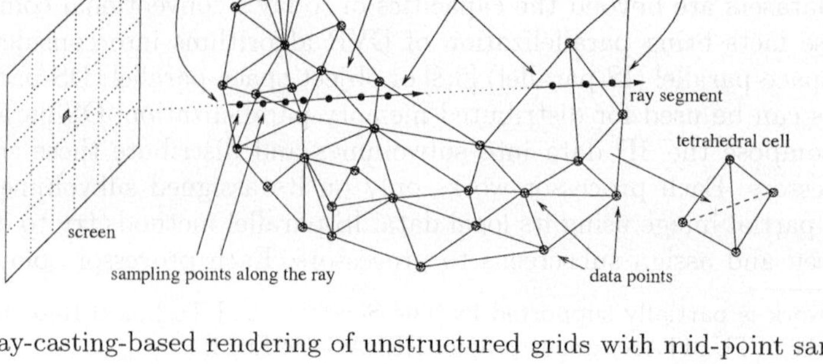

Fig. 1. Ray-casting-based rendering of unstructured grids with mid-point sampling

3 IS-Parallel DVR Algorithm

3.1 View-Independent Preprocessing

The view-independent preprocessing phase, which is performed once at the beginning of the whole visualization process (Fig. 2), performs the operations that are independent of the current visualization parameters. These include retrieval of the data from disk, cell clustering and the initial data distribution. Since the data to be visualized is usually produced by simulations performed on the same parallel machine, it is assumed that the data is already partitioned and stored in the local disks of the processors. Hence, processors can read a subset of cells in parallel.

After the data is read, processors concurrently perform a top-down clustering on their local cells. For this purpose, a graph-partitioning-based clustering approach is followed, where the cells and faces respectively form the vertices and edges of the graph representing the unstructured grid. In the implementation, state-of-the-art graph partitioning tool MeTiS [3] is used to partition this graph and create the cell clusters (subvolumes). Since clustering is performed just once, at the beginning of the whole visualization process, independent of the changing visualization parameters, the cost of cell clustering is almost negligible.

The main idea behind cell clustering is forming groups of close tetrahedral cells and obtaining some volumetric chunks within the data such that the total surface area to be scan-converted is smaller. This way, the computational cost of screen workload calculations during the view-dependent partitioning phase is reduced. Furthermore, since the parallel algorithm works on cell clusters instead of individual tetrahedral cells, the housekeeping work is simplified, number of iterations in some loops are reduced, and some data structures are shortened.

After cell clustering, an initial cluster-to-processor mapping is found. All the following view-dependent preprocessing phases utilize this initial cell cluster mapping. Even if a cell cluster may be temporarily replicated in other processors during the local rendering, it is statically owned by only a single processor. This static owner keeps the cluster's data structures throughout the whole visualization process, and is responsible from sending them to the other processors.

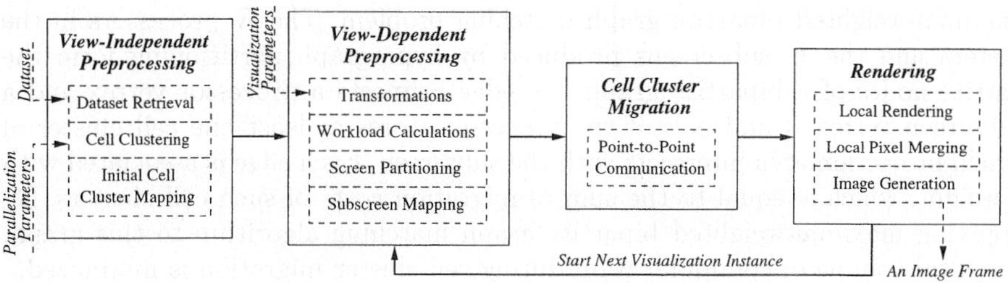

Fig. 2. The proposed IS-parallel DVR algorithm

3.2 View-Dependent Preprocessing

In IS-parallel DVR, the changing visualization parameters at each visualization instance require repartitioning of the screen and assignment of subscreens to processors for a load-balanced rendering. In order to decompose the screen, the rendering-load distribution over the screen pixels should be known beforehand. For this purpose, approximate rendering load of a cell cluster is estimated by summing the areas of its front-facing internal faces. This estimated rendering load for the cell cluster is evenly distributed over the pixels under the projection area of the cell cluster. After this process is repeated for all cell clusters, it becomes possible to know approximately how many samples will be taken along a ray fired from a specific pixel.

Once the workload distribution over the screen is computed, the screen is decomposed into subscreens such that the total load of the pixels in subscreens will be almost equal. Here, the number of subscreens is chosen to be equal to the number of processors, so that each processor is assigned the task of rendering one of the subscreens. In our implementation, for efficiency purposes, an n by n coarse mesh, which forms n^2 screen cells, is imposed over the screen. In this scheme, an individual screen cell corresponds to an atomic task which is assigned to a processor and is completely rendered by that processor. The set of screen cells assigned to the same processor forms a subscreen for the processor. A subscreen is not necessarily composed of geometrically connected screen cells.

We model the the screen partitioning problem as a hypergraph partitioning problem. A hypergraph can be considered as a generalization of a graph, where each hyperedge can connect more than two vertices. In this model, the vertices of the hypergraph correspond to screen cells, that is, a vertex represents the atomic task of rendering a respective screen cell. Each vertex is associated with a weight, which is equal to the total rendering load of the pixels contained in the respective screen cell. Hyperedges of the hypergraph represent the cell clusters. Each hyperedge connects the screen cells which intersect the projection area of the corresponding cell cluster. Each hyperedge is associated with a weight, which is equal to the number of bytes needed in order to store the corresponding cell cluster. By partitioning the hypergraph into equally-weighted parts (subscreens), the model tries to minimize the total replication amount while maintaining a load balance in rendering of subscreens. In the implementation, our hypergraph partitioning tool PaToH [2] is used for partitioning the hypergraph.

Moreover, we formulate the subscreen-to-processor mapping problem as a maximal-weighted bipartite graph matching problem. The K processors in the system and the K subscreens produced by hypergraph partitioning form the partite nodes of a bipartite graph. An edge connects a processor vertex and a subscreen vertex if and only if the processor stores at least one cell cluster of which projection area intersects with the subscreen. Each edge is associated with a weight, which is equal to the sum of migration costs of such cell clusters. By applying maximal-weighted bipartite graph matching algorithm to this graph, the total volume of communication during cell cluster migration is minimized.

3.3 Cell Cluster Migration

After partitioning the screen and mapping subscreens to processors, the processors at which the cell clusters will be replicated are determined. Then, the cell clusters are migrated from their home processors to the new processors through point-to-point communication, according to the replication topology found.

3.4 Rendering

Once the cell cluster migration is complete, processors are ready to render their assigned subscreens in parallel. Most parts of the local rendering is similar to that of the sequential algorithm. The rays are followed throughout the data utilizing the connectivity information, which keeps the neighbor cluster, cell and face ids for the four faces in each cell.

Although it is possible to have non-convex cell clusters as a result of the clustering algorithm, this does not cause an increase in the number of ray segments created. Existence of such non-convexities is eliminated due to replication of the cell clusters. However, the non-convexities in the nature of the dataset still require the use of ray buffers. Since, after the local rendering, all processors have a subimage, an all-to-one communication operation is performed and the whole image frame is generated in one of the processors.

4 Experiments

As the parallel rendering platform, a 24-node PC cluster is used. The processing nodes of the cluster are equipped with 64 Mb of RAM, and are interconnected by a Fast Ethernet switch. Each node contains an Intel Pentium II 400 Mhz processor and runs Debian GNU Linux operating system. The DVR algorithm is developed in C, using MPI as the communication interface.

Each experiment is repeated over three different datasets using five different viewing parameter sets and the average values are reported. In the experiments, each processor is assigned 10 cell clusters, which is an empirically found number. As mentioned before, to make the view-dependent preprocessing overhead affordable, coarse meshes of varying size are imposed over the screen. In all experiments, the proposed hypergraph-partitioning-based (HP-based) model is compared with the previously suggested jagged-partitioning-based (JP-based) model. The details of the JP-based model can be found in [5].

Experiments are conducted over *Blunt Fin*, *Combustion Chamber* and *Oxygen Post* datasets obtained from NASA Research Center. Fig. 3 displays our renderings and the subscreen-to-processor mapping for different models. In each figure, the first image represents the actual rendering obtained using the standard viewing directions. The second and third images show the screen partitioning (by associating each subscreen with a different color) produced by the JP-based and HP-based models, respectively.

The experiments which verify the solution quality are conducted at high number of virtual processors by allocating more than one executable instance per node. Fig. 4 displays the total volume of communication with the varying number

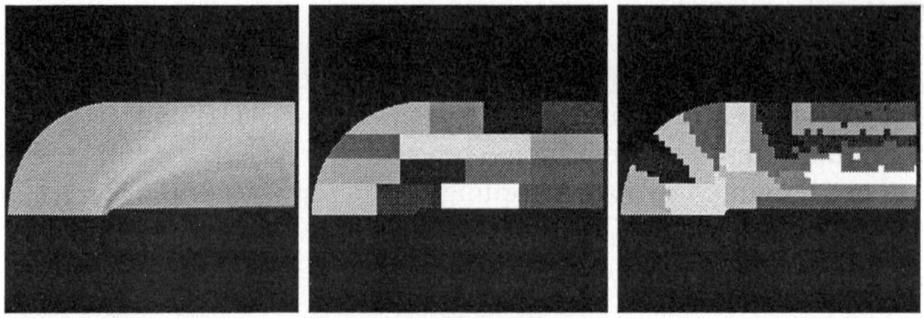

a) The Blunt Fin dataset

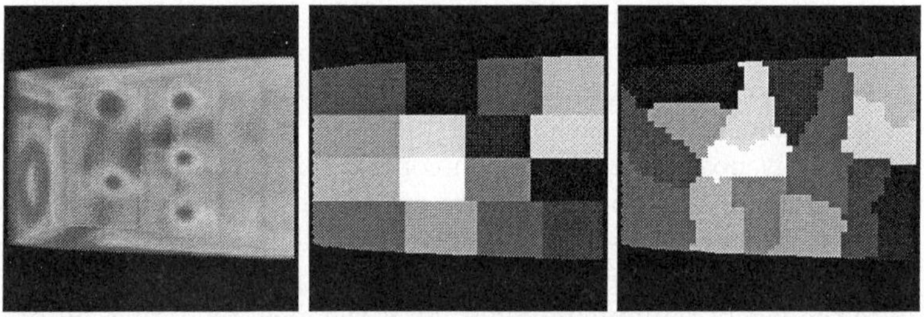

b) The Combustion Chamber dataset

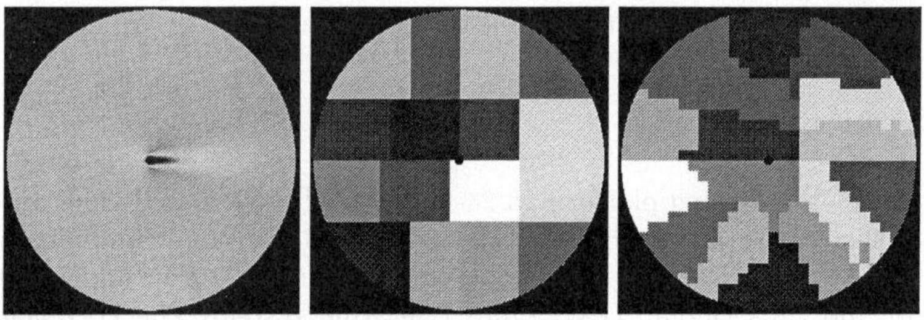

c) The Oxygen Post dataset

Fig. 3. Example renderings and subscreen-to-processor assignments of the datasets

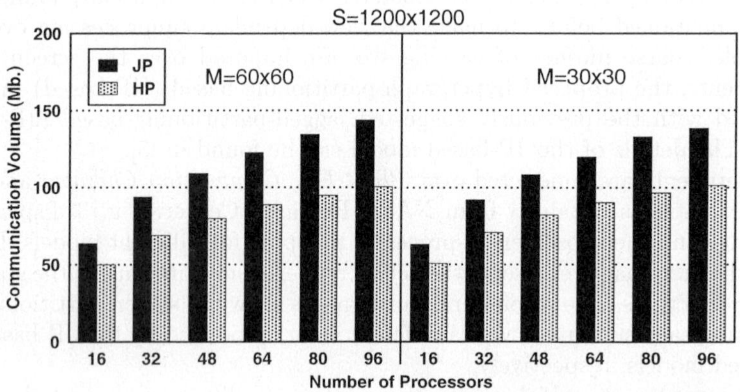

Fig. 4. Total communication volume with the changing number of processors

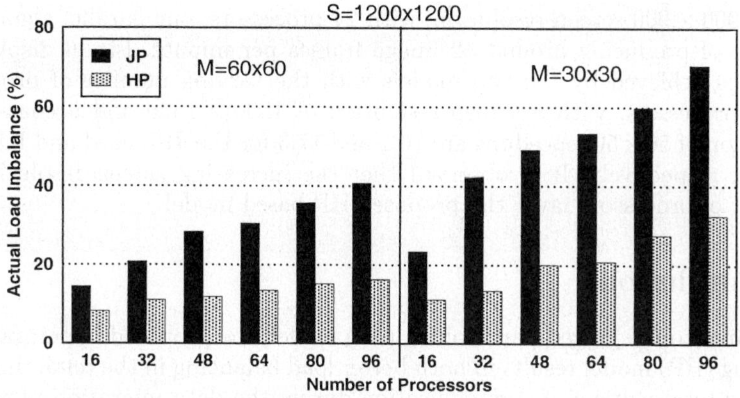

Fig. 5. Load imbalance in local rendering with the changing number of processors

of processors. With a coarse mesh resolution of 60×60, using 96 processors, HP-based model results in around %30 less communication overhead than the JP-based model. When coarse mesh resolution is decreased to 30×30, there occurs a slight decrease in communication volume. This can be explained with the decrease in lengths of subscreen boundaries, and hence the decrease in the amount of overlaps between cell clusters and subscreen boundaries.

Fig. 5 gives the load imbalance rates in local rendering phase. With a coarse mesh resolution of 60×60, using 96 processors, JP-based model results in a load imbalance of 40.7%. With the same parameters, load imbalance values for the HP-based model is 16.3%. When coarse mesh resolution is decreased to 30×30, both models perform worse in load balancing. This is due to the decrease in the number of screen cells, and hence the reduction in solution space.

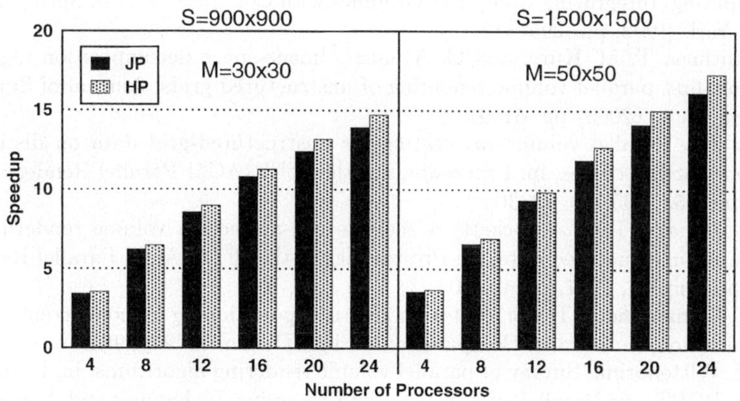

Fig. 6. Speedups at different screen and mesh resolutions

At 900 × 900 screen resolution, with 24 processors, our parallel algorithm is capable of producing around 12 image frames per minute. Fig. 6 displays the speedups achieved by the two models with the varying number of processors. At 24 processors, with a screen resolution of 1500 × 1500 and a coarse mesh resolution of 50 × 50, speedups are 16.1 and 17.3 for the JP-based and HP-based models, respectively. It is observed that the increasing screen resolution and number of processors favor the proposed HP-based model.

5 Conclusions

Compared to the jagged partitioning (JP) model, the proposed hypergraph partitioning (HP) model results in both better load balancing in the rendering phase and less total volume of communication during the data migration phase. The experiments conducted at the available number of processors indicate that HP-based model yields superior speedup values than the JP-based model. We should note that, HP step, which is carried out sequentially on each processor, is the limiting factor on the speedup values. A parallel HP tool, which will probably be implemented in the future, can eliminate this current drawback of our implementation. A nice aspect is that as the new heuristics are developed for HP and the existing HP tools are improved, the solution quality of the proposed model will also improve.

References

1. T. T. Elvins, A survey of algorithms for volume visualization, Computer Graphics (ACM Siggraph Quarterly), 26(3) (1992) pp. 194–201.
2. Ü. V. Çatalyürek and C. Aykanat, PaToH: Partitioning tool for hypergraphs, Technical Report, Department of Computer Engineering, Bilkent University, 1999.
3. G. Karypis and V. Kumar, MeTiS: A software package for partitioning unstructured graphs, partitioning meshes and computing fill-reducing orderings of sparse matrices, Technical Report, University of Minnesota, 1998.
4. K. Koyamada, Fast traversal of irregular volumes, in: T. L. Kunii (Ed.), Visual Computing, Integrating Computer Graphics with Computer Vision, Springer-Verlag New York, 1992, pp. 295–312.
5. H. Kutluca, T. M. Kurc, and C. Aykanat, Image-space decomposition algorithms for sort-first parallel volume rendering of unstructured grids, Journal of Supercomputing, 15(1) (2000) pp. 51–93.
6. K.-L. Ma, Parallel volume ray-casting for unstructured-grid data on distributed-memory architectures, in: Proceedings of the IEEE/ACM Parallel Rendering Symposium '95, 1995, pp. 23–30.
7. K.-L. Ma and T. W. Crockett, A scalable cell-projection volume rendering algorithm for unstructured data, in: Proceedings of the IEEE/ACM Parallel Rendering Symposium '97, 1997, pp. 95–104.
8. M. E. Palmer and S. Taylor, Rotation invariant partitioning for concurrent scientific visualization, in: Parallel Computational Fluid Dynamics '94, 1994.
9. C. M. Wittenbrink, Survey of parallel volume rendering algorithms, in: Proceedings of the PDPTA'98 Parallel and Distributed Processing Techniques and Applications, July 1998, pp. 1329–1336.

Generalization and Localization Based Style Imitation for Grayscale Images

Fatih Nar[1] and Atılım Çetin[2]

[1] Informatics Institute, Middle East Technical University,
fatihnar@ii.metu.edu.tr
[2] Department of Computer Engineering, Bilkent University,
atilim@cs.bilkent.edu.tr

Abstract. An example based rendering (EBR) method based on generalization and localization that uses artificial neural networks (ANN) and k-Nearest Neighbor (k-NN) is proposed. The method involves learning phase and application phase, which means that once a transformation filter is learned, it can be applied to any other image. In learning phase, error back-propagation learning algorithm is used to learn general transformation filter using unfiltered source image and filtered output image. ANNs are usually unable to learn filter-generated textures and brush strokes hence these localized features are stored in a feature instance table for using with k-NN during application phase. In application phase, for any given grayscale image, first ANN is applied then k-NN search is used to retrieve local features from feature instances considering texture continuity to produce desired image. Proposed method is applied up to 40 image filters that are collection of computer-generated and human-generated effects/styles. Good results are obtained when image is composed of localized texture/style features that are only dependent to intensity values of pixel itself and its neighbors.

1 Introduction

In recent years, researchers within computer graphics and computer vision communities put a great effort on example based rendering, non-photorealistic rendering (NPR), and texture synthesis. They use various methods from other disciplines such as machine learning, and image processing. EBR is an useful tool for creating animations and images for various purposes such as imitation of styles, creating educational softwares for children, and creating video games in cartoon world for entertainment with less human effort [8]. These styles/effects, that are aimed to imitate can be human-generated or computer-generated.

Ultimate aim of EBR is creating an analogous image for a given unfiltered image using unfiltered and filtered image pairs. In short, it is style imitation as seen in Figure 1. Ideally the filter learned from an image pair must be sufficient for creating an analogous image for any image even the filter is a complex or non-linear one such as artistic styles or traditional image filters [6].

Varying edge definitions and brush strokes, crossing edge boundaries with varying sizes, textures, randomness, smoothness, and directions are used in different

A. Yazici and C. Şener (Eds.): ISCIS 2003, LNCS 2869, pp. 465–473, 2003.

painting style/effects [8]. These features are sometimes dependent only local features (i.e. intensity values) but sometimes they are also dependent to regional or global features of image, which makes it difficult to learn such filters. In this study, joint statistics of small neighborhoods are used within 3x3 and 5x5 matrix sizes to measure relationships between the unfiltered source and the filtered target image pair.

Unfiltered source image: *A* Filtered output image: *A'* Unfiltered source image: *B* Analogous output image: *B'*

Fig. 1. Transformation filter learned from *A* and *A'* is used to find *B'* from *B*

In learning phase, algorithm takes two images *A* and *A'* where *A* is unfiltered source image and *A'* is the filtered output image and image *A* and image *A'* are pixel wise registered. For the sake of simplicity, grayscale images are used within this study. Learning phase is simply divided into two parts; ANN for generalized learning and feature instance extraction for localized instance based learning. Feed forward artificial neural networks (FFANN) are used to learn transformation filter with the error back-propagation learning algorithm. Feature instances will be retrieved using k-NN algorithm in application phase as explained in section 3. Details of learning algorithm will be explained in section 2.

ANNs has been studied thoroughly in numerous applications and in various problems since mid-80's after the publication of Rumelhart and his colleagues' studies [3]. A FFANN is assembled with an input, an output, and one or more hidden layers. Each layer contains units called neurons that are connected to units in prior layer with certain connection weight (strength) where each unit takes a number of real-valued inputs and generates a single real-valued output, according to an activation function applied to the sum of the inputs [1][2][3].

k-NN is an instance-based learning method and unlike ANN which tries to find generalized rule, k-NN simply stores the training instances for later retrieval. Distance between given pattern and patterns in training instances are evaluated using Euclidian distance metric and smallest *k* of them are taken into consideration [1].

Edge detection, coarse levels, binarisation and similar image-processing operators have been tried with FFANN as input features to enhance training. Since all these operators are explained in introductory chapters of image-processing books [5], so no further detail will be given in the rest of this paper.

Results and example outputs will be given in section 4. Conclusions and future works will be given in section 5.

2 Learning Phase

In learning phase error-backpropagation algorithm is used for training FFANN to find optimum network weights. Input patterns are taken from unfiltered input image *A* and output patterns are taken from filtered image *A'* where two images are pixel wise registered. There are 9 units (3x3 kernel) in input layer and a unit in output layer and there are 21, 17, 13, and 9 units in 4 hidden layers as seen in Figure 2.

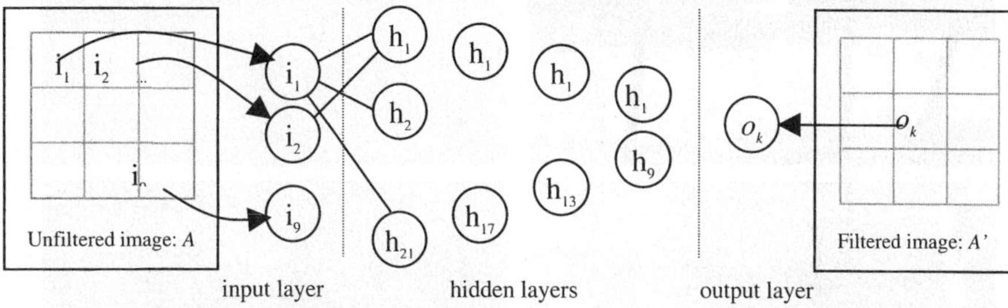

Fig. 2. FFANN structure showing relationship of input and output patterns with images

Image intensity values lay between –1 and +1 where they correspond to black and white accordingly. Incremental (stochastic) training strategy is used with number of 100K patterns that are taken from input and output images in random order where each pixel is used only once unless all pixels are used. Error is calculated using least mean square (LMS) as given in formula 1 where t_k is desired output and o_k is actual output, which are calculated in feed-forward phase.

$$E_d(\vec{w}) = \frac{1}{2} \sum_{k \in outputs} (t_k - o_k)^2 \quad (1)$$

Network weights are initially selected from floating random numbers in the range of –1 and +1. Bipolar o_k = *tanh(.)* is chosen as activation function, and it produces activation values between –1 and +1 which is also in the same range of image's intensity values [2]. Incremental training strategy and bipolar activation function are chosen because they show better convergence and speed properties [4].

Weight update rule for output and hidden layers are given in formula 2 and 3 where η is learning rate and chosen as 0.01 in this study.

$$\Delta w_{jk} = \eta(t_k - o_k)(1 - o_k^2) i_{jk} \quad (2) \qquad \Delta w_{ij} = \eta(1 - o_j^2) x_{ij} \sum_{s \in outputs} \delta_k w_{jk} \quad (3)$$

ANN is applied to several training image pairs that are filtered with 40 different filters for learning transient filter *F*. For some simple effects generalization ability of ANN is sufficient for learning the filter without localization ability of k-NN as seen in Figure 3. Common properties of these filters are that they are relatively simple filters (i.e. there is no texture information that must be learned by ANN). Results of ANN can be enhanced by using extra input features such as gradient flows or coarse level images but experiments shows that it causes ANN to converge harder and total learning and application time is also increased.

Fig. 3. Original image and output images (emboss, inverse, solarize) produced by ANN

ANN is good at generalization but provides very weak results at memorization especially when filter contains extra information such as textures and brush strokes, which cause information-gain in output image. Difference of original image *A* and filtered image *A'* can give us texture information as seen in top right image (*D'*) in Figure 4. Despite ANN cannot help us to memorize that textural information, it is still valuable tool for extracting this texture information better than simply finding *D'*. In bottom right image (Figure 4) you can see image *D"* which is the subtraction of filtered image *A'* and output image *A"* that is produced by ANN. This new difference map *D"*, which acts as texture map for us, is convolved with 5x5 kernel and whenever the value of middle point in kernel is different than zero (or very near to zero), this pattern is stored in indexes *H1* and *H2* (intensities that are taken from *A"*: *H1* and intensities that are taken from *D, D* equals to *D'* or *D"*, itself: *H2*) for later retrieval with k-NN in application phase. In this pattern, 25 intensity values and position of patterns are kept. As you can see in image *D'*, total numbers of patterns that will be stored is much more comparing to image *D"* since image *D'* contains much more nonzero intensity values comparing to image *D"*. Hence memory consumption and query time in application phase is dramatically decreased if image *D"* is used instead of using image *D'* for image pairs *A* and *A'* in Figure 4. So the method proposed in this paper is based on the observation that ANN provides good texture extraction from filtered and unfiltered images for texture synthesis for some cases. In other cases texture map *D'* contains more nonzero intensity values comparing to *D"* so *D'* is used instead of *D"* in such cases.

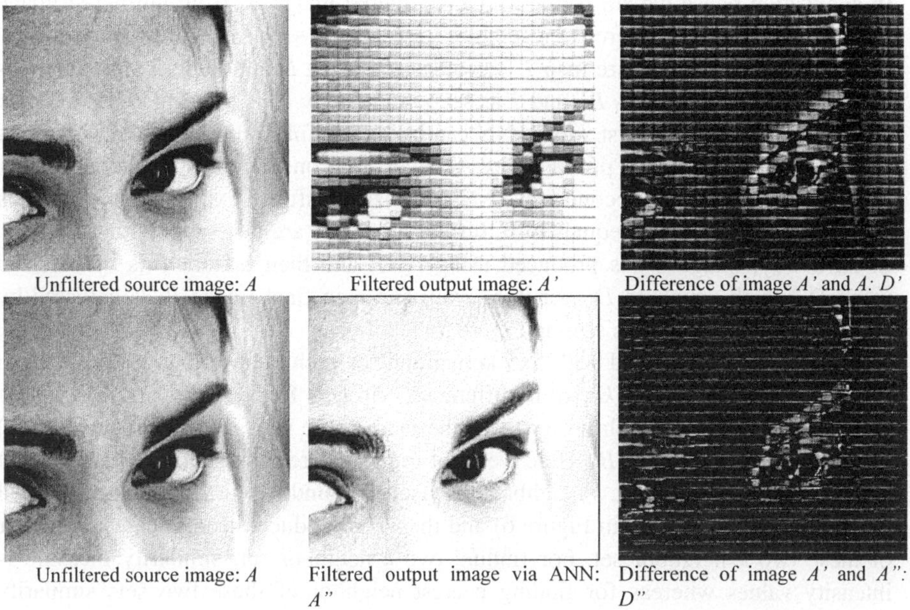

Fig. 4. Creation of training instances (textural patterns) for k-NN using ANN

In this study, training instances are arranged in dynamic arrays using their mean and variance of intensity values (5x5 kernel: 25 intensity values). In k-NN search whenever a new pattern is introduced, its mean value and variance is calculated and neighbor instances are searched according to this mean and variance values within predefined radius (i.e. [calculated mean – radius, calculated mean + radius]) via indexes *H1* and *H2*. This assumption is based on the fact that mean and variance of a new instance is not too much different than mean and variance of its nearest neighbors in training instances. Resultant quality is decreased in small amount but query time is increased considerably.

After learning filter *F*, using ANN and extracting difference (texture) map (appropriate one is selected from *D'* or *D"* texture maps and named as *D*) the problem becomes a texture synthesis problem. Wei-Levoy proposed casual neighborhood for texture synthesis problem [7] and Hertzmann extends this approach for EBR in his image analogies study [6]. Our study is inspired from image analogies study by Hertzmann and latest developments about texture synthesis and makes extension to these studies with generalization ability of ANN.

3 Application Phase

In application phase we are trying to gather filtered image *B'* from unfiltered image *B*. Normally image *B"* (here *B"* resembles to *A"* that is seen in Figure 4) is produced using ANN and then texture map *T* is synthesized using *D* and then final image *B'* is gathered by adding images *B"* and *T* as seen in Figure 5. This filtering operation may occur in three ways. In first way, ANN can be successful to produce target image as seen in Figure 3 so image produced by ANN (*B"*) is considered as *B'* and no further process is necessary. In second way, ANN is unsuccessful to extract texture so *D'* is taken as *D* and *B"* is just equals to *B*, further processes are just same with third way. In third way, image *B"* is produced using ANN and then texture *T* is synthesized using *D* (which equals to *D"* for third way) and then final image *B'* is gathered by adding images *B"* and *T* as seen in Figure 5.

Image *B"* is convolved with 5x5 kernel and for each pattern that are taken from *B"* its *k* nearest neighbor (*k*=16) in difference map *D* is found (using *H1* index). *T* is a texture information which we try to synthesis to merge with *B"* (by image addition) for producing final image *B'*. Here we want to make *T* resembles to *D*. Since *T* must contain continuous texture, *k* neighbor of *T* itself is found (using *H2* index and casual neighborhood [7] as seen in Figure 6) and then *T* is produced using nearest neighbor of these two *k* neighbor set. For finding two *k* neighbor set, similarity measure is intensity values whereas for finding nearest neighbor of these two sets similarity measure is pixels' positions.

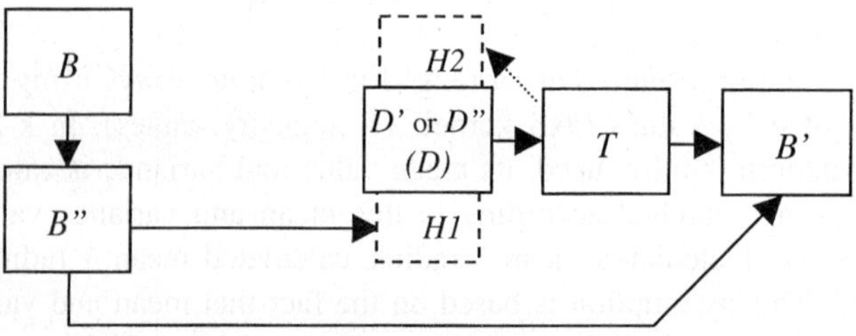

Fig. 5. Process schema of creating image *B'* from *B* using indexes *H1*, *H2* and texture *D*

Pixel intensity value at *P*(*x*, *y*) in image *B'* is *B'*(*x*, *y*) = *B"*(*x*, *y*) + *T*(*x*, *y*) where values less than –1 are set as –1 and values greater than +1 are set as +1. We know the value of *B"*(*x*, *y*) since *B"* = *F*(*B*) or *B*. Only the value we do not know is *T*(*x*, *y*) and it can be found using the nearest neighbor pattern P_{ij} from set *S1* and *S2* where distance metric is position of patterns in *S1* and *S2*. *S1* is found using *k* nearest neighbor pattern of *B"*(*x*, *y*) that exits in $D(x_i, y_i)$ where $i<k$. *S2* is found using *k* nearest casual neighbor pattern of *T*(*x*, *y*) that exists in $T(x_j, y_j)$ where $j<k$.

Above in Figure 6, first image is *T* (target texture map) and other three images are causal neighborhood kernel images. In casual neighborhood search, intensity value of middle point is taken from the training instance where Euclidian distance is minimum. In this study casual neighborhood is used for texture synthesis since it provides texture continuity while preserving pattern similarity [6].

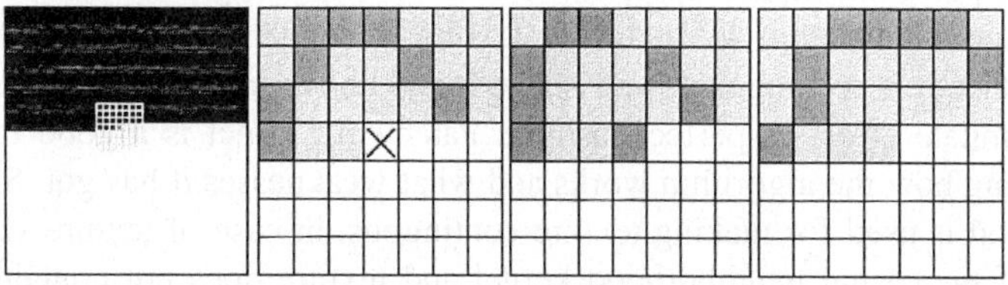

Fig. 6. Casual neighborhood kernel with the size of 7x7 (first 24 pixels are used)

4 Results

Test set is prepared using test images provided by Hertzmann in his web page and using the Adobe Photoshop 6.0.

Fig. 7. Example images (Top: Dorotea, Craquelune; Bottom: Sponge, Film Grain)

Provided method in this paper renders 256x256 grayscale image in 2-3 minutes with PIII-800 (Figure 7). Algorithm is successful at most of the styles/effects within test set, which contains 40 styles/effects and about hundred images.

Unfiltered image   Filtered image (patchwork effect)

Fig. 8. Kernel size problem in imitation of patchwork effect

In Figure 8, patchwork filter is applied that is learned using unfiltered image *A* and filtered image *A'* in Figure 4. Patchwork texture in image *D"* (Figure 4) is in size of 8x10 and since it is rectangular (well-shaped) and above image uses 5x5 kernel size, it fails to imitate effect in perfect fashion. Patchwork effect is a good example for understanding how the algorithm works and what weaknesses it has got. Since casual neighborhood is used for making texture continuous, in case of texture size is larger than size of the casual neighborhood kernel and texture does not containing curvatures it naturally fails to find exact neighborhood pixels [9]. Still it can produce similar outputs but error ratio is increases.

5 Conclusions and Future Works

Combining ANN and k-NN provides good results since they overcome the weakness of each other, however the results indicate that faster and better nearest neighbor search algorithm must be implemented in order to increase the performance of the system (i.e. image pyramids and approximate nearest neighbors) [6]. Proposed method in this paper is based on local features in certain kernel size (i.e. 3x3 and 5x5) hence it produces poor results with textures having large radius or flat shapes like patchwork or effects/styles relying on regional or global features. Iterative texture synthesis methods (based on Markov Random Fields) can be also used for increasing the quality of texture synthesis [9]. Texture continuity versus intensity similarity in texture synthesis process is taken as constant in proposed method and automatic detection of these coefficients is leaved as future work. Proposed method is not suitable for series of images (video) since it does not provide continuity within different images. Currently, the method does not work with color images but adaptation is trivial using RGB channels or luminance instead of pixel's grayscale intensity values. Since only human can quantify the quality of job, success of the proposed algorithm is subjective in some aspects.

Acknowledgments. We would like to thank Ferda Nur ALPASLAN for her guidance and comments and also we would like to thank anonymous reviewers for their valuable suggestions.

References

1. Tom M. Mitchell: Machine Learning, Chapter 4–8. McGraw-Hill series in Computer Science. (1997)
2. John Hertz, Andres Krogh, Richard G. Palmer: Introduction to The Theory of Neural Computation, Chapter 6. Lecture Notes, Vol 1. Santa Fe Institute (1991)
3. D. E. Rumelhart, G.E. Hinton, R. J. Williams: Learning Internal Representations by Error Propagation, pp. 318–362. MIT Press (1986)
4. Dilip Sarkar: Methods to Speed Up Error Back-Propagation Algorithm, Vol 27. ACM Computing Surveys (1995)

5. John J. Russ: The Image Processing Handbook, Chapter 4 and 6. CRC Press (1999)
6. Aaron Hertzmann, Charles E. Jacobs, Nuria Oliver, Brian Curless, David H. Salesin: Image Analogies. Siggraph (2001)
7. Li-Yi Wei, Marc Levoy: Fast Texture Synthesis using Tree-Structured Vector Quantization, Proceedings of SIGGRAPH, (2000)
8. Barbara J. Meier: Painterly Rendering for Animation. Walt Disney Feature Animation (1996)
9. Alexei A. Efros, Thomas K. Leung: Texture Synthesis by Non-parametric Sampling. IEEE International Conference on Computer Vision (1999)

Robot Mimicking: A Visual Approach for Human Machine Interaction

Algan Uskarcı, A. Aydın Alatan, M. Serdar Dindaroğlu, and Aydın Ersak

Department of Electrical-Electronics Engineering
Middle East Technical University
Balgat 06531 Ankara TURKEY
{uskarci, aalatan, e121071, ayersak}@metu.edu.tr

Abstract. The proposed method is the preliminary step for a human-machine interaction system, in which a robot arm mimics the movements of a human arm, visualized through a camera set-up. In order to achieve this goal, the posture of a model joint, which simulates a human arm, is determined by finding the bending and yaw angles from captured images. The image analysis steps consist of preprocessing of noise via median filtering, thresholding and connected component analysis. The relation between the relative positions of these markers can be used to determine the unknown bending and yaw angles of the model joint. This information is further passed to a PUMA 760 robot arm to finalize the goal. The preliminary simulation results are promising to present that the proposed system can be utilized in a real environment in which a human (arm) can be mimicked by a machine with visual sensor.

1 Introduction

One of the most important research fields in the development of successful robotic systems is the Human-Machine Interaction. In the early years of robotics teach pendants and programming were the primary methods for interaction [2]. However, as computer capabilities improve better methods are being developed. Vision based approaches are the most promising among all, since vision is the primary method of interaction among humans [1].

In this paper, we present the preliminary results for a visual posture mimicking system. The system makes use of the captured images of a model joint in order to achieve the same posture for a robot arm with the model joint. This research will form a basis for developing a system, which is able to mimic the arm posture of humans.

The rest of the paper is organized as follows. Section 2 describes the visual processing part of the system. Section 3 describes the robot communication part, which is responsible for controlling the robot by using the data obtained from visual processing part. In section 4, the results obtained during experiments are presented and the last section is devoted to the conclusions and remarks on future work.

A. Yazici and C. Şener (Eds.): ISCIS 2003, LNCS 2869, pp. 474–481, 2003.

2 Visual Analysis

Visual processing of captured images is used to determine the bending and yaw angles of the model joint. The model joint consists of two equal length cylindrical parts (Fig.1). In this model, the lower joint can rotate around the base and an upper one can bend. Thus, one has two parameters for this model joint: a yaw angle and a bending angle. In order to be able to determine these two angles using a visual capture system, two black circular markers are placed at the bottom side of the lower part and one black marker is placed on the upper side of the top part (Fig.1).

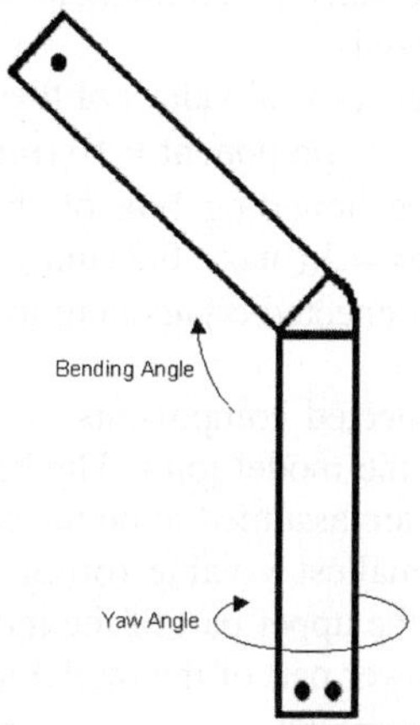

Fig. 1. The Model Joint

2.1 Image Processing for Determining Bending and Yaw Angles

In order to determine the bending and yaw angles of the model joint, first an image of the model joint is captured by using a camera (COHU 4710 model B/W solid state). The captured image is then passed to an application software (written in Visual C++). This software uses Intel's Open Source Computer Vision Library (OpenCV) [7] for image processing and computer vision operations. The major steps in the visual processing stage can be summarized as below:

- A median filter (5-by-5) [3] is applied to the image in order to remove camera and environment noise. A median filter is chosen for noise removal, since a box-car or Gaussian filter blurs the image, which leads to the detection of dots to be more difficult.
- Next, thresholding is applied, based on the pixel values of the image. Although, there are more sophisticated automatic thresholding methods [4], the threshold levels in the simulations are chosen manually after inspecting the environmental effects, such as illumination and background. During the entire experiments, the values for minimum and maximum threshold levels to detect black markers are set to 20 and 80, respectively.
- Thresholding is followed by a connected component analysis [4], in order to determine the connected components within the thresholded image. The connected

component analysis is realized by using 4-connectedness and a pixel value range of –10 to +10 is chosen to determine the homogeneity of neighboring pixels relative to the seed pixel.

- Finally, some of the determined connected components are eliminated in order to determine the set of candidate connected components representing 3 markers on the model joint. Elimination constraints are
  - Area of the connected component for an upper and a lower limit,
  - Ratio of the width of the bounding box of the connected component to the height of the bounding box,
  - Ratio of the area of the connected component to the area of the bounding box (only a lower limit is utilized).

  For a 320x240-pixel image, typical values of these constraints are selected as
  - Area limits of the connected component = 10 (min), 200 (max)
  - Ratio of the width of the bounding box of the connected component to the height of the bounding box = 3 (max), 0.2 (min)
  - Ratio of the area of the connected component to the area of the bounding box = 0.7 (min)

From the set of candidate connected components, 3 of them having the largest area are selected as the markers on the model joint. The centers of the bounding boxes of these 3 connected components are assumed to be the centers of the dots. From these 3 dots, the marker having the smallest y-value (origin is the upper-left corner of the image) is chosen as the dot on the upper part of the model joint and the other two dots are chosen as the ones on the lower part of the model joint.

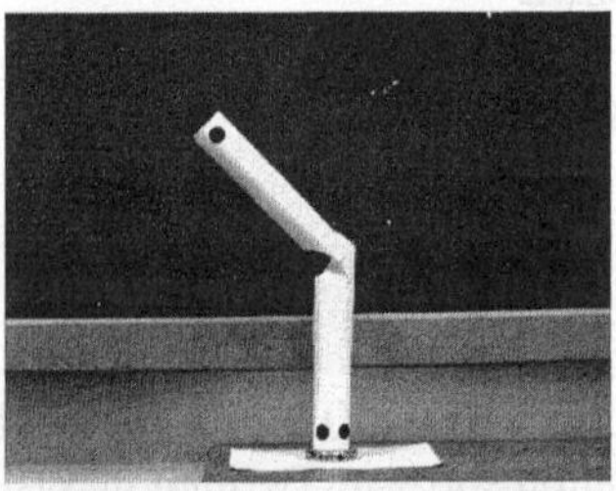

a. Input Image

b. After Thresholding

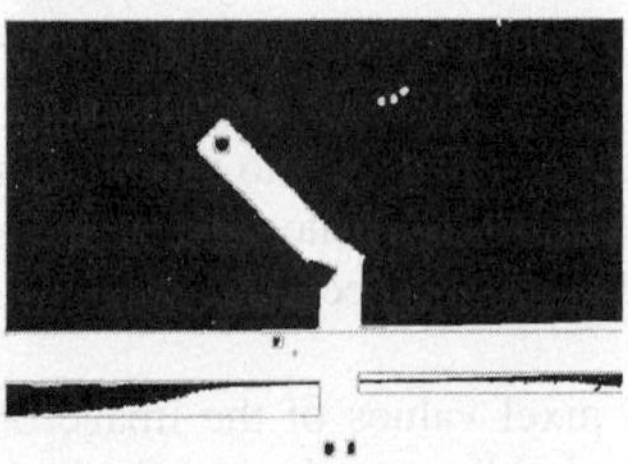

c. After connected-component analysis (all the connected components found are bounded with green boxes.)

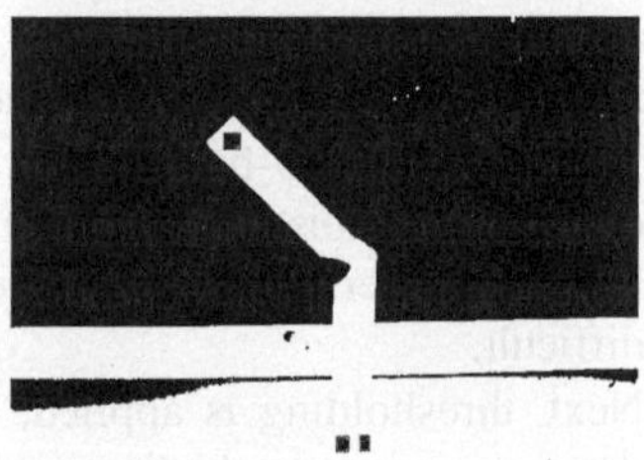

d. The determined markers (The regions with the largest area are chosen as markers and are bounded with red boxes.)

Fig. 2. Steps for Visual Analysis

After the coordinates of the marker are determined, yaw and bending angles of the model joint are determined by using the algorithm in [5]. In this algorithm, first the yaw angle is calculated. Referring to Fig. 3 the variable "N" represents the distance between the lower markers at a zero degree of yaw.

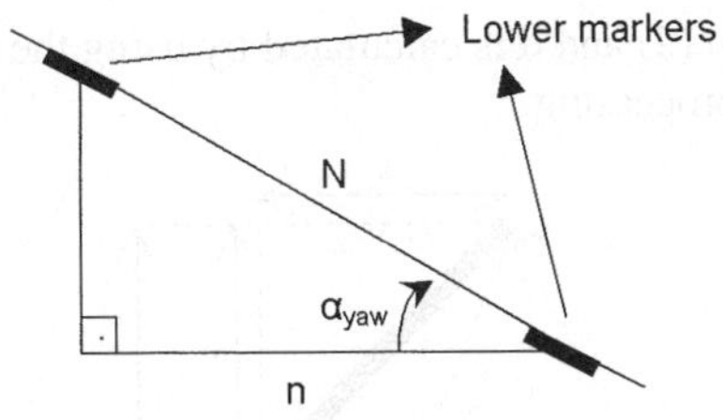

Fig. 3. Calculation of Yaw Degree

Forming a right triangle one can show that

$$\alpha_{yaw} = \cos^{-1}(n/N) \tag{1}$$

where n is the distance between the observed markers at a given yaw angle. Next, the bending angle is determined. Since the image of the model joint will appear skewed for non-zero yaw angles, the bending angle will appear slightly greater than the actual value.

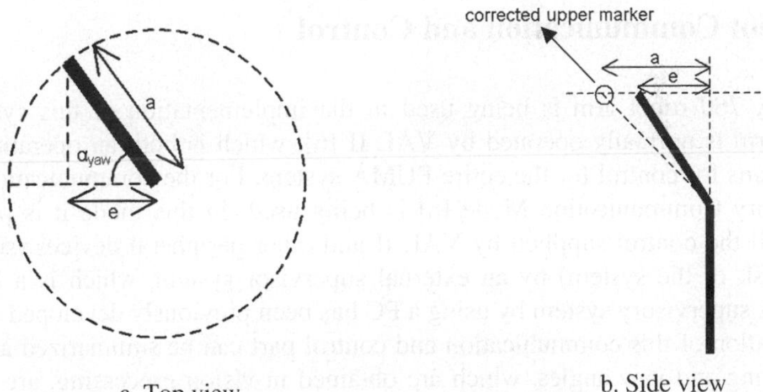

a. Top view b. Side view

Fig. 4. Adjusting Image due to Yaw

Referring to Fig. 4, this error can be corrected by

$$a = e / \cos(\alpha_{yaw}) \tag{2}$$

After the error correction the actual bending angle can be calculated by using the following set of equations. (Fig. 5)

$$\alpha_{bend} = 180 - 2\theta \tag{3}$$

$$\theta = \cos^{-1}(d/c) \tag{4}$$

$$c = a^2 + d^2 \tag{5}$$

where a is calculated in (2) and d is calculated by using the coordinates of the markers determined by image processing.

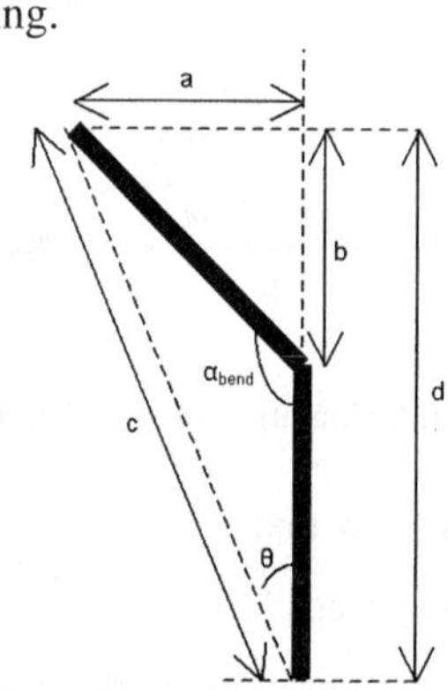

Fig. 5. Calculation of Bending Degree

3 Robot Communication and Control

A PUMA 760 robot arm is being used in the implementation of this system. The PUMA arm is normally operated by VAL II [6], which is both an operating system and a means for control for the entire PUMA system. For the communication method Supervisory Communication Mode [6] is being used. In this mode it is possible to replace all the control supplied by VAL II and other peripheral devices (such as the floppy disk of the system) by an external supervisor system, which is a PC in our system. A supervisory system by using a PC has been previously developed in [6].

The operation of this communication and control part can be summarized as follows: The bending and yaw angles, which are obtained in vision processing, are passed to the robot communication part. By using this data two VAL II commands in the form of "DO DRIVE <joint number>, <angle>, <speed> " are constructed. The parameters passed to the system are the yaw angle for the 1st joint and bending angle for the 2nd joint, since it is assumed that the 1st joint is identical to the rotation of the model joint (i.e. yaw angle) and the 2nd joint is identical to the bending of the model joint (i.e. bending angle). The 3rd joint of PUMA is kept with the same alignment with that of 2nd in order to better visualize the mimicking. Speed parameter gives the percentage speed with respect to the system speed. The commands formed as stated above are then transmitted to the PUMA system through the serial port by using Supervisory Communication Mode.

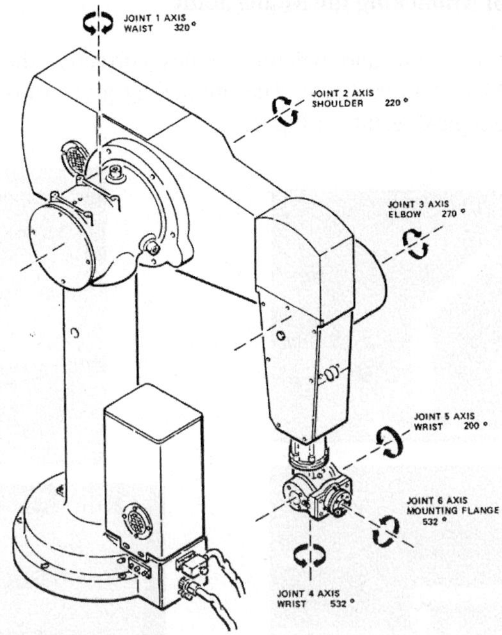

Fig. 6. PUMA 760 Robot Arm

4 Results

The simulations are conducted in two phases. In the first of experiments, the visual information is tested for its performance against angle calculation. In the second part of these experiments, the results of the first part are fed to PUMA 760 robot arm for testing the response for the given inputs.

4.1 Simulations on Determination of Visual Angles

The yaw and bending angles are determined successfully with acceptable errors. After simulations on 25 different images with different yaw and bending angles, the average errors are determined as 1.2 degrees for yaw angle and 3.3 degrees for bending angle. For the same set of experiments, the maximum error was 4.5 degrees for yaw angle and 5.2 degrees for bending angle.

Although the results are successful, it was observed that the system was susceptible to the changes in the background and illumination. The current efforts are making this algorithm robust against illumination and background changes.

4.2 Simulations of Mimicking the Model Joint

After determining the yaw and bending angles correctly, the mimicking step is performed on PUMA 760 robot arm. The mimicking gives satisfying results, as can be seen from some typical results in Figure 7.

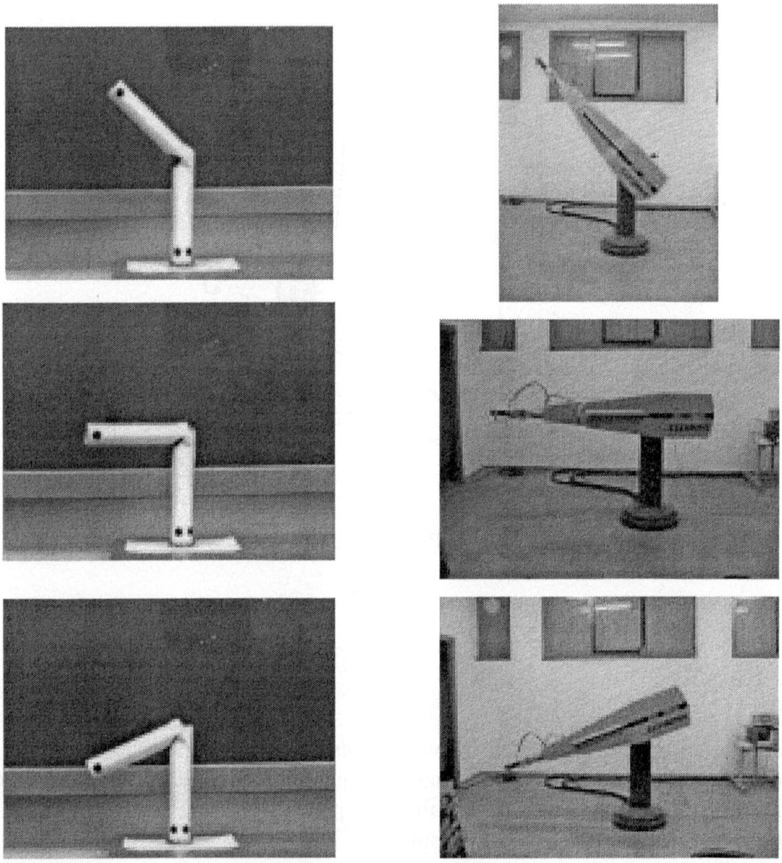

Fig. 7. Example Results for Mimicking

5 Conclusions and Future Works

Considering the errors obtained while estimating the angles during the tests, it can be stated that the system is successful in determining the yaw and bending angles especially in controlled environments, which can be the case in industrial applications. It is also observed that the mimicking, that is realized by PUMA 760 robot arm, is also visually satisfying.

As a future work it is intended to implement this system by using a human arm instead of a model joint. Moreover, the system may be looped in order to work in real time by using a video stream, instead of still images. In order to accomplish these objectives the visual analysis should be improved to decrease the susceptibility to the changes in illumination and background, as well as computational complexity should be further decreased for real time performance.

References

1. V. I. Pavlovic, R. Sharma, T. S. Huang; "Visual Interpretation of Hand Gestures for Human-Computer Interaction: A Review", IEEE Transactions on Pattern Analysis and Machine Intelligence, Vol. 19, No. 7, pp. 677–695, July 1997
2. S. Iba, J.M.V. Weghe, C.J.J. Paredis, and P.K. Khosla; "An Architecture for Gesture-Based Control of Mobile Robots", Proceedings of the IEEE/RSJ International Conference on Intelligent Robots and Systems (IROS'99), Vol. 2, pp. 851–857, October, 1999
3. J.S. Lim; "Two-Dimensional Signal and Image Processing", Prentice Hall, 1990
4. R. Jain, R. Kasturi, B.G. Schunck; "Machine Vision", McGraw Hill, 1995
5. S.C. Arseneau, R.J. Nicholls, M. Farooq, A. Hopkinson; "Robotic Mimicking Control System", Proceedings of the 44th IEEE Midwest Symposium, Vol. 2, pp.547-550, 2001
6. M. S. Dindaro•lu; "Control of PUMA Mark II Robot with an External Computer", M.S. Thesis, Middle East Technical University, Ankara, Turkey, 2002
7. Intel's Open Source Computer Vision Library (OpenCV), http://www.intel.com/research/mrl/research/opencv

Wavelet Packet Based Digital Watermarking for Remote Sensing Image Compression

Seong-Yun Cho[1] and Su-Young Han[2]

[1] Dept. of Digital Media, Anyang University,
Anyang 5-dong, Manan-gu Anyang-si, Kyunggi-do, Korea, 708-113
scho@aycc.anyang.ac.kr

[2] Dept. of Electronic Engineeriing, Hanyang University,
17 Haengdang-dong, Sungdong-gu Seoul, Korea, 133-791
yejiwon@ihanyang.ac.kr

Abstract. In this paper, a new watermark algorithm that based on wavelet packet transform is proposed for the watermark of remote sensing images, which include many high frequency components. The proposed watermark algorithm is used in the high frequency component of image and applies watermark to the overall subband that include the lowest frequency band. And the watermark is embedded on original image after selecting the significant wavelet packet coefficient. For selecting significant coefficients that apply watermark, zerotree is applied to packet transform using CPSO (Coefficient Partitioning Scanning Order) for imperceptibly and robustness. From the experimental result, the proposed algorithm shows better invisibility and robustness performance compare with conventional watermark methods. Especially, it demonstrates better robustness for high image compression in the remote sensing images application.

1 Introduction

Digital watermark denotes information that is imperceptibly and robustly embedded within still images or moving pictures for protect copyrights [1]. So watermarking in the wavelet domain allows precisely to control the location of the watermark, it is very useful in the invisibility and robustness aspect. In the wavelet transform based watermark technique, the watermark is embedded in the subbands that except the lowest frequency band [2]. However, because the image compression is usually lossy compression that eliminates all the high frequency components, the studies that the watermark is embedded in the lowest frequency band have been proceeded for high image compression. But this elastic change by the watermark embedding in the lowest frequency band causes damages of the original image.

Because the high altitude images such as an aerial photograph and a satellite photograph are mainly composed by high frequency components, a new watermark algorithm, inserts watermark into all subband that include the lowest frequency band, is needed for robustness and invisibility

A. Yazici and C. Şener (Eds.): ISCIS 2003, LNCS 2869, pp. 482–489, 2003.

To resolve this problem, wavelet packet based digital watermark algorithm is suggested in this research. So wavelet packet transform analyze adaptively signal of each frequency band contrary to wavelet transform which is recursively decomposed in the low frequency band, it is more suitable for non-stationary signal analysis such as texture image that is easily recognized in the remote sensing images. The wavelet packet transform shows better performance than the conventional wavelet transform in texture images [3]. Because the large coefficients are abstracted from the lowest frequency band as well as high frequency bands after the wavelet packet transform, watermark can be embedded in the overall band without any quality loss of image and keep its robustness against lossy image compression.

In this paper, a new wavelet packet transform based watermark is proposed for satellite photograph or other texture images, which include many high frequency components. For selecting significant coefficients that apply watermark, zerotree is applied to wavelet packet transform using CPSO (coefficient partitioning scanning order) for imperceptibly and robustness. This paper is organized as follows; In section 2, the watermark creation process for this research is explained. The algorithm for embedding watermark and the processes of CPSO are defined in section 3. Detecting process of the watermark is explained section 4. The improvements in the invisibility and robustness of the proposed algorithm over the conventional algorithm are demonstrated by the experiment result in section 5. Finally, the results are summarized, some technical issues are discussed, and some suggestions and further studies are discussed in section 6 as a conclusion.

2 Watermark Creation

A mono image is used for watermark in this research. In general, a logo, seal or signature is used for watermark to prove copyright and these are presented as a binary image.

For the prevention of deformation or detection of watermark, a watermark is scrambled using pseudo-random sequence that has deterministic random characteristics and statistical measurements such as Equation (1).

$$w = \{w(k), k = 1, 2, ..., L, L = M \times N\}. \tag{1}$$

Where k is relocated by pseudo-random sequence and L is the size of binary image and w is binary image sequence for watermark.

3 Watermark Embedding

Early watermarks are embedded in the perceptually insignificant coefficient region for preventing recognition of their existence. But these watermarks are easily damaged or eliminated by image compressions or other image processing techniques. On that account, watermark has to be embedded in the perceptually significant coefficient region and the significant coefficient selecting process has to be concerned for watermark embedding. Moreover, this watermark has to be embedded over fullbands within the limit of original image quality for robustness. In the proposed algorithm in this research, watermark embedding process is composed as following sequences; the wavelet packet transform of original image, CPSO for selecting the perceptually significant coefficients, watermark embedding and inverse wavelet packet transform.

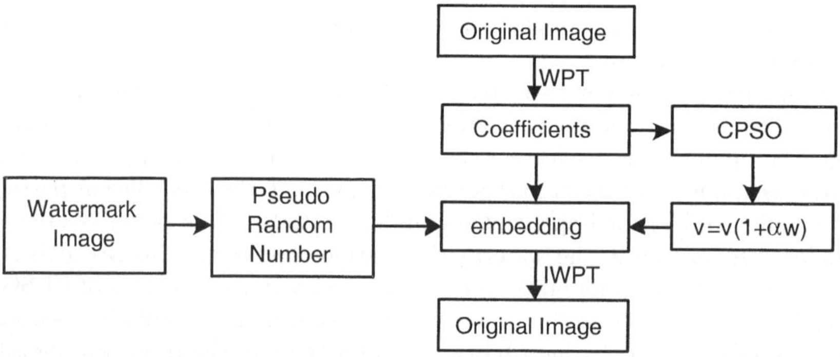

Fig. 1. Watermark embedding processing using wavelet packet transform and CPSO

3.1 Wavelet Packet Transform of Original Image

First of all, input image is decomposed into wavelet packet using 9-7 tap biorthogonal filter and first-order entropy [4].

After the wavelet packet transform has done, each coefficient is partitioned regard to its split information and essentiality of each coefficient. During these processes, CPSO, which use the relationship between each bandwidth, is defined for applying zerotree algorithm to the wavelet packet transform.

3.2 CPSO for Classification of Coefficients

For selecting coefficients embedded by watermark, zerotree method is applied to wavelet packet coefficients. Zerotree algorithm has been mainly used in the wavelet image compression and extened to SPIHT(Set Partitioning In Hierarchical Tree). Zerotree algorithm can search the the large and major coefficients fast and progressively [5] [6].

However, in the wavelet packet transform, zerotree cannot be directly applied. Contrary to the dyadic wavelet transform where all of the parent nodes have always 4 children nodes which have same frequency space, wavelet packet transform is randomly decomposed such as Fig. 2.

CPSO is defined for applying the zerotree algorithm to the wavelet packet transforms. It determines the scan order of significant coefficients depending on its split information and the essentiality of each coefficient. CPSO is defined as the next three conditions.

CPSO0: If child subband S is more decomposed than band P, which is related with the parent node, it does not have a child node. This bandwidth finds out the significant coefficients through the raster scan after finishing the P band threshold scanning as shown in the Figs. 2-a and 2-b.

CPSO4: If child subband S is not decomposed, it has 4 children nodes. It is described in Fig. 2-c.

CPSO1: If child sub-band S, in the higher resolution than P band of parent node, is decomposed into 4 subbands, each coefficient located in the same space of the subband becomes a child node. It is described in Fig. 2-d.

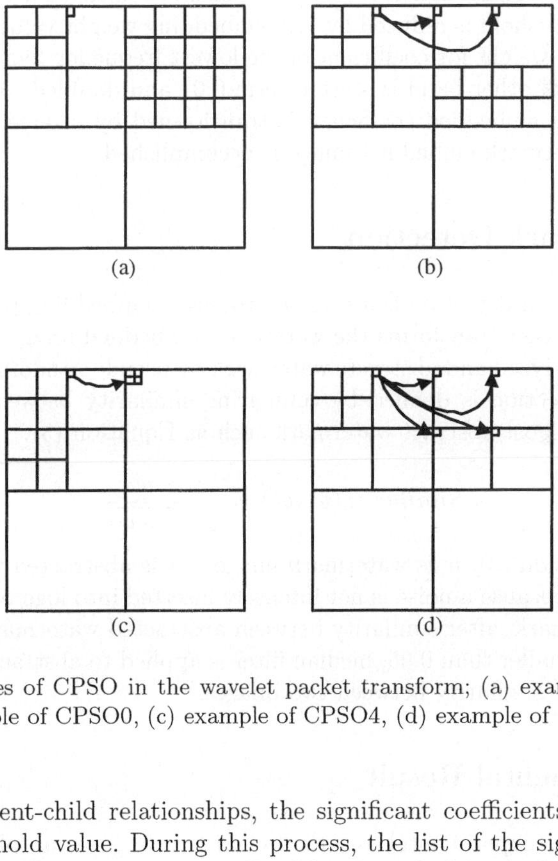

Fig. 2. Examples of CPSO in the wavelet packet transform; (a) example of CPSO0, (b) other example of CPSO0, (c) example of CPSO4, (d) example of CPSO1

By the parent-child relationships, the significant coefficients are identified with the threshold value. During this process, the list of the significant coefficients is saved, which locate in overall subbands including the lowest frequency band. Watermark is embedded in the significant coefficients.

Contrary to in the dyadic wavelet transform, the significant coefficients locate in each subband including high frequency band, so embedding this coefficients prevents the quality of the original image from degrading and brings a robust watermarking.

3.3 Watermark Method Using CPSO Coefficients

Watermark is embedded to wavelet packet coefficient, which selected by CPSO using Equation (2). Equation (2) is used for embedding watermark adaptively based on the selected wavelet packet coefficient. That is, in case of large wavelet packet coefficients, a large α value is embedded and in case of small wavelet packet coefficient, a small α value is embedded. The reason for this watermark embedding, generally, large value is insensible to quantity of addition compare with the small value.

$$v = v(1 + \alpha w) \tag{2}$$

v is a selected coefficient to embedding watermark, w is a watermark and α is an embedding weight. When the wavelet packet coefficients are identified with CPSO, since threshold is reduced by 1/2, embedding weight value, α, is doubled. The embedding weight for coefficient of the lowest frequency band, α, is set 0.04 and coefficient of other band is started form 0.01 and doubled. As a next stage, after watermark embedded coefficient is transformed by inverse wavelet packet transform, watermark embedded image is accomplished.

4 Watermark Detection

Overall watermark detection is a reverse process of embedding process. That is, after wavelet packet transforms the watermark embedded image, watermark information is analyzed and abstracts watermark by pseudo-random sequence. The criterion of detection is defined by comparing similarity between pre-abstract watermark and post-abstract watermark such as Equation (3).

$$Similarity(w, w*) = \frac{w \times w*}{\sqrt{w * \times w*}} \tag{3}$$

In the equation (3), w is watermark image, $w*$ is abstracted watermark.

Especially, because a noise is not intensely inserted into logo or signature image as a watermark, after similarity between abstracted watermark and original watermark is smaller than 0.95, median filter is applied to abstracted watermark and recalculates similarity between two images.

5 Experimental Result

In this section, experimental results for 512 x 512 aerial photograph images, sample-1 (see Figure 3) and sample-2 (see Figure 4) are summarized in Table 1 for comparing other result. These samples are collected from www.spaceimaging.com web site, which has supplied most advanced satellite and aerial images. These kind images are usually composed simplified and recursive geometrical structures such as rectangular, circles, lines and groups of points by high altitude view. A logo, as shown in Figure 5, is used for watermark image.

And two-dimensional separable length 9-7 biorthonormal wavelet filters are used for wavelet packet decomposition. After apply coefficient-partitioning scanning order, wavelet packet coefficients are selected for watermark embedding.

Invisibility and robustness of watermark is used for measurement of performance in this research. PSNR is used for performance of the invisibility after embedding watermark. Similarity using equation (3) is used for performance of the robustness. Other watermark algorithms, such as Xia [2] and Cox [7] are also used for comparing performance at the same condition with proposed algorithm.

5.1 Invisibility

Fig. 6 and Fig. 7 are watermark embedded images using the proposed algorithm. As shown in the two figures, it is impossible to distinguish in perceptually whether watermark is embedded in these images. After embedding watermark to original images, PSNR are calculated for observing image distortion as shown in Table 1. From PSNR in the Table 1, damages of image qualities are not recognized after applying the proposed algorithm for watermark.

Fig. 3. Satellite image as sample-1

Fig. 4. Satellite image as sample-2

Fig. 5. Watermark image

5.2 Robustness

JPEG and conventional wavelet image compression are applied to proposed watermark-embedded image for robustness check against image compression.

Fig. 6. Watermark embedded image of sample-1

Fig. 7. Watermark embedded image of sample-2

Table 1. PSNR of watermark embedded images

	Cox	Xia	Proposed Algorithm
sample-1	39.30	40.19	44.86
sample-2	38.78	38.97	42.54

SPIHT is used for wavelet image compression in this experiment. Experimental result of robustness is shown in table 2. As shown in Table 2, over 90% of watermark image is survived from high image compression.

Table 2. Similarity of JPEG/SPIHT lossy compression

JPEG	sample-1	sample-2	SPIHT	sample-1	sample-2
15%	0.941858	0.904097	15%	0.954368	0.920145
25%	0.984392	0.959219	25%	0.991023	0.964587
50%	0.993924	0.979618	50%	0.997851	0.982561
75%	1.000000	0.996111	75%	1.000000	0.999325

As represented in Table 2, the proposed wavelet packet transform algorithm demonstrates good robustness.

6 Conclusion

In this paper, a new watermarking algorithm is proposed for aerial photograph images using wavelet packet transform. Proposed watermark algorithm is used in high frequency component of image and apply watermark to the overall subband that include the lowest frequency band. And the watermark is embedded on original image after selecting the significant wavelet packet coefficients using CPSO. Moreover, according to the characteristic of selected coefficients for each subband, each different embedding weight is used for invisibility and robustness of watermark image.

From the experimental result, the proposed algorithm shows better invisibility and robustness performance with comparing with conventional watermark methods. Especially, it demonstrates better robustness for high image compression in the remote sensing images such as aerial photos.

A new wavelet packet transform based watermark algorithm is concerned for moving picture as further study.

References

1. Christophe D., J. Delaigle, B. Macq: Invisibility and Application Functionalities in Perceptual Watermarking - An Overview. Proceedings of the IEEE, 90(1) (20002)
2. Xia X., C. Boncelet, G. Arce: A multiresolutional watermark for digital images. IEEE Int. Conf. on Image Processing, 1. (1997) 548–557
3. Han S., S. Cho: Wavelet Packet Image Coder Using Coefficients Partitioning for Remote Sensing Images. lpPRIA2003 (1st Iberian Conference on Pattern Recognition and Image Analysis)
4. Coifman R., M. Wickerhauser: Entropy-based algorithms for best basis selection. IEEE Trans. on Information Theory, 38(2) (1992) 713–718
5. Shapiro J.: Embedded image coding using zerotree wavelet coefficients. IEEE Trans. on Signal Processing, 41 (1993) 3445–3462
6. Said A., W. Pearlman: A new fast and efficient image codec based on set partitioning in hierarchical trees. IEEE Trans. on Circuits and Systems for Video Tech., 6 (1996) 243–250
7. Cox I., J. Kilian, T. Leighton and T. Shamoon: Secure spread spectrum watermarking for multimedia. IEEE Trans. on Image Processing, 6(12) (1997) 1673–1687

Facial Expression Recognition Based upon Gabor-Wavelets Based Enhanced Fisher Model

Sung-Oh Lee[1], Yong-Guk Kim[2*], and Gwi-Tae Park[1]

[1] Department of Electrical Engineering,
Korea University, Seoul, Korea
[2] School of Computer Engineering,
Sejong University, Seoul, Korea
ykim@sejong.ac.kr

Abstract. This work deals with how the machine classifies human facial expressions, which has been a challenging problem for many researchers from the diverse areas. The facial expression recognition system mainly consists of two cascade stages: the representation method for the facial images at the front and the facial emotion classifier at the back. The Gabor-wavelets based method has shown promising performance because of its efficient representation and biological implication. Here we focus on the classification method to obtain high recognition rate of facial expressions. Results suggest that enhanced Fisher discrimination model, which had been used for the face recognition task, outperformed Principal Component Analysis (PCA) based classifier (or the neural network) with the 93% correction rate, when it is combined with the Gabor representation.

1 Introduction

The human face is a great communication device, because facial expressions of humans are so diverse and subtle, and yet are immediately recognized by observers. Although the number of facial expressions that humans could express appears to be endless, long ago Charles Darwin [3] establishes that there are six prototypical (or basic) facial expressions, which are universal across human ethnicities and cultures: *surprise, fear, sadness, anger, disgust and happiness* as shown in Fig. 1. Such foundation provides a convenient framework, by which we test and compare different facial expression recognition systems. Accurate measurement of facial actions has many potential applications such as intelligent human-computer interaction (HCI), entertainment devices, psychiatry [5] and neurology.

To represent facial expression images effectively, several methods have been proposed such PCA, ICA (Independent Component Analysis), Gabor representation, Optic flow, and geometrical tracking method [4, 6]. Among them, the Gabor representation has been favored among many researchers because of its better performance and biological implication [1, 7, 12]. In the present study, we compare the performance between Gabor and non-Gabor cases. After the representation stage in the system, it classifies the facial emotion of the incoming facial image in the next stage. This classification also impacts on the overall performance of the facial

* The corresponding author

A. Yazici and C. Şener (Eds.): ISCIS 2003, LNCS 2869, pp. 490–496, 2003.

expression recognition system. The typical classifier for this purpose has been the neural network. However, other classifiers are also used, such as PCA and SVM (Support Vector Machine).

Fig. 1. A neutral facial expression and six prototypical facial expressions (surprise, fear, sadness, anger, disgust, happiness)

Previous study has shown that the enhanced Fisher discrimination model (EFM) is very effective in a face recognition task [9]. Moreover, when it is combined with the Gabor representation, the face recognition performance is improved greatly. Given that there is evidence that Gabor representation is effective for the facial expression image, we thought that Gabor representation with the EFM could be used effectively in the facial expression task as well.

The remainder of this paper is structured as follows. In section 2 we briefly describe the facial expression database and normalization process. Section 3 contains Gabor wavelet representation for the facial expression images. Classifiers such as PCA and EFM are introduced in section 4. And mathematical derivations are described. In section 6, we compare the performance between several classifiers for the facial expression recognition. Discussion and conclusions will be given in section 7.

2 The Facial Expression Image Database and Normalization of the Image

There are several facial expression databases released by researchers. We have used Cohn-Kanade facial expression database [6], which is becoming a standard. And so, it allows us to compare the facial expression recognition performances between the results from the different laboratories. In the database, each facial expression is recorded as a video sequence. For this study, we chose the maximally expressed image as a basic expression and cropped the face area in the image (88 x 88 pixels) as shown in Fig. 1. There were two kinds of normalization: the first one was on geometrical normalization and the second one was on illumination level of the facial image. We manually clicked the center points of two eyes and the mouth, and then the image was warped by referencing the predetermined three reference points. For the second normalization, the histogram equalization eliminated face relative intensity information. By doing so, we could get the higher recognition rate.

3 Gabor Wavelets Representation for the Facial Expression Images

Gabor wavelets representation was applied to the 2D space by Daugman [1]. Since then, it has been popular method for representing faces, fingerprints and facial expressions. Since the Gabor wavelets consists of orientation component as well as spatial frequency components, they have an advantage in representing any object in an image, compared to the conventional edge detectors, which tends to focus on orientation of the object. In our study, we used five frequencies (from 0 to 4) and eight orientations at each image point within the grid (22 x 22), that drawn over the cropped facial image.

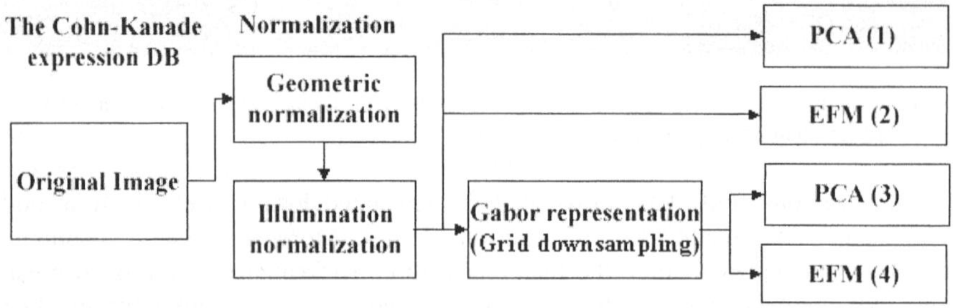

Fig. 2. The block diagram of the facial expression recognition system

4 PCA and EFM Classifiers

4.1 PCA

PCA generates a set of orthonormal basis vectors, known as principal components (PCs) that maximize the scatter of all the projected samples. Let $X \in R^N$ be a random vector representing an image, where N is the dimensionality of the corresponding image space. The covariance matrix of X is defined as follows:

$$\Sigma X = E\{[X - E(X)][X - E(X)]^t\} \quad (1)$$

where $E()$ is the expectation operator t denotes the transpose operation $\Sigma X \in R^{NXN}$. The PCA of a random vector X factorizes the covariance matrix ΣX into the following forms:

$$\Sigma X = \Phi \Lambda \Phi^t \quad (2)$$

where $\Phi = [\phi_1 \phi_2 ... \phi_N] \in R^{NXN}$ is the orthonormal eigenvector matrix; $\Lambda = diag\{\lambda_1, \lambda_2, ..., \lambda_N\} \in R^{NXN}$ is the diagonal eigenvalue matrix with diagonal elements in decreasing order ($\lambda_1, \lambda_2, ... \lambda_N$). Then the first m leading eigenvectors define matrix P

$$P = [\phi_1, \phi_2, ..., \phi_m] \quad (3)$$

An application of PCA is the dimensionality reduction

$$Y = P^t X \quad (4)$$

The lower dimensional vector $Y \in R^m$ captures the most expressive features of the original data X as shown at the top row of Fig. 3[11].

4.2 EFM (Enhanced Fisher Linear Discrimination Model)

We present in this section an EFM that determines the dimensionalities for the reduced image space [8]. Let Y be a random vector representing the lower dimensional feature. Let $w_1, w_2, ..., w_L$ and $N_1, N_2, ..., N_L$ denote the classes and the number of images in each class, respectively. Let $M_1, M_2, ..., M_L$ and M be the mean of the classes and the grand mean. The within-and between-class covariance matrices $\sum w$ and $\sum b$ are defined as follows:

$$\sum w = \sum_{i=1}^{L} P(w_i) E\{(Y - M_i)(Y - M_i)' \mid w_i\} \tag{5}$$

$$\sum b = \sum_{i=1}^{L} P(w_i)(M_i - M)(M_i - M)' \tag{6}$$

EFM first diagonalizes the within-class covariance matrix $\sum w$

$$\sum w \Xi = \Xi \Gamma \text{ and } \Xi' \Xi = I \tag{7}$$

$$\Gamma^{-1/2} \Xi' \sum w \Xi \Gamma^{-1/2} = I \tag{8}$$

where Ξ, Γ are the eigenvector and the diagonal eigenvalue matrices of $\sum w$. EFM proceeds then to compute the between-class covariance matrix as follows:

$$\Gamma^{-1/2} \Xi' \sum b \Xi \Gamma^{-1/2} = K_b \tag{9}$$

Diagonalize the new between-class covariance matrix K_b

$$K_b \Theta = \Theta \Delta \text{ and } \Theta' \Theta = I \tag{10}$$

where Θ, Δ are the eigenvector and the diagonal eigenvalue matrices of K_b. The overall transformation matrix of EFM is now defined as follows:

$$T = \Xi \Gamma^{-1/2} \Theta \tag{11}$$

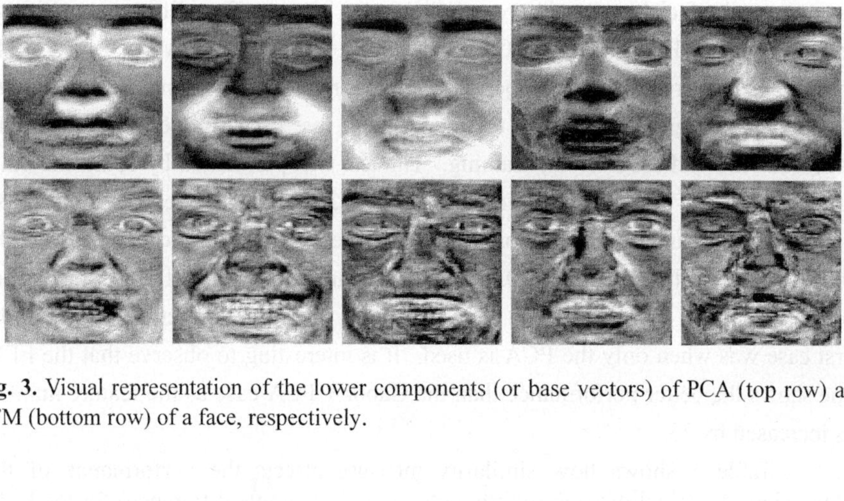

Fig. 3. Visual representation of the lower components (or base vectors) of PCA (top row) and EFM (bottom row) of a face, respectively.

The bottom row of Fig. 2 is shown the 5 lower EFM components from left to right. Notice that the EFM images contain more high spatial frequencies than the PCA images.

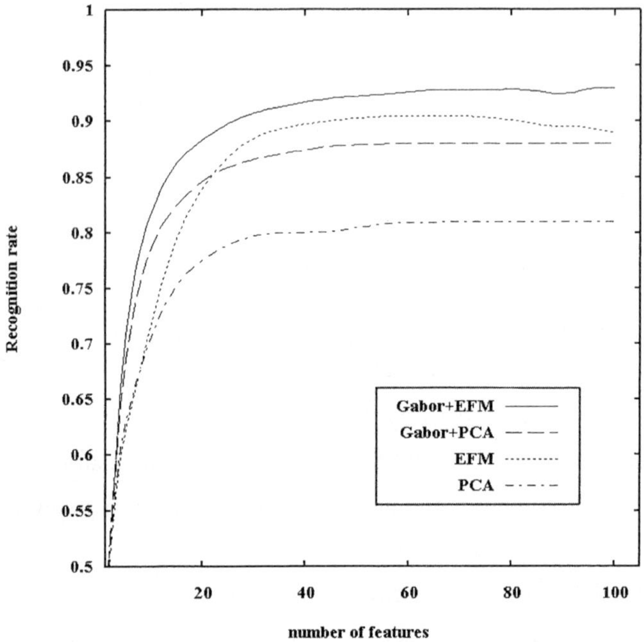

Fig. 4. Performance Comparison between four cases (PCA, EFM, Gabor + PCA, Gabor + EFM).

5 Performance Comparison

We compare the facial expression recognition rates between four different conditions: pure PCA, pure EFM, Gabor + PCA, and Gabor + EFM as shown in Fig. 4. The horizontal axis represents the number of features (or components) and the vertical one indicates the recognition rate. In this experiment, we first sampled the half of the image database and used for the training. The test was performed by using the other half of the images. And we repeated these tests for 20 times and averaged the results.

Notice that the recognition rate approaches to the saturation point when the number of the feature is about 50. The best result was obtained when the Gabor representation was combined with the EFM with the 93% correction, whereas the worst case was when only the PCA is used. It is interesting to observe that the EFM alone shows the better performance than the Gabor + PCA case as the feature number was increased by 25.

Table 1 shows how similarity measure affects the performance of the system. Here, L_2 (Euclidian) is slightly better than L_1 (Simple difference) for the EFM and Gabor + EFM cases. Table 2 is a confusion matrix where we can look up how an expression is confused with the others. For instance, sadness is easily confused with anger, whereas surprise is a distinctive expression. And often, the sadness, anger and fear expression cannot distinguish with the neutral expression. Moreover, happiness and surprise are the easiest expression to recognize than the others.

Table 1. Two different similarity measures (k=80)

(%)	PCA	EFM	Gabor +PCA	Gabor +EFM
L1	84	89	87	92
L2	81	90	87	93

Table 2. Confusion Matrix (Gabor + EFM, L2)

(%)	Neutral	Surprise	Fear	Sadness	Anger	Disgust	Happiness
Neutral	98	0	0	2	0	0	0
Surprise	0	100	0	0	0	0	0
Fear	15	0	79	1	1	0	4
Sadness	24	0	0	67	9	0	0
Anger	14	0	0	11	71	3	0
Disgust	2	0	0	0	1	97	0
Happiness	2	0	0	0	0	0	98

6 Discussion and Conclusions

The work introduces the EFM for the facial expression recognition task. It turns out that its performance was higher than the PCA case. In particular, when the EFM was combined with the Gabor representation, it is even better than the EFM alone. The EFM was originally derived for the face recognition task. Our results suggest that it can be successfully applied to the facial expression case. It is known that human capability to classify human facial emotions is about 90% correction [2]. The best result with the EFM was 93%, which is even higher than human's capability. We are developing an automatic facial expression system, in which the whole processes will be carried out without any human intervention.

References

1. J. Daugman, Uncertainty relationship for resolution in space, spatial frequency, and orientation optimized by two-dimensional visual cortical filters. Journal of the Optical Society of America A, 2: 1160–1169, 1985.
2. M. Dailey, G. Cottrell, and C. Padgett, EMPATH: A neural network that categorizes facial expressions, Journal of Cognitive Neuroscience, 13, 513–532, 2002.
3. C. Darwin, *The expression of emotions in man and animals.* John Murray, London, 1872.
4. G. Donato, M. Bartlett, J. Hager, P. Ekman and T. Sejnowski, Classifying facial actions, IEEE PAMI, 21, 10, 974–989, 1999.
5. P. Ekman and W. Friesen, *Unmasking the Face. A guide to recognizing emotions from facial clues.* Palo Alto. Consulting Psychologists Press, 1975
6. T. Kanade, J. Cohn, and Y. Tian, Comprehensive database for facial expression analysis, Proc. Int'l Conf Face and Gesture Recognition, 46–53, 2000.

7. M. Lades, J. Vorbruggen, J. Buhmann, L. Lange, C. von der Malsburg, R. Wurz, and W. Konen, Distortion invariant object recognition in the dynamic link architecture, IEEE Computers, 42, 300–311, 1993.
8. C. Liu and H. Wechsler, Robust coding schemes for indexing and retrieval from large face databases, IEEE Image Processing, 9, 1, 132–137, 2000.
9. C. Liu and H. Wechsler, Gabor feature based classification using the enhanced Fisher linear discriminant model for face recognition, IEEE Image Processing, 11, 4, 467–476, 2002.
10. Y. Tian , T. Kanade and J. Cohn, Recognizing action units for facial expression analysis, IEEE PAMI, 23, 2, 97–115, 2001.
11. M. Turk and A. Pentland, Face recognition using eigenfaces, Proc IEEE Conf in Comp Vision and Pattern Recognition, 586–591, 1991.
12. Z. Zhang, M. Lyons, M. Schuster, and S. Akamatsu, Comparison between geometry-based and Gabor-based expression recognition using multi-layer perceptron, Proc. Int'l Conf Face and Gesture Recognition, 26–39, 1998.

Image Sequence Stabilization Using Membership Selective Fuzzy Filtering

M. Kemal Güllü and Sarp Ertürk

Department of Electronics & Telecommunications Engineering, University of Kocaeli, Veziroglu Campus, Izmit 41040, Turkey
{kemalg,sertur}@kou.edu.tr

Abstract. Image sequence stabilization aims to remove unwanted fluctuations from an image sequence. This paper proposes a novel stabilization system making use of a fuzzy filter constructed by dynamic system based estimator definition with a fuzzy corrector. The stabilization system selectively switches between a pre-defined set of membership functions so as to improve gross movement tracking and stabilization performance. The stabilization results of the proposed system are compared with results of the Super SteadyShot stabilization system incorporated into SONY® camcorders.

1 Introduction

An important problem in image sequences captured by hand held digital cameras is originated by the fluctuations caused due to unwanted camera motions during video capture. Image stabilization is performed to prevent the affect of these fluctuations. Image stabilization is nowadays commonly used or likely to be used soon in contemporary systems such as hand-held cameras, 3G mobile phones and robot-camera applications.

Motions encountered in image sequences can be classified into two types: global frame motion and local object motion. The global frame motion is of main interest for the image stabilization system as it reflects the movements of the imaging system or framework. The stabilization system typically aims to remove undesired fluctuations encountered in the global frame motion while retaining long-term intentional movements [1]. Hence, it is possible to break up the frame motion into desired frame movements and unwanted fluctuations.

The image stabilization system typically consists of two parts, namely the motion estimation and motion correction systems. The motion estimation system is responsible for obtaining interframe motion parameters. The motion correction system resolves the fluctuation components and accomplishes stabilization. The efficiency of the image stabilization system depends on the accuracy of the motion estimation system, as any error in the motion estimation system directly affects the stabilization system performance [1]. Various techniques for image sequence stabilization have been proposed, such as motion vector integration [2], DFT filtering

A. Yazici and C. Şener (Eds.): ISCIS 2003, LNCS 2869, pp. 497–504, 2003.

based frame position smoothing [1], Kalman filtering based stabilization [3], and Fuzzy adaptive Kalman filtering based stabilization [4]. In the latter case, Fuzzy adaptation of the Kalman filter is utilized to improve stabilization performance, as fuzzy adaptation has proven to outperform classical techniques. This paper proposes image sequence stabilization by directly utilizing a Fuzzy Filter to suppress high frequency components of absolute frame positions obtained by the accumulation of interframe motion vectors.

2 Fuzzy Filtering

Fuzzy logic based systems have been used extensively in image and signal processing applications in recent years. Fuzzy systems provide an effective and smart approach to many nonlinear and uncertain systems. An application of fuzzy logic in image and signal processing for instance is noise filtering. In this paper, fuzzy logic is used in an estimator structure referred to as a fuzzy filter, to stabilize the fluctuations of image frame positions.

2.1 Fuzzy Estimation

In this section, the structure of the estimator used for stabilization is explained. Fuzzy logic has been used as correction function of the estimator in a similar approach to [5].

A standard discrete time-invariant system can be defined by the process and observation equations

$$x_{k+1} = f(x_k) + w_k \tag{1}$$

$$z_k = h(x_k) + v_k \tag{2}$$

where k is the time index, x_k is the state vector, z_k is the measurement vector, v_k is the measurement noise and w_k is the process noise. To find an estimate $\hat{x}_k$ to the discrete time signal, the commonly used estimator architecture known as the recursive predictor-corrector is given by

$$\hat{x}_k = \hat{f}(\hat{x}_{k-1}) + g(z_k, \hat{x}_{k-1}) \tag{3}$$

where $\hat{f}(.)$ shows an estimate of $f(.)$ which maps the state from one time step to the next, and $g(.)$ is the correction function of the system.

The fuzzy estimator structure, which estimates the stabilized frame position by a constant velocity camera model [3], can be constructed as

$$\hat{x}_k^- = \hat{x}_{k-1}^+ + T\hat{v}_{k-1} \tag{4}$$

$$\hat{x}_k^+ = \hat{x}_k^- + g\left(z_k, \hat{x}_k^-\right) \tag{5}$$

where k is the time index, $\hat{x}_k^-$ is the a priori estimate of x at time k, $\hat{x}_k^+$ is the a posteriori estimate of x at time k, T is the update period of the estimator, z_k is the noisy image sequence frame position and $\hat{v}$ is an estimate of the rate of change of frame motion speed, which is typically obtained from

$$\hat{V}_{k-1} = \left(\hat{x}_{k-1}^+ - \hat{x}_{k-2}^+\right)/T \tag{6}$$

The correction function $g(.)$ typically has an uncertain mathematical model as instantaneous fluctuations are unknown. In this paper it is proposed to implement the correction function $g(.)$ by a fuzzy system. As the correction function uses fuzzy logic, the estimator structure is referred to as a fuzzy filter.

2.2 Filter Parameters

The structure used for the fuzzy correction system is displayed in Figure 1. The implemented correction system has two inputs and one output. The input variables are given by

$$I1_k = z_k - \hat{x}_k^- \tag{7}$$

$$I2_k = I1_k - I1_{k-1} \tag{8}$$

where input 1 ($I1$) depends on the difference between the k-th index of unfiltered image sequence frame positions and the a priori estimate $\hat{x}_k^-$. Input 2 ($I2$) is calculated from the difference between current and previous indexes of input 1.

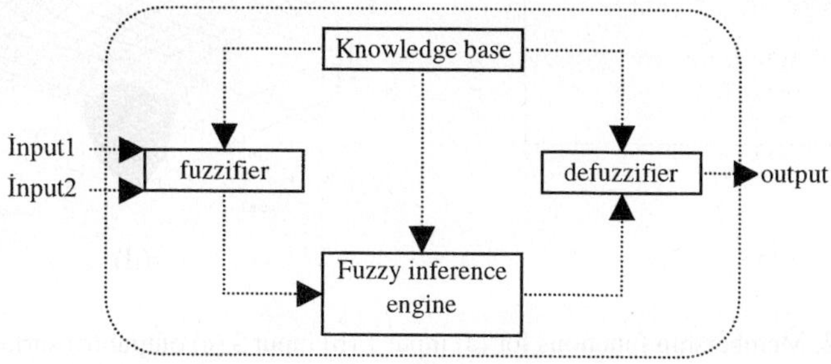

Fig. 1. Fuzzy correction system block diagram.

The shape and parameter selection of membership functions (MF) depends directly on the designer's experience, as there is no inherent way to select membership functions. In the proposed system five Gaussian MFs are used for each input and output, as they are thought to be more appropriate for the desired task. A Gaussian MF is entirely specified by the two parameters $\{c,\sigma\}$, where c represents the MFs mean (centre location) and the standard deviation σ determines the width. A Gaussian membership function can be expressed as

$$y = gaussian(x;c,\sigma) = e^{-\frac{1}{2}\left(\frac{x-c}{\sigma}\right)^2} \tag{9}$$

In the design of the fuzzy system, membership functions and the rule base play key roles for optimal system performance. In the implemented stabilization system, input and output membership functions are adjusted off-hand to obtain the best results. The utilized membership functions are displayed in Figure 2. The constructed rule base containing 25 rules is shown in Table 1.

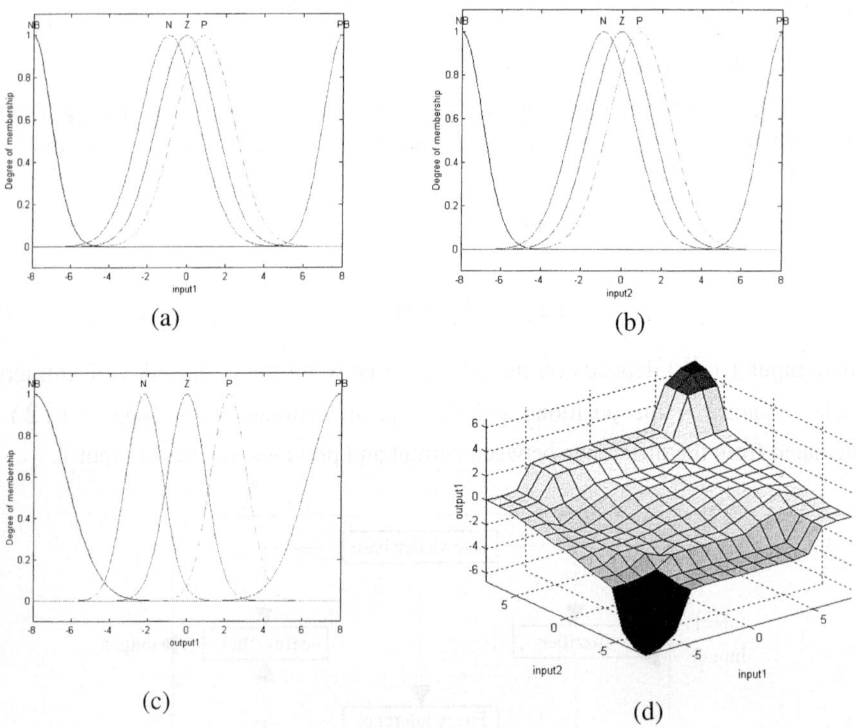

Fig. 2. Membership functions for (a) input 1 (b) input 2 (c) output (d) surface

Table 1. Rule base for the fuzzy filter

		Input2				
		NB	**N**	**Z**	**P**	**PB**
Input1	**NB**	NB	N	N	Z	Z
	N	N	N	Z	Z	P
	Z	N	Z	Z	Z	P
	P	N	Z	Z	P	P
	PB	Z	Z	P	P	PB

*NB = negative big, N = negative, Z = zero, P = positive, PB = positive big

Large fluctuations in the frame position signal can obstruct optimum working conditions for the fuzzy filter. Hence, these fluctuations are preliminary reduced by a mean operation accomplished by the so called preprocess unit. The preprocess unit calculates mean values using present and past two values of the frame position vector, as shown in equation (10).

$$z_{k-1} = (a_k + 2a_{k-1} + a_{k-2})/4 \tag{10}$$

Raw frame positions before and after preprocessing are denoted as a_k and z_k respectively.

In order to have the fuzzy filter operate successfully with a limited number of membership functions, every membership function has to be defined to comprise a limited range. However, if the membership function ranges are limited for optimum operation it is sometimes possible for the input values to exceed the total range of the pre-defined fuzzy filter membership functions. This will largely reduce the performance unless precautions are taken. To prevent this problem, it is proposed in this paper to use 7 separate pre-defined output MF sets. The output MF set utilized by the system is selected from between the 7 possible alternatives according to the rate of change of undesired fluctuations.

In order to introduce selective alternation of membership function sets, the positions of the two membership functions directly affecting the operation of the fuzzy filter, namely the negative (N) and positive (P) MFs, are varied. The position of membership function centre locations with respect to each other directly determines the operation of the fuzzy filter. If the distance between membership function centre locations is increased the fuzzy filter will track global frame positions more closely, but the stabilization intensity will decrease. On the contrary, if the distance between membership function centre locations is reduced, the fuzzy filter will not track global movements as closely but the stabilization performance will increase. The intervals used for the membership functions are shown in Figure 3.

3 Simulation Results

Test sequences have been captured by a digital camcorder mounted on a remote controlled model vehicle, navigating on rough terrain. As it was desired to compare stabilization results of the proposed system with Super SteadyShot results available on the SONY® camcorder, two sequences have been captured one with the SteadyShot system active and one with the SteadyShot system disabled. The model vehicle was started at the same position and has been navigating on a similar path (slightly changed due to terrain structure). The absolute frame positions of the sequence captured with SteadyShot disabled are processed with the proposed fuzzy filter based stabilization system. Figure 4 displays the frame positions of the sequence stabilized with the proposed fuzzy-filter based stabilization system and the sequence captured with SteadyShot enabled. Although there is an offset in the long-term displacements resulting from the vehicle taking slightly different routes due to the rough terrain structure, similarities show that the captured sequences are comparable. It is clearly seen in Figure 4 that the proposed fuzzy filtering based stabilization system has less high frequency components and hence provides improved stabilization.

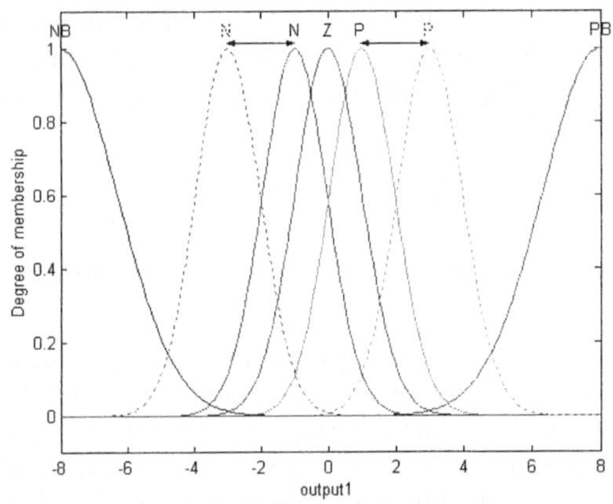

Fig. 3. Changing range between output membership functions centre locations

Figure 5 displays the magnitude spectra of stabilized image sequences using the proposed Fuzzy filter based stabilization system and SONY® Super SteadyShot respectively. It is seen from the magnitude spectra that the proposed fuzzy filter based stabilization system results in lower frequency components, thus achieves a smoother absolute frame displacements and hence provides preferable stabilization performance.

4 Conclusions

A fuzzy filtering based image sequence stabilization system has been proposed in this paper. Absolute image frame displacements are defined by a constant camera velocity model dynamic system and a fuzzy based correction function is utilized. The stabilization system performance is improved by adding selectiveness for output membership functions between a pre-defined set of functions. Stabilization results are compared with the Super SteadyShot system supplied with SONY® camcorders and it is shown that successful stabilization results are achieved.

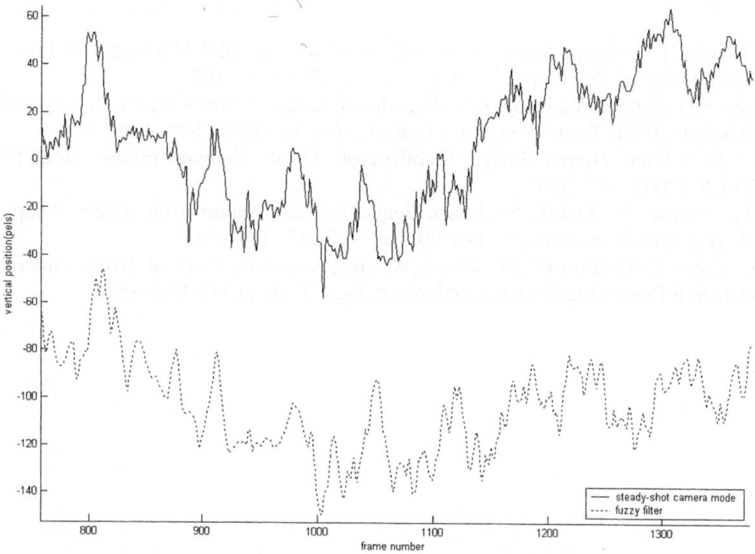

Fig. 4. Output frame position vectors of the steady-shot mode of the digital camera and fuzzy filtered normal mode

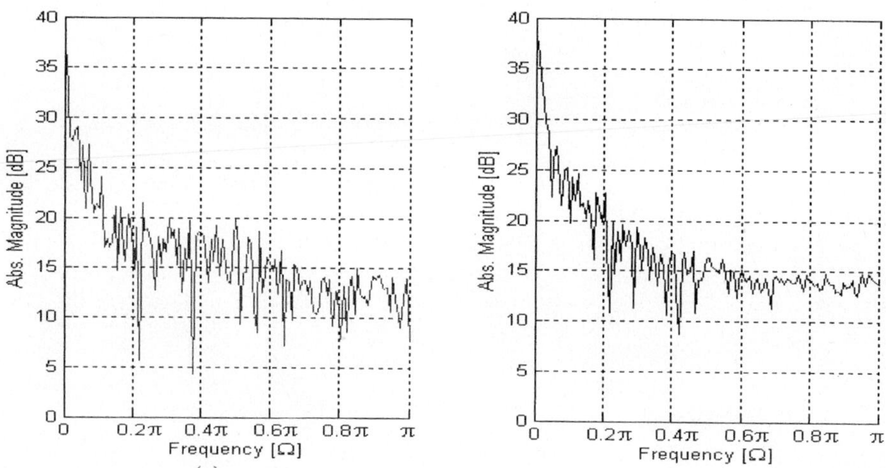

(a) (b)

Fig. 5. Magnitude spectra of frame positions (a) SONY® Super SteadyShot (b) Proposed fuzzy filter stabilization.

References

1. Ertürk, S. Dennis, T.J. : Image Sequence Stabilization Based on DFT Filtering, IEE Proc. on Image Vision and Signal Processing", Vol. 147, No. 2, (2000) 95–102.
2. Ko, S.J., Lee, S.H., Jeon S.W., Kang, E.S. :Fast digital image stabilizer based on gray-coded bit-plane matching, IEEE Trans. Consum. Electron., Vol. 45, (1999) 598–603.
3. Ertürk, S.: Real-Time Digital Image Stabilization Using Kalman Filters, Real-Time Imaging, Vol. 8, (2002) 317–328.
4. Güllü, M.K., Yaman, E., Ertürk, S.: Image Sequence Stabilisation using Fuzzy Adaptive Kalman Filtering, Electronics Letters, Vol. 39, No. 5, (2003) 429–431.
5. Simon, D.: Fuzzy Estimation of DC Motor Winding Currents, Proc. of North American Fuzzy Information Processing Society Conference, New York, (1999) 859–863.

Texture Segmentation Using the Mixtures of Principal Component Analyzers

Mohamed E.M. Musa[1], Robert P.W. Duin[2], Dick de Ridder[2], and Volkan Atalay[3]

[1] Department of Computer Engineering, Cankaya University, Ankara, Turkey
memmusa@cankaya.edu.tr
[2] Pattern Recognition Group, Faculty of Applied Physics, Delft University of Technology, The Netherlands
[3] Department of Computer Engineering, Middle East Technical University, Ankara, Turkey

Abstract. The problem of segmenting an image into several modalities representing different textures can be modelled using Gaussian mixtures. Moreover, texture image patches when translated, rotated or scaled lie in low dimensional subspaces of the high-dimensional space spanned by the grey values. These two aspects make the mixture of local subspace models worth consideration for segmenting this type of images. In recent years a number of mixtures of local PCA models have been proposed. Most of these models require the user to set the number of subspaces and subspace dimensionalities. To make the model autonomous, we propose a greedy EM algorithm to find a suboptimal number of subspaces, besides using a global retained variance ratio to estimate for each subspace the dimensionality that retains the given variability ratio. We provide experimental results for testing the proposed method on texture segmentation.

1 Introduction

Image data can often be described in a much lower number of parameters than the pixels in the original image, due to the large redundancy in ordinary images and the fact that neighouring pixels are highly correlated. Representing image as points in a high dimensional space does not allow easy exploitation of this redundancy. Structured images can more naturally be represented by subspaces, with points in the subspace corresponding to slightly translated, rotated, scaled etc. version of the same image. The subspace then becomes an invariant description of an image (or image patch). Moreover, when the image contains different structures, e.g., it may have more than one texture, one subspace may poorly represent the whole image. One way to solve this problem is to use a mixture of subspaces.

In recent years, several methods to train a mixture of principal component analyzer (PCA) subspaces have been proposed and applied (see [12] for review). The PCA subspace models proposed in literature have three main problems:

A. Yazici and C. Şener (Eds.): ISCIS 2003, LNCS 2869, pp. 505–512, 2003.

1. There is no standard method to specify the optimal number of subspaces.
2. There is no standard method for the EM algorithm initialization, nor a standard method to help the algorithm to escape the local maxima.
3. There is no standard method to specify the optimal dimensionality for each subspace.

Previously, we have proposed a method for solving these problems, and tested it on two classification problems [10,11]. In order to test our model on a different domain and to have visual results for the performance of the proposed model, in this study, we test the model on the texture segmentation problem. The paper is organized as follows: Section 2 explains the probabilistic PCA. Section 3 describes our training method. Section 4 presents and discusses the experimental results. We end the paper with some concluding remarks in Section 5.

2 Probabilistic Principal Component Analyzer

Tipping and Bishop found a probabilistic formulation of PCA by viewing it as a latent variable problem in which a d-dimensional observed data vector $\mathbf{y}$ can be described in terms of an m-dimensional latent vector $\mathbf{x}$ [12] :

$$\mathbf{y} = \mathbf{A}\mathbf{x} + \boldsymbol{\mu} + \mathbf{w} \tag{1}$$

where $\mathbf{A}$ is a $d{\times}m$ matrix, $\boldsymbol{\mu} \in \mathbb{R}^d$ is the data mean and $\mathbf{w} \in \mathbb{R}^d$ is an independent Gaussian noise with a diagonal covariance matrix $\sigma^2\mathbf{I}$. The probability of the observed data vector $\mathbf{y}$ is:

$$p(\mathbf{y}) = (2\pi)^{-d/2}|\mathbf{C}|^{-1/2}\exp\left(-\frac{1}{2}(\mathbf{y}-\boldsymbol{\mu})^T\mathbf{C}^{-1}(\mathbf{y}-\boldsymbol{\mu})\right) \tag{2}$$

where $\mathbf{C}$ is the model covariance matrix given by:

$$\mathbf{C} = \mathbf{A}\mathbf{A}^T + \sigma^2\mathbf{I} \tag{3}$$

Using a Gaussian prior (zero mean, unit standard deviation) over the latent variables $\mathbf{x}$, an EM algorithm can be developed to find the parameters $\boldsymbol{\mu}, \sigma^2$ and $\mathbf{A}$. Furthermore, the algorithm can be quite naturally extended to find mixtures of such subspace model, by having a set of parameters ($\boldsymbol{\mu}^i$, $\mathbf{A}^i$ and σ^i) for each subspace i and re-estimating $p(\mathbf{y}|i)$ and the prior probabilities for each, $p(i)$, in each step of the EM algorithm.

2.1 Subspace Dimensionality and Noise

Intuitively, the model partitions the input space into subspace of signal and noise (σ^2 in Eqn. 3). As the variability in the minor $d-m$ dimensions is hypothetically considered noise only, the eigenvalues that result from the covariance matrix diagonalization, can be used to estimate the noise level. Tipping and Bishop have shown that the maximum likelihood estimate for the noise variance is given by [12] :

$$\sigma^2 = \frac{1}{d-m} \sum_{k=m+1}^{d} \lambda_k, \tag{4}$$

where $\{\lambda_k\}_{m+1}^{d}$ are the $d-m$ smallest eigenvalues.

In line with the conclusion of our previous paper [10], which indicates that the noise level could be used to determine subspace dimensionality, Meinicke and Ritter have given the same suggestion [8]. A PPCA model that has a hypothesized noise level and estimated dimensionality (VD-PPCA, for "variable dimensionality") is advantageous over the one that has a hypothesized fixed dimensionality and estimated noise (FD-PPCA). In the conventional PCA, the user can input a retained variance ratio (let us call it α), for which the system calculates the dimensionality that preserves the given variability ratio. This could also be used with a VD-PPCA model. Moreover, using validation methods, the system could calculate a suboptimal value for α from the given training data, for the underlying application. This suboptimal value has special importance, as it allows the model autonomously estimate the proper dimensionality for each subspace. Therefore, in our proposed VD-PPCA model, we use σ^2 for noise estimation in the subspace covariance matrix Eqn. 3 and a *global* constant retained variance ratio (α) for the dimensionality estimation of the subspaces; i.e. the dimensionality that retains α ratio of the local variability.

3 Greedy EM for Mixture of PPCA (MPPCA) Training

In training a mixture of PPCA (MPPCA) model, the user faces a number of choices: the number of subspaces to look for, the number of dimensions per subspace to use and the way in which the EM algorithm is initialized to avoid local minima. In this section we describe our algorithm which alleviate these choices. Recent theoretical developments [1,7], have shown that the likelihood of finite mixture models is approximately concave as a function of the number of components in the mixture. Accordingly, we have developed and tested a greedy EM algorithm for VD-MPPCA training controlled by likelihood changes [11]. Verbeek et. al. have also investigated greedy learning of Gaussian mixtures [13]. Their experimental results showed that greedy EM outperforms standard EM.

Algorithm 1 outlines our proposed greedy VD-MPPCA training algorithm. The algorithm starts by calculating one subspace parameters for the entire training data set (step 2). Then the algorithm goes into a greedy cycle of increasing the number of subspaces iteratively. This greedy cycle consists of two main parts: [I] finding a hard cluster as an initial estimate for the new subspace (steps 5 through 9). [II] fitting the new subspace and the old subspaces softly together by the EM algorithm (step 10).

An EM algorithm (soft clustering) initialized by a hard clustering algorithm is the state of the art for mixture model training. However, which hard clustering

Algorithm 1 Greedy Training Algorithm

1: input D (training data set) and α (ratio of variance to retain)
2: estimate one VD-PPCA subspace parameters ($\boldsymbol{\mu}^1$,$\mathbf{A}^1$ and σ^1), with a dimensionality that retains α of the variability in D
3: $k \leftarrow 1$
4: **repeat**
5: $\quad \forall i, N_i = \{x$: x among the $|D|/k+1$ points that have highest probabilities for subspace $i\}$
6: $\quad F = D \backslash (\cup N_i)$
7: $\quad$ find a new mean $\boldsymbol{\mu}^*$ in F using Dasgupta algorithm (explained in the text).
8: $\quad$ run the k-means algorithm for $\boldsymbol{\mu}*$ and $\{\boldsymbol{\mu}^i\}_1^k$ in original data space to find the closest points to $\boldsymbol{\mu}^*$ (S')
9: $\quad$ from S' estimate one VD-MPPCA subspace parameters, ($\boldsymbol{\mu}^{k+1}$,$\mathbf{A}^{k+1}$ and σ^{k+1}), with a subspace dimensionality that retains α of the variability in S'
10: $\quad$ fit the $k+1$ subspaces using the EM algorithm
11: **until** stopping criterion met
12: re-fit all subspaces dimensionalities to retain α of their variability
13: fit the model using the EM algorithm

method to use with which EM version is still an open question. Intuitively, a suitable hard clustering method for a greedy EM might also be a greedy one. Dasgupta designed a hard clustering algorithm that works greedily to find Gaussian Mixture means [2] . Dasgupta's algorithm maps the data to a random subspace of size $\mathcal{O}(\log k)$ dimensions and search for the Gaussians means in this subspace. Dasgupta's algorithm allocates the Gaussians one after the other. The point that has the smallest hyper sphere to enclose specific number of points, in the subspace is considered to be a clue for a Gaussian mean. To find the other Gaussian means using the same criterion, the high-density points of the recently found Gaussian are removed. Being greedy algorithm working in a subspace, we found it very similar to our greedy EM. Therefore we included Dasgupta's algorithm in our greedy algorithm. We use Dasgupta's algorithm to find new mean center each time we need to increase the number of subspaces in the mixture. As we remove the high density points of the available Gaussians by step 5 and 6, the version of Dasgupt's algorithm used here is just for finding the mean of the most condensed area in F. Other hard clustering methods like k-means could be used for this purpose [6,4] and we do not argue that our method is the best.

Subspaces change their local variability during EM iterations in step 10. For this reason, in step 12 we re-estimate all subspaces dimensionalities, to fit the criterion of preserving α ratio of the local variability. As step 12 is done in a hard fashion, in step 13 we re-run the EM again to ensure soft fitting.

4 Application: Image Segmentation

Natural texture images from the Brodatz album are artificially combined (using a cross-shaped mask) to create 2-texture images and scaled to a range [0 1]. The

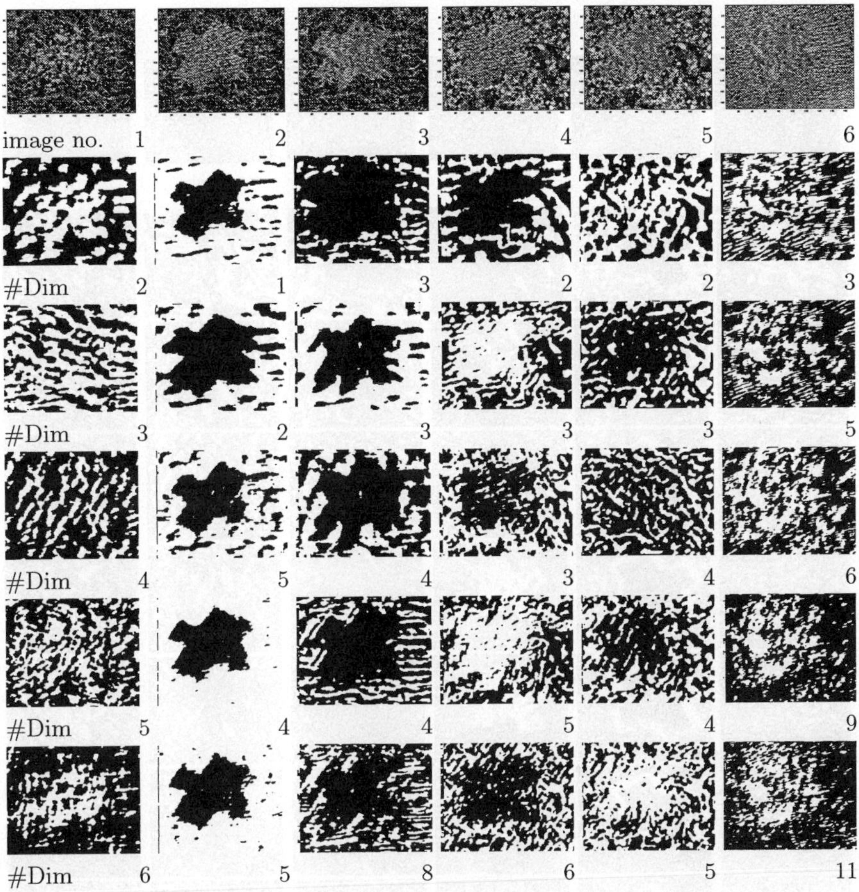

Fig. 1. Segmentation results for VD-MPPCA model where the number of subspaces is two in all experiments. Each row shows a different experiment with different α value in the following order: 0.15 , 0.20 , 0.25 ,0.30,0.35 and 0.40. The average dimensionality for the subspaces is shown under each segmented image.

images are shown in the first row of Figure 1. The training data consists of 1500 image batches extracted from the combined images, where the length of the batch side is 20 pixels. The entire data set is pre-processed by PCA to remove noise direction. 70 dimensions are left from the original 400 dimensions. For inverting the covariance matrices and taking their square root, a slight regularization is used by adding 0.01 to σ^2 (see Eqn. 3). The segmentation is done by assigning each central pixel of an image batch the label of that subspace i for which $p(\mathbf{y}|i)$ is highest. The performance of both ICA and PCA mixtures on the same images is reported in [3], where each model was containing two 2-dimensional subspaces.

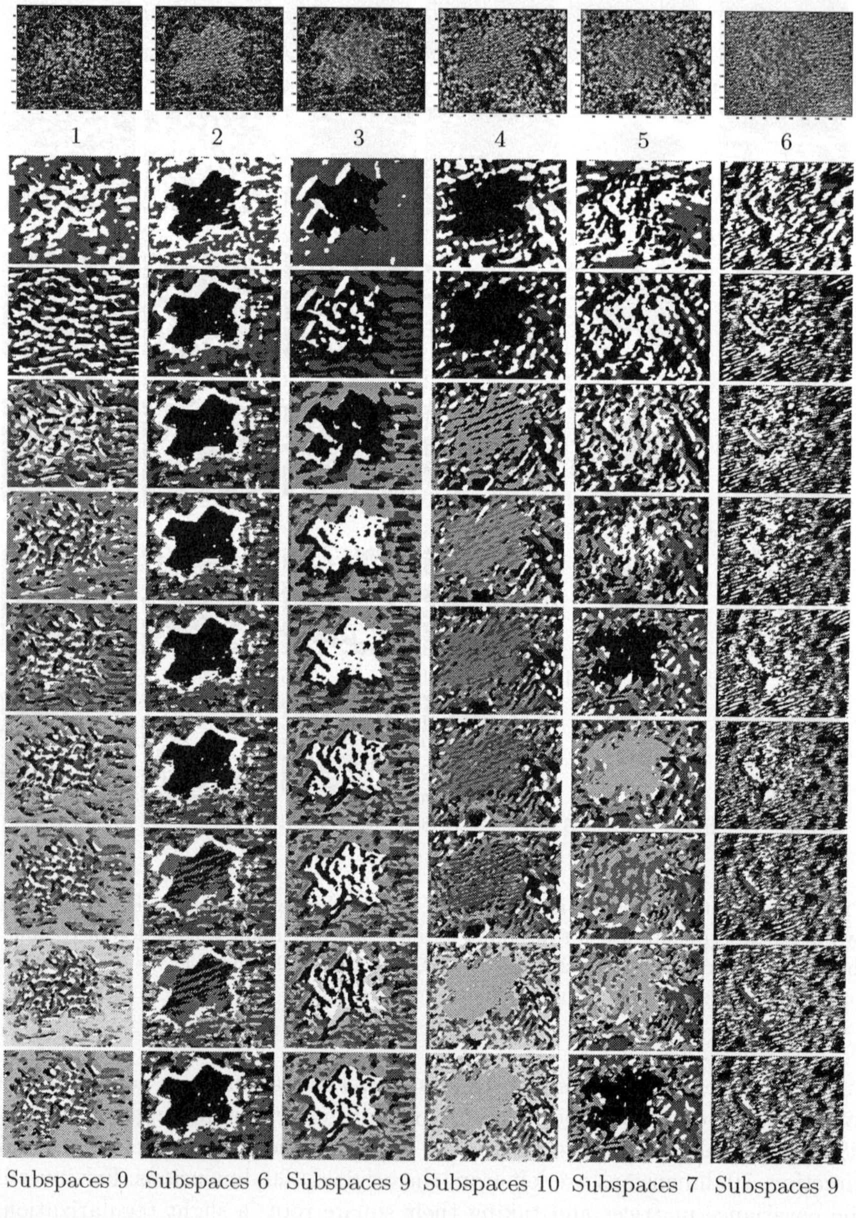

Fig. 2. The second row through the eighth row show the segmentation results of 3 subspaces through 10 subspaces. The last row shows the best segmentation result based on maximum likelihood criterion-the selected number of subspaces is shown under each segmented image.

5 Discussion

Figure 1 shows the resulting segmentations, found by two subspaces VD-MPPCA model. It is clear the result is poor, even for higher α values; i.e., higher subspace dimensionality, there is no obvious improvement. Some parts of the segmented images show that the model subspaces tend to model general image features, such as dark areas, rather than image textures. Moreover, many textures seem to have nonlinear manifold, and therefore need to be modelled by more than one subspace. From these we inferred that restricting the number of subspaces to two is the main reason behind the poor performance. A model with excess number of subspaces may satisfy the need for more subspaces of some textures and can have some subspaces dedicated to the common image features. To test this, we re-ran the experiments with the number of subspaces 3 through 10. As the previous set of experiments show no significant improvement by increasing the retained variance ratio (α), in these experiments we set α to 0.15.

Figure 2 shows the results of the second set of experiments. The second row shows the result of the first experiment in which the number of subspaces is 3, the third row shows the result of 4 subspaces, and then each subsequent row has one additional subspace. It is clear that the model succeeds in segmenting some images, by having more than one subspace to model one texture. Image 2 shows interesting result as the white subspace marked the boundary area clearly. In image 5, the red subspace model the dark area in one texture, it is clear that this area has different manifold than the other part of the texture and need to be modelled by a separate subspace. For all the ten different subspace settings, image 6, the most difficult image, shows almost the same bad segmentation result.

To see the automatic performance of the model, the last row in Figure 2 shows the best segmentation result based on the highest likelihood criterion. In our previous experiment, we base the number of subspaces selection entirely on this criterion; i.e., we stop increasing the number of subspaces when there is no significance change in the likelihood [11].

6 Conclusion

We describe a greedy EM algorithm for training a Mixture of Probabilistic Principal Component Analyzers. According to a global retained variance ratio, α, the algorithm determines for each principal subspace the dimensionality that retains a ratio α of the local variability.

We apply the model to the texture segmentation problem. It is clear from the experiments that increasing the number of subspaces beyond the number of textures in the image, is more efficient than increasing subspaces dimensionalities. The manifold of one texture seems be local and low dimensional. However, there is no reason to consider it globally linear, i.e., we may need more than one subspace to model one texture. Moreover, the common image features, like dark areas and the boundary pixels also play great role in pushing one-subspace-for-one-texture to get suck in some local maximas. These are the main reasons behind one-subspace-for-one-texture poor performance. The experiments reported in [3], showed that a two 2-dimensional ICA mixture model has better performance than a two 2-dimensional PCA mixture model which leads one to wonder about the performance of a variable-number-of-subspaces ICA mixtures on the same problem.

It is clear that MPPCA is not the ideal solution for this problem. However, the model may be useful to be plugged in a larger segmentation system for some specific phase or task in the system.

References

1. Cadez, I., Smyth P., 2000. On model selection and concavity for finite mixture models. Symp. On Information theory (ISIT).
2. Dasgupta, S., 1999. Learning mixtures of Gaussians. Proc. IEEE Symposium on Foundation of Computer Science.
3. de Ridder, D., Kittler, J,, Duin, R., 2000. Probabilistic PCA and ICA subspace mixture models for image segmentation. Proc. 11th British Machine Vision Conference (BMVC 2000), page 112–121, Bristol, UK.
4. de Ridder, D., 2001. Adaptive methods of image processing. Doc. dissertation, Faculty of Applied Science, Delft University of Technology.
5. Hinton, G., Dayan, P., Revow, M., 1997 Modeling the manifolds of images of handwritten digits. IEEE Trans. on Neural Networks. 10(3):65–74.
6. Kambhatla, N., 1995. Local models & Gaussian mixture models for statistical data processing. Doc. dissertation, Oregon Graduate Inst. of Science & Tech.
7. Li, J., and Barron, A., 2000. Mixture density estimation. Advances in Neural Inf. Proc. Systems, 12, MIT Press, Cambridge.
8. Meinicke, P., Ritter, H., 2001. Resolution-based Complexity control for Gaussian mixture models. Neural Comp. 13(2):453–475.
9. Moghaddam, B., Pentland, A., 1997. Probabilistic visual learning for object representation. IEEE Trans. PAMI 19(7). 696–710.
10. Musa, M., Duin, R., de Ridder, D., 2001. An enhanced EM algorithm for mixture of probabilistic principal component analysis. ICANN 2001 Workshop on Kernel & subspace Methods for computer Vision.
11. Musa, M., Duin, R., de Ridder, D., 2003. Almost automomous training of mixtures of principal component analyzers. Submittend to Pattern Rec. Let.
12. Tipping, M., Bishop, C., 1999. Mixtures of principal component analyzers. Neural Comp. 11(2):443–482.
13. Verbeek, J., Vlassis, N., Krose, B., 2003. Efficient greedy learning of Gaussian mixture models. Neural Comp. 15(2):469–485.

Comparison of Feature Sets Using Multimedia Translation

Pınar Duygulu[1], Özge Can Özcanlı[2], and Norman Papernick[1]

[1] School of Computer Science, Carnegie Mellon University, Informedia Project, Pittsburgh, PA, USA
{pinar, norm}@cs.cmu.edu

[2] Dept. of Computer Engineering, Middle East Technical University, Ankara, Turkey
{ozge}@ceng.metu.edu.tr

Abstract. Feature selection is very important for many computer vision applications. However, it is hard to find a good measure for the comparison. In this study, feature sets are compared using the translation model of object recognition which is motivated by the availablity of large annotated data sets. Image regions are linked to words using a model which is inspired by machine translation. Word prediction performance is used to evaluate large numbers of images.

1 Introduction

Due to the developing technology, there are many available sources where images and text occur together: there is a huge amount of data on the web, where images occur with a surrounding text; with OCR technology it is possible to extract the text from images; and above all, almost all the images have captions which can be used as annotations. Also, there are several large image collections (e.g. Corel data set, most museum image collections,the web archive) where each image is manually annotated with some descriptive text. Using text and images together helps disambiguation in image analysis and also makes several interesting applications possible, including better clustering, search, auto-annotation and auto-illustration [4,5,9].

In the annotated image collections, although it is known that the annotation words are associated with the image, the correspondence between the words and the image regions are unknown. There are some methods that are proposed to solve the correspondence problem [4,12,14]. We consider the problem of finding such correspondences as the translation of image regions to words, similar to the translation of text from one language to another [9,10].

As in many problems, feature selection plays an important role in translating image regions to words. In this study, we investigate the effect of feature sets on the performance of linking image regions to words. Two different feature sets are compared. One is a set of descriptors chosen from MPEG-7 feature extraction schemes, since it is mostly used for content based image retrieval tasks; and the other one is a set obtained by combining most of the descriptive and helpful features chosen heuristically for their adequacy to the task.

A. Yazici and C. Şener (Eds.): ISCIS 2003, LNCS 2869, pp. 513–520, 2003.

In Section 2, the idea of translating image regions to words will be explained. The features used in the experiments will be described in Section 3. Section 4 will present the measurement strategies for comparing the performences. Then, in Section 5 experimental results will be shown. Section 6 will discuss the results.

2 Multimedia Translation

Learning a lexicon from data is a standard problem in machine translation literature [7,13]. Typically, lexicons are learned from a type of data set known as an aligned bitext. Assuming an unknown one-to-one correspondence between words, coming up with a joint probability distribution linking words in two languages is a missing data problem [7] and can be dealt by application of the Expectation Maximization (EM) algorithm [8].

There is an analogy between learning a lexicon for machine translation and learning a correspondence model for associating words with image regions. Data sets consisting of annotated images are similar to aligned bitexts. There is a set of images, consisting of a number of regions and a set of associated words. We vector-quantize the set of features representing an image region. Each region then gets a single label (blob token). The problem is then to construct a probability table that links the blob tokens with word tokens. This is solved using EM which iterates between the two steps: (i) use an estimate of the probability table to predict correspondences; (ii)then use the correspondences to refine the estimate of the probability table.

Once learned, the correspondences are used to predict words corresponding to particular image regions (region naming), or words associated with whole images (auto-annotation) [10,4]. Region naming is a model of object recognition, and auto-annotation may help to organize and access large collections of images. The details of the approach can be found in [9,10].

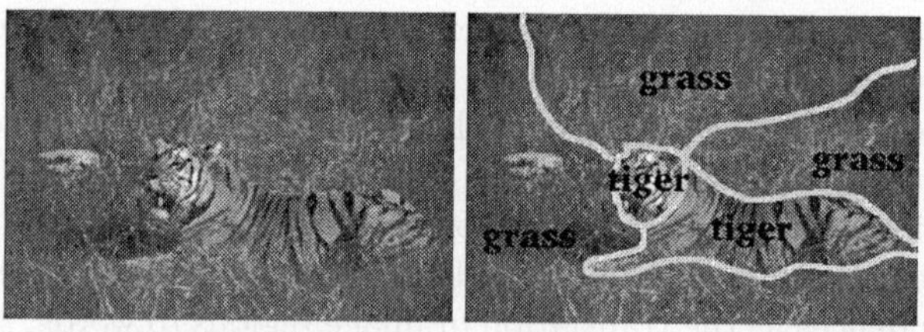

tiger cat grass

Fig. 1. In the annotated image collections (e.g., Corel stock photographs), each image is annotated with some descriptive text. Although it is known that the annotation words are associated with the image, the correspondence between the words and the image regions are unknown. With the proposed approach, image regions are linked to words with a method inspired by machine translation. **Left:** an example image with annotated keywords, **right:** the result where image regions are linked with words.

3 Feature Sets Compared

3.1 Feature Set 1

The first set is a combination of some descriptive and helpful features selected from the features used in many applications: size (1 feature);position (2 features);color (6 features); and texture (12 features). Therefore, a feature vector of size 21 is formed to represent each region. Size is represented by the portion of the image covered by the region. Position is represented by the coordinates (x, y) of the region's center of gravity in relation to the image dimensions. Color is represented using the mean and variance of the RGB color space. Texture is represented by using the mean of twelve oriented energy filters aligned in 30 degree increments.

3.2 Feature Set 2 – MPEG-7 Feature Extraction Schemes

MPEG-7 [3] is a world-wide standardization attempt in representing visual content. It provides many descriptors to extract various features from multimedia data and it aims efficient, configurable storage and access tools. In this study, we chose the following descriptors from the visual content description set of MPEG-7: edge histogram (80 features); color layout (12 features); dominant color (4 features); region shape (35 features); and scalable color (64 features) descriptors. As a result, a feature vector of size 195 is formed to represent each region. The dominant color descriptor is the RGB values and the percentage of the dominant colors in each region. The scalable color descriptor is a color histogram in the HSV color space, which is encoded by a Haar transform. The number of coefficients is chosen to be 64 in this study. Color layout descriptor specifies the spatial distribution of colors in the Y, Cr, Cb color space and all 12 features of it are put into the feature vector. The Region shape descriptor utilizes a set of ART (Angular Radial Transform) coefficients which is a 2D complex transform defined on a unit disk in polar coordinates. Lastly, edge histogram descriptor represents the spatial distribution of four directional edges and one non-directional edge, by encoding the histogram in 80 bins. The feature extraction schemes of each descriptor are explained in detail in [11].

4 Measuring the Performance

Correspondence performance can be measured by visually inspecting the images. However, it requires human judgment and this form of manual evaluation is not practical for large number of images. An alternative way is to compute the annotation performance. Using annotation performance, it is not known whether the word is predicted for the correct blob. However, it is an automatic process allowing the evaluation of large number of images. Furthermore, if the annotations are incorrect, the correspondences will not be correct either. Therefore, annotation performance is a plausible proxy.

Annotation performance is measured by comparing the predicted words with the words that are actually present as an annotation keyword in the image. Two measures are used to compare the annotation performance over all of the images. The first measure is the Kullback Liebler divergence between the target distribution and the predicted distribution. Since the target distribution is not known, to compute KL divergence it is assumed that in the target distribution the actual words are predicted uniformly, and all the other words are not predicted. The second measure is the word prediction measure which is defined as the ratio of the number of words predicted correctly (r) to the number of actual keywords (n). For example, if there are three keywords, `sky`, `water`, and `sun`, then n=3, and we allow the model to predict 3 words for that image. The range of this score is from 0 to 1.

The results are also compared as a function of words. For each word in the vocabulary, recall and precision is computed for comparison. **Recall** is defined as the number of correct predictions over number of actual occurence of the word in the data, and **precision** is defined as the number of correct predictions over all predictions.

5 Experimental Results

In this study, the Corel data set, [1] which is a very large collection of stock photographs, is used. It consists of a diverse set of real scene images, and each image is annotated with a few keywords. In this study, we use 3175 images for training and 1081 images for testing. Each image is segmented using Normalized Cuts segmentation [15]. Then, the features of each region are extracted using both sets. In order to map the feature vectors onto a finite number of blob tokens, first the feature vectors of the regions obtained from all the images in the training set are shifted and scaled to have zero mean and unit variance. Then, these vectors are clustered using the k-means algorithm, with the total number of clusters $k = 500$.

The translation probability table is initialized with the co-occurrences of words and blobs. Then EM algorithm is applied to learn the final translation table.

For region naming, the word with the highest probability is chosen for each blob. Figure 2 shows some example results from the test set. As explained in Section 4, it is very hard to measure the correspondence performance on a large set. Visually inspecting every image and counting the number of correct matches is not feasible. Also, it is not easy to create a ground truth set, since one region may correspond to many words (e.g., both `cat` and `tiger`) or due to segmentation errors, it may not be possible to label a region with a single word. Therefore, we use annotation performance as a proxy.

To annotate an image, the word posteriors for all the blobs in the image are merged into one, and the first n words with the highest probability (where n is the number of actual keywords) are predicted. The predicted words are

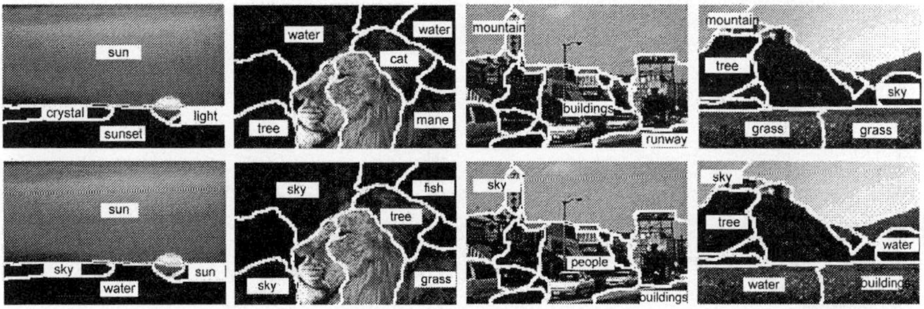

Fig. 2. Predicted words for some example images. **Top:** using *Feature set 1*, **bottom** using *Feature set 2*.

Table 1. Comparison of annotation measures for two different feature sets. **Left:** feature set 1, **right:** feature set 2. The results are compared on training and test sets using Kullback Liebler divergence between the target distribution and the predicted distribution (KL) and using the word prediction measure (PR). For KL smaller numbers are better, for PR larger numbers are better.

	Feature set 1		Feature set 2	
	training	test	training	test
PR	0.3802	0.2719	0.3679	0.2663
KL	2.7488	4.6267	2.7934	4.6529

compared with the actual keywords to measure the performance of the system as explained in Section 4.

Table 2 shows the word prediction measure and KL divergence between the target distribution and predicted distribution on training and test sets for both feature sets. Results show that *Feature set 1* have better annotation performance than *Feature set 2*. Figure 3 compares the feature sets using recall and precision values on training and test sets. A can be seen from the figure *Feature set 1* predicts more words with higher recall and/or precision values.

We also experiment with the effect of each individual feature. Table 2 compares the features using prediction measure and KL divergence and Figure 4 uses recall and precision values for comparison. The results show that energy filters give the best results. Although MPEG-7 uses more complicated color features, mean and variance of RGB values give the best results among the color features.

6 Discussion and Future Directions

Feature set selection is very important for many computer vision applications. However, it is hard to find a good measure for the comparison. In this study, feature sets are compared using the translation model of object recognition. This approach allows us to evaluate large number of images.

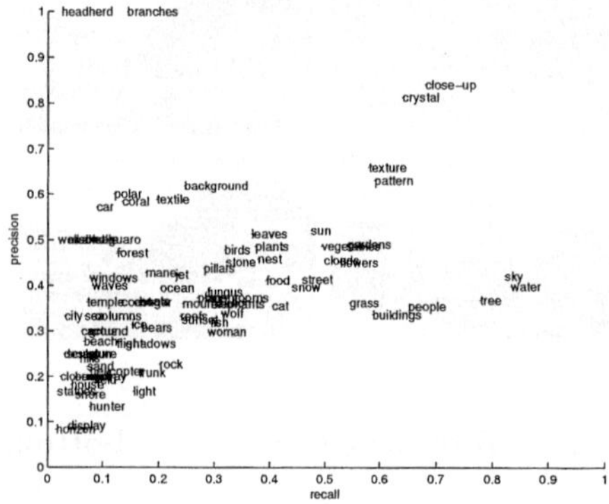

(a) Feature set 1 - training

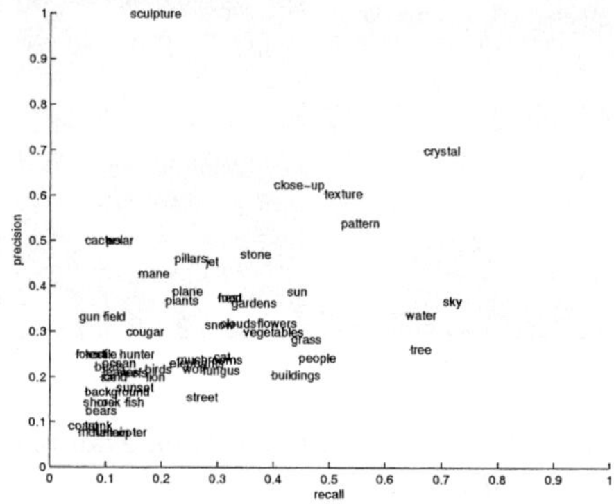

(b) Feature set 1 - test

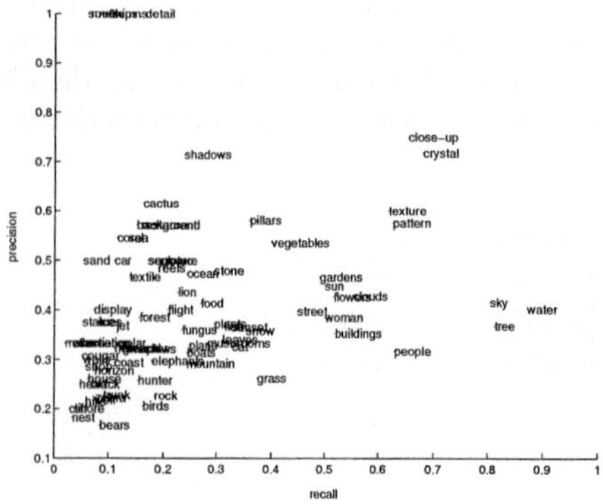

(c) Feature set 2 - training

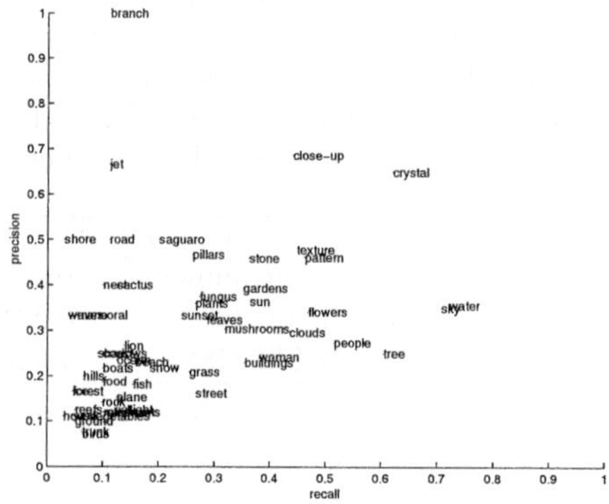

(b) Feature set 2 - test

Fig. 3. Comparison of feature sets using recall and precision values on training and test sets. **Recall** is the number of correct predictions over number of actual occurence of the word in the data, and **precision** is the number of correct predictions over all predictions.

Table 2. Comparison of annotation measures for different color features. The features are sorted in descending order according to their prediction measures.

	Prediction Measure	KL Divergence
Energy filters	0.3991	2.6290
RGB mean and variance	0.3630	2.8342
Scalable Color	0.3520	2.8595
Dominant Color	0.3455	2.8924
Color Layout	0.3441	2.9215
Edge histogram	0.3151	3.0577

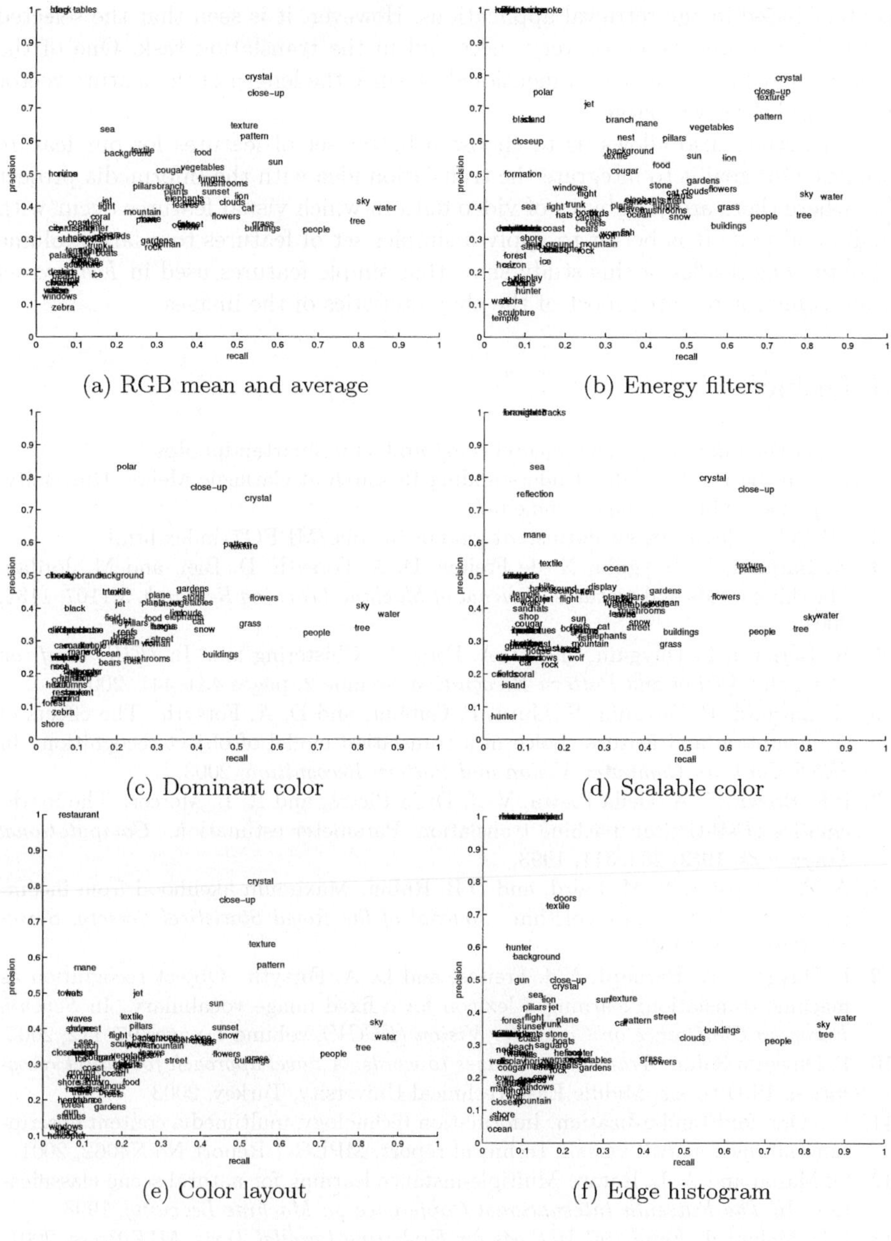

(a) RGB mean and average (b) Energy filters (c) Dominant color (d) Scalable color (e) Color layout (f) Edge histogram

Fig. 4. Comparison of features using recall and precision values.

In [6] subsets of a feature set, which is very similar to Feature set 1, are compared. In this study, we extend this approach to compare two different feature sets. One of the goals was to test MPEG-7 features that are commonly used in content based image retrieval applications. However, it is seen that the selected MPEG-7 features were not very successful in the translation task. One of the reasons may be the curse of dimensionality, since the length of the feature vector for MPEG-7 set was large.

This study also allows us to choose a better set of features for our feature studies. Our goal is to integrate the translation idea with the Informedia project [2], where there are terrabytes of video data in which visual features occur with audio and text. It is better to apply a simpler set of features to a large volume of data. The results of this study show that simple features used in *Feature set 1* are sufficient to catch most of the characteristics of the images.

References

1. Corel Data Set. http://www.corel.com/products/clipartandphotos.
2. Informedia Digital Video Understanding Research at Carnegie Mellon University. http://www.informedia.cs.cmu.edu/.
3. MPEG-7 . http://www.darmstadt.gmd.de/mobile/MPEG7/index.html.
4. K. Barnard, P. Duygulu, N. de Freitas, D. A. Forsyth, D. Blei, and M. Jordan. Matching words and pictures. *Journal of Machine Learning Research*, 3:1107–1135, 2003.
5. K. Barnard, P. Duygulu, and D. A. Forsyth. Clustering art. In *IEEE Conf. on Computer Vision and Pattern Recognition*, volume 2, pages 434–441, 2001.
6. K. Barnard, P. Duygulu, R. Guru, P. Gabbur, and D. A. Forsyth. The effects of segmentation and feature choice in a translation model of object recognition. In *IEEE Conf. on Computer Vision and Pattern Recognition*, 2003.
7. P.F. Brown, S. A. Della Pietra, V. J. Della Pietra, and R. L. Mercer. The mathematics of statistical machine translation: Parameter estimation. *Computational Linguistics*, 19(2):263–311, 1993.
8. A. P. Dempster, N. M. Laird, and D.B. Rubin. Maximum likelihood from incomplete data via the em algorithm. *Journal of the Royal Statistical Society, Series B*, 1(39):1–38, 1977.
9. P. Duygulu, K. Barnard, N.d. Freitas, and D. A. Forsyth. Object recognition as machine translation: learning a lexicon for a fixed image vocabulary. In *Seventh European Conference on Computer Vision (ECCV)*, volume 4, pages 97–112, 2002.
10. P. Duygulu-Sahin. *Translating Images to words: A novel approach for object recognition.* PhD thesis, Middle East Technical University, Turkey, 2003.
11. Int. Org. for Standardization. Information technology, multimedia content description interface, part 3 visual. Technical report, MPEG-7 Report No:N4062, 2001.
12. O. Maron and A. L. Ratan. Multiple-instance learning for natural scene classification. In *The Fifteenth International Conference on Machine Learning*, 1998.
13. I. D. Melamed. *Empirical Methods for Exploiting Parallel Texts.* MIT Press, 2001.
14. Y. Mori, H. Takahashi, and R. Oka. Image-to-word transformation based on dividing and vector quantizing images with words. In *First International Workshop on Multimedia Intelligent Storage and Retrieval Management*, 1999.
15. J. Shi and J. Malik. Normalized cuts and image segmentation. *IEEE Transactions on Pattern Analysis and Machine Intelligence*, 22(8):888–905, 2000.

Estimating Distributions in Genetic Algorithms

Onur Dikmen, H. Levent Akın, and Ethem Alpaydın

Department of Computer Engineering, Boğaziçi University,
TR-34342 Istanbul, Turkey
{onuro, akin, alpaydin}@boun.edu.tr

Abstract. The canonical operators of genetic algorithms, i.e., mutation and crossover, have nondeterministic effects on the population.They use information from only one or two fit individuals and risk deforming the chromosomes of fit individuals and cause an interruption in the progression. Estimation of Distribution Algorithms (EDAs) use probabilistic models rather than mutation and crossover, to guide the progression of genetic algorithms by placing a density over all fit individuals and sampling from this density. EDA therefore makes better use of the fitness information of the previous generation and promise faster convergence without losing any schemata. We consider parametric, nonparametric, and semiparametric models for density estimation in the EDA template with continuous genes. We compare these methods with standard backpropagation and GA proper in the problem of training a multilayer perceptron which is a complex nonlinear estimator. Our results indicate that our algorithms perform definitely better than the proper genetic algorithm (GA) on every problem and can find better solutions than those of backpropagation in training a MLP.

1 Introduction

Genetic algorithms (GA) are optimization methods which are based on generating a sequence of populations of individuals such that the goodness of the individuals, as measured by a fitness function, increase with passing generations. GA is composed of alternating two steps: 1) Evaluating the fitness of a population of individuals and choosing the fit, and 2) Generating candidate new individuals of possibly higher fitness to replace the unfit. In the second step, the canonical operators are mutation and crossover. Mutation adds a random vector to a fit individual to search for its vicinity for possible improvement, and crossover aims to combine the good characteristics of two fit individuals, i.e., parents.

In a recent line of research, methods to avoid using crossover and mutation operators have been developed. These methods are based on the estimation of probability distribution and called *Estimation of Distribution Algorithms* (EDA). EDA first estimates the probability distribution of fit individuals. Then, new individuals are generated by taking samples from this distribution. These steps are repeated until a stopping criterion is reached. The advantage of EDA is that it uses *all* fit individuals of the population in estimating a density, whereas

A. Yazici and C. Şener (Eds.): ISCIS 2003, LNCS 2869, pp. 521–528, 2003.

mutation uses only one and crossover uses two fit individuals. This allows a better approximation of the fitness landscape and therefore a faster convergence.

The organization of this paper is as follows: In Section 2, we give a literature survey of EDA algorithms. In Section 3, we discuss our approach which generalizes EDA to the continuous domain. The results of our experiments are presented in Section 4. In Section 5 we conclude and discuss possible future work.

2 Estimation of Distribution Algorithms

EDA consists of two steps: 1) Fitting a probability density to the selected fit individuals, and 2) Sampling from this density to replace the unfit with possibly fitter individuals. When new individuals are generated by sampling from the distribution representing fit individuals, we are likely to get individuals with high fitness. Mutation uses only one fit individual and crossover typically uses only two parents; but when an algorithm fits a probability distribution on all fit individuals, it makes better use of the fitness information of the previous generation.

Different instantiations of EDA use different probabilistic models to represent the fit individuals. Past work on EDA use binary genes and thus require estimating and sampling from a multivariate Bernoulli distribution. A full multivariate distribution with a long chromosome has many parameters. To make the task easier, simplifying assumptions are made. Allowing partial dependencies, if the bits are not fully dependent, one can represent the probability distribution with a Bayesian network. In this way, it is possible to obtain a factorized representation of the probability distribution. Such a representation is simple and hence is easier to understand, store, and sample from. There are three classes of EDA according to the probabilistic models they use.

The first class of EDA algorithms assume no dependency between genes. UMDA (Univariate Marginal Distribution Algorithm) [7] estimates the distribution by calculating univariate marginal frequencies of bits in the set of selected individuals. PBIL (Population-based Incremental Learning Algorithm) algorithm [1] replaces the population matrix with a probability vector, which shifts toward the selected individuals by using Hebbian learning.

The second class of EDA algorithms allow partial dependency: MIMIC (Mutual Information Maximization for Input Clustering) [4] is a greedy algorithm which searches for the best permutation between the variables and finds the probability distribution in chain form with a unique condition variable. Baluja and Davies [2] model the selected individuals with dependency trees. The best model can be found with a polynomial time maximal branching algorithm and it is guaranteed to be optimal. BMDA (Bivariate Marginal Distribution Algorithm) [9] evaluates dependencies of bit pairs. The algorithm calculates conditional probabilities of every position pair using univariate and bivariate marginal frequencies. Dependencies are found using Pearson's chi-square statistic and a dependency graph is constructed. New individuals are generated using univariate frequencies for independent bits and conditional frequencies for dependent bits.

The third class of EDA algorithms can model full dependencies and thus are the most general: FDA (Factorization Distribution Algorithm) [8], assumes that the probability can be written as a product of marginal frequencies. Given an additively decomposed function and a factorization of the probability distribution, it calculates the probabilities by multiplying relevant conditional probabilities. The Bayesian Optimization Algorithm (BOA), proposed by Pelikan et al. [10], makes use of a Bayesian network to encode the joint probability distribution. The network is constructed imcrementally using the Bayesian Dirichlet metric. New individuals are generated using the joint distribution encoded by the network. A Bayesian network can model full dependencies but constructing a Bayesian network from data and calculating the joint probabilities are costly.

Bosman and Thirens [5] adjusted existing EDA techniques to solve problems with continuous domains and called their algorithm Iterated Density Estimation Evolutionary Algorithm (IDEA). A probability density function (pdf) is selected and its parameters are estimated. New individuals are generated by taking samples from this pdf. They used three distributions: the parametric normal distribution and histogram and normal kernels (Parzen windows) which are nonparametric distributions. Our work and IDEA are similar but they are developed independently. We represent the promising solutions with parametric and nonparametric densities and generalize this to semiparametric normal mixture densities which include the other two densities as its two special extreme cases. After our work was completed, we learned that a version of IDEA with semiparametric densities was also proposed [6].

3 Methodology

The three methods for density estimation are parametric, semiparametric, and nonparametric. In the case where inputs are continuous, the simplest and most widely used distribution is the normal (Gaussian) distribution which has two sufficient statistics, mean and covariance. The normal distribution, additional to its simplicity and its analytical tractability, is also a good approximation to many naturally occurring phenomena.

In the parametric case, there is only one density that models the whole sample. In the nonparametric case, there are as many densities as there are instances in the sample. The semiparametric case is a mixture model with k component densities, k being between one and the sample size; in these two extremes, the semiparametric case degenerates to the parametric and nonparametric cases respectively.

In our algorithms, truncation (elitist) selection is used. In truncation selection, the best subset of the population is used to estimate the density and remains unchanged; the rest of the population, the unfit, are replaced by newly generated individuals sampled from the density. The size of this set is determined by the selection rate, τ. In a population of size N, $\lfloor N - \tau N \rfloor$ new individuals are sampled from the new estimated density and the remaining fit are copied as they are. The algorithms continue alternating these two steps of estimation and sampling, until there is no significant change in parameters, or some prespecified number of generations take place.

3.1 Parametric Distribution

This method assumes that the selected fit individuals of a population come from a single multivariate normal distribution whose dimensionality is given by the length of the chromosome. In a multivariate normal distribution, only means, variances, and covariances need be estimated to completely describe the distribution.

If $\boldsymbol{x}$ has a d-variate normal distribution with mean vector $\boldsymbol{\mu}$ and covariance matrix $\boldsymbol{\Sigma}$, its density is given by

$$p(\boldsymbol{x}) = \frac{1}{(\sqrt{2\pi})^d |\boldsymbol{\Sigma}|^{1/2}} \exp\left[-\frac{1}{2}(\boldsymbol{x}-\boldsymbol{\mu})^T \boldsymbol{\Sigma}^{-1}(\boldsymbol{x}-\boldsymbol{\mu})\right] \quad (1)$$

denoted as as $p(\boldsymbol{x}) \sim \mathcal{N}_d(\boldsymbol{\mu},\boldsymbol{\Sigma})$. The term $(\boldsymbol{x}-\boldsymbol{\mu})^T \boldsymbol{\Sigma}^{-1}(\boldsymbol{x}-\boldsymbol{\mu})$ in the exponent of the multivariate density is the squared generalized distance from $\boldsymbol{x}$ to $\boldsymbol{\mu}$, also called the Mahalanobis distance.

To estimate the normal distribution from the new generation, we use the maximum likelihood estimates of $\boldsymbol{\mu}$ and $\boldsymbol{\Sigma}$, denoted by $\bar{\boldsymbol{x}}$ and $\boldsymbol{S}$. Once these are estimated, the distribution is fully specified and we sample new individuals for the next generation from it. To sample from an arbitrary multivariate distribution, the approach is to generate first a multivariate standard distribution (zero mean, unit variance, zero covariance) and then translate it by the mean, rotate, and scale it by the matrix obtained by applying Cholesky decomposition on the covariance matrix.

3.2 Semiparametric Distribution

The normal density is unimodal (has one peak) and thus assumes that the fitness function has only one maximum. This is a very restrictive assumption and of course if this is the case, there are easier ways to optimize such a function. The mixture model is a semiparametric distribution and a mixture of normal densities allows approximating a density with multiple peaks and thus learn a fitness function with many maxima. Each component of the mixture is called a *group* or *cluster* and learning such a mixture is also called *clustering*.

The mixture density is written as

$$p(\boldsymbol{x}) = \sum_{i=1}^{k} P(G_i) p(\boldsymbol{x}|G_i) \quad (2)$$

where G_i are the components or clusters and k is their number. $P(G_i)$ is the prior probability of cluster i. In the case of a normal mixture, each component is a normal density with its own mean vector and a covariance matrix. To overcome the curse of dimesionality and to have a reasonable number of parameters, we assume that the components share a common diagonal covariance matrix. So the pdf of each cluster becomes $p(\boldsymbol{x}|G_i) \sim \mathcal{N}_d(\boldsymbol{\mu}_i, \boldsymbol{\Sigma}_d)$.

The two steps of EDA are the same as in the parametric case. Fitting a normal mixture to a sample is done by *k-means clustering*. After clustering, a normal distribution is fit on each cluster and parameters of these distributions $(\bar{\boldsymbol{x}}_i, \boldsymbol{S}_d, \hat{P}(G_i))$ are calculated. A common diagonal covariance matrix, $\boldsymbol{S}_d$ with equal variances on all dimensions allows us to use the Euclidean distance for similarity. To generate a new individual from this mixture of distributions, first, a cluster is selected for sampling with probability $\hat{P}(G_i)$. Then the multivariate normal distribution belonging to that cluster is sampled to obtain the new individual chromosome.

Any clustering algorithm can be used in the algorithm, e.g., Expectation-Maximization (EM), Self-Organizing Maps (SOM) and k-means. When EM is used, sampling is done with the full covariance matrix and better results are obtained, but the complexity of the overall algorithm is seriously increased. SOM and k-means use Euclidean distance and therefore use hyperspherical Gaussians.

3.3 Nonparametric Distribution

When the distribution is not sufficiently regular such that it cannot be modeled by a mixture model with small number of clusters, one needs to resort to a nonparametric approach where no simplifying assumptions are made. The nonparametric approach fits a normal distribution on each of the instance points representing the selected fit individuals; this is also known as Parzen windows. This distribution is good for representing local features of the population. These normal distributions are identical, i.e. their covariance matrices are common. The common covariance matrix has zero entries off the diagonal (zero covariances) and there are variances on the diagonal. As the standard deviation of variable j, s_j is used, and it is calculated by dividing the range in dimension j to a constant times the number of selected individuals. In this distribution, mean vectors are the actual selected individuals, $\boldsymbol{X}^i, i = 1..\lfloor \tau N \rfloor$. Note that this is equivalent to the semiparametric approach with $k = \lfloor \tau N \rfloor$ and $P(G_i) = 1/\lfloor \tau N \rfloor$.

The density of the nonparametric distribution is given by

$$p(\boldsymbol{x}) = \sum_{i=1}^{\lfloor \tau N \rfloor} p(\boldsymbol{X}^i) \tag{3}$$

where $p(\boldsymbol{X}^i) \sim \mathcal{N}_d(\boldsymbol{X}^i, \boldsymbol{S})$.

To sample from this distribution, for each variable j a random individual is chosen from the set of selected individuals and a univariate normal sampling is done with $\boldsymbol{X}^i_j$ as mean and s_j as standard deviation. This approach does not take the dependencies between variables into account, because the covariances of variables are taken as zero and sampling is done on each variable independently.

4 Experiments and Results

We compared our approaches with GA proper on the problem of estimating the weights of a Multilayer Perceptron (MLP). A MLP with one hidden layer of sigmoid units is a complex, nonlinear system with many parameters, and a successful estimation of the MLP weights would indicate the applicability of our EDA approach in real life, nonlinear estimation problems in pattern recognition, control, optimization, etc. We also compared our results with those of backpropagation which is based on gradient descent used to train MLP. The MLPs have a fixed structure, i.e., number of hidden units, and in our representation, every weight of the MLP constitutes a gene in the chromosome. The negative of the error rate (misclassification percentage for classification, mean squared error for regression) of the MLP, phenotype decoded from a gene string, is used as the fitness of that individual. We consider both regression and classification problems and used several standard data sets from the UCI repository [3] to test our algorithms: Iris, Monks and Sonar data sets for classification, Bumpreg, Sine and Boston data sets for regression.

The number of hidden units is a parameter of the program, just as the population size and stopping criterion. According to the number of hidden units, the length of the gene string is calculated and each gene of each individual is initialized with a real value between -10 and 10. A separate test set for each problem is not used in fitness evaluations, but only is used to measure the generalization performance, which is what is reported in the tables and figures below. To compare the performances of the algorithms for statistical significance, we use two-sample t test. Table 1 shows the test error rates of algorithms on different data sets. On Bumpreg data set, the parametric distribution outperforms the other algorithms. It is better than the semiparametric distribution with a 95% confidence level. The confidence level is more than 99.9% for the other algorithms. On Sine data set, the parametric approach performs the best. It is better than MLP with backpropagation with 97.5% significance and the other algorithms with at least 99.9%. On Boston data set, MLP with backpropagation outperforms all other methods with 99.9% significance.

Table 1. Error rates of algorithms on test sets of different data sets. Bold values indicate statistically significant superiority.

Data set	GA	Parametric	Semiparametric	Nonparametric	Backpropagation
Bumpreg	1.408±0.321	**0.871±0.003**	0.878±0.011	0.885±0.005	0.896±0.0004
Sine	0.340±0.064	**0.037±0.053**	0.145±0.043	0.190±0.048	0.152±0.159
Boston	0.513±0.065	0.195±0.020	0.422±0.055	0.337±0.020	**0.163±0.009**
Iris	0.257±0.178	**0.04±0.013**	**0.051±0.016**	0.064±0.021	0.067±0
Sonar	0.235±0.026	0.226±0.029	**0±0**	0.195±0.026	0.175±0.019
Monks1	0.312±0.024	0.288±0.037	**0±0**	0.297±0.023	0.143±0.107

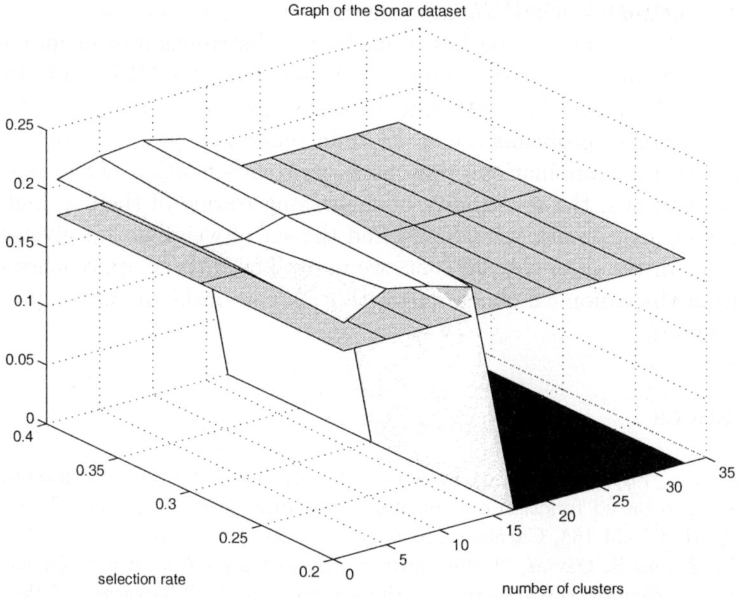

Fig. 1. Error rate of the semiparametric approach versus the number of clusters and the selection rate on Sonar data set. The flat surface is the error rate of MLP trained with backpropagation.

On Iris data set, the parametric approach has the lowest test error rate, but it is not better than the semiparametric approach significantly. These two algorithms are better than the others with high confidence levels. On Sonar and Monks1 data sets, the semiparametric approach definitely outperforms the other algorithms with more than 99.9% confidence. The error rate of the semiparametric method versus the number of clusters and the selection proportion of the fit individuals is shown in Figure 1.

5 Conclusions

In this paper, our main concern is to eliminate the canonical operators of genetic algorithms whose effects on population are unpredictable. They produce fitter individuals because they produce semi-random individuals and the fitter of them are selected. These operators can also deform the chromosomes of fit individuals and cause an interruption in the progression. Estimation of Distribution Algorithms (EDA) place a distribution over the selected individuals and generate new individuals according to this distribution. Because the distribution is estimated using all fit individuals, the new candidate individuals are generated using more information, as opposed to mutation and crossover which make use of one or two fit individuals respectively. We generalize the previous EDA approach from binary to continuous genes. We used the EDA template and used three types of probability estimation approaches to model the distribution of fit individuals.

The algorithms are tested on finding the weights of a MLP, on both regression and classification data sets. On regression problems, our algorithms work well. Classification problems are easier than regression problems because there are more weight combinations that have zero classification error. Since there are more solutions, the probability of converging to one of them is higher. Our semiparametric approach was able to find the set of weights that give zero classification error on all of the data sets we used. These three approaches perform better than the canonical genetic algorithm on the problems whose parameters are continuous.

References

1. Baluja, S., "Population-based incremental learning: A method for integrating genetic search based function optimization and competitive learning", Technical Report CMU-CS-94-163, Carnegie Mellon University, Pittsburgh, PA, 1994.
2. Baluja, S. and S. Davies, "Using optimal dependency-trees for combinatorial optimization: Learning the structure of the search space", *Proceedings of the 14th International Conference on Machine Learning*, pp. 30–38, Morgan Kaufmann, 1997.
3. Blake, C. L. and C. J. Merz, *UCI Repository of machine learning databases*, 1998, http://www.ics.uci.edu/~mlearn/MLRepository.html
4. de Bonet, J. S., C. L. Isbell, Jr. and P. Viola, "MIMIC: Finding optima by estimating probability densities", *Advances in Neural Information Processing Systems*, Vol. 9, p. 424, The MIT Press, 1997.
5. Bosman, P. A. N. and D. Thierens, "Continuous iterated density estimation evolutionary algorithms within the IDEA framework", *Optimization By Building and Using Probabilistic Models OBUPM Workshop at the Genetic and Evolutionary Computation Conference GECCO-2000*, pp. 197–200, 2000.
6. Bosman, P. A. N. and D. Thierens, "Advancing Continuous IDEAs with Mixture Distributions and Factorization Selection Metrics", *Proceedings of the Optimization by Building and Using Probabilistic Models OBUPM Workshop at the Genetic and Evolutionary Computation Conference GECCO-2001*, pp. 208–212, 2001.
7. Mühlenbein, H., "The equation for response to selection and its use for prediction", *Evolutionary Computation*, Vol. 5, pp. 303–346, 1998.
8. Mühlenbein, H., T. Mahning and A. Ochoa, "Schemata, distributions and graphical models in evolutionary optimization", *Journal of Heuristics*, Vol.5, pp.215–247, 1999.
9. Pelikan, M. and H. Mühlenbein, "The bivariate marginal distribution algorithm", *Advances in Soft Computing – Engineering Design and Manufacturing*, pp. 521–535, Springer-Verlag, London, 1999.
10. Pelikan, M., D. E. Goldberg and E. Cantú-Paz, "BOA: The Bayesian optimization algorithm", *Proceedings of the Genetic and Evolutionary Computation Conference GECCO-99*, Vol. I, pp. 525–532, Morgan Kaufmann Publishers, San Fransisco, CA, Orlando, FL, 13–17 1999.

All Bids for One and One Does for All: Market-Driven Multi-agent Collaboration in Robot Soccer Domain

Hatice Köse, Çetin Meriçli, Kemal Kaplan, and H. Levent Akın

Boğaziçi University
Department of Computer Engineering
34342 Bebek, Istanbul, TURKEY
{kose, cetin.mericli, kaplanke, akin}@boun.edu.tr

Abstract. In this paper, a novel market-driven collaborative task allocation algorithm called "Collaboration by competition / cooperation" for the robot soccer domain is proposed and implemented. In robot soccer, two teams of robots compete with each other to win the match. For the benefit of the team, the robots should work collaboratively, whenever possible. The market-driven approach applies the basic properties of free market economy to a team of robots for increasing the profit of the team as much as possible. The experimental results show that the approach is robust and flexible and the developed team is more succcessful than its opponents.

Keywords: Market-driven, multi-agent, collaboration, robot soccer.

1 Introduction

Multi-robot teams, in which robots cooperate with each other and/or with human beings, become more popular as their performance are shown to be better, more reliable and more flexible than single robots, in a variety of tasks (see [1,2] for many papers about cooperative robotics). Unfortunately there are still a limited number of applications in this area, and many of these are about toy problems or limited implementations of applicable problems due to the difficulty of the general problem.

Robotic soccer as first proposed by Mackworth [3] is a challenging research domain that is particularly appropriate for studying a large spectrum of issues of relevance to the development of teams consisting of completely autonomous robots. It has an environment with a complex and dynamic nature, where there are many important problems, like team localization, planning, task allocation, and multi-robot coordination, which can not be solved trivially.

One of the notable applications in robot soccer is multi-agent based perception for team localization; [4,5] work on multi-robot localization. Algorithms have also been introduced for multi-robot perception and object (e.g. ball) tracking [6,7,8]. Another approach combines local maps constructed by extended Kalman filter, and transform these to the overall map in only one iteration [9,10]. Several studies were done on map construction which requires an optimum positioning of all the team members [11] to gather the maximum amount of information about the environment for constructing the best map [12]. In many of the limited multi-agent applications in this area, robot

A. Yazici and C. Şener (Eds.): ISCIS 2003, LNCS 2869, pp. 529–536, 2003.

coordination is typically not implemented since it is found to be costly for a real-time application. Many teams tend to use simple mechanisms that are far from realizing the full potential of collaborative team work.

The market driven methodology have been used to solve several problems in multi-robot systems. It is used in [13,14] for robot coordination. The work in [15] introduces the approach to multi-robot exploration. Implementations are successful, however domains like agricultural areas are not dynamic and do not require fast task allocation, planning and coordination as in robot soccer, since the environment is almost static, and not as complex.

In order to address the challenging dynamic collaborative task allocation problem for multi-agent robotic soccer, this paper proposes a novel approach called "Collaboration by competition / cooperation" based on the free market driven method.

The organization of the paper is as follows: In the second section, the market-driven method is defined. The third section makes a brief introduction to robot soccer. In the fourth section detailed information about the proposed approach can be found. In the fifth section, results of the application of the proposed approach are presented. In the last section, conclusions and suggestions for future work are given.

2 Market-Driven Method

The main goal in the free-markets is maximizing the overall profit of the system. If each participant in the market tries to maximize its profit, as a result of this, the overall profit for the system is expected to increase. The idea of the market-driven method for multi-robot teams is based on the interaction of the robots among themselves in a distributed fashion for trading work, power and information and hence "Collaboration by competition / cooperation". In general, there is an overall goal of the team (i.e., building the map of an unknown planet, harvesting an agricultural area, sweeping buried landmines in a particular area, etc..). Some entity outside of the team is assumed to offer a payoff for that goal. The overall goal of the system is decomposed into smaller tasks and an auction is performed for each of these tasks. In each auction, the participant robots (who are able to communicate among themselves) calculate their estimated cost for accomplishing that task and offer a price to the auctioneer. At the end of the auction, the bidder with the lowest offered price will be given the right of execution of the task and receives its revenue on behalf of the auctioneer. There are many possible actions that can be taken. A robot may open another auction for selling a task that it won from another auction, two or more robots may cooperatively work and get a task which is hard to accomplish by a single robot, or for a heterogeneous system, robots with different sensors/actuators may cooperate by resource sharing (for example, a small robot with a camera may guide a large robot without a vision system for carrying a heavy load).

In order to implement the strategy, a cost function is defined for mapping a set of resources (required energy, required time, etc...) to a real number and the net profit is calculated by subtracting the estimated cost for accomplishing the task from the revenue of the task. For example, in Eq.1 an estimated cost is calculated from the time required for the robot to cover the distance, and align itself according to the task, and the clearance of range which is used to avoid objects on the path between the robot and the task. Here suitably chosen μ_i's act as weights to show the importance of each issue in the overall cost.

$$C_{es} = \mu_1 . t_{dist} + \mu_2 . t_{align} \quad (1)$$

3 The Robot Soccer Domain

In robot soccer, teams of robots play matches against each other, and the team with the highest goal score wins the match as in real soccer. Here, image processing, locomotion, localization, and planning are the main problems.

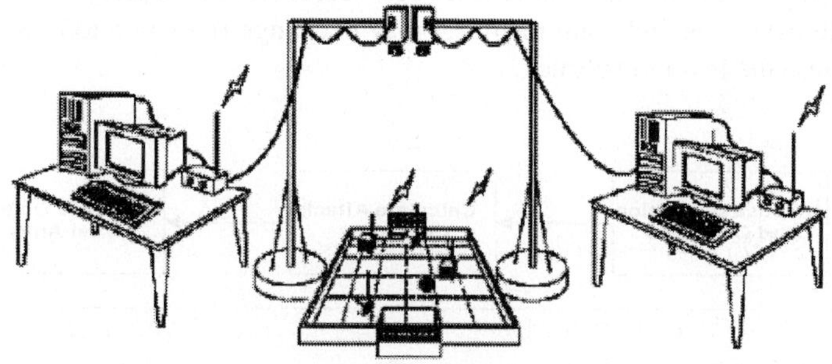

Fig. 1. The MIROSOT environment

Federation of International Robot-soccer Association (FIRA) is one of the associations for international robot soccer [16] where wheeled and legged robots compete in the official games. MIROSOT is one of the categories for these robots. The main part of the MIROSOT soccer system is the remote host computer where the controller is located (Figure 1). The controller processes the input from the vision system. The output of the controller is the communication data package which is sent to the robots through the RF module. The robots first process the package to extract the commands sent to them, which in our case, includes only the left and right wheel velocity information. Then the robot transmits this information to its motor drivers. The work proposed in this paper is a part of the *Robot Idman Yurdu* soccer project [17].

4 The Proposed Approach

The market-driven approach can be applied to several open issues including dynamic task allocation in robot soccer where depending on the strategies, generally there is a pool of predefined roles and a set of possible tasks for each role. These roles, depending on the number of players in each team, can be attacker, defender, midfielder, etc. There are typically two tasks assigned for these roles: shoot or pass to a team member.

Initially, each team member calculates its costs, including the cost of moving, aligning itself suitably for the task, and the cost of object avoidance. The calculated costs are shared among the team members. As shown in Figure 2, after sorting the costs, each team member gets the appropriate role from the pool according to its rank in the ordered costs list (e.g. the member with the lowest defense cost becomes the defender whereas the member with the lowest attack cost becomes the primary attacker). Each role is assigned to exactly one team member. The miscalculation of a cost may lead the team to a wrong role allocation; therefore, the team members may behave unsuitably for the current situation until the next update is performed. The overall effect of this wrong task allocation on the team depends on the length of the update period. A long period may cause the team members to behave inappropriately to their situations for a long time but on the other hand, a short period of update may cause oscillation in the role assignment when two or more team members have close cost values (Due to sensory errors, the costs will oscillate over time and team members may exchange roles in a too fast manner). This may cause the team to be stuck.

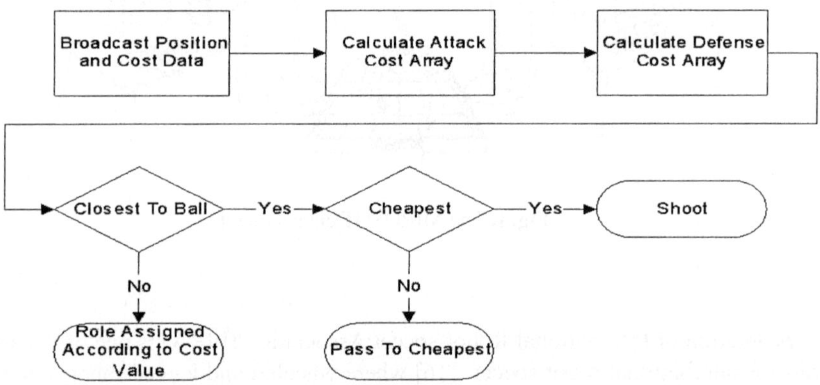

Fig. 2. Flow chart for task assignment

In robot soccer, the most important task is scoring a goal. Consequently, the ball becomes the most important object to be tracked and controlled. It should be kicked to the opponent's goal successfully while preventing the opponent team from scoring. To provide the control of the ball and prevent the opponent team from scoring, all individuals in the team are encouraged to get the ball, and shoot it towards opponent goal whenever reasonable. For example, when there is another robot between the robot who posesses the ball and the opponent goal, a shoot may not be successful. In such a case, it might be more appropriate for that robot not to take the risk and pass the ball to another team member who can score.

After the primary attacker is assigned according to the attacking costs, the one with the lowest defense cost is assigned as defender, and it tries to take the best position between the ball and its own goal area to avoid any possible opponent team scores. The rest of the team are assigned their roles according to cost values, the robot with second good cost would serve as secondary attacker which would help the primary attacker in case of failure of a shoot, or completing an attack by having the ball after the ball is bounced from some obstacle on its way to the goal area. So it would place itself symmetric to the position of the ball to meet with the ball easily if it bounces back, the remaining robot is assigned as the third attacker, it tries to go to the ball, to help the other attackers incase of any failure.

After the initial assignment, each member looks for another team member who can do this task for less cost by opening an auction on that task. If any robot can do this task with a lower cost, the task is assigned to that robot; therefore, the cost is decreased. The remaining robots behave according to their assigned roles. Since each robot has the cost information of all members of the team and the role assignment rules only depends on these cost values, each robot can decide for which task it is the most suitable. This process can be called as "Role Selection" instead of "Role Assignment". If one robot failes to accomplish its task required by its current role, the task remains incompleted and can possibly be taken by another robot in the next auction.

The cost functions used in the implementations are as follows:

$$C_{ES} = \mu_1.t_{dist} + \mu_2.t_{align} + \mu_2.clear_{goal} \tag{2}$$

$$C_{bidder} = C_{ES} + \mu_4.clear_{ball} \tag{3}$$

$$C_{auctioneer} = C_{ES} \tag{4}$$

$$C_{defender} = \mu_5.t_{dist} + \mu_6.t_{align} + \mu_7.clear_{defense} \tag{5}$$

where C_{ES} is the estimated score cost, t_{dist} the time required to move for specified distance, t_{align} the time required to align for specified amount, μ_i the weights of several parameters to mention their relative importance in the total cost function, $clear_{goal}$ clearance from the robot to goal area-for object avoidance, $clear_{ball}$ clearance from the robot to ball-for object avoidance, $clear_{defense}$ clearance from the robot to the middle point on the line between the middle point of own goal and the ball-for object avoidance, C_{bidder} the estimated cost for bidder, $C_{auctioneer}$ estimated cost for auctioneer, $C_{defender}$ estimated cost for defender.

The game plan can be changed simply by changing the cost functions in order to define the relative importance of defensive behavior over offensive behavior, and this gives a greater flexibility in planning, which is not possible with the current algorithms.

5 Tests and Results

5.1 Test Environment

The proposed approach is implemented on *Teambots*, which is a multi-robot simulator designed for multi-agent applications [18]. In this study, it is used to simulate multi-agent behavior of MIROSOT teams, since their multi-agent structure is similar. For locomotion, a potential field based method which is trained with genetic algorithms is used to get a smooth movement. Notice that while keeping the general market-driven idea, many different game strategies, tasks and scenarios can be developed. In this work, one of these is implemented to show the power of the method. The developed $MarketTeam$ (team of robots controlled by market-driven strategy) played against three teams with various strategies. $RIYTeam$ has a simple bidding mechanism based on the distance to ball for task allocation, and uses a potential field based method which is trained by genetic algorithms as $MarketTeam$ to move after tasks are allocated [19]. $AIKHomoG$ uses dynamic role assignment for strategy and potential fields for movement. $Kechze$ uses dynamic role assignment for strategy and geometric calculations as the assignment criteria.

5.2 Metrics

In order to assess the performance of the team, six metrics were designed and calculated during the experiments. *Average Distance Ratio* is the ratio of the sum of the distances of opponent players to the ball to the sum of the distances of our players to the ball. For the next three metrics called *Ball is on our side*, *Ball is on center* and *Ball is on opponent side* which measure the utilization of the field, the game field is divided into three sections. "Our side" is the semicircle with a radius of $9R$ centered in the middle of our goal, the "opponent side" is the similar semicircle on the other side of the field and "center" is defined as the remaining area of the field. Here, R is the radius of a robot. The remaining two metrics are the *Average of Our Scores* and *Average of Opponent Scores*.

5.3 Results

30 matches were played against each team, and the results are given in Table 1. It is seen that the games mainly take place in the center. The $MarketTeam$ was successful in keeping the ball away from its own goal area more often than the opponent teams since the *Ball is on opponent side* metric is always greater than *Ball is on our side* metric. Similarly *Average of Our Scores* is significantly greater than *Average of Opponent Scores* against all the opponents showing that the proposed approach leads to consistent wins against teams with different strategies.

Table 1. Experimental results

Opponent Team	Avg. Dist Ratio	Ball is on our side(%)	Ball is on center(%)	Ball is on opp. side(%)	Avg. Our Score	Avg. Opp. Score
AIKHomoG	0.77	21.09	49.29	29.62	1.20	0.10
RIYTeam	1.53	20.08	52.92	26.99	0.77	0.10
Kechze	1.13	21.55	51.32	27.13	1.43	0.23

6 Conclusions

Robot soccer is one of the new test beds for multi-agent domain, with its highly complex, dynamic and noisy nature bringing more limitations and complexity as being a real-time application. The proposed approach is used for robot coordination in this domain for the first time in this work. The market-based idea provides highly efficient resource sharing including the sharing of physical resources such as computational power and sensors, and informational resources such as a map of the environment, or global location of any mission-related object. This mechanism gives a task to the most appropriate robot, which has the minimum estimated cost to accomplish that task, and forces the robot to finish its task successfully. Otherwise, the robot is penalized by losing the job and paying off a penalty cost. This provides good behavior coordination in between the individual team members, and avoids possible conflicts, which are disastrous problems between team members (e.g. two team members may compete for the ball, they block each other and consequently nobody could access the ball). Besides the simplicity of cost calculation, communication and task allocation allow fast playing which is a must for real-time games. With better low level behaviors such as alignment and shooting and new tasks to be used for defenders, the success would be improved. The results show that system has high performance besides being fast. Also dynamic task allocation due to the situation changes in the game makes the approach adaptive and suitable for real-time events, where the team always has a plan B according to the situation; it becomes defensive or offensive according to the location of the ball and mode of the game. The distributed nature of the approach avoids single point failures common to centralized approaches, and even if some of the robots are injured or lost the team continues to work, and the assigned goals of lost robots are handled and accomplished by the remaining robots, eventually. So the system is highly robust.

Extending both the physical and the informational resources of the robot by trading with team mates allows robots to develop higher level plans and therefore, behave in a more intelligent way. In this way, get the full benefit of 'team spirit' which is the core idea of multi-agent research.

When this implementation is carried to real physical world, the noise existing in the real world and limitations of physical devices might affect the sensors and cause miscalculations of cost functions so role changing between teammates which are in similar positions may be too fast and cause oscillations as described before. This would be effectively avoided by using suitable time stamps which forces the team members to keep their role at least for a limited duration of time.

The main possible disadvantage of market-driven task allocation for robotic soccer domain is the time taken by the auctioning process. Time requirement constraints for auctioning might be satisfied by setting appropriate limits on auction duration and time-out for auctioneer values.

As a future work, usage of the market-driven idea in multi-agent localization and perception would be done.

Acknowledgements. This project is supported by the Boğaziçi University Foundation and by Boğaziçi University Research Fund project 03A101D.

References

1. A. Saffiotti, "Proceedings Workshop WS7 Cooperative Robotics," IROS 2002, *IEEE/RSJ International Conference on Intelligent Robots and Systems,* September 30-October 4, 2002.
2. I. Ribeiro and A. Saffiotti (Eds), *Lecture Notes from European Summer School on Cooperative Robotics,* 2–7 September, 2002.
3. A. K. Mackworth, "On seeing robots". In A. Basu and X. Li, (Eds.). *Computer Vision: Systems, Theory, and Applications*, World Scientific Press, Singapore, pp. 1–13, 1993.
4. D. Fox, W. Burgard, H. Kruppa, and S. Thrun, *A Monte Carlo Algorithm for Multi-Robot Localization,* CMU-CS-99-120, March 1999.
5. A.W. Stroupe, T. Balch, "Collaborative Probabilistic Constraint Based Landmark Localization," *Proceedings of the 2002 IEEE/RSJ Intl. Conference on Intelligent Robots and Systems,* Page: 447–452, EPFL, Lausanne, Switzerland, October 2002.
6. M. Dietl, J.S. Gutmann and B. Nebel "Cooperative Sensing in Dynamic Environments," In Proc. of the *IEEE/RSJ International Conference on Intelligent Robots and Systems (IROS 2001),* Maui, Hawaii, 2001.
7. D. Schultz, W. Burgard, D. Fox and A.B. Cremers "Tracking Multiple Moving Objects with a Mobile Robot," In Proc. of the *IEEE Computer Society Conference on Computer Vision and Pattern Recognition (CVPR 2001),* Kauwai, Hawaii, 2001.
8. T. Schmitt, R. Hanek, S. Buck, and M. Beetz, "Cooperative Probabilistic State Estimation for Vision-based Autonomous Mobile Robots," In Proc. of the *IEEE Intl. Conf. on Intelligent Robots and Systems (IROS 2001),* Maui, Hawaii, 2001.
9. J. E. Guivant and E. M. Nebot, "Optimization of the Simultaneous Localization and Map-Building Algorithm for Real-Time Implementation," *IEEE Transactions on Robotics and Automation,* Vol.17, No.3, Page: 242–257, June 2001.
10. G. Dissanayake, P. Newman, S. Clark, H.F. Durrant-Whyte, and M. Csorba, "A Solution to the Simultaneous Localization and Map Building (SLAM) Problem," *IEEE Transactions on Robotics and Automation,* Vol. 17, No. 3, June 2001.
11. A. W. Stroupe, *Mission-Driven Collaborative Observation and Localization,* Thesis Proposal, The Robotics Institute Carnegie Mellon University, December 2001.
12. J. Borenstein, H.R. Everett, and L. Feng, *Navigating Mobile Robots, Systems and Techniques,* A. K. Peters, Ltd., Wellesley, MA, 1996.
13. M. B. Dias, and A. Stenz, *A Free Market Architecture for Coordinating Multiple Robots,* CMU-RI-TR-99-42, December 1999.
14. M. B. Dias, and A. Stenz, *A Market Approach to Multi-robot Coordination,* CMU-RI-TR-01-26, August 2001.
15. R. Zlot, A. Stenz, M. B. Dias, and S. Thayer, "Multi-Robot Exploration Controlled by a Market Economy," Proceedings of the *IEEE International Conference on Robotics and Automation,* May 2002.
16. FIRA *http://www.fira.net/,* 2003.
17. Robot Idman Yurdu, *http://robot.cmpe.boun.edu.tr/riy/riy.php,* 2003.
18. T. Balch, "Teambots, " *http://www.cs.cmu.edu/ trb/TeamBots/Domains/SoccerBots,* 2000.
19. K. Kaplan, *Design and Implementation of fast controllers for Mobile Robots,* Master Thesis, Bogazici University, January 2003.

Fuzzy Variance Analysis Model

Mahdi Jalili-Kharaajoo and Farhad Besharati

Control & Intelligent Processing Center of Excellence
Department of Electrical & Computer Engineering
University of Tehran, Iran
{mahdijalili,fbesarati}@ece.ut.ac.ir

Abstract. In this paper, a fuzzy variance analysis model with interaction between explanatory variables using Tanaka's model is investigated. A linear programming model is formulated for measuring the value of response factors, based on Tanaka's model. The proposed model measures both values of response factors, as well as their interactions.

1 Introduction

Variance analysis is one of the most used statistical tools by engineers and scientists, which shows the dependency of different terms on a variable [1,2]. In the analysis of some of variables there is interaction between them that causes significant effects on them. A considerable issue about variance analysis is that the relationship between the variables should be as a crisp value. When we have to use expert knowledge, which is usually fuzzy, we need fuzzy variance analysis model. In the fuzzy variance analysis model, mostly, input and output data have fuzzy values and the relationship between them is fuzzy.
Tanaka presented a Fuzzy Linear Programming model in 1982 [3]. Then a possibilitic Linear Programming model was proposed by Tanaka in order to perform data analysis [4,5,6]. In this paper a modified Tanaka's model is proposed and a fuzzy variance analysis model with interaction explanatory variables is investigated. A linear programming model is formulated for measuring the value of response factors based on Tanaka's model. The proposed model measures both values of response factors, as well as their interactions.

2 Tanaka's Model

2.1 Structure of the Model

Model of a linear fuzzy function can be represented as the following

$$\widetilde{Y}_1 = \widetilde{A}_1 x_{1i} + \ldots + \widetilde{A} x_{ni} = \widetilde{A} x_i \qquad (1)$$

where x_i is the vector of independence variables (crisp) and $\widetilde{A}$ is the model parameters (fuzzy). We assume that $\widetilde{A}_j$ is expressed as

A. Yazici and C. Şener (Eds.): ISCIS 2003, LNCS 2869, pp. 537–544, 2003.

$$\mu_{\tilde{A}_j}(\alpha_j) = \begin{cases} 1 - \dfrac{|x_j - \alpha_j|}{C_j}; \alpha_j - C_j \le \alpha_j \le \alpha_j - C_j \\ 0 \quad\quad\quad\quad otherwise \end{cases} \tag{2}$$

where $\mu_{\tilde{A}_j}(\alpha_j)$, α_j and C_j are membership functions, center and width of the fuzzy value respectively. Therefore,

$$\mu_{\tilde{Y}_j}(y) = \begin{cases} 1 - \dfrac{|y - X_i^t|}{C^t |X_i|}; X \ne 0 \\ 1 \quad\quad\quad\quad \mathrm{X} \ne 0, \mathrm{y} \ne 0 \\ 0 \quad\quad\quad\quad \mathrm{X} = 0, \mathrm{y} = 0 \end{cases} \tag{3}$$

where $\mu_{\tilde{Y}_j}(y)$ is the membership function of $\tilde{Y}_j$.

Tanaka, using minimization of

$$Min \sum_i C_j \tag{4}$$

and applying the sets *h*, in which the membership function is greater than h, i.e.

$$\tilde{Y}_i^h = \{y / \mu_{\tilde{Y}}(y) \ge h\} \tag{5}$$

$$\tilde{Y}_i^{*h} = \{y / \mu_{\tilde{Y}}^{\ *}(y) \ge h\} \tag{6}$$

has formulated Tanaka's model as

$$\begin{aligned} & Min \sum_j C_j \\ & subject\ to: \\ & \alpha^t X_i + (1-H) C^t |X_i| \ge y_i + (1-H) e_i \ . \\ & -\alpha^t X_i + (1-H) C^t |X_i| \ge -y_i + (1-H) e_i ; i = 1,..., p \\ & \mathrm{C_j} \ge 0; j = 1,..., x \end{aligned} \tag{7}$$

Using the model (7) the linear fuzzy regression coefficients with the fuzzy width can be calculated. The main assumption of the above model is the independence of the variables. It is clear that in the model, we can not calculate the interaction between the variables. In the next section we will explain the interaction of variable and propose a proper model for that.

2.2 Analysis of Fuzzy Variance for the Variables with Interaction

For the analysis of interaction between the variables, one of the most efficient methods is the variance analysis that is formulated as

$$y_{ijk} = \mu + \tau_i + \beta_j + (\tau\beta)_{ij} + \varepsilon_{ijk} \tag{8}$$

The following example shows the interaction problem:
Example [7]. The maximum output voltage of a specific battery depends on the type of the material used to construct the battery and the temperature of environment. The result of some experiments on different materials and temperatures are obtained as shown in Table 1. The tolerance of the maximum of voltage is shown in Table 2. From variance analysis, there is interaction between the type of material and the temperature that the output voltage depends on this interaction.

Table 1. Maximum output voltage.

	Temperature (C°)		
Type of the material	**50**	**65**	**80**
1	124.75	57.25	57.5
2	155.75	119.75	49.5
3	144	145.75	85.5

Table 2. Tolerance of the maximum output voltage.

	Temperature (C°)		
Type of the material	**50**	**65**	**80**
1	43.35	23.6	26.85
2	23.19	12.66	19.26
3	25.97	22.54	19.28

3 Fuzzy Variance Analysis Model

In the variance analysis problem, the general formulation can be as the following

$$\begin{aligned} Y_{ijk..v} &= \mu+(x_1)_i+(x_2)_j+(x_3)_k+...+(x_{n-1})_s+(x_n)_t \\ &+(x_1x_2)_{ij}+...+(x_1x_n)_{it}+(x_2x_3)_{jk}+...+(x_2x_n)_{jt}+... \\ &+(x_{n-1}x_n)_{st}+(x_1x_2x_3)_{ijk}+...+(x_1x_2..x_n)_{ij..t}+\varepsilon_{ijk..v} \end{aligned} \tag{9}$$

Based on Tanaka's method in the fuzzy case the error of observations can be neglected. Therefore,

$$\begin{aligned} \tilde{Y}_{ijk...v} &= \tilde{\mu}+(\tilde{x}_1)_i+(\tilde{x}_2)_j+(\tilde{x}_3)_k+...+(\tilde{x}_{n-1})_s+(\tilde{x}_n)_t \\ &+(\tilde{x}_1\tilde{x}_2)_{ij}+...+(\tilde{x}_1\tilde{x}_n)_{it}+(\tilde{x}_2\tilde{x}_3)_{jk}+...+(\tilde{x}_2\tilde{x}_n)_{jt}+... \\ &+(\tilde{x}_{n-1}\tilde{x}_n)_{st}+(\tilde{x}_1\tilde{x}_2\tilde{x}_3)_{ijk}+...+(\tilde{x}_1\tilde{x}_2...\tilde{x}_n)_{ij...t} \end{aligned} \tag{10}$$

In the sake of simplicity, in here only two variables are considered

$$\tilde{Y}_{ij} = \tilde{\mu}+(\tilde{x}_1)_i+(\tilde{x}_2)_j+(\tilde{x}_1\tilde{x}_2)_{ij} \tag{11}$$

If the above variables are symmetrical triangular variables with m and c as medium and width respectively, then

$$
\begin{aligned}
&\widetilde{\mu} = (\mu^m, \mu^c) \\
&(\widetilde{x}_1)_i = ((x_1)_i^m, (x_1)_i^c) \\
&(\widetilde{x}_2) j = ((x_2)_j^m, (x_2)_j^c) \\
&(\widetilde{x}_1 \widetilde{x}_2)_{ij} = ((x_1 x_2)_{ij}^m, (x_1 x_2)_{ij}^c)
\end{aligned} \tag{12}
$$

For the practical values, $\widetilde{Y}_{ij}$ can be defined as

$$\widetilde{Y}_{ij} = (Y_{ij}^m, e_{ij}) \tag{13}$$

$$\widetilde{Y}_{ij}^{\;*} = (\widetilde{Y}^{*m}_{ij}, \widetilde{Y}^{*c}_{ij}) \tag{14}$$

where

$$\widetilde{Y}_{ij}^{\;*m} = \mu^m + (x_1)^m{}_i + (x_2)^m{}_j + (x_1 x_2)^m{}_{ij} \tag{15}$$

$$\widetilde{Y}_{ij}^{\;*c} = \mu^c + (x_1)^c{}_i + (x_2)^c{}_j + (x_1 x_2)^c{}_{ij} \tag{16}$$

According to extension principle [8]:

$$
\mu_{\widetilde{Y}_{ij}}(y) = \begin{cases}
1 - \dfrac{\left| Y_{ij}^m - \mu^m - (x_1)^m{}_i - (x_2)^m{}_j - (x_1 x_2)_{ij}^m \right| = A}{\left| \mu^m + (x_1)^c{}_i + (x_2)^c{}_j + (x_1 x_2)_{ij}^c \right| = B} \\
; \mu^c + (x_1)^c{}_i + (x_2)^c{}_j + (x_1 x_2)_{ij}^c \neq 0 \\
1 \quad ; \quad \mathrm{B} = 0, \mathrm{A} = 0 \\
0 \quad ; \quad \mathrm{B} = 0, \mathrm{A} \neq 0
\end{cases} \tag{17}
$$

in which $\mu_{\widetilde{Y}_{ij}}(y)$ will be zero if the numerator is greater than the denominator *(A>B)*.

We assume that $\overline{h}_i$ expresses the regression degree. In the following equations h is a value such that an expert one uses for expression of the fitness of regression.

$$\widetilde{Y}_i^{\,h} = (y / \mu_{\widetilde{Y}_i}(y) \geq h) \tag{18}$$

$$\widetilde{Y}_i^{\,*h} = (y / \mu_{\widetilde{Y}^*{}_i}(y) \geq h) \tag{19}$$

The membership function of $\widetilde{Y}_{ij}$ is defined as follows

$$\mu_{\widetilde{Y}_{ij}}(y) = 1 - \frac{\left| y_{ij}^m - y \right|}{e_{ij}} \tag{20}$$

In order to fit $\widetilde{Y}_{ij}^*$ to the main data, $\widetilde{Y}_{ij}$, further, we will use h as the regression surface. It is remarkable that $\overline{h}_i$ is the maximum value of h such that $\widetilde{Y}_{ij} \subset \widetilde{Y}_{ij}^*$ (Figure 1). In Figure 1:

$$\frac{1}{1-\bar{h}_{ij}}=\frac{e_{ij}}{V}\Rightarrow V=e_{ij}(1-\bar{h}_{ij})$$

$$\frac{1}{1-\bar{h}_{ij}}=\frac{k}{\mu^{c}+(x_1)^{c}{}_{i}+(x_2)^{c}{}_{j}+(x_1x_2)^{c}_{ij}} \tag{21}$$
$$\Rightarrow k=(1-\bar{h}_{ij})(\mu^{c}+(x_1)^{c}{}_{i}+(x_2)^{c}{}_{j}+(x_1x_2)^{c}_{ij})$$

$$\begin{aligned}K=V+\left|Y^{m}_{ij}-\mu^{m}-(x_1)^{m}{}_{i}-(x_2)^{m}{}_{j}-(x_1x_2)^{m}_{ij}\right|=\\ e_{ij}(1-\bar{h}_{ij})+\left|Y^{m}_{ij}-\mu^{m}-(x_1)^{m}{}_{i}-(x_2)^{m}{}_{j}-(x_1x_2)^{m}_{ij}\right|\end{aligned} \tag{22}$$

Using (21) and (22)

$$\begin{aligned}(1-\bar{h}_{ij})(\mu^{c}+(x_1)^{c}{}_{i}+(x_2)^{c}{}_{j}+(x_1x_2)^{c}_{ij})=e_{ij}(1-\bar{h}_{ij})\\ +\left|Y^{m}_{ij}-\mu^{m}-(x_1)^{m}{}_{i}-(x_2)^{m}{}_{j}-(x_1x_2)^{m}_{ij}\right|\end{aligned}$$

So,

$$\begin{aligned}(1-\bar{h}_{ij})(\mu^{c}+(x_1)^{c}{}_{i}+(x_2)^{c}{}_{j}+(x_1x_2)^{c}_{ij}-e_{ij})=\\ \left|Y^{m}_{ij}-\mu^{m}-(x_1)^{m}{}_{i}-(x_2)^{m}{}_{j}-(x_1x_2)^{m}_{ij}\right|\end{aligned}$$

Using the above equations

$$\bar{h}_{ij}=1-\frac{\left|Y^{m}_{ij}-\mu^{m}-(x_1)^{m}{}_{i}-(x_2)^{m}{}_{j}-(x_1x_2)^{m}_{ij}\right|}{\mu^{c}+(x_1)^{c}{}_{i}+(x_2)^{c}{}_{j}+(x_1x_2)^{c}_{ij})-e_{ij}} \tag{23}$$

J is the uncertainty of the model as

$$J=\sum_{i=1}^{a}\sum_{j=1}^{b}(\mu^{c}+(x_1)^{c}{}_{i}+(x_2)^{c}{}_{j}+(x_1x_2)^{c}_{ij}). \tag{24}$$

According to Tanaka's model J should be minimized, so

$$Min\ J\quad;\quad such\ that: \bar{h}_{ij}>H \tag{25}$$

In the above, H is presented by decision maker.
Using expression of $\bar{h}_{ij}>H$ as

$$Min\ \sum_{i=1}^{a}\sum_{j=1}^{b}(\mu^{c}+(x_1)^{c}{}_{i}+(x_2)^{c}{}_{j}+(x_1x_2)^{c}_{ij})$$

such that:

$$1-\frac{\left|Y^{m}_{ij}-\mu^{m}-(x_1)^{m}{}_{i}-(x_2)^{m}{}_{j}-(x_1x_2)^{m}_{ij}\right|}{\mu^{c}+(x_1)^{c}{}_{i}+(x_2)^{c}{}_{j}+(x_1x_2)^{c}_{ij})-e_{ij}}\geq H;\forall i,j \tag{26}$$

$$\mu^{c}\geq 0,(x_1)^{c}_{i}\geq 0,(x_2)^{c}_{j}\geq 0,(x_1x_2)^{c}_{ij}\geq 0$$

$$\mu^{m}_{ij}\geq 0,(x_1)^{m}_{i}\geq 0,(x_2)^{m}_{j}\geq 0,(x_1x_2)^{m}_{ij}\geq 0,\forall i,j$$

We can formulate the model as

$$\begin{aligned}
& Min \sum_{i=1}^{a}\sum_{j=1}^{b}(\mu^c + (x_1)^c{}_i + (x_2)^c{}_j + (x_1x_2)^c_{ij}) \\
& such\ that: \\
& (1-H)(\mu^c + (x_1)^c{}_i + (x_2)^c{}_j + (x_1x_2)^c_{ij}) \\
& +(\mu^m + (x_1)^m{}_i + (x_2)^m{}_j + (x_1x_2)^m_{ij}) \geq Y^m_{ij} + (1-H)e_{ij} \\
& (1-H)(\mu^c + (x_1)^c{}_i + (x_2)^c{}_j + (x_1x_2)^c_{ij}) \\
& -(\mu^m + (x_1)^m{}_i + (x_2)^m{}_j + (x_1x_2)^m_{ij}) \geq Y^m_{ij} + (1-H)e_{ij} \\
& \mu^c \geq 0, (x_1)^c_i \geq 0, (x_2)^c_j \geq 0, (x_1x_2)^c_{ij} \geq 0 \\
& \mu^m_{ij} \geq 0, (x_1)^m_i \geq 0, (x_2)^m_j \geq 0, (x_1x_2)^m_{ij} \geq 0, \forall i,j
\end{aligned} \quad . (27)$$

Thus, using (27) the effects of a variable on the other variables and their interaction can be calculated.

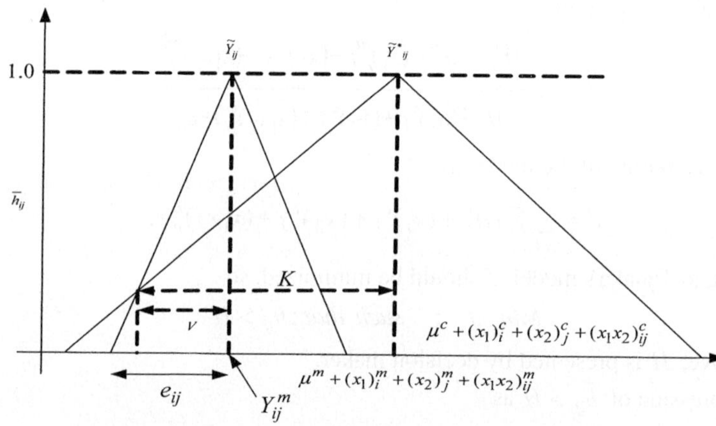

Fig. 1. Degree of fitting $\widetilde{Y}_{ij}$ to given fuzzy datum $\widetilde{Y}^*_{ij}$.

4 Application of the Model

In this section the proposed model is applied to the example introduced in the section 2. The problem can be formulated as

$$Min \quad \sum_{i=1}^{3}\sum_{j=1}^{3}(\mu^{c}+(M)^{c}{}_{i}+(T)^{c}{}_{j}+(TM)^{c}_{ij})$$

$$such \quad that:$$

$$(1-H)(\mu^{c}+(M)^{c}{}_{i}+(T)^{c}{}_{j}+(TM)^{c}_{ij})$$

$$+(\mu^{m}+(M)^{m}{}_{i}+(T)^{m}{}_{j}+(TM)^{m}_{ij})\geq Y^{m}_{ij}+(1-H)e_{ij}$$

$$(1-H)(\mu^{c}+(M)^{c}{}_{i}+(T)^{c}{}_{j}+(TM)^{c}_{ij})$$

$$-(\mu^{m}+(M)^{m}{}_{i}+(T)^{m}{}_{j}+(TM)^{m}_{ij})\geq Y^{m}_{ij}+(1-H)e_{ij}$$

$$\mu^{c}\geq 0,(M)^{c}_{i}\geq 0,(T)^{c}_{j}\geq 0,(TM)^{c}_{ij}\geq 0$$

$$\mu^{m}_{ij}\geq 0,(M)^{m}_{i}\geq 0,(T)^{m}_{j}\geq 0,(TM)^{m}_{ij}=free$$

$$\forall i=1,2,3 \quad ; \quad j=1,2,3$$

In the above, the following parameters have been used (the indices *c* and *m* are used for the fuzzy values with a symmetrical triangular membership functions with *m* as a medium and *c* as the width of that):

$\tilde{\mu}=(\mu^{c},\mu^{m})$: Overall average effect

$\tilde{M}_{i}=(M_{i}^{c},M_{i}^{m})$: Effect of the ith material

$\tilde{T}_{j}=(T_{j}^{c},T_{j}^{m})$: Effect of the jth temperature

$(TM)_{ij}=((TM)^{m}_{ij},(TM)^{c}_{ij})$: Interaction between $\tilde{T}_{i}$ and $\tilde{M}_{j}$.

Y^{m}_{ij}: The average maximum voltage of a battery with i[th] material in the jth temperature.

e^{m}_{ij}: The tolerance of maximum voltage of a battery with i[th] material in the jth temperature.

For this problem the input data are presented in Table 3. In the case of $H=0.05$, the values of the model using GMAS package are shown in Table 4.

Table 3. Model input data in the form of (e_{ij},y_{ij}).

	Temperature (C°)		
Type of the material	**50**	**65**	**80**
1	(43.35,124.75)	(23.6,57.25)	(26.85,57.5)
2	(23.19,155.75)	(12.66,119.75)	(19.26,49.5)
3	(25.97,144)	(22.54,145.75)	(19.28,85.5)

5 Conclusion

The model introduced by Tanaka is not able to show the interaction between the variables, which is very important in the actual problems. In this paper a new fuzzy variance analysis model was introduced to express the interaction between fuzzy variables. The proposed model was applied to an example to show its ability to express the interaction between the variables.

Table 4. Interaction between the variables.

variable	value
μ^c	26.85
$(TM)_{11}^c$	16.5
$(TM)_{11}^m$	134.75
$(TM)_{12}^m$	54.162
$(TM)_{13}^m$	57.5
$(TM)_{21}^m$	151.323
$(TM)_{22}^m$	106.269
$(TM)_{23}^m$	42.289
$(TM)_{31}^m$	143.164
$(TM)_{32}^m$	141.655
$(TM)_{33}^m$	78.308

References

[1] Chang, Y.H.O. and Ayyub, B.M., Fuzzy regression model- a comparative assessment, *Fuzzy sets and systems*, 119, pp.187–203, 2001.

[2] Wang, H.F. and Tsaur, R.C., Insight of a fuzzy regression model, *Fuzzy sets and systems*, 112, pp.355–369, 2001. [3] Tanaka H., S. Uejima, K. Asai, Fuzzy linear model, fuzzy linear regression model, *IEEE Trans. System Man Cybernetics*, 12, pp.903–907, 1982.

[4] Tanaka H., Fuzzy data analysis by possibilistic linear models, *Fuzzy Sets and Systems*, 24, pp.363–375, 1987.

[5] Tanaka H., J. Watada, Possibilistic linear systems and their application to the linear regression model, *Fuzzy Sets and Systems*, 27, pp.275–289, 1988.

[6] Tanaka H., H. Ishibuchi, Identification of possibilistic linear systems by quadratic membership functions of fuzzy parameters, *Fuzzy Sets and Systems*, 41, pp.145–160, 1991.

[7] Montgomery, D.C., *Design and analysis of experiment*, John Wiley & Sons, 1997.

[8] L.A. Zadeh, The concept of a linguistic variable and its application to approximate reasoning, *J. Inform. Sci.,* 8, pp.199–249, 1975.

Effects of the Trajectory Planning on the Model Based Predictive Robotic Manipulator Control

Fevzullah Temurtas[1], Hasan Temurtas[2], Nejat Yumusak[1], and Cemil Oz[1]

[1] Sakarya University, Department of Computer Engineering, Adapazari, Turkey
[2] Dumlupınar University, Department of Electric - Electronic Engineering, Kutahya, Turkey

Abstract. In this study, the application of the single input single output (SISO) neural generalized predictive control (NGPC) and SISO generalized predictive control (GPC) of a three joint robotic manipulator are presented. The sinusoidal and cubic trajectory principles were used for position reference and velocity reference trajectories. NGPC-SISO algorithm performs better than GPC-SISO algorithm for both trajectories. The GPC-SISO robotic manipulator control results have better values in the case of the sinusoidal trajectory, but the NGPC-SISO robotic manipulator control results for both the cubic and sinusoidal trajectory are almost similar.

1 Introduction

In recent years, robotic manipulators have been used increasingly in the manufacturing sector and in applications involving hazardous environments for increasing productivity, efficiency, and worker safety. The use of conventional linear control techniques limits the basic dynamic performance of manipulators. The dynamic characteristics of general spatial manipulators are highly nonlinear functions of the positions and velocities of the manipulator elements. And the dynamic performance characteristics of manipulators are degraded by the inertial properties of the objects being manipulated. Dynamic control of the manipulator is realized by generating the necessary inputs (torque/voltage) which supply the motion of the manipulator joints according to desired position and velocity references and applying these inputs to the joints [1-4].

One of the applied manipulator control techniques is Generalized Predictive Control (GPC) [4,5]. GPC had been originally developed with linear plant predictor model which leads to a formulation that can be solved analytically. If a nonlinear model is used, a nonlinear optimization algorithm is necessary. This affects the computational efficiency and performance by which the control inputs are determined. For nonlinear systems, the ability of the GPC to make accurate predictions can be enhanced if a neural network is used to learn the dynamics of the system instead of standard nonlinear modeling techniques [6,7].

A priori information needed for manipulator control analysis and manipulator design is a set of closed form differential equations describing the dynamic behavior of the manipulators. Various approaches are available to formulate the robot arm dynamics, such as Lagrange-Euler, Newton-Euler and Recursive Lagrange [8,9]. In

A. Yazici and C. Şener (Eds.): ISCIS 2003, LNCS 2869, pp. 545–552, 2003.

this study, Lagrange-Euler is used for dynamics modeling of the three joints robotic manipulator. Furthermore, by adding the effects of the joint frictions and loads to the Lagrange-Euler equation sets, the simulation results are performed for the most general situations.

2 Generalized Predictive Control

Generalized Predictive Control (GPC) belongs to the class of digital control methods called Model-Based Predictive control (MBPC) [10,11]. GPC is known to control non-minimum phase plants, open-loop unstable plants and plants with variable or unknown dead time. It is also robust with respect to modeling errors, over and under parameterization, and sensor noise [10,11].

The GPC system for the robotic manipulator can be seen in Figure 1.a. It consists of three components, the robotic manipulator's simulator, controller and parameter estimator. In the GPC-SISO method, one independent GPC- SISO algorithm is used for each individual joint, as seen in the Figure 1.b. In the Figure 1, *u* is input, *y* is a predicted output, y_r is the reference output. The parameter estimation algorithm used in the GPC-SISO is Recursive Least Squares. The computational issues of the GPC are addressed in [10,11].

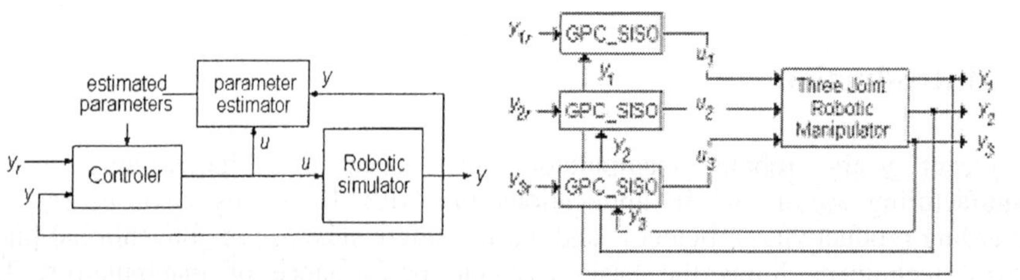

(a) (b)

Fig. 1. Block diagram of the GPC system (a) and application of GPC-SISO algorithm (b)

3 Neural Generalized Predictive Control

In this paper, Neural Generalized Predictive Control (NGPC) [6,7] is proposed for the three joint robotic manipulator as seen in Figure 2.a. It consists of four components, the robotic manipulator or its simulator, a tracking reference signal that specifies the desired trajectory of the manipulator, a neural network for prediction, and the Cost Function Minimization (CFM) algorithm that determines the input needed to produce the desired trajectory of the manipulator. In the NGPC-SISO method, one independent NGPC- SISO algorithm is used for each individual joint as seen in the Figure 2.b. In the Figure 2, torque, *u*, is the control input to the manipulator system and the trajectory, *y*, is the output, *ym* is the reference output and *yn* is the predicted output of the neural network.

The NGPC algorithm operates in two modes, prediction and control. For realizing this aim, a double pole double throw switching is used. The CFM algorithm produces an output which is either used as an input to the robotic manipulator or the manipulator's neural network model. The switch position is set to the robotic manipulator when the CFM algorithm has solved for the best input, *u(n)*, that will minimize a specified cost function. Between samples, the switching position is set to the manipulator's neural network model where the CFM algorithm uses this model to calculate the next control input, *u(n+1)*, from predictions of the response from the manipulator's model. Once the cost function is minimized, this input is passed to the manipulator. The minimization algorithm used in the NGPC-SISO is Newton-Raphson. The computational issues of the NGPC are addressed in [7].

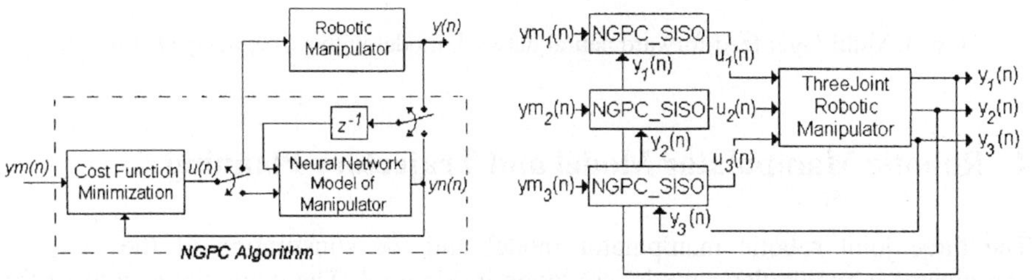

(a) (b)

Fig. 2. Block diagram of the NGPC system (a) and application of NGPC-SISO algorithm (b)

3.1 Robotic Manipulator Neural Network Model

A multi-layer feed-forward network (MLFN) with tapped time delays was used for the robotic manipulator neural network model. The network structure shown in Figure 3 depicts the SISO structure with the linear model embedded into the weights. The torque, *u*, is the control input to the manipulator system and the trajectory, *y*, is the output. The inputs to the network are torque, past values of the torque, and the past values of the manipulator's trajectory. The network has a single hidden layer with multiple hidden layer nodes and a single output node. Equations which used in the neural network model are shown in (1), (2), and (3). As seen from equations, the activation functions for the hidden layer nodes is tangent-sigmoid transfer function and used as activation function for hidden layer and the activation function for the output node is linear transfer function. The back propagation algorithm was used for training of neural network model [12].

$$net_j(n) = b_j + \sum_{i=0}^{n_d} w_{j,i} u(n-i) + \sum_{i=1}^{d_d} w_{j,i+n_d} y(n-i) \tag{1}$$

$$O_j(n) = f\left(net_j(n)\right) = \frac{e^{net_j(n)} - e^{-net_j(n)}}{e^{net_j(n)} + e^{-net_j(n)}} = 1 - \frac{2}{1 + e^{2 \cdot net_j(n)}} \tag{2}$$

$$yn(n) = b + \sum_{j=0}^{hid-1} w_j O_j(n) \tag{3}$$

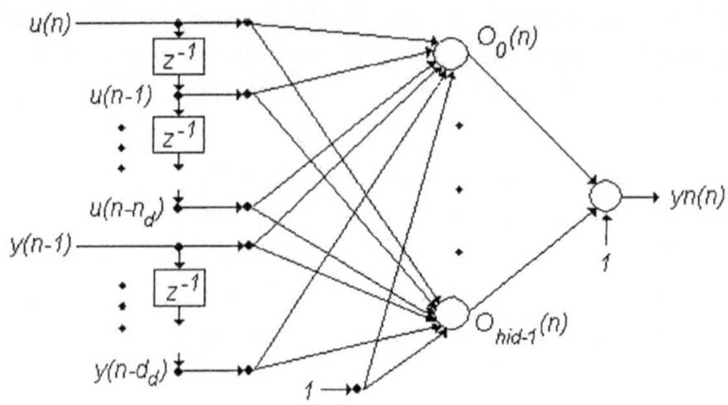

Fig. 3. Multi-layer feed-forward neural network model with a time delayed structure

4 Robotic Manipulator Model and Trajectory Planning

The three joint robotic manipulator model and the constitution of the (x, y, z) coordinates in manipulator model are given in Figure 4. The main dimensions of this model can be seen in the same figure. Equations which used for the (x, y, z) coordinates of robotic manipulator are given in (4), (5), and (6).

$$x = (l_1 + l_2 Cos\theta_2 + l_3 Sin(\theta_2 + \theta_3)) Cos\theta_1 \tag{4}$$

$$y = (l_1 + l_2 Cos\theta_2 + l_3 Sin(\theta_2 + \theta_3)) Sin\theta_1 \tag{5}$$

$$z = l_2 Sin\theta_2 - l_3 Cos(\theta_2 + \theta_3) \tag{6}$$

where, l_1, l_2, and l_3 are the lengths of the limb 1, limb 2, and limb 3 respectively and θ_1, θ_2, and θ_3 are the angular positions of the joint 1, joint 2, and joint 3 respectively.

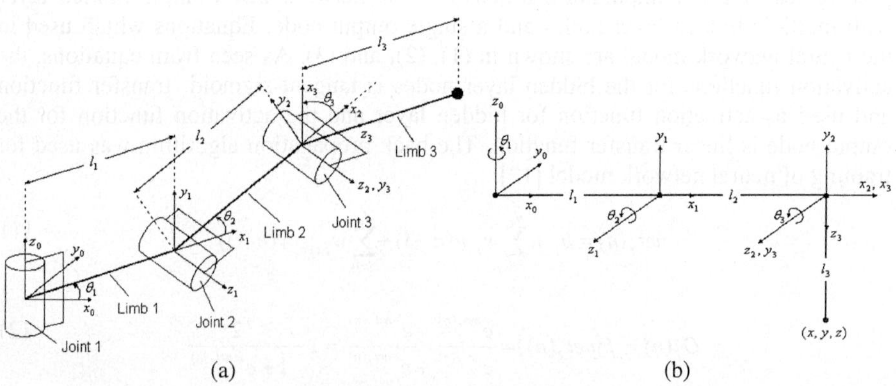

Fig. 4. Robotic manipulator model (a) and constitution of the x,y,z coordinates (b)

To perform the useful tasks, a robot arm must move from an admissible initial position/orientation to an admissible final position/orientation. This requires that the robot arm's configurations at both the initial and final positions must be known before the planning of the motion trajectory [4]. In this study, position reference and velocity reference trajectories for each limb are determined according to the sinusoidal and cubic trajectories principles to control the manipulator simulator. Equations for the sinusoidal and cubic trajectory are shown in (7), (8) respectively.

$$\theta_i(t) = (\frac{\theta_{if}+\theta_{i0}}{2}) - (\frac{\theta_{if}-\theta_{i0}}{2})\, Cos\,(\frac{\pi\, t}{t_f}) \tag{7}$$

$$\theta_i(t) = \theta_{i0} + \frac{3}{t_f^2}(\theta_{if}-\theta_{i0})t^2 - \frac{2}{t_f^3}(\theta_{if}-\theta_{i0})\,t^3 \tag{8}$$

where, $\theta_i(t)$ is the angular position of the joint i at time t, θ_{i0} is the initial angular position of the joint i at time t_0 and θ_{if} is the final angular position of the joint i at time t_f.

5 Simulation Parameters

A three joints robotic manipulator system has three inputs and three outputs. Inputs are the torques applied to the joints and outputs are the velocities of the joints. In this study, the three joints robotic manipulator system is controlled according to SISO control methods. In these control methods one independent SISO algorithm is used for each individual joint, The robotic arm dynamics are interactive, but, these interactions influence the individual joint velocities. Because of these influences, there is no obstruction at the using of the three independent SISO algorithms [4].

GPC-SISO and NGPC-SISO following control states and values were used.

The control states;

A: There is only friction effects

B: There are friction and falling load effects

The control values;

- Torques applied to joints are bounded by *umin* = *-225 Nm* , *umax* = *+225 Nm.*
- The Coulomb friction and viscous friction effects were *0.5 Nt.m* and *1.0 Nt.m/rad.s-1* respectively for control states with friction [13].
- Total simulation time is *1 s.* and total step number is *500.*
- The robotic manipulator caries *10 Kg* load at the state of falling load. And the load is falling in step *300* (at time *0.6 s*).
- Runge-Kutta integration number for each step is *4.*
- Each joint angle is changing from *0 rd* to *0.78539816 rd* during the simulation.

6 Results and Discussions

Some sample control results of the three joints robotic manipulator which use GPC_SISO and NGPC_SISO algorithms are given in the Figure 5 and Figure 6 respectively. Comparison of the GPC_SISO and NGPC_SISO algorithms control results are summarized and demonstrated in the table 1, and table 2.

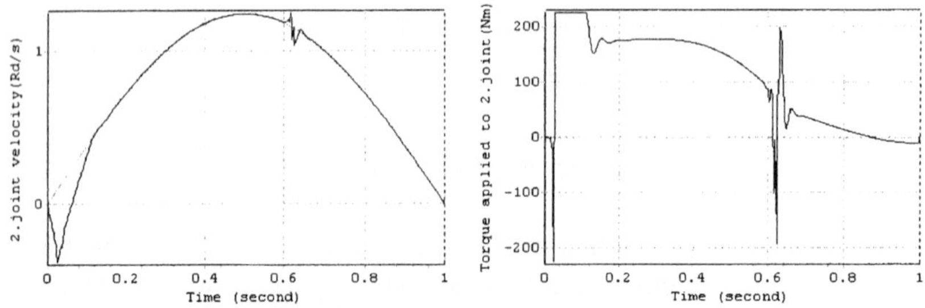

(Sinusoidal trajectory)

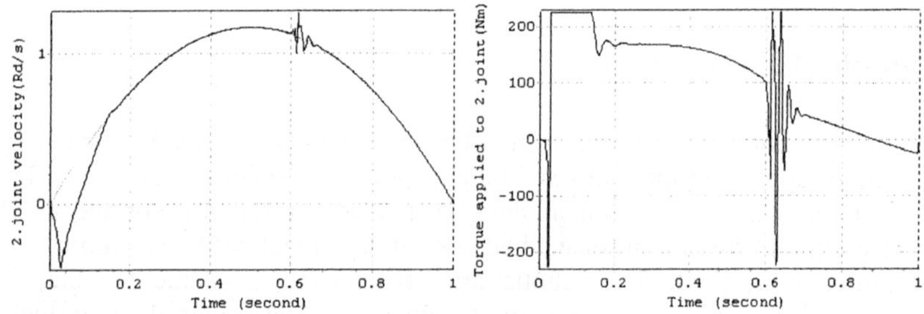

(Cubic trajectory)

Fig. 5. Sample control results of the three joint manipulator controlled by GPC_SISO algorithms for joint 2 at the state of falling load

As seen in the Figure 5 and 6, torque and angular velocity graphics are much smooth in the NGPC-SISO that those in the GPC-SISO for both sinusoidal and cubic trajectory. So, motion of the manipulator is more smooth and flexible in the NGPC-SISO for both trajectory principles. In the Figure 5, it is seen that the influence of load change to the GPC-SISO is less in the case of sinusoidal trajectory. In the NGPC-SISO, influence of the load change is almost similar for both trajectories as seen in the Figure 6. From the same figures, it can be seen easily that the influence of load change to the NGPC-SISO is less than that of the GPC-SISO. These results mean that GPC-SISO is more stable to the load changes in the case of sinusoidal trajectory and NGPC-SISO is more stable than GPC-SISO to the load changes for both trajectories. And as seen in the table 1 and table 2, angle location errors, and x, y, z axis errors of the end point have smaller values when sinusoidal trajectory is used in the GPC-SISO robotic manipulator control. This means that the sinusoidal trajectory is more suitable than the cubic trajectory for the GPC-SISO robotic manipulator control. And these errors are generally similar in both the cubic trajectory and the sinusoidal trajectory for the NGPC-SISO robotic manipulator control. This means that the cubic trajectory and the sinusoidal trajectory are similar for the NGPC-SISO robotic manipulator control. From same tables it can be seen that, these values for the NGPC-SISO are less than that of the GPC-SISO for both trajectories

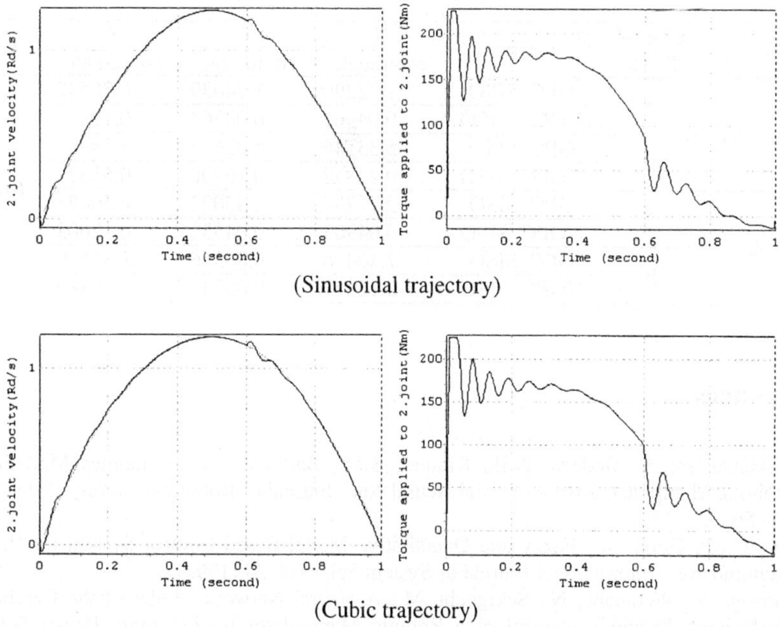

Fig. 6. Sample control results of the three joint manipulator controlled by NGPC_SISO algorithms for joint 2 at the state of falling load

Table 1. Angle location errors

Trajectory	Control States	Control	1.Joint	2.Joint	3.Joint	Unit
Sinusoidal	A	GPC_SISO	0.000014	-0.007872	-0.001717	(Rd)
		NGPC_SISO	0.000013	0.000187	-0.000062	
	B	GPC_SISO	-0.000246	-0.023795	0.004551	
		NGPC_SISO	0.000058	0.000911	0.000017	
Cubic	A	GPC_SISO	-0.000265	-0.011869	0.002915	
		NGPC_SISO	0.000003	0.000213	-0.000063	
	B	GPC_SISO	-0.000483	-0.032949	0.005548	
		NGPC_SISO	0.000045	0.000552	0.000004	

Based on the simulation results shown in the figures and tables, it is seen that NGPC-SISO algorithm performs better than GPC-SISO algorithm for the both trajectory principles. This can be because of that the robotic manipulator is a non-linear system and NGPC-SISO is non-linear system model while GPC-SISO is linear system model. The sinusoidal trajectory gives better results for GPC-SISO robotic manipulator control and the both trajectories give similar results for NGPC-SISO robotic manipulator control. This means that, different trajectories can be suitable for different model based robotic manipulator control methods.

Table 2. *x, y, z* axis errors of the end point

Trajectory	Control States	Control	X coordinate	Y coordinate	Z coordinate	Unit
Sinusoidal	A	GPC_SISO	1.72290	1.74039	-6.28542	(mm)
		NGPC_SISO	-0.04962	-0.03366	0.10838	
	B	GPC_SISO	5.33146	5.02667	-15.19982	
		NGPC_SISO	-0.23858	-0.16706	0.65377	
Cubic	A	GPC_SISO	2.77757	2.45022	-7.30423	
		NGPC_SISO	-0.04903	-0.04559	0.12603	
	B	GPC_SISO	7.40406	6.80366	-21.39159	
		NGPC_SISO	-0.15047	-0.09541	0.39389	

References

1. Eskandarian, A., Bedewi, N.E., Kramer, B.M., Barbera, A.J.: Dynamics Modeling of Robotic Manip. using An Artif.icial Neural Net., Journal of Robotic Systems, 11(1) (1994) 41–56
2. De, N.M., Gorez, R.: Fuzzy and Quantitative Model-Based Control System for Robotic Manipulators, International Journal of System Sci., Vol. 24 (1993)
3. Hosogi, S., Watanabe, N., Sekiguchi, M.: A Neural Network Model of the Cerebellum Performing Dynamic Control of a Robotic Manipulator by Learning, Fujitsi Sci. and Technical Journal, Vol. 29 (1993)
4. Oz, C. Phd. Thesis, Sakarya University, Institute of Science, Adapazari (1998)
5. Hu, H., Gu, D., Generalized Predictive Control of an Industrial Mobile Robot, IASTED International Conference, Intelligent Systems And Control, Santa Barbara, California, USA, October 28–30 (1999), 234–240
6. Soloway, D., Haley, P.J.: Neural Generalized Predictive Control: A Newton-Raphson Implementation, Proceedings of the IEEE CCA/ISIC/CACSD, IEEE Paper No. ISIAC-TA5.2 (1996)
7. Soloway, D., Haley, P.J.: Neural Generalized Predictive Control: A Newton-Raphson Implementation, NASA Technical Memorandum 110244, Langley Research Center, Hampton, Virginia (1997)
8. Silver, W. M.: On the Equivalence of Lagrangian and Newton-Euler Dynamics for Manipulators, The International Journal of Robotics Research, Vol. 1(2) (1982) 60–70
9. Lee, C. S. G.: Robot Arm Kinematics- Dynamics, and Control, Computer, Vol. 15 (12) (1982) 62–80
10. Clarke, D.W., Mohtadi, C., Tuffs, P.C.: Generalized Predictive Control - Part 1: The Basic Algorithm, Automatica, Vol. 23 (1987) 137–148
11. Clarke, D.W., Mohtadi, C., Tuffs, P.C. :Generalized Predictive Control - Part 2: The Basic Algorithm, Automatica, Vol.23 (1987) 149–163
12. Haykin, S.: Neural Networks, A Comprehensive Foundation, Macmillan Publishing Company, Englewood Cliffs, N.J. (1994)
13. Seraji, H.: A New Approach to Adaptive Control of Manipulators, Journal of Dynamic Systems, Measurement, and Control, Vol. 109, pp. (1987) 193–202.

Financial Time Series Prediction Using Mixture of Experts

M. Serdar Yumlu[1], Fikret S. Gurgen[1], and Nesrin Okay[2]

[1] Bogazici University, Department of Computer Engineering,
34342 Bebek Istanbul, Turkey
yumlu2@yahoo.com, gurgen@boun.edu.tr
http://www.cmpe.boun.edu.tr

[2] Bogazici University, Department of Management,
34342 Bebek Istanbul, Turkey
okay@boun.edu.tr

Abstract. This paper investigates the use of artificial neural networks (ANN) in risk estimation of asset returns. Istanbul Stock Exchange (ISE) index (XU100) is studied with a *mixture of experts* ANN architecture using daily data over a 12-year period. Results are compared to feed-forward neural networks, multilayer perceptron (MLP) and radial basis function (RBF) networks and recurrent neural networks (RNN). They are also compared to widely accepted Exponential Generalized Autoregressive Conditional Heteroskedasticity (EGARCH) volatility model. These results suggest that mixture of experts (MoE) have the strength to capture the volatility in index return series and prepares a valuable basis for financial decision making.

1 Introduction

Financial Time Series Prediction (FTSP) aims to find underlying patterns, trends, cycles and forecast future using historical and currently observable data. Forecasting is finding an approximate mapping function between the input and the output data. ANNs are one of the most innovative approaches to prediction problems and in this study we propose a *mixture of experts* to capture the data and its predictive content.

Predicting time series preserves conditional dependence, therefor we use a financial database dependent on historical and current observations. In the market, not all of the information is publicly available. *Efficient Market Hypothesis* (EMH) states that all methods of deciding when to buy and sell, over a particular time period and using past prices to evaluate the decisions, are inferior to the strategy of buying at the beginning of the period and selling at its conclusion (Fama, 1970). The alternative approach, widely accepted by the traders' environment, is the belief that the stock market is predictable in the sense of technical and fundamental analysis methods. We, in this study support the view that EMH is non predictive for analysis of ISE and show the use of NN in predicting financial time series [1, 2].

A. Yazici and C. Şener (Eds.): ISCIS 2003, LNCS 2869, pp. 553–560, 2003.

Generalized Autoregressive Conditional Heteroskedasticity (GARCH) models have been studied many times in the literature. Dorffner and Schittenkopf has studied about financial time series prediction mentioning several neural network architectures including both feed-forward and recurrent neural networks with mixture density network models on non-linear GARCH modeling of historical volatility [1, 2]. As Chan presented Sharpe Ratio maximization can be used as a performance measure and Fourier based recurrent network architectures may have signal generation power [3]. Hellstrom in his studies introduced new concepts about data selection procedure related to the field of financial time series prediction and new performance measures such as Theil coefficient etc [4]. Profit based network training and guidelines for time series prediction has been introduced by Yao [5].

The remainder of this paper proceeds as follows: in the second section, volatility forecasting has been introduced. In the third section we have described our data and the model architecture proposed to capture the data as well as the statistical characteristics of the stock market series. The fourth section describes the results according to the performance and benchmark measures that we have used in this study to compare with other models. Final section concludes the study with future work.

2 Financial Time Series and Volatility

Stock prices vary with changes in volatilities of the underlying risk factor and as a consequence, accurate prediction of future stock prices requires a forecast of asset return's volatility.

Financial time series exhibit time dependent heteroskedastic variance known as conditional variance (volatility) that is not directly an observable feature.

A volatility model [6], proposed in this paper, is used to forecast risk, and return of assets. These forecasts are used in market risk management, portfolio selection, market timing etc. and by other financial decision makers. Therefore, predictability of the volatility is important: a portfolio manager may want to sell a stock or a portfolio before the market becomes too volatile or a trader may want to know the expected volatility to give the right decision while buying or selling a stock. A risk manager has the right to know that his portfolio may likely to decline in near future. None of the players want a volatile market; estimating the volatility of asset returns, which is a basic risk factor component of the stock market, gives valuable information for the future risk in the market and this will make the players to consider the expected high or low volatility in the market.

In the literature there are numerous studies and approaches to estimate volatilities using historical asset returns. Time dependent variance was first proposed by Engle [6] who used past asset returns to model heteroskedastic behavior with Autoregressive Conditional Heteroskedasticity (ARCH) process. Bollerslev [7] generalized this approach offering Generalized Autoregressive Conditional Heteroskedasticity (GARCH) model where conditional variances are governed by a linear autoregressive process of past squared returns and variances.

However, both of these models lack in modeling a volatility fact that is known as the effect of the sign of the innovations called "*leverage effect*". For this purpose, we adopt an asymmetric extension of the GARCH, proposed by Nelson [8] as Exponential Generalized Autoregressive Conditional Heteroskedasticity (EGARCH) model.

$$\log(h_t) = \omega + \beta \log(h_{t-1}) + \gamma \frac{\epsilon_{t-1}}{\sqrt{h_{t-1}}} + \alpha \left[\frac{|\epsilon_{t-1}|}{\sqrt{h_{t-1}}} - \sqrt{\frac{2}{\pi}} \right] \tag{1}$$

ω, α, β and γ are constant parameters. EGARCH considers modeling the sign effect besides using past squared innovations and past variances. Engle and Ng has measured the impact of news on volatility models by employing especially EGARCH models [9]. Application and testing of EGARCH for the Turkish stock market was first done by Okay [10, 11] who concluded that EGARCH performs better than a GARCH model.

3 Data and Model Architecture

Data used in this paper consist of 2946 daily observations of XU100 index of ISE market covering a 12-year period, from 12 January 1990 to 26 April 2002. Besides the index closing values, four supporting series: USD dollar rate, simple turkish interest rate, turkish interbank rate, turkish money supply rate have been studied as helper series to find the underlying non-linear relationship, the unknown patterns and the effects of these series over the volatility of the index return series.

In order to use the data effectively in ANN processing, first we have to keep the series in a constant range by applying normalization. The index price series (y_t) is transformed into continuously compounded return series (r_t) by the formula given below to obtain an accepted stationary series.

$$r_t = \ln(y_t / y_{t-1}) \tag{2}$$

Several statistical characteristics of asset returns have emerged throughout the years and these have been confirmed by numerous studies done by volatility modeling for predicting financial time series [11, 13].

Table 1 reports the statistics for XU100 index return series, obtained from ISE database. The sample period, containing 2945 daily return observations, is from January 12, 1990 to April 26, 2002. The results show that XU100 is negatively skewed, and the kurtosis which is a measure of the thickness of the tails, is very high. Jarque-Bera test statistic rejects the null hypothesis of normal distribution (Bera) [12]. ARCH (5) tests the ARCH effects using Engle's [6] test.

Financial markets in Turkey are chaotic and show non-linearity with very high noise because of the political indeterminate structure and instability of the economy. Any news, any rumor may cause sudden volatile movements making

Table 1. Summary statistics for the daily returns of XU100

XU100 index statistics (12/01/1990 - 26/04/2002)						
Size	Mean	Variance	Skewness	Kurtosis	Min	Max
2945	0.002	0.001	0.130	5.727	-0.2	0.171
Autocorrelations and ARCH test results						
Q(5)	Q(10)	$Q^2(5)$	$Q^2(10)$	ARCH(5)	J.Bera (p-value)	
40.61	56.922	415.784	551.324	272.544	918.253	
0.1122	0.0138	0.1425	0.0676		0.00	

Q (5), and Q^2 (5) are the Ljung-Box statistics of the autocorrelation of residuals and squared residuals respectively, J-B is the Jarque-Bera statistic for normality test.

market volatility a very difficult and a complex problem with all hidden but effecting factors [13].

For this reason, in this study, we developed a *mixture of experts* based forecasting method for financial time series prediction. A neural network's performance besides its model is dependent on the quality and relevance of the data. For this purpose, we divide the data set into three parts: train, validation and test sets which have 1857, 795 and 294 elements respectively. We train our data using the train data set, validate the model parameters using the validation set and use the production (test) data set for testing the performance of the MoE model and compare our results with MLP, RBF and RNN networks.

MLP is the most popular type of neural network, inspired from the simple model of biological neuron structures in the human body nervous system. Backpropogation associated multiplayer network is reintroduced by Rumelhart, Hinton, Williams and individually by Parker (1986) which is turned out to be the neural analog of the steepest descent algorithm of Werbos (1974).

A general d input, h hidden unit and one output MLP type neural network is formulized as follows:

$$y(x) = s\left(\sum_{j=1}^{h} V_j \times s\left(\sum_{i=1}^{d} w_{ji}x_i + w_{j0}\right) + V_0\right) \tag{3}$$

"s" is a typical sigmoid function. w and V are the weights, parameters of the system.

RBF based networks were first used to solve function approximation, interpolation problems. Instead of using sigmoid as an activation function, RBF uses Gaussian curves to fit the underlying model in the data. RBF tries to find mean and variance parameters of these curves.

In mixture of experts modeling, first the data is clustered into groups using Expectation Maximization algorithm. The number of centers is equal to the number of hidden units in the neural network architecture. Each group is assumed to have a gaussian distribution and the initial calculated mean and variances of the groups are optimized using Backpropogation through over each local expert according to the mean square error (MSE) measure. Trained each local expert specializes in its region and the outputs of these local experts are merged through the gating expert which considers the input pattern at the same time processing the outputs of each local expert. Hidden neuron units in the architecture are gaussian hidden units, and this makes the system apply piecewise linear approximation.

3.1 Mixture of Experts Architecture

Mixture of experts proposed by Jacobs [14] is one of the ways of combining multiple learners. It seems like voting, but the mechanism, which gives votes to each expert, is not stable over all the patterns in *mixture of experts* and it considers the input pattern while giving decisions. *Mixture of experts* consists of two modules. Numerous learners (experts) which work in parallel using the same input pattern make up the first module and the second module is the gating expert which determines the output using the outputs of local experts regarding the input pattern.

All experts are trained on all patterns in parallel and the gate expert is trained using the outputs of experts and this gate expert acts as a function of computing the proper weights for each expert to be used for the final weighted decision using the input pattern as a feature in parallel with local experts.

Different experts are allowed to specialize on local regions. Each local expert learns training patterns from different regions and these are combined in the gate expert. This modular architecture of *mixture of experts* provides piecewise linear approximation in financial time series prediction. The architecture of the *mixture of experts* can be seen in Fig. 1.

As shown in the Fig. 1, posterior probability is shown as follows:

$$P\left(y|x,\phi\right) = \sum_j P\left(y|x,\theta_j\right) a_j\left(x\right) \tag{4}$$

$P\left(y|x,\theta_j\right)$ represents the output of the local experts. Each local expert is specialized in its region. $a_j\left(x\right)$ form the weights of the each local expert to form the final decision.

4 Results

As we stated before a neural network's performance besides its model is dependent on the quality and relevance of the data. The data selection procedure is one of the most important components of an NN processing. In this study, we are working on four different series besides XU100. Sliding windows technique that is taking the last n elements in the series as an input is only applied to XU100 and USD series. All the series is used as an input to NN processing and

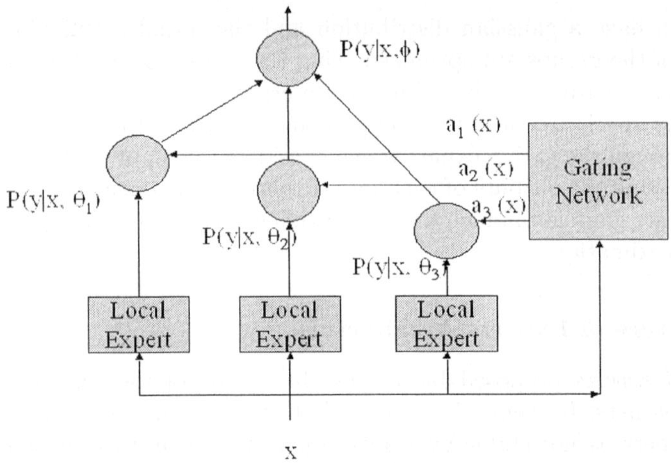

Fig. 1. The architecture of the mixture of experts is shown in the figure. Below module contains several local experts that are also neural networks in themselves. The above module is the gating expert network, which acts as a function computing the proper weights for each expert regarding the input pattern.

one-time-ahead forecast is the expected output of the NN. We are studying on real-valued series and the outputs are also real-valued forecasts. In this study we have chosen a 12-year period of XU100 between 01/01/1990 and 26/04/2002. A seven lag windowed series is trained using 20 hidden units for each network model we have used. ISE shows different distributional effects between 1990 and 1998 because of the indeterminate economical structure, so we tested our models with a smaller and more predictable data set from 01/01/1998 to 26/04/2002 using 15 hidden units in our models. Mean square error (MSE) is used as an error function during the training phase. However for testing the out-of-sample performance and the adequacy of the model we have used several performance metrics. The reported results in Table 2 and Table 3 are obtained from the production data set. Hit rate (H_R) shows the percentage of the correct predictions of the direction of the market. Positive hit rate (H_R^+) is the percentage of the correct predictions during the increasing market and the negative hit rate (H_R^-) is the opposite. Root mean square error ($RMSE$), mean absolute error (MAE) and correlation (ζ) measures the ability of the model to capture the data.

MoE and RNN have outperformed remaining models except in H_R^- measure. In H_R^-, RBF have the best results during 1998 and 2002. RNN is the best if you consider MSE and its derivations, and MoE is the best when you look at the correct direction predictions at H_R. The experimental results suggest that localized NN models has the strength to capture the underlying model in the data series and is able to infer knowledge that can be used during trading and risk management. For the data set in Table 2, train, validation and test data sets have 649, 277 and 102 elements respectively.

Table 2. Performance comparison of NN models with 15 hidden units and EGARCH. (01/01/1998 - 26/04/2002)

	MoE	MLP	RBF	RNN	EGARCH
H_R	89	51.4	68.6	58	51.3
H_R^+	100	47	55.4	56.9	69.5
H_R^-	87	56.9	92.1	58.8	35.9
MSE	0.139	1.064	0.165	0.101	0.174
$RMSE$	0.308	0.943	0.339	0.28	0.318
MAE	0.373	1.032	0.407	0.318	0.417
ζ	0.849	0.324	0.727	0.796	0.037

Table 3 shows the metrics obtained using the whole data set from 1990 to 2002. Because of large fluctuations associated with volatile economic environment in Turkey, make the models (MoE, MLP, RBF, RNN and EGARCH) unable to capture the data. Again MoE has superior to its rivals, but RBF shows close results to MoE outperforming the rest of the models.

Table 3. Performance comparison of NN models with 20 hidden units and EGARCH. (01/01/1990 - 26/04/2002)

	MoE	MLP	RBF	RNN	EGARCH
H_R	62.2	53.8	62.2	52.4	40.4
H_R^+	100	49.1	100	47.8	67.1
H_R^-	60.9	59.8	60.9	57.9	29.8
MSE	0.499	0.988	0.503	0.912	0.129
$RMSE$	0.629	0.906	0.632	0.862	0.287
MAE	0.706	0.994	0.71	0.955	0.359
ζ	0.546	0.347	0.532	0.378	0.021

5 Future Work and Conclusion

In this study, we have demonstrated that traditional simple neural networks such as MLP cannot capture the financial time series data and they are not suitable for modeling risk. But, MoE model of network divides the data into segments that are dealt with local experts and it merges the results using a gating network which gives a more successful and an applicable result in order to give decision while trading. Also RBF as a localized network and RNN cannot outperform MoE using both data sets. This study have shown that one of the most accepted traditional conditional variance model, EGARCH, although is not giving very encoring results, may cope with the neural network methods mentioned.

According to the experimental results localized NN models are suitable for financial time series prediction. Further to this study, volatility and *Value at Risk* (VaR) comparisons may be incorporated and also intraday data may be used for volatility modeling.

References

1. Schittenkopf C., Dorffner G.: Risk Neutral Density Extraction from Option Prices: Improved Pricing with Mixture Density Networks (1999)
2. Tino P., Schittenkopf C., Dorffner G.: Volatility Trading via Temporal Pattern Recognition in Quantized Financial Time Series (2000)
3. Chan L., GAO X.: An Algorithm for Trading and Portfolio Management Using Q-learning and Sharpe Ratio Maximization, in proceedings of International Conference on Neural Information Processing, ICONIP 2000, Taejon, Korea, 832–837
4. Hellstrom T., Holmstrom K.: Predictable Pattern in Stock Returns, Technical Report Series, IMA-TOM (1997–09)
5. Yao J.T., Tan C.L.: Guidelines for Financial Forecasting with Neural Networks (2001)
6. Engle R.: Autoregressive Conditional Heteroskedasticity with estimates of the variance of United Kingdom inflation, Econometrica. 50 (1982) 987–1007
7. Bollerslev T.: Generalized Autoregressive Conditional Heteroskedasticity, Journal of Econometrics. 31 (1986) 307–327
8. Nelson D.: Conditional Heteroskedasticity in asset returns: a new approach, Econometrica. 59 (1991) 349–370
9. Engle R.F., Ng V.K.: Measuring and Testing the Impact of News on Volatility, The Journal of Finance, Vol. 48, Issue 5 (Dec., 1993) 1749–1778
10. Okay, N., Asymmetric Volatility Dynamics: Evidence From The Istanbul Stock Exchange, Business & Economics for the 21st Century, Volume II, B&ESI. (1998) 207–216
11. Okay, N., Evidence For Conditional Heteroskedasticity in Turkish Stock Returns, Readings Book of the 1998 ABA National Conference. (1998) 241–247
12. Bera A.K.,Higgins M.L., Arch Models. Properties, Estimation and testing. Journal of Economic Surveys. 7 (1993) 305–362
13. Okay,N. Dynamic predictability of the Istanbul Stock Exchange Market using a Vector Autoregressive Model. Bogazici Journal, 12 31–56
14. Jacobs R.A., Jordan M.I., Nowlan S.J., Hinton G.E.: Adaptive mixture of local experts, Neural Computation, Vol. 3. (1991) 79–87

Design and Usage of a New Benchmark Problem for Genetic Programming

Emin Erkan Korkmaz[1] and Göktürk Üçoluk[2]

[1] Computer Engineering Department
Middle East Technical University
06531, Ankara, TURKEY
korkmaz@metu.edu.tr,
http://www.ceng.metu.edu.tr/~{}korkmaz

[2] Computer Engineering Department
Middle East Technical University
06531, Ankara, TURKEY
ucoluk@metu.edu.tr,
http://www.ceng.metu.edu.tr/~{}ucoluk

Abstract. Not so many benchmark problems have been proposed in the area of *Genetic Programming* (GP). In this study, a new artificial benchmark problem is designed for GP. The different parameters that can be used to tune the difficulty of the problem are analyzed. Also, the initial experimental results obtained on different instances of the problem are presented.

1 Introduction

Benchmark Problems are important in order to judge the effectiveness of a new approach proposed in a research area. It is possible to get more insight about the contribution of a methodology by using a tunable benchmark problem. Not so many benchmark problems have been proposed in the area of *Genetic Programming* (GP). However, there are some problems widely used by different GP researchers. Usually, the results obtained in these commonly used domains are presented in order to denote the effectiveness of an approach. The problem of programming an artificial ant to follow the *Santa Fe trail* [5], the symbolic regression problems [4] and the N-parity problem [2,1,8,9] are example real world domains which have been used as benchmark problems in GP.

However, using a real-world domain as a benchmark problem has certain drawbacks. It is usually difficult to tune a real-world problem. The different instances of the problem can be disproportionate with each other in terms of difficulty and the size of the search space. The results obtained on a specific instance of the problem might be misleading in terms of the general behavior of the methodology used. Hence the usage of a tunable artificial benchmark problem gains importance for testing the effectiveness of a method.

This paper presents the design and usage of a new benchmark problem for GP. In the following section, previous work in the area is presented. Then, in

A. Yazici and C. Şener (Eds.): ISCIS 2003, LNCS 2869, pp. 561–567, 2003.

section 3, the design of the problem is introduced. In section 4, the initial experimental results obtained on different instances of the problem are presented. The experiments are carried out in order to determine the behavior of GP on the problem. Lastly, in section 5, the conclusion is given.

2 Related Work

As noted in the previous section, it is difficult to find benchmark problems designed for GP. However certain attempts do exist in the literature. For instance, in [7], certain problems which can be used as benchmark tests are proposed.

The most notable work in the area is the benchmark problem proposed in [6]. The formalization used by [6] shares some characteristics with the *Royal Road Problem.* This is a commonly used benchmark problem for tuning the genetic parameters in the field of GA, [3]. The benchmark problem proposed in [6] is an important attempt to transfer the issues addressed in creation of the Royal Road Problem, to the field of GP. These issues focus on the important aspects needed to consider a problem as a benchmark for the evolutionary computation research. The goal is to define a problem, which

- possesses a controllable level of difficulty,
- has clearly defined building blocks,
- can be reduced to various instances to be used to tune the genetic parameters.

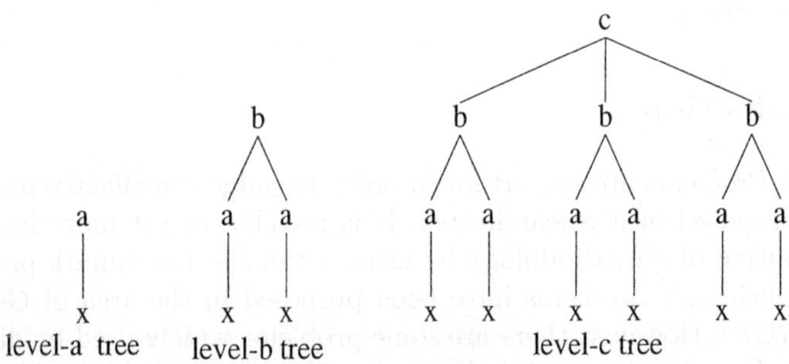

Fig. 1. Perfect trees of different levels.

The formalization in [6] is based on the definition of a *"perfect tree"* of some depth. For instance a level-a tree is perfect when its root is the function a with a single child. Similarly a perfect level-b tree's root should be function b having two perfect level-a trees as children. Certainly a perfect level-c tree will have three perfect level-b trees connected to root c and so on. The terminal set consists of a single element x. Note that the series of functions $a, b, c, d...$ are defined with increasing arity. The perfect trees of levels a, b and c are presented in Figure 1.

The raw fitness of a tree is defined as the score of its root. On the other side the score of each function is calculated by adding the weighted scores of its children. The weight is a constant larger than one ($FullBonus$) if a child is a perfect tree of the appropriate level. When the child is not a perfect tree, the weight turns out to be a constant smaller or equal to one (*Penalty* or *Partialbonus*) depending on the child's configuration. If the child has the correct root *Partialbonus* is used. However, if the root of the child is incorrect too, *Penalty* is used as the weight. If the root itself is the correct root of a perfect tree, then the obtained score is multiplied by *CompleteBonus*. It is stated that typical values that can be used are: $FullBonus = 2, PartialBonus = 1, Penalty = \frac{1}{3}$, and $CompleteBonus = 2$. It is suggested that perfect trees of different depths can be used as benchmark problems for GP.

The proposed definition in [6] has certain drawbacks. It can be claimed that the most important factor that effects the performance of GP is the *deception* of the problem at hand. This notion can be observed in a variety of real world domains. In such domains, the genetic search is easily misled to a local optimum by the building blocks and such problems are called *deceptive problems*. Hence a qualified benchmark problem should provide a mechanism which has control over the deceptiveness of the problem. Deception usually appears as an outcome of *epistasis*. In other words, the interdependency among the subparts of the chromosome should have an influence on the global fitness of the chromosome. However, the formalization provided by [6] enables each child to contribute to the global fitness independent of other children. Furthermore, since the functions are defined with increasing arity, the search space increases rapidly for high levels. The problem is too difficult after level d and e. On the other hand, levels a, b and c are too simple. It is possible for the solution to appear in the initial random population in these levels. Lastly using more than one constant makes the definition unnecessarily complicated.

3 A New Benchmark Problem

Considering the drawbacks mentioned in the previous section, it has been decided to simplify and reorganize the definition of perfect tree. The aim is to obtain a tunable benchmark problem where epistasis can easily be controlled.

The new perfect tree is defined to be a full binary tree of some depth. The function set consists of n functions with arity two ($F = \{X_1, X_2, ..X_n\}$). The terminal set consists of a single terminal element t, ($T = \{t\}$). The raw fitness of a tree is again defined as the score of its root. The fitness of a terminal node is simply defined as 1. The fitness of an internal node is defined as the sum of the fitness values of its two children. The two constraints used to create epistasis for the problem are the following.

When the children of an internal node are not terminal elements:

(i) The index of the parent function should be smaller than the index of its children.
(ii) The index of the right-hand child should be larger than the index of the left-hand child.

The fitness function for an internal node is defined as:

$$f(P) = \begin{cases} f(C_1) + f(C_2) & (i) \\ C_{epis} \cdot f(C_1) + f(C_2) & (ii) \\ f(C_1) + C_{epis} \cdot f(C_2) & (iii) \\ C_{epis} \cdot f(C_1) + C_{epis} \cdot f(C_2) & (iv) \end{cases} \tag{1}$$

In Equation 1, part (i) is chosen if both of the children are terminal elements or none of the constraints are violated. If the first constraint is violated by any child, the fitness of that child is multiplied with a constant smaller than one. This constant is called the *epistasis constant* (C_{epis}). Parts (ii) and (iii) in Equation 1 reflect this situation. Lastly part (iv) is used when both of the children violate the first constraint or when the second constraint cannot be achieved.

Note that these two constraints create interdependency among the subparts of a chromosome. When the epistasis constant is decreased the interdependency increases. It becomes impossible for a subpart of the chromosome to contribute to the global fitness independent of other parts. A well-fit chromosome can easily be ruined when a node that violates a constraint appears after a recombination operation. Hence, fitnesses of similar chromosomes might differ remarkably and the search space becomes discontinuous. What is more is that, when the function set is kept small, it becomes more probable to be stuck in a local minima. Note that the index of the functions has to increase in the down direction of a chromosome. Therefore a wrong choice close to the root might make it impossible to form a perfect tree.

Note that three different parameters exist for tuning the difficulty of the benchmark problem proposed. The first parameter is the depth of perfect tree to be searched. The epistasis constant (C_epis) and the size of the function set are the other two parameters which can be used to tune the problem.

4 Experimental Results

The experiments are carried out by using a perfect tree with a fixed depth of four. Increasing the depth of the perfect tree results an exponential enlargement in the search space. Therefore, such a moderate size is chosen. The change in the performance of GP is observed based on the other two parameters; namely the epistasis constant and the size of the function set.

In figure 4, a possible solution for depth four is given. Note that seven different functions have been used to build the solution and other solutions would exist if a larger function set is used.

Consider the two parameters for controlling the difficulty of the problem. When you enlarge the function set, the number of possible solutions increases, hence it becomes easier to reach to a solution in the search space. On the other side when the epistasis constant is decreased the interdependency increases and it turns out to be more difficult to reach to the solution. Two different sets of experiments are carried out in order to get insight about the behavior of GP on the benchmark problem. In the first phase, the function set is fixed and the behavior is observed based on the change in the epistasis constant. Then in the

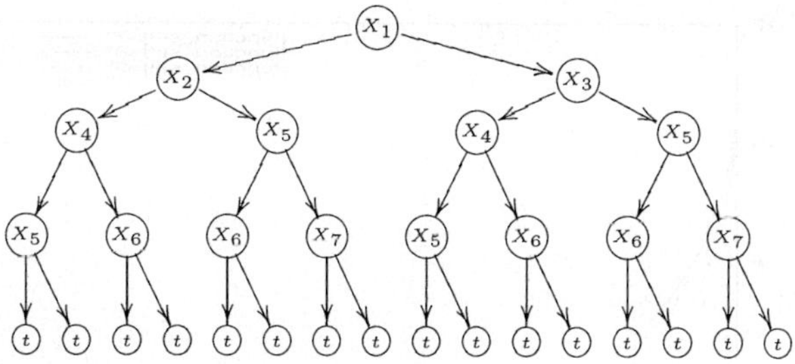

Fig. 2. A possible solution of depth four.

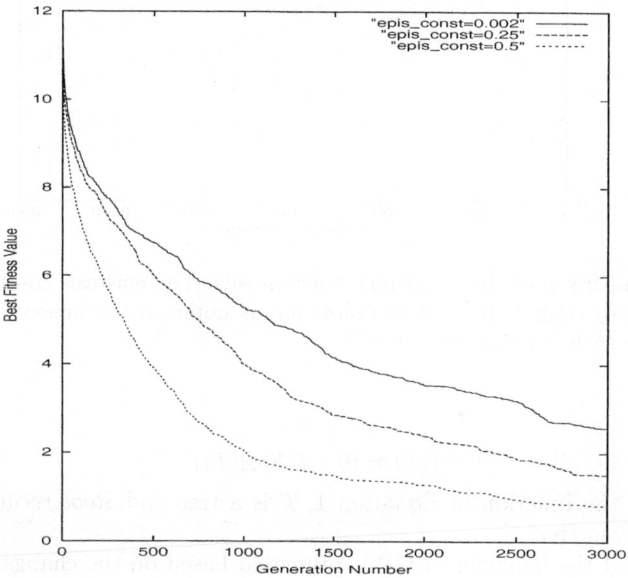

Fig. 3. Comparison of three different epistasis constants. The size of the function set used is 8 for all of the three trials. Best fitness means obtained throughout 100 runs are presented for each epistasis constant.

second phase the reverse procedure is carried out and different function sets are used with a fixed epistasis constant.

The same genetic parameters are used for the two phases and these parameters are set as follows

- Population size = 100
- Crossover at function point fraction = 0.1
- Crossover at any point fraction = 0.7
- Reproduction fraction = 0.1
- Mutation fraction = 0.1
- Number of Generations = 3000
- Selection Method: Fitness Proportional.

The results are obtained by using the average of 100 different runs. Note that the largest value that can be obtained by the fitness function proposed in Equation 1 evaluates to 16 for the perfect tree of depth four. If the best fitness value is to be set as zero, then the fitness function would be

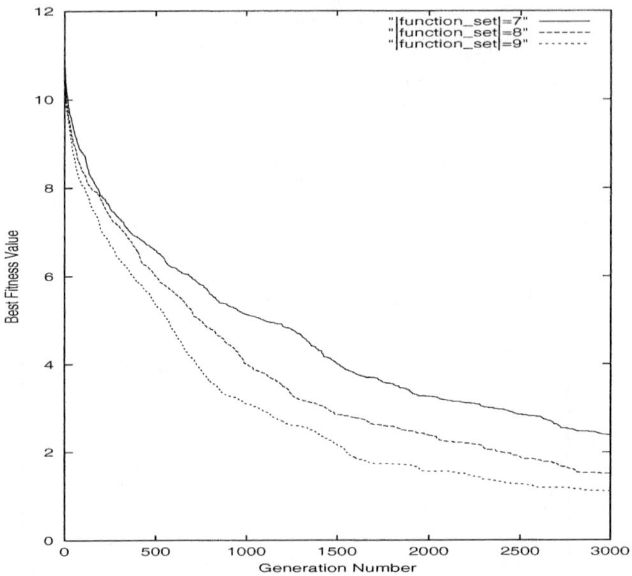

Fig. 4. Comparison of three different function sets. The epistasis constant used for all of the three trials is 0.25. Best fitness means obtained throughout 100 runs are presented for each function set.

$$\hat{f}(T) = 16 - f(Root(T)), \tag{2}$$

where f is the function in Equation 1, T is a tree and *Root* returns the root node of a given tree.

In figure 4 the behavior of GP is presented based on the change in epistasis constant. The presented graphs are the output of three different constants; 0.5, 0.25 and 0.002. The last constant is chosen to be close to zero and as seen in the figure the worst performance is obtained with this constant. The constant 0.5 can be considered to be quite high and GP has the best performance in this instance. Also a third constant is chosen (0.25) in between the difficult and easy instances. As seen in the figure, it is possible to obtain instances with different difficulty levels based on the epistasis constant used. It is observed that the change in performance related to the change in epistasis constant is quite uniform.

In figure 4, the epistasis constant is fixed as 0.25 and the effect of the function set size on the performance of GP is analyzed. The three function sets used for the trials are $F = \{X_1, X_2, ..., X_7\}$, $F = \{X_1, X_2, ..., X_7, X_8\}$ and $F = \{X_1, X_2, ..., X_7, X_8, X_9\}$. As seen in the figure, function set size can be used as a parameter which would change the performance of GP on the problem. A change in this parameter is observed to have a gradual effect on the result and does not lead to a chaotic/disproportional behavior. This is also an asset compared to the work of [6].

5 Conclusion

The goal of this research was to design a tunable benchmark problem which can be used to judge the effectiveness of different methodologies in the field of GP. We have developed a problem where the tree shape has effect on the evaluation function. The proposed problem is inspired by the work of [6] and has certain common characteristics with the definition proposed by [6]. However, it is claimed that it is quite easier to tune and obtain different difficulty levels with the new definition proposed in this study. The experimental results verify that it is possible to obtain different instances which are quite proportionate with respect to each other in terms of difficulty. It is possible to get more insight about the effectiveness of a GP methodology and observe the behavior of the method against the change in epistasis and deception by using the different instances of the problem proposed.

References

1. Chellapilla, K. A Preliminary Investigation into Evolving Modular Programs without Subtree Crossover. Genetic Programming 1998: *Proceedings of the Third Annual Conference*
2. Chris Gathercole and Peter Ross. Tackling the Boolean Even N Parity Problem with Genetic Programming and Limited-Error Fitness. Genetic Programming 1997: *Proceedings of the Second Annual Conference*, pp. 119–127, Stanford University, CA, USA, 1997.
3. Janes, T. A Description of Holland's Royal Road Function. *Evolutionary Computation*, 2(4), pp. 409-415, 1994.
4. Koza, J. R. Genetic Programming. On the Programming of Computers by Means of Natural Selection. *The MIT Press*, London. 1992.
5. W. B. Langdon. Better Trained Ants. *Late Breaking Papers at EuroGP'98: the First European Workshop on Genetic Programming*, Paris, France, 1998.
6. W.F. Punch, D. Zongker and E.D. Goodman. The Royal Tree Problem, a Benchmark for Single and Multi-population Genetic Programming. Appears *in Advances in Genetic Programming g 2*, MIT Press, pg 299-316, 1996.
7. Tackett, W. A. *Recombination, Selection and the Genetic Construction of Computer Programs.* PhD thesis, University of Southern California, April 1994.
8. Terence Soule and James A. Foster. Code Size and Depth Flows in Genetic Programming. Genetic Programming 1997: *Proceedings of the Second Annual Conference*, Stanford University, CA, USA, pp. 313–320, 1997.
9. Man Leung Wong and Kwong Sak Leung. Evolving Recursive Functions for the Even-Parity Problem Using Genetic Programming. *Advances in Genetic Programming 2*, MIT Press, pp. 221–240, 1996.

A New Approach Based on Recurrent Neural Networks for System Identification

Adem Kalinli and Seref Sagiroglu

Erciyes University, Engineering Faculty
Computer Engineering Department, Kayseri, Turkey.
{kalinlia, SS}@erciyes.edu.tr

Abstract. This paper introduces a new approach based on artificial neural networks (ANNs) to identify a number of linear dynamic systems with single recurrent neural model. The structure of single neural model is capable of dealing with systems up to a given maximum number. Single recurrent neural model is trained by the backpropagation with momentum. Total nine systems from first to third orders have been used to validate the approach presented in this work. The results have shown that the recurrent single neural model is capable of identifying a number of systems successfully. The approach presented in this work provides simplicity, accuracy and compactness to system identification.

1 Introduction

Recurrent neural networks (RNNs) with dynamic memories are suitable for representing dynamic systems due to their dynamic structure. These networks have been recently applied for system identification [1-9]. A special type of RNNs is the Elman network. Elman net had failed in identifying second order linear systems [5,6,9]. A number of modifications of the network have been presented to improve the efficiency [3-9].

A great deal of works in the literature has been devoted to identify single system with single model or single system with multi-model. A number of approaches to system identification have been generally introduced to improve single model efficiency [1-14]. In the approaches, good results were achieved but the complexity in designing the identifiers has been increased. Sagiroglu and Kalinli have been recently presented a new approach for multi-system identification with single feedforward neural identifier [15].

This paper introduces a new and simple approach based on Elman network for identifying a number of systems having different orders, parameters and behaviours with single neural identifier. Moreover, Elman network does not only identify second order system but also third order linear systems.

The paper has four main sections. Section 2 briefly introduces a special type of RNNs. Section 3 discusses the identification of linear dynamic systems and the proposed approach. The simulations were given in Section 4. The work is concluded in Section 5.

A. Yazici and C. Şener (Eds.): ISCIS 2003, LNCS 2869, pp. 568–575, 2003.

2 Elman Network

Fig. 1 depicts the original Elman network having three layers of neurons. The first layer consists of two different groups of neurons. These are the group of external input neurons and the group of internal input neurons also called context units. The inputs to the context units are the outputs of the hidden neurons. The outputs of the context units and the external input neurons are the inputs to the hidden neurons. Context units are also known as memory units as they store the previous output of the hidden neurons. In the Elman net, the values of the feedback connection weights have to be fixed by the user if the standard BP algorithm is employed to train the network and usually their strengths are fixed at 1.0 [2-4].

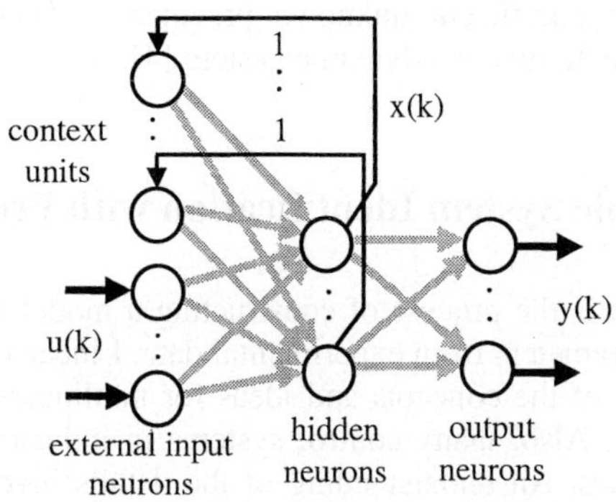

Fig. 1. Structure of the original Elman network

In Fig.1, the external inputs to the network are represented by U(k) and the network outputs, by Y(k). The activations of the hidden units are X(k). From Fig.1 it can be seen that the following equations hold:

$$\mathbf{X}(k) = \mathbf{F}\left\{\mathbf{W}^{xx}\mathbf{X}(k\text{ - }1),\ \mathbf{W}^{xu}\mathbf{U}(k)\right\} \tag{1}$$

$$\mathbf{Y}(k) = \mathbf{W}^{yx}\mathbf{X}(k) \tag{2}$$

where $\mathbf{W}^{xx}$, $\mathbf{W}^{xu}$ and $\mathbf{W}^{yx}$ are the weight matrices and $\mathbf{F}$ is a non-linear vector function. In particular, when linear hidden units are adopted and the biases of the hidden and output units are zero, Eqns (1) and (2) become

$$\mathbf{X}(k) = \mathbf{W}^{xx}\mathbf{X}(k\text{ - }1) + \mathbf{W}^{xu}\mathbf{U}(k) \tag{3}$$

$$\mathbf{Y}(k) = \mathbf{W}^{yx}\mathbf{X}(k) \tag{4}$$

If inputs U(k) are delayed by one step before they are sent to the input units, Eqns (3) and (4) become

$$\mathbf{X}(k) = \mathbf{W}^{xx}\mathbf{X}(k\text{ - }1) + \mathbf{W}^{xu}\mathbf{U}(k-1) \tag{5}$$

$$\mathbf{Y}(k) = \mathbf{W}^{yx}\mathbf{X}(k) \tag{6}$$

Eqns (5) and (6) are standard state-space descriptions of dynamic systems. The order of the model depends on the number of states, which is also the number of hidden units.

When the network is used to model single-input single-output systems, only one unit is needed in the input layer and the output layer. For such networks Eqns (5) and (6) can be expanded into the following:

$$\begin{aligned} y(k) = {} & A_1 y(k-1) + A_2 y(k-2) + \ldots + A_n y(k-n) \\ & + B_1 u(k-1) + B_2 u(k-2) + \ldots + B_m u(k-m) \end{aligned} \tag{7}$$

where A_i and B_j are coefficient unknown parameters. Therefore, theoretically an Elman network is able to model a dynamic system [4].

3 Linear Dynamic System Identification with Proposed Approach

System identification is the process of constructing a model for an unknown system and estimating its parameters from experimental data. Linear systems are important in many respects. Most of the concepts and ideas for nonlinearity can be simplified in the form of linearity. Also, many control systems in industry are still being solved using linear techniques. An understanding of the details involved in the linear case allows the direct extension to solve nonlinear problems.

The input-output characteristics of the system will generally change rapidly or even discontinuously when the environment changes. If single identification model is used, it will have to adapt itself to the new environment before appropriate control action can be taken. In linear systems, such adaptation is possible, but the slowness of adaptation may result in a large transient error. Simpler model is always desired for both to identify the different environments as well as to control them rapidly. This paper presents a simpler model for system identification.

For linear time-invariant plants with unknown parameters, the most general use of input-output equation is written as in Eqn (7). Identifying a linear system means obtaining the coefficients in the equation. A common method for identifying dynamic plant behaviour is to train a neural identifier to minimise the error between the plant and the identifier outputs [1-6].

In this work, the new approach is also based on the same method. Instead of identifying one system with only one identifier, a number of systems (multi-system) are identified using only one neural identifier. Fig.2 shows the present neural identifier in diagrammatic form for multi-system identification. The input-output relationship of p number of linear dynamic systems is identified with single neural identifier given in Fig.2. The system identification approach is based on an adaptation with the tapped-delay line technique to increase its versatility and simplicity. The only knowledge required for the systems to be identified within one model is the number of systems. The neural identifier used in this work can be represented as:

$$Y\left(y_1(.),..,y_p(.)\right) = A1y_1(.) + A2y_2(.) + ... + APy_p(.) + B1u(.) \tag{8}$$

where *Y*(.) depicts the identifier outputs. *A1, A2,..., AP* and *B1* represent the coefficients belonging to different systems having different orders. However, it is reasonable to assume the number of systems *p* can be estimated. In this work *p* was chosen as 3.

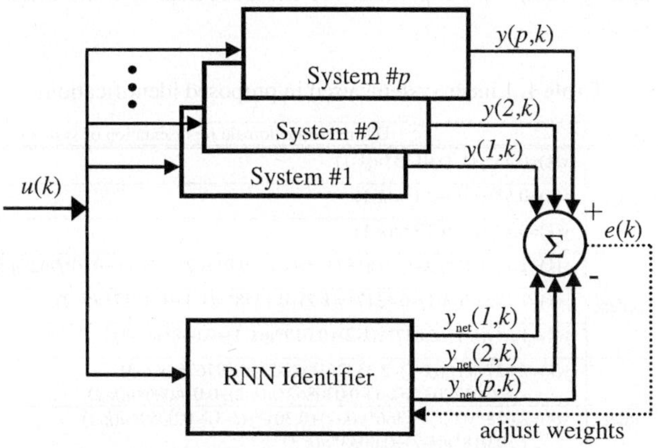

Fig. 2. RNN identifier for multi-system identification

Identifying multi linear systems means achieving the coefficients giving in Eqn (8) with the help of single neural identifier. For example, Eqn (8) becomes Eqn (9) when three of second order systems are identified with one neural identifier.

$$\begin{aligned} Y\left(y_1(k), y_2(k), y_3(k)\right) = {} & A1_1 y_1(k-1) + A1_2 y_1(k-2) + A2_1 y_2(k-1) + A2_2 y_2(k-2) \\ & + A3_1 y_3(k-1) + A3_2 y_3(k-2) + B1_1 u(k-1) + B1_2 u(k-2) \end{aligned} \tag{9}$$

For further identifications, the general formula given in Eqn(8) must be reorganised according to the number of systems to be identified. Throughout this work, the RNN identifier is trained in a supervised mode. The differences between the outputs of the neural identifier and the outputs of the systems are being used to modify the connection weights by the backpropagation with momentum (BPM) algorithm [16].

RNN identifiers are sufficiently trained until the root mean square (RMS) error has been reduced to below a preset threshold. The RMS error is defined as

$$RMS\ error = \left[\frac{1}{s}\sum_{k=1}^{s}\frac{1}{p}\sum_{i=1}^{p}\left[y(i,k) - y_{net}(i,k)\right]^2\right]^{1/2} \tag{10}$$

where s is the number input sequence, p is the number of systems to be identified, $y(i,k)$ and $y_{net}(i,k)$, respectively, are the system#i and the ith output of the RNN at time k.

4 Simulation Results

A number of computer simulations were carried out to test the proposed identification scheme based on Elman network. The structure of single neural identifier trained by the BPM. Total nine systems (plants) given in Table 1 were used to test the new approach presented in this work. The systems given in Table 1, by system#1-#3, system#4-#6 and system#7-#9 represent the first, second, and the third order systems, respectively.

Table 1. Linear systems used in proposed identifications

System	Orders	Discrete-time domain representation of systems
#1		$y(k)=0.75*y(k-1)+0.25*u(k-1)$
#2	1st order	$y(k)=0.5*y(k-1)+0.1*u(k-1)$
#3		$y(k)=0.4*y(k-1)+0.3*u(k-1)$
#4		$y(k)=1.752821*y(k-1)-0.818731*y(k-2)+0.011698*u(k-1)+0.010942*u(k-2)$
#5	2nd order	$y(k)=1.1953*y(k-1)-0.4317*y(k-2)+0.1348*u(k-1)+0.1017*u(k-2)$
#6		$y(k)=1.8*y(k-1)-0.837*y(k-2)+0.019*u(k-1)+0.018*u(k-2)$
#7		$y(k)=2.627771*y(k-1)-2.333261*y(k-2)+0.697676*y(k-3) + 0.017203*u(k-1)-0.030862*u(k-2)+0.014086*u(k-3)$
#8	3rd order	$y(k)=2.038*y(k-1)-1.366*y(k-2)+0.301*y(k-3)+0.0059*u(k-1) -0.018*u(k-2)+0.0033*u(k-3)$
#9		$y(k)=2.0549*y(k-1)-1.3524*y(k-2)+0.2894*y(k-3)+0.0049*u(k-1)+0.0032*u(k-2)$

The thirteen neural identifiers used throughout the simulations had one neuron in the input and six neurons in the hidden and context units. Each system is represented with one neuron in the output layer. All neurons employed in the neural identifiers had linear activation functions. The learning (•) and the momentum (β) coefficients of the BPM were taken between 0.0001 and 0.8. Throughout the simulations, neural identifiers were trained until sufficient results have been achieved. The identifier parameters given in this article were found after at least 20 trails. It was observed that maximum 100,000 iterations were sufficient. The training and test data files with 200 data points were obtained by applying uniform sequences $u(k)\in[-1.0,1.0]$, k=1,...,199,200. At the beginning of a training session, the weights of the neural connections were initialised to small random values in the range [-0.2, 0.2]. The sampling period was 0.1s in all systems.

RNN identifiers (RNN#1-#3, #4-#7 and #9-#12) were firstly trained to identify each system individually. In order to examine the proposed approach, the single neural identifiers (RNN#4, #8, #12 and #13) were used to identify three systems together with the same or different orders with single model.

Tables 2, 3 and 4 show the simulation results obtained from the RNN identifiers for the first, the second and the third order linear dynamic systems, respectively. Each table demonstrates the same order system or systems. The simulation results obtained from RNN#13 identifier for three systems having different orders are given in Table 5. The responses belonging to the systems and the neural identifier are illustrated in Fig.3. The parameters given in Tables 2-5 were found after many trials as stated earlier. From our experience on the parameters, we can clearly point out that the neural identifier performance is very sensitive to the values of β and η (please see reference [16] for more details about the parameters). The selecting appropriate parameters of Elman network becomes crucial to achieve better performance.

As reported in [5,6,9], original Elman network had failed in identifying the second order linear systems. In this work, Elman network has been successfully trained and performed well. This shows the capability of Elman network for identifying linear dynamic systems. In addition to this capability, the Elman network can identify not only individual system but also multi-system successfully.

Table 2. Results obtained from identification of first order linear systems

RNN	System	No. of Sys.	η	β	RMS Error	Average RMS Error
#1	#1	One	0.002	0.015	0.005941	-
#2	#2	One	0.002	0.015	0.005428	-
#3	#3	One	0.002	0.015	0.007019	-
#4	#1 #2 #3	Three	0.002	0.002	0.016476 0.004355 0.007387	0.009406

Table 3. Results obtained from identification of second order linear systems

RNN	System	No of Sys.	η	β	RMS Error	Average RMS Error
#5	#4	One	0.05	0.05	0.056812	-
#6	#5	One	0.01	0.015	0.028961	-
#7	#6	One	0.002	0.002	0.032905	-
#8	#4 #5 #6	Three	0.0005	0.0005	0.029660 0.049646 0.072767	0.050691

Table 4. Results obtained from identification of third order linear systems

RNN	System	No. of Sys.	η	β	RMS Error	Average RMS Error
#9	#7	One	0.02	0.02	0.005476	-
#10	#8	One	0.02	0.02	0.028389	-
#11	#9	One	0.01	0.02	0.028919	-
#12	#7 #8 #9	Three	0.0005	0.0005	0.004876 0.021333 0.025175	0.017128

Table 5. Results obtained from identification of first, second and third order linear systems

RNN	System	No. of Sys.	η	β	RMS Error	Average RMS Error
#13	#1 #4 #7	Three	0.002	0.002	0.006813 0.042686 0.004116	0.017872

5 Conclusions

This paper successfully presents the approach based on RNNs to identify multiple systems with only one RNN identifier. Results of thirteen RNN identifiers have shown that single neural identifier is capable of identifying single and multiple linear systems. RNN identifiers even perform multi-system identification better than single system identification. The approach presented in this work provides simplicity, accuracy and compactness to system identification.

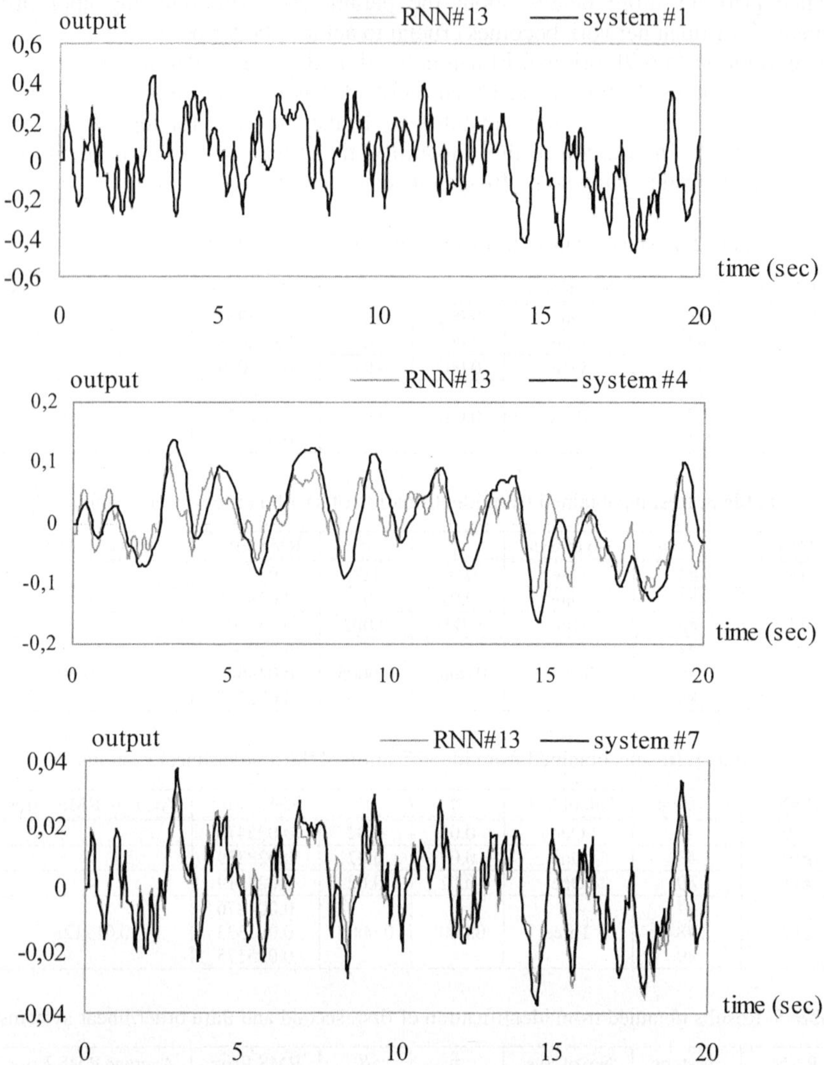

Fig. 3. Responses of single RNN identifier for three different order systems

It is observed from the simulations that the proposed identifier is more sensitive to the both η and β parameters. Smaller parameters are better for single and multi-system identifications. Selecting proper neurons in the hidden and context units are also crucial. So configuring Elman network suitably provides better performance for single and multi-system identifications.

If the new approach had been extended to control applications, it would provide simplicity, and it might bring new directions to the system designers dealing with modelling and control applications. The authors will focus on this extension in the future work.

References

1. Pham, D.T., Liu, X.: Neural Networks for Identification, Prediction and Control, 4th Ed. Springer Verlag (1999)
2. Pham, D.T., Liu, X.: Identification of Linear and Nonlinear Dynamic Systems Using Recurrent Neural Networks. Artificial Intelligence in Engineering, Vol.8. (1993) 90–97
3. Elman, J.L.: Finding Structure in Time. Cognitive Science, Vol.14. (1990) 179–211
4. Liu, X.: Modelling and Prediction Using Neural Networks. PhD Thesis, University of Wales College of Cardiff, Cardiff, UK, (1993)
5. Pham, D.T., Liu, X.: Training of Elman Networks and Dynamic System Modelling. Int. J. Systems Science, Vol.27, No.2 (1996) 221–226
6. Pham, D.T., Karaboga, D.: Training Elman and Jordan Networks for System Identification Using Genetic Algorithms. Artificial Intelligence in Engineering, Vol.13 (1999) 107–117
7. Karaboga, D., Kalinli, A.: Training Recurrent Neural Networks Using Tabu Search Algorithm. 5th Turkish Symposium on Artificial Intelligence and Neural Networks (TAINN'1996), Turkey, (1996) 293–298
8. Kalinli, A., Karaboga, D.: Training Recurrent Neural Networks Using Parallel Tabu Search Algorithm. (in Turkish), 11th Turkish Symposium on Artificial Intelligence and Neural Networks (TAINN'2002), Istanbul, Turkey (2002) 261–270
9. Pham, D.T., Karaboga, D.: Intelligent Optimisation Techniques: Genetic Algorithms, Tabu Search, Simulated Annealing and Neural Networks. Advanced Manufacturing Series, Springer-Verlag, London (2000)
10. Narendra, K.S., Balakrishnan, J., Ciliz, M.K.: Adaptation and Learning Using Multiple Models, Switching, and Tuning. IEEE Control Systems Magazine, Vol.15, No.3 (1995) 37–51
11. Narendra, K.S., Balakrishnan, J.: Adaptive Control Using Multiple Models. IEEE Trans on Automatic Control, Vol.42, No.2 (1997) 171–187
12. Gundala, R., Hoo, K.A., Piovoso, M.J.: Multiple Model Adaptive Control Design for a Multiple-Input Multiple-Output Chemical Reactor. Ind. & Eng. Chem. Res., Vol.39 (2000) 1554–1564
13. Galván, J.B., Pérez-Ilzarbe, M.J.: Two Neural Networks for Solving the Linear System Identification Problem. Proceedings of the IEEE Int. Conf. on Neural Networks, (1994) 3226–3231
14. Sagiroglu, S.: Identification Of Lineer Systems Using Multi-Layer Perceptrons, Proceedings of ISCIS XI, 6-8 November, Antalya, Turkey, Vol.2, (1996), 517–526
15. Sagiroglu, S., Kalinli, A.: A New Approach Based on Artificial Neural Networks for Multi-system Identification, TAINN 2003, 2–4 July 2003, Çanakkale, Turkey.
16. Rumelhart, D.E., McClelland, J.L.: Parallel Distributed Processing: Explorations in the Microstructure of Cognition, Vol.1, MIT Press, Cambridge, Massachusetts, (1986)

The Real-Time Development and Deployment of a Cooperative Multi-UAV System

Ali Haydar Göktoğan[1], Salah Sukkarieh, Gürçe Işikyildiz, Eric Nettleton, Matthew Ridley, Jong-Hyuk Kim, Jeremy Randle, and Stuart Wishart[2]

[1] Australian Centre for Field Robotics
School of Aerospace, Mechanical and Mechatronic Engineering
The Rose Street Building J04
The University of Sydney, NSW 2006, Australia
agoktogan@acfr.usyd.edu.au,
http://www.acfr.usyd.edu.au
[2] BAE Systems, Australia

Abstract. This paper presents a systems view of the Autonomous Navigation and Sensing Experimental Research (ANSER) project. ANSER is one of the most advanced UAV projects of its kind, which is aimed at demonstrating Decentralised Data Fusion (DDF) and Simultaneous Localisation and Map (SLAM) building on multiple cooperative UAVs. The demonstration of DDF and SLAM require both navigation and terrain sensors to be carried onboard by the UAVs. These include an INS/GPS navigation system, millimeter wave (MMW) radar, and both a single vision node and a vision node augmented with a laser system. This paper presents the implementation of the algorithms, sensors and platforms, along with their interaction to address this demonstration. Furthermore, the paper will present the high fidelity real time simulator which is implemented to thoroughly test all algorithms and sensors before actual implementation in the environment.

1 Introduction

The aim of the Autonomous Navigation and Sensing Experimental Research (ANSER) project is to demonstrate novel algorithms in the area of Decentralised Data Fusion (DDF) and Simultaneous Localisation and Map (SLAM) building on multiple, cooperative UAVs.

DDF is an architecture which allows for the ability to decentralise estimation algorithms across multiple sensing nodes so that there is no common failure point. The architecture also provides the ability for scalable and modular data fusion systems thus providing solutions to many network-centric problems which are currently being faced. The paradigm uses a Kalman filter (or more commonly its information form equivalent) in its decentralised form so that local sensor nodes have global knowledge.

One such data estimation problem is distributed target tracking. In this scenario multiple sensor nodes are tracking multiple targets. In most forms a centralised architecture is implemented. However using the DDF paradigm allows

A. Yazici and C. Şener (Eds.): ISCIS 2003, LNCS 2869, pp. 576–583, 2003.

for not only a distributed network but also a decentralised one, thus allowing nodes to come in and out of the network in run time.

Another example is the implementation of SLAM. In the single vehicle case, SLAM is an algorithm which allows for the simultaneous building up of an environment map, and the use of this map to then localise the vehicle within it. This is true autonomous navigation since no a priori information about the map or vehicle location is required. In the distributed multi-vehicle case, the map between vehicles is shared, better improving the its quality and the quality of the vehicle locations. Applying DDF to this navigation structure then further allows for decentralised paradigm to be applied.

In the literature there are numerous innovative research approaches to DDF and SLAM. However the algorithms have been demonstrated on static sensor networks [6] or robotic platforms with the slow and/or simple dynamics [1] [3]. Performing these algorithms and architectures on multiple UAVs is a very challenging exercise [13].

UAVs pose a difficult platform to work on. They have both complex and very high dynamics and flight tests are both expensive and are high risk operations. Any hardware or software system failure may have catastrophic results in any UAV experiment.

In this paper we present a system's view of the ANSER project. Section 2 will first introduce the fundamental concepts of both DDF and SLAM. In section 3 the UAVs are presented. Both the navigation and terrain sensors will be presented in section 4. The communication framework CommLibX, and real-time multi UAV simulator, mission control and ground station systems will be presented in section 5. This is an important part of the system since it is used to test all electronic hardware, software modules, their interoperatability and algorithms implemented in the system [5]. Finally the conclusion and further work is provided in section 6.

2 Decentralised Data Fusion

A Decentralised Data Fusion (DDF) system comprises of a network of sensor nodes each incorporating a sensor together with local processing and communication capabilities. Each node runs its own local data fusion algorithm and communicates information to other nodes in its neighbourhood. Nodes fuse incoming information with local estimates to produce a global picture of the state of the world. This strategy results in a network of sensor nodes in which the fusion process is decentralised. A general decentralised data fusion system can be characterised by three basic constraints [6]:

1. There is no single central fusion centre and no node should be central to the operation of the network.
2. There is no common communications facility - communications must be kept on a strictly node-to-node basis.
3. Each node has knowledge only of its immediate neighbours - there is no global knowledge of the network topology.

These constraints combine to ensure that there is no single element that is critical to the operation of the network. If any node or communication link should fail, the result is a gradual degradation in network performance rather than catastrophic failure.

The conventional structure for multi-sensor systems requires that all sensors send observation information back to a single central point for fusion. This has some advantages in that all information is known at a single point and so, in principle, fusion is based on the best possible information. However centralised structures also have a number of undesirable characteristics: Using a centralised resource for fusion creates both computational and communication bottlenecks as the system increases in size. This limits the ability of a system to scale to large numbers of sensors. A second key problem is that a central fusion site makes the whole system vulnerable to catastrophic failure of the fusion processor.

The decentralised system architecture implemented in this research [8] offers a number of advantages over conventional centralised or hierarchical architectures:

- **Scalability:** Eliminating the central fusion centre and any common communication facility ensures that the system is scalable as there are no limits imposed by centralised computational bottlenecks or lack of communication bandwidth.
- **Survivability:** Ensuring that no node is central and that no global knowledge of the network topology is required for fusion means that the system can be made survivable to the on-line loss (or addition) of sensing nodes and to dynamic changes in the network structure.
- **Modularity:** As all fusion processes must take place locally at each sensor site and no global knowledge of the network is required *a priori*, nodes can be constructed and programmed in a modular fashion.

2.1 Decentralised Applications

The DDF architecture is initially applied to the problem of tracking multiple ground targets using a network of airborne sensing platforms [11]. The objective of this problem is for the sensing nodes on each platform to build a composite global picture of targets in an environment using both local sensor observations and information communicated from other platforms in a decentralised manner. This is accomplished by integrating the terrain sensing payload on each aircraft with local processing and communication facilities to form a sensing node. A decentralised network of these nodes can then be formed, where the sensing nodes communicate directly in terms of target information to have a local estimate using global information. This communication has a number of positive effects:

- The extra information available to nodes through the communicated information improves the quality of the estimates.
- The robustness of a DDF architecture to 'node failure' is equivalent in the airborne tracking problem to 'aircraft failure'. If an aircraft is damaged or

destroyed, the information it gathered is not lost in a DDF network as it has been communicated to all other vehicles.
- The picture of all targets in a region is available to all aircraft in the DDF network as soon as any single platform visits that area. Aircraft can therefore have a picture of targets in an area that they have not yet visited.

Simultaneous Localisation and Map building (SLAM) for a robotic platform is a process of building a map of the surrounding environment while simultaneously using this map to localise [2]. The DDF architecture is used for decentralising SLAM.

The UAV uses a terrain sensor to make relative observations to stationary features or landmarks in the environment. As these observations are relative to the vehicle, an error in the platform pose results in a corresponding error in the landmark location. Over time, the entire map becomes correlated through the motion of the vehicle. For a single platform using the SLAM algorithm to decrease its location uncertainty, it must revisit features it has seen previously. However, with multiple platforms it is possible to share information and so generate a more accurate map and location estimate. Indeed, if certain platforms are directed to revisit shared features, then there will be significant location estimate improvements for all platforms.

3 The UAV

The Brumby MkIII UAVs are the robotic platforms used in the ANSER project. The Brumby UAV has been developed over the past six years at The University of Sydney, Australia. In order to meet an increasing payload weight requirement for the research projects, the Brumby UAVs have incorporated a number of changes. Currently we have three different models as shown in table 1. They are designed as test beds for various navigation algorithms, payload sensors and real time distributed data fusion. They offer a large payload volume, a speed range of 55-100Knots, a payload mass of over 13kg and over 1 hour of flight capability.

The Brumby UAVs are delta winged, pusher aircrafts. The pusher design leaves a clear space in the front for sensors which provides unobstructed view. The Brumby airframe is modular in construction to enable the replacement or upgrade of each component. Each payload position is provided with 24V power and an Ethernet and/or CAN (Controller Area Network) connection to the other onboard systems. The airframe is also capable of carrying a specially designed gimballed scanner that enable radar or laser sensors to be scanned across the ground.

4 Sensors

The sensor are grouped as either flight or payload sensors. Flight sensors provide data to be used to monitor and control the UAV. Flight sensors include an Inertial Measurement Module (IMU), Global Positioning Sensor (GPS). Payload

Table 1. Brumby Mk I-II-III UAV specifications

	Mk I	Mk II	Mk III
MTOW	25kg	30kg	45kg
Wing Span	2.3m	2.8m	2.9m
Engine	74cc	80cc	150cc
Power	5Hp	5.5Hp	16Hp
Max Speed	100 Knots	100 Knots	100 Knots

sensors are those used for target detection from the terrain for DDF target tracking and SLAM. Each payload sensor has its own PC104+ based processing and ethernet and/or CAN based communication module.

Fig. 1. Optionally either MMW radar or Laser/Vision payloads can be mounted in the nose cone of the Brumby Mark-III UAV. The vision camera is located under the fuselage

Vision Payload: Each UAV is equiped with a vision payload which is capable of detecting artificial targets on the ground. The vision payload consists of a 266MHz PC104+ computer with frame grabber . An image stream of size 384x288 @ 50Hz is obtained by extracting the odd and even fields of an interlaced stream of size 384x576 @ 25Hz. For DDF picture compilation flights, the vision node must assimilate both the navigation solution of the platform and raw sensor data into the information matrix and vectors, for use with the information filter as defined in [7].

Laser/Vision Payload: Laser/Vision payload which is also called a Secondary Imaging System (SIS) consists of a laser range finder and a complete vision system. Although the vision payload would provide accurate bearing measurement, its range measurement is very poor if the target size is known. In this payload, the vision system is suplemented with the laser range finder for accurate range measurement.

Radar Payload: It is important for DDF that at least one of the platform carries a sensor which returns Range, Bearing and Elevation (RBE) of the ground targets [12][9]. We have developed a 77GHz millimeter wave radar operating on a frequency modulated continuous-wave (FMCW) principle. The whole MMW radar unit is mounted on an attitude-stabilizing gimbal to keep the grazing angle of the radar beam fixed. The gimbal has two axes of freedom; one along the roll and the other on the pitch axis. The gimbal is controlled in real time to counter the motion of the UAV on these axes [4]. The scanning mirror on top of the gimbal reflects the transmitted and received signals to and from the horn antenna of the MMW radar. Received radar signals are processed by dual ADSP-21060 SHARC Digital Signal Processor (DSP) for real-time feature extraction [4] [10].

5 System Software Components

CommLibX: The high dynamics nature of the UAV requires both real-time monitoring and control software systems. Each UAV carries a PC104+ based Flight Control Computer (FCC) performing real-time navigation, guidance and flight control. The FCC uses the QNX real-time kernel and communicates with the ground control station via wireless radio modem and with other on board computer nodes via ethernet and/or CAN based local network. UAVs communicate between each other via radio ethernet. The sensor nodes run different OS; Vision and Laser/Vision nodes use Linux while radar uses WinNT. This variety of OS is due to availability of driver support that was available. As communication appears to be a challenging problem, it is solved with a novel communication framework, *CommLibX*. CommLibX is developed to address OS and transport layer independent multi channel real-time communication [5].

RMUS: Every software and hardware unit running in the UAV experiments must be tested thoroughly. Individual of-line testing of these units may not be sufficient. Their real-time inter and intra-operateability with real hardware must be tested. A *Real-time Multi-UAV Simulator* (RMUS) has been developed to address these problems. RMUS can be used both in real-time hardware-in-the-loop (HIL) and off-line simulations. It is a flexible distributed simulation architecture designed to address multi-UAV experiments. Details of the RMUS architecture, CommLibX framework and their applications in various multi-UAV experiments can be found in [5].

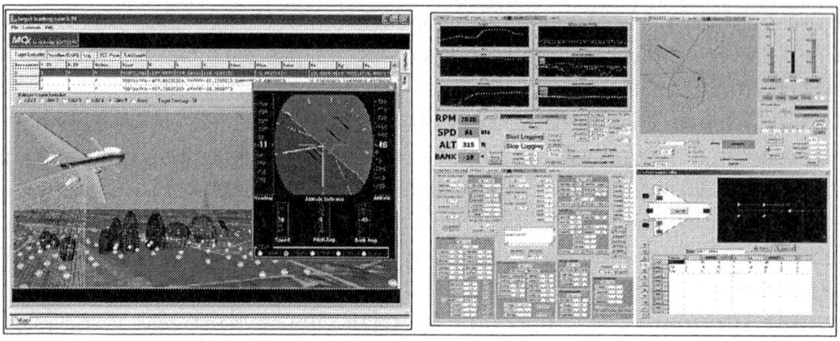

Fig. 2. Mission Control System (left) has been developed on the RMUS architecture. Ground Station System (right) allows real-time display and log all telemetered UAV data.

MCX: RMUS architecture allows us to develop real-time on-line applications. The *Mission Control System*(MCX) is an RMUS based application which is used to monitor multiple UAV locations, attitude, paths, sensor frustums and target location estimates in real-time. The logging and replay function along with the interactive 3D display on MCX makes it possible to look at the scene from any angle before, during and after the flight tests.

Ground Station: Each UAV has its own *Ground Station* (GS) system in the ground control center. The purpose of the GS is to display and log all telemetered data of its associated UAV in real-time. GS with its utility programs can replay the logged flight for further off-line analysis of the flight mission and UAV performance.

6 Conclusion and Future Work

This paper has presented a summary of the DDF architecture, picture compilation and SLAM algorithms and some of the major system components of the ANSER project.

In the current phase of the project, five Brumby Mk III UAVs have been built and tested. So far more than 40 successful flight missions have been performed for data collection. We also successfully demonstrated real-time DDF picture compilation on multi-UAVs. Multi-UAV SLAM is demonstrated on real-time simulation with real flight data.

Demonstration of real-time multi-UAV SLAM is scheduled for late 2003. Four UAVs will be flown simultaneously for this demonstration. The Brumby UAV airframe development continues for new models for larger and heavier payload capacity. In the RMUS environment we are currently testing the application of the DDF architecture for decentralised multi-UAV coordinated control.

Acknowledgements. The authors wish to thank BAE Systems for their support in providing funding and systems engineering towards this project. Also, thanks to Alan Trinder from ACFR for his assistance with the UAV construction.

References

1. Gamini Dissanayake, Hugh Durrant-Whyte, and Tim Bailey. A computationally efficient solution to the simultaneous localisation and map building (slam) problem. In *IEEE International Conference on Robotics and Automation 2000*, pages 1009–1014, San Francisco CA, 2000.
2. M. Dissanayake, P. Newman, H. Durrant-Whyte, S. Clark, and M. Csorba. An experimental and theoretical investigation into simultaneous localisation and map building. In *6th International Symposium on Experimental Robotics*, pages 171–180, Sydney, 1999.
3. Hugh Durrant-Whyte, Somajyoti Majumder, Marc de Battista, and Steve Scheding. A bayesian algorithm for simultaneous localisation and map building. In *10th International Symposium of Robotics Research - ISRR 2001*, Lorne, Victoria, Australia, 2001.
4. Ali Haydar Göktoğan, Graham Brooker, , and Salah Sukkarieh. A compact millimeter wave radar sensor for unmanned air vehicles. In *Field and Service Robotics, FSR'03*, Lake Yamanaka, Japan, 2003.
5. Ali Haydar Göktoğan, Eric Nettleton, Matthew Ridley, and Salah Sukkarieh. Real time multi-uav simulator. In *IEEE International Conference on Robotics and Automation*, Taipei, Taiwan, 2003.
6. S. Grime and H. Durrant-Whyte. Data fusion in decentralized sensor networks. *Control Engineering Practice*, 2, No 5:849–863, 1994.
7. E. Nettleton and H. Durrant-Whyte. Delayed and asequent data in decentralised sensing networks. In G.T. McKee and P.S. Schenker, editors, *Sensor Fusion and Decentralised Control in Robotic Systems IV*, volume Proc. SPIE, pages 1–9, 2001.
8. E. Nettleton, H. Durrant-Whyte, and S. Sukkarieh. A robust architecture for decentralised data fusion. In *International Conference on Advanced Robotics*, 2003.
9. Eric W. Nettleton, Hugh F. Durrant-Whyte, Peter W. Gibbens, and Ali Haydar Göktoğan. Multiple platform localisation and map building. In G.T. McKee Schenker and P.S., editors, *Sensor Fusion and Decentralised Control in Robotic Stystems III*, volume 4196, pages 337–347, Boston,USA, 2000.
10. Matthew Ridley, Ali Haydar Göktoğan, Graham Brooker, and Salah Sukkarieh. Sensor nodes for decentralised data fusion with multiple uninhabited air vehicles. In *The 2nd International Workshop on Information Processing in Sensor Networks (IPSN'03)*, Palo Alto, California, USA, 2003.
11. S. Sukkarieh, E. Nettleton, J. Kim, M. Ridley, A. Goktoğan, and H. Durrant-Whyte. The ANSER project - multi-UAV data fusion. *IJRR (to appear)*, 2003.
12. Salah Sukkarieh, Ali Haydar Göktoğan, Jong-Hyuk Kim, Eric Nettleton, Jeremy Randle, Matthew Ridley, Stuart Wishart, and Hugh Durrant-Whyte. Cooperative data fusion and control amongst multiple uninhabited air vehicles. In *ISER 2002 Seventh International Symposium on Experimental Robotics*, 2002.
13. Salah Sukkarieh, Eric Nettleton, Jong-Hyuk Kim, Matthew Ridley, Ali Haydar Göktoğan, and Hugh Durrant-Whyte. The anser project-multi uav data fusion. *Internatioal Journal of Robotics Research*, 2002.

The Modular Genetic Algorithm: Exploiting Regularities in the Problem Space

Ozlem O. Garibay, Ivan I. Garibay, and Annie S. Wu

University of Central Florida
School of Electrical Engineering and Computer Science
P.O. Box 162362, Orlando, FL 32816-2362
{ozlem,igaribay,aswu}@cs.ucf.edu

Abstract. We introduce the modular genetic algorithm (MGA). The modular genetic algorithm is a search algorithm designed for a class of problems pervasive throughout nature and engineering: problems with modularity and regularity in their solutions. We hypothesize that genetic search algorithms with explicit mechanisms to exploit regularity and modularity on the problem space would not only outperform conventional genetic search, but also scale better for this problem class. In this paper we present experimental evidence in support of our hypothesis. In our experiments, we compare a limited version of the modular genetic algorithm with a canonical genetic algorithm (GA) applied to the checkerboard-pattern discovery problem for search spaces of sizes 2^{32}, 2^{128}, and 2^{512}. We observe that the MGA significantly outperforms the GA for high complexities. More importantly, while the performance of the GA drops 22.50% when the complexity of the problem increases, the MGA performance drops only 11.38%. These results indicate that the MGA has a strong scalability property for problems with regularity and modularity in their solutions.

1 Introduction

According to the NFL theorem (Wolpert & Macready 1995), a search algorithm that outperforms every other on every problem does not exist. What does exist, however, are algorithms that are very good for a particular class of problems. Modularity, or the concept of forming and reusing high-level building blocks from lower-level building blocks, is pervasive in nature: atoms form molecules, molecules are the basic components of cellular organization, cells form organs, and so on. Most importantly, modularity and regularity are also present in the way we organize our ideas—books are made of chapters, chapters of paragraphs and paragraphs of sentences—; and the way we conceive solutions—designs are made of components and subcomponents; computational systems are made of programs, programs are made of reusable routines, etc. Due to the pervasiveness of modularity and regularity in the way that nature self-organizes and also in the way that we tend to engineer solutions to problems, we believe that it is important to investigate algorithms that explicitly work on modular and regular search spaces.

A. Yazici and C. Şener (Eds.): ISCIS 2003, LNCS 2869, pp. 584–591, 2003.

The concept of modularity has been studied extensively in complex systems design and analysis in general, and in evolutionary computation in particular (Happel & Murre 1994, O'Reilly 1996, Angeline & Pollack 1993, Boers & Kuiper 1992, Wagner 1995, Angeline & Pollack 1994, DeJong & Oates 2002). Recently, there has been a surge of interest in modularity in the evolutionary computation community as a way to improve the "innovativeness" and the scalability of evolutionary search. For instance see (Garibay & Wu 2003, Koza, Streeter & Keane 2003, Hu, Goodman et al. 2003). In our perspective, modularity not only implies the hierarchical organization of components from one level of complexity into the next, but also the ability to freely reuse components. It is this component reuse that gives rise to regular and repetitive organizational patterns.

Evolutionary algorithms, such as genetic algorithm are thought to be good at processing building blocks to assemble solutions (Holland 1975, Goldberg 1989). In this paper, we introduce an evolutionary algorithm explicitly designed to work in highly regular and modular search spaces. We call this algorithm the *Modular Genetic Algorithm* (MGA). We envision the MGA as an algorithm that extends the GA's ability to work with building blocks by explicitly encouraging the formation of modules and the reuse of these modules. To this end, our MGA design accounts for two important features: the use of a representation that exploits regular and modular search spaces, and the use of mechanisms for automatic module discovery and encapsulation. The MGA implemented for this paper uses only the first feature. We leave the automatic module discovery and encapsulation for future work on the MGA.

The objective of this paper is to compare the performance and scalability of evolutionary algorithms with and without modularity-aware representations when applied to a modular and regular problem: the checkerboard-pattern discovery problem. We hypothesize that for a regular and modular problem space, evolutionary algorithms with explicit mechanism to handle regularity and modularity should outperform evolutionary algorithms not explicitly designed to do so. More importantly, we also expect that for these kinds of problems, modularity-aware algorithms scale to higher complexities better than algorithms with no modularity-awareness. As an initial test of our hypothesis, we compare the simple GA with no explicit modularity with an MGA with a representation explicitly designed to exploit regularities on the problem space. We compare these algorithms on three instances of the checkerboard-pattern discovery problem of increasing complexity. Experimental studies show that our hypothesis holds true for this problem. In effect, we observe that the MGA significantly outperforms the GA for higher complexity intances of our test problem. While the performance of the GA drops 22.50% when the complexity of the problem increases, the MGA performance drops only 11.38%. These results seem to indicate that the MGA has a strong scalability property for problems with regularity and modularity on their solutions.

2 The Checkerboard-Pattern Discovery Problem

After a brief survey in the evolutionary computation community, we were unable to find a widely accepted benchmark problem for algorithms that exploit regularity and modularity. As a result we design our own: the *scalable checkerboard-pattern discovery problem*. The objective of this problem is to discover the target pattern of white and black squares arranged in a checkerboard of size $N \times M$. The fitness evaluation for a candidate solution is simply the number of correctly matched (white or black) squares. A solution with a perfect match achieves a maximum fitness of $N \times M$ while a solution with no matches to the target has a fitness of zero. In Figure 1 (A) and (B), we see an example of a target and a candidate solution with 20 wrongly placed squares and a sub-optimal fitness of $8 \times 16 - 20 = 108$. Figure 1 (C) and (D) shows and example of a target and a candidate solution with a perfect match. We designed this simple problem to explicitly provide an environment rich in regularity and modularity (handcrafted patterns) to be our scalable initial test problem for the Modular GA as seen in Figure 1. We can scale up the complexity of these problems by simply increasing

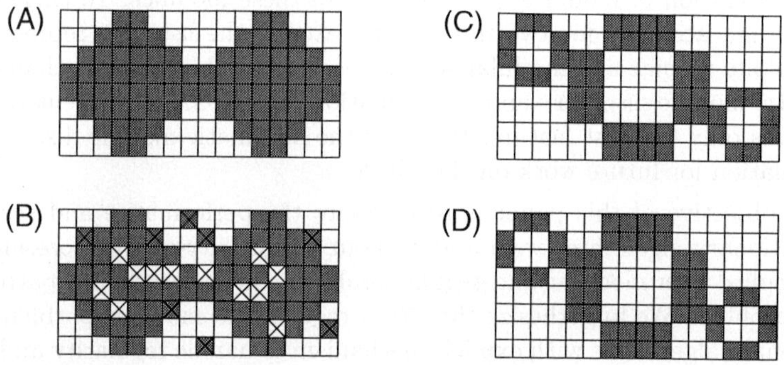

Fig. 1. Examples of target **(A)** and candidate **(B)** solutions for a checkerboard-pattern discovery problem of size 8×16. The fitness of the candidate solution is 108 because there are 20 un-matched squares (marked with an X). The maximum fitness possible for this instance is $8 \times 16 = 128$. Target **(C)** and candidate with optimal solution **(D)** for a checkerboard-pattern discovery problem of size 8×16.

the size of the checkerboard. We can increase the complexity but keep constant the amount of regularity by keeping the number of components in each pattern constant. Figure 2 shows the three instances of the checkerboard-pattern discovery problem used on this paper: 4x8(A), 8x16(B), and 16x32(C). The search space for this three problems increase exponentially in size 2^{32}(A), 2^{128}(B), and 2^{512}(C), while the amount of regularity on the pattern is kept constant: four black and four white square areas.

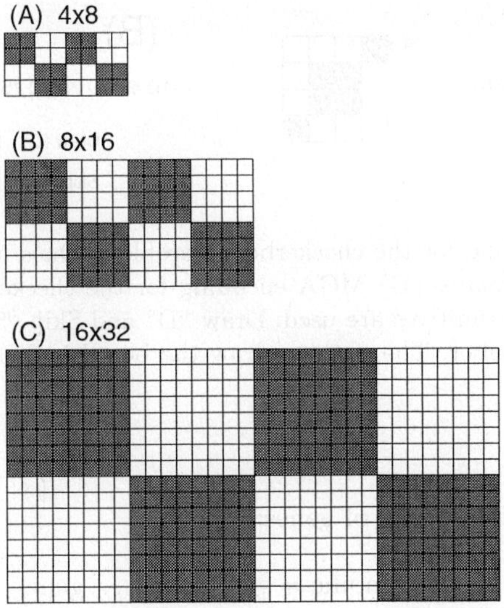

Fig. 2. The target pattern for the checkerboard-pattern discovery problem used in all experiments on this paper. This pattern is scaled up in size 4x8(A), 8x16(B), and 16x32(C), to increase the complexity of the problem while keeping the pattern constant: four black and four white big squares. The search space's sizes increase exponentially: 2^{32}(A), 2^{128}(B), and 2^{512}(C).

3 Comparing Representations with and without Explicit Modularity Awareness

3.1 No Modularity: Genetic Algorithm

As an example of an evolutionary algorithm with no explicit mechanisms to exploit modularity on the search space we use a simple binary genetic algorithm. The encoding of the problem is shown in Figure 3 (A). We represent each square of the board with one bit: one for black and zero for white.

3.2 Repetitive Modularity: Modular Genetic Algorithm

We consider two features to be key to for the MGA's success: it needs a representation that exploits regular and modular problem spaces, and it needs mechanisms for automatic module discovery and encapsulation. In this paper we study an MGA with only the first feature. A simple implementation of such representation is described below.

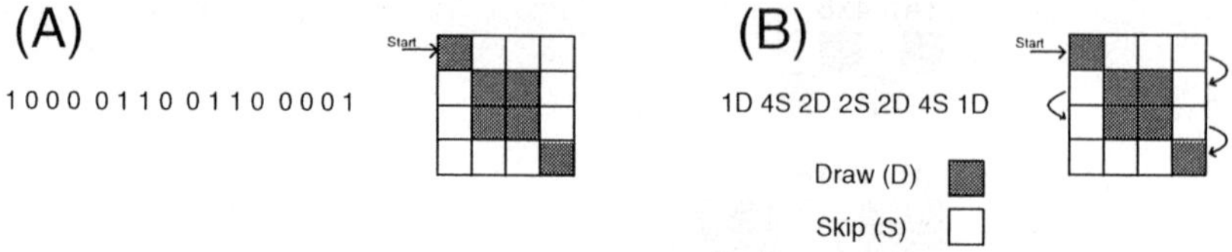

Fig. 3. **(A)** GA encoding for the checkerboard problem. Ones indicate black squares; zeros indicate white squares.**(B)** MGA encoding for the checkerboard problem. Two functional predefined primitives are used: Draw "D" and Skip "S". They are preceded by their repetition number. The path to draw the board is fixed as indicated by the arrows.

A MGA genome is a string of genes:

$$\text{MGA-Genome} = \text{gene}_1\text{gene}_2 \dots \text{gene}_i$$

with each gene being of the form:

$$gene_i = \langle \text{number-of-repetitions}_i, \text{function}_i() \rangle$$

and gene_i being interpreted as:

$$gene_i = \underbrace{\text{function}_i()\text{function}_i() \dots \text{function}_i()}_{\text{number-of-repetitions}_i}$$

This is a functional representation with each gene being prefixed by its gene expression value. The gene expression value specifies the number of times a gene is expressed or executed. This representation requires a set of initial predefined functions. For the checkerboard-pattern discovery problem, the set of initial functions is $\{D(), S()\}$. The *draw* function, D(), paints the current square black then moves to the next square. The *skip* function, S(), skips to the next square without painting any square. Functions are prefixed by their number of repetitions. For example the string $2D4S1D2S$ is interpreted as $DDSSSSDSS$, where 2D = DD, 4S = SSSS, and so on. The path to follow in the checkerboard is predefined, hence there is no need for directional primitives such as right() or left(). As a result, the draw() and skip() primitives are sound and complete for our checkerboard-pattern discovery problem. A MGA representation of the checkerboard problem is shown in Figure 3 (B).

4 Experiments

4.1 Objectives

We compare the GA with the Modular GA and observe if the simple MGA implementation has a positive impact on the search performance and scalability for the checkerboard-pattern discovery problem. We perform three experiments comparing this two algorithms with the following problem sizes: 4×8, 8×16, and 16×32. The target pattern for all the runs is the same and it is shown in Figure 2. The following parameters are kept constant throughout all the experiments: 20 runs, two-point crossover, crossover rate of 0.7, mutation rate of 0.001, standard fitness proportional selection, and a population size of 1000. Each experiment was run until population convergence: 500 generations for the 4×8 board size, 1000 generations for the 8×16, and 2000 generations for the 16×32. Initialization is performed at random: a random binary string for the GA and random string of genes for the MGA. The GA uses a standard binary alphabet. Each random gene for the MGA is a repetition number randomly picked from the interval $[0, N/2]$ (for a problem of size $N \times 2N$). This random repetition number is paired with a symbol randomly picked from the MGA alphabet $\{S, D\}$. The GA uses bit-flip mutation. Mutation for the MGA changes both parts of the gene: the number of repetitions and the symbol from its alphabet. Crossover for the GA is canonical, for the MGA crossover is allowed only to act between genes with no gene splitting allowed.

4.2 Results

The performance is measured as the best fitness obtained by an algorithm on its final generation averaged over 20 runs. Fitness is computed as described on Section 2. Complexity is measured in terms of the size of the space being searched by the algorithms. Figure 4 shows that the GA and the MGA perform similarly for problems of size 4×8, 8×16, but the MGA significantly outperforms the GA on the high complexity case: problem of size 16×32. Figure 5 plots the performance versus complexity. We observe that, for the GA, this curve drops sharply in the last increase in complexity, while, for the MGA, the curve decreases more steadily. This plot indicates that the MGA scales better than the GA for this problem. In fact, while GA performance decreases by 22.50% from the 4×8 to the 16×32 problem, the MGA performance decreases by only half that amount, 11.38%, as shown in Table 1.

Table 1. Percentages of performance drops for the GA and MGA as the complexity of the problem is increased. GA and MGA both drop their performances around 3.5% on a increase of search space size from $2^{4\times 8}$ to $2^{8\times 16}$. Interestingly, for the increase of search space size from $2^{4\times 8}$ to $2^{16\times 32}$ the GA drops in performance a substantial 22% while the MGA drop only around half of that amount: 11%.

	Performance Drop (% of fitness decrease)	
Complexity increase (in search space size)	**GA**	**MGA**
from $2^{4\times 8}$ to $2^{8\times 16}$	3.48%	3.68%
from $2^{4\times 8}$ to $2^{16\times 32}$	22.50%	11.38%

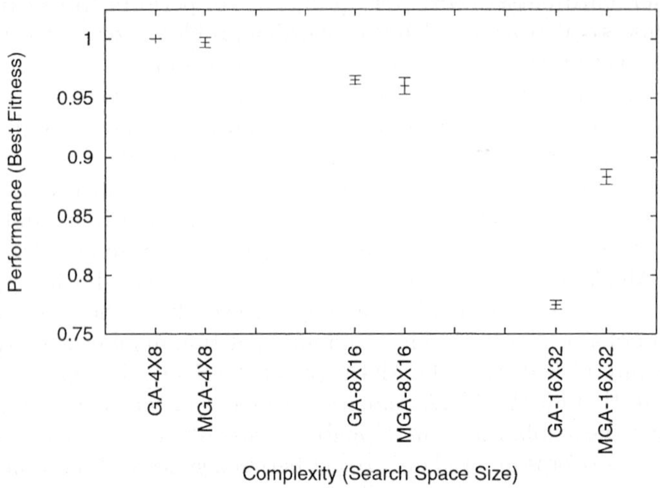

Fig. 4. GA vs. MGA performance comparison I: performance is measured as the best fitness of the last generation averaged over 20 runs and shown with 95% confidence intervals. (Left) GA vs. MGA on the checkerboard-pattern discovery problem of size 4×8. (Center) GA vs. MGA for the same problem size of 8×16 and (Right) for size 16×32. MGA and GA have equivalent performance for low and medium complexity, but MGA significantly outperform GA on the high complexity case.

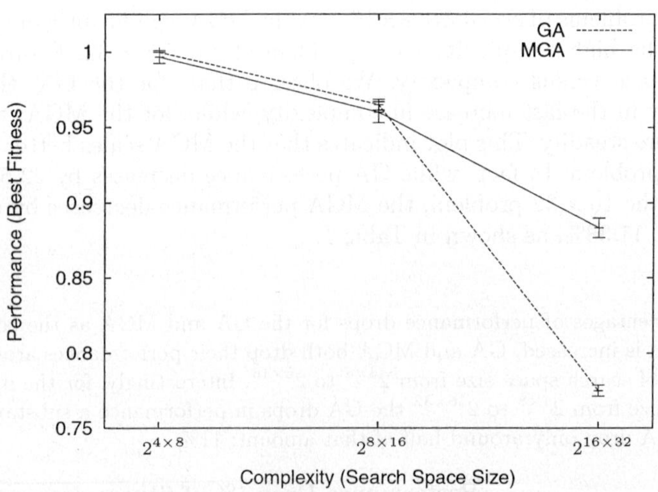

Fig. 5. GA vs. MGA performance comparison II: performance is measured as the best fitness of the last generation averaged over 20 runs and shown with 95% confidence intervals. The performance of the GA decreases sharply as complexity increases. The performance of the MGA decreases less dramatically. This graphic suggests that the MGA scales better than the GA for the checkerboard-pattern discovery problem.

5 Conclusions

We introduce the *Modular Genetic Algorithm* in this paper. This algorithm is designed for problem spaces with a high degree of modularity and regularity. We hypothesize that the MGA will outperform conventional genetic search and scale better for the class of problems with significant degree of modularity and regularity on their solutions. We provide experimental results that support our hypothesis on a well defined problem: the checkerboard-pattern discovery problem. Our results show that the MGA significantly outperforms a basic GA for the highest complexity case tested (16×32). For the lower complexity cases (4×8 and 8×16) their performance are comparable. These results indicate that the MGA scales much better than the GA for this problem class. We find these first results very encouraging and revealing. A simple change from a binary representation that exhaustively enumerates every element of the solution being described, to a more functional representation geared towards creating modules and exploiting repetitions can bring a large benefit in terms of both performance and scalability to the evolutionary search.

References

Angeline, P. J. & Pollack, J. (1993), Evolutionary module adquisition, *in* 'Proceedings of the second annual conference on evolutionary programming', pp. 154–163.

Angeline, P. J. & Pollack, J. (1994), Coevolving high-level representations, *in* 'Proceedings of Artificial Life III', pp. 55–71.

Boers, E. J. W. & Kuiper, H. (1992), Biological metaphors and the design of modular artificial neural networks, Master's thesis, Leiden University.

DeJong, E. D. & Oates, T. (2002), A coevolutionary approach to representation development, *in* 'Proc. of the ICML-2002 WS on develop. of repres.', p. ??

Garibay, I. I. & Wu, A. S. (2003), Cross-fertilization between proteomics and computational synthesis, *in* '2003 AAAI Spring Symposium Series', pp. 67–74.

Goldberg, D. E. (1989), *Genetic algorithms in search, optimization, and machine learning*, Addison Wesley.

Happel, B. L. M. & Murre, J. M. J. (1994), 'The design and evaluation of modular neural network architectures', *Neural Networks* **7**, 985–1004.

Holland, J. H. (1975), *Adaptation in Natural and Artificial Systems*, University of Michigan Press, Ann Arbor, MI.

Hu, J., Goodman, E. et al. (2003), HFC: a continuing EA framework for scalable evolutionary synthesis, *in* '2003 AAAI Spring Symposium Series', pp. 106–113.

Koza, J., Streeter, M. & Keane, M. (2003), Automated synthesis by means of genetic programming, *in* '2003 AAAI Spring Symposium Series', pp. 138–145.

O'Reilly, U. (1996), Investigating the generality of automatically defined functions, *in* 'Proceedings of the first annual conference on genetic programming', pp. 351–356.

Wagner, G. P. (1995), Adaptation and the modular design of organisms, *in* 'Proceedings of the european conference on artificial intelligence', pp. 317–328.

Wolpert, D. H. & Macready, W. G. (1995), No free lunch theorems for search, Technical Report SFI-TR-95-02-010, The Santa Fe Institute, Santa Fe, NM.

A Realistic Success Criterion for Discourse Segmentation

Meltem Turhan Yöndem and Göktürk Üçoluk

Dept of Computer Eng.,
Middle East Tech. Univ. 06531
Ankara, Turkey
{mturhan,ucoluk}@ceng.metu.edu.tr

Abstract. In this study, compared to the existing one, a more realistic evaluation method for discourse segmentation is introduced. It is believed that discourse segmentation is a fuzzy task [Pas96]. Human subjects may agree on different discourse boundaries, with high agreement among them. In the existing method a threshold value is calculated and sentences that marked by that many subjects are decided as real boundaries and other marks are not been considered. Furthermore automatically discovered boundaries, in case of being misplaced, are treated as a strict failure, disregarding the proximity wrt to the human found boundaries. The proposed method overcomes these shortcomings, and credits the fuzziness of the human subjects' decisions as well as tolerates misplacements of the automated discovery. The proposed method is tunable from crisp/harsh to fuzzy/tolerant on human decision as well as automated discovery handling.

1 Introduction

This study is about evaluation of the success of programs that divides large volumes of text into a certain number of utterances that form coherent units called *Discourse Segments*. It is widely accepted that discourse is structured. Many experiments support this statement [Gro92,Gro86,Hir93,Lit95,Man88, Pol88,Web91]. Naive subjects also agree on the discourse boundaries of a given text.

The first step is to represent the segment boundary information decided by human subjects in a natural way. It is quite a common technique to ask a group of subjects to read a given text and then indicate the sentences where a new context (discourse) starts. Following this, usually a statistical analysis of the results is carried out to decide whether there is an agreement among the subjects about each candidate boundary. Then, having the boundaries at hand, computer generated boundaries are tested against them, and by this way a decision about the quality of the computer segmentation is made.

Most of the current works use crisp methods in deciding about the success of the boundary discovery. This, of course leads to non realistic evaluations where

A. Yazici and C. Şener (Eds.): ISCIS 2003, LNCS 2869, pp. 592–600, 2003.

near-miss cases receive the same discrediting as complete misses. Furthermore, the fuzziness steaming from disagreements among human subjects are also not handled. There exist a minor number of previous work that pinpoint this issue and propose solutions [Bee97,Pev94]. This work proposes a new evaluation scheme claiming to be a solution to all such aspects.

2 Discourse Segmentation

The hypothetical line between the discourse segments is named as *discourse boundary*. The following example is a portion of some Turkish corpus used and the human subjects' decision about the boundaries. *(Leading smilies before each sentence reflect the count of agreement and intend to aid the visualization of where the boundaries are.)*

Emine bir aralık bu oyundan usandı. (marked as a boundary by 0 subjects)
After some time Emine got bored of this game.
Kamer'in kucağından inip taşlığın sonundaki bahçeye koştu. (0 subject)
Getting from Kamer's lap, she run to the garden at the end of the stone courtyard.
☺☺☺☺ İstanbul'un Kıztaşı taraflarında dededen kalma bir konaktı. (4 subjects)
It was a mansion in İstanbul by Kıztaşı, inherited from grandfather.
Annesi, babası, ağabeyi bir tarafta, teyzesi, eniştesi,ablası öbür tarafta otururlardı. (0 subjects)
On one side her mother, father and brother, on the other side her aunt, uncle in law and sister used to lie.
Bahçe iki ailenindi. (0 subjects)
The garden belonged to the two families.
☺☺☺☺ Fakat hikayemizi anlattığımız sıralarda kadınlar erkekten kaçardı. (4 subjects)
But at the time we were telling our story, women used to run away from men.
☺ Bu, ne demek diyeceksin. (1 subjects)
what does this mean, you ask?
☺ Evet, sevgili küçük okuyucum, kadınlarla erkeklerin hayatları ayrı geçer, babalar, kardeşler ve çok yakınlarla ancak akşamları buluşulurdu. (1 subjects)
Yes, dear fellow reader, women and men lived life separately; it was only in the evenings that fathers, brothers and close relatives were met with.
Erkekler çoğu vakitlerini evin selamlık denilen bir bölümünde geçirirlerdi. (0 subjects)
Men used to spend most of their time in a part of the house called the selamlık.
Kadınların oturdukları bölümün adı haremdi. (0 subjects)
The part in which women used to live was called the harem.
Mutfak kapısı bahçeye açıldığından, üstelik aşçı da erkek olduğundan, kadınlardan pek oraya çıkan olmazdı. (0 subjects)
Since the kitchen door opened to the garden and also because the cook was a man, women did not usually enter there.
☺☺☺☺☺☺☺ Emine taflanlı yollarda koştu, bahçenin ortasındaki uzun servinin çevresini birkaç kere dolandı. (7 subjects)
Emine ran on the flowered roads, went around the tree in the middle of the garden a couple of times.
☺ Hava oldukça serindi. (1 subject)
It was quite chilly.
Aşçı Yaver ağa, mutfak kapısından başını uzatıtı. (0 subjects)
The cook Yaver ağa looked through the kitchen door.

3 Existing Evaluation Method

The method can be summerized as:

- Statistically determine what makes a human subjects' boundary decision reliable.

- Nominate all such reliable boundaries to be the *real boundaries.*
- Consider all boundaries discovered by the automated process that match exactly with real boundares as success points. Consider all other automaticaly discovered points as failures.

As the concept of reliable boundary is major to this method, it is worth to look into it in greater details. In the following subsection you will find the statistical procedure used so far in the existing method to discover the reliable boundaries.

3.1 Statistical Analysis: Cochran's Q Method

This section is a brief summary of the Cochran's Q method used to judge the agreement between the subjects on segment boundaries. Passonneau & Litman [Pas96,Pas97] used this method to judge their subject's agreement. The advantage of this method is that it gives the number of agreements necessary for a variable to be considered as the needed class, in this case a boundary. In order to find the number of agreements necessary, usually a partial Cochran's Q method is used.

In this kind of agreement calculation, the distribution of 1's (indicating there is a boundary before the sentence) and 0's (indicating there is no boundary before the sentence) in the subjects' responses are tested against the null hypothesis that the agreement was by chance. A good example for such a calculation of an English corpus can be found in [Pas96].

$$Q = \frac{k(k-1)\sum_{j=1}^{k}\left(G_j - \sum_{j=1}^{k} G_j^*\right)^2}{k\sum_{i=1}^{N} L_i - \sum_{i=1}^{N} L_i^2} \tag{1}$$

where

G_j : total number of boundaries in the jth column
G^* : mean of the G_j
L_i : total number of boundaries in the ith row

As an example, the Q calculated for a human segmentation of a corpus of 3691 sentences from which the above given extract was taken yielded a Q value of 16931. Chi-square values indicated that the result would be significant when Q had a value greater than 45. In this case, the Q value was greater than this value for $p = 0.001$, which means that the probability of accidental agreement among subjects is less than 0.001 for this narrative; that is, the agreement is so high that it could not occur by chance.

The next issue is to determine the required number of subject agreements to consider a sentence as a boundary. Similar to Passonneau [Pas96], and other similar studies do this by partitioning Q into distinct components for each possible G_i (0 to *total number of subjects*). The boundaries of any discourse can be decided by partially calculating Cochran's Q. By this way, it is statistically possible to determine the required minimal number of subjects to agree on a single sentence with accidental occurrence probability lesser than the calculated p value. All of the sentences marked as boundary by that minimal number or more human subjects will be considered as boundaries in subsequent analyses of the corpus.

3.2 Short Commings of the Existing Evaluation Method

The following cases explains the need for more realistic discourse segmentation evaluation method.

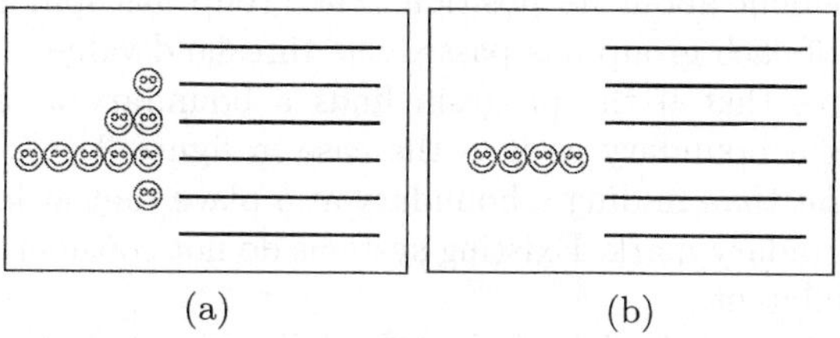

Fig. 1. A case of more information content

The existing evaluation method would consider sentence 4 (third bar in the figure) as a boundary in both figure 1 (a) and figure 1 (b). There will be no difference in the credits received for both cases if the automated boundary discovery hits/misses this boundary. But we believe that there is more clue about the boundary in (a) with respect to (b) since much more human subjects agreed that there is a boundary in that vicinity.

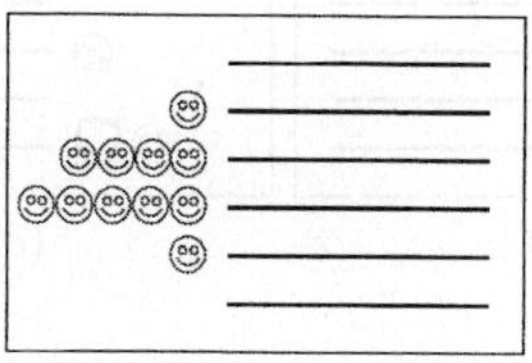

Fig. 2. A case of two peeks in the same vicinity

Consider the human subjects' agreements are as in the figure 2. If sentences 3 is accepted as a boundary then 4 is also a boundary. This is so because the existing system cares only about the number of subjects that marked a sentence as boundary to be above a constant threshold in order to accept it as a boundary. But, obviously there is only one boundary which the subjects could not come

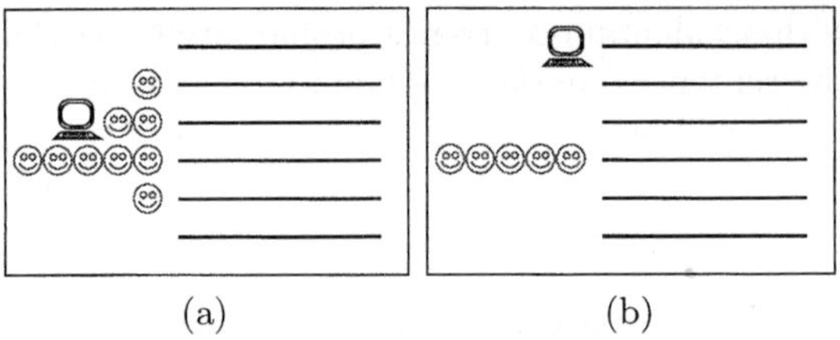

Fig. 3. A case of week vs. strong disagreement of human and computer

to a unified agreement about its position. The group has split into two groups where the count of each group has passed the threshold value.

We also believe that if the program finds a boundary at a sentence that no subject marks a boundary as it is the case in figure 3 (b), that should be considered different than finding a boundary at a place that at least some of the subjects put a boundary mark. Existing systems do not consider figure 3 (a) and Figure 3 (b) as different.

Summing up, we are basicly facing the following problems which are ill-treated in the existing systems:

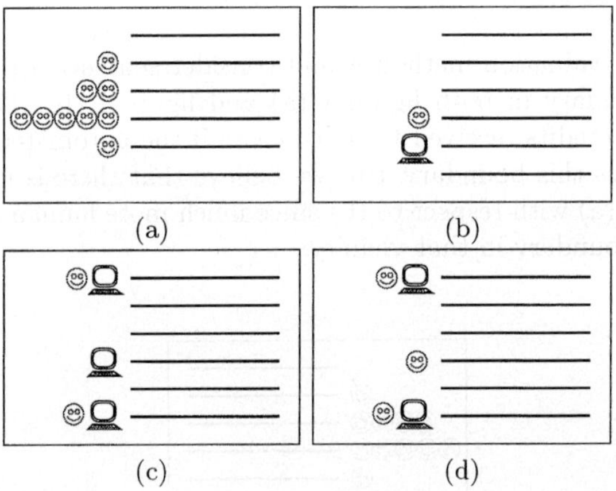

Fig. 4. Currently ill-treated cases

- The human segmenters do not always agree on a boundary (figure 4 (a))
- The automated segmentation process does not always hit the boundary even if it is crisp. (figure 4 (b))
- Occasionally the automated segmentation process may
  - create additional boundaries (we will name these as *fantom*) (figure 3) (figure 4 (c))
  - or omit the existence of a boundary. (figure 4)(figure 4 (d))

4 Proposed Evaluation Method

The idea is to set up a system which considers boundaries as islands of the distributions. We name these islands as *clusters*. A clustering algorithm based on statistical values determines the cluster formations in the results of the human subjects segmentation. The boundary decisions of the automated system which fall into the close vicinity of those clusters are considered to be a distribution about a single boundary (similar to the case of human subjects) and the quality of the judgment of the automated process is assessed by an distribution versus distribution evaluation.

Placements of phantom boundaries (claimed boundaries of the automated system which are not in the close vicinity of a cluster) are punished proportional to their distance from the nearest cluster.

The proposed system has adjustable parameters which control the crispness of this treatment. These are explained below, along with the algorithm.

4.1 Evaluation Algorithm

Let us assume the following:

- S human subject participated the segmentation.
- $h(i)$ is the discrete distribution value of the count of human subjects that agree there is a segmentation boundary at the end of line i of a given text. *If* $h(3)$ *is 5 this will mean that 5 individual have agreed that there is a segmentation boundary before the 5 th sentence.*
- $c(i)$ is the discrete boolean distribution, generated by a computer segmentation system, that yields *true* if the existence of a segmentation boundary claimed before line i of the text, and a $false$ if no boundary there exists. $c(3)$ *is true if the computer segmentation system is claiming the existence of a boundary before the 3rd sentence.*
- Let N number of sentence exist in the text.

4.2 Step 1: Determine Clusters of h

Clusters are subranges of [1,N]. We define

$$cluster_k \triangleq \langle cluster_k.lower, cluster_k.upper \rangle$$

So that

- $cluster$ denotes the count of clusters.
- $cluster_k.lower \leq cluster_k.upper$
- $cluster_k.upper < cluster_{k+1}.lower$ for $k = 1, \ldots, cluster$
- $(x \in cluster) \triangleq (cluster_k.lower \leq x \leq cluster_k.upper)$
- $\forall s,\ s \in cluster_k,\ similarity\_measure(i, cluster_k, h) < expected\_similarity(cluster_k, h)$

The last item, which defines the criterion of being a member of a cluster is based on two functions: *similarity_measure* and *expected_similarity*. Literally the second imposes a quantified level of similarity based on the portion of h falling into the cluster, and the first is a quantified measure of similarity of a candidate point with respect to a cluster.

This recursive definition of a cluster can be implemented in various ways. We propose a very simple $\mathcal{O}(n)$ algorithm based on two parameters:

chain_strength A maximum allowed value of $\mid s_1 - s_2 \mid$ such that $\forall s,\ s_1 < s < s_2,\ h(s) = 0$ and $s_{1,2} \in cluster_m$

minimal_peak An empirical value such that $\forall k \exists s, s \in cluster_k,\ s \geq$ minimal_peak.

Clustering algorithm

```
find_clusters(cluster, h, N, chain_weekness, minimal_peak) ←
{
  k ← 0
  s ← 1
  candidate_exists ← false
  for s ← 1...N do
    {
      if h(s) > 1 then
                    if ¬candidate_exists
                      then { candidate_exists ← TRUE
                             candidate_start ← s
                             weekness ← 0
                             has_minimal_peak ← (h(s) ≥ minimal_peak) }
                      else
                        if ¬has_minimal_peak ∧ h(s) ≥ minimal_peak
                          then has_minimal_peak ← TRUE
                          else
                            if weekness = chain_strength
                              then
                                if has_minimal_peak
                                  then { k ← k + 1
                                         cluster_k.lower ← candidate_start
                                         cluster_k.upper ← s − weekness }
                                  else candidate_exists ← FALSE
    }}
```

This algorithm is based on the assumption that at least a gap of size chain_strength exists between successive clusters. If that is not the case then a more elaborated clustering algorithm must be employed.

Note that is is quite possible that some of the human data gets ignored and does not become a part of a cluster.

4.3 Step 2: Evaluating Performance of c

Now having to hand the clusters we propose the following evaluation formula for the performance of a computer segmentation c:

$$success(c) = \mathcal{P}(c) - \mathcal{N}(c)$$

where $\mathcal{P}(c)$ is some calculated positive value awarding the success points and $\mathcal{N}(c)$ is some subtracted positive value punishing the failure points.

The following is proposed for $\mathcal{P}(c)$

$$\mathcal{P}(c) \triangleq \frac{1}{cluster \cdot S} \cdot \sum_{k=1}^{cluster} \sum_{s=low(k)}^{up(k)} \sum_{q=low(k)}^{up(k)} \frac{h(s) \cdot c(q)}{s - q + 1^{\alpha}}$$

Here $up(k)$ and $low(k)$ are either the limits of $cluster_k$ or a narrowed down version of them based on the statistical properties of the h distribution in the range of $cluster_k$. α is an exponent value in the range of $1 \leq \alpha \leq 2$ that we will name as *hardness*.

$$low(k) \triangleq \max(\mu_k - \beta\sigma_k, cluster_k.lower)$$
$$up(k) \triangleq \min(\mu_k + \beta\sigma_k, cluster_k.upper)$$

Where μ_k and σ_k are defined as the mean and standard deviation of the distribution in the range of $cluster_k$, respectively. β is a parameter that controls the *crispness* of the success evaluation. The bigger β is the fuzzier the evaluation gets.

For the punishment term that is going to be introduced for the cases of phantom boundaries the fallowing is proposed. This is a linear function of the distance of all phantom boundaries from the mid point of their nearest clusters. Assuming a minimal punishment of value P_{min} and a maximal of P_{max} the $\mathcal{N}(c)$ term can be expressed as

$$\mathcal{N}(c) \triangleq \sum_{k=1}^{cluster-1} \sum_{q=low(k)}^{up(k)} \frac{P_{min} - P_{max}}{2up(k)} \cdot 2q - low(k+1) - up(k) + P_{max}$$

5 Conclusion

We are proposing a more realistic approach to the evaluation of an automated discourse segmentation. The following are the problems of discourse segmentation which are not handled properly and delicately in the existing approach:

- Discourse segmentation is a fuzzy task and human responses should be kept as close to natural as possible without forcing this information to harsh and crisp representations. Not doing so causes information loss and extremely oversimplifies the evaluation.
- Automated segmentation is just an approximation to human intelligence. It is easily misled in weak circumstances especially in cases where human segmenters have not come to a full agreement, either.

A new method is proposed to overcome the injustice of the existing method. The new method has the following advantages:

- It is cognitively more similar to the human way of success evaluation.
- Almost all the boundary information marked by human subjects are kept and considered.
- A tunable metric for closeness of two distribution, namely the ones of human subjects and the automated process, is introduced. This is believed to increase the fairness of the evaluation.
- Phantom boundaries claimed by an automated process is punished by a severeness criterion which is based on the distance from the nearest real boundary.

References

[Bee97] Beeferman, D., 'A Probabilistic Error Metric for Segmentation Algorithms', *Unpublished notes*, `http://www.dougb.com/research.html`, 1997.

[Gro86] Grosz B., Sidner, C., 'Attention Intention and Structure of Discourse: A Review', *Computational Linguistics*, Vol. 12, No. 3, pp. 175–204, 1986.

[Gro92] B. Grosz, J. Hirschberg, 'Some Intentional Characteristics of Discourse Structure', *Proceedings of the International Conference on Spoken Language Processing*, pp. 429–432, 1992.

[Hir93] Hirschberg, J., Litman, D., 'Empirical Studies on the Disambiguation', *Computational Linguistics*, Vol. 19, No. 3, pp. 501–530, 1993.

[Lit95] Litman, D., J., Passonneau, R., 'Combining Multiple Knowledge Sources for Discourse Segmentation', *33rd Annual Meeting of Association for Computational Linguistics*, pp. 108–115, 1995.

[Man88] Mann, W.C., Thompson, S.A., 'Rhetorical Structure Theory: Towards a Functional Theory of Text Organization', Text, Vol. 8, pp. 243–281, 1988.

[Pas96] Passonneau, R., Litman, D.J., 'Empirical Analysis of Three Dimensions of Spoken Language: Segmentation, Coherence and Linguistic Device', ed. Hovy, E., Scott, D., Computational and Conversational Discourse, pp. 161–194, Springer Verlag, 1996.

[Pas97] Passonneau, R., Litman, D.J., 'Discourse Segmentation by Human and Automated Means', Computational Linguistics, Vol. 23, No. 1, 1997.

[Pev94] Pevzner, L., Hearst M., 'A Critique and Improvement of an Evaluation Metric for text Segmentation' *Computational Linguistics*, Vol. 21, No. 1, pp. 19–36, 1997.

[Pol88] Polanyi, L., 'A Formal Model of the Structure of Discourse', Journal of Pragmatics, Vol. 12, pp. 601–638, 1988.

[Web91] Webber, B. L., 'Structure and Ostension in the Interpretation of Discourse Deixis', Language and Cognitive Processes, Vol. 6, No. 2, pp. 107–135, 1991.

Nonlinear Filtering Design Using Dynamic Neural Networks with Fast Training

Yasar Becerikli

Kocaeli University, Computer Engineering Depart., Izmit Turkey
becer@kou.edu.tr

Abstract. This paper presents nonlinear filtering using dynamic neural networks (DNNs). In addition, the general usage of linear filtering structure is given. DNN which has a quasi-linear structure has been effectively used as a filter with fast training algorithm such as Levenberg-Marquardt method. The test results are shown that the performance of DNN as linear and nonlinear filters is satisfactory.

1 Introduction

The purpose of filtering is to remove undesired signals or equivalently to obtain desired signals. In this paper, the deterministic filters are studied. Real world signals are often nonlinear. These filters are especially very important in communication, modern control and nonlinear signal processing areas etc. In recent, nonlinear filtering is used some special application [1], [2]. A simple nonlinear filter (that means the dynamical perceptron) which is suitable for processing nonlinear signals can be used. DNN has good nonlinearity properties. For nonlinear filter implementation, dynamic neural networks (DNNs) have been used [3]-[6]. These DNNs can be trained by a gradient based algorithm such as Levenberg-Marquardt (LM) etc. [3]-[10]

2 Nonlinear Filter (NLF) Concept

Linear filters as a fundamental tool are often used in signal processing, control, modeling and prediction etc. applications. Since the linear filters have simple and efficient mathematical statements, these filters can be easily designed and applied. But, the existence of nonlinear systems in some applications, the use of linear filters is got difficult. Therefore, the importance of nonlinear filters can be understood for this point of view. In this study, continuous-time deterministic nonlinear filters (NLFs) are studied. In addition to this, nonlinear digital filters are widely used in many applications [1]. The structure of NLF is considered as follows,

$$\frac{dx}{dt} = f(x(t), p, u(t)) \quad , x(t_0) = x_0 \tag{1}$$

$$y(t) = h(x(t)) \tag{2}$$

A. Yazici and C. Şener (Eds.): ISCIS 2003, LNCS 2869, pp. 601–610, 2003.

where $x(t) \in R^n$ is the state variable vector function, $u(t) \in R^l$ is the input vector function, $p \in R^m$ is the parameter vector, $f(.) \in R^n$ is the nonlinear vector function and $h.(.) \in R^q$ is the nonlinear output vector function of NLF. f(.) and h(.) vector functions are fundamental function for the filter structure. In addition, $x_0 \in R^n$ are the initial conditions of the NLF. The behaviors of NLF are strictly dependent the initial conditions.

In this study, the mass-spring system as physical system is used as nonlinear filter structure below,

$$\ddot{x} - a\dot{x} + b(1 + cx)x = u(t) \tag{3}$$

where **x** is the horizontal deviation, **a** is the damping coefficient, **b** and **c** are nonlinearity parameters and u(t) is control function. Our purpose is to implement in that structure filter with DNN.

In addition to this, the linear filters are realized with DNNs. For this, a second order band pass filter (BPF) is used. This BPF has two important parameters which are band-with (BW) and center frequency.(w_0) Besides, the quality factor (Q) is an important characteristic parameter which depends on w_0 and BW. The transfer function of this type filter is given,

$$H(s) = \frac{\left(w_0/Q\right)s}{s^2 + \left(w_0/Q\right)s + w_0^2} \tag{4}$$

where BW=w_0/W. This filter is implemented with adjustable parameters, w_0 and BW using DNN.

3 The Dynamic Neural Network Model Structure

By a dynamic neural network we mean a network with unconstrained connectivity and with dynamical elements in the processing units. This can be contrasted three simpler network architectures: 1) in which connectivity is constrained to be feedforward and there are no dynamics in the processing units. Feedforward/algebraic networks are the workhorse of neural network applications. 2).In which feedback connections are allowed but dynamics in processing units are not. Networks of this type have been used for several symbolic processing tasks [11]-[13]. 3.)In which the connectivity is constrained to be feedforward but dynamical elements are included. For example, the output of the unit nonlinearity can be passed through a filter before serving as input the other, downstream, units [14].

The computational model for dynamic neural networks (DNNs) with two-neuron two-input/outputs that we have used is shown in Fig. 1. In general, there are $\boldsymbol{l}$ input signals (these can be time-varying) and $\boldsymbol{n}$ dynamic neural network units. The units have dynamics associated with them, as indicated, and they receive inputs from themselves and all other units. The output of a unit $\boldsymbol{y_i}$ is a general sigmoidal function $\boldsymbol{h(x_i, \gamma_i\ \beta_i)}$ of a state variable $\boldsymbol{x_i}$ associated with the unit. The output of the network (**m** output $\mathbf{z_i}$) is a linear weighted sum of the unit outputs. Weights $\boldsymbol{p_{ij}}$ are associated with the connections from input signals $\boldsymbol{j}$ to units $\boldsymbol{i}$, $\boldsymbol{w_{ij}}$ with interunit connections from $\boldsymbol{j}$ to *i*, and q_{ij} with connections from units *i* to the output summing element. For clarity, we only consider the case of one network input *u* and one network output z. The extension to multiple inputs and outputs (MIMO) and multiple units is straightforward (Fig. 2).

The general computational model is summarized in the following equations:

$$z_i = \sum_{j=1}^{n} q_{ij} y_j \quad , \quad y_i = h_i(x_i, \gamma_i, \beta_i) = \frac{1}{1+\exp[-(\gamma_i x_i + \beta_i)]} \tag{5, 6}$$

$$\dot{x}_i = \frac{1}{T_i}[-x_i + \sum_{j=1}^{n} w_{ij} y_j + \sum_{j=1}^{l} p_{ij} u_j + b_i] = f(.) \quad , \quad x_i(0) = x_{i0} \tag{7}$$

Because of the dynamics, initial conditions on the state variables $x_i(0)$ must be specified. Most work in neural networks allows for bias or threshold weights with processing units. They are not explicitly shown above, but equivalent to weights from a constant unity input signal.

This model is similar to some in the existing literature including [4],[15]-[17]. Differences exist in the treatment of inputs, in the form and relative placement of the nonlinearity. Other researchers have also used similar models for network with feedback connections, but have simplified the continuous-time dynamical aspect. Tsung [18] adopts a first order finite difference approximation to Eq.(7), and Williams and Zipser [19] use non- dynamical units (equivalent to T_i=0).

Given a set of parameters, initial conditions, and input trajectories, the set of equations (6) and (7) can be numerically integrated from t=0 to some desired final time t_f. This will produce trajectories over time for the state variables x_i and the internal outputs y_i. From these, the trajectory for *z* can be obtained. Point and periodic attractors can be realized. In practice, stability problems appear to rarely arise. The Eqs. (6) and (7) are a set of first-order nonlinear differential equations. We have used the fifth order Runge-Kutta method [20]. The integration time step has to be commensurate with the temporal scale of dynamics, determined the time constants T_i. In our work, we have specified a lower bound on T_i and have used a fixed integration time step of some fraction (e.g.,1/10) of this bound. Fig. 3 shows example of state space trajectories for two-unit networks with one constant unity input. The network parameters were:

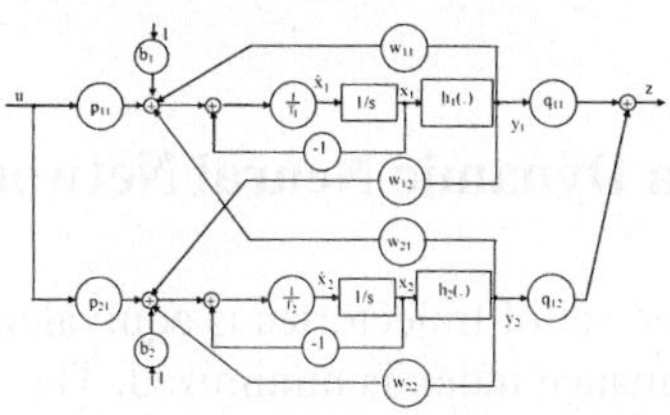

Fig. 1. State diagram of a two-unit SISO DNN

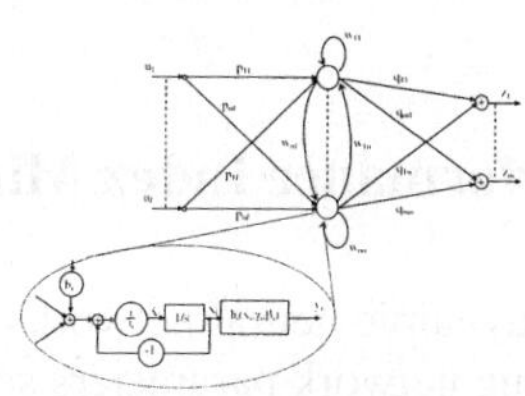

Fig. 2. General DNN model structure

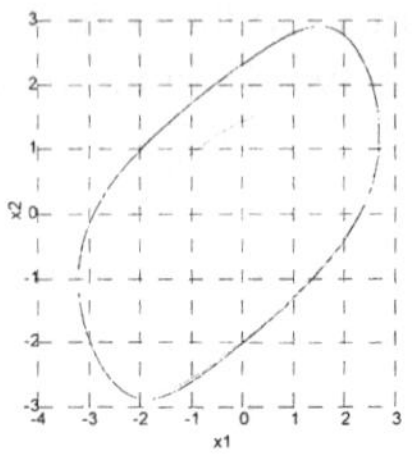

Fig. 3. State space trajectory of a DNN (periodic attractor)

$p=\begin{bmatrix}3\\-5\end{bmatrix}$, $w=\begin{bmatrix}0 & -10\\10 & 0\end{bmatrix}$, $q=\begin{bmatrix}1\\1\end{bmatrix}$, $T=\begin{bmatrix}2 & 0\\0 & 1\end{bmatrix}$. Initial conditions in the case were $\boldsymbol{x}_1(\mathbf{0})$=1.0, $\boldsymbol{x}_2$(0)=1.0. The network converges to a periodic attractor or limit cycle. The parameters for the network were adapted from [18], although due to differences in models network behavior is not identical. The integration time step was 0.01.

We consider a particular application of dynamic neural networks: trajectory tracking for process simulation That is, we desire to configure the network so that its output initial conditions and input trajectories have been specified, but all the parameters **p**, **w**, **q**, **γ**, **β** and **T** are adjustable (in this paper we do not discuss the issue of determining model structure, such as the number of neural network units). A performance index can be associated with the network for this task. For example:

$$J=\frac{1}{2}\int_0^{t_f}[z(t)-zd(t)]^T[z(t)-zd(t)]dt \tag{8}$$

It is easiest to think of ***zd***(t) and *z*(t) as actual and modeled process responses, but in fact this formulation can serve many other purposes. For example, we can conceive of a dynamical neural network parameter estimator, where we would like the output of the network at time $\boldsymbol{t_f}$ to equal some relevant parameter (e.g.,a time constant or gain) associated with the process that generated the data. In this case the performance index would simply be $\frac{1}{2}[z_i(t_f)-zd_i(t_f)]^2$. Applications of feedforward networks to the parameter estimation of dynamical systems are described in [21]-[23]. The formulation is also easily extended to the case where multiple target trajectories, e.g., corresponding to different input trajectories and initial process conditions, are given.

4 Performance Index Minimization in Dynamic Neural Networks

Training dynamic neural networks to mimic a given set of trajectories is equivalent to determining network parameters so that the performance index is minimized. This is a dynamic nonlinear optimization problem. Our focus in this paper has been on gradient-based algorithms for solving this problem. Abstractly, the algorithms consist of iterating the following three steps: 1.) Simulate the dynamic neural network from specified initial conditions, using specified input trajectories. This requires the solution of the n differential equations (7) with current network parameter values. 2.) Compute the performance index gradients given the target trajectory. 3.) Compute new network parameters. These steps are repeated until the performance index is sufficiently small. Initially, all parameters are set to specified or randomly-generated values. In this section, we discuss two approaches each to Steps 2 and 3: gradient computation and parameter updating.

We require the computation of gradients or sensitivities of the performance index with respect to the various parameters: $\frac{\partial E}{\partial p_{ij}}, \frac{\partial E}{\partial w_{ij}}, \frac{\partial E}{\partial T_i}$ etc.. An expression for the output weight gradients is readily obtained by differentiating Eqs.(8) and (5):

$$\frac{\partial J}{\partial q_{ij}} = \int_0^{t_f} [z_i(t) - zd_i(t)] \frac{\partial z_i}{\partial q_{ij}} dt = \int_0^{t_f} e_i(t) y_j dt \tag{9}$$

The simulation of the dynamic neural network gives us the trajectories $z(t)$ and $y_i(t)$, from which the above expression can be evaluated. The remaining gradients require the solution of additional sets of linear differential equations. Two methods which are forward and adjoint sensitivity analysis can be used. Here the second one used is described below.

Adjoint Sensitivity Analysis: The forward sensitivity analysis approach results from viewing dynamic network training as the minimization of performance index (8) subject to the constraints imposed by Eq. (7). Efficient another approach to solving constrained optimization problems is based on the use of Lagrange variables. Under this formulation, an alternative "Adjoint" method for sensitivity computation can be derived [24]-[26]. A new dynamical system is defined with adjoint state variables λ_i:

$$-\dot{\lambda}_i = -\frac{1}{T_i}\lambda_i + \frac{1}{T_i}\sum_j w_{ij} y_j' \lambda_j + e_i(t) \sum_j q_{ij} y_j' \ , \quad \lambda_i(t_f) = 0 \tag{10}$$

The size of adjoint vector is **n** and is independent of network parameters. There are **n** quadratures for computing the sensitivities. The integration of the differential equations must be performed backwards in time, from t_f to 0. We have used 5th order Runga-Kutta-Butcher integration rule [20]. Let $\boldsymbol{p}$ be a vector containing all network parameters. Then, the cost gradients w.r.t. parameters are given by the following quadratures;

$$\frac{\partial J}{\partial p} = \int_0^{t_f} \left(\frac{\partial f}{\partial p}\right)^T \lambda dt \tag{11}$$

Some of the cost gradients as in [24]-[26] are as bellows;

$$\frac{\partial J}{\partial w_{ij}} = \int_0^{t_f} \frac{\lambda_i y_j}{T_i} dt, \ \frac{\partial J}{\partial b_i} = \int_0^{t_f} \frac{\lambda_i}{T_i} dt \qquad \frac{\partial J}{\partial T_i} = -\int_0^{t_f} \frac{\lambda_i}{T_i^2}[-x_i + \sum_{j=1}^{n} w_{ij} y_j + \sum_{j=1}^{1} p_{ij} u_j + b_i] dt \tag{12, 13}$$

$$\frac{\partial J}{\partial \gamma_j} = \int_0^{t_f} (\sum_i \frac{\lambda_i}{T_i} w_{ij}) x_j h_j (1 - h_j) dt \tag{14}$$

All other gradients can be easily derived.

Equation (10) specifies final conditions. The integration must therefore be performed backwards in time, from t_f to 0. A general backwards integration capability is likely to require a more sophisticated approach.

The published literature on the adjoint method and dynamic networks is small. Pearlmutter [16],[24]-[27] describes an approach to trajectory learning that is similar to ours. Barhen, Toomarian and Gulati [17] give a theoretical treatment of the adjoint method for training dynamic neural networks to desired steady-state attractors. The complexities of backward integration are not addressed in either. The examples discussed in [16] employ constant inputs, a special case in which the first-order integration scheme used appears to suffice.

Constrained Levenberg-Marquardt Algorithm: We would like to find values for the ***m*** parameters $\tilde{p}$ (this can be considered as a vector obtained by concatenating ***p***, ***w*** and ***T***, etc) for which the quadratic performance index between network trajectory *z*(t) and desired trajectory ***zd***(t) is minimized. We assume that, at each iteration, gradients of the performance index **J** with respect to all network parameters have been computed. Here we describe an algorithm we have used for updating parameter values based on this gradient information.

A simple gradient-descent approach can be applied to update parameters:

$$\Delta\tilde{p} = -\eta \nabla_{\tilde{p}} J \tag{15}$$

where η is a step size parameter. Gradient descent is used in the majority neural network applications, usually under the banner of "backpropagation''.

Instead of simple gradient method, we used the well-known Levenberg-Marquardt technique [20],[28]. The extension consists of the incorporation of a method for handling constraints on parameter values. This Levenberg Marquardt (LM) algorithm has been used extensively for parameter estimation in linear continuous-time systems (a nonlinear parameter estimation problem).

The parameter update is computed as:

$$\Delta\tilde{p} = -\left[\hat{H} + \mu I\right]^{-1} \nabla_{\tilde{p}} J \tag{16}$$

I is the ***mxm*** identity matrix, and $\hat{H}$ is an approximation to the Hessian matrix of the response (the matrix of second derivatives of *z* with respect to $\tilde{p}$). The exact Hessian is computationally prohibitive. The Levenberg-Marquardt scheme approximates it as;

$$\frac{\partial^2 z}{\partial \tilde{p}_i \partial \tilde{p}_j} \cong \left[\frac{\partial z}{\partial \tilde{p}_i}\right]\left[\frac{\partial z}{\partial \tilde{p}_j}\right]^T \tag{17}$$

μ in Eq. (16) is a parameter that controls the parameter step size and the extent to which second-order information influences the update. For large μ, Eq. (16) essentially implements a gradient-descent rule. μ is updated automatically by the algorithm based on the error history. Thus the Levenberg-Marquartd algorithm implements a continuously varying hybrid of gradient descent and an approximate second order optimization.

This algorithm is recommended for small and medium-sized systems. For significantly larger systems, the matrix inversion in Eq. (16) requires careful treatment. Singular value decomposition and iterative inversion techniques are available (and in fact have been employed in the neural networks community) and these should facilitate scale-up.

It can be shown that the exact system Hessian can be computed economically using both the adjoint and response gradients [29]. Thus by performing both the forward and adjoint sensitivity analyses, an exact Newton method can be implemented at substantially lower cost than that involved in the "forward'' computation of exact second derivatives.

5 Filter Design with DNN

In this study, Equ. (3) has been used as a nonlinear filter (NLF). For linear filter (LF), Equ. (4) will be used. DNN and desired filter are trained as in Fig. 4.

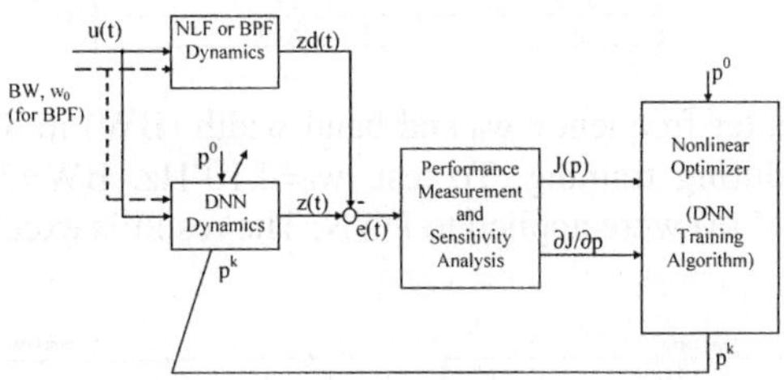

Fig. 4. Schematic diagram of DNN training as NLF and BPF

6 Simulation Results

In the simulation, for target NLF, a=0.6, b=3 and c=1/3 were selected, and the input function as in Fig. 5 is used for adjusting the DNN parameters.

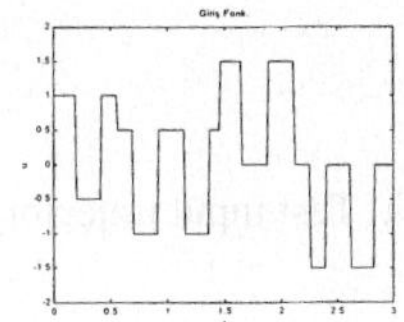

Fig. 5. Input function for NLF training with DNN

DNN parameters were randomly selected, but its initial conditions were used the same as NLF. After the training, to test the DNN filter performance, another input as in Fig. 6 (a) is applied to both converged DNN and original NLF. DNN and NLF outputs are shown in Fig. 6 (b). As the last example, DNN was used as BPF using some values (w_0,BW) as indicated in Table 1 and the input in Fig. 5.

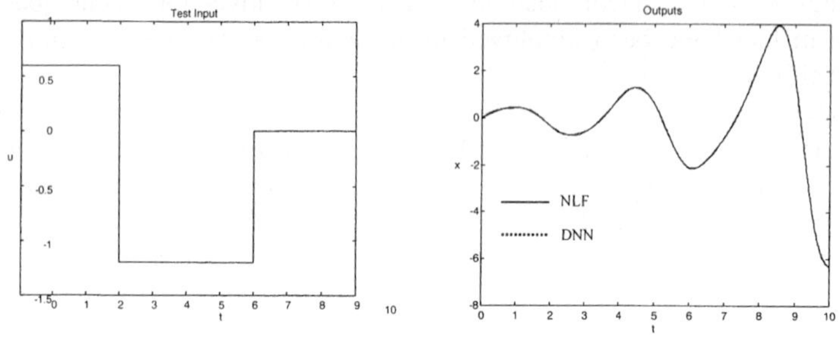

Fig. 6. NLF testing for DNN (a) Test input trajectory (b) DNN and NLF outputs

Table 1. BPF parameters used for training DNN as BPF

BW(rd/sec)	w_0(rd/sec)
2.10^3	10^4
10^3	5.10^4
5.10^2	10^5
10^2	5.10^5

The values of center frequency w_0 and band width (BW) in **Table 1** were used to be mixed in time during training. To test, w_0=2.10^4Hz, BW=750Hz and the input trajectory as in Fig. 7 (a) were applied to DNN. The result is excellent shown in Fig. 7 (b)

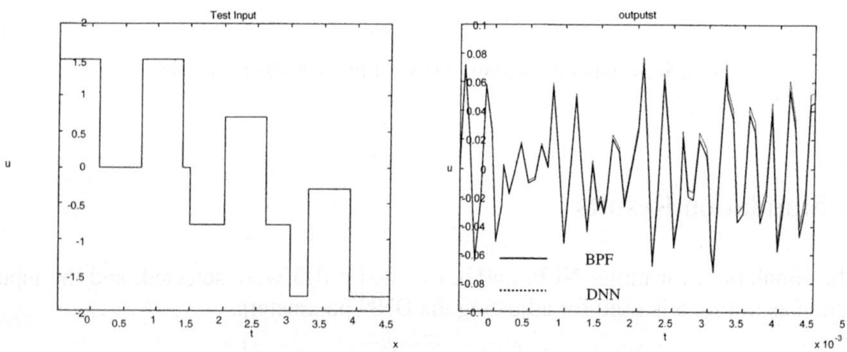

Fig. 7. Testing of DNN as BPF (a) Test input trajectory (b) DNN and BPF outputs

7 Conclusions

It I shown that analog linear and nonlinear filters can be implemented with DNN. A novel class of algorithm that combine the updating scheme with nonlinear approximate second order gradient descent class of algorithm which is LM has been proposed for training DNN as filter. Any nonlinear physical dynamic system such as nonlinear filter used above can be captured by DNN. Simulation results show that the dynamic network structure can grow more accurate by dynamic neuron approximators.

High order linear and nonlinear filters can be considered to be implemented.

References

[1]. Pitas, I., "Nonlinear Digital Filters, Principles and Applications", Kluwer Academic Publishers, 1990.

[2]. Khalil, H.K., "Nonlinear Systems", Prentice-Hall, Inc., 1996.

[3]. Hopfield, J.J., "Neural networks and physical systems with emergent collective computational abilities.'' *Proc. of the National Academy of Sciences*, 79, pp. 2554–2558, 1982.

[4]. J.J., Hopfield, J.J., "Neurons with graded response have collective computational properties like those of two-state neurons.'' *Proc. of the National Academy of Sciences*, 81, pp. 3088–3092, 1984.

[5]. Konar, A.F., and Samad, T., "Dynamic Neural Networks", *Technical Report SSDC-92-I 4152-2, Honeywell Technology Center, 3660 Technology Drive*, Minneapolis, MN 55418, 1992.

[6]. Konar, A.F., Becerikli, Y., and Samad, T., "Trajectory Tracking with Dynamic Neural Networks", *Proc. of the 1997 IEEE Int. Sym. On Intelligent Control (ISIC'97)*, Ýstanbul 1997.

[7]. Lippmann, R.P., "An Introduction to Computing with Neural Nets", IEEE, ASSP Magazine, pp.4–22, 1987.

[8]. Haykin, S., "Neural Networks, A Comprehensive Foundation", Prentice-Hall, Inc., 1999.

[9]. Cichocki, A., and Unbehauen, R.,: "Neural Networks for Optimization and Signal Processing", John Wiley & Sons. Ltd. & B.G. Teubner, 1993.

[10]. Scales, L.E.,: "Introduction to Nonlinear Optimization", Springer-Verlag New York Inc., 1985.

[11]. Jordan, M.I., "Attractor dynamics and parallelism in connectionist sequential machine.'' *Proc. of the Eighth Annual Conference of Cognitive Science Society.* Hillsdale, N.J.: Lawrence Erlbaum Associates, 1986.

[12]. Elman, J.L., "Finding Structure in Time''. *Technical Report 8801, Center for Research in Language*, University of California, San Diego, La Jolla, CA 92093, 1988.

[13]. Servan-Schreiber, D., Cleeremans, A., and McClellans, J.L. "Encoding Sequential Structure in Simple Recurrent Networks.'' *Technical Report CMU-CS-88-183, School of Computer Science*, Carnegie Mellon University, Pittsburg, PA 15213, 1988.

[14]. Morris, A.J., "On artificial neural networks in process engineering.'' *IEE Proc. Pt. D. Control Theory and Applications,* 1992

[15]. Pineda, F., "Generalization of backpropagation to recurrent and higher order neural networks.'' *Proc. of the IEEE International Conference on Neural Networks*, 1987

[16]. Pearlmutter, B., "Learning state space trajectories in recurrent neural networks.'' *Neural Computation*, 1, pp. 263–269, 1989.

[17]. Barhen, J., Toomarian, N., and Gulati, S., "Adjoint operator algorithms for faster learning in dynamical neural networks''. *In Advances in Neural Information Processing Systems* 2, D.S. Touretzky (Ed.) San Mateo, Ca.: Morgan Kaufmann, 1990.

[18]. Tsung, F-S. "Learning in recurrent finite difference networks. In Connectionist Models:'' *Proceedings of the 1990 Summer School, D.S. Touretzky et al. (Eds.) San Mateo, Ca.: Morgan Kaufmann*, 1990.

[19]. Williams, R.J. and Zipser, D., "A Learning Algorithm for Continually Running Fully Recurrent Neural Networks.'' *ICS Report 8805, Institute for Cognitive Science*, University of California, San Diego, La Jolla, Ca. 92093, 1988.
[20]. Chapra, S.C., and Canale, R:P., "Numerical Methods for Engineers", *McGraw-Hill, Inc.*, 1989.
[21]. Samad, T., and Mathur, A., "System Identification with neural Networks.'' *Technical Report CSDD-89-I4920-2, Honeywell SSDC, 3660 Technology Drive*, Minneapolis, MN 55418, 1988.
[22]. Samad, T., and Mathur, A., "Parameter estimation for process control with neural networks.'' *International Journal of Approximate Reasoning*, 1992.
[23]. Konar, A.F., and Samad, T., "Hybrid Neural Network/ Algorithmic System Identification.'' *Technical Report SSDC-91-I4051-1, Honeywell SSDC, 3660 Technology Drive*, Minneapolis, MN 55418, 1991.
[24]. Konar, A.F., and Samad, T., "Dynamic Neural Networks.'' *Technical report SSDC-92-I 4142-2, Honeywell Technology Center*, 3660 Technology Drive, Minneapolis, MN 55418, 1992
[25]. Becerikli, Y., "Neuro-Optimal Control", *Ph.D Thesis, Sakarya University, Sakarya*, Turkey, 1998
[26]. Becerikli, Y., Konar, A.F. and Samad, T., "Intelligent optimal control with dynamic neural networks" Neural Networks, vol.16(2), pp.251–259, March, 2003
[27]. Leistritz, L, Galicki, M, Witte, H., and Kochs, E., "Training Trajectories by Continuous Recurrent Multilayer Networks", IEEE Trans. on Neural Networks, Vol.13, no.2, March 2002
[28]. Marquardt, D.W:, "An algorithm for least-squares estimation of nonlinear parameters'' *J. Soc. Ind. Appl. Math.*, 11, pp. 431–441, 1963.
[29]. Konar, A.F., "Gradient and curvature in nonlinear identification.'' *Proc. Honeywell Advanced Control Workshop*, January 21–22, 1991.

Prediction of Protein Subcellular Localization Based on Primary Sequence Data*

Mert Özarar[1], Volkan Atalay[1], and Rengül Çetin Atalay[2]

[1] Dept. of Computer Eng., Middle East Technical University, Ankara, TURKEY
{ozarar,volkan}@ceng.metu.edu.tr,

[2] Dept. of Molecular Biology and Genetics, Bilkent University, Ankara, TURKEY
rengul@bilkent.edu.tr,

Abstract. This paper describes a system called *prediction of protein subcellular localization (P2SL)* that predicts the subcellular localization of proteins in eukaryotic organisms based on the amino acid content of primary sequences using amino acid order. Our approach for prediction is to find the most frequent motifs for each protein (class) based on clustering and then to use these most frequent motifs as features for classification. This approach allows a classification independent of the length of the sequence. Another important property of the approach is to provide a means to perform reverse analysis and analysis to extract rules. In addition to these and more importantly, we describe the use of a new encoding scheme for the amino acids that conserves biological function based on *point of accepted mutations (PAM)* substitution matrix. We present preliminary results of our system on a two class (dichotomy) classifier. However, it can be extended to multiple classes with some modifications.

1 Introduction

Eukaryotic cells are subdivided into functionally separate membrane enclosed compartments. Each compartment and its vicinity contain functionally linked proteins related to the activity of that cell compartment [1]. In an eukaryotic cell, each protein is targeted to its specific cell localization where it is functionally active. Large scale genome analysis provides high number of putative genes to be characterized. Therefore, prediction of the subcellular localization of a newly identified protein is invaluable for the characterization of its function. Furthermore, studying subcellular localization is useful for understanding the disease mechanisms and developing novel drugs. If the rules for the prediction were biologically interpretable, this knowledge could help in designing artificial proteins with desired properties. Hence, a fully automatic and reliable prediction system for protein subcellular localization would be very useful.

* This work was supported by the Turkish Academy of Sciences to R.Ç.A. (in the framework of the Young Scientist Award Program-RCA/TÜBA-GEBİP/2001-2-3).

A. Yazici and C. Şener (Eds.): ISCIS 2003, LNCS 2869, pp. 611–618, 2003.

The aim of this work is to design and develop a system called *prediction of protein subcellular localization (P2SL)* that predicts the subcellular localization of proteins in eukaryotic organisms based on the amino acid content of primary sequences. The amino acid composition in the full or partial sequences can be taken as a global feature and the order may represent the local features such as the sequence order of amino acids that are found in protein sequence motifs [2]. In this paper, we are interested in the prediction using only local features. Our approach for prediction is to find the most frequent (hopefully the most significant) motifs for each protein (class) based on clustering and then to use these most frequent motifs as features for classification. This approach allows a classification independent of the length of the sequence. Another important property of the approach is to provide a means to perform reverse analysis and analysis to extract rules. In addition to these and more importantly, we describe the use of a new encoding scheme for the amino acids that conserves biological function based on *point of accepted mutations (PAM)* substitution matrix [3]. *PAM* is used to score aligned peptide sequences to determine the similarity of these sequences. The scores in *PAM* are derived by comparing aligned sequences of proteins with known homology and determining the observed. By using *PAM* substitution matrix, we believe that we are able to represent the chemical differences of each amino acid in protein sequences. In the literature, each amino acid is traditionally represented in binary form independent of their chemical properties. In this study, we present preliminary results of our system on a two class (dichotomy) classifier. However, it can be extended to multiple classes with some modifications.

The manuscript is organized as follows. In Section 2, we indicate the related studies. The data and computational methods used in this study are presented in Section 3. Experiments and comments on the results are then explained in the subsequent section. Finally, the eventual improvements are indicated together with conclusions and future work.

2 Related Work

Several attempts have been made to predict protein subcellular localization. Most of these prediction methods can be classified into two categories: one is based on the recognition of protein N-terminal sorting signals and the other is based on amino acid composition.

PSORT was developed based on rules for various sequence features of known protein sorting signals [4]. iPSORT was developed based on a decision tree with an amino acid index rule and an alphabet indexing and pattern rule [5]. TargetP was developed based on neural networks and achieved high prediction accuracy [6]. There are several studies to predict the specific localizations. MitoProt was developed for analyzing mitochondrial proteins and MitoProt II was for predicting the mitochondrial ones [7]. MTS prediction was based on hidden Markov models for mTPs [8]. SignalP was developed based on neural networks for SP prediction [9]. ChloroP was developed based on neural networks for chloroplast targeting peptide prediction [10]. SortPred was developed for using both neural networks and hidden Markov models for four class problem of subcellular localization [11]. The prediction accuracy of SortPred is 86.4% for plant and 91.3% for non-plant, while the accuracy of TargetP and iPSORT is 85.3% and 84.5%, respectively for plant and 90% and 88%, respectively for non-plant. Among them, PSORT and iPSORT use global features, on the other hand MitoProt and MTS use local features. TargetP, SignalP, ChloroP and SortPred use both global and local features.

A combination of clustering followed by classification seems to be the most important aspect of this study. *P2SL* dichotomizer prediction results are very promising compared to the experimental results indicated in the literature. Our ultimate goal is to design a system that performs predictions only on human proteins yielding comparable results with TargetP.

When compared to the studies in the literature,

- we use windows (motifs) similar to the work by Emanuelsson et.al. [6],
- we use self organizing maps (SOM) similar to the work by Cai et.al. [12],
- we use a novel encoding scheme based on PAM [13].

3 Methods

The main idea for the prediction of protein subcellular localization using local features is based on finding the substrings which are common for a protein class and infrequent for the other classes. Such substrings are called as motifs. We use a self organizing map for this purpose. For an unknown input sequence, we determine which motifs exist and the sequence is classified according to this information. The flow diagram of *P2SL* is illustrated in Figure 1. The input to the system is amino acid sequences. The sequences are extracted from this data. The primary sequence is then decomposed into substrings. Each substring is encoded with *PAM250* [13] substitution matrix. We apply clustering on the encoded substring via a self organizing map. During the training phase, motifs for each class are determined. Throughout the test phase, when the substrings of an unknown input sequence is given, according to the winning nodes in the self organizing map, we form a binary vector which indicates the existence of motifs of a particular class in the input. k-nearest neighborhood classifier is then applied to this binary vector to determine the label of the unknown protein.

3.1 Data Representation

Protein sequences are strings of arbitrary size and amino acids correspond to the letters in a protein sequence. Let $\hat{X}$ represent a protein sequence whose length is $len(\hat{X})$. $\hat{X}$ can be decomposed into substrings of some fixed length, κ. If $\kappa < len(\hat{X})$, there are exactly $(len(\hat{X}) - \kappa + 1)$ substrings in $\hat{X}$. $\hat{X}(j : m + j)$ then denotes j^{th} substring in a protein sequence $\hat{X}$. In order to perform further computational analysis, we need to encode the amino acids. Although, the most

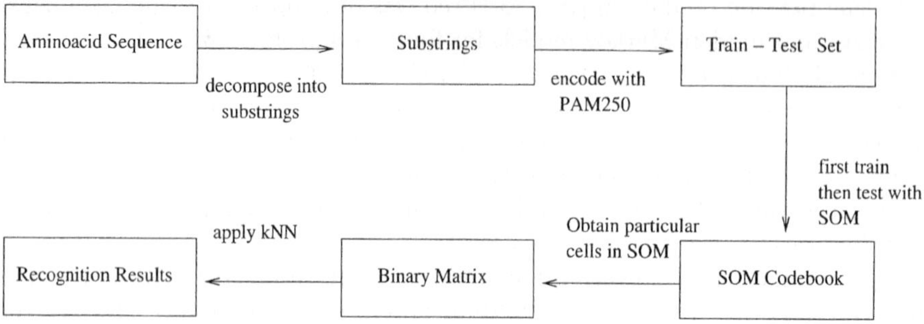

Fig. 1. Flow diagram of *P2SL*.

popular way of encoding reported in the literature is to represent each amino acid in binary form, in this study, we make use of substitution matrices. While aligning two protein sequences, certain methods are used to score the alignment of one residue against another. Substitution matrices indicate score values for this purpose. We employ *PAM250* scoring matrix to encode an amino acid. In the rest of the manuscript, X denotes a *PAM* encoded protein sequence $\hat{X}$.

The frequencies of these mutations are in this table as a "log odds-matrix" where:

$$M_{ij} = 10(\log 10\ R_{ij}),$$

In this equation, M_{ij} is the matrix element and R_{ij} is the probability of that substitution as observed in the database, divided by the normalized frequency of occurence for amino acid i. All of the number are rounded to the nearest integer. The base 10 log is used so that the numbers can be added to determine the score of a compared set of sequences, rather than multiplied.

3.2 Clustering

We use a self organizing map (SOM) for clustering. SOM is an unsupervised artificial neural network model that relates similar input vectors to the same region of a map of nodes or neurons [14]. Topological organization of neurons in SOM is its essential feature, since it does a topological ordering of the input. SOM is often used to categorize and interpret data, by mapping a high-dimensional input data to a lower dimensional space which is usually 2. Each input data is composed of a vector of elements. The map is an array of nodes which are also called neurons and it is often laid out in a rectangular or hexagonal lattice. Each node has an associated reference vector of the same size as input feature vectors. Input vectors are compared with these reference vectors. There are two phases of a SOM: training and testing. For training, all the input vectors, one at a time are presented to the network. Each input vector is compared to weight vectors associated with every neuron. The neuron having the weight vector with the smallest difference to the current input vector becomes the winning neuron. The weight vector of this winning neuron and those of the neighboring neurons as well are then updated in the direction of the input vector. Note that in this training scheme similar input vectors are mapped to nodes that are close together on the map. This, in fact generates both the topological ordering and clustering properties of a SOM. In the training phase, there is no update in the weight vectors and therefore we are only interested to determine to which of the nodes (cluster) the input data is mapped.

In our system, clustering occurs during training and in this phase substrings are topologically grouped. The problem of finding motifs of a protein class turns out to finding the nodes specific to a class. At the end of training, these nodes are found by simply looking at the difference of the number of substrings of two classes assigned to each node. "assigned" is used in the sense that for an input vector X, SOM cell i is the winning node.

Let $c_i^{\mathcal{X}}$ and $c_i^{\mathcal{Y}}$ denote the cardinal of the set of substrings of class $\mathcal{X}$ and class $\mathcal{Y}$, respectively assigned to the cell i. If the size of the two dimensional SOM is m by n, then there are $m \times n$ nodes. The difference of substrings of the two classes assigned to cell i is then

$$\Delta c_i^{\mathcal{X}} = (c_i^{\mathcal{X}} - c_i^{\mathcal{Y}}) \text{ and } \Delta c_i^{\mathcal{Y}} = -\Delta c_i^{\mathcal{X}} = (c_i^{\mathcal{Y}} - c_i^{\mathcal{X}})$$

Let the sets of SOM nodes to which motifs of class $\mathcal{X}$ and $\mathcal{Y}$ are assisgned during the training phase be $P^{\mathcal{X}}$ and $P^{\mathcal{Y}}$, respectively. $P^{\mathcal{X}}$ and $P^{\mathcal{Y}}$ are determined as follows. If $\Delta c_i^{\mathcal{X}} > \tau^{\mathcal{X}}$ then $i \in P^{\mathcal{X}}$, otherwise i is not in $P^{\mathcal{X}}$ where $\tau^{\mathcal{X}}$ is a threshold value emprically determined. Similarly, If $\Delta c_j^{\mathcal{Y}} > \tau^{\mathcal{Y}}$ then $j \in P^{\mathcal{Y}}$, otherwise j is not in $P^{\mathcal{Y}}$. Remark that we choose $\tau^{\mathcal{X}}$ and $\tau^{\mathcal{Y}}$ such that there are equal number s of elements in $P^{\mathcal{X}}$ and $P^{\mathcal{Y}}$.

3.3 Classification

The k nearest neighbor (kNN) classification method is one of the most popular classification methods in pattern recognition. In kNN, the class label of an unknown sample is determined by the majority of class labels of the k nearest training samples to the unknown sample. Nearest neighbor method using only one nearest training sample is called 1-Nearest Neighbor (1NN) method. On the other hand, that using $k > 1$ nearest training samples is called k-nearest neighbor (kNN) method. Compared to linear or quadratic classifers, the nearest neighbor method is more effective for a complex distribution of samples. On the other hand, kNN method requires more computational cost than 1NN method.

After clustering, the next step is classification. For this purpose, for each training input X a binary vector Z of $2s$ elements is formed as follows. The elements $0, \dots, s-1$ represent class $\mathcal{X}$ while those $s, \dots, 2s-1$ represent class $\mathcal{Y}$. If the winning node corresponding to input substring $X(j : j+\kappa)$ is l^{th} element of $P^{\mathcal{X}}$, then $Z(l) = 1$. Similarly, for class $\mathcal{Y}$, if the winning node corresponding to input substring $X(j : j+\kappa)$ is l^{th} element of $P^{\mathcal{Y}}$, then $Z(s+l) = 1$. Note that final form of Z is obtained after processing all of the available substrings in a protein sequence X.

Assume that Z' represents the binary vector for a protein sequence in the training set and Z for that in the test set. For each protein i in the test set, Hamming distance between corresponding Z_i and Z'_j (for all of the elements in the training set) is calculated. Then, k proteins of the training set having the least Hamming distance to Z_i is checked. Suppose that among those k protein sequences, there are q proteins belonging to class $\mathcal{X}$ and r proteins belonging to class $\mathcal{Y}$. Hence, $q+r=k$. Then, a voting mechanism takes place: if $q > r$, then the ith element of the test set is classified as of class $\mathcal{X}$. If $r > q$, then the ith element of the test set is classified as class of $\mathcal{Y}$. Since, the k is chosen as an odd value, there is no chance of $q = r$.

4 Material, Results, and Discussions

In our experiments, we first employ our method to a previously published data set [6]. By using this data set, we have generated four data subsets (classes), signal peptide containing proteins (SP class), nuclear proteins (NP class), cytosolic proteins (CP class) and mitochondrial proteins (MP class), of which only two (SP and NP) are used in this study. Both classes are represented in *Fasta* format.

From each class, 40 proteins are randomly chosen for training from the input data. Randomly chosen 20 proteins from each class exclusive of those in the training set are used for testing. Substrings of size $\kappa = 30$ are extracted from the protein sequences. Therefore, 18815 SP substrings and 23290 NP substrings are formed. For the self organizing map, SOM-PAK [15] is used as a computational tool. We have tried different map sizes, topologies and neighborhood functions. Experiments yield that a SOM with map size 25x25, randomly initialization, rectangular topology and Gaussian neighborhood function gives better results for our problem. Both ordering and fine-tuning training is used with 10000 and 50000 epochs, respectively. Figure 2 shows the difference of histograms of SOM nodes after the training phase. The peaks are obvious for both classes, but the important nodes are the ones in which a high number of samples exists for one class yet not a significant value exists for the other class. For example, the difference value for node (0,0) is approximately 40. This shows that unless there are cells with lower difference values, it shall not be treated as a particular node for both classes. However, for instance, the frequency difference between SP and NP is approximately 90 for the node (24,0) and it is one of the specific cells for the SP class.

By keeping the thresholds ($\tau^{\mathcal{X}} = \tau^{\mathcal{Y}}$) as 20, (16,7), (14,5), (16,8), (17,4), (17,8), (12,8), (17,5), (18,9), (19,9), (19,6), (15,8), (17,7), (13,8), (19,8), (18,7), (14,4), (17,11), (18,3), (15,7), (0,19) represent the particular set of cells for class NP and (24,0), (15,0), (0,3), (7,19), (6,21), (16,0), (9,4), (24,19), (24,21), (3,10), (6,22), (21,0), (5,2), (8,0), (5,3), (9,24), (4,9), (4,24), (6,24), (9,0) represent the specific set of nodes for class SP. The k value is taken as 5, for kNN and 100% accuracy is obtained from the test results. The test set ratio over training set ratio is 1/4 which is quite large for a pattern recognition experiment. This shows that our methodology is meaningful even though the sample size is small.

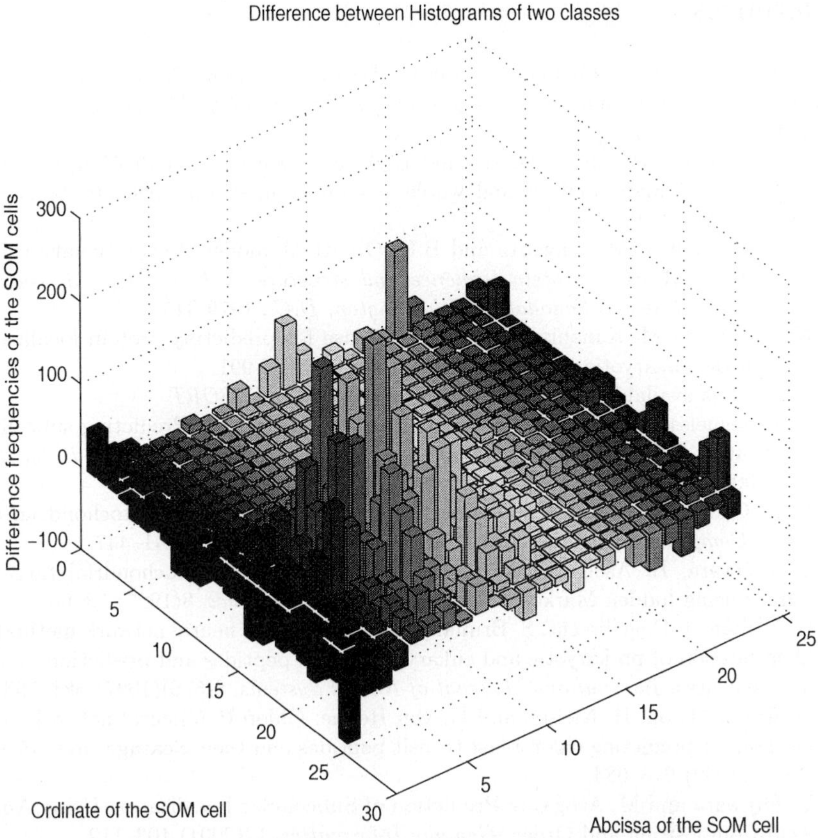

Fig. 2. Difference of histograms of SOM cells for SP and NP classes.

5 Conclusion

We describe *P2SL* for the prediction of protein subcellular localization sites using amino acid order. It achieves higher prediction accuracy than the previous two class classifiers. Our clustering strategy is training self organizing maps and using kNN for classification purposes. In order to extract features from amino acid sequences, *PAM250* scoring matrix is used. This preserves the biological meaning of each independent amino acid found in protein subcellular targeting sequence motifs. Our classification strategy is based on choosing the dominant vectors which are extracted by clustering. As the next step, we intend to increase the number of classes to 4 rather than 2. Cytoplasmic and mitochondrial classes shall be added. More samples should be used for training the SOM. Futhermore, another classifier such as multilayer perceptrons can be employed together with kNN to obtain better results. In addition to these, SOM clustering can be useful for rule extraction and reverse analysis.

References

1. C. van Vliet, E.C. Thomas, A. Merino-Trigo, R.D. Teasdale, P.A. Gleeson: Intracellular sorting and transport of proteins. *Prog Biophys Mol Biol.*, 83(1)(2003) 1–45.
2. F. Corpet, F. Servant, J. Gouzy and D. Kahn: ProDom and ProDom-CG: tools for protein domain analysis and whole genome comparisons. *Nucleic Acids Res.*, 28(2000) 267–269.
3. M.O. Dayhoff, R.M. Schwartz and B.C. Orcutt: A model of evolutionary change in proteins. *Atlas of protein sequence and structure. Vol. 5, Suppl. 3. National Biomedical Research Foundation, Washington, D.C.*, 1979 345–352.
4. K. Nakai and M. Kanehisa: A knowledge base for predicting protein localization sites in the eukaryotic cells, *Genomics*, 14(1992) 897–991.
5. iPSORT is available at: *http://hypothesiscreator.net/iPSORT*
6. O. Emanuelsson, H. Nielsen, S. Brunak and G. von Heijne: Predicting subcellular localization of proteins based on their N-terminal amino acid sequence, *J.Mol.Biol.*, 300(2000) 1005–1016.
7. M.G. Claros: MitoProt: a Macintosh application for studying mitochondrial proteins, *Computer Applications in the Biosciences* 11(4)(1995) 441–447.
8. Y. Fujiwara, H. Asogawa and K. Nakai: Prediction of mitochondrial targeting signals using hidden Markov models, *Genome Informatics*, 8(1997) 53–60.
9. H. Nielsen, J. Engelbrecht, S. Brunak, G. von Heijne: A neural network method for identification of prokaryotic and eukaryotic signal peptides and prediction of their cleavage sites, *International Journal of Neural Systems*, 8(5–6)(1997) 581–599.
10. O. Emanuelsson, H. Nielsen and G. von Heijne: ChloroP, a neural network-based method for predicting chloroplast transit peptides and their cleavage sites, *Protein Sci.*, 8(1999) 978–984.
11. Y. Fujiwara and M. Asogawa: Prediction of Subcellular Localization Using Amino Acid Composition and Order, *Genome Informatics*, 12(2001) 103–112.
12. Y. Cai, X. Liu, K. Chou: Artificial neural network model for predicting protein subcellular location, *Computers and Chemistry*, 26(2002) 179–182.
13. S.F. Altschul: Amino acid substitution matrices from an information theoretic perspective, *J. Mol. Biol.*, 219(1991) 555–565.
14. T. Kohonen: The self-organizing map. *Proceedings of the IEEE*, 78(9)(1990) 1464–1480.
15. The SOMPAK package is available at: *http://www.cis.hut.fi/nnrc/papers/*

Implementing Agent Communication for a Multi-agent Simulation Infrastructure on HLA

Erek Göktürk and Faruk Polat

Department of Computer Engineering, Middle East Technical University,
İnönü Bulvarı, 06531, Ankara, Turkey
{erek, polat}@ceng.metu.edu.tr

Abstract. Multi-agent simulation is gaining popularity due to its intuitiveness and ability in coping with domain complexity. HLA, being a distributed simulation architecture standard, is a good candidate for implementing a multi-agent simulation infrastructure on, provided that agent communication can be implemented. In this paper, we present a layered approach to the agent communication, followed by a discussion of implementing the lowest two layers of this approach using HLA and the agent communication language KQML in the context of a multi-agent simulation.

1 Introduction

A multi-agent architecture is defined as one in which decisions and reasoning are distributed among the agents. This distribution of processes creates an intuitive style of modeling, when considered from a simulation perspective. Modeling using multi-agency helps tackling with the domain complexity by allowing one to separately study the structure of components that make up the system and the interactions between these components which create the domain's dynamics [1].

Communication plays a key role in the multi-agent systems. The agents have to encode information and their attitudes regarding it using a language. The design of a multi-agent system is influenced by the structure and assumptions behind the agent communication language from two aspects: The social structure of the agents and the implications of language on the architecture of the resultant multi-agent system.

High Level Architecture (HLA) is a distributed simulation standard (IEEE 1516) that aims at interoperable and component-based reusable simulations. HLA can be used as an infrastructure to build multi-agent simulations on, to foster its interoperability concept thereby allowing a multi-agent simulation to act itself as a component in a bigger simulation. In order to build a multi-agent simulation using HLA, an agent communication scheme must be developed.

In this paper, we draw upon a layered approach to the agent communication, followed by a discussion of implementing the lowest two layers of this approach using the HLA and the agent communication language KQML in the context of a multi-agent simulation. A basic implementation demonstrating the concepts

A. Yazici and C. Şener (Eds.): ISCIS 2003, LNCS 2869, pp. 619–626, 2003.

is realized using the Run-Time Infrastructure (RTI) implementation of Defense Modeling and Simulation Office of Department of Defense of USA. Implementing KQML in a multi-agent simulation seems most likely be considered when the agents are considerably deliberative, and the deliberative functions include reasoning that uses communication explicitly. There are alternatives to KQML as an agent communication language, but the choice of KQML is not arbitrary: It is due to the fact that KQML puts less restrictions on the policies and leaves more room for the designer's preferences, when compared to its major alternative, the FIPA Abstract Architecture.

This work is refined in some part from the experience gained in a 3D multi-agent simulation of commando operations project, called SAVMOS, being carried on in the Modeling and Simulation Laboratory co-established by METU and the Turkish Armed Forces.

The rest of the paper is organized as follows: Next section two chapters are on agent communication languages and their implications on the multi-agent system architecture. In the following section, we discuss how to realize a simulation consisting of agents that communicate using an agent communication language, KQML. The last section is conclusion and contains our final comments.

2 Agent Communication

By definition of the multi-agent systems, agent communication plays a crucial role as the only way of coordination between the problem solving entities, the agents. The communication between the agents take place either explicitly, that is by agents issuing communication actions and sending messages to other agents, or implicitly by agents having the results of their actions perceived by other agents. Without explicit communication, coordination becomes the very hard problem of opponent modeling, which is not a problem to be tackled for most of the practical multi-agent system implementations.

For decades, the state of the art in modeling communication systems has been the use of layers whose functions and interfaces are more or less well-defined. In the literature, we see that agent communication is also structured in layers [2] [3]. We take an approach similar to the one in the FIPA Abstract Architecture, and propose a three layered model.

The highest layer is the *content layer*. In the content layer, the information intended to be passed between the agents is expressed in a content language such as Knowledge Interchange Format (KIF) or Semantic Language (SL), using an ontology known by both participants of the communication.

Below the content layer is the *communication language* layer, in which the content received from the upper layer is encapsulated using an agent communication language (ACL) such as KQML or FIPA-ACL [4] [5]. Usually, these agent communication languages contain performatives, which are said to stem from the speech-act theory [6]. The ACL message also contains information such as the names of the sender and receiver agents as well as interaction protocol related fields, ontology and the content language used.

As the lowest layer, just above the actual information transfer such as a network connection, IPC or a middleware such as HLA, we observe the *transport layer* whose task is to handle the specific transfer related issues, such as converting the ACL message in a form transferable over the actual connection, converting agent names to transport addresses and encapsulating the ACL message with the sender and receiver transport addresses and the ACL type.

3 Implications of ACLs on MA System Architecture

The agent communication languages have an influence on the structure of social interactions in the multi-agent system they are used in. Moreover, the model assumed at ACL's design for the social interactions that will take place using the ACL has influence on the design of it, so the assumed model necessarily have implications for the realizations. This resembles the fact that social interactions in a society both influences and is influenced by the natural language the members of the society speak.

In the FIPA-ACL case, the architectural design assumptions supporting the agent communication are made explicit through the FIPA Abstract Architecture Specification. In their architecture, ACL is relieved from the task of finding other agents, their properties, and services provided by some entities which are not necessarily agents, by defining directory services separately from the agents. The designers of the architecture is also aware that these directories may be implemented by some special agents, yet they also put the note that discovering and communicating in such a case is a problem that's outside the scope of the FIPA Abstract Architecture Specification document. By this way, FIPA abstracts and excludes some functions that's being accomplished by certain performatives in KQML from its agent communication language FIPA-ACL.

In KQML, the architectural assumptions are not made explicit, rather they're implied in the specification. The KQML agents get to know of each other by exchanging advertisements. There are special agents in a KQML speaking agent society called the facilitators. These facilitators resemble the directories in FIPA and can act as mediators between the agents. There exists some performatives in KQML, which are said to not be speech acts in the pure sense, to assist this mediation [7]. KQML relies on the multi-agent system implementation to handle the details of agent and facilitator discovery mechanisms and requires only agents to have the ability to discover other agents. It should also be added that the transport details, e.g. addressing is said to be left outside KQML, yet KQML performatives register and transport-address requires the agent to record the transport address the KQML message come from, introducing the transport details into their semantics and blur the distinction between the transport and the communication layers.

KQML-Lite should also be mentioned here, as an attempt to merge FIPA and KQML specifications [8]. Although KQML-Lite is meant to be light, it adds more performatives from the FIPA communicative acts library to the performative set of KQML. KQML-Lite also calls for standardization of the services offered by the facilitator agents, thereby emphasizing the correlation between KQML implied architecture and FIPA Abstract Architecture. Furthermore, in an attempt to establish a better separation between the transport and communication layers, KQML-Lite defines a layer above the KQML expression and calls it the transmittal layer, whose output is again in the form of a KQML message but restricted to use only the networking and facilitation performatives, and performatives related to agent execution control.

4 Implementing KQML

The title of this section is deliberately chosen to remind the reader that an ACL is not an interpreted or a compiled language, and cannot have an implementation per se [9]. What we mean by implementing KQML is implementing an architecture in which agents may communicate respecting the semantics of KQML performatives as defined in [7], building on top of HLA architecture.

The first architectural entity to be mapped onto HLA is the concept of agents. From the KQML perspective, agents are computational entities carrying unique names and causing some KQML messages be sent. So it's pretty obvious that the agents will be mapped onto federates. The agents should be able to find out about at least the presence of other agents in the runtime environment, thus we need to design a way so that agents discover other agents. This can be accomplished by making agent executing federates publish agent objects to RTI, and subscribe to agent class so that the RTI will inform them of new agents or deleted ones. Discovering in this sense does not mean that federates can discover abilities of agents, to do that takes sending perhaps several KQML messages for querying agent abilities. Furthermore, RTI assigns names to the created objects, names which are unique in the scope of a federation, so using these names as the agent symbolic names relieves the designer of the problem of ensuring unique agent names.

The other architectural entity is a KQML message. A KQML message is nothing but a piece of transient data to be transferred between the agents. Since the agents are executed by federates in our HLA based architecture, the KQML messages are to be perceived as data passed between the federates. It must be noted that semantically this data is sent from an agent to an agent, but architecturally the message is to be passed between federates. We assume that the exchanged KQML data is a somewhat encoded form of the KQML message, that all the federates know how to decode and parse it.

KQML designers have made some assumptions about the transport layer that will carry the KQML messages. These assumptions are:

1. Agents are connected by unidirectional communication links that carry discrete messages. These links may have a non-zero message transport delay associated with them.
2. When an agent receives a message, it knows from which incoming link the message arrived. When an agent sends a message, it may direct the message to a particular outgoing link.

3. Messages to a single destination arrive in the order they were sent.
4. Message delivery is reliable.

Straightforward ones first: The ability of transferring data between agents which is mentioned in the first assumption is trivially satisfied by HLA's ability to transfer data between the federates. Furthermore, the fourth assumption is about the delivery of messages and HLA RTI is defined to be configurable about using reliable transport for interactions and attribute updates. So these two assumptions create no problem.

Two major difficulties is that the first assumption, combined with the second one, calls for point-to-point links between the agents, and the third assumption calls for send-order reception of messages. These two have no immediate counterpart solutions in HLA, so various alternative solutions have been studied on. The following two subsections cover the solutions we devised.

4.1 Point-to-Point Links Problem

Providing point-to-point links between the agents in the multi-agent architecture defined over the HLA is difficult due to HLA's policy of preventing federates being aware of each other directly. This implies that the links we talk about are simulated links between the agent HLA objects, wherever their execution may be taking place. It turns out that one may use Data Distribution Management (DDM) quite effectively for the purpose of limiting the distribution of the message to only the relevant federates. The use of DDM is postponed to the end of this subsection.

The first way of transporting KQML messages between the federates that execute the communicating parties is using the interactions. In this method, all federates publish and subscribe to a *KQMLMessage* interaction class. When a federate wants to send a message on behalf of an agent it simulates, the message along with the source and destination agent names is encoded into a KQMLMessage interaction and sent. Without DDM, this interaction is received by all federates and the federate simulating the destination agent may easily deduce that it should handle the message.

The second way of transporting KQML messages is using the object attribute update mechanisms of HLA. One can either use this method in a push or pull communication scheme. Pull communication scheme is relatively more simple than the push scheme. In the pull scheme, a *MessageUttered* attribute is defined for the Agent HLA object class. All federates that simulate an agent publish an instance of this class for all agents they simulate, and subscribe to this class to get the messages other agents produce. Whenever a federate wants to send a message, it encodes the message and updates the MessageUttered attribute of the agent instance, and, having subscribed, all other federates receive this attribute update and decode the message to see if its destination is an agent they simulate.

The push scheme uses a *MessageReceived* attribute defined in the Agent class, and HLA's object attribute ownership management facilities. In this scheme, as in the pull case, all federates publish an instance of the Agent class and subscribe to the Agent class to get the attribute updates for the MessageReceived attribute. When a federate wants to send a message on behalf of an agent it simulates, it first acquires the ownership of the MessageReceived attribute of the agent which is the destination of the message. When acquisition is completed, the message is sent by updating the value of the attribute, thereby causing all federates to receive the message and decode to see if it is for an agent they simulate.

As it's most easily seen in the last scheme, these methods of transporting the KQML message are not very efficient due to the fact that all federates receive all messages, whether it is relevant for them or not. This is surely not desirable, instead we conceive of point-to-point links as being between the corresponding parties, and not causing any load for others that may be present in the communication network. As said before, this inefficiency is due to HLA's design. The solution proposed by the standard is use of DDM services. We applied the DDM services to the mentioned solutions. To use DDM, a routing space is created and every agent in the simulation is given a different region in this space. All the federates simulating agents publish, for every agent they simulate, the region of the agent through an instance of an Agent HLA object class. All federates also subscribe to the Agent HLA object class so that all federates can access the regions of any agent present.

In the case of employing DDM when interactions are used for delivery, all federates subscribe to the interaction class KQMLMessage with a region that covers the union of all regions of the agents it is simulating. When a message is to be sent, the sending federate sends the interaction to the target agent's region, and DDM routes the interaction to the only relevant federate.

When the pull scheme is used with DDM, a federate subscribes to the MessageUttered attribute with a region that is the union of all regions of the agents it simulates, as in the interaction case. Whenever a federate, on behalf of an agent, wants to send a message, it first makes the source agent's MessageUttered attribute visible to the federate simulating the destination agent by changing the publication region of the MessageUttered attribute to cover the destination agent's region. Then the source agent's object intance's attribute is updated and the message gets transferred. The push scheme is similar with the extra step of acquiring the attribute ownership.

4.2 Send-Order Reception Problem

The third transport assumption of KQML calls for send-order reception of messages. This mechanism has no immediate equivalent in the HLA architecture: The HLA architecture supports receive-order or time-stamp-order message transport. We devised two solutions, both using time to make messages arrive in send-order, one defining the flow of time in terms of the messages created by all agents (or federates we may say) in a federation, and the other relying on the physical nature of message generation.

The first solution defines the flow of simulation time in terms of messages generated throughout the federation. All federates work in optimistic time management mode, thereby observing all the events in their simulated future by issuing FLUSH QUEUE REQUEST service of RTI. When a federate generates a message, it increments its simulation time by a fixed amount. When it receives messages, it tries to increment its time to the time of the latest message it received. This solution creates problems with DDM though, since it depends on all federates receiving all events in the future to update their time, and DDM effectively prevents this by providing true point-to-point links (Fig. 1 shows diagrammatically). It is possible to use a separate event for the coordination purpose, and using such a small event may be justified taking the size of messages to be delivered into consideration.

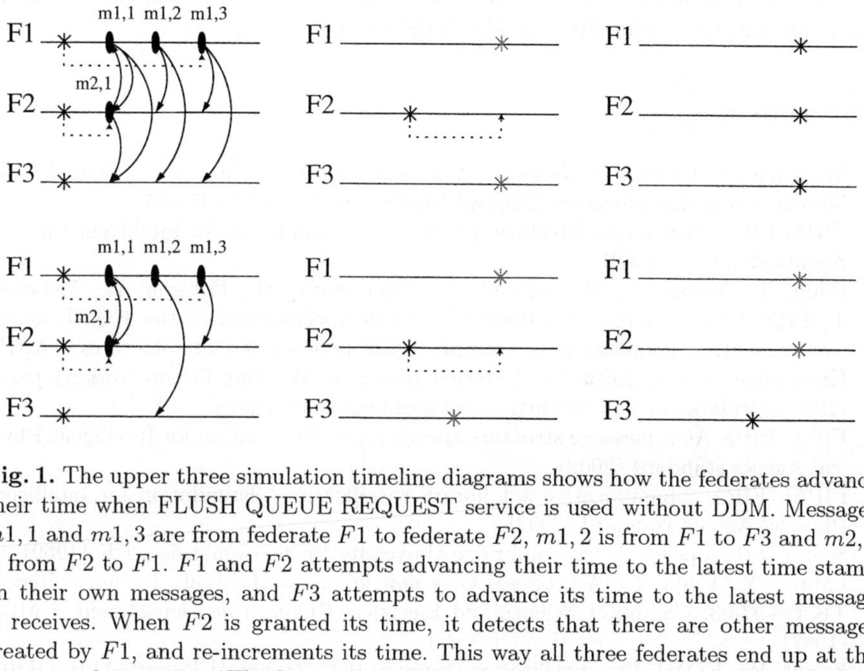

Fig. 1. The upper three simulation timeline diagrams shows how the federates advance their time when FLUSH QUEUE REQUEST service is used without DDM. Messages $m1, 1$ and $m1, 3$ are from federate $F1$ to federate $F2$, $m1, 2$ is from $F1$ to $F3$ and $m2, 1$ is from $F2$ to $F1$. $F1$ and $F2$ attempts advancing their time to the latest time stamp on their own messages, and $F3$ attempts to advance its time to the latest message it receives. When $F2$ is granted its time, it detects that there are other messages created by $F1$, and re-increments its time. This way all three federates end up at the same simulation time. The lower three diagrams show the case when DDM is used. DDM effectively prevents federate $F3$ gaining the necessary information about $m1, 3$, therefore federates $F1$ and $F2$ get stuck in time advancing state.

The other solution is to assume that in a simulation, time has a physical meaning and using time as merely a mechanism for synchronization would render the federation's reuse and interoperability. In such a view of time, creating a message is a physical action that takes some amount of time to accomplish. This implies that either all the messages created by an agent have different time stamps, or the number of messages created with the same time stamp is limited, and that not receiving the messages until an agent's local time, which may considerably differ from agent to agent in a distributed simulation, passes the message creation simulated time.

5 Conclusion

HLA, being a standard for distributed simulation architecture, is destined to provide better support for the use of agent technology since agent-based modeling is gaining popularity. Agent communication languages may be of importance as tools to build upon the data transport medium of HLA for agent based simulations. We believe that this paper presents one solution to the agent communication issue, using the language KQML.

Of the solutions described in this paper, we believe that using interactions with DDM provides the most elegant solution. This belief is empirical, and further analysis need to be made in order to defend one method against other. Further studies include analysis of such design decisions and implementing the FIPA architecture using HLA as the transport medium.

References

1. Marcenac, P., Giroux, S.: Geamas: A generic architecture for agent-oriented simulations of complex processes. Applied Intelligence **8** (1998) 247–267
2. FIPA: FIPA abstract architecture specification. Foundation for Intelligent Physical Agents standard (2002)
3. Finin, T., Weber, J., Wiederhold, G., Genesereth, M., Fritzson, R., McGuire, J., Pelavin, R., Shapiro, S., Beck, C.: Draft specification of the KQML agent-communication language plus example agent policies and architectures. ARPA Knowledge Sharing Initiative, External Interfaces Working Group working paper (1993) Available in web site http://www.cs.umbc.edu/kqml/.
4. FIPA: FIPA ACL message structure specification. Foundation for Intelligent Physical Agents standard (2002)
5. FIPA: FIPA communicative act library specification. Foundation for Intelligent Physical Agents standard (2002)
6. Searle, J.R.: Speech Acts. Cambridge University Press, Cambridge, UK (1969)
7. Labrou, Y., Finin, T.: A proposal for a new kqml specification. Technical Report TR CS-97-03, Computer Science and Electrical Engineering Department, UMBC (1997)
8. Kogut, P.: KQML lite specification, revision 0.3. Technical Report ALP-TR/03, Lockheed Martin Mission Systems (1998)
9. Labrou, Y., Finin, T.: Semantics and conversations for an agent communication language. In Huhns, M.N., Singh, M.P., eds.: Readings in Agents. Morgan Kaufmann, San Francisco, CA, USA (1997) 235–242

Improved POCS-Based De-blocking Algorithm for Block-Transform Compressed Images*

Yoon Kim[1], Chun-Su Park[1], Kyunghun Jang[2], and Sung-Jea Ko[1]

[1] Department of Electronics Engineering, Korea University, Anam-Dong, Sungbuk-Ku, Seoul 136-701, Korea.
{ykim, cspark, sjko}@dali.korea.ac.kr

[2] i-Networking Lab. Samsung Advanced Institute of Technology, Suwon, Korea
khjang@samsung.com

Abstract. This paper presents a postprocessing technique based on the theory of projections onto convex sets (POCS) to reduce the blocking artifacts in low bit rate BDCT-coded images. In the block discrete cosine transform (BDCT), the image is divided into a grid of non-overlapped 8×8 blocks, and then each block is coded separately. Thus, a block, which is shifted one pixel diagonally from the original grid of BDCT, will include the boundary of the original 8×8 block. If blocking artifacts are introduced along the block boundary, the frequency characteristics of this shifted block will be different from those of the original block. Therefore, a comparison of frequency characteristics of these two overlapping blocks can detect the undesired high-frequency components, mainly caused by the blocking artifacts. By eliminating these undesired high-frequency components adaptively considering the local statistical properties of the image, robust smoothing projection operator can be obtained. Computer simulation results indicate that the proposed scheme provides better visual performance than conventional postprocessing algorithms.

1 Introduction

Image compression techniques based on BDCT have been popularly used for both still and moving image coding standards, such as JPEG [1], H.26x [2], and MPEG [3]. In BDCT, an image is partitioned into spatially adjoining blocks, each of which is processed independently without considering the inter-block correlation. At low bits rates, image compression based on BDCT inevitably produces the blocking artifacts. Various algorithms have been proposed to improve the quality of block-coded images in the decoder without increasing the bit rate. Among them, iterative approaches based upon the theory of POCS have been widely used for blocking artifacts reduction [4,5] and error concealment [6].

In this paper, based on the theory of POCS, we propose a new postprocessing technique to reduce the blocking artifacts in BDCT-coded images. In BDCT,

* This work is supported by a grant from Korea University and Samsung Advanced Institute of Technology.

A. Yazici and C. Şener (Eds.): ISCIS 2003, LNCS 2869, pp. 627–634, 2003.

the image is divided into a grid of non-overlapped 8×8 blocks, and then each block is coded separately. Consider a block that is shifted one pixel diagonally from the 8×8 original grid. Since this shifted block includes boundaries of the original 8×8 block, the two overlapping blocks will have different frequency characteristics due to the blocking artifacts along the block boundaries. Based on these characteristics, we introduce a novel closed convex set and its projection operator in the DCT domain based on the theory of POCS to reduce blocking artifacts effectively.

The rest of this paper is organized as follows. In the next section, conventional postprocessing algorithms based on the theory of POCS are briefly introduced. The proposed postprocessing scheme is presented in Sect. 3. Sect. 4 presents and discusses the experimental results. Finally, our conclusions are given in Sect. 5.

2 Conventional Postprocessing Techniques Based on the Theory of POCS

The theory of projections onto convex sets (POCS) is a special case of the composite mapping algorithms for image restoration. It is known that the postprocessing techniques based on the theory of POCS satisfy two requirements [4, 5,7]: First, the closed convex sets, which capture the properties of the image free from the blocking artifacts and close to the original image, should be defined. Second, the projection operators onto them are derived.

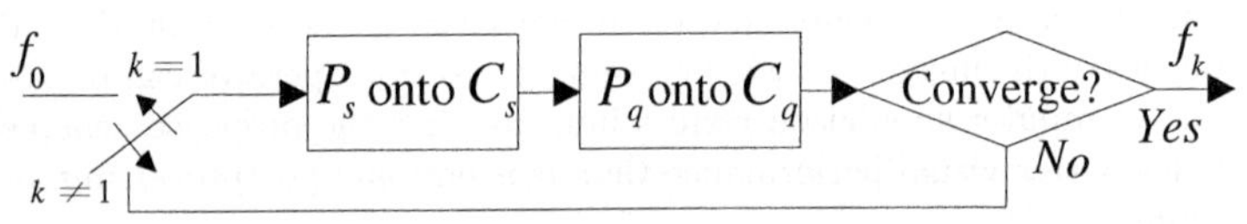

Fig. 1. Block diagram of the postprocessing technique based on the theory of POCS

Zakhor [4] first introduced an iterative algorithm using the theory of POCS for the reduction of blocking artifacts of block DCT-coded images. In this approach, a decoded image is reconstructed by the iterative projections onto two constraint sets. Generally, these constraint sets can be classified into either *smoothness constrain set* (SCS, C_s) and *quantization constraint set* (QCS, C_q) (Fig. 1). The projection P_s onto SCS bandlimits the image in the horizontal and vertical directions in order to reduce directional blocking artifacts. On the other hand, in common the QCS is defined as the quantization interval for the original DCT coefficient. Since the quantization parameters are transmitted from the encoder, the quantization interval for each DCT coefficient is already known to the decoder. And its projection operator P_q moves the DCT coefficient into the quantization interval. In [5,7,8], the SCSs are proposed and the same quantization constraint utilized in Zakhor's method is used.

3 Proposed Smoothness Constraint Set and Its Projection for the Reducing of Blocking Artifacts

Next, we introduce a method to reduce the blocking artifacts effectively by analyzing frequency characteristics of the original block and the shifted block which is one pixel diagonally apart from the original block. To do this, we propose the smoothness constraint set and its projection operator in the DCT domain.

First, let us denote an $mN \times nN$ input image and its pixel by $\boldsymbol{f}$ and $f(k,l)$, respectively, where (k,l) is the pixel coordinate. Also, let $\boldsymbol{f}_{A_{ij}}$ and $\boldsymbol{f}_{B_{ij}}$ be sets consisting of N^2 elements representing pixels in each $N \times N$ block, given by

$$\boldsymbol{f}_{A_{ij}} = \{a_{ij}(0,0), \cdots, a_{ij}(N-1,N-1)\}, \tag{1}$$

$$\boldsymbol{f}_{B_{ij}} = \{b_{ij}(0,0), \cdots, b_{ij}(N-1,N-1)\}, \tag{2}$$

where $a_{ij}(x,y) = f(iN+x, jN+y)$, $b_{ij}(x,y) = f(iN+x+1, jN+y+1)$, $i = 0, \cdots, (m-2)$, and $j = 0, \cdots, (n-2)$, respectively.

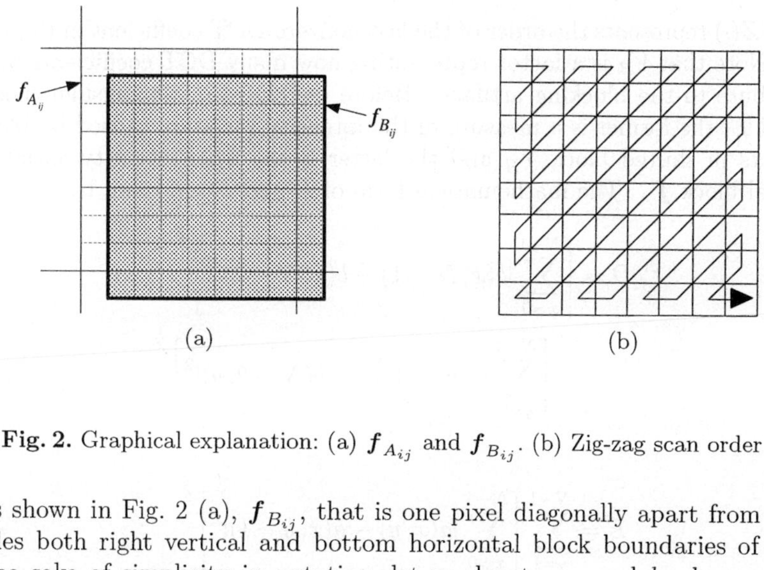

Fig. 2. Graphical explanation: (a) $\boldsymbol{f}_{A_{ij}}$ and $\boldsymbol{f}_{B_{ij}}$. (b) Zig-zag scan order

As shown in Fig. 2 (a), $\boldsymbol{f}_{B_{ij}}$, that is one pixel diagonally apart from $\boldsymbol{f}_{A_{ij}}$, includes both right vertical and bottom horizontal block boundaries of $\boldsymbol{f}_{A_{ij}}$. For the sake of simplicity in notation, let us denote a_{ij} and b_{ij} by a and b, respectively. And let the DCT of $a(x,y)$ and $b(x,y)$ be $A(u,v)$ and $B(u,v)$, respectively. Then, we have

$$A(u,v) = \alpha(u)\alpha(v) \sum_{x=0}^{N-1} \sum_{y=0}^{N-1} a(x,y) \times \cos[\frac{\pi(2x+1)u}{2N}] \cos[\frac{\pi(2y+1)v}{2N}], \tag{3}$$

$$B(u,v) = \alpha(u)\alpha(v) \sum_{x=0}^{N-1} \sum_{y=0}^{N-1} b(x,y) \times \cos[\frac{\pi(2x+1)u}{2N}] \cos[\frac{\pi(2y+1)v}{2N}], \tag{4}$$

where

$$\alpha(k) = \begin{cases} \sqrt{\frac{1}{N}}, & k = 0, \\ \sqrt{\frac{2}{N}}, & \text{otherwise.} \end{cases} \tag{5}$$

To reduce the blocking artifacts in the decoded image, we use the frequency characteristics of B. If nonzero coefficients of B occur at higher order in the zig-zag scan (See Fig. 2 (b)) than the highest nonzero valued location of A, those coefficients correspond to high frequencies caused by the blocking artifacts. In order to eliminate these high frequencies, we propose a POCS-based de-blocking algorithm using the smoothness constraint set and its projection operator as follows:

Let us define closed convex set C_B as

$$C_B = \{\boldsymbol{f} | \boldsymbol{f}_B \subset \boldsymbol{f}, NZ(B) \leq K_B\}, \tag{6}$$

where

$$K_B = NZ(A) + V_B, \tag{7}$$

and $NZ(\cdot)$ represents the order of the last nonzero DCT coefficient in the zig-zag scan. Note that V_B is a factor representing how many DCT coefficients of B do contribute to the blocking artifacts. Before defining V_B, we consider measures D and E, the former is a measure of the intensity variation caused by blocking artifacts in shifted block $\boldsymbol{f}_B$ and the latter is the total intensity variation in original block $\boldsymbol{f}_A$. The mathematical form of D and E are given by

$$D = \left[\sum_{x=0}^{N-1} |b(x, N-1) - b(x, N-2)|^2\right]^{\frac{1}{2}} + \left[\sum_{y=0}^{N-1} |b(N-1, y) - b(N-2, y)|^2\right]^{\frac{1}{2}}, \tag{8}$$

and

$$E = \sum_{y=1}^{N-1} \left[\sum_{x=0}^{N-1} |a(x, y) - a(x, y-1)|^2\right]^{\frac{1}{2}} + \sum_{x=1}^{N-1} \left[\sum_{y=0}^{N-1} |a(x, y) - a(x-1, y)|^2\right]^{\frac{1}{2}}. \tag{9}$$

Define $\tilde{E} = \frac{E}{N-1}$ for scaling. It is obvious that when D is smaller than $\tilde{E}$, blocking artifacts do not exist and $V_B = N^2 - NZ(A)$. As D increases, blocking artifacts increase, while V_B decreases. A function representing the above property is given by

$$V_B = round\left\{\left[1 - \max\left(\frac{D - \tilde{E}}{D + \tilde{E}}, 0\right)\right] \cdot \left[N^2 - NZ\left(A\right)\right]\right\}, \tag{10}$$

where, $max(\cdot,\cdot)$ is larger one between two values, and $round(c)$ is the integer value closest to c.

By observing the smoothness constraint set defined above, the projection operator onto that set can be easily found as follows: By discarding the nonzero coefficients of B at higher orders than the predetermined value K_B, we can obtain the projected element $\hat{B}$.

Given a decoded image $\boldsymbol{f}_0$, we determine $mN \times nN$ closed convex set C_q's by using the quantization level for each DCT coefficient of the block. Then, we use the closed convex set C_B in (6). Then, the projection operator onto smoothness constraint set is applied. Note that this computation is performed for all of the $(m-1)\times(n-1)$ smoothness constraint set $C_{B_{ij}}$'s. Next, the projection operator onto quantization constraint set is applied [4] to generate the postprocessed image $\boldsymbol{f}_1$. This procedure is iteratively performed to obtain the postprocessed image $\boldsymbol{f}_k$.

4 Experimental Results

In this section, the performance of four postprocessing techniques, namely, Zakhor's [4], Yang's [5], Paek's [8], and the proposed technique is evaluated on still images including "LENA", "ZELDA", "CAMERA", "BRIDGE", and etc. "LENA" and "ZELDA" images contain low-frequency components and smooth area, while "CAMERA" and "BRIDGE" images contain high-frequency components and edge area. Thus, we will be able to examine how much the high-frequency components in the original image affect the performance, and the robustness of the content of the input images. Several decoded images, with visible blocking artifacts, are obtained by JPEG [1] with the same quantization table as shown in Table 1.

Table 1. Quantization table

50	60	70	70	90	120	255	255
60	60	70	96	130	255	255	255
70	70	80	120	200	255	255	255
70	96	120	145	255	255	255	255
90	130	200	255	255	255	255	255
120	255	255	255	255	255	255	255
255	255	255	255	255	255	255	255
255	255	255	255	255	255	255	255

In Fig. 3, the PSNR performance of the proposed technique is compared with those of other techniques, with iteration increasing. One iteration of postprocessing is carried out by applying two projection operators first onto C_s and next onto C_q, as described in the previous section. As shown in Fig. 3, it is observed that the proposed technique converges, regardless of the input images, and can

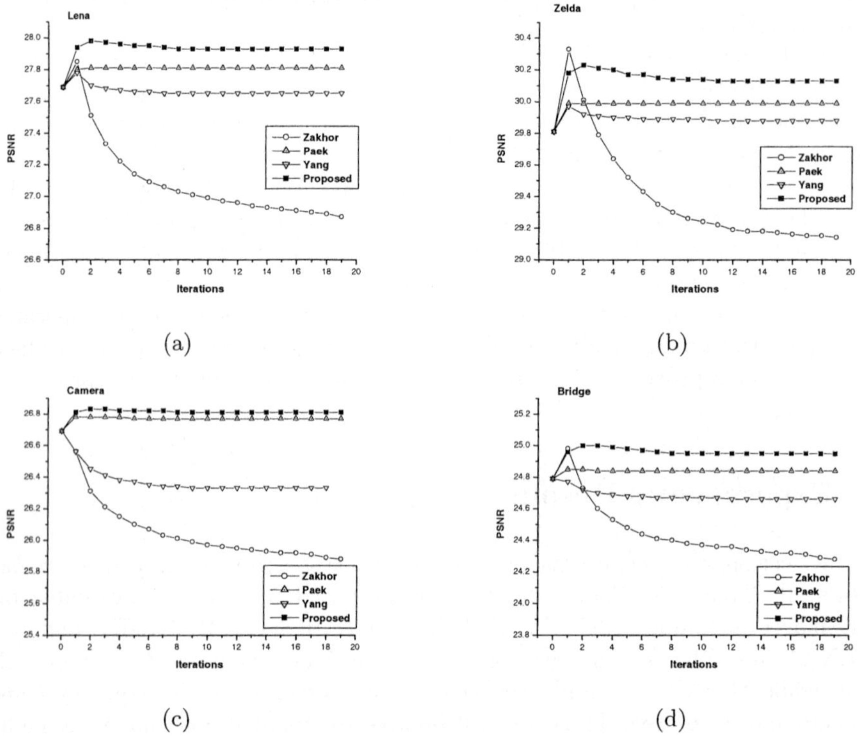

Fig. 3. PSNR performance variations on four decoded images. (a) "LENA" image. (b) "ZELDA" image. (c) "CAMERA" image. (d) "BRIDGE" image

be easily implemented. From Fig. 3, we can see that the Zakhor's technique fails to converge, in terms of the theory of POCS. Also, the performance of the proposed technique is better than those of Yang's and Paek's techniques in terms of the PSNR. Thus, it is believed that our technique is robust to the input images, in terms of convergence behavior and performance improvement.

To make a comparison of the subjective quality more clear, we present enlarged photographs of the details of "LENA" in Fig. 4. As shown in Fig. 4, although Zakhor's technique alleviated the blocking artifacts, it yields an excessively smoothed image due to the use of a global low-pass filter. Fig. 4 reveal that the blocking artifacts are alleviated more effectively by the proposed technique than the other techniques. It is also observed that edges are preserved very faithfully by the proposed technique. Similar results are also observed on the other three test images. Hence the proposed smoothness constraint set and its projection operator are properly defined, providing good performance in terms of both the PSNR and subjective quality.

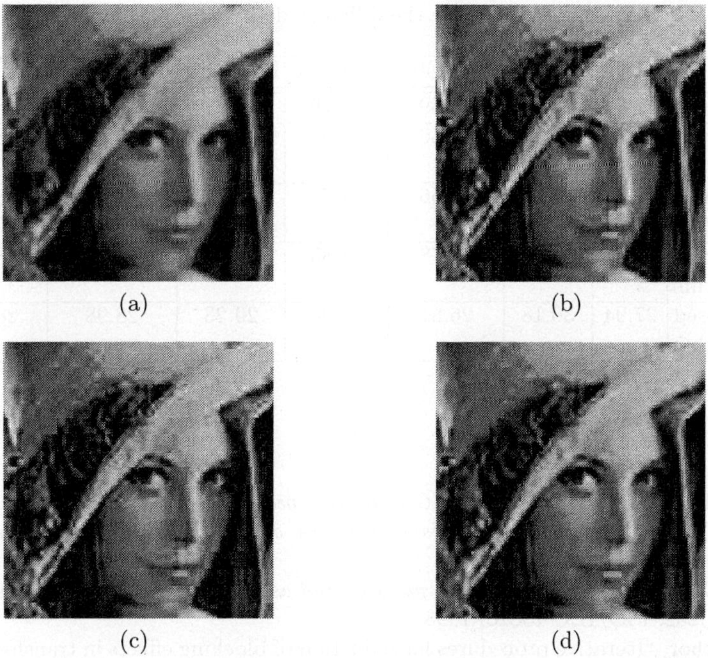

Fig. 4. Comparison of subjective quality on "LENA". Post-processed images: (a) Zakhor's algorithm. (b) Yang's algorithm.(c) Paek's algorithm. (d) The proposed method

In Table 2, the PSNR performance of the proposed technique is compared with those of Zakhor's, Yang's, and Paek's techniques. The simulation results show that the performance of the proposed algorithm is better than those of other algorithms.

5 Conclusions

In this paper, based on the theory of POCS, we proposed a postprocessing visual enhancement technique to reduce the blocking artifacts in BDCT-coded images. The novel smoothness constraint set and its projection operator were introduced. By using two overlapping blocks each of which is one pixel apart from the other, we can detect undesired high-frequency components mainly caused by the blocking artifacts. By eliminating these undesired high-frequency components adaptively, we obtained the robust smoothing projection operator. Computer simulation results indicate that the performance of the proposed scheme performs better than conventional postprocessing schemes.

Table 2. PSNR for the different de-blocking methods

	LENA	ZELDA	CAMERA	BRIDGE	PEPPER	BARBARA	CHURCH
JPEG	27.68	29.81	26.69	24.79	28.84	28.43	28.44
Zakhor's algorithm	27.85	30.33	26.56	24.98	29.27	29.13	28.77
Yang's algorithm	27.78	29.97	26.56	24.77	28.71	28.96	28.35
Paek's algorithm	27.80	29.99	26.78	24.85	29.01	28.64	28.22
Proposed algorithm	27.94	30.18	26.81	24.96	29.23	28.98	28.74

References

1. ISO/IEC/JTC1/SC1/WG8 *JPEG technical specification*, vol. Revision 8, 1990.
2. ITU-T *Video codec for audiovisual services at px64kbps*, vol. Recommendation H.261, 1993.
3. I. JTC1/SC29 *Coding of moving pictures and association audio*, vol. Recommendation H.262: ISO/IEC 13818, 1993.
4. A. Zakhor, "Iterative procedures for reduction of blocking effects in transform image coding," *IEEE Trans. on Circuits Syst. Video Technol.*, vol. 2, pp. 91–95, Mar. 1992.
5. Y. Yang, N. P. Galatsanos, and A. K. Katsaggelos, "Regularized reconstruction to reduce blocking artifacts of block discrete cosine transform compressed images," *IEEE Trans. on Circuits Syst. Video Technol.*, vol. 3, pp. 421–432, Dec. 1993.
6. H. Sun and W. Kwok, "Concealment of damaged block transform coded images using projections onto convex sets," *IEEE Trans. Image Processing*, vol. 4, pp. 470–477, Apr. 1995.
7. Y. Yang, N. P. Galatsanos, and A. K. Katsaggelos, "Projection-based spatially adaptive reconstruction of block-transform compressed images," *IEEE Trans. on Circuits Syst. Video Technol.*, vol. 5, pp. 298–304, Aug. 1995.
8. H. Paek, R. C. Kim, and S. U. Lee, "On the pocs-based postprocessing technique to reduce the blocking artifacts in transform coded images," *IEEE Trans. on Circuits Syst. Video Technol.*, vol. 8, pp. 358–367, June 1998.

Lossy Network Performance of a Rate-Control Algorithm for Video Streaming Applications

Aylin Kantarcı[1] and Turhan Tunalı[2]

[1]Computer Engineering Department, Ege University, Bornova, Izmir, Turkey
kantarci@bornova.ege.edu.tr

[2]International Computer Institute, Ege University, Bornova, Izmir, Turkey
tunali@ube.ege.edu.tr

Abstract. In this paper, we present performance results of our previously developed rate control algorithm under various controlled packet loss rates. Since IP has no QoS support for real-time delivery of multimedia data, QoS control service has to be provided by the applications. Unlike traditional rate control approaches that take into account only the loss statistics, our algorithm integrated receiver buffer status into the feedback messages from the clients. Under various packet loss rates, we compared our approach to traditional two watermark approach and observed that our algorithm is more robust to varying network conditions.

1 Introduction

Traditional Internet applications owe their stability to the congestion control and avoidance algorithms implemented in TCP, the dominant transport protocol of the Internet. Based on additive increase multiplicative decrease (AIMD) principle, TCP employs a window based congestion control approach. The congestion control mechanism incorporated into TCP probes for available bandwidth by slowly increasing a congestion window. When one or more packets get lost, it reduces the congestion window multiplicatively by a factor of two.

However, TCP is not suitable for real-time audio and video transmission. One of the reasons is that reliability and ordering semantics of TCP increases end-to-end delays and delay variations. Another reason is the aggressiveness of the windows based congestion control mechanism of TCP. Every lost packet results in a decrease in the transmission rate by a factor of two. This sharp decrease leads to unpleasant display qualities. On the other hand, multimedia applications can tolerate loss to some extent. Per packet acknowledgement strategy is another reason that makes TCP unsuitable for multimedia streaming. Acknowledgement packets introduce a large bandwidth overhead to high bandwidth multimedia applications [1].

Due to the above reasons, UDP is preferred over TCP as the transport protocol for real-time multimedia streams. However, UDP has no support for Quality of Service (QoS), which expresses the requirements of multimedia applications in terms of parameters such as throughput, loss, delay and jitter. Also, UDP has no provision for

A. Yazici and C. Şener (Eds.): ISCIS 2003, LNCS 2869, pp. 635–642, 2003.

congestion control. Fluctuations in network load may adversely affect the performance of the multimedia applications. Another problem is that high bandwidth requirement of multimedia applications with no congestion control mechanism, may lead to the starvation of TCP applications. Therefore, it is essential to implement a congestion control mechanism running on top of UDP[1, 2].

The other fact is that UDP has no support for real-time data. Due to this fact, IETF has developed new transport protocols for streaming applications. One of the proposed protocols is Real-time Transport Protocol, RTP. RTP is an application layer protocol based on UDP. It supports many payload types such as MPEG-1, MPEG-2, MPEG-4, H.261, H.263, JPEG, etc. RTP offers no mechanisms for reliability and ordering facilities. These issues are left to application developer. Although RTP has been designed specifically for multicast applications, is well suited to unicast applications. RTP has no mechanism for QoS control. Instead, it is accompanied with another protocol called Real-time Control Protocol, RTCP to convey statistical information about the QoS parameters such as loss, delay and jitter. It is the responsibility of applications to perform rate control using RTCP reports [3].

Earlier studies on guaranteeing a certain level of QoS were based on mechanisms such as admission control and resource reservation. These mechanisms assume that resource requirement of multimedia applications known a priori and use worst case resource usage scenarios which lead to resource underutilization. Differentiated or prioritized services at network switches may also be used to provide a certain level of QoS with the applications [1]. Later, it is observed that adjusting the resource usage according to the existing network conditions is more appropriate. This approach is preferred to the previously proposed mechanisms based on admission control and resource reservation because it leads to better utilization of available network resources, which change dynamically. Additionally, this approach is well suited to the nature of multimedia applications, which allow the media rate and quality can be changed over a wide range. In literature, this approach is called *rate control* [4].

In this study, we implemented a rate control mechanism [6] for video streaming of MPEG-1 data on Solaris 2.8 platform and demonstrated the behavior of our rate control algorithm in lossy networks using a WAN simulation package, CLOUD. Most of the rate control mechanisms in literature [1] employ only loss statistics for adaptation. In our work, buffer status has been incorporated into the rate control algorithm in addition to loss statistics.

This paper is organized as follows: In Section 2 our rate control algorithm is described in detail. Performance results are given in Section 3. Finally, Section 4 is the conclusion.

2 The Rate Control Algorithm

Our rate-control algorithm is developed in [5, 6]. In this study, we examine the robustness of our algorithm under varying network conditions. This section of the paper summarizes some of the design principles of our algorithm.

Some features of our system are as follows:

1. Videos are pre-encoded at multiple rates, namely 100Kbps, 200 Kbps, 500 Kbps and 1000 Kbps. Videos are transmitted in unicast manner. Each video file is associated with a meta data file that describes the structure of the video. The metafiles are useful to facilitate application layer framing and to adjust data rate. Meta files store information about the frame types, frame sizes, GOP statistics, sequence statistics and packet interval values for different adjustment levels.
2. We employed source based rate control with a probe based approach for bandwidth detection. Receivers send their feedback on congestion status via RTCP reports. The server then adjusts its rate properly. In non-congested state, the sender probes for extra bandwidth by switching to a better quality video and monitors RTCP loss statistics. As long as no congestion is detected, probing experiments continue. When congestion occurs the previous version of the video is switched back.
3. In addition to loss statistics, buffer status has been incorporated into the rate control algorithm.
4. A rate shaping mechanism with frame dropping filter approach [3] has been implemented. The frame dropping filter omits frames from the GOP pattern to be sent according to the importance of different frame types.

Our adaptation policy is based on three observed variables, namely congestion level, receiver buffer level and the rate of change in receiver buffer level.

Congestion level is monitored through loss rate statistics reported in RTCP feedback messages. Table 1 shows the congestion levels in the system according to the loss fraction field in RTCP reports. In the uncongested state, the sender progressively increases its transmission rate in an additive manner. In congested state, the sender progressively reduces its transmission rate in a more aggressively additive manner than in the mildly congested state. In the severely congested state, the rate is reduced multiplicatively to alleviate the congestion in the network.

Table 1. Congestion Classes

Congestion Status	**Loss %**
NONCONGESTED	0-5
MILDLY CONGESTED	5-15
CONGESTED	15-50
SEVERELY CONGESTED	50-

At the client side, two parameters have been taken into account to determine the buffer status and are sent regularly to the server over a UDP channel. The first one is ttp, the duration of video currently present in the buffer. The second on is dttp, the rate of change in ttp. We determine three dttp regions. First region includes the negative dttp values, which corresponds to decrease in buffer level. The second region corresponds to the case when the dttp is between 0 and 1. In the third region, dttp values are greater than 1, which we assume that dttp is above 1.

We divided our buffer space into zones as follows: We set four points for our receiver buffer. Byte-overflow (byte-ovfl) is the top most level above which the receiver buffer enters a physical overflow region. Next comes time-to-play-overflow (ttp-ovfl) point set in terms of seconds. Note that byte-ovfl must be higher than highest quality video data rate multiplied by ttp-ovfl. Next what we call adjust threshold (adj-thr) is a point somewhere in the adjustable region. Next comes ttp-unfl, which determines the underflow region. We try to keep the buffer level around adj-thr level.

The rate control module at the server side reacts to the feedback messages by changing the video quality in accordance with the loss, ttp and dttp parameters. Video quality is changed in a seamless manner by switching to a video encoded at another rate, by dropping/adding frames from the current GOP pattern and by increasing/decreasing packet interval values between consecutive packets.

Each video in the system is stored at multiple encoding rates. Currently, four encoding rates, namely 100 Kbps, 200 Kbps, 500 Kbps and 1000 Kbps, are supported. Frame dropping/adding is performed by taking into consideration the dependencies among different frame types and the smoothness of the video stream.

Each encoding rate and GOP pattern adjustment level pair corresponds to a different video rate in the network. With these pairs, a grid may be formed where y axis and x axis correspond to encoding bit rate and GOP pattern adjustment levels respectively. Moving down along the y axis and right along the x axis reduces the video rate in the network. Various paths can be followed to change the rate of video in the network. Among all possible paths, we chose three of them to be used in different congestion and buffering conditions given in Fig. 1. In *linear* movement, effective data rate changes in an approximately linear fashion. Depending on the current state, any *linear* movement adaptation may involve frame discard rate or encoding date rate however, the latter change is much less infrequent. In *cubical* movement, depending on the current state, effective data rate changes either in additive or multiplicative manner. In *diagonal* movement, effective data rate changes in a multiplicative manner.

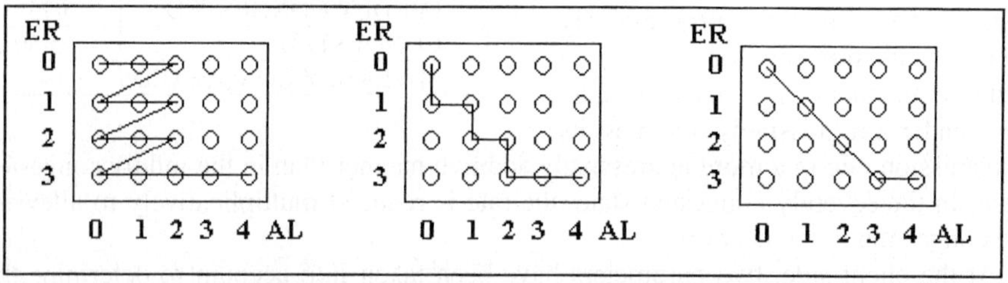

Fig. 1. Linear, cubical and diagonal movements

When the metadata files are being prepared, packetization module is executed for each encoding rate and adjustment level to determine the number of packets to be transmitted per video file. For each encoding rate and adjustment level, video duration is divided by the number of packets to calculate the transmission interval between successive packets during delivery. For flexibility, we used five packet interval values for each encoding rate and adjustment level pair. Packet intervals determined by using actual packet counts correspond to MEDIUM value of the packet interval. The other four values are obtained by dividing the interval between MEDIUM values of subsequent adjustment levels into four sub-intervals. The first and second values after the MEDIUM value of adjustment level k is called MEDIUM-HIGH and HIGH values of adjustment level k, respectively. The third and fourth values are LOW and MEDIUM-LOW values for adjustment level k+1, respectively. The proper packet interval is selected according to the severity of the congestion level and client buffer level. For example, in uncongested state and when the buffer level is low, LOW values of packet intervals are used to increase the buffer level in a shorter time period.

3 Performance Results

We tested our rate control algorithm by using CLOUD simulation software that simulates actual WAN environment by dropping packets received from the server in accordance with a given loss pattern.

We collected performance results under regular loss patterns and with a congested network scenario. Fig. 2 illustrates the loss conditions that we used in our experiments. Fig. 2.a, 2.b and 2.c shows the cases where the average loss rate is at a constant level in uncongested state and Fig 2.d illustrates a congested network.

When the loss rate is 1% and 3%, the system is in uncongested state. Therefore, rate control algorithm takes into account only the buffering conditions at the receiver side. Transmission starts at the encoding rate of 200 Kbps with a frame rate of 10 fps. Probing experiments show that the network is able to support higher quality. Therefore, the encoding rate and frame rate are increased to 1000 Kbps and 30 fps, respectively, which represents the highest video quality. Transmission of high quality video results in higher number of packets with larger end-to-end delay with respect to the case with lower video quality. After the prebuffering period, the client starts to consume the video. As the end-to-end delay increases due to transmission of large number of packets, it is observed that the consumption rate from the buffer becomes larger than incoming packet rate to the buffer. The goal of the adaptation algorithm is to keep the ttp values above adj-thr(=55 sec) as long as possible and react to congestion in the network. Shortly after the display begins, the ttp value falls below the adj-thr and packet loss is reported. The adaptation algorithm reacts by decreasing the video quality to 500 Kbps. When the loss rate is 1%, at time t=350, t=466 and t=510 sec., buffer level falls below the adj_thr (Fig. 4.a). At these points, encoding rate is reduced to increase the buffer level above adj_thr (Fig. 3.a). Reducing the encoding rate decreases network load. This is shown in the bps graph in Fig. 2.a. When the load decreases, delay also decreases and buffer level increases at a higher rate. Fig. 3 shows that, in all loss cases, frame level is changed more frequently than the encoding rate. When the average loss rate is 3%, more packets get lost in the network and consequently, buffer level drops more frequently below adh-thr(Fig. 4.b). Fig. 3.b shows that the encoding rate decreases to 200 Kbps to keep the buffer level at the desired level. In conjunction with the reduction in the encoding rate, network load decreases to 200 Kbps in average as given in Fig. 2.b.

The case with the average loss rate of 5% corresponds to the behavior of algorithm at the boundary point between the uncongested and mildly congested states. With this loss rate, loss statistics start to contribute to the rate control decisions when the instantaneous loss rate exceeds 5%. A regular loss pattern of 5% causes quick decreases in buffer occupancy . Our algorithm uses a trick to prevent the buffer from draining. When the buffer level is under ttp_unfl and the system is in uncongested state, packet interval is reduced to the smallest value of the prevailing encoding rate

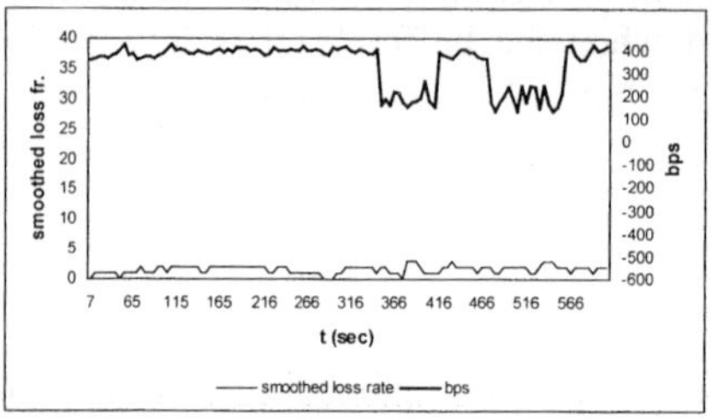

(a) loss= 1%

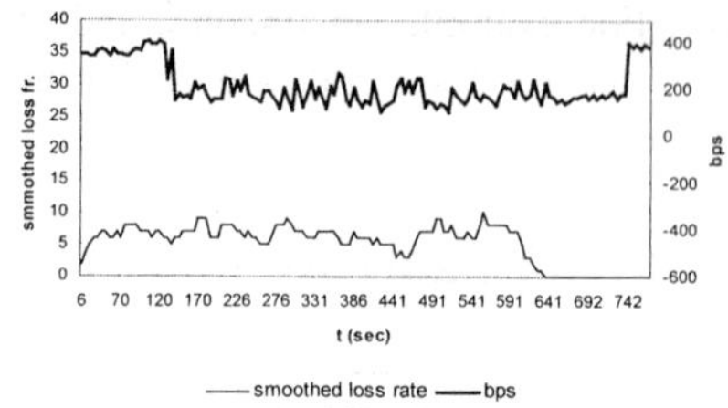

(b) loss = 2%

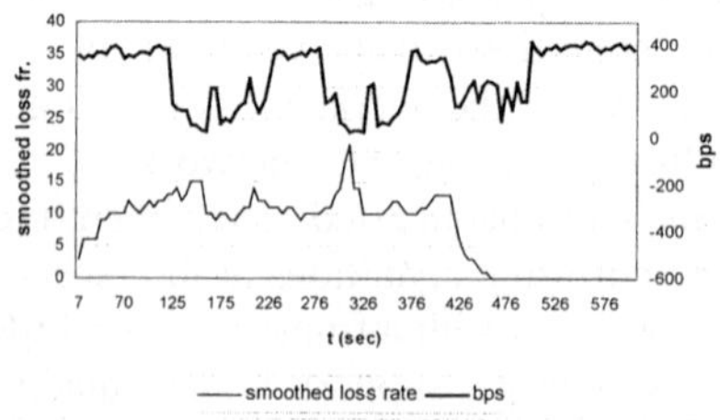

(c) loss= 5%

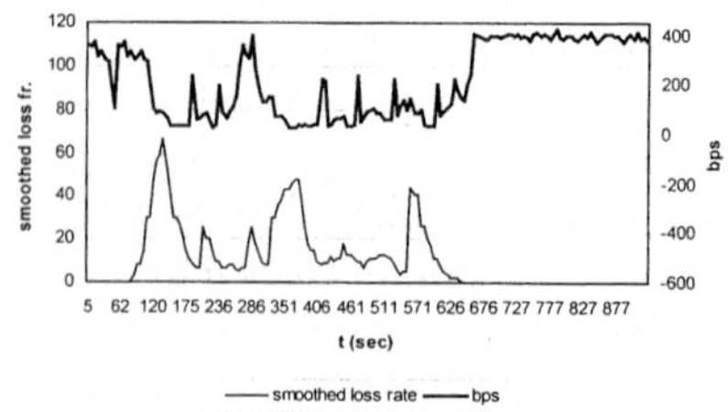

(d) congestion scenario

Fig. 2. Regular loss and congestion scenarios used in the experiments. Loss percentage is the integer part after dividing the loss fraction by 256.

until the buffer occupancy rises above adj_thr. High increases of ttp values given in Fig. 4.c reflects this behavior of our rate control algorithm. When the loss rate is 5%, an oscillating pattern is observed for the encoding rate. In conjunction with losses and decreases in buffer levels under adj_thr, encoding rate is decreased to 100 Kbps. The trick with packet interval values increases the ttp value above adj_thr and subsequently encoding rate is increased to its highest value for a period of time. This cycle is repeated during the playout of the video as shown in Fig. 3.c.

We also conducted experiments with regular loss patterns at loss rates higher than 10%. In those cases, encoding rate and frame rate decreased to the lowest values. More packets got lost in the network and buffer quickly drained, resulting in interrupts during the playout.

Fig. 2.d shows a variable loss pattern that we used in our experiments. The system is subjected to periods of congestion (t=90-200 sec, t=351-406 sec, t=550-626 sec).and periods of low loss values (Fig. 3.d). During congestion periods, ER values are quickly set to 100 Kbps and frame rates dropped to 1 fps. During uncongestion periods, video quality is increased to higher encoding rates and frame rates. When Figure 4.d is examined, the trick with packet interval values again prevents the buffer from draining when the loss rate is low.

In conclusion, when Fig. 4 is examined, it is seen that at low values of loss, ttp values are almost constant. Packet interval values are also almost constant indicating a stable network traffic. As the loss values increase, buffer occupancy decreases sharply. As a result of the switching between various encoding rates and frame rates, packet interval values show variation.

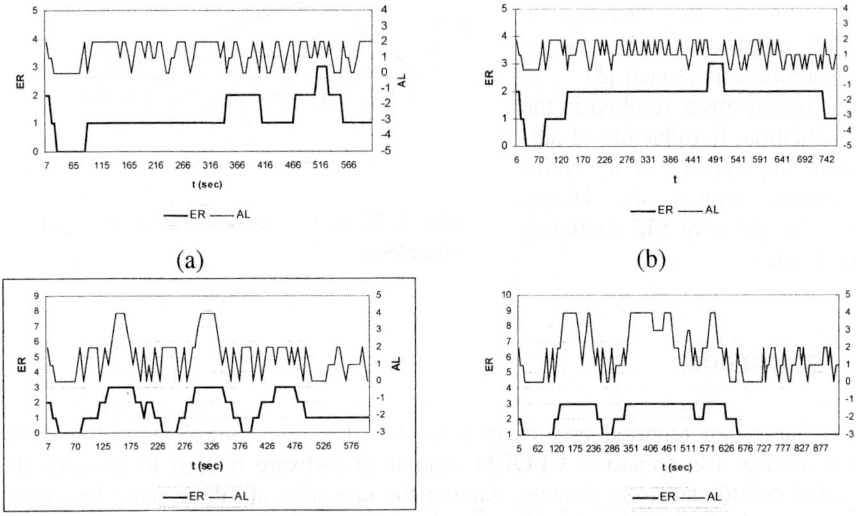

Fig. 3. ER/AL diagrams corresponding to the loss scenarios given in Fig. 2.

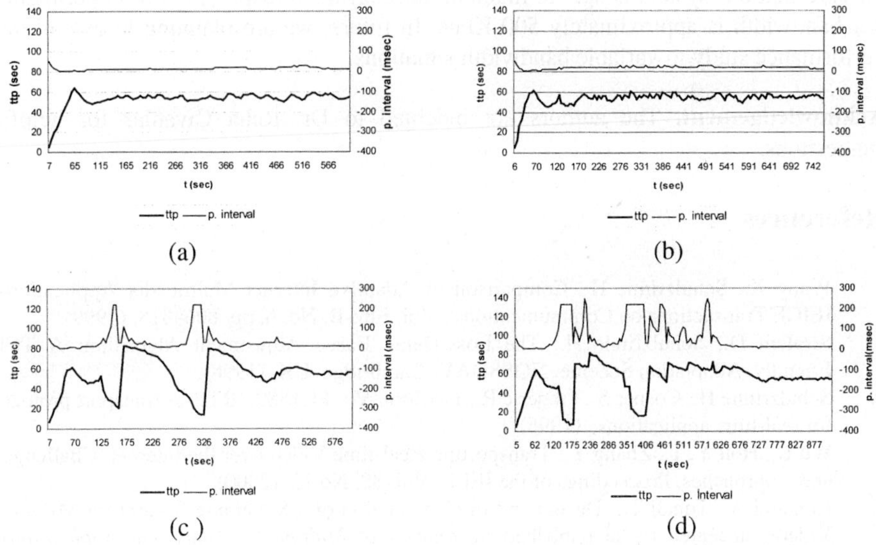

Fig. 4. Buffer levels and packet interval values for the loss patterns given in Fig. 2

We also compared the performance of our adaptation module with a traditional rate control algorithm with no consideration of buffer occupancy. Fig. 5 shows the buffer occupancy for the latter case. With the traditional rate control, buffer quickly drains leading to interruption in the display. In addition, employment of a simple two watermark approach [5] in buffer management resulted in the same situation. Introduction of adj-thr and employment of a control mechanism related to adj-thr enabled to preserve the continuity of the display.

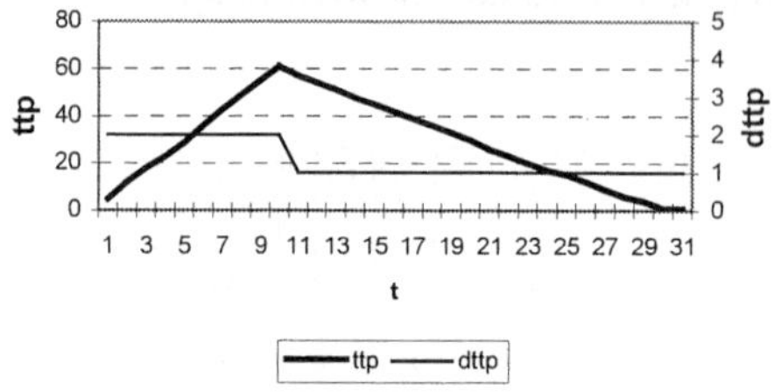

Fig. 5. Buffer level when buffer status is not considered

4 Conclusion

In this paper, we reported performance results of a rate control algorithm under various packet loss scenarios. CLOUD simulation software is used to generate the simulated end-to-end lossy channel. Among the scenarios are three fixed loss rates. We have gradually increased the loss rate to find out the breaking point. We have observed that our system is able to provide uninterrupted display even if we experience a fixed continuous loss rate of 10%. The varying loss rate scenario we have reported also involves burst losses of relatively long intervals, yet we still observe that our system is able to maintain uninterrupted display. In our experiments, our bandwidth is approximately 500 Kbps. In future, we are planning to extend this performance study to variable bandwidth situations.

Acknowledgement. The authors are indebted to Dr. Reha Cıvanlar for helpful suggestions.

References

1. Wang X., Schulzrinne H.: Comparison of Adaptive Internet Multimedia Applications, IEICE Transactions on Communications , Vol. E82-B, No. 6, pp. 806–818, (1999).
2. Sisalem D., Schulzrinne H.: The Loss-Delay Based Adjustment Algorithm: A TCP Friendly Adaptation Scheme, NOSSDAV, Cambridge, UK, (1998).
3. Schulzrinne H., Cosner S., Frederic R., Jacobson V.: FC1889: RTP: A transport protocol for real-time applications, (1996).
4. Wu D., Hou Y. T., Zhang Y.: Transporting Real-time Video over the Internet: Challenges and Approaches, Proceedings of the IEEE, Vol. 88, No.12 ,(2000).
5. Kantarci A., Tunali T.; Design and Implementation of a Streaming System for MPEG-1 Videos, accepted to be published in *Journal of Multimedia Tools and Applications*, Kluwer Academics.
6. Tunali T., Kantarci A., Özbek N.: , Robust Quality Adaptation for Internet Video Streaming in Heterogenous Networks, Journal of Multimedia Tools and Applications, in review.

A Hierarchical Architecture for a Scalable Multicast

Abderrahim Benslimane and Omar Moussaoui

Laboratoire d'Informatique d'Avignon LIA
339 chemin des Meinajaries
BP 1228 – 84911 Avignon cedex 9
benslimane@lia.univ-avignon.fr

Abstract. Multimedia applications, such as videoconferences, require an efficient management of the Quality of Service (QoS) and consist of a great number of participants. In order to support such applications, we propose a hierarchical architecture allowing efficient communication between disjoint local groups. To connect these groups, we use a shared-based tree method. For an effective evaluation, we compare it to a source-based tree method. With NS-2 simulations, we show that the two methods are better than the direct architecture. Shared-based tree method performs well when using dynamically several rendezvous points instead of unique and static point. The performances are the reduction of used bandwidth and the communications delays.

1 Introduction

The demand for multimedia which combines audio, video and data streams over a network is rapidly increasing. Some of the more popular real-time interactive applictions are teleconferencing, tele-teaching, games, white boards, etc. Multimedia applications require in general a considerable amount of bandwidth and a great number of participants. Multicast is regarded as a promising solution for group multimedia applications. It allows to reduce considerably the costs of communication (i.e., a single sender to several receivers or several senders to several receivers).
Several multicast protocols were proposed in the literature. However, the majority of them are not scalable. Indeed, these protocols are badly adapted to the networks of great dimension like Internet. Techniques based on hierarchical trees represent very promising solutions. Nevertheless, studies are primarily related to only theoretical aspects without taking account implementation.
In addition to the need of scalability, group based multimedia applications also demand stringent QoS requirements such as the minimum end-to-end delay, jitter delay and the efficient use of bandwidth. Several works was proposed to support QoS in networks. They concern the network functionalities of low levels (scheduling, traffic management, etc). The development of routing sensitive to QoS attracted less attention, although it is essential for the multimedia applications.
In this work, we propose a scalable multicast protocol supporting QoS. Indeed, we use hierarchical trees, rendezvous points and criteria on QoS to connect multicast

A. Yazici and C. Şener (Eds.): ISCIS 2003, LNCS 2869, pp. 643–650, 2003.

group members which are geographically located in the Internet. Whereas work in [4] use rendezvous points in static way our protocol determinates rendezvous points in a dynamic way.

The rest of the paper is organized as follow. In section 2, we give an overview of the multicast trees and protocols. Section 3, describes the conception of the hierarchical architecture. In section 4, we give a simulation with NS-2. Finally, we give a conclusion.

2 Multicast and QoS Overview

With the introduction of multimedia applications requiring guaranties of QoS, the multicast problem becomes more challenging. Efficiency of multicast protocols depends strongly on the underlying tree. Moreover, QoS guarantee depends on the architecture of the communication (i.e. subsequent network) and the used multicast protocol.

2.1 Multicast Tree

Multicast trees can be classified in two categories: shared trees and source-specific trees [6, 7]. A specific tree is built starting from a given source, so that it is necessary to build several trees for the same multicast group if this group contains several sources. It is unidirectional tree from the source to the receivers. On the other hand, a shared tree is established once to connect all multicast group members. Thus, it is bidirectional tree: there is no distinction between sources and receivers. The difference between the two types of tree relates to the number of states required to maintain the tree. The three principal types of tree are described in the following:

- The Shorter path tree, called SPT, is currently the most used. Each leaf of a tree is connected to the source by using shortest path. By construction, delays of this type of tree are minimal. However, use of resources with SPT trees is not economic. For each source there is a specific tree. Moreover, each branch is built independently of the other by unicast routing, without worrying about the proximity of nodes of the same group multicast.
- The Steiner tree is a shared tree allowing to connect the group members through a given graph by minimizing the used resources. The construction of Steiner tree is an NP-hard problem, which makes it extremely difficult to be implemented in a network of great scale. By construction, Steiner trees are optimal with respect to the cost (i.e. use of resources).
- The Core Based Tree (CBT) is extremely simple but it requires the knowledge of the rendezvous point (RP). To connect a leaf node to the multicast tree, it is enough to connect it to the RP with the shortest path (by using the subjacent unicast routing). The performances of CBT trees depend on the node where the RP is placed. However, RP are in general static (fixed once by the manager).

Table 1, gives some characteristics of the previous types of multicast trees. Results are issued from the above remarks and from simulation results given in [6, 7].

Table 1. Principal multicast trees

	SPT	CBT	Steiner
Complexity	low	low	high
Dynamic	good	good	bad
Cost	important	medium	low
Nb states	θ (*G.S*)	θ (*G*)	θ (*G*)
Delay	low	medium	medium
concentration	low	strong	strong

Thus, Steiner trees are particularly interesting from theoretical point of view because they allow to reduce considerably resources (number of links and states in the routers) used by a group multicast. Because they not allow a dynamic management and they are too complex to conceive, Steiner trees are not used currently. SPT trees are used for their simplicity and their excellent performances for multimedia applications (low delays and low concentration). Nevertheless, this type of tree consumes many resources. CBT trees seem an intermediate solution compared to Steiner and SPT trees. Delays can be rather good if PR is well placed. The use of resources is well reduced compared to SPT tree in the case of groups having several sources.

2.2 Multicast Protocols

In this section, we focus on the Internet protocols. Most of the currently deployed multicast protocols (i.e., DVMRP, PIM, MOSPF) build one shortest path multicast tree per sender, the tree being rooted at the sender's sub-network.

- DVMRP protocol: Distance Vector Multicast Routing Protocol (DVMRP) [8] uses a Reverse Path Multicast algorithm (RPM). It consists on the construction of a multicast tree where datagrams are sent by a source S to the members of the group.
- PIM protocol: PIM (Protocol Independent Multicast) works in two distinct modes which can be used together:
    - *Dense mode*: PIM-DM [3] is similar to DVMRP but uses routing tables of the underlying unicast protocol. It allows to build SPT trees by broadcasting and then pruning of the useless branches.
    - *Sparse mode*: PIM-SM [4] allows to build CBT or SPT trees. Rendezvous points are fixed administratively at the time of the configuration of the routers.

  Sparse mode is more economic in term of signalization exchanges or number of stored states when the group is slightly distributed in the network. On the contrary, the dense mode is well adapted when the group members are strongly concentrated in the network.

- MOSPF Protocol: MOSPF [5] is an extension of the unicast protocol OSPF (Open Shortest Path First). It builds only SPT trees. Each router has a topological vision of the network and the location of each member of the multicast group allows to build a representation of SPT tree.

The major limitation of existing multicast protocols lies in the fact that they are badly adapted to large scale networks like the Internet. Moreover, all these above protocols do not take into account all the requirements of good multicast routing protocol such as end-to-end delay, and bandwidth. To overcome these limitations, we propose a hierarchical architecture allowing efficient communication between group multicast members and supporting guaranties of QoS. The architecture consists on grouping members, according to their localization and to their response to the QoS requirements of the application, into disjoint groups. We use two different methods to connect these groups. The first one, presented in this paper, consists on using the concept of source-based tree. Whereas work in [4] use rendezvous points in static way, our protocol determinates rendezvous points in a dynamic way. The second one, considered in the simulation, consists on using a source-based tree method to connect groups between them. These architectures allow a scalable multicast that is sensitive to QoS.

3 Hierarchical Architecture for Multicast Group

Hierarchical trees are particularly interesting to support multicast in the wide-area networks. For this raison, we are interested in the shared-based tree.
So, we consider a multicast group M constituted of N processes distributed geographically on inter-connected different networks. These processes have different identities and communicate between them toward the Internet. Moreover, they participate at the same multimedia application such as videoconferencing. Communication between two processes can take different path.

3.1 Local Group Construction

Considering the high number of participants in multicast group M, it appears essential to divide them into local groups according to their concentration in the various areas of the Internet to ensure QoS. This decomposition allows to use efficiently the bandwidth, to reduce the consumption of resources, to optimize the delay and to ensure communications between processes. The construction of local groups was introduced by A. Benslimane and A. Abouaissa [1] in a logical way. Their algorithm supposes that processes communicate between them via virtual channels. In this work, we use real paths, i.e. physical links existing between the hosts and routers participating in the multicast group. To build these local groups, we construct a neighboring set and transit set for each process. A neighboring set is constructed according to a Time To Live value and a threshold value. A transit group is constructed according to the neighboring set and the capabilities of processing and buffering of media units of each process. After having constructed the transit groups the processes proceed to the grouping in local groups. Each local group elects its local server. Thus, the multicast group M is divided into local sub-groups. Each element of M belongs to only one local group. The communication in the group may pass trough the server. In other term, a process communicates with the other participants of the multicast group only through the server of its local group. The complete description of these algorithms is given in [2].

3.2 Hierarchical Tree Construction between Servers

Now, let us consider that K local groups are built and each one has its local server. Let $\Gamma=\{S_1, .., S_K\}$ the set of these local servers which can be distributed in different networks. Remark that the number of these servers can be very high. Moreover, in a videoconference several sources can belong to the same multicast group. Consequently, it is necessary to build a multicast tree which allows to link these servers while reducing the participants of the multicast group. So, we propose the use of core-based tree, called RDV (RenDezVous) hierarchical architecture. In this work, we determine the rendezvous points in dynamic way. Moreover, we propose the use of several rendezvous points to avoid the congestion problem of the traffic when only one rendezvous point is used.

Algorithm description:

We suppose that $S_p \in \Gamma$ is the local server of the group where is located the first source which want to broadcast media units to the other members of the multicast group M. This server represents the first rendezvous point RP_l. Given a threshold delay D' that is selected by taking account of the network extent.
At the beginning, RP_1 does not have any information on the addresses of the other servers. Consequently, it broadcasts hop by hop an initialization message *INIT*(RP_1, *adrG*, *TTL*) including the address of the rendezvous point RP_l, a time to live TTL and group multicast address adrG. All members of M that are not servers delete the received message. However, each local server S_i sends an acknowledge message *ACK*(S_i, RP_1) to RP_1. When RP_1 receives acknowledgement message from S_i, it computes the round-trip delay rd_1. If this delay is smaller than the threshold D', it selects the server S_i and puts it in its autonomous domain DA_1 (a set of processes). Then, it stores in $\overline{S}$ all other servers which are not in its domain DA_1: $\overline{S}=\Gamma-DA_1$. After construction of DA_1, RP_1 stores the computed delay between it and each server S_i of $\overline{S}$ in a matrix *MAT*, allowing to store the round-trip delays between the elements of $\overline{S}$ and the existing rendezvous points in the multicast tree, in order to determinate the next rendezvous point (Table 2). Then, it sends the message *SUCCESSOR*(S_i, RP_1, $\overline{S}$, *MAT*) to the nearest server S_i which does not belong to its domain DA_1. In other

words, that which is linked to RP_1 by a path having the smallest value of round-trip delay rd_{1i}, strictly higher than D', and which belongs to $\overline{S}$.

Table 2. Round-trip delays between rendezvous points and servers of S

RP\ S	S_i	S_j	S_k	S_l
RP_1	rd_{1i}	rd_{1j}	rd_{1k}	rd_{1l}
RP_2	rd_{2i}	rd_{2i}	rd_{2i}	rd_{2i}
…				

When a local server S_i receives message *SUCCESSOR*(S_i, RP_p, $\overline{S}$, *MAT*), it understands that it constitutes a new rendezvous point, we noted RP_2. The new rendezvous point RP_2 play the role of initiating server of the set $\overline{S}$: the set of servers which are not in the domain of RP_1. Thanks to the message SUCCESSOR, RP_2 knows the addresses of all processes in $\overline{S}$, then it sends to them message *JOIN*(RP_2, S_j) in unicast way. When server S_j receives this message, it replies with *ACK*(S_j, RP_2) to RP_2. Then, RP_2 computes the minimum round-trip delays between it and elements of $\overline{S}$ and carries out the following operations:

- It select all servers of $\overline{S}$ having a round-trip delay smaller or equal to the threshold D' and puts them in its autonomous domain DA_2.
- It removes from $\overline{S}$ the selected servers: $\overline{S}=\overline{S}-DA_2$.
- It removes the columns of the matrix MAT corresponding to the elements of its domain DA_2.
- It adds a line in MAT to store the minimum round-trip delays between it and all servers of $\overline{S}$: those which do not belong to any domain.
- It searches the smallest value of delays in MAT and takes the couple (RP_p, S_q) corresponding to this value. Thus, we determined dynamically the next rendezvous point S_q, among the servers of $\overline{S}$, which father is RP_p that is a rendezvous point already created. In other term, S_q is a server of the set $\overline{S}$ and it is the nearest to the existing rendezvous point RP_p while taking the round-trip delay as metric.
- It sends message *SUCCESSOR*(S_q, RP_p, $\overline{S}$, *MAT*) to the new rendezvous point S_q, noted RP_3.
- Finally, RP_2 joins members of its domain DA_2 and its rendezvous point father RP_1 toward the SPT tree which root is RP_2.

After the new rendezvous point RP_3 receives the message *SUCCESSOR*(S_q, RP_p, $\overline{S}$, *MAT*), it makes the same thing as RP_2 and so on until emptiness of $\overline{S}$. In other words, until all servers are connected to the multicast tree.

4 Simulations and Analysis

In these simulations, we are interested with the scalability problem that arises when multimedia applications in multicast groups are to be executed. The way with which the communication is done between participants influences the guarantee of QoS and the scalability. So, for these raisons we focus the analysis on the communication between local groups. So, to compare our methods with other, we implement a specific-source tree, called LDS (Link Direct Shortest path) hierarchical architecture. This method allows to connect a group where there is a source to all other groups directly. We, also, compare them to a DIRet architecture DIR.

We consider a connected graph constituted of 2000 nodes which are set in a matrix of 5000x5000 and linked between them in a random way. We choose 8 sources of multimedia stream located randomly in 50 sub-groups. As a metrics, we use the shortest path with a given TTL=5 hops to consider the delay. Moreover, for each group a node with a smallest identity number is chosen as a local server.
For RDV, we have selected five local servers as rendezvous points RP. Then all other local servers are connected to these RP.
For LDS (Direct links between servers), we connected directly, each local server of the group where is located one source to all others.
For DIR, we used the shortest paths between each source and the other nodes.
Simulation parameters are: simulation time is 100(s), generation rate of each source is 200 (media units/s) and media unit size is 500 bytes. The scheduling of multimedia multicast for each source is as follows: source 1 from 0 s to 80 s, source 2 from 10 s to 80 s, source 3 from 20 s to 80 s, source 4 from 30 s to 80 s, source 5 from 50 s to 80 s, source 6 from 60 s to 80 s, source 7 from 70 s to 80 s, source 8 from 70 s to 100 s.

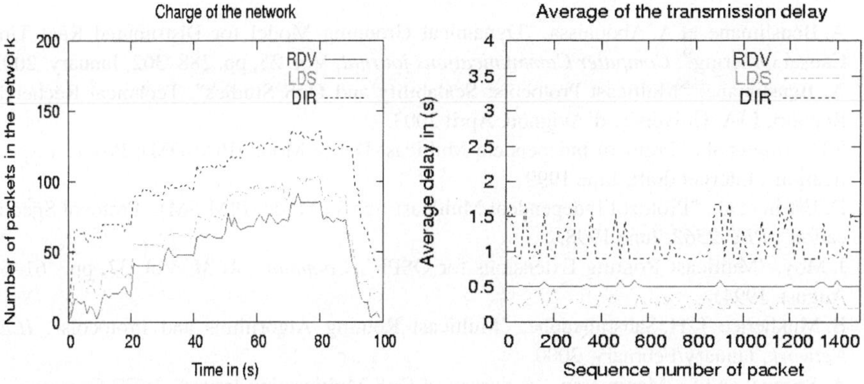

a. Charge of the network. b. Average of the transmission delay.

Fig. 1. Simulation example on a network of 2000

Thanks to NS-2, we generate three files corresponding to the three architectures. To interpret obtained results, we counted, at each 0.1 s, the number of packets in the network (Figure 1.a). The number of packets in the network depends on the number of multicast sources. In curves corresponding to the network load, we observe that the number of packets is very high between 70(s) and 80 (s) because the 8 sources, broadcast streams at the same time.

Also, we computed the average of transfer delay for each packet, from its emission by a source until its arrival to all destinations (Figure 1.b). The average of transfer delay of a packet is the time necessary so that this packet is delivered by all receivers of the multicast group (i.e., total transmission time of all copies of the same packet sent by a source in the network).

5 Conclusion

We have described different types of multicast trees and existing multicast protocols dedicated to the Internet network. As we have shown, these protocols are limited when we consider scalability and QoS requirements for multimedia applications. To overcome these limitations, we have proposed a decomposition of the system to local groups according to the neighboring set, the capabilities of processing and buffering of media units of each process. In this paper, we are interested to the communication path between local groups. We show that when using shared-based tree with dynamic rendezvous points, the performances are better compared to source-based tree or direct connection. So, delays and resources use are reduced. Our purpose is confirmed by NS-2 simulations.

References

1. A. Benslimane et A. Abouaissa, "Dynamical Grouping Model for Distrubuted Real Time Causal Ordering", *Computer Communications journal*, Vol. 25, pp. 288–302, January 2002.
2. A. Benslimane, "Multicast Protocols: Scalability and QoS Studies", Technical Recherche Repport, LIA, Université d'Avignon, April 2003.
3. S.Deering et al., "Protocol Independent Multicast-Dense Mode (PIM-DM): Protocol Specification", Internet draft, June 1999.
4. D. Estrin et al., "Protocol Independent Multicast-Sparse Mode (PIM-SM): Protocol Specification", *RFC 2362*, June 1998.
5. J. Moy, "Multicast Routing Extensions for OSPF", *Commun. ACM*, Vol. 37, pp. 61–66, August 1994.
6. B. Mukherjee L.H. Sahsrabuddhe, "Multicast Routing Algorithms and Protocols", *IEEE Network*, January/February 2000.
7. A. Striegel and G. Manimaran, "A Survey of QoS Multicasting Issues", IEEE Communications Magazine, June 2002, pp. 82–87.
8. D. Waitzman and C. Partridge, "Distance Vector Multicast Routing Protocol", *RFC 1075*, November 1988.

Effect of the Generation of MPEG-Frames within a GOP on Queueing Performance

J.C. Lopez-Ardao, M. Fernandez-Veiga, R.F. Rodriguez-Rubio,
C. Lopez-Garcia, A. Suarez-Gonzalez, and D. Teijeiro-Ruiz

Telematics Engineering Department, University of Vigo (Spain)
ETSET Telecomunicacion, Campus Universitario
36200 Vigo (Spain)
{jardao, mveiga, rrubio, candido, asuarez, diego}@det.uvigo.es

Abstract. MPEG video traffic is expected to represent most of the load in the future high-speed networks. Adequate traffic models for MPEG *Variable Bit-Rate* (VBR) video are important for network design, performance evaluation, admission control and resource allocation.
It is well-known that VBR video exhibits long-range correlations over arbitrarily long time-scales, a phenomenon usually referred to as *Long-Range Dependence* (LRD).
Many models for VBR video traffic have been proposed in the literature. However, while the correlation between *Groups of Pictures* (GOPs) has been widely analyzed in literature, little effort has been devoted up to now to the generation of the different frame-types within a MPEG GOP. Due to the difficulty and complexity involved in this issue, this is often neglected even though it is a fundamental characteristic of MPEG traffic and it might have an important impact on queueing performance. In fact, many works avoid to descend to the frame level proposing models for the GOP process.
In this paper, we analyze the impact on queueing performance of different solutions proposed in the literature for generating the different types of MPEG frames within a GOP (these solutions have never been compared and analyzed jointly). In this way, we can be in a good position to use the best model for MPEG in terms of simplicity, computational efficiency and queueing performance, depending on the performance metric to study (loss rate, mean delay and jitter).

1 Introduction

MPEG video traffic is expected to represent most of the load in the future high-speed networks. So, adequate traffic models for MPEG *Variable Bit-Rate* (VBR) video are important for network design, performance evaluation, admission control and resource allocation.

The output of a MPEG encoder consists of a deterministic periodic sequence of encoded frames where the period is called GOP (Group of Pictures). A GOP contains three different types of frames: one I-frame (like JPEG, achieved after

A. Yazici and C. Şener (Eds.): ISCIS 2003, LNCS 2869, pp. 651–658, 2003.

removing the spatial redundancy within a still image) and several P- and B-frames, which are encoded adding motion compensation with respect to the previous I-frame.

It is well-known that VBR video traffic is characterized by a high burstiness and a strong positive correlation. These properties were found to be induced by the presence of a characteristic inherent to VBR video traffic, called *self-similarity*. This characteristic involves long-range correlations over arbitrarily long time-scales, a phenomenon usually referred to as *Long-Range Dependence* (LRD) [1]. LRD is mainly characterized by an ACF with a hyperbolic decay.

Many models for VBR video traffic have been proposed in the literature. In Section 2 we describe their main characteristics. However, while inter-GOP correlation has been widely analyzed in literature [2], [3], [4], little effort has been devoted up to now to the generation of the different frame-types within a MPEG GOP. This issue is often neglected even though it is a fundamental characteristic of MPEG traffic and it might have an important impact on queueing performance [4], [5]. In fact, many works avoid to descend to the frame level and propose models only for the GOP process [6], [7].

Different solutions have been proposed in the literature, but these have never been compared and analyzed jointly. So, this is the main goal of this work.

The paper is organized as follows: Section 2 starts classifying the different video models proposed in the literature and discussing their advantages and drawbacks. Also the problem of generating frames within a MPEG GOP and the solutions proposed are dealt. In Section 3 we show the main results related to queueing performance. Finally, Section 4 summarizes the main conclusions of this study.

2 On VBR Video Modeling

Depending on how the relevant time-scales are captured, the VBR video models proposed in the literature (see [8] for a survey) can be classified into two types: hierarchical and non-hierarchical.

Hierarchical models typically consider two time-scales: scene or activity level (time-scale of minutes) and GOP/frame (time-scale of milliseconds/seconds) [9], [10], [6]. Scene changes occur when the mean of the bit-rate process changes significantly as a result of a considerable change in picture content (camera cuts). Hierarchical models have several well-known drawbacks. On the one hand, the scene layer adds complexity to the model and, on the other hand, the model has an important subjective component in the scene detection process [11]

Non-hierarchical models consider only the GOP/frame level. For this reason, only those models based on stochastic processes that incorporate inherently a wide range of time-scales are valid. In this field, the use of self-similar processes in video traffic modeling [2], [12], [3], [5], [11] has a clear advantage over the traditional use of Markovian or Autoregressive processes [13], [9], [7], since the former models ignore the correlations beyond a particular lag intending to keep the analytical tractability, and so it is said that they exhibit *Short-Range Dependence* (SRD). But their validity is in doubt because modeling LRD through SRD processes requires many parameters. In other words, it is well-known that it is necessary a sum of infinite exponentials to match a hyperbolic function.

The requirement to use few parameters is important because they must be estimated from the empirical data. Each estimate incurs a certain amount of error and, on the other hand, a video traffic model should be independent of any empirical data, and so it is very important that its parameters have physical meaningful.

For this reason, the rise of self-similar processes for video traffic modeling purposes has been essential due to their capability to exhibit LRD over all time-scales by making use of few parameters (*parsimonious modeling*).

In any case, the impact of the LRD on queueing performance depends much on the length of the busy period (the number of the relevant correlations that interact at the queue) and so this effect can be less important when the utilization is low or with small buffers [14], [15], [16].

However, though this discussion is not within the scope of this paper, it seems clear that, if it is feasible, the use of a simple, parsimonious and efficient model based on self-similar processes (or, in general, exhibiting LRD) will permit to achieve better estimations of the system performance. Furthermore, the model will neither depend on particular and hypothetical assumptions about the load or the buffer sizes, nor on the subjectivity of the scene detection. In order to reinforce this statement, in [11] it is shown that the hyperbolic decay ($k^{-\beta}$) is the best match for the ACF of the different frame-types of many commonly used MPEG-encoded video sequences.

As for the choice of the type of LRD processes, we opt to use Gaussian FARIMA(1,d,0) processes for simplicity reasons (only two parameters: the AR(1) coefficient for SRD and d for LRD, with $H = d + 0.5 = 1 - \beta/2$) and computational cost (using the fast generation method proposed in [17]).

Queuing performance depends not only on the correlation structure, but also on the marginal distribution [14], [16]. In this respect, Huang *et al.* [3] demonstrated that Gaussian processes enjoy the attractive advantage that their marginal distribution (parameters included) can be changed by a sufficiently regular transformation without modifying their LRD structure. Nevertheless, this transformation induces a slightly decrease of the magnitude of the SRD. However, the use of Gaussian FARIMA(1,d,0) processes permit to easily overcome this inconvenience by adequately adjusting the AR component.

An extensive study in [4] concludes that Lognormal or Gamma distributions are an useful approximation of the histograms of the I, P, and B frame sizes for a wide range of MPEG video sequences. Similar results are found for the GOP sizes. We use Lognormal distributions for efficiency reasons.

2.1 On Generating MPEG Frames within a GOP

An important work in this field is due to Lombardo *et al.* [5], that obtains the conditional distribution of P- and B-frames sizes, given an I-frame size. However, this model requires a huge computational cost and it is little flexible. We will focus on other more efficient and simpler solutions for generating MPEG frames within a GOP.

In [3] and [12], three different distribution transformations for each frame-type, $h_I(x)$, $h_P(x)$ and $h_B(x)$, are applied to a background LRD process that matches the empirical ACF of the I-frame sizes (inter-GOP correlation). We will refer to it as **solution HUA**.

Krunz *et al.* [10] propose a hierarchical model where the inter-GOP correlation is only taken into account for the I-frames. P- and B-frames are modeled by two independent processes of i.i.d. random variables with Lognormal distribution. We will refer to it as **solution KRU**.

Rose [18] uses a background process that matches the inter-GOP correlation to obtain a GOP-size process. The frames sizes are computed by multiplying the GOP size by a scaling factor. The scaling factor for each frame-type is the quotient between the mean frame-size for that type and the mean GOP-size. With this simple method, P-frames (and B-frames) have the same size in every GOP, and so the frame-by-frame correlation is lost. We will refer to this solution as **solution ROS**.

Finally, Ansari *et al.* [11] propose to use three independent processes matching the ACFs $R_I(k)$, $R_P(k)$ and $R_B(k)$ of each frame-size process, $I(n)$, $P(n)$ and $B(n)$. We will refer to it as **solution ANS**.

3 Queueing Performance

Although the validation of a source model requires distribution and autocorrelation fitting, the ultimate validity of a model must be determined by its performance predictions in comparison to empirical data.

In the literature, VBR video traffic models are commonly used to predict the queueing performance at a switch. The system used is a single-server FIFO queue with finite buffer size. The capability of the server (bits per second), or its utilization factor, and the buffer size are system variables.

In order to analyze the aforementioned solutions for generating the different types of MPEG frames within a GOP, we have made exhaustive trace-driven simulation experiments. The video frames, whose sizes are object of modeling, arrive at switch at a constant rate (25 frames per second in our case). When the buffer limit is reached, new arrivals are dropped.

Given that "goodness" of a traffic model may depend on the metric under study, we analyze three important performance measures (statistics) of the system: loss probability, mean delay ($\mathrm{E}[T_i]$) and jitter ($\mathrm{E}[T_i - T_{i-1}]$).

For the sake of brevity, in this paper we present only the results for the empirical MPEG encoded data *The Simpsons*, although the considerations and conclusions are valid for all the traces we have analyzed[1]. The trace consists of 40.000 frames which is equivalent to approximately half an hour (at a rate of 25 frames per second). The GOP length is 12 (IBBPBBPBBPBB).

[1] The traces were courtesy of Dr. O. Rose [4]

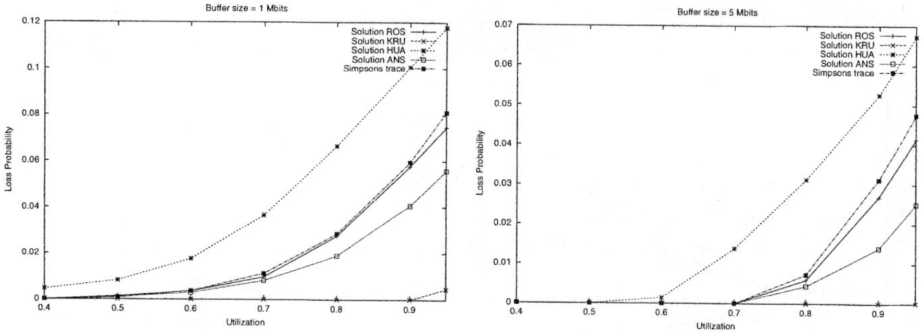

Fig. 1. Loss probability results

3.1 Loss Probability

Regarding the estimated loss probabilities, the results are very interesting (see Figure 1). Curiously, the solution **ROS** achieves very good predictions, clearly better than the other solutions. The solution **ANS** always underestimates the loss rate, although it does not work bad for low and moderate utilization. Nevertheless, the other two solutions work really bad. The solution **HUA** gives rise to a very high loss rates, indicating that the method for inducing the intra-GOP correlation is not suitable. Finally, the solution **KRU** hardly generates losses, confirming that modeling just the inter-GOP correlation, in this case through the I-frame sizes, even capturing all the marginal distributions, leads to a very poor model for loss-rate predictions.

These results indicate that the GOP-size process is dominant for loss performance. That is, loss rates will be better predicted by the solution that best matches the PDF and the ACF of the GOP-size process, and also takes into account the intra-GOP correlation, even by means of simple averaging factors. It does not seem necessary to devote efforts to capturing the correlation behaviors of the size of each frame-type.

3.2 Mean Delay

For mean delays, the results are slightly different (see Figure 2). Now both the solution **ROS** and the solution **ANS** work well enough, although the solution **ROS** goes on being slightly better. Specifically, it is the best option for small and moderate buffer sizes. The predictions of both solutions get worse when buffer size is increased, whereas the solution **HUA** obtains better and better predictions as buffer size and/or utilization is increased. In fact, for infinite buffer the predictions are very accurate.

Results for the solution **KRU** are not shown in the graphics because of its extremely poor predictions (very low mean delays) due to the reasons cited in the previous section.

In short, when the queue size is not very large, a good approximation consists of modeling only the GOP-size process and introducing the intra-GOP correla-

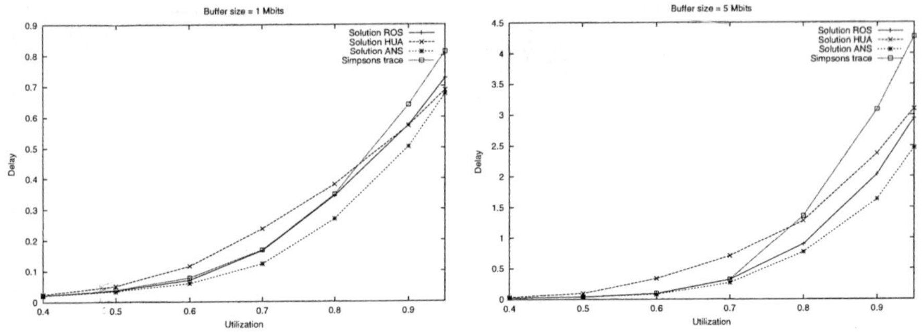

Fig. 2. Mean Delay results

tion by simple averaging. Alternatively, adequately capturing the correlation structure of each type of frame also provides acceptable performance results. However, when queue size is very large, and so the correlation structure is much more relevant to performance, the results suggest that the GOP-size process loses relevance in favor of the intra-GOP correlation, and so another method for characterizing this type of correlation is necessary. Perhaps, that is the reason why the interpendence introduced by using the same background process in the solution **HUA** provides the best results for the largest queue sizes.

3.3 Jitter

Jitter depends on the difference in size between consecutive frames. So, P-frames, and mainly B-frames, play a fundamental role owing to the relative number of these in comparison to I-frames. Properly characterizing the ACF and PDF of the B-frame sizes is still more important because they are sent consecutively. For this reason, the solution **ANS** is clearly the best.

Instead, the solutions **ROS** or **KRU** can never be valid. The former loses the frame-by-frame correlation, introducing several consecutive frames of identical size in the same GOP, so leading to many zero-jitter samples. Simulation results (see Figure 3) demonstrate that jitter is grossly underestimated. On the other hand, the solution **KRU** removes both the intra-GOP correlation and the autocorrelation of each frame-type, and so it is expected that jitter predictions are highly overestimated as the simulation results demonstrate.

The solution **HUA** obtains similar predictions to those of the solution **ROS**, also due to the fact that the empirical P- and B-frame correlations are not captured. However, as the utilization and the buffer size is increased, slightly better and better predictions are evidenced, perhaps for similar reasons to those cited in the mean-delay case.

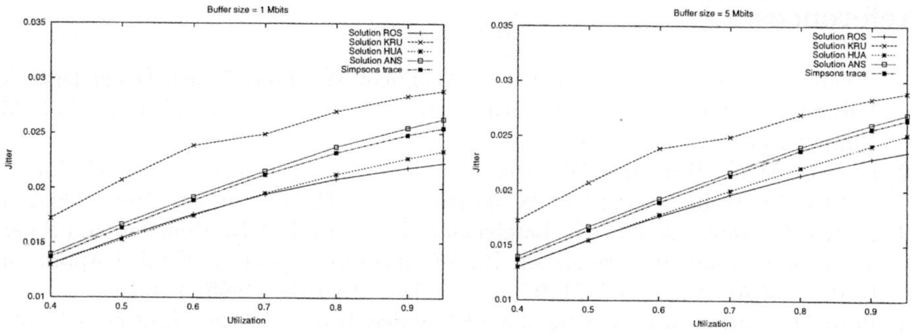

Fig. 3. Jitter results

4 Conclusions

Many models for VBR video traffic have been proposed in the literature. However, while inter-GOP correlation has been widely analyzed in literature, little effort has been devoted up to now to the generation of the different frame-types within a MPEG GOP.

In this paper we have analyzed different solutions proposed in the literature GOP. The results showed us that the suitability of a model depends much on the performance metric to estimate.

For loss rate, the results indicate that the GOP-size process is dominant, and so the best option is the one that best matches the PDF and the ACF of the GOP-size process, but also taking into account the intra-GOP correlation, even by means of simple averaging factors applied to the GOP sizes. It does not seem necessary to devote efforts to capturing the correlation behaviors of the size of each frame-type.

For mean delay, when the queue size is not very large, the GOP-size process and obtaining the MPEG frame sizes by means of averaging factors are the best option again. However, when the queue size is very large, and so the correlation structure dominates performance, the results suggest that the GOP-size process loses relevance in favor of the intra-GOP correlation, and so another method for characterizing this type of correlation might be necessary.

For jitter, adequately characterizing the ACF and PDF of the B-frames is very important because they are sent consecutively. Again, when the utilization and the buffer size are increased, intra-GOP correlation gains relevance.

However, regardless of the target performance metric, adequately capturing the distribution and the correlation structure of each type of frame provides acceptable predictions and it is a reasonable compromise solution in those scenarios where the intra-GOP correlation is not important enough, that is, as utilization and buffer size increase, the predictions lose accuracy.

References

1. Beran, J., Shreman, R., Taqqu M.S., Willinger W.: Long-Range Dependence in Variable-Bit-Rate Video Traffic. IEEE Transactions on Communications Vol. 43, Num. 2-4 (1995) 1566–1579.
2. Garrett, M.W., Willinger, W.: Analysis, Modeling and Generation of Self-Similar VBR Video Traffic. In Proc. of ACM SIGCOMM '94, London, UK (1994) 269–280.
3. Huang, C., Devetsikiotis, M., Lambadaris, I., Kayevol, A.R: Modeling and Simulation of Self-Similar Variable Bit Rate Compressed Video: A Unified Approach. In Proc. of ACM SIGCOMM '95, Cambridge, MA USA (1995) 114–125.
4. Rose, O.: Statistical Properties of MPEG Video Traffic and their Impact on Traffic Modeling in ATM Systems. In Proc. of the 20th Annual Conference on Local Computer Networks, Minneapolis, MN (1995) 397–406.
5. Lombardo A., Morabito G., Palazzo., Schembra, G.: MPEG Traffic Generation Matching Intra- and Inter-GoP Correlation. Simulation, Vol. 47, Num. 2 (2001)
6. Jelenkovic, P.R., Lazar, A.A, Semret, N.: The Effect of Multiple Time Scales and Subexponentiality of MPEG Video Streams on Queueing Behavior. IEEE Journal on Selected Areas in Communications, Vol. 43, Num. 2-4 (1995) 1566–1579
7. Frey, M., Nguyen-Quang, S.: A Gamma-Based Framework for Modeling Variable-Rate MPEG Video Sources: the GOP GBAR Model. IEEE/ACM Transactions on Networking, Vol. 8, Num. 6 (2000) 710–719.
8. Izquierdo, M.R., Reeves, D.S: A Survey of Statistical Source Models for Variable-Bit-Rate Compressed Video. Multimedia Systems, Vol. 7 (1999) 199–213.
9. Heyman D.P., Lakshman, T.V.: Source Models for VBR Broadcast-Video Traffic. IEEE/ACM Transactions on Networking, Vol. 4, Num. 1 (1996) 40–48
10. Krunz, M., Tripathi, S.K.: On the Characterization of VBR MPEG Streams. In Proc. of ACM SIGMETRICS '97, Seattle, WA (1997) 192–202.
11. Ansari N., Liu H., Shi Y.Q.: On Modeling MPEG Video Traffics. IEEE Transactions on Broadcasting, Vol. 48, Num. 4 (2002) 337–347.
12. Enssle, J.: Modeling of Short- and Long-Term Properties of VBR MPEG-Compressed Video in ATM Networks. In Proc. of the 1995 Silicon Valley Networking Conference & Exposition, San Jose, CA (1995) 95–107.
13. Melamed, B., Pendarakis D.: A TES-Based Model for compressed Star Wars Video. In Proc. of IEEE GLOBECOM '94 (1994) 120–126
14. Grossglauser, M, Bolot, J.-C.: On the Relevance of Long-Range Dependence in Network Traffic. In Proc. of ACM SIGCOMM '96, Stanford University, CA (1996) 15–24
15. Heyman, D.P., Lakshman, T.V.: What Are the Implications of Long-Range Dependence for VBR-Video Traffic Engineering?. IEEE/ACM Transactions on Networking, Vol. 4, Num. 3 (1996) 301–317.
16. Ryu B.K., Elwalid A.: The Importance of Long-Range Dependence of VBR Video Traffic in ATM Traffic Engineering: Myths and Realities. In Proc. of ACM SIGCOMM '96, Stanford University, CA (1996) 3–14
17. López-Ardao, J.C., Suárez-González A., López-García, C., Fernández-Veiga, M., Rodríguez-Rubio, R.: On the use of self-similar processes in network simulation. ACM Transactions on Modeling and Computer Simulation, Vol. 10 Num. 2 (2000) 125–151.
18. Rose, O.: Simple and Efficient Models for Variable Bit Rate MPEG Video Traffic. Performance Evaluation, Vol. 30 (1997) 69–85

Multiple Description Coding for Image Data Hiding in the Spatial Domain

Mohsen Ashourian[1] and Yo-Sung Ho[2]

[1] Azad University of Iran, Majlesi Branch
P.O. Box 86315-111, Isfahan, Iran
mohsena@iaumajlesi.ac.ir

[2] Kwangju Institute of Science and Technology (K-JIST)
1 Oryong-dong Puk-gu, Kwangju, 500-712, Korea
hoyo@kjist.ac.kr

Abstract. In this paper, we develop a robust image data hiding scheme based on multiple description coding of the signature image. At the transmitter, the signature image is encoded by balanced two-description scalar quantizers in the wavelet transform domain. The information of the two descriptions are embedded in the host image in the spatial domain with a masking factor derived from the gradient of the image intensity values. At the receiver, the multiple description decoder combines the information of each description and reconstructs the original signature image. We experiment the proposed scheme for embedding a gray-scale signature image of 128×128 pixels size in the spatial domain of the gray-scale host image of 512×512 pixels. Simulation results show that data embedding based on multiple description coding has low visible distortions in the host image and robustness to various signal processing and geometrical attacks, such as addition of noise, quantization, cropping and down-sampling.

1 Introduction

Various digital data hiding methods have been developed for multimedia services, where a significant amount of signature data is embedded in the host signal. The hidden data should be recoverable even after the host data has undergone some signal processing operations, such as image compression. It should also be retrieved only by those authorized [1].

The main problem of image hiding in another host image is a large amount of data that requires a special data embedding method with high capacity as well as transparency and robustness. Chae and Manjunath used the discrete wavelet transform (DWT) for embedding a signature image into another image, which has high visible distortion in the smooth area of the host image [2]. It is possible to improve their scheme by employing the human visual system (HVS) model in the process of information embedding [3,4]; however, exact adjustment of the HVS model is not easy in many applications. As another approach for improving the robustness of data embedding, Mukherjee et. al. [5] designed a joint source-channel coding scheme for hiding

A. Yazici and C. Şener (Eds.): ISCIS 2003, LNCS 2869, pp. 659–666, 2003.

a signature video in a video sequence. However, the channel optimized quantizer is not suitable in image hiding applications, where intentional or non-intentional manipulations, are variable and not known in advance.

In this paper, we suggest to use a multiple description coding method for encoding the signature image. Multiple description coding (MDC) is a joint source-channel coding technique where the source is encoded by multiple descriptions, so that there is some redundancy among descriptions [6,7]. These descriptions are transmitted over separate channels. Figure 1 shows the block diagram of MDC. At the receiver, the multiple description decoder combines the information of each description and reconstructs the original signal. It can decode only one channel, when data on the other channel is highly corrupted; otherwise, it can combine the received information from both channels.

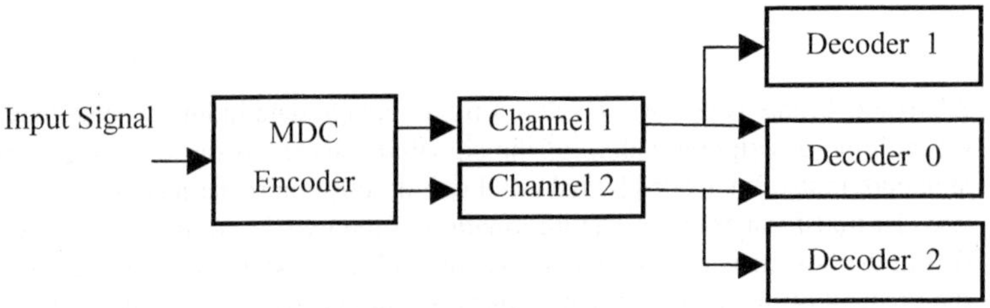

Fig. 1. Multiple description source coding

The design of the MD scalar quantizer was pioneered by Vaishampyan [8], and a method for designing of the MD lattice vector quantizer was introduced by Kelner et. al. [9]. In this paper, we encode the signature image using a two-description scalar quantizer of image subbands. The main advantage of encoding the signature image by two descriptions and embedding these descriptors in the host signal is that with an appropriate strategy, we can reconstruct a good approximation of the signature signal, even when the host signal is severely attacked.

In Section 2, we explain the encoding process of the signature image using MDC, and we describe the process of embedding information and tests on performance evaluation of the system in the following sections.

2 Signature Image Encoding

In the first stage for signature encoding, we decompose the signature image using the Haar wavelet transform, resulting in four subbands usually referred to as LL, LH, HL and HH.

Except for the lowest frequency subband (LL), the probability density function (PDF) for other subbands can be closely approximated with the Laplacian distribution. Although the LL subband does not follow any fixed PDF, it contains the most important visual information. We use a phase scrambling operation to change the PDF of this band to a nearly Gaussian shape [10]. Figure 2 gives the block schematic of the phase scrambling method. As shown in Figure 2, the fast Fourier transform

(FFT) operation is performed on the subband and then a pseudo-random noise is added to the phase of its transformed coefficients. The added random phase could be considered as an additional secret key between the transmitter and the registered receiver.

We encode the subbands using a PDF-optimized two-description scalar quantizer, assuming the Laplacian distribution for high frequency bands and the Gaussian distribution for the LL subband after phase scrambling. The index assignment method is shown in Fig. 3.

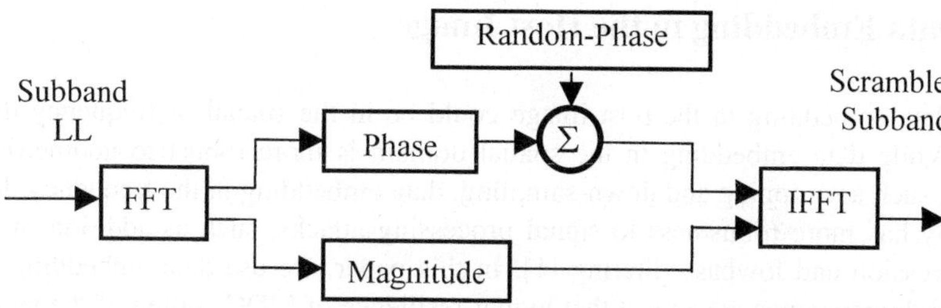

Fig. 2. Phase-Scrambling of lowest frequency subband

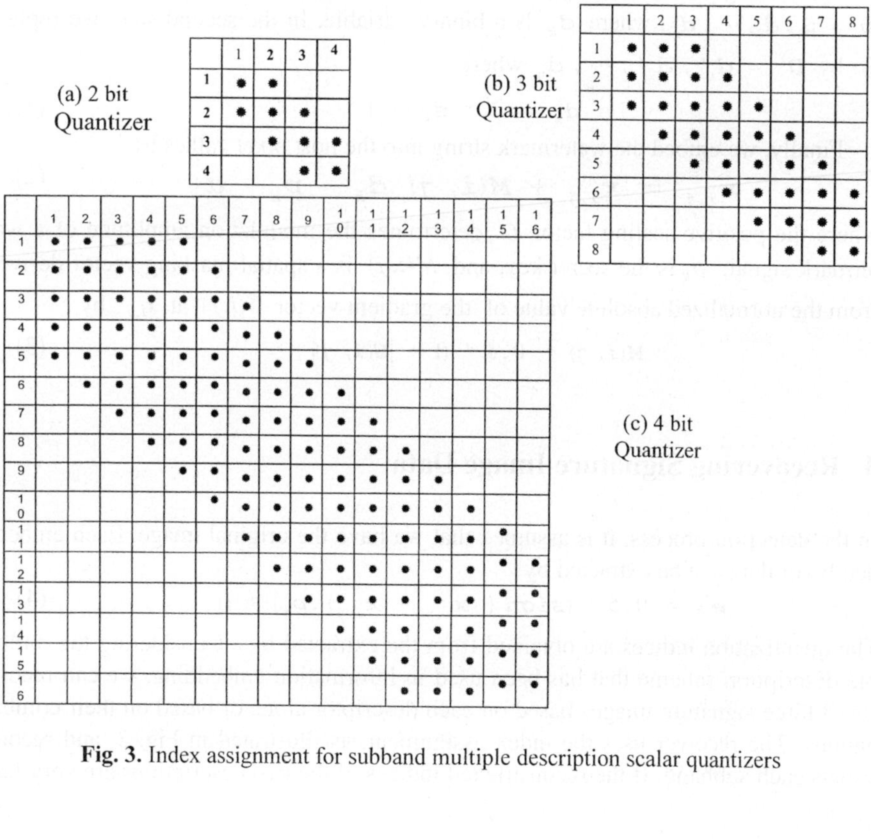

Fig. 3. Index assignment for subband multiple description scalar quantizers

In this paper, we have set the encoding bit-rate at three bit per sample (bps), and obtained PSNR value over 31 dB for different tested images, which is satisfactory in image hiding applications. We use an integer bit-allocation among subbands based on their energies. The information of subband energies (15 bits) can be sent as side information or it can be encoded with a highly robust error correction method and embedded in the host image. We use the folded binary code (FBC) for representing output indices of quantizer to have higher error resilience.

3 Data Embedding in the Host Image

The data embedding in the host image could be in the spatial or frequency domain [1]. While data embedding in the spatial domain is more robust to geometrical attacks, such as cropping and down-sampling, data embedding in the frequency domain usually has more robustness to signal processing attacks, such as addition of noise, compression and lowpass filtering [1]. In this paper, we use data embedding in the spatial domain since we expect that higher resilience of MDC coding of the signature signal can help the data embedding scheme to survive the signal processing attacks.

In order to embed output indices of the signature image into pixel values ($x_{i,j}$) of the host image, we scramble and arrange these indices as a binary sequence: $D = d_1, d_2, \cdots, d_n$, where d_k is a binary variable. In the second step, we replace D by $D' = d_1', d_2', \cdots, d_n'$ where

$$d_k' = 2 * d_k - 1 \tag{1}$$

Finally, we embed the watermark string into the host pixel values by

$$\hat{x}_{i,j} = x_{i,j} + M(i,j) \cdot d_k' \cdot p_k \cdot \alpha \tag{2}$$

where the positive scaling factor α determines the modulation amplitude of a watermark signal, p_k is the secret key, and $M(i,j)$ is a spatial masking vector derived from the normalized absolute value of the gradient vector $G(i,j)$ at $x_{i,j}$ by

$$M(i,j) = 0.5 * (1 + |G(i,j)|) \tag{3}$$

4 Recovering Signature Image Data

In the detection process, it is assumed that we have the original image. Each embedded bit of data can be extracted by

$$e_k' = 0.5 * (sign\{(\hat{x}_{i,j} - x_{i,j}) \cdot p_k\} + 1) \tag{4}$$

The quantization indices are obtained from the extracted bits. Considering the multiple description scheme that has been used in information embedding, we can reconstruct three signature images based on each descriptor alone or based on their combinations. The receiver uses the index assignment, as illustrated in Fig. 3, and reconstructs each subband. If the reconstructed indices of the two descriptions are very far, we assume that one of the two descriptions has highly been corrupted by noise; therefore, by comparing the MSE value of the original host image and the reconstructed one in the area contains those descriptions, we can decide which index should be selected.

5 Experimental Results and Analysis

In our scheme, the host image should be at least 6 times larger size than the signature image, because we use two descriptions with three bits per pixel quantization. We use a gray-scale host image of 512×512 pixels and signature image of 128×128 pixels size. Two images, "Barbara" and "Baboon", are used as signature images, and the image "Lena" is used as the host image.

Figure 4 shows PSNR values for the Lena image with different embedding factors. From Figure 4, we can observe that PSNR values are above 34 dB for embedding factor α below 15. We choose $\alpha = 15$ for our experiments, because we consider it as the maximum embedding factor with nearly low visible distortion. Figure 5 shows the two reconstructed signature images with the same embedding factors ($\alpha = 15$).

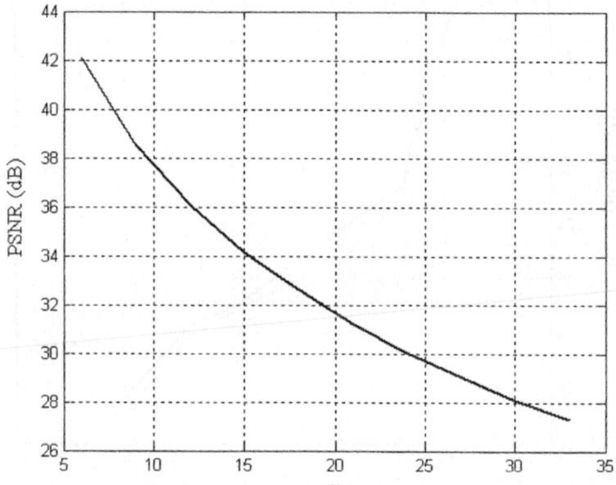

Fig. 4. Effect of embedding modulation factor (α) on PSNR of the host image

In order to evaluate the system performance, we calculate PSNR values of the reconstructed signature images. The system can be applied to applications such as hiding logo images for copyright protection, where the presence or absence of the signature is important more than the quality of the reconstructed image. In these applications, we usually set a threshold to decide on the amount of the cross correlation between the recovered signature and the original signature [1]. However, in this paper, we concentrate only on image hiding applications and provide PSNR values of reconstructed images.

Robustness to Gaussian Noise: We add Gaussian noises of different variances to the normalized host signal after signature embedding. Figures 6 show the PSNR of signature images for the additive noises with different variances. We conclude from

Figure 6 that for certain range of noise, our scheme demonstrates good performance in resisting Gaussian noise for data-hiding application.

(a) Barbara (b)Baboon

Fig. 5. Samples of reconstructed signature images

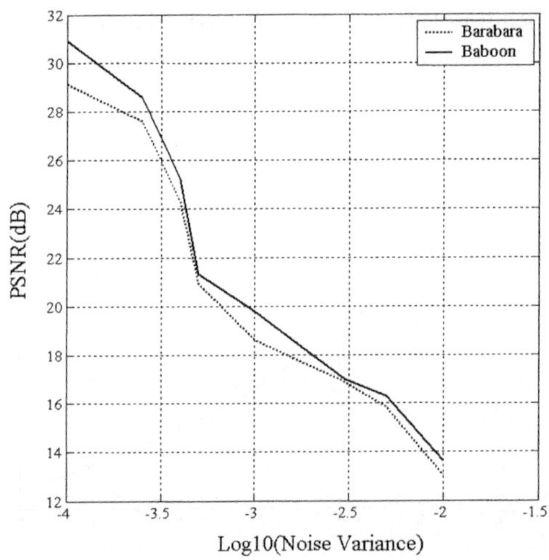

Fig. 6. PSNR variation of recovered signature image due to additive Gaussian noise

Resistance to JPEG Compression: The JPEG lossy compression algorithm with different quality factors (Q) is tested. Figure 7 shows the PSNR variation for different Q factors. As shown in Figure 7, the PSNR values drop sharply for Q smaller than 70.

Resistance to Median and Gaussian filtering: Median and Gaussian filters of 3×3 mask size are implemented on the host image after embedding the signature. The PSNR of recovered signature are shown in Table 1.

Resistance to Cropping: Table 2 shows PSNR values when some parts of the host image corners are cropped. We fill the cropped area with the average value of remaining part of the image. Considerably good resistance is due to the existence of two descriptors in the image and scrambling of embedded information, which makes it possible to reconstruct the signature image information in the cropped area from the available descriptor in the non-cropped area.

Resistance to Down-sampling: Due to loss of information in the down-sampling process, the host image cannot be recovered perfectly after up-sampling. However, it is possible to recover the signature image from those pixels available in the host image, as the two descriptions of the signature image information are scrambled and distributed in the host image. Table 3 lists PSNR values after several down-sampling processes.

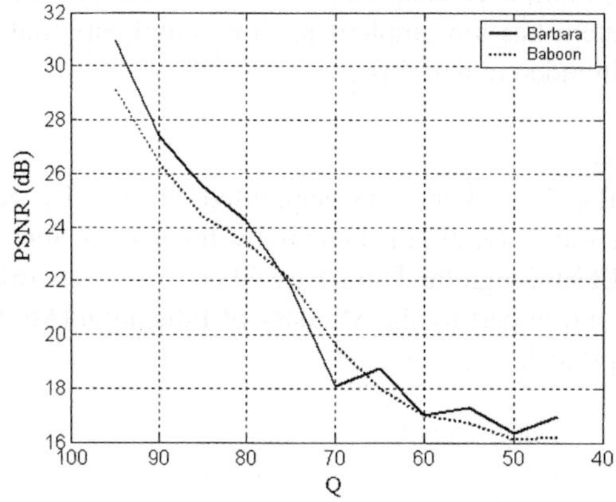

Fig. 7. PSNR variation of recovered signature image due to JPEG-compression of the host image

Table 1. PSNR (dB) values of the recovered signature images after implementing median and Gaussian filters on the host image

	Median Filter	Gaussian Filter
Barbara	17.90	24.80
Baboon	17.65	23.82

Table 2. PSNR (dB) values of the recovered signature image for different percentage of cropping the host image

	5%	10%	15%	20%
Barbara	21.28	19.42	18.60	17.92
Baboon	24.15	21.60	20.10	18.90

Table 3. PSNR (dB) values of the recovered signature image after different amount of down-sampling the host image

	1/2	1/4	1/8
Barbara	20.18	16.1	15.2
Baboon	21.03	14.3	13.7

6 Conclusions

We have presented a new scheme for embedding a gray-scale image into another gray-scale host image. The signature encoding is based on multiple description sub-band image coding, and the embedding process is performed the spatial domain. The proposed system needs the original host image for recovering the signature at the receiver; however, it is possible to use the system as a blind data hiding scheme by embedding the signature information in the texture area of the host image. We evaluate the reconstructed signature image quality when the host undergone various signal processing and geometrical attacks. The results show the system has good robustness. The developed system has low implementation complexity and can be extended for embedding video in video in real time.

Acknowledgements. This work was supported in part by Kwangju Institute of Science and Technology (K-JIST), in part by the Korea Science and Engineering Foundation (KOSEF) through the Ultra-Fast Fiber-Optic Networks (UFON) Research Center at K-JIST, and in part by the Ministry of Education (MOE) through the Brain Korea 21 (BK21) project.

References

1. Petitcolas F.A.P., Anderson R.J., and Kuhn, M.G.: Information Hiding-a Survey. Proceedings of the IEEE, Vol. 87, No.7, (1999) 1062–1078.
2. Chae, J.J., and Manjunath, B.S.: A Robust Embedded Data from Wavelet Coefficients. Proc. of SPIE, Storage and Retrieval for Image and Video Databases VI, (1998) 308–317.
3. Wolfgang R.B., Podilchuk C.I., and Delp E.J.: Perceptual watermarks for digital images and video. Proceedings of the IEEE, Vol. 87, No. 7, (1999) 1108–1126.
4. Swanson M.D., Zhu B., and Tewfik A.H.: Transparent Robust Image Watermarking. In Proceeding of the IEEE International Conference on Image Processing, Vol.2, (1997) 676–679.
5. Mukherjee, D., Chae, J.J., Mitra, S.K., and Manjunath, B.S.: A Source and Channel-Coding Framework for Vector-Based Data Hiding in Video. IEEE Trans. on Circuits and System for Video Technology. Vol. 10, No. 6 , (2000) 630–645.
6. El-Gamal A.A., and Cover, T.M.: Achievable Rates for Multiple Description. IEEE Trans. on Information Theory, Vol. 28, No. 11, (1982) 851–857.
7. Goyal, V.K.: Multiple Description Coding: Compression Meets the Network. IEEE Signal Processing Magazine, Vo.18, Issue 5, (2001)74–93.
8. Vaishampayan V.A.: Design of Multiple Description Scalar Quantizers. IEEE Trans. on Information Theory, Vol. 39 , No.5, (1993) 821–834.
9. Kelner J.A., Goyal V.K., and Kovacevic J.: Multiple description lattice vector quantization: variations and extensions. Data Compression Conference, (2000) 480–489.
10. Kuo C.C.J., and Hung C.H.: Robust Coding Technique-Transform Encryption Coding for Noisy Communication. Optical Eng., Vol. 32, No. 1, (1993) 150–153.

POCS-Based Enhancement of De-interlaced Video

Kang-Sun Choi, Jun-Ki Cho, Min-Cheol Hwang, and Sung-Jea Ko

Korea University, Anam-Dong Sungbuk-Ku, Seoul, Korea,
kschoi@dali.korea.ac.kr

Abstract. To convert an interlaced video into a progressive one effectively, de-interlacing techniques have been developed. However, existing de-interlacing techniques can not perfectly remove high frequency alias components inherently existing in the interlaced video. In this paper, based on the theory of POCS, we propose a video enhancement technique to improve the visual quality of de-interlaced video. We introduce novel constraint sets that are suitable for the characteristics of de-interlaced video and derive the projection operators for those sets. These projection operators using multiframes can reduce high frequency alias components of the de-interlaced video effectively. Extensive computer simulations show that the proposed method significantly improve the quality of the de-interlaced video by restoring the meaningful frequency information of the original progressive video.

1 Introduction

Television pictures are broadcast in an interlaced format which has the purpose of reducing both bandwidth required and large area flicker. However, TV pictures suffer from uncomfortable visual artifacts such as edge flicker, interline flicker, and line crawling, caused by high frequency alias components, the inherent nature of the interlaced scanning process, arising on the progressive-to-interlaced conversion. In spite of these inherent problems, the interlaced scan may still be employed in view of compatibility with existing TV and camera systems.

De-interlacing, a picture format conversion from interlaced to progressive picture, has been widely used to reduce the visual effects of those artifacts. Moreover, HDTV systems support the progressive scan to improve the visual quality. A number of techniques have so far been proposed to estimate the missing parity for the interlaced-to-progressive scan conversion [1,2,3,4,5]. Most advanced approaches to de-interlacing is motion compensation based de-interlacing [3,4, 5] in which interpolation is performed along the motion trajectory. The motion compensation may be useful to get high resolution and flicker-free pictures in motion area. In [5], the missing field reconstructed with the same parity fields of the neighboring frames. Thus, a pre-filter for interpolating missing lines was not required. However, the existing de-interlacing techniques can not perfectly correct the high frequency components which are degraded by the alias components inherently existing in the interlaced video.

A. Yazici and C. Şener (Eds.): ISCIS 2003, LNCS 2869, pp. 667–674, 2003.

In this paper, we propose a novel postprocessing scheme based on the POCS for enhancement of de-interlaced video sequence. Since the de-interlacing process can be considered as recovery of the high frequency components, we can further improve the de-interlaced video by removing the alias components remaining after the de-interlacing process. A de-interlaced video obtained through existing de-interlacing methods is characterized that it contains at least a half of the original video, alternative parity fields, which includes perfect details, i.e., precise high frequency components. Thus, the adjacent frames of a particular frame can keep additional frequency information to restore the frame more precisely. Effective extracting this information from the neighboring frames and incorporating it into the current frame can improve the de-interlaced video. We introduce several constraint sets suitable for the characteristics of de-interlaced video and derive the related projection operators which enhance high frequency components in a particular frame with the frequency components of the neighboring frames. This allows us to impose additional constraints on a particular frame and correct detail information more precisely with information of the adjacent frames. It is notable that the proposed enhancement algorithm can improve de-interlaced video obtained by any de-interlacing techniques.

The paper is organized as follows. In the following Sect., the conventional postprocessing algorithms based on the theory of POCS are briefly introduced. The proposed postprocessing scheme including the constraint sets and the corresponding projection operators is presented in Sect. 3. Section 4 presents and discusses the experimental results. Finally, our conclusions are given in Sect. 5.

2 Iterative Approaches Based on the Theory of POCS

Before introducing the proposed postprocessing technique, we review the POCS which is a special case of the composite mapping algorithm for image restoration.

Assume that every known property of the original image $\mathbf{f}$ can be formulated into a corresponding closed convex subset in Hilbert space $\mathcal{H}$ [6]. For example, n known properties of the original image $\mathbf{f}$ generate n well-defined closed convex sets C_i, $i = 1, 2, \cdots, n$, and necessarily, the original image $\mathbf{f}$ should be included in all the C_i's and also the intersection of all the C_i's, C^*, i.e.,

$$\mathbf{f} \in C^* = \bigcap_{i=1}^{n} C_i. \tag{1}$$

It is clear that the intersection C^* is a closed and convex set, and any element in C^* satisfies n given properties. Thus, the problem of restoring the original image from its n properties is equivalent to finding at least one point belonging to C^*. The iteration

$$\mathbf{f}_k = P_n P_{n-1} \cdots P_2 P_1 \mathbf{f}_{k-1}, \quad k = 1, 2, \cdots \tag{2}$$

will converge to a limiting point $\mathbf{f}^*$ on the intersection C^*, as $k \to \infty$, for an arbitrary initial element $\mathbf{f}_0$ in $\mathcal{H}$ where P_i, the projection operator onto C_i, is given by

$$\|\mathbf{f} - P_i\mathbf{f}\| = \min_{\mathbf{g} \in C_i} \|\mathbf{f} - \mathbf{g}\|. \tag{3}$$

It is known that postprocessing techniques based on the theory of POCS satisfy two requirements: First, the closed convex sets, which capture the properties of the original image, are defined. Second, it is necessary to derive the projection operators onto them.

In the existing de-blocking algorithms using POCS [7,8,9], the iterative algorithm defined two constraints on the coded image: smoothness constraint (C_s) and quantization constraint (C_q). The smoothness constraint bandlimits the image in the horizontal and vertical directions in order to reduce both directional high-frequency artifacts. Since the decision level of the quantizer applied to each DCT coefficient is known when an encoded image is decoded, the quantization constraint ensures that the DCT coefficients of the processed image remain in their original quantization regions. If the constraints can be defined as closed convex sets with corresponding projectors, then the theory of POCS ensures the convergence of the coded image to an image that belongs to the intersection of the convex sets.

3 Proposed Constraint Sets and Projection Operators

In this Sect., we first briefly consider the characteristics of de-interlaced video. Then, we propose the upper and lower bounds of DCT coefficients and the corresponding projection operator, which are suitable for the characteristics of de-interlaced video. In addition, the iterative algorithm to improve video quality is presented.

In [10], it is seen that when a progressive image is converted into an interlaced image, the vertical spectrum of the image is distorted by alias within only high frequency components. From this point of view, the de-interlacing is defined as a processing of recovery of the high frequency alias components. Thus, the de-interlaced video obtained by the existing de-interlacing techniques can be further improved by correcting the alias components remaining after the de-interlacing.

Video has a temporal dimension that can lead to better reconstruction if utilized effectively. Since each de-interlaced frame has at least a half of the original progressive picture with precise details alternatively, the neighboring frames of a particular frame can keep additional frequency information to restore frequency components of the frame more precisely.

Based on these considerations, we propose a POCS-based method modifying the high frequency alias components. As explained in the previous Sect., POCS-based enhancement methods must define constraint sets. In the blocking-artifact reduction problem, the well-known constraint set is the quantization-bound information. There, however, is no quantization-bound in the process of de-interlacing. Instead, we define a DCT-coefficient constraint bound with the DCT coefficients of the motion compensated neighboring frames.

Let us consider successive de-interlaced frames, $\mathbf{f}(n-1)$, $\mathbf{f}(n)$, and $\mathbf{f}(n+1)$, and assume that the given field at time n, $\mathbf{p}(n)$, is odd parity, where n is a frame number. First, $\mathbf{f}(n)$ is divided into non-overlapping blocks, $\mathbf{b}_{ij}(n)$'s, where i and j are the horizontal and vertical indices of the block, respectively. Denote BDCT$(\cdot)$ and $\mathrm{M}_{n_1}^{n_2}(\cdot)$ as the block-DCT and the motion compensation mapping operator from the frame n_1 to n_2, respectively. Thus, $\mathrm{M}_n^{n-1}(\mathbf{b}_{ij}(n))$ and $\mathrm{M}_n^{n+1}(\mathbf{b}_{ij}(n))$ represent motion compensated blocks within the frames $n-1$ and $n+1$, respectively. If the motion estimation is believed to be accurate, we can write

$$\mathrm{BDCT}(\mathrm{M}_n^{n-1}(\mathbf{b}_{ij}(n))) \approx \mathrm{BDCT}(\mathbf{b}_{ij}(n)) \approx \mathrm{BDCT}(\mathrm{M}_n^{n+1}(\mathbf{b}_{ij}(n))). \tag{4}$$

For the simple notation, we denote $\mathrm{BDCT}(\mathbf{b}_{ij}(n))$ and $\mathrm{M}_n^{n-1}(\mathbf{b}_{ij}(n))$ as $\mathbf{B}_{ij}$ and $\mathbf{b}_{ij}^{-1}$, respectively. Therefore, (4) can be rewritten as

$$\mathbf{B}_{ij}^{-1} \approx \mathbf{B}_{ij} \approx \mathbf{B}_{ij}^{+1}. \tag{5}$$

Denoting $B_{ij,kl}$ and $B_{ij,kl}^{-1}$ as the kl^{th} coordinate DCT coefficients within $\mathbf{B}_{ij}$ and $\mathbf{B}_{ij}^{-1}$, respectively, we define the constraint set for each coefficient $B_{ij,kl}$ as

$$C_1 = \{c \mid B_{ij,kl} - \alpha \leq c \leq \ B_{ij,kl} + \alpha\}, \tag{6}$$

where $\alpha = \min(|B_{ij,kl} - B_{ij,kl}^{-1}|,\ |B_{ij,kl} - B_{ij,kl}^{+1}|)$.

We propose a projection operator P_{C_1} which maps each coefficient $B_{ij,kl}$ onto the constraint set C_1 as

$$P_{C_1}(B_{ij,kl}) = \begin{cases} \beta, & \text{if } \beta \in C_1, \\ B_{ij,kl} - \alpha, & \text{if } |\beta - (B_{ij,kl} - \alpha)| < |\beta - (B_{ij,kl} + \alpha)|, \\ B_{ij,kl} + \alpha, & \text{otherwise,} \end{cases} \tag{7}$$

where β is equivalent to the average value of $B_{ij,kl}^{-1}$, $B_{ij,kl}$, and $B_{ij,kl}^{+1}$.

It is worth noting that modifying any DCT coefficient of a block affects the whole pixels including the block boundaries in the block. Even though we configure the bounds of each DCT coefficient carefully by C_1, the modification can deteriorate the quality of the block. To avoid this deterioration, we propose a smoothness constraint set using information about the continuity between block boundaries.

Let $Q_u(\cdot)$ be a linear operator such that $Q_u(\mathbf{b}_{ij})$ represents the upper boundary of $\mathbf{b}_{ij}$ adjacent to $\mathbf{b}_{i(j-1)}$. Similarly, $Q_d(\cdot)$, $Q_l(\cdot)$, and $Q_r(\cdot)$ are defined as the lower, left, and right boundaries. Then, the boundary constraint set for each block is defined as

$$C_2 = \{\mathbf{b}'_{ij} \mid D_{ij}(\mathbf{b}'_{ij}) \leq D_{ij}(\mathbf{b}_{ij})\}, \tag{8}$$

where $D_{ij}(\cdot)$ represents the boundary difference between a block and the neighboring blocks of the ij^{th} block as

$$D_{ij}(\mathbf{b}) = \|Q_u(\mathbf{b}) - Q_d(\mathbf{b}_{i(j-1)})\| + \|Q_d(\mathbf{b}) - Q_u(\mathbf{b}_{i(j+1)})\| \\ + \|Q_l(\mathbf{b}) - Q_r(\mathbf{b}_{(i-1)j})\| + \|Q_r(\mathbf{b}) - Q_l(\mathbf{b}_{(i+1)j})\|. \tag{9}$$

To satisfy both C_1 and C_2, the projection operator P_{C_2} embeds P_{C_1} as in (10) so that the result of P_{C_1} should be projected onto C_2.

$$P_{C_2}(B_{ij,kl}) = \begin{cases} P_{C_1}(B_{ij,kl}), & \text{if } \mathbf{b}''_{ij} \in C_2, \\ B_{ij,kl}, & \text{otherwise,} \end{cases} \tag{10}$$

where $\mathbf{b}''_{ij}$ is an inverse discrete cosine transformed (IDCTed) block of $\mathbf{B}_{ij}$ except that $P_{C_1}(B_{ij,kl})$ is used for the kl^{th} DCT coefficient instead of $B_{ij,kl}$.

The third constraint set, C_3, reflects the original interlaced video as in (11) by P_{C_3} replicating the corresponding field with the original parity field.

$$C_3 = \{\mathbf{f}' \mid \mathbf{p}' = \mathbf{p}\}, \tag{11}$$

where $\mathbf{p}$ and $\mathbf{p}'$ represent the original parity field and the corresponding field of a frame $\mathbf{f}'$.

Next, we summarize the iterative procedure using the proposed projections for improving the de-interlaced video.

1. Initialize n with 1.
2. Choose a reference frame n to be reconstructed and its adjacent frames $n-1$ and $n+1$.
3. For each block $\mathbf{b}_{ij}$, find $\mathbf{b}_{ij}^{-1}$ and $\mathbf{b}_{ij}^{+1}$ from the adjacent frames, which are located on the motion trajectories of $\mathbf{b}_{ij}$.
4. Each DCT coefficient $B_{ij,kl}$ in the high frequency band of $\mathbf{B}_{ij}$ is updated by P_{C_2}.
5. Reconstruct a IDCTed block, $\mathbf{b}''_{ij}$, with the updated coefficients $P_{C_2}(B_{ij,kl})$'s.
6. Through $P_{C_3}(\mathbf{f})$, restore the original parity field.
7. Increase n by 1 and go to Step 2 until all frames are reconstructed.
8. Stop, if the stopping criterion is reached; else go to Step 1.

4 Experimental Results

The proposed POCS-based enhancement method starts with an initial de-interlaced video obtained through existing de-interlacing algorithms. To test the performance of the proposed algorithm, three initial de-interlaced videos are obtained by using "the spatial temporal edge-based line average (STELA)" [2], "the bi-directional de-interlacing algorithm using motion compensated field interpolation (BDMCFI)" [5], and "the time-recursive de-interlacing algorithm (TRD)" [4] which is the conventional motion compensated de-interlacing.

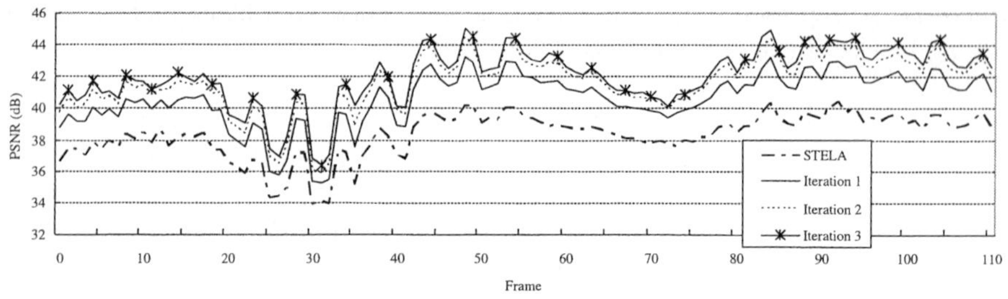

Fig. 1. PSNR variations at different iterations of the proposed algorithm on the "News" sequence obtained by STELA.

As an objective measure of the improvement made by the proposed POCS-based technique, the peak signal-to-noise ratio (PSNR) is used. Figure 1 shows that the objective quality of the "News" sequence de-interlaced by STELA become gradually improved as employing the proposed algorithm iteratively.

For the comparison of the subjective visual quality, we also present magnified photographs of the details of the 70th frame of the "Table Tennis" sequence in Fig. 2. Impulsive noise at face and hands yielded in the de-interlacing process is reduced by iterating the proposed algorithm and restoring a image close to the original image.

(a) (b) (c)

Fig. 2. Comparison of subjective quality on the 70th frame of the "Table Tennis" sequence. (a) Original subregion. (b) Result of STELA with (a). (c) Result of the proposed algorithm with (b) at the 5th iteration.

Figure 3 exhibits magnified subregion of the 196th frame of the "News" sequence. Since the subregion is located in the center of the frame and ballet dancers within it are moving quickly, the subregion must be a region of interest. The proposed video enhancement method produces an image near the original one from very degraded image which is mainly caused by using incorrect motion information in the de-interlacing process, and thus, the subjective visual quality of the frame is significantly improved.

(a) (b) (c)

Fig. 3. Comparison of subjective quality on the 196th frame of the "News" sequence. (a) Original subregion. (b) Result of BDMCFI with (a). (c) Result of the proposed algorithm with (b) at the 1st iteration.

Table 1 summarizes the average PSNR performance of the proposed algorithm for various de-interlaced videos. In most cases, the average PSNR qualities are gradually improved, particularly at the first iteration by 1∼2 dB, and show the convergence behavior.

Table 1. Average PSNR Improvement at Different Iterations of the Proposed Algorithm.

Sequence		Iteration					
		0	1	2	3	4	5
Table Tennis	STELA	29.35	30.75	31.20	31.38	31.44	31.45
	BDMCI	33.24	33.91	34.22	34.39	34.49	34.54
	TRD	24.38	24.54	24.57	24.57	24.55	24.53
Beach	STELA	36.93	39.05	39.63	39.75	39.73	39.68
	BDMCI	40.27	40.80	40.98	41.05	41.05	41.03
	TRD	35.19	35.97	36.25	36.34	36.37	36.37
News	STELA	38.24	40.53	41.49	41.95	42.20	42.35
	BDMCI	38.10	39.12	39.80	40.31	40.70	41.02
	TRD	35.78	36.69	37.12	37.33	37.45	37.54

5 Conclusions

In this paper, based on the theory of POCS, we proposed a video enhancement technique to improve the visual quality of a de-interlaced video. Considering the characteristics of de-interlaced video, we introduced novel constraint sets utilizing multiframes and derived the related projection operators. These projection operators can enhance high frequency components of de-interlaced video with those of the motion-compensated neighboring frames. Through simulations, we showed that the proposed video enhancement method significantly improve the visual quality of the de-interlaced video by restoring the meaningful frequency information of the original progressive video.

References

1. Haavisto, P., Neuvo, Y., Juhola, J.: Motion adaptive scan rate up-conversion. Multidimensional Systems and Signal Processing **3** (1992) 1113–130
2. Lee, M.H., Kim, J.H., Lee, J.S., Ryu, K.K., Song, D.I.: A new algorithm for interlaced to progressive scan conversion based on directional correlations ant its IC design. IEEE Trans. on Consumer Electronics **40** (1994) 119–129
3. Kwon, S.K., Seo, K.S., Kim, J.K., Kim, Y.G.: A motion-adaptive de-interlacing method. IEEE Trans. on Consumer Electronics **38** (1992) 145–149
4. Wang, F.M., Anastassiou, D., Netravali, A.N.: Time-recursive deinterlacing for idtv and pyramid coding. Signal Process. : Image Commun. (1990) 365–374
5. Jung, Y.Y., Choi, B.T., Park, Y.J., Ko, S.J.: An effective de-interlacing technique using motion compensated interpolation. IEEE Trans. on Consumer Electronics **46** (2000) 460–466
6. Youla, D., Webb, H.: Image restoration by the method of convex projections: Part I-Theory. IEEE Trans. on Medical Imaging **MI-1** (1982) 81–94
7. Yang, Y., Galatsanos, N.P., Katsaggelos, A.K.: Projection-based spatially adaptive reconstruction of block-transform compressed images. IEEE Trans. on Image Processing **4** (1995) 896–908
8. Zakhor, A.: Iterative procedures for reduction of blocking effects in transform image coding. IEEE Trans. on Circuits Syst. Video Technol. **2** (1992) 91–95
9. Paek, H., Kim, R.C., Lee, S.U.: On the POCS-based postprocessing technique to reduce the blocking artifacts in transform coded images. IEEE Trans. on Circuits Syst. Video Technol. **8** (1998) 358–367
10. Sugiyama, K., Nakamura, H.: A method of de-interlacing with motion compensated interpolation. IEEE Trans. on Consumer Electronics **45** (1999) 611–616

A New Construction Algorithm for Symmetrical Reversible Variable-Length Codes from the Huffman Code

Wook-Hyun Jeong and Yo-Sung Ho

Kwangju Institute of Science and Technology (K-JIST)
1 Oryong-dong, Puk-gu, Kwangju, 500-712, Korea
{whjeong, hoyo}@kjist.ac.kr
http://vclab.kjist.ac.kr

Abstract. Variable-length codes (VLCs) improve coding performance using statistical characteristics of source symbols; however, VLCs have disastrous effects from bit errors in noisy transmission environments. In order to overcome problems with VLCs, reversible variable-length codes (RVLCs) have been introduced as one of the error resilience tools due to their error recovering capability for corrupted video streams. Still, existing RVLCs are complicated in the design and have some rooms for improvement in coding efficiency. In this paper, we propose a new design method for a symmetrical RVLC from the optimal Huffman code table. The proposed algorithm has a simpler construction process and also demonstrates an improved performance in terms of the average codeword length than other symmetrical RVLC algorithms.

1 Introduction

Most image and video coding schemes have used VLCs, such as the Huffman code [1] or the arithmetic code [2], to improve compression efficiency. However, VLCs are so sensitive to bit errors and packet losses, along with predictive coding. If there is a bit error in the VLC bitstream, we have to discard all the ensuing data until the resynchronization marker.

In recent years, the reversible variable-length code (RVLC) has been introduced in order to reduce the effect of channel errors in the compressed bitstream. In RVLC with the resynchronization marker, we can decode the bitstream both in the forward and backward directions and recover unaffected video data as much as possible from the received bitstream. Thus, RVLC has received extensive attention as one of the error resilience tools, during the development of new video coding standards, such as MPEG-4 and H.263+, which require enhanced error control capabilities for mobile applications.

RVLC can be categorized into two different classes, symmetrical and asymmetrical codes, according to their bit patterns. The symmetrical RVLC employs the same code table for decoding both in the forward and backward directions. Although the asymmetrical RVLC offers better coding efficiency than the symmetrical RVLC owing to more flexible code assignment, the asymmetrical RVLC

A. Yazici and C. Şener (Eds.): ISCIS 2003, LNCS 2869, pp. 675–682, 2003.

requires two separate coding tables. While MPEG-4 includes an asymmetrical RVLC, H.263+ employs a symmetrical RVLC [3], [4].

After Takishima *et al.* [5] proposed the first work for constructing a symmetrical RVLC from a given Huffman code, Tsai *et al.* [6] improved the symmetrical RVLC construction algorithm and reduced the average codeword length. However, these algorithms should find symmetrical codewords on a full binary Huffman tree and precalculate the number of available symmetrical codewords at each level before constructing the symmetrical RVLC. Moreover, the overall design procedure for the symmetrical RVLC requires high complexity due to adapting precalculated values at each level to the given Huffman table, and some restrictions are imposed during this adaptation process. Consequently, symmetrical codewords can be missed at some levels.

In this paper, we propose a new algorithm to construct a symmetrical RVLC based on the optimal Huffman code table. When we find symmetrical codewords on one side of the binary Huffman tree, we simplify the adaptation process to the given Huffman table. In addition, the proposed adaptation process can contribute to reducing the average codeword length since any effective symmetrical codewords cannot be missed.

2 The Proposed RVLC Algorithm

2.1 Search for Symmetrical Codewords

Fig. 1 (a) illustrates an example of the binary Huffman tree. Starting from the root node, we assign '0' and '1' to the left and right branches of the tree. The leaves of the tree are only allowed to be codewords so that the Huffman code satisfies the prefix condition. However, the allocation of '0' and '1' to the left and right branches from the root node is arbitrary. Therefore, we can obtain another Huffman code, as shown in Fig. 1 (b), that has the same average codeword length as that of Huffman code in Fig. 1 (a); this interchange of '0' and '1' is equivalent to the bit inversion operation in the original Huffman codewords.

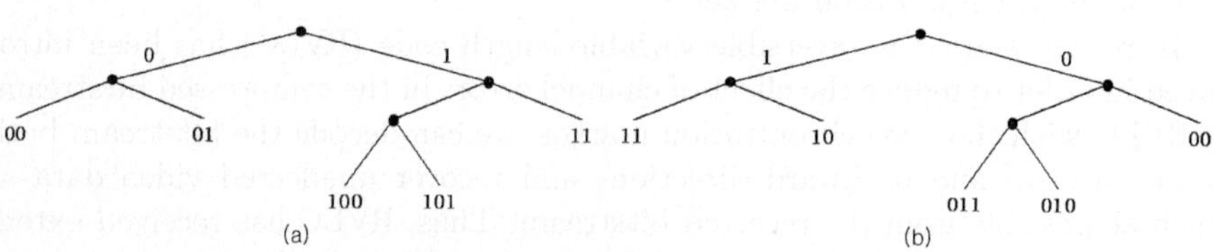

Fig. 1. Binary Huffman trees

RVLCs have to satisfy not only the prefix condition but also the suffix condition to be decoded in both the forward and backward directions instantaneously. For the symmetrical RVLC, however, the prefix condition leads to the suffix condition due to the symmetrical bit-pattern property. This symmetry property provides another advantage. If all the bits of the chosen symmetrical codeword are inversed, we can obtain another symmetrical codeword which has the same length and satisfies both the prefix and suffix conditions. For example, in Fig. 1 (a) and (b), we can derive symmetrical codewords '11' and '101' from '00' and '010' through bit inversion, respectively.

In order to use this property, we search for symmetrical codewords in the left half region of the binary Huffman tree, especially assigned to '0'. In this region, we find $\lceil S/2 \rceil$, not S, candidates of symmetrical codewords where S is the number of given symbols and $\lceil x \rceil$ is the smallest integer larger than or equal to x. A target symmetrical RVLC for S is composed of the already selected symmetrical codewords on the left half tree and their bit-inversed versions existing on the other side of the binary tree [7].

The number $m_H(l)$ of all symmetrical codewords at level l on the left half tree is

$$m_H(l) = 2^{\lfloor (l+1)/2 \rfloor - 1} \tag{1}$$

Let $C(l)$ denote the set containing all symmetrical codewords at level l in a half region. Then,

$$C(1) = \{0\}, \qquad C(2) = \{00\} \tag{2}$$

$$C(l) = \{ \ l\text{-}bit \ \ codewords \ \ for \ \ 2 \cdot e \ \ and \ \ (2^{l-1} - 2) - 2 \cdot e, \\ where \ \ e \in C(l-2) \ \} \ \text{ for } \ l \geq 3 \tag{3}$$

Fig. 2 depicts the distribution of symmetrical candidates on a half binary tree assigned to '0' from (1)-(3) and also shows integer values corresponding to the symmetrical codewords at each level.

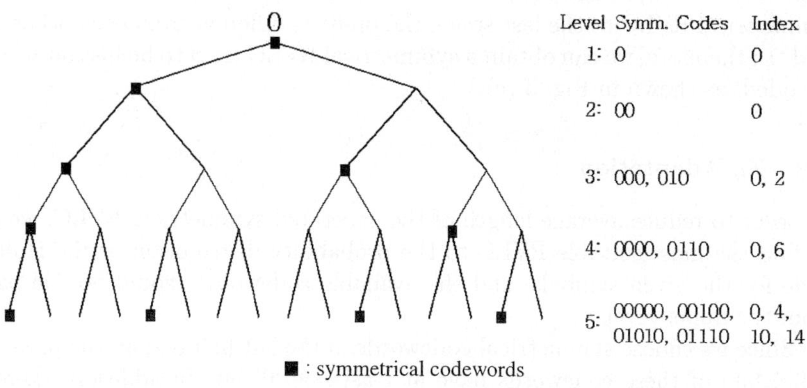

Fig. 2. Distribution of symmetrical codewords on a half binary tree

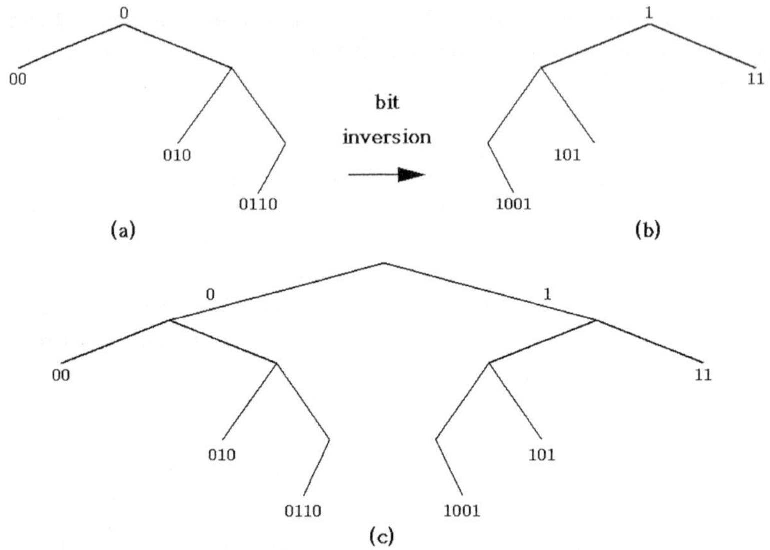

Fig. 3. (a) Unique decodablity of symmetrical codewords already chosen in the left region (b) Unique decodablity of bit inversed vergion in the right region (c) Unique decodable symmetrical RVLC

The prefix condition is the necessary and the sufficient condition for the uniquely docodable code. When we pick up symmetrical codewords on a half binary tree that satisfy the prefix condition by removing codewords that violate the prefix condition, the resulting RVLC is instantaneously decodable. If these codewords are uniquely decoded solely in one side region in Fig. 3 (a), reciprocal codewords generated by bit-inversion can also be uniquely decodable only in the other side region associated with '1' in Fig. 3 (b). When the originally chosen codewords for $\lceil S/2 \rceil$ and bit-inversed codewords for $\lceil S/2 \rceil$ are combined into the symmetrical RVLC at the last stage, the prefix is different from each other as '0' and '1'; therefore, we can obtain a symmetrical RVLC for S to be instantaneously decoded, as shown in Fig. 3 (c).

2.2 $\mathbf{Z_L}$ Adaptation

In order to reduce average length of the generated symmetrical RVLC, we need to find the most suitable RVLC to the probability distribution or the Huffman code for the given symbols, and the available codewords should not be passed from the upper level.

Since we choose symmetrical codewords in the left half region, the prefix and suffix bits of these codewords have at least one '0' bit. In addition, there are symmetrical codewords that consist of all '0' bits at each level, as shown in Fig 2. We define these codewords as $\mathbf{Z_L}$s at level L. For $\mathbf{Z_L}$, we should consider the following two situations.

1) If $\mathbf{Z_L}$ is chosen, the number of '0' bits in the prefix or the suffix of each selected symmetrical codeword in the left half region, except $\mathbf{Z_L}$, is less than L due to the elimination process. For instance, the selection of '000', $\mathbf{Z_3}$, leads that the prefix or the suffix of the other symmetrical codewords are determined to be only '0' or '00'. In other words, the choice of $\mathbf{Z_L}$ can control the number of target symmetrical RVLCs at each level.
2) Since bit-inversed symmetrical codewords are included in the target RVLC, we can obtain the codeword composed of L '1' bits for $\mathbf{Z_L}$. Thus, these two codewords are added to level L in the result. If $\mathbf{Z_L}$ is selected carefully at a proper upper level L to be suitable for the distribution of occurrence probabilities of symbols, the average length can be reduced successfully.

In this paper, we propose $\mathbf{Z_L}$ adaptation to construct a symmetrical RVLC from the optimal Huffman code table [7]. In $\mathbf{Z_L}$ adaptation, L is determined in such a way that the bit length of $\mathbf{Z_L}$ equals to L_{min}, which is defined as the bit length of the shortest codeword in the given Huffman code, opposed to L_{max}, the bit length of the largest one. $\mathbf{Z_L}$ adaptation allocates $\mathbf{Z_L}$ and L '1'bit codeword from the most probable symbol successively so that we can obtain more efficient symmetrical RVLC.

We summarize the proposed construction procedure for the symmetrical RVLC below.

1) In the left half region of the binary Huffman tree, $\mathbf{Z_L}$ is determined. The bit length of $\mathbf{Z_L}$ is selected to be the same as that of the shortest Huffman code, L_{min}. For instance, if a given Huffman code starts from a 2-bit codeword, which means that L_{min} is 2, simply '00' is selected.
2) Until symmetrical codewords are selected as many as $\lceil S/2 \rceil$, all available symmetrical codewords are chosen from the highest level. All the selection processes are followed by the elimination of codewords that violate the prefix condition.
3) Combining the already chosen symmetrical codewords and their bit-inversed codewords, we can obtain a target symmetrical RVLC to be instantaneously decoded.

Hence, the number $m(l)$ of effective symmetrical codewords at level l for $\lceil S/2 \rceil$ on a half binary tree is

$$m(l) = m_H(l) - \sum_{l} v_z(l) - \sum_{i=1}^{L-1} v_{ci}(l) \tag{4}$$

where $v_z(l)$ indicates the number of codewords causing the violation of the prefix condition at level l from the choice of $\mathbf{Z_L}$, and $v_{ci}(l)$ represents the number of codewords to be deleted from the previous selection of symmetrical codewords. In addition, L and i denote the bit length of $\mathbf{Z_L}$ and the number of '0' bits on the prefix or the suffix of the previous chosen codeword, respectively.

In Eq. (4), $v_z(l)$ is given by

(i) $v_z = 1$, when $l < 2L + 1$,
(ii) $v_z = m_H(l - 2L)$, when $2L+1 \leq l$,

and $v_{ci}(l)$ is expressed by

(i) $v_{ci} = 1$, when $2L' + 1 - i < l < 2L' + 1$,
(ii) $v_{ci}(l) = m_H(l - 2L')$, when $2L'+1 \leq l$,

where L' is the bit length of the already selected symmetrical codeword at the upper level.

3 Experimental Results and Analysis

In order to evaluate the proposed algorithm, we compare the performance of the proposed algorithm with that of existing RVLC algorithms in terms of the computational complexity of the construction process and coding efficiency.

3.1 Complexity of the Construction Process

Conventional RVLC schemes [5], [6] construct symmetrical RVLCs based on the Huffman binary tree as many as S. After the precomputation of the number of available symmetrical codewords at each level, from L_{min} to L_{max}, they repeat the adaptation and search process, whose complexity is $O(N^2 \cdot (\sqrt{2})^N) \mid_{N=S}$.

However, the proposed scheme constructs a symmetrical RVLC on a half binary tree as many as $\lceil S/2 \rceil$. After the decision of $\mathbf{Z_L}$, we search for RVLCs until a half of S. Then, we finish the design of the code by bit inversion. The complexity of the proposed RVLC scheme is $O(N^2 \cdot (\sqrt[4]{2})^N) \mid_{N=S}$. The proposed algorithm reduces the number of symbols and the search range by half. This reduction makes a significant difference of complexity between the existing and new design algorithms, which is about $O((\sqrt[4]{2})^N) \mid_{N=S}$ or $(1.19)^S$.

3.2 Coding Performance

Table 1 lists codeword assignments for the English alphabet with symmetrical RVLCs designed by Takishima's [5], Tsai's [6], and the proposed algorithms, and compares their coding performances in terms of the average codeword length. In Table 1, C1, C2, and C3 are generated by the Huffman, Takishima's, and Tsai's algorithms, respectively.

Results of C2 and C3 indicate that their algorithms do not find all available symmetrical codewords at Level 8 and Level 9 despite the existence of other effective candidates at those levels, owing to meet the restriction condition at Level 7. In addition, we observe that the unavoidable limitation occurs at Level 3, the most probable symbol location. There are four effective codewords at Level 3; nevertheless, two available codewords are omitted because the bit length of RVLC should be bounded to that of the Huffman code.

Table 1. Comparison of coding performance for the English alphabet

Occurrence Probability		Huffman C1		Takishima's algorithm : C2		Tsai's algorithm : C3		Proposed algorithm : C4	
		L	codeword	L	codeword	L	codeword	L	codeword
E	0.14878570	3	001	3	000	3	010	3	000 ($\mathbf{Z}_3$)
T	0.09354149	3	110	3	111	3	101	3	111
A	0.08833733	4	0000	4	0110	4	0110	3	010
O	0.07245796	4	0100	4	1001	4	1001	3	101
R	0.06872164	4	0101	5	00100	4	0000	4	0110
N	0.06498532	4	0110	5	11011	4	1111	4	1001
H	0.05831331	4	1000	5	01010	5	01110	5	00100
I	0.05644515	4	1001	5	10101	5	10001	5	11011
S	0.05537763	4	1010	5	01110	5	00100	5	01110
D	0.04376834	5	00010	5	10001	5	11011	5	10001
L	0.04123298	5	00011	6	001100	6	011110	6	001100
U	0.02762209	5	10110	6	110011	6	100001	6	110011
P	0.02575393	5	10111	6	010010	6	001100	6	011110
F	0.02455297	5	11100	6	101101	6	110011	6	100001
M	0.02361889	5	11110	6	011110	7	0111110	7	0010100
C	0.02081665	5	11111	6	100001	7	1000001	7	1101011
W	0.01868161	6	011100	7	0010100	7	0010100	7	0011100
G	0.01521216	6	011101	7	1101011	7	1101011	7	1100011
Y	0.01521216	6	011110	7	0011100	7	0011100	7	0111110
B	0.01267680	6	011111	7	1100011	7	1100011	7	1000001
V	0.01160928	6	111011	7	0100010	7	0001000	8	00111100
K	0.00867360	7	1110100	7	1011101	7	1110111	8	11000011
X	0.00146784	8	11101011	8	00111100	8	01111110	8	01111110
J	0.00080064	9	111010101	9	001010100	9	011111110	8	10000001
Q	0.00080064	10	1110101000	10	0010110100	10	0111111110	9	011111110
Z	0.00053376	10	1110101001	10	1101001011	10	1000000001	9	100000001
Average length		4.15572392		4.69655649		4.60728507		**4.46463681**	

In Table 1, C4 is designed by the proposed method. Experimental results show that the average codeword length of C4 is about 5.2% and 3.2% shorter than those of C2 and C3, respectively. Moreover, C4 is composed of pairs of bit inversion, $\mathbf{Z}_3$ and '111', which are the shortest in target symmetrical RVLC, are assigned to the most probable symbols by $\mathbf{Z}_\mathbf{L}$ adaptation, and attainable symmetrical candidates are not missed at any levels.

Table 2 shows a comparison of characteristics of the proposed symmetrical RVLC with existing symmetrical RVLCs. In Table 2, the proposed algorithm is superior to the conventional algorithm in relation to three factors: maximum codeword length, minimum codeword length, and the number of symmetrical codewords at the highest level $n_{Huff}(L_{min})$, where $n_{Huff}(i)$ is the number of Huffman codewords having a length i. These factors can affect the average codeword length and the coding performance significantly.

Table 2. Comparison of code characteristics

Type of Code	Max. Length	Min. Length	Number of Codewords at L_{min}
Huffman Code	L_{max}	L_{min}	$n_{Huff}(L_{min})$
Conventional Symm. RVLC	$\geq L_{max}$	L_{min}	$\leq n_{Huff}(L_{min})$
Proposed Symm. RVLC	$\leq L_{max}$	$\leq L_{min}$	$\geq n_{Huff}(L_{min})$

4 Conclusions

In this paper, we have proposed a new algorithm to design a symmetrical reversible variable-length code (RVLC) from the optimal Huffman code table. After we find symmetrical codewords in the left region of the given binary Huffman tree with $\mathbf{Z_L}$ adaptation more efficiently, we use bit inversion to generate a symmetrical RVLC. Bit inversion and $\mathbf{Z_L}$ adaptation resolve the variation problem and simplify the construction process, efficiently reducing the average codeword length. Experimental results demonstrate that the proposed RVLC algorithm improves the performance over existing RVLC algorithms.

Acknowledgments. This work was supported in part by Kwangju Institute of Science and Technology, in part by the Korea Science and Engineering Foundation (KOSEF) through the Ultra-Fast Fiber-Optic Networks (UFON) Research Center at K-JIST, and in part by the Ministry of Education (MOE) through the Brain Korea 21 (BK21) project.

References

1. Huffman, D. : A method for the construction of minimum redundancy codes, Proc. Inst. Radio Engr., Vol. 40, Sept. (1952) 1098–1101
2. Rissanen, J. J. and Langdon. Jr., G. G. : Arithmetic Coding, IBM J. Res. Develop., 23, (1979) 149–162
3. ISO/IEC 14496–2 : Information Technology – Coding of audio/video objects, Final Draft Int. Std., Part 2 : Visual, Oct. (1998)
4. ITU-T Rec. H.263 : Video coding for low bit rate communications, Annex V, (2000)
5. Takishima, Y., Wada, M., and Murakami, H. : Reversible variable length codes, IEEE Transactions on Communications, Vol. 43, Feb. (1995) 158–162
6. Tsai, C. W. and Wu, J. L. : A modified symmetrical reversible variable length code and its theoretical bounds, IEEE Transactions on Information Theory, Vol. 47, Sept. (2001) 2543–2548
7. Jeong, W. H. and Ho, Y. S. : Design of symmetrical reversible variable-length codes from the Huffman code, Picture Coding Symposium (2003) 135–138

A Solution to the Composition Problem in Object-Based Video Coding

Jeong-Woo Lee and Yo-Sung Ho

Kwangju Institute of Science and Technology (K-JIST)
1 Oryong-dong, Puk-gu, Kwangju, 500-712, Korea
{jeongwoo, hoyo}@kjist.ac.kr
http://vclab.kjist.ac.kr/

Abstract. In this paper, we introduce the composition problem associated with object-based video coding and propose a solution to this problem. Although the object-based rate control algorithm can provide the overall coding gain, it may create the composition problem due to different temporal resolutions in object encoding. By checking shape changes of video objects, we can minimize the possibility of the composition problem at the encoder. At the decoder, we can also apply hole detection and recovery algorithms to eliminate the effect of the composition problem to the human visual system.

1 Introduction

In MPEG-4 video coding [1], there are three types of coding scenarios. The first one is the simple frame-based coding. The second one is an object-based coding, where the temporal rates of all objects are constrained to be the same, but the bit allocation is performed at the object level. The third one is also an object-based coding, but the temporal rate of each object may vary. In each coding mode, we should consider trade-offs between spatial and temporal qualities to improve the overall coding efficiency. In the object-based framework, we have a freedom to choose different frameskip factors and corresponding quantization parameters for the objects in the scene.

However, the existing MPEG-4 rate control algorithms [2,3] do not address the case of coding several objects at different temporal rates. In other words, the objects in the current frame are either all coded or all skipped. As shown in Fig. 1, we can choose a different frameskip factor and corresponding quantization parameters for each object in the object-based coding framework.

Although an object-based rate allocation algorithm can provide a potential coding gain, it also makes the problem complicated significantly since we must track the individual time instant when each object is coded. The second difficulty to develop the object-based framework is a matter of procedure. It is not clear how we can determine the set of frameskip factors and quantization parameters; one possible approach is to break the main problem into smaller sub-problems [4]. The third difficulty in coding objects at different temporal rates is due to the composition problem, because holes may appear in the reconstructed frame

A. Yazici and C. Şener (Eds.): ISCIS 2003, LNCS 2869, pp. 683–690, 2003.

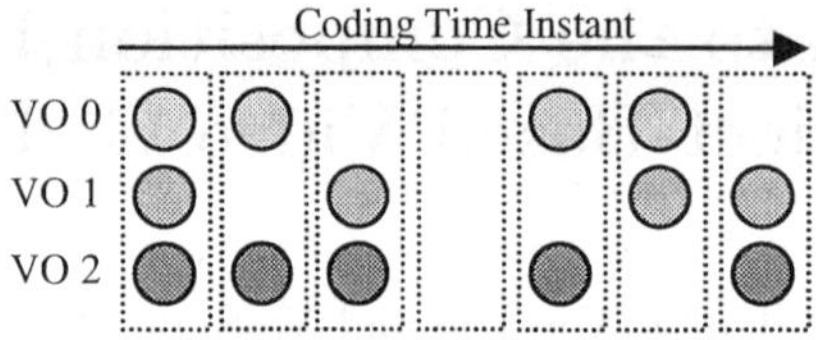

Fig. 1. Object-based coding framework

when objects are encoded at different temporal rates [5]. This can easily be avoided if all the objects in the current frame are constrained to have the same temporal rate, i.e., a *fixed* temporal rate. However, in order to fully explore the potential coding gain of object-based video coding, a different temporal rate for each object, i.e., *variable* temporal rates, should be allowed.

In this paper, after we describe the concept of the composition problem, we propose a solution to this problem both at the encoder and the decoder sides. While we can minimize the composition problem at the encoder, we can try to eliminate the problem at the decoder. For this objective, the encoder detects changes in the object boundaries over time and the decoder employs hole detection and recovery algorithms. Although the idea of detecting changes in object shape boundaries over time minimizes the effect on the average PSNR values in the combined objects [6], it does not consider the sensitivity of the human visual system. In other words, we should note that due to the sensitivity of the human visual system, holes may be easily detected even though they do not impact the average PSNR value significantly. In addition, there was no rate control algorithm that effectively utilizes this information for object-based coding.

This paper is organized as follows. Section 2 describes the concept of the composition problem. Section 3 provides new ideas to solve the composition problem at the encoding and the decoding parts. After we present simulation results to evaluate the performance of the proposed algorithms in Section 4, we draw conclusions of this work in Section 5.

2 Composition Problem

Fig. 2 illustrates the composition problem with the FOREMAN sequence that has two objects: foreground and background. The left image shows the decoded and composited sequence for the case when both objects are encoded at 30Hz. The right image shows the decoded and composited sequence when the foreground is encoded at 30Hz and the background at 15Hz.

When all objects are encoded at the same temporal resolution, there is no problem during the object composition for image reconstruction at the decoder, i.e., all pixels in the reconstructed frame are well-defined. However, the composition problem can occur if objects are encoded at different temporal rates. When the shapes of object boundaries are changing in the scene and these objects are encoded at different temporal rates, we may have some undefined pixels or holes

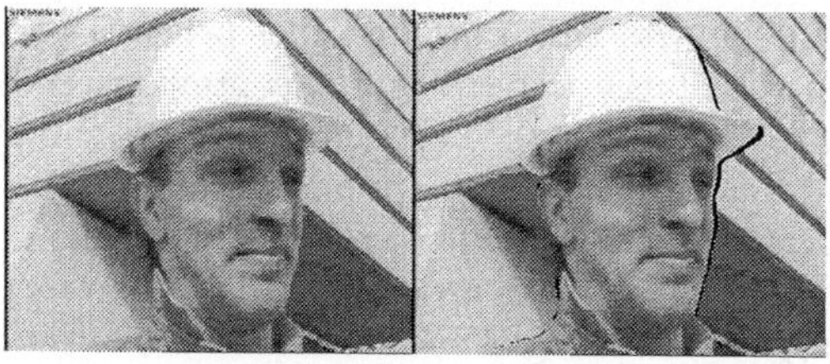

Fig. 2. Illustration of the composition problem

in the reconstructed frame. These holes are created due to the movement of one object without updating adjacent or overlapping objects. The holes are uncovered areas in the scene that cannot be associated with any previous information; therefore, those pixels are not well-defined. The holes are disappeared when objects are resynchronized, i.e., when both the background and the foreground objects are coded at the same time instant.

3 Solution to Composition Problem

3.1 Encoding Part: Minimization Process

In order to resolve the composition problem, we can try to minimize the possibility of the problem at the encoder. For this objective, we need to define the shape change of each object over time to identify its boundary information.

A well-known measure for the shape difference is the Hamming distance, which counts the number of different pixels between two shapes. Fig. 3(a) illustrates the concept of the Hamming distance.

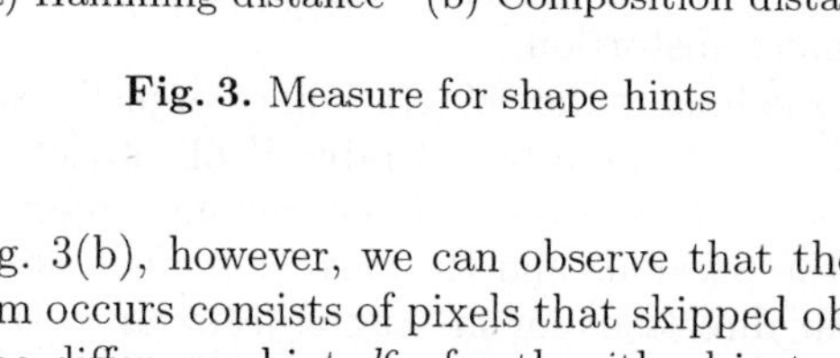

(a) Hamming distance (b) Composition distance

Fig. 3. Measure for shape hints

As shown in Fig. 3(b), however, we can observe that the region where the composition problem occurs consists of pixels that skipped objects do not cover. Therefore, the shape difference hint $d^c_{j,i}$ for the jth object at the current time index i is defined by

$$d^c_{j,i} = |A_{j,p} - A_{j,c}| \tag{1}$$

where $A_{j,c}$ and $A_{j,p}$ be sets that contain pixel positions of the segmentation map of the jth object at the current and the previous coding time instants, respectively. The sign '−' implies the *difference* of the set and $|\cdot|$ is the *cardinality* of the set. We note that all operations are performed by the set operation.

We then normalize the shape difference hint $d^c_{j,i}$ by the number of pixels in the object. The value of '0' indicates no change, while the value of '1' implies that the object is moving very fast. Fig. 4 shows shape hints of the AKIYO sequence, which indicate very small movement of objects. Since the shape hint is a good indicator of object movement, we can use it for the object-based allocation of variable temporal resolutions.

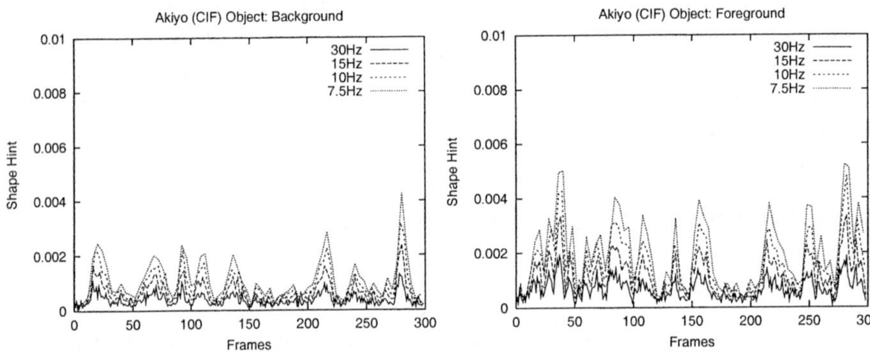

(a) Background (b) Foreground

Fig. 4. Shape hints for AKIYO

Based on the proposed measure, we can employ a simple algorithm to predict and avoid the problems at the encoder [5]. First of all, we need to determine existence of stationary objects, either rectangular background objects that cover the entire frame or arbitrarily shaped objects that do not move. Since we need to have at least two moving objects for the composition problem, we can apply any object-based rate allocation algorithm to the encoding process. In order to determine whether movement of the non-stationary objects is tolerable or not, we compare each shape hint to an empirically determined threshold value. If the threshold value is exceeded by any shape hint, we conclude that the composed scene contains too much distortion.

Although the shape hint of the non-stationary objects exceeds the threshold value, movement of objects may be tolerable if all objects move in the same direction. In order to test directions of the moving objects, we calculate the difference between the previous and the current segmentation maps. Although we consider only four directions for moving objects, any other methods can be employed to detect more detailed directions of the moving objects.

Fig. 5 explain how shape hints are used and how object-based rate allocation is performed. After shape hints for all objects are calculated by (1), collections of the extracted hints are passed into an analyzer where we estimate whether the

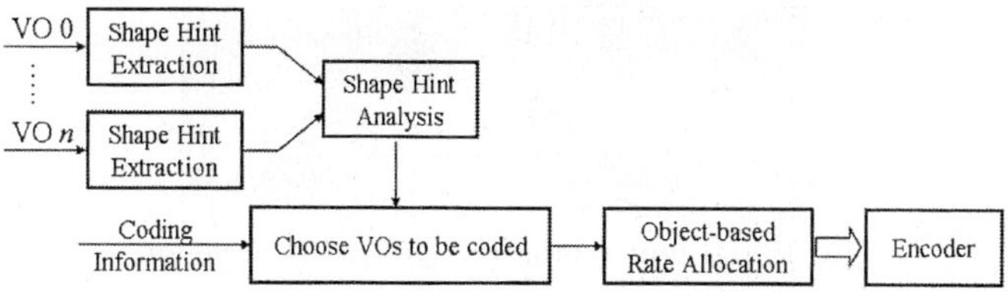

Fig. 5. Encoding process to reduce the composition problem

composition problem can occur at the decoder or not. Consequently, the possible coded object set M_L is determined based on values of shape hints and directions of the moving objects as well as the buffer occupancy [4]. For example, we do not allow variable temporal rates for those objects that move to the opposite direction each other.

3.2 Decoding Part: Elimination Process

If movement of shape boundaries is small, any hole in the reconstructed frame is negligible and does not effect the overall PSNR value significantly. However, we should note that due to the sensitivity of the human visual system, the hole may easily be detected. In order to overcome this problem, we can reduce its visual effect by recovering any undefined pixel values at the decoder.

In order to eliminate the visual effect of holes in the scene, we first check the existence of the holes and then delete hole regions. Fig. 6 illustrates how to detect holes in the reconstructed frame with the rectangular background object.

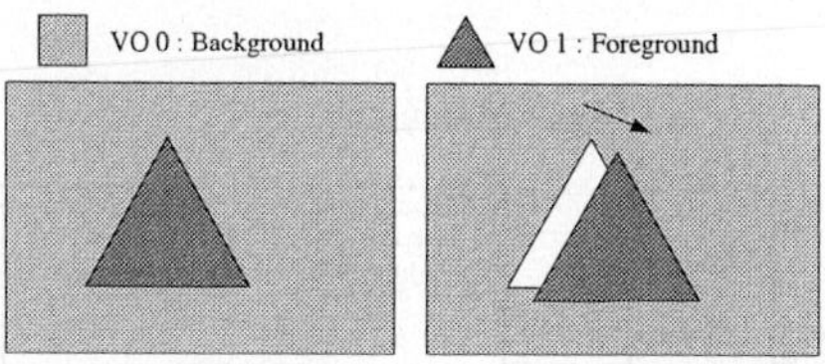

(a) Previous frame (b) Current frame

Fig. 6. Frame recovery with a rectangular background object

Let $A_{j,d}$ be the difference between $A_{j,p}$ and $A_{j,c}$. The set H_i representing hole regions in the reconstructed frame at the time index i is calculated by

$$H_i = \bigcup_{j=0}^{M-1} [A_{j,d} - \bigcup_{k=0,k\neq j}^{M-1} A_{k,c}] \tag{2}$$

where M is the number of objects. If the jth object is skipped, $A_{j,d}$ is empty.

If the reconstructed frame consists of arbitrarily-shaped objects without the background object, the proposed algorithm can detect the hole region indicated

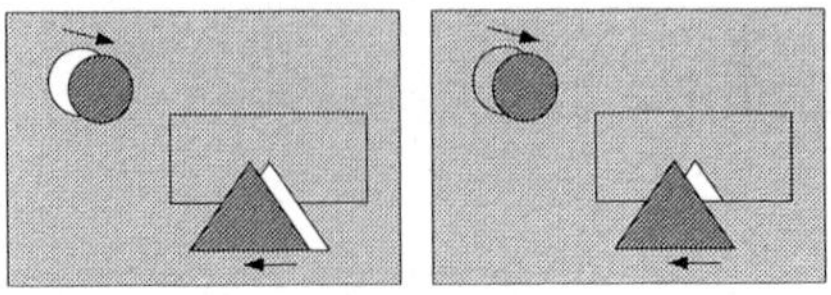

(a) Initial hole region (b) Desired hole region

Fig. 7. Detection of the hole region

by the white space in Fig. 7(a). In order to detect the exact hole region, as shown in Fig. 7(b), we impose same restrictions on the hole detection algorithm.

For the set H_i, an element is discarded if there is no element of skipped objects within the search range around the pixel position of the element. Because the possibility of the composition problem is already reduced at the encoder, it is not necessary to select a wide search range. The search range empirically determined in our experiment is eight. When the object has a background, we do not need the search range.

Once we detect holes in the reconstructed frame, we need to recover the pixel values within the holes. When one object is coded and the other is skipped in the frame, because the coded object has the original shape of the object, changes of the coded object result in visual degradation. Therefore, the pixels within the holes must be recovered from the region of the skipped objects.

In order to recover pixel values in those holes, we use the Euclidean distance measure between pixels within the holes and pixels in the segmentation plane of the skipped objects. Each pixel within the holes is replaced by the pixel in the shape boundary of the skipped object that has the minimum distance between the pixel in the holes and the pixel in the skipped object.

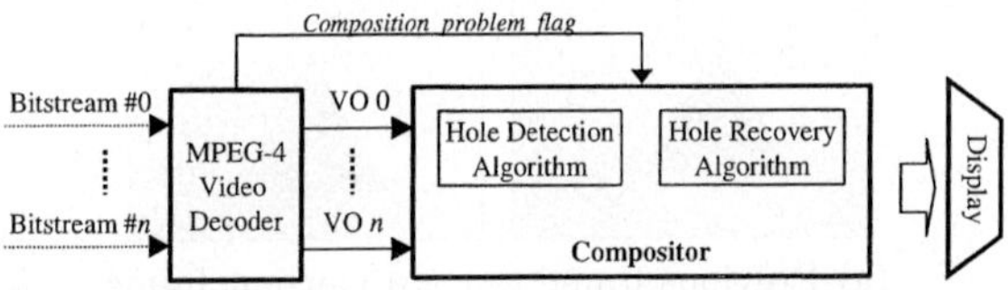

Fig. 8. Decoding process to reduce the composition problem

Fig. 8 shows the block diagram of the decoding process to reduce the composition problem. During the decoding process, each bitstream is decoded at the current decoding time. If there is no data to be decoded at the current time for the case of the skipped object, the object at the current time is replicated by the object at the previous decoding time. If all objects are decoded, the *composition_problem_flag* is set to be 0 and the reconstructed frame is directly displayed with no additional process. If the value of *composition_problem_flag* is 1, however, we apply the hole detection and recovery algorithm because of the composition problem at the reconstructed frame.

4 Experimental Results

In order to evaluate the performance of the proposed algorithm, we have tested the FOREMAN and COASTGUARD sequences. We have also applied the object-based rate allocation algorithm [4].

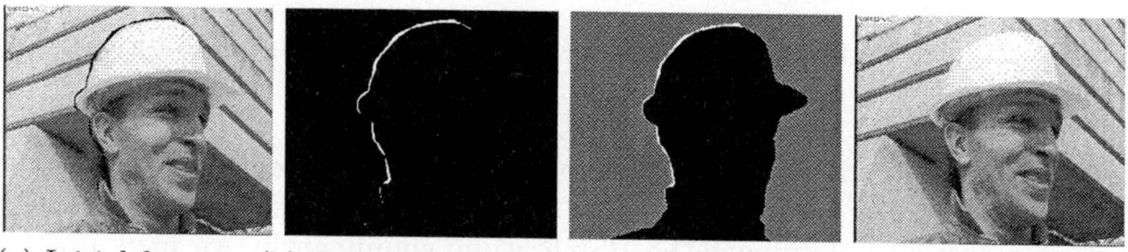

(a) Initial frame (b) Detected holes (c) Skipped object (d) Recovered frame

Fig. 9. Performance for a frame with a full-rectangular object

Fig. 9 shows an example of the composition problem generated by the foreground and background objects. If two objects construct the whole frame, as in the FOREMAN sequence, existence of the background object can be easily detected. Fig. 10 is another example of the composition problem generated by an arbitrarily-shaped object with no background object. Our test is conducted on two video objects (VO1 and VO2) of the COASTGUARD sequence. VO1 is a large boat with some motion and a complex shape, while VO2 is a small boat. VO2 moves in the opposite direction to VO1.

The white area in Fig. 9(b) shows the result of the hole detection algorithm by (2). The shaded or gray areas in Fig. 9(c) show the skipped object in the current frame. Undefined pixel values are recovered by the pixel values at the boundaries of the skipped object. Fig. 9(d) shows the result of the proposed hole recovery algorithm. As shown in Fig. 9(d), there is no problem with the object composition and no picture quality degradation is observed.

Fig. 10(b) shows the detected holes when the search range is not applied. In Fig. 10(b), the white and grey areas represent the detected holes and the skipped object, respectively. The pixel values in the white area should be recovered from the grey area. However, there exist some areas that can be against the human visual system when there is no background object. Fig. 10(d) and Fig. 10(e) show the results of the hole detection algorithm with the restriction and its reconstructed frame, respectively. These results indicate that the reconstructed frame is more comfortable to human eyes when the hole regions are recovered within the search range.

5 Conclusions

In this paper, we have proposed a solution to overcome the composition problem that can be generated in object-based video coding schemes. We define a shape hint measure to compute the change in the object shape over time and detect the

(a) Initial frame (b) Without restriction (c) With restriction (d) Recovered frame

Fig. 10. Performance for a frame without a full-rectangular object

direction of the moving object. The proposed idea is applied to the rate control part of the encoding process. Although any holes in the reconstructed frame are negligible and do not impact the PSNR value significantly, we have proposed the hole detection and recovery algorithm to minimize the effect of the visual distortion from the object composition problem. The proposed hole detection algorithm can be applied irrespective of existence of the background object.

Acknowledgments. This work was supported in part by Kwangju Institute of Science and Technology, in part by the Korea Science and Engineering Foundation (KOSEF) through the Ultra-Fast Fiber-Optic Networks (UFON) Research Center at K-JIST, and in part by the Ministry of Education (MOE) through the Brain Korea 21 (BK21) project.

References

1. ISO/IEC 14496–2 (MPEG-4 Video):Information Technology – Coding of Audio/Video Objects,(1998)
2. Vetro, A., Sun, H., and Wang, Y. :MPEG-4 Rate Control for Multiple Video Objects, IEEE Trans. Circuits Syst. Video Technol., Vol. 9, (1999) 186–199
3. Lee, J.W., Vetro, A., Wang, Y., and Ho, Y.S. :Bit Allocation for MPEG-4 Video Coding with Spatio-Temporal Trade-offs, IEEE Trans. on CSVT, Vol. 13, June (2003) 488–502
4. Lee, J.W., Vetro, A., Wang, Y., and Ho, Y.S. :MPEG-4 Video Object-based Rate Allocation with Variable Temporal Rates, ICIP, Sept. (2002) 701–704
5. Vetro, A. and Sun, H. :Encoding and Transcoding of Multiple Video Objects with Variable Temporal Resolution, Proc. IEEE Int'l Symp. on Circuits and Systems, May (2000)
6. Vetro, A., Sun, H., and Wang, Y. :Object-based Transcoding for Adaptable Video Content Delivery. IEEE Trans. on CSVT, Vol. 11, (2001) 387–401

Real-Time Advanced Contrast Enhancement Algorithm

Tae-Chan Kim[1], Chang-Won Huh[2], Meejoung Kim[1], Bong-Young Chung[2], and Soo-Won Kim[1]

[1] ASIC Design Lab., Dept. of Electronics Eng., Korea University, Anam-Dong, Sungbuk-Ku, Seoul 136-701, Korea.
{taechan, kmj, ksw}@asic.korea.ac.kr

[2] System LSI Business, Samsung Electronics Co. Ltd, San#24, Nongseo-Ri, Kiheung-Eup, Yongin-City, Kyunggi-Do, Korea.
{cs.huh, bychung}@samsung.com

Abstract. The image quality enhancement based on digital signal processing (DSP) has been addressed as one of the crucial issues in digital display technology and market. Since real-time digital imaging should be controlled in limited speed and bits, colored motion pictures with digital display generally generate many problems such as limited operating speed of algorithm and gamut range of expressed color compared to analog cathode ray tube (CRT) display. Especially, the contrast enhancement with limited values sometimes may result in overpassing contrast limit. The changes of hue and saturation cause a damage of color nature of original image. Moreover, the abruptly changed gain during contrast enhancement causes the flickering problem as time passes. This paper introduces the image contrast enhancement algorithm named Advanced Contrast Enhancement (ACE) with adaptive and recursive method which operates at 135MHz, SXGA, keeps the color tone of original image, and prevents gain from an abrupt change. The chip with ACE algorithm will be useful not only for general imaging but also for special treatment such as medical imaging to detect problems in human body pictures such as X-ray picture, ultrasound, and CT in real-time.

1 Introduction

Recently, display market trend changes fast from CRT display, a kind of analog format, to flat panel display (FPD), a kind of digital format. Development of digital technologies makes it possible to implement signal processing by DSP technology, which was used to be implemented by analog technology. Moreover, image quality based on DSP has been highlighted in display technology and market.

Image enhancement is a general procedure processing an image to generate a more suitable processed image than the original one. Therefore, the improvement of high image quality and of high speedy system in displayer has been highly needed and studied for real-time image enhancement of colored motion pictures.

A. Yazici and C. Şener (Eds.): ISCIS 2003, LNCS 2869, pp. 691–698, 2003.

Various algorithms have been introduced for this purpose [1] - [8]. Nowadays, most original images are generally processed with these algorithms and the processed images are displayed on such as LCD monitor and PDP.

One of these algorithms is the contrast enhancement [1] - [4]. The goal of contrast enhancement is to increase the visibility of images. In general, this kind of real-time contrast enhancement technology uses contrast stretching or histogram equalization technology with various algorithms [1], [5] - [6]. The contrast enhancement methods can usually be classified into two areas: intensity-based and feature-based techniques. The former is a kind of transformation applied to a whole image such as contrast stretching and generally uses linear or nonlinear function such as square, exponential, and logarithmic function as a transformation. While the latter, which is a popular method, is the histogram equalization, which is related to the probability of the occurrence of each gray level. The contrast at each gray level is proportional to the amplification of the image histogram.

It is important that the techniques mentioned above should neither create nor destroy image information. Especially, contrast enhancement should keep the color tone of natural image. However, different from gray images, the changes of red, green, and blue (RGB) ratio can cause over a contrast enhancement, and consequently induce the changes of hue and saturation level, which can cause damages of color nature of the original image such as discolored and gloomy result. In addition, the abrupt change of gain during contrast enhancement effects on the flickering problem as time passes. To minimize all of these defects of contrast enhancement, a more efficient new algorithm is highly demanded.

In this paper, we introduce a real-time image algorithm named Advanced Contrast Enhancement (ACE). The proposed algorithm keeps original image tone and doesn't cause the abrupt change of contrast gain. With this merit, it can be usually used in a flat panel display. Perceptually the saturation value of color seems like being enhanced even though hue and saturation values are not changed. Therefore we can expect not only a contrast enhancement but also vivid color of the image through the proposed algorithm. Moreover, the chip with the ACE algorithm can be applied to not only the area of general image but also the area of medical image where the enhanced pictures make it easy to detect problems of body image in real-time.

2 Architecture

The real-time contrast enhancement illustrated in this paper is implemented in SXGA at 135MHz clock frequency for colored motion picture. The gamma function operating at 135MHz and based on statistics is proposed for the real-time equalization rather than a general histogram equalization methodology which is used for a contrast equalization.

2.1 RGB to YCbCr and Vice Versa

There are a lot of color models and the RGB model is the most popular one. The RGB system matches well with a human eye since the human eye is very perceptive to red, green, and blue even though these kinds of color models are not well suited for describing colors in practical interpretation. Therefore, it is necessary to select and derive a suitable color model from the RGB model so as to enhance the contrast. One of the choices is the YCbCr color model because it is generally used in video systems. The YCbCr color model was developed as a part of ITU-R BT.601 of digital component video standards.

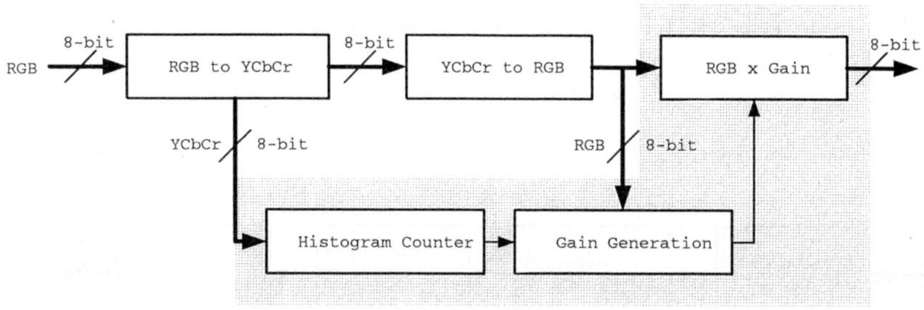

Fig. 1. Block diagram of ACE algorithm.

Fig. 1 shows the block diagram of ACE algorithm proposed in this paper. The processing steps are as follows: First, the RGB pixel data are converted to the YCbCr data which enhance luminance area. Second, all Y data, which are luminance and contrast factor in the YCbCr model in previous and current frames, are counted for histogram equalization. Then the spatially adaptive and recursive contrast enhancement process is applied. Finally, the processed R'G'B' data come out. The detailed procedure is as follows. The 8-bit RGB data are changed to the luminance and chrominance (YCbCr) data with 8-bits given by the following equations for histogram calculation of contrast as illustrated in Fig. 1 [7]. There are usually limited ranges in YCbCr color models for SDTV and HDTV such as 16–235 and 16–240 in 8-bits. However, if the R'G'B' data have a range of 0–255 in computer systems, 8-bit YCbCr and R'G'B' data can be denoted with 0–255 levels with the below equations. Note that 8-bit YCbCr and R'G'B' data should be expressed within 0–255 levels to avoid underflow and overflow wrap-around problems.

$$Y = 0.257 \times R + 0.504 \times G + 0.098 \times B + 16 \tag{1}$$

$$C_b = -0.148 \times R - 0.291 \times G + 0.439 \times B + 128 \tag{2}$$

$$C_r = 0.439 \times R - 0.368 \times G - 0.071 \times B + 128 \tag{3}$$

Since the luminance factor, the Y data, in the YCbCr model is the contrast factor to calculate equalization, only Y data are counted and multiplied by the gain from gamma factors. Then the 8-bit YCbCr data are changed to the 8-bit RGB data for equalized RGB value given by the following equations [7].

$$R = 1.164 \times (Y - 16) + 1.596 \times (C_r - 128) \tag{4}$$

$$G = 1.164 \times (Y - 16) - 0.813 \times (C_r - 128) - 0.391 \times (C_b - 128) \tag{5}$$

$$B = 1.164 \times (Y - 16) + 2.018 \times (C_b - 128) \tag{6}$$

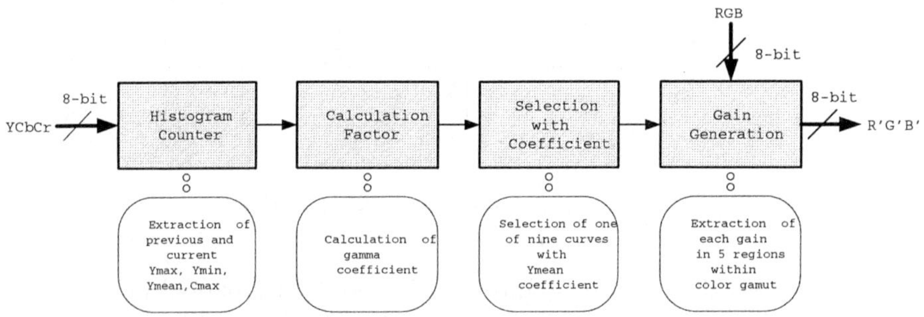

Fig. 2. Gain generation architecture.

2.2 Gain Generation

Fig. 2 shows the detailed architecture of gain generation part that is shown in the block diagram of Fig. 1. In order to equalize contrast, the YCbCr goes to Histogram Counter block which calculates maximum data of luminance(Ymax), minimum data of luminance(Ymin), mean data of luminance(Ymean), and maximum data of chrominance(Cmax) in previous and current frames. The adaptive and recursive coefficients needed for calculation of gamma function come from Calculator Factor block and the most suitable gamma waveform is selected with the coefficients in Selection with Coefficient block. Gamma function gain is obtained from Gain Generation block, which adaptively optimizes the gain that does not deviate from the range of gamut.

2.3 Adaptive and Recursive Gain Control

Fig. 3 is the flow chart illustrating adaptive and recursive gain control algorithm. To prevent flickering problem of motion picture caused by the abrupt gain change

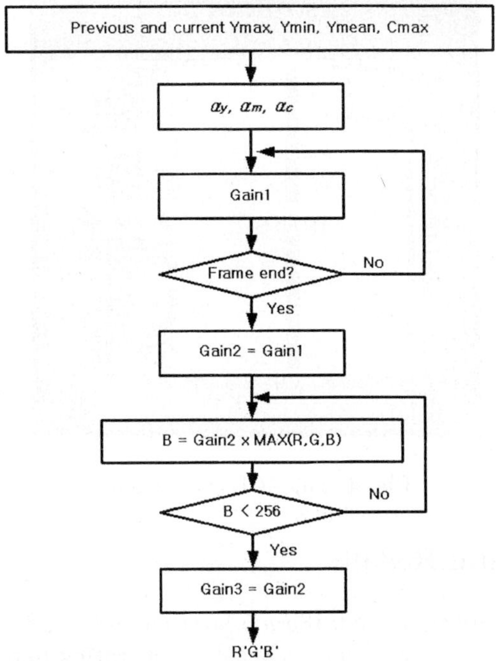

Fig. 3. Flow chart of adaptive and recursive gain control.

of gamma function as time passes, we must find the maximum and mean ratio values of luminance α_y and α_m and maximum ratio value of chrominance α_c in previous and current frames. Note that these factors are obtained adaptively and recursively because these factors are adaptively changed and optimized at each frame according to the mean value of luminance(Ymean) in the current frame and the abrupt gain change is recursively controlled with the previous and current data ratio.

Next, we need to find the first gain, Gain1, within the range of gamut preventing flickering problem with α_y, α_m, and α_c and select the most suitable gain according to the mean value of luminance, Ymean. The range of gamut here maintains hue, saturation value, and color tone of natural image. Gain1 is adaptively and recursively controlled to be included in the range of gamut. The second gain, Gain2, comes from Gain1 after one frame is ended and is controlled by new Gain1 at each frame. The Gain2 is multiplied by each RGB value. If the multiplied result value is above 255, the gain should be adaptively optimized again. Finally, the last gain, Gain3, is replaced by the optimized gain, Gain2. This algorithm gives an excellent performance improvement even though a few gates are needed.

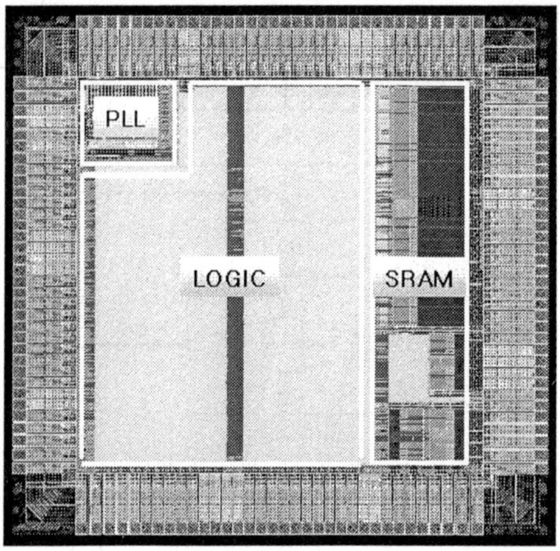

Fig. 4. The ACE chip layout.

3 Experimental Results

The ACE chip is fabricated in a $0.18\mu m$ 5-layer metal CMOS technology. It consists of 350,000 gates and consumes 800mW at operating frequency of 135MHz and occupies about $9mm^2$. The layout of the chip is shown in Fig. 4.

3.1 Comparison of Original Value with Changed Value

Fig. 5 consists of two graphs: (a) an applied gamma S-curve used in this experiment and (b) RGB value with the S-curve as time passes. There are many kinds of gamma curves. We, however, hope to suppress the value in low and high regions of full regions in Fig. 5(a) to reduce noise in low and high regions, and enhance the value only in middle region. Therefore we select S-curve among many kinds of gamma curves. Fig. 5(b) shows the differences between an original input and the processed images after equalizing the original image, especially in middle region. We can find the enhanced image in middle region. The differences between them become larger where the gamma function gain becomes more effective while it keeps smooth not abrupt as time passes within the range of gamut. Note that the processed image value keeps within 0–255. This means the proposed algorithm successfully operates within gamut.

3.2 Comparison of Original Image with Processed Image

Fig. 6 shows the comparison of an original natural image with the processed one after equalizing the original one with the gamma function of S-curve shown in Fig. 5 by the proposed ACE algorithm. We can find the contrast of processed image is enhanced especially in middle region. Figs. 6(b) and 6(d) are the image histograms of the original image and the processed one. We can find the distribution of histogram in Fig. 6(d) becomes widen than that in Fig. 6(b). This

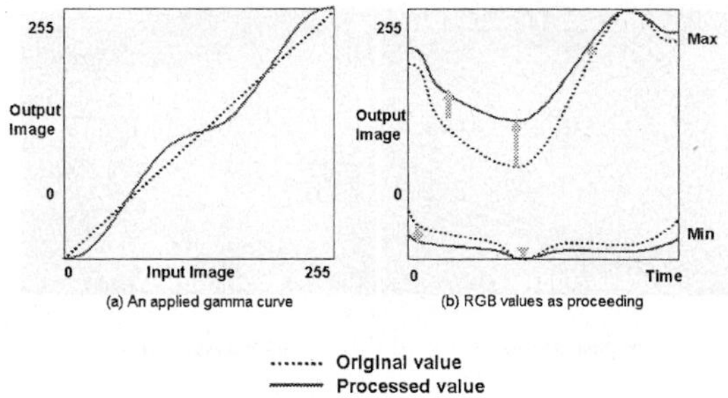

Fig. 5. An applied gamma curve and RGB values.

means the proposed algorithm is successfully equalized with the gamma function of S-curve in Fig. 5. Fig. 7 shows the comparison of an original medical image of body with the processed one after equalizing the original one such as the Fig. 6.

We can get better images with the proposed algorithm compared to original images. The processed images are dramatically enhanced in the contrast while maintained within color gamut range. The experimental results show that the contrast enhancement process with the ACE algorithm does not alter the values of hue and saturation of an image. Hence the overall color perception can be kept. Moreover, the proposed algorithm controls the abrupt change of motion pictures. Therefore, this ACE algorithm can be applied to not only the area of general picture but also the area of medical picture in real-time such as X-ray, ultrasound, and CT.

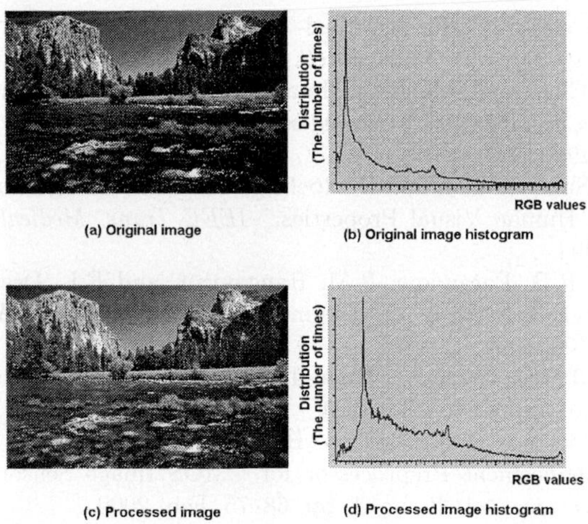

Fig. 6. The original and processed natural images.

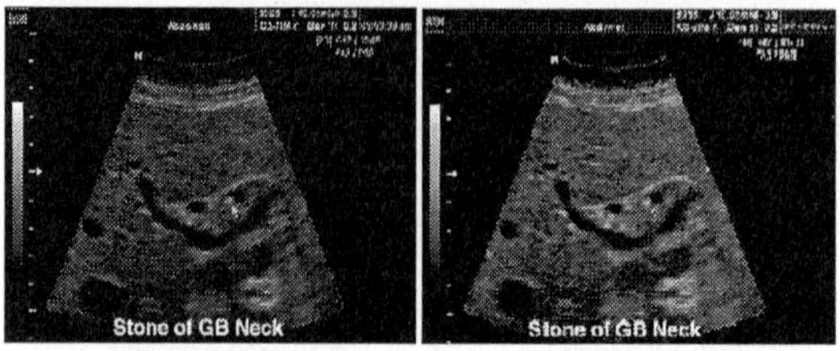

(a) Original image (b) Processed image

Fig. 7. The original and processed medical images.

4 Conclusions

In this paper, we proposed the adaptive and recursive Advanced Contrast Enhancement algorithm and described the architecture of it. The proposed algorithm operates at 135MHz, SXGA, keeps the color tone of original image, and prevents the abrupt gain change. The experimental results show that the contrast equalization in colored motion pictures perfectly operates by the ACE algorithm. For instance, the real-time image qualities of real contrast enhancement and perceptional color enhancement are dramatically improved. Therefore, the ACE algorithm can be applied to not only general imaging but also special treatment such as medical imaging so as to find out some problems in body pictures in real-time.

References

1. P.M. Narendra and R.C. Fitch, "Real-Time Adaptive Contrast Enhancement," *IEEE Trans. Pattern Anal. Mach. Intell.*, vol. PAMI-3, no. 6, pp. 665–661, 1981.
2. H. Zhu, F.H.Y. Chan, and F.K. Lam, "Image Contrast Enhancement by Constrained Local Histogram Equalization," *Computer Vision and Image Understanding*, vol. 73, no. 2, pp. 281–290, 1999.
3. T.-L. Ji, M.K. Sundareshan, and H. Roehrig, "Adaptive Image Contrast Enhancement Based on Human Visual Properties," *IEEE Trans. Medical Imaging*, 13(4), pp. 573–586, 1994.
4. W.M. Morrow, R.B. Paranjape, R.M. Rangayyan, and E.L. Desautels, "Region-Based Contrast Enhancement of Mammograms," *IEEE Trans. Medical Imaging*, 11(3), pp. 392–406, 1992.
5. R.E. Woods and R.C. Gonzalez, "Real-Time Digital Image Enhancement," *IEEE Proc.*, vol. 69, no. 5, pp. 643–654, 1981.
6. Yun-Ho Jung, Jae-Seok Kim, Bong-Soo Hur, and Moon Gi Kang, "Design of Real-time Image Enhancement Preprocessor for CMOS Image Sensor," *IEEE Trans. Consumer Electronics*, vol. 46, no. 1, pp. 68–75, Feb. 2000.
7. Keith and Jack, *Video Demystified : A Handbook for the Digital Engineer*, Butterworth–Heinemann, Chapter 1–3, pp. 1–34, 2001.
8. R.C. Gonzalez and R.E. Wood, *Digital Image Processing*, Addison–Wesley, Chapter 1–6, pp. 1–348, 2002.

A Video Watermarking Algorithm Based on the Human Visual System Properties

Ji-Young Moon[1] and Yo-Sung Ho[2]

[1] Samsung Electronics Co., LTD
416, Maetan3-dong, Paldal-gu, Suwon-si, Gyenggi-do, Korea
jiyoung.moon@samsung.com

[2] Kwangju Institute of Science and Technology(K-JIST)
1 Oryoung-dong, Puk-gu, Kwangju, 500-712, Korea
hoyo@kjist.ac.kr

Abstract. In this paper, we propose a new video watermarking algorithm based on the human visual system (HVS) properties to find effective locations in video sequences for robust and imperceptible watermarks. In particular, we define a new HVS-optimized global masking map for hiding watermark signals by combining the frequency masking, the spatial masking, and the motion masking effects of HVS. In this paper, we generate the watermark by the bit-wise exclusive-OR operation of a logo image and a random sequence, and we embed the watermark in the uncompressed video sequence. The amount of inserted watermarks is controlled by the peak-signal-to-noise ratio of the watermarked frame. Experimental results demonstrate that the proposed method is imperceptible and robust against various attacks with a good watermark capacity.

1 Introduction

In recent days, digital video can easily be reproduced and widely distributed over various transmission networks. However, these attractive properties of the digital video lead to serious problems related to copyright protection.

Now that digital watermarking has become an active research area for the digital video copyright protection, several video watermarking algorithms have been proposed. Most of them embed watermark signals in each frame of the video sequence using still-frame image watermarking techniques [1], which would allow inheriting robustness of the two-dimensional approaches. However, they are vulnerable to averaging attacks, where consecutive frames are averaged to remove embedded watermarks. In addition, a simple extension of the image watermarking technique for video watermarking does not consider temporal correlation along the time axis or movement between the consecutive image frames. Other watermarking techniques embed the watermark signal in the DCT domain for the MPEG-2 compression [2]. However, they are not fully exploited in various video codecs. Furthermore, due to the bit rate constraint, only few DCT coefficients of the watermark can be embedded per image block.

A. Yazici and C. Şener (Eds.): ISCIS 2003, LNCS 2869, pp. 699–706, 2003.

In this paper, we propose a new video watermarking method based on the characteristics of the human visual system (HVS). In order to design a general watermarking scheme, we insert the watermark signals in the uncompressed video sequence; therefore, our watermarking method is independent of the coding scheme and the compression ratio.

One of the important goals of watermarking techniques is to embed some useful information in the original content as much as possible, while maintaining invisibility of that information; thus, we consider the HVS characteristics carefully in our design. In this paper, we propose a new HVS-optimized weighting map in order to hide the watermark effectively by combining the frequency masking, the spatial masking, and the motion masking effects of HVS.

2 The Global Masking Map

2.1 Frequency Masking

Our frequency masking operation is based on the Watson's visual model, defined in the DCT domain [3]. After we divide the image I into 8x8 pixel blocks $I[x,y]_k$, where $x, y = 0, 1, \dots, 7$ and k is the block number, each block is transformed into the DCT domain. Then, we use the frequency sensitivity table [4], which contains the smallest magnitude of each DCT coefficient in the block that is perceptible in the absence of any masking noise. Thus, a smaller value in the table indicates that the eye is more sensitive to the frequency component.

In the absence of masking noise in the frequency domain, we can find a visibility threshold value that is the minimum level below which the signal is not perceptible. The visibility threshold is defined by

$$t_{th}[i,j]_k = t[i,j][\frac{\tilde{I}[0,0]_k}{\tilde{I}_{avg}[0,0]}]^{\alpha} \tag{1}$$

where $\tilde{I}[0,0]_k$ is the DC coefficient of the kth block in the original image, $\tilde{I}_{avg}[0,0]$ is the average of the DC coefficients in the image, and α is a constant. In our experiment, we set $\alpha = 0.649$ empirically. The frequency masking function is also defined by

$$\tilde{F}[i,j]_k = t_{th}[i,j] \cdot max\{1, [\frac{|\tilde{I}[i,j]_k|}{\tilde{I}_{th}[i,j]_k}]^{w}\} \tag{2}$$

where $\tilde{I}[i,j]_k$ is the DCT coefficients of the kth block and w is a constant.

The frequency masking function is shown in Figure 1(a), where we choose $w = 0.7$ for the slope of the line. When $\tilde{I}[i,j]_k$ are larger than $t_{th}[i,j]_k$, the signal threshold values at all frequencies lie along the straight line, which means that the masking effect occurs. Figure 1(c) shows the result of the frequency masking for the *Foreman* sequence.

(a) (b) (c)

Fig. 1. Frequency masking : (a) Frequency masking function (b) Original frame (c) Frequency masking result

2.2 Spatial Masking

The main purpose of the edge map in the proposed watermarking algorithm is to extract connected edges in each image frame. In this paper, we control the contrast of images before the edge detection operation to obtain a good spatial masking map from the following lightness function, proposed by Schreiber [5]:

$$S[x,y] = 1 + 99\frac{log(1 + I[x,y] \cdot a) - log(1+a)}{log(1+100a) - log(1+a)} \tag{3}$$

where $I[x,y]$ is the luminance value of the original frame. Schreiber indicated that $a = 0.05$ provides a well-adapted luminance scale. After we apply the lightness function, we extract important edges to find the spatial masking effect.

(a) (b) (c)

Fig. 2. Spatial masking and Motion masking : (a) Spatial masking only using the edge detection (b) Spatial masking using the edge detection after controlling contrast of image (c) Motion masking result

Figure 2(a) is the result of the spatial masking using the edge detection operation, and Figure 2(b) is the result of the proposed spatial masking, where we control the contrast of images. In Figure 2, we can observe that Figure 2(b) is better; that is, Figure 2(b) has less spurious edges than Figure 2(a).

2.3 Motion Masking

A video watermarking method can exploit the structural characteristics of the video sequence. After we find displacement parts in the successive image frames, we can apply a suitable filter to extract image contours. Figure 2(c) shows the result of the motion masking, where high values are assigned in the face part because of large motion changes.

2.4 Global Masking Map Modeling

In this paper, we define the global masking map by combining the above frequency, spatial, and motion masking effects together after normalization. In other words, the global masking map G is obtained by

$$G = F + S + M \tag{4}$$

where F is the frequency masking, S is the spatial masking, and M is the motion masking, respectively. Figure 3 shows simulation results with the global masking; Figure 3(a) is obtained by the previous method, and Figure 3(b) is obtained by the proposed method. We can see that Figure 3(b) is more effective than Figure 3(a); that is, we can insert more watermarks effectively using the proposed global masking map more than the previous one.

(a) (b)

Fig. 3. Global masking result: (a) The previous method (b) The proposed method

3 Watermarking System

3.1 Watermarking Embedding System

Figure 4 shows the block diagram of the proposed watermarking scheme, where we perform the exclusive OR operation of a random sequence X_1 and a gray-level logo image X_2 as the watermark W.

1. Divide the test data into non-overlapping 8x8 pixel blocks.
2. Obtain the frequency masking, the spatial masking, and the motion masking factors for each image block, respectively.

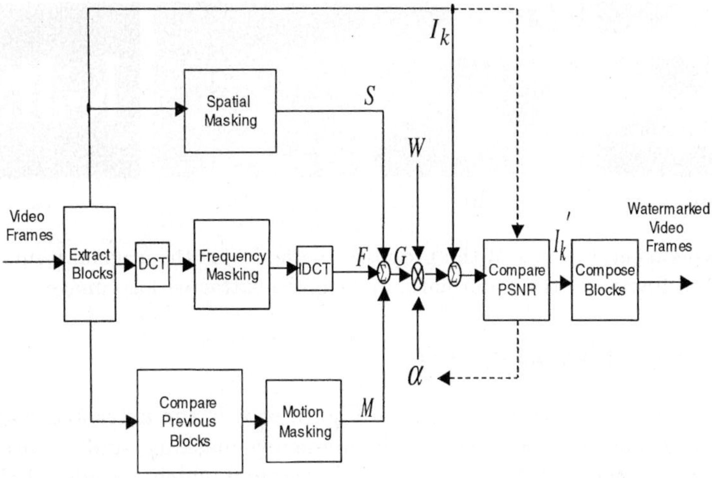

Fig. 4. Proposed watermarking method

3. Generate the global masking map G by combining the frequency masking, spatial masking, and motion masking factors after normalization.
4. Add the watermark weighted by G to the original frame I:

$$I' = I + \alpha \cdot G \cdot W \tag{5}$$

   where the control parameter α is initially set to 1.
5. Find the peak-signal-to-noise ratio(PSNR) of the watermarked frame to control the parameter α: if PSNR is higher than the target, we increase α; otherwise, we decrease α.

3.2 Watermarking Extraction System

1. The original frame I is subtracted from the watermarked frame I':

$$I' - I = G \cdot W^* \tag{6}$$

2. We perform the exclusive OR operation as follows:

$$G \cdot W^* \bigoplus X_1 = X_2^* \tag{7}$$

   where X_2^* is the extracted logo image.

4 Experimental Results and Analysis

4.1 Invisibility Test

Figure 5 shows the experimental result of the proposed method of the *Foreman* test frame. Figure 5(a) is the original frame, and Figure 5(b) is the watermarked frame. The watermarked frame appears visually identical to the original. Figure 5(c) is the watermark for each frame. It is scaled to gray levels for display, and has the same size as the original frame. Figure 5(d) is the extracted logo.

Fig. 5. Experimental results of the proposed method : (a) the original frame, (b) the watermarked frame, (c) the watermark, and (d) the extracted logo image

4.2 Watermark Capacity Test

Figure 6(a) is the watermarked frame. Figure 6(b) is the extracted watermark from the previous methods using only frequency masking, and Figure 6(c) is the extracted watermark from the proposed method which considered the three masking effects. We can observe that Figure 6(c) is more effective in terms of watermark capacity, compared to Figure 6(b).

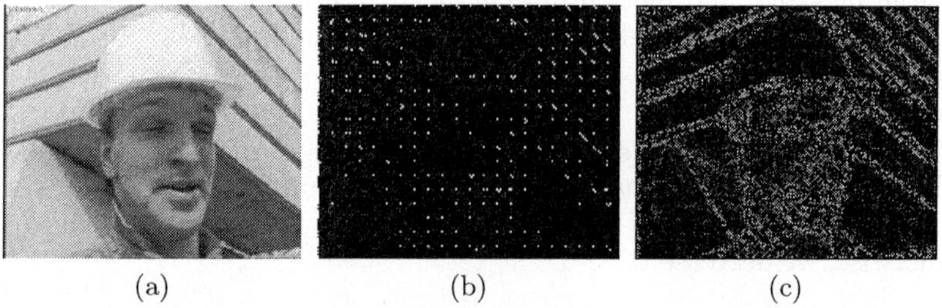

Fig. 6. Watermark Capacity Test : (a) Watermarked frame, (b) Extracted watermark from frequency masking, (c) Extracted watermark from the proposed method

4.3 Robustness Test

Robustness Test on MPEG-2. The test was on three different bit rates: 5 Mbps, 3 Mbps, and 2.5 Mbps. The watermarked frames have been coded and decoded again at different bit rates. Figure 7 shows the extracted logo images at those bit rates. All logo images have been detected only with slight degradation of image quality, but we can see that the performance of the proposed method is not invalidated.

Robustness Test on Re-encoding. We can see that the watermark can always be extracted from the watermarked video frames compressed by MPEG-2 repeatedly. Figure 8 shows the extracted logo images at the different bit rates after MPEG-2 re-encoding.

(a) (b) (c)

Fig. 7. Extracted images after MPEG-2 test : (a) 5 Mbps, (b) 3 Mbps, (c) 2.5 Mbps

(a) (b) (c)

Fig. 8. Extracted images after re-encoding : (a) 5 Mbps, (b) 3 Mbps, (c) 2.5 Mbps

Robustness Test on Frame Cropping. Figure 9(a) is the watermarked frame and Figure 9(b) is the cropped version of Figure 9(a). The missing parts are then replaced by the same parts from the original unwatermarked frame, as shown in Figure 9(c). Figure 9(d) is the extracted logo image after the cropping attack. We can extract the logo image only with small quality degradations from the cropping attack.

(a) (b) (c) (d)

Fig. 9. Experimental results to frame cropping : (a) the watermarked frame, (b) the cropped version of (a), (c) the replaced version, (d) the extracted logo image

5 Conclusions

In this paper, we propose a new masking model for video watermarking based on the characteristics of the human visual system(HVS). In order to design the general watermarking scheme, we embed the watermark signals in the uncompressed video sequence. In this paper, we define an HVS-optimized global masking map for the best trade-off between invisibility and robustness. We generate the global masking map by combining the frequency, the spatial and the motion masking effects. After embedding the watermark signal using the information from the global masking map, we control the amount of watermarks with the control parameters. Experimental results show that the proposed method is imperceptible to human eyes, and also good in terms of watermark capacity. In addition, our method is robust against the various attacks, such as MPEG-2 coding, MPEG-2 re-encoding, and frame cropping. We have observed that the logo images under those attacks are extracted properly only with slight degradation of image quality.

Acknowledgments. This work was supported in part by Kwangju Institute of Science and Technology, in part by the Korea Science and Engineering Foundation (KOSEF) through the Ultra-Fast Fiber-Optic Networks (UFON) Research Center at K-JIST, and in part by the Ministry of Education (MOE) through the Brain Korea 21 (BK21) project.

References

1. Hsu, C.T.: Digital watermarking for images and videos. Ph. D. dissertation, Commun, Multimedia Lab., National Taiwan Univ. (1997)
2. Hartung, F. and Girod, B.: Digital watermarking of raw and compressed video. Proc. SPIE Digital Compression Technologies and Systems for Video Commun, vol. 2952, Oct. (1996) 205–213
3. Watson, A.B.: DCT quantization matrices optimized for individual images. Human Vision, Visual processing, and Digital Display IV, SPIE-1913 (1993) 202–216
4. Peterson, H.A., Peng, H., Morgan, J.H., and Pennebaker, W.B.: Quantization of color image components in the DCT domain. Human Vision, Visual Processing, and Digital Display. Proc. SPIE (1991) 210–222
5. Schreiber, W.F.: Image processing for quality improvement, Proc. IEEE, vol. 66, Dec. (1978) 1640–1651

Network-Aware Video Redundancy Coding with Scene-Adaptation for H.263+ Video*

Jae-Young Pyun[1], Jae-Hwan Jeong[1], Kwang-Il Ji[1], Kyunghun Jang[2], and Sung-Jea Ko[1]

[1] Department of Electronics Engineering, Korea University
5-1 Anam-Dong, Sungbuk-ku, Seoul 136-701, Korea
{jypyun, meeso2, lanian, sjko}@dali.korea.ac.kr

[2] i-Networking Lab. Samsung Advanced Institute of Technology, Suwon, Korea
khjang@samsung.com

Abstract. This paper introduces a new error-resilient mechanism based on video redundancy coding (VRC) of H.263 Version 2, formerly known as H.263+. VRC is a mechanism to achieve temporal error resilience in error-prone environments. However, VRC is not suitable for the time-varying error-prone channel. The proposed network-aware VRC mechanism adaptively changes the prediction structure with multiple threads according to the channel status. Also, scene-adaptiveness is incorporated with the network-aware VRC to reduce the motion-jerkiness occurred by an abrupt scene change. Simulation results show that the proposed adaptive VRC mechanism does not only utilize network resources efficiently, but also reduce the fluctuation of the video quality.

1 Introduction

Video communication over bit-rate-limited and error-prone channels such as packet networks and wireless links requires both high compression and high error resilience. VRC is one of error-resilient encoding mechanisms to suppress the temporal error propagation [4,5]. Input video frames in the VRC mechanism are partitioned into separate groups called "threads", and frames in each thread are coded without using other threads for prediction. VRC can confine the picture quality degradation to only one thread when a transmission error occurs. However, restricting the prediction domain can reduce the coding efficiency. In other words, a better reconstructed picture quality can be achieved at the expense of coding efficiency. The existing prediction structure of VRC is not adaptively adjusted according to the time-varying error-prone channel status and does not consider the scene characteristics of the sequences at an encoder.

To solve these problems, in this paper, we propose two adaptive VRC (AVRC) mechanisms. One is channel-adaptive VRC which chooses VRC parameters by using channel status information, provided that back channel messages can

* This work is supported by a grant from Korea University and Samsung Advanced Institute of Technology.

A. Yazici and C. Şener (Eds.): ISCIS 2003, LNCS 2869, pp. 707–714, 2003.

be conveyed within reasonable round-trip periods of time. Real Time Protocol (RTP) is required for the support of multi-thread structure of VRC [3]. In RTP/UDP/IP transmission environments, the channel information can be reported to the sender in the receiver reports of the Real Time Control Protocol (RTCP) [2]. This mechanism is always available, because RTCP is mandatory if RTP is used. Thus, channel-adaptive VRC using RTCP does not need any additional traffic load to get channel information. The conveyed channel information such as packet loss ratio and burst loss length is used to determine the number of threads and the frame rate per thread. The other mechanism is scene-adaptive VRC that can reduce the quality fluctuation and unsmoothness occurred by the abrupt scene change. When scene change occurs at sync-frame, VRC tends to yield the consecutive frame skipping. However, the proposed scene-adaptive VRC can alleviate this problem by changing the number of frames per thread.

This paper is organized as follows. The error-resilience features of the conventional VRC are described in Sect. 2. Sect. 3 presents our proposed channel and scene adaptive VRC mechanisms. Experimental results and conclusions are given in Sect. 3 and 4, respectively.

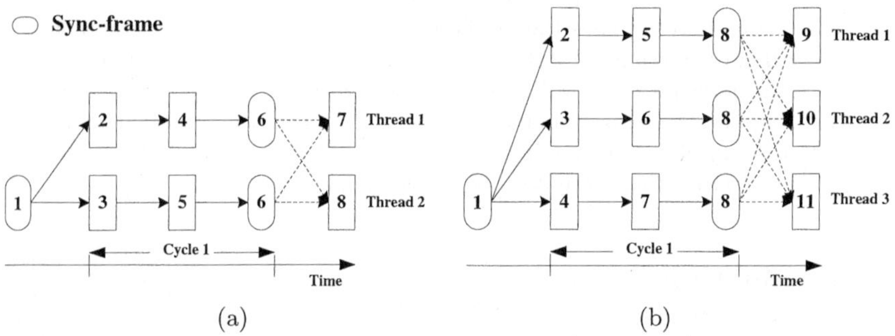

Fig. 1. Illustration of VRC. (a) N_{th}:N_{frm}=2:3. (b) N_{th}:N_{frm}=3:3

2 Video Redundancy Coding in H.263+

VRC sends at least two threads of P-frames simultaneously, and each P-frame of the thread depends on the earlier P-frame but not on any information of the other thread(s). Pictures are arranged in threads in an interleaved manner as shown Fig. 1. The multi-thread structure is controlled by the number of threads N_{th} and the number of frames per thread N_{frm}, which determines the synchronization frequency $f_{sync} = N_{th} \times (N_{frm} - 1) + 1$. Fig. 1 shows that 2:3 and 3:3 (for N_{th}:N_{frm}) are illustrated, respectively. At the end of each cycle, redundant sync-frames are encoded. All threads are started from the sync-frame and ended into another sync-frame. If one thread is damaged, the other threads remain intact and can be decoded and displayed. If packet losses have not occurred, then the sync-frame contents of thread 1 can be used and those of other threads can be discarded (and similarly for other threads) at the transport stack. This is accomplished by an RTP payload format optimized for the optional modes of H.263+ [3]. Thus, RTP/RTCP protocol stack is essential to implement the VRC.

3 Proposed Adaptive Video Redundancy Coding

Fig. 2 presents the block diagram of our proposed AVRC system. Using RTCP feedback messages including current channel information, we determine VRC parameters, N_{th} and N_{frm}, according to the current network status. These VRC parameters can be recalculated by scene-adaptive VRC to alleviate the consecutive frame skipping problem occurred by the abrupt scene change. To detect the abrupt scene change the scene-adaptive VRC has the pre-analysis procedure which analyzes frames in the buffer before encoding [7].

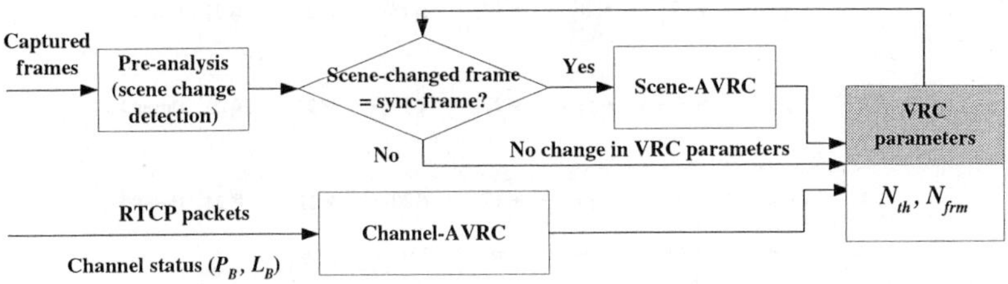

Fig. 2. The proposed Adaptive VRC system

3.1 Scene-Adaptive Video Redundancy Coding

As a scene changes abruptly, since statistical characteristics of the current picture are very different from the previous, statistical information of the previous picture cannot be used for motion estimation of the future frame. To prevent the intra-coded bit rates from exceeding the maximum buffer size, the encoder must cease generating bits by skipping frames thereby causing an interruption to the smoothness of the video [1]. However, if the scene-changed frame is the sync-frame in VRC, frames are skipped consecutively as shown in Fig. 3 (a). When 8th frame is the sync-frame as well as a scene-changed frame, six frames are consecutively skipped owing to three sync-frames if two frames are supposed to be skipped for a scene-changed frame. Thus, cycle 2 starts with the 15th frame in VRC mechanism. If the abrupt scene change occurs, the scene-adaptive VRC determines whether the scene-changed frame is a sync-frame or not. If it is the sync-frame, the algorithm increases the current N_{frm} by one, and subtracts one from the next N_{frm}. Fig. 3 (b) shows the reorganized multi-thread structure in scene-adaptive VRC. After 8th frame is encoded, two frames are skipped. Then, 11th and 14th frames are encoded with the reference frame 6 and 7, respectively.

Note that frames are not skipped consecutively, and thus the unsmoothness of the video sequence are reduced.

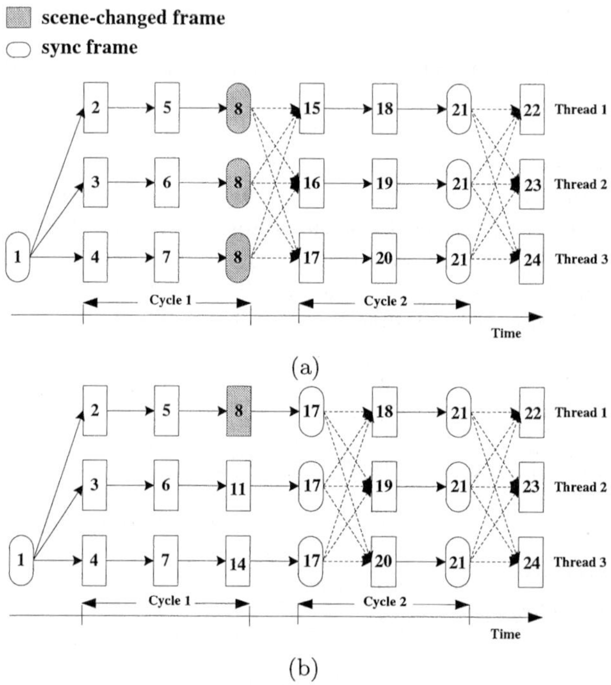

Fig. 3. Reorganized frame encoding structure to reduce the motion-jerkiness in scene-adaptive VRC. (a) Scene-change occurred in sync-frame. (b) Reorganized frame encoding structure in scene-adaptive VRC

3.2 Channel-Adaptive Video Redundancy Coding

The packet loss behavior in the lossy networks can be explained reasonably well with a two-state Markov chain [6]. The two states are state G (good), where packets are received correctly and timely, and state B (bad), where packets are lost either due to network congestion or due to exceeding the maximum allowed transmission delay. This model is described by the transition probabilities P_{GB} from state G to B and P_{BG} from state B to G. We use the average loss probability $P_B = Pr(B) = P_{GB}/(P_{GB}+P_{BG})$ and the average burst length $L_B = 1/P_{BG}$ which is the average number of consecutively lost packets. This model can represent the bursty packet loss characteristics of the error-prone network. Receiver analyzes the arrived RTP streaming packets, and reports two channel information P_B and L_B to the sender. We assume the following two conditions to design channel-adaptive VRC using P_B and L_B:

1. All threads should not be damaged consecutively by the packet losses. Since the sync-frame of the undamaged thread can be used for recovery, at least one of N_{th} threads is necessary to stop error propagation within one cycle. Moreover, consecutive losses of N_{th} frames cause the serious motion-jerkiness and make the recovery of the next frames difficult.
2. The number of lost frames should be less than two in each thread. We consider that this loss condition is desirable to achieve the good perceptual video quality.

First, we determine the number of threads N_{th}. To find out N_{th} satisfying the first assumption, let $g(k)$ denote the probability that k packets are lost consecutively. i.e., $g(k) = Pr(1^k 0|0)$, where '1' is packet loss and '0' is packet arrival with success. In our model, in state B all packets are lost ('1'), while in state G all packets are received ('0'), yielding

$$g(k) = \begin{cases} 1 - P_{GB} & \text{if } k{=}0 \\ P_{GB}(1 - P_{BG})^{k-1} P_{BG} & \text{otherwise.} \end{cases} \tag{1}$$

Now, we find out N_{th} to achieve the target loss probability P_{tar} of $g(k)$. N_{th} is derived by using the following equation,

$$\arg \min_k (g(k) \leq P_{tar}). \tag{2}$$

The number of threads is determined as $N_{th} = min(max(N_{th}^{min}, k), N_{th}^{max})$, where N_{th}^{min} and N_{th}^{max} are the minimum and maximum number of N_{th}, respectively. That is, the probability that all threads are consecutively damaged is less than P_{tar}, when a frame is packetized into a packet.

Second, we determine the number of frames N_{frm} in a thread. To satisfy two assumptions described above, $\frac{N_{th}-1}{N_{th}} \cdot \frac{1}{N_{frm}} = P_B$ is formulated. Therefore, N_{frm} can be represented with the following equation:

$$N_{frm} = \min \left\{ \max \left(N_{frm}^{\min}, \left\lceil \frac{N_{th} - 1}{N_{th} \cdot P_B} \right\rceil \right), N_{frm}^{\max} \right\}, \tag{3}$$

where N_{frm}^{min} and N_{frm}^{max} are the minimum and maximum number of N_{frm}, respectively. When each RTCP receiver report is arrived at the sender, N_{th} and N_{frm} are determined, and they are used for the new multi-thread structure starting from the next cycle. Consequently, the channel-adaptive VRC can provide the robust video transmission over variable-error-rate channels.

4 Experimental Results

Our AVRC scheme has been implemented in a H.263+ standard codec. Four experiment sequences are generated by concatenating two different scenes for scene-adaptive VRC. For example, the experiment sequence "Test 2" is a concatenation of *Mother & daughter* and *News*. A fixed bit rate of 64 Kbps, a fixed

Table 1. PSNR results of VRC and scene-adaptive VRC methods

Test Num.	Seq. Name	N_{th}: N_{frm}	Avg. of PSNR		STD. of PSNR	
			VRC	Scene-AVRC	VRC	Scene-AVRC
1	*Miss America*	2:5	31.310	31.316	4.467	4.460
	M & D	3:3	30.543	30.947	5.30	4.838
2	*M & D*	2:5	28.744	28.856	3.886	3.825
	News	3:3	27.594	27.801	4.153	3.926
3	*Akiyo*	2:5	27.808	28.009	1.971	1.669
	Bream	3:3	26.644	27.062	1.985	1.274
4	*Bream*	2:5	25.483	26.231	5.319	4.488
	Container	3:3	23.892	25.383	5.972	4.651

Table 2. Performance comparison between VRC and AVRC methods in the 1st experiment. (N_{th}^{min}=2, N_{th}^{max}=4, N_{frm}^{min}=2, N_{frm}^{max}=5, P_{tar}=0.001, average RTT=300ms)

Measured values	Channel status		2:5 VRC	4:5 VRC	Proposed AVRC
	Time [sec]	P_B:L_B			
P_e	0 – 110	0.05:1.5	0.134	0.023	0.107
	110 – 220	0.15:1.5	0.303	0.105	0.194
	220 – 330	0.05:1.5	0.114	0.023	0.077
	Total average		0.184	0.050	0.126
Avg. of PSNR	0 – 110	0.05:1.5	30.020	29.78	30.13
	110 – 220	0.15:1.5	26.831	27.551	27.327
	220 – 330	0.05:1.5	28.424	28.409	28.569
	Total average		28.425	28.579	28.674
R_E [Kbps]	Total average		74.033	77.933	76.033

frame rate of 20 fps, and QCIF sized sequences were used for the experiments. For these sequences, the scene changes occupy at the sync-frame of both 2:5 VRC and 3:3 VRC structure. First, we present the comparison between the VRC and the proposed scene-adaptive VRC method. Table 1 shows that the proposed scene-adaptive VRC performs better results than VRC in terms of both average and standard deviation of PSNR of three test sequences, "Tests 2, 3, and 4". The scene-adaptive VRC has similar PSNR results with VRC for "Test 1", since the second scene in "Test 1" has moderate motion. Fig. 4 illustrates the PSNR results of both VRC and scene-adaptive VRC on the test sequence "Test 2". It is observed that the motion jerkiness problem caused by the consecutive frame skipping of VRC is alleviated.

Second, we show the experimental results of VRC and channel-adaptive VRC. For our experiments, we generate a test sequence consisting of 8 sequences, i.e., *Miss America, Mother & daughter, News, Akiyo, Bream, Container, Foreman, and Trevor*. It is looped for the duration of 330 seconds to prevent the influence of the random nature of the packet loss generator. To evaluate the performance of the channel-adaptive VRC, we use three performance measures such as the

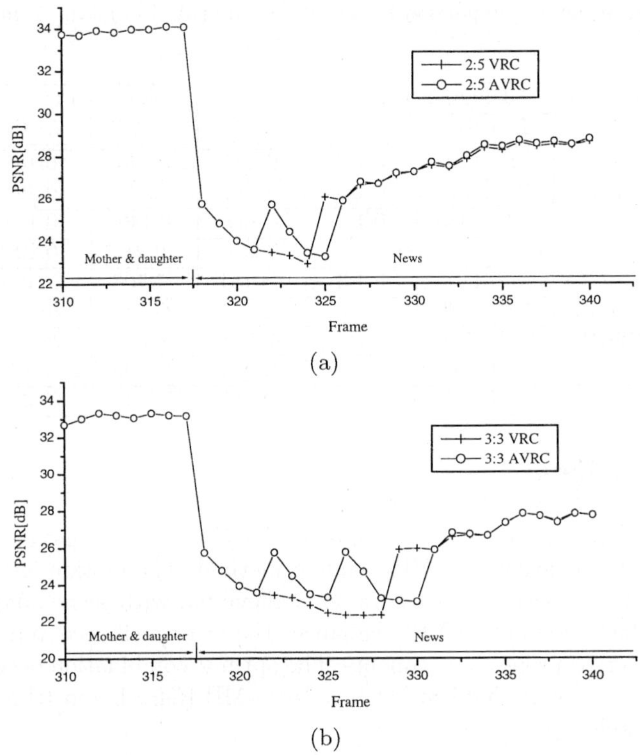

Fig. 4. The comparison of the quality smoothness between VRC and scene-adaptive VRC for the sequence "Test 2". (a) N_{th}:N_{frm}=2:5. (b) N_{th}:N_{frm}=3:3

probability P_e that all threads are damaged, the average of PSNR, and the average of encoded bit rates R_E. The initial network status are set by P_B of 0.05 and L_B of 1.5, and is altered by P_B of 0.15 and L_B of 1.5 during the second simulation period (110–220 seconds). In addition, the sender transmits periodically a RTCP sender report to the receiver every one second. Table 2 shows that 4:5 VRC exhibits a smaller P_e than other schemes for the first simulation period (0–110 seconds), while it produces the worst coding efficiency R_E. Even though 2:5 VRC has a good coding efficiency, it has the worst error-resilience feature. Thus, every thread can be easily damaged, and the error propagates beyond one cycle. However, the proposed AVRC maintains the perceptual video quality while adapting to the channel characteristics.

Additional experiment shows how the error-resilience property of AVRC reacts to the increased packet losses. We can see that the AVRC technique is effective for protecting the video quality from degradation caused by packet loss and achieving good perceptual picture quality over time-varying network conditions as described in Table 3.

Table 3. Performance comparison between VRC and AVRC methods in the 2nd experiment

Measured values	Channel status		2:5 VRC	4:5 VRC	Proposed AVRC
	Time[sec]	P_B:L_B			
P_e	0 – 110	0.1:3	0.224	0.176	0.188
	110 – 220	0.2:3	0.372	0.308	0.283
	220 – 330	0.1:3	0.187	0.146	0.194
	Total average		0.261	0.21	0.222
Avg. of PSNR	0 – 110	0.1:3	28.151	27.703	28.027
	110 – 220	0.2:3	24.041	25.041	26.624
	220 – 330	0.1:3	26.668	26.922	26.675
	Total average		26.501	26.559	27.104
R_E [Kbps]	Total average		74.045	77.939	76.237

5 Conclusions

In this paper, we showed that our proposed AVRC mechanism has a superior performance to the conventional VRC coding method. The motion-jerkiness problem occurred by a scene-changed frame is alleviated with scene-adaptive VRC. Moreover, channel-adaptive VRC enhances the error resilience and coding efficiency in the error-prone environments. The optimal combination between AVRC and other resilience mechanisms such as Intra-MB Refresh and RPS will be our further research topic.

References

1. ITU-T/SG-15 Video Coding Experts Group, Video codec test model, TMN8, 1997.
2. H. Schulzrinne, S. Casner, and V. Jacobson, "RTP: A Transport Protocol for Real-Time Applications," *RFC 1889*, Jan. 1996.
3. C. Bormann, L. Cline, G. Deisher, T. Gardos, C. Maciocco, D. Neweel, J. Ott, G. Sullivan, S. Wenger, and C. Zhu, "RTP payload format for the 1998 version of ITU-T Rec. H.263 video(H.263+)," *RFC 2429*, Oct. 1998.
4. S. Wenger, G. Knorr, J. Ott, and F. Kossentini, "Error resilience support in H.263+," *IEEE Trans. Circuits Syst. Video Technol.*, vol. 8, no. 6, pp. 867–877, Nov. 1998.
5. Y. G. Kim, J. W. Kim, and C.-C. Jay Kuo, "Network-Aware Error Control using Smooth and Fast Rate Adaption Mechanism for TCP-friendly Internet Video," in *Proc. International Computer Communications and Networks (ICCN)*, pp. 320–325, 2000.
6. D. Wu, Y.T. Hou, B. Li, W. Zhu, Y.Q. Zhang, H.J. Chao, and H.J.Chao, "An End-to-end approach for optimal mode selection in Internet video communication: Theory and application," *IEEE J. Select. Areas Commun.*, vol. 18, pp. 977–995, Jun. 2000.
7. H. J. Song and K. M. Lee, "Adaptive rate control algorithms for low-bit-rate video under the networks supporting bandwidth renegotiation," *Signal Process.:Image Commun.*, vol. 17, no. 10, pp. 759–779, Nov. 2002.

Scheduling Mixed Traffic under Earliest-Deadline-First Algorithm

Yeonseung Ryu

Department of Computer Software, Myongji University
Nam-dong, Yongin, Kyongki-do, Korea
ysryu@mju.ac.kr

Abstract. Recently, real-time packet schedulers based on *Earliest Deadline First* (EDF) policy have been extensively studied to support end-to-end bounded delay for real-time traffic. However, the packet scheduler could not guarantee the QoS requirements of real-time traffic since it receives a number of non-real-time traffic for the purpose of management and control. In this paper, we study a packet scheduling scheme servicing non-real-time traffic using the available time of link (i.e. *slack time*). Proposed scheme assigns the deadline to non-real-time packets on-line and services them under EDF policy. Since proposed scheme services the non-real-time traffic when the link bandwidth is not used, it can guarantee the schedulability of real-time flows.

Keywords: Packet scheduling, Real-time scheduling, Slack stealing

1 Introduction

Today's network switches have to service a mix of *real-time* and *non-real-time* traffic. Even though the switches service only real-time communications, the nodes in the network can receive a number of request messages for the purpose of management. For example, manager software at the network management center can periodically send SNMP messages to query MIB data stored on the node or can send ICMP messages for Ping, and so on. The request messages to setup the real-time flows also could affect the guaranteed transmission of existing real-time traffic if a number of requests arrive at the same time. Therefore, if we do not consider non-real-time traffic in the real-time packet scheduling scheme, the schedulability of real-time traffic could be violated by non-real-time traffic.

The problem of scheduling hybrid traffic, consisting of real-time and non-real-time traffic, has been considered in a number of literatures. In [16], *Rate-Controlled Static Priority* (RCSP) was presented. A RCSP scheduler consists of multiple prioritized FCFS queues and services packets using a non-preemptive static-priority discipline: which non-preemptively chooses packets in FCFS order from the highest-priority non-empty queue. Non-real-time packets have the lowest static priority and are serviced only when there are no real-time packets. While RCSP can provide service guarantees to real-time flows at a *low cost*, it

A. Yazici and C. Şener (Eds.): ISCIS 2003, LNCS 2869, pp. 715–722, 2003.

cannot provide high-performance to non-real-time traffic. In [8], *Rotating Combined Queueing* (RCQ) was proposed. RCQ uses frame-based scheduling, where each connection is allocated some number of packet slots in a fixed frame time. RCQ can provide good performance to non-real-time traffic by allowing bursty traffic to utilize unused bandwidth. However, it cannot efficiently support communications with low delay bounds requirements since the worst-case packet delay is coupled to the frame size.

Recently real-time packet schedulers based on *Earliest Deadline First* (EDF) policy have been extensively studied to support end-to-end bounded delay for real-time traffic [10,6,4,5,1,17]. In [10], a general necessary and sufficient schedulability (deadline guarantee) condition of EDF was obtained for flows with traffic regulation assumption. The EDF algorithm is regarded the best choice since it has been proven to be optimal and achieve full resource utilization [11].

Although EDF is an optimal algorithm, it cannot deal with a mix of task sets, consisting of real-time and non-real-time tasks, since it assumes that all tasks must have hard deadline requirements. To schedule non-real-time tasks (aperiodic tasks) under EDF algorithm, various server mechanisms have been investigated by [15,7,2,12,14,13]. In [7], the authors proposed *Deadline Deferrable Server* (DDS), which services non-real-time tasks periodically with higher priority. The DDS mechanism provides the non-real-time tasks with fast response time while guaranteeing the real-time requirements of real-time tasks. It is known, however, that its implementation has high run-time overhead. In [2], the authors proposed *Total Bandwidth Server* (TBS) mechanism. The TBS assigns a suitable deadline, which is determined by calculating the available processing time (i.e. *slack time*), to the aperiodic task. Then aperiodic task is scheduled according to the EDF algorithm along with real-time tasks.

In this work, we study a packet scheduling scheme which services a mix of non-real-time and real-time traffic under EDF scheduling algorithm. Goals of this work are to:

- guarantee the real-time constraints (end-to-end bounded delay) of the real-time flows.
- service the non-real-time traffic at a low cost while not hurting schedulability of the real-time flows that are already guaranteed.

Our work is based on the TBS scheme. Proposed method assigns the deadline to non-real-time packet by calculating the slack time on-line and services the non-real-time packet along with the real-time packet using EDF algorithm. Since it services the non-real-time traffic when the link bandwidth is not used, it can guarantee the schedulability of the real-time flows. In proposed scheme, the time complexity for calculation of slack time and deadline assignment to the non-real-time packet is $O(1)$ and thus the scheduling of non-real-time traffic can be performed at a low cost. Deadlines of the non-real-time packets are determnied by traffic parameters of the real-time flows and link utilization due to real-time flows. Through the experiments, we investigate the length of deadlines of the non-real-time packets and examine the responsiveness of non-real-time traffic.

The rest of this paper is organized as follows. In Section 2, we give the overviews of the real-time packet scheduling model and our assumptions. In Section 3, we provide an efficient method for calculating the slack time on-line and assignment of the deadline to the non-real-time packets. Section 4 presents the experimental results to investigate the responsiveness of the non-real-time flows. The conclusions of this paper are given in Section 5.

2 Real-Time Packet Scheduling Model

Recently a number of analytical models for Earliest Deadline First (EDF) scheduling were proposed to provide delay bounds for real-time communications [10,6,4,5,1]. The real-time flows have real-time constraints, such as end-to-end bounded delay. We assume that flow setup protocol such as RSVP is used to provide guaranteed service to the real-time flows. After establishing a flow i, a packet j of flow i arriving at each node has deadline, d_i. The real-time packets are serviced by EDF scheduling policy. The EDF scheduler selects the real-time packet with the earliest deadline for transmission. In general, the EDF scheduler assigns each arriving packet a deadline, computed as the sum of the arrival time at the scheduler and the delay bound. Let d_i be a local delay bound of flow i and $a_{i,j}$ be an arrival time of a packet j of flow i at the scheduler, respectively. Then the deadline of packet j of flow i is assigned as

$$D_{i,j} = a_{i,j} + d_i \tag{1}$$

The EDF scheduler needs to know the condition that must hold at the scheduler such that delay bound violations of real-time flows do not occur. These conditions are referred to as *schedulability conditions*. In [10], the authors presented necessary and sufficient schedulability conditions for a single node under which a set of delay bounds can be met.

Since a network traffic could be distorted and local schedulability conditions will be violated, two mechanisms have been proposed to enforce that traffic entering a packet scheduler conforms to the given traffic constraint function. One mechanism is a *traffic policer* which rejects traffic if it does not comply to traffic constraint function. The other is a *rate controller*, which temporarily buffers packets to ensure that traffic entering the scheduler queue conforms to traffic constraint function. The idea of per-node traffic shaping called RC-EDF (Rate-Controlled EDF) was proposed [6,3]. In [6], the authors showed that with identical shapers at each node along a flows' path, EDF can provide end-to-end delay bounds.

Traffic constraint functions can be derived from deterministic traffic models that characterize the worst-case traffic by a small set of parameters. Let $A_i[s, t]$ be the amount of traffic (measured in bits/second) from flow i arriving over interval $[s, t]$. We assume that $A_i[t] = A_i[0, t]$. Let $A_i^*(t)$ be a right continuous subadditive function. $A_i^*(t)$ is said to be an envelope of flow $A_i[t]$, if for all times $s > 0$ and for all $t \geq 0$ we have

$$A_i[s,t] \leq A_i^*(t-s) \tag{2}$$

where $A_i^*(t) = 0$ for all $t < 0$. For example, the traffic constraint function for the (σ, ρ)-model is given by $A_i^*(t) = \sigma_i + \rho_i t$, where σ_i is a burst parameter and ρ_i is a rate parameter of flow i.

Let $R = \{1, 2, ..., N\}$ be a set of real-time flows, where flow $i \in R$ is characterized by the traffic constraint function. Then the schedulability condition for EDF scheduler is given as follows [10,5]:

Theorem 1 *The set R is EDF-schedulable if and only if for all $t \geq 0$*

$$\sum_{i \in R} A_i^*(t - d_i) \leq ct \tag{3}$$

where c is the capacity (maximum rate) of the link (bits/second).

Informally the theorem states that the real-time flows are EDF-schedulable iif the sum of the time for transmitting the real-time traffic that arrived with deadline before or at time t does not exceed the available time in the interval [0, t].

We assume that each node has a rate controller, such as RC-EDF, to ensure that traffic entering the EDF scheduler queue conforms to traffic constraint function, $A_i^*(t)$. In this work, we assume that the real-time traffic is characterized by the (σ, ρ)-model.

3 Scheduling Non-real-time Packets under EDF

3.1 Analysis of Slack Time

After real-time flows are determined to be schedulable under EDF, we can service non-real-time packets using unused link capacity. The available time to use link at a given time is called *slack time*. If we can calculate the slack time on-line and assign the deadline to non-real-time packets using the slack time, then non-real-time traffic can be serviced without hurting the real-time requirements of real-time traffic. We define *utilization factor* of non-real-time flows, U_R, as

$$1 - \frac{1}{c} \sum_{i \in R} \rho_i. \tag{4}$$

For example, $U_R = 0.1$ means that the available link bandwidth for non-real-time flows is at most 10% of the total link bandwidth since the link utilization due to current admitted real-time flows is 90%. We assume $0 < U_R < 1$. The following theorem gives the amount of slack time at a given time.

Theorem 2 *For any $t \geq 0$, the time interval $[t, t + t_1]$ where*

$$t_1 = \frac{x + \xi_R}{U_R} \tag{5}$$

contains at least x amount of slack time, where

$$\xi_R = \frac{1}{c}\sum_{i \in R}(\sigma_i - \rho_i d_i) \quad (6)$$

Proof: We prove the theorem by contradiction. Let us assume that the amount of slack time in $[t, t+t_1]$ is smaller than x. Then there must be a deadline miss before $t+t_1$ if we add a link use time x into the interval $[t, t+t_1]$. Furthermore, from a certain time $t' < t+t_1$, only real-time packets ready at t' or later and having deadline less than or equal to $t+t_1$ are transmitted. Let C be the total transmission time demanded by these real-time packets. Since there is a violation at $t+t_1$, it must be $C > t+t_1-t'$. Moreover,

$$C \leq \frac{1}{c}\sum_{i \in R} A_i^*(t+t_1-t'-d_i) + x = \frac{1}{c}\sum_{i \in R}(\sigma_i + \rho_i(t+t_1-t'-d_i)) + x \quad (7)$$

$$\leq \frac{1}{c}\sum_{i \in R}\rho_i(t+t_1-t') + \frac{1}{c}\sum_{i \in R}(\sigma_i - \rho_i d_i) + x \quad (8)$$

Thus,

$$(1 - \frac{1}{c}\sum_{i \in R}\rho_i)(t+t_1-t') < \frac{1}{c}\sum_{i \in R}(\sigma_i - \rho_i d_i) + x \quad (9)$$

$$t+t_1-t' < \frac{x}{U_R} + \frac{\frac{1}{c}\sum_{i \in R}(\sigma_i - \rho_i d_i)}{U_R} \quad (10)$$

Since $t_1 = \frac{x+\xi_R}{U_R}$, it is followed by $t < t'$, which leads to a contradiction. Therefore, there is at least x amount of slack time in the interval $[t, t+t_1]$ where $t_1 = \frac{x+\xi_R}{U_R}$. □

3.2 Deadline Assignment for Non-real-time Packets

Consider that a non-real-time packet i requesting T_i transmission time arrives at time s_i. In order to service packet i, at least T_i amount of slack time is needed. From the theorem 2, there is slack time of T_i in the interval $[s_i, s_i+t_1]$ where $t_1 = \frac{T_i+\xi_R}{U_R}$. Therefore, we can assign

$$max\{s_i, f_{prev}\} + \frac{T_i + \xi_R}{U_R} \quad (11)$$

as its deadline, where f_{prev} is the time at which the previous non-real-time packet is finished. If a non-real-time packet has arrived before the completion of a previous non-real-time packet, we can assign its deadline using f_{prev} just after the completion of the previous packet. Then the EDF scheduler can schedule the non-real-time packet along with real-time packets according to EDF policy while guaranting that no deadline of real-time traffic will be missed.

The time complexity for deadline assignment is $O(1)$, because we can keep track of ξ_R and U_R which are calculated only using the real-time traffic which are already guaranteed. Therefore, the overhead is practically negligible.

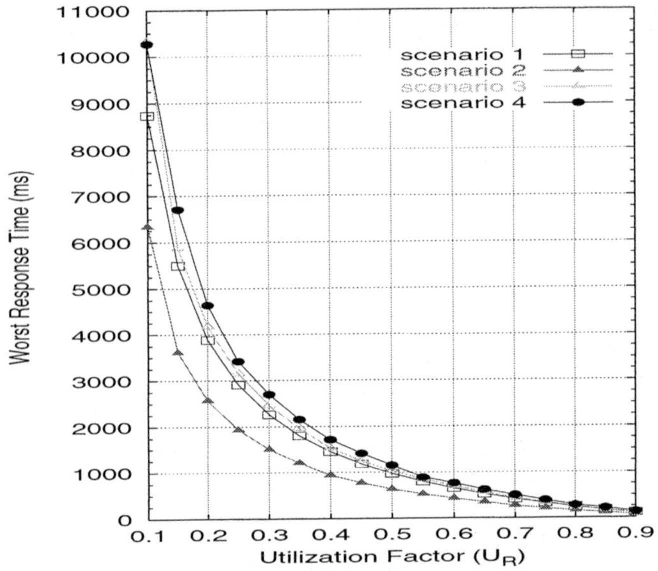

Fig. 1. Experiment result

4 Experiments

In this section, we have performed experiments in order to investigate the responsiveness of non-real-time flows given a set of admitted real-time flows. When a non-real-time packet i requesting T_i transmission time arrives, its response time is $\frac{T_i+\xi_R}{U_R}$ if there is no previous non-real-time packet or previous non-real-time packet was already transmitted. The response time of non-real-time traffic is mainly determnied by traffic parameters of real-time flows and link utilization due to real-time flows.

To understand how real-time traffic parameters affect the responsiveness of non-real-time traffic, several experiments have been performed by changing the real-time traffic parameters and the load of real-time traffic. The first scenario of our experiments generates real-time traffic which is charaterized by $\sigma = 10000$ bits and $\rho = 10000$ bps. This traffic parameters represent audio-like traffic. In the second scenario, for video-like traffic, we take the value of σ and ρ of 1 Mbits and 1.5 Mbps, respectively. In the third scenario, we increase the value of burst parameter, σ, to 1.6 Mbits but do not change rate parameter (i.e. $\rho = 1.5$ Mbps). In the fourth scenario, we generate mixed traffic patterns including audio-like traffic and video-like traffic. We take $\rho = 10^p Kbps$, where p is uniformly distributed in [1, 3]. And we take $\sigma = r * \rho Kb$, where r is uniformly distributed in [0.8, 1.6]. We take a delay requirement $d = 10^s * 30ms$, where s is uniformly distributed in [0, 0.52], thus d ranging in [30ms, 100ms]. The generated traffic patterns include the typical video and audio traffic [9].

In all the experiments, we compute the worst response time (i.e. deadline) of non-real-time packet using Equation (11) with varying the utilization factor (U_R). U_R means the available fraction for non-real-time traffic of the total link capacity. We assume the link has a capacity of 155 Mbps.

Figure 1 illustrates the results of our experiments. All the scenarios exhibit a similar performance. Notice that for utilization factor is greater than about 0.8, the worst response time is less than about 200 ms. It may be tolerable response time for a single node. However, performance becomes poor as the utilization factor tends to 0.0 (i.e. the link utilization of real-time traffic tends to 100%). We can find that the worst response time becomes large (> 1 sec) when the link utilization of real-time traffic begins to be greater than 60%.

We should note that the non-real-time packet's deadline is derived from the worst-case assumption of real-time traffic parameters. However, real-time traffic do not always arrive as the worst-case and thus there may be more slack time than it is calculated. Hence, the non-real-time packet is mostly serviced much earlier than its deadline. If we want the worst response time be smaller, then we need to increase utilization factor (i.e. decrease the link utilization due to real-time traffic by limiting the maximum number of admitted real-time flows). In practice, therefore, we consider tradeoff between the maximum number of admitted real-time flows and the worst response time of non-real-time flows.

5 Conclusion

Recently a number of real-time packet scheduling algorithms based on *Earliest Deadline First* (EDF) policy have been studied in order to provide end-to-end bounded delay guarantees for real-time traffic. Even though the switches service only real-time communications, they usually receive a number of non-real-time messages for the purpose of management. This could lead to violation of schedulability of guaranteed real-time flows. Therefore, we need a mechanism considering non-real-time traffic in the EDF-based real-time packet scheduler.

In this paper, we presented a packet scheduling scheme which services a mix of non-real-time and real-time traffic under EDF scheduling algorithm. We have developed an analytical method for obtaining the amount of *the slack time* at a given time assuming that the real-time traffic is characterized by (σ, ρ)-model. Proposed method assigns a deadline to the non-real-time packet by calculating the slack time on-line and services the non-real-time packet along with the real-time packet using EDF algorithm. In proposed scheme, the time complexity for calculation of the slack time and deadline assignment to the non-real-time packet is $O(1)$ and thus the scheduling of non-real-time traffic can be performed *at a low cost*. Moreover, it can guarantee the schedulability of the real-time flows because it services non-real-time traffic only when the link bandwidth is not used by real-time traffic.

In proposed method, deadlines of the non-real-time packets are determined by characteristic of real-time traffic and link utilization factor. The simulation study reveals that the responsiveness of the non-real-time flows is highly dependent on the link utilization due to real-time traffic. We also found that the response time of the non-real-flows can be improved by controlling the number of admitted real-time flows.

References

1. M. Andrews. Probabilistic end-to-end delay bounds for earliest deadline first scheduling. In *IEEE INFOCOM*, 2000.
2. G. Buttazzo and F. Sensini. Optimal deadline assignment for scheduling soft aperiodic tasks in hard real-time environments. *IEEE Trans. on Computers.*, 48(10):1035–1052, 1999.
3. F. Chiussi and V. Sivaraman. Achieving high utilization in guaranteed services networks using early deadline first scheduling. In *IEEE/IFIP International Workshop on Quality of Service (IWQoS '98)*, 1998.
4. Domenico Ferrari and Dinesh C. Verma. A scheme for real-time channel establishment in wide-area networks. *IEEE Journal on Selected Areas in Communications*, 8(3):368–379, 1990.
5. Victor Firoiu, James F. Kurose, and Donald F. Towsley. Efficient admission control for EDF schedulers. In *INFOCOM (1)*, pages 310–317, 1997.
6. Leonidas Georgiadis, Roch Guérin, Vinod Peris, and Kumar N. Sivarajan. Efficient network QoS provisioning based on per node traffic shaping. *IEEE/ACM Transactions on Networking*, 4(4):482–501, 1996.
7. T.M. Ghazalie and T.P. Baker. Aperiodic servers in a deadline scheduling environment. *The Journal of Real-Time Systems*, 9:21–36, 1995.
8. Jae H. Kim and Andrew A. Chien. Rotating combined queueing (RCQ): Bandwidth and latency guarantees in low-cost, high-performance networks. In *ISCA*, pages 226–236, 1996.
9. Edward W. Knightly, Dallas E. Wrege, Jorg Liebeherr, and Hui Zhang. Fundamental limits and tradeoffs of providing deterministic guarantees to VBR video traffic. In *Measurement and Modeling of Computer Systems*, pages 98–107, 1995.
10. Jörg Liebeherr, Dallas E. Wrege, and Domenico Ferrari. Exact admission control for networks with a bounded delay service. *IEEE/ACM Transactions on Networking*, 4(6):885–901, 1996.
11. C.L. Liu and J.W. Layland. Scheduling algorithms for multiprogramming in a hard real-time environment. *Journal of the ACM*, 20(1):46–61, 1973.
12. I. Ripoll, A. Crespo, and A. Garcia-Fornes. An optimal algorithm for scheduling soft aperiodic tasks in dynamic-priority preemptive systems. *IEEE Trans. on Software Engineering*, 23(6):388–400, 1996.
13. Yeonseung Ryu. Considering non-real-time traffic in real-time packet scheduler. *Lecture Notes in Computer Science*, 2515:216–228, November 2002.
14. Marco Spuri and Giorgio C. Buttazzo. Scheduling aperiodic tasks in dynamic priority systems. *Real-Time Systems*, 10(2):179–210, 1996.
15. J.K. Strosnider, J.P. Lehoczky, and L. Sha. The deferrable server algorithm for enhanced aperiodic responsiveness in hard realtime environments. *IEEE Trans. Computers*, 44(1):7391, 1995.
16. Hui Zhang and Domenico Ferrari. Rate-controlled static-priority queueing. In *INFOCOM (1)*, pages 227–236, 1993.
17. K. Zhu, Y. Zhuang, and Y. Viniotis. Achieving end-to-end delay bounds by edf scheduling without traffic shaping. In *IEEE INFOCOM*, April 2001.

Fast Mode Decision for H.264 with Variable Motion Block Sizes

Jeyun Lee and Byeungwoo Jeon

School of Information and Computer Engineering, Sungkyunkwan University
300 Chunchun-dong, Jangan-gu, Suwon, 440-746, KOREA
jeyun22@ece.skku.ac.kr, bjeon@yurim.skku.ac.kr

Abstract. The new emerging video coding standard H.264 employs variable block size motion compensation using multiple references with quarter-pel motion vector accuracy. This scheme is a key feature to accomplish higher coding gain, however, also a decisive factor that increases overall computational complexity. To overcome this, we propose a novel fast mode decision scheme suited for variable block sizes by classifying coding modes based on rate-distortion cost. The experimental results show that the proposed method provides significant reduction in computational complexity without any noticeable coding loss and additional operations.

1 Introduction

It is known that H.264 [1] provides up to 50% additional bit-rate reduction over the MPEG-4 SP (Simple Profile) at the same coding quality. However, in return, it requires higher complexity than MPEG-4 SP by a factor of 16 in its encoding process [2]. Particularly, the coding tools of H.264 - variable block size motion compensation, multiple reference frames, and quarter-pel motion vector accuracy significantly increase the coding gain. Its adaptive coding structure further increases the encoding complexity as well. The variable block sizes for motion compensation are shown in Fig. 1. For each macroblock, proper motion vectors are estimated after investigating all forms of variable block sizes shown in Fig. 1 where MxN (e.g. 16x8) indicates the unit of motion compensation. In the case of 8x8 submode, a macroblock is divided into four 8x8 regions and each 8x8 block can independently have any submode of 8x8, 8x4, 4x8, and 4x4. Each block of size 8x8 or larger can refer to either the same or different reference picture. The maximum number of possible reference pictures depends on its application, so on H.264 level constraints [1]. H.264 supports the motion vector with quarter-pel accuracy, therefore, all of the possible reference pictures are interpolated by a factor of four before suitable motion vectors in MxN blocks in Fig. 1 are estimated. This procedure is accomplished by considerable computation and processing time. Since inappropriate selection of the best motion vector, reference frame, and macroblock type leads to huge degradation of coding efficiency, the decision process is to be carefully designed. Hence, H.264 employs RD-optimization method introduced in [3]. Briefly speaking, the RD-optimization method in H.264 is to make the best selection among the multiple

A. Yazici and C. Şener (Eds.): ISCIS 2003, LNCS 2869, pp. 723–730, 2003.

possibilities of representation based on rate–distortion. This technique provides bit-rate reduction up to about 10% [2].

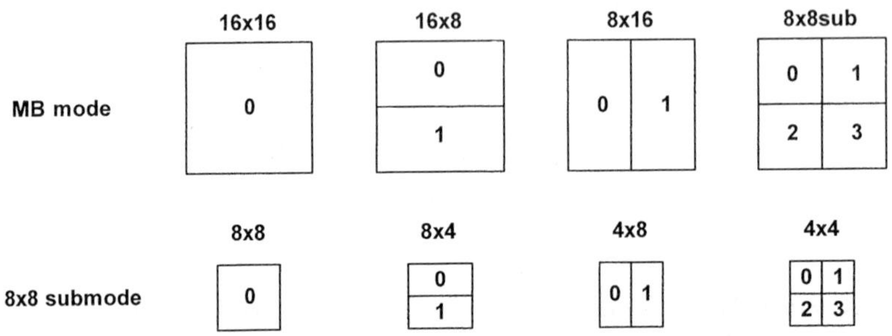

Fig. 1. The variable block size motion segmentation in H.264

2 Fast Mode Decision

Mode decision is relatively more complex and important as compared with the process of selecting motion vectors or reference frames. There are seven macroblock modes: SKIP, MB16x16, MB16x8, MB8x16, SUB8x8, INT4x4, and INT16x16. The SKIP mode is defined as the case where the motion vector is (0,0) or the same as its predictive motion vector, and integer transform coefficients of motion-compensated residual signal are all zeros. Both macroblock modes of INT4x4 and INT16x16 have spatial prediction modes: INT4x4 has nine directional modes with 4x4 block size, and INT16x16 has four modes of DC, horizontal, vertical, and plane prediction with 16x16 block size [1]. To choose the best mode out of many combinations above, RDcost values for all macroblock modes are computed using the amounts of encoded bits and distortion. Following, the mode which has the minimum RDcost is chosen to be the best macroblock mode. Therefore, in order to obtain the RDcost values, integer transform, quantization, and entropy coding have to be performed for every macroblock mode. The RDcost value can be calculated by a distortion model using a Lagrangian coefficient. The equation for computing RDcost, J_{Mode} is given as [1]:

$$J_{Mode} = D + \lambda_{Mode} R \tag{1}$$

where D is the distortion measured as the sum of squared difference between original and reconstructed images, λ_{Mode} is the Lagrange constant, $\lambda_{Mode} = 0.85 \times 2^{Qp/3}$, Qp is the quantization parameter, and R is the rate representing total number of bits associated with coded motion vectors, reference frames, residual signal, and other coding syntaxes in MB with regard to the coding mode. As mentioned above, the computation of RDcost demands huge computational complexity. Therefore, required is a more efficient way of mode decision such as determining the best mode at the earliest stage possible so to omit computing RDcost as much as possible. Hence, we propose a fast mode decision method which makes early mode decision possible for inter macroblock mode and lets the routine of computation of RDcost omitted for intra mode whenever it is possible. The flowchart of proposed mode decision is given in Fig. 2 which is explained as follows.

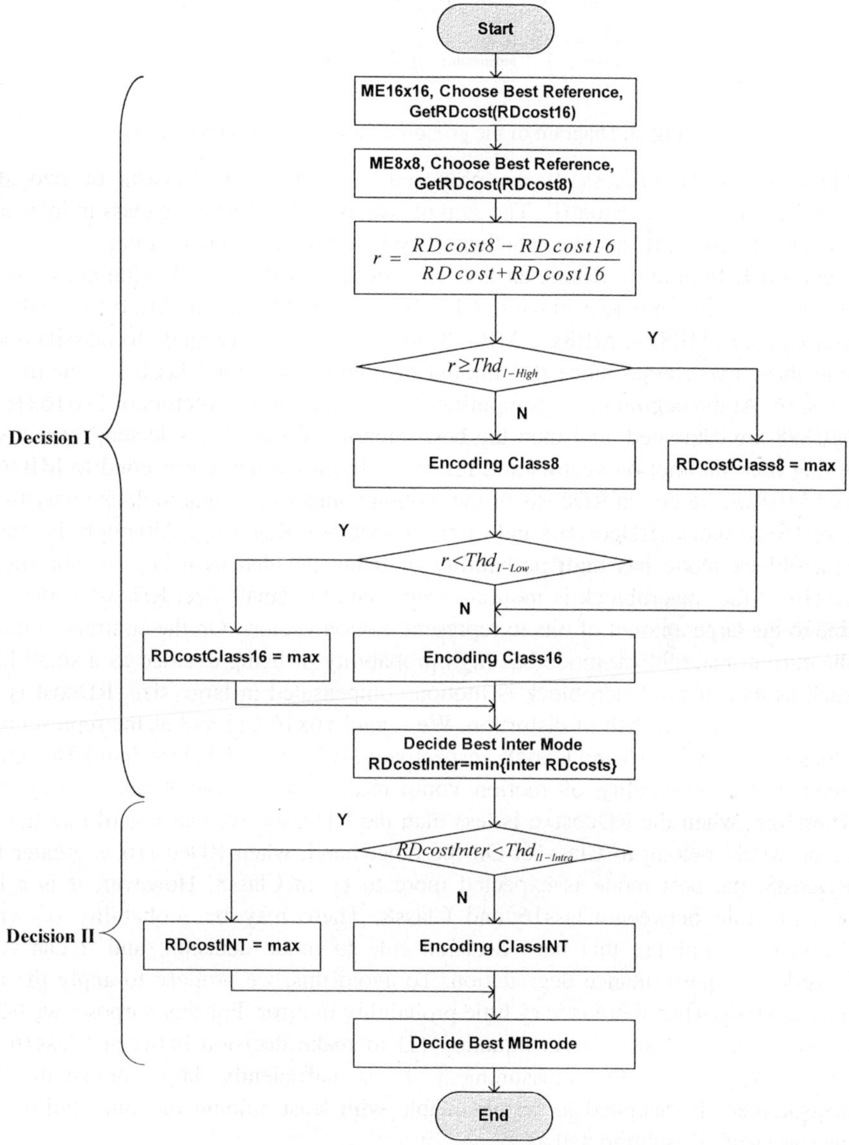

Fig. 2. Flow chart of the proposed fast mode decision method

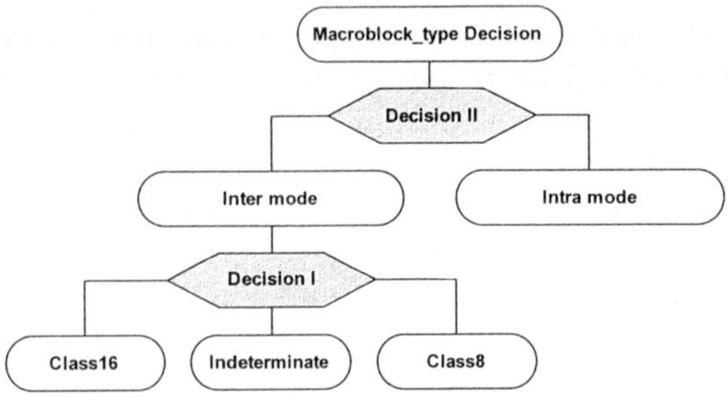

Fig. 3. Diagram of the proposed fast mode decision method

Fig.3 shows the process of the proposed method which consists of two steps: 'Decision I' and 'Decision II'. The step of 'Decision I' selects one class in inter mode classes. 'Decision II' decides whether to try encoding intra mode or not.

Decision I: In order to decide an inter macroblock mode at the beginning, we divide the inter modes into two classes: Class16={SKIP, MB16x16, MB16x8, MB8x16} and Class8={MB8x8, MB8x4, MB4x8, MB4x4}. It is reasonable to classify modes into these two classes since the amount of computation for Class8 is four times of Class16. At the beginning of computing RDcost, the motion vectors of MB16x16 and MB8x8 are estimated, and then the best reference frames are selected, respectively. Using both the motion vectors and reference frames which correspond to MB16x16 and MB8x8, we obtain RDcosts of the motion compensated macroblock consisting of size 16x16 block (RDcost16) and of size 8x8 block(RDcost8). Although the current macroblock mode has high probability of being decided as a large block such as 16x16, if the macroblock is motion-compensated in small size, RDcost is increased due to the large amount of bits to represent motion vectors. On the contrary, although the current macroblock mode has high probability of being decided as a small block such as 4x4, if the macroblock is motion-compensated in large size, RDcost is also increased due to growth of distortion. We regard 16x16 and 8x8 as the representative block sizes of Class16 and Class8, respectively. If RDcost16 is less than RDcost8, we assume that probability of motion compensation with large block is very high. Therefore, when the RDcost16 is less than the RDcost8, we can regard that the best mode would belong to Class16. On the other hand, when RDcost16 is greater than RDcost8, the best mode is expected more to be in Class8. However, it is a hard decision rule between Class16 and Class8. There may be probability of wrong decision in applying this hard decision rule to mode decision, and it can cause considerable performance degradation. To avoid this, we propose to apply the hard decision only when there is very little probability of error. For this purpose, we define r as the measurement as in equation (2) to make decision between Class16 and Class8 only when the measurement r is sufficiently large or small. This measurement is designed to be obtainable with least amount of computation. The measurement r is computed as:

$$r = \frac{RDcost8 - RDcost16}{RDcost8 + RDcost16} \qquad (2)$$

Fig. 4 shows the probability of decision error with regard to r. In Fig. 4, negative r means that the best mode is expected to be in Class8, however the true best mode is found as belonging to Class16. On the other hands, positive r indicates that we decide Class16, however, the best mode is in Class8. As shown in Fig. 4, the more closely r approaches origin, the higher the probability of mode decision error becomes. To minimize the error, we divide r into three regions: Class8, Class16 and the indeterminate. When r is less than '$Thd_{I\text{-}Low}$', we choose Class8, and when r is greater than '$Thd_{I\text{-}High}$', Class16 is selected. In the case of 'otherwise', we don't make any decision which we call "the indeterminate", and in this case, all coding modes are tested without early decision. The thresholds '$Thd_{I\text{-}Low}$', '$Thd_{I\text{-}High}$' are determined as following:

$$Thd_{I-Low} = mean - \frac{std}{2},\ Thd_{I-High} = mean + \frac{std}{2}, \tag{3}$$

where *std* is standard deviation of r for given quantization parameter, Qp.
According to the Chebyshev's inequality [4], probability that a Gaussian random variable exists within 1/2 standard deviation from its mean is nearly 0.4. However the probability distribution of decision error in Fig. 4 is sharper than the Gaussian. Besides, the true probability within '$Thd_{I\text{-}Low}$' and '$Thd_{I\text{-}High}$' is more than 55%. Therefore, these threshold values are useful to minimize error and performance degradation.

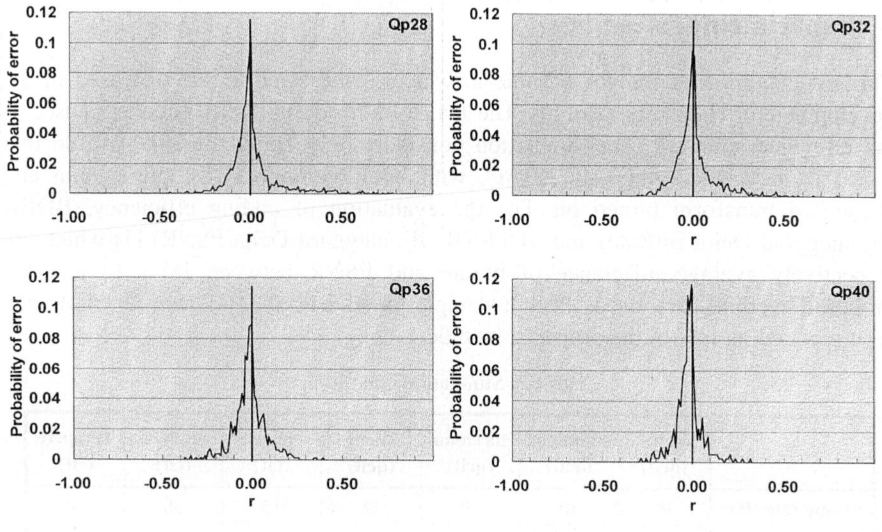

Fig. 4. Probability distribution of decision error with RDcost with regard to quantization parameter (foreman sequence)

Decision II: To attain high coding efficiency, H.264 tries also encoding intra mode at every macroblock. In the case of intra coding mode, ClassINT={INT4x4, INT16x16}, mode decision is quite complex as well as inter mode because of various directional prediction modes in spatial domain. In many cases, RDcost of best inter mode is much less than RDcost of best intra mode in the same macroblock of P-picture due to high correlation between frames. Based on this observation, if the RDcost of the best inter mode is less than a threshold '$Thd_{II\text{-}Intra}$', we can omit the routine of trying the intra modes. To obtain the threshold value, we estimate the pdfs of best inter and intra mode according to RDcost from sequences in Table 2. However, because the pdfs of sequences are quit different with each other and these shapes are also complex, for simplicity's sake, we assume that the pdf is Gaussian distribution and then '$Thd_{II\text{-}Intra}$' is obtained based on maximum likelihood decision theory. Table 1 shows each threshold value for mode decision with regard to different Qp values. These values are computed through training experiment with sequences in Table 2.

Table 1. Thresholds for fast mode decison with regard to Qp (Quantization parameter)

Threshold \ Qp	28	32	36	40
$Thd_{I\text{-}Low}$	-0.0848	-0.0789	-0.0719	-0.0734
$Thd_{I\text{-}High}$	0.0051	0.0002	-0.0090	-0.0163
$Thd_{II\text{-}Intra}$	14069.84	25546.31	45274.67	75555.79

3 Experimental Results

The test condition is shown in Table 2, which is the same as the one used in the development of H.264 standard [5]. The JM (Joint Model) 6.1d [6] encoder is used as the reference software. The simulation considers only H.264 baseline profile that contains no B slice and no CABAC, with both option of RD optimization and Hadamard transform turned on. For the evaluation of coding efficiency, BDBR (Bjonteggrad Delta BitRate) and BDPSNR (Bjonteggard Delta PSNR) [7] which are respectively average difference of bitrate and PSNR between JM 6.1d and the proposed method, are used. Both (+) sign in BDBR and (-) sign in BDPSNR represent coding loss of the proposed method.

Table 2. Simulation condition

	news (qcif)	**container (qcif)**	**foreman (qcif)**	**silent (qcif)**	**paris (cif)**	**mobile (cif)**	**Tempete (cif)**
Frame rate (Hz)	10	10	10	15	15	30	30
Total frames	100	100	100	150	150	300	250
Qp	28, 32, 36, 40						
Coding option used	R-D optimization, Hadamard transform IPPP structure, CAVLC, no error tools						
Codec	JM 6.1d encoder						

Table 3 shows the results of the proposed fast mode decision. R indicates the average computational saving in terms of the number of calculating RDcost, and REF means the JM 6.1d encoder. The average computational saving is given as:

$$R = \frac{\#RDcost\{REF\} - \#RDcost\{proposed\}}{\#RDcost\{REF\}} \times 100\ [\%] \tag{4}$$

Table 3. Experimental results of the proposed fast mode decision

Sequence	Decision I			Decision II			Total		
	R [%]	BDBR [%]	BDPSNR [%]	R [%]	BDBR [%]	BDPSNR [%]	R [%]	BDBR [%]	BDPSNR [%]
container	15.23	0.51	-0.03	52.99	1.79	-0.09	68.28	2.88	-0.14
foreman	14.22	1.08	-0.06	51.32	3.16	-0.17	65.50	4.38	-0.23
news	14.92	1.11	-0.06	51.83	0.94	-0.05	66.78	2.51	-0.14
mobile	13.35	0.79	-0.03	30.29	0.25	-0.01	43.53	1.21	-0.05
silent	14.93	1.53	-0.07	54.48	2.12	-0.10	69.37	2.83	-0.13
paris	14.71	1.44	-0.07	49.57	0.79	-0.04	77.20	1.95	-0.10
tempete	13.95	0.56	-0.02	44.56	0.85	-0.04	58.44	1.60	-0.07
Average	14.47	1.00	-0.05	47.86	1.41	-0.07	64.16	2.48	-0.12

The ratio of reduced counts of RDcost is about 14% for the decision I and 48% for the decision II. The total computational saving when both decision steps are active is about 64%, while BDBR loss is only 2.5%. In Table 3, the computational saving gain for both mobile and tempete sequences is slightly low. Because tempete has many frames of leaves having fast and rotary motion, and mobile has complex motion such as rotation, repetition of upward and downward movement, and camera panning, therefore, RDcost is higher than '$Thd_{II\text{-}Intra}$' in most of cases. Hence, in tempete and mobile, the skipped number of computing RDcosts is less than others. At the same frame rate, it is easily observed that the proposed method can achieve more computational saving in the sequence having relatively simple motion.

4 Conclusion

In this paper, we proposed a method capable of selective early discarding of some coding modes in RDcost computation. In H.264 with variable block size motion compensation, the procedure of mode decision critically affects the overall performance gain of an encoder. Since the method of RD optimization which is implemented in JM 6.1d for mode decision requires high computation, we proposed an efficient fast mode decision method. The proposed fast mode decision algorithm provides considerable reduction of the number of RDcost calculation and computational complexity. The current research is using static threshold values which are hard to adapt to the characteristic of sequence. In addition, the threshold values are obtained by the statistical data from several sequences in advance. Hence, if the statistical data turn out to be very much different from the true estimate, it can cause considerable performance degradation. Therefore, more smart method should be investigated to further improve accuracy of proper threshold values for given sequence.

Acknowledgement. This work was supported by Korea Research Foundation Grant(KRF-2002-041-D00405).

Reference

1. Joint Video Team (JVT) of ISO/IEC MPEG & ITU-T VCEG: Draft ITU-T Recommendation and Final Draft International Standard of Joint Video Specification (ITU-T Rec. H.264 | ISO/IEC 14496-10 AVC), Doc. JVT-G050r1 (2003)
2. Minhua Zhou: Evaluation and Simplification of H.26L Baseline Coding Tools, ITU-T Q.6/16, Doc. #JVT-B030 (2002)
3. G. Sullivan and T. Wiegand: Rate-Distortion Optimization for Video Compression, Draft for submission to IEEE Signal Proc. Magazine, Vol.15 pp74–90 (1998)
4. Rodger E. Ziemer: Elements of engineering probability & statistics, Prentice Hall, NJ (1997)
5. G. Sullivan, G. Bjontegaard: Recommended Simulation Common Conditions for H.26L Coding Efficiency Experiments on Low-Resolution Progressive-scan Source Material, ITU-T Q.6/16, Doc. #VCEG-N81 (2001)
6. http://bs.hhi.de/~suehring/tml/download/jm61d.zip
7. G. Bjontegaard: Calculation of Average PSNR Differences between RD-curves, ITU-T Q.6/16, Doc. #VCEG-M33 (2001)

An Optimal Scheduling Algorithm for Stream Based Parallel Video Processing

D. Turgay Altılar[1] and Yakup Paker[2]

[1] Dept. of Computer Engineering, İstanbul Technical University
Ayazağa Campus, Maslak, 34457, İstanbul Turkey
altilar@itu.edu.tr

[2] Dept. of Computer Science, Queen Mary, University of London
Mile End Road, E1 4NS, London, United Kingdom
paker@dcs.qmul.ac.uk

Abstract. We present a new optimal scheduling algorithm called Periodic Write-Read-Compute (PWRC) scheduling for stream based parallel video processing. Although PWRC scheduling exploits the properties of the video data, it is applicable to any type of periodic data over which a data independent application is to run. The PWRC algorithm is designed considering a bus based parallel architecture allowing point-to-point communication between host and workers. The PWRC requires a high level atomic write-read command for data transmission which can be created in various ways. The analysis of the PWRC provides information either to form a parallel video processing system or to predict the overall performance of an existing system in order to meet real-time requirements of video processing.

1 Introduction

A parallel video processing system can be thought as a real-time processing system with periodic data input. We believe that scheduling for such a system should exploit input-output characteristics in order to cope with real-time requirements. Input data for such a real-time system naturally possess continuity and periodicity features. In this paper, we dealt with data independent computations over video streams, i.e., computation time is proportional with the data size. Continuity and periodicity of input and output decoupled with data independency of the application provide us with a base to define an optimal scheduling algorithm.

The performance of a scheduling algorithm relies upon both the architectural properties of the system such as I/O bandwidth, processor power, memory size, and the properties of the application such as data dependency, data partitioning. For example the need of consecutive frames makes a great difference in the design of scheduling algorithms for video processing. In this paper, we dealt with only stream based video processing algoritms. Initial results of such algorthms is discussed in [3]. Scheduling for frame by frame processing were given in another

A. Yazici and C. Şener (Eds.): ISCIS 2003, LNCS 2869, pp. 731–738, 2003.

paper[2]. However, our approach is the same for both: utilising both I/O channels and processors while minimising the response time.

Given a number of cost models [1],[4],[5],[6],[7], and [8] the analysis of the proposed schemes has been inspired from a recent paper of Lee and Hamdi [6] comprising generic units and definitions for a cost model. Having the same cost model parameters will also provide us with a common base to compare our algorithm with theirs.

In this paper, we will show that for a given system and algorithm, a scheduling method can be defined and the overall system performance can be predicted. Since a scheduling scheme could be defined according to system architecture and algorithm variables, parallel processing architecture variables such as processor power and bus rate can also be calculated, for a given algorithm and a given scheduling method.

The proposed scheduling algorithm relies upon an indivisible write-and-read command to access continuous data storage medium. The considered parallel processing environment has a write-and-read command, which can be implemented as a high level atomic command. The algorithms mentioned in this paper were designed, developed and analysed for a bus based parallel system having a client-server model running Single Program Multiple Data (SPMD) type programs. The target architecture is a client-server based parallel system having a point-to-point communication between the server and client processors. A typical hardware configuration comprises a server processor, a frame buffer and a number of client processors connected via a high speed I/O bus and a signal bus. Data transfer occurs over the high speed I/O bus to and from the frame buffer. The frame buffer is the medium that a video stream is written via an input device such as video player or camera. Processed data is also written to the frame buffer. No communication or data transfer exists between client processors. A client is allowed to read/write data from/to the frame buffer under the control of the server.

The rest of the paper is organised as follows: Section 2 introduces the cost model with reference to Lee and Hamdi [6]. PWRC Scheduling is defined, discussed, analysed and performance comparisons are given in Section 3. Section 4 explains the use of the PWRC to decide system parameters of a parallel system to be build. Paper ends with conclusions and further research.

2 A Scheduling Scheme

For a loosely coupled, client-server type programming environment, Lee and Hamdi presented a performance prediction model for a parallel image processing system running convolution in a recent paper [6]. The application they considered is an image convolution program running over a network of workstations in a "Host-Node" (client-server) manner. The number of workstations, n, in order to achieve the minimum execution time and the approximate value of maximum speed-up, S, for parallel execution are given as follows:

$$n = \frac{M^2\gamma}{\alpha/K + \beta} + 1 \qquad S \approx \frac{M^2\gamma}{2(\alpha/K + \beta)} \tag{1}$$

where M is the width of coefficient matrix to be used for convolution, γ is computing time per pixel, α is latency time, β is data transmission time per byte and K is data packet size.

For a given data of size of P bytes, the communication time is is defined by $T_{comm} = \lceil P/K \rceil \alpha + P\beta$. The sub-image computation time is declared as $N^2 M^2 \gamma / n$, where N^2 is the size of the image matrix.

Input/output time is longer than the processing time per processor. Therefore, processors are likely to queue up for input/output which yield long idle durations for processors. The scheme aims at the full utilisation of the I/O channel without paying much attention to the utilisation of CPUs (Fig.1a). Although the I/O channel (or host CPU dispatching the partitioned data) is being kept busy throughout the process, the processors are not highly utilised (Fig.1a). Even if execution time could be made equal to the sum of I/O durations of all of the other processors, waiting for data between cycles introduces an idle duration T_{idle} for a system with n client processors:

$$T_{idle} = \ (n-1) \ x \ data \ read \ time \ per \ processor$$

This duration becomes very significant with finer granularity. This scheduling scheme does not consider continuous and periodic nature of the video sequences. Processing with a frame starts after the previous one. Waiting between frames introduces idle durations for processors. The approach that we adopt is to minimise the idle duration of processors, if not to totally eliminate it.

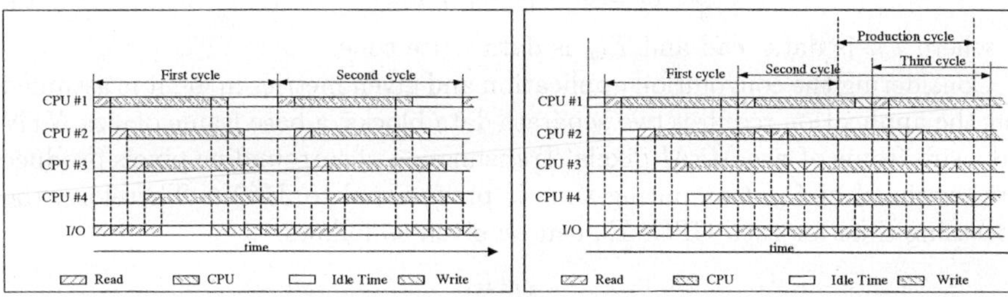

Fig. 1. Processor and I/O channel uses for 4 processors for a)Lee&Hamdi b)PWRC

3 Periodic Write-Read-Compute Scheduling

The PWRC aims to increase the utilisation of the processors while keeping the I/O channel fully occupied by exploiting the continuity and periodicity of the input data. In order to keep a processor as busy as possible in such a parallel system, a processor should receive the new data just after it sends (writes back) processed data. An indivisible write-read mechanism could be implemented even at high level programming. Since the processors are supplied with new data as soon as it writes the previous result, the I/O channel will be released and processing will start immediately. If the processing times for the processors are overlapped with the I/O channel accesses of the other processors, full utilisation of the processors and the I/O channel will be achieved. A timing diagram for 4 processors running under the proposed scheduling scheme is sketched in Fig.1b. Except for the very first cycle of the processing, which is negligible considering the whole process the I/O channel is kept fully utilised. Given the timing diagram in Fig.1b , the utilisation of processing units are at their maximum and the I/O channel is also fully utilised after the first cycle.

3.1 Performance of the PWRC Scheduling

We are going to consider two metrics to compare the performance of two scheduling methods: cycle time and production time. The cycle time is dominated by the total data transmission (read and write) time required by the client processors for processing systems since I/O is dominant. The production time is as the same as the cycle time for Lee and Hamdi's method (Fig.1a) However, in PWRC, production time corresponds to lifetime of a frame in parallel processing system(Fig.1b). Accepting that data transmission time per processing unit is the same for every processor, cycle time, T_{cycle}, and computation time, T_c, for n processors are defined as follows:

$$T_{cycle} = n(T_{dr} + T_{dw}) \tag{2}$$

$$T_c = (n-1)(T_{dr} + T_{dw}) \tag{3}$$

where T_{dr} is data read and T_{dw} is data write time.

Considering the convolution application and given metrics in [6], it is assumed that the application requires two separate data blocks: a base frame of size NxN and a sub-frame of size MxM pixels. Transmission of surrounding pixels produce data overhead of O_d. Computing time is propotional to M^2N^2. Therefore, the processing time for each CPU, T_c, can be given as follows:

$$T_c = \frac{M^2N^2}{n}\gamma \tag{4}$$

Data read T_{dr} and data write T_{dw} durations are:

$$T_{dr} = \frac{M^2}{K}\alpha + M^2\beta + \frac{N^2+O_d}{nK}\alpha + \frac{N^2+O_d}{n}\beta \tag{5}$$

$$T_{dw} = \frac{N^2}{nK}\alpha + \frac{N^2}{n}\beta \tag{6}$$

Substituting Eq.4, Eq.5 and Eq.6 in Eq.3 and solving for n, we obtain

$$n^2(\alpha + M^2\beta) + n\left(\left(\frac{N^2+O_d}{K} - 1\right)\alpha + \left(2N^2 + O_d - M^2\right)\beta\right) - \left(\left(2N^2+O_d\right)\left(\frac{\alpha}{K}+\beta\right) + M^2N^2\gamma\right) = 0 \tag{7}$$

The roots of such a second degree equation can be given as follows:

$$n_{1,2} = -\left(\frac{\left(\frac{2N^2+O_d}{K}-1\right)\alpha + \left(2N^2+O_d-M^2\right)\beta}{2(\alpha+M^2\beta)}\right)$$

$$\pm\sqrt{\left(\frac{\left(\frac{2N^2+O_d}{K}-1\right)\alpha + (2N^2+O_d-M^2)\beta}{2(\alpha+M^2\beta)}\right)^2 + \frac{\left((2N^2+O_d)\left(\frac{\alpha}{K}+\beta\right)+M^2N^2\gamma\right)}{\alpha+M^2\beta}} \quad (8)$$

The positive valued of n shows the required number of processors. Although the value of O_d depends on the number of partitions, i.e. n, an iterative computation for n and O_d beginning with the upper bound of O_d yields a solution. The value of O_d is at most 10-20% of the actual data size.

A numerical example is given below to compare the performance of the PWRC algorithm with the one proposed in [6]. For a group of given typical values for a convolution process; $N = 1024pixels$ (of bytes, i.e., grey-level), $M = 11pixels$, $K = 1024bytes$, $\alpha = 2ms$, $\beta = 2\mu s$, and $\gamma = 2\mu s$, 63 processors (partitions) are required for the best performance with respect to Lee and Hamdi's equation. However, we find that this figure dramatically falls to 32 processors (partitions) if PWRC is used under the same conditions.

4 Deciding System Hardware Architecture Parameters

On the other hand, it would be sufficient to send the coefficient matrix once in the cases of video processing processes. If the coefficient matrix is sent once, every factor related to the coefficient matrix size would be ignored. Assuming that the upper values are close to the actual values and $O_d \ll N^2$ read and data write time could be defined as follows:

$$T_{dr} = \left(\frac{N^2}{n}\right)\left(\frac{\alpha}{K}+\beta\right) \qquad and \qquad T_{dw} = \left(\frac{N^2}{n}\right)\left(\frac{\alpha}{K}+\beta\right)$$

Having the above equations, n can be computed as follows:

$$n = \frac{1}{2}M^2\frac{\gamma}{(\frac{\alpha}{K}+\beta)}+1 \quad (9)$$

Eq.9 indicates the relation among the number of processors, the coefficient matrix size and the system coefficients. Surprisingly, the number of processors becomes independent of the size of the image. Eq.9 also indicates that the minimum execution times can be achieved by using half of the processors with PWRC. We defined the system architectural constants under a single name "Coefficient of Architecture", i.e., C_a and compute the speed-up value for a parallel system having n processors as follows:

$$S = \frac{1}{2}M^2C_a + 1 \quad (10)$$

The speed-up value is also independent of the number of processors in the system. However, both Eq.9 and Eq.10 includes hidden interdependences. Considering Fig.1b and having the same assumptions given above we can derive T_{cycle} and compute it in another way:

$$T_{cycle} = T_{dw} + T_c + T_{dr} = \frac{N^2}{n}\left(2\left(\frac{\alpha}{K} + \beta\right) + M^2\gamma\right) \quad (11)$$

Since α, β, and K are communication related parameters, we defined "Coefficient of Communication" ,i.e. C_c, by those parameters. Thus, the number of processors became:

$$n = \frac{N^2}{T_{cycle}}\left(2\left(\frac{\alpha}{K} + \beta\right) + M^2\gamma\right) = \frac{N^2}{T_{cycle}}(C_c + M^2\gamma) \quad (12)$$

When Eq.12 is solved for T_{cycle}

$$T_{cycle} = \frac{N^2}{n}(C_c + M^2\gamma) \quad (13)$$

If a processing system, with typical values N=1024 pixels (of bytes, i.e., grey-level), $M = 11pixels$, $K = 1024bytes$, $\alpha = 2ms$, $\beta = 2\mu s$, and $\gamma = 2\mu s$, runs to achieve computation performance of $T_{cycle} = 10seconds$, 25 client processors would be sufficient. For a video processing system with 32 client processors, the above given application would run for a single frame in 8.1875 seconds, i.e. $T_{cycle} = 8.1875seconds$. It is obvious that these values are far from the real-time processing constraint of 40 ms per frame for PAL standard. Even an increase in the number of processors would not allow this system to run in real time. The bandwidth of the system for transferring data is not sufficient for the given typical characteristic values. The time elapsed to transmit (read and write) the frame by neglecting the overhead is defined as:

$$T_{transmission} = N^2 C_c \quad (14)$$

$T_{transmission} = 8seconds$ for the above example. Therefore, a more powerful data transmission system is required to provide real-time processing. Actually a parallel system connected via a high speed bus or a dedicated network would provide the required system characteristics for a real-time processing system, i.e., $T_{transmission} = 40ms$. To design such a system, utilising both I/O channel and processors, and running in real-time, one should calculate the number of processors by Eq.12 for a given system and application parameters providing $T_{transmission} = 40ms$.

The number of processors required for real time video processing, i.e., achieving a processing rate of 25 frames/second, with respect to the system parameters (C_c and γ) for different values of M^2 and N^2 are given in Fig.2a for $M^2 = 9$ and $N^2 = 288x360$; Fig.2b for $M^2 = 25$ and $N^2 = 288x360$; and Fig.3 for $M^2 = 9$ and $N^2 = 576x720$.

Fig.4a and Fig.4b show the value of C_c with respect to real system parameters of α, the latency time and β, data transmission time per byte. The comparison of the two graphs shows that the impact of the latency time is dominant as well as the packet size in determining the system communication parameter, C_c.

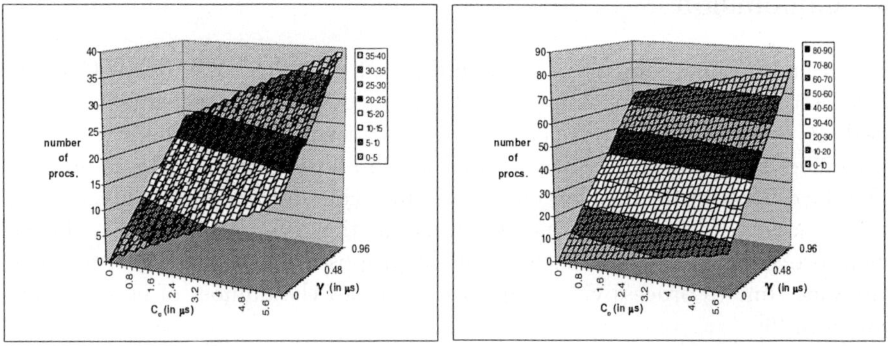

(a) (b)

Fig. 2. Number of processors wrt C_c and γ for N^2=288x360 a)M^2=9 b)M^2=25

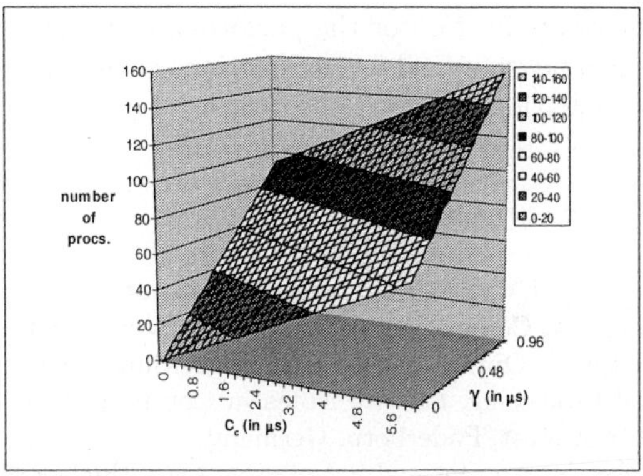

Fig. 3. Number of processors wrt C_c and γ for N^2=576x720 M^2=9

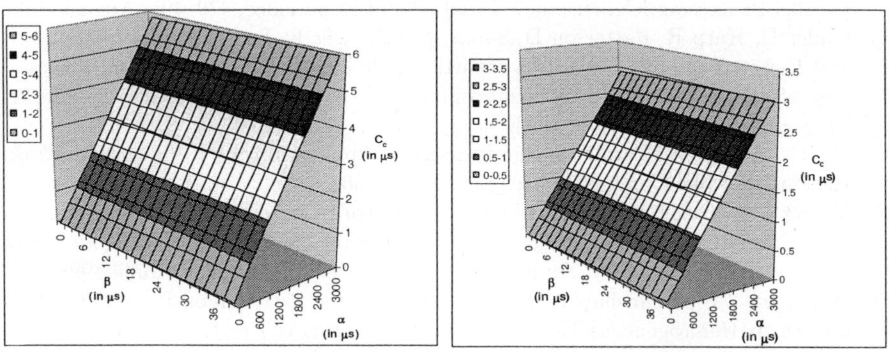

(a) (b)

Fig. 4. C_c wrt α and β for a)K=1024 bytes b)K=2048 bytes

5 Conclusion

A new and optimal scheduling algorithm called Periodic Write-Read- Compute (PWRC) scheduling algorithm for real time video processing is defined and analysed. It requires a high level atomic write-read command. Since it is easy to implement such an indivisible command in high level programming, it does not introduce a new problem. The generic system architecture is based upon a client-server model having point-to- point communication between the host and every client processor. It has been shown that the proposed scheduling algorithm takes the same time to process video sequence with half the number of processors required in [6].

Further analysis of the PWRC scheduling algorithm yields a number of equations expressing the dependencies of the system characteristics, a communication constant, C_c, a processing constant γ, an architectural constanti, C_a and application characteristics such as the size of the frame and width of the surrounding pixel frame. It is shown that either a parallel video processing system can be built up for a given type of application or the performance of an established parallel processing system can be examined for applications with different characteristics by the use of these equations.

References

1. Agrawal R, Jagadish H V, Partitioning Techniques for Large-Grained Parallelism, IEEE Transactions on Computers, Vol.37, No.12, December,1988.
2. Altilar D T, Paker Y, Optimal Scheduling Algorithms for Communication Constrained Parallel Processing, Lecture Notes in Computer Science 2400, Euro-Par 2002, 27th – 30th August, Paderborn, Germany.
3. Altilar D T, Paker Y, An Optimal Scheduling Algorithm for Parallel Video Processing, Proceedings of International Conference on Multimedia Computing and Systems'98, Austin Texas USA, 245–258, July 1998.
4. Crandall P. E., Quinn M. J., A Partitioning Advisory System for Networked Data-parallel Processing, Concurrency: Practice and Experience, 479–495, August 1995.
5. Culler D, Karp R, Patterson D, Sahay A, Schauser K, Santos E, Subramonian R and Eicken T, LogP: Towards a realistic mode of parallel computation, Proceedings of 4th ACM SIGPLAN Symposium on Principles and Practices of Parallel Programming, Vol.28, May 1993.
6. Lee C., Hamdi M., Parallel Image Processing Applications on a Network of Workstations, Parallel Computing, 21 (1995), 137–160.
7. Moritz C A, Frank M, LoGPC: Modeling Network Contention in Message-Passing Programs, ACM Joint International Conference on Measurement and Modeling of Computer Systems, ACM Sigmetrics/Performance 98, Wisconsin, June 1998.
8. Weissman J.B., Grimshaw A. S., A Framework for Partitioning Parallel Computations in Heterogeneous Environments, Concurrency: Practice and Experience, Vol.7(5),455–478,August 1995.

A Practical Approach for Constructing a Parallel Network Simulator*

Yue Li[1], Depei Qian[1], and Wenjie Zhang[2]

[1] Department of Computer Science and Engineering, Xi'an Jiaotong University, 710049 Xi'an, P.R.China
{yuelichina, depei}@263.net

[2] Institute of Computing Technology, Chinese Academy of Science, 100080 Beijing, P.R.China
zwj@ict.ac.cn

Abstract. Network simulation is widely used in network research to evaluate the performance of network protocols. With the development of computer networks, network models grow in size and complexity, so execution time of simulation can be unbearably long. In this paper, we present a practical approach to construct a parallel network simulator which is based on the popular sequential network simulator *ns*. Parallel discrete event simulation (PDES) techniques are applied to modify the event scheduling mechanism in ns. Some necessary extensions are also made to ns model library. Performance measures including speedup and memory consumption are evaluated at last.

1 Introduction

With the development of computer networks, scale of network models is increasing and more details are incorporated in the models. This makes execution time of simulation unbearably long. Parallel discrete event simulation (PDES) techniques [1] can provide a solution by dividing large simulation model into sub-models and executing them in a parallel fashion, which can be expected to run more efficiently.

NS [2] is a sequential open source network simulator, which is widely used in network research. A large number of legacy simulation models exist using this simulator. In this paper, we propose an approach to construct a ns-based parallel network simulator which runs on network of workstations. We use PDES techniques to modify the sequential event scheduling mechanism in ns, and make some necessary extensions to its model library. Performance results show that significant speedup can be obtained with minor modifications to the model description script for parallel execution.

* This work was supported by the National Key Basic Research Program of China (973) under grant No. G1999032710.

A. Yazici and C. Şener (Eds.): ISCIS 2003, LNCS 2869, pp. 739–746, 2003.

2 Background

PDES can be considered as a collection of sequential discrete event simulations, each called a logical process (LP). The original event list is partitioned into sub-lists according to certain rules and each sub-list is assigned to a LP. If LP still adopts the sequential event scheduling mechanism, out-of-order event processing may happen. This is a well known issue in PDES, namely time synchronization [1]. Time synchronization mechanisms can be fell into two main categories: conservative synchronization and optimistic synchronization.

Conservative synchronization is based on blocking. The rationale is that no LP can process an event until it can be proven that no other earlier events can be received from any other LPs, that is, an event must be proven to be *safe* before it can be processed. One of the early conservative synchronization mechanisms is *null message* algorithm [3]. It assumes that the connection topology of LPs is fixed and communication system is FIFO. Another conservative mechanism is designed based on bulk synchronous parallel model (BSP) [4]. A global synchronization is involved to determine the events that are safe to process. In this mechanism, each LP cycles through following steps:

- Global synchronization, computes a lower bound on time stamp (LBTS) of messages it might later receive;
- Processes the events with time stamp not exceeding LBTS.

Barrier synchronization can be adopted to achieve global synchronization. To compute LBTS, the concept of *lookahead* is important, which is the smallest amount of simulation time that must elapse between an event occurrence in one LP and its effect on another LP. The value of lookahead depends on the specific model being simulated.

Optimistic synchronization was proposed to avoid blocking. The rationale is that LP can forward its local simulation clock *bravely*, if any causal error occurs a mechanism called *roll back* corrects it.

Both synchronization mechanisms have deficiency and the choice vary with different applications. In general if the model has good lookahead characteristics, conservative mechanism can be the choice.

NS provides substantial support for simulation of TCP, routing and multicast protocols over wired and wireless networks. A general simulation scenario includes generation of network topology and *logical connections* between data source and sink. Performance data can be collected from simulation results.

3 Architecture of the Parallel Network Simulator

The parallel network simulator is based on ns as mentioned before. Fig. 1 illustrates its architecture. The ns model library which is composed of varieties of network protocol models and traffic models can be divided into layers, namely physical link layer, network layer, transport layer and application layer, similar to the TCP/IP protocol stack. Network models can be constructed with the model library. In the parallel network simulator, the model being simulated is divided into sub-models and each sub-model is assigned to one ns instance. An optimal partitioning should be a trade-off between lookahead and load balance. In order to keep the memory requirement for each ns instance as small as possible, only the portion of model being simulated is defined on the corresponding ns instance, so certain extensions to the original model library are needed. In Fig. 1 for example, distant link model has been added to the physical link layer to link the nodes resided on different ns instances. Specific extensions to the network layer and transport layer are also needed for similar reason. In Sect. 5 we will describe the extensions in detail.

Event scheduling in the parallel network simulator is performed by a component called simulation engine (SE) which is composed of three modules: event scheduler, time synchronization and communication interface, as shown in Fig. 1. The event queue consists of internal events and external events, the former are produced by local sub-model, the latter are received from other ns instances via communication interface. Event scheduler extracts the event with the earliest time stamp from event queue and handles it, messages may be sent to other ns instance via communication interface. When there is no safe event to process, event scheduler will invoke correlative primitives in time synchronization module to start a barrier synchronization and LBTS computation. A new execution round can be started as soon as the computation results are successfully returned. We will describe the corresponding details in Sect. 4. Communication interface is a set of APIs which are responsible for messages exchange between ns instances, MPICH for example. It achieves reliable delivery and frees the system from communication deadlock. Two kinds of messages exist in the system: event messages and synchronous messages. The former are the actual external events to be handled by a ns instance, and the latter are the messages for barrier synchronization.

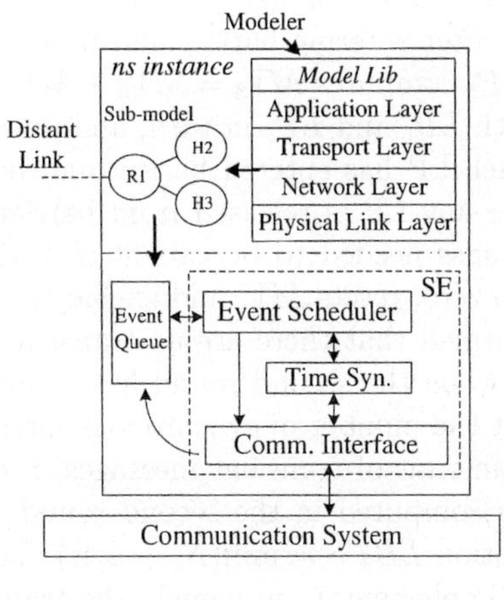

Fig. 1. Architecture of the parallel network simulator

4 Barrier Synchronization and LBTS Computation

In order to compute LBTS, *transient messages* must be taken into consideration. A transient message is defined as the event message which has been sent but has not yet been received by its destination. An incorrect (e.g. larger) LBTS value may be computed if transient messages are not taken into account.

It can be observed from the two-step processing cycle of LP in Sect. 2 that event messages generated in one cycle are not eligible for processing until next cycle. The execution loop of SE is illustrated as follow. Here N_i denotes the time stamp of next event for LP_i and LA_i denotes the lookahead of LP_i.

```
while(there are events to process) {
    receive messages generated in previous cycle;
    catch transient messages;
    LBTS = min (Ni + LAi);
    process events with time stamp <= LBTS;
}
```

Several algorithms were proposed for barrier synchronization, such as broadcast barrier, tree barrier and butterfly barrier [5]. To catch transient messages a mechanism to detect the presence of transient messages should be provided, in [6] an approach based on message counters was proposed, in which LP maintains two counters, one for the number of event messages sent by it before barrier, another for the number of event messages received. The deficiency is that excessive transient messages can result in high overhead. We propose to use vector counters instead of send/receive counters in butterfly barrier, which ensures that all transient messages can be caught after two round of exchange. The detail is described as follow.

LP_i maintains a vector called MV_i. If LP_i sends an event message to LP_k, it computes $MV_i[k] = MV_i[k] + 1 (i \neq k)$. If LP_i receives an event message, it computes $MV_i[i] = MV_i[i] - 1$. LPs exchange their MV in a butterfly style [5]. Taking 8 LPs (LP_0, $LP_1 \ldots LP_7$) context as an example, in the first round LP_3 first sends MV_3 to LP_2 after entering barrier and waits for the reply from LP_2. After receiving MV_2, LP_3 computes $MV_3 = MV_3 + MV_2$. Then LP_3 carries out the same operations with LP_1 and LP_7 in turn, and finishes this round. Now it can be affirmed that each LP has entered barrier and no more event messages will be generated before any LP is released from barrier. In the second round LP_i has transient messages needed to be caught if $MV_i[i] > 0$. So LP_i waits for $MV_i[i]$ decreasing to zero, resets MV_i and exchanges MV_i with corresponding LPs. It can be confirmed that there are no transient messages remained in communication system when the second round has completed. From the above it can be concluded that the number of synchronous messages will never exceed $2n \log n$ despite of the amount of transient messages, n denotes the number of LPs. The LBTS can be computed in the second round of the algorithm mentioned above, from equation $LBTS = \min(N_i + LA_i)$. The lookahead is a fixed constant in the current implementation, namely the transmission time plus the smallest link delay over all distant links.

5 Extensions to the Model Library

5.1 Physical Link Layer

The physical link layer mainly consists of network node models and link models to construct network topology. We add distant link model to this layer to define distant link between the nodes which reside on different ns instances. The distant link model inherits from the original link model in ns, with attributes like bandwidth, delay and queue management policy. Since remote end node of the distant link is not defined locally, the local end node and an identifier should be specified for defining a distant link. During initialization, distant links defined on different ns instances with the same identifier are considered to be connected. When a data packet is transfered over a distant link in simulation, it is clear that an event message holding the packet is sent from one ns instance to another.

5.2 Network Layer

In the default routing strategy of ns routes are computed centrally using global knowledge of network topology. In the parallel network simulator only a portion of network model is defined on each ns instance, so it cannot work in parallel context. In addition huge amount of memory space can be consumed when conducting large-scale network simulation using ns. The bottleneck is identified to be routing tables after careful investigation. This is because routing table on each simulated network node must have a routing entry to every other node, which makes memory space required $O(N^2)$, where N is the number of simulated nodes in the topology.

In fact, if a network is large the nodes are usually organized into a hierarchy. We adopt a hierarchical routing strategy in the parallel network simulator. Fig. 2 (left) illustrates a hierarchical topology (two level), in which network nodes are partitioned into four separate clusters. Each node has its own address in the form of $A.B$, here A denotes cluster and B denotes node within the cluster. By applying the hierarchical routing strategy the size of routing table can be reduced, therefore reducing memory space required in simulation. During parallel simulation, each ns instance computes local intra-cluster routes independently. In addition inter-cluster routes can be computed using knowledge of a virtual inter-cluster topology (shown in Fig. 2 right) constructed on each ns instance through exchanging routing messages. Thus routing information about whole network can be obtained. Details of this hierarchical routing strategy can be found in [7].

5.3 Transport Layer

The transport layer mainly consists of TCP and UDP models, including many variants. When a user sets up network model it is necessary to define a logical connection between specific data source and sink, for example $ns connect $Tcp-Source $TcpSink. A main function of this instruction is to include port numbers

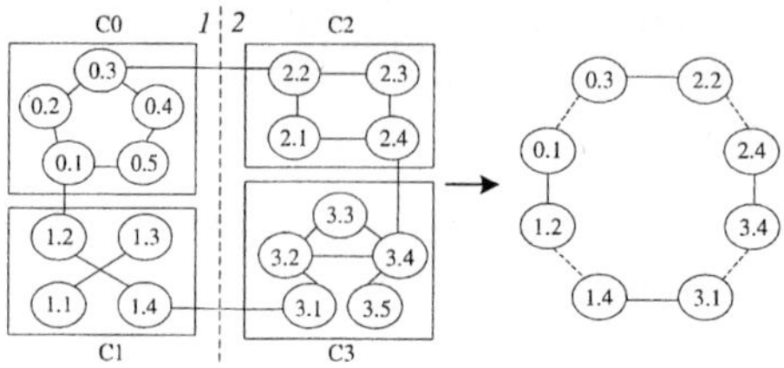

Fig. 2. Hierarchical routing

of the source and sink into data packets. Now consider the situation in parallel simulation, if source and sink reside on different ns instances, remote end point of the logical connection cannot be specified using the instruction above. To solve the problem we bind the remote end point to an explicit port and the port number is designated by user. When building a remote logical connection, user can specify the destination node address and the port number in the form $ns connect $LocalTcpSrc $DstNodeAddr $DstPort.

6 Limitation

At present not all models in ns are supported by the parallel network simulator. This is because of extensive use of global variables and zero simulation time interactions in some protocol implementation. For example, to model multicast behavior ns maintains a global table of multicast groups. But when simulation runs on network of workstations, method must be applied to ensure consistence of multicast group information on each ns instance. The most straightforward way is to implement with message exchange, but this can result in a zero simulation time interaction between message sender and receiver and result in poor performance. To support parallel execution of such models substantial modifications are needed. Because of these problems only a part of models (e.g. IP, UDP and TCP) are supported presently.

7 Related Work

Several research projects have focused on parallel network simulation in recent years. A C-based parallel simulation language 'Parsec' has been developed in UCLA, which supports multiple synchronization algorithms. GloMoSim [8] which is a network model library especially for wireless network, runs on top of Parsec. Researchers in Georgia Tech have developed a Telecommunication Description Language (TED). Simulators using TED to set up network models run on top of GTW [9] for parallel execution. Both these systems require users to learn new languages to describe their models, so neither of them has been widely used. By contrast our work is based on a widely used sequential network simulator and provides a simple way to reuse existing network models.

Ferenci presents a generic parallel simulation architecture [10] which is based on RTI-KIT and model proxy. RTI-KIT is a library to support development of DARPA High Level Architecture (HLA) software. Model proxy can provide an approach to define certain interaction rules among federates in HLA. On the basis of this architecture, a parallel version of ns is implemented. The drawback is that it demands excessive efforts to simulation user. For example the routing paths must be computed and established by simulation user. This will be a heavy burden if the network model is very large in scale. While we adopt the hierarchical routing strategy to extend ns model library, users only need to specify a few simple configurations. Good scalability can be achieved.

8 Performance Analysis

Our experimental platform consists of four workstations (PIII 1.13 GHz processor and 1.5GB memory each) connected by 100Mbps Ethernet. We use the topology generator *itm* available with ns to generate benchmark model with 160 network nodes, 40 nodes on each workstation. A number of local and remote logical connections are also defined in the model. The speedup results obtained for comparison of sequential and parallel simulations with different model configurations are shown in Table 1. The time in Table 1 is the actual run time of simulation, excluding the time for initialization and model starting-up. Speedup increases as the value of lookahead increases, since larger LBTS can be computed in the process cycle so that LP can find more safe events to handle. In addition, when the number of local logical connections increases, speedup also increases. The reason is that LPs are more heavily loaded, so more work can be done while LBTS is fixed.

Table 1. Speedup results

Lookahead (ms)	8			13			20		
Number of local logical connections	2	6	10	2	6	10	2	6	10
Sequential execution (s)	660	816	958	642	795	933	620	776	915
Parallel execution (s)	376	343	374	310	307	340	279	276	313
Speedup	1.76	2.38	2.56	2.07	2.59	2.74	2.22	2.81	2.92

As mentioned before, we adopt hierarchical routing strategy in the parallel network simulator to support large-scale network simulation. We have generated models with 1000 to 10,000 nodes. Memory space consumed in these simulations is shown in Fig. 3. Curve 1 illustrates the experiment results from execution on a single workstation using the default routing strategy of ns. Curve 2 shows the execution results from parallel simulation. The values of curve 2 are the total amount of memory space consumed on all four workstations.

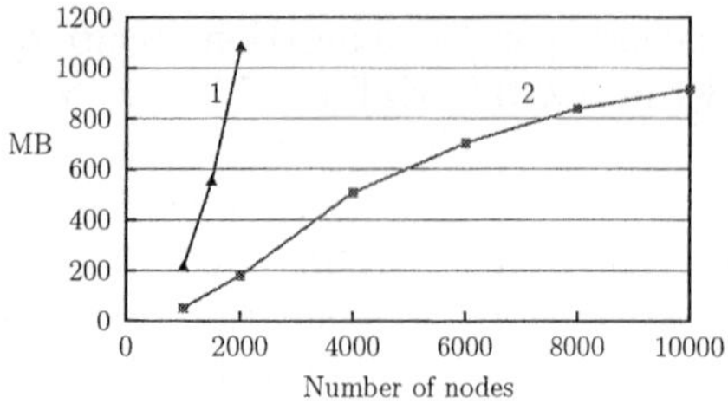

Fig. 3. Experiment results of model scale

9 Conclusion

Network simulation is playing a more and more important role in research of network protocols and control algorithms. To meet the needs of simulating large-scale complex networks while minimizing the efforts in learning the usage of a new simulation system, we propose a practical approach for constructing a parallel network simulator based on the popular sequential network simulator ns. Since only limited modifications have been made to ns, network models can run on parallel platform with minor changes to the input script. This is very encouraging to the current ns users.

References

1. Fujimoto R. Parallel discrete event simulation. Communications of ACM, 1990, 33(10):30–53
2. Kevin Fall. ns Manual. A Collaboration between researchers at UC Berkeley, 2002, LBL, USC/ISI, July 1
3. Chandy K. M. J. Misra. Distributed simulation: A case study in design and verification of distributed programs. IEEE Tran. on Software Engineering, 1979, SE-5(5): 440–452
4. L G Valient. A bridging model for parallel computation. Communications of ACM, 1990, 33(8):103–111
5. Eugene D. The butterfly barrier. International Journal of Parallel Programming. 1986, 15(4):295–307
6. Fujimoto R. Parallel and distributed simulation. Winter Simulation Conference Proceedings. 1999, 122–131
7. LI Yue, QIAN Depei. Improvement of Hierarchical Routing Protocol in the Network Simulator, Accepted by Journal of system simulation
8. Bagrodia R. M. Gerla. GloMoSim: A library for the parallel simulation of large wireless networks. Workshop on Parallel and Distributed Simulation 1998, 154–161
9. Das S. R. R. Fujimoto. GTW: A Time Warp system for shared memory multiprocessors. Winter Simulation Conference Proceedings, 1994, 1332–1339
10. L. Ferenci. An Approach for Federating Parallel Simulators. Workshop on Parallel and Distributed Simulation 2001, 63–70

Distributed Multicast Routing for Efficient Group Key Management

John Felix C[1] and Valli S[2]

Anna University, College of Engineering, Guindy Chennai 600 025 TN INDIA
johnfelix@cs.annauniv.edu
valli@annauniv.edu

Abstract. Multicast is an evolving technology for efficient transmission for one-to-many and many-to-many communications. The successful deployment of secure multicast model needs to be more distributed rather than the current centralized approach. In this work, a distributed approach in multicast routing is proposed which enhances the group key management schemes over a large-scale network. Existing work prove that group key management is vulnerable due to latency and complexity involved in multicast transmission. This model is designed to reduce latency and distribute the complexity. The assumptions based on which this work was implemented are discussed.

1 Introduction

Multicasting is the technology for an efficient one-to-many or many-to-many communications, which is extensively used for collaborative multimedia applications such as multiparty conferencing, distance learning etc. The primitive goal is to achieve better utilization of available network resources by substantially reducing the traffic load at the source. Current model was developed, by giving more importance to factors such as reliability and scalability [6], which make the current time-constrained applications difficult to adapt to the current service model. This work focuses on a distributed routing scheme, which supports the security mechanism namely group key management. The major factor that affects the deployment of group key management is latency and complexity [1]. These factors make group key management vulnerable and make multicast a no choice for most ISPs. Based on the earlier research works on multicast security [1], it can be concluded that group key management combined with access control is the best approach for providing multicast security. These mechanisms increase the complexity and thereby latency in the multicast transmission, which are the issues in the multicast model.

2 Existing Work

Earlier work was focused on routing in a single dimension, tree routed schemes, which make the network unstable when security mechanisms where implemented in them. Lolus [1] uses a hierarchy of security key agents, which form sub-groups

A. Yazici and C. Şener (Eds.): ISCIS 2003, LNCS 2869, pp. 747–754, 2003.

with the tree leaves as hosts. Sub-groups are independent of every other sub group in the tree. Wong [12] recent model implements group key management through hierarchical keys instead of hierarchy of key agents, which was used in Lolus [1]. Rekeying was done using user oriented, group oriented and key oriented strategies. Wong's approach was to reduce N, the number of encryptions and transmissions required for rekeying. The value of N is approximately log(s), where s is the multicast group size. The model discussed in this paper is an underlying routing architecture for the Wong's model.

3 Distributed Routing

This model focuses on time-constrained applications rather than error-sensitive applications. Reliability is compromised in order to achieve reduce latency and distribute the complexity. Therefore, retransmission of packets don't occur, error is detected and corrected only at the physical layer through FEC techniques. Retransmission of packets in a time constrained application is waste of resource at the network entities. Late arrived packets have no importance, as the packets' play-out time is not the current time. Since there is no re-transmission in the model, there is no necessity to acknowledge the received packets. Absence of retransmission and acknowledgment will greatly reduce the multicast complexity and traffic load [5], but will also increase the error-rate at the receiver, which can be ignored due to the current standards in the transmission medium.

3.1 Design Parameters

This model defines routing architecture in a two-dimensional approach. First dimension of routing is implemented over an partially complete bi-directional graph. This graph forms the backbone of the multicast routing. The multicast graph contains a number of Multicast Access Control (MAC) routers, which are responsible for management of the multicast graph. A MAC in the graph is functionally independent of every other MAC in the multicast graph. This model uses minimum diameter approach for generating graph. A MAC in the graph has a shortest path to every other MAC in the multicast backbone network, which is an immediate MAC neighbor. The MACs maintains a spanning tree that covers all the MACs in the multicast backbone network. The links in the spanned tree are defined as active links in the graph. Non-MAC functionality is to provide a shortest path route between two MACs or else it is removed from the multicast backbone network. The shortest path between MACs ensures a very low latency to the domain they manage. The number of MACs in the graph is proportional to induced latency in the graph.

Domain of the MAC is the second dimension of routing, which uses the traditional tree approach routing.The domain of the MAC consists of all the Non-MAC immediate neighbors to a MAC and all the hosts controlled by the Non-MAC as leaf nodes. MAC acts as the central core of the multicast tree, which has hosts as leaf nodes and Non-MACs as the parent nodes for the leaf nodes. A MAC has responsibility of updating its routing database depending

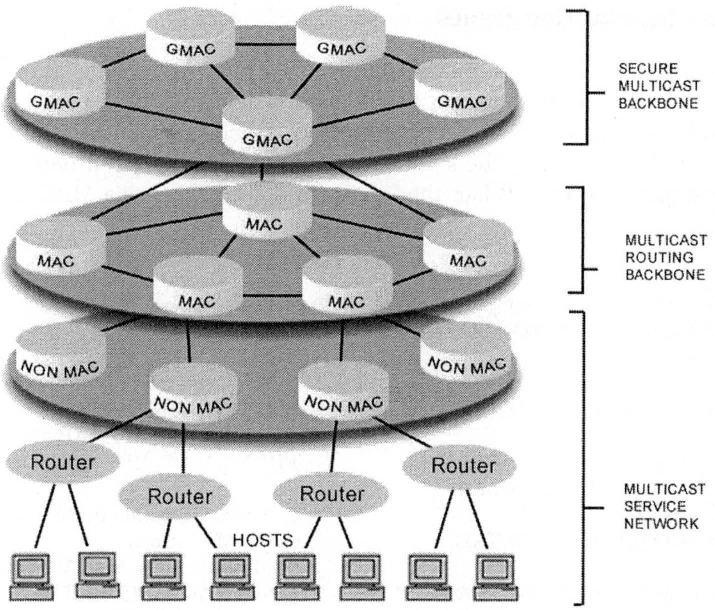

Fig. 1. Distributed Routing Architecture

upon the non-MACs in its domain. Routing database for the second dimension of the architecture has path information for the shared tree, which the MAC manages. Two types of Non-MACs exist in the second dimension of the routing scheme, such that a non-MAC can be a multicast enabled or disabled router.

If overhead at a MAC is increased over a threshold, at this point the MAC will induce a high latency. At this scenario, a non-MAC will switch to become a MAC if it has enough resources to manage MAC functions. As the overhead at a MAC is due to increase in hosts in the particular domain of the MAC, this will drive the ISP to enable a Non-MAC to a MAC dynamically. Dynamic properties of the model will allow good deployment of network management and adapt to changing conditions in the Internet environment and the network resources. This property also provides some fault tolerance to some extent.

In this approach, redundancy is increased due to presence of cyclic path in the graph. Therefore, it is the responsibility of the MAC to eliminate duplicate packets due to the cyclic paths. Each edge in the graph is a link between two MACs in the multicast backbone network. To eliminate duplicate packets, a link is defined either as a active or passive link. A receiver MAC is responsible for making a link either passive or active link. A link is made passive if the MAC receives a duplicate packet through the link. The passive link will not be used for any more forwarding of packets, as the active link is the best low delay path towards the receiver MAC. A passive link is periodically refreshed to check whether the passive link is better path than the current active link towards a receiver MAC.

3.2 Implementation Issues

This implementation of the distributed routing mechanisms has many issues to deal with. The joining node can be of three types, namely, a router can either join a MAC graph network as a MAC or to a specific MACs domain where it is the non-MAC spanned to the shared tree and the third type of network node is which can join as a host. When the joining node functions as a MAC is discussed as case 1.

```
1. [Join Operation of MAC]
Send Join Request JREQ(MAC_IP)
to all neighbor MAC
Receive Join Confirmation
JCONF(MAC_IP, SHORT_PATH)

2. [Join operation of a Non-MAC]
If Non-MAC Multicast enabled
Send JREQ(IP)
Send JREQ(IP, HOST_IP_TAB)
Else
Receive JCONF(MAC_IP, SHARED_TREE)
Update ROUTING_TAB -> JCONF
Update SHARED_TREE -> JREQ

3. [Join operation of a Host]
Send JREQ(IP) to all
immediate access router
If Router NOT in group
Initiate Step 2
Else
Send Host Add Request JADD(IP, HOST_IP)

4. [Leave Operation of MAC]
If SHARED_TREE = empty
Send PRUNE(MAC_IP)
to all neighbor MAC
[On Receive of PRUNE]
Delete MAC_ROUT_TAB ->
PRUNE(MAC_ IP)

5. [Leave Operation from
a Non-MAC Host]
Send Leave Request MLVE(IP)
Delete MAC_SHARED_TREE
-> MLVE

6. [Defining Link as Active or Passive]
Receive IP Packet >> RPACKET
If RPACKET already RECEIVED
Send Make Passive MPAS(MAC_IP)
[On the Sender MAC]
Update MAC_ROU_TAB -> MPAS
Delay t
Increase t expotentially
```

Case 1. In this scenario a router joins the multicast group as a MAC. The joining router sends a join request JREQ to every other immediate MAC neighbors. All the immediate MACs respond with join confirmation JCONF which updates the routing database of the MAC. MAC maintains a routing table for storing every shortest path to all immediate routers in the multicast backbone graph. The MAC will adapt dynamically to its available resources by adding or eliminating some entries in the multicast routing database. Elimination in done only to passive links entries in the MAC routing database.

Case 2. In the second case of join operation, the joining node is non-MAC and will have to be spanned to the shared tree managed by a MAC domain, which is second dimension routing of the model. The MAC responds to the join request JREQ from the Non-MAC by sending a join confirmation signal JCONF. Join confirmation will find a shortest sub-optimal path that exist in the shared tree form the MAC towards the joining Non-MAC. If the joining non-MAC is multicast enabled then the JREQ contains only the IP information of the joining node, but in case the joining router is multicast disabled then the JREQ contains IP information of the router and all hosts under the Non-MAC. This information will update the routing database in the MAC, which maintain the IP information for all routers, and hosts in its domain.

Case 3. If joining network entity is a host, then it is added to the second dimension of the routing scheme i.e. the shared tree managed by a MAC domain. The host will send a Unicast JREQ to the immediate access router in its network, which will initiate a non-MAC join operation. In case the immediate router is already a member of the shared tree and is multicast disabled, it will send a Unicast packet to the MAC defining the IP information of the joining host. The MAC on receiving the update packet will span the host to the existing shared tree of its domain.

4 Multicast Security

Existing multicast service model raises deployment issues in multicast security. The senders or receivers failed to authenticate before joining the group. Moreover, any host can join the group as a receiver or sender, which makes the multicast vulnerable to eaves dropping and attacks such as Denial of Service, theft of service. These threats can be well defended using group key management and access control mechanisms.

4.1 Design Objectives

In multicast group key management, encrypting the data with a shared key provides confidentiality. Encryption of the multicast traffic is done using a symmetric key and all the authorized users of the multicast group are given the decryption key. Issues regarding group key management get complicated as the group membership is dynamically changed due to newly joining and leaving hosts in the group. When a new member joins the group, the new group key can be sent to the new members using the old key. Matters' get complicated only when a leave operation is taking place. The naive approach is to re-compute the keys on every leave operation and new key is distributed to all the receivers in the group. This is not optimal since each leave operation requires N different encryptions and transmissions. This model emphasize on reducing N by distributing the host and grouping them in domain controlled by MAC.

Distributed two-dimensional routing, supports the security mechanisms such as group key management, access control schemes at an optimum level. Similar to the multicast routing, the group key management uses a traditional tree approach for distributing the keys. Group key management uses the MAC as a key distribution center (KDC) for the domain it controls. In this model, GMAC (Gateway multicast access control) is a MAC that is capable of supporting the multicast backbone graph at the transport layer. Therefore, GMAC controls all the Non-GMACs in the domain of the GMAC. Non-GMACs are MACs, which can support the multicast backbone graph at the network layer. The GMACs in the multicast backbone graph form a secure backbone for the multicast model. Each GMAC is responsible for distributing the keys to its domain independent of every other GMAC. In the multicast backbone graph network, no security is required at this dimension since any hosts such as a sender or receiver cannot join directly to multicast backbone network. Therefore GMACs are independent and requires no centralized control for graph management.

5 Analysis

The objective of the model is to reduce N, the number of encryptions and transmissions done by a key distribution center by distributing the overhead independently. Rekeying in a conventional approach requires N encryptions and transmission, where N is the group size. This model divides N independently by use of m MAC modes. Therefore rekeying is done only to the domain of the MAC. A discrete event simulator was used for the simulation. The simulation dynamically changed the network topology. This dynamic property of the network topology is required to analyze the multicast graph backbone of the first dimension routing scheme. Every node existence in the topology is dependent upon a probability ranged over uniform distribution. The assumption based on which this property is performed is that network cannot be partitioned. Occurrence of join/leave operation of hosts is ranged over normal distribution.

5.1 Complexity

The simulation process probed the complexity incurred at the node of a MAC. Initial complexity at the MAC node was high compared to IP multicast. The complexity as shown in figure 2a increases proportionally with the group size until it reaches the threshold (T) of the MAC. At this point, the MAC splits its domain by initializing a new MAC, to share its overhead. MAC's domain size (n) decreases by the new MAC's domain size (m). IP multicast complexity of the centralized node increases linearly with-respect to the group size of the multicast tree. Analysis of complexity with help of delay characteristics of the model revealed more properties.

5.2 Delay

The latency of the packet forwarded is proportional to the current MAC's domain size (n), which will not exceed the latency (Md) when T is the domain size and Md is the maximum delay for a MAC. Another important consideration for latency is the sub-optimality of paths in the shared tree maintained by the MAC for its second dimension routing domain. It is important to note that latency is not affected by the actual group size (N) where N is the summation of domain size n for every MAC node in the graph.

The domain size of MAC (n) is dependent upon the maximum threshold or overhead the MAC can service without degrading service to higher layers. Average delay incurred in this model is proportional with the number of MAC

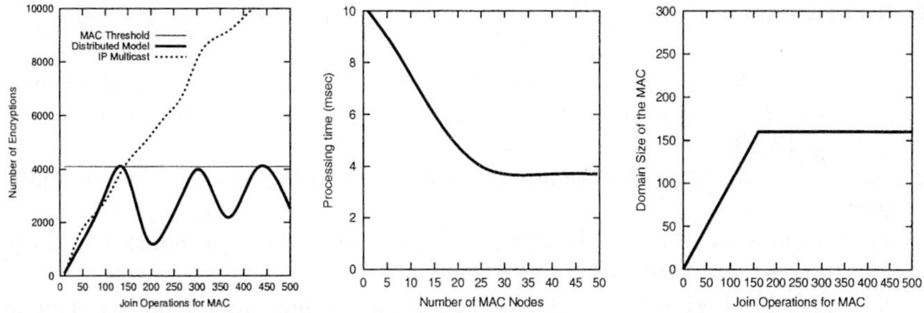

Fig. 2. a. MAC Domain Split-up at Threshold b. Delay is proportional to No. of MACs c. Increased scalability until threshold is reached

nodes in the multicast network backbone as shown in figure 2b. Network locality of the MAC nodes affects the MACs routing database requirements. The dynamic property of the network topology requires regular updates to the routing database. Locality of node decides the number of immediate neighbor MACs to each other MAC in the topology. Network locality also affects the complexity of join/leave operations. MACs, which exist very remotely relative to the multicast group, will have more stress in link and the nodes of its neighbor MACs , whereas a Non-MAC, which is within the domain of another MAC, will join as MAC with very less complexity.

5.3 Scalability

Scalability is dependent on the maximum domain size of the MAC (T), which is predetermined by the model. Scalability is limited to the point at which no new MAC can be initialized and the current MAC's domain size has reached the threshold (T) as shown in figure 2c. However, the model provides a fair scalability feature until (threshold) T of the domain is reached and the actual group size (N) is not the domain size of the MAC (n).

6 Conclusion

This routing model supports the deployment of the security and network management schemes such as group key management, access control and packet authentication schemes. Security in multicast content distribution has matured over the years, but there remain issues, which still needs solution. This model reduces latency but if the error-rate in the transmission medium is high then the Quality of Service will be poor compared to IP multicast since the model doesn't support reliability mechanisms except for FEC techniques. Analysis of the model revealed that distribution of complexity requires more number of active participants as MACs so that overhead is shared. Though this model provides transparency in deployment but it still requires ISPs to enable routers to support multicast. It can be concluded that multicast requires a protocol stack similar to unicast, which obtains support from all the layers.

References

1. Matthew J. Moyer, Josyula R. Rao, and Pankaj Rohatgi, "A Survey of Security Issues in multicast transmission", IEEE Network Magazine, Vol. 13 No. 6, November 1999 pp 12–23.
2. Jack Snowyink, "A Lower bound for Multicast key distribution", IEEE INFOCOM 2001.
3. Y. H. Chu, S. G. Rao and H. Zhang, "A case for end system multicast", in proc. ACM Sigmetrics, Santa Clara, CA, June 2000.
4. N.G.Duffield, J. Horowitz, F.Lo.Presti, "Adaptive multicast topology inference", IEEE INFOCOM 2001
5. S. Deering, D. Estrin, D. Farinacci, V. Jacobson and L Lei, "The PIM Architecture for wide area multicast" IEEE/ACM Transactions on Networking, Vol. 4, No. 2 April 1996, pp 153–162.
6. T.Ballardie, P. Francis, and J. Crowcroft, "Core Based Trees (CBT): An Architecture for scalable multicast routing" ACM Sigcomm 1995
7. K. Almeroth, "The Evolution of Multicast: From the Mbone to Inter-domain multicast to internet2 deployment" IEEE Network Magazine, Vol. 14 No. 1, January 2000 pp 10–30.
8. Kin-Ching Chan and S.H Gary Chan, "Distributed server approach for large-scale secure multicast",IEEE Journal of selected areas of communication. Vol 20. No. 8, October 2002, pp 1500–1510.
9. D. Maughan, M. Schertler, M. Schneider and J. Tuner, " Internet security association and key management protocol" in RFC 2048, April 1998
10. Robert Beverly, "Wide Area IP Multicast Traffic Characterization", IEEE Network, Vol. 17, No. 1, Jan 2003 pp 8–15.
11. Paul Judge and Mostafa Ammar,"Security Issues and solutions in Multicast content distribution: A Survey", IEEE Network Magazine, Vol. 17, No. 1, January 2003 pp 30–36.
12. Chung Kei Wong, Mohamed Gouda and Simon S. Lam, "Secure group communication using key graphs", IEEE/ACM Transactions on Networking, Vol. 8 No. 1, Feburary 2000 pp 16–30.

Multi-threshold Guard Channel Policy for Next Generation Wireless Networks

Hamid Beigy and M.R. Meybodi*

Soft Computing Laboratory
Computer Engineering Department
Amirkabir University of Technology
Tehran, Iran
{beigy, meybodi}@ce.aut.ac.ir

Abstract. In this paper, we consider the call admission problem in next generation wireless networks, which must handles multi-media traffics. We give an algorithm, which finds the optimal number of guard channels, which minimizes the overall blocking probability calls with lowest level of QoS in a multi-cell cellular network subject to the hard constraint on the blocking probabilities of other calls.

1 Introduction

The next generation wireless networks are expected to eventually carry multi-media traffics. In order to support such wide range of traffics on a network, the network must be capable of satisfying various quality of service (QoS) requirements. The satisfying QoS means that the various traffics should get predictable service from the available resources in the network. Since wireless spectrum remains as the prime limited resource in the next generation networks, hence, it is necessary to develop mechanisms that can provide effective bandwidth management while satisfying the QoS requirement for incoming calls. In order to maintain the QoS requirements, call admission control is needed. The call admission control policies determine whether a call should be either accepted or rejected at the base station and assign the required channel(s) to the admitted call. Several call admission control policies have been proposed to reduce the dropping of voice calls in wireless networks [1,2,3,4,5]. However, little attention is paid to wireless multi-media networks. In what follows, we review some of proposed call admission policy in the cellular networks.

The simplest call admission control policy is called *guard channel* policy (GC), which reserves a subset of channels, called *guard channels*, allocated to the cell for sole use of handoff calls [1]. Whenever the channel occupancy exceeds a certain threshold, this policy rejects new calls until the channel occupancy goes below the threshold. This policy accepts handoff calls as long as channels are available. If only the dropping probability of handoff calls is considered, the

* This work is partially supported by Iranian Telecommunication Research Center (ITRC), Tehran, Iran.

A. Yazici and C. Şener (Eds.): ISCIS 2003, LNCS 2869, pp. 755–762, 2003.

guard channel policy gives very good performance, but the blocking probability of new calls is degraded to a great extent. In order to have more control on both the dropping probability of handoff calls and the blocking probability of new calls, *limited fractional guard channel policy* (LFG) is proposed [3]. The LFG policy reserves non-integral number of guard channels for handoff calls. In [5], *uniform fractional guard channel policy* (UFG) is introduced, which accepts new calls with a fixed probability. It is shown that, the UFG policy performs better than GC policy in low handoff traffic conditions. In [6,7], a multi-media cellular network with two traffic classes are considered and the call admission problem is formulated as a semi-Markov decision process problem and Q-learning [6] and neuro-dynamic programming [7] are used for finding the optimal policy.

All of the above mentioned call admission control policies consider only one threshold to decide for accepting/rejecting of new calls. These policies fail when there is several classes of traffics with different level of QoS. In such cases, we need multi-threshold policy, which provides different thresholds for different classes. In [8], *dual-threshold reservation* (DTR) scheme is given for integrated voice/data wireless networks. In this scheme, three classes of calls in ascending order of level of QoS are considered which are data calls (both new and handoff calls), new voice calls and handoff voice calls. The basic idea behind the DTR scheme is to use two thresholds, one for reserving channels for handoff voice, while the other is used to block data traffic into the network in order to preserve the voice performance in terms of handoff dropping and call blocking probabilities. The equations for blocking probabilities of DTR are derived and the effect of different values for number of guard channels on dropping and blocking probabilities are plotted, but no algorithm for finding the optimal number of guard channels is given. In [9], a *two-threshold guard channel* (TTGC) policy, which uses two sets of guard channels, is introduced in which three classes of traffics in ascending order of level of QoS are considered. The limiting behavior of TTGC policy is analyzed under stationary traffic and an algorithm for finding the minimum number of channels in each cell in order to maintain the QoS for all classes of calls. In [10], a prioritized channel assignment algorithm is given which maintains the level of QoS for different classes of calls. This channel assignment algorithm uses the TTGC as call admission control policy.

In this paper, we extend the idea given in [11] for single cell case to the multi-cell cellular networks and introduce a channel assignment algorithm for multi-cellular networks consisting of several clusters, where a typical cluster m contains N_m cells. We give an optimal algorithm that divides the channel set allocated to the network into N_m disjoint channel sets, where each channel set is allocated to one cell in the cluster. Then, the channel set of each cell is divided into N subsets. The objective is to find the optimal value for thresholds, which minimize the overall blocking probability of the lowest priority class of calls subject to the hard constraint other calls. By applying our algorithm to each cluster in the system, the channel assignment is obtained for the whole network.

The rest of this paper is organized as follows: Section 2 presents the limiting behavior of multi-threshold guard channel policyunder stationary traffics. Section 3 gives an algorithm to find the optimal value of thresholds in multi-cell system and section 4 concludes the paper.

2 Multi-threshold Guard Channel Policy

In [11], the multi-threshold guard channel policy (MTGC) is introduced. In this policy, we considered network cells with N classes of traffics $W = \{w_1, \ldots, w_N\}$ and C full duplex channels. Each traffic class w_i (for $1 \leq i \leq N$) consists of a stream of statistically identical calls with Poisson arrival at rate λ_i and independent identical exponentially distributed call holding times with mean $1/\mu_i$. Every call requests only one channel. Class k (for $k = 1, 2 \ldots, N$) has a level of QoS, q_k, which must be satisfied. Without loss of generality, it is assumed that $q_1 \geq q_2 \geq \ldots \geq q_N$. Thus, the priority of calls for class k (for $k = 1, 2 \ldots, N-1$) is less than the priority of calls for class $(k+1)$. Let $\Lambda_k = \sum_{j=k+1}^{N} \lambda_j$, $\alpha_k = \frac{\Lambda_k}{\Lambda_0}$, $\mu^{-1} = \sum_{j=1}^{N} \mu_j^{-1}$, and $\rho = \frac{\Lambda_0}{\mu}$. We consider a cell in isolation. The state of a particular cell at time t is defined to be the number of busy channels in that cell, which is denoted by $c(t)$. In order to provide the specified level of QoS for calls of each class, channels which are allocated to the given cell are partitioned into (N) subsets. In order to partition the channel sets, $(N-1)$ thresholds, $T_1, \ldots, T_{N-1}$ $(0 < T_1 \leq T_2 \leq \ldots \leq T_{N-1})$ are defined. For the sake of simplicity, two additional fixed thresholds $T_0 = -1$ and $T_N = C$ are used. The procedure for accepting calls in MTGC policy, as shown in figure 1. In the MTGC policy,

```
if (Call of Class k) then
    if (c(t) < T_k ) then
        accept call
    else
        reject call
    end if
end if
```

Fig. 1. Multi-threshold guard channel policy.

$\{c(t)|t \geq 0\}$ is a continuous-time Markov chain (birth-death process) with states $0, 1, \ldots, C$. The state transition diagram of a particular cell in the network, which has C full duplex channels and uses MTGC policy as shown in figure 2.

From structure of the Markov chain, we can easily write down the solution to the steady-state balance equations. Define the steady state probability

$$P_n = \lim_{t \to \infty} \text{Prob}[c(t) = n] \qquad n = 0, 1, \ldots, T_N. \tag{1}$$

By writing down the equilibrium equations for the steady-state probabilities P_n $(n = 0, 1, \ldots, T_N)$, we obtain the following expression for P_n $(T_k < n \leq T_{k+1})$.

$$P_n = P_0 \frac{(\rho\alpha_k)^n}{n!} \prod_{j=1}^{k} \left(\frac{\alpha_{j-1}}{\alpha_j} \right)^{T_j}, \tag{2}$$

where P_0 is the probability that all channels are free and obtained from equation $\sum_{n=0}^{C} P_n = 1$ and can be expressed by the following expression.

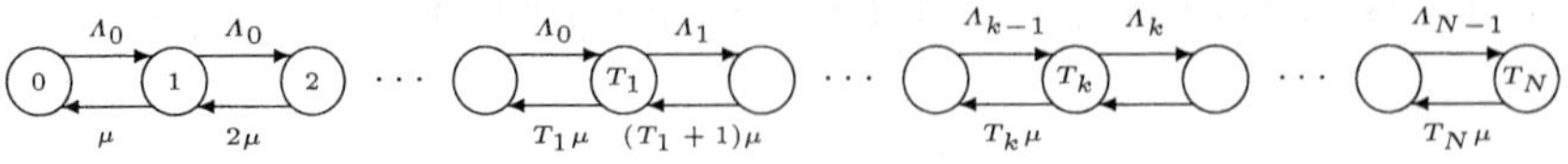

Fig. 2. Markov chain model of cell for multi-threshold guard channel policy.

$$P_0 = \left[\sum_{k=0}^{N-1} \prod_{j=1}^{k} \left(\frac{\alpha_{j-1}}{\alpha_j} \right)^{T_j} \sum_{n=T_k+1}^{T_{k+1}} \frac{(\rho\alpha_k)^n}{n!} \right]^{-1}. \tag{3}$$

Define T as $[T_0, T_1, \ldots, T_N]$, e_j as the unit $((N+1) \times 1)$ vector with 1 as the jth element and the rest zero and E_i^j as $\sum_{k=i}^{j} e_k$. Thus, the blocking probability of class N is equal to

$$B_N(T) = \prod_{i=1}^{N-1} \left(\frac{\alpha_{i-1}}{\alpha_i} \right)^{T_i} \frac{(\rho\alpha_{N-1})^{T_N}}{T_N!} P_0. \tag{4}$$

Similarly , the blocking probability of class k $(K < N)$ is given by

$$B_k(T) = \sum_{j=k}^{N-1} \prod_{i=1}^{j} \left(\frac{\alpha_{i-1}}{\alpha_i} \right)^{T_i} \sum_{n=T_j+1}^{T_{j+1}} \frac{(\rho\alpha_j)^n}{n!} P_0. \tag{5}$$

$B_k(.)$ has interesting properties some of which are listed below. The proof of these properties are given in [12].

Property 1. For any given value of T, we have $B_k(T) \geq B_{k+1}(T)$.

Property 2. For any given value of T, $B_k(.)$ is a monotonically decreasing function of T_k.

Property 3. For any given value of T, $B_k(.)$ is a monotonically increasing function of T_j $(j < k)$.

Property 4. For any given values of T, $B_k(.)$ is a monotonically increasing function of T_j $(j > k)$.

3 Optimal Channel Assignment in Multi-cell Networks

In this section, we extend the idea given in [11] for single cell case to the multi-cell cellular networks and introduce a channel assignment algorithm for networks consisting of several clusters, where a typical cluster m contains N_m cells. Assume that a total of C full duplex channels are allocated to the whole network and hence to each cluster. Under our channel assignment scheme, the allocated channels will be divided into N_m disjoint channel sets, where each channel set is allocated to one cell in the cluster. Then, the channel set of each cell is divided into N subsets. By applying our algorithm to each cluster in the system, the channel assignment is obtained for the whole network. Assume the exponential channel holding time and Poisson arrivals for each call as in section 2. Let $\Lambda = \sum_{i=1}^{N_m} \lambda_1^i$ be the total arrival rate of class 1 traffics over all cells in cluster m and λ_1^i is the arrival rate of class 1 calls in cell i of cluster m. Define the overall blocking probability of class 1 traffics by

$$B = \sum_{i=1}^{N_m} \frac{\lambda_1^i}{\Lambda_n} B_1^i(T), \tag{6}$$

where $B_1^i(T^i)$ is the blocking probability of class 1 traffics in cell i when C^i channels are allocated to that cell and T^i is the set of thresholds for that cell. The objective is to find the optimal value for T^i $(i = 1, 2, \ldots, N_m)$, which minimizes B subject to the hard constraint other calls. This problem is formulated as the following non-linear optimization problem.

Problem 1. Minimize the overall blocking probability of class 1 traffics, B, subject to the following hard constraints.

$$B_k^i(T^i) \leq q_k \qquad \text{for} \quad k = 2, \ldots, N, \tag{7}$$

$$\sum_{i=1}^{N_m} C^i = C, \tag{8}$$

for all cells $i = 1, 2, \ldots, N_m$ in cluster m.

In what follows, we propose an algorithm for solving problem 1. This algorithm uses the convexity[1] property of B_1 with respect to T_N (property 5).

Property 5. If thresholds T are fixed, then $B_1(T)$ is convex in T_N provided that $\frac{\rho\alpha_{N-1}}{T_N+1} < 1$.

Using property 5, it is evident that by adding more channels to a cell while the level of QoS are fixed, the blocking probability of class 1 traffics is decreased. An optimal solution of the problem 1 is found by exploiting the convexity property of B_1. Initially for each cell i, the smallest number of channels required to satisfy the

[1] A function $f(z)$ defined on the set of integers $Z = \{z | z \text{ is an integer}\}$ is called convex if its first differences are increasing. That is, $f(z)$ is convex if $f(z) - f(z+1) \leq f(z-1) - f(z)$ for all $z \in Z$.

given QoS is found. To do this, we use algorithm given in [12] to find the minimum channels for each cell. Then the remaining channels, if any, are allocated to cells one by one. Let γ_i denotes the potential amount of decrement in B_1^i brought by allocation of an additional channel to cell i. Note that the additional channel can be used in any of N subsets. In order to find the usage of the additional channel, the algorithm given in [11] is used. The potential amount of decrement in B_1^i are computed for all cell i (for $i = 1, 2, \ldots, N_m$) according to the following equation.

$$\gamma_i = \frac{\lambda_1^i}{\Lambda} \left[B_1^i(T^{*i}) - B_1^i \left(T^{*i} + e_N \right) \right].$$

Note that γ_i is always positive. Then a cell with the largest potential decrease in B_1 is found among all cells in the cluster and an additional channel is assigned to it. This procedure is repeated until all available channels C in the cluster are used. Algorithm given in figure 3 summarizes this procedure.

Algorithm MultiCell-MinBlock
    Use algorithm in [12] for all cells.
    set $S \leftarrow C - \sum_{i=1}^{N_m} C^i$
    if $S = 0$ **then** terminate. T is optimal.
    if S ¡ 0 **then** terminate. C channels cannot satisfy the specified QoS.
    for $i \leftarrow 1$ **to** N_m **do**
        Use algorithm given in [11] for cell i with C^i and $C^i + 1$ channels.
        set $\gamma_i \leftarrow \frac{\lambda_1^i}{\Lambda} \left[B_1^i(T^i) - B_1^i(T^i + e_N) \right]$.
    end for
    for $i \leftarrow 1$ **to** S **do**
        set $j \leftarrow \text{argmax}_i \gamma_i$.
        set $C^j \leftarrow C^j + 1$.
        set $\gamma_j \leftarrow \frac{\lambda_1^j}{\Lambda} \left[B_1^j(T^j) - B_1^i(T^j + e_N) \right]$.
    end for
    $\{T^i | i = 1, 2, \ldots, N_m\}$ is the optimal solution.
end Algorithm

Fig. 3. Multi-cell channel assignment algorithm

Theorem 1. *Algorithm given in figure 3 finds the optimal solution of problem 1.*

Proof. The initial assignment is an undominated solution, in the sense that it uses the minimum number of channels to satisfy constraints (7). This assignment results the maximum value of B subject to constraints (7). Then the algorithm assigns channels one by one to cells which results the largest decrement in blocking probability of new calls. This strategy results the optimal solution. Let j_i be the index of the cell with the largest decrement in B at step i (for $i = 1, 2, \ldots, S$). Assume that there is another strategy which is optimal and at step i chooses cell

$k_i \neq j_i$. Thus, there is $\delta_i \geq 0$ for which we have $\gamma_{k_i} = \gamma_{j_i} - \delta_i$. Then interchanging cell j_i with cell k_i results in assignment

$$B_N^{k_i} = \sum_{l=1}^{N_m} \frac{\lambda_1^l}{\Lambda} B_1^l(T^l).$$

By subtracting B^{k_i} from B^{j_i}, we obtain

$$B^{j_i} - B^{k_i} = \delta_i.$$

Repeating this procedure for S steps, we obtain

$$\sum_{i=1}^{S} \left[B^{j_i} - B^{k_i}\right] = \sum_{i=1}^{S} \delta_i,$$

which is positive. Thus, no index other than the index with the largest value of γ_i would results in the optimal solution. Hence, the proposed cell selection mechanism minimizes the value of B subject to the hard constraints (7) and results in the optimal solution.

3.1 Numerical Example

Consider a cellular system with clusters having 4 cells. Assume that a total of 80 full duplex channels are available in this system. The level of QoS for different classes are 0.05, 0.035, 0.02, and 0.01, respectively. The call arrival rates, which are normalized to the call holding time, are given in table 1. The result of algorithm 3 is given in table 2.

Table 1. The traffic parameters of cellular network

Cell	Λ_0	Λ_1	Λ_2	Λ_3
1	14	9	5	2
2	14	10	5	3
3	30	28	18	5
4	18	12	9	5

4 Conclusions

In this paper, we studied the problem of call admission control in the next generation cellular mobile networks, which supports multi-classes of services. We introduced a multi-threshold guard channel policy and derived blocking probabilities of the network. Then we proposed an optimal prioritized channel assignment for multi-class services multi-cellular networks.

Table 2. The result of channel assignment for multi-cell system

Cell	T_1 T_2 T_3 T_4	B_1	B_2	B_3	B_4
1	12 13 13 15	0.180902	0.025208	0.025208	0.002966
2	14 15 15 17	0.131336	0.023735	0.023735	0.00356
3	21 22 22 24	0.119553	0.024871	0.024871	0.004288
4	22 22 22 24	0.016902	0.016902	0.016902	0.002914

References

1. D. Hong and S. Rappaport, "Traffic Modelling and Performance Analysis for Cellular Mobile Radio Telephone Systems with Priotrized and Nonpriotorized Handoffs Procedure," *IEEE Transactions on Vehicular Technology*, vol. 35, pp. 77–92, Aug. 1986.
2. S. Oh and D. Tcha, "Priotrized Channel Assignment in a Cellular Radio Network," *IEEE Transactions on Communications*, vol. 40, pp. 1259–1269, July 1992.
3. R. Ramjee, D. Towsley, and R. Nagarajan, "On Optimal Call Admission Control in Cellular Networks," *Wireless Networks*, vol. 3, pp. 29–41, 1997.
4. G. Haring, R. Marie, R. Puigjaner, and K. Trivedi, "Loss Formulas and Their Application to Optimization for Cellular Networks," *IEEE Transactions on Vehicular Technology*, vol. 50, pp. 664–673, May 2001.
5. H. Beigy and M. R. Meybodi, "Uniform Fractional Guard Channel," in *Proceedings of Sixth World Multiconference on Systemmics, Cybernetics and Informatics, Orlando, USA*, July 2002.
6. S.-M. Senouci, A.-L. Beylot, and G. Pujolle, "A Dynamic Q-Learning-Based Call Admission Control for Multimedia Cellular Networks," in *Proceedings of the 3rd IEEE International Conference in Mobile and Wireless Communication Networks, MWCN'2001, Recife, Brazil*, pp. 37–43, Aug. 2001.
7. S.-M. Senouci, A.-L. Beylot, and G. Pujolle, "Call Admission Control for Multimedia Cellular Networks Using Neuro-Dynamic Programming," in *Proceedings of the IFIP Networking, NETWORKING'02, Pisa, Italy*, May 2002.
8. L. Yin, B. Li, Z. Zhang, and Y. Lin, "Performance analysis of a dual-threshold reservation (DTR) scheme for voice/data integrated mobile wireless networks ," in *Proceedings of the IEEE Wireless Communications and Networking Confernce, WCNC. 2000*, pp. 258–262, Sept. 2000.
9. H. Beigy and M. R. Meybodi, "An Optimal Prioritized Channel Assignment Scheme for Using in Mobile Transaction Environments," in *Proceedings of 8th Annual International Computer Society of Iran Computer Conference CSICC-2003, Mashhad, Iran*, pp. 66–74, Feb. 2003.
10. H. Beigy and M. R. Meybodi, "An Optimal Channel Assignment Scheme," in *Proceedings of 3th Iranian Conference on Electrical Engineering, ICEE-03, Shiraz, Iran*, vol. 2, pp. 634–641, 2003.
11. H. Beigy and M. R. Meybodi, "A General Call Admission Policy for Next Generation Wireless Networks," in *Accepted for Presentation and will be Appeared in Proceedings of the second International Symposium on Telecommunications (IST2003), Isfahan, Iran*, Aug. 2003.
12. H. Beigy and M. R. Meybodi, "A General Call Admission Policy for Next Generation Wireless Networks," Tech. Rep. TR-CE-2003-003, Computer Engineering Department, Amirkabir University of Technology, Tehran, Iran, 2003.

Application of Fiat-Shamir Identification Protocol to Design of a Secure Mobile Agent System

Seongyeol Kim[1], Okbin Lee[2], Yeijin Lee[3], Yongeun Bae[3], and Ilyong Chung[3*]

[1] School of Computer and Information, Ulsan College, Ulsan, 682-090, Korea
`kimsy@mail.ulsan-c.ac.kr`

[2] Dept. of Computer Science, Chungbuk University, Cheongju, 361-763, Korea
`lobin@mogent.net`

[3] Dept. of Computer Science, Chosun University, Kwangju, 501-759, Korea
`iyc@chosun.ac.kr`

Abstract. Even though an agent system contributes largely to mobile computing on distributed network environment, it has a number of significant security problems. In this paper, we analyze security attacks to this system presented by NIST[3]. In order to protect it from them, we suggest a security protocol for a mobile agent system by employing Identity-based key distribution and digital multi-signature scheme. To solve the problems described on NIST, securities of mobile agent and agent platform should be accomplished. Comparing with other protocols, our protocol performs both of these securities, while other protocols mention only one of them. Also, it is designed to guarantee the liveness of agent, and to detect message modification immediately by verifying the execution of agent correctly.

1 Introduction

Due to the progress of distributed technology[2] paradigms for drawing up network-based application have been gradually developed. Among these paradigms, the mobile agent paradigm extending the concept of Code-on-Demand model has drawn considerable attentions since it has many advantages from the aspects of system level, middleware and user-level.

In a mobile agent system, its executable code that is not depended upon a specific system performs tasks during traversal between systems. This system has characteristics of the mobile code executed in JAVA applet, and furthermore, has characteristics of travelling lots of systems and of being mobile in its own when needed. So it is more efficient than the previous models by providing low cost of communication, better asynchronous interaction, and improved flexibility. However, since it has to execute a code coming from the exterior system and this code is exposed thoroughly to the executing environment, this mobile agent system has been faced with serious security problems since the birth.

* Corresponding Author: Ilyong Chung (`iyc@chosun.ac.kr`)

A. Yazici and C. Şener (Eds.): ISCIS 2003, LNCS 2869, pp. 763–770, 2003.

In this paper, we analyze security attacks to this system presented by NIST[3]. To solve the problems described on NIST, securities of mobile agent and agent platforms should be accomplished. Vigna et al[4] presents a structure of protecting an agent by transmitting the execution status of agent to a verifier and this verifier would audit it. However, this method would be expensive since a significant amount of network resources would be utilized and execution codes would be expanded. Bennet et al[5] also proposes a Proof Verification, but it was evaluated to be inappropriate for application. In Baek et al[6], the problems seen in [4] and [5] can be solved. An agent is protected by performing a security system using routing information on a agent and information on execution status obtained from digital signatures and audit tools. However, a drawback of this method is that modification activities done by agents can be audited only at the final stage. Since immediate detection of these activities is not performed, a system can take unnecessary overheads and lengths of signature becomes longer owing to repeated usage of signature.

A few access methods to protect a mobile agent have been suggested - the first method that does not allow a sufficient amount of time for attackers to analyze the code[7], the second that encrypta an agent where it is located on the perfect environment TPE(tamper-proof environment)[8], the third that enables the execution of the agent encrypted with the key generated by time and environment of server[9]. Although a security protocol for a server against unauthorized agents was suggested while ignoring the danger of server to an agent[10], these systems do not provide mutual authentication between an agent and a server.

In this paper, we propose a new protocol to solve the security issues for mobile agent systems by employing the digital multi-signature and Identity-based key distribution scheme. In Identity(ID)-based cryptographic system, there are a public key ID and a secrete key that corresponds to this ID, where a secret key can be generated only at the key distribution center[11]. Since an ID is used as a public key, authentication of the public key is not needed. Furthermore, the electronic signature that plays an important role in an exchange of electronic document satisfies fixing signature length, allowing verification, detection of tampering, maintaining confidentiality and commonality[12], and has accomplished a multi-signature scheme. Also, our protocol can verify an interim signature and the number of communications for a signature is smaller.

2 Design of the Security Protocol for Mobile Agent Systems

The security protocol proposed in this paper obtains secure communications by using one-time password between hosts for each section through Identity-based key distribution rather than maintaining a public key directory. It generates multi-signature on the mobile code and verifies results of the previous step when migrating to next server. Then, the executable code and resulting data can be protected and unauthorized tampering can be detected in real time. Moreover, malicious disposal of agent and unauthorized copying can be detected by monitoring the migration condition of agent at the agent management center. Fig.1 illustrates an interaction of factors required for executing this protocol and Table 1 shows the notation used in this Chapter.

2.1 Registration (Agent-Server Registration and Key Distribution)

All agent platforms should be registered ahead in order to execute services in mobile agent systems. When a request of registration from an AP is called, the AMC generates a key according to the following method, distributes it to agent platforms and registers it.

(1) Select two large prime numbers, p and q, and calculate N = p × q.
(2) Compute $\varphi(N)$ = (p-1)(q-1) and e with gcd(e, $\varphi(N)$) = 1.
(3) Compute d with ed = 1 mod $\varphi(N)$.
(4) Select g that is a primitive root both in $GF(p) and GF(q)$.
(5) Compute the values S_i and S_{ij} $(1 \leq j \leq k)$, k_{ix} for AP_i.

$S_i = {AP_i}^d$ mod N
I_{ij} = f(AP$_i$, j) ($j = 1, 2, ..., k$)
${I_{ij}}^{-1} = {S_{ij}}^2$ mod N, $(\exists\, I_{ij},\ \ I_{ij} \in QR_N)$[1]
k_{ix} , where $1 \leq k_{ix} \leq k$, $I_{ij} \in QR_N$

(6) Register AP_i at the agent-sever DB and store p, q securely
(7) Distribute the key using smart card containing the following factors

$$(N, e, g, S_i, f, h, S_{i1}, ..., S_{ik}, k_{i1}, ..., k_{ix}, AP_1, ..., AP_m, AMC)$$

$k_{i1}, .., k_{ix}$ is a series of j that ${I_{ij}}^{-1}$ is a quadratic residue. When the key is renewed in the future, a new key is received using this session key between AP_i and the AMC and the smart card key is updated.

2.2 CreateAgent

When a agent is created at the homeplace, the AP$_H$ let the AMC inform this creation and conduct security management. For these purposes, the procedure is designed as follows.

(1) The migration path of agent is generated as follows.
A_route = AP$_1$ ∥ AP$_2$ ∥ ... ∥ AP$_n$
(2) A sign value is setup with executable code of agent and multi-signature which are yet null state.
A_sign = H$_H$ = f(A_code) A_code, A_sign ∈ MA
(3) $k_{H,AMC}$ is created by generating a session key shared with AMC according to registration process.

[1] quadratic residue for modulus N

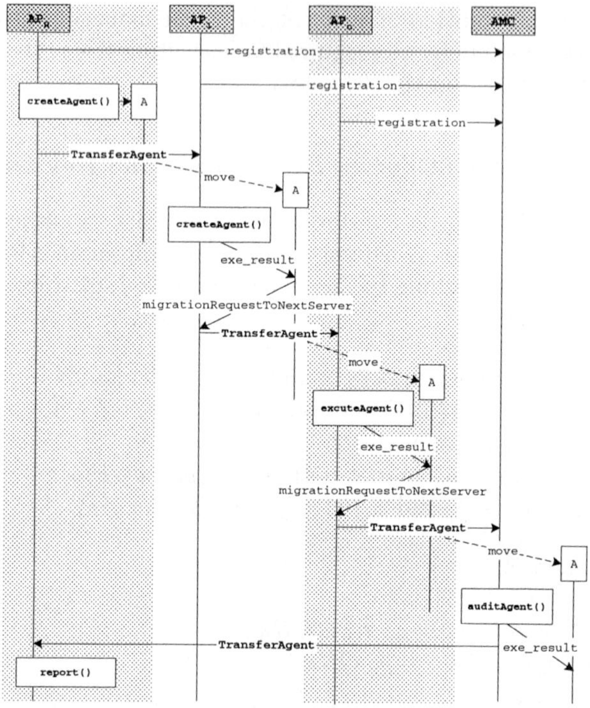

Fig. 1. Interaction of factors required for execution

(4) $k_{H,1}$ shared with AP_1 in which an agent is executed for the first time, is created.

(5) Agent code and path information are sent to the AMC as follows.
$AP_H \rightarrow AMC : E_{k_{H,AMC}}(MA\ ,\ t1_H)$

(6) A signature is generated as follows.

$$X_H = R_H{}^2 \bmod N$$
$$(e_{H1}\ , \ldots\ , e_{Hk}\ ) = h\ (A\_route,\ A\_exe\_results,\ H_H\ ,\ X_H)$$
$$Y_H = R_H \prod_{e_{Hj}=1} S_{Hj} \bmod N\ ,\quad j = 1, 2, \ldots, k$$
$$A\_sign = (H_H,\ X_H,\ k_H,\ Y_H)\ ,\quad A\_sign \in MA$$

(7) AP_H transmits the data to AP_1.
$AP_H \rightarrow AP_1 : E_{k_{H,1}}\ (MA\ ,\ t1_H)$

Generation of a session key between AP_i and AP_j. The session key of AP_i and AP_j is generated by applying Diffie-Hellman key exchange method.

(1) AP_i selects a random number $R_i \in Z_N$.

(2) AP_i calculates C_i and send it to AP_j.
$C_i = g^{R_i} \bmod N$

Table 1. Notatio used in this protocol

Notations	Explanation
AMC	Agent Management Center
AP_i	ID of the i th agent platform on migration path of agent
AP_H	Home Place of Agent
MA	Mobile Agent. This is a set of { A_name , A_code , A_route , A_exe_results , A_sign }
A_route	Migration Path of Agent
A_name	Name of Agent
A_exe_results	Result of executing an agent
A_code	Executable code of Agent
A_sign	multi-signature for result of executing an agent
f , h	public unilateral function
Hm	Hash values of agent code created by APm
$k_{i,j}$	Session key between AP_i and AP_j
Ek(M)	Message M is encrypted with the key k
R_i	The random number generated by AP_i
$R_{i,j}$	The random number generated by AP_i to transmit to AP_j
$t1_i$, $t2_i$	Timestamp generated by AP_i

(3) After AP_j selects a random number R_j, calculates C_j and send it to AP_i.
$C_j = g^{R_j} \bmod N$

(4) AP_i computes the session key shared with AP_j
$k_{i,j} = (C_j)^{R_i} \bmod N = g^{R_i \cdot R_j} \bmod N$

(5) AP_j computes the session key shared with , as follows.
$k_{i,j} = (C_i)^{R_j} \bmod N = g^{R_i \cdot R_j} \bmod N$

2.3 ExecuteAgent

When an agent migrates to AP_{i+1} , a host treats this agent as one thread.

(1) AP_i executes a mobile agent and then it makes $\log_i$, and renews A_exe_results

$\log_i = E_{k_{i,AMC}}$ (A_exe_results$_i$, $t2_i$)
A_exe_results$_i$ = A_exe_results$_{i-1}$ || $\log_i$

The results of execution should be protected from other agent platforms and finally be verified by the AMC.

(2) A signature is made as follows.

$R_i \in Z_N$
$X_i = {R_i}^2 X_{i-1} \bmod N$, $(i = 1, 2, \ldots, k)$
$(e_{il}, \ldots, e_{ik})$ = h(A_route, A_exe_results$_i$, X_i, H_H)
$$Y_i = Y_{i-1} R_i \prod_{e_{ij}=1} S_{ij} \bmod N \ , \ (j = 1, 2, \ldots, k)$$
A_sign = $(H_H, X_H, k_H, X_1, k_1, X_2, k_2, \ldots, X_i, k_i, Y_i)$

2.4 TransferAgent

When an agent is transmitted at AP_H, or a migration request made at AP_i and an agent migrates to AP_{i+1}, TransferAgent procedure is accomplished between AP_i(or AP_H) and AP_{i+1}. It is designed to guarantee that no security problems have occurred in agent's performance.

(1) $AP_{i,i+1}$, the session key of AP_i and AP_{i+1}, is generated.
(2) AP_{i+1} to receive an agent generates the session key $k_{i+1,AMC}$ shared with the AMC.
(3) AP_i transmits the sign for results of execution and agent code to AP_{i+1}.
$AP_i \rightarrow AP_{i+1} : E_{k_{i,i+1}}(MA, t1_i)$
(4) AP_{i+1} can verify the signature written by previous AP as follows.

$$I_{xj} = f(AP_x, j),\ (x = 1, 2, \ldots, i\ ,\ j = 1, 2, \ldots, k)$$
$$(e_{i1}, \ldots, e_{ik}) = h(A\_route,\ A\_exe\_results_i,\ X_i,\ H_H)$$
$$X_i = Y_i^2 \prod_{x=1}^{i} \prod_{e_{ij}=1} I_{xj} \bmod N,\ (j = 1, 2, \ldots, k)$$

If X_i obtained from the fourth step of this procedure is equal to X_i in A_sign, the result would be effective.
(5) When the verification is correct, AP_{i+1} execute this agent, but if incorrect, AP_{i+1} reports immediately to the AMC.

2.5 AuditAgent

The AMC knows the migration path according to $AP_H \rightarrow AMC : E_{k_{H,AMC}}(MA, t2_H)$ performed at the procedure of CreateAgent. Moreover, each time an agent migrates, a session key is shared with AP_i , the AMC can detect it until an agent stop. When an agent normally travels the planned path and arrives at the AMC, the entire processes of signing can be verified as follows.

$$I_{ij} = f(AP_i, j)$$
$$(e_{i1}, \ldots, e_{ik}) = h(A\_route,\ A\_exe\_results_i,\ X_i,\ H_H)$$
$$X_i = Y_i^2 \prod_{x=1}^{i} \prod_{e_{ij}=1} I_{ij} \bmod N,\ ,\ (x = 1, 2, \ldots, n\ ,\ j = 1, 2, \ldots, k)$$

Since $A\_exe\_results = log_1 \parallel \ldots \parallel log_n$ and $log_i = E_{k_{i,AMC}}(A\_exe\_result, t1_i)$, the result of execution recorded by each server can be deciphered. And then this deciphered data is ciphered with $k_{H,AMC}$ and transmitted to home. Finally, the mobile agent reports to home and terminates execution.

3 Analysis of the Proposed Protocol

Table 2 shows analysis of our protocol compared with other schemes such as Hole method[7], Whlhelm-Stamann method[8], Riordan-Schneier method[9], Baek method[6], in terms of security features.

Table 2. Table of session key in AMC

schemes / matters	[7]	[8]	[9]	[6]	proposed protocol
protection method	time limited and code mixture	hardware	environmetal key	repeated simple signature	information hiding and muli-signature
cryptography method	asynchronous	asynchronous	asynchronous	asynchronous	synchronous by ID key
authentication method	unidirectional	unidirectional	unidirectional	unidirectional	bidirectional
liveness	×	×	×	partially supported	○
confidentiality	○	○	○	not described but supported	○
integrity	×	×	×	not described but supported	○
preventing repudiation	×	×	×	○	○
The result of execution is opened	oepn	open	open	open	secret

Our protocol can satisfy security requirements - bi-directional authentication, confidentiality, integrity and nonrepudiation and solves the drawback of [6], which constructs a long signature. It is designed to take measures when an illegal tampering against an agent occurred. Employing this scheme, it is able to protect an agent and data efficiently and to guarantee the liveness of an agent.

4 Conclusions

In this paper, we propose the security protocol for a mobile agent system using Identity-based on key distribution and Fiat-Shamir digital signature in order to authenticate between agent and server, to protect the resulting data, and to guarantee liveness of an agent. It is able to do interim verification so that it would not have unnecessary overheads. Identity-based cryptography can be applied in key distribution and digital signature, and have advantages of simplification of key management and of fast signature compared with the public key mechanism. The following are the summary of the characteristics of the proposed protocol. The first characteristic is the structure of simplifying key management. This not only can overcome problems related to directory management for the public key mechanism but also has an advantage to setup a new onetime session key every time. Secondly, it provides security services - authentication, confidentiality, integrity, and nonrepudiation and prevention of replay attack. In this system, one's own data is never exposed to any other APs by ciphering execution result. Each AP can confirm integrity of agent code, path information, and status information through a verification process before it executes the arrived agent. It immediately reports to the AMC in case that some problems occur. And the repudiation service can be offered by using digital signature. Thirdly, liveness of an agent can be guaranteed. The AMC receives A_route generated by each AP at every hop of agent migration and then the AMC monitors unauthorized termination done by an arbitrary AP. Fourth, the result of execution should be protected. Problems related to agent behaviors by reading the results of execution obtained from previous steps or by modifying them illegeally are solved.

This security model premises that an agent will migrate along the planned path. Later this method, if the mobile platform is determined at the time of migration, should consider management of locations for remote access and recording an active list of APs.

References

1. Dale, J. and Mamdani, E., "Open Standards for Interoperating Agent-Based Systems," In Software FOCUS, Wiley, 2001.
2. Poslad, S. and Calisti, M., "Towards Improved Trust and Security in FIPA Agent Platforms," Autonomous Agents 2000 Workshop on Deception, Fraud and Trust in Agent Societies, Spain, 2000.
3. Jansen, W. and Karygiannis, T., "Mobile Agent Security," NIST Special Publication 800–19, 1998.
4. Vigna, G., "Protecting Mobile Agents through Tracing," Mobile Object Systems ECOOP Workshop, 1997.
5. Bennet, S. Y., "A Sanctuary for Mobile Agents," DARPA Workshop on Foundations for Secure Mobile Code Workshop, pp.26–28, 1997.
6. Baek, J. and Lee, D., "Security of Mobile Agent Using Digital Signature and Audit trail," Proc. of KISS Fall Conference, Vol. 24, No.2, KISS, 1997.
7. Hohl, F., "An approach to solve the problem of malicious hosts," Universitat Stuttgart, Fakultat Informatik, Fakultatsbericht Nr., 1997.3.
8. Wilhelm, U. G. and Stamann, S., "Protecting the Itinerary of Mobile Agents." Proc. of the ECOOP Workshop on Distributed Object Security, pp.135–145, INRIA, France, 1998.
9. Riordan, J. and Schneier, B., "Environmental Key Generation towards Clueless Agents," Mobile Agents and Security, pp.15–24, Springer-Verlag, 1998.
10. Ordille, J., "When agents roam, who can you trust?," Proc. of the First Conference on Emerging Technologies and Applications in Communications, Porland, May 1996.
11. Shamir, A., Identity-based cryptosystem and signature scheme," Advances in Cryptology, Springer-Verlag, pp.47–57, 1985.
12. Kim, S. and Won, D., "A Study on the Special Digital Signature Systems," KIISC, Vol.6, No.2, pp.21–32, 1996.
13. Gang, C., "A study on the digital multisignature scheme and applications," Ph.D. dissertation, Chungnam National Univ., Taejon, Korea, 1993.

Neural Network Based Optical Network Restoration with Multiple Classes of Traffic

Demeter Gökışık and Semih Bilgen

Electrical and Electronics Engineering Department, METU, Ankara, 06531 Turkey.
Phone: +90 312 210 2319 Fax: +90 312 210 1261
demeter_gokisik@yahoo.com bilgen@metu.edu.tr

Abstract. Neural-network-based optical network restoration is illustrated over an example in which multiple classes of traffic are considered. Over the pre-planned primary and backup capacity, optimal routing and wavelength assignment is carried out. In case of a network failure, protection routes and optimum flow values on these protection routes are extracted from a previously trained feed-forward neural network which is distributed over the optical data communications network.

Keywords: optical networks, wavelength division multiplexing, restoration, neural networks.

1 Introduction

Optical networks provide a large communication capacity which needs to be managed effectively. Restoration of failed facilities after network failures is a significant problem of network management.

The purpose of this work is to illustrate the operation of a neural-network-based restoration method [1, 2] over an example that involves traffic from two classes of security (secure – insecure) and three classes of reliability (path protected, link protected and unprotected). The restoration method combines a previously defined distributed routing algorithm [3] with needs introduced for different types of users in terms of security restrictions and survivability needs.

2 Spare Capacity Assignment

User specific static optimal design of a %100 mesh survivable optical network is handled using Integer Linear Programming. The basic approach is similar to that proposed by [4] but here, traffic that belongs to all three classes of reliability and secure as well as insecure users is aggregated.

2.1 Input Parameters

Peak Demand Values of Users. Maximum number of sessions that can be requested between each network node is input to the system.

A. Yazici and C. Şener (Eds.): ISCIS 2003, LNCS 2869, pp. 771–778, 2003.

Reliability Classification of Users. Users will specify their reliability needs demanding link protection (which implies that traffic on a failed link will be restored using alternative connections between its two end-points), path protection (which implies that traffic on an end-to-end path that has become inoperable due to any link failure, will be restored using alternative paths between the end-points of the failed path) or best effort failure recovery for which no capacity is arranged before failure. Restored traffic will be routed on paths with different lengths depending on the class to which the user belongs. Restoration times will also depend on user classes.

Failure Type. Single link failures are considered only. It is assumed that cost-effective restoration of single link failures is sufficient essentially due to asynchronous failure characteristics. From a practical point of view, it is clear that restorability of multiple link failures simultaneously would increase overall network cost. Single link failures will be sensed by the WDM layer upon loss of light.

Security Classification of Users. Users are categorized as secure and insecure according to their security properties. Insecure user protection paths are forbidden to traverse the nodes equipped with optical amplifiers if these nodes are traversed by secure protection traffic.

2.2 Minimized and Evaluated Items

Cost of Spare and Working Capacity. Working and spare capacity needed for supplying %100 restoration to demanding users and satisfying peak user requirements will be minimized. The designed network will satisfy peak requirements of different types of users. In capacity calculations, stub release which is the usage of channels on unbroken links of the failed paths is taken care of. User groups generating secure and insecure traffic and requiring different protection levels as path protection, link protection and no protection are introduced. Primary path selection divides the requested sessions equally between shortest paths. Insecure traffic can not traverse predetermined nodes which are equipped with optical amplifiers.

3 Restoration Applying Multi Layer Feed-Forward Neural Network

The method considered here depends on keeping the information needed for restoration in the network, in compressed form utilizing the abilities of multi layer feed-forward networks for data compression and generalization. The basic characteristics of the approach are as follows:

- Input to the first layer (input) neurons in an OXC in case of any single link failure consists of:

- Identification of failed link (2 neurons)
- Demand units in path protected connections initiated by this OXC that are lost due to the failure. (One neuron for secure sessions and one neuron for insecure sessions

per affected demand pair considering all demand pairs starting from this node; adds up to 2*3 = 6 neurons for the case in Fig. 1.)

- If the failing link is attached to this OXC, demand units that are lost in link protected connections, initiated by any OXC. (The same neurons as in the previous paragraph, implying that for the case in Fig. 1, only 8 input neurons are sufficient.)

• Output from the final layer (output) neurons at a node consists of :

- Restoration path ids as determined in spare capacity planning. (One neuron per restoration path.)
- Secure and insecure demand units restored on this path (2 neurons per restoration path)

• The number of hidden neurons per OXC is determined by trial and error as the minimum that enables proper training convergence. (Only one is sufficient for the case in Fig. 1.)
• For propagation delays during protection path selection, a duration will be predefined for data to settle down between neurons.
• Only single link failures are considered so the network is not trained for generalizing from trained inputs but for memorizing and compressing optimum protection route and flow data.
• No extra communication links are required for signaling among OXCs. The existing links including planned spare capacity will be sufficient for distribution of failure alarm indication signals and neuron outputs.

In Fig. 1, the big circles denote OXCs, the inner square nodes represent input neurons related with that Label Switch Router(LSR)/OXC interface, the inner circular nodes are hidden layer neurons related with the overall operation of the network and the inner elliptical nodes represent output neurons related with the operation of that LSR/OXC interface.

As a link failure occurs, the closest OXCs will notice the failure first because of light loss and they will broadcast an indication frame to inform other OXCs.

Details of operation have been explained elsewhere [1, 2].For the network in Fig. 1, capacity is designed for maximum 2 secure and 2 insecure path protected sessions between the nodes. Primary path selection divides the requested sessions equally between shortest paths. Insecure traffic can not traverse node 1 as it is equipped with optical amplifiers, but it may start or end in it.

4 Restoration Performance

Minimum Congestion Routing Algorithm (MCgR) [3] is employed for routing and wavelength assignment. MCgR is a distributed algorithm which proceeds by broadcasting shortest paths computed by each node to each destination. The number of available channels on each link, as well as the total number of nodes and available wavelength converters along a path are used for calculating path costs in determining shortest paths. Wavelength conversion requirement is minimized by McGR during working path selection. Full wavelength conversion capacity is assumed for restoration path wavelength assignment. Number of wavelengths that would be sufficient for primary paths is precalculated and deployed in the network for operation where primary path selection divides the requested sessions equally between shortest paths. Spare capacity needed for supplying %100 restoration to demanding users and satisfying peak user requirements is minimized.

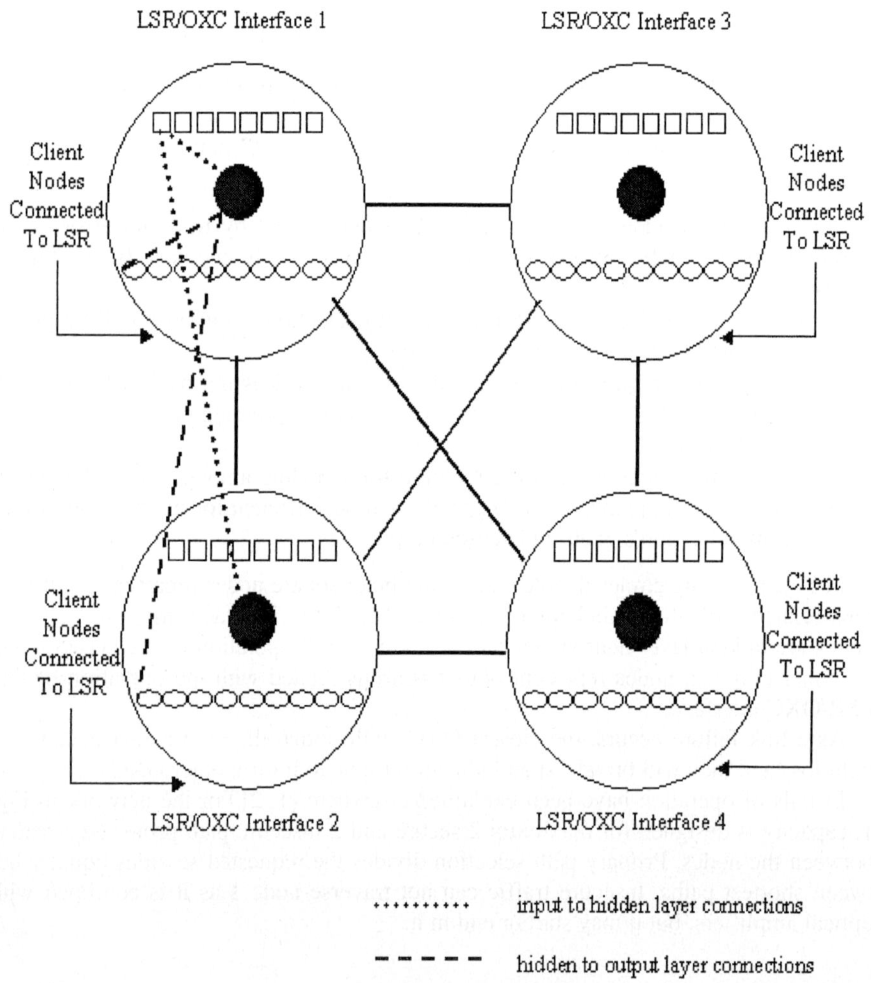

Fig. 1. 4-Node Sample Network Topology

The feed-forward neural network is trained using Levenberg-Marquardt back-propagation training method. Training is managed offline and the weights obtained are deployed in the network. Restoration employing 3-layer feed-forward neural network has been evaluated over various networks [1, 2]. For the network in Fig. 2, ca pacity was designed to be sufficient for a maximum of two path protected secure and two path protected insecure sessions between the pairs. Results in Table 1 are obtained with simulation.

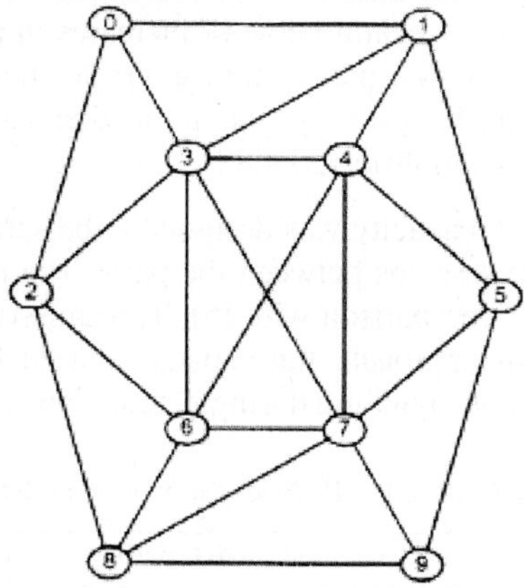

Fig. 2. 10-Node Sample Network Topology

Table 1. Restoration Performance for 10-Node Network with Secure and Insecure Sessions

Parameter Name	Parameter Setting	Simulation Result
Session interarrival time at a node	200 s	
Signal transmission rate	140 Mbps	
Propagation speed	c	
Link Length	1000 km	
Assumed protocol logic overhead at a node	0	
Nodes equipped with optical amplifiers	0,4,8	
Neural Network Configuration	# input neurons per node : 20 # hidden layer neurons per node : 2 # output neurons per node : 36 neuron transfer function : sigmoid	
Physical network redundancy	0.40	
Average primary path length for secure path protected traffic		1.74 hops
Average restoration path length for secure path protected traffic		3.66 hops
Average primary path length for insecure path protected traffic		1.74 hops
Average restoration path length for insecure path protected traffic		4.22 hops
Restorability for single link failures		%100
Restoration path finding duration		96.66 ms
Total data communicated for neural network operation in case of a single link failure		(# input neurons per network node + # hidden layer neurons per node) * (float size) * (number of nodes) = (20+2)*4*10 = 880 Bytes

Presence of insecure demand increases the information that must be taught to the neural network, and the size of neural network increases in number of neurons in the layers. Insecure traffic restoration path length is greater than the secure traffic path length because insecure traffic primary and protection paths can not traverse the nodes equipped with optical amplifiers, 0,4,8 for this case.

For the network in Fig.2, capacity was designed to be sufficient for a maximum of two path protected, secure sessions between the pairs. The results in Table 2 are obtained with simulation, for comparison with [5]. Transmission rate is still taken to be 140 Mbps, because in our approach, the capacity placed for restoration can completely be used for restoration signaling during neural network operation.

Table 2. Restoration Performance for 10-Node Network with Settings Comparable to [5]

Parameter Name	Parameter Setting	Simulation Result
Signal transmission rate	140 Mbps	
Propagation speed	0.6 c	
Link Length	1 km	
Assumed protocol logic overhead at a node	0	
Neural Network Configuration	# input neurons per network node : 11 # hidden layer neurons per network node : 1 # output neurons per network node : 12 neuron transfer function : sigmoid	
Physical network redundancy	0.27	
Average primary path length for path protected traffic		1.74 hops
Average restoration path length for path protected traffic		3.66 hops
Restorability for single link failures		%100
Restoration path finding duration		3 times total propagation and transmission delays : 3*9*(1km / 0.6c + 250 μs) = 3*9*(5.5 μs + 250 μs) = 6.88 ms
Total data communicated for neural network operation in case of a single link failure		(# input neurons per network node + # hidden layer neurons per node) * (float size) * (number of nodes) = (11+1)*4*10 = 480 Bytes

5 Method Evaluation

The proposed method is evaluated as follows:

Data kept at network nodes for optimum backup path finding is embedded in a feed-forward neural network distributed over the data communications network. In case of a failure, neurons distributed over the data communications network must cooperate. This causes all nodes in the data communication network become critical in a degree directly proportional to the number of hidden layer neurons they have. This situation is healed by the fact that a feed-forward neural network has redundant capacity. Furthermore, the functioning of a neuron is not affected by the state of neurons to which it is not connected. Depending on different neural network topologies, importance of each network node may be controlled.

Table 3. Restoration Performance Reported in [5] for 10-Node Network

Parameter Name	**Parameter Setting**	**Results Reported in [5]**
Signal transmission rate	64 kbps	
Propagation speed	0.6 c	
Link Length	1 km	
Protocol logic overhead at a node	0.5 –1 ms	
Physical network redundancy [5]	0.27	
Restorability for single link failures [5]		%100
Restoration path finding duration [5]		Minimum: 28 ms Average: 78.66 ms Maximum: 235 ms

As the restoration path finding duration is directly related to the maximum total processing and link delays in the network, it is bounded and reasonable. Every node keeps the part of overall neural network that is directly related to its operation, thus processing is distributed among network nodes.

Restoration path finding phase necessitates that all type of demands (i.e. path protected, link protected, secure and insecure) wait for equal amount of time until nodes determine protection paths directly related to themselves. That is why there can be no service differentiation for these different traffic types considering the time elapsed until protection paths are found.

Application can be generalized to different routing schemes different capacity design approaches.

Data kept in the network is compressed. Data compression capabilities of feed-forward neural networks have been exemplified in the literature [6].

Utilization of neural networks for data storage and extraction makes easier to reach the protection route and flow data in comparison to a global search in a database especially when the number of parameters that specialize the protection route increase (i.e further detailed client types) [6].

For neural network communication, spare capacity placed during the capacity calculation phase is used. These links are used for restored traffic after the neural network operation is completed. Furthermore, the multi layer feed-forward network exhibits a great degree of robustness or fault tolerance because of built-in redundancy. Damage to a few neurons or links thus need not impair overall performance significantly [7].

Neural network sizing may be a problem depending on the training method and capacity of tool used. As training is a one-time effort to be spent prior to operation, this is not considered to be a critical limitation.

6 Conclusions

Different user requirements including security levels, optical channel level path protected, link protected, and best effort failure recovery cases are handled both in terms of capacity planning and dynamic distributed routing and restoration.

Users with different security characteristics that define a constraint on nodes traversed are taken care of in two different groups of secure and insecure users.

References

1. D.Gökışık, Distributed Restoration in Optical Networks Using Feed-Forward Neural Networks, PhD Thesis, Middle East Technical University, January 2003
2. D.Gökışık, S.Bilgen, "Distributed Restoration in Optical Networks Using Feed-Forward Neural Networks", Submitted to Optical Network Management , Kluwer, 2003
3. O.Başbuğoğlu, S.Bilgen, "A Distributed Minimal Congestion Routing Algorithm for WDM Networks, " ISCIS XIV, pp.18–20, October 1999
4. R.Irachko, M.H.McGregor, "Optimal Capacity Placement for Path Restoration in STN or ATM Mesh Survivable Networks," IEEE/ACM Transactions on Networking, Vol.6, No.3, pp.325–336, June 1998
5. R.Iraschko, W.D.Grover, "A Highly Efficient Path-Restoration Protocol for Management of Optical Network Transport Integrity," IEEE Journal on Selected Areas in Communications, Vol. 18 No.5, pp.779–794, May 2000
6. M.R.Berthold, F.Sudweeks, S.Newton, R.Coyne, "Clustering on the Net: Applying an autoassociative neural network to computer-mediated discussions," http://jcmc.huji.ac.il/vol2/issue4/berthold.html#Berthold97
7. M.S.Chen, "Analysis and Design of Multi Layer Perceptron Using Polynomial BasisFunctions," PHD submitted to University of Texas, Arlington, 1996

Network Level Congestion Control in Mobile Wireless Networks: 3G and Beyond

Seungcheon Kim

Dept. of Information and Communication Engineering, Hansung University, Seoul, Korea.
iluqu@hotmail.com

Abstract. The key problem that is expected in the future mobile wireless networks is related with the mobility effect on the network data traffic, which may cause the performance degradation and congestion. This paper explores the mobility effect on the delay and congestion when the future mobile wireless networks have become the whole IP based networks and introduces a network level congestion control based on the Explicit Congestion Notification (ECN) broadcasting in the wireless sub networks. The simulation results are provided to show the performance improvement when the proposed scheme's adopted.

1 Introduction

The future mobile wireless networks, or 3G and beyond mobile wireless networks are expected to provide the mobile multimedia services supporting user mobility fully based on Mobile IP [1][2]. When the mobile wireless network has become IP switched, more sophisticated network control mechanisms are necessary to guarantee the quality of multimedia services considering the mobility effect on the network [3][4].

When it comes to the traffic management in the mobile wireless networks, currently we don't have any other choices rather than relying on the window control of the end host to regulate their data rate in case of congestion. Related to TCP improvement in the wireless networks, some methods like Snoop, I-TCP and Fast Retransmit etc [5], have been proposed. However, even though they are all focusing on the improvement of TCP in the wireless networks, they are mainly dealing with the retransmission task of TCP. That means all of those works rarely resolve the congestion in the wireless networks. In the wireless environment, where the mobile station moves around, we need something more to catch and react on congestion in addition to the TCP window control [6].

Having that in mind, a network level congestion control scheme in the mobile wireless networks is introduced with an exploration about the mobility effect on the delay and congestion. Then the simulation results are introduced to see the performance improvement and the increase of the network stability when the proposed scheme's adopted.

A. Yazici and C. Şener (Eds.): ISCIS 2003, LNCS 2869, pp. 779–785, 2003.

2 Mobility Effect on Delay and Congestion

When we think about the number of mobile stations in a certain subnet at time '*t*', we can say that the subnet is composed of two types of mobile stations, one of which is the mobile station that continues to communicate in that subnet from the first time when it started to communicate. The other one is the mobile station that comes from other subnet and still holds the connection. Let's call the former as a resident mobile station and the latter as a migratory mobile station. Assuming that the number of migratory mobile stations is proportional with the probability '*p*', the number of resident mobile stations is proportional with the probability '*1-p*'. Thus we can say the number of mobile stations in a certain subnet, N_t, is described like this.

$$N_t = pN_t + (1-p)N_t$$

And the average data arrival rate will be $\lambda_t = \lambda_i N_t$ in case that the data rate of each mobile station is λ_i. The response time of the mobile station is different depending on the mobile station's type. For example, if a mobile station comes from other subnet, it will have the increased return path and the response time will increase. If the mobile station is staying in the subnet originally, then the response time will be shorter than the migratory one's. Considering these, we can say that the response time distribution in a certain subnet can be described like this.

$$f_\tau(x) = p\mu_1 e^{-\mu_1 x} + (1-p)\mu_2 e^{-\mu_2 x}$$

In this equation, μ_1 represent the average response time of the migratory mobile station with the probability of p and μ_2 is for the resident mobile station with the probability of *1-p*.

For the calculation of the average response time of the mobile station in the subnet, we can use *M/G/1* queuing and the average service time will be shown like this.

$$E[T] = E[\tau] + \frac{\lambda E[\tau^2]}{2(1-\lambda E[\tau])} \tag{1}$$

$$E[\tau] = \int_0^\infty x f_\tau(x)dx = \frac{p}{\mu_1} + \frac{1-p}{\mu_2} \tag{2}$$

$$E[\tau^2] = \int_0^\infty x^2 f_\tau(x)dx = 2\left(\frac{p}{\mu_1^2} + \frac{1-p}{\mu_2^2}\right) \tag{3}$$

From the equations (1), (2) and (3), we can get the average response time of the mobile stations as shown in the Fig. 1. To get this result, the average response times of mobile stations in the subnet are assumed as 0.1 second for the migratory mobile stations and 0.01second for the resident mobile stations.

As shown in Fig. 1, we can see that the average response time of the mobile station in the subnet is growing as the whole data arrival rate increases and the probability of the migratory mobile station in the subnet increases, which can be explained by the triangular route of the mobile station. [2] In the situation that the response time increases, it becomes very hard for the mobile station to regulate its data rate according to the TCP ACK/NAK and also the probability of the congestion will

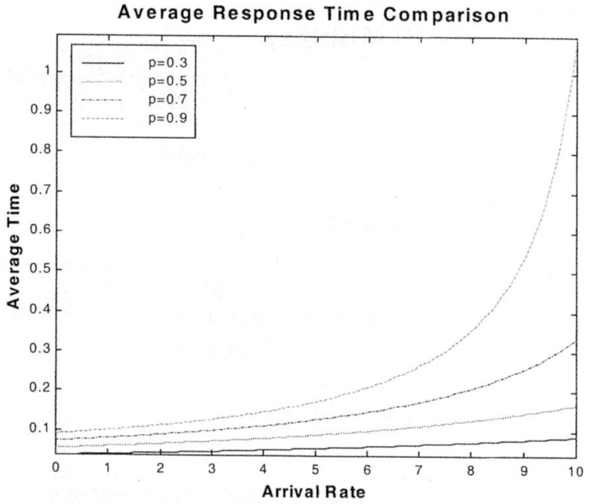

Fig. 1. Average response time with variation of the migratory mobile stations

increase mostly in the connecting routers. It can also be interpreted that the average response time of the whole traffic in a subnet is mainly affected by the data rate and the probability of the migratory mobile stations in the subnet.

As a result we need a subsidiary congestion control mechanism in the mobile access subnet in addition to TCP's window control. That scheme must prevent the mobile subnet from going into congestion and help all the mobile stations to keep as much performance as the subnet can support.

3 ECN Broadcasting in Local Sub-networks

The very good candidate for the congestion control in the mobile wireless networks can be the Explicit Congestion Notification (ECN) [7], which is now being considered to be used in Internet. The ECN provides a mechanism for intermediate routers to send early congestion feedback to the source before actual packet losses happen. The routers monitor their queue length. If the queue length exceeds a threshold, the router marks the Congestion Experienced bit in the IP header. Upon the reception of a marked packet, the receiver marks the ECN Echo bit in the TCP header of the acknowledgement to send the congestion feedback back to the source. Then the source can reduce the data rate on receiving the message.

However, in the mobile wireless networks, where the mobility can affect the delay and the congestion as shown in the previous section, the return path of the mobile station can be varied. Mostly the return path of the migratory mobile stations will increase because the returning packets will take the detour to the source. And the easily congested part of the mobile wireless networks would be the sub domain router (SDR) or the foreign agent (FA) router. When it experiences congestion, all

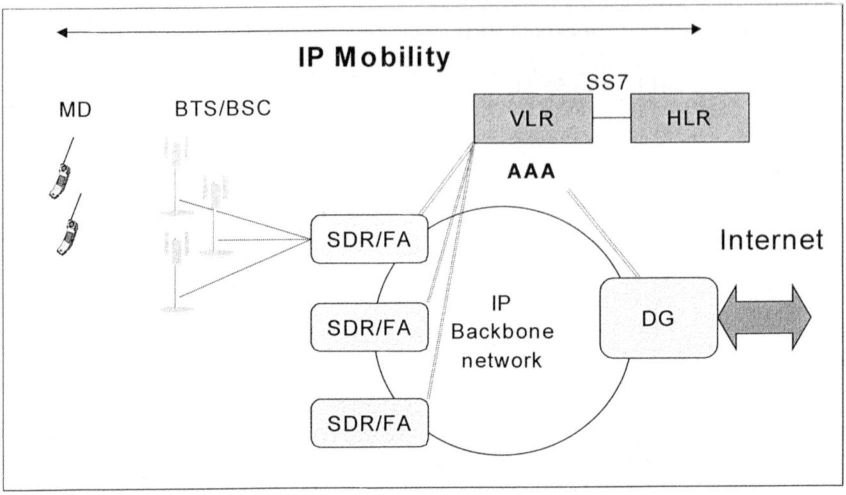

MD: Mobile Device
BTS: Base transceiver system
BSC: Base station controller
FS: Frame selection

SDR/FA: Sub domain router/Foreign agent
DG/HA: Domain gateway/Home agent
HLR: Home location register
VLR: Visitor location register
AAA: Authentication authorization accounting server

Fig. 2. Future Mobile Wireless Network Architecture

destinations that have received packets passing through it have to return a message to the each source to inform the congestion. Consequently ECN alone cannot be effective in resolving congestion in the mobile wireless networks.

Here, we propose the ECN broadcasting SDR or FA of the wireless access network. The future mobile wireless networks will be composed of mobile access networks as shown in Fig.2. And each access network is managed by SDR or FA. When the ECN broadcasting is adopted in SDR or FA, the congestion information can be broadcasted on the congestion of the corresponding local access network. For an example, if the congestion happened in the local access network, that information could be returned to the mobile station after the corresponding receiver of each mobile station sent the packet with congestion experienced bit set. That will definitely cause the performance degradation of the communication in the local wireless access network. However, if the ECN is broadcasted in the local wireless network using backward congestion radio channel, all the mobile stations could react on congestion promptly no matter how long the return path of each mobile station is. In addition, the broadcasting is an advantageous feature in wireless radio network and IP network.

4 Simulation Results

Simulations are done with OPNET MIL3 v6.0. In the simulations, we assumed that all the data traffic of the wireless subnet goes to Internet through the SDR or FA that can deal with traffic amount to Internet with a bandwidth allowance and manage the mobility with the ability of forwarding the data to the corresponding mobile terminals. And the all mobile terminals are assumed to have the sliding window and slow start to regulate the traffic amount of the end terminal based on the time-out and NAK received. The response time of the migratory mobile station is assumed to be delayed in Internet due to the mobility support based on Mobile IP. All other simulation details are followings.

- Link Speed: 10Kbps
- SR/FA router Buffer Size: 10 packets
- One way packet delivery time of mobile station: 1sec
- Packet return time of a migratory mobile station: 3sec
- Max. window size in sliding window: 64 packets
- Source data rate: 0.1~10 packets/s
- Packet time-out in sliding window: 5sec
- ECN threshold in SR/FA router: 7packets
- Proportional variation of the new and existing mobile stations: 0.1~0.9

Figure (a) and (b) in Fig.3 show the throughput comparisons between when the ECN broadcasting is adopted and when only ECN is adopted. From each result, we can see that the throughput has been improved when ECN broadcasting is adopted. This improvement was found mostly after the congestion was encountered around 1 packet/sec of source data rate, which shows the proposed ECN broadcasting scheme has performed more properly after the congestion.

The packet drop rate in SDR/FA with only ECN goes up sharply as source data rate increases as shown in Fig.3 (d). Instead when the ECN broadcasting is adopted, the packet drop rate in SDR/FA is relatively low as in Fig.3 (d) and this can be managed by handling the threshold of ECN in the SDR/FA router buffer. Therefore, we can expect that the mobile subnet that is linked through one SDR/FA to the Internet can be more stable when the ECN broadcasting is adopted in the SDR/FA.

5 Conclusions

To provide the Internet service in the future mobile wireless networks, it's necessary to consider the network level assistance to keep end-to-end throughput better and network stable. In accordance with these requirements, ECN could be the solution for resolving and avoiding the network congestion. However, since the mobility has an effect on delay and congestion together, ECN alone cannot be the best solution for the congestion in the mobile wireless networks. In this paper, we have proposed the ECN broadcasting to utilize the advantages of IP and radio access networks. The proposed ECN broadcasting can be the easy and simple way to resolve the congestion when it is adopted in subnet router or FA router. This paper also has shown the performance improvement with simulation results. Judging from these results, the proposed scheme, ECN broadcasting is expected to become a fairly good solution in reducing congestion in mobile wireless subnet and improve the throughput of the Internet service in wireless IP networks.

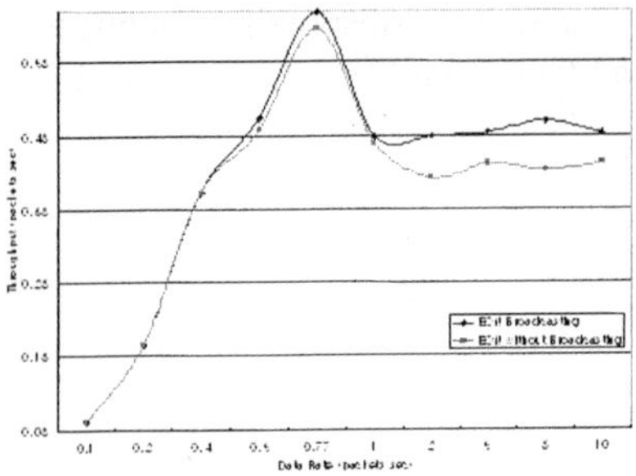

(a) Throughput comparison with p=0.4

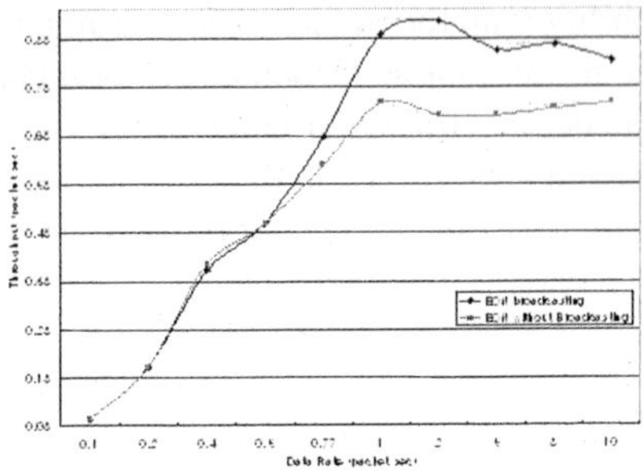

(b)Throughput comparison with p=0.9

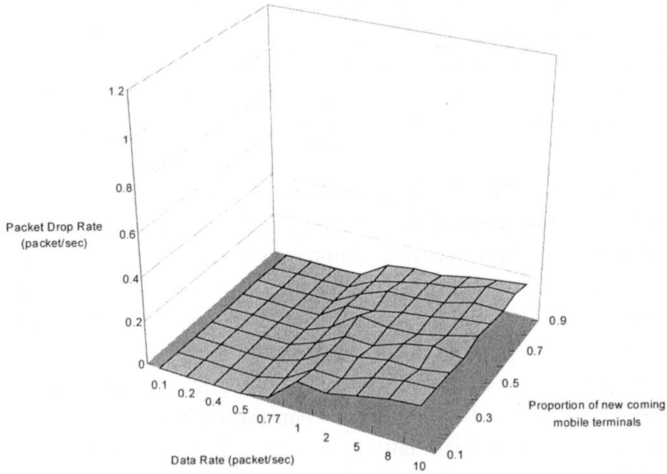

(c) Packet drop rate with ECN broadcasting

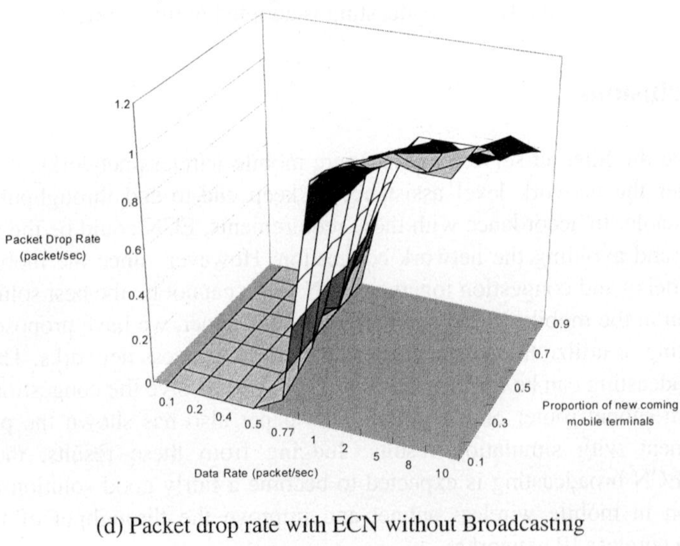

(d) Packet drop rate with ECN without Broadcasting

Fig. 3. Simulation Results

Still more research is necessary in comparing the performances when the traffic types are various in the mobile wireless networks and the service priority has to be considered in the future research work.

Acknowledgement. This Research was financially supported by Hansung University in the year of 2003.

References

[1] Girish Patel, Steven Dennett, "The 3GPP and 3GPP2 Movements Toward and All-IP Mobile Network", IEEE Personal Communications, August 2000, pp 62–64.

[2] James D. Solomon, "Mobile IP: The Internet Unplugged", PTR Prentice Hall,1998, Upper Saddle River, New Jersey 07458.

[3] Balakrishna H, Kats, Seshan S, "A Comparison of Mechanism for Improving TCP Performance over Wireless Link", ACM SIGCOMM, August 1996.

[4] Ramachandran R., et al, "IP-Based Access Network Infrastructure for Next-Generation Wireless Data Networks", IEEE Personal Communications, August 2000, pp 34–41.

[5] Caceres, R., and Iftode, L., "Improving the Performance of Reliable Transport Protocols in Mobile Computing Environments", IEEE Journal on Selected Area in Communications, 13(5), June 1995.

[6] Adbi R. M., Seshadri M., "Control and Management in Next-Generation Networks: Challenges and Opportunities", IEEE Communication Magazine, September 2000, pp 94–102.

[7] K. Ramakrishnan and S. Floyd, ``A Proposal to add Explicit Congestion Notification (ECN) to IP," *RFC 2481*, January 1999.

Network Dependability: An Availability Measure in N-Tier Client/Server Architecture

Flávia Estélia Silva Coelho[1], Jacques Philippe Sauvé[2], Cláudia Jacy Barenco Abbas[3], and Luis Javier García Villalba[4]

[1] Catholic University of Brasília, Dept. Computer Science, Brasília-DF, Brazil
fcoelho@ucb.br
[2] Fed. Univ. of Campina Grande, Dept. Systems and Computation, Campina G.-PB, Brazil
jacques@dsc.ufcg.edu.br
[3] University of Brasilia, Dept. Electrical Engineering, LabRedes, Brasília-DF, Brazil
barenco@redes.unb.br
[4] Complutense Univ. of Madrid, Dept. Computer Systems and Programming, Madrid, Spain
javiergv@sip.ucm.es

Abstract. Published work on computer network reliability frequently uses availability as a dependability measure. However, although several ways of defining availability have been proposed, none capture the overall level of service obtained by client hosts in a modern n-tier client/server architecture. We propose such a measure by calculating the fraction of client hosts receiving complete services from the network. We also extend a published efficient heuristic method for calculating availability to take into account our new proposed measure. The end result is a procedure of polynomial complexity $O(n_t^4)$, where n_t is the total number of components (hosts, links and interconnection equipment) in the network.

1 Introduction

Computer networks must provide infrastructure that meets requirements imposed by the applications necessities. One of the main performance measures of interest is availability [1]. This measure is especially important in applications such as e-commerce, banking transaction systems, etc., where the mission-critical role of applications is evident. Today, the main possibility of deploying applications is through the use of an n-tier client/server architecture [2]. Especially popular is the 3-tier architecture composed of the user services tier (client hosts), the middle tier (web servers, application servers, directory services servers, etc.) and the data tier (corporate database servers, mail servers, etc.). The middle tier is also frequently called the *business tier*, since this is where *business application logic* mostly executes. Other than corporate servers accessed by all clients, other servers may exist: these are departmental servers, frequently used by workgroups for file storage and print services. It must be noted that whereas departmental servers are accessed by client hosts in a particular workgroup, corporate servers in the business and data tiers are accessed by all, or most, client hosts in the network. In the context of such corporate networks, a particular client host obtains services from many servers. In order for a particular client host to obtain *full services* from the network, the following

A. Yazici and C. Şener (Eds.): ISCIS 2003, LNCS 2869, pp. 786–793, 2003.

connectivity restrictions must be obeyed (all connectivity restrictions mentioned below are bi-directional):

1. The client host must have access to its departmental servers; this would be necessary for file sharing or other workgroup applications, for example.
2. The client host must have access to corporate servers from the middle tier; this would be necessary so that the main application business logic could execute.
3. Corporate servers in the middle tier must have access to each other; this is necessary so that, for example, a web server can locate a service through a directory server, create a business object on an application server and call its business methods.
4. Corporate servers in the middle tier must have access to corporate servers in the data tier; for example, this would be necessary whenever a business object executing in an application server (middle tier) needs persistence services from a database server (data tier).

The failure of hosts (clients or servers), interconnection equipment and communication links can all affect these connectivities and thus decrease the availability of the client hosts' access to services. Several availability measures have been proposed in the literature: probability of network connectivity [3, 4, 5], the probability of all operational devices accessing a particular device [3], the number of device pairs that can communicate [3, 4, 5] and the number of devices that can communicate with a particular device [3]. We claim that a new way of measuring availability must be found. The issue must be examined from the user population point of view since this is what better reflects the effect failures have on the business. Since a network only exists to offer services to its user population, the effect of failures on the user population must be captured. Disconnecting a single user certainly is not as important as disconnecting a database server affecting all users. What does it mean to say that "the network is 99.95% available"? We claim that availability should measure the fraction of the user population receiving full network services, on average. In the next section, we formally define a new measure of availability in computer networks based on the n-tier client/server architecture. After that, we present an efficient (polynomial complexity) heuristic method for calculating the new availability measure. Numerical results for particular topological configuration are present follow.

2 A New Measure of Availability in Computer Networks

We consider the following network components are in our study: hosts (clients, departmental servers, middle tier corporate servers and data tier corporate servers), interconnection equipment (switches, routers, hubs, etc.) and individual links. We use the following notation, shown in table 1, in defining the new availability measure.

In order to define the new availability measure, we use several matrices described below. In this paper we use the term *adjacent* in a graph-theoretic sense. Two components are *adjacent* if they are directly connected by a communication link. The components thus considered are hosts and interconnection equipment. The *Original Adjacency Matrix* between hosts and interconnection equipment is defined as follows:

OAM = $[oam_{ij}]$ is a matrix of order $(n_h + n_i)$ x $(n_h + n_i)$, where $1 \le i, j \le (n_h + n_{eq})$. The components are organized in the matrix in the following order: n_c, n_{ds}, n_{mcs}, n_{dcs}, n_i. A component of matrix is defined as follows: $oam_{ij} = 1$ if component i is adjacent to component j, $oam_{ij} = 0$ otherwise. Observe that the components are numbered in the following order: clients, departmental servers, middle tier corporate servers, data tier corporate servers and interconnection equipment.

Table 1. Notation.

Symbol	Meaning
n_t	Total number of components $(n_h + n_l + n_i)$
n_c	Number of clients
n_{ds}	Number of departamental servers
n_{mcs}	Number of middle tier corporate servers
n_{dcs}	Number of data tier corporate servers
n_l	Number of individual communication links
n_i	Number of interconnection equipaments
n_h	Total number of hosts $(n_c + n_{ds} + n_{mcs} + n_{dcs})$
n_f	Number of failure states in the network
C	Client
Sd	Departamental server
Smc	Middle tier corporate server
Sdc	Data tier corporate server
L	Individual link
Eq	Interconnection equipment
DS_i	Set of departmental servers for client I
DS	Set of all departmental servers
OAM	Original adjacency matrix
SAM^s	Adjacency matrix for a particular failure state s
DCM^i	Desired connectivity matrix for client I
SCM^s	Actual connectivity matrix for a particular failure state
s	Particular failure state

The *Desired Connectivity Matrix* (for a particular client) is the key to defining the new availability measure. It represents the partial connectivities required between host components so that a client may obtain full services from the network. Since each client host has particular needs, as far a connectivity is required, this matrix must be defined for each of the n_c client hosts. This matrix is structured in the following order: n_c, n_{ds}, n_{mcs}, n_{dcs} and includes only hosts, since only these are ultimately accessed to obtain network services. In this matrix hosts are numbered in the following order: clients, departmental servers, middle tier corporate servers and data tier corporate servers. Let $DCM^i = [dcm^i_{jk}]$ be a matrix of order n_h x n_h, where $1 \le i \le n_c$, $1 \le j, k \le n_h$, the desired connectivity matrix for client i. The value of dcm^i_{jk} can be 0 or 1, depending on the connectivity need between two hosts j and k in order to satisfy the needs of client i. When dcm^i_{jk} is 0, hosts j and k need not be connected for client i to receive services from the network. In other words, should a failure disconnect hosts j and k (or should these hosts themselves fail), the availability of services for client i will not be affected. The case where dcm^i_{jk} is 1 indicates the opposite situation where client i will no longer be obtaining full services from the network. It is also clear that, as far as client *i* is concerned, the availability of services for other clients is of no concern. The matrices DCM^i are thus independent of one another.

Our approach is completely general, in the sense that any Desired Connectivity Matrix may be defined. The remainder of this paper uses a three-tier architecture as an example. For such an architecture, we may obtain the values of $[dcm^i_{jk}]$, as shown in the table 2. In order to calculate the fraction of clients receiving full services from the network, we must compare the actual connectivities between hosts to the desired connectivities. Actual connectivities between hosts are subject to the effects of failure in the hosts themselves, in the interconnection equipment and in individual communication links. I order to factor in the effect of such failures, we consider the network's *failure states*. The network can be in one of several failure states. A failure state indicates a set of failed components. That is, a particular failure state consists of one or more failed components. The sets {}, {1}, {2}, ..., {1, 2}, {1, 3}..., {1, 2, 3}, etc. where {i} means that component *i* has failed are examples of failure states.

We use an adjacency matrix for each failure state to represent the adjacencies between hosts and interconnection equipments representing the effects of failures for the given failure state. Let $SAM^s = [sam^s_{ij}]$ be the adjacency matrix for a failure state s. This matrix has the same structure as the Original Adjacency Matrix. The matrix is of order $(n_h + n_i) \times (n_h + n_i)$, where $1 \le s \le n_f$, $1 \le i, j \le (n_h + n_i)$, as follows: $sam_{ij} = 1$ if component *i* is adjacent to component *j*, $oam_{ij} = 0$ otherwise.

Table 2. Values of $[dcm^i_{jk}]$.

mcd^i_{jk}	*Restrictions*	*Meaning*
mcd^i_{kj}	$j > k, 1 \le j \le n_h, 1 \le k \le n_h$	Bi-directional connectivity is necessary
1	$j = k = I$	Client i must be connected to itself (that is, client i must be operational)
0	$1 \le j \le n_c, j \le k \le n_h, j \ne I$	The connectivity of other clients hosts is of no interest to client *I*
0	$j = i, 1 < k \le n_c$	Client *i* need not be connected to other clients
1	$j = i, n_c + 1 \le k \le n_c + n_{ds}, Sd_k \in DS_i$	Client i must be connected to all its departmental servers, where $DS_i = \{k \mid Sd_k$ is a departmental server for client i$\}$. (Sd_k is the k-th departmental server)
1	$j = i, n_c + n_{ds} + 1 \le k \le n_c + n_{ds} + n_{mcs}$	Client *i* must be connected to all middle tier corporate servers
0	$j = i, n_c + n_{ds} + n_{mcs} + 1 \le k \le n_h$	Client i need not be connected to data tier corporate servers
0	$n_c + 1 \le j \le n_c + n_{ds}, j < k \le n_h$	Departmental servers need not be connected between themselves, or to corporate servers in the middle or data tiers
1	$n_c + n_{ds} + 1 \le k \le n_c + n_{ds} + n_{mcs}$	Middle tier corporate servers must connected to each other and to data tier corporate servers
0	$n_c + n_{ds} + n_{mcs} + 1 \le j \le n_h$	Data tier servers need not be connected to each other

We now represent actual connectivities between network hosts, for a particular failure state using an Actual Connectivity Matrix. This matrix is obtained by evaluating the effect of failures for that particular state and how these failures disconnect hosts from one another. Let $SCM^s = [scm^s_{ij}]$, where $1 \leq s \leq n_f$, $1 \leq i, j \leq n_h$. SCM^s is of order n_h x n_h and is structured similarly to the Desired Connectivity Matrix. The values scm^s_{ij} are obtained,as shown as follows: $scm^s_{ij} = 1$ if host i is connected to host j, $scm^s_{ij} = 0$ otherwise. With these 4 matrices in hand (OAM, SAM^s, DCM^i, SCM^s), we are now ready to define the new availability measure for a network based on an n-tier client/server architecture. We consider all possible failure states. In a network with n_t components susceptible to failure, there are 2^{nt} possible failure states. The failure states are denoted by S_k, where $1 \leq k \leq 2^n t$. S_k represents the k-th failure state, where $S_1 = \phi$, $S_2 = \{1\}$, $S_3 = \{2\}$ and so on. Thus, S_1 corresponds to the state without failure and $S_2^{n\ t}$ corresponds to the state where all components have failed. State S_k occurs with probability $P(S_k) = \prod^{n_t}_{i=1} p_i\ (q_i/p_i)^{T_i(S_k)}$ where p_i $(1 \leq i \leq n_t)$ is the probability of component i being operational, $q_i = 1 - p_i$, and the value of $T_i(S_k)$ is shown as follows: $T_i(S_k) = 1$, if component i is operational in state S_k, $T_i(S_k) = 0$ otherwise. Finally, the new network availability measure, that is the fraction of client hosts receiving full network services, is given by $A = \sum^{2^{n_c}}_{k=1} P(S_k)A(S_k)$ where $A(S_k)$ is the fraction of clients receiving full services in failure state S_k, as shown as follows: A $= [\sum^{n_c}_{i=1} A_i(S_k)]/n_c$ where $A_i(S_k)$ indicates whether client i is receiving full network services in failure state S_k: $A_i(S_k) = 1$ if DCM^i AND $SCM^{S_k} = DCM^i$, $A_i(S_k) = 0$ otherwise. In this last equation, *AND* is a Boolean operation and must be realized cell by cell to compare the Desired Connectivity Matrix for client i (DCM^i) and the Actual Connectivity Matrix for failure state S_k (SCM^{Sk}). Thus, DCM^i AND $SCM^{Sk} = DCM^i$, if and only if dcm^i_{jt} AND $scm^{S\ k}_{jt} = dcm^i_{jt}$ $\forall\ 1 \leq j, t \leq n_h$. In this case, connectivities for client i are satisfied and it is receiving full services from the network in failure state S_k. Evaluating network availability by considering all 2^{nt} possible failure states results in an algorithm with exponential complexity and thus imposes serious restrictions on the size of the network considered. [5] presents a detailed study concerning the difficulty of calculating traditional availability measures. In the next section, we present a heuristic method for evaluating network availability using the measure introduced above. Only the most probable failure states are considered and the algorithm has polynomial complexity.

3 Efficient Evaluation Method for the Availability Measure

The straightforward evaluation of the new availability measure, A, has computational complexity $O(2^{nt})$, since all failure states must be considered. We seek a heuristic method which would allow its approximate calculation in polynomial time. Such a method can be found in [6] and is based on enumerating the *most probable* failure states. The mathematical model used is as follows: a computer network is represented by a non-directed graph G = (V, E) with $n_v = n_h + n_i$ vertices (one vertex for each host and interconnection equipment) and n_l edges (one for each bi-directional communication link). V is a finite set of vertices $V = \{v_1, v_2, ..., vn_v\}$ and E is a finite set of edges $E = \{e_1, e_2, ..., en_l\}$ where each edge is identified by a pair of vertices, $e_k = (v_a, v_b)$, where $1 \leq k \leq n_i$ and $1 \leq a, b \leq n_v$ and $v_a, v_b \in V$. Proper loops, $a = (v_a, v_a)$, are permitted. Specifically, we have, $V = \{C_1, ..., Cn_c, Sd_1, ..., Sdn_{ds}, Smc_1, ..., Smcn_{mcs}, Sdc_1, ..., Sdcn_{dcs}, Eq_1, ..., Eqn_i\}$ and $E = \{e_1, ..., en_l\}$. Vertices and edges may be in one of two states: operational or failed. Intermediate states, such as one in which component performance is degraded, are not considered. To each component (vertex or edge) i is associated a probability p_i of being in the operational state. $q_i = 1 - p_i$ is the probability of this same component being in the failed state. These states change at random and are independent of one another. Finally, the components are ordered such that $R_1 \geq R_2 \geq ... \geq Rn_t$, where $R_i = q_i/p_i$. To determine the most probable network failure states, the states are generated in decreasing order of probability according to a failure state generation algorithm given in [6]. For the n_m most probable failure states, S_k, where $1 \leq k \leq n_m$, we have $P(S_1) \geq P(S_2) \geq ... \geq P(Sn_m)$. The value of n_m may be chosen in several ways: as a fixed value, as a fraction of all states, as a function of the total number of components, or in such a way as to obtain a desired level of precision while calculating network availability. Since only most probable states are considered, it would be useful to obtain upper (A_{sup}) and lower (A_{inf}) bounds for the availability measure, A. [6] shows how to do this as follows. Let M be an arbitrary performance measure, and let $M(S_k)$ be its value when the network is in failure state S_k. This measure must be such as to obey the following relation given by: $M(S_{2^{n_t}}) \leq M(S_k) \leq M(S_1)$, where $1 \leq k \leq 2^{n_t}$. In other words, network performance is best in state S_1, when the network is fully operational and is worse in state $S_{2^{n_t}}$, when all components have failed. We can thus obtain an upper bound by using the measure $M(S_1)$ for all states not considered in the enumeration and we can obtain a lower bound by using the measure $M(S_{2^{n_t}})$ for all states not considered in the enumeration. For the proposed availability measure, A, we have the next expressions: $A_{inf} = \Sigma^{n_m}_{k=1} P(S_k)A(S_k) + (1 - \Sigma^{n_m}_{k=1} P(S_k))A(S_{2^{n_t}})$ and $A_{sup} = \Sigma^{n_m}_{k=1} P(S_k)A(S_k) + (1 - \Sigma^{n_m}_{k=1} P(S_k))A(S_1)$. Since in state $S_{2^{n_t}}$ all components have failed, we have $A(S_{2^{n_t}}) = 0$. Further, in state S_1 no component has failed and we have $A(S_1) = 1$. Then, $A_{inf} = \Sigma^{n_m}_{k=1} P(S_k)A(S_k)$ and $A_{sup} = \Sigma^{n_m}_{k=1} P(S_k)A(S_k) + (1 - \Sigma^{n_m}_{k=1} P(S_k))$. We are ready to give the algorithm for calculating the upper and lower bounds for network availability.

Purpose: calculate upper and lower bounds for the availability of a network based on a n-tier client/server architecture, that is, the fraction of client hosts receiving full network services.

Input: number of clients, number of departmental servers, number of middle tier corporate servers, number of data tier corporate servers, total number of components, type of each component and its probability of failure (in increasing order of probability), list of departmental servers and the clients it serves, list of adjacencies between hosts and interconnection equipment.

Output: upper and lower bounds for the network availability by considering the n_m most probable network failure states.

```
EVALUATE NETWORK AVAILABILITY {
obtain_clients_for_deparmental_servers();
obtain_original_adjacency_matrix();
obtain_desired_adjacency_matrix_for_clients();
S1=ϕ;
calculate_probability_of_first_failure_state();
execute_algorithm_ORDER(); /* gives nm most probable states and their
probability */
lower_bound = 0;
cumulative_state_probability = 0;
from i = 1 to nm do
        {
        generate_adjacency_matrix_for_i-th_failure_state( );
        execute_transitive_closure_algorithm ( );
        generate_connectivity_matrix_for_i-h_network_failure_state( );
        clients_ok =
        calculate_N_of_clients_with_full_network_service_in_state_i( );
        low_bound = low_bound + (clients_ok/N_clients) * prob_state[i];
        cumulative_state_prob = cumulative_state_prob + prob_state[i];
        }
        upper_bound = lower_bound + (1 - cumulative_state_probability);
}
```

We may now obtain the computational complexity of every step in the algorithm, as shown in table 3. Since the value of n_t is larger than the values of n_{ds}, n_c, n_h, n_i, the computational complexity of the algorithm is $O(n_m n_t^3 + n_m n_t \log n_m)$. Since n_m is usually chosen as a linear function of n_t, we have complexity $O(n_t^4)$. Thus, our heuristic algorithm has polynomial computational complexity and may be used to calculate the availability of much larger networks than would be the case with a standard exponential complexity algorithm. The heuristic method was used to evaluate network availability for several 3-tier configuration topologies. Experimental results are given in [7].

Table 3. Computational Complexity of Proposed Algorithm.

Step	Complexity
Obtain clients for departamental servers	$O(n_{ds})$
Obtain original adjacency matriz	$O[(n_h + n_i)^2]$
Obtain desired adjacency matrix for clients	$O(n_c n_h^2)$
Calculate probability of first failure state	$O(n_t)$
Execute algorithm ORDER	$O(n_t^2 n_m + n_t n_m \log n_m)$
Generate adjacency matrix for I-th failure state for *most probable states* (*mps*)	$O[n_m(n_h + n_i)^2]$
Execute transitive closure algorithm	$O[n_m(n_h + n_i)^3]$
Generate connectivity matrix for I-th network failure state for *mps*	$O[n_m(n_h + n_i)^2]$
Calculate number of clients with full network service in state I for *mps*	$O(n_m n_c n_h^2)$

4 Conclusions

When we started researching the current problem, we were investigating network design methodologies. Network design deals with finding appropriate network solutions (architectures, topologies, equipment, protocols, etc.) in order to meet certain design constraints such as cost and performance. Among performance goals are those dealing with delay, throughput and availability. Although techniques dealing with delay and throughput are well-solved, we found that the same could not be said about availability. In particular, we found that availability measures suggested in the literature did not address the problem from the "business" point of view. In other words, what should it mean for a network to be 99.97% available?

Our first contribution is thus to offer a new measure of availability that has direct significance to the business: the fraction of clients receiving full network services. We claim that such a measure is easily understandable by network operators, network administrators, mid-level and top-level management and is thus preferable to other measures used to date. The measure has been formally defined and an efficient, polynomial-time, heuristic method was produced for calculating the new measure. This is our second contribution. Experimental results have confirmed the expected behavior of the availability measure as various network parameters change.

Further work includes the introduction of the heuristic method in a general network design tool. So far, we can only analyze a given network. It would be beneficial to find ways of *designing* networks to meet given availability criteria. For example, it is possible to factor our method in the work of [8, 9]. The heuristic method is especially suited to this task since the enumeration of most probable failure states indicates where the most critical failure points are located (this information is part of the failure state definition). Another direction would be to take into account mechanisms that inherently improve availability, such a the Spanning Tree Protocol, dynamic routing, HSRP (*Hot Standby Routing Protocol*) and *DLD* (*Deterministic Load Distribution*).

As a final note, observe that the method proposed is not only applicable to n-tier architectures, although its applicability for such architectures shows that modern networks can be adequately handled by the method.

Acknowledgements. L. J. García-Villalba's work is supported by the Spanish Ministry of Science and Technology under Projects TIC2000-0735 and TIC2002-04516-C03-03. This author would like to express his appreciation to the Programa Complutense del Amo for providing him a grant to stay at IBM Research Division. Part of this work was done while he was with the Information Storage Group at the IBM Almaden Research Center (San Jose, California, USA).

References

1. High System Availability. Product Bulletin. Cisco Systems, 1999.
2. J. Edwards. *3-Tier Server/Client at Work.* John Wiley & Sons, 1999.
3. M. O. Ball. *Computing Network Reliability.* Operations Research, Vol. 27, 1979.
4. P. Kubat. *Estimation of Reliability for Communication Computer Networks – Simulation/Analytic Approach.* IEEE Transactions on Communications, Vol. 37, 1989.
5. M. O. Ball. *Complexity of Network Reliability Computations.* Networks, Vol. 10, 1980.
6. V. K. Li and J. A. Silvester. *Performance Analysis of Networks with Unreliable Components.* IEEE Transactions on Communications, Vol. 32, 1984.
7. F. E. Coelho Silva. *Avaliação de Disponibilidade de Redes de Computadores Baseadas na Arquitetura Cliente/Servidor em n Camadas.* Master's Thesis, Universidade Federal da Paraíba, 2000.
8. S Pierre et al. *A Tabu-Search Approach for Designing Computer-Network Topologies with Unreliable Components.* IEEE Transactions on Reliability, Vol. 46, 1997.
9. A. Balakrishnan et al. *Designing Hierarchical Survivable Networks.* Operations Research, Vol. 46, 1998.

One-Time Passwords: Security Analysis Using BAN Logic and Integrating with Smartcard Authentication

Kemal Bicakci and Nazife Baykal

Middle East Technical University, Informatics Institute
06531 Ankara, Turkey
{bicakci,baykal}@ii.metu.edu.tr

Abstract. In this paper we make a formal analysis of one-time password protocols using BAN logic and provide some guidelines to integrate securely one-time passwords with smartcard based authentication. We also propose some extensions to the BAN logic to facilitate analyzing hash chain based authentication protocols.

1 Introduction

Authentication is not an easy problem. In the security literature many protocols have been published and at a later time weaknesses and flaws were discovered in them. This leads security scientists to establish better guidelines for protocol design and analysis.

The most popular approach to analyze authentication protocols is through the use of logic. The first such logic and the best known one is the BAN logic, named after its inventors Mike Burrows, Martin Abadi, and Roger Needham [1]. The BAN logic provides a formal method of reasoning about the beliefs of participants in a security protocol. It reasons about what is reasonable for a participant to believe, given sight of certain messages.

BAN logic was used succesfully to find the flaws in some security protocols e.g. CCITT X.509 protocol [2]. On the other hand it has also its own limitations. According to Meadows [5], "it is unlikely that any formal method will be able to model all aspects of a protocol, and thus it is unlikely that any formal method will be able to detect or prevent all types of protocol flaws". We do not want to go into the details but refer to some references for these limitations [3] [5].

Organization of this paper. What we would like to do instead is to give a short background information on the BAN logic itself first in section 2 and then start analyzing one-time password (OTP) protocols using this tool in section 3. Even if armored with cryptography, traditional passwords can be easily attacked. This is why one-time passwords where each password is only used once and replay kinds of attacks are avoided is considered to be a viable alternative or supplement for software authentication.[1] OTP protocols have been proposed in the past but

[1] Another popular approach that is resistant to replay is smartcard authentication. It is a more expensive solution based on specialized hardware.

A. Yazici and C. Şener (Eds.): ISCIS 2003, LNCS 2869, pp. 794–801, 2003.

we are unaware of any previous work on formal analysis of OTP protocols. Our analysis will be a valuable one in "formally" specifying the weaknesses of current OTP protocols. This might also lead the research on designing more powerful alternatives. In section 4, we will provide some guidelines when we need to integrate one-time passwords with a smartcard based authentication protocol in order to have a "survivable" authentication framework. What do we mean by "survivable" will be also explained in this section. In section 5, we end by summing up our work and discussing future possibilities for research.

2 Summary of BAN Logic

In this section we would like to summarize the BAN logic. For a more comprehensive treatment we recommend the original papers [1] [4].

The key idea in BAN logic is that we will believe that a message is authentic if it is fresh and encrypted with a relevant key. Notice that this belief in fact means that the underlying crypto algorithms used for encryption is secure. It also demonstrates the difference between the motivations of protocol analyzer and crypto-analyst.

The constructs of the logic can be expressed using the following notations:

$A| \equiv X$: A is entitled to believe X.
$A| \sim X$: A once said X.
$A| \Rightarrow X$: A has jurisdiction over X (A is authority on X and is to be trusted).
$A \lhd X$: A sees X.
$\sharp X$: X is fresh.
X_K: X is encrypted using the key K.
$\rightarrow^K A$: K is A's public key (K^{-1} is only known by A).

These constructs can be manipulated by using the following postulates:

Message-meaning rule (for public key cryptography): States that if A sees a message encrypted under K^{-1} and K is the public key of B, then A will believe that the message was once said by B.

$$\frac{A \lhd X_{K^{-1}}, A| \equiv \rightarrow^K B}{A| \equiv B| \sim X}$$

Nonce-verification rule: States that if a participant once said a message and the message is fresh, then that participant still believes it.

$$\frac{A| \equiv \sharp X, A| \equiv B| \sim X}{A| \equiv B| \equiv X}$$

Jurisdiction rule: States that if a participant believes something and is an authority on that matter, then he or she should be believed.

$$\frac{A| \equiv B| \Rightarrow X, A| \equiv B| \equiv X}{A| \equiv X}$$

Note that the statements on the top are the conditions and the one on the bottom is the result. There are a number of further postulates but for space limitations we prefer to give only the most important ones here.

3 Verifying One-Time Password Protocols Using BAN Logic

One other external assumption (and a limitation) of BAN logic is that we assume the password is not available to anyone who might use it in an unauthorized manner. However there are several ways in which your password may be snooped directly on the client machine while you are typing [6]. No matter how sophisticated they are, none of the software authentication methods based on traditional passwords can safeguard against the attacks on insecure client machines where the only way to be authenticated securely is through the use of one-time passwords. Since each OTP we use is valid for only one time, the OTP that is snooped is not useful afterwards.

Our goal in this section is to analyze one-time password (OTP) protocols using BAN logic. The most popular one-time password protocol, S/KEY system [11] built on top of Lamport's hash chain idea [12] will be analyzed in the subsection 3.3 after a required extension to the logic is proposed.

The second viable OTP approach, the signature chain based one-time password (SCOTP) [2] protocol [6] is analyzed first after providing a brief introductory information.

3.1 Description of SCOTP Protocol

We will summarize the operation of SCOTP protocol here. For detailed information please consult to [6].

Definition: Let algorithm S be a signing algorithm in a signature scheme (e.g. RSA) where d is the private key and the corresponding public key is already known by the server. $S_d^N(x)$ denotes that we apply the signing algorithm S recursively N times to the initial input x. As seen below, recursive applications result in a signature chain (a chain of infinite length OTPs) originated from the initial input x:

$$x, S_d(x), S_d^2(x), S_d^3(x), ..., S_d^N(x), S_d^{N+1}(x), ...$$

By utilizing a signature chain (SC), the SCOTP protocol works as follows:
Initialization:

1. The user generates a public key-private key pair, registers himself to the server and sends securely his public key to the server.
2. The server and the user agree on the seed value to be used (This seed value does not need to be secret and can be generated from the public key by both parties individually. See the second guideline in subsection 4.3).

[2] The SCOTP protocol is based on our earlier work of [7].

3. The server keeps a table for each user which stores
   - user's ID
   - user's public key
   - OTP sequence number (initially zero)
   - Previous OTP (initially the seed value)
4. The user generates any number of OTPs he wishes from the seed value by constructing a SC using his private key and prints out them in a piece of paper. The user can update his OTP list anytime without communicating with the server by computing more elements in the infinite length SC e.g. when the OTPs are about to finish.

Operation:

1. The user sends his ID to the server.
2. The server finds the entry for the ID the user has entered in the authentication file and sends the current value of OTP sequence number to the user.
3. The user enters the OTP with the sequence number the server has requested.
4. The server verifies the OTP by the user's public key, if it is correct then authentication succeeds, it updates the previous OTP with the one the user has entered and also increment the OTP sequence number. If the OTP is not correct then the authentication fails, it sends a warning message to the user.

3.2 Verifying SCOTP Protocol

The analysis of a given protocol in the BAN logic can be performed in three steps:

- The idealized protocol is derived from the original one.
- The goals of the authentication protocol is formalized and assumptions about the initial state are written.
- Apply the postulates of the logic to discover the beliefs held by the participants.

We can express the SCOTP protocol in standard notation as follows:

Message 1: $A \to S : ID_A$
Message 2: $S \to A : SEQ_A$
Message 3: $A \to S : (R_{SEQ_A})_{K_A^{-1}}$

In BAN logic, the cleartext communication is omitted. So the protocol in idealized form can be written as:

$A \to S : (N_A)_{K_A^{-1}}$

The goal of SCOTP protocol is $S| \equiv A| \equiv N_A$ (one-way authentication only, not a mutual authentication). It is important to realize that this is a weaker goal than most other authentication protocols where the protocol is completed when two parties agreed on the value of secret key K.

As the assumptions, first it makes sense to accept that the server (S) has received securely (and therefore believes) the public key of A. In BAN notation, this is written as $S| \equiv \rightarrow^{K_A} A$.

Secondly we assume that the user A did not previously sign the value N_A and therefore N_A can be accepted as fresh. SCOTP protocol ensures that in the previous runs of the protocol user A did not sign the current value of N_A but it is also vital to ensure this in a situation where the same public key is reused for other purposes. We will say more on this issue in the next section.

The final step is very straigtforward. By applying the message-meaning rule we can show $S| \equiv A| \sim N_A$. Then we can apply the nonce-verification rule and proves that $S| \equiv A| \equiv N_A$.

As stated in [6], SCOTP protocol does not protect against active attacks such as "man in the middle" and "hijacking connection" attack. We observe that this is due to the weaker goal the protocol accomplishes. To safeguard against these more sophisticated attacks we need stronger achievements: e.g. S and A should believe in sharing the same secret key K so that all the communication between them can be performed in an encrypted tunnel thereby eliminates the risk of hijacked connection.

As the final note of this subsection, we agree with [6] in the recommendation of complementing SCOTP (or any other one-time password protocol) with protocols like SSH [8] to be protected against active network attacks.

3.3 Verification of S/KEY OTP Protocol

In S/KEY [11], a hash chain of length N is constructed by applying recursively a hash function $h()$ to a initial seed value (s).

$$K^N = h^N(s) = \underbrace{h(h(h(...h(s)...)))}_{Ntimes}$$

The last element K^N resembles the public key in public key cryptography so the message-meaning rule and the nonce-verification rule of the BAN logic can be restated as follows: (Note: the parameter i can take value between 1 and $N-1$)

$$\frac{A \triangleleft K^i, A| \equiv \rightarrow^{K^N} B}{A| \equiv B| \sim K^i}$$

$$\frac{A| \equiv \sharp K^i, A| \equiv B| \sim K^i}{A| \equiv B| \equiv K^i}$$

Now similar to SCOTP protocol, the authentication goal ($S| \equiv A| \equiv K^i$) can be proved by applying above postulates successively.

4 Integrating SCOTP with a Smartcard Based Authentication Protocol

4.1 The Reason for Integration

We have seen that traditional passwords by itself does not provide the security level most systems require that is why National Institute of Standards and Technology (NIST) defines a strong authentication to be characterized by the use of at least two kinds of evidence at least one of which is resistant to replay [9]. This motivates to use special hardware (smart tokens - smart cards) for the authentication framework because the only method not relying on special hardware resistant to replay is one-time passwords which is not a very convenient solution.

In a recent conference, Ahn and Shin [10] presented a token-based architecture for e-health systems. Their main contribution is the design of framework to make the authentication service "scalable" for adopting smart tokens using different technologies. However, we claim that survivability is more important than scalability in mission-critical systems like health information systems where there is a significant risk in locations where there is no smartcard reader available such as on an airplane or in a foreign country. For instance, suppose that a minister gets sick while he is in a formal visit to a foreign country, his doctor traveling with him needs to reach his patient record but there is not any smart card reader to use for authentication.

One practical solution to the aforementioned problem is to complement smartcard based authentication system with one-time passwords (OTPs). Then the system would work as follows:

OTPs are written down on a piece of paper and carried in the pocket. In order to be authenticated using devices without a proper smart card reader, users enter the correct OTP manually. This is somehow an inconvenience for the user but that inconvenience is worth in order to be authenticated securely and reach critical information in most medical emergency scenarios. The inconvenience of OTPs in fact is useful to facilitate secure authentication using smart tokens in the usual procedure.

4.2 Alternatives for Integration

One-time password alternatives for the integration are as follows:

- use S/KEY in its original form.
- sign the last element of the hash chain in S/KEY.
- use SCOTP protocol.

The first alternative is based on a shared secret between the user and the server and has some security wekanesses such as off-line dictionary attacks. (The hash chain is derived by using the password (shared secret) as the seed value.)

Most smartcard based authentication protocols use public key cryptography where the greatest advantage is to avoid shared secrets between participants.

The server uses only the user's "public" key for verification therefore the risk of compromised or hostile servers is eliminated. Since we have a public key infrastructure available used for smartcart based authentication, it is a reasonable idea to use the same infrastructure for one-time passwords as well.

While both of the last two alternatives provides a secure solution, SCOTP protocol is a more convenient one since it can generate infinite number of OTPs without requiring the user to interact with the server. Another advantage of SCOTP is; from any incorrectly revealed OTP, unspent OTPs cannot be calculated therefore for secure operation the protocol does not assume the user is careful enough to enter the correct OTP in each authentication. (This feature can be obtained without applying hashing if a signature scheme which does not have the "message recovery" property is used. [6])

Note that, some of the guidelines we will provide in the next subsection can also be applied to the second alternative as well.

4.3 Integrating SCOTP

In [13], one of the principles for public key protocols was: "avoid using the same key for two different purposes". The reason for this principle is best illustrated by an example in [3]. Let us adapt the attack in that example to our case.

Suppose we use the same key for smart card authentication and for generating the signature chain. In smartcard authentication, usually the server asks the user to sign a random challenge to identify him. If an attacker asks the user to sign the OTP that was just used, then he can get a valid OTP to be useful for the next authentication (If the Lamport's hash chain is used and the attacker gets the user to sign the last element of the hash chain, then the situation is worse; the attacker gets a list of valid OTPs).

The easiest solution to this attack is the one which Anderson and Needham recommended [13]; use different keys for these two different tasks.

If we need to use the same key for these two tasks for some reasons (e.g. to save users having to carry two different cards or to save the server to store two public keys for the same user), then the following guidelines will help for secure operation:

1. Choose a signature scheme which does not have the message recovery property and do not apply hash algorithm before signing in constructing the signature chain. In smartcard authentication the random challenge is hashed before signing so any signature the attacker can get is not useful in SCOTP protocol.
2. If the public key (or the certificate) is to be used as the seed value (then of course we need hashing before signing), the first valid OTP should be the second element in the signature chain because the first element can be obtained by the attacker by getting the user sign the hash of the public key. However the second element can not be obtained if the first guideline is conformed.

5 Conclusions and Future Work

In this paper, using the BAN logic we analyzed OTP protocols. We see that the (proven) authentication goal of these protocols is a weaker one and this is the formal reason of these protocols' vulnerability to active attacks such as "man in the middle" and hijacking connection". We also give some guidelines for secure integration of smartcard authentication with one-time passwords. These guidelines will help us to assure one of the assumptions (freshness of OTPs) we have made in our formal analysis.

Hash chains are useful constructions and find applications in some other authentication protocols other than S/KEY [14,15]. By the help of extensions we have proposed, it will be possible to perform the security analysis of these protocols. Another promising future work is to analyze the security of hybrid solutions like SSH supplemented with OTPs. Designing an OTP protocol with a stronger authentication goal is the last future work we suggest in this paper.

References

1. M. Burrows, M. Abadi, R. Needham: A logic of authentication. ACM Transactions on Computer Systems, 8(1):18–36, February 1990.
2. CCITT X509 and ISO 9594–8: The Directory – Authentication Framework CCITT Blue Book, Geneva, March 1988.
3. Ross Anderson: Security Engineering. Wiley Computer Publishing, 2001.
4. M. Burrows, M. Abadi, R. Needham: A logic of authentication. In Proc. of the Royal Society of London volume 426, 1989, pp 233–271.
5. C. Meadows: Formal verification of cryptography protocols. ASIACRYPT 1994.
6. K. Bicakci, N. Baykal: Improving the Security and Flexibility of One-Time Passwords by Signature Chains. In submission to Turkish Journal of Electrical Engineering and Computer Sciences.
7. Kemal Bicakci, Nazife Baykal: Infinite Length Hash Chains and Their Applications. In Proc. of IEEE 11th International Workshops on Enabling Technologies (WETICE 2002), Pittsburgh, USA.
8. T. Ylonen: SSH – Secure login connections over the Internet. In Proc. of 6th USENIX Security Symposium, July 1996.
9. NIST FIBS 190: Guidelines for the Use of Advanced Authentication Technology Alternatives. September 1994.
10. G. Ahn, D, Shin: Towards Scalable Authentication in Health Services. In Proc. of IEEE 11th International Workshops on Enabling Technologies (WETICE 2002).
11. N. Haller: The S/Key One-Time Password System. Proc. of the Symposium on Network and Distributed Systems Security, Internet Society, CA, February 1994.
12. Leslie Lamport: Password authentication with insecure communication. Communications of the ACM, 24(11): 770–772, November 1981.
13. R. Anderson, R. Needham: Robustness principles for public key protocols. CRYPT 1995.
14. N. Asokan, G.Tsudik, and M. Waidner: Server-supported signatures. Journal of Computer Security, vol. 5., no. 1, 1997.
15. K. Bicakci, N. Baykal: A New Efficient Server Assisted Signature Scheme for Pervasive Computing. To Appear in the Proceedings of the 1st International Conference on Security in Pervasive Computing (SPC 2003), LNCS 2802, Springer, 2003.

Design and Implementation of a Secure Group Communication Protocol on a Fault Tolerant Ring

Özgür Sağlam[1,2], Mehmet E. Dalkılıç[2], and Kayhan Erciyeş[2]

[1] BEKO Elektronik R&D Center, Alsancak, İzmir, Turkey
OzgurS@beko.com.tr
[2] International Computer Institute Ege University Bornova, Izmir, Turkey
{dalkilic,erciyes}@ube.ege.edu.tr

Abstract. In this paper, we describe a secure group communication protocol for a fault-tolerant synchronous ring. Our protocol, named Secure Synchronous Ring Protocol (SSRP), integrates a secure group communication facility into an existing scalable, fault-tolerant ring protocol. SSRP is a hierarchical group communication protocol that employs Cliques GDH contributory key management protocol and Diffie-Hellman encryption algorithm. Security related functions and group communication functions are integrated into a single layer guaranteeing that not only the application messages of the group, but also the messages related to the group communication layer are protected. A novel fault-tolerant leader election algorithm and a proof of Virtual Synchrony semantics on SSRP are also given.

1 Introduction

Industrial and military applications that require the communication of information within a group are becoming an indispensable part of the modern computing. Security, in addition to reliability and high-availability, is one of the main characteristics of these group communication based applications. However, providing security for group communication is a complex task especially in the presence of network and node failures. The main issue in secure group communication is the key management. Since group has a variable view, changing dynamically as new members join or leave the group during the group's lifetime, a key management policy should have the ability to handle these dynamic operations. Moreover it should preserve the group communication secrecy independently from these changes. One approach relies on a single entity that is responsible for generating the group key and distributing it to the entire group. Such a scheme is open to the single point of failure problem. Kerberos [13] is an example of this scheme. Another key management approach selects a group member to generate new keys and distribute them to the other group members. This makes the system fault tolerant in the case of crashes and partitions since a new member will be selected to regenerate the group. Different from the above, there exists a contributory key management scheme. Steer et al. [11], Burmester and Desmedt [5], Group Diffie-Hellman (GDH) [12] and Tree-based GDH [8] key management protocols are examples of this scheme. All of these are based on 2-party Diffie-Hellman

A. Yazici and C. Şener (Eds.): ISCIS 2003, LNCS 2869, pp. 802–810, 2003.

key exchange protocol extended to the multi-party case. Contributory key agreement is suitable for peer to peer communication groups. There are some systems implementing security concepts over group communication environment. These are SecureRing [7] project at UCSB, the Horus/Ensemble [10] work at Cornell and SecureSpread [2] project at Johns Hopkins University. The Ensemble security work is the state of-the-art in secure reliable group communication and addresses problems such as group keys and re-keying [3]. Ensemble uses PGP authentication, which is not contributory. SecureSpread is a recent project on secure group communication where a secure communication layer between the Spread group communication deamon and the application layer is implemented. Different from Ensemble, it uses a group key structure that is contributory. The used structure is from Cliques Toolkit [12][8], using 2-Party Diffie-Hellman key exchange protocol extended to multi-party case.

In this study, we describe a system called Secure Synchronous Ring Protocol (SSRP) that relies on integrating a proven contributory key management protocol entity into the group communication protocol, which is developed by Tunali and Erciye• [14][6]. This entity is in the communication layer and is completely independent from the layers above. The main goal of the work is to develop a fault tolerant, scalable, synchronous, real-time and secure distributed system. These properties allow the system to be suitable for large groups needing secrecy in the group messages. By integrating a security capability into the group communication layer, it is guaranteed that not only the application messages of the group, but also the corresponding information related with the group communication layer is protected from the outside attacks. The reduction in the total messaging needs to construct a secure group communication is another advantage in terms of bandwidth usage. In this study, only the attacks from the outside of the group are considered.

The rest of the paper is as follows. Section 2 outlines the hierarchical, fault-tolerant ring protocol [14] and the Cliques [4] protocol suite which is designed for group key management into dynamic groups. Section 3 presents the Secure Synchronous Ring Protocol (SSRP) with membership operations, leader selection algorithm, and the proof of virtual synchrony semantics. The conclusions are given in Section 4.

2 Background

The Hierarchical Fault Tolerant Ring Protocol is designed for distributed real-time systems [14] and it is a synchronous, hierarchical and scalable communication protocol that may be used for group management as shown in Fig.1. There are three entities within the protocol having dedicated responsibilities throughout this hierarchy named as *node*, *representative* and *leader*. Each sub ring (i.e. a cluster) consists of one controller called the *representative* and a limited number of *nodes*. Controller is a generic name for representatives at any level. Representative is responsible for connecting the corresponding cluster, called the *inner ring*, to the one step higher level ring called the *outer ring*. Also group membership operations of the cluster are its responsibilities. Representative releases an empty token at each period of time. The token passes through the ring and related fields are filled with requested information by the nodes and the token returns to the representative. The resultant token is passed to the higher level cluster when an empty token of this level reaches the representative. Group communication processes in the higher level are the same with that of lower level. The controller of this level is called the *leader*. It has the same responsibilities on its cluster as the representative. This hierarchical structure based on nodes, representatives and leader can be built on *n* levels based on the group size and communication and computation overheads without loss of generality.

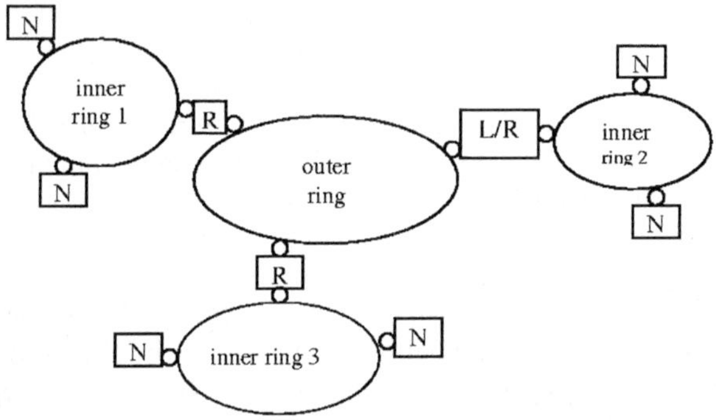

Fig. 1. The Ring Protocol with two level communication hierarchy [14]

It is possible to build various distributed applications on this architecture. At the lowest level, the distributed clock synchronization is built since the system model is synchronous. In the clock synchronization algorithm, the controller periodically requests clock information from the nodes and upon receipt of the clock information, the controller decides on the new clock value and dictates this to the whole system via the cluster representatives. Above the clock level, the distributed scheduler operates similar to the clock synchronization module [1]. In the group membership layer, the processes may belong to a particular group that is defined independent of the cluster topology. At each time period, a token is released to the first member of that ring by the controller. Node fills the token with the available information and passes it to the next member of the current view of the cluster. As long as a crash does not occur, the token returns back to the controller. In the case of failures, the protocol rebuilds the system and starts functioning again. When the token circulation is not finished in a certain time, then the controller starts to rebuild the view of the cluster by extracting the crashed node(s) by polling the current view. When the controller crashes, the partitioned cluster starts the leader election algorithm and determines the new controller of the cluster. Then, partitioned cluster rejoins the group through the new controller.

The membership management of this protocol is based on Virtual Synchrony model (VS) [15]. VS states that when a message is sent to the group, only the group members that are in the view of the group when the message was originally sent can receive the message. This property is a must for a group when building a strictly secure group communication system.

Cliques is a protocol suite designed for implementing group key management into dynamic groups. It consists of proven key management protocols each having different performance values [4]. Toolkit assumes an underlying reliable group communication system that provides reliable broadcast, message ordering and group membership services. GDH [12] is one of the contributory key management protocols implemented in Cliques. It is computationally expensive but yields better performance in terms of bandwidth usage. It is also appropriate for ring based systems. GDH provides key independence and perfect forward secrecy and was proven secure to passive outside attacks. Active outsider attacks are not addressed in this protocol, however, active attacks can be prevented by the use of public key signatures. If all the group members know the public keys of each other, they can check the received messages by decrypting the signature with the public key of the expected sender. If signature is not verified, the message is simply ignored [4].

3 Secure Synchronous Ring Protocol (SSRP)

For SSRP, GDH protocol which has least bandwidth usage when handling group membership operations [4] is selected from the methods in the Cliques Toolkit. The management structure of the GDH is much like a ring application and GDH also supports handling the group key management operations via a controller. In the ring protocol, the group membership operations are performed independently in each ring. Similar to Iolus [9], the individual group keys are calculated by each ring. This provides scalability for large groups having hundreds of members. SSRP protocol calculates group key independently for each cluster while handling the group membership operations such as member join/leave, mass join/leave and group join/leave. The leader and the representatives are not only responsible for managing the cluster's membership operations but also managing the contribution process of GDH when generating the cluster key of each view. Here the inner ring messages are decrypted with the inner ring key and again encrypted with the outer ring key. However, this operation requires decryption/encryption of whole data which increases the computation costs. Instead, the approach proposed in [9] can be implemented in SSRP for this situation, since each cluster has independent group membership management [14].

3.1 Membership Operations

The following operations are provided by SSRP:

Member addition: The initial case is that there is only one entity waiting to add new members to the group. This entity is the leader. Leader accepts a finite number of members as representatives. After this, new joining requests by the nodes are served by the representatives until they reach a specific count. When joining the nth member, total messaging need of this membership operation is $n + 3$.

Member leave: The GDH member leave protocol [12] is implemented without any modification. When a member leaves the cluster having n members, total messaging need of this membership operation is n.

Mass join: As suggested in [12], the chained implementation of controller based GDH single member join operation is used for mass join. When m new members join n member cluster, total messaging need of this membership operation is $n + 3m + 1$.

Mass leave: The GDH mass leave protocol [12] is implemented without any modification. When m members leave the cluster having n members, the total messaging need of this membership operation is n.

Group join and group leave: In SSRP, group join operations are carried out by the representative of the cluster. The group join operation is simply the member join operation of the representative into the outer ring controlled by the leader. Since each cluster has independent membership management, outer ring membership does not effect the inner ring operations. The same logic is applied to the group leave operation. In this case, member leave operation is applied on the representative of the cluster requesting to leave. Note that, since SSRP uses GDH for member addition, member leave, mass join and mass leave operations, the computation complexity and the security properties declared in [12] are preserved in SSRP.

3.2 The Representative Finite State Machine

The simplified finite state machine diagram of the representative for single layer is shown in Fig.2 with the following states:

Wait Period: In this state, the representative runs its timer in order to keep track of the token to be released for each data circulation period of the system.

Wait Data: The representative waits for the token to be filled by its group members in this state. If the filled token is received back in a bounded time, then the representative sets its state to *Wait Period* in order to start the next token circulation for the next period.

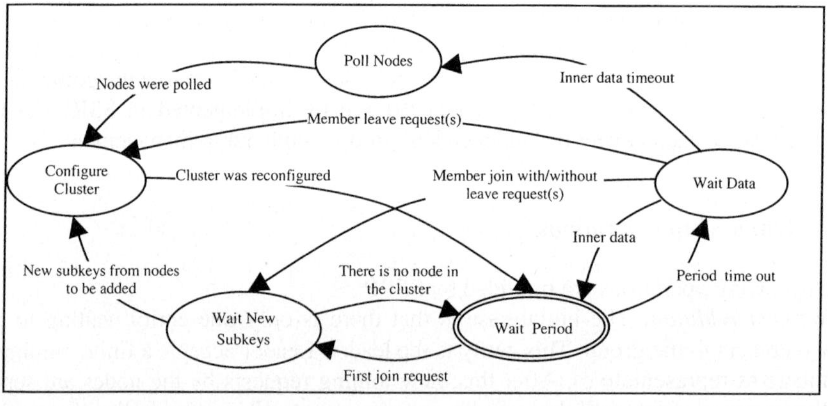

Fig. 2. Simplified FSM diagram of an SSRP representative

This is the normal communication loop of the SSRP. If the filled token is not received back in a bounded time, then the representative starts searching the ring to exclude the problematic node(s) from the group and sets its state to *Poll Nodes*. During the normal group communication operation, the new joining requests from the outside and the leave requests from the ring are held in request queues generated by the representative. If there are any join requests without leave requests in the request queues, the corresponding join protocol (mass or member join) is executed and the representative sets its state to *Wait New Subkeys*. If there are also any leave requests in addition to join requests then, first the subkeys of the leaving nodes are removed from the current subkeys list and the representative updates the resulting list with its new private key. After that, join protocol is started using these new subkeys to join the new members. In this case again, the next state is *Wait New Subkeys*. If there are only leave requests while in this state, then the representative starts the member/mass leave protocol. It removes the subkeys of leaving nodes from the current subkeys list and updates the resulting list with its new private key. The next state is set to *Configure Cluster*.

Wait New Subkeys: According to the controller based GDH member join and mass join protocols, controller of the group sends the last received subkeys that are defined in [12] to the new joining member(s) and it waits the updated values by the new members in the way that is defined in GDH protocol definitions. As the controller of this group, representative waits updated subkeys from the nodes to be added in this state. If these keys are not received within a bounded time, representative returns to the *Wait Period* state.

Polling Nodes: To find the crashed node(s), the representative polls the ring nodes and excludes the member(s) from the view which does not respond to this polling message within a bounded time. It removes the subkeys of the crashed nodes from the current subkeys list and updates the resulting list with its new private key. The next state is set to the *Configure Cluster*.

Configure Cluster: In this state, representative contributes its private key to the received or generated new subkeys. The resulting subkeys list is then replaced in a configuration token and sent to the ring members. Each ring member receiving this token then calculates the group key of the new group view that is to be shared among the ring members. Then the new group view is set up and the representative sets its state to *Wait Period* to run the SSRP protocol for this view.

3.3 SSRP Leader Election Algorithm

Assuming the existence of a distributed clock synchronization service, we developed a leader election algorithm based on timers. Each node runs a timer checking the liveliness of the controller. Each time a node receives a token or a polling message, it resets its timer since the origin of these messages in the SSRP protocol is always the controller. The first node that has a timeout will declare itself as the new controller. Timeout value, T_i which reflects node$_i$'s distance from the controller is different for each node. The Equation for T_i is given below where T_{clock} is the current clock value and *OFFSET* is the expected time for the new controller to reconfigure the ring.

$$T_i = T_{clock} + (id_i * OFFSET) \quad \text{and} \quad OFFSET > \frac{nT_p + T_{config}}{2n}$$

3.4 Proof of Virtual Synchrony Semantics on SSRP

In this section, we show that the SSRP protocol preserves the virtual synchrony semantics that are pointed in [3] and defined in [15].

1. Self Inclusion: If a node installs a view v then it is a member of this view. Because the only way the node can receive the token t updating the group view is that its address should be known by the preceeding ring member in order to send the token. This is possible if the representative places the information of this node into the current view since it controls the group view operations in SSRP.

2. Local Monotonicity: If a node installs a view v^+ after installing a view v then the identifier of v^+ is greater than the identifier of v. In SSRP, it is impossible to install a view more than once since the view installing operation is started by the representative once per view change occurring in the group.

3. Sending View Delivery: The new view installing operation is started only when the data token is received back by the representative at *Wait Data* state or at *Wait Period* state when there is no node in the cluster. So, if data is circulating through the ring, it is guarenteed that there will be no view change until the data is received by all the nodes that are members of the view in which the data has been sent.

4. Delivery Integrity: If a node receives a message from a token in a view, there is always at least one member, whose index number in the ring is lower than this node, that transmits this token in the same view before the node receives it. The reason is that the data is transmitted by tokens and tokens are always unicast among the ring members in one direction.

5. No Duplication: A message is not sent twice. Each token circulation has a unique number and the only source that creates this token is the representative.

6. Self Delivery: All ring members except the controllers (i.e. representatives and leader) has to direct the received token to the next member within a bounded time.

7. Transitional Set: In SSRP if a node n_1 and n_2 install a new view, then n_1 is in the transitional set of the n_2 if and only if n_1's previous view is identical to n_2's previous view. Consider the case that n_1 is not in the previous view of n_2. This case is valid if n_1 is one of the new members requesting the join to the group since it is not possible to add n_1 into the current view without changing the view id. That is, the representative stops the token circulation and configures the view by adding the new members including n_1 so that the previous view of n_2 does not include n_1. Then n_1 is not included in the transitional set of n_2.

8. Virtual Synchrony: From sending view delivery property, in SSRP, tokens are released by the representative and they are received by all nodes of the view that tokens are sent in. Then, if two nodes are included in any two consecutive views they see the same set of messages in both views. All messages are delivered in total order since the messages are delivered by tokens circulating in one direction. So every member receives the messages in the same order.

4 Conclusions

In this work, we described a group communication protocol, SSRP, having a built in security implementation which maintains a group key shared among the group members for any membership operation. This protocol supports virtual synchrony semantics and has the security properties of GDH. Integrating GDH and the ring protocol does not increase the communication complexity of the resulting design compared with the ring protocol and integration process is easy. This integrated protocol increases the system security by combining the security protocol and application data. Also we introduce a leader election algorithm for SSRP assuming clock synchronization service of the ring protocol. The protocol is fully fault tolerant in case of multiple crashes. Because adding security service does not degrade the communication performance, this protocol is suitable for wide area networks. SSRP protocol has the advantage of less bandwidth usage because GDH has low message complexity and also in SSRP, group membership and key generation operations are integrated, reducing the overall communication complexity. Hierarchical construction also makes this design suitable for large groups (>100) since group operations are carried out in parallel within subrings. As a future work, we plan on improving the SSRP protocol by adding authentication service into the key management process.

References

1. Akay, O., Erciyes, K.: A Dynamic Load Balancing Model For A Distributed System. Mathematical and Computational Applications,Vol. 8 No. 3 (2003) 353–363
2. Amir, Y., et. al.: Secure Group Communication in Asynchronous Networks with Failures: Integration and Experiments. Proceedings of the 20th IEEE International Conference on Distributed Computing Systems (2000) 330–343
3. Amir, Y., et al.: Exploring Robustness in Group Key Agreement. Proc. of the 21st Int'l. Conf. on Distributed Computing Systems --ICDCS'01 (2001) 399–408
4. Amir, Y., et al.: On the Performance of Group Key Agreement Protocols. Proc. of 22nd Int'l. Conf. on Distributed Computing Systems --ICDCS'02 (2002) 463–464
5. Burmester, M., Y. Desmedt, Y.: A Secure and Efficient Conference Key Distribution System. Advances in Cryptology – EUROCRYPT'94 (1994) 275–286
6. Erciyeş, K.: Implementation of A Scalable Ring Protocol for Fault Tolerance in Distributed Real-Time Systems. Proc. of 6th Symp. On Comp. Networks –BAS 2001 (2001) 188–197
7. Kihlstrom, K.P., Moser, L. E., Melliar-Smith, P.M.: The Secure Ring Protocols for Securing Group Communication. Proc. of the IEEE 31st Hawaii International Conference on System Sciences, Vol. 3 (1998) 317–326
8. Kim, Y., Perring, A., Tsudik G.: Simple and Fault-tolerant Key Agreement for Dynamic Collaborative Groups. 7th ACM Conf. on Comp. & Communication Security (2000) 235–244
9. Mittra, S.: Iolus: A Framework for Scalable Secure Multicasting. Proceedings of the ACM SIGCOMM'97 (1997) 277–288
10. Rodeh, O., Birman, K., Hayden, M., Xiao, Z., Dolev, D.: Ensemble Security. Tech. Rep. TR98-1703, Cornell University, Dept. of Computer Science (1998).
11. Steer, D., Strawczynski, L., Diffie, W., Wiener, M.: A Secure Audio Teleconference System. Advances in Cryptology – Lecture Notes in Computer Science (1990) 520–528

12. Steiner, M., Tsudik, G., Waidner, M.: Key Agreement in Dynamic Peer Groups. IEEE Trans. on Parallel and Distributed Systems. Vol. 11. No. 8 (2000) 769–781
13. Steiner, J.G., Neuman, C., Schiller, J.I.: Kerberos: An Authentication Service for Open Network Systems. Usenix Winter Conference (1988) 191–202
14. Tunalı, T., Erciyeş, K., Soysert, Z.: A Hierarchical Fault-Tolerant Ring Protocol For A Distributed Real-Time System. Special issue of Parallel and Distributed Computing Practices on Parallel and Distributed Real-Time Systems, Vol. 2, No. 1 (2000) 33–44
15. Vitenberg, R., Keidar, I., Chockler, G.V., Dolev, D.: Group Communication Specifications: A Comprehensive Study. Tech. Rep. CS0964, Comp. Sci. Dept., Technion (1999)

A New Role-Based Delegation Model Using Sub-role Hierarchies†

HyungHyo Lee[1], YoungRok Lee[2], and BongHam Noh[2]

[1] Div. of Information and EC, Wonkwang University, Iksan, 570-749, Korea
hlee@wonkwang.ac.kr

[2] Dept. of Computer Science, Chonnam National University, Gwangju, 500-757, Korea
{yrlee, bongnam}@chonnam.ac.kr

Abstract. Delegation in computer systems plays an important role in relieving security officer's management efforts, especially in a large-scale, highly decentralized environment. By distributing management authorities to a number of delegatees, scalable and manageable security management functionality can be achieved. Recently, a number of researches are proposed to incorporate delegation concept into Role-Based Access Control(RBAC) model, which is becoming a promising model for enterprise environment with various organization structures. In this paper, we propose a new role-based delegation model using sub-role hierarchies supporting restricted inheritance functionality, in which security administrator can easily control permission inheritance behavior using sub-roles. Also, we describe how role-based user-to-user, role-to-role delegations are accomplished in the proposed model and analyze our delegation model against various delegation characteristics.

1 Introduction

The basic idea behind delegation is that some active entity in a system delegates authority to another active entity to carry out some functions on behalf of the former[4]. Delegation can be defined as a trust-based authority transfer among users, and it be used as a basis for distributed network and systems management. In the mean time, Role-Based Access Control(RBAC) model is becoming a promising model for enterprise environments with various organization structures. In RBAC model, permissions are associated with roles, and users are made members of appropriate roles based on their responsibilities and qualifications, acquiring the permissions of these roles[1].

Recently, a number of research activities are published to incorporate delegation concept into RBAC model[3,4,10]. RBDM0[3] and RDM2000[10] are precursors of delegation-enhanced RBAC models that focus on user-to-user, total delegation. But there would be a security breach of least privilege principle since they only support total delegation, and they entail an increased overhead for multiple delegation due to user to user delegation.

† This work was supported by University IT Research Center Project and partially by Wonkwang University in 2002

A. Yazici and C. Şener (Eds.): ISCIS 2003, LNCS 2869, pp. 811–818, 2003.

In this paper, in order to address those problems, we propose a new role-based delegation model using sub-role hierarchies. In addition to the restricted permission inheritance, sub-role hierarchies can be used to support various delegation types such as total/partial delegation, user-to-user/role-to-role delegation, etc. Also, we describe how role-based user-to-user, role-to-role, total and partial delegations are accomplished in the proposed model and analyze our delegation model against various delegation characteristics.

The rest of this paper is organized as follows. Section 2 describes related work for role-based delegation. In Section 3, we briefly reviewed sub-role hierarchies, a key component of our delegation model. Section 4 presents how user-to-user and role-to-role delegations can be achieved using sub-role hierarchies and analyze our delegation model against various delegation characteristics. Section 5 concludes this paper and outlined our further work.

2 Related Work

Barka and Sandhu proposed RBDM0 model[3,4]. They developed a simple role-based delegation model and explored some issues including revocation, delegation with hierarchical roles, permission-based partial delegation and multi-step delegation. One limitation of RBDM0 is that it does not address the relationships among each component of a delegation, which is a critical notion to the delegation model[10]. RDM2000 is to address user-to-user delegation supporting role hierarchies and multi-step delegation in role-based systems[10]. In RDM2000, a new relation called delegation relation is defined, and some components and constraints needed to support delegation and revocation are proposed.

While RBDM0[4] and RDM2000[10] are simple but practical role-based delegation models, they only support user-to-user, total delegation. User-to-user delegation gets security administrator to perform user assignment operations if a delegating user to delegate a role to all members of another role at the same time, which can be easily done by role-to-role delegation. In addition, in role-based delegation models like RBDM0 and RDM2000, only total delegation is possible since the unit of delegation is the role itself. But total delegation may breach the need to know security principle if some permissions of a delegating role need not be delegated.

3 Role Hierarchies Providing Restricted Permission Inheritance

In this section, the components and characteristics of sub-role hierarchies, a key component of our role-based delegation model, are briefly reviewed.

3.1 Roles and Sub-roles

A role is a job function in the organization that describes the authority and responsibility conferred on a user assigned to the role[2]. Administrators can create roles according to the job functions performed in their organizations. This is very intuitive and efficient approach except unconditional permission inheritance. In RBAC models, a senior role inherits the permissions of all its junior roles. This property may breach the least privilege principle, one of the main security principles RBAC models support[2]. In order to address this drawback, we divide a role into a number of *sub-roles* based on the characteristics of *job functions* and the *degree of inheritance*. Figure 1 shows a proposed sub-role concept compared with an original or *macro* role.

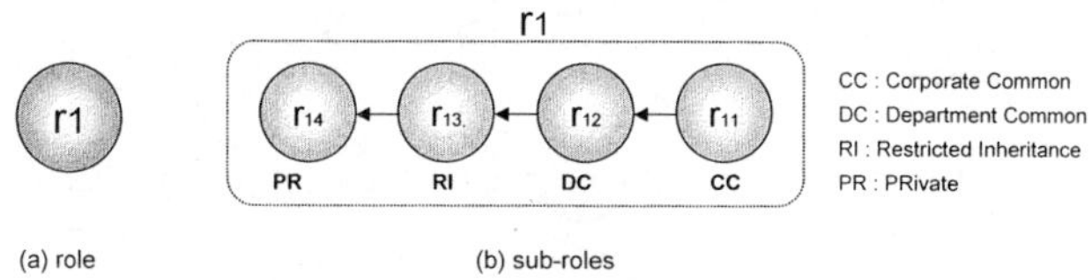

Fig. 1. Sub-role concept for corporate environment

In Figure 1, *r1* means a role and it is divided into sub-roles considering corporation environment which consists of several departments and job positions. We categorize sub-roles as *Corporate Common*(CC) roles, *Department Common*(DC) roles, *Restricted Inheritance*(RI) roles and *PRivate*(PR) sub-roles based on their functional and inheritance properties. Sub-roles have characteristics in terms of inheritance as follows(Table 1).

Table 1. Categrorization of sub-roles and their characteristics

Sub-role category	Degree of Inheritance	Characteristics of assigned permissions to sub-roles
Corporate Common (CC)	Unconditional inheritance	- permissions allowed to all members in a corporation - includes junior roles' permissions in a CC role hierarchy
Department Common (DC)	Unconditional inheritance	- permissions allowed to all members of a specific department - includes junior roles' permission in DC role hierarchy
Restricted Inheritance (RI)	Restricted inheritance	- permissions may or may not be inherited to its senior roles in RI role hierarchy - security administrator specify the roles to which permissions are restrictively inherited
Private (PR)	No inheritance	- permissions only allowed to directly assigned users - no inheritance to any other roles

3.2 User Assignment

Figure 2 illustrates how users are assigned to roles in the sub-role hierarchies. Figure 2 (a) shows a user-role assignment in a traditional role hierarchy and (b) depicts a user-role assignment in the proposed model. Solid lines in Figure 2 indicate permission inheritance, while a dotted line denotes restricted inheritance. For example, both $r_{11} \rightarrow r_{21}$ and $r_{12} \rightarrow r_{22}$ relations indicate that the permissions of the junior roles are unconditionally inherited to its seniors, respectively. But, $r_{13} \rightarrow r_{23}$ (a dotted line) shows restricted inheritance relation in which permissions of sub-role(r_{13}) are inherited only to designated its senior roles, in this example, r_{23}. Finally, r_{14} and r_{24} are private roles and no permission inheritance occurs between two private roles. Users can be assigned to only private sub-roles(In section 4.2.2, this constraint is mitigated to support user-to-user partial delegation).

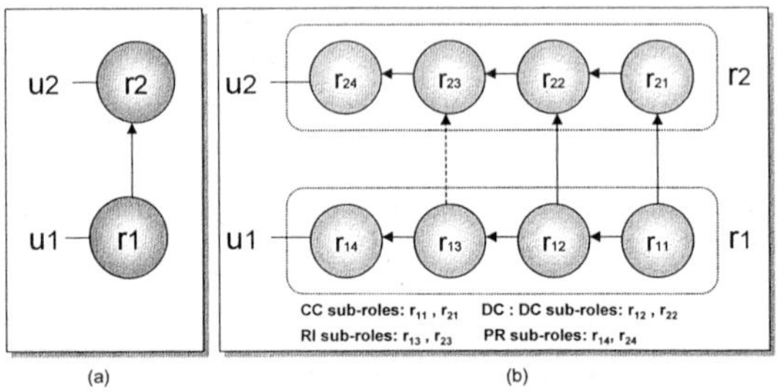

Fig. 2. Comparison of user-role assignment

3.3 Permission Inheritance in Sub-role Hierarchies

There are two kinds of sub-role hierarchies: *horizontal* and *vertical*. Horizontal sub-role hierarchy(i.e., *job position plane*) is a partially ordered relation between sub-roles which are divided from the same macro role, and only unconditional permission inheritance exists between sub-roles. Vertical sub-role hierarchy(i.e., *job function plane*) is a partially ordered relation between sub-roles in the same sub-role category(i.e., CC, DC, RI, PR sub-roles) but in different macro roles, and both unconditional and restricted inheritance exit in it. Sub-roles in RI category need to specify the sub-roles to which their permissions should be inherited. Only the specified sub-roles in RI hierarchy can inherit the permissions of their junior sub-roles.

In Figure 3, even if sub-role r_{i3} belongs to *General Manager* role, a senior role to *Manager* role, the permissions of r_{j3} are not inherited to r_{i3}.

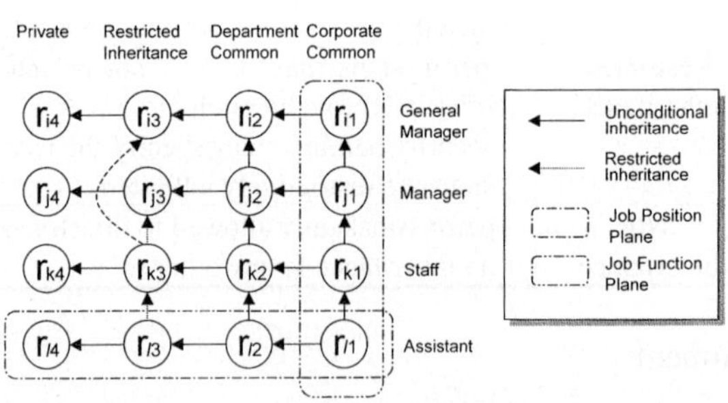

Fig. 3. Example of sub-role hierarchies

4 Delegations Using Sub-role Hierarchies

Delegation in computer systems can be done in various methods, such as user to user, user to machine, and perhaps even machine to user[6,7,8,9]. As far as the author knows, every research on role-based delegation is based on user to user delegation, in which a delegating user, a member of a delegating role, assigns a delegated user to the delegating role. Why role-based delegation researches do not support role to role delegation even if such delegation type is useful? The problem steams from the *granularity of delegation* the original role hierarchy support. Role to role delegation in the role hierarchy *may* form a cycle and as a result, all users assigned to roles in the cycle share the same permissions because all the permissions of a delegating role are delegated to the delegated roles(i.e., total delegation). This may cause a unintended or a unwanted permission flow in the role hierarchy, which only supports unconditional inheritance.

In terms of the granularity of delegation, sub-roles provide a fine-grained delegation vehicle to security administrators. Sub-roles enables security administrators to delegate some of the permissions of a delegating role(i.e., partial delegation) to a delegated user through user to user delegation method.

4.1 User to User Delegation

Recent researches on role-based delegation mainly focused on user-to-user delegation[3,4]. However user-to-user delegation in previous work can only support total delegation, that is all permissions of the delegating role are delegated to the delegated user. But in our model, depending on assigning a delegated user to which delegation sub-role, security administrator can conduct partial or total delegation. For example, if a user is assigned to the private sub-role of a delegating role, all permissions of the delegating sub-roles is delegated to the user. But, if a user is assigned to sub-roles other than private sub-role, the permissions of the delegating sub-roles except private sub-role are delegated to the delegated user.

4.1.1 Total Delegation

Total delegation means delegating all of the permissions that are assigned to the delegating role. In the proposed model, *user-to-user total* delegation can be achieved by assigning a user to the private sub-role of the delegation role. In figure 4 (a), a user *u*, an original member of role *staff*, can be a delegated member of role *manager* by being assigned to the private sub-role of the delegation role *manager*. As a result, since a private sub-role inherits all the permissions of its junior sub-roles in the same job position plane, the user *u* can perform all permissions of both roles, *staff* and *manager*.

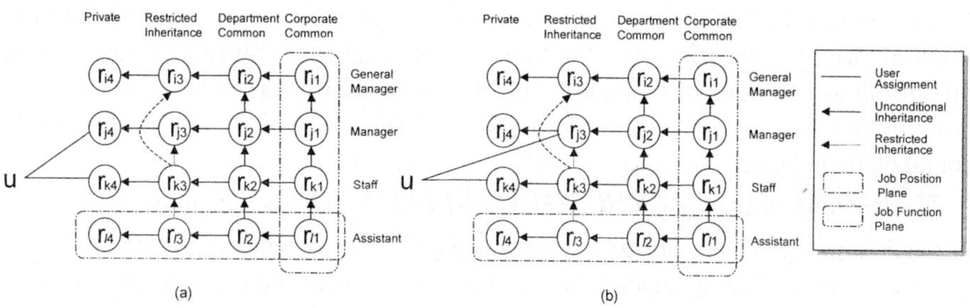

Fig. 4. Example of user-to-user total/partial delegation

Definition 1. A *user-to-user total delegation* relation authorizes user-to-user total delegation in the sub-role hierarchies:

U2U_TOTAL_DELEGATION $\subseteq \boldsymbol{R}_{PR} \times \boldsymbol{R}_{PR}$, where $\boldsymbol{R}_{PR}$ is a set of private sub-roles.

The meaning of $(r_x, r_y) \in$ ***U2U_TOTAL_DELEGATION*** where $r_x, r_y \notin \boldsymbol{R}_{PR}$ is that security administrator can assign a user, say *u*, in the set *users*(r_y) to private sub-role r_x, which is senior to r_y.

4.1.2 Partial Delegation

Partial delegation means only the subsets of the delegating role's permissions are delegated to the delegated role. In the proposed model, *user-to-user partial* delegation can be conducted by assigning a user to the non-private sub-role of the delegating role. In order to support user-to-user partial delegation, the constraint which restricts the assignment of a user only to the private sub-role should be modified. In figure 4 (b), a user *u*, an original member of role *staff*, can be a delegated member of role *manager* by being assigned to the sub-role, for example r_{j3}, of the delegation role *manager*. As a result, only the permissions assigned to the junior roles of r_{j3}, that is r_{j1} and r_{j2}, are delegated to the user *u*.

Like **Definition 1**, a *user-to-user partial delegation* relation, ***U2U_PARTIAL_DELEGATION*** is defined, but we omit its formal definition due to space limitation. The meaning of $(r_x, r_y) \in$ ***U2U_PARTIAL_DELEGATION*** where $r_x \notin \boldsymbol{R}_{PR}$ is that a user, say *u*, in the set *users*(r_y) can be assigned by security administrator to a non-private sub-role r_x, which is in higher job position plane than that of r_y.

4.2 Role to Role Delegation

In some situations, role-to-role delegation is useful when security administrator wants to delegate a role to all members of a delegated role[10]. For example, a delegating user may need to delegate a role to all members of another role *at the same time*. A role-to-role delegation would be an answer to such needs.

4.2.1 Total Delegation

In the sub-role hierarchies, role-to-role delegation is achieved by creating a *delegation link* from a delegating sub-role to a delegated sub-role. Since a private sub-role inherits all permissions of its junior sub-roles on the same horizontal plane, a delegation link from the private sub-role to a delegated sub-role which is on the lower horizontal plane indicates a role-to-role total delegation(Figure 5 (a)).

The meaning of $(r_x, r_y) \in$ ***R2R_TOTAL_DELEGATION*** is that all the permissions of the delegating private sub-role r_x are delegated to the delegated private sub-role r_y. After role-to-role total delegation, all members of the delegated role are authorized to perform all the permission of the delegating role in a single delegation operation. This method is a simple but not trivial solution for the shortcomings of user-to-user delegation model mentioned in [10].

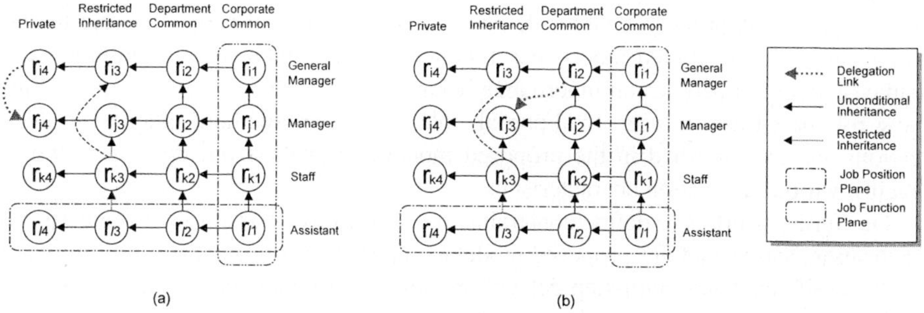

Fig. 5. Example of role-to-role total/partial delegation

4.2.2 Partial Delegation

Like user-to-user delegation, partial delegation is supported in our model, while it can not or very limitedly be supported in previous role-based delegation models. Delegation link from sub-roles other than private sub-role to a delegated role indicates a role-to-role partial delegation (Figure 5 (b)).

The meaning of $(r_x, r_y) \in$ ***R2R_PARTIAL_DELEGATION*** where $r_x \notin \boldsymbol{R}_{PR}$ is that subset of the permissions of the delegating non-private sub-role r_x are delegated to the delegated sub-role r_y.

4.3 Comparison

Table 2 summarizes the characteristics of role-based delegation models, and the criteria are from [4]. Currently, the proposed model does not support a multi-step delegation and a self-acted delegation characteristics, which enable ordinary users can activate a delegation.

Table 2. Comparion among role-based delegation models

Criteria \ Delegation models		Proposed model	RDM2000	RBDM0
Delegation types	user-to-user	○	○	○
	role-to-role	○	×	×
Totality	total	○	○	○
	partial	○	×	×
Levels of delegation	single-step	○	○	○
	multi-step	×	○	○
Administration		agent-acted	self-acted	self-acted

5 Conclusions and Future Work

In this paper, we propose a new role-based delegation model using sub-role hierarchies supporting restricted inheritance functionality, in which security administrator can easily control permission inheritance behavior using sub-roles. Also, we describe how role-based user-to-user, total/partial, role-to-role with/without inheritance delegations are accomplished in the proposed model and analyze our delegation model against various delegation characteristics.

Our further work is to define constraints for various role-based role delegation and revocation, and extend our proposed model to support other delegation characteristics such as self-acted and multi-step delegation. Also, the development of administration facilities of our model is needed.

References

1. Ravi S. Sandhu, "Rational for the RBAC96 Family of Access Control Models," In Proceedings of 1st ACM Workshop on Role-Based Access control, ACM, Article No. 9, 1996.
2. Ravi S. Sandhu, Edward J. Coyne, Hal L. Feinstein and Charles E. Youman, "Role-based access control model," IEEE Computer, Volume 29, February 1996, pages 38–47.
3. Ezedin Barka and Ravi S. Sandhu, "A Role-based Delegation Model and Some Extensions," Proceedings of 16th Annual Computer Security Application Conference, Sheraton New Orleans, Dec. 11–15, 2000.
4. Ezedin Barka and Ravi S. Sandhu, "Framework for Role-Based Delegation Models," Proceedings of 23rd National Information Systems Security Conference, Baltimore, Oct. 16–19, 2000, pages 101–114.
5. Ravi S. Sandhu, Venkata Bhamidipati, Qamar Munawer, "The ARBAC97 model for role-based administration of roles," ACM Transactions on Information and System Security, Volume 2, Issue 1, 1999, pages 105–135.
6. Henry M. Gladny, "Access Control for Large Collections," ACM Transactions on Information Systems, Volume 15. Issue 2, April 1997, Pages 154–194.
7. Martin Abadi, Michael Burrows, Butler Lampson and Gordon Plotkin, "A Calculus for Access Control in Distributed Systems," ACM Transactions on Programming Languages and Systems, Volumn 15, Issue 4, September 1993, pages 706–734.
8. Morrie Gasser, and Ellen McDermott, "An Architecture for practical Delegation in a Distributed System," 1990 IEEE Computer Society Symposium on Research in Security and Privacy, Oakland, CA. May 7–9, 1990.
9. Vijay Varadharajan, Philip Allen, and Stewart Black, "An Analysis of the Proxy Problem in Distributed systems," IEEE Symposium on Research in Security and Privacy, Oakland, CA 1991.
10. Longhua Zhang, Gail-Joon Ahn, Bei-Tseng Chu, "A rule-based framework for role based delegation," ACM Workshop on Role Based Access Control, Proceedings of the Sixth ACM Symposium on Access Control Models and Technologies, Chantilly, Virginia, United States, May 3-4, 2001, pages 153–162.

POLICE: A Novel Policy Framework

Taner Dursun[1] and Bülent Örencik[2]

[1]TÜBİTAK UEKAE
PK 21 41470 Kocaeli, Turkey
tdursun@uekae.tubitak.gov.tr
[2]İstanbul Technical University
Maslak, İstanbul, Turkey
orencik@cs.itu.edu.tr

Abstract. In this paper we present a complete policy-based framework, composed of a policy specification language and its deployment and management models for policy distribution. The Police policy language provides a common means of specifying every kind of policies that may be involved in management of distributed systems. It supports obligations and permissions. The Police policies contain event triggered action sets for policy-based management of distributed systems. Other key concepts of the framework include domains used to group objects, and distributed conflict handling.

1 Introduction

The difficulties encountered in the management of distributed systems have led to the prominence of research in the area of policy-based management. In this paper we present a framework for specifying and managing policies in a policy life cycle. In conjunction with a policy specification language, the framework permits integrated administration of policies with automated deployment. Our model also introduces a novel distributed conflict detection mechanism.

Remainder of this paper is organized as follows. Section 2 describes the Police language and then in Section 3 the deployment model that is capable of enforcing the specified Police policies is presented. The conflict detection and resolution issues provided within our model are discussed in Section 4. Section 5 includes evaluation of the related work from literature. The last section presents our conclusions.

2 POLICE Policy Specification Language

To facilitate policy management activities it is necessary to use a policy language easily understandable by human administrators in conjunction with an integrated toolkit for the deployment, enforcement and coordination of policies within the system. The versatility of policy for use in system management depends a lot on the descriptive power of the policy language.

POLICE framework has an object-oriented language for specifying both **security** and **management policies** for distributed systems. Unlike many other policy specification notations, uniform enforcement for all kind of policies makes the Police framework simpler. Another simplicity provided within Police framework is integrating condition and event concepts used separately in Literature (see Sect. 3.3).

A. Yazici and C. Şener (Eds.): ISCIS 2003, LNCS 2869, pp. 819–827, 2003.

We use the term **actor** to refer to users, principals or automated manager components, which have management responsibility. Actors access **target objects** (resources or service), by invoking their methods.

```
authorisation policy:
    cando policyName {
          [actor    domain - scope expression;]
          target    domain - scope expression;
          action  : action list;
          while   : constraint expression;
    }
obligation policy:
    mustdo policyName {
          [actor    domain - scope expression;]
          target    domain - scope expression;
          action  : action list;
          when    : constraint expressions;
    }
constraint expression :
(time expressions|condition expressions|event expressions|ALWAYS|NEVER)*
```

Fig. 1. Police policy syntax

The syntax of a Police policy is shown in Fig.1. There may be actions executed automatically by hidden actors such as the system's itself (Impersonal Policy). Hence, the actor fields are optional. The **action** part can be extended to include any kind of statements composed of method calls on local or remote objects.

Limiting the applicability of a policy, constraint clauses could be based on a particular time period, attribute values of objects or several events. In contrast to the many other policy languages [3, 4, 5], all policies specified in Police can be event-triggered. Events can be simple, i.e. an internal timer event, or an external event notified by monitoring service components.

We use two basic policy types: *authorizations* and obligations. In Literature, these two classes can be further divided into positive and negative policies [1, 2]. However, we eliminate negative policies to handle policy conflicts easily. Although negative policies complicate enforcement process, there are reasons to support them. Negative authorization policies, for example, can be used to temporarily remove access rights from actors if the need arises. Instead of negative policies, Police uses constraint keywords like NEVER and, ALWAYS to restrict some actions. Actually our philosophy is based-on "Permission-Based Regime" in which prohibition is the default unless explicitly permitted. The keywords specified above can be used only to narrow scope of policies in terms of actors.

```
cando Login ( actor A, target T, TInterval validTI,int maxLogoff) {
   action T.login ();
   while time.within(validTI)   and A.logoffToday <= maxLogoff;
}
Login loginPolicy = new Login(/student/grade4, LabPC/blue,0900-1700,10);
```

The policy states that all students from grade 4 are permitted to login to computer named blue, but only between 09:00 and 17:00 and only if the number of attempts per day is no more than 10.

Authorization (cando) Policies are designed to give permissions to actors to run some actions on other system objects. They are conceptually enforced near the actor instead of target objects to be affected by the operations actor performed. The previous figure presents a view of the language.
Obligation (mustdo) Policies define what actions an actor must do if the conditions specified in the policy are met or certain events occur. The obligation policies do not depend on authorization policies. This means that if the conditions for an obligation policy are met, the action will performed immediately without checking if there is any authorization policy allowing the actor to run this action.

3 POLICE Policy Deployment Framework Components

An overview of the policy deployment model is shown in Fig. 2. Policy Server acts as the interface to policy management, which stores compiled policy classes, distributes them and supports policy management coordination. Policy Management Service creates deployment objects. Policy Deployment Service coordinates the distribution of the deployment objects to the PEP's.

3.1 Management Console and Policy Programming IDE

The Management Console (MC) provides a graphical interface for specifying, reviewing and modifying policies. Being integrated with Domain Service and Police Compiler, the MC helps the administrator to define valid policies conforming to both object model of the whole system and the language syntax. Our policy management console will also include a policy-programming tool. As using this IDE tool, the administrators can manipulate policies of the system as if they write a code to be run on a distributed system. As relying on the Police language, the programming language of this IDE will support loop, if-else statements, and many other structures of an ordinary computer programming language. We call the language as **Police Interface Language** (PIL), since its statements will be interpreted into Police policies. We also plan to use visual components in programs written in PIL to allow administrator to create their custom interfaces. A **Command- Line Window** will also be provided to enter commands to the Policy Management Server for interactive management

3.2 Policy Distributions and Enforcement

In our model, the enforcement agents, termed **Policy Controllers (PC**s) are responsible for enforcement of both authorization and obligation type policies. Both cando and mustdo policies are distributed in the same **uniform** way to the PCs near the actors that it makes our architecture simpler.

Policy Management Service generates a **deployment object** for each policy that Policy Deployment Service distributes to its enforcement platforms. The deployment objects distributed to PEPs, are merged into related PC. Normally, each actor is in a scope of at least one **PC**, which enforces all policies defined for that actor object. A **PC** controls all the actors at its location and enforces all policies relating to its actors. Being primarily a stationary agent, each PC normally enforces many policies and controls the behaviors of many different actors in the domain for which this PC is responsible. Policy Deployment Service creates the deployment objects and sends to appropriate **PC**s. **PC**s analyze the deployment objects they receive and enlarge their behavior according to the content of them.

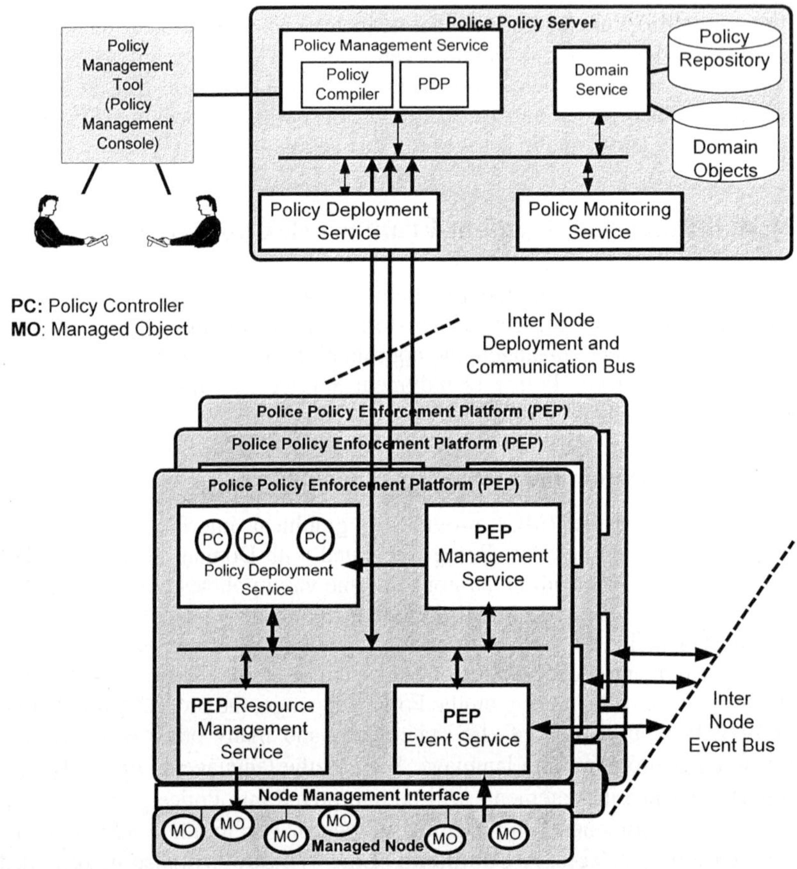

Fig. 2. Architecture of Police framework

```
UserObject a=new UserObject (aAksoy, Ahmet, AKSOY, ...);
DomainService.addElement ( "\user\student\", a);
Actor actor1 = new Actor("\user\ student\aAksoy");

while (HostA.noUserLogin){

   actor1 cando HostA.method1( );
   actor1 cando HostB.method2( );
}
for ( Target trg in [ target1, taget2,....., targetn]){
   trg cando HostB.method3( );
}
```

Fig. 3. Sample statements written in PIL

In the PEP architecture, the **Resource Controller** intercepts all access requests of the actors and redirects to concerned PC to check whether the access is permitted, as shown in Fig. 4. This PC will check that the constraints of authorization policies are fulfilled. Whereas in case of obligation policies, PCs wait for the signal from Event Service indicating that the constraints are fulfilled before enforcing the actors

3.3 Event Service and Policy Gauge

The **Event Service** collects and composes events from the managed nodes, and forwards them to the registered **PC**s executing policies. The **ES** is an integrated service spread through the distributed system nodes via the **Inter-Node Event Bus**.

The constraint sections of the Police policies are implemented as event-statements composed of system-events and pseudo-events. In order to express event statements, we adopt complicated event expressions from the **Policy Definition Language** (PDL) [6], defining several operators to derive complex events from primitive events.

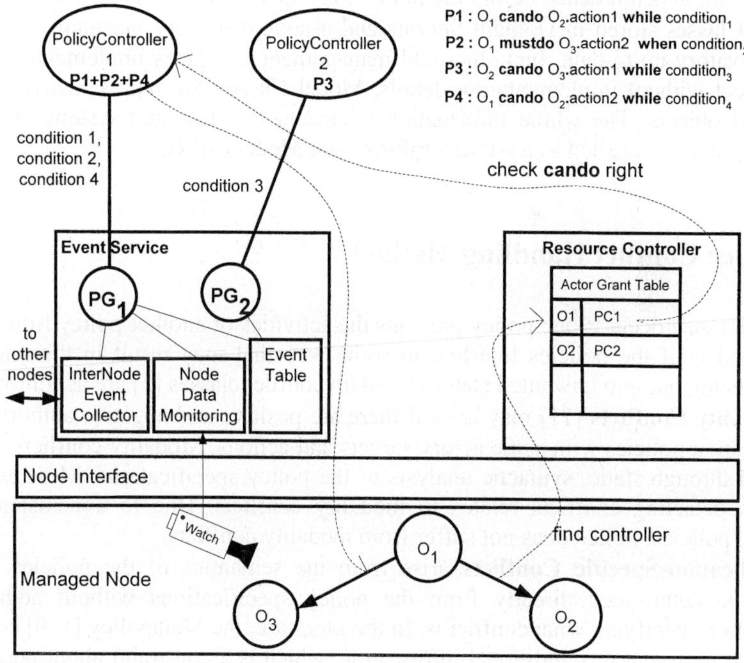

Fig. 4. Interaction between PCs, Resource Controller and Event Service

The pseudo-events are created to observe attributes of the managed system's objects and occur when these attributes reach at specified value ranges. The sophisticated time period conditions can also be implemented as pseudo-events. The constraint part statements are named **Policy Gauges**. Unlike other policy specification languages, Police uses event-triggers for both authorization and obligation policies.

After a **PC** registers with the Event Service (**ES**), the policy gauge expression is created and continuously evaluated. When the output of the gauge is true, the ES triggers the related PC. So, there is no need the PC to evaluate its policies whether the conditions are met to execute them. Since, the **ES** already performs this task for **PC**s.

While a gauge is active, if related policy is a **cando-**type, the **actors** can perform actions if they attempt, otherwise nothing will happen. In case of the **mustdo-type policy,** the activation of the gauge causes the **PC** to enforce the actors of the policy to do actions of the policy and deactivation of gauges stop the actors.

The superiority of our enforcement architecture is catching prohibited actions at the source, before these actions consume some system resources. In Ponder model, for example, actions are checked at target-side to determine whether the actors are allowed to perform them. In contrast, the Police philosophy is to assign a **policeman** for each **actor** in the system, not to set up defense lines around the resources against **any** actor. We control the actions at their sources before they are started.

Police policies can be defined over domains[1] or individual objects. Policy Management Server must to have a priori knowledge of the interfaces of the target objects with which it deals, before the policies are specified. This is achieved with the **Model Classe**s stored in Domain Service and a node discovery mechanism keeping this repository up-to-date. Including real management interfaces implemented by the real object without implementation details, Model Classes are representatives of the managed objects. The whole information related to the managed system, stored in Domain Service is called as System's Information Model (SIM).

4 Police Conflict Handling Method

A conflict may occur if one policy prevents the activities of another policy from being performed or if the policies interfere in some way that may result in the managed objects being put into unwanted states [1]. Main conflict classes [1] are as follow:

Modality Conflicts [11] may arise if there are positive and negative authorization or obligation policies with same actors, targets and actions. Modality conflicts can be detected through static, syntactic analysis of the policy specifications. Most existing work in detecting conflicts relates to modality conflicts. Due to nonexistence of negative policies, Police does not suffer from modality conflicts.

Application-Specific Conflicts arise from the semantics of the policies. They cannot be determined directly from the policy specifications without additional information specifying what conflict is. In the literature, the Metapolicy [1, 9] concept is used to represent this additional information, which is a constraint about permitted policies (policies about policies). In [11], it is claimed that if there is not common object of two policies (disjoint policies) there is no possibility of conflict too. But, we think that this assumption is not true for some application-specific conflicts. There may be implicit relationships between objects and consequently between policies applied to them. This may cause application-specific conflicts implicitly.

Metapolicy-based approach cannot always fulfill the requirements to solve the problem of application-specific conflicts. Since, the administrator must specify metapolicies for all possible runtime situations, which may result in conflicts. It is almost impossible for the administrators to overlook all implicit relatsionships may cause conflicts in the system being managed. Moreover, in many cases, the fact that there are policies related to each other does not mean a conflict will occur at runtime.

In contrast to working groups using meta-policy concept to solve application-specific conflicts, we have developed a novel policy conflict detection mechanism based on the relationships between the objects of the system to be managed. On considering these associations among actors or targets, the relationships between the policies to be enforced on these objects can also be determined. Because, object relationships implicitly show the relationships of policies applied to them. The Policy Controllers investigate the likelihood of conflicts at runtime by analysing the relations between policies. Then, they enforce their actors according to this analysis.

5 Related Work

Most of groups working on policy based management of network and distributed systems follow the IETF approach [4] Moreover, unlike the Police framework, which is independent of application domains, the majority of them concentrate on a specific area, primarily quality of service or access control management [3,4,7]. In the IETF policy framework [4], only limited types of policies can be pushed into PEP.

Supporting domains, roles, and policy reuse, Ponder is a language, for specifying management and security policies [10]. It also employs events but only for triggering obligation policies, and constraints for controlling the enforcement of policies. Unlike our approach, authorisation and obligation policies are enforced by diffrent type of agents. Policy deployment objects carry platform-dependent classes. Although it is claimed, their deployment framework [5] does not include enough support to use in management of distributed systems. Although Ponder also supports static analysis of policies [11], static analysis repeated after each policy specification results in long delay while the amount of policies grows. Ponder employs meta-policies to prevent application-specific conflicts.

In [12], the main focus is conflicts in multi-agent systems in which agents share and carry out tasks collaboratively. While the agents perform the tasks, possible conflicts caused by dependencies between the tasks can be solved by using policies specified for the agents. We evaluate that the model used to solve the conflicted tasks mentioned in [12] can also be employed in policy-based management systems to detect and solve the conflicted policies. Moreover, our "object relations" concept may provide an infrastructure needed in multi-agent systems. Associations between the tasks they define are similar to our concept of relationships between managed objects.

6 Conclusions and Future Work

This paper introduces a framework fulfilling most of the requirements of comprehensive policy-based management. Thereby, it offers a novel conflict-handling model based on object associations. In our work, we designed a deployment model, which is application domain-independent. Introducing the "Model Class" logic for the managed resources allows Police policies to be deployed to any kind of platform.

In order to obtain a general policy model suitable for any application domain, more complex policies (policy as code) that is much harder to analyze for consistency should be chosen. Many groups [3, 7] have tended to follow the IETF approach (policy as object), leading to policies that are easier to analyze. But keeping policy specification simple causes several limitations. For some closed systems, which have static, rigid structure, these simple policies may be adequate. Nevertheless, it is inevitable to consider more complex policies, even their analysis is so hard.

In the consistency analysis field, a complete solution or standard meeting all requirements of both policy as code and policy as object fashions has not appeared yet. In our work, however, we propose a way for conflict detection, which is independent of the policy complexity. Thus, without taking care of how policies will be analyzed, more complexity can be merged into policy. We are currently working on prototype implementation. Areas requiring further research are as follow:

- Enhancing the language, to enable the expression of concepts such as action sequences, conditional branching and looping,
- Investigation for an effective inter-agent communication mechanism to be employed inter-PC and inter-ES communication,
- Research for developing an application-domain-independent model for the object associations,
- Using intelligent enforcement agents to handle conflicts and indirect (implicit) object associations,
- Examination of how the proposed model meets the requirements of various management domians, and work in practical applications,
- Using mobile agent paradigm [13] within policy deployment process to increase autonomy.

References

1. Moffett J.D: "Policy Hierarchies for Distributed Systems Management", IEEE JSAC Special Issue on Network Management, Vol 11, No. 9 (1993)
2. E. Lupu, M. Sloman: "Conflicts in Policy-based Distributed Systems Management", IEEE Trans. On Software Engineering, Vol 25. No 6: 852–869, (1999)
3. G.N. Stone, B. Lundy, and G.G. Xie. Network Policy Languages: A Survey and a New Approach. IEEE Network Magazine, 15(8) ,(2001) 10–21
4. R. Yavatkar, D. Pendarakis, and R. Guerin. A Framework for Policy-based Admission Control. RFC 2753, Intel, IBM, U. of Pensylvania, (2000)
5. N.Dulay, E.Lupu, M.Sloman, N.Damianou, A Policy Deployment Model for the Ponder Language, IEEE/IFIP International Symp. on Integrated Network Management, (2001)
6. Lobo, J., R. Bhatia, and S. Naqvi. A Policy Description Language. In Proc. of AAAI, Orlando, Florida, USA (1999)
7. T. Hamada, P. Czezowski, T. Chujo, "Policy-based Management for Enterprise and Carrier IP Networking", FUJITSU Sci. Tech. J.,36,2. (2000) 128–139
8. D.C. Verma: Simplifying Network Administration Using Policy-Based Management, IEEE Network, Policy based management special issue (2002) 34–39
9. M. Sloman, E. Lupu, Security and Management Policy Specification, IEEE Network March/April 2002 Policy based management special issue (2002) 10–19
10. Damianou, N., N. Dulay, E. Lupu, and M. Sloman. Ponder: A Language for Specifying Security and Management Policies for Distributed Systems. Research Report DoC 2000/1, Imperial College of Sci. Tech. and Medicine, Department of Computing, London (2000)

11. M.Sloman, "Policy Specification for Programmable Networks," First Int. Working Conf. Active Networks (1999)
12. T. Wagner, J. Shapiro, et al: Multi-Level Conflict in Multi-Agent Systems, Proc. of AAAI Workshop on Negotiation in Multi-Agent Systems (1999)
13. V. A. Pham, A. Karmouch: Mobile Software Agents: An overview, IEEE Communication Magazine (1998) 26–37

Covert Channel Detection in the ICMP Payload Using Support Vector Machine

Taeshik Sohn, Jongsub Moon, Sangjin Lee, Dong Hoon Lee, and Jongin Lim

Center for Information Security Technologies, Korea University,
1-ga, Anam-dong, Sungbuk-gu, Seoul, Korea
{743zh2k, jsmoon, sanjin, donghlee, jilim}@korea.ac.kr

Abstract. ICMP traffic is ubiquitous to almost TCP/IP based network. As such, many network devices consider ICMP traffic to be benign and will allow it to pass through, unmolested. So, attackers can generate arbitrary information tunneling in the payload of ICMP packets. To detect a ICMP covert channel, we used SVM which has excellent performance in pattern classification problems. Our experiments showed that the proposed method could detect the ICMP covert channel from normal ICMP traffic using SVM.

1 Introduction

Currently, internet environment has many problems in information security as its network is increasing rapidly. So, various solutions for security protection such as IDS, firewall, ESM, VPN have been evolved. Although these solutions were widely used, they have yet much vulnerability due to the problems of the protocol itself. One of the vulnerability is the possibility of hidden channel creation. The hidden channels are defined as the communication channel used in a process which transmits information by some methods violating the system's security policy. This channel is used for transmitting special information to processes or users prevented from accessing the information[1]. In this paper, we analyze the method which transmits the hidden data using the ICMP protocol payload. To detect the ICMP covert channel, we used SVM, which is known as a kind of the Universal Feed Foreword Network proposed by Vapnik in 1995, is efficient to complex pattern recognition and classification. Specially, it has the best solution for the classification problems[2][3].

The rest of this paper are organized as follows: Section 2 addresses related work of Covert Channel. Section 3 describes the background of SVM. Our detection approach is explained in section 4. Experiments are explained in section 5, followed by conclusions and future work in section 6.

2 Related Work

A security analysis for TCP/IP is found in [4]. Paper[5] and [6] describe works related to the various covert channel establishments. A general survey of

A. Yazici and C. Şener (Eds.): ISCIS 2003, LNCS 2869, pp. 828–835, 2003.

information-hiding techniques is described in "Information Hiding - A Survey." John Mchugh[5] provides a wealthy of information on analyzing a system for covert channels in "Covert Channel Analysis." Specially, "Covert Channels in the TCP/IP Protocol Suite"[6], Craig Rowland describes the possibility of passing covert data in the IP identification field, the initial sequence number field and the TCP acknowledge sequence number field. He programmed a simple proof-of-concept, raw socket implementation. "Covert Messaging Through TCP Timestamps"[7], describes a tunnel using timestamp field in TCP header. "Loki: ICMP Tunneling, daemon9, Pharack Magazine, Volume 6, Issue 49, article 6 of 16"[8] describes the possibility of generating covert channel in a ICMP protocol.

3 Support Vector Machine

3.1 Background

The SVM is based on the idea of structural risk minimization, which minimizes the generalization error, i.e. true error on unseen examples. The number of free parameters used in the SVM depends on the margin that divides the data points into classes but not on the number of input features, thus the SVM does not require a reduction in the number of features in order to avoid overfitting. The SVM provides a generic mechanism to fit the data within a surface of a hyperplane of a class through the use of a kernel function. The user may provide a kernel function, such as a linear, polynomial, or sigmoid curve, to the SVM during the training process, which selects support vectors along the surface of the function. This capability allows classifying a broader range of problems. The primary advantage of SVM is binary classification and regression that it provides to a classifier with a minimal VC(Vapnik Chervonenkis)-dimension, which implies low expected probability of generalization errors [2][3].

3.2 SVM for Classification

In this section we review some basic ideas of SVM. For the details about SVM for classification and nonlinear function estimation, see [2][3][9][10]

Given the training data set $\{(x_i, d_i)\}_{i=1}^{l}$, with input data $x_i \in R^N$ and corresponding binary class labels $d_i \in \{-1, 1\}$, the SVM classifier formulation starts from the following assumption. The classes represent by subset $d_i = 1$ and $d_i = -1$ are linearly separable, where $^{\exists}w \in R^N,\ b \in R$ such that

$$\begin{cases} w^T x_i + b > 0 \text{ for } d_i = +1 \\ w^T x_i + b < 0 \text{ for } d_i = -1 \end{cases} \tag{1}$$

The goal of SVM is to find an optimal hyperplane for which the margin of separation ,ρ, is maximized. The margin of separation ,ρ, is defined by the separation between the separating hyperplane and the closest data point. If the optimal hyperplane is defined by $w^T + b_0 = 0$, then the function $g(x) = w^T x + b_0$

gives a measure of the distance from x to the optimal hyperplane. Support Vectors are defined by data points $x^{(s)}$ that lie the closest to the decision surface. For a support vector $x^{(s)}$ and the canonical optimal hyperplane g, we have

$$r = \frac{g(x^s)}{||w_0||} = \begin{cases} +1/||w_0|| \text{ for } d^{(s)} = +1 \\ -1/||w_0|| \text{ for } d^{(s)} = -1. \end{cases} \tag{2}$$

Since, the margin of separation $\rho \propto \frac{1}{\|w_0\|}$. Thus, $\|w_0\|$ should be minimal to achieve the maximal separation margin. Mathematical formulation for finding the canonical optimal separation hyperplane given the training data set $\{(x_i, d_i)\}_{i=1}^{l}$, solve the following quadratic problem

$$\begin{cases} \text{minimize } \tau(w,\xi) = \frac{1}{2}\|w\|^2 + c\sum_{i=1}^{l}\xi_i \\ \text{subject to } d_i(w^T x_i + b) \geq 1 - \xi_i \text{ for } \xi_i \geq 0,\, i = 1, ..., l \end{cases} \tag{3}$$

Note that the global minimum of above problem must exist, because $\phi(w) = \frac{1}{2}\|w_0\|^2$ is convex in w and the constrains are linear in w and b. This constrained optimization problem is dealt with by introducing Lagrange multipliers $\alpha_i \geq 0$ and a Lagrangian function given by

$$L(w, b, \xi; \alpha, \nu) = \tau(w, \xi) - \sum_{i=1}^{l} \alpha_i [d_i(w_i^T x_i + b) - 1 + \xi_k] - \sum_{i=1}^{l} \nu_i \xi_i \tag{4}$$

$$\frac{\partial L}{\partial w} = 0 \Longleftrightarrow w - \sum_{i=1}^{l} \alpha_i d_i x_i \;\; (\therefore w = \sum_{i=1}^{l} \alpha_i d_i x_i) \tag{5}$$

$$\frac{\partial L}{\partial b} = 0 \Longleftrightarrow w - \sum_{i=1}^{l} \alpha_i d_i = 0 \tag{6}$$

$$\frac{\partial L}{\partial \xi_k} = 0, \text{ for } 0 \leq \alpha_i \leq c\, ,\, k = 1, ..., l \tag{7}$$

The solution vector thus has an expansion in terms of a subset of the training patterns, namely those patterns whose α_i is non-zero, called(we previous defined) *Support Vectors.* By the Karush-Kuhn-Tucker complementarity conditions, we have,

$$\alpha_i [d_i(w^T x_i + b) - 1] = 0 \text{ for } i = 1, ..., N \tag{8}$$

by substituting $(5), (6)$ and (7) into L(equation (4)), find multipliers α_i which

$$\text{maximize } \Theta(\alpha) = \sum_{i=1}^{l} \alpha_i - \frac{1}{2} \sum_{i=1}^{l} \sum_{j=1}^{l} \alpha_i \alpha_j d_i d_j < x_i \cdot x_j > \tag{9}$$

$$\text{subject to } 0 \leq \alpha_i \leq c, \ i = 1, ..., l \text{ and } \sum_{i=1}^{l} \alpha_i y_i = 0 \tag{10}$$

The hyperplane decision function can thus be written as

$$f(x) = sgn\left(\sum_{i=1}^{l} y_i \alpha_i \cdot (x \cdot x_i) + b \right) \tag{11}$$

where b is computed using (8).

To construct the SVM, the optimal hyperplane algorithm has to be argumented by a method for computing dot products in feature spaces nonlinearly related to input space. The basic idea is to map the data into some other dot product space (called the feature space) F via a nonlinear map ϕ, and to perform the above linear algorithm in F, i.e nonseparable data $\{(x_i, d_i)\}_{i=1}^{l}$, where $x_i \in R^N, \ d_i \in \{+1, -1\}$, preprocess the data with,

$$\phi : R^N \to F, \ x \mapsto \phi(x) \text{ where } l \ll \mathsf{dimension}(F) \tag{12}$$

Here w and x_i are not calculated. According to Mercer's theorem,

$$\langle \phi(x_i), \phi(x_j) \rangle = K(x_i, x_j) \tag{13}$$

and $K(x, y)$ can be computed easily on the input space. Finally the nonlinear SVM classifier becomes

$$f(x) = sgn\left(\sum_{i=1}^{l} \alpha_i d_i K(x_i, x) + b \right) \tag{14}$$

4 ICMP Covert Channel Detection

4.1 An Overview of ICMP Covert Channel

ICMP type 0x0 specifies an ICMP echo reply and type 0x8 indicates an ICMP echo request. This is what the ping program does. This ping traffic is ubiquitous to almost every TCP/IP based network and subnetwork. As such, many networks consider ping traffic to be benign and will allow it to pass through, unmolested. ICMP echo packets also have the option to include a payload. This data section is used when the record route option is specified, or the more common case, usually the default to store timing information to determine round-trip times. Although the payload is often timing information, there is no check by any device as to the content of the data. So, as it turns out, this amount of data can also be arbitrary in content as well[8]. The arbitrary contents of the payload can have various data according to the message types of ICMP protocol and kinds of the operating system(OS). In case of the normal ICMP packet, it has insignificant values or null values and so on. Namely, therein can lie the covert channels.

4.2 Proposing the Detection Method of ICMP Covert Channel

In this paper, we propose a model to detect covert channel in the ICMP payload. The payload of ICMP packets have generally null values or several characteristics dependent on the OS such as Windows, Linux and Solaris as illustrated in Table 1. At this time, the characteristic of payload of each OS is normally the same or it has the successive change of one byte in the payload. The rest 4 bytes of ICMP header are dependent on the each ICMP message type. Thus, we propose the detection method of ICMP covert channel using SVM with the characteristic of ICMP packet payload and the 4 bytes of ICMP header described above. First, we collect normal ICMP packets using a packet capturing tool like tcpdump and abnormal ICMP packets generated by covert channel tool like Loki2[8]. Then we preprocess the collected raw packets such as ICMP payload(13 dimensions) and ICMP payload plus the rest 4 bytes of ICMP header(15 dimensions) as illustrated in Figure 1. One dimension of preprocessed data is comprised of

Table 1. The Characteristic of ICMP payload

	ICMP Payload
Null Packet	0000 0000 0000 0000 0000 0000 0000 0000 0000 0000 0000 0000 0000
Win Packet	0900 6162 6364 6566 6768 696a 6b6c 6d6e 6f70 7172 7374 7576 7761
Solaris Packet	50ec f53d 048f 0700 0809 0a0b 0c0d 0e0f 1011 1213 1415 1617 1819
Linux Packet	9077 063e 2dbd 0400 0809 0a0b 0c0d 0e0f 1011 1213 1415 1617 1819

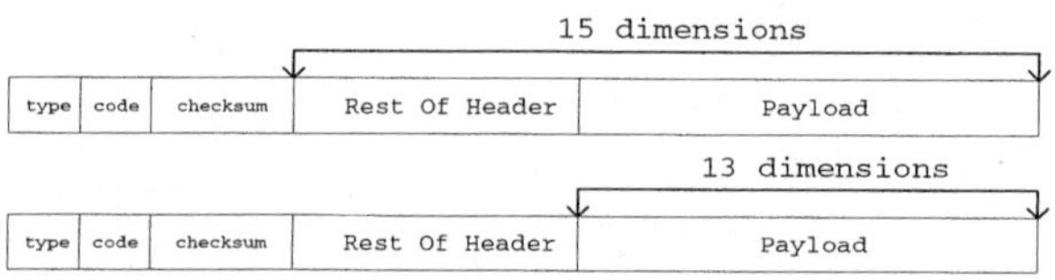

Fig. 1. The features of SVM

two bytes of raw packet. So, 26bytes ICMP payload is 13 dimension and the rest of header(4bytes) + 26bytes ICMP payload is 15 dimension. At this time, the preprocessed packets are classified as a training data set and a test data set. Each dimension, which means one input feature in SVM, is converted to decimal value, that is, the hexa values of 16bits(2bytes) are rearranged by the integer value of decimal in the raw dump values of packet. Finally, we learn the SVM using training data set and classified test data set with the SVM classifier[11].

5 Experiment

5.1 Experiment Methods

The SVM data is first comprised of two data sets : a training data set and a test data set. Also these data sets consist of the training set1, training set2 and test set1, test set2 as followed in Table 2. We preprocessed the raw packet

Table 2. SVM Training Data Set and Test Data Set

Data Set	Training Set1(Total 4000)	Training Set2(Total 4000)
Normal Packet	All typed ICMP packet(2000)	OS based ICMP packet(2000)
Abnormal Packet	Loki packet (2000)	Loki packet (2000)
Data Set	Test Set1 (Total 1000)	Test Set2 (Total 1000)
Normal Packet	All typed ICMP packet(250) + OS based ICMP packet(250)	All typed ICMP packet(250) + OS based ICMP packet(250)
Abnormal Packet	Loki packets(500)	Loki packets(500)

values in order to make training data and testing data in the SVM. Through the preprocessing, the feature is determined. The determined features are comprised of two cases : a 15 dimension including the rest 4bytes of packet header and packet payload and a 13 dimension including only the payload of packet. Each training data set is comprised of 4000 packets. Training set1 data has general ICMP packets collected by CIST server(Our Institute Web Server). Training set2 data has ICMP packets based on the characteristic of operating systems(Linux, Solaris, Windows). Also, abnormal packets are generated by Loki2 tool. Each training set contains 2000 abnormal packets. Next, the test set1 and the test set2 consist of 500 normal packets and 500 abnormal packets. Here, the normal packets of the test set have 250 general ICMP packets and 250 OS dependent packets. The abnormal packets of the test set have packets which are forged using Loki2 tool. SVM detection tool used here is the freeware package mySVM[11]. To compare the detection performance, we used the two SVM kernels : linear, polynomial type.

Table 3. The experiment results of ICMP covert channel detection

Training Set	Kernel	Features	Test Set1 FP	Test Set1 FN	Test Set1 TC	Test Set2 FP	Test Set2 FN	Test Set2 TC
Training Set1	Linear	13	2.5	0.4	97.1	0.7	0.7	98.6
		15	1.1	0.8	98.1	0	0.6	99.4
	Polynomial	13	0.2	0.6	99.2	0	0.8	99.2
		15	0.8	0.6	98.6	0	0.8	99.2
Training Set2	Linear	13	24.3	0.8	74.9	12.1	1.6	86.3
		15	0	0.8	99.2	0	0.6	99.4
	Polynomial	13	3.8	0.6	95.6	2.5	1.0	96.5
		15	0.8	0.6	98.6	0	0.2	99.8

*The degree of Polynomial Kernel = 3, FP = False Positive(%), FN = False Negative(%), TC = Total Correctness(%)

5.2 Experiment Results

In the detection experiments of the ICMP covert channel using an SVM, the learning data set is classified as training set1 and training set2 according to the characteristic of the ICMP payload. We analyzed the detection results of each test set1 and test set2 as the two SVM kernel functions and the variation of the number of features. Table 3 shows overall experiment results. The resultant graph of covert channel detection using training set 1 is shown in Figure 2 and the resultant graph of covert channel detection using training set 2 is illustrated Figure 3. In case of the SVM training set, we can see that it is more efficient to classify the abnormal packets by assuming all the general types of ICMP packets are normal(The detection rate of Training set1 is 98.68%). Also, we can see in table 4 that detection performance is better in a 15 dimension and is best in polynomial kernel with degree of 3.

In this paper, we proposed the SVM method with some features of ICMP. Such an SVM could detect ICMP covert channel with the correction rate of nearly 99%(As illustrated in Table 4).

Table 4. The experiment results of each parameter(%)

	TR1	TR2	KR1	KR2	F13	F15
Detection(%)	98.68	93.79	94.13	98.34	93.43	99.04

*TR1 = Training Set1, TR2 = Training Set2, KR1 = Linear, KR2 = Polynomial, F13 = 13 Features, F15 = 15 Features

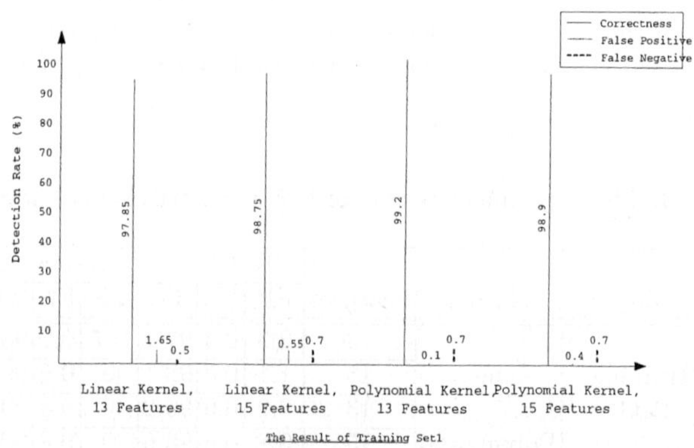

Fig. 2. The results of Training Set1

6 Conclusion and Future Work

Covert channel attacks are an increasingly potential threat to Internet environments. We did not yet have the best solution for covert channel detection. The goal of this paper was to propose the detection method for ICMP covert channels with SVM among the many covert channels. The preprocessing for SVM learning to detect a covert channel consisted of two cases: one case includes only an ICMP payload and the other case includes an ICMP payload and the remaining 4 bytes of the ICMP header. We classified training sets into training set 1 with generally used ICMP packets and training set 2 with ICMP packets based on the characteristic of the operating system. Also, the experiment environment has been subjected to informal tests in a laboratory test bed. The experiment results show that under these conditions, the detection provided by the SVM learning described the high correction rate as illustrated in Table 4.

Future work will include the expansion of training sets, test sets and the experiments for various kernels which can be use for performance improvement and some of its constraint parameters.

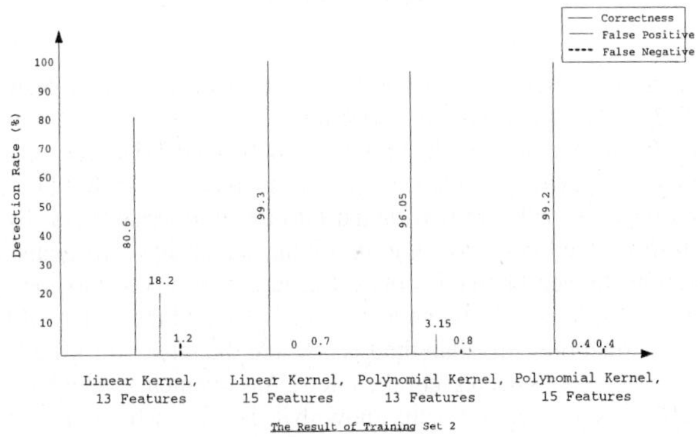

Fig. 3. The results of Training Set2

References

1. U.S. Department Of Defence, "Trusted Computer System Criteria.",1985
2. Vapnik V., "The Nature of Statistical Learning Theory", Springer-Verlag, 1995.
3. Bueges C J C., "A Tutorial on Support Vector Machines for Patter Recognition.", Data Mining and Knowledge Discovery, Boston, 1988.
4. S.M. Bellovin, "Security Problems in the TCP/IP protocol suite", Computer Communication Reviews,19(2):32–48, April 1989
5. John McHugh, "Covert Channel Analysis", Portland State University, 1995
6. Craig H. Rowland, "Covert Channels in the TCP/IP protocol suite", First Monday, 1996
7. John Giffin, "Covert Messaging Through TCP Timestamps", PET2002
8. Daemon9, "Loki: ICMP Tunneling", Pharack Magazine, Volume 6, Issue 49
9. Cristianini N., "An Introduction to Support Vector Machines.", Cambridge University press, 2000.
10. S. Mukkamala, G. Janowski, A. H. Sung, "Intrusion Detection Using Neural Networks and Support Vector Machines", IEEE IJCNN, May 2002, pp.1702–1707.
11. Joachmims T,"mySVM – a Support Vector Machine", Univerity Dortmund

An Efficient Location Area Design Scheme to Minimize Registration Signalling Traffic in Wireless Systems

Ümit Aslıhak[1] and Feza Buzluca[2]

[1] Turkish War Colleges, War Gaming and Simulation Centre, Yenilevent Istanbul, Turkey
uaslihak@harpak.tsk.mil.tr
[2] Istanbul Technical University, Electrical - Electronics Faculty, Dept. of Computer Engineering, Maslak, 34469 Istanbul, Turkey
buzluca@cs.itu.edu.tr

Abstract. In this paper, a new static traffic-based location area design scheme named ETB-LAD (enhanced TB-LAD) for wireless systems is proposed. This scheme is an enhancement on the previously published TB-LAD scheme. In the new method, the expected intercell movement patterns of mobiles are determined and then the cells are partitioned into location areas (LAs) by applying the new traffic-based cell grouping algorithm, which has two goals. First, the cell pairs with higher intercell mobile traffic are grouped into the same LA. Second, the LAs, in which the neighbour cells have higher intercell traffic, allowed to include more cells than the LAs, where the intercell traffic is low. The aim of the scheme is to decrement the inter-LA movements, which create registration traffic. Experimental results show that the new scheme performs better than the TB-LAD and proximity based location area design (PB-LAD) schemes in the sense that it can reduce the location updates.

1 Introduction

One of the main problems in mobile computing is the tracking of the current location of the users (mobiles). When a connection needs to be established for a particular user, the network has to determine the user's exact location within the cell granularity. Location management involves two operations: The operation of informing the network about the current location of the mobile user is known as *location registration*, and the operation of determining the location of the mobile user is called *terminal paging* [1].

Mobility tracking expends the limited resources of the wireless network. Beside the bandwidth used for registration and terminal paging, power is also consumed from portable devices. Frequent signalling may also result in degradation of Quality of Service, due to interferences. Therefore, the goal of location management is to minimize the signalling traffic [2].

Current networks use location area (LA)-based management techniques. The coverage area is partitioned into a number of LAs, each containing a group of cells. While a mobile is moving from one LA to another, it reports its new LA by a registration process. An LA may *static* or *dynamic*. A static LA consists of a group of cells that are permanently assigned to that LA, and is fixed for all mobiles. On the other hand, dy

A. Yazici and C. Şener (Eds.): ISCIS 2003, LNCS 2869, pp. 836–843, 2003.

namic LAs [3], [4] are created for each mobile during a registration process based on mobility and call patterns of the user. Although signalling traffic can be reduced by using dynamic LAs they impose higher computation and separate data storage of LAs for each mobile. As a result, most of the current cellular systems use static LAs.

Two main factors affecting the signalling traffic are the number of cells in an LA and the cell-partitioning technique [5]. When the number of cells in an LA is high, the registration traffic decreases, but the paging traffic increases [6]. On the other hand, for smaller LAs, the registration traffic increases, but the paging traffic decreases. The cell-partitioning technique is also very important. If the LAs are designed such that the inter-LA mobile traffic is reduced, the registration traffic decreases for the same LA size.

In this paper, we propose a new static location area design scheme named ETB-LAD (Enhanced TB-LAD), which is an enhancement on previously published Traffic-based location area design (TB-LAD) technique [7]. In TB-LAD technique, the intercell traffic prediction and traffic-based cell grouping schemes are used consecutively to partition the cells into LAs. The neighbour cells with higher intercell traffic are assigned to the same LAs, to decrease the inter-LA movements of mobiles. But in this technique the proper number of cells in a LA is not determined.

Our ETB-LAD scheme differs significantly from the TB-LAD scheme by explicitly taking into account the number of cells in an LA. The intercell traffic predictions are used by the traffic-based cell grouping scheme to group cells into LAs and also to determine the proper number of cells in an LA. The LAs, in which the neighbour cells have higher intercell traffic, may include more cells than the LAs, where the intercell traffic is low. We try to increment the intra-LA movements of mobiles in order to decrement the inter-LA movements, which create registration traffic.

In the remainder of the paper we analyze the new location area design scheme ETB-LAD and show that it reduces the registration traffic compared to other two static location area design schemes, namely the proximity-based location area design (PB-LAD) and the traffic-based location area design (TB-LAD) scheme.

2 Proximity-Based and Traffic-Based Location Area Design

In the *proximity-based static* LAD (PB-LAD) cells are grouped into static LAs based on proximity. The cells close to each other are grouped into LAs such that all of the cells belong to one and only one LA. In Fig. 1a, five-cell static LAs are created by using the PB-LAD technique. Each hexagon represents a cell and bold lines along the cell borders separate the LAs. In Fig. 1a, if a mobile moves between points a and b following the highway, it crosses the LA borders five times. Hence, this mobile needs to register five times when we use the PB-LAD scheme as shown in Fig. 1a.

In the *traffic-based static* LAD (TB-LAD) [7], cells are grouped according to the expected intercell mobility patterns, such that the cell pairs with higher intercell mobile traffic are grouped into the same LA. The goal of the scheme is to reduce the inter-LA movements of mobiles. The same scenario in Fig. 1b is also used to explain how TB-LAD technique reduces the number of inter-LA movements. When we use the TB-LAD scheme, the mobile moving between points a and b crosses an LA boundary only once.

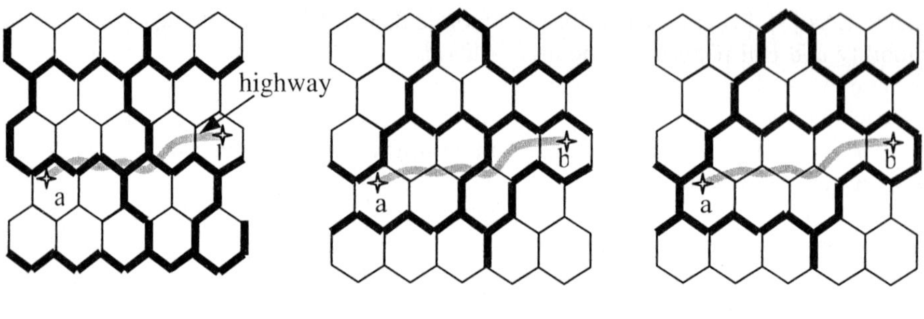

a) Proximity-based LAD **b)** Traffic-based LAD **c) Enhanced** TB-LAD

Fig. 1. Comparison of three static LAD schemes

3 The Enhanced Traffic-Based LA Design Scheme (ETB-LAD)

In this section we develop a new static location area design scheme, named ETB-LAD that is an enhanced version of the previously published TB-LAD scheme. The main difference between ETB-LAD and TB-LAD is that, in TB-LAD the proper number of cells in an LA (the size of LA) is not determined. For all LAs, the same predefined maximum value is used to limit the number of their member cells. On the other hand, in ETB-LAD different limit values are applied to LAs according to the traffic between their neighbour cells. The LAs, in which the neighbour cells have higher intercell traffic, may include more cells than the LAs, where the intercell traffic is low. So we can keep more cell pairs, with high intercell traffic, in the same LA. As it is shown in Fig. 1c, the LA that covers the highway has more cells than the others if the ETB-LAD is used. It causes that the mobile moving between points a and b stays in the same LA and does not create a registration traffic.

Because the paper reports an enhanced version of the TB-LAD scheme, for easy comparison we shall retain and use/quote most of the notations adopted by Cayirci and Akyildiz [7] in their development and analysis of the TB-LAD scheme, and adopt the same framework as used by them.

3.1 The Formulation of the Scheme

First step for the ETB-LAD is to determine the expected amount of mobile movements between neighbour cells. The intercell traffic of mobiles is predicted by examining the roads (highways, railroads, streets, footpaths, etc.) since mobiles generally move on roads. The expected traffic t_{kij} from cell i of LA k to its neighbour cell j is computed from

$$t_{kij} = \sum_{z=1}^{r_{kij}} d_{kijz}, \tag{1}$$

where

d_{kijz} is the traffic density of road z between cell i of LA k and cell j, and
r_{kij} is the total number of roads between cell i of LA k and cell j.

The traffic density d_{kijz} of each road can be determined by observing the traffic for a long period of time, e.g. a year. Since this method may be impractical, a so-called *density look up table* can be build by using the type and surface characteristics of a road. This table contains the d_{kijz} values, which are the number of vehicles expected per unit of time on a road z between cell i of LA k and cell j.

The second step of the ETB-LAD scheme is determining two threshold values t_L and t_H, namely the low and high thresholds by examining the expected intercell traffic (t_{kij}) values. These two thresholds partition the set of expected intercell traffic values into three categories. If an intercell traffic is greater than t_H, it is interpreted as 'high', similarly traffic values under the t_L are interpreted as 'low', and at last, traffic values between the thresholds are 'normal'. These categories are used to determine the maximum size of an LA as it is shown in (4).

The objective of our ETB-LAD scheme is to design LAs such that the number β_m of inter-LA movements of the mobiles is minimised. The expected value of β_m can be predicted by using the road data as follows:

$$\beta_t = \sum_{k=1}^{l} \sum_{i=1}^{\eta_k} \sum_{j \in S'_k} t_{kij} , \tag{2}$$

where
β_t is the expected value of β_m,
t_{kij} is traffic between cell i of LA k and cell j,
S_k' is the set of cells which are not members of LA k,
η_k is the number of cells in LA k, and
l is the number of LAs.

In order to minimize β_t, we maximize the expected intra-LA area traffic φ_t determined from:

$$\varphi_t = \sum_{k=1}^{l} \sum_{i=1}^{\eta_k} \sum_{j \in S_k} t_{kij} , \tag{3}$$

where S_k is the set of cells which are members of LA k.

Our objective function is

$$\text{maximise } \varphi_t \tag{4}$$

subject to

$$1 \le \eta_k \le \eta_{kmax} , \quad \eta_{kmax} = \begin{cases} \eta_{max} + 2 & \text{if } t_{kmin} \ge t_H \\ \eta_{max} & \text{if } t_{kmin} < t_H \text{ and } t_{kmin} \ge t_L \\ \eta_{max} - 2 & \text{if } t_{kmin} < t_L \end{cases} \quad \text{for } k = 1, \dots, l ,$$

where

η_{max} is the maximum number of cells in an LA, in which the smallest intercell traffic is between thresholds values t_L and t_H,
η_{kmax} is the maximum number of cells in LA k, η_k is the number of cells in LA k,
t_{kmin} is the smallest intercell traffic in LA k. It is defined as $t_{kmin} = \min\{t_{kij}\}$ for $i, j \in S_k$.

As it is shown in (4), an a LA may include two more cells than another LA, if its smallest intercell traffic is 'high' (over t_H) and the smallest intercell traffic in the other

LA is 'normal'. In this paper, increment/decrement value that is used two determine the maximum LA size, is 2. The optimal value depends on the characteristics of the metropolitan area. Determination of this value is left as a further study.

3.2 The Algorithm for ETB-LAD

In [7] it has been proven that the optimal TB-LAD under the condition of the maximisation of intra-LA traffic is NP-complete. Therefore we designed the approximation algorithm in Fig. 2

1. Create a list of neighboring cells for each cell. The list of neighboring cells must satisfy $t_{i,m} \leq t_{i,m+1}$ where $t_{i,m}$ is the traffic from cell i for which the list is prepared, to its neighbor m in the list.
2. Create an ordered list of cells in which $t_{i,1} \leq t_{i+1,1}$ where $t_{i,1}$ is the traffic between the cell i in the list and the first cell in its list of neighboring cells.
3. Initialize all the cells as 'NOT INCLUDED'.
4. Determine the low (t_L) and high (t_H) threshold values by examing the intercell traffic values.
5. Initialize current LA number $i \leftarrow 1$.
6. Repeat until there is no cell that is 'NOT INCLUDED'.
   - 6.1. Construct a new LA ai.
   - 6.2. Initialize the number l_{ai} of cells for ai, $l_{ai} \leftarrow 1$.
   - 6.3. Include the highest ordered 'NOT INCLUDED' cell c_{lai} from the cell list.
   - 6.4. Mark c_{lai} as 'INCLUDED'.
   - 6.5. Initialize flag $done \leftarrow$ 'FALSE'.
   - 6.6. Repeat until there is no more cell which is in the neighbors list of one of the cells included for ai and 'NOT INCLUDED' or $done$ = 'TRUE'.
     - 6.6.1. Find a new 'NOT INCLUDED' cell c_{new} with highest $t_{m,cnew}$ from the neighbor lists of the cells included for ai.
     - 6.6.2. $$\eta_{kmax} = \begin{cases} \eta_{max} + 2 & \text{if } t_{m,cnew} \geq t_H \\ \eta_{max} & \text{if } t_{m,cnew} < t_H \text{ and } t_{m,cnew} \geq t_L \\ \eta_{max} - 2 & \text{if } t_{m,cnew} < t_L \end{cases}$$
     - 6.6.3. If $l_{ai} \geq \eta_{kmax}$ then $done \leftarrow$ 'TRUE'
     - 6.6.4. else
       - 6.6.4.1. Include c_{new} into ai, Mark c_{new} as 'INCLUDED'.
       - 6.6.4.2. Increment l_{ai}, $l_{ai} \leftarrow l_{ai} + 1$.
       - 6.6.4.3. If $l_{ai} \geq \eta_{kmax}$ then $done \leftarrow$ 'TRUE'
   - 6.7. Increment i, $i \leftarrow i+1$.

Fig. 2. The approximation algorithm

Using the algorithm in Fig. 2, we first create a list of neighbours for each cell. The neighbour cells are ordered according to the predicted traffic between the neighbour cells and the list heads, i.e., the cell for which the neighbour list is created. Then, we order these lists according to the traffic between the list heads and the first neighbours in the lists. All of the cells are initialized as 'NOT INCLUDED'. Then we determine two threshold values t_L and t_H by examining the intercell traffic values. A loop iterates until all of the cells are included. In each iteration, the first "NOT INCLUDED" cell from the cell list is selected and a new LA is created with this cell. Then, an inner loop finds the neighbour with the highest predicted traffic from the neighbour lists of the cells that are included for the current LA. The predicted intercell traffic of this neighbour is used to calculate the maximum number of cells for the current LA. If the number of cells is not reached this maximum number the new cell is included into the current LA. The inner loop terminates when there is no neighbour that can be included or the maximum number of cells is reached for the current LA.

3.3 Experimental Results

We compare the performance of ETB-LAD to TB-LAD and PB-LAD by using two sets of experiments. For easy comparison we used the same experiments and data sets as in [7]. In the first set of experiments, road data are used to compute intercell traffic in a real metropolitan area. These data are obtained from a scanned hardcopy map and can be downloaded from the website: http://users.ece.gatech.edu/erdal/metropol1.txt .

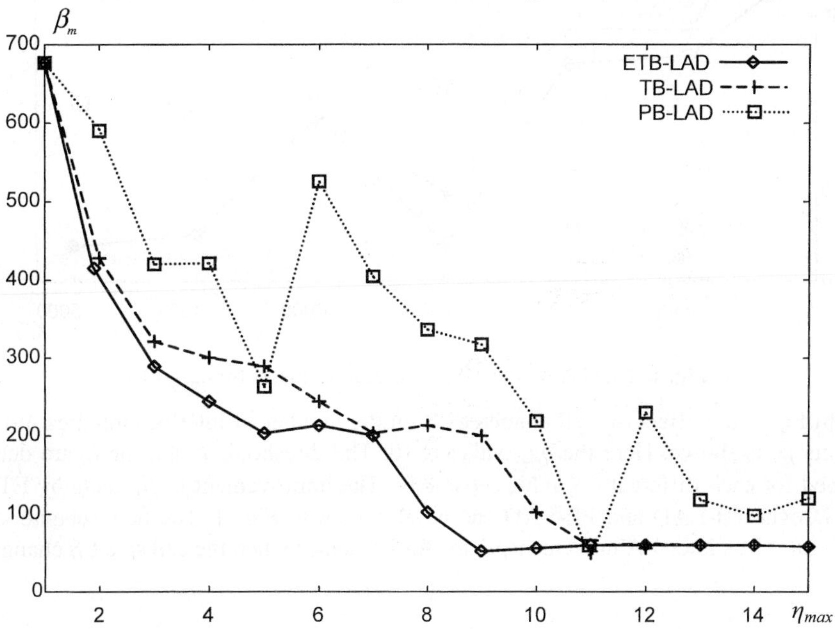

Fig. 3. Number of interlocation area movements for CS = 3500 m

Then, we run ETB-LAD, TB-LAD and PB-LAD techniques to design the LAs. In the second sets of experiments, we used mobility data about 56 real people, living in the same metropolitan area. They have different professions and different mobility characteristics. We trace the movements of the interviewed people by using their mobility data on the LAs designed by ETB-LAD, TB-LAD and PB-LAD and count the number of inter-LA movements, then compare the results.

In Fig. 3 the effect of η_{max} on the number of interlocation area movements β_m is shown. Here the diameter of cells (cell size – *CS*) is 3500m. The low and high thresholds for expected intercell traffic values are determined as $t_L = 50$ and $t_H = 200$ respectively. As it shown in Fig. 3 the new ETB-LAD scheme performs better than TB-LAD and PB-LAD because it generates less the inter-LA movements. If maximum number of cells η_{max} is greater than 11, ETB-LAD and TB-LAD schemes produce same results. The reason is that the digitized map used in the experiment can contain limited number of cells if the CS=3500m. Incrementing the size of the LAs decreases the number of possible LAs in the coverage area. Therefore two traffic-based LAD schemes produce same results.

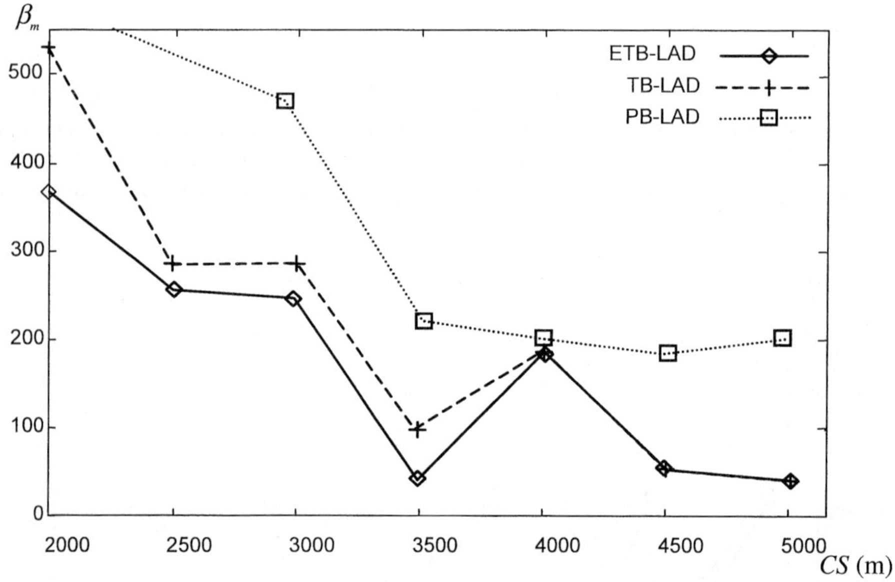

Fig. 4. Number of interlocation area movements for $\eta_{max} = 10$

In Fig. 4 the effect of Cell diameter *CS* on the number of interlocation area movements β_m is shown. Here the η_{max} value is 10. The thresholds t_L and the t_H are determined for each different *CS* value separately. The improvement in β_m made by ETB-LAD over TB-LAD and PB-LAD can be also seen in Fig. 4. The new scheme still generates less inter-LA movements than other schemes when the cell size *CS* changes.

4 Conclusion

This paper has considered and addressed the issue, partitioning the coverage are into a number of LAs, each containing a group of cells, such that the registration traffic is minimised. We developed and analyzed a new static traffic-based location area design scheme named ETB-LAD (enhanced TB-LAD), which is an enhanced version of previously published traffic-based location area design (TB-LAD) technique. The new

ETB-LAD scheme differs significantly from the TB-LAD scheme by explicitly taking into account the proper number of cells in an LA. The LAs, with higher intercell traffic are allowed to include more cells than the LAs, where the intercell traffic is low. As a result, the intra-LA movements of mobiles are increased in order to decrement the inter-LA movements, which create registration traffic.

We have shown in this paper that the ETB-LAD scheme performs better than the TB-LAD and PB-LAD schemes in the sense that it can partition a metropolitan area into LAs, such that the registration traffic generated by mobiles, is reduced. Our method can be applied easily to cellular wireless networks to reduce the location update costs, without special mobile devices are needed.

References

1. Wong,V.W.-S., Leung, V.C.M.: Location Management for Next-Generation Personal Communications Networks. IEEE Network Magazine, Vol.38. (2000) 18–24
2. Subrata, R., Zomaya, A.Y.: Location Management in Mobile Computing. Proceedings of the ACS/IEEE International Conference on Computer Systems and Applications, Beirut (2001) 287–289
3. Araujo, L.P., de Marca, J.R.B.: Paging and Location Update Algorithms for Cellular Systems. IEEE Transactions On Vehicular Technology, Vol.49. (2000) 1606–1614
4. H.-W. Hwang, H.-W., Chang, M.-F., Tseng, C.-C.: A Direction Based Location Update Scheme with a Line-Paging Strategy for PCS Networks. IEEE Comm. Letters. Vol. 4 (2000) 149–151
5. Saraydar, C.U., Kelly, O.E., Rose, C.: One-Dimensional Location Area Design. IEEE Transactions On Vehicular Technology. Vol. 49. (2000) 1626–1632
6. Wang, W., Akyildiz, I.F., Stüber, G.L.: An Optimal Paging Scheme for Minimizing Signaling Costs Under Delay Bounds. IEEE Communications Letters. Vol. 5. (2001) 43–45
7. Cayirci, E., Akyildiz, I.F.: Optimal Location Area Design to Minimize Registration Signalling Traffic in Wireless Systems. IEEE Transactions On Mobile Computing, Vol. 2. (2003) 76–85

A Simple Pipelined Scheduling for Input-Queued Switches

Sang-Ho Lee[1] and Dong-Ryeol Shin[2]

[1] Samsung Electronics, System LSI Division, Korea,
sangho74.lee@samsung.com,
http://www.samsung.com

[2] Sungkyunkwan University, Network Research Laboratory, Korea
drshin@ece.skku.ac.kr,
http://nova.skku.ac.kr

Abstract. Input-queued switch is useful for high bandwidth switches and routers because of lower complexity and fewer circuits than output-queued switch. However, it suffers HOL-blocking, which limits the throughput to 58%. To overcome HOL-blocking problem, many input-queued switches are controlled by sophisticated scheduling algorithms at centralized schedulers which restrict the design of the switch architecture. In this paper, we propose a simple scheduler called Pipelined and Prioritized Round Robin(PPRR) which is intrinsically distributed by each input-port. An iterative prioritized round robin scheduling algorithm in a pipelined fashion is provided. The proposed algorithm has less complexity and yet comparable performance with respect to other algorithms such as iSLIP and RPA. The effectiveness of PPRR is demonstrated with simulations under uniform and bursty traffic conditions.

1 Introduction

Input-queued switch with a FIFO queue in each input-port suffers the HOL-blocking problem which limits the throughput to 58% [1]. A lot of scheduling algorithms have been suggested to improve the throughput. In order to overcome the performance reduction due to HOL-blocking, separate queues are required at each input-port for different output-ports called Virtual Output Queue(VOQ).

The recently appeared algorithm is based on bipartite matching problem, known either as a maximum weighted matching (MWM) or a maximum sized matching (MSM), depending on the value of weight. MWM find the matching that provides maximum total weight. MSM selects the match containing the maximum number of pairs. It is a special case of the MWM with same weight.

One of MWM policies , Reservation with Preemption Acknowledgement (RPA)[2] belongs to MWM, whereas PIM and iSLIP are typical examples of MSM.

PIM is a three-phase scheduling algorithm which uses parallelism, randomness, and iteration to achieve higher throughput. The switch is very efficient and its throughput can reach 98% in four iterations. Some variations of PIM such as iSLIP appeared recently [3, 4], which leads to the optimal and fair usage of the

A. Yazici and C. Şener (Eds.): ISCIS 2003, LNCS 2869, pp. 844–851, 2003.

switch bandwidth under a variety of traffic patterns. Unfortunately, these policies are not simple to implement, requiring a computational complexity, $O(N^2 logN)$ [5].

RPA is based on reservation rounds where input ports indicate their urgency, possibly overwriting less urgent request by other input ports, and an acknowledgement round to select actual transfer toward desired output ports. RPA is able to deal with multiple traffic classes and its complexity is $O(N^2)$ [5].

In this paper, we propose a different approach to three-steps matching used in PIM and iSLIP or reservation scheme, RPA.

The arbitration in this paper is solved by applying pipelined and prioritized round robin scheme rather than bipartite method, maximum matching, reservation-acknowledge method. Simulation results show that the proposed approach achieves good performances in simple architecture, less complexity, which compares favorably with other algorithms such as iSLIP and RPA.

This paper is organized as follows.Section 2 gives a basic principle of the proposed scheduling method. Section 3 shows the discussion and comparison of results obtained through the simulations. A simple hardware implementations is covered in section 4. Section 5 provides concluding remarks.

2 Proposed Scheduling Algorithm

2.1 Motivation

We propose an architecture called Pipelined and Prioritized Round Robin (PPRR) Scheduler which is an input-port controller that includes a cell scheduler to avoid HOL-blocking and to reduce delay or jitter. The algorithm in PPRR is simple. Like other VOQ-based scheduling methods, PPRR maintains multiple virtual queues at the input port for each output.

In an iSLIP if two or more cells routed to the same output in a time slot interval, three steps are used to resolve the conflict among inputs using input and output control units and round robin pointer. A recently proposed method, RPA has a similar idea but different scheduling scheme compared to PPRR.

Actually PPRR does not require a bipartite matching among input and output ports. PRRR instead composes of two parts. The first one is to maintain multiple virtual queues, which is the same as iSLIP and RPA. The second one is sequential comparison like RPA but the scheduling is completed with one reservation round to reduce complexity, whose scheduling algorithm is based on Prioritized Round Robin(PRR). One of important issues here is the implementation complexity. Most proposed schedulers are implemented as centralized modules. The size of switch is restricted by centralized scheduler. PPRR scheduling is distributed at each input port. This guarantees the simplicity of implementation.

2.2 Prioritized Round Robin

The incoming cells wait in the buffer of its own designated output port, i.e., virtual output queue. The input scheduler selects a virtual queue and transmits a next cell in the header of selected virtual queue into crossbar switch. The scheduling algorithm is based on Prioritized Round Robin(PRR). To apply PRR, each VQ has a priority counter depending on the queue length or waiting time and counting up as many as its priority weight at each time slot. The priority depends on the queue length, queue occupancy time, or some weights. To avoid HOL-blocking, each scheduler should not select the same destined VQ among input ports. The schedulers in the PRR scheduling do not schedule simultaneously but sequentially among input ports. This algorithm is implemented with N schedulers interconnecting the N input ports which determine the input-output port matches in a round robin and sequential manner. One input scheduler compares N VOQs to select one with highest priority. The next input scheduler then compares N-1 VOQs with which have been previously unselected VOQ index, and continues this procedure until the final input scheduler reaches. It is of centralized type and takes time to calculate, which may be significant computational burden at high speed switch.

2.3 Pipelined PRR

We propose a Pipelined PRR (PPRR) to reduce scheduling time and complexity. Each input port compares its own VOQs and selects a VOQ index of higher priority and forwards VOQ index with lower value to the next input port. In order to share temporary scheduling information between neighboring input schedulers, each input port is connected with its neighbor in a ring structure. The input-port has two operation modes, called master mode and slave mode. At any scheduling time, only one input can be a master and the others become slave. To guarantee the fairness among input ports, the master is determined by round robin. Fig.1 shows interconnection and its operation.

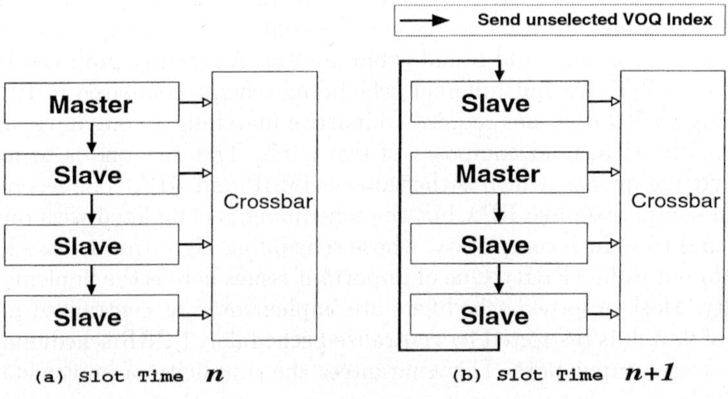

Fig. 1. PPRR's interconnection and it's operation

Let i and k be index of input port and output port, respectively, and p(i, k) a priority of VOQ corresponding to output port k and input port i. The master and slave operations are shown in the following pseudo code. The output port index is denoted by VOQ index.

Pseudo code of Master Operation

```
/*** Initialize Register, PR ***/
PR.PRIORITY = 0;    PR.INDEX = 0;

/** Start Schedule **/
for(k=1; k =<N; k++) {
    AR.PRIORITY = p(MY_INDEX, k);     /* Load VOQ's priority & index */
    AR.INDEX = k;
    if (AR.PRIORITY > PR.PRIORITY) {
        VQO <== AR.INDEX ;            /* Send unselected index */
        PR.PRIORITY = AR.PRIORITY;
        PR.PRIORITY = AR.INDEX;
    } else {
        VQO <== PR.INDEX;             /* Send unselected index */
    }
}
```

Pseudo code of Slave Operation

```
/*** Initialize Register, PR ***/
PR.PRIORITY = 0;        PR.INDEX = 0;

/** Start Schedule **/
while (TRUE) {
    wait_VQI_receive_event();         /* Wait receive event */
    AR.INDEX <== VQI;                 /* Receive output index */
    AR.PRIORITY = p(my_id, AR.INDEX);
    if (AR.PRIORITY > PR.PRIORITY) {
        VQO <== AR.INDEX ;            /* Send unselected index */
        PR.PRIORITY = AR.PRIORITY;
        PR.INDEX = AR.INDEX;
    } else {
        VQO <== PR.INDEX;             /* Send unselected index */
    }
}
```

At a start, the master compares priorities between two VOQs, taking higher one as a temporary selected index of VOQ and transfers an unselected output port index to the next slave input port. Repeat the comparison between temporary chosen VOQ and next VOQ within the same input port until the final winner is selected.

When a VOQ index arrives at the next slave input port, the input port scheduler compares the priority of previously indexed VOQ considered as higher priority up to previous comparison with the priority of the VOQs corresponding to the index received from the former, and selects higher priority (winner) and transfer the index of the VOQ with lower priority to the next input port.

At each comparison, the winner is kept and the loser is transferred to the next input port scheduler. During new comparison is made in the former input port scheduler, the next input port scheduler performs the comparison based on the information from previous input scheduler which is actually an output port index of loser. This comparison and the final selection of the VOQ continue until no more comparison is made. Fig. 2 shows this scheduling operation in the case of 4x4 switch.

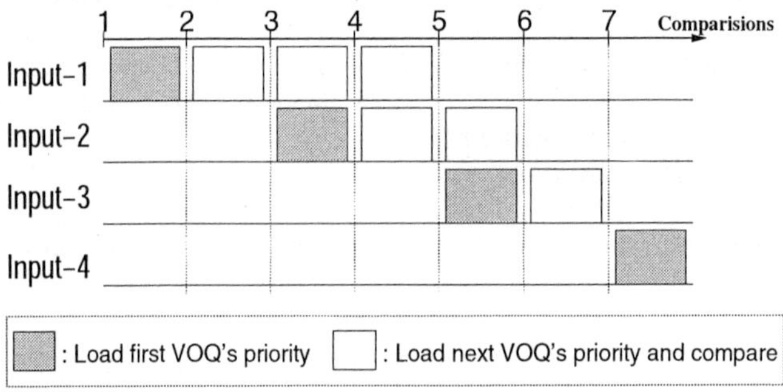

Fig. 2. Comparision Sequence

For 4x4 switch, only 7 mini slots (7 operations), which are smaller than normal scheduling slots shown Fig.1, are required. This comparing can be implemented as a simple logic which is composed of loading, comparison and forwarding. It can be extended to NxN switch case. We need only 2N-1 computations for NxN switch due to pipelined operations whose complexity is thus, which is much simpler compared with iSLIP.

When a scheduling completes, the current master input port returns a slave mode and one of slave input ports gets into the new master mode. This scheduling procedure continues to operate in a round robin fashion with one slot time.

3 Simulation

3.1 Simulation Model

Simulation is performed under a variety of workloads on a 16 by 16 switch. To evaluate the performance of the proposed algorithm, we compare it with iSLIP with 4-iteration and RPA in which the priority of each cell is defined by weighted fair queueing algorithm.

We consider two input traffic models:

a) Uniform traffic : cells arrive with bernoulli arrival process, the cell output-ports are selected with random independently

b) Bursty traffic : cells arrive with on-off arrival process modulated by a two-state Markov chain with destinations uniformly distributed over all outputs

For simplicity, a priority within each input-port is assigned based on the time already spent in the queue by the cell at the queue head (i.e., oldest cell first scheme).

3.2 Delay Performance

Fig. 3 shows the curves of the average cell delay normalized to the output queue cell delay values for three different input-queued switches. The delay performance is worse than RPA, which is due to transient delay at a start and priority assignment, but slightly better performance than iSLIP as shown in Fig. 3.

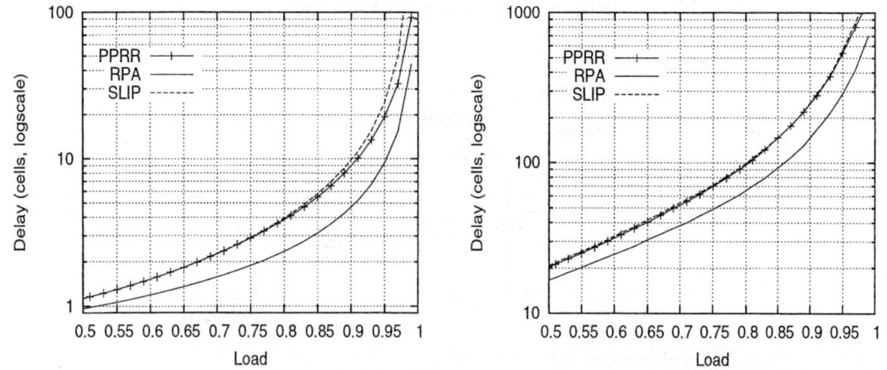

(a)Under uniform traffic (b)Under bursty traffic

Fig. 3. Delay Performance

3.3 Throughput

The throughput of the proposed scheduler is better than iSLIP as shown in Fig. 4. RPA provide the highest throughput under both traffic.

4 Implementation

We describes a simple hardware structure of a PPRR scheduler. As shown in Fig. 5, each PPRR scheduler has a comparator to compare with two priorities of VOQs. These priorities are loaded into a passive register (PR) and a active register (AR). PR loads priority from memory block. This priority corresponds to the VOQ which has the number from MUX.

In the master mode, MUX transfers numbers generated from counter. In the slave mode, the MUX transfers a number from VQI.

After each comparison, the higher priority and it's corresponding VOQ's number is feedback to PR. The number with lose VOQ is transferred to VQO.

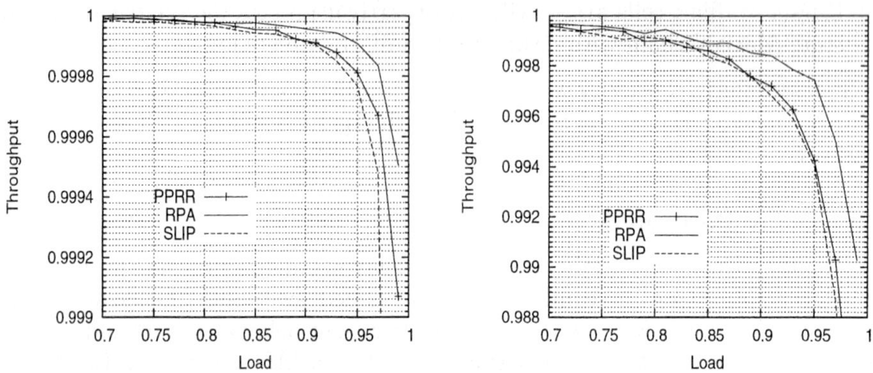

(a)Under uniform traffic (b)Under bersty traffic

Fig. 4. Troughput Performance

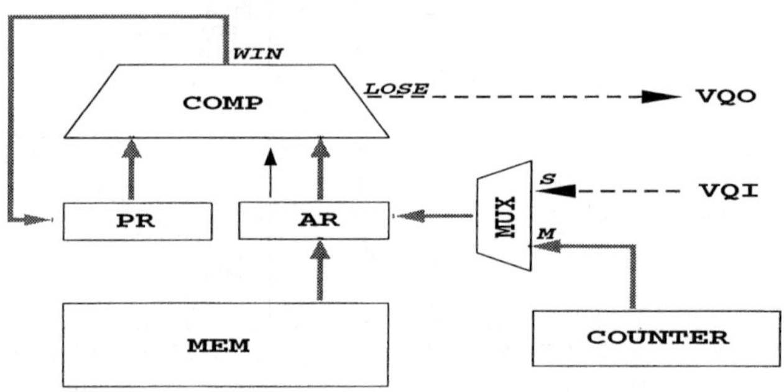

Fig. 5. PPRR's interconnection and it's operation

5 Conclusion

A highly efficient scheduling algorithm for overcoming HOL-blocking in an input-queued switch has been proposed. Its main feature is a distributed arbitration between input controllers in a pipelined weighted round robin manner rather than bipartite matching between input and output controllers. The implementation is simpler in the sense of no information transfer between input and output controllers. The performance such as throughput and delay shows better or comparable performance under uniform and bursty traffic comparing with alternative scheduling methods.

References

1. M. Karol, M. Hluchyj, S. Morgan : Input versus output queueing on a space division switch, IEEE Transactions on Commumnication, vol.35 (1987) 1347–1356

2. Ajmone Marsan M., Bianco A., Leonardi E. : RPA: a simple efficient and flexible policy for input buffered ATM switches, IEEE Communication Letters, vol.1 (1997) 83–86
3. T. Anderson, S. Owicki, I. Saxe, C. Thacker : High speed switch scheduling for local area networks, ACM Transactions on Computer Systems, vol.11 (1993) 1871–1894
4. Mckeon N., Mekkittikul A.: A practcal scheduling algorithm to achieve 100% throughput in input-queued switches, Proceedings of IEEE INFOCOM'98, vol. 2 (1998) 792–799
5. Ajmone Marsan M., Bianco A., E. Filippi: A comparision of input queuing cell switch architecture, Proceedings of IEEE INFOCOM'01, (2001)

Transport Protocol Mechanisms for Wireless Networking: A Review and Comparative Simulation Study

Alper Kanak and Öznur Özkasap

Koç University, Department of Computer Engineering, Istanbul, Turkey
{akanak, oozkasap}@ku.edu.tr

Abstract. Increasing popularity of wireless services has triggered the need for efficient wireless transport mechanisms. TCP, being the reliable transport level protocol widely used in wired network world, was not designed with heterogeneity in mind. The problem with the adaptation of TCP to the evolving wireless settings is because of the assumption that packet loss and unusual delays are mainly caused by congestion. TCP originally assumes that packet loss is very small. On the other hand, wireless links often suffer from high bit error rates and broken connectivity due to handoffs. A range of schemes, namely end-to-end, split-connection and link-layer protocols, has been proposed to improve the performance of transport mechanisms, in particular TCP, on wireless settings. In this study, we examine these mechanisms for wireless transport, and discuss our comparative simulation results of end-to-end TCP versions (Tahoe, Reno, NewReno and SACK) in various network settings including wireless LANs and wired-cum-wireless scenarios.

Keywords: TCP, wireless transport protocols, end-to-end protocols, split-connection protocols, wired-cum-wireless.

1 Introduction

With the growth and increasing popularity of wireless services, need for efficient wireless connections to the existing network infrastructures will be become crucial in future internetworks. TCP, being the reliable transport level protocol widely used in wired network world, was not designed with heterogeneity in mind. As an example, when a data packet is lost, in a wired network it is relatively safe to assume that this is most likely due to congestion, that is, too many packets are contending for network resources. However, when a wireless link or sub-network is involved it could as well be because of bad reception at the location of the user.

It is not unusual today, and will certainly become increasingly more common in forthcoming years, that a given TCP connection would pass through networks with varying latency and bandwidth characteristics. For example, it may pass through a network with high latency/low bandwidth (e.g. a wireless WAN) and then through a low latency/high bandwidth (wired) network. The problem with the adaptation of TCP to the evolving wireless settings is because of the assumption that packet loss and unusual delays are mainly caused by congestion. TCP is thus tuned to adapt to such congestion losses by slowing down the amount of data it transmits. It shrinks its

A. Yazici and C. Şener (Eds.): ISCIS 2003, LNCS 2869, pp. 852–859, 2003.

transmission window and backs off its retransmission timer, thus reducing the load and congestion on the network. However, in wireless networks, packet loss is often caused due to other factors besides congestion. Wireless channels often suffer from high bit error rates and broken connectivity due to handoffs. Moreover, the Bit Error Rate (BER) may vary continuously during a session. Unfortunately, TCP assumes that these losses are due to congestion and invokes its congestion control algorithms. Consequently, effects of packet losses in wireless links on TCP performance and enhancements to the classical TCP versions are significant research topics to study. Based on the studies in this area, a question to be answered would be "Would TCP, in particular, be the transport layer of preference for a wired-cum-wireless world?"

A range of schemes has been proposed to improve the performance of transport mechanisms, in particular TCP, on wireless settings. They can be broadly categorized into three groups: end-to-end protocols, split-connection protocols and link-layer protocols. These approaches are revisited in the next section. In this study, we examine mechanisms for wireless transport, and conduct simulations and analysis of end-to-end TCP versions (Tahoe, Reno, NewReno and SACK) for various network settings including wireless LANs and wired-cum-wireless scenarios. Tahoe is an old TCP protocol that is rarely used currently. It implements slow start algorithm and has no fast recovery algorithm. In TCP Reno, the fast retransmit operation has been modified to include fast recovery. It prevents the communication path from going empty after fast retransmit, thereby avoiding the need to slow start to refill it after a single packet loss. Reno significantly improves the behavior of Tahoe when a single packet is dropped from a window of data, but can suffer from performance problems when multiple packets are dropped from a window of data. The NewReno TCP includes a small change to Reno algorithm at the sender that eliminates Reno's wait for a retransmit timer when multiple packets are lost from a window. NewReno can recover without a retransmission timeout. The TCP SACK uses the TCP Extensions for high performance. The congestion control algorithms are a conservative extension of Reno's congestion control. SACK differs from Reno when multiple packets dropped from a window of data. During fast recovery, SACK maintains a variable called pipe that represents the estimated number of packets outstanding in the path. The sender only sends new or retransmitted data when the estimated number of packets in the path is less than the congestion window [1].

The outline of the paper is as follows. In Section 2, we review mechanisms for wireless transport, namely end-to-end protocols, split-connection protocols and link-layer protocols. Section 3 gives details of our simulation study and analysis results on various network settings. Section 3.1 discusses comparisons of TCP performances over wired and wireless LAN scenarios. Section 3.2 and 3.3 discuss results for end-to-end protocols and split-connection protocols in wired-cum-wireless scenarios respectively. Finally, our conclusions and future work are stated in Section 4.

2 Review of Mechanisms for Wireless Transport

In contrast to wired LANs, a wireless LAN exhibits typical characteristics, such as low and highly variable throughput, high and highly variable latency, bursty and random packet losses unrelated to congestion, irregular blackouts, and asymmetric uplink and downlink channels. Under such conditions, when packets are lost due to errors other than congestion, this leads to unnecessary reduction in end-to-end throughput and hence degraded performance. In order to improve the transport protocol performance, in particular TCP, in wireless settings, two methods are common in systems experiencing packet loss:

- Hiding any non-congestion-related losses from the TCP sender which therefore requires no changes to existing sender implementations.
- Attempt to make the sender aware of existence of the wireless hops and realize that some packets losses are not due to congestion

For implementing these methods, several schemes are proposed which can be examined in three broad categories, namely, *end-to-end protocols* where sender is aware of the wireless link, *link layer protocols* that provide local reliability, and *split-connection scheme* where the connection is partitioned into two, wired and wireless, at the base station [2]. Next, we review these approaches.

2.1 End-to-End Protocols

End-to-end protocols, in which the sender is aware of the wireless link, retain a single TCP connection from sender to receiver and they handle losses through the use of selective acknowledgements (SACKs). This allows the sender to recover from losses within a window without resorting to timeout. This scheme performs well with TCP SACK but also applicable for Tahoe and Reno protocols.

The common TCP implementation currently employed on the Internet is Reno TCP. Reno TCP algorithm uses a combination of slow-start, congestion avoidance, fast retransmit and fast recovery methods. It utilizes cumulative acknowledgments for providing reliable delivery. NewReno TCP is an extended version of Reno TCP which is proposed for improving performance after multiple packet losses. SACK protocols add selective acknowledgments allowing the sender to handle multiple losses within a window of outstanding data more efficiently. Another approach referred to as explicit loss notification (ELN) is used to prevent unnecessary throttles applied to congestion window.

2.2 Data Link Layer Protocols

Proposals in this category are based on the following argument: Since the problem of high link error rates in a wireless environment lies at the physical layer, the data link layer (LL) has more control over it than any other layer and can sense a problem faster. Hence, the problem can be solved at the LL that aims to offer a good communication channel to the layers above, in particular to TCP. This does not require any change on current TCP implementations. The way to do this is to ensure reliable delivery of packets at all times, for example using an Automatic Repeat reQuest (ARQ) scheme. However, studies have shown that this could lead to degraded performance. This is because TCP also attempts to ensure reliable transmission, thus leading to a lot of duplicate effort. If such a solution is to be accepted, it has to be tightly coupled with TCP.

The most prominent proposal in this category is the SNOOP protocol [3]. SNOOP lies in an intermediate position between the end-to-end and split-connection proposals, trying to utilize the ability of a LL protocol to respond fast, and at the same time using the available information to keep TCP "happy" with the existing network connection. For example, SNOOP would favor local LL retransmissions instead of TCP retransmissions. This is achievable because a SNOOP agent would be aware of duplicate acknowledgments traveling from the receiver to the sender and suppress them, locally re-transmitting the potentially lost segment instead. Without SNOOP, the receipt of a certain number of duplicate acknowledgments would have caused a TCP segment retransmission.

2.3 Split-Connection Protocols

The basic idea behind the proposals in this category, such as Indirect TCP (I-TCP) [4], is that since there exist two completely different classes of sub-networks, namely wired and wireless, each TCP connection could be split into two connections at the point where the two sub-networks meet. As an example, suppose a mobile user browses a conventional web site using his laptop. The TCP connection will be split into two: one between the mobile host and the base station and one between the base station and the web server. The advantage is that TCP implementation in the sender does not need to be modified to deal with the enhanced functionality required for the wireless hop. The best transport protocol for each type of network can be utilized. This is very similar to using a HTTP proxy server. Splitting the TCP connection is essentially the technique used under the Wireless Application Protocol (WAP) architecture. The most significant disadvantage of splitting TCP connections is the loss of end-to-end semantics of TCP. In addition, the performance may also be degraded by the fact that it could end up splitting a particular connection several times, if different combinations of sub-networks are involved. Handoffs are also not handled as efficiently, and crashes in the base station result in TCP connection termination.

3 Simulation Results

The underlying platform for our simulation model is ns-2 network simulator [5]. Wireless model in ns-2 supports the effectiveness of mobile nodes by different routing mechanisms, routing protocols, network components, movement/traffic scenario generation and transmission protocols. Among the ad-hoc routing protocols currently available for mobile networking in ns-2, we chose DSR (dynamic source routing) as the routing agent. The DSR agent checks every data packet for source-route information. It forwards the packet as per the routing information. In case it does not find routing information in the packet, it provides the source route if route is known, or caches the packet and sends out route queries if route to destination is not known. Routing queries, always triggered by a data packet with no route to its destination, are initially broadcast to all neighbors. Route replies are sent back either by intermediate nodes or the destination node, to the source, if it can find routing info for the destination in the route query. Simulation parameters common to all set of runs are frequency of 2.4GHz, 802.11b Mac layer, 10Mbps channel, 100m distance between neighbor nodes in the topology, RED queue management algorithm, and 1400 byte-packet size with sender's rate of 200 packets per second. Versions of TCP protocols simulated are Tahoe, Reno, NewReno and SACK.

3.1 Comparison of TCP Performances over Wired and Wireless LAN Scenarios

Scenario 1: Simple two-node connection: The first scenario consists of a pair of nodes communicating either in wireless or wired settings that is used to simulate wireless LAN without collision. This is because there is only a pair of nodes communicating, and no additional node exists which could affect the communication. Besides, note that there is an error model on the link which is described when discussing our simulation results. The second set is for the two nodes connected via a wired link.

The measurement metrics are throughput and queue delay. Queue delay measurement is accomplished as follows: Suppose that a packet p is to be sent. There are two events associated: E1 and E2. E1 is scheduled to occur when the current sending operation has completed and E2 represents the packet arrival event. Here E1 is associated with a *Queue* object of ns-2, and queue delay is the time difference between these two events. On the other hand, average queue delay is calculated by tracing a set of packets during a time period. RED is used as the queuing algorithm, and buffer size is varied by using ns-2 arguments while we kept the buffer sizes of both sender and receiver the same.

According to the throughput results in Fig. 1 where x-axis represents the number of lost packets in a congestion window, SACK performs better in terms of throughput among all TCP versions while Tahoe has the lowest throughput values. The reason is that SACK uses a selective acknowledge and pipe scheme to ensure that when packets are dropped, the congestion window will recover fast. Thus the average throughput will be improved. Now let's consider the effect of buffer size on delay and throughput. As shown in Fig. 2, when the buffer size increases, different TCP versions have almost the same performance on average queue delay. However, we observed that the distinction of throughput for different TCP versions when buffer size increases is relatively large (Fig.3). The NewReno and SACK performs better than Tahoe and Reno. The reason is that when buffer size is small, multiple packets will be dropped. Tahoe and Reno has no fast recovery algorithm for dealing with multiple drops. Thus the TCP congestion window drops rapidly, hence leading low throughput. We observed similar results in wired connection as well (because of the page limitation, we do not include these graphs).

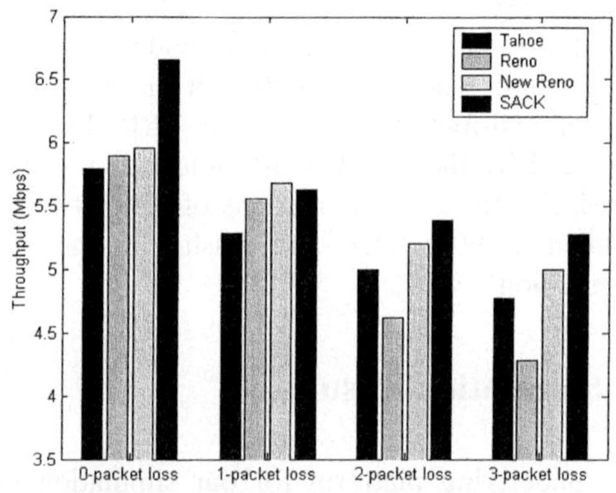

Fig. 1. Throughput for n-packet losses in simple wireless scenario

Scenario 2: Wireless N-node model: The second scenario is a wireless N-node model as illustrated in Fig. 4, which is used to simulate a wireless LAN with collisions. The network size N changes from 10 to 50. When the network size increases, the collisions become more frequent. Fig. 5 shows throughput analysis results as the network size increases for TCP versions. We observe that all four curves have the same trend of decrease when node number increases. The reason is that if node number increases, due to collisions taking place frequently, it becomes harder and harder to establish a connection link for each pair. However, SACK still presents the best performance among all. This is due to the fast recovery and fast retransmission algorithms implemented in SACK. Even when collisions occur and multiple packets are dropped, fast recovery algorithm could help TCP link to maintain a relatively good performance.

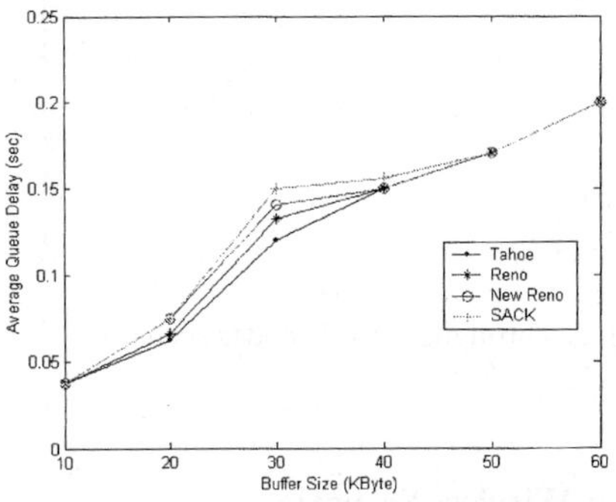

Fig. 2. Average queue delay as a function of buffer size in simple wireless scenario

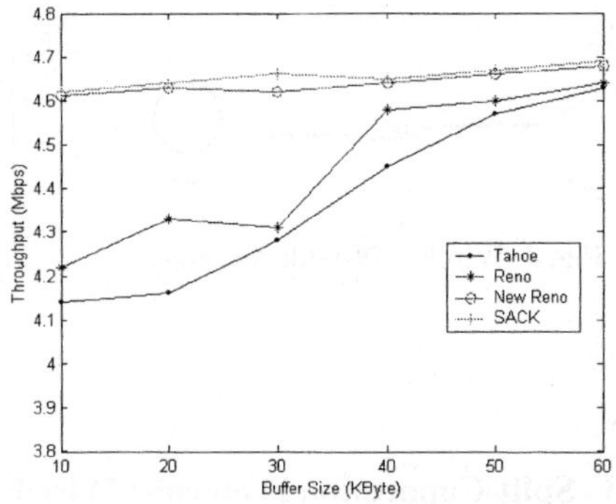

Fig. 3. Throughput as a function of buffer size in simple wireless scenario

3.2 End-to-End Protocols: Wired-Cum-Wireless Scenario

TCP has been optimized over the years for wired networks. With the proliferation of wireless networking, TCP has to perform well in heterogeneous infrastructures, which exhibit different characteristics than the wired ones such as random segment corruption over wireless links. Several improvement proposals attempt to lessen TCP's inefficiencies in a wired-cum-wireless environment. In order to simulate the end-to-end schemes, we have constructed the topology shown in Fig. 6. Node 1 sends ftp packets to every node in the system without caring the link on the way to the destination. That could be either a wireless or wired link. End-to-end protocol maintains a single TCP connection from sender to receiver and attempts to make TCP aware of wireless losses so that it can deal with them. Protocols handle losses through the use of some form of selective acknowledgements (SACKs). As mentioned before, this allows the sender to recover from losses within a window without needing to timeout. Thus, end-to-end schemes involve modifying the TCP implementation in the sender to make it "wireless" aware. This may not always be feasible and is a potential problem for widespread implementation of end-to-end schemes.

Note that, in this scenario, a real base station is not constructed at node 3 but a non-mobile node is inserted to simulate the end-to-end protocol. In fact, there may be a base station to manage the communication among mobile nodes. End-to-end protocols do not worry about the communication path between the sender and the receiver even if there is a base station on the way. In other words, the mobile nodes in our simulation act as a base station. We construct a scenario with a base station for split-connection protocols, and evaluate combined performance results in the next section.

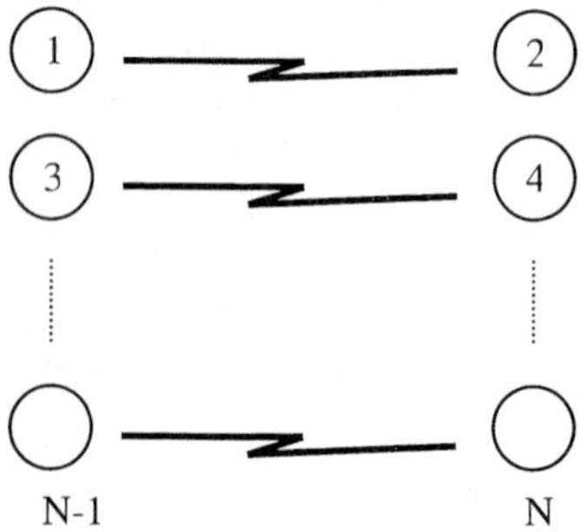

Fig. 4. Wireless N-node topology

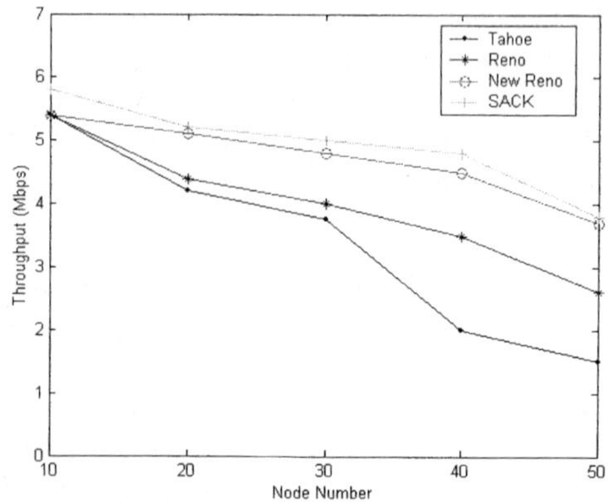

Fig. 5. Throughput for N nodes scenario

3.3 Split-Connection Protocols: Wired-Cum-Wireless Scenario

In this scenario, we replace node 3 in Fig.6 with a base station to split the connection into wired and wireless parts. In other words, both parts are communicating via the base station. The nodes connected to each other via wired links are aware of the wireless link on the other end. Split-connection protocols hide the unreliability of the wireless link from the sender by terminating the TCP connection at the base station and using a separate protocol from the base station to the mobile host. This has the advantage that the TCP implementation in the sender does not need to be modified.

Throughput analysis results of end-to-end and split-connection cases for different error rates are given in Fig. 7. The rates represent the ratio of erroneous bits over the whole packet. For instance, 1/256 means there is 1 erroneous bit for every 256 bit in a packet. In all cases, SACK shows better performance in lossy wireless links. For high error rates, splitting schemes may perform better compared to end-to-end counterparts. Reno is the weakest protocol in all cases. As shown in Fig. 8, we observe that the bigger the queue size of the link, less congestion will occur and performance would be better. When queue size increases, a large proportion of total error is due to non-congestion losses. This is because of the fact that as the queue size on the link increases, the probability of congestion would decrease. Hence the throughput does not change much. Among all TCP versions simulated, SACK protocols perform better. Likewise, end-to-end case with TCP Reno shows degraded performance among the others.

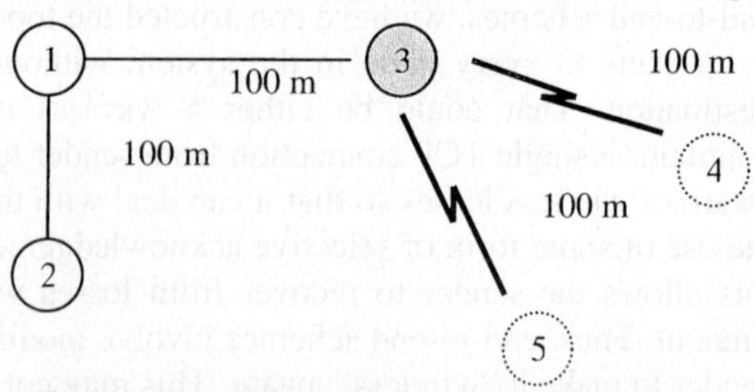

Fig. 6. Simulation topology for end-to-end and split connection protocols

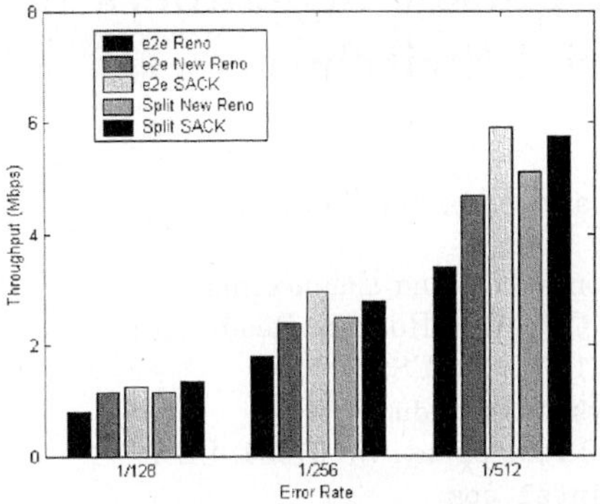

Fig. 7. Throughput analysis of end-to-end and split protocols as a function of error rate

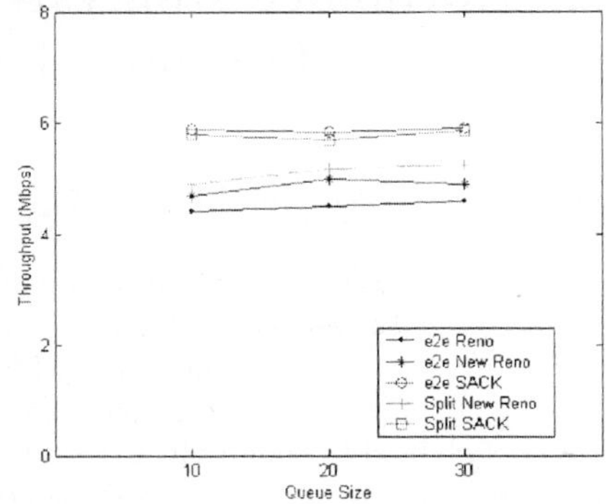

Fig. 8. Throughput analysis of end-to-end and split protocols as a function of queue size

4 Conclusions

In this study, we review three main approaches for transport mechanisms of wireless networking, namely end-to-end, split-connection and link-layer methods together with our comparative simulation results. Our simulation study yields some conclusions about the performance of end-to-end and split-connection transport protocol mechanisms particularly in wireless local area network settings. We conclude that, among the simulated TCP versions, TCP SACK has the best performance. When the buffer size increases, different TCP versions show almost the same trend on average queue delay, but the difference is apparent on average throughput behavior. In particular, for wireless multi-node model, throughputs of all TCP versions are inversely proportional to the node number. We have also simulated wired-cum-wireless scenarios for both end-to-end and split connection mechanisms and found out that TCP SACK performs best in both cases in terms of throughput versus different error rates and queue sizes. According to results, TCP SACK with end-to-end protocols performs a little better than the TCP SACK with split-connection protocols. An area for further study would be simulating and analyzing link-layer protocols and ELN schemes. There are also other solutions within this area such as WTCP (wireless TCP) or TCP-aware protocols that can be studied on the same network scenarios.

References

1. K. Fall and S. Floyd, Comparisons of Tahoe, Reno, and SACK TCP, ftp://ftp.ee.lbl.gov/papers/sack.ps.Z, December 1995.
2. H. Barakrishnan, V. N. Padmanabban, S. Seshan, R. H. Katz, A comparison of mechanisms for improving TCP performance over wireless links,Proc. *ACM SIGCOMM*, 1996.
3. H. Balakrishnan, S. Seshan, and R.H. Katz. Improving Reliable Transport and Handoff Performance in Cellular Wireless Networks. *ACM WirelessNetworks*, 1(4), December 1995.
4. A. Bakre and B. R. Badrinath. I-TCP: Indirect TCP for Mobile Hosts. In *Proc. 15th International Conf. on Distributed Computing Systems (ICDCS)*, May 1995.
5. K.Fall and K. Varadhan, NS Notes and Document. February 25, 2000.

Performance Analysis of Packet Schedulers in High-Speed Serial Switches

Oleg Gusak[1], Neal Oliver[2], and Khosrow Sohraby[1]

[1] School of Interdisciplinary Computing and Engineering,
University of Missouri-Kansas City 5100 Rockhill Road,
Kansas City, MO 64110-2499, USA
{gusako, sohrabyk}@umkc.edu

[2] Intel Corporation, 1515 Route 10 Parsippany, NJ 07054, USA
Neal.Oliver@intel.com

Abstract. In this work we examine the performance of arbitration algorithms for core high-speed serial switches (HSSS). Taking Infiniband as an example, experimental results show that, for a homogeneous network load, the average queuing delay for the switch output ports under the weighted round-robin (WRR) algorithm defined for InfiniBand is similar to the average queuing delay resulting from the largest delay-first (LDF) or first-in-first-out (FIFO) algorithms. For a 4-port switch, when the average load is high (close to 95% of the network capacity) and unbalanced with respect to the WRR weights, the difference in average delay between WRR and LDF or FIFO is large. However, for a 20-port switch and the same high unbalanced average network load, this difference is less than half of that of the 4-port switch. Further, the average queuing delay difference between WRR and LDF or FIFO diminishes quickly as the average load decreases. Hence, even for a fairly high average load, LDF or FIFO can be suggested for arbitration in core HSSS.

1 Introduction

Due to the growing number of network applications and their demands on network resources, Quality of Service (QoS) issues are continuing to receive research attention [1, 2, 3, 4, 5, 6, 7, 8, 9]. In this work we concentrate on QoS guarantees which can be provided by high-speed serial switches such as Infiniband [10], PCI-Express/Advanced Switching [11], serial RIO [12], etc. In our experiments we consider an Infiniband architecture (IBA) network in which QoS may be supported through the mechanism of virtual lanes (VLs) associated with each output port of an IBA node and arbitrated by a pre-emptive scheduling algorithm layered on top of a weighted round-robin algorithm.

In this work, we characterize network nodes as edge nodes (i.e., nodes which connect terminal devices to the network) or core nodes (i.e., switches which interconnect edge nodes), and observe the behavior of the WRR algorithm in the core nodes. In other words, we examine the behavior of WRR in core nodes which polices traffic shaped by WRR in edge nodes. The goal of this analysis

A. Yazici and C. Şener (Eds.): ISCIS 2003, LNCS 2869, pp. 860–868, 2003.

is to compare the performance of WRR to relatively simple algorithms, such as largest delay-first (LDF) and first-in-first-out (FIFO).

We simulate a simple IBA network consisting of four traffic sources and a single switch. We assume that every node of the network adopts the same weights for a particular VL. The results of experiments for various traffic parameters show that, when the average network load is balanced, the difference in average delay for WRR and LDF or FIFO is small. On the other hand, when the average network load is 95% of the network capacity and the average load is unbalanced with respect to the WRR weights, this difference is substantial. However, for a 20-port switch and the same high unbalanced average network load, this difference is less than half of the delay observed in the 4-port switch. We also observed that the square coefficient of variation of the queuing delay in switch output ports is larger for WRR than for FIFO or LDF.

In the next section, we briefly discuss the mechanism of virtual lanes and describe the network configuration used in our experiments. The results of experiments are given in section 3 and in section 4 we conclude.

2 InfiniBand Architecture and Experiment Setup

In an IBA network, each node may have one or more communication ports which can send and receive data concurrently. Each port has its own set of input and output queues associated with virtual lanes of the port. It is assumed that VLs are numbered starting from 0. The maximum number of VLs supported by an IBA port is 16. All IBA ports support VL 0 and VL 15. VL 0 is the default VL used for data transfer and VL 15 is used for network management and has priority over other VLs. We remark that IBA documentation does not specify QoS levels but mentions that VLs are one of the mechanisms which can be used to provide QoS guarantees [10].

When an IBA output port supports more than two VLs, all VLs except VL 15 are arbitrated by a two-level process consisting of preemptive scheduling layered upon weighted round robin. In this process, all VLs are divided into high and low priority sets. A VL with the same index can be a member of both sets. Arbitration between the two sets is done with a high priority counter, which is increased every time a packet is sent from a high priority VL. When the counter reaches a predefined limit or there are no available packets in the queues associated with the high priority VLs, the low priority set becomes active. The counter is reset every time that the low priority set becomes active. The VLs of each set are arbitrated by a weighted-round robin algorithm. In this algorithm, each VL has an associated weight corresponding to the number of bytes that can be continuously sent from this VL until control is given to another VL of the set. A detailed description of the algorithm and Infiniband architecture can be found in [10].

In our simulation model, we implemented a simplified version of the VL arbitration process in which only one priority level is used. In this simplified process, only the WRR algorithm, acting upon VLs 0 through 14, is important.

We set $w_i = 5p(i+1)$, where w_i is the weight of VL i, $i = 0, 1, \ldots, 14$, and p is the average size of the packets transmitted over the network.

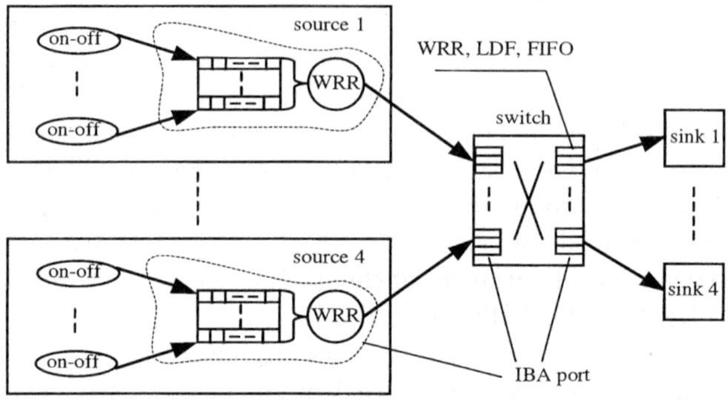

Fig. 1. Simulated network

The simulated network is shown in Fig. 1 and consists of four nodes generating packet flows to the network, a four-port input-output queuing switch (see [13] for a survey of high-speed switching techniques), and four sink nodes. We assume that all point-to-point links connecting network nodes have the same bandwidth of 2.5 Gb (see [10] for the link characteristics adopted by IBA). Every source node has 16 on-off packet sources corresponding to 16 VLs of the source node. The destination address of a packet is randomly drawn from set $\{1, 2, 3, 4\}$ according to a uniform distribution. Queues of the output ports of the source nodes are arbitrated by the WRR having weights defined in the previous paragraph.

Input queues of the switch are served in the order of VL indices associated with the queues. When the queue currently holding the right of transmission has a packet to send, the packet is transmitted and the right of transmission is passed to the next queue. If the queue currently holding the right of transmission does not have a packet to send, the right of transmission is immediately passed to the next queue. We assume that the relay time of a packet from an input to an output port of the switch (i.e., the switching slot) is equal to the average transmission time of a packet over a link connected to a port of the switch. We also assume that packets of the input ports selected for relaying in a given switching slot are transferred to the output ports at the end of the switching slot. Note that, in a single slot, at most four packets (i.e., at most one packet from each port) can be relayed to the output ports. Since in this work we concentrate on the output queues of the switch, we assume that the switching fabric is capable of relaying at most four packets to the output ports regardless of their destination port number. In other words, if more than one packet is destined to the same port, all of them can be transmitted to the same port in a single slot. See [2, 7] for research related to blocking in input-queuing packet switches. As a result of this assumption, a higher load is imposed on the output queues than would be the case when blocking of the packets destined to the same output port can occur.

Queues of a switch output port are arbitrated either by WRR with the same weights as in the source nodes, by LDF in which the packet having largest delay is transmitted first, or by FIFO, where all packets entering an output port are queued in a single queue. Note that in all cases, packets destined to VL 15 are enqueued in a separate queue, which has priority over other queues.

In the next section, we discuss the results of experiments with the IBA network and compare the behavior of WRR versus LDF and FIFO algorithms on VL arbitration.

3 Simulation Results

We implemented the simulation model of Fig. 1 in OPNET [14]. In all experiments, the size of the data packets follows an exponential distribution with the mean equal to 1024 bytes. The interarrival time of packets generated in the on

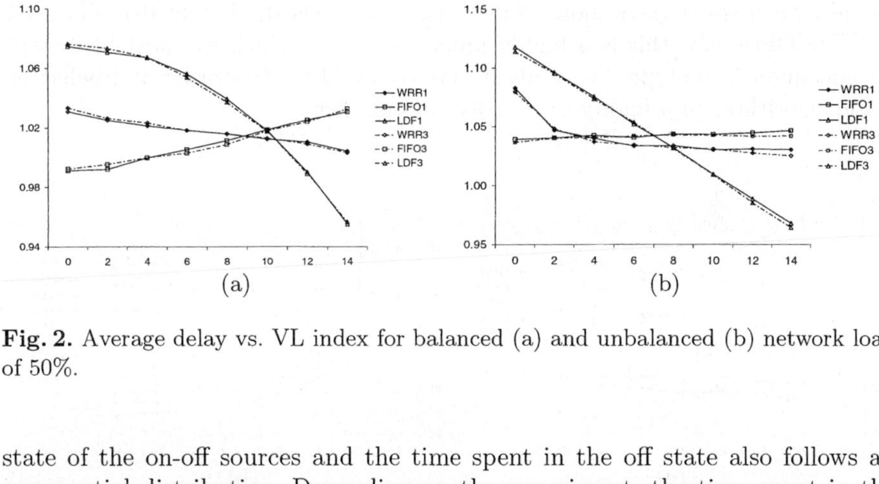

(a) (b)

Fig. 2. Average delay vs. VL index for balanced (a) and unbalanced (b) network load of 50%.

state of the on-off sources and the time spent in the off state also follows an exponential distribution. Depending on the experiment, the time spent in the on state follows an exponential or a hyperexponential distribution of order two. The probability density function of the hyperexponential distribution of order two is given by [15, p.399]

$$f(t) = p\mu_1 e^{-\mu_1 t} + (1-p)\mu_2 e^{-\mu_2 t},$$

where $0 \leq p \leq 1$, $1/\mu_1$ and $1/\mu_2$ are the means of the first and the second exponential distributions respectively. We use the hyperexponential distribution with balanced means, i.e., $p/\mu_1 = (1-p)/\mu_2$. Hence, if the mean of the hyperexponential distribution is m and the square coefficient of variation is S_c^{on}, p, μ_1, and μ_2 are given by

$$p = \frac{1}{2}\left(1 - \sqrt{\frac{S_c^{on} - 1}{S_c^{on} + 1}}\right), \; \mu_1 = \frac{2p}{m}, \; \mu_2 = \frac{2(1-p)}{m}.$$

In our experiments we set S_c^{on} equal to 2 or 3.

We consider two types of load imposed to VLs. In the first case, which we call balanced load, $l_i = l \cdot i$ for $i = 1, 2 \ldots, 14$, where l_i is the average load imposed to VL i, and l is the load imposed to VL 0 and VL 15. Note that $l_i = \frac{a}{a+b}\lambda_i$, where a and b are the mean times spent in the on and off states respectively, and $1/\lambda_i$ is the mean interarrival time of packets generated by source i in the on state. In the second case, which we call unbalanced load, $l_i = C \cdot l$, $i = 0, 1, \ldots, 15$, where C is a constant. In all experiments, we set $a = b$. Hence, $l_i = \frac{1}{2}\lambda_i$. For balanced and unbalanced average network load, we choose l and C such that the average load is 50% (moderate load) or 95% (high load) of the capacity of the link connecting a source to the switch. Observe that the balanced load scenario corresponds to the case in which the flow average arrival rates are in agreement with the weights of WRR. On the contrary, in unbalanced load scenario, lower indexed VLs are highly overloaded, whereas higher indexed VLs are underloaded. For instance, when the average load is 95% of the link capacity, average arrival rate to VL 0 is 7.6 times higher than the bandwidth allocated to it. Moreover, average peak arrival rate in this case is more than 15 times exceeds the bandwidth allocated to VL 0. Obviously, this is a highly unbalanced load which we most likely will not encounter in real life. We study it here to reveal relative order and behavior of the algorithms in a highly unfriendly environment.

(a) (b)

Fig. 3. Average delay vs. VL index for balanced (a) and unbalanced (b) network load of 95%.

In the first set of experiments, we compare the average queuing delay in the switch in which output queues are served using WRR, LDF, and FIFO when the average network load is moderate. In Fig. 2(a), we plot average queuing delay versus queue index for the case when the average network load is balanced. Results of Fig. 2(b) correspond to the case when the average network load is unbalanced. Note that, on all figures, the reported average queuing delay is normalized with respect to the average packet transmission time. In all figures, the indices of WRR, FIFO, and LDF (i.e., 1, 2, and 3) correspond to the value of S_c^{on}. The 95% confidence intervals for the results of Fig. 2 do not exceed 1%.

According to our assumption on the switching fabric, the packets that are relayed from input to output ports of the switch in a given slot are enqueued to the output port queues at the end of the slot. As a result of this assumption, packets residing in the queues of a port may have equal waiting times. When the queues are arbitrated by LDF and more than one packet have the largest delay, priority is given to the packet of a higher indexed queue. Hence, as can be seen on Fig. 2, the average queueing delay for LDF in VL 0 is larger than in VL 14. We remark that, when the average network load is moderate, the average queuing delay is small (about the average packet transmission time) and is insensitive to S_c^{on}. For unbalanced average network load, the difference in average queuing delay between WRR and FIFO is within 1.6%, except for VL 0 for which the difference is 4%. The difference in average queuing delay between WRR and LDF does not exceed 6.1%. Note that, for an unbalanced average network load, the average load imposed on VL 0 is 3.9 times larger than the link bandwidth allocated to it. However, we do not observe large average queuing delay for VL 0 since the average network load imposed to VLs $3, 4, \ldots, 14$ is below the bandwidth allocated to them.

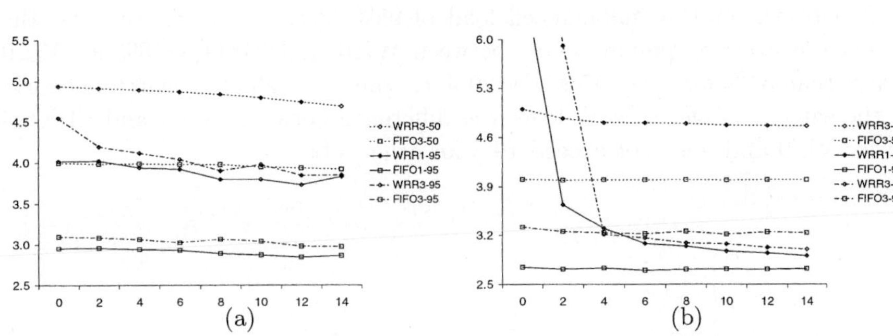

Fig. 4. S_c of queuing delay vs. VL index for balanced (a) and unbalanced (b) network load.

In Fig. 3, we give results of experiments for the case where the average network load is 95% of the link capacity. The 95% confidence intervals for the results of Fig. 3 do not exceed 10% for WRR (except for the results of VL 0, for which the confidence intervals are within 15%) and 9% for FIFO. Since the difference between the average queuing delay for FIFO and LDF is small, we plot results for LDF only for the case of balanced load and $S_c^{on} = 1$ (see Fig. 3(a)).

Firstly, we remark that, in all experiments, the average queuing delay is significantly larger than for the case of a moderate average load. Secondly, when the average load is balanced, the difference in the average queuing delay for WRR and FIFO is less than 9.5% for $S_c^{on} = 1$ and is less than 7.6% for $S_c^{on} = 2$ and

$S_c^{on} = 3$. On the other hand, when the average load is unbalanced, the difference in the average queuing delay between WRR and FIFO is 74% for VL 0 and is less than 46% for other VLs. Note also that, for WRR, the average queuing delay for VL 0 is large (116 for $S_c^{on} = 1$, 127 for $S_c^{on} = 2$, and 137 for $S_c^{on} = 3$) compared to the average queuing delay in other VLs. The average queuing delay for VL 0 arbitrated by WRR is large because VL 0 is significantly overloaded (see discussion on page 864). In general, for WRR or FIFO, the average queuing delay is larger for $S_c^{on} = 2$ than for $S_c^{on} = 1$, and is larger for $S_c^{on} = 3$ than for $S_c^{on} = 2$.

In Fig. 5, we give results for the case when the average network load is unbalanced and is 90% of the link capacity. The 95% confidence intervals for the results of Fig. 3 are within 6% for FIFO and within 5% for WRR except for VL 0, for which the confidence intervals are within 11%.

We remark that the difference in average queuing delay between WRR and FIFO is significantly smaller (especially for VL 0) than for an average load of 95%. When S_c^{on} is 1 or 2, the difference is 53% for VL 0 and does not exceed 18% for other VLs. When $S_c^{on} = 3$, the difference is 58% for VL 0 and is less than 21% for other VLs.

We also carried out experiments for a larger number of traffic sources and a larger number of ports in the switch. For instance, for 8 data sources, an 8-port switch network, and an unbalanced load of 95% of the network capacity, the difference in average queuing delay between WRR and FIFO is 68% for VL 0 and less than 31% for other VLs. For 20 data sources, a 20-port switch network, and the same average network load, the difference between WRR and FIFO is 57% for VL 0 and does not exceed 19% for other VLs.

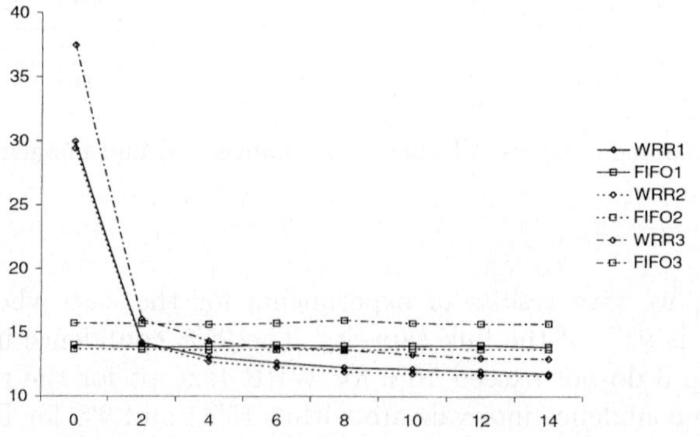

Fig. 5. Average queuing delay vs. VL index for unbalanced average network load of 90%

In Fig 4, we give results for the square coefficient of variation, S_c, of the queuing delay for balanced (a) and unbalanced (b) average network load. We remark that, in each experiment, S_c is larger for WRR than for FIFO or LDF. Note that we plot results only for WRR and FIFO since the difference in S_c for FIFO and LDF is small. We also remark that, for moderate average network load, for a particular queuing algorithm, the difference in S_c for different values of S_c^{on} is negligible. Hence, for moderate average network load we plot results for S_c only for the case of $S_c^{on} = 3$. It is interesting to note that, for balanced and unbalanced average network load, for a particular queuing algorithm and value of S_c^{on}, S_c is larger for the moderate average network load than for the high average load, excluding results of WRR for VL 0 and VL 2 when the average network load is high. For WRR, S_c for VL 0 (not shown on Fig. 4 (b)) is 7 when $S_c^{on} = 1$ and is 11 when $S_c^{on} = 3$.

4 Concluding Remarks

In this work, we examined queuing delay experienced by packets under VL arbitration in an InfiniBand switch. We compared WRR to LDF and FIFO arbitration algorithms for various average network loads (moderate and high, balanced and unbalanced) and various values of S_c^{on}. The results of experiments show that, when the average load to VLs is balanced with respect to weights of WRR, the difference in average queuing delay between WRR and LDF or FIFO is small even for a fairly high load. When the average network load is unbalanced and is 95% of the network capacity, the difference in average queuing delay between WRR and LDF or FIFO is large. However, this difference diminishes quickly when the network load gets smaller. The difference in average queuing delay between WRR and FIFO is also smaller for large numbers of traffic sources and switch ports. When the average load is high, the average queuing delay for WRR, LDF or FIFO is larger for larger values of S_c^{on}. We also observed that, in a particular experiment, S_c is larger for WRR than for FIFO or LDF.

In summary, assuming that, in the edge nodes of an IBA network, the average load imposed to a VL does not significantly exceed the network bandwidth allocated for the VL, FIFO or LDF may be used instead of WRR for VL arbitration in core InfiniBand nodes. Future work may focus on examining the average queuing delay of WRR, FIFO, and LDF for heterogeneous sources and network parameters. Also, of particular interest may be an analysis of the queuing delay experienced by packets as they traverse more than one core node.

References

1. H. Zhang, "Service disciplines for guaranteed performance service in packet-switching networks," *Proceedings of the IEEE*, vol. 83, no. 10, pp. 1374–1396, 1995.
2. R. Guérin and K.N. Sirvarajan, "Delay and throughput performance of speeded-up input-queueing packet switches," TR, IBM, 1997, http://www.seas.upenn.edu/ tcom502/references/ISRpaper.pdf.

3. N.G. Duffield, T.V. Lakshman, and D. Stiliadis, "On adaptive bandwidth sharing with rate guarantees," in *Proceedings of INFOCOM'98*, San Francisco, CA, 1998, pp. 1122–1130.
4. I. Stoica and H. Zhang, "Providing guaranteed services without per flow management," in *Proceedings of ACM SIGCOMM'99*, Boston, MA, 1999, pp. 81–94.
5. T. Nandagopal, N. Venkitaraman, R. Sivakumar, and V. Bharghavan, "Delay differentiation and adaptation in core stateless networks," in *Proceedings of INFOCOM'00*, Tel-Aviv, Israel, 2000, pp. 421–430.
6. J. Wang and Y. Levy, "Managing performance using weighted round-robin," in *Proceedings of ISCC'00*, Antibes-Juan les Pins, France, 2000.
7. A.S. Diwan, R. Guérin, and K.N. Sivarajan, "Performance analysis of speeded-up high-speed packet switches," *J. of High Speed Networks*, vol. 10, no. 3, pp. 161–186, 2001.
8. R. Guérin and V. Pla, "Aggregation and conformance in differentiated service networks: a case study," *Computer Communication Review*, vol. 31, no. 1, pp. 21–32, 2001.
9. Y. Xu and R. Guerin, "Individual QoS versus aggregate QoS: a loss performance study," TR, University of Pennsylvania, 2001.
10. *InfiniBand architecture specification*, 2000, http://www.infinibandta.org/specs.
11. Advanced Switching for the PCI Express* Architecture, Intel Corporation, 2002, http://www.intel.com/design/network/papers/25173701.pdf.
12. RapidIO: The Interconnect Architecture for High Performance Embedded Systems, Rapid IO Trade Association, 2003, http://www.rapidio.org/data/tech/techwhitepaper_rev3.pdf.
13. H. Ahmadi and W.E. Denzel, "A survey of modern high-performance switching techniques," *IEEE J. on Selected Areas in Communications*, vol. 7, no. 7, pp. 1091–1103, 1989.
14. *OPNET Modeler, the network simulation power tool, ver. 8.0.C*, 2001, http://www.opnet.com.
15. H.C. Tijms, *Stochastic modelling and analysis: a computational approach*, Wiley series in probability and statistics. Wiley, Great Britain, 1986.

Practical Security Improvement of PKCS#5

Sanghoon Song[1], Taekyoung Kwon[1], and Ki Song Yoon[2]

[1] School of Computer Engineering, Sejong University, Seoul 143-747, Korea
song,tkwon@sejong.ac.kr
[2] Internet Computing Department, Electronics and Telecommunications Research Institute, Daejeon, Korea

Abstract. A public key infrastructure (PKI) is being deployed in a field of network security. PKCS#5 is one of the most popular standards in PKI framework, intended for the practical implementation of password-based cryptography. So, the PKCS#5 encryption must be useful for general software applications within multimedia systems. However, it has a critical weak point in terms of security such as being vulnerable to off-line attacks due to the password-derived encryption key. In this paper, we observe a practical and simple method to improve security of the PKCS#5 encryption without modifying the installed base. The idea is to hide a *salt* by exploiting several existing schemes.

1 Introduction

A need for a PKI is growing rapidly in a field of securing multimedia applications. PKCS#5 is one of the most popular standards in PKI framework. It was intended for the practical implementation of password-based cryptography so as to protect sensitive information such as private keys in software [15,16]. Accordingly, it offers various tools such as key derivation functions, encryption schemes, and message-authentication schemes based on a human memorable password of low entropy. So, the PKCS#5 encryption must be useful for general software-based applications within multimedia systems. However, it has a critical weak point in terms of security such as being vulnerable to off-line attacks due to the weakness of password-derived encryption keys [4]. In this paper, we provide a simple and practical method to improve security of the PKCS#5 encryption in a way of manipulating a *salt*. Note that the salt is traditionally used for the benefits such as (1) disallowing adversaries to pre-compute all the keys corresponding to a dictionary of passwords, and (2) minimizing the possibility of selecting the same key [15]. This paper adds one more benefit such as (3) preventing off-line attacks without modifying the installed base. For the purpose, we exploit several existing schemes with considering practical implementations in software.

This paper is organized as follows: In Section 2 we will describe preliminaries. In Section 3 we will show basic idea and generic model. Section 4 and 5 respectively describes two concrete methods for the proposed model. Section 6 discusses security and efficiency, and Section 7 concludes this paper.

A. Yazici and C. Şener (Eds.): ISCIS 2003, LNCS 2869, pp. 869–876, 2003.

2 Preliminaries

Notation will be borrowed conveniently from [15], [11], and [7].

2.1 PKCS#5

PKCS#5 is a password-based cryptography standard in which various useful tools are provided, including the following [15]:

Salt and Iteration Count. A salt is denoted by s while a counter by o. The counter is for increasing the cost of producing keys from passwords. Here s is required at least 64 bits in length for security reasons while o 1000 iterations.

Key Derivation Functions. PBKDF (password-based key derivation functions) is specified to derive a key dk from a password π. Let $dkLen$ denote the required key length. Then $dk \leftarrow \mathcal{F}(\pi, s, o, dkLen)$ implies that a PBKDF $\mathcal{F}()$ outputs dk in length of $dkLen$ [15].

Encryption Schemes. Two encryption schemes are specified, depending on PBKDF, as PBES (password-based encryption schemes). Let $E_{dk}()$ and $D_{dk}()$ denote encryption and decryption functions respectively. A typical application is a private key protection method, where the message contains private key information, as in PKCS#8 [16].

2.2 PKCS#5 Vulnerability

Security of PBES is dependent upon the underlying PBKDF and cipher methods, meaning that a password of low entropy could make PKCS#5 vulnerable to off-line attacks. This is because s and o are saved in plain text form, and the deterministic encoding method is used in PKCS#5 [15]. As a typical example, the following attack works in a small space of passwords. Let $\varepsilon \leftarrow E_{dk}(sk)$ denote that a private key sk is encrypted with PBES. A user, usr, stores the values, $\langle s, o, dkLen, \varepsilon, \mathcal{C}\rangle$, where $\mathcal{C}$ denotes a X.509 certificate [5]. An adversary, adv, who compromised user's device and captured the values $\langle s, o, dkLen, \varepsilon, \mathcal{C}\rangle$, can attempt to decrypt ε using a dictionary of likely passwords, π'.

$$dk' \leftarrow \mathcal{F}(\pi', s, o, dkLen)$$
$$sk' \leftarrow D_{dk'}(\varepsilon)$$

If sk' is not decoded correctly, adv can discard the wrong guess. Otherwise, adv attempts to sign an arbitrary message m with the decrypted key sk' and verify the signed message with $\mathcal{C}$. Provided that the signature is invalid, adv can discard the wrong guess again. adv repeats this procedure until a correct guess is found. This is a typical form of off-line attacks on the PKCS#5 encryption.

2.3 Related Methods

A tamper-resistant hardware device must be promising but it is still expensive when we consider its deployment in practice [2]. So, we assume the installed hardware is a user-controlled and software-dependent device for running multimedia applications, for example, a desktop computer, notebook, handheld, etc. PKCS#5 is necessary in that sense. Due to the weakness of the PKCS#5 encryption, several software-only methods were developed specifically for encrypting a private key in a secure way. They include a private key download method [13], a software smart card [3], a networked cryptographic device [11], and a robust software token [9]. All of them exploit network connectivity for security improvement. However, the first stores all user credentials in a center server, while the others discard PKCS#5.

3 Proposed Generic Model

3.1 Basic Idea

Our idea[1] is very simple and straightforward in improving the robustness of PKCS#5 without modifying its basic structure. It starts from the fact that a random salt with sufficient length has already enough entropy to prevent off-line attacks in PKCS#5. That is, the weak point of PKCS#5 can be overcome if the salt is maintained securely. So, we claim that *the security requirement of the salt must be at least equal to the required security of the encrypted data.*

3.2 Encrypting Salt

For securing the salt, we do not require tamper-resistance of a storage device. Instead, we exploit network connectivity to the trusted server for considering practical deployment. The existing networked schemes can be applied in that sense [13,11]. A generic model for securing the salt is as follows:

- The PKCS#5 values, $\langle s, o, dkLen, \varepsilon, \mathcal{C} \rangle$, are given to a user-controlled device, dvc, where usr remembers π. We assume ε is an encrypted private key of a user such that $\varepsilon = E_{dk}(sk_{\mathsf{usr}})$ where dk is derived by PBKDF [15].
- dvc computes the following for π and s. Here κ denotes a security parameter such that $\kappa = 160$ while $h_1()$ a random oracle and $\oplus$ exclusive-OR [1].
  $u \leftarrow_R \{0,1\}^{\kappa}$
  $c \leftarrow h_1(u, \pi) \oplus s$
- The value c is manipulated to be read by a trusted server, svr, only. For example, it may be encrypted under a public key of svr.
- dvc stores $\langle u, o, dkLen, \varepsilon, \mathcal{C} \rangle$ in its local memory and erases $\langle \pi, s, c \rangle$.
- dvc and svr communicate with each other for recovering s, so as to derive dk and decrypt ε.

[1] One of the authors presented the basic idea in [8]. This work is extended from it.

usr		dvc		svr
Type a password				
	$\xrightarrow{\pi}$			
		Request salt		
			$\xrightarrow{\mathcal{R}_q(\pi)}$	
				Abort if $\mathcal{R}_q(\pi)$ is incorrect Otherwise respond with salt
			$\xleftarrow{\mathcal{R}_s(s)}$	
		Decrypt data		

Fig. 1. Protocol for Generic Model

Here $\leftarrow_R$ means that the left value was chosen at random. The random oracle $h_1(u, \pi)$ can be replaced by a strong one-way hash function that outputs a random-looking data in length κ. Note that adv cannot obtain s without c. That is, security is assured simply by encrypting s with a secret key, $h_1(u, \pi)$, while its plain form and verifiable data are removed from dvc. A cooperation between dvc and svr, is necessary for recovering s such that $s = h_1(u, \pi) \oplus c$. A protocol for the generic model is depicted in Figure 1.

3.3 Generic Protocol

The protocol between dvc and svr must satisfy the followings except for the case that both dvc and svr are compromised:

- A request, $\mathcal{R}_q(\pi)$, should not leak any information about π, even to svr.
- A response, $\mathcal{R}_s(s)$, should not leak any information about s to adv.

For concrete implementation, the existing networked schemes will be applied in the following sections [3,11,13]. Firstly we will utilize a password-based authentication protocol[2] being discussed by the IEEE P1363 Standard Working Group in Method 1 [4]. Among those protocols, AMP is considered to be the most efficient one, so we will utilize one of its family as an example in Method 1 [7]. Also we will utilize the networked cryptographic device as another example in Method 2 [11]. Note that both schemes will be modified for satisfying our goals mentioned above. Let $\langle pk_{\mathsf{svr}}, sk_{\mathsf{svr}} \rangle$ denote svr's public key pair while $\langle pk_{\mathsf{usr}}, sk_{\mathsf{usr}} \rangle$ usr's public key pair in both protocol descriptions.

4 Method 1

Method 1 is inspired by Perlman and Kaufman's private key download method, so the related protocol, TP-AMP (Three-Pass AMP), is applied [10,13]. Other protocols, SPEKE, SRP, PAK and AMP, can be applied as well [4,6,7,12,14].

[2] Password security has been studied for more than thirty years and there have been a great amount of work. Currently the IEEE P1363 Standard Working Group is working on strong password protocols including SPEKE, SRP, PAK and AMP [4].

usr	dvc		svr
$\xrightarrow{\pi}$			
	$x \leftarrow_R Z_q$		
	$\mu \leftarrow f(u, \pi)$		
	$\mathcal{G}_1 \leftarrow g^x \mu$		
	$id \leftarrow \mathcal{C}$	$\xrightarrow{id, \mathcal{G}_1}$	
			$\mathcal{B} \leftarrow \frac{\mathcal{G}_1}{\mu}$
			if $\neg$ACCEPTABLE($\mathcal{B}$) then abort
			otherwise, $y \leftarrow_R Z_q$
	$\upsilon \leftarrow h_1(u, \pi)$		$\mathcal{G}_2 \leftarrow (\mathcal{B}\nu)^y$
	$\varpi \leftarrow (x + \upsilon)^{-1}(x + 1) \bmod q$		$\beta \leftarrow (\mathcal{B}g)^y$
			$\rho \leftarrow h_2(id, \mathcal{G}_1, \mathcal{G}_2, \beta)$
			$\eta \leftarrow \rho \oplus c$
		$\xleftarrow{\mathcal{G}_2, \eta}$	
	$\alpha \leftarrow \mathcal{G}_2{}^{\varpi}$		
	$\rho \leftarrow h_2(id, \mathcal{G}_1, \mathcal{G}_2, \alpha)$		
	$s \leftarrow \rho \oplus \eta \oplus \upsilon$		
	$dk \leftarrow \mathcal{F}(\pi, s, o, dkLen)$		
	$sk_{\mathsf{usr}} \leftarrow D_{dk}(\varepsilon)$		
	return sk_{usr}		

Fig. 2. Protocol for Method 1

4.1 Three-Pass Authenticated Key Agreement via Memorable Passwords

The advantage of the IEEE P1363.2 protocols is that they do not require server's authentic public key [7,4]. The protocol, TP-AMP, is a hybrid variant of AMP combined with PAK to achieve three message passes with less computation [7, 10,12]. Let g be a generator of a q-order subgroup of Z_p^*. We assume p be a secure prime integer [7] such that $(p-1)/2q$ is also prime or each prime factor of $(p-1)/2q$ is larger than a prime integer q where $q \leftarrow_R \{0,1\}^\kappa$. These values may be chosen and distributed by the server entity. We assume $f()$ is a function to the q-order subgroup G_q and ACCEPTABLE() is a function to check its validity [10]. Let us omit mod p for convenience when it is clear from the context.

4.2 Device Initialization and Registration

Firstly usr types π and subsequently dvc computes the followings.

$$
\begin{aligned}
&u \leftarrow_R \{0,1\}^\kappa \\
&c \leftarrow h_1(u, \pi) \oplus s \\
&\nu \leftarrow g^{h_1(u,\pi)} \\
&\mu \leftarrow f(u, \pi)
\end{aligned}
$$

dvc registers $\langle c, \nu, \mu \rangle$ to svr, with id derived from $\mathcal{C}$. The values $\langle u, o, \varepsilon, dkLen, \mathcal{C} \rangle$ and $\langle g, p, q \rangle$ are saved in stable storage of dvc while all the other values must be deleted from it. Then svr saves $\langle id, c, \nu, \mu \rangle$ in its storage device.

4.3 Protocol Run: Method 1

Figure 2 depicts the concrete protocol run of Method 1.

- Firstly dvc chooses x at random from Z_q^* and computes $\mathcal{G}_1 = g^x\mu$ by getting $\mu = f(u, \pi)$. Then dvc sends the values, $\langle id, \mathcal{G}_1\rangle$, to svr and computes the followings; $\upsilon = h_1(u, \pi)$ and $\varpi = (x + \upsilon)^{-1}(x + 1) \bmod q$.
- Secondly svr computes $\mathcal{B} = \frac{\mathcal{G}_1}{\mu}$ and checks its validity. ACCEPTABLE($\mathcal{B}$) may return false if $\mathcal{B} \notin G_q$. Then svr aborts, otherwise chooses y at random from Z_q^* and computes $\mathcal{G}_2 = (\mathcal{B}\nu)^y$, $\beta = (\mathcal{B}g)^y$, and $\rho = h_2(id, \mathcal{G}_1, \mathcal{G}_2, \beta)$. Then svr replies with $\langle \mathcal{G}_2, \eta\rangle$ by computing $\eta = \rho \oplus c$.
- Finally dvc computes $\alpha = \mathcal{G}_2{}^{\varpi}$, $\rho = h_2(id, \mathcal{G}_1, \mathcal{G}_2, \alpha)$, $s = \rho \oplus \eta \oplus \upsilon$ and $dk = \mathcal{F}(\pi, s, o, dkLen)$, and returns sk_{usr} such that $sk_{\mathsf{usr}} = D_{dk}(\varepsilon)$.

Note that message 1 corresponds to $\mathcal{R}_q(\pi)$ while message 2 corresponds to $\mathcal{R}_s(s)$ of our generic model in Figure 1. Also note that the third message of TP-AMP is not used in Method 1 because of the generic model. However, we could add the third message for explicit authentication to the server.

5 Method 2

5.1 Networked Cryptographic Devices

Networked cryptographic devices proposed by MacKenzie and Reiter [11] needs server's authentic public key. The basic idea of this paper was motivated by this scheme. Preliminary work with this scheme can be found from [9].

5.2 Device Initialization

Firstly usr types π and subsequently dvc computes the followings.

$$\begin{aligned} u &\leftarrow_R \{0,1\}^\kappa \\ a &\leftarrow_R \{0,1\}^\kappa \\ c &\leftarrow h_1(u,\pi) \oplus s \\ b &\leftarrow h_2(u,\pi) \\ \tau &= E_{pk_{\mathsf{svr}}}(a,b,c) \end{aligned}$$

The values $\langle u, o, \varepsilon, dkLen, \mathcal{C}\rangle$ and $\langle a, \tau, pk_{\mathsf{svr}}\rangle$ are saved in stable storage of dvc while all the other values must be deleted from it. Note that usr does not need to register to svr. Also note that we modified b so as to make $\mathcal{R}_q(\pi)$ leak no information about π to svr because svr will read b on protocol run.

5.3 Protocol Run: Method 2

Figure 3 depicts the concrete protocol run of Method 2.

- dvc computes $\beta = h_2(u, \pi)$ and chooses ρ at random from $\{0,1\}^\kappa$. Then dvc computes $\gamma = E_{pk_{\mathsf{svr}}}(\beta, \rho)$ and $\delta = \mathsf{mac}_a(\gamma, \tau)$ where mac denotes a message authentication code. dvc sends svr $\langle \gamma, \delta, \tau\rangle$ and computes $\upsilon = h_1(u, \pi)$.

usr		dvc		svr
	$\xrightarrow{\pi}$			
		$\beta \leftarrow h_2(u, \pi)$ $\rho \leftarrow_R \{0,1\}^\kappa$ $\gamma \leftarrow E_{pk_{\mathsf{svr}}}(\beta, \rho)$ $\delta \leftarrow \mathsf{mac}_a(\gamma, \tau)$		
			$\xrightarrow{\gamma, \delta, \tau}$	
		$\upsilon \leftarrow h_1(u, \pi)$		$\langle a, b, c\rangle \leftarrow D_{sk_{\mathsf{svr}}(\tau)}$ abort if $\mathsf{mac}_a(\gamma, \tau) \neq \delta$ $\langle \beta, \rho\rangle \leftarrow D_{sk_{\mathsf{svr}}(\gamma)}$ abort if $(\beta \neq b)$ $\eta \leftarrow \rho \oplus c$
			$\xleftarrow{\eta}$	
		$s \leftarrow \rho \oplus \eta \oplus \upsilon$ $dk \leftarrow \mathcal{F}(\pi, s, o, dkLen)$ $sk_{\mathsf{usr}} \leftarrow D_{dk}(\varepsilon)$ return sk_{usr}		

Fig. 3. Protocol for Method 2

- svr decrypts τ to get $\langle a, b, c\rangle$ and aborts if $\mathsf{mac}_a(\gamma, \tau) \neq \delta$. svr decrypts γ and aborts if $\beta \neq b$. Then svr computes $\eta = \rho \oplus c$ and sends this to dvc.
- dvc computes $s = \rho \oplus \eta \oplus \upsilon$ and $dk = \mathcal{F}(\pi, s, o, dkLen)$, and returns sk_{usr} such that $sk_{\mathsf{usr}} = D_{dk}(\varepsilon)$.

Note that message 1 corresponds to $\mathcal{R}_q(\pi)$ while message 2 corresponds to $\mathcal{R}_s(s)$ of our generic model in Figure 1.

6 Discussion

Two concrete schemes must meet the goal of the generic model. Security of s was simply assured by the base schemes [7,10,11]. Let us denote by $Adv(S)$ the classes of adversaries who succeed in capturing S where $S \subseteq \{\mathsf{dvc}, \pi, sk_{\mathsf{svr}}\}$. We say $Adv(S_1) \subseteq Adv(S_2)$ if $S_1 \subseteq S_2$, in the same way as in [11]. Both methods are secure against $Adv(\{\mathsf{dvc}\})$ and $Adv(\{sk_{\mathsf{svr}}, \pi\})$. Note that $Adv(\{sk_{\mathsf{svr}}\})$ is not a threat, meaning that they are independent of $Adv(\{\pi\})$. However, $Adv(\{\mathsf{dvc}, sk_{\mathsf{svr}}\})$ can be transformed to $Adv(\{\mathsf{dvc}, sk_{\mathsf{svr}}, \pi\})$ in polynomial time. That is, s is recovered by off-line attacks only for the case that both dvc and svr are compromised.

As for the performance issues, the proposed methods do not add any expensive operations to the base schemes. Instead the networked cryptographic device scheme reduces its costs for ρ, η, and $M()$ [11] by applying to our generic model. Consequently, we can say the idea of hiding salt by networked approaches is more effective than expected.

7 Conclusion

In this paper, we studied useful methods to improve security of the PKCS#5 encryption that is essential for various multimedia applications. The proposed generic model is simple but effective without modifying the installed base. The existing schemes can be applied to our generic model simply in software.

References

1. M. Bellare and P. Rogaway, "Entity authentication and key distribution," *Advances in Cryptology – Crypto'93*, Springer-Verlag, 1993.
2. S. Brands, *Rethinking public key infrastructures and digital certificates*, The MIT Press, p.11 and pp.219–224, 2000.
3. D. Hoover, B. Kausik, "Software smart cards via cryptographic camouflage," In Proceedings of the *IEEE Symposium on Security and Privacy*, 1999, *http://www.arcot.com* .
4. IEEE P1363.2, " Standard Specifications for Public Key Cryptography: Password-based Techniques," *http://grouper.ieee.org/groups/1363/passwdPK/index.html*, May 2002.
5. ISO/IEC 9594–8, "Information technology – Open Systems Interconnection – The Directory: Authentication framework," *International Organization for Standardization*, 1995.
6. D. Jablon, "Strong password-only authenticated key exchange," *ACM Computer Communications Review*, vol.26, no.5, pp.5–26, 1996.
7. T. Kwon, "Authentication and key agreement via memorable passwords," In Proceedings of the *ISOC Network and Distributed System Security Symposium*, February 2001.
8. T. Kwon, S. Lee, Y. Choi, and H. Kim, "Hybrid networked cryptographic devices in practice," IEICE Transactions on Communications, pp.1832–1834, Vol. E85-B, No.9, September 2002.
9. T. Kwon, "Robust Software Tokens – Yet another method for securing user's digital identity," *Information Security and Privacy – ACISP 2003*, Lecture Notes in Computer Science, Vol. 2727, Springer-Verlag, July 2003. An extended and revised version can be found at `http://dasan.sejong.ac.kr/~tkwon/research/rst.pdf`.
10. T. Kwon, "AMP – Authenticated key agreement via Memorable Passwords," More information can be found at `http://dasan.sejong.ac.kr/~tkwon/amp.html`.
11. P. MacKenzie and M. Reiter, "Networked cryptographic devices resilient to capture," In Proceedings of the *IEEE Symposium on Security and Privacy*, 2001, a full and updated version is DIMACS Technical Report 2001–19, May 2001.
12. P. MacKenzie, "The PAK suite: Protocols for Password-Authenticated Key Exchange," Submission to IEEE P1363.2, April 2002
13. R. Perlman and C. Kaufman, "Secure password-based protocol for downloading a private key," In Proceedings of the *ISOC Network and Distributed System Security Symposium*, February 1999.
14. T. Wu, "Secure remote password protocol," In *Network and Distributed System Security Symposium*, 1998
15. PKCS#5, Password-based cryptography standard, RSA Laboratories Standard Specification, Version 2.0, 1999.
16. PKCS#8, Private-key information syntax standard, RSA Laboratories Standard Specification, Version 2.0, 1999.

Access Network Mobility Management*

Sang-Hwan Jung[1], Do-Hyeon Kim[2], and You-Ze Cho[3]

[1] LG Electronics, 431-080 Hoyeuo-dong, Anyang, South Korea illusion@lge.com
[2] Dept. of Information & Communications, Cheonan University
115 Anseo-dong, Cheonan, South Korea
dhkim@cheonan.ac.kr
[3] School of Electronic and Electrical Engineering, Kyungpook National University,
Sankyeog-dong, Taegu, South Korea yzcho@ee.knu.ac.kr

Abstract. *Recently, many micro-mobility-supporting protocols have been suggested, such as the regional registration protocol and Cellular IP. In these protocols, mobility is mainly managed by the mobile node itself when it moves within an access node. However, these protocols often have a long registration delay based on variations in the advertisement message broadcasting period and registration message transmission period. Furthermore, various problems, including radio resource wastage and an increased network load, can also occur with these protocols. Accordingly, the current paper proposes the ANMM (Access Network Mobility Management) protocol as an improved and efficient protocol for supporting micro-mobility in an access network. To realize the ANMM protocol, an effective adaptation method is proposed for link-layer handoff information along with a tunneling scheme between an access node and the gateway in an access network. As such, the ANMM protocol is able to reduce the registration delay, signaling overhead, and radio resource wastage.*

1 Introduction

Various micro-mobility-supporting protocols have already been suggested, including the regional registration protocol and Cellular IP. In these protocols, mobility is mainly managed by a mobile node when it moves within an access node(or local domain). As such, a mobile node manages its own mobility based on receiving an agent advertisement message from the access network. Alternatively, it periodically transmits a registration message to an access node [1-5].

However, these protocols can have a long registration delay due to variations in the broadcasting period of an agent advertisement message or transmission period of a registration message. As a result, this long registration delay causes an increase in the total handoff delay and packet loss delivered to the mobile node. Furthermore, radio resources are wasted due to message exchanges through the radio section between the mobile node and the access network [1,5].

* University fundamental Research Program supported by Ministry of Information & Communication in republic of Korea. This work was in part supported by the KOSEF (contract number: R01-1999-000-00239-0) and the BK21 project

A. Yazici and C. Şener (Eds.): ISCIS 2003, LNCS 2869, pp. 877–884, 2003.

Accordingly, the current paper proposes ANMM(Access Network Mobility Management) as an improved and efficient protocol for supporting micro-mobility in an access network. The proposed protocol offers a method of local mobility management within an access network when a mobile node moves within the same access network. The proposed protocol uses the handoff information from the link-layer instead of an agent advertisement message and registration request message between the access node and the mobile node. Plus, an efficient tunneling scheme is adopted to transfer the data between an access node and the gateway in the access network. ANMM also supports macro-mobility, including the movement of a node between access networks, using Mobile IP. Consequently, the proposed protocol can reduce the registration delay, packet loss, signaling overhead, and radio resource wastage.

The rest of the paper is organized as follows: Section 2 proposes the idea of ANMM and the basic assumption. Section 3 presents the network architecture model and the protocol stack for ANMM. Section 4 illustrates the registration and handoff procedure for supporting the micro-mobility and the macro-mobility. Section 5 compares the performance of mobility supporting protocols regarding the registration delay, throughput and packet loss. Section 6 gives some final conclusions.

2 Basic Concept of ANMM

ANMM is based on Mobile IP as the standard protocol for supporting IP macro-mobility. As shown in Fig. 1, ANMM creates a new access network between a foreign agent and a mobile node within the basic Mobile IP network. As such, it provides a solution to the micro-mobility problem of an access network supporting its own mobility management. The macro-mobility between a home agent and the gateway uses Mobile IP, whereas the micro-mobility in a wireless access network uses ANMM as the new protocol.

The main difference between ANMM and other micro-mobility protocols is that the access node leads the registration procedure instead of the mobile node. As such, the access node, rather than the mobile node, creates and transmits the registration message to the gateway for mobility management in the access network. The access node then detects the movement of the mobile node using the handoff information in the link-layer. As a result, the agent advertisement message and registration request message between the access node and the mobile node are eliminated, as the handoff information in the link-layer performs this function based on the link-layer address of the mobile node and the identification of the old access node. In addition, a fast handoff can also be spontaneously supported in the IP-layer.

And, an appropriate adaptation method is proposed as a tunneling method between an access node and the gateway in the access network. To support efficient micro-mobility management in an access network, ANMM only considers foreign agent care-of addresses, as with a co-located care-of address, the termination point of a tunnel is a mobile node, therefore, radio resources can be wasted because the encapsulation packet is transmitted via a wireless link.

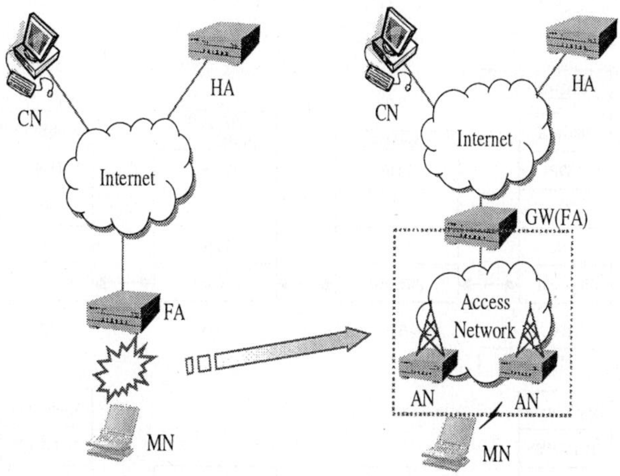

Fig. 1. Basic idea of ANMM protocol

ANMM uses link-layer handoff information for an IP-layer fast handoff. The link-layer information considered is the link-layer address of the mobile node and identification of the old access node. The link-layer handoff information triggers an IP-layer handoff, while the identification of the old access node notifies the new access node whether the mobile node is moving within the access network or moving between access networks. If the mobile node is moving within the access network an ANMM registration is processed using the identification of the old access node.

A network-initiation fast handoff involves a shorter registration delay compared to a mobile-initiation fast handoff because the process of sending an agent advertisement message is eliminated. Therefore, ANMM uses a network-initiation fast handoff for an IP-layer fast handoff.

3 Network Architecture Model for ANMM Protocol

The ANMM network architecture model is introduced a wireless access network between a foreign agent and a mobile node to extend the network architecture. A wireless access network consists of mobility management entities, including access nodes and a gateway, and interior routers for packet routing within the access network. In ANMM, an access node and gateway are introduced as new functional entities for supporting mobility management. The access node fulfills a basic function as a router, while also supporting ANMM. In addition, an air interface is added to the access node. The gateway, as an extension to the foreign agent function in Mobile IP, also has an ANMM support function. In addition, the gateway forwards data packets destined for the mobile node to the access node using tunneling.

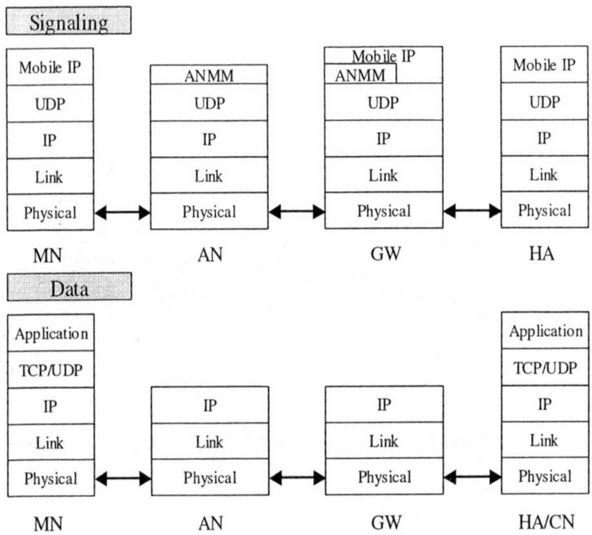

Fig. 2. Protocol stack of ANMM protocol

Fig. 2 shows the protocol stack of the signaling plane and data plane for the ANMM protocol. When comparing the protocol stack of the signaling plane with the Mobile IP protocol stack, a mobile node and home agent have identical protocol stacks without modification. This means a mobile node and home agent operate independently within the ANMM protocol.

4 Registration and Handoff Procedure for ANMM

There are two types of registration procedure. One is the ANMM registration procedure for supporting micro-mobility, while the other is the Mobile IP registration procedure for supporting macro-mobility. In the case of ANMM registration, the mobile node does not need to transmit any handoff messages because the access network itself manages the mobility of the mobile node. The ANMM registration list is maintained in a soft state, and no new signaling message is required to maintain the ANMM registration list because it reuses the Mobile IP Binding Update Message. Accordingly, the ANMM protocol can reduce the signaling overhead compared with other micro-mobility supporting protocols. Fig. 3 shows the ANMM registration signaling flows for supporting micro-mobility.

The new access node checks the old access node identification delivered from the link-layer immediately after the link-layer handoff has been completed and decides where the old access node belongs.

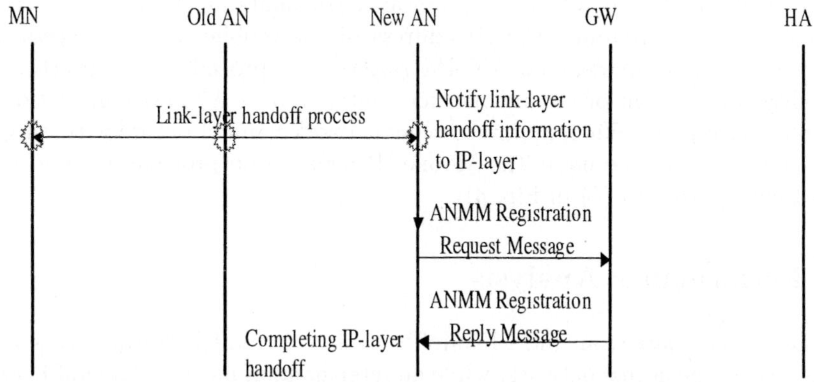

Fig. 3. ANMM registration signaling flows for supporting micro-mobility

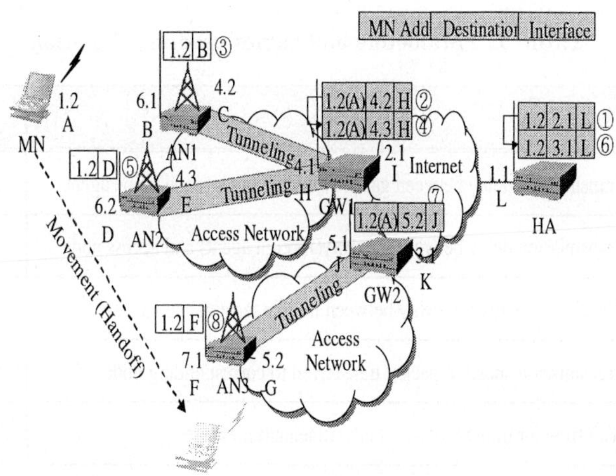

Fig. 4. Example of handoff in ANMM protocol

When an intra-access-network handoff occurs at access node 2 with a continuously moving mobile node, the mobile node will not detect a handoff because the agent advertisement message broadcast by access node 2 contains the same care-of address as previously broadcast by access node 1. Only the access node can detect a handoff using the link-layer handoff information, and then transmits an ANMM Registration Request Message containing the link-layer address of the mobile node to gateway 1.

After receiving this message, gateway 1 looks up the ANMM registration list and modifies the entry to match the received link-layer address (step (4) in Fig. 4). Based on this modification, the termination point of the tunnel used to forward packets to the mobile node changes from access node 1 to access node 2. As such, the access network manages the mobility of the mobile node by itself. After the list modification, gateway 1 transmits an ANMM Registration Reply Message containing the IP address of the mobile node to access node 2, which then completes the ANMM registration procedure by inserting the mobility information of the mobile node into its own ANMM registration list (step (5) in Fig. 4). When an inter-access-network handoff occurs with on-going movement of a mobile node, the Mobile IP registration procedure is performed repeatedly (steps (6)-(8) in Fig. 4).

5 Performance Analysis

In the current paper, an intra-handoff means a handoff between access nodes within the same access network, while an inter-handoff means a handoff between access nodes in different access networks.

Table 1. Parameters and values used in simulation

Parameter	Meaning	Value
D_1	Transmission delay between gateway(foreign agent) and home agent	200ms
D_2	Transmission delay between gateway(foreign agent) and access node	10ms
D_3	Wireless transmission delay between mobile terminal and access node	20ms
R	Transmission speed of packet transferred to corresponding node	50 packets/sec
α	Wait time for transfer of agent advertisement message	$0< \alpha <3$sec

The simulation assumed a hard-handoff and used the parameters including the transmission delay and packet rate are shown below in table 1. D1 represents the typical transmission delay between the countries, which was lower than 200ms. D2 represents the typical MAN delay, which was lower than 10ms. D3 represents the transmission delay in the wireless section, which was lower than 20ms considering interleaving in cdma2000. R was used as the packet rate for VoIP, which was typically 50 packets/sec.

Fig. 5 shows a performance comparison of mobility management protocols as regards mobility. With the proposed ANMM protocol, a fast handoff is realized

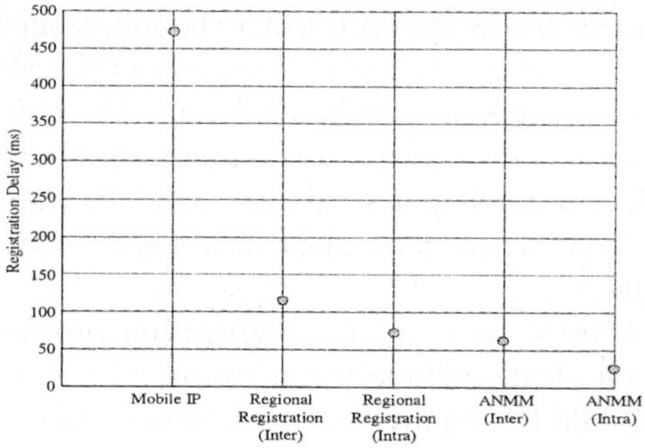

(a) Registration delay

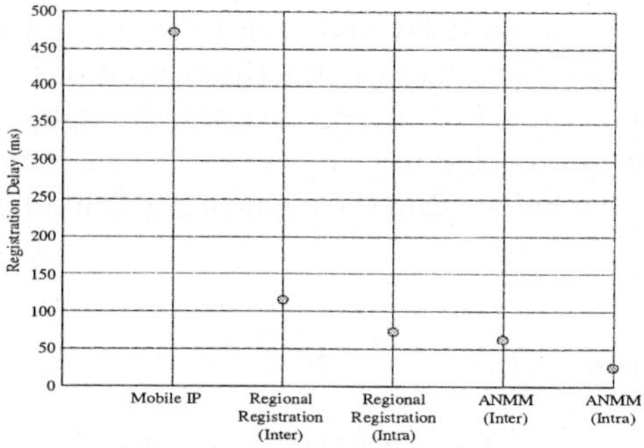

(b) Packet loss

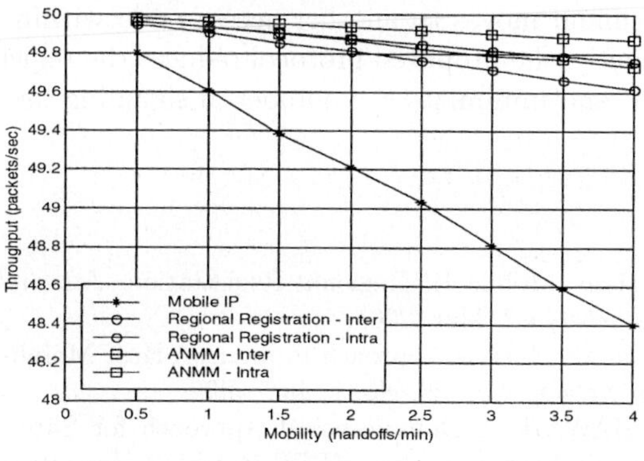

(c) Throughput

Fig. 5. Results of performance comparison of mobility management protocols naturally based on the access network using the link-layer handoff information for its own mobility management. The performance of the Mobile IP and regional registration protocol applying a fast handoff using the link-layer handoff information was analyzed for an appropriate comparison. Here, Inter expresses the case where the ratio of inter-handoffs to intra-handoffs was about 1:10, whereas Intra expresses the case where movement of a mobile node is limited within a single access network.

The proposed ANMM and regional registration protocol performed better than the existing physical architecture in terms of the registration delay, as shown in Fig. 5. Mobile IP required about a 480ms registration delay, whereas ANMM and the regional registration protocol required less than 120 ms for the location registration. For an intra handoff, ANMM was similar to the regional registration protocol, yet exhibited a better performance for an inter handoff.

Although the registration delay and packet loss are independent of mobility, the throughput depends on it. As such, the throughput of Mobile IP abruptly decreased as the mobility increased. In contrast, the throughput of ANMM and the regional registration protocol slowly decreased. When comparing the throughput, ANMM performed better than the regional registration protocol for an inter handoff.

6 Conclusions

The current paper proposed the ANMM protocol to solve the micro-mobility problem in a wireless access network based on the IP protocol. The ANMM protocol supports a fast handover using the handover information in the link layer. The proposed protocol processes a speedy handover registration procedure when a mobile terminal moves to another access node within a wireless access network. Consequently, the proposed protocol reduces the registration delay and signaling overhead, and minimizes the number of signaling messages.

References

1. E. Gustafsson et al. Mobile IP Regional Registration. *Internet Draft, draft-ietf-mobileip-reg-tunnel-04.txt*, Mar, 2001.
2. A. Valko, Cellular IP: A New Approach to Internet Host Mobility.*ACM Computer Communication Review*, Vol. 29, No. 1, Jan. 1999.
3. Ramjee et al., HAWAII: A Domain-based Approach for Supporting Mobility in Wide Area Wireless Networks. *Proc. IEEE ICNP'99*, Nov. 1999.
4. S. Das et al., TeleMIP: Telecommunication Enhanced Mobile IP Architecture for Fast Intra-Domain Mobility. *IEEE Personal Communications*, pp. 50–58, TBD, Aug. 2000.
5. K. E. Malki et al., Low Latency Handoff Mobile IPv4. *Internet Draft draft-ietf-mobileip-lowlatency-handoffs-v4-01.txt*, May 2001.

Design of a Log Server for Distributed and Large-Scale Server Environments

Attila Özgit, Burak Dayıoğlu, Erhan Anuk, İnan Kanbur, Ozan Alptekin, and Umut Ermiş

{ozgit,dayioglu}@metu.edu.tr
{erhan.anuk,inan.kanbur,ozan.alptekin,
umut.ermis}@ceng.metu.edu.tr

Abstract. Collection, storage and analysis of multiple hosts' audit trails in a distributed manner are known as a major requirement, as well as a major challenge for enterprise-scale computing environments. To ease these tasks, and to provide a central management facility, a software-suit, named as "Log-Hunter" has been developed. Log-Hunter is a secure distributed log server system which involves log collection and consolidation in a large-scale environment having multiple hosts that keeps at least one audit trail. This architecture also eases the inspection and monitoring of the audit trails generated on multiple hosts. By consolidating all the audit trails on a centralized server, it significantly reduces the manpower requirement, and also provides secure log storage for inspection of log entries as it becomes necessary. This paper presents the functional specifications, architecture and some preliminary performance results of the Log-Hunter.

1 Introduction

In large scale computing environments, keeping audit trails on a centralized server is a crucial task. Besides many other aspects, these audit trails are very important in terms of security and recovery related issues [1,2]. However, in an enterprise network accommodating many hosts, keeping track of all audit trails is a difficult and challenging problem. On the other hand, inspection of audit trails on every single host is both inappropriate and time consuming.

Collecting audit trails from their hosts at the time they are generated, and consolidating them into a centralized server in a real-time manner seems to be the best solution. Since audit trails on different hosts are naturally kept in different formats, it is also a good idea to have a common log format for consolidation. Storing these consolidated audit trails on a non-volatile media (such as WORM) increases the integrity. Finally, all the hosts are desired to communicate with the log consolidation server in a secure way, and time synchronization must be held between all the hosts and the central log consolidation server.

With the motivation of these ideas, a log server have been designed and implemented. We call this software as "Log-Hunter", which is a secure distributed log server system for large-scale enterprise environments.

A. Yazici and C. Şener (Eds.): ISCIS 2003, LNCS 2869, pp. 885–891, 2003.

2 Log Hunter's Functional Specifications

Log-Hunter architecture has the following major features:

- Keeps integrity of audit trails collected from different hosts on a network with a synchronized timestamp.
- Supports platform independence. It runs on all Unix and MS Windows environments. It can also be easily tailored for proprietary platforms.
- Delivers collected audit trails in an efficient and secure way to a centralized log consolidation server.
- Provides secure storage of consolidated data in a hierarchical manner on conventional RDBMS running on disk along with a copy on non-volatile (WORM) media to keep a secure backup copy.
- Provides services to compare secure copies of log entries on non-volatile media with those on RDBMS.
- Provides services to support analysis/correlation of stored log entries.
- Provides a plug-in structure for handling new types of audit trails.

3 System Architecture

Log-Hunter consists of three main modules: Agent–subagent Module, Secure Channel Module and Consolidation Server Module. Fig. 1 depicts the general structure of the system.
The overall architecture involves one central log consolidation server and multiple instances of log collection and communication agents that are to be installed on every host that keeps at least one audit trail. The central log consolidation server collects all the audit trails coming from the agents through a secure channel [3]. In order to provide unique and synchronized log timestamps, all software components are time synchronized by using Network Time Protocol (NTP).

3.1 Agent Module

The main duty of Agent–subagent module is to collect audit trails on different hosts of a network and to send these log records to the consolidation server. Since an enterprise network may contain multiple hosts with different operating systems like NT or UNIX, Agent-subagent module is designed to run in both Windows and UNIX environments. On every host in the network there are a single agent and one or more subagents communicating with their superior agent.

Each subagent watches the log file associated with it, and upon arrival of a log record at that file, fetches the newly coming log record. After formatting the log record with the common log format, the subagent sends it to the agent [4].

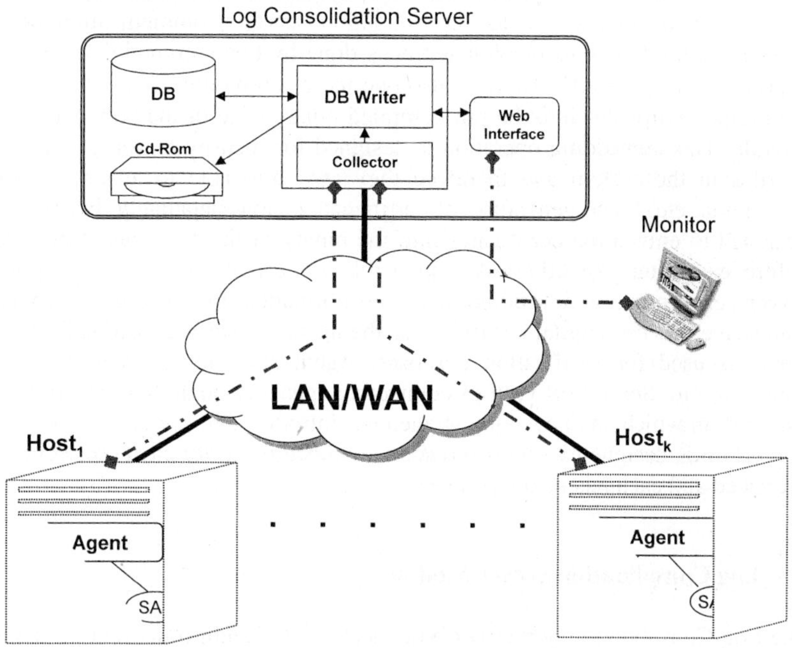

Fig. 1. General Structure of the Log Hunter

In UNIX environments, the sub-agents are designed as shared objects consisting of common function interfaces. All the sub-agents are placed in a previously identified directory, and the agent loads all the available sub-agents in that directory at start-up time using UNIX dynamic library functions. On Windows platforms sub-agents are designed as dynamic link libraries. As in UNIX environments they reside in a predefined directory. They are loaded and used by functions in Win-32 API.
The agent collects all the records coming from its subagents, and sends those records to the log consolidation server through a secure channel. Agents are designed in a multi-threaded architecture. In this architecture, agent is the mother process, and subagents run as separate threads of that agent. Every agent is extendible through dynamic loading of subagents. In case of a new type of audit trail to be considered, a new subagent can be installed and dynamically loaded to watch a particular log file. This plug-in approach eliminates the need to install and run multiple different programs to handle every different audit trail format.

3.2 Secure Channel Module

Communication between the agents and the log consolidation server is done through SSL (Secure Socket Layer) protocol, which ensures the security of log transfer between an agent and the log consolidation server. SSL encrypts data and ensures its integrity. Whenever an agent is to be installed on some host, a digital certificate is generated for authentication purposes on both sides of the communicating entities, i.e. between an agent and the log consolidation server. Communication between the agents and the log consolidation server is done by two sub-modules, *AgentPort and ServerPort*, respectively. There is also one more sub-module, *inserter*, which embeds the digital certificates into the pre-compiled binary code of the both agent and server module. This embedding operation is designed for security reasons; certificates exist as files in the system and therefore they are vulnerable to attacks, modification, replication, etc. Since generation of certificates is done separately, inserter module is designed to embed the certificates into the binary of the agent and server codes just before execution. AgentPort is responsible for establishing the connection to the server, encrypting and sending common formatted log records. Throughout the handshake process, digital certificate of the agent, which is embedded into binary of agent, is used for verification purposes. Agent also authenticates the server it is connecting to. ServerPort verifies connecting agents through their certificates and the list it has in which any new coming agents is introduced to server using web interface. ServerPort is designed in multi-threaded architecture, so for each connection a thread is created and each has its own queue.

3.3 Log Consolidation Server Module

The Log Consolidation Server (***LCS***) collects all the audit trails sent by the agents in that environment. Those collected log entries are stored in a relational database, and at the same time, they are written onto non-volatile media to obtain a secure copy. Moreover, for the purposes of displaying and analyzing the stored log entries as well as controlling Log Hunter system configuration, a web interface has been developed.

LCS has two sub-modules. One of them includes the tasks of collecting, inserting into the database, and writing onto non-volatile storage of the collected audit trails (a similar approach can be found in [5]). The other one is the web interface sub-module.

Collecting, inserting and writing processes are done in this order for a single log entry. However, handling incoming log records without any loss, internal multiple queues exist for keeping up with bursty traffic. For security reasons, all of these processing are confined in a single process address space. The mother process creates and uses multiple threads for each of these processing jobs.

3.3.1 Log Sub-module

Log Sub-module is responsible for collecting and inserting log entries into the database, and writing them onto non-volatile storage.

When the Log Sub-Module is started main thread of the program creates three threads for the tasks of database insertion, writing onto CD and accepting new agent connections. The thread that accepts new secure connections is created first, and then database insertion thread is created.

DBWriter thread created by the main process does database insertion. It gets collected audit trails from queues of the threads listening to the agents. DBWriter thread searches all queues for new audit trails and if finds some, inserts them into the database. Before inserting it, DBWriter thread checks the integrity of the information of audit trail by the pre-inserted agent and subagent information in database. In any error situation, audit trails are written into associated log files. The other job that is done by the DBWriter is to calculate the time of writing a cluster of audit trails, and then triggers the thread responsible for writing onto CD.

TCPListener is the thread that deals with agent connections. It listens to a specified port and creates a new thread for any coming requests named as Collector threads. Each connected agent has a separate Collector thread. First of all, a secure communication channel should be established before sending log records. It requires any agent that will be added to the system should be introduced to LCS by using services through the web interface, such as giving new id number and creating new digital certificate for new incoming agent. Any host that has not been introduced to LCS yet would not be able to connect to the system. Any incoming connection request is examined by the ServerPort (*see sec3.2)* inside the Collector thread, which controls the digital certificate of the connecting peer and compares its information with the pre-stored information in the database. By the creation collector thread, a new queue space from memory is allocated for incoming log records. If the authentication and verification checks are successful, Collector thread starts to receive the log records sent by the agent. After fetching log records, Collector thread puts them into its own queue for later manipulations. These collector queues are shared memory used by Collector threads and DBWriter thread. In other words, there is a producer-consumer relationship between Collector threads and DBWriter threads. When agent cuts the connection, associated Collector thread kills itself.

Another thread of the main process is for writing received audit trails into CD, which is CDWriter thread. This thread is created by main thread at the start of execution. DBWriter triggers CDWriter thread according to whether a condition is satisfied or not which is the number of audit trails in a cluster. First job done by CDWriter thread is to write the audit trails into a file. After CDWriter thread changes this file into "ISO" file and triggers the CD-writing process for writing ISO formatted file into CD. This thread is also change CD related information in the database according to the result of burning CD process.

3.3.2 Web Sub-module

Web interface is designed for the purposes of displaying, analyzing the stored log entries and controlling Log Hunter system configuration. PHP is used for creating connection to database and querying '*LOG*' table in the database. In this module, search pages are designed according to selected criteria. Besides these, an instant monitoring page showing the last 2 minutes of inserted audit trails into LOG table is provided. This monitoring page refreshes itself at every n seconds, which is a user-configurable parameter. For implementation of Web Sub-Module, Apache Web Server is installed in the Consolidation Server.

4 Summary and Results

The preliminary results obtained from the experiments done on a 10 Mbps Ethernet Network are summarized in the following tables.

Table 1. Consolidation Server (Pentium III 800 MHz, 512 MB SD-RAM)

Duration: 60 min. Log Entry Size: 1074 B # Of Agents: 5 # of SAs: 2/Agent	Agent-1 (Windows)		Agent-2 (Windows)		Agent-4 (Linux)		Agent-5 (Linux)		Server (Linux)
	SA-1	SA-2	SA-1	SA-2	SA-3	SA-4	SA-3	SA-4	
Generated/Received Log Entries	69,098	35,884	87,125	35,899	55,328	63,028	54,934	54,435	455,731
# of Log records Generated-Received/sec	19.194	9.968	24.201	9.972	15.369	17.508	15.259	15.121	**126.59**
Wait Time Lower Bound (sec)	0.9	1	0.9	1	0.9	0.9	0.9	0.9	-
Wait Time Upper Bound (sec)	1.1	1	1.1	1	1.1	1.1	1.1	1.1	-
Burst Record Count	20	10	25	10	15	17	15	15	-
Average Memory Usage	6 MB		6 MB		1.8 MB		1.8 MB		46 MB
Average Processor Usage	1%		1%		1%		1%		71.8%

Table 2. Consolidation Server (Pentium 4 2.0 GHz, 1 GB RD- RAM)

Duration: 60 min. Log Entry Size: 1074 B # of Agents: 5 # of SAs: 2/Agent	Agent-1 (Windows)		Agent-2 (Windows)		Agent-4 (Linux)		Agent-5 (Linux)		Server (Linux)
	SA-1	SA-2	SA-1	SA-2	SA-3	SA-4	SA-3	SA-4	
Generated/Received Log Entries	250,248	42,189	280,519	35,255	165,983	128,441	163,802	165,931	1,232,368
# of Log records Generated-Received/sec	69.513	11.719	77.922	9.793	46.106	35.678	45.501	46.092	**342.32**
Wait Time Lower Bound (sec)	0.9	1	0.9	1	0.9	0.9	0.9	0.9	-
Wait Time Upper Bound (sec)	1.1	1	1.1	1	1.1	1.1	1.1	1.1	-
Burst Record Count	70	12	78	10	45	35	45	46	-
Average Memory Usage	8 MB		8 MB		3.4 MB		3.4 MB		46 MB
Average Processor Usage	1%		1%		1%		1%		73.4%

In these experiments, subagents are synthetically constructed to measure the peak performance. Each sub-agent is programmed in such a way, that they wait for a random amount of time uniformly distributed between *wait-time-lower-bound* and *wait-time-upper-bound*, and then they generate a burst of records specified by the *burst-record-count*. Sub-agents' parameters are chosen to be "aggressive" rather than being realistic, in order for observing the limits of processing.
It has been observed that agent-subagent modules consume very little resource (processing time and memory) on their respective hosts.
The maximum processing rate of logs has been found as 342 logs/sec on second configuration (Table-2). The major bottleneck of the server is observed on I/O subsystem, which can easily be enhanced by using SCSI disks, RAID subsystem, appropriate kernel parameters etc.
As a near-feature work, experiments will be carried out on a resource-rich hardware for the log server. In parallel to experimentation, the software will be enhanced by adding heartbeat and fail-recovery features among agents and the log consolidation server.

References

[1] S. E. Hansen and E. T. Atkins, "Automated System Monitoring and Notification With Swatch", Proceedings of the Seventh Systems Administration Conference (LISA VII), 1993.

[2] S. Axelsson, U. Lindqvist, U. Gustafson and E. Jonsson, "An Approach to UNIX Security Logging", Proc. 21st National Information Systems Security Conference, 1998, pp. 62–75.

[3] B. Schneier and J. Kelsey, "Secure Audit Logs to Support Computer Forensics", In ACM Transactions on Information and System Security, Vol. 2, No. 2, May 1999, pp. 159–176, USA.

[4] M. Bishop, "A Standard Audit Trail Format", In Proc. 18th National Information Systems Security Conference", 1995, pp. 136–145.

[5] C.J. Antonelli, M. Undy and P. Honeyman, "The Packet Vault: Secure Storage of Network Data", In Proceedings of the USENIX Workshop on Intrusion Detection and Network Monitoring, April 1999, USA.

[6] John Kelsey and Bruce Schneier, "Minimizing Bandwidth for Remote Access to Cryptographically Protected Audit Logs", in Proceedings of Recent Advances in Intrusion Detection, 1999.

On Fair Bandwidth Sharing with RED

Diego Teijeiro-Ruiz, José-Carlos López-Ardao, Manuel Fernández-Veiga, Cándido López-García, Andrés Suárez-Gonzalez, Raúl-Fernando Rodríguez-Rubio, and Pablo Argibay-Losada

Telematics Engineering Department, University of Vigo (Spain)
ETSET Telecomunicacion, Campus Universitario
36200 Vigo (Spain)
{diego, jardao, mveiga, candido, asuarez, rrubio, pargibay}@det.uvigo.es

Abstract. One weakness of the RED algorithm typical of routers in the current Internet is that it allows unfair bandwidth sharing when a mixture of traffic types shares a link. This unfairness is caused by the fact that, at any given time, RED imposes the same loss probability on all flows, regardless of their bandwidths.
In this paper, we propose Random Rate-Control RED (RRC-RED), a modified version of RED. RRC-RED uses per-active-flow accounting to enforce on each flow a loss rate than depends on the flow's own rate.
This papers shows than RRC-RED provides better protection than RED and its variants to solve that problems (like FRED, CHOKe or RED-PD), and, moreover, it is easier to implement and lighter in complexity.

1 Introduction

The spectacular growth of Internet during the decade has made congestion control one of the most active research fields. Congestion is mainly caused by the lack or under-use of three essential resources in network nodes: buffer space, bandwidth and processing capacity.

To deal with congestion, TCP uses an end-to-end mechanism where the sending TCP entity adjust its sending rate according to the information obtained monitoring the connection itself.

In Drop-Tail routers - a queueing discipline where the last arrival will be the first candidate to be sacrificed - packet discarding due to buffer overflow represents an implicit congestion notification. The main problem with this kind of queue management policy is finally the inexistence of any specific step to avoid congestion, since packet discarding only occurs when congestion is already a reality.

A simple solution to this problem could be *Random Drop* [1], although it must be combined with some other mechanism to early notify whichever detected congestion risk in order to take the right preventive actions. This has led to what is called AQM (Active Queue Management).

AQM techniques are based on routers detecting the incipient congestion early, and advertising end-hosts to slow their sending rate before packets begin to be dropped. AQM results are smaller mean queue sizes and, consequently, smaller end-to-end delays.

The most popular AQM techniques are ECN (Explicit Congestion Notification) [2] and RED (Random Early Detection) [3]. We shall focus in the latter because its

A. Yazici and C. Şener (Eds.): ISCIS 2003, LNCS 2869, pp. 892–899, 2003.

widespread use today, and the advantage of needing no modifications at all in the host-end comunication software, where (TCP) sources will continue working the standard way after detecting the loss of a packet.

RED's main goal is to discard packets from a particular flow proportionally to its bandwidth use. This should imply a fair share of the remaining bandwidth [3].

However, situations revealing some kind of RED misbehaviour have been identified. In [5], for example, authors highlight the fact that when several TCP connections have different buffer occupancy in a RED router, dropping packets proportionally does not always guarantee fair bandwidth share.This problem may be aggravated by the presence of UDP flows, because this kind of traffic ignores congestion control signals. Also, in [4] the authors point out that RED increases the packet dropping probability, so if a packet is dropped when a connection is in the slow-start process, it will suffer specially to recover its transmission window.

Over the last few years some solutions have been proposed to mitigate this undesirable RED behaviour. In [5] a modification called Flow RED (FRED) adds some per flow state information to the basic mechanism to prioritize those flows with smaller queue occupancy, and to control those users that do not react to congestion signals. Nevertheless, FRED's improvements are not predictable and depend strongly on the flows' arrival times.

Another interesting solution is the CHOKe algorithm [6], where every time a new packet arrives, another one from the queue is chosen randomly, and if both belong to the same flow, both are discarded. This algorithm is based on the assumption that the more active a flow is the more the packets it will have in the queue. However, CHOKe does not work properly when the number of flows is high, or in the presence of UDP flows.

Finally, Floyd's solution - RED with Preferential Dropping [7] - combines some of the previous ideas. In RED-PD, RED's drop history is used to identify the flows getting most of the bandwith, because, due to the probabilistic nature of the drops, discarded packets can be considered random samples of the incoming traffic [8]. With this information, and a RTT estimation, the flows using more bandwidth than allowed are identified and penalized until they come back into the right range.

In this paper we propose a new algorithm based on RED, called *Random Control Rate - RED* (RRC-RED), which obtains a reasonable bandwidth fair share, even better than some of the previous solutions, but with the advantage of being a very simple solution, with less complexity and adding little per flow state information at routers.

The paper is organized as follows: In section 2, RED's basics and its main drawbacks are reviewed. In Section 3 we describe the proposed algorithm and some implementation details. Performance evaluation is treated in section 4. And, finally, Section 5 summarizes the work presented and some conclusion remarks.

2 RED Algorithm

The RED algorithm tries to early detect the congestion, and to do so it uses a particular average queue size estimation (avg) and some threshold values. To calculate avg it uses a low-pass filter based on an EWMA estimator (*Exponential Weighted Moving Average*) over the instantaneous size of the queue ($inst_{queue}$) every time a packet arrives at the node:

$$avg = avg * w_q + inst_{queue} * (1 - w_q) \tag{1}$$

where w_q is a configuration parameter.

If the average queue size is below a lower threshold (min_{th}), the newly arrived packet is never discarded. When the average queue size exceeds min_{th}, but is smaller than an upper threshold (max_{th}), RED drops the packet with some probability P_{drop}. This probability grows proportionally to the average queue size (avg), according to:

$$P_{drop} = (avg - min_{th})/(max_{th} - min_{th}) * P_{max} \tag{2}$$

When the average queue size exceeds the upper limit, max_{th}, the incoming packet will be discarded with probability 1.

This way, RED can detect an incipient and persistent congestion, besides allowing routers to detect transient bursts.

Finally, random packet drop in RED avoids the undesirable effect of global sinchronization.

2.1 RED Drawbacks

As we have pointed out earlier, RED's main goal is to implement a packet dropping strategy that arises from the bandwidth consumption proportionality among the different packet flows sharing the buffer. This is achieved by discarding any incoming packet with the same probability (assuminging that the average queue size does not change significantly). This way, connections with greater rates will also have greater percentange of discarded packets.

However, from a connection point of view, the instantaneous packet dropping rate during a short period of time is independent of its bandwidth use. When there is risk of congestion, that is, the average queue size exceeds min_{th}, the dropping probability has a non zero value for every connection, contributing to a non-fair share of the link bandwidth. In [5] some possible reasons are identified:

- The fact that every connection see the same loss rate implies that even the connection that receives much less bandwidth than it should will suffer from losses. Moreover, such unfairly treated connection will eventually also have to reduce its transmission window to half the current size if one of its packets is discarded.
- The acceptance of a new packet implies an increase in the dropping probability of future packets in the other connections, even when those consume less bandwidth. This causes undesirable temporary drops that break the proportionality rule above mentioned, even between identical flows.
- If a particular connection does not obey to congestion signals, this may lead to a collective high drop rate, and represents a clear proof of the RED incapability to offer fair bandwidth share to adaptive connections in presence of aggresive users, even when congestion is not severe.

3 RRC-RED Algorithm (*RED with Random Rate-Control)*

Our algorithm (*RED with Random Rate-Control*) represents another attempt to improve bandwidth fairness when RED is used. Against other solutions, the main new feature of

RRC-RED lies in its simple flow rate estimation method. Then, at the time to discard a packet, estimated flow rates will determine among a number of randomly chosen flows from which one we must eliminate the packet.

Flows rate estimations will only be calculated at the time to (early) discard a packet, and is computed dividing the number of bytes sent by a particular flow by the time such flow has been sending data.

Thus, the main difference between RED and RRC-RED concerns to the packet that must be discarded, not to the decision or opportunity to take the dropping action. While RED discards the incoming packet, RRC-RED compares the average rate of the flow this packet belongs to with those of **N-1** other flows randomly chosen among the ones which have a packet enqueued at that time, discarding the last arrived packet from the flow with the largest flow rate at that moment. Choosing the last arrived packet is well suited for TCP, because doing so avoids unnnecesary retransmissions, as well as for UDP, because the flows sending at a higher rate will have their packets discarded with more probability as they will trigger the early drop algorithm more often. Moreover, if the flow the eliminated packet belongs to appears more than once in the randomly selected **N** set, the algorithm discards, if possible, many packets as times it was selected.

The algorithm accumulates the number of bytes sent by each flow, and the rates estimations only occurs when a packet has to be discarded by the RED algorithm. Thus the complexity that the algorithm adds to RED is very small. Moreover, these calculations, as well as RED does, can be done in parallel with packet delivery without having a significant influence in the processing capacity of the router.

After many simulations, we have observed that increasing N does not improve significantly the results obtained, moreover if we think about maintainning in a low level the computational load of the algorithm In fact, only by taking two flows randomly, RED is improved with a minor increase of the complexity.

In section 4 we present the results obtained with our algorithm in different situations, compared to RED and to different solutions proposed in the literature.

4 RRC-RED Evaluation

In this section we present the results obtained with the proposed algorithm in several scenarios, and compare its performance with the ones achieved by RED and the other mentioned solutions. We have used the **Network Simulator** to draw the results. To

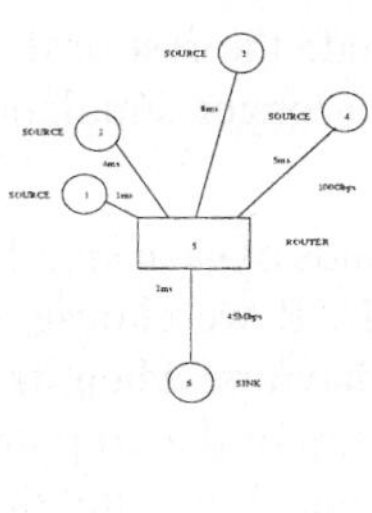

Fig. 1. Scene 1

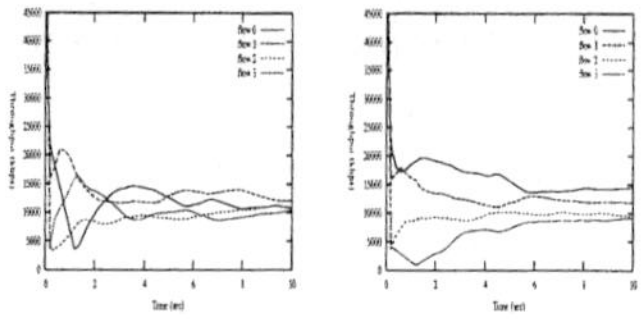

(a) RRC-RED (b) RED

Fig. 2. Comparación entre RRC-RED y RED

make the comparisons easy, we will evaluate RRC-RED performance using the same network scenario described in [3], and represented in Figure 1: Four TCP conections, with different RTTs and start times, are considered. Windows' sizes are limited by the smaller link capacity and by RTT, and they will have, respectively, 33, 67, 112 and 78 packets. Simulations have been made with a fixed packet length of 1000 bytes. And inside the router, the buffer size is 1000 packets, $min_{th} = 30$, $max_{th} = 80$, $w_q = 0.002$, and $max_p = 1/10$. As in [3], the start times of the flows are separated 20 miliseconds, and we assume that all sources have always data to send. In Figure 2 we can see a comparison between RED and RRC-RED. As this figure shows, RRC-RED rapidly reaches a situation where the four flows have very similar throughputs. On the contrary, RED is unable to reduce the rate of the first flow (flow 0) once this has accomodated its window size: in RED, the first flow arriving at the router uses all the resources, so it fixes its window size to take the most of that capacity; nevertheless, the rest of the flows, which will appear every 20 ms, will see a much smaller bandwidth, because in that moment flow 0 is monopolizing the link. With this situation the random drop mechanism begins to work, having a bigger impact on the flows still at the slow-start phase, since they still are adjusting their window size. It is obvious that when this point is reached, as shown in figure 2, it is difficult to reduce the most active flow rate, and to increase the rate of the less active ones, so the rate differences among all the flows are significant. Our algorithm tries to avoid, as much as possible, this undesirable effect, so fairness in bandwidth share can be reached soon. This speed of convergence does not discriminate between long-lived or short-lived connections, offering a fair share whatever the situation is, something that RED can not do satisfactorily.

In the next comparison we include the rest of the proposals (RED-PD, FRED and CHOKe), but use 8 TCP flows in a longer simulation with the same scenenario (we duplicate the original 4 sources).

In figure 3 we show the last seconds of each simulation, where we can observe again the right performance of RRC-RED. If we choose any flow and follow its evolution over time, we can observe these behaviors: when its throughput is high, it is probable that sooner or later it will be the victim of the dropping algorithm, so its rate will begin to descend slowly. After reducing enough its rate, this flow will not be the goal of the discards for a period of time, so its rate will increase again while other flows see their

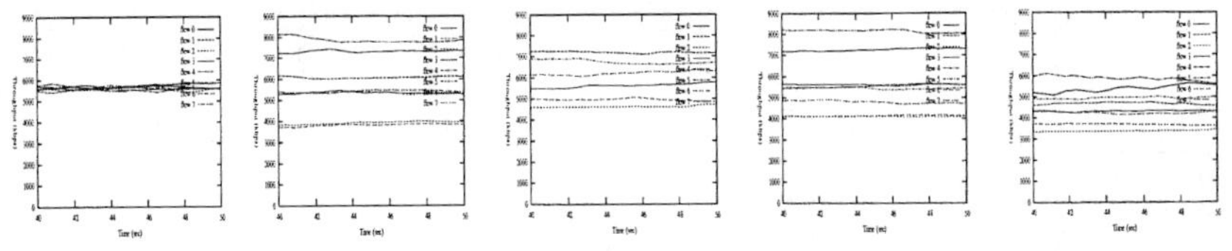

(a) RRC-RED (b) RED (c) RED-PD (d) FRED (e) CHOKe

Fig. 3. Comparison between RRC-RED, RED, RED-PD, FRED y CHOKe

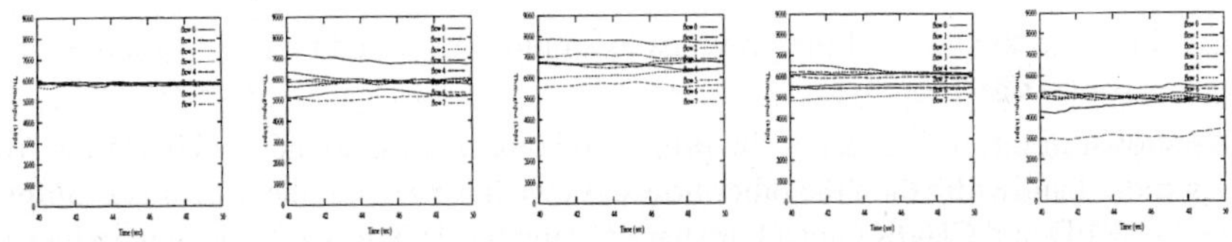

(a) RRC-RED (b) RED (c) RED-PD (d) FRED (e) CHOKe

Fig. 4. Comparison with identical flows

rates reduced. This way, each flow's rate will be fluctuating slightly with time, depending on which state it is.

The rate control of each flow in RRC-RED manintains very close the throughput values, something that the rest of the tested solutions could not achieve. In the graphics of figure 3, we can see how RED's algorithm experiments the same problems as in the previous example. And something similar happens to RED-PD and FRED. FRED hardly improves RED's performance, while RED-PD, although it is slightly better, penalizes flow 0 from the beginning with a very tiny window. The only solution that works reasonably well is CHOKe, although the fairness is clearly worse than with RRC-RED and, besides, it discards an important number of packets. In another interesting experiment, we play with a number n of identical sources (8 in this example). We use the same topology as in the previous cases, but now the starting times are separated 0.5 secs, all the windows have the same size (100 packets), and the delay introduced by the link is always 2 ms. Looking at figure 4, we can observe the right evolution of RRC-RED over time. While disciplines such as RED or RED-PD reach a steady state, this does not occur to RRC-RED, where the most active flows are forced to reduce their rate, allowing the less active flows to get more bandwidth. Here we can see the failure of CHOKe when it tries to make rates look similar. We also see FRED's nice performance. Up to now, we have only compared TCP flows. Let us look at the results obtained in presence of UDP flows, which are unresponsive to any congestion control mechanism. In this example,

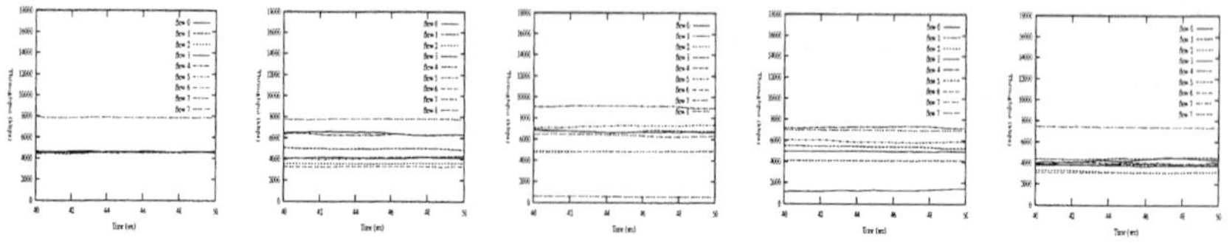

(a) RRC-RED (b) RED (c) RED-PD (d) FRED (e) CHOKe

Fig. 5. Comparison with TCP and UDP flows

we use the same topology of the previous examples but we add an UDP source which generates packets of 1000 bytes.

As shown in figure 5, none of the proposed solutions can avoid the UDP flow from getting more bandwidth than the other flows. As we have seen in the previous examples, only RRC-RED and CHOKe get a fair share among the TCP flows while they reduce the UDP flow rate as much as possible. Again, the main difference between RRC-RED and CHOKe is that the latter discards much more packets from the TCP flows, firing more retransmissions. To conclude with the simulation study, we present in table 1 the results obtained when we have a large number of flows competing for the bandwidth, because as we explained in the introduction, some of the algorithms proved here did not work fine with a large number of flows. We use again the mean deviation of the flows' throughput to show the performance of each algorithm. Finnally, we will comment some details

Table 1. Large # of flows

Algorithm	RRC-RED	RED	RED-PD	FRED	CHOKE
M.Deviation (10^3)	4.14	33.24	40.07	18.35	6.69

about the complexity of the studied algorithms. RRC-RED adds only one arithmetic operation, with two variables per flow, every time the algorithm is executed, and one two arithmetic operations and one comparison in an early drop. FRED, unlike RRC-RED, mantains two variables per flow, making 8 comparisons and 6 arithmetic operations more than RED, each time a packet is enqueued and dequeued. RED-PD uses a list where the last drops from each flow in some period of time are stored, which can contribute to a large increase of the information stored in a router when the number of flows and/or the number of drops is high. Lastly, CHOKe is the lighter solution because it does not need per flow information and it only does one more comparison than RED.

5 Conclusions

The problem of congestion control in the current Internet has been broadly studied during the last years. One of the most successful solutions in this area has been RED. However, in several situations, RED has revealed itself as a mechanism incapable of guaranteing bandwidth's fair share. There have been a number of proposals to attenuate this malfunction, but none of them revolve this satisfactorily. In this paper we present a new algorithm, RRC-RED, a mechanism that uses a rate estimator of the incoming flows to detect those consuming more bandwidth, and, thus, to discard preferably packets from those flows, in order to control the bandwidth they receive and to guarantee a fair share among all the present flows. By means of simulation, we have tested the proposed algorithm, and it has been compared with other solutions proposed in literature.

References

1. A. Mankin, K. K. Ramakrishnam., editors for the IETF Performance and Congestion Control Working Group, Gateway Congestion Control Survey, RFC 1254 (1991)
2. Floyd., S. TCP and Explicit Congestion Notification. *ACM Computer Communication Review* (1994), vol. 24, 10–23
3. S. Floyd y V. Jacobson. Random Early Detection Gateways for Congestion Avoidance. *IEEE/ACM Transactions on Networking* (1993), vol. 1, 397–413
4. M. May, C. Diot, B. Lyles. Reasons not to Deploy RED, en *Proceedings of the IEEE/IFIP IWQoS* (1999)
5. D. Lin and R. Morris, Dynamics of Random Early Detection, en *Proceeding of ACM Sigcomm* ACM, (1997) 127–137
6. R. Pan, B. Prabhakar, and K. Psounis. CHOKe, A Stateless Active Queue Management Scheme for Approximating Fair Bandwidth Allocation. In IEEE INFOCOM (2000)
7. Ratul Mahajan and Sally Floyd, RED with Preferential Dropping (RED-PD).E n Proc. ACM 9th International Conference on Network Protocols (ICNP) (2001)
8. S. Floyd and K. Fall. Router mechanisms to support end-to-end congestion control. LBL Technical Report (1997)

PES: A System for Parallelized Fitness Evaluation of Evolutionary Methods

Onur Soysal, Erkin Bahçeci, and Erol Şahin

Kovan research group
Department of Computer Engineering
Middle East Technical University
06531 Ankara, Turkey
{soysal, erkinb, erol}@ceng.metu.edu.tr
http://kovan.ceng.metu.edu.tr

Abstract. The paper reports the development of a software platform, named PES (Parallelized Evolution System), that parallelizes the fitness evaluations of evolutionary methods over multiple computers connected via a network. The platform creates an infrastructure that allows the dispatching of fitness evaluations onto a group of computers, running both Windows or Linux operating systems, parallelizing the evolutionary process. PES is based on the PVM (Parallel Virtual Machine) library and consists of two components; (1) a server component, named PES-Server, that executes the basic evolutionary method, the management of the communication with the client computers, and (2) a client component, named PES-Client, that executes programs to evaluate a single individual and return the fitness back to the server. Performance of PES is tested for the problem of evolving behaviors for a swarm of mobile robots simulated as physics-based models, and the speed-up characteristics are analyzed.

1 Introduction

Evolutionary Robotics[6] is a new approach for designing autonomous robots. It considers autonomous robots as artificial organisms that can be selectively "bred" based on their fitness for the tasks that they are being designed for. An active research track in Evolutionary Robotics is the development of behaviors for simulated robot systems. In these studies, the goal is to evolve controllers that use the sensory information of the robot to control robot's actuators such that the robot accomplishes a desired task. Initially a population of genotypes that encode the controllers is given. Then the robots are simulated under the control of the controller specified by the genotype and its fitness is evaluated. The fittest controllers are then allowed to reproduce as defined by a set of genetic operators, and the process is repeated. Evolving behaviors in simulated robot systems require large amounts of computational power, mainly due to the evaluation of different individuals. Therefore the computational requirements of

A. Yazici and C. Şener (Eds.): ISCIS 2003, LNCS 2869, pp. 900–907, 2003.

using evolutionary methods tend to be proportional to the computational requirements of evaluating a single individual. This creates a major bottleneck for evolutionary methods.

Recently there have been projects[3,5] that aim to create platforms that can use the idle processing power of computer systems that are connected over a network. SETI@home[3] is a scientific experiment that uses Internet-connected computers in the Search for Extraterrestrial Intelligence (SETI). The downloaded program runs as a background task or a screen-saver getting chunks of radio telescope data from a server and performing a computation intensive processing of the data to seek signs of artificial signals and reporting the results back to the server. This platform made it possible for the SETI project to utilize a total computing power that equals or surpasses supercomputers.

This paper reports the development of a platform, named *PES* (Parallellized Evolution System), that parallelizes an evolutionary method on a group of computers connected via a network. In the next section, we describe PES and its specifications. Section 2 describes the implementation of PES, explaining server and client components of the system. Section 3 analyzes the speed-ups obtained using PES for the problem of evolving behaviors for a swarm of simulated mobile robots. Section 4 summarizes the results and discusses the shortcomings of the system and future development directions of the system.

2 PES

PES[1] is a platform to parallelize evolutionary methods on a group of computers connected via a network. It separates the fitness evaluation of genotypes from other tasks (such as selection and reproduction) and distributes these evaluations onto a group of computers to be processed in parallel. PES consists of two components; (1) a server component, named PES-Server, that executes the evolutionary method, the management of the communication with the client computers, and (2) a client component, named PES-Client, that executes programs to evaluate a single individual and return the fitness back to the server. Figure 1 shows the structure of a PES system.

PES provides the user with an easy interface that relieves him from dealing with the communication between server and client processes. PES-Client is developed for both Windows and Linux, enabling the PES system to harvest computational power from computers running either of these operating systems. An easy-to-use framework for implementing evolutionary methods, and the interoperability of the system distinguishes PES from other systems available and makes it a valuable tool for evolutionary methods with large computational requirements.

PES uses PVM (Parallel Virtual Machine)[4][2], a widely utilized message passing library in distributed and parallel programming studies, for communi-

[1] Documentation and source code of PES is freely available at http://kovan.ceng.metu.edu.tr/software/PES/.

[2] Available at http://www.csm.ornl.gov/pvm/pvm_home.html.

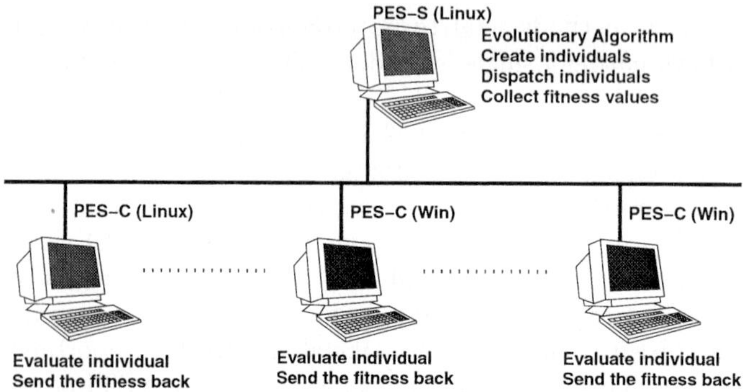

Fig. 1. Sketch of PES system is shown. The PES-Server runs on a Linux machine and handles the management of the evolutionary method. It executes the selection and reproduction of the individuals (genotypes) which are then dispatched to a group of PES-Clients (running both Windows and Linux systems). The individuals are then evaluated by the clients and their fitnesses are sent back to the server.

cation between the server and the clients. We have also considered MPI[2] as an alternative to PVM. MPI is a newer standard that is being developed by multiprocessor machine manufacturers and is more efficient. However PVM is more suitable for our purposes since (1) it is available in source code as free software and is ported to many computer systems ranging from laptops to CRAY supercomputers, (2) it is inter-operable, i.e. different architectures running PVM can be mixed in a single application, (3) it does not assume a static architecture of processors and is robust against failures of individual processors.

PES wraps and improves PVM functionality. It implements a time-out mechanism to detect processes that have crashed or have entered an infinite loop. It provides *ping*, *data* and *result* message facilities. Ping messages are used to check the state of client processes. Data messages are used to send task information to client processes and result packages are used to carry fitness information from clients.

Now we will describe the PES-Server and PES-Clients.

2.1 PES-Server

PES-Server provides a generic structure to implement evolutionary methods. This structure is based on Goldberg's basic Genetic Algorithm[1] and is designed to be easily modified and used by programmers. The structure assumes that fitness values are calculated externally. In its minimal form, it supports tournament selection, multi-point cross-over and multi-point mutation operators.

PES-Server maintains a list of potential clients (computers with PES-Client installed), as specified by their IP numbers. Using this list, the server executes an evolutionary method and dispatches the fitness evaluations of the individuals to the available clients. The assignment passes the location of the executable to be run on the client as well as the parameters that represent that particular individual and the initial conditions for the evaluation. Then it waits for the clients to complete the fitness evaluation and get the computed fitness values back.

PES-Server contains fault detection and recovery facilities. Using the *ping* facility the server can detect clients that have crashed and assign the uncompleted tasks to other clients. In its current implementation, the server waits for the results of fitness evaluations from all the individuals in a generation before dispatching the individuals from the next generation.

2.2 PES-Client

PES-Client acts as a wrapper to handle the communication of the clients with the server. It fetches and runs a given executable (to evaluate a given individual) with a given set of parameters. It returns the fitness evaluations, and other data back to the server.

Client processes contain a loop that accepts, executes and sends results of tasks. Client processes reply to *ping* signals sent by the PES-Server to check their status. Crashed processes are detected through this mechanism.

PES-Clients are developed for single processor PC platforms running Windows and Linux operating systems. Note that to use clients with both operating systems the fitness evaluating program should be compilable on both systems. In its current implementation, these clients have the fitness evaluation component embedded within them to simplify the communication. Yet, once the clients are installed, the fitness evaluation component of the system can be updated using *scp* (secure copy) utility from the server.

3 Experimental Results

The PES platform is developed as part of our work within the Swarm-bots project[3] [7,8], for evolving behaviors for a simulated swarm of mobile robots. We have conducted experiments to evolve behaviors for clustering a swarm of robots and analyzed the speed-up and efficiency of the PES system in this task.

The swarm of robots and their environment are modeled using ODE (Open Dynamics Engine), a physics-based simulation library, Figure 2(a). The parameters of this simulation and parameters of the controller (network weights) are passed to the PES-Client from the PES-Server. The simulator constructs the world and runs it, by solving differential dynamic equations. Movements of the robots are determined by their controller as specified by the genotype. This controller uses the sensors of the robots and moves the robots for 2000 time steps. Then a fitness value is computed based on a measure of clustering achieved. This fitness value is then returned to PES-Server, Figure 2(b).

[3] More information can be found at http://www.swarm-bots.org.

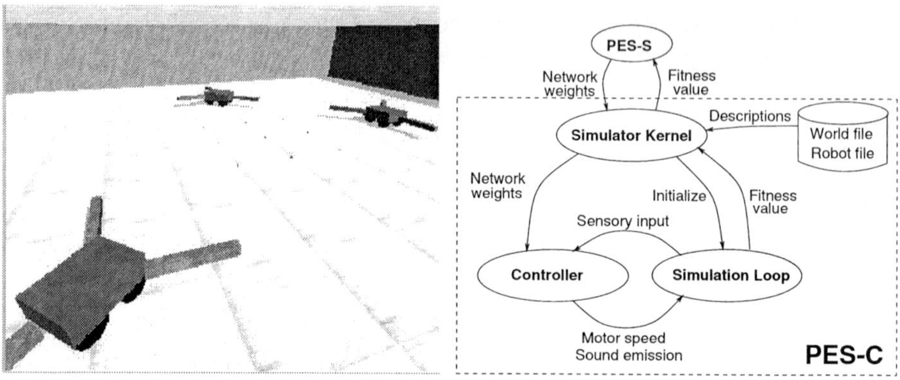

(a) (b)

Fig. 2. **(a)** A snapshot of the environment being simulated: Three mobile robots, distributed in an arena are enclosed by walls, can be seen. The rods emanating out of the robot bodies visualize the proximity sensing capabilities of the robots. **(b)** Architecture of PES-Client being used.

3.1 The Experimental Set-up

We have installed PES-Clients to 12 PC's of a student laboratory at the Computer Engineering Department of Middle East Technical University, Ankara, Turkey. During the experiments, these computers were being used by other users and each of them had different workloads that varied in time. The population size is set as 48, requiring that 48 fitness evaluations take place during each generation. 30 generations were evolved.

Figure 3 plots the load of the 12 processors in time, during the evaluation of five generations. PES-Server waits for fitness evaluations of all the individuals in a generation before the selection and reproduction of the individuals of the next generation. In the plot, the vertical lines separate the generations. Within each generation, 48 fitness evaluations are calculated, which are visible as dark diamonds or dark horizontally stretched hexagons. It can be seen that the fitness evaluation time varies between different cases. There are two major causes of this. First, each processor has a different and varying workload depending on the other users of that computer. Second, the physics-based simulation of the swarm of robots slows down dramatically as robots collide with each other and the walls in the environment. As a result, the computation required by different simulations vary drastically.

In order to analyze the speed-ups achieved through the use of the PES system and its efficiency, we have repeated the evolution experiment using 1, 2, 3, 6 and 12 processors. The data obtained is used to compute the following two measures:

$$S_p = \frac{\text{Time required for single machine}}{\text{Time required for p machines}}$$

$$E_p = \frac{\text{Speed-up with p processors}}{\text{p}}$$

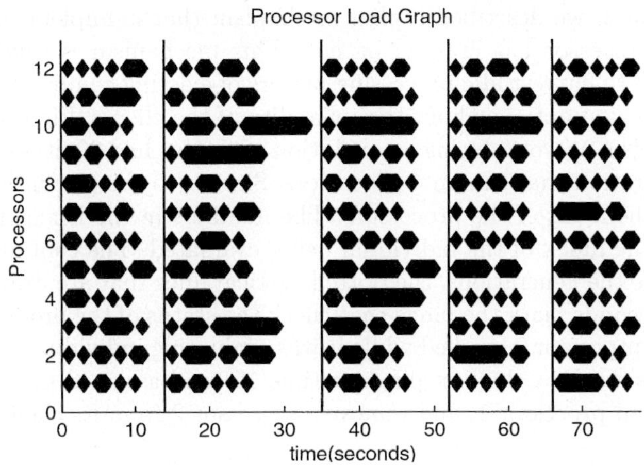

Fig. 3. The load of the 12 processors during 5 generations of evolution. See text for discussion.

The results are plotted in Figure 4(a,b). Ideally S_p should be linear to number of processors and E_p should be 1. The deviance is a result of the requirement that all individuals need to be evaluated before moving on to the next generation. As a consequence of this, after the dispatching of the last individual in a generation, all-but-one of the processors has to wait for the last processor to finish its evaluation. This causes a decrease in the speed-up and efficiency plots. Note that, apart from the number of processors, these measures also depend on two other factors: (1) the ratio of total number of fitness evaluations in a generation to the number of processors, (2) the average duration of fitness evaluations and their variance.

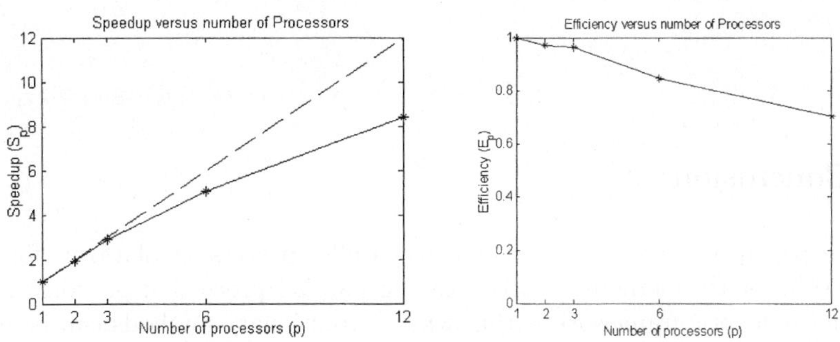

(a) (b)

Fig. 4. **(a)** Speed-up is plotted against number of processors. **(b)** Efficiency is plotted against number of processors.

In Section 2, we described a ping mechanism that is implemented to check whether a processor has crashed or not. This mechanism is crucial since we envision PES to harvest idle processing powers of existing computer systems and cannot make assumptions about the reliability of the clients. Figure 5 shows the ping mechanism at work during an evolution where we had 20 fitness evaluations in each generation that run on 4 processors. Similar to the plot in Figure 3, this plot shows the loads of the processors. The numbers in the hexagons are labels that shows the index of the individual being evaluated. The continuous vertical bars separate the generations. the dotted vertical lines that are drawn at 15, 30, 45, and 60 seconds mark the pings that check the status of the processors. In this experiment, processor 2 crashed while it was evaluating individual 1. PES-Server detected this crash at the first ping (at time 15) and assigned the evaluation of individual 1 to processor 1, and removed processor 2 from its client list.

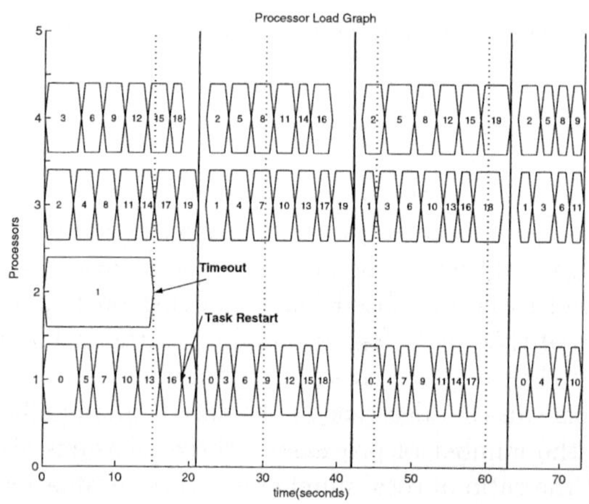

Fig. 5. Load of each processor during a run in which a processor fails. See text for discussion.

4 Conclusion

In this paper, we have reported a new parallel processing platform for running evolutionary methods. Unlike existing parallel processing platforms, PES provides a generic framework within which evolutionary methods can be easily implemented. PES provides an interface which relieves its user from the details of communication and the status of the clients. PES adds better fault tolerance mechanisms to PVM allowing crashed processes to be detected. The user only needs to program a separate client program with a few constraints and should customize the server program to meet its requirements while leaving the rest to PES.

The analysis showed that although evolutionary methods lend themselves easily to parallelization, non-incremental selection and reproduction (that is the selection and reproduction occurring only after all the individuals are evaluated) is a major source of wasting processing time. The use of incremental selection and reproduction methods would eliminate this problem.

Acknowledgments. This work was partially funded by the SWARM-BOTS project, a Future and Emerging Technologies project (IST-FET) of the European Community, under grant IST-2000-31010. The information provided is the sole responsibility of the authors and does not reflect the Community's opinion. The Community is not responsible for any use that might be made of data appearing in this publication.

This work is also funded by Middle East Technical University within the "Sanal Robot Kolonisi" project under grant BAP-2003-07-2-00-01.

References

1. Goldberg D. E., *Genetic Algorithms in Search, Optimization, and Machine Learning.* Reading, MA: Addison-Wesley, 1989.
2. Hempel, R., *The MPI Standard for Message Passing.* High–Performance Computing and Networking, International Conference and Exhibition, Proceedings, Volume II: Networking and Tools. Ed. Gentzsch, Wolfgang and Harms, Uwe. 247–252,1994.SV, LNCS vol797, 1994.
3. Korpela E., Werthimer D., Anderson D., Cobb J., Lebofsky M., *SETI@home: An Experiment in Public-Resource Computing* Communications of the ACM, Vol. 45 No. 11, pp. 56–61, November, 2002.
4. Kowalik J. (ed), *PVM: Parallel Virtual Machine: A Users' Guide and Tutorial for Networked Parallel Computing.* MIT Press Scientific and Engineering Computation, 1994.
5. Mukherjee S., Mustafi J., Chaudhuri A., *Grid Computing: The Future of Distributed Computing for High Performance Scientific and Business Applications* Lecture Notes in Computer Science, Vol. 2571, pp 339–342, 2002.
6. Nolfi S., Floreano D., *Evolutionary Robotics: The Biology, Intelligence, and Technology of Self-Organizing Machines*, MIT Press/Bradford Books, 2000.
7. Şahin E., Labella T.H., Trianni V., Deneubourg J.-L., Rasse P., Floreano D., Gambardella L.M., Mondada F., Nolfi S., Dorigo M., *SWARM-BOT: Pattern Formation in a Swarm of Self-Assembling Mobile Robots.* In A. El Kamel, K. Mellouli, and P. Borne, editors, Proceedings of the IEEE International Conference on Systems, Man and Cybernetics, Hammamet, Tunisia, October 6–9, 2002. Piscataway, NJ: IEEE Press.
8. Trianni V., Labella Th.H., Gross R., Sahin E., Rasse Ph., Deneubourg J.-L. and Dorigo M. *Evolving Aggregation in a Robotics Swarm.* Accepted to the European Conference on Artificial Life (ECAL'03), 2003.
9. Vinschen C., Faylor C., Delorie D. J., Humblet P., Noer G., *Cygwin User's Guide.*

Design and Evaluation of a Cache Coherence Adapter for the SMP Nodes Interconnected via Xcent-Net¶

Sangman Moh[1], Jae-Hong Shim[1], Yang-Dong Lee[1], Jeong-A Lee[2], and Beom-Joon Cho[2]

[1]School of Internet Eng.,
smmoh@chosun.ac.kr
[2]School of Computer Eng.,
Chosun Univ.
375 Seoseok-dong, Dong-gu, Gwangju, 501-759 Korea

Abstract. This paper presents the design and evaluation of a cache coherence adapter for the cache-coherent non-uniform memory access multiprocessor system in which symmetric multiprocessor (SMP) nodes are interconnected via Xcent-Net. The SMP node is a 4-way symmetric multiprocessor subsystem based on the Intel Xeon processors, and Xcent-Net is a dual, adaptive-routed, virtual cut-through multistage interconnection network composed of hierarchical crossbar routers. The cache coherence adapter contains a directory and a remote access cache to support the directory-based cache coherence protocol customized for the SMP nodes on Xcent-Net. For any cache design, cache size and cache line size are crucial design parameters in terms of performance and implementation, and thus they are extensively evaluated. According to the simulation results, it is shown that a 128-Mbyte remote access cache with 64-byte lines is the best choice, where the average data access latency is 9.4 μs and the effective bandwidth is 6.8 Mbytes/s per node.

1 Introduction

Scalable multiprocessor systems are suitable for general-purpose multiuser applications. A non-uniform memory access (NUMA) multiprocessor is a shared memory system in which the access time varies with the location of memory words. As a variation of NUMA architecture, a cache-coherent non-uniform memory access (CC-NUMA) model is defined with distributed shared memory and cache coherence mechanism [1-2]. A major concern of CC-NUMA is the cache-coherent memory access transparent to all the processors [3-5]. Latency tolerance for remote memory access is also a major limitation of CC-NUMA systems [6].

A CC-NUMA system with symmetric multiprocessor (SMP) nodes is a hierarchically structured multiprocessor machine, which has two layers of architecture: SMP and CC-NUMA models. In such a system, since SMP nodes are interconnected via an interconnection network, the access time to remote memories is longer than that to the local memory. In most SMP-based CC-NUMA multiprocessor systems, a direc-

¶ This study was supported in part by research funds from Chosun University, 2003.

A. Yazici and C. Şener (Eds.): ISCIS 2003, LNCS 2869, pp. 908–915, 2003.

tory-based adapter is used for internode cache coherence since the systems have many processors and general interconnection topologies [3, 7].

Off-the-shelf commodity SMPs are more popular in the commercial marketplace [8]. Moreover, well-developed system interconnects provide higher performance with scalability. For CC-NUMA multiprocessor systems with the commodity SMPs and well-developed interconnection networks, the specialized cache coherence adapter does enable high-performance, system-wide data accesses with better programmability. Some research prototypes and commercial systems of SMP-based CC-NUMA multiprocessors have been developed [9-12]. They typically use commodity microprocessors available in the marketplace.

In this paper, we present the design and evaluation of a cache coherence adapter for an SMP-based CC-NUMA multiprocessor system, where the SMP nodes are interconnected via Xcent-Net. Xcent-Net [13] is a dual, adaptive-routed, virtual cut-through multistage interconnection network composed of hierarchical crossbar routers. In particular, the adaptive routing and dual-network topology of Xcent-Net help the cache coherence protocol to guarantee deadlock-free data delivery and minimal queueing delay. The cache coherence adapter was evaluated by using the DEVSim++ simulator [14] which is a discrete event simulator providing a framework for modeling and simulation. The design parameters of cache size and cache line size are extensively evaluated because they are crucial factors in cache design in terms of performance and implementation. According to the simulation results, it is quantitatively shown that a 128-Mbyte remote access cache with 64-byte lines is the best choice.

The rest of the paper is organized as follows: The design of the cache coherence adapter is presented in the following section. The corresponding cache coherence protocol is also described. In section 3, the methodology and results of modeling, simulation and evaluation are given and discussed. The modeling and simulation based on the DEVSim++ simulator are described, and the evaluation of design parameters is subsequently discussed in terms of memory access performance. Finally, conclusions are discussed in section 4.

2 Design of the Cache Coherent Adapter and Protocol

The target system is an SMP-based CC-NUMA multiprocessor computer as shown in Fig. 1 that can be extended up to 16 SMP nodes. Xcent-Net with dual subnetworks is used to provide multiple paths and high bandwidth. The SMP node is a 4-way symmetric multiprocessor based on Intel Xeon processors.

Xcent-Net [8] consists of dual subnetworks: upper and lower subnetworks. Each subnetwork is a packet-switched hierarchical crossbar network which can interconnect up to 128 nodes by connecting routers hierarchically. Virtual cut-though adaptive routing and source synchronous clocking are effectively used to boost up the network performance. The node connected to Xcent-Net can take up to 1,066 Mbytes/sec of network bandwidth through dedicated full-duplex ports.

The SMP node consists of up to four Intel Xeon processors [15], memory modules, input/output devices, and a cache coherence adapter. The processor contains a 4-

way set-associative, 512-Kbyte, write-back second-level (L2) cache with 32-byte lines. The cache coherence adapter is the specialized hardware suitable for the SMP nodes on Xcent-Net. It consists of a full-map directory (DIR), a directory controller, a remote access cache (RAC), an RAC controller, and bus and network interfaces.

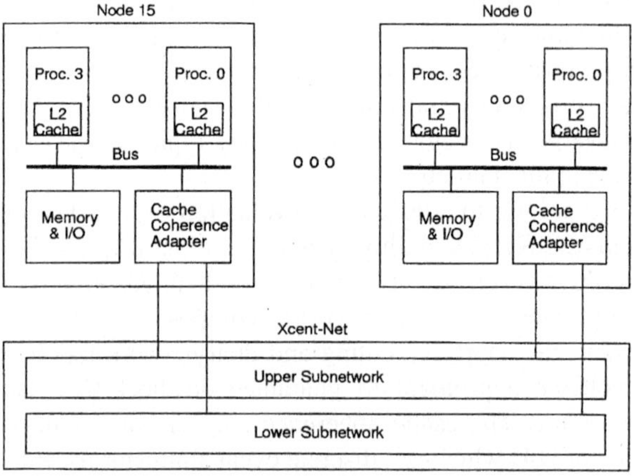

Fig. 1. The SMP-based CC-NUMA system using Xcent-Net.

Fig. 2 shows the organization of the directory and the RAC. Each line in the full-map directory consists of 16 bit-map pointers and a 2-bit state. Practically, only 15 bit-map pointers are required for full-map pointing because the directory does not maintain the caching state of the home node. Each pointer P_i in the directory line j (for the memory block j) is a 1-bit vector which represents whether the node i has a copy of the designated memory block j. RAC is a direct-mapped write-back cache. Each RAC line consists of a tag, a state, a data block and an error control code (ECC). The tag contains the most significant bits of a remote memory address.

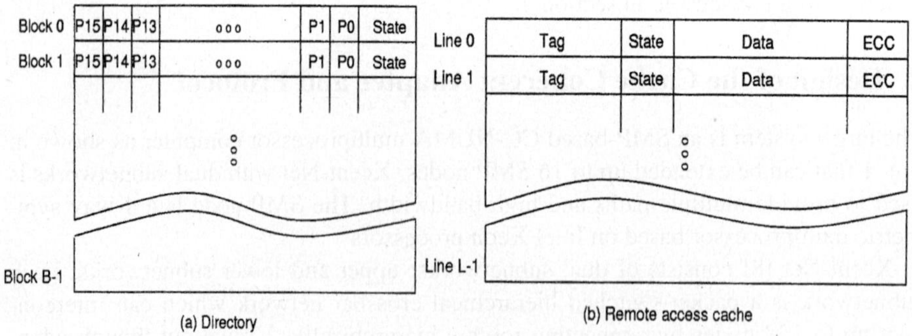

Fig. 2. Organization of the directory and the remote access cache.

All accesses to the same address are serialized at the home node. The full-map directory in the home node is the serialization point of all memory accesses, no matter which node accesses the memory block. The node holding the ownership of a memory block provides up-to-date data to the requesting node directly. Ghost sharing due to the replacement of a shared block without notification is allowed in the system. In the target system, the directory does not maintain the caching state of local copies in the L2 caches within the same node. Locked operations of remote memory locations are also supported by the RAC.

The processor with the L2 cache issues various bus transactions which affect the cache coherence protocol in our SMP-based CC-NUMA multiprocessor system. The bus transactions are summarized in Table 1. Six network transactions are defined, which support internode cache-coherent accesses through Xcent-Net. The Xcent-Net transactions are summarized in Table 2. Each network transaction begins with a request operation and ends with a reply operation. The reply operation can turn in a negative acknowledgement to inform the request node of error and retry information.

Table 1. Bus transactions.

Transaction name	Abbr.	Meaning
Read invalidate line	BRIL	Read a line and invalidate other copies
Invalidate line	BIL	Invalidate other copies
Read line	BRL	Read a line
Write line	BWL	Write a line
Locked read	BLR	Locked memory read
Locked write	BLW	Locked memory write

Table 2. Xcent-Net transactions.

Transaction name	Abbr.	Meaning
Coherent read	NCR	Read a read-only shared copy
Exclusive read	NER	Read a writable exclusive copy
Uncached read	NUR	Read the most up-to-date data with uncached attribute
Invalidate	NIV	Invalidate a cached copy
Write-back	NWB	Write back a dirty (modified) block
Uncached write	NUW	Write data into home memory with uncached attribute

Each entry in the directory has one of three states: uncached (U), shared (S), and dirty (D). The state transition diagram of the directory is shown in Fig. 3. Not only bus transactions but also network transactions cause the state transition of the directory. Each state transition makes subsequent operations, a series of bus and network transactions, be followed. The state transition and operation of the directory are tightly related with the L2 caches and the remote access caches.

As far as remote memory addresses are concerned, inclusion property is preserved between the L2 caches and the remote access cache in the same node. Each line in the remote access cache has one of three states: invalid (I), shared (S), and dirty (D). The remote access cache is a kind of third-level cache in memory hierarchy. Fig. 4 shows the state transition diagram of the remote access cache. Like the directory, the state transition in the remote access cache is also caused by bus and network transactions. Each state transition makes subsequent operations be followed. As mentioned earlier, the locked read-modify-write sequence of a remote memory location is supported by the remote access cache.

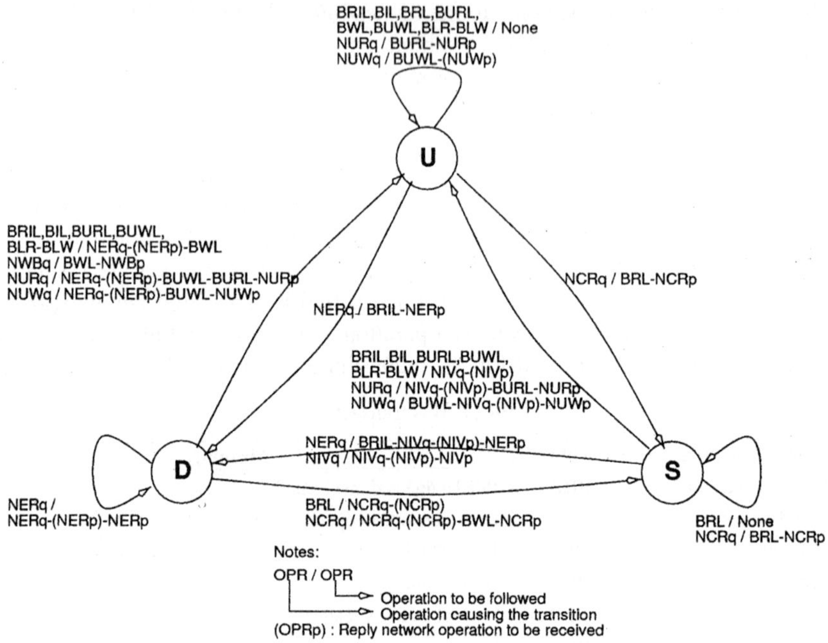

Fig. 3. State transition diagram of the directory.

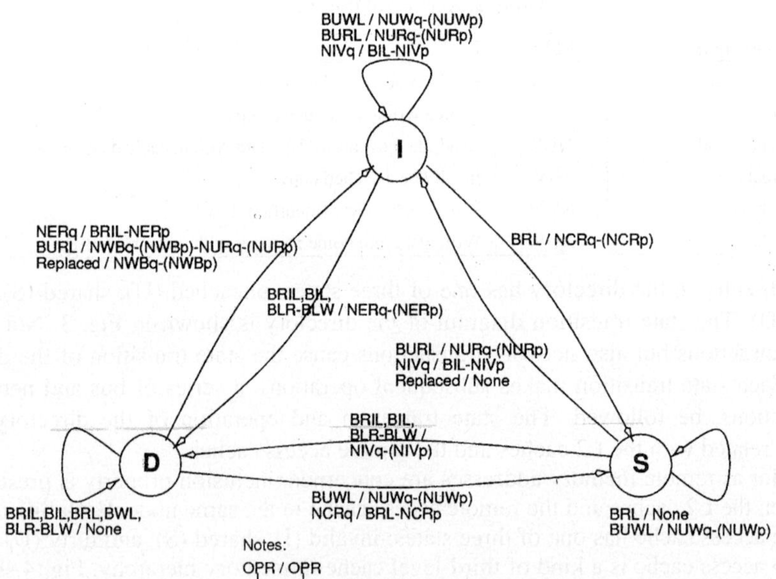

Fig. 4. State transition diagram of the remote access cache.

3 Evaluation of Data Access Performance

Discrete event simulation has been used extensively in computer performance evaluation [16]. When temporal issues of systems are significant, discrete event modeling and simulation can be considered as the good solution. In this section, we evaluate the cache coherence adapter by using the DEVSim++ simulator [14] that is a discrete event simulator providing a framework for modeling and simulation. The goal of our evaluation work is to determine the optimal values of design parameters like the RAC size and the RAC line size, which make our design be suitable for SMP nodes on Xcent-Net. In general, in terms of performance and implementation, cache size and cache line size are crucial design parameters in cache design. In addition, the data access latency and bandwidth are used as the most important performance metrics for network-based systems. We establish the model and simulate it under the system configuration with eight nodes. It can be assumed that the probabilistic distribution of query generation interval is approximately exponential [17].

Fig. 5 shows the average data access latency versus the RAC size for four RAC line sizes given. If the RAC line size is less than or equal to 64 bytes, the average latency increases slowly as the RAC size increases. Note here that the L2 cache of the processor is 512-Kbyte write-back cache with 32-byte lines. On the other hand, if the RAC line size is grater than or equal to 128 bytes, the average latency decreases slowly as the RAC size increases. In case of the RAC line size of 256 bytes that is not shown in Fig. 5, the latency is hundreds of microseconds and decreases slowly as the RAC size increases.

Fig. 6 shows the average data access latency versus the RAC line size for four RAC sizes given. In case of the RAC size of 128 Mbytes, Fig. 6 reveals a minimum latency when the RAC line size is 64 bytes. If the RAC size is 512 Mbytes, the minimum latency is shown when the RAC line size is 128 bytes. That is, the RAC line size with minimal latency varies along with the RAC size as observed in Fig. 6. Note that when the RAC line size is 256 bytes, the average latency is hundreds of microseconds.

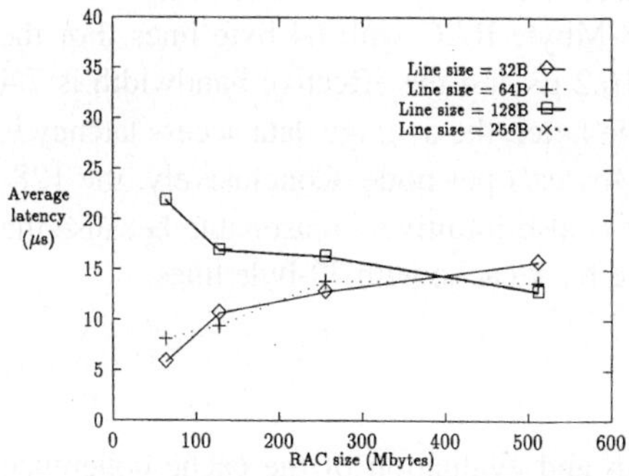

Fig. 5. Average latency versus RAC size.

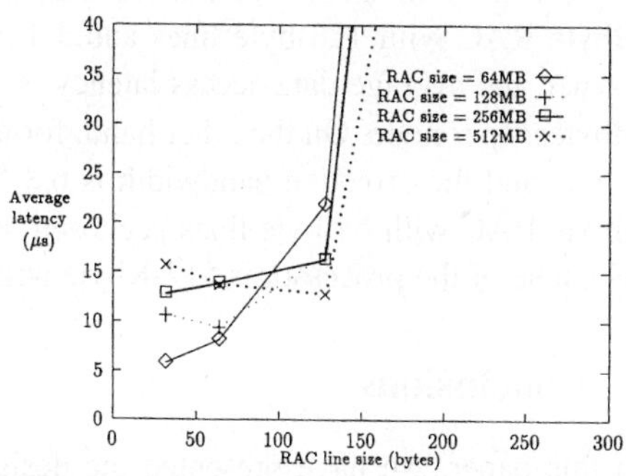

Fig. 6. Average latency versus RAC line size.

Fig. 7 shows the effective node bandwidth versus the RAC size for four RAC line sizes. If the RAC line size is less than or equal to 64 bytes, the effective bandwidth per node decreases as the RAC size increases. On the other hand, if the RAC line size is grater than or equal to 128 bytes, the effective bandwidth per node increases as the RAC size increases. In case of the RAC line size of 256 bytes, the effective bandwidth per node is much smaller compared to the others. This is due to the side effect of a long RAC line, which includes long fetch delay, degree of locality, and false sharing. According to the trend revealed in Fig. 7, the bandwidth deviation between two RAC sizes of 128 and 256 Mbytes is relatively small compared to the others.

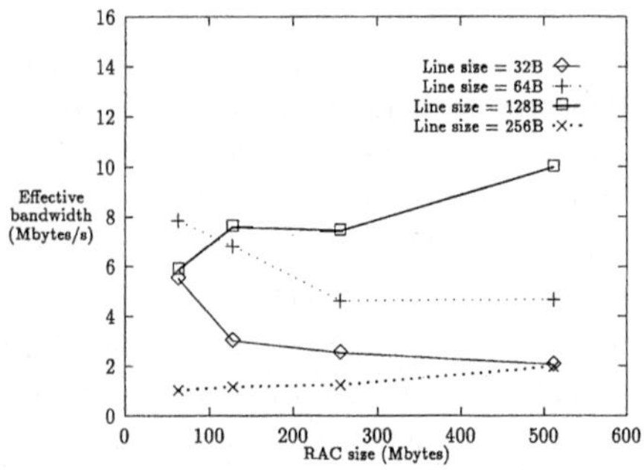

Fig. 7. Node bandwidth versus RAC size.

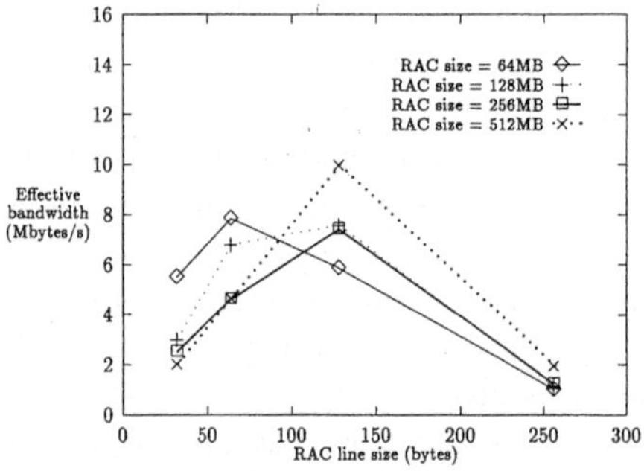

Fig. 8. Node bandwidth versus RAC line size.

Fig. 8 shows the effective node bandwidth versus the RAC line size for four RAC sizes selected. For all cases of the RAC sizes from 64 to 512 Mbytes, either 64- or 128-byte line is the best choice in terms of effective node bandwidth. That is, the effective bandwidth per node is maximized when the RAC line size is either 64 or 128 bytes. In particular, when the RAC line size is 128 bytes, the maximum effective bandwidth is accomplished for three RAC sizes of 128, 256 and 512 Mbytes. Only for the RAC size of 64 Mbytes, the maximum effective bandwidth per node is shown when the RAC line size is 64 bytes. In case of the RAC line size of 256 bytes, the effective bandwidth per node is much smaller compared to the others because of the unavoidable side effect as shown in Fig. 7.

According to the simulation results, there are two possible candidates: a 256-Mbyte RAC with 128-byte lines and a 128-Mbyte RAC with 64-byte lines. For the former, the average data access latency is 16.2 μs and the effective bandwidth is 7.4 Mbytes/s per node. On the other hand, for the latter, the average data access latency is 9.4 μs and the effective bandwidth is 6.8 Mbytes/s per node. Conclusively, the 128-Mbyte RAC with 64-byte lines is chosen. It is also intuitively reasonable because the L2 cache of the processor is 512-Kbyte write-back cache with 32-byte lines.

4 Conclusions

In this paper, we have presented the design and evaluation of the cache coherence adapter for the SMP-based CC-NUMA multiprocessor system on Xcent-Net. The cache coherence adapter consists of the directory and the remote access cache to support the directory-based internode cache coherence protocol which has been also newly designed in this paper. In order to determine the RAC size and the RAC line size, we have evaluated the cache coherence adapter in terms of data access performance by using the DEVSim++ simulator. Due to the simulation results, the 128-Mbyte remote access cache with 64-byte lines is the best choice. For the choice, the average data access latency is 9.4 μs and the effective bandwidth is 6.8 Mbytes/s per node.

References

1. Hwang, K.: Advanced Computer Architecture: Parallelism, Scalability, Programmability. McGraq-Hill, Inc., New York (1993) 3–32
2. Protic, J., Tomasevic, M., Milutinovic, V.: An Overview of Distributed Shared Memory. In: Protic, J., Tomasevic, M., Milutinovic, V. (eds.): Distributed Shared Memory: Concepts and Systems. IEEE Computer Society Press, Los Alamitos, California (1998) 12–41
3. Lilja, D. J.: Cache Coherence in Large-Scale Shared-Memory Multiprocessors: Issues and Comparisons. ACM Computing Surveys, Vol. 25 (1993) 303–338
4. Tomasevic, M., Milutinovic, V.: Hardware Solutions for Cache Coherence in Shared-Memory Multiprocessor Systems. In: Tomasevic, M., Milutinovic, V. (eds.): The Cache Coherence Problem in Shared-Memory Multiprocessors: Hardware Solutions. IEEE Computer Society Press, Los Alamitos, California (1993) 57–67
5. Field, A. J., Harrison, P.G.: A Fixed-Point Model of a Distributed Consistency Protocol. In: Baccelli, F., Jean-Marie, A., Mitrani, I. (eds.): Quantitative Methods in Parallel Systems. Springer-Verlag, Distributed Shared Memory: Concepts and Systems. IEEE Computer Society Press (1995) 237–247
6. Agarwal, A., Simoni, R., Hennessy, J., Horowitz, M.: An Evaluation of Directory Schemes for Cache Coherence. Proc. 15th Int. Symp. on Computer Architecture (1988) 280–289
7. Chaiken, D., Fields, C., Kurihara, K., Agarwal, A.: Directory-Based Cache Coherence in Large-Scale Multiprocessors. IEEE Computer, Vol. 23 (1990) 49–58
8. Intel Corporation, Intel Server Products, http://developer.intel.com/design/servers/buildingblocks/ (2003)
9. Lenoski, D., Laudon, J., Gharachorloo, K., Gupta, A., Hennessy, J.: The Directory-Based Cache Coherence Protocol for the DASH Multiprocessor. Proc. of 17th Int. Symp. on Computer Architecture (1990) 148–159
10. Lenoski D., Weber, W.-D.: Scalable Shared-Memory Multiprocessing. Morgan Kaufmann Publishers, San Francisco, California (1995) 173–203
11. Lovett T., Clapp, R.: STiNG: A CC-NUMA Computer System for the Commercial Marketplace. Proc. of 23th Int. Symp. on Computer Architecture (1996) 308–317
12. Laudon J., Lenoski, D.: The SGI Origin: A ccNUMA Highly Scalable Server. Proc. of 24th Int. Symp. on Computer Architecture (1997) 241–251
13. Park, K., Han, J.-S., Sim, W.-S., Hahn, W.-J.: Xcent-Net: A Hierarchical Crossbar Network for a Cluster-Based Parallel Architecture. Proc. of 8th Int. Conf. on Parallel and Distributed Computing and Systems (1996) 139–141
14. Kim, T. G.: DEVSim++ User's Manual. Ver. 1.0, Computer Engineering Research Lab., KAIST (1994)
15. Intel Corporation, The Intel Xeon Processor Family, http://developer.intel.com/design/Xeon/ (2003)
16. Heidelberger, P., Lavenberg, S. S.: Computer Performance Evaluation Methodology. IEEE Trans. on Computers, Vol. 33 (1984) 1195–1220
17. Allen, A. O.: Probability, Statistics, and Queueing Theory with Computer Science Applications. 2nd Ed., Academic Press (1990)

Low Cost Coherence Protocol for DSM Systems with Processor Consistency[1]

Jerzy Brzeziński and Michał Szychowiak

Institute of Computing Science
Poznań University of Technology
Piotrowo 3a, 60-965 Poznań, POLAND
phone: +48 61 665 28 09, fax: +48 61 877 15 25

{Jerzy.Brzezinski,Michal.Szychowiak}@cs.put.poznan.pl

Abstract. Modern Distributed Shared Memory (DSM) systems offer high speed application processing by allowing to use relaxed consistency models, such as *processor consistency*. Unfortunately, most of the existing coherence protocols implementing relaxed consistency in multiprocessors or loosely couples clusters use *write-update* strategy which incurs large communication overhead, and therefore is impractical for most distributed applications. This paper presents a new *home-based* coherence protocol for DSM systems with processor consistency. The protocol uses *local invalidation* paradigm introducing little overhead. No additional invalidation messages are required; all coherence information is piggybacked to update messages.

1 Introduction

Distributed Shared Memory (DSM) is a virtual memory space available for distributed processes interacting by sharing common objects maintained by the DSM system. One of the most important issues in designing DSM systems is efficiency. In practice a replication mechanism is used to increase the efficiency of the DSM object access by allowing several processes to concurrently access local replicas of the shared object. However, concurrent existence of several replicas of the same shared object requires consistency management. The coherence protocol synchronizes each access to replicas accordingly to the DSM consistency criterion. There are several DSM consistency models with different properties proposed in the literature atomic [8], sequential [14], causal [1], PRAM [11], processor [2] and release consistency [3], among others. Some of the consistency models provide stronger guarantees about synchronization of replica values than other models. On the other hand, the more relaxed the consistency, the more concurrency for shared object access is allowed, resulting in better efficiency of the DSM system.A simple strategy for implementing coherency protocols is to use *write-update* schema, which ensures propagation of every modification of a given object to all its replicas ([1], [4], [5], [11], [12], [15]). The exact protocols differ in the scope of the replication, or in use of communication paradigms (as *write-broadcast* [1]). However, the write-update strategy turns to be very message intensive

[1] This work has been partially supported by the State Committee for Scientific Research grant no. 7T11C 036 21

A. Yazici and C. Şener (Eds.): ISCIS 2003, LNCS 2869, pp. 916–925, 2003.

and therefore impractical for many applications, especially in object-based DSM systems, where the read-to-write ratio is typically low. Moreover, as the goal of proposing relaxed consistency models was to increase the performance of DSM systems, the implementation of the coherence protocol should not incur large overhead. This motivates investigations for new coherency protocols implementing relaxed consistency models DSM with reduced overhead.

An alternative to the write-update strategy is the *write-invalidate* one. In this approach, a write operation on a replica of a given object is required to eventually mark other available replicas of this object as outdated (*invalid*). The actual update is only performed on demand of read access to an invalidated replica (read miss). After the invalidation several subsequent writes can be performed without the need for any communication. As the invalidation-based coherence protocols incur lower overhead of the write operation, they are a better solution for implementation of relaxed consistency models.

This paper presents a new coherence protocol for the processor consistency model, PCG ([2],[6]). PCG is probably the most relaxed consistency model allowing full transparency of the coherence operation from the point of view of the application process, and still useful for solving several classes of computational problems (see [9] as an example). To the best of our knowledge this is the first invalidation-based coherence protocol for the processor consistency model, and therefore it fully allows to exploit the efficiency of the model[2]. Moreover, the communication overhead of the proposed protocol is additionally reduced as no explicit invalidation messages are transmitted. Only *local invalidation* operations are performed to maintain the consistency, relying on the information received with update messages. The concept of local invalidation was formerly proposed in [10] to track causal precedence of memory access; however, the invalidation condition proposed there does not apply to processor consistency model. Furthermore, the protocol of [10] results in invalidating more objects than strictly necessary, in contrary to the one proposed here.

This paper is organized as follows. In Section 2 we define the system model. Section 3 details the new coherence protocol. The protocol is proven correct in Section 4. Some concluding remarks are given in Section 5.

2 Basic Definitions

2.1 System Model

The DSM system is a distributed system composed of a finite set P of sequential processes $P_1, P_2, ..., P_n$ that can access a finite set O of shared objects. Each shared object consists of its current state (*object value*) and *object methods* which read and modify the object state. Shared object x is identified by its system-wide unique identifier denoted $x.id$. The current value of x is denoted $x.value$. In this paper we consider only *read-write* objects, i.e. we distinguish two operations on shared objects: read access

[2] An invalidation-based protocol has also been implemented in Dash [6], but the consistency model used there is incomparable to PCG.

and write access. We denote by $r_i(x)v$ that the read operation returns value v of x, and by $w_i(x)v$ that the write operation stores value v to x. Each write access results in a new object value of x.

The replication mechanism is typically used to increase the efficiency of the DSM object access by allowing each process to locally access a replica of the object. However, concurrent access to different replicas of the same shared object requires consistency management. The coherence protocol synchronizes each access to replicas accordingly to the DSM consistency criterion. This protocol performs all communication necessary for the interprocess synchronization via message-passing. In this paper we assume the communication to be reliable, i.e. no message is ever lost or corrupted.

2.2 Processor Consistency

In this work we investigate *processor consistency* (PCG), first proposed by Goodman in [7], and further formalized by Ahamad et al. in [2]. This consistency model is sufficient for several classes of distributed algorithms but requires weaker synchronization than atomic, sequential or causal consistency, thus allowing for more concurrency and efficiency. It guarantees that all processes accessing a set of shared objects will perceive the same order of modifications of each single object, additionally respecting the local order of write operation performed by each process. More formally, PCG execution of access operations respects PRAM consistency ([11]) and cache consistency ([6]), as defined below.

Let *local history* H_i denote the set of all access operations to shared objects issued by P_i, *history* H denote the set of all operations issued by the system ($H = \bigcup_{i=1..n} H_i$), *write history* HW denote the set of all write operations ($HW \subset H$), and finally $H|x$ denote the set of all write operations performed on x ($H|x \subset H$). By $\rightarrow_i$ we denote the local order relation of operations issued by process P_i.

Definition 1 PRAM consistency (Pipelined RAM, [11])

Execution of access operations is *PRAM consistent* if for each P_i there exists a serialization $\mapsto_i$ of the set $H_i \cup HW$ such that:

$$\forall_{o^1, o^2 \in H_i \cup HW} \left(\exists_{j=1..n} \; o^1 \rightarrow_j o^2 \Rightarrow o^1 \mapsto_i o^2 \right)$$

Following from that definition, PRAM consistency preserves the local order of operations of each process. The order of operations issued by different processes may be arbitrary.

Definition 2 Cache consistency (coherence, [6])

Execution of access operations is *cache consistent* if for each P_i there exists a serialization $\mapsto_i$ of the set $H_i \cup HW$ satisfying:

$$\underset{x \in O}{\forall} \; \underset{w^1, w^2 \in HW \cap H|x}{\forall} \left(\underset{i=1..n}{\forall} w^1 \mapsto_i w^2 \vee \underset{i=1..n}{\forall} w^2 \mapsto_i w^1 \right)$$

The above definition requires cache consistency to ensure for each process the same order of operations on every shared object.

Definition 3 Processor consistency (PCG, [2])

Execution of access operations is *processor consistent* if for each P_i there exists a serialization $\mapsto_i$ of the set $H_i \cup HW$ that preserves both PRAM consistency and cache consistency. We shall call this serialization the *processor order*.

3 The Coherence Protocol

Here we propose a brand new coherence protocol, named PCGp. The PCGp protocol uses the *write-invalidate* strategy and ensures that all local reads reflect the processor order of object modifications by invalidating all potentially outdated replicas. If, at any time, process P_i updates object x, it determines all locally stored replicas of objects that could have possibly been modified before x, and denies any further access to them (invalidates), preventing P_i from reading inconsistent values. Any access request issued to an invalidated replica of x results in fetching its up-to-date value from a *master replica* of x. The process holding a master replica of x is called x's *owner* and shall be denoted for simplicity *x.owner*. According to the *home-based* approach, the protocol statically distributes the ownership of shared objects among all processes (*static ownership*), i.e. the *x.owner* is assigned a priori and never changes (alternatively, it is called *home-node* of x). From now on, we shall assume that there is a home-node for each object x, and the identity of *x.owner* is known.

The PCGp protocol introduces 3 different states of an object replica: writable (denoted WR), read-only (RO), and invalid (INV). The current state of x shall be denoted *x.state*. Only the master replica can have the WR state, and this state enables the owner to perform instantaneously any write or read access to that replica. Meanwhile, every process is allowed to instantaneously read the value of any local RO replica. However, the write access to any RO replica requires additional coherence operations. Meanwhile, the INV state indicates that the object is not available locally for any access. Thus, an access to the INV replica requires the coherence protocol to fetch the value of the master replica of the accessed object and update the local replica.

Each process P_i manages a vector clock VT_i. A vector clock is a well-known mechanism used to track the dependency of events in distributed systems [13]. Here it is intended to track the local precedence of write operations performed by distinct processes. The i-th component of the VT_i increases with each write access performed by P_i. Moreover, replica x has been assigned a scalar timestamp denoted by *x.ts*. This timestamp is used to reflect the modification time of the local replica of x, and is updated on each write operation performed to that replica. In order to keep the master replica up-to-date, the home-node (*x.owner*) collects modifications performed by other processes, however such writes do not increase *x.ts*.

There are four basic procedures invoked by the protocol at P_i:

- $inc_i(VT_i)$ – increments $VT_i[i]$;
- $local\_invalidate_i(X)$ – invalidates all replicas with identifiers belonging to the set X, i.e. for all x:: $x.id \in X$ performs: $x.state$:=INV and $x.ts := VT_i[i]$;
- $owned\_by_i(j) := \{\ x.id :: x.owner = j\ \}$ – returns the set of identifiers of object replicas locally available at P_i owned by a given process P_j;
- $modified\_since_i(t) := \{\ x.id :: x.ts > t\ \}$ – returns the set of identifiers of object replicas at P_i having modification timestamps newer than given t; during communication with some process P_j this procedure is used to detect objects possibly overwritten or invalidated recently by P_i – in fact, P_j can be interested only in modifications of objects not owned by itself, since the master replicas are always kept up-to-date, therefore P_i will actually use another set:$outdated_i(t, j) := modified\_since_i(t) \setminus owned\_by_i(j)$.

Actually, each process P_i manages two vector clocks: VT_i – which j-th value reflects the number of modifications performed by P_j and known to P_i (P_i will use this value to ask P_j for more recent modifications); and $VTsent_i$ – which j-th value reflects the number of modifications performed by P_i which has already been communicated to P_j (P_i will use this value to remember the latest modification P_j can be aware of).

Actions of the PCGp protocol are formally presented in Fig. 1 and can be described by the following rules:

Rule 1) If process P_i wants to access object x available locally (i.e. in any other state than INV) for reading, the read operation is performed instantaneously.

Rule 2) If P_i wants to access a WR replica of x for writing, the write operation is performed instantaneously.

Rule 3) If P_i wishes to gain a read access to object x unavailable locally ($x.state$=INV), i.e. a *read-fault* occurs, the protocol sends request message REQ(i, $x.id$, $VT_i[x.owner]$) to $x.owner$, say P_k. The owner sends back update message R_UPD(x, $VT_k[k]$, INVset), where INVset contains identifiers of objects modified by P_k since $VT_i[k]$ (which was received in REQ), and possibly not yet updated by P_i (excluding objects owned by P_i and the requested x, as x is going to be updated on receipt of the R_UPD message) i.e.: INVset:=$outdated_k(VT_i[k],i)\setminus\{x.id\}$. On receipt of R_UPD, first $local\_invalidate_i$(INVset) is processed. A local replica of x is created with the value received in R_UPD and state set to RO. Finally, the requested read operation is performed.

Rule 4) If P_i wishes to perform a write access to a replica of x in either INV or RO state (i.e. a *write-fault* occurs), the protocol issues a write request W_UPD(i, x, $VT_i[i]$, INVset) to $x.owner$ – P_k. The INVset contains identifiers of objects modified by P_i since the previous update sent to P_k, i.e. INVset := $outdated_i(VTsent_i[k], k)$. On this request, P_k performs $local\_invalidate_k$(INVset) and sends back to P_i an acknowledgment message ACK(t), where t is the current timestamp of the master replica of x. Then, $w_i(x)v$ is performed and P_i's clock is advanced with $inc(VT_i)$. The local replica of x at P_i is timestamped with t.

```
on ri(x)v :                   if  x.state = INV
                                  send REQ(i,x.id,VTi[x.owner]) to x.owner
                                  wait for R_UPD(x,t,INVset)
                                  local_invalidatei(INVset)
                                  VTi[x.owner] := t
                                  x.state:=RO
                              return x.value

on wi(x)v :                   inc(VTi)
                              x.value := v
                              if  x.state ≠ WR
                                  INVset := outdatedi(VTsenti[x.owner],x.owner)
                                  send W_UPD(i,x,VTi[i],INVset) to x.owner
                                  wait for ACK(t)
                                  x.ts := t
                                  VTsenti[x.owner] := VTi[i]
                              else
                                  x.ts := VTi[i]

on REQ(j,x,t) :               INVset := outdatedi(t,j)\{x.id}
                              send R_UPD(x, VTi[i],INVset) to j
                              VTsenti[j] := VTi[i]

on W_UPD(j,x,t,INVset) :      inc(VTi)
                              local_invalidatei(INVset)
                              VTi[j] := t
                              find y such that y.id=x.id
                                  y.value := x.value
                              send ACK(y.ts) to j
```

Fig. 1. PCGp protocol operations

Fig. 2 presents a sample execution of the coherence protocol operations in a system of 3 processes P_1, P_2 and P_3 sharing 2 different objects x, y, both owned by P_2. P_2 initializes the values of x and y to 0 with $w_2(x)0$ and $w_2(y)0$ operations, resulting in two subsequent $inc(VT_2)$. Note that the value of VT_2 is shown on the Figure below the two write operations. After that, a read request from P_1 arrives at P_2. At this moment, P_2 determines the set $oudated_2(VT_2[1]{=}0) = modified\_since_2(0)\backslash\varnothing$ returning $\{x.id, y.id\}$, and responds with R_UPD(y, $VT_2[2]{=}2$, INVset=$\{x.id\}$). The id of y is not included in the INVset because y is being updated. On receipt of that message, P_1 invalidates x and updates the sender position of its own vector clock $VT_1[2]$ to 2. That value is be used to compose the next request message to P_2. In the sample execution, P_2 also receives W_UPD(y, $VT_3[3]{=}0$, INVset=$\varnothing$) from P_3. This message causes the update of *y.value* and $VT_2[3]$. However, *y.ts* remains unchanged. Finally, two read accesses are invoked on P_1: the first one, $r_1(x)$, is issued to the previously invalidated x, while the second, $r_1(y)$, is performed locally on currently available replica of y. Note that value 0 of y has not been invalidated during the update of x. This is due to the fact that *y.ts* remains equal to 2 at *y.owner*, indicating that the local value of y at P_1 is still processor consistent. It can be easily seen in this example that the processor consistent operation $r_1(y)0$ is not causally consistent (also not sequentially consistent).

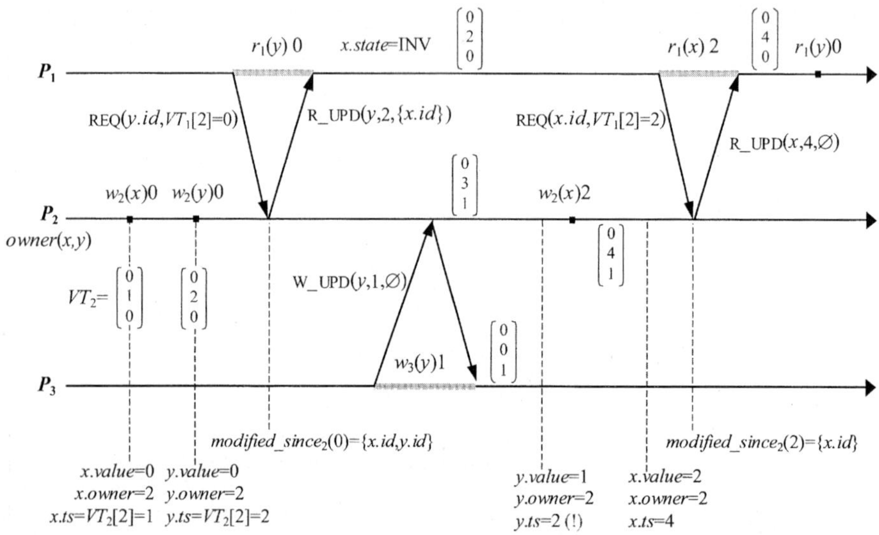

Fig. 2. A sample execution of protocol operations

4 Correctness of the Protocol

We argue that the coherence protocol presented in Section 3 always maintains the shared memory in a state which is processor consistent. To prove this claim we shall show that in any execution of access operations the PCGp protocol serializes the operations in the processor order. First, we remark that in a given execution of PCGp protocol on P_i there is exactly one total ordering $\to_i$ of H_i (as processes are sequential). There can be, however, several serializations $\mapsto_i$ of $H_i \cup HW$ possible.

Definition 4 Legal serialization

Serialization $\mapsto_i$ of $H_i \cup HW$ is legal if it preserves local ordering $\to_i$ ($\to_i \subseteq \mapsto_i$), i.e.:

$$\forall_{o^1, o^2 \in H_i} \quad o^1 \to_i o^2 \Rightarrow o^1 \mapsto_i o^2$$

In the rest of this section, for each $H_i \cup HW$ we choose arbitrarily a serialization that is legal and can be constructed by extending $\to_i$ with results of reception of R_UPD and W_UPD messages processed in a given execution of PCGp. We denote it by $\looparrowright_i$. We show that such serializations preserve both PRAM and cache consistency, i.e. fulfill the processor consistency condition of Definition 3. We start by proving that each $\looparrowright_i$ preserves cache consistency. By $o_i^t(x)$ we denote an operation on x performed by P_i at time t.

Lemma 1 If P_k is the home-node for object x ($x.owner=k$), then:

$$\underset{w^1,w^2\in HW\cap H|x}{\forall}\ \underset{i=1..n}{\forall}\ w^1 \looparrowright_i w^2 \Leftrightarrow w^1 \looparrowright_k w^2$$

Proof. 1) First, let us consider two writes $w^1=w_i(x)a$ and $w^2=w_i(x)b$ issued to x by the same process. The case $i=k$ is trivial, therefore we assume $i\neq k$. In PCGp, every write $w_i(x)$ issued to a non-master replica requires to update the master replica at the home node and every update must be acknowledged before issuing next $w_i(x)$. Therefore, the order of any two write operations in $\looparrowright_k$ agrees with the local order of the issuer, i.e.: $w_i(x)a \rightarrow_i w_i(x)b \Leftrightarrow w_i(x)a \looparrowright_k w_i(x)b$, and from this $w_i(x)a \looparrowright_i w_i(x)b \Leftrightarrow w_i(x)a \looparrowright_k w_i(x)b$.

2) Now, let us consider $w^1=w_j(x)a$, $w^2=w_i(x)b$ and $w_j(x)a \looparrowright_i w_i(x)b$. The result of any $w_j^{t'}(x)v$, for $j\neq i\neq k$, is made visible to P_i in PCGp only by reception of R_UPD during $r_i^{t''}(x)v$, where $t''>t'$, possible only if x was invalidated at P_i before t''. Operation $r_i^{t''}(x)v$ will therefore return a value brought from master replica of x, enforcing ordering which conforms to $\looparrowright_k$.

Yet again, we have $w_j(x)a \looparrowright_i w_i(x)b \Leftrightarrow w_j(x)a \looparrowright_k w_i(x)b$. □

Lemma 2 Serialization $\looparrowright_i$ preserves cache consistency, according to Definition 2.

Proof. Let us consider any $x\in O$, and any two $w^1,w^2\in HW\cap H|x$, and assume $w^1\looparrowright_k w^2$ where $k=x.owner$. From Lemma 1, $\looparrowright_i$ agrees with $\looparrowright_k$, i.e.: $w^1\looparrowright_i w^2$, for any $i=1..n$, and this ensures cache consistency. □

Lemma 3 Serialization $\looparrowright_i$ preserves PRAM consistency, according to Definition 1.

Proof. Let us consider $o^1,o^2\in H_i\cup HW$, where $o^1=o_j(x)b$ and $o^2=o_j(y)c$ such that $o^1\rightarrow_j o^2$. To prove the claim we shall show that $o^1\looparrowright_i o^2$. We consider the following cases:

1) $i=j$: as $\looparrowright_i$ is legal, the claim follows from Definition 4;

2) $x=y$: from Lemma 2, $\looparrowright_i$ preserves cache consistency, thus for all $i=1..n$: $o^1\looparrowright_i o^2$;

3) $i\neq j$ and $x\neq y$: we have $o^1=w_j^{t'}(x)b$ and $o^2=w_j^{t''}(y)c$, where $t'<t''$, as a consequence of $w_j^{t'}(x)b\rightarrow_j w_j^{t''}(y)c$. Let a be the previous value of x read by P_i. We prove the claim by contradiction – we assume that the order of o^1 and o^2 is reversed on P_i, i.e. $w_j^{t'}(x)b\rightarrow_j w_j^{t''}(y)c \wedge w_j^{t''}(y)c \looparrowright_i w_j^{t'}(x)b$. Such inverse order is possible if there exists $r_i^{t^{**}}(x)a$ such that $w_j^{t''}(y)c \looparrowright_i r_i^{t^*}(y)c \rightarrow_i r_i^{t^{**}}(x)a \looparrowright_i w_j^{t'}(x)b$. It follows from $w_j^{t''}(y)c \looparrowright_i r_i^{t^*}(y)c$ that P_i reads value c of y updated by R_UPD message received prior to time t^*. The INVset carried in that message must contain x, as $w_j^{t'}(x)b\rightarrow_j w_j^{t''}(y)c$ (from our assumption). From Rule 3) of the PCGp protocol description, x is invalidated then. Therefore, the first subsequent $r_i(x)$ will cause the PCGp protocol to update x from the master replica of x. Because $w_j^{t'}(x)b$ was performed at time t':: $t'<t''<t^*$, the master replica value at time t^* reflects the $w_j^{t'}(x)b$ (the master replica value can currently be b

or more recent, but not a any more). So, $r_i^{t^*}(y)c \rightarrow_i r_i^{t^{**}}(x)a$ is impossible in PCGp for any $t^{**}>t^*$, and this contradicts the assumption. □

Theorem 1 PCGp implements the processor consistency, according to Definition 3.

Proof. Let $\mapsto_i = \leadsto_i$ for each $i=1..n$. It follows directly from Lemma 2 and Lemma 3 that $\mapsto_i$ preserves processor consistency. The protocol does not provide stronger consistency, neither causal or sequential. The example on Fig. 2 shows operation $r_1(y)0$ performed by the protocol, which is not causally consistent and not sequentially consistent. □

5 Conclusions

The coherence protocol PCGp proposed in this paper is the first invalidation-based protocol for processor consistency PCG. It uses local invalidation paradigm to reduce the overhead of coherence communication, preserving processor consistency at low cost. No invalidation messages are sent, all coherence information is piggybacked to update messages send on read misses.

The presented approach allows further several interesting extensions, concerning reliability issues for instance. Currently, we are designing an extension of the PCGp protocol aimed at providing fault-tolerance of the DSM system in spite of multiple node and link failures. Another open issue is the relaxation of the wait for acknowledgment condition, which may additionally increase the efficiency of the protocol.

References

[1] M. Ahamad, P.W. Hutto and R. John, "Implementing and Programming Causal Distributed Shared Memory", Proc. *11th Int'l Conf. on Distributed Computing*, May 1991, pp. 274–281.

[2] M. Ahamad, R. A. Bazzi, R. John, P. Kohli, and G. Neiger, "The power of processor consistency", Technical Report GIT-CC-92/34, Georgia Institute of Technology, Atlanta, December 1992.

[3] C. Amza, A. L. Cox, S. Dwarkadas, P. Keleher, H. Lu, R. Rajamony, W. Yu and W. Zwaenepoel, "TreadMarks: Shared Memory Computing on Networks of Workstations", *IEEE Computer*, 29(2), February 1996, pp. 18–28.

[4] C. Amza, A. L. Cox, and W. Zwaenepoel, "Data Replication Strategies for Fault Tolerance and Availability on Commodity Clusters", Proc. *Int'l Conf. on Dependable Systems and Networks (DSN2000)*, June 2000.

[5] R. Christodoulopoulou, R. Azimi and A. Bilas, "Dynamic data replication: An approach to providing fault-tolerant shared memory clusters", Proc. *9th IEEE Symposium on High-Performance Computer Architecture (HPCA9)*, February 2003.

[6] K. Gharachorloo, D. Lenoski, J. Laudon, P. Gibbons, A. Gupta and J. Hannessy, "Memory Consistency and Event Ordering in Scalable Shared-Memory Multiprocessors", Proc. *17th Int'l Symposium on Computer Architecture*, May 1990, pp. 15–26.

[7] J. R. Goodman, "Cache consistency and sequential consistency", Technical Report 61, IEEE Scalable Coherent Interface Working Group, March 1989.

[8] M. Herlihy and J. Wing, "Linearizability: A Correctness Condition for Concurrent Object", *ACM Transactions on Programming Languages and Systems*, 12(3), July 1990, pp. 463–492.
[9] L. Higham and J. Kawash, "Bounds for Mutual Exclusion with only Processor Consistency", Proc. *14th Int'l Symposium on Distributed Computing (DISC2000)*, October 2000, LNCS 1914, Springer, pp. 44–58.
[10] R. John and M. Ahamad, "Causal Memory: Implementation, Programming Support and Experiences", Technical Report GITCC-93/10, Georgia Institute of Technology, 1993.
[11] R. J. Lipton and J. S. Sandberg, "PRAM: a Scalable Shared Memory", Technical Report CS-TR-180-88, Princeton University, September 1988.
[12] M. C. Little and S. K. Shrivastava, "Integrating Group Communication with Transactions for Implementing Persistent Replicated Objects", Lecture Notes in Computer Science vol. 1752, 2000, pp. 238–249.
[13] F. Mattern, "Time and Global States of Distributed Systems", Proc. *Int'l Workshop on Parallel and Distributed Algorithms*, 1988.
[14] M. Raynal, "Sequential Consistency as Lazy Linearizability", Technical Report PI-1437, IRISA Rennes, January 2002.
[15] J. S. Sandberg, "Design of PRAM Network", Technical Report CS-TR-254-90, Princeton Univ., April 1990.

Minimizing Communication Cost in Fine-Grain Partitioning of Sparse Matrices*

Bora Uçar and Cevdet Aykanat

Department of Computer Engineering, Bilkent University, 06800, Ankara, Turkey
{ubora,aykanat}@cs.bilkent.edu.tr

Abstract. We show a two-phase approach for minimizing various communication-cost metrics in fine-grain partitioning of sparse matrices for parallel processing. In the first phase, we obtain a partitioning with the existing tools on the matrix to determine computational loads of the processor. In the second phase, we try to minimize the communication-cost metrics. For this purpose, we develop communication-hypergraph and partitioning models. We experimentally evaluate the contributions on a PC cluster.

1 Introduction

Repeated matrix-vector multiplications (SpMxV) $y = Ax$ that involve the same large, sparse, structurally symmetric or nonsymmetric square or rectangular matrix are kernel operations in various iterative solvers. Efficient parallelization of these solvers requires matrix A to be partitioned among the processors in such a way that communication overhead is kept low while maintaining computational load balance. Because of possible dense vector operations, some of these methods require symmetric partitioning on the input and output vectors, i.e, conformal partitioning on x and y. However, quite a few of these methods allow unsymmetric partitionings, i.e., x and y may have different partitionings. The standard graph partitioning model has been widely used for one-dimensional (1D) partitioning of sparse matrices. Recently, Çatalyürek and Aykanat [3,4] and others [9,10,11] demonstrated some flaws and limitations of this model and developed alternatives. As noted in [10], most of the existing models consider minimizing the total communication volume. Depending on the machine architecture and the problem characteristics, communication overhead due to message latency may be a bottleneck as well [8]. Furthermore, maximum communication volume and latency handled by a single processor may also have crucial impacts on the parallel performance. In our previous work [17], we addressed these four communication-cost metrics in 1D partitioning of sparse matrices.

The literature on 2D matrix partitioning is rare. The 2D checkerboard partitioning approaches proposed in [12,15,16] are suitable for dense matrices or sparse matrices with structured nonzero patterns that are difficult to exploit. In

* This work was partially supported by The Scientific and Technical Research Council of Turkey under project EEEAG-199E013

A. Yazici and C. Şener (Eds.): ISCIS 2003, LNCS 2869, pp. 926–933, 2003.

particular, these approaches do not exploit sparsity to reduce the communication volume. Çatalyürek and Aykanat [3,6,7] proposed hypergraph models for 2D *coarse-grain* and *fine-grain* sparse matrix partitionings. In the *coarse-grain* model, a matrix is partitioned in a checkerboard-like style. In the *fine-grain* model, a matrix is partitioned on nonzero basis. The *fine-grain* model is reported to achieve better partitionings than the other models in terms of the total communication volume metric [6]. However, it also generates worse partitionings than the other models in terms of the total number of messages metric [6]. In this work, we adopt our two phase approach [17] to minimize the four communication-cost metrics in the fine-grain partitioning of sparse matrices. We show how to apply our *communication hypergraph model* to obtain unsymmetric partitioning and develop novel models to obtain symmetric partitioning.

2 Preliminaries

A hypergraph $\mathcal{H} = (\mathcal{V}, \mathcal{N})$ is defined as a set of vertices $\mathcal{V}$ and a set of nets. Every net n_i is a subset of vertices. Let d_j denote the number of nets containing a vertex v_j. Weights can be associated with vertices. $\Pi = \{\mathcal{V}_1, \cdots, \mathcal{V}_K\}$ is a K-way vertex partition of $\mathcal{H} = (\mathcal{V}, \mathcal{N})$ if each part $\mathcal{V}_k$ is non-empty, parts are pairwise disjoint, and the union of parts gives $\mathcal{V}$. In Π, a net is said to *connect* a part if it has at least one vertex in that part. *Connectivity* λ_i of a net n_i denotes the number of parts connected by n_i. A net n_j is said to be cut if $\lambda_j > 1$ and uncut otherwise. The set of cut and uncut nets are called external and internal nets, respectively. In Π, the weight of a part is the sum of the weights of the vertices in that part. In the hypergraph partitioning problem, the objective is to minimize the cutsize:

$$cutsize(\Pi) = \sum_{n_i \in \mathcal{N}} (\lambda_i - 1). \tag{1}$$

This objective is referred to as the *connectivity−1 cutsize* metric [14]. The partitioning constraint is to satisfy a balancing constraint on the part weights, i.e.,

$$W_{max} \leq (1 + \epsilon) W_{avg} \tag{2}$$

where W_{max} is the weight of the part with the maximum weight and W_{avg} is the average part weight, and ϵ is an imbalance ratio. This problem is NP-hard [14].

A recent variant of the above problem is called *multi-constraint hypergraph partitioning* [3,7,13]. In this problem, a vertex has a vector of weights. The partitioning objective is the same as above, however, the partitioning constraint is to satisfy a set of balancing constraints, one for each type of the weights.

In the fine-grain hypergraph model of Çatalyürek and Aykanat [6], an $M \times N$ matrix A with Z nonzeros is represented as a hypergraph $\mathcal{H} = (\mathcal{V}, \mathcal{N})$ with $|\mathcal{V}| = Z$ vertices and $|\mathcal{N}| = M + N$ nets for 2D partitioning. There exists one vertex v_{ij} for each nonzero a_{ij}. There exists one net m_i for each row i and one net n_j for each column j. Each row-net m_i and column-net n_j contain all vertices v_{i*} and v_{*j}, respectively. Each vertex v_{ij} corresponds to scalar multiplication $a_{ij} x_j$. Hence, the computational weight associated with a vertex is 1. Each row-net m_i represents the dependency of y_i on the scalar multiplications with a_{i*}'s. Each column-net n_j represents the dependency of scalar multiplications with a_{*j}'s on x_j. With this model, the problem of 2D partitioning a matrix among K processors reduces to the K-way hypergraph partitioning problem. In this model, minimizing the cutsize while maintaining the balance on the part weights corresponds to minimizing the total communication volume and maintaining the balance on the computational loads of the processors. An external column-net represents the communication volume requirement on a x-vector entry. This communication occurs in *expand phase*, just before the scalar multiplications. An external row-net represents the communication volume requirement on a y-vector entry. This communication occurs in *fold phase*, just after the scalar multiplications. Çatalyürek and Aykanat [6] assign the responsibility of expanding x_i and folding y_i to the processor that holds a_{ii} to obtain symmetric partitioning. Note that for the unsymmetric partitioning case, one can assign x_i to any processor holding a nonzero in column i without any additional communication-volume overhead. A similar opportunity exists for y_i. In the symmetric partitioning case, however, x_i and y_i may be assigned to a processor holding nonzeros both in the row and column i. In this work, we try to exploit the freedom in assigning vector elements to address the four communication-cost metrics.

A 10×10 matrix with 37 nonzeros and its 4-way fine-grain partitioning is given in Fig. 1(a). In the figure, the partitioning is given by the processor numbers for each nonzero. The computational load balance is achieved by assigning 9, 10, 9, and 9 nonzeros to processors in order.

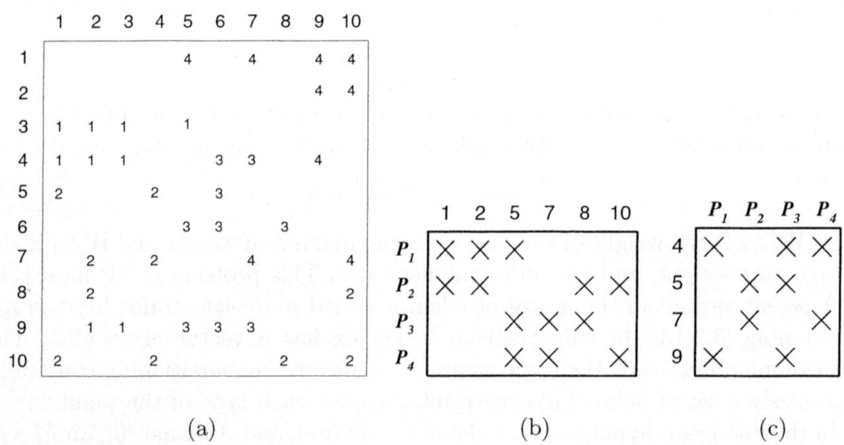

Fig. 1. (a) A 10×10 matrix and a 4-way partitioning, (b) communication matrix C_x, and (c) communication matrix C_y

3 Minimizing the Communication Cost

Given a K-way fine-grain partitioning of a matrix, we identify two sets of rows and columns; *internal and coupling*. The internal rows or columns have nonzeros only in one part. The coupling rows or columns have nonzeros in more than one part. The set of x-vector entries that are associated with the coupling columns, referred to here as x_C, necessitate communication. Similarly, the set of y-vector entries that are associated with the coupling rows, referred to here as y_C, necessitate communication. Note that when symmetric partitioning requirement arises we add to x_C those x-vector entries whose corresponding entries are in y_C and vice versa. The proposed approach considers partitioning of these x_C and y_C vector entries to reduce the total message count and the maximum communication volume per processor. The other vector entries are needed by only one processor and should be assigned to the respective processors to avoid redundant communication. The approach may increase the total volume of communication of the given partitioning by at most $\max\{|x_C|, |y_C|\}$. We propose constructing two matrices C_x and C_y, referred to here as *communication matrices*, that summarize the communication on x- and y-vector entries, respectively. Matrix C_x has K rows and $|x_C|$ columns. For each row k we insert a nonzero in column j if processor P_k has nonzeros in column corresponding to $x_C[j]$ in the fine-grain partitioning. Hence, the rows of C_x correspond to processors in such a way that the nonzeros in the row k identify the subset of x_C-vector entries that are needed by processor P_k. Matrix C_y is constructed similarly. This time we put processors in columns and y_C entries in rows. Figure 1(b) and (c) show communication matrices C_x and C_y for the sample matrix given in (a).

3.1 Unsymmetric Partitioning Model

We use *row-net* and *column-net* hypergraph models for representing C_x and C_y, respectively. In the row-net hypergraph model, matrix C_x is represented as hypergraph $\mathcal{H}_x$ for columnwise partitioning. The vertex and net sets of $\mathcal{H}_x$ correspond to the columns and rows of matrix C_x, respectively. There exist one vertex v_j and one net n_i for each column j and row i, respectively. Net n_i contains the vertices corresponding to the columns which have a nonzero in row i. That is, $v_j \in n_i$ if $C_x[i,j] \neq 0$. In the column-net hypergraph model $\mathcal{H}_y$ of C_y, the vertex and net sets correspond to the rows and columns of the matrix C_y, respectively, with similar construction. Figure 2(a) and (b) show communication hypergraphs $\mathcal{H}_x$ and $\mathcal{H}_y$.

A K-way partition on the vertices of $\mathcal{H}_x$ induces a processor assignment for the expand operations. Similarly, a K-way partition on the vertices of $\mathcal{H}_y$ induces a processor assignment for the fold operations. In unsymmetric partitioning case, these two assignment can be found independently. In [17] we showed how to obtain such independent partitionings in order to minimize the four communication-cost metrics. The results of that work are immediately applicable to this case.

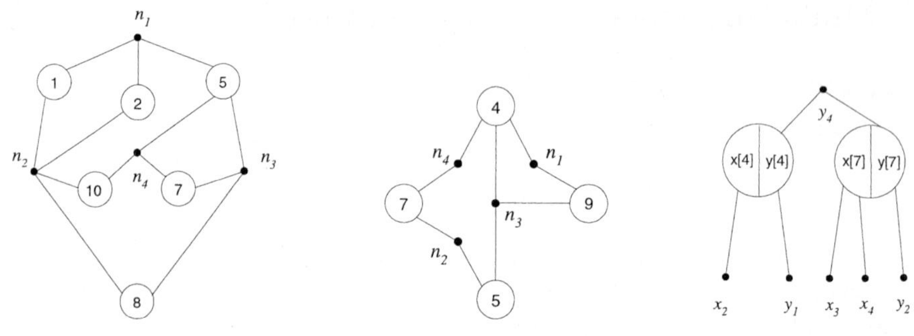

(a) (b) (c)

Fig. 2. Communication hypergraphs: (a) $\mathcal{H}_x$, (b) $\mathcal{H}_y$, and (c) a portion of $\mathcal{H}$

3.2 Symmetric Partitioning Model

When we require symmetric partitioning on vectors x and y, the partitionings on $\mathcal{H}_x$ and $\mathcal{H}_y$ can not be obtained independently. Therefore, we combine hypergraphs $\mathcal{H}_x$ and $\mathcal{H}_y$ into a single hypergraph $\mathcal{H}$ as follows. For each part P_k, we create two nets x_k and y_k. For each $x_C[i]$ and $y_C[i]$ pair, we create a single vertex v_i. For each net x_k, we insert v_i into its vertex list if processor P_k needs $x_C[i]$. For each y_k, we insert v_j into its vertex list if processor P_k contributes to $y_C[j]$. We show vertices v_4 and v_7 of $\mathcal{H}$ in Fig. 2(c). Since communication occurs in two distinct phases, vertices have two weights associated with them. The first weight of a vertex v_i is the communication volume requirement incurred by $x_C[i]$; hence we associate weight $d_i - 1$ with the vertex v_i. The second weight of a vertex v_i is the communication volume requirement incurred by $y_C[i]$; as in [17] we associate a unit weight of 1 with each v_i.

In a K-way partition of $\mathcal{H}$, an x_k-type net connecting λ_{xk} parts necessitates $\lambda_{xk} - 1$ messages to be sent to processor P_k during the expand phase. The sum of these values thus represents the total number of messages sent during the expand phase. Similarly, a y_k-type net connecting λ_{yk} parts necessitates $\lambda_{yk} - 1$ messages to be sent by P_k during the fold phase. The sum of these values represents the total number of messages sent during the fold phase. The sum of the *connectivity* $- 1$ values for all nets thus represents the total number of messages. Therefore, by minimizing the objective function in Eq. 1, partitioning $\mathcal{H}$ minimizes the total number of messages. The vertices in part $\mathcal{V}_k$ represent the x-vector entries to be expanded and the respective y-vector entries to be folded by processor P_k. The load of the expand operations are exactly represented by the first components of the vertex weights if for each $v_i \in \mathcal{V}_k$ we have $v_i \in x_k$. If, however, $v_i \notin x_k$, the weight of a vertex for the expand phase will be one less than the required. We hope these shortages to occur, in some extent, for every processor to cancel the diverse effects on the communication-volume load balance. The weighting scheme for the fold operations is adopted with the rationale that every $y_C[i]$ assigned to a processor P_k will relieve P_k from sending a unit-volume message. If the net sizes are close to each other then this scheme will prove to be a reasonable one. As a result, balancing part sizes for the two set of weights, e.g., satisfying Eq. 2, will relate to balancing the communication-volume loads of processors in the expand and the fold phases, separately. For the minimization of the maximum number of messages per processor metric we do not spend explicit effort. We merely rely on its loose correlation with the total number of messages metric.

In the above discussion, each net is associated with a certain part and hence a processor. This association is not defined in the standard hypergraph partitioning problem. We can enforce this association by adding K special vertices, one for each processor P_k, and inserting those vertices to the nets x_k and y_k. Fixing those special vertices to the respective parts and using *partitioning with fixed vertices* feature of hypergraph partitioning tools [1,5] we can obtain the specified partitioning on $\mathcal{H}$. However, existing tools do not handle fixed vertices within multi-constraint framework. Therefore, instead of obtaining balance on the communication-volume loads of processors in the expand and the fold phases separately, we add up the weights of vertices and try to obtain balance on aggregate communication-volume loads of processors.

4 Experiments

We have conducted experiments on the matrices given in Table 1. In the table, N and NNZ show, respectively, the dimension of the matrix and the number of nonzeros. The `Srl.Time` column lists the timings for serial SpMxV operations in milliseconds. We used PaToH [5] library to obtain 24-way fine-grain partitionings on the test matrices. In all partitioning instances, the computational-load imbalance were below 7 percent. `Part.Mthd` give the partitioning method applied: `PTH` refers to the fine-grain partitioning of Çatalyürek and Aykanat [6], `CHy` refers to partitioning the communication hypergraphs with fixed vertices and aggregate vertex weights. For these two methods, we give timings under column `Part.Time`, in seconds. For each partitioning method, we dissect the communication requirements into the expand and fold phases. For each phase, we give the total communication volume, the maximum communication volume handled by a single processor, the total number of messages, and the maximum number of messages per processor under columns `tV`, `xV`, `tM`, and `xM`, respectively. In order to see whether the improvements achieved by method `CHy` in the given performance metrics hold in practice, we also give timings, the best among 20 runs, for parallel SpMxV operations, in milliseconds, under column `Prll.Time`. All timings are obtained on machines equipped with 400 MHz Intel Pentium II processor and 64 MB RAM running Linux kernel 2.4.14 and Debian GNU/Linux 3.0 distribution. The parallel SpMxV routines are implemented using LAM/MPI 6.5.6 [2]. To compare our method against `PTH`, we opted for obtaining symmetric partitioning. For each matrix, we run `PTH` 20 times starting from different random seeds and selected the partition which gives the minimum in total communication volume metric. Then, we constructed the communication hypergraph with respect to `PTH`'s best partitioning and run `CHy` 20 times, again starting from different random seeds, and selected the partition which gives the minimum in total number of messages metric. Timings for these partitioning methods are for a single run. In all cases, running CHy adds at most half of the time required by PTH to the framework of fine-grain partitioning.

In all of the partitioning instances, CHy reduces the total number of messages to somewhere between 0.47 (*fom12*) and 0.74 (*CO9*) of PTH. In all partitioning instances, CHy increases the total communication volume to somewhere between 1.32 (*creb*) and 1.86 (*pds20*) of PTH. This is expected, because a vertex v_i may be assigned to a part $\mathcal{V}_k$ while P_k does not need any of $x_C[i]$ or $y_C[i]$. However, reductions in parallel running times are seen for all matrices except *lpl1*. The highest speed-up achieved by PTH and CHy is 5.96 and 6.38, respectively, on *fxm3*.

Table 1. Communication patterns and running times for 24-way parallel SpMxV

Matrix	Size		Part.		Expand Phase				Fold Phase				Prll.	Srl.
	N	*NNZ*	Mthd	Time	tV	xV	tM	xM	tV	xV	tM	xM	Time	Time
CO9	10789	249205	PTH	11.43	2477	524	290	21	4889	473	358	22	4.55	12.54
			CHy	0.66	5121	318	223	22	7367	714	259	18	4.05	
creb	9648	398806	PTH	26.71	9344	750	490	23	12660	871	504	23	6.64	19.30
			CHy	2.51	13047	715	313	23	16157	1068	341	20	5.92	
ex3s1	17443	679857	PTH	48.88	7964	602	312	22	26434	1762	356	20	8.39	33.52
			CHy	13.58	19537	1128	195	23	36347	2252	270	16	7.91	
fom12	24284	329068	PTH	22.07	7409	559	228	23	21208	1143	228	13	5.03	19.86
			CHy	13.76	16713	983	96	10	28151	1541	119	8	4.03	
fxm3	41340	765526	PTH	37.73	1843	279	212	23	2662	282	236	17	6.39	38.13
			CHy	0.29	3299	215	142	16	4027	456	156	15	5.97	
lpl1	39951	541217	PTH	27.04	7646	1062	226	20	13752	961	253	17	5.73	29.81
			CHy	5.09	15079	892	166	22	20582	1507	186	12	5.83	
mod2	34774	604910	PTH	32.83	5015	845	267	23	9421	1135	278	22	6.92	30.81
			CHy	2.18	10523	656	181	23	14142	1517	198	17	5.92	
pds20	33874	320196	PTH	18.65	5373	557	299	23	13548	956	317	19	5.23	17.82
			CHy	6.09	14066	794	177	18	21302	1436	201	13	4.95	
pltex	26894	269736	PTH	14.29	1883	172	167	16	7065	508	273	20	4.27	14.64
			CHy	1.11	4533	311	89	16	8828	782	139	10	3.63	
world	34506	582064	PTH	30.84	4934	794	300	23	9710	1295	316	23	7.35	29.63
			CHy	2.50	10679	656	181	23	14854	1745	205	18	6.05	

5 Conclusion and Future Work

We showed a two-phase approach that encapsulates various communication-cost metrics in 2D partitioning of sparse matrices. We developed models to obtain symmetric and unsymmetric partitioning on input and output vectors. We tested performance of the proposed models on practical implementations. In this work, a sophisticated hypergraph partitioning tool that can handle fixed vertices in the context of multi-constraint partitioning was needed. Since the existing tools do not handle this type of partitioning, we are considering to develop such a method.

References

1. Charles J. Alpert, Andrew E. Caldwell, Andrew B. Kahng, and Igor L. Markov. Hypergraph partitioning with fixed vertices. *IEEE Transactions on Computer-Aided Design*, 19(2):267–272, 2000.
2. Greg Burns, Raja Daoud, and James Vaigl. LAM: an open cluster environment for MPI. In John W. Ross, editor, *Proceedings of Supercomputing Symposium '94*, pages 379–386. University of Toronto, 1994.
3. Ü. V. Çatalyürek. *Hypergraph Models for Sparse Matrix Partitioning and Reordering*. PhD thesis, Bilkent Univ., Computer Eng. and Information Sci., Nov 1999.
4. Ü. V. Çatalyürek and C. Aykanat. Hypergraph-partitioning based decomposition for parallel sparse-matrix vector multiplication. *IEEE Transactions on Parallel and Distributed Systems*, 10(7):673–693, 1999.
5. Ü. V. Çatalyürek and C. Aykanat. PaToH: A multilevel hypergraph partitioning tool, ver. 3.0. Tech. Rep. BU-CE-9915, Computer Eng. Dept., Bilkent Univ., 1999.
6. Ü. V. Çatalyürek and Cevdet Aykanat. A fine-grain hypergraph model for 2d decomposition of sparse matrices. In *Proceedings of International Parallel and Distributed Processing Symposium (IPDPS), 8th International Workshop on Solving Irregularly structured Problems in Parallel (Irregular 2001)*, April 2001.
7. Ü. V. Çatalyürek and Cevdet Aykanat. A hypergraph-partitioning approach for coarse-grain decomposition. In *Proceedings of Scientific Computing 2001 (SC2001)*, pages 10–16, Denver, Colorado, November 2001.
8. J. J. Dongarra and T. H. Dunigan. Message-passing performance of various computers. *Concurrency—Practice and Experience*, 9(10):915–926, 1997.
9. B. Hendrickson. Graph partitioning and parallel solvers: has the emperor no clothes? *Lecture Notes in Computer Science*, 1457:218–225, 1998.
10. B. Hendrickson and T. G. Kolda. Graph partitioning models for parallel computing. *Parallel Computing*, 26:1519–1534, 2000.
11. B. Hendrickson and T. G. Kolda. Partitioning rectangular and structurally unsymmetric sparse matrices for parallel processing. *SIAM Journal on Scientific Computing*, 21(6):2048–2072, 2000.
12. B. Hendrickson, R. Leland, and S. Plimpton. An efficient parallel algorithm for matrix-vector multiplication. *Int. J. High Speed Comput.*, 7(1):73–88, 1995.
13. G. Karypis and V. Kumar. Multilevel algorithms for multi-constraint hypergraph partitioning. Tech. Rep. 99-034, University of Minnesota, Dept. Computer Science/Army HPC Research Center, Minneapolis, MN 55455, November 1998.
14. T. Lengauer. *Combinatorial Algorithms for Integrated Circuit Layout*. Wiley–Teubner, Chichester, U.K., 1990.
15. J. G. Lewis, D. G. Payne, and R. A. van de Geijn. Matrix-vector multiplication and conjugate gradient algorithms on distributed memory computers. In *Proceedings of the Scalable High Performance Computing Conference*, 1994.
16. A. T. Ogielski and W. Aiello. Sparse matrix computations on parallel processor arrays. *SIAM Journal on Numerical Analysis*, 1993.
17. Bora Uçar and Cevdet Aykanat. Encapsulating multiple communication-cost metrics in partitioning sparse rectangular matrices for parallel matrix-vector multiplies. *Siam J. Sci. Comput.*, Submitted to, 2002.

Scalability and Robustness of Pull-Based Anti-entropy Distribution Model

Öznur Özkasap

Koç University, Department of Computer Engineering, Istanbul, Turkey
oozkasap@ku.edu.tr

Abstract. There are several alternative mechanisms for disseminating information among a group of participants in a distributed environment. An efficient model is to use epidemic algorithms that involve pair-wise propagation of information. These algorithms are based on the theory of epidemics which studies the spreading of infectious diseases through a population. Epidemic protocols are simple, scale well and robust again common failures, and provide eventual consistency as well. They have been mainly utilized in a large set of applications for resolving inconsistencies in distributed database updates, failure detection, reliable multicasting, network news distribution, scalable system management, and resource discovery. A popular distribution model based on the theory of epidemics is the anti-entropy. In this study, we focus on pull-based anti-entropy model used for multicast reliability as a case study, demonstrate its scalability and robustness, and give our comparative simulation results discussing the performance of the approach on a range of typical scenarios.

Keywords: Epidemic algorithms, pull-based anti-entropy, loss recovery for multicast, Bimodal Multicast.

1 Introduction

There are several alternative mechanisms for disseminating updates/information among a group of participants in a distributed environment. Unicast involves the transmission of a separate message for each participant. Both multicast and broadcast can be effectively used with push mode of dissemination, and both modes would be very efficient if the underlying network supports them. Otherwise, flooding for broadcast or application-level dissemination trees for multicast can be utilized. Another alternative is to use epidemic algorithms that involve pair-wise propagation of updates. Epidemic algorithms are based on the theory of epidemics which studies the spreading of infectious diseases through a population. Epidemic communication mechanisms were first proposed for spreading updates in a replicated database [1]. The aim in this case is to infect all replicas with new updates as fast as possible.

Epidemic protocols are simple, scale well and robust again common failures, and provide eventual consistency as well. They combine benefits of efficiency in hierarchical data dissemination with robustness in flooding protocols. Epidemic communication allows temporary inconsistencies in shared data among participants, in ex-

A. Yazici and C. Şener (Eds.): ISCIS 2003, LNCS 2869, pp. 934–941, 2003.

change for low-overhead implementation. Information changes are spread throughout the participants without incurring the latency and bursty communication that are typical for systems achieving a strong form of consistency. In fact, this is especially important for large systems, where failure is common, communication latency is high and applications may contain hundreds or thousands of participants. Epidemic or gossip style of communication has been used for several purposes. Examples include large-scale direct mail systems [2], group membership tracking [3], support for replicated services [4], deciding when a message can be garbage collected [5], failure detection [6], loss recovery in reliable multicast [7], and distributed information management [8].

A popular distribution model based on the theory of epidemics is the *anti-entropy* [9]. According to the terminology of epidemiology, a site holding information or an update it is willing to share is called *infective*. A site is called *susceptible* if it has not yet received an update. In the anti-entropy process, non-faulty sites are always either susceptible or infective. In this model, a site P picks another site Q at random, and exchanges updates with Q. For exchanging updates, there are three approaches [10]:

- *Push approach*: P only propagates its updates to Q. In this case, updates can be propagated only by infective sites. If many sites are infective, the probability of each one selecting a susceptible site is relatively small. As a result, a particular site may remain susceptible for a long period simply because it is not selected by an infective site. Hence, this property limits the speed of spreading updates.
- *Pull approach*: P only gets new updates from Q. When several sites are infective, this approach works better. In this case, spreading updates is triggered by susceptible sites. It would be highly possible that such a site will contact an infective one to pull in the updates and become infective as well.
- *Push-pull approach*: This is a hybrid of pull and push approaches where P and Q send updates to each other.

One of the fundamental results of epidemic theory shows that simple epidemics eventually infect the entire population. If there is a single infective site at the beginning, updates will eventually be spread across all sites using either form of anti-entropy. Full infection is achieved in expected time proportional to the logarithm of the population size.

In this study, we focus on pull-based anti-entropy model for reliability of multicast communication, and demonstrate its scalability and robustness. We give our comparative simulation results discussing the performance of the model on a range of typical scenarios. Our case study, namely Bimodal Multicast protocol [11], utilizes the model for multicast loss recovery. Periodically, every site chooses another site at random and exchanges information to see any differences and achieve consistency. The information exchanged includes some form of message history of the group members.

The paper is organized as follows. Section 2 describes the concept of multicast loss recovery and our case study of using pull-based anti-entropy for this purpose. Section 3 presents simulation settings, analysis and results of our study. Section 4 summarizes conclusions and discusses future work.

2 Pull-Based Anti-entropy for Multicast Reliability

Loss recovery is an essential part of a multicast service offering reliability. Overall, the key issue is to reduce the number of feedback messages that are returned to the sender. In the *nonhierarchical feedback control* approach [10], a model that has been adopted by several wide-area applications is referred to as *feedback suppression*. A well-known example is SRM protocol [12]. In SRM, when a receiver detects that it missed a message, it multicasts its feedback to the rest of the group. Multicasting feedback allows another group to suppress its own feedback. A receiver lacking a message schedules a feedback with some random delay. There are a number of other alternatives such as *forward error correction* (FEC) as utilized by PGM reliable multicast protocol [13] for ensuring reliability as well. Further discussion on the approaches for loss recovery and scalability in multicasting is given in our prior study [14] where large-scale behavior of epidemic loss recovery is analyzed on network topologies consisting of around thousand nodes.

Our case study for evaluating the behavior of pull-based anti-entropy model, Bimodal Multicast [11], or Pbcast (Probabilistic Multicast) for short, is a novel option in the spectrum of multicast protocols that offers throughput stability, scalability and a bimodal delivery guarantee as the key properties. The protocol is inspired by prior work on epidemic protocols [1], Muse protocol for network news distribution [15], and the lazy transactional replication method of [4]. Bimodal Multicast has been shown to exhibit stable throughput under failure scenarios that are common on real large-scale networks [11]. In contrast, this kind of behavior can cause other reliable multicast protocols to exhibit unstable throughput. Bimodal Multicast consists of two sub-protocols, namely an *optimistic dissemination* protocol, and a *two-phase anti-entropy* protocol.

The former is a best-effort, push mode, hierarchical multicast used to efficiently deliver a multicast message to its destinations. This phase is unreliable and does not attempt to recover a possible message loss. If IP multicast is available in the underlying system, it can be used for this purpose. Otherwise, a randomized dissemination protocol can play this role.

The second stage of the protocol is responsible for message loss recovery. It is based on a pull-based anti-entropy protocol that detects and corrects inconsistencies in a system by continuous gossiping. The two-phase anti-entropy protocol progresses through unsynchronized rounds. In each round:

- Every group member randomly selects another group member and sends a digest of its message history. This is called a *gossip message*.
- The receiving group member compares the digest with its own message history. Then, if it is lacking a message, it requests the message from the gossiping process. This message is called *solicitation*, or *retransmission request*.
- Upon receiving the solicitation, the gossiping process retransmits the requested message to the process sending this request.

Details and the theory behind the anti-entropy protocol are given in [11] for the interested reader.

3 Simulations, Analysis, and Results

We have developed a simulation model for Bimodal Multicast protocol and its pull-based anti-entropy mechanism on ns-2 network simulator [16]. The simulation model consists of three modules: unreliable data dissemination using IP multicast protocol, pull-based anti-entropy protocol, and FIFO message ordering for applications. Details of our implementation are given in [17]. In this section, we first describe the simulation settings, and then discuss results demonstrating the scalability and robustness of the dissemination model.

3.1 Simulation Settings

The simulation scenarios consist of two representative cases, namely transit-stub dense topologies, and clusters connected by a bottleneck link. Transit-stub topologies approximate the structure of the Internet that can be viewed as a collection of interconnected routing domains where each domain can be classified as either a stub or a transit domain. Stub domains correspond to interconnected LANs and the transit domains model WAN or MANs [18]. The first scenario of transit-stub dense topologies is considered for various group sizes where all nodes are members of the multicast group. A certain link noise probability is set on every link that forms a randomized system-wide noise. An example application for this scenario would be a multicast based distance education session in a wide area setting consisting of multiple local campus networks, where one server would multicast the content to most of the nodes in the network. The second case includes scenarios where LANs connected by long distance links and networks where routers with limited bandwidth connect group members. Such configurations are common in today's networks as well. With these in mind, we constructed topologies with fully-connected clusters, and a single link connecting those clusters. All nodes are members of the multicast group where there is one sender located on the first cluster. There is 1% intra-cluster noise formed in both clusters, and a varying high drop rate is injected on the link connecting the clusters which make it to behave as a bottleneck link. We obtain our results from several runs of simulations, each run consisting of a sequence of 35000 multicast data messages transmitted by the sender.

3.2 Loss Recovery Overhead, Scalability, and Robustness for Anti-entropy

We investigate loss recovery overhead distribution of Bimodal Multicast on the scenarios mentioned in the previous section. For the transit-stub dense topologies, message rate of the multicast source is 50 messages per second. Fig.1 shows request messages received by each receiver in the multicast group for group and network sizes of 40 and 120, and system-wide noise rate of 0.01 on all links. It is observed that the load of overhead traffic is balanced over group members, a desirable property that avoids overloading one member or a portion of members with high overhead traffic. Increasing participant size does not have a significant effect on the distribution only causing a negligible increase in the number of requests received by each group re-

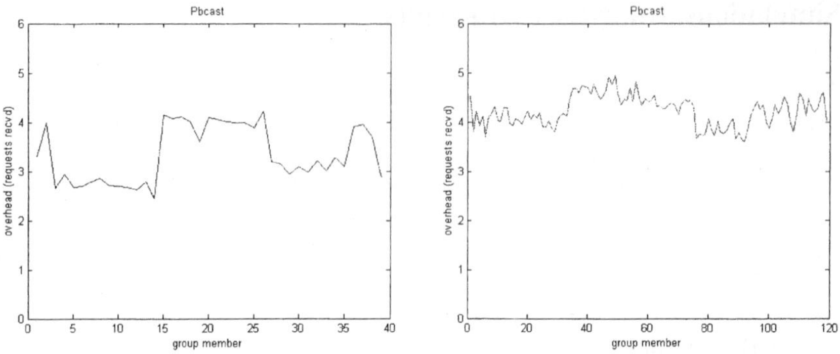

Fig. 1. Request messages received by each group member, Bimodal Multicast, transit-stub dense, noise rate: 0.01

ceiver. Likewise, Fig.2 demonstrates analysis results where system wide-noise rate is increased to 0.1. It is obvious that increasing noise rate by a multiple of 10 on every link would increase the number of message drops experienced on the network. In fact, when compared with Fig.1, overhead does not increase linearly with the noise rate, and on a typical member, the number of overhead messages remains almost constant and even decrease in some cases as group size scales up. Comparative simulation results with nonhierarchical feedback control approach for this scenario are given in section 3.3.

For clustered topologies, message rate of the multicast source is 100 messages per second. Fig.3 shows request messages received by each receiver in the multicast group where group size is 60 and 120 respectively for two different bottleneck noise (25% and 50%). The first half of the group members reside in cluster 1 and the rest in cluster 2. Due to the high bottleneck noise rate, a large percentage of messages get dropped during transmission from cluster 1 to cluster 2. The resultant overhead distribution on group members shows the effect of bottleneck noise where the members in the first cluster take a major part in the loss recovery process. However, the over

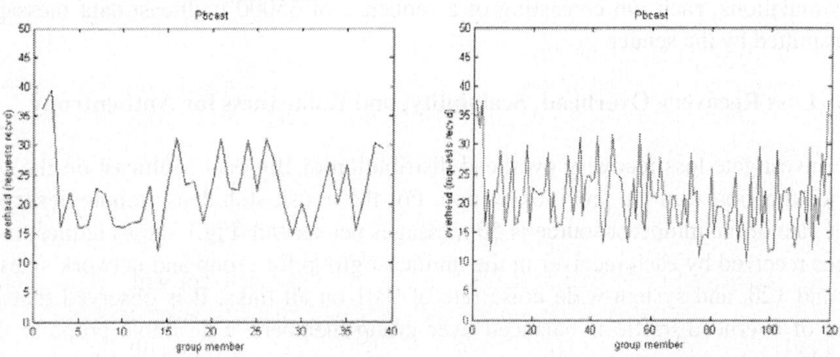

Fig. 2. Request messages received by each group member, Bimodal Multicast, transit-stub dense, noise rate: 0.1

head on group members within clusters is balanced and even decreases as group size doubles from 60 to 120.

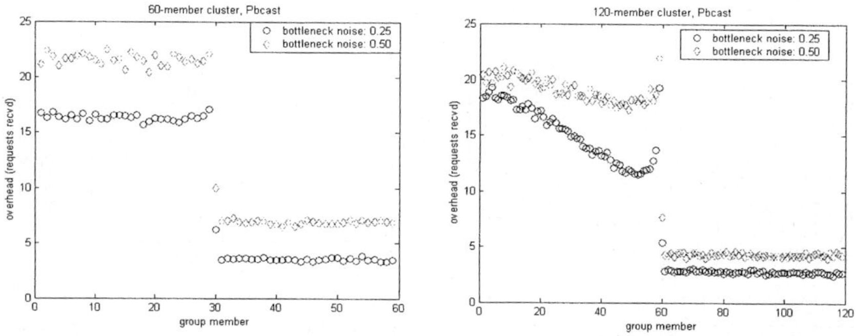

Fig. 3. Request messages received/group member, Bimodal Multicast, clustered networks

We explore the impact of an increase in group size, and randomized noise over network links on transit-stub topologies. Fig.4 shows average loss recovery overhead in the form of requests received and sent on all receivers of the multicast group where system-wide noise rate and group size vary. As group size increases, protocol overheads remain stable. On the other hand, the effect of increasing noise rate by a multiple of 10 (1% to 10%) on all links has been measured. In particular, overhead percentage in the form of request messages received causes a slight increase which is below linear. These two observations indicate the scalability of the pull-based anti-entropy loss recovery as group size and noise rate expand.

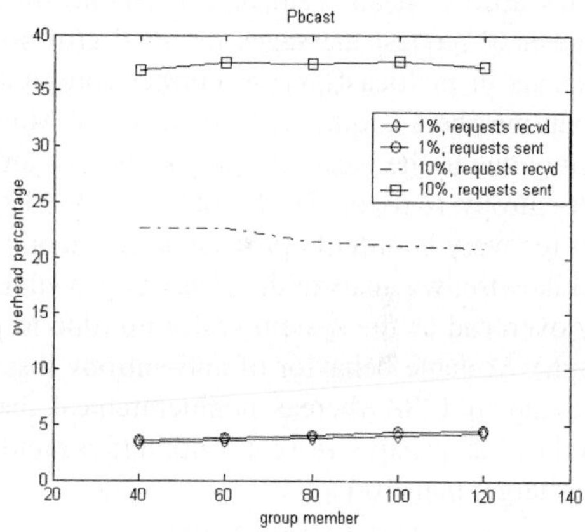

Fig. 4. Overhead percentage vs group size, transit-stub dense

3.3 Comparison with Nonhierarchical Feedback Control

Recent studies [19,20,11] have shown that, for the SRM protocol with its nonhierarchical feedback control mechanism for loss recovery, random packet loss can trigger high rates of overhead messages. In addition, this overhead grows with the size of the system. For examining this effect, and demonstrating the superiority of anti-entropy as a method for multicast loss recovery, we have conducted a set of simulations by using SRM's feedback control model. On transit-stub dense scenarios, comparative analysis results for Bimodal Multicast and SRM are displayed in Fig.5, left and right,

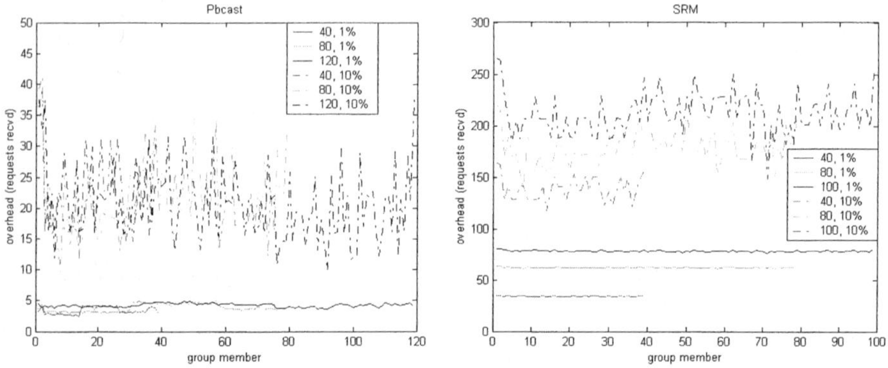

Fig. 5. Overhead for protocols, transit-stub dense: a) Bimodal Multicast, b) SRM.

respectively. For a fixed noise rate on links (either 1% or 10%), when group size scales up, overheads remain very stable for Bimodal Multicast, whereas for SRM number of request messages received grows with an increase of the number of participants in multicast group. Furthermore, number of request messages received by group members is quite low for Bimodal Multicast when compared to SRM. This is mainly due to the pair-wise propagation of information among group members when anti-entropy is used. On the other hand, SRM uses multicast dissemination during loss recovery in order to provide high reliability.

Likewise, we analyze the effect of growth in system-wide noise on the loss recovery overhead as the system scales up (due to page limitation, we do not include this graph). Scalable behavior of anti-entropy loss recovery has been observed for group sizes up to 120, whereas nonhierarchical feedback control reveals increase in the overhead as group size scales up, and a rapid increase has been observed for group sizes larger than 100.

4 Conclusions and Future Work

Anti-entropy distribution model provides eventual data consistency, scalability, and independence from communication topologies. It also transparently handles failures and can work with minimal connectivity. This study yields conclusions on scalability and robustness of pull-based anti-entropy distribution model used for reliable multicasting as a case study. Transit-stub dense topologies, and clusters connected by a bottleneck link are the representative scenarios analyzed. We show that anti-entropy loss recovery produces balanced overhead distribution among group receivers and it is scalable with an increase in group size, multicast message rate and system-wide noise rate. Comparison of the model with nonhierarchical feedback control has been conducted as well. As a further research direction, scalability and robustness of multicast loss recovery would be indispensable for multicast services over wireless networks as well [21]. Wireless multicast applications cover a wide range including mobile commerce, distance education, location-based services, and military command

and control. These applications would especially benefit from multicast communication support with efficient provision of reliability guarantees.

References

1. Demers, A., Greene, D., Hauser, C., Irish, W., Larson, J., Shenker, S., Sturgis, H., Swinehart, D. and Terry, D., Epidemic Algorithms for Replicated Database Maintenance, Proc. of the Sixth ACM Symp. on Principles of Distributed Computing, 1–12p, 1987.
2. Birrell, A.D., Levin, R., Needham, R.M. and Schroeder, M.D., Grapevine, An Exercise in Distributed Computing, Communications of the ACM, 25(4), 260–274p, 1982.
3. Golding, R.A. and Taylor K., Group Membership in the Epidemic Style, Technical Report, UCSC-CRL-92-13, University of California at Santa Cruz, 1992.
4. Ladin, R., Lishov, B., Shrira, L. and Ghemawat, S., Providing Availability using Lazy Replication, ACM Transactions on Computer Systems, 10(4), 360–391p, 1992.
5. Guo, K., Scalable Message Stability Detection Protocols, Ph.D. dissertation, Cornell University Dept. of Computer Science, 1998.
6. van Renesse, R., Minsky, Y. and Hayden, M., A Gossip-style Failure Detection Service, Proceedings of Middleware'98, 55–70p, 1998.
7. Xiao, Z. and Birman, KP., 2001, A Randomized Error Recovery Algorithm for Reliable Multicast, Proceedings, IEEE Infocom 2001.
8. van Renesse, R., Birman, K.P., Vogels, W., Astrolabe: A Robust and Scalable Technology for Distributed System Monitoring, Management, and Data Mining, ACM Transactions on Computer Systems, Vol. 21, No. 2, pp. 164–206, May 2003.
9. Bailey, N.T.J., The Mathematical Theory of Infectious Diseases and its Applications, second edition, Hafner Press, 1975.
10. Tanenbaum, A.S. and van Steen, M., Distributed Systems: Principles and Paradigms, Prentice Hall, ISBN 0-13-088893-1, 2002.
11. Birman, K.P., Hayden, M., Ozkasap, O., Xiao, Z., Budiu, M. and Minsky, Y., Bimodal Multicast, ACM Transactions on Computer Systems, 17(2), 41–88p., May 1999.
12. Floyd, S., Jacobson, V., Liu, C., McCanne, S. and Zhang, L., A Reliable Multicast Framework for Light-weight Sessions and Application Level Framing, IEEE/ACM Transactions on Networking, 5(6), 784–803p., 1997.
13. Gemmell, J., Montgomery, T., Speakman, T., Bhaskar, N., and Crowcroft, J., The PGM Reliable Multicast Protocol, IEEE Network, Jan/Feb 2003.
14. Ozkasap, O., Large-Scale Behavior of End-to-end Epidemic Message Loss Recovery, QofIS2002, Zurich, LNCS, Springer Verlag, Vol.: 2511, pp. 25–35, October 2002.
15. Lidl, K., Osborne, J. and Malcome, J., Drinking from the Firehose: Multicast USENET News, USENIX Winter 1994, 33–45p., 1994.
16. Bajaj, S., Breslau, L., Estrin, D., et al., Improving Simulation for Network Research, USC Computer Science Dept. Technical Report 99–702, 1999.
17. Ozkasap, O., Scalability, Throughput Stability and Efficient Buffering in Reliable Multicast Protocols, Technical Report, TR2000-1827, Dept. Comp. Sci., Cornell University, 2000.
18. Calvert, K., Doar, M., and Zegura, E.W., Modeling Internet Topology. IEEE Communications Magazine, June 1997.
19. Liu, C., Error Recovery in Scalable Reliable Multicast, Ph.D. dissertation, University of Southern California, 1997.
20. Lucas, M., Efficient Data Distribution in Large-Scale Multicast Networks, Ph.D. dissertation, Dept. of Computer Science, University of Virginia, 1998.
21. Varshney, U., Multicast over Wireless Networks, Communications of the ACM, vol.45, no.12, pp.31–37, December 2002.

Extended Partial Path Heuristic for Real-Time Staging in Oversubscribed Networks

Mohammed Eltayeb[1], Atakan Doğan[2], and Füsun Özgüner[1]

[1] Department of Electrical Engineering, The Ohio State University, 2015 Neil Avenue, Columbus, Ohio 43210, USA

{eltayeb, ozguner}@ee.eng.ohio-state.edu

[2] Department of Electrical and Electronics Engineering, Anadolu University, 26470 Eskisehir, Turkey

atdogan@anadolu.edu.tr

Abstract. In this paper we propose the use of the PPH as a base for an offline schedule method to detect unsatisfiable requests in a staging system. This property allows a reduction in the overhead of transferring data-items with deadlines in a real-time environment, through paths rearrangement. The EPP heuristic allows early detection of eventually, non-satisfied, requests based on their urgencies. Early detection and dropping of these requests also reduces the latencies of the satisfied requests. We show analytically and experimentally that the performance of the EPP heuristic is at least equivalent to the previous PPH proposed for data-staging problem in real-time environments.

1 Introduction

In today's world of advanced technology, numerous amounts of scientific distributed applications are emerging as critical part of the community needs. The proliferation of the Internet, the development of wireless and satellite systems and networks, the advent of high performance computing and the advancement in measurements and imaging instrumentations have all created the opportunity for the development of modern distributed services in several fields. These advancements have also created and inspired new approaches to support the transportation, management, access, and analysis of large-scale data objects by potentially large number of end points. The *Data Staging* problem, for example, has gained its importance recently with the emergence of a class of new applications by which relatively large scale blocks of information is to be transferred from one location to another across a network of limited resources in real-time fashion. The data staging problem requires the design of efficient methods and schemes for transferring data blocks or objects to different destinations to mitigate the effect of consumption of network resources in case of scarcity of these resources. The real-time aspects of the distributed applications utilizing a data staging system can further complicate the data staging problem. The challenge, then, becomes meeting requests deadlines in scarce resource environments.

A. Yazici and C. Şener (Eds.): ISCIS 2003, LNCS 2869, pp. 942–951, 2003.

The BADD program [1] is an example of a system that adds real-time constraints to the staging problem. Other applications for the data staging problem with real-time constraints and requirements include bioinformatics [4], distributed weather prediction systems [5], real-time distributed computing [6], etc. The data management problem that was addressed by the BADD program presented a mathematical model for a simplified data staging problem. Static scheduling heuristics were then developed to provide near optimal solutions to a problem that is proven NP-hard.

To the best of our knowledge, the static scheduling method presented in [1] and the accompanied heuristics is the only work in literature that discusses the specifics of this problem. The heuristics proposed for the static scheduling are the *Partial Path Heuristic* (PPH) and the *Full Path Heuristic* (FPH) and are based on a greedy, expensive algorithm (Dijkstra's multiple-source, shortest path algorithm [7].) Both heuristics adopt a strategy by which all data requests are considered simultaneously and the shortest path for each request is found as if the request is the only one present in the system. Conflicting requests are then resolved with the goal of maximizing the weighted sum of the priorities of all potentially satisfiable requests. The PPH attempts to achieve this goal by strictly following a specific cost function throughout the request path for each hop. This can result in a number of inefficient transfers for some requests due to other competing requests. Also, as we shall see later in this paper, PPH may result in many interleaved transfers of several different requests. This case results in increased overhead for the centralized unit, which executes the schedule. The FPH proposed in the same paper resolves this issue at the cost of overall performance as shall be seen.

Our *Extended Partial Path Heuristic* (EPP) combines the PPH and the FPH features and attempts to reduce the transfer overhead (and the algorithm complexity,) yet maintain high performance. The basic idea is to compute an extended path for transferring data objects based on the cost function. The EPP runs an offline schedule for detecting unsatisfiable requests and re-arrange (based on the offline schedule) the steps of transmission to achieve high performance.

2 System Model

When large blocks of data or information in a data staging system are requested by many potential end-points or destinations, the availability of these blocks at or near potential requesting sites in the network is a desired property of the system. These data blocks (also will be interchangeably referred to as data objects in this paper) may be generated or stored at a specific source location(s). Staging the data from a source to a destination, in this case, is defined as moving a data object in its entirety from one point to intermediate points along the path to the final destination. The intermediate points will act like *proxies* for the data object. It is assumed that a staged data-item will remain in the intermediate node until it is delivered to the final destination. The data objects may be kept in the intermediate locations for two main reasons. The first is to provide a level of redundancy for the application. The second reason is to improve the efficiency of the system by allowing scattered potential requests benefit from the current transfer of the data object rather than re-establishing a new transfer for each incoming request.

Our assumptions for the system model are provided as follows: First, a network of machines constituting the data-staging system is modeled as a collection of nodes and edges. Each node (machine) can be a source of data or a destination as well as an intermediate point. The network is assumed irregular and any node can have a different degree of connectivity. The nodes can assume different values of temporary storage capacity (cache) and the edges (links) connecting nodes will also vary in bandwidth. A *request* r_i is the instance by which a specific data object (sometimes referred to as *data-item* I_i) is to be acquired by a specific destination or end-node. The *destination* D_i of the request r_i is typically a machine by which the requested data-item is processed. There could be one or more destinations for a specific data-item. The *source* S_i of a request is the node or machine in the network by which the data-item is stored or generated. It is also possible to have many such points for the data-item. As a result, several requests for a particular data-item, which is stored at a specific node, may result. These requests will be transferred to different destinations and may be obtained from different sources. We will assume an abstract by which requests arrive at a centralized scheduler. Destination nodes and source nodes can both initiate requests. We will assume a destination-based initiation. Hence, request r_i is defined with the following tuple: (D_i, I_i, d_i, P_i), where, d_i is the deadline associated with the request and P_i is its priority. To the schedulers, a request is mainly composed of source(s), a destination, a data-time, a deadline and a priority. We assume that all sources of a particular data-item are known to the scheduler (i.e., data-item's storage locations or generation tasks are already mapped to machines in the network.) The data-item sizes are known and assumed to be considerably large. The deadline of the request represents the vitality of the data-item to the destination or its usefulness in case of real-time applications. This value indicates the time by which the data-item associated with the request must reach its destination. Normally, the request initiator assigns deadlines. Finally, each request r_i can have a priority value P_i based on the priority assigned to request initiator. A more detailed description of the system model can be found in [1].

Since our transmission scheme is assumed to be a staging scheme by which the data-time is transferred to intermediate machines along the path until final destination, the scheduler must implement an efficient algorithm to manage transfers of data-item to destination based on the requests' individual urgencies and priorities. Also the algorithm should be able to provide a way to maximize the number of deadlines met by data-transfers in case of contention for resources along the assigned paths.

3 Overview of PPH and FPH

The PPH and FPH heuristics proposed in [1] are built around the greedy expensive Dijkstra's multiple-source shortest path algorithm. First, the Dijkstra's algorithm discovers a shortest path from a set of source nodes to a specific destination node for each request. Then the *cost* for transferring each request is determined. The cost is a function that basically incorporates the priority and the urgency of the request as its deadline approaches. Once the cost of each request is determined, the scheduling algorithm schedules the request with the "minimum cost" and allows the transfer from its source location to the next (intermediate) node along the path. For the partial path heuristic (PPH), Dijkstra's algorithm is repeatedly invoked after each data-transfer. This is basically to find alternative paths for the requests and is necessary because each transfer of a data-item results in resource consumption at the intermediate node. The PPH is composed of the following steps for each iteration: (1) For a given set of requests, repeat steps from 2 to 5 until all requests are serviced, (2) Run Dijkstra's multiple-source shortest path algorithm to compute a shortest path for each request, (3) For all eligible requests, compute the value of a cost function, (4) Pick up the request with minimum cost and transfer to next node on the path, (5) Update the system parameters.

The PPH attempts to maximize the number (or the weight) of requests that are completely serviced by delivering the data-item to its destination before the deadline. A request in this case is said to be *satisfied.* The PPH computes the cost value of all requests at each schedule step[1]. The PPH is greedy in the sense that the least cost request will always be selected first for the transmission. Hence and due the fact that other requests will also compete for transmission as their deadlines approach, it is possible that another request gets selected next (because of attaining the minimum cost.) This will result in transferring the newly selected request rather than the initial request, which was scheduled prior to this new request. Because of that, it is possible for a request be deemed unsatisfiable even after it is been transferred for many hops. The FPH was proposed to avoid the scenario in which an initially satisfiable minimum-cost request is dropped after several data transfer steps. In the FPH an initially selected request will be scheduled for a transfer for the entire path length, rather than just one hop as in PPH. This will ensure its satisfiability. Other requests will not be served until this request is delivered to its final destination. We can realize here that, although initially selected requests will be satisfied, it is also possible that many other requests miss their deadlines. This is due to the increase of the requests' urgencies as time passes. This will be shown later in our mathematical analysis.

4 The Extended Partial Path

In this section, we present the EPP heuristic. Fig. 1 shows the main functions of the EPP. In step 1, the function "Compute_offline_schedule()" is a call to the PPH with the following two assumptions: one, the system has infinite resources so repetitive calls of Dijkstra's algorithm is not needed as in PPH. Two, the urgencies of the requests are used as the cost values. This assumption aims towards detecting the satisfiability of the request in an environment that favors requests based on their deadlines. The execution of function Compute_offline_schedule() returns all unsatisfiable requests that will be excluded from the schedule via a call to Drop_non_satisfiables(), which is step 2 in EPP. The heuristic then iterates the following steps: step 3 is to check the existence of pending requests. Steps 4 and 5 compute the cost of all existing requests and extract the minimum cost request via calls to Compute_cost_function() and Find_next_cost(), respectively. The result of

---

[1] Schedule step assigns a resource to a given request at a given time. It is formally defined later in the paper.

```
1. Compute_offline_schedule();
2. Drop_non_satisfiables();
3. While (requests_exist) {
4.   Compute_cost_function();
5.   Find_next_cost();
6.   Construc_extended_path(next_to_min);
7.   Transfer_on_extended_path();
8.   Call_Dijkstra(); }
```

Fig. 1. Details of the EPP heuristic. The PPH implemented is in the function Compute_offline_schedule() which calls the Dijkstra's algorithm only once.

those two calls is a value "next_to_min" which is the cost value next to the minimum cost. Step 6 of the heuristic uses this value to construct the extension of the path. The extended path is the path that is composed of the next hops of a length equal to or less than next_to_min. Step 7 transfers the data-time along the constructed extension and updates the system parameters including new storage capacities. In step 8, Dijkstra's algorithm is called based on the newly updated parameters to find alternative paths.

It is worthwhile to emphasize that the EPP heuristic runs the Dijkstra's algorithm to find the shortest paths for the requests only at the beginning of each extension (rather than at every hop). In addition, EPP runs PPH with aforementioned assumptions to discover and exclude requests that cannot be satisfied, thus giving more chances to the actually satisfiable requests.

The EPP heuristic is based on the fact that rearranging data-transfers to produce extended step (i.e., one with many hops instead of only one hop as in PPH) will not only reduce transmission overhead for the centralized scheduling unit but also create fewer transmission phases or steps for a request. We will show later that under some assumptions the re-arrangements and collection of transmission steps for requests in the EPP heuristic will not impair the general performance relative to the PPH, which is based on strictly scheduling according to the cost function.

Fig. 2 shows an example of a request system for an offline schedule generation for four requests r_1, r_2, r_3, and r_4. For the purpose of simplifying, we assume equal priorities for requests and adopt a cost function that represents the cost of a request as the urgency of the request (the difference between the deadline and the length of the remaining path). In this example, the length of the path between any two nodes is assumed to be one time unit. In addition, the initial deadlines for the given requests are respectively: 15, 20, 35, and 10 units, and the initial paths are 10, 11, 11, and 3 units. As we can see from Fig. 2 that request r_2 is not satisfied even with the partial path scheduling. Furthermore, we can realize that if we exclude the "falling" request r_2 we can schedule request r_1 for 7 consecutive stages (i.e., 7 hops) before scheduling another request. The reduction is not only on the times Dijkstra's algorithm is run but also the overhead on the schedule in re-establishing transmission phases between different requests, in addition the network overhead.

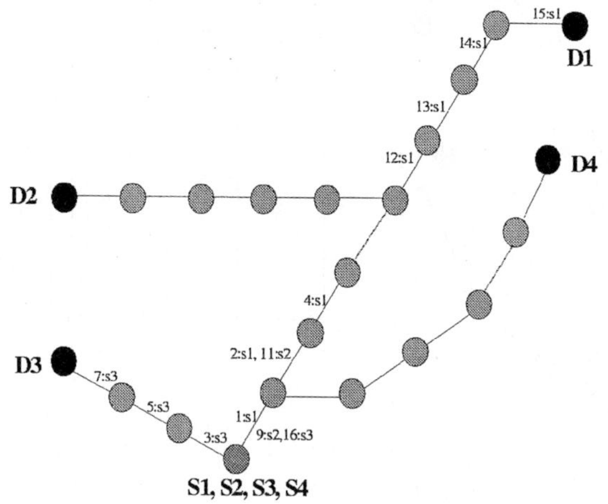

Step	Urgency			
	r_1	r_2	r_3	r_4
1	5	9	24	7
2	5	8	23	6
3	5	7	22	5
4	4	6	21	5
5	4	5	20	4
6	3	4	19	4
7	3	3	18	3
8	2	2	17	3
9	2	1	16	-
10	1	1	15	-
11	1	0	14	-
	0	0	13	-
	0	-1	12	-
	↓		↓	

Fig. 2. The left figure shows an example for partial path schedule where r_i represents a request from source S_i to destination D_i. On the right, the computation of urgencies (deadline – remaining length) as the partial path offline schedule is built is presented.

The extended partial schedule resulting from the example above is shown in Fig. 3. Aggressive extended path schedules attempt to maximize the partial paths. Basically, the most urgent request is allowed to advance until the next request is a must serve case. This is found to be beneficent when the network is stable in general and also is found to work fine for concurrent scheduling [8]. We offer next a simplified discrete analysis of the EPP followed by a theorem and a corollary for the relation between PPH and EPP schedules.

5 EPP Analysis

In order for us to present the theorem about EPP, we need to provide some definitions and lemmas that will assist us in formulating the proof. We assume for simplification purposes that the network links are uniform and the delays incurred by the requests are equivalent in all links. The base of this assumption is the fact that if the data-item sizes are large and comparatively equivalent to each other the delay incurred in transmitting the data-item is dependant on the link speed. We also assume that the deadlines assigned to requests are integer multiple of the lengths of their paths. These two assumptions allow us provide a discrete model for the derivation of the lemmas and the theorem. Our EPP considers the urgency of the request as the function that represents the request. The priorities of the requests could be incorporated to provide a more specific function. We start first by the following articulating definitions:

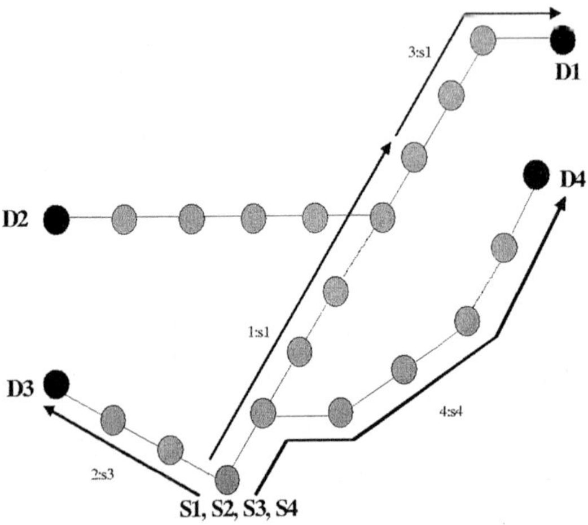

Step	Urgency			
	r1	r2	r3	r4
1	5	-	24	7
2	5		17	0
3	2		14	0
4	2		11	-
	-		↓	-

Fig. 3. The left figure shows the extended partial paths of the example. It shows the transmission steps of all requests after dropping r_2. On the right, urgencies of the requests as they approach their destinations are presented.

Definition 1. (urgency) We define the urgency of a request r_i at time t as; $U_g(r_i,t) \equiv [D(r_i)-t]-P_l(r_i,t)$, where $D(r_i)$ is the deadline of the request and $P_l(r_i,t)$ is the path length of request r_i at time $t \geq 0$ which is the total time elapsed from the start of the data staging in the network.

Definition 2. (the total set) The set S = { r_i }, is the total set of all requests present during a period $[t_0,t_n]$; called the scheduling period. We assume set S does not change during this period.

Definition 3. (schedule step)**:** We say a schedule step of length $[t_a,t_b]$ is performed on r_i iff ∃ r_i ∈ S (the total set) such that r_i is transmitted for one hop of a length (t_b-t_a) >0 along the path $P_l(r_i,t_a)$ while no other request in S is transmitted. The times t_a and t_b are the start time of data transfer and the finish time of data transfer respectively.

Definition 4. (satisfiability) A request r_i ∈ S is satisfied by a schedule step iff ∃ a schedule step that is performed on r_i such that $P_l(r_i,t)$ $=0$ at time t and $U_g(r_i,t) \geq$ 0. The request is dropped otherwise, i.e. $P_l(r_i,t)$ >0 and $U_g(r_i,t)$ <0.

Definition 5. (schedule) A schedule is a sequence of schedule steps performed on requests $r_i \in T \subset S$ such that all requests in S are either satisfied or dropped during the scheduling period.

Definition 6. (competing requests) Two requests r_i and r_j are said to be competing during the period $[t_a, t_b]$, iff $U_g(r_i, t_a) = U_g(r_j, t_a)$ and $P_l(r_i, t)$, $P_l(r_j, t) > 0$ $\forall\ t \in [t_a, t_b]$. The requests are said to be zero competing iff they are competing with zero urgency values. A group of competing requests is formed if any two that belong to the group are themselves competing.

Definition 7. (selection process) A random selection is performed on a group of competing requests iff a schedule step is performed randomly on one of them.

Lemma 1. (urgency reduction) Iff a schedule step of length $[t_a, t_b]$ is performed on request r_i, then, $U_g(r_i, t_a) = U_g(r_i, t_b)$ and $U_g(r_j, t_a) > U_g(r_j, t_b)$, $\forall\ r_i, r_j \in S$ and $r_i \neq r_j$.

Lemma 2. (dropping condition): A request r_i is dropped iff a schedule step is performed on request $r_u \in S$, $r_u \neq r_i$ and r_i is zero competing with at least one request r_j

Lemma 3. (competing steps): Two requests r_i and r_j with urgencies $U_g(r_i, t_0) > U_g(r_j, t_0)$ at time $t = t_0$, if reach a competing point at $t_p > t_0$ then number of schedule steps performed on r_j prior to t_p is given by $\dfrac{U_g(r_i, t_0) - U_g(r_j, t_0)}{t_b - t_a}$, where $(t_b - t_a)$ is the size of the schedule step.

Lemma 4. (maximum reduction): A requests r_i that is competing at time t_p with request r_j, if reaches a zero competing point with it at time $t_u \geq t_p$, will have at most $\dfrac{U_g(r_i, t_p)}{t_b - t_a}$ schedule steps performed on either request prior to t_u, where $(t_b - t_a)$ is the size of the schedule steps.

Lemma 5. (path incrementing) If request r_i is zero competing in a schedule performed on a total set S with given path lengths then, if the path of r_i is incremented during the scheduling period r_i will also reach a zero competing point during the scheduling period.

Theorem 1. (general case)**:** For a stable system of data staging (i.e., stable network and non-changing request conditions), the number of satisfied requests in a schedule generated by the EPP is larger than the number of satisfied requests in PPH in general.

Corollary 1. (special case) For a stable system of data staging, if no path change is encountered (e.g. the case of tree networks) and if non-random selection process is adopted for the schedule, then a request that is satisfied by the PPH is also satisfied by the EPP.

6 Simulation Results

The simulation was performed on an environment of 30 nodes forming an irregular network. Each node represents a machine with fixed capacity of 1unit of storage and each is connected to at most three other nodes. The delay across the links was uniformly set to 20 units of time and. The experiment includes running random generated requests on random topologies. The results shown in Table 1 and Table 2 represent the behavior of both PPH and EPP in this environment. It is clear from the tables that EPP was always superior to PPH. Table 1 shows the performance when the deadlines of all requests are set to a constant 5000 unit of time (250 times the link length) and the load of the system is altered from 50 to 600 requests. It is clear that at heavy load EPP outperforms PPH by a big margin due to its ability to schedule on long extensions. Table 2 shows the deadline response for both EPP and PPH fixing the load to 100 requests and altering the uniform deadlines of the requests. The EPP also demonstrated superiority in such environment with the given inputs.

Table 1. The performance of the EPP and the PPH when deadline is fixed for all requests at 5000 time unit (250 times the link delay)

Load	50	100	200	300	400	600
PPH Satisfiability (%)	100	94	42	27		0.167
EPP Satisfiability (%)	100	100	57	39		19.66

Table 2. The performance of the EPP and the PPH when deadline is fixed for all requests at 5000 time unit (250 times the link delay)

Deadline	1000	1500	2000	2500	3000	4000	5000	15000
PPH Satisfiability (%)	0	17	33	44	49	76	94	100
EPP Satisfiability (%)	28	39	53	63	74	95	100	100

7 Conclusions

It was demonstrated in this paper both analytically and experimentally that under certain conditions the PPH is a lower bound of performance for the EPP. With fewer invocations to Dijkstra's EPP will inflict less overhead to the scheduler and will be able to achieve higher performance. Because the PPH attempts continuously to look for other paths for requests, which may satisfy a specific request, this satisfiability will be at the expense of other requests. The EPP is a lower overhead heuristic that efficiently handle requests with equal priorities. If the goal is to maximize a weighted sum of priorities then EPP may have a lower performance than PPH. For this case the EPP must be combined with a mechanism that improves the overall performance by maximizing both the number of satisfied requests and the weighted sum of their priorities. This mechanism is proposed in [8] and referred to as concurrent scheduling. The PPH is expected to have a better performance in a non-stable environment by which dynamically changing network and continuously incoming requests are assumed. The EPP complexity must be further studied in case of a large number of requests at which the offline schedule is of a high complexity.

References

1. Theys, M. T., Beck N., Siegel, H. J., Jurczyk, M.: A Mathematical Model and Scheduling Heuristics for Satisfying Prioritized Data Requests in an Oversubscribed Communication Network. IEEE Trans. Parallel and Distributed Systems, Vol. 11, No. 9, (2000)
2. Jones, P. C., Lowe, T. J., Muller, G., Xu, N., Ye, Y., Zydiak, J. L.: Specially Structured Uncapacitated Facility Location Problem. Operation Research, Vol. 43, No. 4, (1995) 661–669
3. Pinedo, M.: Scheduling Theory, Algorithms and Systems. Prentice Hall, Englewood Cliffs, New Jersey (1995)
4. Lee, J., Tierney, B., Johnston, W.: Data Intensive Distributed Computing: A medical Application Example. Proceedings of the IEEE Supercomputing, (1997)
5. Allcock, B., Foster, I., Nefedova, V., Chervenak, A., Deelman, E., Kesselman, C., Lee, J., Sim, A., Shshani, A., Drach, B., Williams, D.: High Performance Remote Access to Climate Simulation Data: A Challenge Problem for Data Grid Technologies. Argonne National Laboratory, (2001)
6. Shirdhar, B., Dharma, S., Agrawal, P.: Scheduled Pipelined Communication in Distributed Memory Multiprocessors for Real-time Applications. The 18th Annual International Symposium on Computer Architecture, (1991) 222–231
7. Cormen, T., Leiserson, C., Rivest. R.: Introduction to Algorithms. MIT Press, Cambridge, Massachusetts, (1990)
8. Eltayeb, M., Doğan, A., Özgüner, F.: Concurrent Scheduling for Real-time Staging in Oversubscribed networks. The 16th International Conference on Parallel and Distributed Computing Systems, (2003)

Signal Compression Using Growing Cell Structures: A Transformational Approach

Borahan Tümer[1] and Betül Demiröz[1]

Marmara University Faculty of Engineering, Göztepe Campus MB Building 4th floor, 81040 Kadiköy, İstanbul, Turkey
{bora,bdemiroz}@eng.marmara.edu.tr

Abstract. We present an adaptive compression system (ACS) that compresses signals using signal primitives obtained by the self organizing neural architecture growing cell structures (GCS) [6]. We determine the length w_{max} of the primitive that maximizes the compression. We decompose the signal into w_{max}-long segments. Then GCS is trained to adaptively construct categories from segments. A reconstruction of the original signal may be obtained as a sequence of GCS categories with some error. We analyze the performance of ACS using two criteria: CR and PRD. We define CR as the ratio of the memory space required to hold the original signal over that required by the compressed version of the signal. We define PRD as the error between original signal and reconstructed signal from the compressed signal information. CR and PRD counteract providing a trade-off among the compression potential and the reconstruction quality of ACS. We apply ACS to electrocardiogram (ECG) signals.

1 Introduction

With rapidly growing technology new advanced techniques have been developed to record detailed medical data that provides crucial information for human health. For each patient, keeping medical data is vitally important not only for the identification of a current health problem, but also for later use to help accurately identify future health problems. Increasing diversity of medical signals and more sensitive devices achieving more detailed and accurate assessments has brought about large amounts of medical data for each patient. The need to store large amounts of medical data has made signal compression a popular research subject for longer than three decades.

Many signal compression techniques have been proposed in the literature [1, 2,3,4,5,7,8,9,10,11,12,13,15,16,18]. These techniques are mainly classified in two categories: those that directly process the data (direct signal compression techniques) [1,7,8,12], and those that change the processing domain before the compression (transformational methods) [2,5,9,14,15,18]. Direct signal compression techniques are generally more popular than transform methods since they are easier to implement [10]. However, the compression ratio they attain is usually

A. Yazici and C. Şener (Eds.): ISCIS 2003, LNCS 2869, pp. 952–959, 2003.

low or they have to consider a high degradation on the reconstructed signal quality (i.e., high signal reconstruction error) to reach a higher compression ratio. The transform methods may attain higher compression rates with lower reconstruction errors. However, the reason they are not as popular is their computation-intensive nature. The transform methods usually require the computation of eigenvalues and eigenvectors of large matrices. A method with such requirements is presented in [18]. Another such method is Karhunen Loeve transform (KLT). KLT is applied twice in [2]. The first application required the solution of a 3×3 matrix, and the second the solution of a 150×150 matrix.

In this work we present an adaptive compression system (ACS). We base our work on the fact that a signal (especially a periodic signal) consists of signal segments that are used to build categories depending on their similarities [17]. Each category has a representative that may replace, with some error, any signal segment from the corresponding category in the original signal. In the context of ACS, the original signal is a sequence of measurements sampled in time. We decompose the original signal into signal segments by grouping consecutive samples allowing no overlaps and obtain a sequence of signal segments. Using all signal segments we adaptively form a set of categories called an *alphabet* where each category is represented by an *exemplar*. Hence, each exemplar is a member of the alphabet. Each signal segment is associated with the category for which the exemplar of the corresponding category provides the best match.

When all segments in the sequence are presented, a self-organizing neural net architecture called "Growing Cell Structures" (GCS) [6] is used to adaptively obtain the exemplars. Once the alphabet is constructed, we may reconstruct the original signal as a sequence of the exemplars with some reasonable error. Hence, all we need to store to obtain the original signal is the exemplars used in the reconstruction and the sequence of the indices of the alphabet.

In the next section, we proceed with the methodology of the compression. Here, we discuss the three steps of ACS. In Section 3, we present the results obtained in various experiments. Finally in Section 4, we discuss our results and conclude the paper.

2 Adaptive Compression System (ACS)

A signal S is considered to be a sequence $S = s_1 \cdots s_k$ of signal segments $s_i, 1 \leq i \leq k$, where $s_i = [s_{i1} \cdots s_{iw}]^T$ is a vector composed of w time samples. The length of the signal is denoted by $|S|$ and is $|S| = kw$ samples. A self-organizing neural net architecture, GCS [6], groups signal segments s_i composing the original signal into categories γ_js where the exemplar c_j representing a specific category γ_j matches better with all segments S_j associated with the category γ_j than the exemplars of other categories do. The set of the exemplars $\Sigma = \{c_1 \cdots c_p\}$ forms the alphabet used to reconstruct the particular signal S we want compressed. Each $c_j = [c_{j1} \cdots c_{jw}]^T$ is a vector of length w, and is obtained in GCS architecture during the training of GCS. Then we use a sequence $C = c_{j_1} \cdots c_{j_k}$ of alphabet elements to represent the original signal S where each exemplar c_{j_i} replaces the signal segment s_i in S. The transformation of the original signal S into the sequence C of alphabet elements provides a reduction in the memory space used.

The compression is achieved in three steps:

- determine w_{max} and decompose signal into w_{max}-long non-overlapping segments
- decide on the reconstruction quality (i.e., PRD) and determine the alphabet size
- train GCS, construct alphabet, and compute CR and PRD.

In the following subsection, we define CR and PRD, and in the subsequent subsections we discuss the components of ACS.

2.1 Criteria

We define in Equation (1) CR as a function of the number of samples in the original signal S, the window size w, and the number of alphabet elements p:

$$CR = f(S, p, w) = \frac{rS}{i\frac{S}{w} + rpw} \tag{1}$$

where r and i are the numbers of bytes a floating point number and an ASCII character are respectively represented. In the rest of this paper, we will assume a floating point number and a character are represented in four bytes and one byte (i.e., i=1 and r=4), respectively. Hence (1) will become as follows:

$$CR = f(S, p, w) = \frac{4S}{\frac{S}{w} + 4pw} \tag{2}$$

The main goal is to maximize the CR, while maintaining the quality of the reconstruction. We assess the reconstruction quality using the popular error concept "percent root-mean-square difference" or the PRD. Let x_{org} and x_{rec} be the samples in the original and reconstructed signal, respectively. We define the PRD as follows:

$$PRD = \sqrt{\frac{\sum_{i=1}^{n}[x_{org}(i) - x_{rec}(i)]^2}{\sum_{i=1}^{n} x_{org}^2(i)}} \tag{3}$$

To prevent a possible degradation of the reconstruction quality, we attempt to keep the PRD at a minimum level.

2.2 Decomposition

Assume the original periodic signal X is a sequence of n samples $X = [x_1, \cdots, x_n]$. The samples may be recorded from any domain. We decompose the signal into segments s_i of length w where a segment $s_i = [s_{i1} \cdots s_{iw}]^T$ with each entry $s_{ik} = x_{(i-1)w+k}$ is a sequence of samples with a specific length w.

Hence $s_i = [x_{(i-1)w+1} \cdots x_{iw}], 1 \leq i \leq \lceil n/w \rceil$.

At the end of the decomposition, the signal is represented by a sequence $X = [s_1 \cdots s_{\lceil n/w \rceil}]$of segments.

One critical issue is the selection of w. We consider (2) in deciding w. To find w_{max} that maximizes CR, we take the derivative of CR with respect to w, and find w_{ext} at its horizontal tangent, while keeping S and p constant. To see if w_{ext} is a maximum, we check if $\frac{d^2CR}{dw}|_{w=w_{max}} < 0$. Here, we assume the continuity of w, and at the end, we round w_{max} to the nearest integer value since w is defined in a discrete domain. We find w_{max} as follows:

$$w_{max} = w_{ext} = \sqrt{\frac{S}{4p}} \tag{4}$$

The relationship in (4) states for a given input signal (i.e., S is given), we may find w_{max} for any degree of reconstruction quality we determine by p.

2.3 Adaptive Alphabet Construction

The signal is presented to GCS as a sequence of consecutive segments $s_i, 1 \leq i \leq \lceil n/w \rceil$. During the presentation of the signal GCS undergoes a self-organization in which GCS adaptively forms the exemplars $c_j, 1 \leq j \leq p$ from segments s_i. At the end of self-organization, each exemplar $c_j = [c_{j1} \cdots c_{jw}]^T$ represents a category providing the best match for a particular set of segments S_j. The best matching exemplar c_{best} is mathematically defined as follows:

$$c_{best} = \min_j \{ \sum_{k=1}^{w} (c_{jk} - s_{ik})^2 \} \tag{5}$$

Each exemplar c_j within the GCS architecture is adaptively obtained in which each segment in the corresponding set S_j accordingly updates the exemplar c_j. The categorization of a segment s_i to exemplar c_j not only causes a change in c_j but also in the topological neighbors N_{c_j} of c_j. Suppose l_c and l_N are the constant learning parameters corresponding to c_{best} and the set of topological neighbors $N_{c_{best}}$, respectively. Then the update equations are as in (6):

$$\begin{aligned} \triangle w_c &= l_c(s_i - w_c) \\ \triangle w_{N_c} &= l_{N_c}(s_i - w_{N_c}), \end{aligned} \tag{6}$$

where w_c and w_{N_c} are the weight vectors corresponding to c_{best} and $N_{c_{best}}$, respectively. Further information on GCS may be found in [6]. Each exemplar c_j is an element of the alphabet and the associated pattern is stored as a weight vector w_{c_j} within GCS architecture. To construct the alphabet, we extract each vector w_{c_j} and specify the vector as the jth element of the alphabet.

Along with w and S, the number p of alphabet elements determines the quality of the reconstruction. If $p = \lceil n/w \rceil$, then we obtain an error-free reconstruction with no compression. For any $p \leq \lceil n/w \rceil$, a non-zero PRD builds up, and as p decreases, PRD increases. At the other end with $p = 1$, we achieve the maximum compression ratio but with an unacceptably high PRD. Since we assumed to represent p in one byte in (2), $1 \leq p \leq 255$. In Section 3, we show how for a given S and w_{max}, PRD changes with changing p.

3 Results

We used ECG signals (time samples in mV) received from patients suffering from atrial fibrillation in our experiments.

The sampling frequency of the original signal is 1000 samples/sec. The original signal is then filtered to eliminate high-frequency noise such that every fourth sample is used. Hence, signals used in experiments have a frequency of 250 Hz.

In our experiments, we varied S, p, and w within the following ranges, respectively: (1) $25K \leq S \leq 75K$ time samples, (2) $100 \leq p \leq 255$ signal primitives, (3) $6 \leq w \leq 14$ time points. These ranges have been sufficient to establish a good basis for our discussion and conclusions.

For each w in the range specified above, we prepared input signals with S within the range necessary to show that w_{max} maximizes CR as expected and provides $CR = CR_{max}$. Further, to see the effect of the alphabet size p on both CR and PRD we constructed alphabets with 13 different sizes for each given window size.

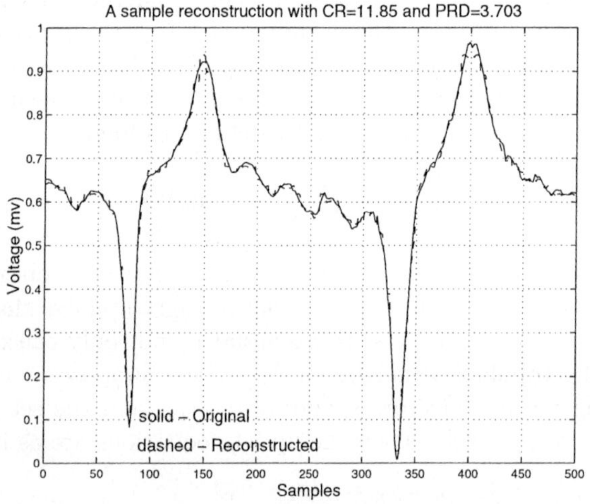

Fig. 1. A sample reconstruction of a signal from its compressed version by ACS

In Fig. 1, an original signal and its reconstructed version from compressed signal information are illustrated. The performance parameters for this experiment are $CR = 11.85$ and $PRD = 3.703$ where $S = 25K$ samples, $w = 6$, and $p = 178$ alphabet elements.

4 Discussion and Conclusions

In this section, we discuss our observations regarding how the w, S and p relate to the performance parameters (CR and PRD) of ACS.

One factor that dominantly determines the compression capacity (assessed by CR) is w. In Section 2.2, we show that the compression potential attains a peak value for $w = w_{max}$. From 4 we see w_{max} grows with S proportionally to its square root and falls as p grows in proportion again to its square root. Fig. 2 illustrates how CR changes with respect to S and w for various p. We see that peaks form for each surface of a specific alphabet size as expected. Further, the smooth rise of the peaks in CR with increasing w and S reflect the dependent nature of w_{max} on both S and p. Smaller alphabets provide higher compression

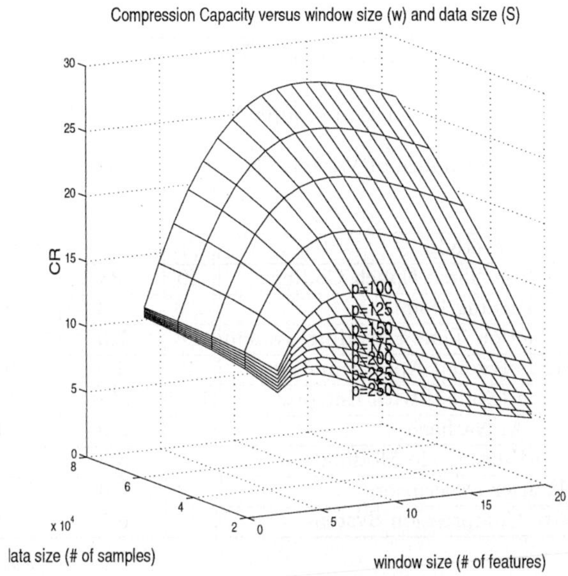

Fig. 2. Compression ratio as a function of data size and window size

ratios. We further see that as the alphabet size grows smaller window sizes generate higher compression ratios. In Fig. 2, we observe that with larger data we attain a higher compression capacity. Finally we can see from Fig. 2 that with larger data we attain a higher CR. The reconstruction quality is heavily depended upon the alphabet size. In Fig. 3, the PRD is illustrated as a function of p at $w = 8$ for various S. For a given w, a larger alphabet represents each segment more accurately providing a smaller PRD whereas an alphabet with less elements results in a larger PRD. Another obvious conclusion we can draw from Fig. 3 is that smaller S generate smaller PRD. The interceptions between the last two lines are formed by the attempts of the optimizer to reduce the alphabet to maximize CR.

Finally, comparing CR performance at a given PRD with other methods in Table 1, we conclude that ACS outperforms other methods. Al-Nashash technique [3] has a better PRD than ACS for a smaller CR. However, their technique

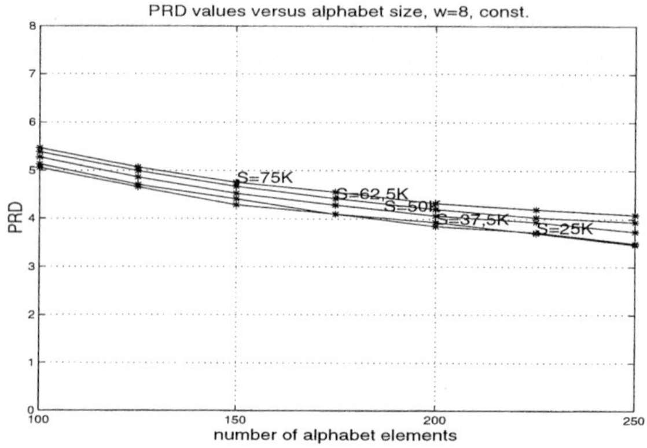

Fig. 3. PRD as a function of alphabet size at $w = 8$

Table 1. Performance of Various Compression Methods

Method	CR	PRD (%)	SF (Hz)
Amplitude Zone Time Epoch Coding	10	28	500
Turning Point	2.0	5.3	500
Coordinate Reduction Time Encoding System	4.8	7.0	200
Scan Along Polygonal Approximation	3.0	4.0	250
Peak Picking (Spline) with Entropy	10.0	14.0	500
Al-Nashash	16	3.0	500
Differential Pulse Code Modulation	7.8	3.5	500
Fourier Descriptors	7.4	7.0	250
Adaptive Compression System	24	6.5	250

involves training of a Hebbian neural network which requires the inclusion of all expected arrhythmias during the training while ACS only needs the signal to compress to get trained. Further the rather simple applicability (i.e., the easy retrieval of the reconstructed signal or any component) and the low computation complexity are other dominating aspects of ACS.

References

1. "J.P. Abenstein and W.J. Tompkins". "New Data Reduction Algorithm for Real Time, ECG Analysis". *"IEEE Transactions on Biomedical Engineering"*, 29:43–48, January 1982.
2. "N. Ahmed, P.J. Milne, and S.G. Harris". "Electrocardiographic Data Compression via Orthogonal Transforms". *"IEEE Transactions on Biomedical Engineering"*, 22:484–487, 1975.
3. "E. Al-Hujazi and H. Al-Nashash". "ECG Data Compression using Hebbian Neural Networks". *"Journal of Medical Engineering and Technology"*, 20(6):211–218, November/December 1996.

4. "G.D. Barlas and E. Skordalakis". "A Novel Family of Compression Algorithms for ECG and Other Semiperiodical, One-dimensional, Biomedical Signals". *"IEEE Transactions on Biomedical Engineering"*, 43(8):820–828, August 1996.
5. "J. Chen and S. Itoh". "A Wavelet Transform-based ECG Compression Guaranteeing desired signal Quality". *"IEEE Transactions on Biomedical Engineering"*, 45(12):1414–1419, December 1998.
6. "B. Fritzke". "Growing Cell Structures-A Self-Organizing Network for Unsupervised and Supervised Learning". *"Neural Networks"*, 7(9):1441–1460, 1994.
7. "B. Furht and A. Perez". "An Adaptive Real-Time ECG Compression Algorithm with Variable Threshold". *"IEEE Transactions on Biomedical Engineering"*, 35(6):489–493, June 1988.
8. "T.S. Ibiyemi". "A Novel Data Compression Technique for ECG Classification". *"Engineering in Medicine"*, 15(1):35–38, 1986.
9. "A. Iwata, Y. Nagasaka, and N. Suzumura". "Data Compression of ECG using Neural Network for Digital Holter Monitor". *"IEEE Engineering in Medicine and Biology Magazine"*, 9(3):53–57, September 1990.
10. "S.M.S. Jalaleddine, C. Hutchens, R.D. Strattan, and W.A. Coberly". "ECG Data Compression Techniques-A Unified Approach". *"IEEE Transactions on Biomedical Engineering"*, 37(4):329–343, April 1990.
11. "N. Krisnamurthy, E. Kresch, S.S. Rao, and Y. Kresh". "Constrained ECG Compression using Best Adapted Wavelet Packet Bases". *"IEEE Signal Processing Letters"*, 3(10):273–275, October 1996.
12. "W.C. Mueller". "Arrhythmia Detection Program for an Algorithm for Ambulatory ECG Monitor". *"Biomedical Science and Instrumentation"*, 14:81–85, 1978.
13. "G. Nave and A. Cohen". "ECG Compression using Long-Term Prediction". *"IEEE Transactions on Biomedical Engineering"*, 40(9):877–885, September 1993.
14. "T.A. De Perez, M.J. Stefanelli, and F. D'Alvano". "ECG Data Compression via Exponential Quantization of the Walsh Spectrum". *"Journal of Clinical Engineering"*, 12:373–378, 1987.
15. "B.R.S. Reddy and I.S.N. Murthy". "ECG Data Compression using Fourier Descriptors". *"IEEE Transactions on Biomedical Engineering"*, 33:428–434, 1986.
16. "S.C. Tai". "ECG Data Compression by Corner Detection". *"Medical and Biological Engineering and Computing"*, 30:584–590, 1992.
17. "M.B. Tumer, L.A. Belfore, and K.Ropella". "a Syntactic Methodology for Automatic Diagnosis by Analysis of Continuous Time Measurements using Hierarchical Signal Representations". *"IEEE Transactions on Systems, Man, and Cybernetics Part B"*, Accepted.
18. "M.E. Womble, J.S. Halliday, S.K. Mitter, M.C. Lancester, and J.H. Triebwasser". "Data Compression for Storing and Transmitting ECGs/VCGs". *"IEEE Transactions on Biomedical Engineering"*, 65(12):702–706, May 1977.

A New Continuous Action-Set Learning Automaton for Function Optimization

Hamid Beigy and M.R. Meybodi

Soft Computing Laboratory
Computer Engineering Department
Amirkabir University of Technology
Tehran, Iran
{beigy, meybodi}@ce.aut.ac.ir

Abstract. In this paper, we study an adaptive random search method based on learning automaton for solving stochastic optimization problems in which only the noise-corrupted value of objective function at any chosen point in the parameter space is available. We first introduce a new continuous action-set learning automaton (CALA) and theoretically study its convergence properties, which implies the convergence to the optimal action. Then we give an algorithm, which needs only one function evaluation in each stage, for optimizing an unknown function.

1 Introduction

Many engineering problems, such as adaptive control, pattern recognition, filtering, and identification, under the proper assumptions can be regarded as the parameter optimization problems. Consider a system with measurements $g(x,\alpha)$ on the performance function $M(\alpha) = \mathrm{E}\left[g(x,\alpha)\right]$, where α is the parameter and x is the observation, the parameter optimization problem is to determine the optimal parameter α^* such that the performance function is extermized. The performance function $M(.)$ may also be a multi-modal function. Many efficient methods like steepest descent method, Newton's method, are available when the gradient ∇M is explicitly available. Usually, due to the lack of sufficient information concerning the structure of the function M or the lack of mathematical intractability, the function M to be optimized is not explicitly known and only noise-corrupted value of the function $M(\alpha)$ at any chosen point α can be observed.

Two important classes of algorithms are available for solving the above problem when only the noise-corrupted observations are available: stochastic approximation based algorithms [1] and learning automata based algorithms [2]. Stochastic approximation algorithms are iterative algorithms in which the gradient of the function M is approximated by a finite difference method, and using the function evaluations obtained at points, which are chosen close to each other [1]. The learning automata are adaptive decision making devices that operating in unknown random environments and progressively improve their performance

A. Yazici and C. Şener (Eds.): ISCIS 2003, LNCS 2869, pp. 960–967, 2003.

via a learning process. Since learning automata theorists study the optimization under uncertainty, the learning automata are very useful for optimization of multi-modal functions when the function is unknown and only noise-corrupted evaluations are available. In these algorithms, a probability density function, which is defined over the parameter space, is used for selecting the next point. The the evaluation signal and the learning algorithm are used by the learning automata (LA) for updating the probability density function at each stage. We want that this probability density function converges to some probability density function where the optimal value of α is chosen with probability as close as to the unity. The distinguishing feature of of the learning is that the probability distribution of $g(x, \alpha)$ is unknown. Methods based on stochastic approximation algorithms and learning automata represent two distinct approaches to the learning problems. Though both approaches involve iterative procedures, updating at every stage is done in the parameter space in the first method, which may result to a local optimum, and in the probability space in the second method. The learning automata methods have two distinct advantages over the stochastic approximation algorithms. The first advantage is that, the action space need not be a metric space because as in the stochastic approximation algorithms in which the new value of the parameter is to be chosen close to the previous value. The second advantage is that the methods based on learning automata lead to global optimization, because at every stage any element of the action set can be chosen. Learning automata are divided into two main groups: finite action-set learning automata (FALA) and continuous action-set learning automata (CALA) based on whether the action set is finite or continuous [3]. FALA has finite number of actions and has been studied extensively. For an $r-$action FALA, the action probability distribution is represented by an $r-$dimensional probability vector that updated by the learning algorithm. In many applications there is need to have large number of actions. The learning automata with too large number of actions converge too slowly. In such applications CALA, whose actions are chosen from real line, are very useful. For CALA, the action probability distribution is represented by a continuous function and this function is updated by learning algorithm at any stage. In the theory of LA, several algorithms for learning optimal parameters have been developed for many discrete and continuous parameters [2,4]. Gullapalli proposed a generalized learning automaton with continuous action set, which uses the context input as well as the reinforcement signal [5]. In [6], a CALA is given and its convergence has been shown. This CALA is used for stochastic optimization and needs two function evaluations in each iteration, irrespective of the dimension of the parameter space. In [7], a team of FALA and CALA is also used for stochastic optimization. In [8], a CALA is given for adaptive control, but no formal study is conducted to explain its behavior.

In this paper, we study an adaptive random search method for finding the global minimum of an unknown function. In the first part of the paper, we introduce a new continuous action-set learning automaton and study its convergence. We state a strong convergence theorem that implies form of optimal performance for CALA. In the second part of the paper, we propose an algorithm, which uses the proposed CALA for stochastic optimization. The proposed algorithm is a constant step size learning algorithm. The proposed algorithm unlike the scheme reported in [6], that requires two function evaluations in each stage, it needs only one function evaluations in each stage which leads to lesser computational overhead. The proposed algorithm is independent of the dimension of the parameter space of the function to be optimized.

The rest of this paper is organized as follows: In section 2, a new continuous action-set learning automaton is given and its behavior is studied. In section 3, an algorithm for stochastic optimization and the experiments are given and section 4 concludes the paper.

2 A New Continuous Action-Set Learning Automaton

In this section, we introduce a new CALA, which will be used later for determining the optimal parameters of call admission control policy in cellular networks. For the proposed learning automaton, we use the Gaussian distribution, $N(\mu, \sigma)$ for selection of actions, which is completely specified by the first and second order moments, μ and σ. Thus, unlike finite action-set learning automaton, we only need to store the mean and variance parameters of the Gaussian distribution. The learning algorithm now updates the mean and variance of the Gaussian distribution at any instant using the evaluation signal β, obtained from the random environment. The evaluation signal, $\beta \in [0,1]$, is a noise-corrupted evaluation signal, which indicates a noise-corrupted observation of function $M(.)$ at the selected action. The evaluation signal β is a random variable whose distribution function coincides almost with the distribution $H(\beta|\alpha)$ that belongs to a family of distributions which depends on the parameter α. Let

$$\begin{aligned} M(\alpha) &= \mathrm{E}[\beta(\alpha)|\alpha] \\ &= \int_{-\infty}^{\infty} \beta(\alpha) dH(\beta|\alpha), \end{aligned}$$

be a penalty function with bound $\mathcal{M}$ corresponding to this family of distributions. We assume that $M(.)$ is measurable and continuously differentiable almost everywhere. The CALA has to minimize $M(.)$ by observing $\beta(\alpha)$. Let (μ_n, σ_n) be the mean and the standard deviation of the Gaussian distribution that represents the action probability of the CALA at instant n. Through the learning algorithm, we ideally want that $\mu_n \to \mu^*$ and $\sigma_n \to 0$ as time tends to infinity.

The interaction between the CALA and the random environment takes place as iterations of the following operations. Iteration n begins by selection of an action α_n by the CALA. This action is generated as a random variable from the Gaussian distribution with parameters μ_n and σ_n. The selected action is applied to the random environment and the learning automaton receives an evaluative signal $\beta(\alpha_n)$, which has the mean value $M(\alpha_n)$, from the environment. Then the learning automaton updates the parameters μ_n and σ_n. Initially $M(.)$ is not known and it is desirable that with interaction of learning automaton and the random environment, the μ and σ converges to their optimal values which results the minimum value of $M(.)$. The learning automaton uses the following rule to update the parameters μ_n and σ_n, thus generating a sequence of random variables μ_n and σ_n.

$$\begin{aligned} \mu_{n+1} &= \mu_n - a\beta(\alpha_n)\sigma_n(\alpha_n - \mu_n), \\ \sigma_{n+1} &= f(\sigma_n), \end{aligned} \tag{1}$$

where a is learning rate and $f(.)$ is a function that produces a random sequence of σ_n (described later). The equation (1) can be written as

$$\mu_{n+1} = \mu_n - a\sigma_n^2 y_n(\alpha_n), \tag{2}$$

where

$$y_n(\alpha_n) = \beta(\alpha_n)\left(\frac{\alpha_n - \mu_n}{\sigma_n}\right). \tag{3}$$

An intuitive explanation for the above updating equations is as follows. We can view the fraction in equation (3) as the normalized noise added to the mean. Since a, β and σ all are positive, the updating equation changes the mean value in the opposite direction of the noise. If the noise is positive, then the learning automaton should update its parameter, so that mean value increased and visa versa. Since $\mathrm{E}[\beta|\alpha]$ is close to unity when α is far from its optimal value and it is close when α is near to the optimal value, thus the learning automaton updates μ with large steps when α is far from its optimal value and with small steps when α is close to its optimal value. This causes a finer quantization of μ near its optimal value and a grain quantization for points far away its optimal value. Thus, we can consider the learning algorithm as a random direction search algorithm with adaptive step sizes.

In what follows, we state the convergence of the proposed learning automaton in stationary environments. The convergence is proved based on the following assumption.

Assumption 1 *The sequence of real numbers $\{\sigma_n\}$ is such that*

$$\sigma_n \geq 0, \qquad \sum_{n=1}^{\infty} \sigma^3 = \infty, \qquad \sum_{n=1}^{\infty} \sigma^4 < \infty.$$

Note that these conditions imply that $\sigma_n \to 0$ as $n \to \infty$. Therefore, in limit, σ_n of Gaussian distribution tends to zero and the action of learning automaton becomes equal to the mean. The condition $\sum_{n=1}^{\infty} \sigma^3 = \infty$ ensures that the sum of increments to the initial mean, μ_0, can be arbitrary large, so that any finite initial value of μ_0 can be transformed into the optimal value μ^*. At the same time, the condition that $\sum_{n=1}^{\infty} \sigma^4 < \infty$ ensures that the variance in μ_n is finite and the mean cannot diverge to infinity.

Assumption 2 *There is a unique real number μ^* such that*

$$M(\mu^*) = \min_{\alpha}(\alpha).$$

This assumption implies that $M(.)$ has unique minimum. Note that this assumption can be relaxed to multi-modal functions. Suppose that $\mathcal{M}$ be the bound on $M(\alpha)$. It is also assumed that $M(\alpha)$ has a finite number of minima inside a compact set and has bounded first and second derivatives with respect to α. Let

$$R(\alpha) = \frac{\partial M(\alpha)}{\partial \alpha}, \tag{4}$$

and

$$S(\alpha) = \frac{\partial M^2(\alpha)}{\partial \alpha^2}, \tag{5}$$

be the first and second derivative of $M(\alpha)$, respectively. Suppose that $\mathcal{R}$ and $\mathcal{S}$ be the bounds on R and S, respectively.

Note that this assumption ensures that there is an optimal action α^* for the learning automaton for which $\mathrm{E}[\beta(\alpha^*)]$ is minimum. Since in limit $\sigma_n \to 0$, then this assumption ensures that there is an optimal mean μ^* for which M is minimized.

Assumption 3 *Suppose that $R(\alpha)$ is linear near μ^*, that is*

$$\sup_{\epsilon \leq |\alpha - \mu^*| \leq \frac{1}{\epsilon}} (\alpha - \mu^*) R(\alpha) > 0, \tag{6}$$

for all $\epsilon > 0$. This assumption is restrictive, because it requires $M(.)$ to be linear in the neighborhood of the optimal action. However, it may be possible to weaken this assumption as has been done in stochastic approximation algorithms, but only at complicating the cost of the analysis, which don't consider it here.

Assumption 4 *Suppose that the noise in the reinforcement signal $\beta(.)$ has a bounded variance, that is*

$$\begin{aligned} \mathrm{E}\left\{[\beta(\alpha) - M(\alpha)]^2\right\} &= \int_{-\infty}^{\infty} [\beta(\alpha) - M(\alpha)]^2 \, dH(\beta|\alpha) \\ &\leq K_1 \left[1 + (\alpha - \mu^*)^2\right] \end{aligned} \tag{7}$$

for some real number $K_1 > 0$.

Given the above assumptions, in what follows, we study the behavior of the proposed CALA. The following theorem states the convergence of the random process defined by (1).

Theorem 1. *Suppose that the assumptions 1-4 hold, μ_0 is finite and there is an optimal value of μ^* for μ. Then if μ_n and σ_n are evolved according to the given learning algorithm, then $\lim_{n\to\infty} \mu_n = \mu^*$ with probability 1.*

Proof. The proof of this theorem is given in [9].

3 Optimization of a Function

In this section, we give an algorithm based on the continuous action-set learning automaton given in section 2, for optimization of an unknown function. The proposed algorithm can be easily extended to multivariate functions by using a cooperative game of CALA with identical payoff. Consider the function $M : \Re \rightarrow \Re$ to be minimized. At any instant n, the automaton chooses an action α_n using the Gaussian distribution $N(\mu_n, \sigma_n)$, where μ_n and σ_n is the mean and the standard deviation, respectively. As before, let $\beta(\alpha)$ denote the noisy function evaluation at point $\alpha \in \Re$ such that $M(\alpha) = \mathrm{E}\left[\frac{\beta(\alpha)-\lambda_2}{\lambda_1}\right]$. This is because of the assumption that β is a bounded and non-negative random variable. The signal $\beta(\alpha)$ is used to update the μ of the Gaussian distribution (equation (1)).

In order to study the behavior of the proposed algorithm, we consider the optimization of the penalized Shubert function, which is borrowed from [6], when the function evaluations are noisy. We assume that only the function evaluations are available. The penalized Shubert function is given below.

$$M(x) = \sum_{i=1}^{5} i\cos((i+1)x+1) + u(x,10,100,2), \tag{8}$$

where u is the penalizing function given by

$$u(x,b,k,m) = \begin{cases} k(x-b)^m & x > b \\ 0 & |x| \le b \\ k(-x-b)^m & x < -b \end{cases} \tag{9}$$

This function has 19 minima within interval $[-10,10]$ where three of them are global minima. The global minimum value of the penalized Shubert function is approximately equal to -12.87 and is attained at points close to -5.9, 0.4, and 6.8. The penalized Shubert function is frequently used as one of the benchmark problems for global optimization problems.

The proposed continuous action-set learning automaton and the automaton proposed in [6] with different initial values of the mean and variance parameters are used for finding the minimum of penalized Shubert function. The algorithm given in [6] is used with the following values of parameters: the penalizing constant C is equal to 5, the lower bound for the variance, $\sigma_l = 0.01$ and the step size $a = 2\times 10^{-4}$. The proposed algorithm is used with $a = 0.01$ and the variance is updated according to the following equation.

$$\sigma_n = \frac{1}{\lfloor \frac{n}{10} \rfloor^{1/3}}$$

The function evaluations are corrupted by a zero mean noise randomly generated in the range [-0.5,0.5] with uniform distribution. The results of simulation for two algorithms are shown in tables 1 and 2. The simulation results show that the mean value of Gaussian distribution used in CALA always converge to a minimum of penalized Shubert function within the interval [-10,10].

Table 1. The simulation results with noise added to the penalized Shubert function evaluations for the algorithm given in [6]

Case	Initial Values μ_0	σ_0	After 8000 iterations μ_{8000}	σ_{8000}	Function value
1	4	6	6.716046	0.1	-12.861304
2	4	10	0.436827	0.1	-12.848987
3	8	5	7.805426	0.1	-3.5772
4	8	3	6.704283	0.1	-12.868272
5	12	6	5.460669	0.1	-8.476369
6	-10	5	-8.107043	0.1	-3.749682
7	-10	6	-7.09686	0.1	-8.507154

Table 2. The simulation results with noise added to the penalized Shubert function evaluations for the proposed algorithm

Case	Initial Values μ_0	σ_0	After 8000 iterations μ_{8000}	σ_{8000}	Function value
1	4	6	2.534	0.01	-3.578
2	4	10	0.4308	0.01	-12.87
3	8	5	5.364	0.01	-8.5
4	8	3	6.72	0.01	-12.87
5	12	6	1.454	0.01	-3.58
6	-10	5	-7.1	0.01	-8.5
7	-10	6	-5.8	0.01	-12.87

By comparing the results of simulations for both algorithms, we conclude that two algorithms have approximately the same accuracy, but the proposed algorithm only requires one function evaluation in each stage, which leads to lesser computational overhead. Figure 1 shows the changes in μ versus n for a typical run. This figure shows that the proposed algorithm converges to a minimum quickly and have oscillations around the minimum point. However, such oscillations could be decreased by using a small step size, which results in decreasing in the rate of convergence.

4 Conclusions

In this paper, we have studied a random search method for solving stochastic optimization problems. We have considered a class of problems where the only available information is a noise-corrupted values of the function. In order to solve such problems, we proposed a new continuous action learning automaton and studied its convergence properties. We stated and proved a strong convergence theorem that implies the optimal performance for the proposed learning automaton. Finally, we given an algorithm for stochastic optimization, which needs only

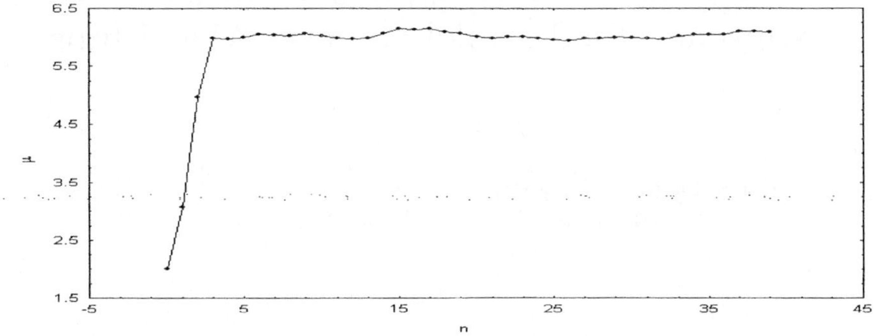

Fig. 1. The convergence of the mean value of the Gaussian distribution.

one function evaluation in each stage, and study its behavior through computer simulations.

References

1. H. J. Kushner and G. G. Yin, *Stochastic Approximation Algorithms and Applications.* Applications of Mathematics, New York: Springer–Verlag, 1997.
2. K. S. Narendra and K. S. Thathachar, *Learning Automata: An Introduction.* New York: Printice-Hall, 1989.
3. M. A. L. Thathachar and P. S. Sastry, "Varieties of Learning Automata: An Overview," *IEEE Transactions on Systems, Man, and Cybernetics-Part B: Cybernetics*, vol. 32, pp. 711–722, Dec. 2002.
4. K. Najim and A. S. Pozyak, "Multimodal Searching technique Based on Learning Automata with Continuous Input and Changing Number of Actions," *IEEE Transactions on Systems, Man, and Cybernetics-Part B: Cybernetics*, vol. 26, pp. 666–673, Aug. 1996.
5. V. Gullapalli, *Reinforcement learning And Its Application on Control.* PhD thesis, Deparqement of Computer and Information Sciences, University of Massachusetts, Amherst, MA, USA, Feb. 1992.
6. G. Santharam and P. S. S. M. A. L. Thathachar, "Continuous Action set Learning Automata for Stochastic Optimization," *Journal of Franklin Institute*, vol. 331B, no. 5, pp. 607–628, 1994.
7. K. Rajaraman and P. S. Sastry, "Stochastic Optimization Over Continuous and Discrete Variables with Applications to Concept Learning Under Noise," *IEEE Transactions on Systems, Man, and Cybernetics-Part A: Systems and Humans*, vol. 29, pp. 542–553, Nov. 1999.
8. G. P. Frost, *Stochastic Optimization of Vehicle Suspension Control Systems Via Learning Auiomata.* PhD thesis, Department of Aeronautical and Automotive Engineering, Loughborough University, Loughborough, Leicestershire, LE81 3TU, UI, Oct. 1998.
9. H. Beigy and M. R. Meybodi, "A New Continuous Action-set Learning Automaton for Function Optimization," Tech. Rep. TR-CE-2003-002, Computer Engineering Department, Amirkabir University of Technology, Tehran, Iran, 2003.

A Selectionless Two-Society Multiple-Deme Approach for Parallel Genetic Algorithms

Adnan Acan

Computer Engineering Dept., Eastern Mediterranean University,
Gazimağusa, T.R.N.C. Mersin 10, TURKEY
adnan.acan@emu.edu.tr

Abstract. A novel multi-deme parallel genetic algorithm approach that eliminates the use of the selection operator by using multiple populations separated into two societies is introduced. Each individual population contains two subpopulations, one in each society, and individuals in one society are superior in fitness to the ones in the other and the size of subpopulations in each society is dynamically determined based on the average fitness value. The fitness-based division of individuals into two social subpopulations is based on the fact that, due to fitness-based selection procedures, most of the recombination operations take place among individuals with an above-average fitness value. Unidirectional synchronous migration of individuals is carried between populations in the same society and in the two societies. The proposed algorithm is applied for the solution of hard numerical and combinatorial optimization problems, and it outperforms the standard genetic algorithm implementation in all trials.

1 Introduction

Genetic algorithms (GAs) are biologically inspired search procedures that have been successfully used for the solution of hard numerical and combinatorial optimization problems. Since their primary introduction by Bremermann and Fraser in 1960s, and their algorithmic development by John Holland in 1975, there has been a great deal on the derivation of various algorithmic alternatives of the standard implementation towards a faster and better localization of optimal solutions. The power and success of GAs are mainly achieved by the diversity of individuals of a population which evolves following the Darwinian principle of "survival of the fittest" [1], [2].

The basic implementation strategy of the genetic algorithms is as follows: Given a problem described by a configuration space and an objective function defined on this space, an initial population of randomly selected individuals is constructed and each individual is evaluated according to the objective function. The objective function value for an individual is referred to its fitness and it is indeed a relative functional performance specifying how well the individual satisfies the optimization criteria. Then, this population is evolved, over a number of generations, by a string manipulation process based on three genetic operators: reproduction, crossover, and mutation.

A. Yazici and C. Şener (Eds.): ISCIS 2003, LNCS 2869, pp. 968–975, 2003.

From the diversity point of view, parallel implementations aim to provide further diversity by employing multiple populations and inter-population migration strategies. The way in which GAs can be parallelized depend on a number of algorithmic considerations such as the fitness calculation mechanism, the number of populations used, the inter-population migration mechanism, and the way the selection method is applied. Depending on how these elements are implemented and inter-mixed, more than ten different methods of parallelizing GAs can be obtained [3], [4]. However, considering the majority of practical applications, one can state that there are three main types of parallel GAs (PGAs): (1) global single-population master-slave PGAs, (2) single-population fine-grained PGAs, and (3) multiple-population coarse-grained PGAs.

In a master-slave PGA there is a single panmictic population stored on a master processor, but the evaluation of fitness is distributed among several slave processors [5]. Fine-grained PGAs consist of one spatially structured population in which individuals are distributed to multiple processors based on a particular neighborhood topology for the purpose of parallelizing the selection of parents, selections of individuals to replace, mating and crossover [6]. Multiple population (or multiple-deme) PGAs are more sophisticated, as they consist of several populations which exchange individuals occasionally, that is called migration and controlled by several parameters [7], [8]. Due to migration, computation time to communication time ratio is relatively high compared to the previous two types of PGAs [9]. A very critical issue in multi-deme PGAs is the amount and frequency of migration operation that is applied synchronously in the majority of this type of PGAs. There is no problem independent migration schedule and there is a critical migration rate at which the maximum performance of a PGA is reached [8]. Deme topology and the individual replacement policies after migration also have significant impact on the convergence rate and the solution quality [10]. The final method to parallelize GAs, hierarchical PGAs, combines multiple demes with master-slave or fine-grained GAs. A hierarchical PGA combines the benefits of its components and can reduce the execution time more than any of the components alone [11].

This paper introduces a novel PGA approach of the multi-deme type such that each deme is a two-level population where the size of each level (subpopulation) is dynamically determined based on the average fitness value. The subpopulations in the two levels of individual demes are combined to form two societies of subpopulations. The idea of dividing a population into two subpopulations based on the average fitness value arises from the following observation: Due to fitness-based selection procedures, most of the individuals taking place in recombination operations are high-fitness individuals. Figure 1 illustrates the ratio of above-average individuals in recombination for three different fitness cases: *a*) individuals with fitness greater than or equal to $Average\_Fitness$ (indicated by the solid straight line), *b*) individuals with fitness greater than or equal to $Average\_Fitness + 0.5(Max\_Fitness - Average\_Fitness)$ (indicated by the dash-dot curve), and *c*) individuals with fitness greater than or equal to $Average\_Fitness + 0.75(Max\_Fitness - Average\_Fitness)$ (indicated by the dotted curve). Note that the ratio of individuals in recombination is 99% for case *a* in all generations, 96% for case *b* in all but very few initial generations, and 75% for case c. These results indicate that, only a very small percentage of individuals having below-average fitness are involved in recombination operations. Consequently, one can put the individuals with above-average fitness into a sub-population (sub-population of superior individuals) which will act as the mating pool and, thereon, can eliminate any fitness-based selection procedure. Obviously, the rest of the individuals of a population are combined into a second sub-population (sub-population of inferior individuals) and a small percentage of parent individuals may be randomly selected for mating from this sub-population. The implementation details of this two-society, two-level multi-deme, and selectionless Parallel Genetic Algorithm (PTSGA) approach are presented in section 2.

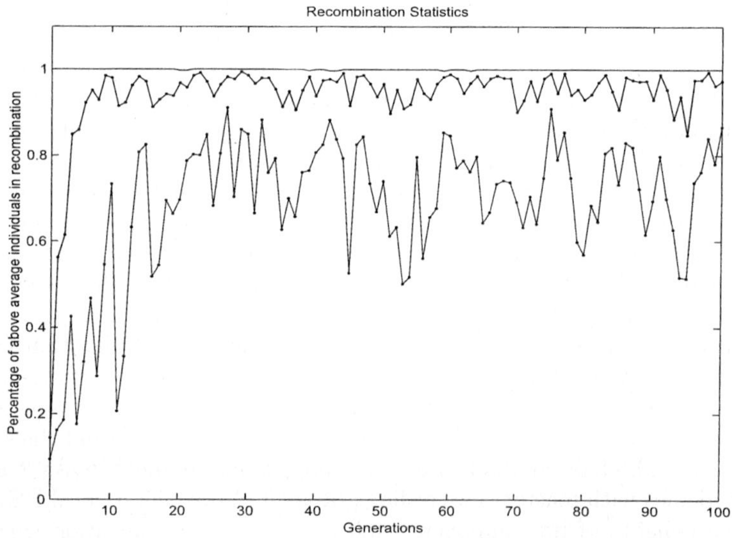

Fig. 1. Percentage of above-average individuals taking place in recombination.

The organization of this paper is as follows. The implementation details of the PTSGA approach is explained in section 2. Section 3 covers the case studies for numerical and combinatorial optimization problems. Comparisons are made with the conventional GAs implementation. Finally, conclusions and future research directions are specified.

2 The Selectionless Two-Society Multiple-Population Approach for Parallel Genetic Algorithms

According to the observations in section 1, individuals having a fitness value greater than or equal to $Average\_Fitness + a_s * (Max\_Fitness - Average\_Fitness)$, where $a_s \leq 1$ are grouped in a sub-population (the first or the top level) and named as the population of superior individuals. The remaining individuals in the population are grouped in another sub-population (the second or the bottom level) and named as the population of inferior individuals. Since most of the recombination operations are taken place between superior individuals, the population of superior individuals is considered as the main mating pool whereas the inferior individuals enter the recombination operations mainly for diversification purposes. Figure 2 illustrates an individual deme architecture and the formation of the two levels (subpopulations) within the population. Based on the two-level scheme, there are three categories of possible mating operations: between superior individuals, between superior and inferior individuals, and between inferior individuals.

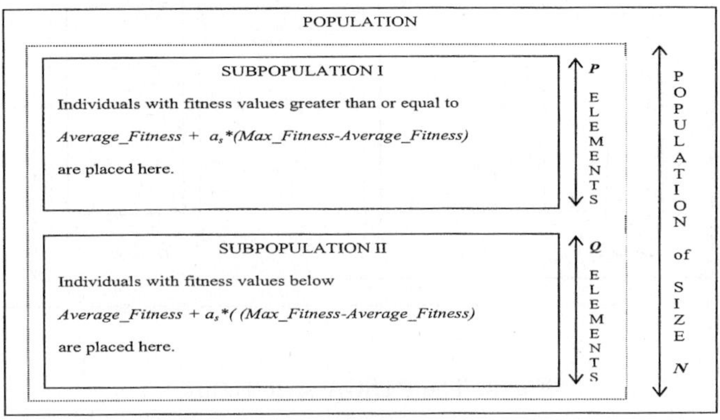

Fig. 2. The two-level deme organization based on average-fitness value.

For both intensification and diversification purposes, which are the main mechanisms for a successful search in evolutionary algorithms, mating of individuals in each of the three categories is carried out in a controlled manner. Note that mating individuals from the sub-population of superiors only will become a mostly intensification approach, whereas excessive recombination of individuals from the sub-population of inferiors may delay the convergence by searching over the hopeless regions of the solution space. As a result of these considerations the following recombination schedule is followed: For a population of N individuals, $k_1\%$ of individuals are selected as the elite individuals of the current generation, $k_2\%$ of individuals are generated through the recombination of randomly selected superior individuals, $k_3\%$ of individuals are generated through the recombination between a superior and an inferior parent, and $k_4\%$ of individuals are generated through the recombination of inferior individuals. The experimentally evaluated values of these coefficients and other GA parameters are given in the next section.

Figure 3 illustrates the PTSGA architecture. There are N individual demes each of which has two subpopulations. Subpopulations in the upper society hold the superior individuals and the subpopulations in the lower society hold the inferior individuals. It is easy to see that the proposed PTSGA architecture is quite appropriate for either fine-grained or coarse-grained parallel implementations.

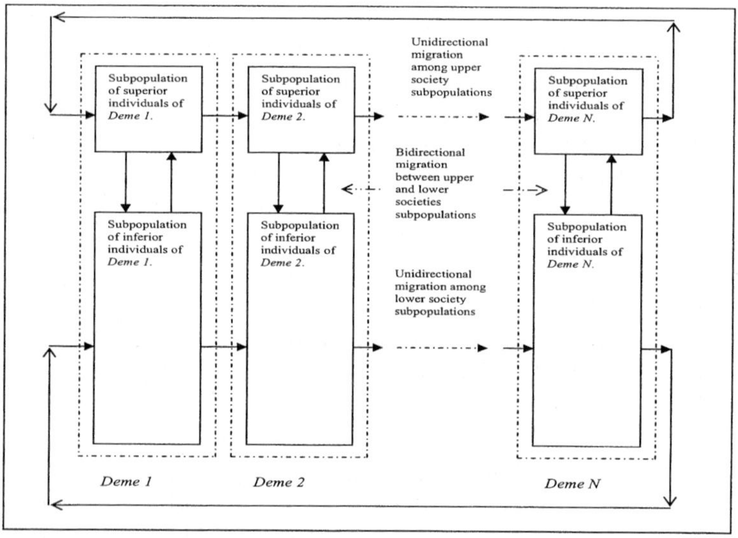

Fig. 3. The PTSGA architecture.

Following the formation of offspring individuals in all demes, unidirectional synchronous migration of individuals takes place between subpopulations in each society and between the subpopulations of each individual deme. Migration between the subpopulations within the same deme is carried out first. In this respect, offspring individuals in the superior level having smaller fitness values than their parents are replaced by better parents. The replaced superior offspring individuals migrate to lower subpopulation and replace the worst-fitness individuals. The second round of migration takes place unidirectionally between subpopulations in the same society. From left-to-right, each subpopulation sends K randomly selected individuals to the subpopulation to its right and receives the same amount of randomly selected individuals from the subpopulation to its left.

3 Two Case Studies

To study the performance of the described PTSGA approach, it is compared with the conventional GAs for the solution of some benchmark problems from numerical and combinatorial optimization fields. Those benchmark numerical optimization problems handled in evaluations are taken from [12] and [13], which are claimed to provide reasonable test cases for the necessary combination of path-oriented and volume-oriented characteristics of a search strategy. For the combinatorial optimization problems, the 100-city symmetric traveling salesman problem, kroA100, taken from [14] is considered as a representative problem instance.

In all experiments, real-valued chromosomes are used for problem representations. Tournament selection and the uniform crossover operator are employed with a crossover rate equal to 0.7, whereas the mutation rate is 0.01. Experiments are carried out using a population size of 500 individuals for conventional GAs, whereas the total number of individuals in the multideme PTSGA approach is also 500, i.e. 500/D in each deme, where D is the number of demes. In this way, total number of individuals in convential GAs and PTSGA are kept the same. For the PTSGA approach, the coefficients a_s, k_1, k_2, k_3, and k_4 determining dynamic fitness range for individuals in the superior level, and the ratio of offspring individuals created by elitism and the three recombination categories, respectively, are experimentally determined as 0.5, 0.2, 0.6, 0.15, and 0.05. The value of K determining the amount of intra-society migration is taken as 15% of subpopulation size. Number of demes, D, is taken as 5 in all experiments. Each experiment is performed 10 times and all the tests were run over 500 generations. In the following worked examples, the results obtained with conventional GAs and the PTSGA approach are compared for relative performance evaluations.

3.1 Performance of PTSGA Approach in Numerical Optimization

Conventional GAs are compared with PTSGA approach for the minimization of functions listed in Table 1. Each function has 20 variables. The best solution found using the conventional GAs and PTSGA approach are given in Table 1. PTSGA provided very close to optimal results in all trials. These results demonstrate the success of the implemented PTSGA strategy for the numerical optimization problems.

Table 1. Performance evalution of conventional GAs and GAs with chromosome reuse for numerical optimization.

Function	Global Opt., n=Num. Vars.	Best Found: Conv. GA		Best Found: Proposed	
		Global Min.	ITER	Global Min.	ITER
Michalewicz	-9.66 ,$n = m = 10$	-8.55	500	-9.56	100
Griewangk	0, $n = 20$	0.0001	380	$1.0e^{-}15$	50
Rastrigin	0, $n = 20$	0.01	200	$1.0e^{-}10$	100
Schwefel	$-n * 418.9829, n = 20$	-8159	400	-8374	100
Ackley's	0, $n = 20$	0.0015	400	$1.0e^{-}12$	80
De Jong (Step)	0, n=20	1	500	0	30

3.2 Performance of the PTSGA Approach in Combinatorial Optimization

To test the performance of the PTSGA approach over a difficult problem of combinatorial type, the 100-city TSP kroA100 is selected. The best found solution for this problem is 21282 obtained using a branch-and-bound algorithm. In the ten experiments performed, the best solution found for this problem using the conventional GAs is 21340 which is obtained in 1000 generations with population size equal to 500. The best solution obtained with the PTSGA approach with 500 individuals, in total, is 21282 which is obtained after 100 generations. Figure 4 shows the relative performance of the PTSGA approach compared to the conventional GAs implementation, the straight line plot shows the results for the PTSGA approach.

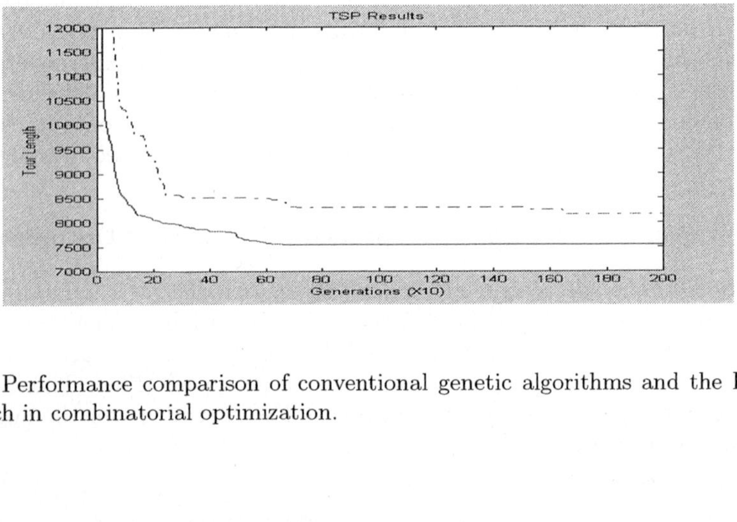

Fig. 4. Performance comparison of conventional genetic algorithms and the PTSGA approach in combinatorial optimization.

4 Conclusions and Future Work

In this paper a novel selectionless, two-level multi-deme, two-society, and parallel GA approach, PTSGA, is introduced. The main ideas behind the proposed method are the elimination of the the selection operator by two-level populations dynamically controlled by the average fitness value and, the migration and individual replacement policies among multiple demes. The implemented algorithm is used to solve difficult numerical and combinatorial optimization problems and its performance is compared with the conventional GAs implementation for representative problem instances. Each problem is solved exactly the same number of times and the best fitness results are analyzed for performance comparisons. All GA parameters are kept unchanged throughout all experiments.

From the results of case studies, for the same population size, it is concluded that the PTSGA approach outperforms the conventional implementation in all trials. Additionally, the PTSGA approach exhibits much better performance for both numerical and combinatorial optimization problems. In fact, problems from these classes are purposely chosen to examine this side of the proposed strategy.

This work requires further investigation from following point of views: Effects of different selection strategies such as roulette-wheel and truncation selection strategies, performance evaluations for other problem classes such as neural network design, speech processing, and face recognition, problem representations involving variable size chromosomes, and applications in genetic programming.

References

1. Goldberg D.E.: Genetic Algorithms in Search, Optimization, and Machine Learning, Addison-Wesley Publishing Company, 1989.
2. Back T.: Evolutionary Algorithms in Theory and Practice, Oxford University Press, 1996.
3. Nowostawski M., Poli R.: Review and Taxonomy of Parallel Genetic Algorithms, Technical Report: CSRP-99-11, The University of Otago, New Zeeland, May 1999.
4. Cantu-Paz E.: A Survey of Parallel Genetic Algorithms, IlliGAL Report, University of Illinois at Urbana-Champaign, USA, 1999.
5. Cantu-Paz E.: Designing Efficient Master-Slave Parallel Genetic Algorithms, IlliGAL Report:97004, University of Illinois at Urbana-Champaign, USA, 1997.
6. Manderick B., Spieesens P.: Fine-Grained Parallel Genetic Algorithms, Proceedings of the Third International Conference on Genetic Algorithms, Schaffer J. D. (ed.), p.428–433, Morgan Kaufmann, CA, 1989.
7. Lin S. -C., Punch W., Goodman E.: Coarse-Grain Parallel Genetic Algorithms: Categorization and New Approaches, IEEE Symposium on Parallel and Distributed Processing, IEEE CS Press, 1994.
8. Cantu-Paz E.: Topologies, Migration Rates, and Multi-Population Parallel Genetic Algorithms, IlliGAL Report:99007, University of Illinois at Urbana-Champaign, USA, 1999.
9. Hauser R., Manner R.: Implementation of Standard Genetic Algorithm on MIMD Machines, Parallel Problem Solving from Nature, PPSN III, p.504–513, Springer-Verlag, 1994.
10. Nowostawski M., Poli R.: A Highly Scalable Parallel Genetic Algorithm Based on Dynamic Deme Reorganization, Technical Report:CSRP-99-12, The University of Otago, New Zeeland, 1999.
11. Lin S. -H., Goodman E. D., Punch W. F.: Investigating Parallel Genetic Algorithms on Job Shop Scheduling Problem, Sixth International Conference on Evolutionary Programming, Angeline P., Renolds R., Eberhart R. (eds.), p. 383–393. Springer-Verlag, 1997.
12. Website: http://www.f.utb.cz/people/zelinka/soma/func.html.
13. Kim, H.S., Cho, S.B: An Efficient genetic algorithm with less fitness valuations by clustering, Proc. of the 2001 IEEE Congress on Evolutionary Computation, p.887–894, Seoul, Korea, May 27–30, (2001).
14. Web-site:
http://www.iwr.uni-heidelberg.de/groups/comopt/software/TSPLIB95/tsp/

Gene Level Concurrency in Genetic Algorithms

Onur Tolga Şehitoğlu and Göktürk Üçoluk

Computer Engineering Department,
METU, Ankara, Turkey,
{onur,ucoluk}@ceng.metu.edu.tr

Abstract. This study describes an alternative concurrency approach in genetic algorithms. Inspiring from implicit parallelism in a physical chromosome, a vertical concurrency is introduced. Proposed gene process model allows genetic algorithms work in encodings independent from the gene position ordering in a chromosome. This feature is used to implement a gene reordering version of genetic algorithm. Further possible models of flexible gene position encodings are discussed.

1 Introduction

Genetic algorithms mimic the evolution in the nature in order to search a solution space for non-trivial problems like optimization problems. They have been successfully applied to many engineering and scientific problems where a polynomial time deterministic algorithm does not exist. They efficiently explore of the search space by using the global information gained during the exploration in a population of individuals.

As genetic algorithms get widely used, parallel genetic algorithms became a major study area. Cantú-Paz classifies parallel genetic algorithms in three groups [1]: In *global parallelism* application of genetic operators and evaluation of individuals are explicitly parallelized. In *coarse grain* and *fine grain* parallelism population is distributed among the processors and only mating within the subpopulations and among the neighbor populations are allowed. Also there are some *hybrid* studies combining these approaches.

In this study a different approach to fine grain parallelism is discussed where each process keeps track of a single gene value of the whole population. Crossover and mutation operations can be done concurrently as single cycle operations providing an implicit parallelism for genetic operators. In addition, operations become independent from the gene ordering making more flexible chromosome encodings possible [2,3].

In the following sections, first the gene process model where each process represents a gene position is introduced. Then application of this model with a gene reordering genetic algorithm [4,3] is described. Then other possible encodings in this model are discussed.

A. Yazici and C. Şener (Eds.): ISCIS 2003, LNCS 2869, pp. 976–983, 2003.

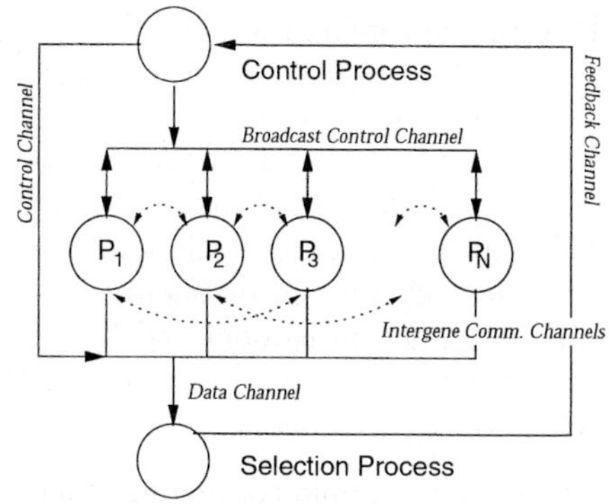

Fig. 1. Architecture of the gene process model

2 Gene Process Model

In the proposed model, each gene position in the phenotype is executed by a separate process. In each process an object keeps the specific genom data of the whole population. These objects are connected to each other and to two other special processes via communication channels. These two special processes are the *Control Process* and the *Selection Process*. Architecture of the model is given in Figure 1.

Execution of the entire model is based on message passing on order preserving and lossless channels. All gene processes and the selection process execute a *receive message — do corresponding action* loop. The control process initiates and supervises the genetic algorithm.

If we represent the ith chromosome in the population as a vector of genes as $\Gamma_i = \langle g_1, g_2, \ldots, g_n \rangle$ where n is the phenotype length, and the population size is m, we can denote the whole population $\mathbf{\Gamma}$ as a vector of chromosomes. A particular gene value in the population is then represented as $\Gamma_{i,j}$ denoting the jth gene of the ith chromosome.

In the proposed architecture, this representation is transposed into a collection of vertical gene vectors instead of a collection of chromosomes. A gene vector Λ_i is the vector containing all gene values in the ith position of the chromosomes of the pool $\Lambda_i = \langle \Gamma_{1,i}, \Gamma_{2,i}, \ldots, \Gamma_{m,i} \rangle$.

All gene processes are identical objects defined by a set of attributes and actions (methods). So a gene process P_i is a tuple:
$P_i = \langle i, \mathsf{pos}, \Lambda, new\Lambda, \mathsf{Broad}, \mathsf{Inport}, \overline{\mathsf{Outports}}, \mathsf{Actions} \rangle$
Where:

- i: Position of the gene implemented by this process in the phenotype.
- pos: Phenotype independent position information. It is used by variable permutation representations and may contain any spatial or hierarchical information. In simple GA implementation it is set to i.
- Λ: Gene vector Λ_i of the current population.

$new\Lambda$: Gene vector Λ_i of the new generation.
Broad: Broadcast command channel to be listened
Inport: Private input channel of the process
Outports: A vector of output ports that this process uses to send data. It includes the data channel flowing through the *selection process*, the inter-gene channels and the broadcast channel. In simple GA implementations only the data channel is sufficient.
Actions: A set of actions. Each action is identified by a named tuple of any arity. When a message of the same pattern is received the corresponding action is executed by the gene process.

A gene process executes a very simple command sequence:
1) Wait for a message in Inport or Broad. 2) Execute the matching action. 3) Go to step 1

Selection process S is similarly a tuple:
$S = \langle \mathbf{\Gamma}, new\mathbf{\Gamma}, \overline{\text{fitnesses}}, \text{Inport}, \text{Outport}, f, \text{Actions} \rangle$
Where:
$\mathbf{\Gamma}$: Data of the entire pool of the current generation.
$new\mathbf{\Gamma}$: Data of the entire pool of the new generation.
fitnesses: Fitnesses calculated for the individuals in the pool
Inport: Input channel to be listened.
Outport: Feedback channel to send results of the selection.
f: Fitness function.
Actions: A set of actions. Similar to gene processes.

Selection process executes the same loop with the gene processes:
The pool data is received from the gene processes. Then the fitness calculation and the selection action is initiated by a message coming from the control process. The selection information is sent back to the control process via the feedback channel.

The control process executes the genetic algorithm loop by sending genetic operator messages to all gene processes, than the fitness calculation message and the selection message to the selection process, in each iteration. Repeating this iteration for many generations will make genetic algorithm work.

3 Simple GA Implementation

In a simple GA implementation a gene process implements the following messages:

`init(`M`)` Initializes the gene vector Λ randomly

$$\Lambda_i \leftarrow random() \text{ for all } i = 1, .., M$$

`mutate(`$prob$`)` All genes in the new population $new\Lambda$ is mutated with a probability of $prob$.

$$new\Lambda_i(t+1) \leftarrow \begin{cases} mutated(new\Lambda_i(t)) & \text{if } random([0,1]) \leq prob \\ new\Lambda_i(t) & \text{otherwise} \end{cases} \quad \text{for all } i = 1, .., M$$

`crossover(`cp`, `$p1$`, `$p2$`)` Parents $p1$ and $p2$ in the current population are crossovered to produce two new offsprings in the new population. cp is the crossover point where offsprings switch parents. ($\bullet$ is used to denote the append operation)

$$newA \leftarrow newA \bullet \langle g_A, g_B \rangle \text{ where } \langle g_A, g_B \rangle = \begin{cases} \langle A_{p1}, A_{p2} \rangle & \text{if } \mathsf{pos} \leq cp \\ \langle A_{p2}, A_{p1} \rangle & \text{otherwise} \end{cases}$$

`uniformcrossover(`$p1$`, `$p2$`,[`$prob$`])` In uniform crossover, offspring value is taken from one of the parents, probabilistically.

$$newA \leftarrow newA \bullet \langle g_A, g_B \rangle \text{ where } \langle g_A, g_B \rangle = \begin{cases} \langle A_{p1}, A_{p2} \rangle & \text{if } random([0,1]) \leq prob \\ \langle A_{p2}, A_{p1} \rangle & \text{otherwise} \end{cases}$$

`senddata()` This messages initiates the sending of the gene information to the selection process so that it could make calculations on this global data. $\mathsf{send}_{datachannel}$`(data(`$i$`, `$newA$`))`

`select(`$List$`)` The control process sends a list of chromosome identifiers to be selected via this message.

$$A \leftarrow \langle newA_k \mid k \in List \rangle \quad ; \quad newA \leftarrow \langle\,\rangle$$

Similar to the gene processes, selection process implements a set of messages as actions. Those messages are received over the same channel from gene processes or control process. This messages are `data(`i`,`L`)`, for getting the data of the ith gene process, `setfitnesses()` for calculating fitnesses over the population, `select(`K`)` to select K element for crossover in the next generation by applying any selection mechanism, `sendselected()` to send the list of selected individuals to the control process back.

After this definitions of messages (or actions) control process executes the following loop:

```
send_broadcast(init(M))
DO {   REPEAT (CrossoverRatio × M) times {
                 A, B ← random(1,M) ; CP ← random(1,N)
                 send_broadcast(crossover(CP,A,B)) }
       send_broadcast(mutate(MutateProb),senddata())
       send_selection(setfitnesses(),select(M),sendselected(M))
       receive_feedback(selected(List))
       send_broadcast(select(List))
} WHILE Maximum number of generations is not reached
```

Most of this communication can be done asynchronously. Only places requiring synchronization are the fitness calculation and the selection process.

4 Gene Reordering GA

Gene reordering genetic algorithm is introduced in [4,3]. It is a linkage learning method and empirically shown to improve online performance of genetic algorithms in deceptive problems.

In gene reordering GA, a single global permutation is considered during the computation. This permutation maps a gene number to a position value in the chromosome encoding. Crossover operations are based on this mapping instead of the original gene ordering in the representation. During the evolution of the genetic algorithm, this global permutation is readjusted by means of statistical analysis on neighboring genes in the population.

Let $\mathbf{\Gamma}$ be the encoding of the problem and Γ_i represent the value of the ith feature in a chromosome. We define a permutation function $p : \{1,\ldots,n\} \mapsto \{1,\ldots,n\}$ so that Γ_i will be considered in the $p(i)^{th}$ position for crossover operation and $\Gamma_{p^{-1}(i)}$ and $\Gamma_{p^{-1}(i+1)}$ values are neighbor gene values with respect to p.

We define a *neighbour-affinity function* for neighbour gene positions in the permutation in its most general form as: $\mathcal{A}_i^p : \{\langle \Gamma_{p^{-1}(i)}, \Gamma_{p^{-1}(i+1)} \rangle\}_{pool} \mapsto [0,1]$

$\mathcal{A}_i^p$ function is based on a statistical analysis of the pool and maps the neighbour values from the pool to an affinity value. The type of the statistical analysis used depends on the problem representation. Examples can be *hamming distance* for binary encoding and *variance* for other numerical encodings.

The next step is to modify the permutation mapping by looking at the results of neighbour-affinity value calculations from the individuals in the current population. We will be calling these values A_i^p. All A_i^p values will be calculated with some period of generation. If an A_i^p value is found to be less then a threshold value τ, these neighbour genes will be considered not to contribute solution well together and the permutation will be changed to separate them. Actually there exist 4 possible affinity cases for each gene position:

1. *Affinity is greater then τ for both neighbours* so current ordering is fine. The gene position in the permutation kept unaltered.
2. *Affinity with left gene is greater than τ but it is less than τ for the right gene*. So left neighbour is fine but we should separate it from the right. So it exchanges position with the left neighbour.
3. *Affinity with left gene is less than τ but it is greater than τ for the right gene*. Similarly it exchanges position with the right neighbour.
4. *Both affinities are less than τ*. Gene is moved to a random position in the permutation.

In this way, modifications in the permutation mappings are kept to be as local as possible.

5 Gene Reordering Genetic Algorithms and Gene Level Concurrency

In *gene reordering genetic algorithms* global ordering of genes with respect to crossover operator is changed by the local decisions to maximize affinity values among the gene positions.

In gene level concurrency, crossover operation is based on the pos attribute of each gene process. So moving a gene in the global permutation is just simply updating the pos values of the gene processes. Since the affinity calculations are done among the neighboring genes, they can be calculated by means of local communications. In this way simple genetic algorithm implementation can be extended into gene reordering genetic algorithm with a few additions.

In the gene reordering genetic algorithm, in addition to simple GA, a gene process includes LeftAffinity and RigthAffinity attributes. Furthermore, $\overline{\mathsf{Outports}}$ includes private ports to the other gene processes.

The new gene process is the following tuple:
$P_i = \langle i, \mathsf{pos}, \Lambda, new\Lambda, \mathsf{Broad}, \mathsf{Inport}, \overline{\mathsf{Outports}}, f, aff, \mathsf{Actions}, \mathsf{LeftAff}, \mathsf{RightAff}\rangle$
Only affinity values to the left and right neighbor processes and the user defined affinity function aff are added. This *neighborhood* is defined as to possess consecutive pos attribute values.

New message and actions are required to calculate and process affinities. Affinity calculation requires the data of the two processes. So each process sends its data to the left neighbor. Left neighbor calculate and set the right affinity and sends it to the right so that it can update the left affinity. When this cycle is completed all affinity values would be known for all gene processes.

The next step is to update the positions based on the affinities obtained. Since the position updates are local in the implementation of the gene reordering genetic algorithm, this decision is left to the gene process. In the sequential implementation this is done deterministically in a linear scan of the permutation. In the concurrent version this is done probabilistically.

Following messages are introduced in order to implement gene reordering GA:

`sendtoleft()` This initiates the gene vector exchange among the neighbors. Each gene process sends its Λ to the left neighbor (having pos-1 position) in a `data(...)` message.

$$\mathsf{send}_{gene(\mathsf{pos}-1)}(\mathtt{data}(i, \Lambda))$$

`data(`k`,`$Neigh\Lambda$`)` Data is available from the right neighbor (having pos+1 position). The gene calculates and updates the right affinity by calling a user defined aff function and sends back the calculated value to its neighbor.

$$\mathsf{RightAff} \leftarrow aff(\Lambda, N\Lambda)$$
$$\mathsf{send}_{gene(\mathsf{pos}+1)}(\mathtt{setaff}(i, \mathsf{RightAff}))$$

`setaff(`k`,`v`)` Left neighbor is sending the calculated affinity. Just set the LeftAff to the value sent.

$$\mathsf{LeftAff} \leftarrow v$$

`moveme(`k`,currpos,topos)` This messages is received by all processes via the broadcast channel since order change of a process may affect positions of all genes. After this change the gene process listens to the channel of its new position. The gene requesting the move, simply updates its position.

$$\mathsf{pos} \leftarrow \begin{cases} \mathsf{topos} & \text{if } \mathsf{currpos} = \mathsf{pos} \\ \mathsf{pos} - 1 & \text{if } \mathsf{currpos} < \mathsf{pos} \text{ and } \mathsf{topos} > \mathsf{pos} \\ \mathsf{pos} + 1 & \text{if } \mathsf{currpos} > \mathsf{pos} \text{ and } \mathsf{topos} < \mathsf{pos} \\ \mathsf{pos} & \text{otherwise} \end{cases}$$

Only `sendtoleft(...)` is initiated by the control process. `data(...)` and `setaff(...)` is generated among the gene processes as a consequence of this message. `moveme(...)` on the other hand is a probabilistically generated message. After a gene process completes a `select(...)` request, it probabilistically (with a probability of $\frac{1}{t}$ for an expected period of t (generations) makes a movement decision and sends a `moveme(...)` message to the broadcast channel.

This decision is based on its left and right neighbor affinities and a threshold value τ, of them. If gene process have good affinities with both neighbors it will not send any message and retain its existing position. If any of the neighbour affinity is below the threshold, it sends a command to move itself into a local or a random position according to the decision specified in Section 4.

After introducing these messages into the gene processes, the only additional update required for the control process is to have a `sendtoleft(...)` message to initiate the affinity calculation in the main loop.

6 Conclusion and Other Possible Architectures

Gene reordering GA is not the only possible architecture that can be implemented in the gene level concurrency model. Since the model eliminates the requirement for a linear fixed order, any non-linear and/or variable topology can be implemented by using it.

For example a matrix notation can be suitable to represent 2-D spatial chromosome encodings (Figure 2(b)). Image processing is a good example for such an application area. The only change required is to have a tuple for the pos attribute. The crossover point is going to be any shape in the 2-D representation. This shape will separate the chromosome into two partitions. So the crossover will decide about a particular gene of a chromosome, considering which partition it belongs to.

So resulting gene process tuple will be:

$$P_i = \langle\langle i_x, i_y\rangle, \langle \mathsf{pos}_x, \mathsf{pos}_y\rangle, \Lambda, new\Lambda, \mathsf{Broad}, \mathsf{Inport}, \overline{\mathsf{Outports}}, \mathsf{Actions}\rangle$$

Any shape description which divides the matrix into two partitions is suitable. It can be a line or any arbitrary shape as long as a function returning a binary choice $partition : Shape \times Position \rightarrow \{0,1\}$ can be defined. Than the crossover can be based on this function.

For example if the shape is a line passing from two points $\langle a_x, a_y\rangle$ and $\langle b_x, b_y\rangle$ the *partition* function can be defined as:

$$partition(\langle a_x, a_y\rangle, \langle \mathsf{pos}_x, \mathsf{pos}_y\rangle) = \begin{cases} \text{if } \mathsf{pos}_y < \frac{b_y - a_y}{b_x - a_x}(\mathsf{pos}_x - a_x) + a_y \ , & 0 \\ \text{otherwise} \ , & 1 \end{cases}$$

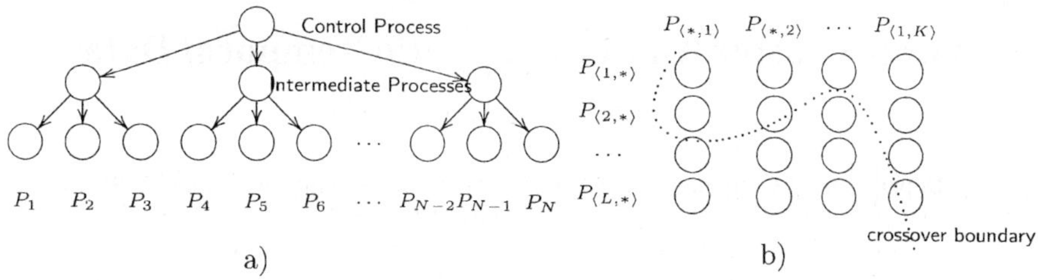

Fig. 2. Possible chromosome representations a) hierarchical representation. b) mesh representation

Another possible extension of the method is the hierarchical chromosome representation shown in (Figure 2(a)). Instead of a single level orientation of gene processes an intermediate level of processes can be inserted between the control process and the gene processes. These processes capture the incoming control messages and generate modified messages through their child processes. This allows different levels of genetic operator and building block interactions possible similar to [5].

In summary, this study describes an alternative way of realizing the implicit concurrency within a physiological chromosome and considering each genotype a separate processing identity. The resulting implementation has an implicit parallelism. This parallelism has been combined with the encoding flexibility of the proposed model. Gene reordering genetic algorithm is an example of this flexibility work. This idea of having each gene position a separate entity can be further expanded to have alternative approaches to genetic algorithm.

References

1. Cantú-Paz, E.: A summary of research on parallel genetic algorithms. Technical Report 95007, IlliGAL (1995)
2. Sehitoglu, O.T.: A concurrent constraint programming approach to genetic algorithms. In Ryan, C., ed.: Graduate Student Workshop, San Francisco (2001) 445–448
3. Şehitoğlu, O.T.: Gene Reordering and Concurrency in Genetic Algorithms. PhD thesis, Computer Engineering Dept, METU, Ankara (2002)
4. Sehitoglu, O.T., Ucoluk, G.: A building block favoring reordering method for gene positions in genetic algorithms. In Spector, L., Goodman, E., eds.: Proc. of the Genetic and Evolutionary Computation Conference (GECCO-2001), San Francisco, Morgan Kaufmann (2001) 571–575
5. Pelikan, M., Goldberg, D.E.: Escaping hierarchical traps with competent genetic algorithms. In Spector, L., Goodman, E., eds.: Proc. of the Genetic and Evolutionary Computation Conference (GECCO-2001), San Francisco, Morgan Kaufmann (2001) 511–518
6. Holland, J.: Adaptation in Natural and Artificial Systems. MIT Press (1975)
7. Harik, G.: Learning Gene Linkage to Efficiently Solve Problems of Bounded Difficulty Using Genetic Algorithms. PhD thesis, University of Michigan (1997)

Fuzzy Cluster Analysis of Spatio-Temporal Data*

Zhijian Liu and Roy George

Department of Computer Science, Clark Atlanta University, Atlanta, GA 30314
rkavil@bellsouth.net

Abstract. The quantities of earth science data collected have necessitated the development of new data mining tools and techniques. Mining this data can produce new insights into weather, climatological and environmental trends that have significance both scientifically and practically. This paper discusses the challenges posed by earth science databases and examines the use of fuzzy K-Means clustering for analyzing such data. It proposes the extension of the fuzzy K-Means clustering algorithm to account for the spatio-temporal nature of such data. The paper introduces an unsupervised fuzzy clustering algorithm, based on the fuzzy K-Means and defines a cluster validity index which is used to determine an optimal number of clusters. It is shown experimentally that the algorithms are able to identify and preserve regions of meteorological interest

1 Introduction

Satellites, weather stations, and sensors are collecting large volumes of geospatial data on a wide range of parameters. Examples of such geospatial data include earth science data describing spatiotemporal phenomena, multi-dimensional sequences of images in geographic regions, the evolution of natural phenomena, etc. However, despite the importance of such geospatial data sets it is only recently that there have been efforts to develop appropriate data mining (DM) and knowledge discovery in databases (KDD) tools and techniques suitable for analysis.

The spatio-temporal domain is complex [1] and characterized by high volumes of data. For example several global landcover/landuse maps have terabytes of information, requiring computationally intense analysis techniques. Interesting signals and data are often masked by stronger signals caused by local effects, such as seasonal variations. The coupling between different regions of the globe also introduces complexities in behavior. These effects make analysis of this data difficult. Non-uniformity in data gathering and sampling sometimes require indirect measurements and interpolation, which lead to the introduction of model artifacts. Formulating geographic knowledge, and applying it to knowledge discovery and data mining is

* This work is partially supported by the Army High Performance Computing Research Center Contract No. DAAD19-01-2-0014 and Army Research Laboratory Contract No. DAAL01-98-2-0065. The content of this work does not reflect the position or policy of the US Army and no official endorsement should be inferred.

A. Yazici and C. Şener (Eds.): ISCIS 2003, LNCS 2869, pp. 984–991, 2003.

also difficult. This level of complexity is evident in Data Mining (DM) and Knowledge Discovery in Databases (KDD) techniques for this domain which have encompassed a wide range of models and techniques [2]. These techniques vary from the visual oriented approach [3], the generation of geographic association rules and sequence rules [4], clustering [5, 6], to combinational approaches [7].

The application of fuzzy logic techniques to data mining and knowledge discovery in the weather domain has several advantages. Imprecision and uncertainty in this domain is present at several levels. Attribute ambiguity occurs when class membership is partial or unclear. Attribute ambiguity is a severe problem in remotely sensed data[8], such as aerial photography, which is often interpreted inconsistently. Spatial vagueness emerges when the sampling resolution is not fine enough to identify boundary locations exactly, where gradual transitions occur between classes, or when there is location uncertainty. Clustering is a technique that helps in the analysis of such large data sets through the definition of regions that have similar properties. However, conventional hard clustering [6] is inappropriate when faced with the ambiguities in weather data measurement. The data often has numerous missing values or errors in measurement, and is the spatial and attribute ambiguities make analysis difficult. Fuzzy clustering is more appropriate for this data with its ability to naturally incorporate these real world issues. The ability to produce soft boundaries permits a improved interpretation capabilities. The development of DM and KDD techniques that can model and incorporate this uncertainty can thus lead to better understanding of such features. Clustering techniques have been widely used in DM and KDD. Fuzzy clustering is an extension of the classical clustering technique and has been used to solve numerous problems in the areas of pattern recognition and fuzzy model identification [12]. A variety of fuzzy clustering methods have been proposed and several of them are based upon distance criteria. Fuzzy K-means Clustering has been widely used for understanding patterns especially where the clusters might overlap. It has been applied to landuse/landcover classification [8], gene cluster identification [9] and the classification of water chemistry data [10]. The weather data, its characteristics, and the preprocessing steps are discussed in Section 2. The application of fuzzy k-means clustering to spatio-temporal data as a data mining technique and a new algorithm for unsupervised fuzzy k-means clustering are described in Section 3. Section 4 examines future directions and concludes the paper.

2 Clustering in the Spatio-Temporal Domain

Clustering is the process by which feature vectors are grouped into clusters based on a similarity measure. The choice of cluster centers (or prototypes) is crucial to the clustering process. The similarity measure should discriminate against feature vectors that are farther away from the cluster center in favor of vectors that are closer. Several different clustering techniques have been introduced by various authors. However, the challenge is in applying them to domain specific problems particularly the identification of similarity measures that are appropriate to the problem. In this effort we report on the application of the fuzzy K-means clustering technique to the spatio-temporal domain.

2.1 Fuzzy K-Means Clustering

The classical K-Means clustering does a hard partition (0 or 1) on the data. The Fuzzy K-Means [14] is a more expressive clustering technique. It computes the degree of membership of a data point in a cluster (μ ε [0,1]). For the spatio-temporal domain this permits flexibility in interpretation of regions that are at the outer limits of a cluster. The hard partition can be viewed as a fuzzy partition with a truth-value of either 0 (false) or 1 (true).

$\overline{X}$, $\overline{Y}$ are the mean of variable X and Y respectively; $\sum(x \cdot y)$ is the sum of the product of all ordered pairs; and n is the number of ordered pairs (data points). $\sum x^2$ is the sum of the squares of all values of the variable X, and $\sum y^2$ is the sum of the squares of all values of the variable Y.

Fuzzy k-means clustering attempts to minimize the within-cluster sum of square errors function under the following conditions:

$$\sum_{k=1}^{c} \mu_{ik} = 1,\ i=1,2,\ldots\ldots,n; \tag{1}$$

$$\sum_{i=1}^{n} \mu_{ik} > 0,\ k = 1,2,\ldots\ldots,c$$

μ is the membership function and $\mu_{ik} \in [0,1]$ $i = 1,2,\ldots\ldots,n;$ c is the cluster number. It is defined by the following objective function:

$$J = \sum_{i=1}^{n} \sum_{k=1}^{c} \mu_{ik}^{\varphi} d^2(x_i, c_k) \tag{2}$$

where n is the number of data points, c is the number of clusters, c_k is the vector representing the centroid of cluster k, x_i is the vector representing individual data point i and $d^2(x_i,c_k)$ is the squared distance between x_i and c_k according to a chosen definition of distance, which for simplicity denoted by d^2_{ik}. φ is the fuzzy exponent and ranges from (1, ∞). It determines the degree of fuzziness of the final solution, i.e. the degree of overlap between groups. With φ =1, the solution is a hard partition. As φ approaches infinity the solution approaches its highest degree of fuzziness.

The minimization of the objective function [15], J, provides the solution for the membership function:

$$\mu_{ik} = \frac{d_{ik}^{-2/(\varphi-1)}}{\sum_{j=1}^{c} d_{ij}^{-2/(\varphi-1)}},\ i=1,2,\ldots\ldots,n;\ k=1,2,\ldots\ldots,c \tag{3}$$

$$c_k = \frac{\sum_{i=1}^{n} \mu_{ik}^{\varphi} x_i}{\sum_{i=1}^{n} \mu_{ik}^{\varphi}}, \; k = 1,2,\ldots, c \tag{4}$$

The Fuzzy K-Means algorithm is initialized by the following:

a: *Choose the number of clusters: k, with 1<k<n.*

b: *Select a value for the fuzziness exponent φ, with $\varphi>1$.*

c: *Choose a definition of distance in the variable-space.*

d: *Select a value for the stopping criterion e (e= 0.001 gives reasonable convergence.)*

The steps of the K-Means algorithm are as below:

Step1: *Initialize $M = \{ \mu_{ik} \} = M^{(0)}$, with random memberships or with memberships from a hard k-means partition.*

Step2: *Start iteration with it =1.*

Step3: *Calculate $C = [11] = C^{(it)}$ using equation [5] and $M^{(it-1)}$*

Step4: *Calculate $M=M^{(it)}$ using equation [4] and $C^{(it)}$. If numerical overflow would occur with d_{ic} close or equal to 0, m_{ic} is set to 1.*

Step5: *Compare $M^{(it)}$ to $M^{(it-1)}$. If $||M^{(it)} - M^{(it-1)}|| < e$, then stop; otherwise it=it+1, go to Step 3.*

In the spatio-temporal domain each data point (in space) may be viewed as a vector consisting of time series parameters. The similarity in this domain may be measured by Pearson's correlation coefficient *p* through using Pearson Distance |1-*p*|. For variables (vectors) *X* and *Y*, Pearson Coefficient of Correlation is defined as

$$p = \frac{\sum(x \cdot y) - n \cdot \overline{X} \cdot \overline{Y}}{\sqrt{(\sum x^2 - n \cdot \overline{X}^2) \cdot (\sum y^2 - n \cdot \overline{Y}^2)}} \tag{5}$$

The initialization of membership function matrix *M* has impact on the resulting clustering, and so multiple runs of clustering should be carried out when random initialization is used.

The spatio-temporal domain for this research effort is weather data. The Navy Operational Global Atmospheric Prediction System (NOGAPS) [11] is a global weather forecasting model. NOGAPS uses conventional observations (surface, rawinsonde, pibal, and aircraft), and various forms of satellite-derived observations. Figures 1 and 2 are the Fuzzy K-Means clustering of temperature and precipitation data. There are 121 measurement points in the region, and the weather parameters are recorded 4 times daily. The contour lines represent height information. The number of clusters, K, is chosen to be five, and the clusters are visualized on the ARCINFO GIS system. . The clusters are expected to have a meteorological explanation, however initial selection of centroids for clusters and cluster number, **K,** have impact on the result grouping.

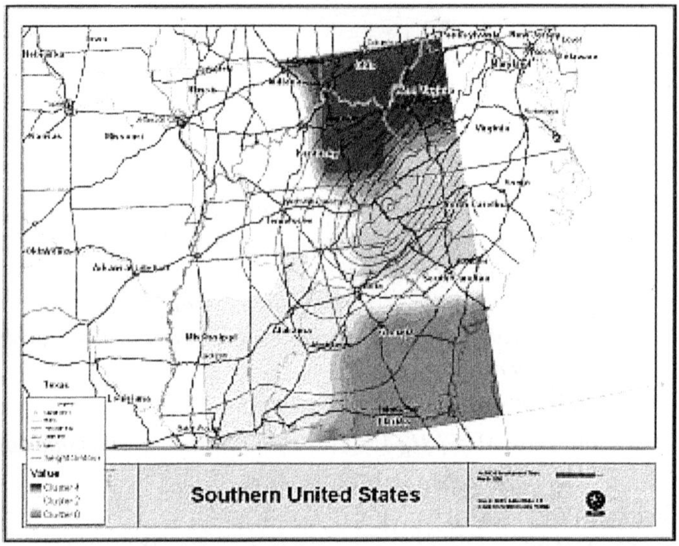

Fig. 1. Fuzzy K-Means clustering for temperature, 5 clusters

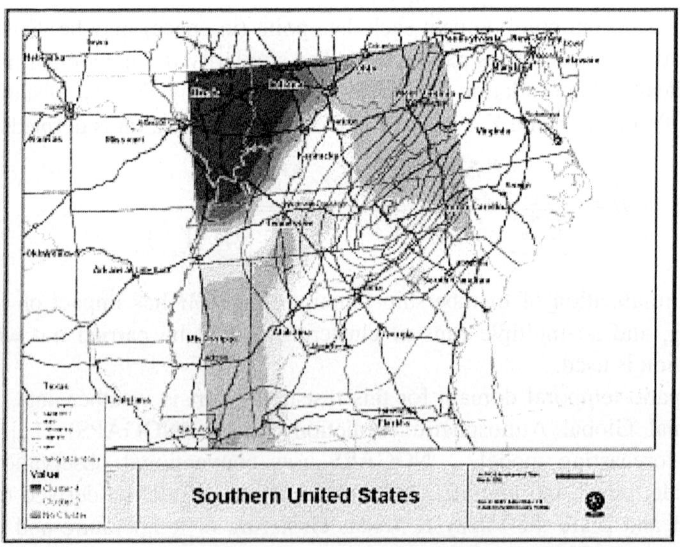

Fig. 2. Fuzzy K-Means clustering for precipitation, 5 clusters

From a domain standpoint (Climatic Atlas of the US, 1931-60), these clusters correspond to known weather features. The weather off the coast of Florida is dominated by a permanent air mass called the Bermuda high. This modifies the weather in

Florida, distinguishing it from the Gulf Coast. The Appalachian range (high elevation) produces modifications in the weather, except in the south-west part of the range, which is more typically affected by the Gulf effects. The weather in the interior is composed of several clusters, however their significance is not completely understood. These multiple clusters are an artifact of the clustering technique that apriori decided that there were 5 clusters in the data. A better solution would be to have an unsupervised clustering approach where the number of clusters is determined either using a domain independent approach or through the use of cluster determining domain knowledge. Both techniques would require the clusters to be validated, in the former case through validity measures or in the latter case through subject matter expertise. The Unsupervised Fuzzy K-Means Clustering technique was developed using the domain independent approach.

2.2 Unsupervised Fuzzy K-Means Clustering (UFKM)

A problem with the K-Means clustering (including fuzzy version) is that the number of clusters, **K**, has to be specified apriori. This creates a problem- a small value of **K**, would aggregate many natural clusters, hiding desirable features. On the other hand a larger value of **K** would result in the creation of several trivial clusters. In either case the clustering does not result in optimal detection of all interesting features, leaving the user to guess the minimal number of clusters that reveal all significant features. Unsupervised clustering may be employed to handle this and a bottom-up version of unsupervised clustering is reported here[16]. A large initial set of **K** clusters are initially assumed by the algorithm. The algorithm eliminates trivial clusters, and merges clusters that are similar at each step. These steps are repeated until the number of clusters is "minimal". A validity index is computed at each step. This validity index is used to decide which stage of clustering is capable of conserving pattern information.

The Unsupervised Fuzzy K-Means algorithm is as follows:

a. Choose the initial number of clusters

($k = \sqrt{n}$ is a good guess, where n is number of data points)

b. Develop a clustering using the Fuzzy K-Means

c. Merge those clusters that satisfy the following rules:

- *Pearson Coefficient of Correlation of their virtual centroids is less than 0.5*

d. Calculate validity index.

e. Repeat step b and c till only two clusters left.

After obtain a series of **clusters** with clustering number ranging from k_0 to 2, an optimal clustering can be chosen according to validity index. The Xie-Beni validity index is used here to determine the optimal number of clusters. It is extended to accommodate the spatio-temporal nature of the data through the incorporation of the Pearson Distance.

$$S = \frac{\sum_{k=1}^{c} \sum_{i=1}^{n} \mu_{ik}^{2}(1 - p_{ik})}{n \min_{j,k}(1 - p_{jk})}, \; j,k = 1,2,\ldots\ldots, c \tag{6}$$

where p_{ik} is pearson coefficient of x_i and c_k, and p_{ik} is pearson coefficient of c_j and c_k. A lower value of S indicates a better clustering.

The initial number of clusters is chosen to be 11, and the UFKM algorithm reduces this number iteratively. The result with 8 clusters gives the optimal validity index- however; the results when shown to meteorologists were not easily explained. It is possible that the 8 clusters reveal microclimatic regions- this issue is still being investigated. A set of 4 clusters derived correspond to the significant climatological regions in the selected region of the US discussed in the previous section.

3 Conclusion

The proliferation of geospatial data sources has necessitated the development of new data mining tools and techniques suitable to this domain. Mining this data can produce new insights into weather and climatological trends that can aid in applications such as operations planning. Data mining techniques can also be used to reveal microclimatic regions that may be used to modify large scale weather models to include locally relevant phenomena. This paper proposed the use of fuzzy clustering to overcome the problem of imprecise and uncertain data found in geographical data sets. Several new contributions are proposed in this paper. The fuzzy k-means clustering methodology was extended to the spatio-temporal domain. Second, a new unsupervised fuzzy clustering algorithm was introduced, and a new cluster validity index that determines the optimal number of clusters was defined. It was shown that the unsupervised clustering can identify and preserve geographically significant features in weather data and global climate data while minimizing the number of clusters.

There are several extensions to this work. The reduction of clusters in UKFM is done through the use of distance measures between cluster centroids. An alternate method of deriving significant clusters would be to use other geographic data sets for cluster validation. We are currently investigating the extension of UKFM through the use of such multi-data sets and initial results are promising. The centroid represents the characteristic properties of a cluster. These characteristic properties may be used to detect microclimatic regions within the area of analysis. The definition and identification of such microclimatic regions is an area that needs further study.

References

1. Gahegan, M., *Data Mining and Knowledge Discovery in the Geographical Domain: Intersection of Geospatial Information and Information Technology.* 2002, National Academies, Computer Science and Telecommunications Board.
2. Roddick, J.F. and M. Spiliopoulou, *A Bibliography of Temporal, Spatial, and Spatio-Temporal Data Mining Research.* SIGKDD Explorations, 1999. **1**(1).
3. Openshaw, S., *The Modifiable Areal Unit Problem.* CATMOG 38, 1984.
4. Koperski, K. and J. Han. *Discovery of Spatial Association Rules in Geographic Information Databases.* in *4th International Symposium on Large Spatial Databases (SSD95).* 1995. Maine.
5. Ester, M., H.-P. Kriegel, and e. al. *A Density Based Algorithm for Discovering Clusters in Large Spatial Databases with Noise.* in *2nd International Conference on Knowledge Discovery and Data Mining (KDD96).* 1996.
6. Steinbach, M., P.N. Tan, and e. al. *Clustering Earth Science Data: Goals, Issues and Results.* in *Fourth KDD Workshop on Mining Scientific Datasets.* 2001.
7. Gahegan, M., M. Wachowicz, and e. al., *The Integration of Geographic Visualization with Knowledge Discovery in Databases and Geocomputation.* Cartography and Geographic Information Systems, 2001.
8. Mohan, B.K., *Integration of IRS-1A L2 data by fuzzy logic approaches for landuse classification.* International Journal of Remote Sensing, 2000. **21**(8): p. 1709–1713.
9. Gasch, A.P. and M.B. Eisen, *Exploring the conditional coregulation of yeast gene expression through fuzzy k-means clustering.* Genome Biology Research, 2002: p. 0059.1–0059.22.
10. Guler, C., G.D. Thyne, and e. al., *Evaluation of graphical and multivariate statistical methods for classification of water chemistry data.* Hydrogeology Journal, 2002. **10**(4): p. 455–474.
11. Baker, N., et al., *The Navy Operational Global Atmospheric Prediction System: A Brief History of Past, Present, and Future Developments .* 1998.
12. Forgy, E., *Cluster analysis of multivariate data: efficiency versus interpretability of classifications.* Biometry, 1965. **21**(785).
13. MacQueen, J.B. *Some methods for classification and analysis of multivariate observations.* in *5th Berkeley Symp. on Probability and Statistics.* 1967. Berkeley.
14. deGruijter, J.J. and A.B. McBratney, *A modified fuzzy k means for predictive classification,* in *Classification and Related Methods of Data Analysis*, H.H. Bock, Editor. 1988, Elsevier Science: Amsterdam. p. 97–104.
15. Bezdek, J.C., *Pattern Recognition with Fuzzy Objective Function Algorithms.* 1981, New York: Plenum Press.
16. Cosic, D. and S. Loncaric. *New methods for cluster selection in unsupervised fuzzy clustering.* in *Proceedings of the 41th Anniversary Conference of KoREMA.* 1996.

Multi-agent Based Integrated Framework for Intra-class Testing of Object-Oriented Software

P. Dhavachelvan[1] and G.V. Uma[2]

[1] Research Scholar, School of Computer Science and Engineering, Anna University, Chennai – 25, Tamilnadu, India
pd_chelvoume@yahoo.co.in
[2]Senior Lecturer, School of Computer Science and Engineering, Anna University, Chennai – 25, Tamilnadu, India
gvuma@annauniv.edu

Abstract. The primary features of the Object-Oriented paradigm lead to develop a complex and compositional testing framework for object-oriented software. Agent technologies facilitate the software testing by virtue of their high-level independency and parallel activation. This paper presents a Multi-Agent based approach to enhance the definition for class testing in object-oriented paradigm. The Integrated framework has been built on two existing testing techniques namely Mutation Testing and Capability Testing. In both the cases, testing is carried out at Autonomous Unit Level (AUL) and Inter-Procedural Level (IPL). Mutation Based Testing-Agent and Capability Assessment Testing-Agent have been developed for performing AUL testing and Method Interaction Testing-Agent has been developed for performing IPL testing.

1 Introduction

The increased size and complexity of software systems has led to the current focus on developing distributed applications that are constructed from component-based systems. A component-based system is composed of both data and functionality and is configurable through parameters at run-time [7][13]. For an object-oriented application, class definitions provide the basic components of a program. Low-level component testing is nothing but the *unit testing*, which is to be performed on the independent units without any interface and interactions [7][13]. This is referred as *Autonomous Unit Level* (AUL) testing and it is true for conventional system testing but not for object oriented systems, since an object (class) is to be considered as an unit. For the purpose of improving the quality of our final product, class testing plays an important role in the stages of software testing and maintenance. Testing a class for its functionality means testing its member. The general members of a class are *data members, constructors and methods.*

Some of the testing techniques used to test conventional programs have been adopted for testing object-oriented programs. *State-based testing* is one of the most popular technique for testing object-oriented classes that covers the entire object

A. Yazici and C. Şener (Eds.): ISCIS 2003, LNCS 2869, pp. 992–999, 2003.

rather than just individual methods and so is much more appropriate for testing objects [13][16][17]. The tests cases generated with state-based testing methods will be used to execute *intra-class testing* but it ignores the program code, and could miss the detection of data members that do not define the state of the object class. Moreover, this technique might not generate all possible sequences of test cases based on the state-transition trees. They are suitable for the classes consist of methods, which don't interact with the outside members.

Data flow testing is also employed in the testing of object-oriented classes. This is not suitable for generating the sequences of messages for testing a class at the *intra-class* level, because such messages could be in an arbitrary order [6][13][16]. Intra-class testing tests the interactions of public methods when they are called in various sequences. Since users of a class may invoke sequences of methods in indeterminate order, we use intra-class testing to increase our confidence that sequences of calls interact properly. However, since the set of possible public method call sequences is infinite, we can only test a subset of this set. In the object-oriented environment, generally the interaction between the methods can be classified as follows.

Case-I

1. Interaction between the methods of same class.
2. Interaction between the methods of same class and program functions.

Case-II

1. Interaction between the methods of different classes.
2. Interaction between the methods of different classes and program functions.

In case-II, interaction between different class members can be referred as *unit-to-unit interaction*. Normally the unit-to-unit interaction is to be examined in the integration-testing phase. But in case-I, the program functions can't be considered as separate units. So, the interaction between the members of a class and program functions must be examined during the unit (object) testing. This is referred as *Inter-Procedure Level* testing (IPL) and it is not a part of the integration testing.

This type of the interaction can also be tested in this Enhanced State-Based integrated approach, by an agent called *Method Interaction Testing-Agent* (MIT-Agent). This gives an efficient cost reduction strategy in Integration Testing.

2 Need for Integration

Considerable research has gone into the development of methods for evaluating how 'good' a test set is for a given program against a given specification. Such criteria are also known as '*Test Adequacy Criteria*' or simply '*Adequacy Criteria*' [10][11][16]. A testing technique may use one or more of these criteria to assess the adequacy of a test set for a given unit and then decide whether to stop testing this unit or to enhance the test set by constructing additional test cases needed to satisfy a criterion. In principle, such criteria and the procedures may also be applied for the assessment of tests for subsystems. However, such an application is likely to be inefficient due to program size, redundant because multiple test teams might test the same part of the code, and incomplete because the large program size might prohibit testers from applying the criteria exhaustively.

Considering the units, which are to be tested prior to integration, we have developed an enhanced model for unit testing. Because of the important role of testing in software process and product quality, an integrated model for unit testing is developed, which compromises two testing techniques – *Mutation Based Testing* and *Capability Assessment Testing*. This model provides a variety of adequacy criteria by developing separate agents and defining their responsibilities in an efficient way.

This development is motivated by the need to assess test sets for subsystems, in which come about due to the complications during the unit testing.

3 Agents-Based System Architecture

Agent Oriented Software Engineering performance is based on three key terms for addressing any problem. They are *Decomposition, Abstraction and Organization* [5]. Agents based frameworks must have the objectives gives one a clear way to decompose the problems into agents. The agents are to be possessed the adaptive behavior, which doesn't need to specify all interactions in advance [4][8].

Agents maintain state. This means that they can potentially model themselves and others. But the important point, computationally, is that the response to a query or function call may be based not just on the state conveyed by the caller, but also based upon other information maintained by the agent from dynamic information sources [3][4]. The aim of this paper is to introduce a *Multi-Agent* based approach for object oriented software class testing.

3.1 Back-Ground Information Needed

- $P = \{ G, C, L \}$: Program to be Tested.
- $G = \{ g_1, g_2, ...g_m \}$: Set of global methods in P.
- $C = \{ c_1, c_2, ...c_n \}$: Set of member functions in the test class in P.
- $L = \{ l_1, l_2, ...l_p \}$: Set of local methods in P.
- f_r = function to be tested where $f_r \varepsilon \{ G \}$ or $f_r \varepsilon \{ C \}$ or $f_r \varepsilon \{ L \}$
  'r' value is such that, $1 \le r \le N$ and $N = n + m + p$.
- $T (f_r)$: Test case of the function f_r generated by MBT-Agent or CAT-Agent.
- $T^{/} (f_r)$: Test case of the function f_r generated by MIT-Agent.

3.2 System Agents – Task Allocation and Implementation

A close relation exists between the different levels of task decomposition and the specification of the interaction between tasks. Each task is assigned to one or more agents. Agents themselves perform one more (sub) tasks, either sequentially or in parallel. [9][15]. For design from scratch, including the design of agents themselves, tasks distinguished within a task hierarchy can be assigned to different agents on the basis of the tasks decomposition: both *complex and primitive* tasks alike. Task allocation at this level is not *one-to-one*: in many situations the same task may be assigned to more than one agent. In other situations, agents already have certain capabilities and characteristics.

3.2.1 Mutation Based Testing (MBT) – Agent

The mutation based testing is a *fault-based* testing strategy that measures the quality/adequacy of testing by examining that whether the test set used in testing can reveal certain types of faults [10]. Mutation testing has been found to be powerful in its error detection effectiveness when compared to other code coverage based criteria for selecting and evaluating test case sets at unit level [11]. The results can help with risk reduction. It does not verify the test completeness. It should be used as an adjunct to other testing techniques. It does not verify pre/post conditions.

In this framework, the mutation testing responsibilities are given to an agent *Mutation Based Testing-Agent* (MBT-Agent) such that, it has to test the functions in the sets G or C or L in an *autonomous fashion*. The following algorithm depicts the principle activities of MBT-Agent.

Algorithm – 1

Given input is 'P'.

1. Define the sets of C, G, L.
2. For each 'f_r',
   - 2.1. Select the type of Mutant for 'f_r' and fix it.
   - 2.2. Check, is there any function call in 'f_r'.
   - 2.3. If there any function call(s) in 'f_r', submit T (f_r) to MIT-Agent. Then *goto* 2.6.
   - 2.4. Else, run T (f_r).
   - 2.5. Observe the output of T (f_r) and record it.
   - 2.6. Repeat from 2.1 for another mutant.
3. Repeat 2 for next f_r.
4. Add the test report to Integrated Test Profile.

3.2.2 Capability Assessment Testing (CAT) – Agent

The Capability assessment testing is a *load based* testing strategy that measures the capacity of software units by examining the functionality of the units at various load conditions. It is mainly used for identifying the limits thereby identifying the deficiencies of the units. Capability assessment testing is an efficient approach for defining the functionality of a unit (particularly loop constructs) when compared to other code coverage based criteria for selecting and evaluating test case sets at unit level. It tests the loops in its workspace, boundary values and out-of-work-space with exception values. Since it can be for analyzing the loops mainly, it can be used as an adjunct to other testing techniques.

In this framework, the capability assessment testing responsibilities are given to an agent *Capability Assessment Testing –Agent* (CAT-Agent) such that, it has to test the functions in the sets G or C or L in an *autonomous fashion*. This agent is to automatically generate structural unit test vectors to achieve full *Modified Condition/Decision Coverage* (MC / DC). The following algorithm depicts the principle activities of CAT-Agent.

Algorithm – 2

Given input is 'P'.

1. Define the sets of C, G, L.
2. For each 'f_r',
   - 2.1. Define the test piece T_p in 'f_r'.
   - 2.2. Define the range of test process for 'T_p'.
   - 2.3. Check, is there any function call in 'f_r'.
   - 2.4. If there any function call in 'f_r', submit T (f_r) to MIT-Agent. Then *goto* 2.7.
   - 2.5. Else, run T (f_r).
   - 2.6. Observe the output of T (f_r) and record it.
   - 2.7. Repeat from 2.1 for another mutant.
3. Repeat 2 for next f_r.
4. Add the test report to Integrated Test Profile.

3.2.3 Methods Interaction Testing (MIT) – Agent

Since the interaction between a class members (methods) and program members (methods) can't be considered as unit-to-unit testing, it has to be tested in the unit test phase itself. In this framework, the method interaction testing is carried-out by an agent *Method Interaction Testing–Agent* (MIT-Agent) such that, it has to test the functions in the sets G or C or L in an *interactive fashion*. Here, the global and local subordinates (program members) of a class member are treated as global and local stubs respectively. The stubs are neither with minimal functionality nor with minimal data manipulation. Since, they are the exact replicas of the actual subordinates, it results in better performance irrespective of its overhead. The following algorithm depicts the principle activities of MIT-Agent.

Algorithm - 3

Given input is 'P' and T (f_r) from MBT-Agent or CAT-Agent.

1. Receive the T (f_r) from MBT-Agent *or* CAT-Agent with its input data specification
2. For each T (f_r),

2.1 Identify the subordinates and generate stubs for T (f_r), that gives T' (f_r).
2.2 Run T' (f_r). And record the output.

3. Repeat 2 for next T' (f_r). , if $r < m$ *or* $r < n$ *or* $r < p$.
4. Add the test report to Integrated Test Profile.

3.2.4 Task Control within and between Agents

Task control knowledge in complex and primitive tasks alike, make it possible to specify an agent's reasoning and acting patterns distributed over the hierarchy of agent components. Each component is assumed to have a discrete time scale. When and how a component will be activated is to be specified [15]. This most often includes the specification of at-least:

- the interaction required to provide the necessary input facts.
- the set of facts for which truth values are sought (target set)

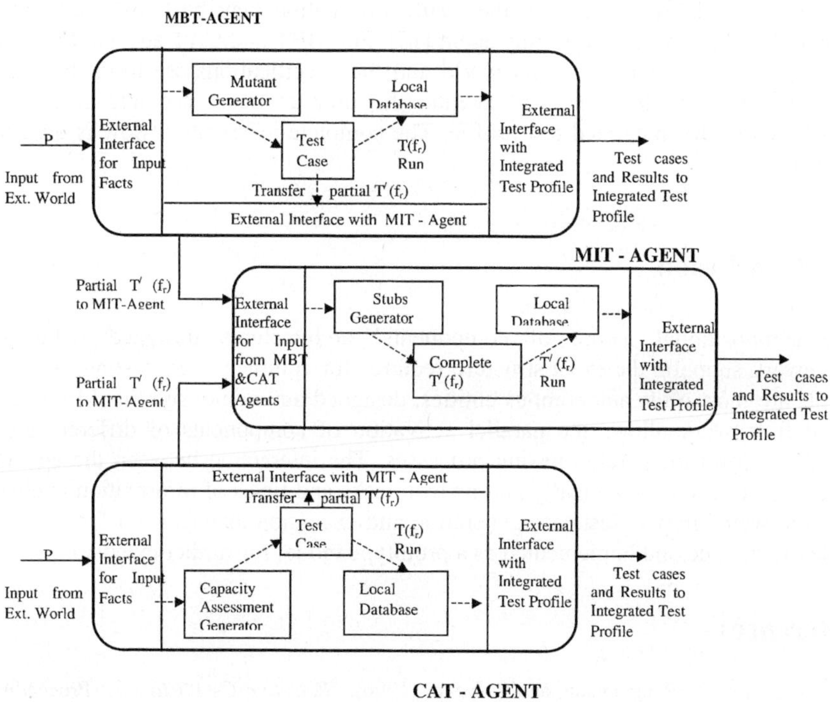

Fig. 1. Multi-agent based Framework

In the MBT-Agent, the local and global task controls are based on the Mutant specifications and Additional stubs requirements respectively. In the CAT-Agent, the local and global task controls are based on the test piece specifications and Additional stubs requirements respectively. For the task control between the agents, minimal global task control is required to initially activate all agents included in task performance. Since the input for MIT-Agent is from MBT and CAT agents, the task control in the MIT-Agent is based on the test case(s) generated either by MBT-Agent or CAT-Agent.

3.2.5 Information Flow within and between Agents

Information exchange within and between agents is based on the information links. Information links support modeling of specific types of interaction. For example, in a given situation, an agent may require specific information to be able to complete a reasoning task. The agent transfers this request as information to one or more other agents through information links. The information requested may, as a result, be transferred back to the agent through other information links. This mechanism is an essential element in modeling communication between agents [3][4][9]. In the fig.1, it is clearly explained that the test cases are formed at intermediate level in MBT and CAT agents (if there is any function call) and it is submitted to the MIT-Agent for further formation and execution. Interaction between an agent and the external world is modeled almost identically from the agents' point of view. For example: an observation of the external world may be modeled as an agent's specific request for information about the external world, transferred to the external world through an information link. As a result of the result information may be transferred through another link back to the requesting agent [15]. For MBT and CAT agents, the input is a test program from the external world and the specifications are from the user to generate the test cases. For all agents, the outputs (test case and results) are transferred to the integrated test profile. The complete information flow is described in the fig.1.

4 Conclusion

The compositional nature of components' architectures designed within the framework supports the exact structure requires for complete class testing. Since the agents are most often autonomous entities, designed autonomously, this Multi-Agent based framework allows the parallel activation of components of different agents there by allows the parallel testing processes. The interaction between the agents is well defined: each agent clearly had its own tasks and types of information exchange required were known. Test case generation and execution management for all agents is clearly defined and implemented as a prototype model for further extension.

References

1. T. Ashok, K. Rangaraajan, and P. Eswar (1996), *"Retesting C++ Classes,"* Proceedings, Ninth International Software Quality Week. Software Research Institute, San Francisco, May 1996.
2. Beizer, Boris, *"Software Testing Techniques"*, Van Nostrand Reinhold, 1990.
3. Brazier, F.M.T. and J. Treur (1994), *"User Centered Knowledge-Based System Design: A formal Modelling Approach"*, In: L. Steels, G. Schreiber and W. Van de Velde(eds.), *"A Future for Knowledge Acquisition"*, Proceedings of the 8th European Knowledge Acquisition Workshop, EKAW-94. Springer-Verlag, Lecture Notes in Artificial Intelligence 867, pp. 283–300.

4. Brazier, F.M.T., P.A.T. Van Eck, J. Treur (1995), *"Modelling Exclusive Access to Liminted Resources within a Multi-Agent Environment: Formal Specification"*, Technical Report, Vrije Universiteit Amsterdam, Department of Mathematics and Computer Science.
5. Charles Petrie.(2001), *"Agent-Oriented Software Engineering"*, Springer-Verlag 2001, Lecture Notes in Artificial Intelligence, pp.58–76.
6. J. Chen and A. Yang (2001), *"Enhance Software Reliability by Combining State-based and Data Flow Testing",* Proc. of the 5th World Multi conference on Systemics, Cybernetics and Informatics (SCI 2001), Volume 1, pp. 354–359. IIIS Press, 2001.
7. Chung, Chi-Ming and Ming-Chi Lee (1992), *"Object-Oriented Programming Testing Methodology"*, published in Proceedings of the Fourth International Conference on Software Engineering and Knowledge Engineering, IEEE Computer Society Press, 15 -20 June 1992, pp. 378–385.
8. Keith S. Decker and Victor R. Lesse (1995), *"Designing a Family of Coordination Algorithms"*, In
9. Proceedings of the First International Conference on Multi-Agent Syystems, pp. 73–80., San Francisco, June-1995. AAAI Press.
10. Langevelde, I.A. Van, A.W. Philipsenand J. Treur (1992), *" Formal Specification of Compositional Architechtures"*, in B. Neumann (ed.), Proceedings of the 10th European Conference on Artificial Intelligence, ECAI'92, John Willey & Sons, Chichester, pp. 272–276.
11. P. Mathur, M. Delamaro, and J. Maldonado (1996), *"Integration testing using interface mutations"*, In *Proceedings of the Seventh International Symposium on Software Reliability Engineering*, pp.112–121. IEEE Computer Society Press, 1996.
12. Márcio E. Delamaro, José C. Maldonado, Aditya P. Mathur(2001), *"Interface Mutation: An Approach for Integration Testing"*, IEEE Transactions on Software Engg, March-2001, vol.27, pp. 228–247.
13. Mary Jean Harrold, John D. McGregor, and Kevin J. Fitzpatrick (1992), *"Incremental Testing of Object-oriented Class Structures", Proceedings, 14th International Conference on Software Engineering*, May 1992. IEEE Computer Society Press, Los Alamitos, Calif. pp.68–80.
14. Robert V. Binder (1996), *"Testing Object-Oriented Software: A Survey",* Journal of Software Testing, Verification and Reliability, vol. 6, pp.125–252, 1996.
15. Sun-Woo Kim, John A. Clark, John A. Mc.Dermid (2001), *"Investigating the effectiveness of object-oriented testing strategies using the mutation method",* Journal on 'Software Testing, Verification and Reliability' vol.11, Number 3, December-2001, pp.207–225.
16. Treur. J. and M. Willems (1995), *"Foraml Notions for Verification of Dynamics of Knowledge-Based Systems",* In: M.C. Rousset and M. Ayel (eds.), Proc. European Symposium on Validation and Verification of KBSs, EUROVAV'95, Chambery.
17. Tsai, Bor-Yuan; Stobart, Simon; Parrington, Norman and Mitchell, Ian (1998), *"Selecting Intra-Class Test Cases Based on State-Based Testing and Data Flow Testing Methods"*, Occasional Paper, CIS-4-98, School of CIS, University of Sunderland, UK, 1998.

Test Case Generation According to the Binary Search Strategy*

Sami Beydeda and Volker Gruhn

University of Leipzig
Department of Computer Science
Chair of Applied Telematics / e-Business
Klostergasse 3
04109 Leipzig, Germany
{sami.beydeda,volker.gruhn}@informatik.uni-leipzig.de
http://www.lpz-ebusiness.de

Abstract. One of the important tasks during software testing is the generation of test cases. Unfortunately, existing approaches to test case generation often have problems limiting their use. A problem of dynamic test case generation approaches, for instance, is that a large number of iterations can be necessary to obtain test cases. This article introduces a formal framework for the application of the well-known search strategy of binary search in path-oriented test case generation and explains the *binary search-based test case generation (BINTEST) algorithm.*

1 Introduction

This article presents a novel approach to automated test case generation. Several approaches have been proposed for test case generation, mainly *random*, *path-oriented*, *goal-oriented* and *intelligent* approaches [8]. Random techniques determine test cases based on assumptions concerning fault distribution (e.g. [2]). Path-oriented techniques generally use control flow information to identify a set of paths to be covered and generate the appropriate test cases for these paths. These techniques can further be classified in *static* and *dynamic* ones. Static techniques are often based on symbolic execution (e.g. [9]), whereas dynamic techniques obtain the necessary data by executing the program under test (e.g. [7]). Goal-oriented techniques identify test cases covering a selected goal such as a statement or branch, irrespective of the path taken (e.g. [8]). Intelligent techniques of automated test case generation rely on complex computations to identify test cases (e.g. [10]). Another classification of automated test case generation techniques can be found in [10].

The algorithm proposed in this article can be classified as a dynamic path-oriented one. Its basic idea is similar to that in [7]. The path to be covered is considered step-by-step, i.e. the goal of covering a path is divided into subgoals, test cases are then searched to fulfill them. The search process, however, differs

* The chair of Applied Telematics / e-Business is endowed by Deutsche Telekom AG.

A. Yazici and C. Şener (Eds.): ISCIS 2003, LNCS 2869, pp. 1000–1007, 2003.

substantially. In [7], the search process is conducted according to a specific error function. In our approach, test cases are determined using binary search, which requires certain assumptions but allows efficient test case generation. Other aspects of the BINTEST approach are covered in [3,4].

2 Terminology

The primary use of the BINTEST algorithm is in testing the methods of a class. Before explaining the BINTEST algorithm, we first formally define the basic terms.

Definition 1. *Let M be the method under test and C the class providing this method. Furthermore, let $a_1, \ldots, a_l$ designate the arguments of M and attributes of C, and D_{a_i} with $1 \leq i \leq l$ be the set of all values which can be assigned to a_i.*

(i) *The* domain *D of M is defined as the cross product $D_{a_1} \times \cdots \times D_{a_l}$,*
(ii) *an* input *of M as an element x in D and*
(iii) *a* test case *x_O as an input which satisfies a testing-relevant objective O.*

The BINTEST algorithm generates test cases with respect to certain paths in the control flow graph of the method to be tested. It attempts to identify for a path P a test case x_P in the method's domain appropriate for the traversal of that path. The traversal of path P thus represents the testing-relevant objective O referred to in Definition 1. A test case x_P is characterized as *traversing* or *covering* a path P if the blocks modeled by nodes constituting P are executed in the sequence prescribed if the arguments of M and attributes of C are set to the values specified by x_P, and M is invoked. The definition below defines some of the basic term required.

Definition 2. *Let M be the method under test.*

(i) *The* control flow graph *G of M is a directed graph (V, E, s, e) where V is a set of nodes, $E \subseteq V^2$ is a set of edges, and $s, e \in V$ are the initial and final node, respectively. The initial and final node in a control flow graph are the only nodes having no predecessor and no successor, respectively.*
(iii) *A* path *P in G is defined as a tuple $(v_1, \ldots, v_m) \in V^m$ of nodes with $(v_j, v_{j+1}) \in E$ for $1 \leq j < m$, v_1 and v_m being the initial node s and final node s of G, respectively.*

The nodes of a control flow graph represent basic blocks within the source code of M, the edges control flow between basic blocks. A *basic block* is a sequence of consecutive statements in which flow of control enters at the beginning and leaves at the end without halting or branching except at the end [1].

3 Test Case Generation Strategy

The BINTEST algorithm employs a strategy similar to that of the test case generation approach in [7]. In both approaches, the path to be covered is not considered as a whole, but rather divided into its basic constituents, which are then considered in the sequence respecting their order on the path. A test case x_P is approached by iteratively generating inputs successively covering each of the edges of P. A particular edge is only traversed by a subset of all possible inputs. The inputs need to fulfill the traversal condition of this edge.

Definition 3. *Let M be the method under test, D its domain and (v_j, v_{j+1}) an edge in its control flow graph. Let furthermore be $\mathbb{B}$ the set of boolean values $\{false, true\}$. The* traversal condition $T_{(v_j,v_{j+1})}$ *of edge (v_j, v_{j+1}) is a function $T_{(v_j,v_{j+1})} : D \rightarrow \mathbb{B}$ defined as*

$$T_{(v_j,v_{j+1})}(x) = \begin{cases} true \text{ if } (v_j, v_{j+1}) \text{ is traversed by } x, \\ false \text{ otherwise.} \end{cases}$$

Traversal conditions associated with edges of a control flow graph link single inputs in the method's domain with paths in its control flow graph. Control flow graphs as introduced so far do not relate inputs of the represented method with paths and we thus cannot determine the path traversed for a certain input.

The BINTEST algorithm receives the initial input x_0 from the tester and evaluates the traversal condition of the first edge (v_1, v_2) of P with respect to this value. Traversal condition $T_{(v_1,v_2)}$ is generally not met for all inputs in D but for values in a certain subset $D_1 \subseteq D$ and the initial input is therefore changed to a value $x_1 \in D_1$ ensuring the traversal of edge (v_1, v_2), i.e. $T_{(v_1,v_2)}(x_1) = true$. In the next step, the traversal condition of the second edge (v_2, v_3) on P is evaluated given that arguments of M and attributes of C are set to the values specified by x_1. Again, $T_{(v_2,v_3)}$ is generally only satisfied by a subset $D_2 \subseteq D_1$ and x_1 needs to be modified if it does not lie in D_2. Hence, $D_2 \subseteq D_1 \subseteq D$. This procedure is continued for all edges on P until either an input is found fulfilling all traversal conditions or a contradiction among these conditions is detected. In such a case, the traversal conditions cannot be fulfilled entirely and the path is infeasible [10].

4 Monotony

The BINTEST algorithm approaches to a test case x_P traversing a path P by iteratively generating a series of inputs $x_0, x_1, x_2, \ldots, x_P$. In such a series, input x_0 is provided by the tester as the initial starting value, the others are calculated by the test case generation algorithm. Let Δ_i be the necessary qualitative modification in order to obtain x_{i+1} from x_i. A possibility to determine Δ_i is using information concerning the monotony behavior of the traversal condition under consideration.

Definition 4. *Let $\leq_X$ and $\leq_Y$ be order relations defined on sets X and Y, respectively, and x, x' be two arbitrary elements in a subset I of X with $x \leq_X x'$. A function $f : X \to Y$ is*

(i) monotone increasing on I *iff* $f(x) \leq_Y f(x')$,
(ii) monotone decreasing on I *iff* $f(x) \geq_Y f(x')$ *and*
(iii) monotone on I *iff it is either monotone increasing or decreasing on* I.

Definition 5. *Let X be a set and 2^X its power set.*

(i) A partition A *of* X *is a subset of* 2^X *with* $\bigcup_{a \in A} = X$ *and* $\forall a_1, a_2 \in A, a_1 \neq a_2 : a_1 \cap a_2 = \emptyset$. *The single sets in* A *are also called* blocks.
(ii) *A function* $f : X \to Y$ *is called* piecewise monotone *iff it is monotone on all blocks in a partition* A.

The notion of monotony describes the behavior of a function in relation to a change of the input. It gives a qualitative indication whether outputs of the function move in the same direction as inputs or in the reverse direction. Considering a traversal condition as a function whose monotony behavior is known, the direction in which the input needs to be moved to satisfy the traversal condition can be determined uniquely. Eventually, a traversal condition might not be monotone on its entire domain. In such a case, consideration has to be restricted to a subset on which it is monotone with the consequence that Δ_i can only be uniquely determined within this subset and might be different in others. Depending on the size of these subsets, they can also be grouped together according to the monotony behavior of the corresponding traversal condition to avoid that test case identification degenerates to linear search. For instance, a traversal condition defined on the set of integer numbers which maps even values to *true* and odd values to *false* is only monotone on subsets containing two elements. Instead of considering these subsets separately, they can be grouped to a family such as $(\{i, i+1\})_{i \text{ is integer}}$ and, since the traversal condition possesses the same monotony behavior on all subsets in the family, the family can be considered as a whole.

However, the monotony behavior of arbitrary traversal conditions is usually not known and suitable means are required to determine it. One solution is to explicitly specify the monotony behavior of the traversal condition associated with each edge in the control flow graph of a method. This solution is obviously undesirable, since the control flow graph of a complex method can have a large number of edges and the effort for monotony behavior specification can be substantial. The solution employed in the context of the BINTEST algorithm is to deduce the monotony behavior of a traversal condition from those of the functions of which the traversal condition is composed. The following lemma gives the formal basis for this.

Lemma 1. *Assume that $(f_k : X_k \to Y_k)_{1 \leq k \leq n}$ is a family of functions, with f_k being piecewise monotone with respect to order relations $\leq_{X_k}$ and $\leq_{Y_k}$, and $Y_k \subseteq X_{k+1}$. Let $F_n : X_1 \to Y_n$ be a function defined as the composition $F_n =$*

$f_n \circ \cdots \circ f_1$. Under this assumption, F_n is also piecewise monotone with respect to order relation $\leq_{X_1}$ defined on its domain and $\leq_{Y_n}$ defined on its codomain.

The proof of this lemma has been omitted due to space restrictions and can be found in [3]. A function is referred to as *atomic* if it cannot be further decomposed. Such a function is typically implemented by the underlying programming language as an operation or by a class or component as a method. The single atomic functions of which a particular traversal condition is composed can technically be determined using tracing. Tracing statements can be inserted into the method under test which are executed immediately prior to the execution of operations and methods corresponding to atomic functions, and the atomic functions constituting a particular traversal condition can be identified.

5 Algorithm

Figure 1 shows the BINTEST algorithm. The BINTEST algorithm requires as input the set of paths, $\mathcal{P}$, to be traversed and computes an appropriate set of test cases, $\mathcal{T}$, as output. The algorithm executes three distinct phases during its execution. These phase are the initialization phase (line 1), the test case generation phase (lines 2–45) and the finalization phase (line 46). The essential phase among them is obviously the test case generation phase. The algorithm executes three nested loops during this phase, which are the following:

Outmost loop. The single paths in $\mathcal{P}$ are considered during respective iterations of the outmost loop (lines 2–45). Each path $P \in \mathcal{P}$ is considered in an iteration, during which set A is initialized (line 3), the second loop is entered to generate an appropriate test case (lines 4–43) and the test case, if any could be generated, is added to $\mathcal{T}$ (lines 44–45). For the path $P = (v_1, \ldots, v_m)$ considered, a set A is constructed including all possible tuples $(I_1, \ldots, I_{m-1})$ with I_j being a block in the partition of $T_{(v_j, v_{j+1})}$'s domain. Block I_j is a subset of the domain of traversal condition $T_{(v_j, v_{j+1})}$ on which it is monotone and in which thus an appropriate test case can be approached to. The traversal of a path requires that all traversal conditions need to be considered in order to identify an input x satisfying all, or formally $\bigwedge_{1 \leq j < m} T_{(v_j, v_{j+1})}(x)$, the sufficient condition for the path's traversal. A block needs therefore to be specified for the traversal condition associated to each edge on the path. An appropriate input x, if it exists, thus necessarily lies in all of these blocks, i.e. $x \in \bigcap_{1 \leq j < m} I_j$.

Middle loop. The single tuples in A are considered during respective iterations of the second loop (lines 4–43). This loop is executed until either a test case has been found covering P or all elements in A have been considered and P is thus infeasible. During an iteration of this loop, an element $(I_1, ..., I_{m-1})$ is selected from A which has not been considered in an iteration before, and D_{cur} and j_{prev} are initialized (lines 5–7). D_{cur} gives the current search interval, whereas j_{prev} gives the index of the traversal condition considered in the previous iteration. After these initialization steps, the third and innermost loop is entered (lines 8–42).

```
1: T = ∅
2: for each path P = (v_1, ..., v_m) ∈ P
3:    A = A_1 × ··· × A_{m-1}, with A_j the partition of T_(v_j,v_{j+1})'s domain, 1 ≤ j ≤ m − 1
4:    repeat
5:       (I_1, ..., I_{m-1}) = an arbitrary element in A not considered before
6:       D_cur = D
7:       j_prev = 0
8:       repeat
9:          x_mid = middle element of D_cur regarding to ≤_D
10:         j_min = least j with x_mid ∉ I_j or T_(v_j,v_{j+1})(x_mid) ≠ true, 0 if j does not exist
11:         if j_min ≠ 0
12:         then
13:            if x_mid ∉ I_{j_min}
14:            then
15:               if x_mid <_D lower boundary of I_j
16:               then Δ = increase
17:               else Δ = decrease
18:            else
19:               if j_min > j_prev
20:               then
21:                  monotony = increasing
22:                  Δ = increase
23:                  D_backup = D_cur
24:               if j_min = j_prev
25:               then
26:                  if monotony = increasing
27:                  then Δ = increase
28:                  else Δ = decrease
29:               if j_min < j_prev
30:               then
31:                  if monotony = increasing
32:                  then Δ = decrease
33:                  else Δ = increase
34:            if Δ = increase
35:            then D_cur = {x ∈ D_cur | x ≰_D x_mid}
36:            else D_cur = {x ∈ D_cur | x ≤_D x_mid}
37:            if D_cur = ∅ and monotony = increasing
38:            then
39:               monotony = decreasing
40:               D_cur = D_backup
41:            j_prev = j_min
42:      until j_min = 0 or D_cur = ∅
43:   until j_min = 0 or all elements in A have been considered
44:   if j_min = 0
45:   then add x to T
46: return T
```

Fig. 1. The BINTEST algorithm.

Innermost loop. The binary search strategy is implemented by the innermost loop, which is executed until either an appropriate test case has been found or the search interval is empty and thus cannot contain an appropriate test case (lines 8–42). The first operation of an iteration is computation of the search interval's middle element x_{mid}. The traversal conditions associated to edges on P are then considered regarding to x_{mid} starting with that of the first edge on P and proceeding with respect to their ordering on P. Each traversal condition is analyzed to determine whether x_{mid} lies in the block specified by the tuple and the traversal condition results *true* for that input. j_{min} gives either the index of the first traversal condition for which one of these conditions is not satisfied, or its has a value of 0 to indicate that both conditions are satisfied for all traversal conditions. In the case of $j_{min} \neq 0$, i.e. P is not covered, lines 13–41 are executed in order to approach to an appropriate input. Otherwise, a test case has been found covering P and the inner two loops are left. The algorithm validates if x_{mid} is in the block $I_{j_{min}}$ specified by $(I_1, ..., I_{m-1})$ and sets Δ accordingly if it does not (lines 15–17). If x_{mid} lies in the block specified, j_{min} necessarily references the first traversal condition which is not satisfied by x_{mid} and the algorithm attempts to approach to an appropriate input (lines 19–33). For this purpose, j_{min} is compared with j_{prev}, the value of j_{min} during the last iteration. j_{min} can be greater, equal to or less than j_{prev}. The first case is given when the traversal condition considered during the last iteration is now satisfied and the algorithm considers in the current iteration the traversal condition associated to one of the next edges on the path (lines 19–23). As the traversal condition is considered for the first time, its monotony behavior is not known and an assumption is made. Based on this assumption Δ is set accordingly and the current search interval is stored in an auxiliary variable to allow the correction of the monotony assumption later. The second case is given when the traversal condition considered during the last iteration is still not fulfilled (lines 24–28). Another iteration is thereby necessary and Δ is set according to the monotony assumption made before. Finally, the third case occurs if a traversal condition satisfied before is not satisfied anymore due to the modification of the input made during the last iteration (lines 29–33). In this case, Δ is set to the reverse of the value assigned to it during the last iteration in order to approach to a value satisfying this traversal condition again. After obtaining Δ, the current search interval is bisected according to x_{mid} and one of the halves is selected with respect to Δ (lines 34–36). The iterations made, however, do not necessarily have to result in a suitable test case. One reason for this can be a wrong monotony assumption. The algorithm handles wrong monotony assumptions by reseting the search interval to that when the monotony assumption has been made and correcting the assumption (lines 37–40). Finally, the index of the traversal condition considered is stored in an auxiliary variable.

Theorem 1. *Let $P = (v_1, \ldots, v_m)$ be the path to be covered. Assume that the domains of the the traversal conditions $T_{(v_j, v_{j+1})}$, $1 \leq j < m$, are each partitioned in at most n blocks. The number of iterations conducted by the BINTEST algorithm to identify a test case covering P is bounded by $O(mn \log |D|)$.*

The proof of this theorem has been omitted due to space restrictions and can be found in [3].

6 Conclusions

We have presented in this article a novel approach for test case generation based on binary search. We are continuing our research on this approach, as it possesses several benefits. One of these benefits is that it can be used to generate test cases of any type as long as a total order exists on the search interval. Furthermore, the success of some existing test case generation techniques often depends on certain parameters and we can encounter the problem of calibration. Our approach does not require parameter calibration. Another aspect is that path-oriented test data generation is often carried out using optimizing techniques. Optimizing techniques can suffer from the problem of local minima or the initial starting point being too far from the solution [6]. Our approach does not suffer from these problems.

One of the applications of the BINTEST algorithm is in testing COTS components [3,5]. We believe that the diverging needs of the two parties involved in the development of a component-based system, component developers and developer of the system, can be met by self-testability. A possibility to achieve component self-testability is to embed a test case generation technique, such as the BINTEST approach, into the component. In this context, we would like to invite the reader to participate in an open discussion started to gain a consensus concerning the problems and open issues in testing components. The contributions received so far can be found at `http://www.stecc.de` and new contributions can be made by email to `sami.beydeda@informatik.uni-leipzig.de`.

References

1. Alfred V. Aho, Ravi Sethi, and Jeffrey D. Ullman. *Compilers, principles, techniques, and tools.* Addison Wesley, 1988.
2. Alberto Avritzer and Elaine J. Weyuker. The automatic generation of load test suites and the assessment of the resulting software. *IEEE Transactions on Software Engineering*, 21(9):705–716, 1995.
3. Sami Beydeda. *The Self-Testing COTS Components (STECC) Method.* PhD thesis, Universität Leipzig, Fakultät für Mathematik und Informatik, 2003.
4. Sami Beydeda and Volker Gruhn. BINTEST – binary search-based test case generation. In *Computer Software and Applications Conference (COMPSAC).* IEEE Computer Society Press, 2003.
5. Sami Beydeda and Volker Gruhn. Merging components and testing tools: The self-testing COTS components (STECC) strategy. In *EUROMICRO Conference Component-based Software Engineering Track.* IEEE Computer Society Press, 2003.
6. Matthew J. Gallagher and V. Lakshmi Narasimhan. Adtest: A test data generation suite for ada software systems. *IEEE Transactions on Software Engineering*, 23(8):473–484, 1997.
7. Bogdan Korel. Automated software test data generation. *IEEE Transactions on Software Engineering*, 16(8):870–879, 1990.
8. Roy P. Pargas, Mary Jean Harrold, and Robert R. Peck. Test-data generation using genetic algorithms. *Software Testing, Verification and Reliability*, 9(4):263–282, 1999.
9. C. Ramamoorthy, S. Ho, and W. Chen. On the automated generation of program test data. *IEEE Transactions on Software Engineering*, SE-2(4):293–300, 1976.
10. Nigel Tracey, John Clark, and Keith Mander. Automated program flaw finding using simulated annealing. In *SIGSOFT International Symposium on Software Testing and Analysis (ISSTA)*, volume 23 of *Software Engineering Notes*, pages 73–81. ACM Press, 1998.

Describing Web Service Architectures through Design-by-Contract

Sea Ling, Iman Poernomo, and Heinz Schmidt

School of Computer Science and Software Engineering,
Monash University, Caulfield East, Victoria, Australia 3145.
{sling,ihp,hws}@csse.monash.edu.au

Abstract. Architectural description languages (ADLs) are used to specify a high-level, compositional view of a software application, specifying how a system is to be composed from coarse-grain components. ADLs usually come equipped with a formal dynamic semantics, facilitating specification and analysis of distributed and event-based systems. In this paper, we describe the Radl [12], an ADL framework that provides both a process and a structural view of web service-based systems. We use Petri-net descriptions to give a dynamic view of business workflow for web service collaboration. We adapt the approach of [14] to define a form of design-by-contract [10] for configuring workflow architectures. This serves as a configuration-level means of constructing safer, more robust systems.

1 Introduction

Business-to-business (B2B) requires software solutions that are business-oriented, mission-critical, scalable and distributed. In meeting these demands, the software engineer can benefit from a formal design methodology. Different methodologies should be employed to design different aspects of a system. For example, UML [11] is useful to describe fine-grain, object-oriented design of individual components of a system.

In this paper, we outline an approach to specification and analysis of *architectural* aspects of middleware-based enterprise systems. These aspects consist of coarse-grain, structural design decisions that need to be made to facilitate quality requirement of the system. Architectural description languages (ADLs) are used to define and analyse architectural designs, as configurations of interoperating components. Generally, this is enabled through the use of a static syntax, for defining configurations of components, and a dynamic semantics, for analysing the behaviour of configurations. The formal nature of ADLs enables us to meet many of the needs of the enterprise at the architectural level. Architectural description can help us understand scalability and distribution issues to (partially) satisfy mission-critical demands.

The past few years has seen the emergence of web services as a B2B enabling technology [7]. In this paper, we will be concerned with workflow architectures that are implemented through configurations of web services.

A. Yazici and C. Şener (Eds.): ISCIS 2003, LNCS 2869, pp. 1008–1018, 2003.

We describe how our ADL, Radl [12], addresses B2B concerns, through the architectural description and analysis of web service based systems. We will be concerned with configurations of web services that implement a required business workflow. A workflow is a specific ordering of work activities across time and place, with a beginning, an end, and clearly defined inputs and outputs. Business workflows are both internal and external to autonomous business entities, defining their means of collaboration. An architecture for web service workflow deployment defines how the workflow's activities are to be organised: their location, hierarchical relationships, structural reuse and compositionality.

Our language can describe these various kinds of deployment, employing a uniform syntax and semantics for description and analysis. We define web service architectures through encapsulating workflows within the ADL. Our approach useful, because it provides us with a single framework in which to 1) design, understand and analyse the overall business-logic of a system, and 2) investigate and specify possible combinations of web service-oriented middleware for a workflow deployment.

Our work also uses a Petri-net semantics. We organise hierarchies of interacting web service workflows, each implementing a reusable, encapsulated business process. For the purposes of modelling, we use an abstract view of a web service, similar that of traditional ADLs for component modelling. We specify web services in terms of both workflows that are needed and public views of workflow that are available for participation. We employ an object-oriented type inference system, defined over web service interface descriptions, to facilitate web service substitutability based on behavioural inheritance. Then, we provide a novel adaption of recent approaches to architectural design-by-contract [13,10] to this context, defining when and how two workflow web services can safely interact with each other. These approaches give us a means of obtaining safer notions of interoperability between workflow architectures.

We proceed as follows. Section 2 provides some required preliminary definitions, summarizing how Petri nets may be used to model workflow. Section 3 defines our ADL for web service description. Section 4 provides a small case study. In section 5, we identify related work and provide concluding remarks.

2 Process Description Using Petri Nets

Petri nets have been widely used for process definition, covering behaviours of sequential execution, non-determinism and/or concurrency. (For a detailed description of Petri nets, see, e.g., [5]).

It is natural to use Petri nets for business process or workflow specification [4]. A workflow is a set of coordinated tasks to fulfill a specific business purpose [16]. In a special class of Petri nets, called Workflow nets (WF-nets) [2], workflow concepts are modelled by Petri net elements: workflow *activities or tasks* are modelled by transitions (graphically depicted by rectangles), *conditions* (precedence relations) modelled by places (depicted by circles), flow directions modelled by directed arcs and *cases* modelled by tokens. Standard workflow building blocks, such as AND-split, AND-join, OR-split and OR-join, have been represented by various net structures. Petri nets are strictly more powerful than the standard workflow graphs, since a number of high-level net classes [8] extend standard Petri nets in ways permitting states to carry complex and structured cases (tokens), and allowing activities to be parametrized, without losing the analytical power of Petri nets.

A Petri net $N = (P, T, F)$ is a *Workflow net (WF-net)* if and only if N has two special places $i \in P$ called *source* (an entry point) and $o \in P$ called *sink* (an exit point), and by adding a transition t^* to N, the short-circuited net $(P, T \cup \{t^*\}, F \cup \{(o, t^*), (t^*, i)\})$ must be strongly connected [1]. We use a contractor example described in [3] to illustrate a WF-net process specification, as shown in Figure 1.

Starting from source `i`, the contractor sends an order to some external subcontractor for a particular product. The `send order` tasks generates three concurrent threads of execution (AND-split): cost statement thread (first task: `prepare cost statement`), customer bill thread (first task: `bill`) and specification thread (first task: `create specification`). The choice (OR-split) structure of the process is illustrated by the checking of customer bill. At state `p1`, after the customer bill is created, the contractor has to make sure it is `okay`. If not, the bill has to be revised in a loop structure. After all three threads have been executed successfully, they will merge through the final task `handle product` that will lead to the sink `o`.

The tasks and process flow specified in Figure 1 are of local interest to the contractor organization and they are *private*. However, some tasks need to communicate and interact with external organizations (e.g. a subcontractor). In [3], these tasks are exposed as *public* methods so that interactions with the subcontractor organization or any other organization is possible. The combination of workflows is an interorganizational workflow [3] comprising several local workflows interacting with each other. The notion of workflow correctness or soundness has also been defined and relates directly to the liveness and boundedness properties of the underlying Petri net graph.

Each local workflow can be viewed as an individual workflow web service. While [3] exposes the public methods as web service interface and hides the internals, in our work we shall distinguish between the *required* interface and the *provided* interface in addition to exposing the protocol of methods' invocation.

Workflows can be enhanced and altered by adding new tasks. To permit such workflow changes and still ensure correctness, a behavioural equivalence property in net structures has been formalized [3] based on branching bisimilarity [6]. Consequently, it is possible to define a notion of inheritance, called projection inheritance, which focuses on the dynamics rather than data and signatures of methods [3].

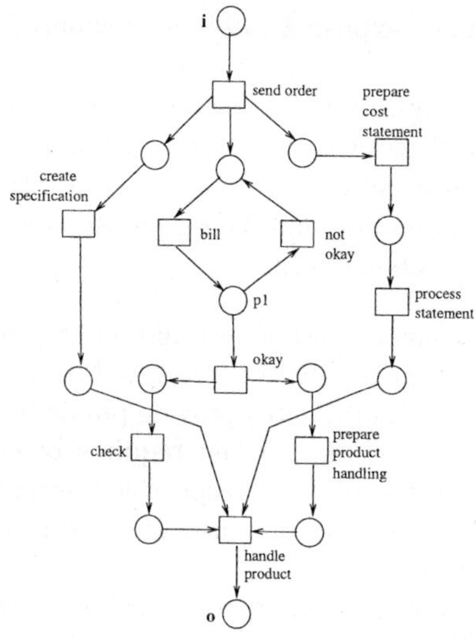

Fig. 1. A WF-net for the contractor.

3 Architectural Description

The Radl ADL [12] was originally described in [14], and has been extended by Ralf Reussner and two of the current authors in [13], to use finite state machines for behavioural and protocol descriptions and interoperability checks, specifically for component-based software.[1] The ADL has been used to model architectures for enterprise systems, by providing representations and semantics that meet enterprise concerns. In previous work, we have investigated .NET component-based architectures, and, in particular, configurations of business-centric .NET components. This paper now extends Radl to use Petri-nets for web-service description. First, we summarize basic aspects of Radl that are relevant to our current purpose. Our language has (semantically equivalent) textual and visual presentations. The former is useful for machine checking. The latter form is useful for human design and comprehension, and, for this reason, in this paper we define Radl in terms of the visual syntax.

3.1 Basic Concepts

Architectural description languages (ADLs) present a compositional, web service-oriented view of software architecture. Our ADL achieves this through modelling configurations of

- *basic kens*, representing web services that are executable and available (for example, web services that have been located by a UDDI server),

[1] Radl is the product of continuing research conducted by the TrustME group at the DSTC and the School of Computer Science and Software Engineering, Monash University.

- *gates*, interfaces of kens, exposing public behavioural information about an associated ken,
- *connections* between required and provided *gates* of kens, the possible types of communication and interaction within a system, and
- *compound kens*, higher-level entities composed of interconnected kens, that may in turn be basic or compound. These specify how a new web service can be built from smaller web services.

Kens and gates are analogous to components and services respectively in Darwin, to web services and ports respectively in C2 and ACME, or to processes and ports in MetaH [9]. As interfaces of kens, gates provide public behavioural descriptions of how a ken can be used, or what a ken requires of other kens in order to function. These two uses of gates result respectively from two types of gates for kens: *provided* and *required* gates. In our case, our interface descriptions take the form of Petri-net workflows.

For the purposes of comprehending configurations, kens can be viewed at various levels of encapsulation. A *black-box* view of a ken does not provide details of how the ken implements the functionality described by the gate interfaces. A *white-box* view of a ken provides such detail. A white-box view of a basic ken consists of a private workflow description, with a mapping between tasks of this description, and the tasks exposed by the gates of the ken. A white-box view of a compound ken provides details of how a ken's functionality is built from configurations of subsidiary kens, each of which in turn is given as a white-box ken. A *grey-box* view of a compound ken provides some – but not necessarily all – details of how a ken's functionality is built from configurations of subsidiary kens. This view given subsidary kens as either white-box or black-box views.

An *architecture* is defined by a set of interconnected kens.

There are two forms of connections between gates: connection mappings and bindings. *Mappings* are hierarchical connections. They may occur between two required gates or two provided gates, where the first gate belongs to a ken that is contained within the second gate's ken. *Bindings* are connections between required and provided gates of kens. They are non-hierarchical, because the kens must at the same level of compositionality: for binding to take place, one ken cannot be contained within the other.

Gates possess a richer language than, say, ports of Darwin [9]:

- A gate is associated with a signature for type checking.
- Gates are instances of gate classes. Consequently, gates are analogous to interface objects, adaptors or wrappers in programming.
- Designers can protect existing functionality within gates, but also it permits the substitutions between existing kens in a configuration, subject to compatibility checks over gates.

These features enable us to provide web services specifications as kens. In particular, multiple interfaces exposed by a web service are simply modelled by a web service ken with multiple gates.

3.2 Protocol between Gates of a Ken

In contrast to most ADLs, we define a public protocol between provided an required gates. Visually, this is represented as a workflow transition between a tasks of separate gates. This provides a description of how tasks, accepted by a required gate, are subsequently sequenced with those tasks that are produced by the required gate. This description provides encapsulation: a black-box view of the ken does not review the details of how this sequencing arises.

The need for public description of interactions between provided and required interfaces does not arise for most ADLs, because these languages are not designed for the purpose of modelling workflow architectures. In these cases, interfaces can be presumed as purely asynchronous and independent of each other. In the case of workflow, this is generally not the case. In the case of the `Subcontractor` example, the workflow between gates specifies that the processing of a specification is required to be completed prior to sending out a cost.

In this way, a ken is given a public workflow through its gates. This provides the architect with compositional constraints that lead to safer designs: whether or not kens may be connected (*compatibility*) and or may be substituted for one another (*substitutibiltiy*) within an architectural configuration. These notions can be formally understood through behavioural equivalence of gate Petri-nets.

3.3 Class-Based Organisation of Architectures

Radl employs object-oriented mechanisms for its definitions, to give us a notion of correct substitutibility between workflow web services. A ken is an instance of a *ken class*, and a gate is an instance of a *gate class*. These kinds of classes may be specialized through object-oriented subclassing. This permits reuse of specifications.

We define an object-oriented type system for architectures in the following manner.

Definition 1 (Ken subtyping). *Let K and K' be two kens classes. Let $\bar{p}^K = [p_1^K, \ldots, p_i^K]$ and $\bar{p}^{K'} = [p_1^{K'}, \ldots, p_j^{K'}]$ denote the provided gates of K and K', respectively. Let $\bar{r}^K = [p_1^K, \ldots, p_i^K]$ and $\bar{r}^{K'} = [p_1^{K'}, \ldots, p_j^{K'}]$ denote the required gates of K and K', respectively. Let wf^K and $wf^{K'}$ denote the public workflow of K and K', respectively. We say K' is a subtype of K, writing $K' \leq K$, when*

$$\begin{aligned} wf^K &\sqsubseteq wf^{K'} \\ \bar{p}^K.wf &\sqsubseteq \bar{p}^{K'}.wf \\ \bar{r}^{K'}.wf &\sqsubseteq \bar{r}^K.wf \end{aligned}$$

These conditions correspond to saying that a ken K' can be substituted for a ken K when

1. The workflow of K is preserved by K' – K' may now involve new tasks, but still permits the original sequencing of tasks of K.

2. K' may provide larger workflows, involving more tasks, but it must at least expose the original functionalities of K.
3. K' can require less interaction with other workflows, but cannot require more than that needed by K.

3.4 Design-by-Contract

The class-based organization forms a kind of design-by-contract [10], adapted to the architectural design level [13]. The requirement for safer connections between web services is satified by assigning interfaces to gates, because validity of connections between web services is determined by type checking.

Within the domain of programming language design, there are convincing arguments for adding further semantic annotations to web service interfaces, to make interface usage safer. Essentially, it is argued that an interface signature alone does not tell us *what* the interface methods are supposed to do, and that this information is necessary to use the interface safely.

This is difficult to achieve in most alternative ADLs. Most ADLs model a component's interface as a signature of required tasks and provided events. A behavioural specification tells us how these tasks and events are related to each other. These ADLs define interface elements to possess no signature or specification, so interoperability between components is understood as a simple binding between interfaces of web services. However, the task of determining whether interfaces *should* be connected is orthogonal to architectural design. This can be acceptable for defining small-scale architectures, where communication between web services is simple (such as Unix scripts which use pipes and filters). Unfortunately, for larger architectures, where complex information is being communicated, this situation leads to increased risk of design failure. This situtation is therefore not satisfactory for modelling large web service based systems.

4 Case Study

In our case study, we use an example of an interorganizational workflow introduced by Aalst [3], involving two business partners: a contractor and a subcontractor. That is, the previous contractor workflow example in Figure 1 is expanded to include communications with a subcontractor. The contractor sends a product order to the subcontractor followed by a detailed product specification. The subcontractor then sends a cost statement to the contractor. Based on the product specification, the subcontractor manufactures the product and sends it to the contractor.

Figure 2 illustrates (a) the contractor workflow web service and (b) the subcontractor workflow web service. Note that the internal structure of Figure 2 corresponds to Figure 1. As in [3], a list of methods is offered to other business domains. We also specify the expected order of execution for these methods, using Petri nets. For example, `send_order` must occur before `create_spec`, and `process_cost` before `handle_product`. These methods corresponds to some

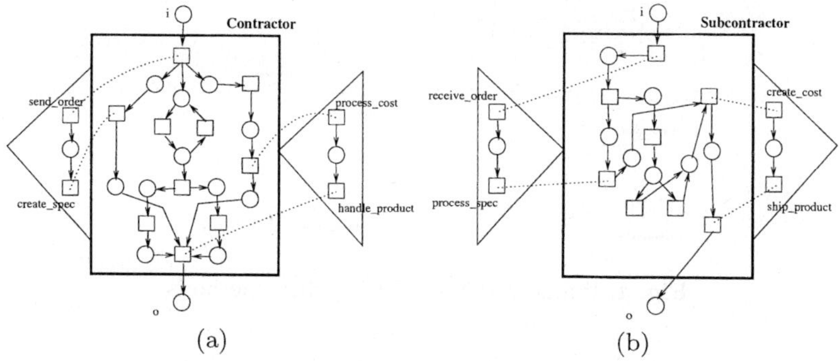

Fig. 2. (a) Contractor workflow. (b) Subcontractor workflow.

tasks within the internal workflow description of the web service, as depicted by the dotted lines in the figures. The description, hidden from the external environment, is the actual workflow to be executed, called the private workflow in [3]. It consists of tasks which are only of local interest.

The contractor's provided gate provides services `process_cost` and `handle_product`, while the subcontractor's provided gate provides `receive_order` and `process_spec`. Workflow methods, associated with these services, expect some form of input data or trigger in order to be executed. The Petri net on the provided gate also outlines the acceptable protocol method execution sequence. Symmetrically, a required gate represents possible connections to other web services that need to perform the services provided. The Petri net on the required gate can be interpreted as an abstraction of the call sequence potentially generated during services provided.

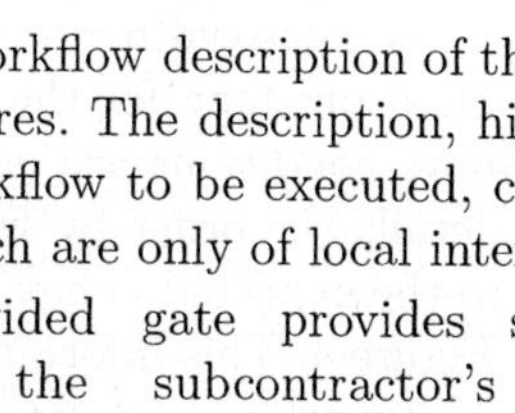

Fig. 3. The interorganizational workflow.

The two web services can be connected through appropriate methods to form an interorganizational workflow as shown in Figure 3. For example, `send_order` sends an order to `receive_order` while `ship_product` ships the product to `handle_product`.

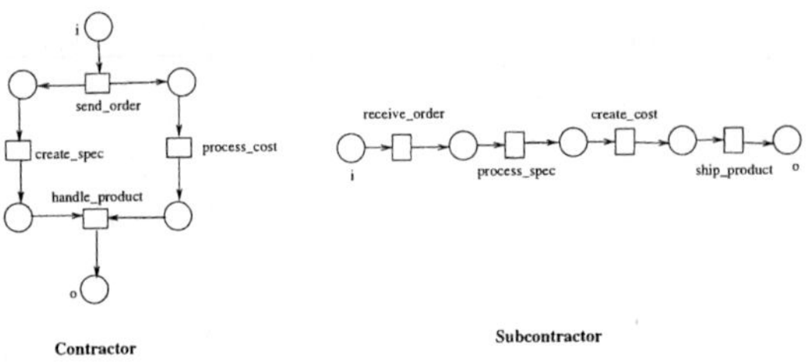

Fig. 4. Public workflows for interface methods

However, connecting the appropriate methods is insufficient to ensure correct workflow execution. The gates must also provide information detailing the relationship between the required net and the provided net of a web service. In fact, `send_order` and `create_spec` must precede `process_cost` and `handle_product` for the contractor web service, while `receive_order` and `process_spec` must be followed by `create_cost` and `ship_product` for the subcontractor web service. A deadlock will occur if the above conditions are not met. The workflow, only visible to the external world, details the order by which the interface methods should be executed. Adhering to the expected behaviour of the web services, the public workflows are shown in Figure 4. This information should be given to the web service users to ensure correct workflow operations.

5 Related Work and Conclusions

Most research on architectural description languages has been primarily concerned with architectures of concurrent, distributed, event-based software. To the best of our knowledge, this paper is the first attempt at using an ADL to describe web service architectures and to address B2B concerns. While addressing many concerns for enterprise design and analysis, this work has not explicitly focused on business-oriented concerns, nor, in particular, the problem of modelling enterprise workflow architectures. Most ADLs involve a dynamic semantics, useful for describing and understanding distribution and concurrency in architectures. However, such languages can be impractical for describing enterprise workflow.

The notable exception is [3], where an ADL with a Petri net semantics was developed, facilitating web service-based organisation and analysis of workflow. Petri nets have been used effectively for workflow description, and tools exist to intergrate Petri net descriptions into implementations in various workflow engines. However, that language is not as rich as traditional ADLs, where language web services are usually specified in terms of provided interfaces, functionality that the web service exposes as services to other web services, and required interfaces, services that the web service can use from other web services.

Object-oriented notions of behavioural subtyping have been investigated in [14]. Our adaptation of this notion to architectures is comparable to that of C2:

both make use of of a behavioural equivalence partial order over web service interfaces.

Our conditions for subtyping are stronger than those of Aalst, because we do not only consider the overall public workflow of a web service, but also the individual workflows defining the provided and required gates.

Our approach emphasizes two issues that are important to enterprise workflow modelling. The first is modelling safer usages between web services by means of design-by-contract in our ADL. The second issue is provision of closer correspondence between dynamic semantics and workflow description in practice. Most ADLs involve a dynamic semantics, useful for describing and understanding distribution and concurrency in architectures. However, such languages can be impractical for describing enterprise workflow. On contrast, Petri nets have a long history of use in describing workflow, and tools exist to integrate Petri net descriptions into implementations in various workflow engines.

Current state-of-the-art in modelling enterprise workflow is to use the BizTalk or Oracle Workflow notations and tools. Also, in the domain of web service workflow description, the WSDL has been proposed as a standard [7]. It is an open area of research to adapt our methods to for these other notations. This should be possible, because Petri nets have been shown to be a good formalism for formally representing many workflow notatins.

References

1. W. van der Aalst. Verification of workflow nets. In *Application and Theory of Petri Nets 1997. 18th International Conference Proceedings*, pages 407–26, LNCS 1248, Springer-Verlag, 1997.
2. W. van der Aalst. The application of Petri nets to workflow management. *The Journal of Circuits, Systems and Computers*, 8(1):21–66, 1998.
3. W. van der Aalst. Inheritance of interorganizational workflows: How to agree to disagree without loosing control. Technical Report BETA Working Papers Serise, WP46, Eindhoven University of Technology, The Netherlands, 2000.
4. W. van der Aalst, J. Desel, and A. Oberweis, editors. *Business Process Management: Models, Techniques and Empirical Studies.* Springer-Verlag, 2000.
5. J. Desel and J. Esparza. *Free Choice Petri Nets.* Cambridge University Press, 1995.
6. R.J. van Glabbeek and W.P. Weijland. Branching time and abstraction in bisimulation semantics. *Journal of the ACM*, 43(3):550–600, 1996.
7. W3C Group. Web services activity site. Web site, W3C, 2002. Available at `http://www.w3.org/2002/ws/`.
8. K. Jensen and G. Rozenberg, editors. *High-Level Petri Nets, Theory and Application.* Springer-Verlag, 1991.
9. Nenad Medvidovic and Richard N. Taylor. A classification and comparison framework for software architecture description languages. *IEEE Transactions on Software Engineering*, 26(1):70–93, Janurary 2000.
10. Bertrand Meyer. *Object-Oriented Software Construction.* Prentice/Hall, 1997.
11. OMG. OMG Unified Modeling Language Specification. Technical report, Object Management Group, 2000.

12. Iman Poernomo, Heinz Schmidt, and Ralf Reussner. The TrustME language site. Web site, DSTC, 2001. Available at `http://www.csse.monash.edu.au/dsse/trustme`.
13. Ralf Reussner, Iman Poernomo, and Heinz Schmidt. Using the trustme tool suite for automatic component protocol adaptation. In Peter M. A. Sloot, Chih Jeng Kenneth Tan, Jack Dongarra, and Alfons G. Hoekstra, editors, *Computational Science - ICCS 2002, International Conference, Amsterdam, The Netherlands, April 21–24, 2002. Proceedings, Part II*, volume 2330 of *Lecture Notes in Computer Science*, pages 854–863. Springer-Verlag, 2002.
14. Heinz Schmidt. Compatibility of interoperable objects. In *Information Systems Interoperability*, pages 143–199. Research Studies Press, Taunton, Somerset, England, 1998.
15. Heinz Schmidt and Ralf Reussner. Automatic component adaptation by concurrent state machine retrofitting. Technical Report 2000/81, Monash University, School of Computer Science and Software Engineering, 2000.
16. Workflow Management Coalition. Workflow management coalition terminology and glossary (WFMC-TC-1011). Technical report, Workflow Management Coalition, Brussals, February 1999.

Modeling Web Systems Using SDL

Joe Abboud Syriani and Nashat Mansour

Computer Science Program, Lebanese American University
P.O. Box: 13-5053, Beirut, Lebanon
{jsyriani, nmansour}@lau.edu.lb

Abstract. We propose modeling the architecture of web systems using the Specification and Description Language (SDL), which is a formal language. SDL is shown to be quite convenient for modeling features of web systems such as hyperlinks, sending and receiving data, and client-server communication. Hence, it facilitates our understanding of web applications. Further, we describe how to test web systems, based on the SDL model, in order to ensure that the implementation conforms to the specification.

1 Introduction

Using web technologies, users can access other documents or data from other servers by sending requests. A client sends a request using a browser and the server responds to the client with the document or data needed. A web system incorporates a web server, network connection, client browser, and a web application. A client browser navigates and renders a web page that can be considered as a document page related to other pages (via hyperlinks) and objects (Database, DOM, etc…). A web application is a client/server software that uses an HTML/XML browser for one or more clients communicating with a web server via HTTP and an application server managing business logic [1].

Web Applications are becoming more complex. Complexity arises due to several factors, such as large number of hyperlinks, communication, interaction, and distributed servers. To manage complexity, web systems are modeled. Modeling allows a software engineer to specify, understand and maintain the architecture of web application more effectively. The Unified Modeling Language (UML) has been used for modeling web applications. Conallen [2] has proposed an extension to the UML that is designed so that web-specific components can be integrated with the rest of the system model, and to exhibit the proper level of abstraction and detail suitable for designers, implementers, and architects of web applications. Kaewkasi and Rivepiboon [3] have also proposed using UML and use case maps to model web applications.

In this paper, we explore the use of the Specification and Description Language (SDL) [4] for modeling the architecture of web systems; SDL is usually used for modeling communication systems. The SDL model allows us to use existing implementation code of SDL specifications. We also propose an improvement to the existing SDL implementation. Further, the model allows us to use existing SDL based techniques for testing and verifying that the implementation conforms to the specification. To demonstrate this advantage, we have used the Testing and Test Control Notation [5].

A. Yazici and C. Şener (Eds.): ISCIS 2003, LNCS 2869, pp. 1019–1026, 2003.

2 Background on SDL

Specification and Description Language (SDL) is used for formal specification and design of systems. It supports reactive, concurrent, real-time and distributed systems [4,6,7]. SDL can be described in terms of its structural and behavioral concepts. The structure of SDL is divided into agents and communication. Agents are composed of systems, blocks and processes, whereas communication is composed of channels and gates. An agent is an extended finite communication state machine that has its own identity, its own signal input queue, its own life cycle and a reactive behavior specification. Three main parts exist on agent declarations: attributes, behavior, and internal structure. System is the entry point of the SDL specification. It includes a set of blocks and channels. Blocks are connected to each other and to environment by channels. A block can contain either a set of processes or a set of block substructures. Processes are used to specify the behavior of the system. Variables store data local to an agent and they are owned by the agent's state machine. They can be private, local, or public. Communication is based on signal exchanges that carry the signal name, user data and sender identification. It requires a complete path from sender to receiver that consists of channels, gates and connections.

Finite state machines describe the behavior of an agent. They consist of states that represent a particular condition in which an agent may consume a signal and transitions that represent the sequence of activities triggered by the consumption of the signal. They are called processes in SDL. A state machine is either in a state waiting for a signal or performing a transition. A transition results in entering a new state or stopping the agent. SDL processes communicate with each other and with the environment by exchanging signals. Each process instance in SDL owns a dedicated input port that allows received signals to be queued until they are consumed or discarded by the process instance owner. SDL supports modeling of non-determinism for transitions, postponing signals, and conditions signals.

A Message Sequence Chart (MSC) describes a specific execution sequence of the system [4]. It shows how messages are passed between the instances. Instances are described by vertical lines that define the temporal ordering of the events related to the instance. An instance represents an SDL block, process or service. Messages represent the interaction between instances or between an instance and the environment. The message is described by a horizontal arrow. Conditions in MSC represent a notion of state, which is represented by a hexagon. An action in MSC is represented by a rectangle and it describes an internal activity of the instance.

3 Modeling Approach

In this section, we describe how SDL can model the main features of the architecture of web applications. These features include: pages, hyperlinks, behavior of the web page on the client side and the server side, and client-server and distributed-server communication. Furthermore, the SDL model allows us to use existing implementation code of SDL specifications and this enables us to use also existing techniques and schemes in SDL for testing and verification [4].

The SDL model of a web application represents all the web pages of the system and their relationships with each other. Each web page is represented by an agent and the hyperlinks between pages are represented by signals. A hyperlink in a Web application represents a navigational path through the system. This relationship is represented in the SDL model with a signal sent through a channel association. The signals may contain parameters. For example, such parameters may contain user name and passwords that are sent within the signals to logon to a server. This link association originates from a client page and points to either a client or a server page.

The procedure embodied in both the client and the server can be modeled using composite states. This is done by modeling the transition from one state to another in order to control the internal procedures of both the client and the server. These steps may contain input signals, output signals, procedure calls, etc… A Message Sequence Chart can be used to model the sequence steps of moving between agents or states. We note that this model helps in verifying the consistency of a web application specification with its requirements.

If a client is accessing a server, a communication signal is fired. Upon receiving this signal, the server should reply back with another signal. The contents of this signal can also be specified. By modeling this system using SDL, we can ensure that this communication is working correctly. This also can be done from one server to multiple servers i.e. hyperlinks, database query, etc.... This feature makes SDL more powerful in comparison with UML, as UML has its strengths in the early phases of software engineering because of its semi-formality; SDL has its advantages mainly in the design phase and subsequent phases [8].

4 Example

We illustrate our modeling approach using a simple web site example that enables a user to login and check his/her account balance. We include only some essential graphical diagrams and omit the textual representation due to space limitation. We assume that the system is built from a client browser and a web server that includes the database. The user can do any of the followings: create a new account, login, logout, or check the account balance. The server will respond to each of these requests by a confirmation, an error, or a variable containing the account balance. In the following subsections, we model the blocks, processes and message sequence charts.

4.1 Blocks

We have two blocks: Client and Server. The block client has two processes: client_manager process that deals with the creation management and client_login that deals with the clients that login. The block server has similar processes. The graphical representation of only the server blocks is given in Figure 1. Note that the channel ch_server_local has only one direction and it cotains no reply or feedback. Also, the create_error message is sent from the server manager to the server login in case an error occurred.

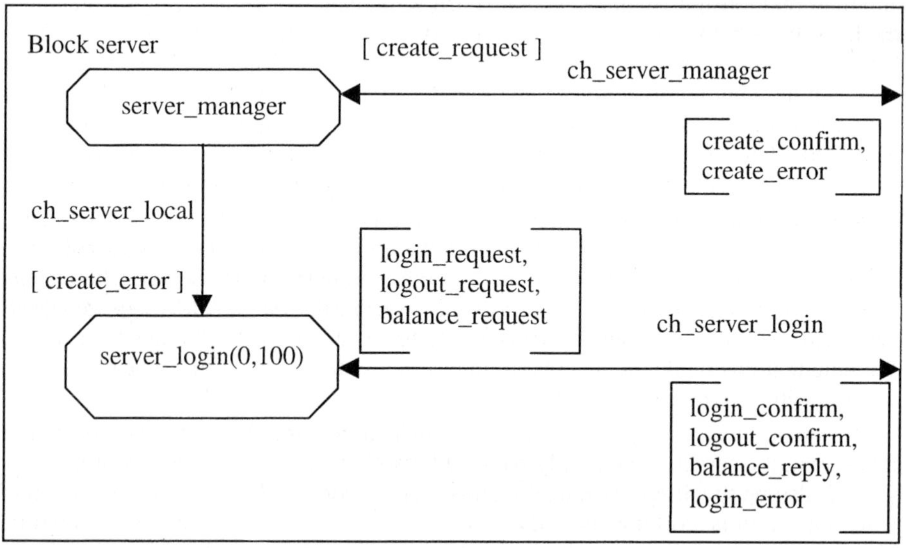

Fig. 1. Graphical representation of the Block server

4.2 Processes

Four processes are derived from the two blocks: client login, client manager, server login and server manager. The client_login process is represented by a finite state machine. It can be in any of the two states: active and idle. Procedures are first declared in the process. The graphical representation of the client login process is given in Figure 2. The client receives a reply from the server: whether the login was successful or not, a logout confirmation, or the balance. When any of these messages are received, the client runs a procedure that mainly contains an HTML file to be rendered by the client browser.

The client_manager process is also represented by a finite state machine. It can be only in one state: idle. One Procedure is declared in this process: user_create_error. This procedure will send an HTML page to the client informing it about a creation error. The client manager can receive a message that creation is done successfully or with error. It can also receive a message that the login failed. If the message is a create confirmation, an output signal about the login confirm is sent to the output. If the message is a login error, a message is sent to the output that a creation is needed. The graphical representation of the client manager process is given in Figure 3. Serve_login and server_manager processes have similarities with those of the client side and are omitted for brevity.

4.3 Message Sequence Chart

Message Sequence Charts (MSC) are used to represent the different requests. In our example, there are four main requests: create request, logout request, login request, and balance request. For brevity, we consider only the login request.

In the login request module, two processes exist: the client login and the server login. The create request module accepts the user request only if the client login and the server login are in the idle state. Then, there is an internal action within the server login to check if the account exists. If it does not exist, the state of the server login remains idle and a login error output will be sent to the client login. If the account exists, the state of both client login and server login becomes active and a login confirmation is sent to the client login and the client login sends to the browser that the client is logged in. The login request MSC is shown in Figure 4 (ignoring the time information which is used in the next section).

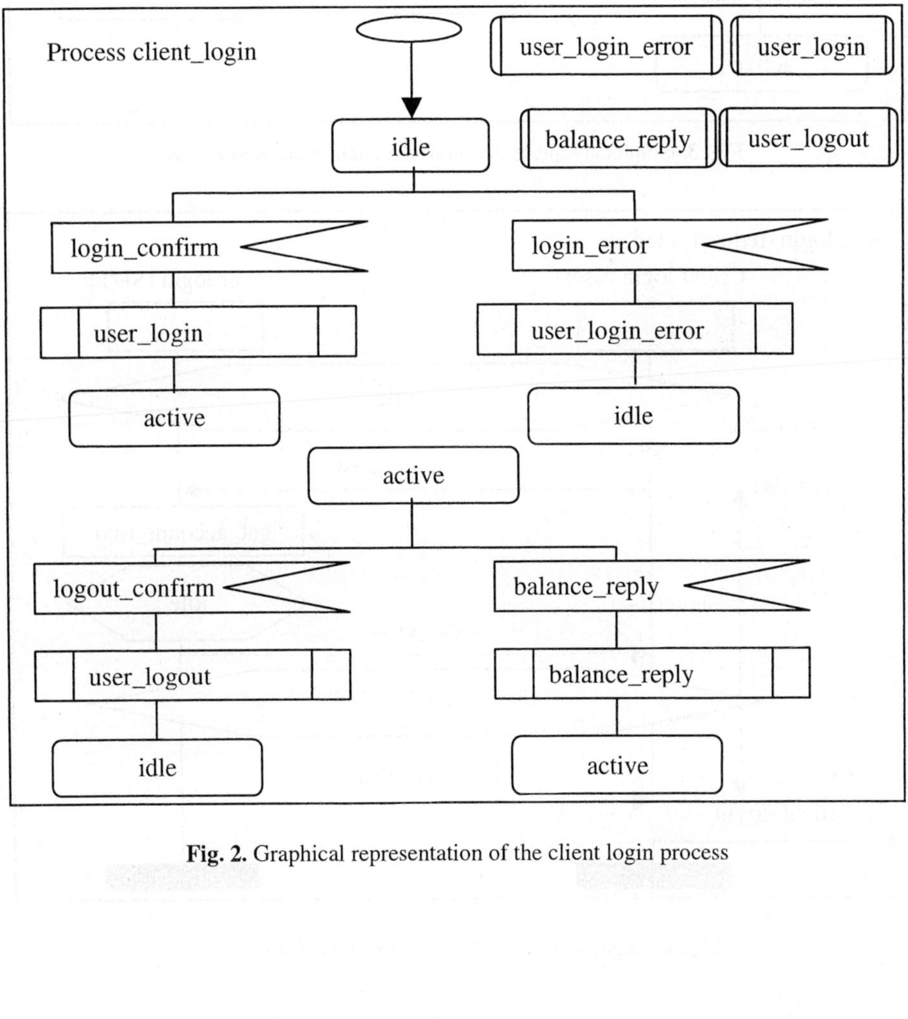

Fig. 2. Graphical representation of the client login process

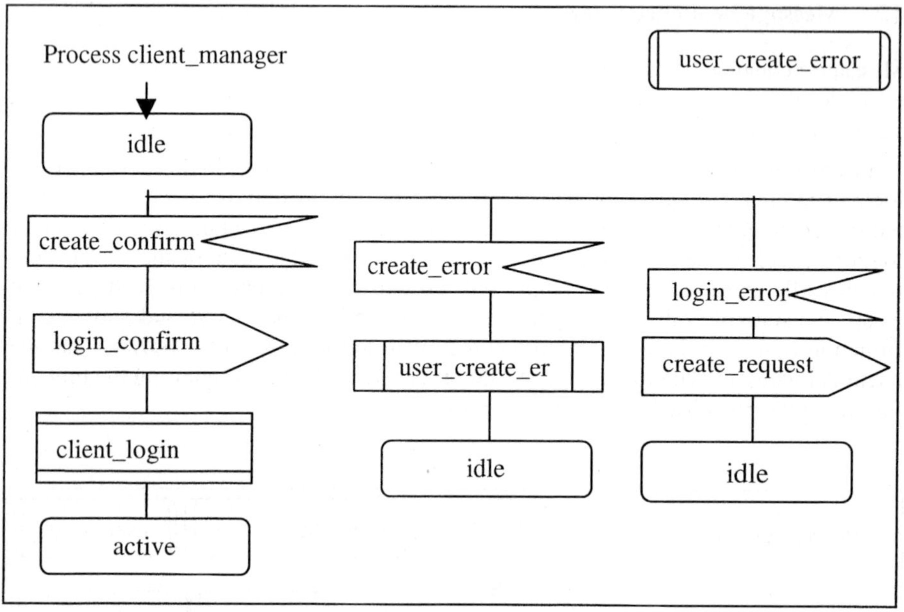

Fig. 3. Graphical representation of the client manager process

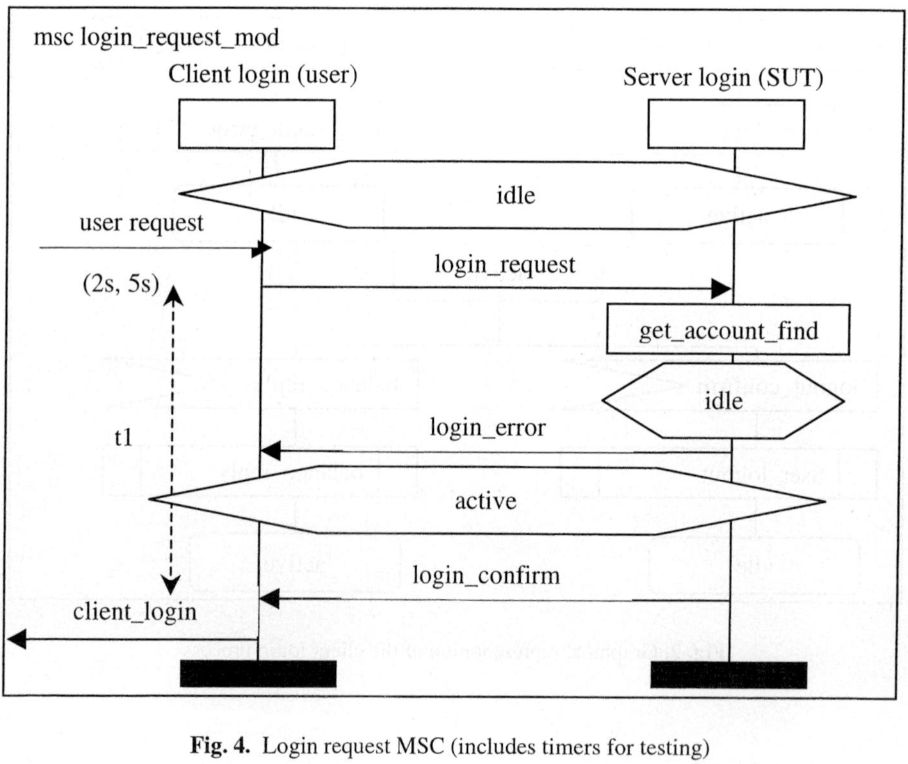

Fig. 4. Login request MSC (includes timers for testing)

5 Testing

In this section, we demonstrate that based on the SDL model of a web system, we are able to generate test cases to verify that the implementation conforms to the specification. We use the existing Testing and Test Control Notation (TTCN) [5]. We have also added timers to our test cases in order to control and measure the response time. We give only one example that shows how to use TTCN-3 to test the login request module.

Figure 4 shows a modification to the MSC representation of the login request by adding time. We have added a time interval where the start event is a send to the server and the end event is a receive from the server. Since two time points are needed, we declare two TTCN timers: t-check_min and t_check_max. In addition, t1 measures the time taken between sending the message and receiving the response. The TTCN-3 code for testing the login request is shown in Figure 5. In this test case, we check the following: if the minimum or maximum time is timed out, the test fails; if the client receives the response of either login_confirm or login_error that satisfies the specification of the web application and within the time interval, the test passes; in case other responses are received, nothing happens until time out.

6 Extending SDL Implementation for Web Systems

SDL basics have been implemented for protocols. The implementation comes with different solutions for the process management and the buffer management [4]. In this section, we propose an improvement to the existing SDL implementation that is relevant for web systems.

Since Web design contains a lot of communication between clients and server(s), a lot of signals are transferred and the server may be busy and might not respond immediately. This issue can be addressed by either minimizing copy operations or by optimizing the process management. Usually when a signal is sent from one process to another, it is copied to the output queue and waits for the input queue of the receiver to release it. We use buffer management to alleviate this problem. The data will be stored on some data queues and the buffer will store the signal identification and related information as well as the reference to the data queues. The buffer stores the data until the transition is finished and it is released to the receiver process instance.

One approach to optimize process management in the context of SDL is the activity thread model. The server model exhibits overhead such as that of synchronous operations including queuing. This is not present in the thread control. However, thread control is based on synchronous communication that makes it incompatible with the SDL model. Instead of transmitting signals to the receiving process instance, the procedure implementing the process instance can be called directly. This will merge scheduling with communication. Concerning the internal communication of the active thread, the sequence of the output and the input constructs result in a sequence of procedure calls that is the activity thread. The activity thread is terminated when the event processed by the SDL process is terminated.

```
timer t_check_min;                              // minimum time
timer t_check_max;                              // maximum time
timer t_measure := 10000;
var float t1;
client_login.send(login_request) ;
t_check_min.start(2);                       // start the minimum time measurement
t_check_max.start(5);                       // start the maximum time measurement
t_measure.start;                            // start the measurement time
alt {
      [] t_check_min.timeout {              // if the minimum time is timed out
            verdict.set(fail);              // test is failed
            mycomponent.stop;}              // stop the component
      [] t_check_max.timeout {              // if the maximum time is timed out
            verdict.set(fail);              // test is failed
            mycomponent.stop;}              // stop the component
      [] client_login.receive(login_confirm) {
            vedict.set(pass);                  // test is passed
            t1 := t_measure.read;              // read the time interval
            t_measure.stop;                    // stop the time measure
            t_check_min.stop;
            t_check_max.stop;}
      [] client_login.receive(login_error) {
            vedict.set(pass);                  // test is passed
            t1 := t_measure.read;              // read the time interval
            t_measure.stop;                    // stop the time measure
            t_check_min.stop;
            t_check_max.stop;}
```

Fig. 5. TTCN-3 code for the login request

7 Conclusion

We have shown how SDL can be used to model web systems. Such modeling allows us to use existing implementation code of SDL specifications. Also, we have demonstrated how to use SDL modeling to test web systems using the TTCN technique.

References

1. Dietel, Dietel, Nieto: E-business & e-commerce how to program, Prentice Hall (2001)
2. Conallen J.: Building Web Applications With UML, Reading, Mass., Addison-Wesley (1999)
3. Kaewkasi, C., Rivepiboon, W.: WWM: A Practical Methodology for Web Application Modeling, Chulalongkorn University, Bangkok, Thailand (2002)
4. Mitschele-Thiel, A.: Systems Engineering with SDL, John Wisley & Sons, LTD (2001)
5. ETSI: Method for Testing and Specification, The Testing and Test Control Notation version 3 (2003)
6. J. Fischer, E. Holz, M. v. Löwis, A. Prinz (2000), *SDL-2000: A Language with a Formal Semantics*, Humboldt-Universität zu Berlin.
7. International Engineering Consortium (2001), *Specification and Description Language (SDL)*, http://www.iec.org, Telelogic.
8. Schwingenschlogl, C., Schonauer, S.: Application and Service Development using UML and SDL, Technische Universitat Munchen (2000)

Software Quality Improvement Model for Small Organizations

Rabih Zeineddine[1, 2] and Nashat Mansour[2]

[1]Central Bank of Lebanon, IT Department, PO Box 11-5544 Beirut, Lebanon,
rzeineddine@terra.net.lb,
[2] Lebanese American University, Computer science Program, PO Box 13-5053 Beirut, Lebanon,
nmansour@lau.edu.lb

Abstract. Small software organizations are not capable of bearing the cost of establishing classical software process improvement programs. In this work, we propose a new software quality improvement model for small organizations (SQIMSO), based on three major issues. Firstly, every improvement program should be wide enough to include the major trends. Secondly, any process quality model should answer the question "How to do things?" Thirdly any suggested quality model should be practical enough to be implemented by small software organizations. SQIMSO also draws upon international quality standards, models, and experiences.

1 Introduction

1.1 Quality and Process Models

Quality models and standards have been developed to improve product quality, satisfy business goals, and standardize software engineering practices and procedures. Their certification have been sought due to management improvement strategies, governments' policies, market competition, and customer's requirements. However, the implementation of quality models and standards involves time and cost overheads that are large, especially for small organizations.

The evolution of international quality models was intended to improve quality and to provide more guidelines for reducing overhead involved. ISO 9001 [1] required establishing, documenting, and maintaining a software process. The Capability Maturity Model (CMM) was intended to improve software processes using a set of recommended practices in a number of key process areas [2,3]. ISO 9000-3 preceded CMM guidance by introducing "Guidelines for the application of ISO 9001 to the development, supply and maintenance of software" [4]. LOGOS tailored CMM Model to suit small organization by addressing documentation overload, layered management, Limited resources and other factors [5]. BOOTSTRAP is a software process assessment and improvement that is based on benchmarking and determination of current achievement levels to assess suitable improvement programs and action planning [6]. The main objectives of the SPICE project were to put the first

A. Yazici and C. Şener (Eds.): ISCIS 2003, LNCS 2869, pp. 1027–1034, 2003.

draft for software process assessment and to conduct early trials [7]. Based on SPICE, a new framework called SPIRE was created [8]. Trying to adapt the SPICE model to small size organizations, SPIRE adapted the language but used the same structure. Extreme Programming (XP) is actually a deliberate and disciplined approach that suits risky projects with dynamic requirements [9]. XP is based on simplicity, continual communication with customer, and rapid feedback mechanisms, and it only suits "small to medium sized teams building software with vague or rapidly changing requirements" [10].

1.2 International and Local Surveys

There have been a number of international surveys concerning international standards and Capability Maturity Models, and their strengths and weaknesses. A survey was done in the United Kingdom by Hall and Wilson [11] about quality system formality, ISO Standards, and quality certification for large-to small-scale software companies. The negative comments on quality certification were: it was irrelevant to quality, less important than having quality infrastructure and culture, just about producing software consistently and was not necessarily for high quality, and not useful without practitioner professionalism and ability. Another survey in Scotland [12] led to similar results; an analyst programmer put it as follows "We have to fill a lot of forms, but it hasn't affected the way I write software, not at all.".

A survey was done in Germany by Stelzer [13] on 21 software houses that were ISO 9001 certified. The objectives were to assess the value of an ISO 9001 certificate for buyers of software and software-related services. The major findings of the survey were as follows: some interpreted standards clauses strictly others very widely; deviations from the standards were not pointed out; a certificate did not guarantee that the quality system fulfilled all ISO 9001 requirements; an ISO 9001 certificate was not an indicator of the quality of the products, the processes, or the quality system; ISO was a way for certification bodies to hold small companies to ransom.

Another survey was done in Europe by Stelzer [14] based on interviews and reports from 36 European software houses. The major findings were as follows: not the technical contents of ISO 9000 made process improvements; the culture created by wide improvement program seemed to be more important; implementing an ISO 9000 quality system was a helpful impetus for a cultural change.

The lessons of the Australian experience surveyed by Wilson [15] can be summarized as follows: lack of understanding of ISO 9000; rigorous and documented processes and procedures do not guarantee quality products; three aspects are important to quality: people, process and product; much of the criticism directed to ISO 9000 was the result of human error resulted from either misinterpretation or misguided management.

We have also carried out a survey in Lebanon to figure out the existing software engineering practices concerning customer-supplier relationship, requirements acquisition processes, development processes, faced problems, standards and models used, and organization's willingness to invest in and initiate quality improvement program. The survey included 32 software companies. The findings of this survey are: small software houses face many problems that compel them to think first how to survive before thinking how to start quality improvement programs. The major factor is economic. Quality systems need good level of qualification, experience, training and probably additional staff, which implies additional cost.

1.3 Objectives

The experiences presented by the local and international surveys lead to the following remarks: (a) product quality or software process quality improvement needs a wide improvement program including building quality culture and quality system infrastructure that will facilitate the implementation process. (b) Nothing is achieved without practitioner professionalism and ability; i.e., provide "know how" and the applicable methods. (c) ISO 9001 certificate is not an indicator of the quality of the products, the processes, or the quality system. (d) Practitioners have to fill a lot of forms, but it hasn't affected the way they write software; thus, procedures and methods should be carefully selected.

Small software organizations face serious problems when dealing with the challenges of existing models because they can not bear the costs. To give small software organizations the chance to have efficient and applicable quality improvement systems a new model should be developed. This model should avoid all the drawbacks and deficiencies of the existing international standards, and should offer quality culture by adding a new factor that helps practitioners implement "what to do" by knowing "how to do". In this work, we propose SQIMSO as a model that suits small software organizations.

2 Software Quality Model for Small Organizations (SQIMSO)

2.1 Purpose and Justification

In SQIMSO, three main critical issues are considered. The first critical issue is that every improvement program should be wide enough to include three main factors which are process quality, product quality, and human resources management. The second issue is that any process quality model should answer the question *"How to do?"*. The third issue is that any suggested quality Model should be practical enough to be implemented by small software organizations for saving cost and time without decreasing the quality turnover level.

Based on international quality standards, models, surveys, and on the local field survey, the new software quality improvement model SQIMSO is introduced. SQIMSO processes model structure is based on SPICE processes model structure but adapted to fit the practices of small organizations. Using a new framework, the processes entirely reestablished based on ISO 9001, ISO 9000-3, CMM, SPICE, SPIRE, software engineering practices, fields studies and surveys findings, and our software engineering field experience. Conceptually, SQIMSO discusses quality improvement strategy from three dimensions that are process, capability, and method. A new factor, methods, is added to facilitate initiating and implementing software process improvements.

SQIMSO is designed for small software organizations that are not capable of bearing the cost of establishing software process improvement programs especially when new people are needed. It offers an improvement program through established and documented standard processes that can be adopted and maintained to ensure quality conformance. It does not expect from the practitioner the knowledge of international standards or quality models practices, and maturity is not required, but is expected to be gained. SQIMSO is designed to offer guidance and suggested actions are explained thoroughly. Mainly, methods are defined to provide guidance and suggest a way of implementation.

Many practitioners need to know how to do things to avoid implementation faults. Although quality model formalism may limit creativity, but until knowledge and skills are attained it is better to have a quality system that tells how to do things. However, since some practitioners like to do things their own way, the "how to do" suggestions remain informative in their nature. The suggested methods are not recipes to be abided by. They provide sufficient guidelines that can be adapted during implementation to suit practical work. Practitioners may add or modify suggested methods, but, elimination is not preferred. However, the practitioner should ensure that the "what to do" requirements are to be achieved.

Further, SQIMSO emphasizes continuous improvement through quality values and culture. It also emphasizes: efficient communication to meet the new designed quality system; teamwork and fair distribution of jobs and responsibilities; empowering employees with necessary knowledge and skills; giving more value to working people as well as software process and the product itself.

2.2 SQIMSO Concepts and Structure

In this section we describe the three components of SQIMSO: process, capability, and method.

Process. A software process can be defined as an environment of capable interrelated resources managing a sequence of activities using appropriate methods and practices to develop a software product that conforms to customers' requirements.

The requirements are not the only input to the process. In addition, supplier objectives add to customer requirements in order to construct the process input. In fact, this factor is important because it is related directly to the process itself and provides guidance for assessors to know what are the limits and restrictions for software process improvements.

Based on ISO TR 15504 (SPICE), SPIRE Model, and other suggested software process improvement frameworks, the software processes in SQIMSO are subdivided into software subprocesses. In SPIRE, subprocesses differ in impact; thus, one can focus on subprocesses that meet business goals. This view is somehow deficient because neglecting some important subprocesses will affect the stability and adequacy of quality models. Another alternative can be to combine subprocesses requirement and to eliminate irrelative parts since we are dealing only with one scale of organizations. In small organizations, it shouldn't be left to practitioners to evaluate and decide what to use and what to ignore. Naturally, the success of a software subprocesses depends on the outcome of its preceding subprocess. Therefore, any hidden neglect may lead to deficiencies and rework. If practice indicates that a subprocess is weak in terms of its practical applicability, this subprocess should be reviewed and adapted to facilitate implementation, instead of avoiding it.

In SQIMSO the Organization processes of the SPIRE model are combined and embedded into other adapted categories to fit small scale. The management process category plays an important role in process categories interaction and control. In order to facilitate determining process requirements and guidance, a practical process framework is established within SQIMSO. The answer to "when to do things?" is reflected in the sequence of customer-supplier and engineering processes. For other processes they provide baselines, when needed, to show process support activities sequence. The overall structure of SQIMSO processes is defined above in Table 1.

Table 1. SQIMSO Model Process Structure

Process Category	Process ID	Process Title
Customer-Supplier	SQIMSO-C	
	SQIMSO-C1	Acquisition
	SQIMSO-C2	Supplier Selection
	SQIMSO-C3	Requirements Elicitation
Engineering	SQIMSO-E	
	SQIMSO-E1	Requirement Analysis and Specification
	SQIMSO-E2	Software Planning
	SQIMSO-E3	Software Design
	SQIMSO-E4	Software Implementation
	SQIMSO-E5	Software Testing & Integration
	SQIMSO-E7	Software Maintenance
Support	SQIMSO-S	
	SQIMSO-S1	Documentation
	SQIMSO-S2	Configuration Management
	SQIMSO-S3	Quality Assurance
	SQIMSO-S4	Joint Review
	SQIMSO-S5	Methods Selection
Management	SQIMSO-M	
	SQIMSO-M1	Project Management
	SQIMSO-M2	Improvement Program
	SQIMSO-M3	Human Resources Management

SQIMSO's Process framework consists of the following elements:

- Purpose and Justification.
- Process Inputs.
- Who is involved?
- What to do?
- How to do?
- Process Outputs.
- What to be ensured?

Capability. Process capability is defined as the range of expected results that can be achieved by following a process or the ability of a process to achieve a required goal. The process capability can be measured by maturity key process areas to determine the level of current capability and maturity achievement. This measurement helps organization's management to develop appropriate quality improvement strategy. the levels of capability and maturity will be used as measurement tools to determine the current status of work environment. Passing from level to another will lead the organization to achieve better process quality results.

Methods. Methods are the procedures, patterns, techniques, metrics, roadmaps, and all other tools used to develop software products that meet customer's requirements and achieve supplier's business objectives. They may be used to develop resources, monitor deficiencies, and enhance engineering and management approaches. Methods answer the important question *"How to do things?"* In order to achieve process and business objectives, methods should be selected, adopted, adapted, and used.

Methods have a great influence on product quality conformity and sometime wrong selection may lead to project failure. They are an essential part of industry's best practices. Methods vary depending on the characteristics of the project. Methods selection may be tedious but this activity should be performed to ensure implementing best practices. Once methods are selected and defined it is the role of quality assurance teams to control methods implementation and to assess and report any deficiencies. Although the methods selection process should be established, maintained, and controlled by software quality teams, developers' input and feedback should also be considered.

3 An Example Processes

In this Section we present one example due to space limitation. We consider the Improvement Program Process (SQIMSO-M2).

Purpose and Justification. The purpose of this process is to explain a way of implementing SQIMSO as an improvement program. This process does not suggest starting improvement program from scratch, but the implementer should understand and consider what exists in his/her organization and determine what are the significant deviations from standard processes. Then, the implementer should assess whether suggested processes could be integrated in the development work.

Process Inputs:

The inputs of this process are: software quality improvement model, organization resources, and capable pilot team.

Who is involved?

Management, pilot team, and software quality assurance members should be involved in this process.

What to do?

- Assign pilot team to study and understand the SQIMSO model
- Identify implementation opportunities

- Define the scope of pilot project and allocate adequate resources
- Conduct pilot project development
- Assess improvements feedback and analyze impact of implementation and lessons learned and report to concerned management
- Setup and conduct training
- Change development process accordingly

How to do?

- Select a project at low risk and assign the development task to credible development team
- Pilot project team should be methodological and systematic, flexible and dynamic, willing to improve, skilled and experienced in software development and maintenance, objective and reasonable
- Pilot project team should identify current activities, roles, authorities and responsibilities, and development process.
- Pilot project should assess improvements and applicability, and identify changes, impacts and necessary training.
- Assessment report should include process changes, affected resources quantitatively, risks and opportunities, strengths and weaknesses, lessons learned and feedback, and conclusion

Process outputs:

The outputs of this process are: adopted and maintained software quality improvement model, product quality, software process quality, and efficient human resources management.

What to be ensured?

- Personal resistance to change is considered and handled
- Status quo analysis is done before implementing the new model
- Weaknesses of the organization are not considered as quality model weaknesses
- Assigning the right credible developers
- Pilot project team is formed from within the organization
- Assessment is not built on current process defensive view
- Resources factors changes and overall turnover are reported objectively
- Software quality assurance team are involved in the pilot project
- Pilot project is given enough time to achieve its purpose
- The improvement program is intended to improve quality and not to misevaluate existing development process

4 Conclusion

Small organizations are not capable of bearing the cost of establishing software process improvement programs, and the existing software process standards or models are not easily applicable. Thus, a practical, and comprehensive quality improvement model is proposed. SQIMSO provides a practical framework that gives small software organizations the opportunity to have a feasible quality improvement model to improve their software product quality and to provide software practitioners with quality culture and skills.

Acknowledgement. We thank the National Council for Scientific Research for partially supporting this work.

References

1. ISO 9001, ANSI/ISO/ASQC Q9001-1994: Quality Systems – Models for Quality Assurance in Design Development, Production, Installation, and Servicing (1994)
2. Paulk M.: How ISO 9001 compares with the CMM? IEEE Software, January (1995) 74–83
3. Paulk M., Curtis B., and Chrisis M., Capability Maturity Model version 1.1, Journal of IEEE Software, July (1993) 18–27
4. ISO 9000-3, International Standards, ISO 9000-3:1991(E): Quality management and quality assurance standards, Part 3, Guidelines for the application of ISO 9001 to the development, supply and maintenance of software (1991)
5. Johnson D. and Brodman J.: Tailoring the CMM for Small Organizations and Small Projects, Elements of Software Process Assessment & Improvement, edited by K. El Emam and N. Madhavji, IEEE Computer Society (1999) 239–257
6. Steinen H., Software Process Assessment and Improvement, Elements of Software Process Assessment & Improvement, edited by K. El Emam and N. Madhavji, Edward Brothers, USA: IEEE Computer Society (1999) 57–75
7. SPICE, The Theory and Practice of Software Improvement and Capability Determination, IEEE Computer Society (1998)
8. Sanders M.: SPIRE Project, Centre for Software Engineering, Dublin, Ireland (1998)
9. Wells D., www.extremeprogramming.org/what.html (2001)
10. Paulk M.: Extreme Programming from a CMM Perspective, IEEE Software, Nov.-Dec. (2001) 19–26
11. Hall T. and Wilson D.: Views of software quality: a report field, IEE Proc. Software Engineering, Vol. 144, No. 2 (1997) 111–118
12. Beirne M., Panteli A., and Ramsay H.: Going soft on quality?: Process management in the Scottish software industry, Software Quality Journal, Vol. 6 (1997) 195–209
13. Stelzer D., Mellis W. and Herzwurm G., A critical look at ISO 9000 software quality management, *Software Quality Journal,* 6 (1997) 65–79
14. Stelzer D., Mellis W. and Herzwurm G., A critical look at ISO 9000 software quality management, *Software Quality Journal,* 6 (1997) 65–79
15. Wilson D.: Software quality assurance in Australia: an update, Software Quality Journal , 6 (1997) 81–87

Representing Variability Issues in Web Applications: A Pattern Approach

Rafael Capilla[1] and N. Yasemin Topaloglu[2]

[1] Department of Informatics and Telematics,
Universidad Rey Juan Carlos, Madrid, Spain
rcapilla@escet.urjc.es

[2] Department of Computer Engineering, Ege University, Izmir, Turkey,
yasemin@bornova.ege.edu.tr

Abstract. Web applications have unique characteristics that require suitable software engineering practices in the development process. In this way, software architectures and pattern-based approaches are suitable design techniques for modeling purposes. But if we want to build sets of similar systems, we need to represent the common and variable aspects of such systems under an architectural point of view. Therefore, representing and managing those variable issues is a goal to achieve when designing similar software applications. In this work we will try to deal with the variability problem from a pattern point of view as well as applying this to web software products.

1 Introduction

At present, Web applications have reached a point that is far beyond from the initial considerations for Web both from the technical and social point of view. The scope and complexity of current Web applications vary from small-scale, short-lived services to large-scale enterprise applications distributed across the Internet and corporate intranets and extranets [15].

The development and maintenance of web applications have special time to market requirements in the sense that they have to be engineered in short periods of time. Often, changes are performed in days or even hours, so we need to have agile development and maintenance processes in order to solve such problems. In order to improve such development and maintenance processes, software architectures (SA) and product line architectures (PLA) are both a good choice because we can represent common and variable points and therefore try to accelerate the maintenance tasks for controlling better the evolution of the system.

Software architectures represent key design decisions that meet the customer requirements in a nice way. A software architecture [4] comprises a set of components and connectors guided and restricted by architectural styles and design patterns. In this way, how to reflect the variable points (i.e.: variation points) in the architecture is an important aspect that should be supported by the basic design elements that con

A. Yazici and C. Şener (Eds.): ISCIS 2003, LNCS 2869, pp. 1035–1042, 2003.

form the architecture. Design patterns and architectural styles are composed in heterogeneous software architectures to reflect and restrict early design decisions as well as try to represent the variability needed to produce similar software systems in an easy way. Sometimes we don't have appropriate representation mechanisms to describe a variation point at the architectural level or at the pattern level. In this work we will try to provide some guidance for representing variable aspects at the design level to be used in the design and development.

In section 2 we will mention some concepts and approaches of using patterns for modeling tasks. In section 3 we will discuss those variability aspects involved in the construction of software systems and how variability can be modeled under a pattern approach. Section 4 provides some conclusions.

2 Pattern Concept for Modeling Software Systems

A pattern is the abstraction of a problem in a specific domain and the representation of a generic solution to be used in different contexts [2]. Since software community adopted the pattern concept, which was introduced by Christopher Alexander [1] for the discipline of architecture, patterns have been employed in various stages of software development.

At present, the most popular usage of patterns in software development is as *design patterns* [14] and *architectural patterns* [8]. Design patterns are descriptions of communicating objects and classes that are customized to solve a general design problem in a particular context. An architectural pattern expresses a fundamental structural organization schema for software systems including the subsystems, their responsibilities and the relationships between them. As these definitions imply, architectural patterns are helpful in structuring a software system into subsystems while design patterns are useful in expressing micro architectures in subsystems.

Modeling plays an important role in any kind of software development, which results in several models of the system at various abstraction levels. In order to facilitate the modeling task, usage of standard notations like UML is preferred. When we consider the web domain, we see that several Web modeling languages, which employ different approaches, have been developed in the last decade like WebML [11], Connalen [12] and OOHDM [23]. Gu et al. [17] proposes an architectural design framework for web applications that defines two aspects of technical architecture of Web applications as the *information architecture* and the *functional architecture*.

Ability to support pattern modeling and ability to support life cycle maintenance due to the ever-changing nature of Web applications are identified as essential requirements for functional architectural representation [16]. Among the available Web modeling languages, patterns are involved explicitly only in OOHDM [23]. In next section we will introduce our approach for modeling variability with patterns and applying this to the functional architecture of web applications.

3 Representing Variability from a Pattern Point of View

3.1 Variability Issues in Software Construction

From an architectural point of view, design patterns and architectural patterns [8] [14] are widely used in the construction of software architectures. One of the main advantages of using software architectures is to employ the same software design for developing a set of systems that share common characteristics. In this way, the variability of a system can be outlined in the architecture through a set of variation points (VP) able to support the differences of a set of similar systems. Additionally, in product-line architectures (PLA) [5], the architecture holds the commonalities of the products while the variation points provide support for different ones. PLA architectures and specifically light-weight approaches [3] are suitable to be used in the web domain [10] and depending when we want to control the evolution of a product over time, we can change the binding time such variation points [6].

The lack of mechanisms to describe clearly the variation points, put barriers in the design process, and many times forwards the variability aspects to the code level. Some proposals from a feature point of view, add quantitative values to variation points by using a simple language [9] in an attempt to improve the FODA features model. Others, [21] propose several notations for representing the variability issues using features. Such as mentioned in [7], there is a need for standard notation and exchange format for describing variability issues.

A variation point is characterized by a reference to the product line, a rationale, a variability rule and a mechanism that specifies how to use the variants in the context and all this information is represented by UML aggregations [22]. In [13], the authors employ the UML notation to model variability in product lines, but the proposed representation don't show with enough detail the information described by the variation points. Something similar occurs in [18] when modeling variation points with a simple graphical notation. But when building software architectures, most of the boxes representing modules or subsystems don't describe which of them hold variation points that later must be mapped to specific software components. Therefore it would be useful to outline which parts of the architecture will need support for variable points as well as describe the internals of such variations.

3.2 Patterns and Variation Points

If we want to model variability issues from an architectural point of view, we will need to represent the variations points at several degrees of detail (e.g.: architectural modules, design patterns or source code) in order to cover the whole life cycle. First of all we need to specify that a particular module, subsystem or component has variation points and later define them making easy the transition from the design level to the implementation one. One problem that rises here is that certain software applications do not follow the object-oriented paradigm (e.g.: web-based applications). In this case, modeling variable points through classes (such as in [19]) and objects that represent object oriented design patterns could be quite difficult. For these reasons it seems to be more practical to describe the variation points employing a not object oriented approach and using a graphical notation suitable for web modeling purposes. Our proposal represents the following information.

1. The component or subsystem that supports variability.
2. A description of the variability supported by a specific component. In this case we need to specify which information about variability issues will be available. From our point of view we believe we need to specify the following aspects:
   a. The name and number of the variation points (VP).
   b. The attributes that characterize each variation point.
   c. The values permitted for each attribute.

Therefore and using a simple graphical notation, the designer knows which modules of the architecture support the variability needed to customize the system and reduces the gap between design and implementation. For instance, the *Whole-Part* pattern [8] aggregates components that all together form a semantic unit (e.g. the parts of a car). The Whole is an aggregated component and encapsulates its components in Parts. The solution provided by this pattern is to introduce a component that encapsulates smaller objects and defines an interface able to access the functionality of the encapsulated objects, acting in this sense as a wrapper. These visible properties of the Parts can be described by a features tree such as the FODA model or similar. Therefore, specific variation points can be attached to the properties of the Parts for representing variability issues. From our point of view, the pattern can be modified to incorporate specific variation points using a graphical notation that represents the information specified in points (2a), (2b) and (2c). This permits to the designers an easy way to communicate the variation points defined in the architectural elements. Figure 1 shows an example of this.

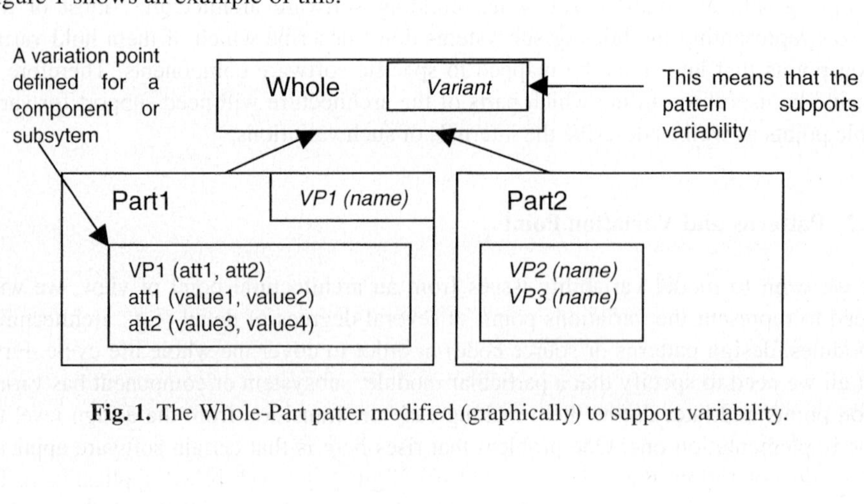

Fig. 1. The Whole-Part patter modified (graphically) to support variability.

This notation can be used in any component or subsystem and applied to several architectural styles or design patterns for representing the variability aspects at the design level. One of the key aspects in our approach when modeling web applications, is to represent structural design decisions but not from an object-oriented point of view. In this way the programming issues of patterns will be implemented by not object oriented languages. In next section we apply our ideas to the web domain.

3.3 Variability with Patterns in Web Applications

Web applications consist of diverse components which include traditional and non traditional software, interpreted scripting languages, plain HTML files, mixtures of HTML and programs, databases, graphical images and complex user interfaces [20].

When modeling web applications, object oriented approaches don't fit well (except in those cases of using specific object oriented web languages such as PYTHON), so OO design techniques are difficult to apply. From an architectural point of view the representation of the variation points of web applications can be modeled using the notation described in section 3.2. In this way, the representation of variation points in web applications is sometimes different than in other kind of software applications, because usually mark-up languages code is mixed with programming or scripting languages. Therefore it results difficult to separate different pieces of code when we want to build appropriate reusable components able to support the variable aspects already defined in the architecture.

In addition, instead of grouping web components by functional parts of the specific web pages we can define several modules or reusable pieces of code that gather a specific functionality based on the language on which they are written and to be used by several web sites. As an example, instead of specific web pages, we can have PHP or JavaScript pieces of code able to be used in several web sites, holding several variable points and serving for different purposes such as: Database access, animated menus, etc.

For instance, in a HTML+PHP web system where a module accesses several types of Databases using PHP functions, such module supports variability and the particular variation points will be the different PHP databases functions (ODBC, SQL, Oracle, etc.) with particular values (e.g.: name of the database, user name, password, etc.). In this case we can model such variability point such as is shown in figures 2a and 2b.

Figure 2 shows a partial view of the architecture in which we have modeled three variation points, which are used in two different components or subsystems of the architecture. The figure represents also a more detailed view of the PHP database component, which exhibits the specific variation point. In this example the variation point *connect* has one attribute (Dbtype) that specifies two types of databases (i.e. *odbc* and *sql*) and performs the connection to the specific database. Besides, the implementation language could be also specified in the values of the attributes for each variation point.

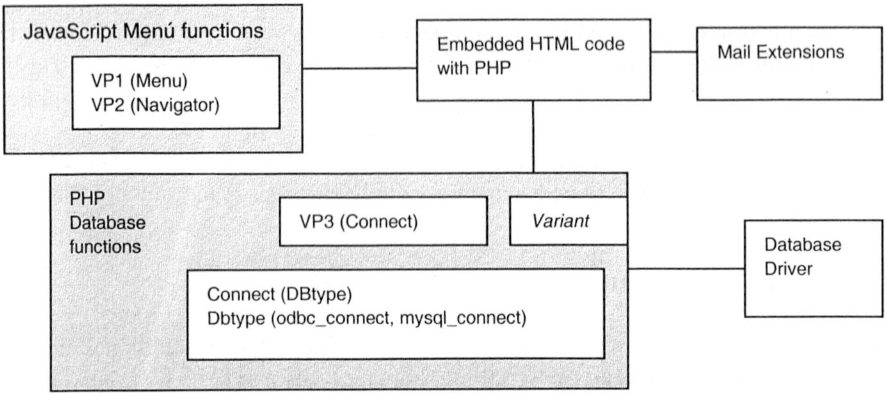

Fig. 2. Partial view of a software architecture representing variation points at the design level.

Another example can be modeled when employing the *Model-View-Controller* (MVC) architectural pattern [8]. This pattern decomposes an interactive application in three components. The *Model* contains the functionality and data. The *Controller* receives the user inputs and sends these as requests to the Model or to the View. Finally, the *View* displays information to the user in several forms.

The increasing demand of more complex web applications that use more sophisticated GUI environments makes more complex the design of such applications. In this way the MVC pattern can be used for modeling web applications by the separation of concerns of its parts. Therefore, the *View* and the *Controller* of the MVC pattern can be associated to the presentation layer of a web system, whereas the *Model* supports the functionality of the business logic.

Dynamic web applications will receive the inputs in the *Controller* (e.g.: HTTP requests) and translate these to the Model that processes the client's requests. Once the model has processed the requests, the server returns the answer (e.g.: the data or the response) to the View. As an example for supporting the variability in this model, several variations points can be defined at different Views or in several logic units supported by the Model. For instance, we could have variation points in the View for showing the same information in different types of HTML tables with a number of variants (e.g.: color, columns, rows, etc.) or generating different types of menus for clicking the options by the Controller. Also, several logic units in the Model can hold variation points such as customized mail functions, or database access among others.

Figure 3 shows an example of the MVC pattern describing variation points for web based applications. In the picture, views and controller are part of the presentation layer whereas the model, what the system does, belongs to the business layer of the web system. In figure 3 we have represented two variation points that correspond for two different views of the same data that is, an HTML TABLE and a graph. Additionally, the model of the MVC patterns holds a third variation point belonging to the business logic of the web application. In this way, we have the same variation point of figure 2 that accesses several databases through a PHP module.

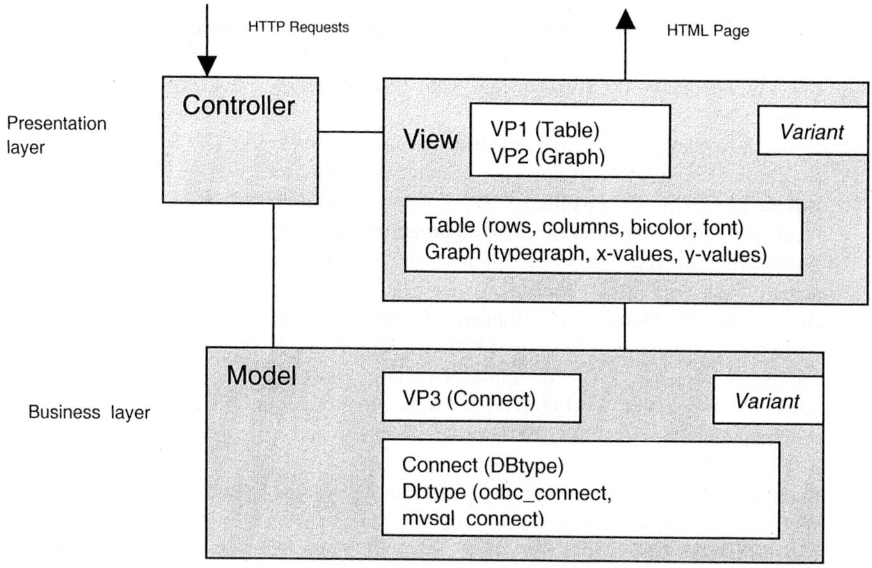

Fig. 3. Representation of variation points using the MVC pattern for web systems.

4 Conclusions

Supporting variability is a common need of all software systems today. However, special quality attributes of Web applications and the frequency of new releases make this need more explicit and critical for Web applications software. But when modeling software systems, some of them such as web-based ones, need not object oriented approaches when we want to design them employing architectural approaches. Therefore, suitable representation formalism is needed by designers to outline variability issues that can be translated in an easy way to code. In this case, the use of patterns as an abstraction of a problem in a specific domain to be used in different contexts is a good choice for modeling suitable designs. In this paper, we have showed how architectural and design patterns can be used to describe in a more accurate manner the variability issues that we want to model in a design process. The proposed notation represents the variability information in a simple and straightforward manner and also is suitable for non-object oriented approaches. As a result of this work, we can model and represent and communicate the variation points in an easy way to be understood by designers and developers. This aspect results key to control better the maintenance and evolution processes that need a redesign of certain parts of a system.

References

1. Alexander, C.: The Timeless Way of Building. Oxford University Press, New York (1979)
2. Appleton, B.: Patterns and Software: Essential Concepts and Terminology. http://www.cmcrossroads.com/bradapp/docs/patterns-intro.html

3. Bandinelli, S.: Light-weight Product Family Engineering. 4th International Workshop on Software Product-Family Engineering. Bilbao, Spain (2001) 327–331
4. Bass, L., Clements, P., Kazman.: Software Architecture in Practice, Addison-Wesley, 2nd Edition (2003)
5. Bass, L., Northrop, L: Software Product Lines, Addison-Wesley (2002)
6. Bosch, J., Design & Use of Software Architectures, Addison -Wesley (2000)
7. Bosch, J., Florijn, G., Greefhorst, D., Kuusela, J., Onbbink, J. H., Pohl, K.: Variability Issues in Software Product Lines. 4th International Workshop on Software Product-Family Engineering. Lecture Notes in Computer Science, Vol. 2290. Springer-Verlag, Berlin Heidelberg New York (2002) 13–21
8. Buschmann, F., Meunier, R., Rohnert, H., Sommerland, P., Stal, M.: Pattern-Oriented Software Architecture. A System of Patterns, John Wiley & Sons, New York (1996)
9. Capilla, R., Dueñas, J. C.: Modelling Variability with Features in Distributed Architectures. 4th International Workshop on Software Product-Family Engineering. Lecture Notes in Computer Science, Vol. 2290. Springer-Verlag, Berlin Heidelberg New York (2002) 319–329
10. Capilla, R., Dueñas, J. C.: Light-weight Product Lines for Evolution and Maintenance of Web Sites. 7th IEEE Conference on Software Maintenance and Reegineering, Benevento, Italy (2003) 53–62
11. Ceri, S., Freternali, P., Bongio, A.: Web Modelling Language (WebML): A Modelling Language for Designing Web Sites. WWW9 Conference, Amsterdam (2000)
12. Connallen, J.:Modelling Web Application Architectures with UML. Communications of the ACM. 42 (10) (1999).
13. Dobrica, L., Niemelä, E.: Using UML Notation to Model Variability in Product Line Architectures, International Workshop on Software Variability Management, ICSE'03, Portland, Oregon, USA, (2003) 8–13
14. Gamma, E., Helm, R., Johnson, R., Vlissides, J.: Design Patterns, Addison-Wesley (1995)
15. Ginige, A., Marugesan, S.: Web Engineering: An Introduction. IEEE Multimedia, January/March (2001) 14–17
16. Gu, A., Henderson-Sellers, B., Lowe, D.: Web Modelling Languages: The Gap Between Requirements and Current Exemplars. The Eighth Australian WWW Conference (2002)
17. Gu, A., Lowe, D., Henderson-Sellers, B.: Linking Modelling Capabilities and Abstraction Levels: The Key to Web System Architectural Integrity. WWW'2002: The Eleventh International World Wide Web Conference, Hawaii, USA (2002)
18. Jacobson, I., Griss, M., Johnsson, P.: Software Reuse. Architecture, Process and Organization for Business Success, ACM Press (1997)
19. Keepence, B., Mannion, M.: Using Patterns to Model Variability in Product Lines, IEEE Software, July/August (1999) 102–108
20. Offutt, J.: Quality Attributes of Web Software Applications, IEEE Software, March/April (2002), 25–32
21. Robak, S.: Feature Modeling Notations for System Families, International Workshop on Software Variability Management, ICSE'03, Portland, Oregon, USA, (2003) 58–62
22. Salicki, S., Farcet, N.: Expression and Usage of the Variability in the Software Product Lines. 4th International Workshop on Software Product-Family Engineering. Lecture Notes in Computer Science, Vol. 2290. Springer-Verlag, Berlin Heidelberg New York (2002) 304–318
23. Schawbe, D., Rossi, G., Barbrosa S.: Abstraction, Composition and Lay-out Definition Mechanisms in OOHDM, in Cruz,I.F., Maks, J. and Wittenburg, K. (eds.) Proceedings of the ACM Workshop on effective Abstractions in Multimedia, San Fransisco, CA (1995)

Modeling and Analysis of Service Interactions in Service-Oriented Software

Woo Jin Lee

Dept. of Computer Science, Kyungpook National University, Sankyuk-dong, Buk-gu, Daegu, South Korea
{woojin}@knu.ac.kr

Abstract. As the Internet usage increases rapidly, an earnest desire for flexible software applications grows larger for reflecting diverse users' demands, for handling evolution of software applications, and for treating pressure of short-term development cycle. In this trend of flexible software, service-oriented software concept is introduced, in which a system is considered as a set of flexible or distributed services. In service-oriented software approach, it is necessary to provide an analysis environment for abnormal service interactions as well as to provide a service execution framework. In this paper, we provide an approach for modeling and analyzing service interactions by using Petri nets. As a case study, feature interactions in the telecommunication literature are discussed as an example of service-oriented software approach.

1 Introduction

The Internet age has ushered in a new era of highly dynamic and agile organizations that must be in a constant state of evolution if they are to compete and survive in an increasingly global marketplace. This era poses significantly new problems for software development, characterized by a shift in emphasis from producing a system in product view to the need to produce services in customer view [1]. Also, the need of satisfying personalized requirements, reuse of software services, and management of software evolution are emerged. The trend of service-oriented software can be seen in service-based software [1], web services [2], and intelligent network [3], and so on. Service-oriented software is a new software development approach in which services are configured to meet a specific set of requirements at a point in time, executed and discarded. The concept of web services represents emerging technologies to reuse software as services over the Internet by wrapping underlying computing models using XML. Intelligent networks appeared to provide an environment for rapid service creation and deployment in telecommunication software systems.

In the service-oriented software approach, a system can be shown as a collection of services, which may be performed in different and distributed platforms. In order to apply service-oriented software concept to a practical application, there are two main problems to be solved. The one is to support a flexible execution framework for easily introducing a new service, for providing a service customization and composition

A. Yazici and C. Şener (Eds.): ISCIS 2003, LNCS 2869, pp. 1043–1050, 2003.

environment, and for dynamically executing customized services. The other is to provide methods and tools for statically and dynamically checking inconsistent or abnormal conflicts among services. In this paper, we focus on the methods for analyzing consistency and completeness of services and abnormal interactions among services. Since the study of service-oriented software is in the beginning stage, there are few related works for modeling and analysis of service-oriented software. As a similar research, there has been studied for feature interactions [3] in telecommunication software systems. However, these works are restricted and dedicated to a specific telecommunication framework. Therefore, service-oriented software approach needs a more generalized and broaden concept of service than the one of telecommunication software.

In order to analyze abnormal service interaction in service-oriented software, at first, each service is described in a formal notation. Most of existing graphic formal methods such as Finite State Machine, Statechart [10], Petri nets [5] have weakness for dealing with such service features as independence from other services, distributed processing, and composition of other services. And although rule-based approach and logic approach can deal with the compositional feature, they are difficult to understand and describe service behaviors and they have drawbacks in maintaining the independence of distributed services and in efficiently analyzing service conflicts. Therefore, in this paper, we propose a new Petri net formalism, *Service-oriented Modular Petri nets (SMPN)*, in which each service is independently described and managed, and service models can be easily composed. Since service interaction occurs when introducing a new service into a system as well as when customers dynamically change or customize their services on their demands, service analysis should be performed in static and dynamic manner. Service interaction analysis is performed in compositional approach after checking consistency and completeness of each service.

The rest of the paper is organized as follows. Section 2 defines the properties of service-oriented software and provides an overview of its supporting environment. Section 3 provides a method for describing services in Service-oriented Modular Petri nets. Section 4 provides analysis techniques of abnormal interactions among services. In Section 5, a case study for modeling and solving feature interaction problems [3] is provided with illustrative examples. Finally, in Section 6, we provide a conclusion and future work.

2 Service-Oriented Software Environment

Most software engineering techniques are conventional supply-side methods, driven by technological advance. This approach works well for systems with rigid boundaries of concern, such as embedded systems, but it is inappropriate to flexible software systems where system boundaries are not fixed and subject to constant urgent change, such as Internet-based applications [4]. For enhancing flexibility of a software, service-oriented framework in which a service is a basic building unit for being created, customized, deployed, evolved, and discarded in a customer-oriented and demand-led viewpoint is introduced. Services may have an atomic functionality or may be composed out of smaller ones (and so on recursively), procured and paid for on demand, when needed. Also, services perform their functionality by interacting with other services. In users' and service providers' viewpoints, service-oriented software has such features as easy introduction and customization, dynamic service management, and platform-transparent execution.

For efficiently managing development and execution environment of service-oriented software, four main components such as service creation environment, service customization environment, service execution environment, and static and dynamic interaction analysis techniques, as shown in Figure 1, are needed.

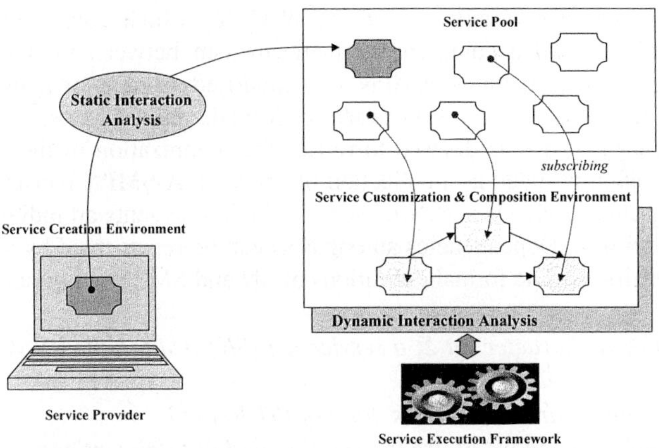

Fig. 1. Overview of Service-oriented Software Environment

Service creation environment provides an environment in which service providers create a new service and add it into the service pool after statically checking abnormal interactions against all existing services. Service providers take advantage of this environment to catch up customers' demands with agility. Through the service customization process, customers can have a differentiated service according to their own requirements and it is necessary to dynamically check the abnormal interaction among customized services. Since services are transparent to locations and execution platforms, service execution framework can be considered as logically distributed computing engine and it provides flexibility for service evolution operations such as dynamic customization, replacement, and discard of services. Since each service is created in the partial viewpoints and it may be designed to interact with other services, the consistency and completeness of a service should be checked. When a new service is introduced into a system, it is necessary to rigorously check whether it properly operates or not and whether it normally interacts with other services or not. Also, during customization process or composition process of services, abnormal interaction among customized services should be checked dynamically. Among the four main components, this paper focuses on the static and dynamic interaction analysis part since flexibility of service-oriented software can be acquired by logically guaranteeing normal interaction among services through formal analysis methods.

3 Modeling of Service-Oriented Software Systems

In order to analyze the interaction among services, behaviors of each service and interactive behaviors between services should be described in a formal notation since a service is a basic building unit in a service-oriented software. Each service should be independently described in a single model for efficiently handling customization and evolution of a service independently. As a formalism of service-oriented software system, we choose Petri net formalism since it is suitable for describing distributed features of services and it has several analysis techniques. However, since Petri nets have weakness in representing modularity, we introduce a new modular Petri nets, named *Service-oriented Modular Petri nets (SMPN)*, which complements service-oriented modularity and a communication mechanism between modules using the labels of places and transitions. SMPN is a modified version of Constraint-based Modular Petri nets [4], which was proposed for formalizing use cases.

The structure of SMPN is devised to reflect the organization of the flexible software system, which is stated as a collection of services. A SMPN consists of a set of logically integrated service nets (SN_i), each of which represents an individual service model with Petri nets. Dependencies among SNs can be represented by shared places and shared transitions. The formal definitions of SN and SMPN are given as follows.

Definition 1 *For a character set Σ, a service net (SN) is a 6-tuple SN = (P, T, F, G, L, M_0), where*

- *P, T, and M_0 are the same as those of P/T Net [5],*
- *F represents the set of arc information and arc descriptions which indicate the amount and type of a token flow,*
- *G is the set of guard expressions in transitions,*
- *$L : P \cup T \rightarrow \Sigma^*$ is a label function that associates a distinct label taken from strings (Σ^*) with each place and transition of P and T, respectively.*

Definition 2 *Service-oriented Modular Petri nets (SMPN) are defined as SMPN = { SN_i | i = 1...n} satisfying the following conditions:*

- *P_i, T_i, and F_i should be disjoint for SN_i,*
- *The same label should not be used for both places and transitions,*
- *M_0 for shared places should be the same.*

In SMPN model, each service is described in an independent model. Since each service model has a single or multiple control threads, a service model is described as an iterative form. Figure 2 shows a SMPN model of the basic call processing (BCP) model [6] is composed of three service nets. Figure 2 (a) and (b) show service nets of originating and terminating parties, respectively. Figure 2(c) describes a process of connection establishment between an originating party and a terminating party. In order to perform a functionality of a service, resources such as hardware, software, and devices are utilized. Behaviors of a service are closely related with the resources of the system. When resources are shared with several services, a service may not occur due to the lack of available resources. In Figure 2, **Resource** place represents the resource of a telephone system, which has a single capacity for processing a call at a time.

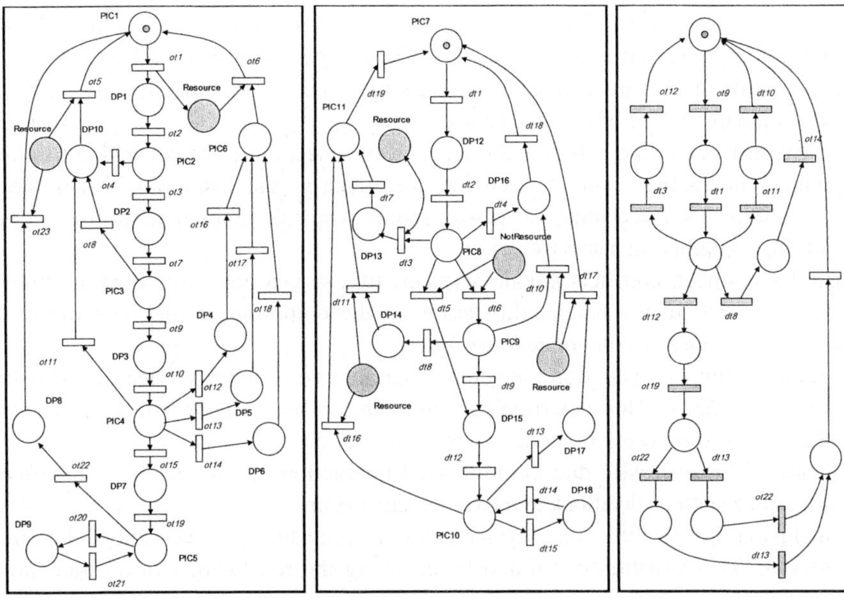

(a) a service net of an originating party (b) a service net of a terminating party (c) interactions of two parties

Fig. 2. The SMPN model of the BCP model

4 Service Interaction Analysis

The goals of service interaction analysis are to check consistency and completeness of each service and to check abnormal interactions among services in off-line or on-line manner. Service interaction analysis is performed when introducing a new service into a system as well as when customers dynamically change or customize their services on their demands. Before checking service interaction analysis, service models are composed with the basic system model. Service models are merged by combining shared places (or shared transitions) with the same label into a composed place (or a composed transition). In the composed model, a reachability graph is generated for checking abnormal situations such as deadlock, livelock, unreachable transitions, and so on.

Service interaction analysis is mainly composed of consistency analysis for a service net and conflict analysis among service nets. For checking consistency of a single service, a service net is composed to the basic model. In the reachability analysis of the composed model, there are following types of inconsistency.

- deadlock : the behavior of a service may cause the basic services to be blocked. In worst case, a system does not work any more. Deadlock situations can be easily found by checking a dead marking.
- livelock : due to the abnormal interaction with the basic service, a system may fall into a trap or an infinite loop. Livelock situations can be found by checking a loop without containing the initial marking. Once in a while, livelock may be intentionally added into a service net.
- meaningless service : the functionality of a service will not occur due to unintended interaction. This service has no effect in the behaviors of a system. Meaningless service situations can be found by checking the reachability of transitions contained in a service net.

In order to check conflicts among services, two service nets are combined into a composed model. In the reachability graph of the composed model, conflict types among services may be categorized as follows.

- non-deterministic situation : at some situation, two or more services are simultaneously enabled. Non-deterministic situation can be found by checking whether there exists a marking that has two or more branches.
- deadlock or livelock : due to unintended interactions among services, abnormal situations such as deadlock and livelock can occur.
- inclusion of a service : one service can not occur due to prevention of the other service. This situation can found by checking the reachability of all transitions contained service nets.

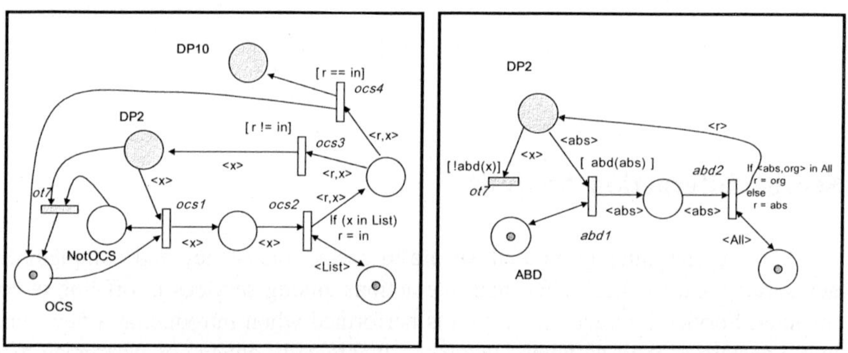

(a) Originating Call Screen Service (b) Abbreviated Dialing Service

Fig. 3. Service nets of OCS and ABD services

5 Case Study

In intelligent networks, telecommunication systems are enhanced by a large and steadily growing number of supplementary services such as CF (Call Forwarding), CW (Call Waiting), OCS (Originating Call Screen), ABD (Abbreviated Dialing), TCS (Terminating Call Screen) and so on. In this section, we describe OCS and ABD services in SMPN and check abnormal interactions among them. Since each telecommunication service is performed its behavior by interacting with BCP model via DP nodes, it is independently described as a service net by sharing DP places of the BCP model. Figure 3 shows the examples of describing OCS and ABD services. An OCS service checks whether the screening list includes a dialed number or not. And ABD service translates an abbreviated number into the registered phone number if it is registered previously. Otherwise, it returns the input number via DP2.

The consistency and completeness analysis for general properties can be more efficiently applied to the Petri net slices [7] than SMPN model. Since a SMPN model has shared places that are similar to global variables, it is difficult to analyze a SMPN model in a modular approach. The Petri net slices have only shared transitions, which are obtained by restructuring the SMPN model in the perspective of control threads. Figure 4 shows the example of Petri net Slices generated from the composed model of the originating party of BCP, OCS, and ABD services. For simplicity, we omitted the guard conditions in Figure 4. Each slice has its own control token and is performed its behavior by synchronizing with other slices via shared transitions.

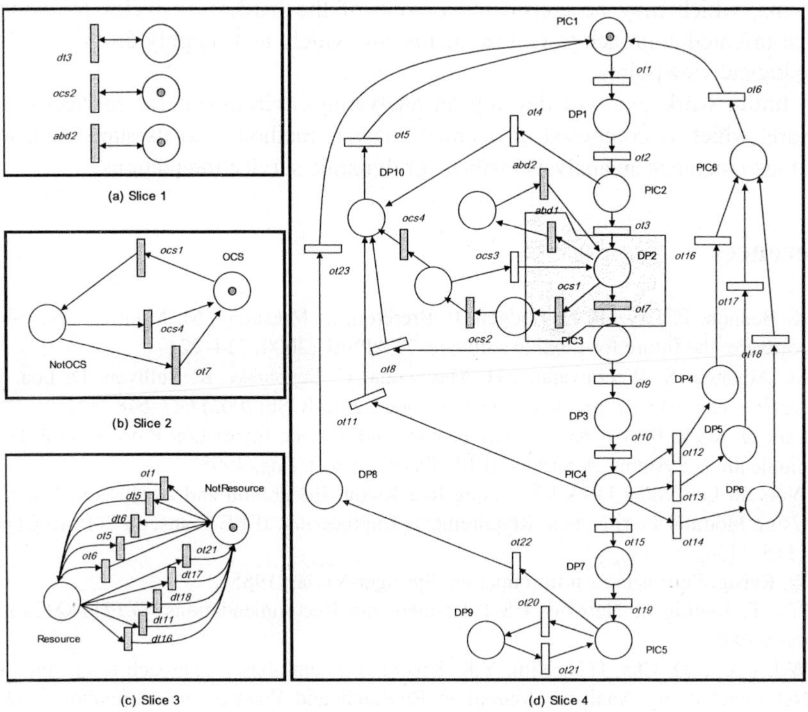

Fig. 4. Petri nets Slices of the SMPN model shown in Fig. 2

A SMPN model is said to be inconsistent if there exists a set of transitions that are never enabled. This type of flaws is analogous to an unreachable code in programs. Since services are expected to reflect genuine needs, it is reasonable to require that SMPNs do not contain transitions that are never enabled. Another type of inconsistency occurs when there are deadlocks. These inconsistencies can be detectable by generating a compositional reachability graph (RG) of Petri net slices. In compositional analysis, after each slice is locally analyzed by generating its local RG, a pair of slices are composed and analyzed incrementally. For example, in local analysis of slice 4, we can find a situation which *ocs1*, *abd1*, and *ot7* transitions can be enabled in non-deterministic order, as shown in the shaded box of Figure 4. That is, since OCS service and ABD service can be performed in arbitrary order, it is possible that the OCS function has no effect on the abbreviated form of a screening number.

6 Conclusion and Future Work

We have described the service-oriented software approach and proposed a general framework for modeling and analyzing services and service interactions by using a modular Petri nets. In the present circumstance that the service-oriented concept is gradually accepted and applied in the Internet-based applications, service interaction problems, which may be considered as one of the hardest obstacles for applying service-oriented approach to real problems, are widely and roughly discussed even if in the logical viewpoints.

As future work, we will develop an analyzing environment for service-oriented software, which is composed of detailed analysis methods and its supporting tools. And it also includes an analysis method for dynamic service interactions.

References

1. K. Bennett, P. Layzell, D. Budgen, P. Brereton, L. Macaulay, M. Munro: Service-based software: the future for flexible software. 7th APSEC(2000) 214–221
2. M. Aoyama, S. Weerawarana, H. Maruyama, C. Szyperski, K. Sullivan, D. Lea: Web services engineering: promises and challenges. 24rd ICSE(2002) 647–648
3. Dirk O. Keck, Paul J. Kuehn: The Feature and Service Interaction Problem in Telecommunications Systems: A Survey. IEEE Trans. on Soft. Eng.(1998)
4. Woo Jin Lee, Sung Deok Cha, Yong Rae Kwon: Integration and Analysis of Use Cases Using Modular Petri Nets in Requirements Engineering. IEEE Trans. on Soft. Eng.(1998) 1115–1130
5. W. Reisig, Petri nets : An Introduction. Springer-Verlag(1985)
6. ITU-T, Intelligent Network CS-1 Refinements Recommendations. Q.1211-Q1215 Geneva(1995)
7. W.J. Lee, S.D. Cha, H.N. Kim, Y.R. Kwon: A Slicing-based approach to enhance Petri Net Reachability Analysis. Journal of Research and Practice in Information Technology(2000) 131–143
8. G. Piccinelli, M. Salle, C. Zirpins: Service-oriented modeling for e-business applications components. Tenth IEEE International Workshops on WET ICE(2001) 12–17
9. P. Layzell: Addressing the software evolution crisis through a service-oriented view of software: a roadmap for software engineering and maintenance research. IEEE International Conference on Software Maintenance (2001)
10. D. Harel: Statecharts : A Visual Formalism for Complex Systems. Science of Computer Programming(1987)

Designing Reusable Web-Applications by Employing Enterprise Frameworks

Marius Dragomiroiu[1], Robert Gyorodi[2], Ioan Salomie[1], and Cornelia Gyorodi[2]

[1] University of Limerick, ECE Department, Limerick, Ireland
[2] University of Oradea, Computer Science Department, Oradea, Romania
{marius.dragomiroiu, robert.gyorodi}@ul.ie

Abstract. Given the complexity of web-applications, the associated development process should focus on improving their reusability and flexibility. Enterprise Frameworks encapsulate reusable, tailorable software solutions as a collection of collaborative components, assuring integration of new components and reducing the complexity of the systems. The paper presents a development process of enterprise frameworks for web-applications and proposes a compositional design pattern targeting to increase framework flexibility and reusability.

1 Introduction

Building web-applications is a complex and time–consuming process. Web-applications typically evolve over time, by domain extensions or by an evolution in the quality of provided services. Therefore, the development process should focus on improving reusability and flexibility of the application in order to reduce the resources and time spent for it's building, maintaining or extending. A solution to meet these concerns is carried out by employing software frameworks in the development process. Enterprise Frameworks ensure reuse not only for building blocks but also for entire system architectures including their design [1]. Unfortunately, due to the complexity of the development process, Enterprise Frameworks do not always fulfil their promises. Therefore, this paper proposes an approach in developing enterprise frameworks for web-applications aiming to improve their reusability and flexibility.

The remainder of the paper is structured as follows: section two presents the application domain together with architectural analysis, section three describes the development approach of the enterprise framework, and section four summarizes the benefits of the proposed enterprise framework design. The paper concludes in section five.

2 Domain Analysis

Domain analysis identifies domain main features by capturing and organizing the associated domain knowledge. For architectural design, decomposing and organizing the domain functionalities in layers is an effective mean for managing complexity [2]. The domain layering is based on both the architectural and functional decomposition.

A. Yazici and C. Şener (Eds.): ISCIS 2003, LNCS 2869, pp. 1051–1059, 2003.

Generally, a web application domain can be decomposed at least in three architectural layers, according to the model-view-controller architectural pattern.

1. Presentation Layer – models the look and feel of the application. Typically, this layer contains components such as: *html pages, jsp pages, applets* and *frames.*
2. Model Layer – defines and implements the core concept of the business. This layer is specific to any application business domain.
3. Control Layer – defines and implements the navigational mechanism of the application, by interacting with the model and presentation layers. It contains server-side components that handle *http* requests and generate the associated responses.

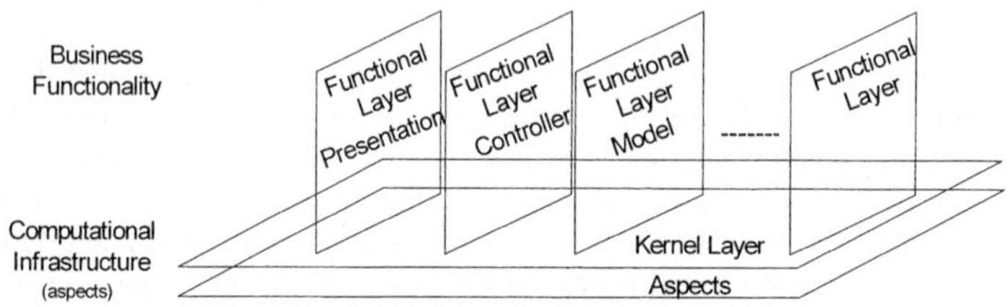

Fig. 1. Domain decomposition into layers

Based on the types of functionalities embodied, the MVC domain layers can be further decomposed. Components that interact with other legacy applications, persistent data storages or hardware devices, and also components located in different nodes (in case of distributed systems) can be structured into new layers. For example the Model Layer can be split into a *Business Logic Layer* – which defines and implements the business logic of the domain and a *Data Access Layer* – which is in charge of manipulating the persistent data needed in the business model.

2.1 Computational Infrastructure

Another issue of the domain analysis that must be addressed is the separation of *business functionality* from the *computational infrastructure*. The business functionality, expressed by *functional components*, addresses the business domain requirements. On the other hand, the *computational infrastructure*, addressing system non-functional requirements like security, load balancing, fault tolerance, communication and other services tied to the system infrastructure, is modelled by *infrastructure components*, also known as *aspects* [3]. The mixture of *business functionality* with the *infrastructure* generates design artefacts difficult to understand, limits reuse and forces re-engineering of the framework in order to meet new requirements. Separation of the *business functionality* from the *computational infrastructure* allows the reuse of the *infrastructure* and at the same time promotes flexibility of the *business functionality*. As a result, enterprise frameworks that address different business domains can use the same computational infrastructure, while the business functionality can use other infrastructures with minor or no changes in business components.

The computational infrastructure can be also divided into layers. An intermediate layer, named *Kernel Layer*, can be introduced between the computational layer and the business functionality. The *Kernel Layer* defines and implements the framework internal services that are independent from the business domain.

2.2 Designing the Business Functionality

The design of business functionality is an incremental process carried out in a set of steps, from requirements analysis to identification of framework components and their collaboration model. These steps depicted in Fig 2 can be described as follows.

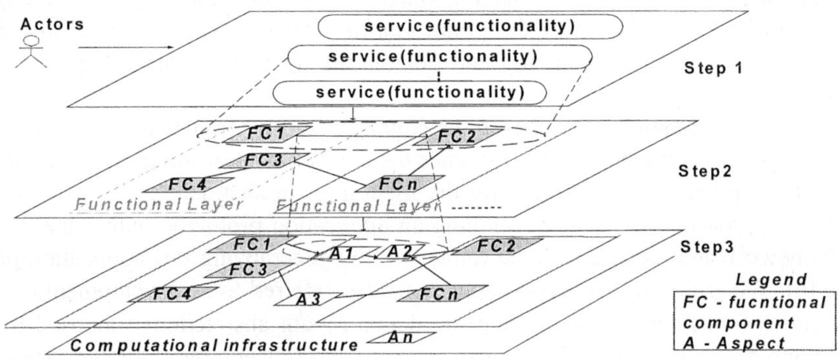

Fig. 2. Design Stratification

The first step deals with the identification of the framework functionalities based on the business requirements. The actors (clients) together with the set of services provided to them are identified out from the business requirements.

The second step provides a conceptual organization of service's components into domain layers. The service functionalities come out from the interaction of components arranged into the domain layers, as is emphasised in Fig. 2. As a result of organizing the service's components into layers new domain layers can be identified.

In the last step, the infrastructure components and the framework internal services needed in the interaction of the business components are determined.

3 Enterprise Framework Development Process

By considering the separation between the functional components and computational infrastructure as well as the decomposition of business functionality into layers, the development process is structured in the following three steps: (i) implementation of the computational infrastructure without referring to the business functionality, (ii) implementation of the business functionality according to domain decomposition and independent from the computational infrastructure; and then (iii) design a flexible interaction mechanism between the business functionality and infrastructure [4].

3.1 Developing the Computational Infrastructure

Depending on the chosen computational infrastructure, its design can be more or less complex. In some cases most of the computational infrastructure is "provided" by the programming language, or by the technology employed (EJB, RMI, CCM, etc). Otherwise, during the framework development, the computational infrastructure should be implemented before and independent of the business functionality.

3.2 Developing the Business Functionality

Our approach in developing of business functionality focuses on improving the enterprise framework flexibility by designing a *utility framework* for each identified domain layer, which assures an easy and flexible management of the enterprise framework.

There are two main approaches in developing a (utility) framework summarized as follows: (i) top-down approach – assumes the development of the framework directly from domain analysis by identifying the main domain abstractions [5] and (ii) bottom–up approach – starts by developing an application prototype within the domain of framework and then defines the framework by generalizing this application prototype [6]. We argue for the second approach, also referred to as development by *generalization*, considering that finding the domain main abstractions, imposed by the top-down approach is a difficult process in the case of complex domain. Thus, the framework's variability points (hot-spots) are identified by generalizing the structure of the existing prototype application classes. At this stage application specific parts have to be identified and separated from those common to all applications within the domain, process carried out together with the domain experts.

The framework development process incorporates design patterns and principles like *separation principle* [7], separation of component interface from implementation, provision of loose coupling among components, *role oriented interfaces* [8], etc.

The design of each utility framework can employ specific design solutions according to their addressed functionality.

The design of Control Layer Framework (CLF) for the Control Layer incorporates the *Front Controller pattern* and the *Intercepting Filter pattern* [9]. The Front Controller pattern provides a single access point to services and reduces the amount of redundant code in an application. The Intercepting Filter pattern is used for preprocessing client requests in a standard manner. The filter components are controlled declaratively using a *deployment descriptor*. The solution allows adding or removing the filter components at run time, without affecting the application.

The design of Data Access Layer Framework (DALF) for the Data Access Layer is in accordance with the *Data Access Object pattern* [9]. This pattern provides a flexible solution for encapsulating the access to the data storage.

The design of the Presentation Layer Framework (PLF) for the Presentation Layer is based on the *View Helper Objects* and the *Template pages*. The View Helper

Objects are used for collecting and formatting the information that should be displayed, while template pages reduce the html code.

Utility Frameworks (UF) are independent one from another, thus the development process of utility frameworks can take place in parallel. Nevertheless the development of utility frameworks has to be guided by the latter composition among them, since service functionality is modeled through composition with parts of functionality from different utility frameworks.

3.3 Framework Composition (Integration)

The enterprise framework for web-applications is defined as a composition of the utility frameworks together with the computational infrastructure.

Composition of Utility Frameworks. The composition of utility frameworks makes up the business functionality of the enterprise framework. Each utility framework models distinct parts of services' functionality, as it is outlined in the previous sections by separation of the domain in distinct layers.

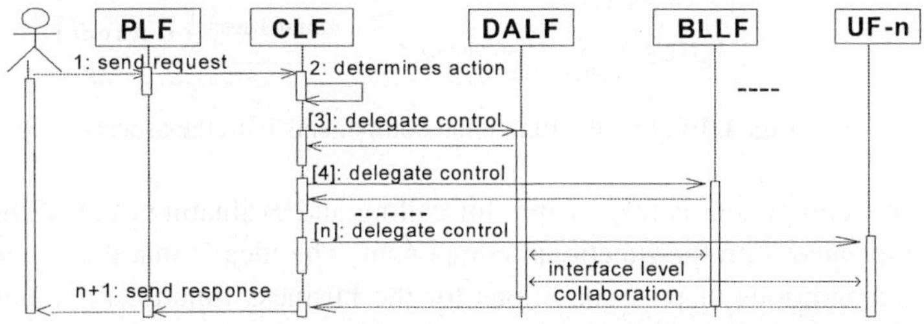

Fig. 3. Utility Framework Interaction – Workflow Control

A centralized framework composition process is proposed, promoting at the same time a high degree of flexibility in interaction among frameworks. This process, illustrated in Fig. 3, can be summarized as follows. The Control Layer Framework (CLF) initiates the collaboration among utility frameworks and assures the main control of the application workflow by instantiating a set of cooperation components. It handles *http* requests and delegates the control to the other utility frameworks. After the execution of the request, the CLF generates the response passing the control to the PLF.

A higher degree of flexibility in framework composition can be achieved by loose coupling within the framework interaction, using interfaces and abstract classes. To avoid the tight coupling between CLF and the rest of the utility frameworks, each utility framework incorporates the *Abstract Factory* design pattern [10] that defines an abstract class in charge of the creation of framework components. In this way the CLF delegates the creation of a framework component to the abstract factory class of the corresponding utility framework. The abstract factory class returns the interface of the instantiated component to the CLF. Furthermore, the collaborations among the utility frameworks are realized at interface level. This assures that the framework component implementation technology (JavaBeans, EJB, CCM) is transparent for the framework collaboration processes. The advantage of using Abstract Factory is evident especially when an entire implementation of a utility framework is subject to change. In this case, all the modifications take place in that utility framework and in its abstract factory class, rather than involving other utility frameworks. For instance, consider an application that deals with persistent data management. In case of changing the type of the persistent data storage using this aforementioned approach modifications are required only in the corresponding utility framework.

Composition of Functionality with Computational Infrastructure. The binding between the *functional component* and the *infrastructure components,* also referred to as *aspects,* is achieved through a *Proxy Bridge Component* (proxy).

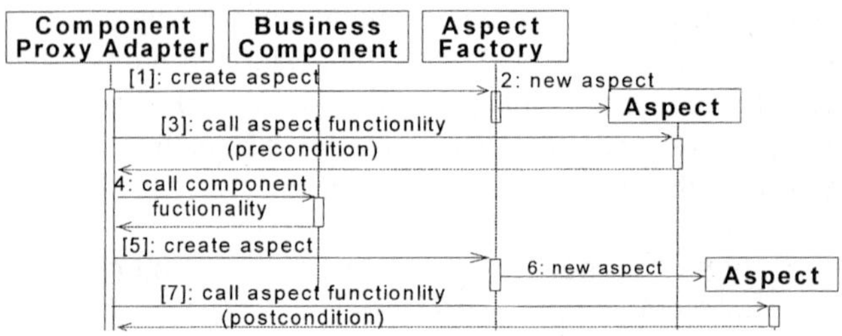

Fig. 4. Binding the functional components with the aspects

The proxy component is responsible for calling and evaluating each of the *aspects* that are associated with the functional component. The idea is that the *aspects* represent the preconditions or post-conditions for the business functionality. Before executing the business functionality, the proxy component evaluates the precondition by calling the aspects components. In case the pre-conditions succeed, the proxy calls the component's functionality [11]. Once execution is completed, the proxy will evaluate the post-condition by calling the associated aspects, see Fig. 4.

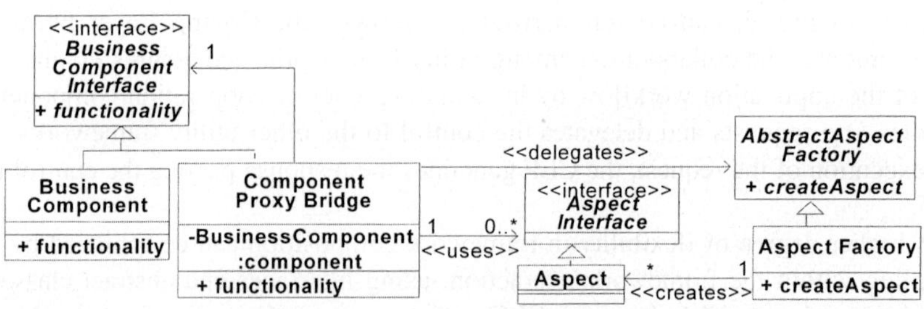

Fig. 5. Proxy-Adapter Pattern Structure

The paper introduces the *Proxy Adaptor* pattern in order to improve the interaction flexibility among the business functionality, the computational infrastructure and the proxy component. The pattern is defined as a combination of the *Decorator* pattern [10] and the *Abstract Factory* pattern. The Decorator pattern is used for defining the proxy component, while the Abstract Factory pattern deals with instantiation of the aspects. Therefore, each proxy is a representative for a business component. The proxy implements an interface identical to the one of the business component it represents. Any calls to the proxy component is packaged with the necessary pre and post conditions and forwarded to the business component. The proxy evaluates the pre and the post conditions by delegating the creation of the corresponding aspects to an Abstract Factory. The Factory class return the aspect interface to the proxy component. The structure of the pattern is illustrated in the Fig. 5. The benefits of using this pattern can be summarized as follows:

- Assures independency between the business functionality and the infrastructure.
- Functional components and aspects are transparent form the proxy component.
- Reduces the amount of redundant code, since the proxy component is defined for a *family* of business components (components with the same interface).

4 Evaluation and Design Benefits

The performance of the framework design is expressed in terms of reusability and flexibility in generating new custom applications within the addressed domain. To outline the benefits of the presented methodology in designing web-applications we present the results of the evaluation, detailed in [12], of three Virtual Learning Environment variants: a hard-wired VLE application, a VLE-MVC framework (Model-View-Controller architectural pattern) and the VLE Framework (VLEF). The first two variants of the VLE can be considered as the evolution towards the VLEF. The values presented are approximated and resulted from an empirical calculus. Note that the differences are in the architecture and not in the functionality of the system. The business functionality is similar in all three versions. Table 1 emphasis the set of metrics that determines the quality attributes (reusability, flexibility and extensibility).

Table 1. Metrics' Values

Metric Name/ Description	Hard-Wired VLE	VLE-MVC	VLEF
Design Size (DSC) –Total number of classes in the system	54	90	129
Number of hierarchies (NOH)	1	3	5
Number of inheritances (NOI) - Number of classes that use inheritances (incl. interfaces)	1	20	43
Number of Direct Class Coupling (NDCC) – classes that are directly related by attributes declaration or by instantiation	4	3	2.7
Number of Loosely Coupling Classes (NLCC) – number of distinct classes that use instance of other classes by employing delegation, or by using only their interfaces	0.2	0.8	1.3
Data Access Metric (DAM) - This metric is the ratio of the number of private, protected attributes to the total number of attributes declared in the class. A metrics closer to 1 is preferred.	0.8	0.9	1

The values, presented in Table 1, emphasize the advantages of VLEF over the other two VLE versions by the following: (i) increasing the number of classes by separating the class functionalities into different classes, providing more flexibility in adapting the framework component functionality; (ii) increasing the number of loose couplings among components while decreasing the number of direct component couplings and (iii) increasing the plug-in points (interfaces) for future extension or adaptation.

The benefits of the presented framework design can be summarised as follows:

- The computational infrastructure and the business functionality are loosely coupled and can be independently reused.
- Decomposition of the domain into layers provides an easier way to maintain and extend the framework. The design of utility frameworks and the interaction among them provide a higher level of flexibility to the enterprise framework.

5 Conclusions

The paper emphasises that any web-application domain can be decomposed and layered to match their business's requirements. By separating the business domain from the computational infrastructure, we show how to develop the enterprise framework to manage dependencies and reduce coupling between them.

A particularly important issue is defining the enterprise framework as a composition of utility frameworks on one side, and the composition of business functionality and computational infrastructure on the other side. Using Abstract Factory Method and a loose coupling among utility frameworks allows replacing an entire domain layer without having to change the rest of the enterprise framework. The paper also defines the proxy-adapter pattern as a flexible solution in binding the business functionality with computational infrastructure. The presented approach generates reusable and highly flexible enterprise framework solutions for custom web applications.

References

1. Fayad, M.and Hamu, D.: Enterprise Frameworks: Guidelines for Selection. ACM, Vol. 32/No1, Art No. 4 (2000)
2. Baumer, D., Gryczan, G., Knoll, R., Lilienthal, C., Riehle, D. and Zullighoven, H.: Framework Development Layering in large System. ACM Vol. 40/No. 10, (1997), 52–59
3. Fayad, M., Hamu, D. and Brugali, D.: Enterprise Framework Characteristics, Criteria, and Challenges. ACM, Vol. 43/No. 10, (2000), 39–46
4. Mili, H., Fayad, Brugali, D., Hamu, D. and Dori, D.: Enterprise Frameworks: issues and research direction. Software–Practice and Experience, Vol. 32, (2002), 801–832
5. Akist M., Tekinerdogan B. and Marcelloni F.: Developing Object-Oriented Frameworks Using Domain Models, ACM, Vol. 32, Art No. 11, (2000).
6. Schmid H.: Systematic Framework Design by Generalization. ACM, Vol. 40, (1997), 48–51

7. Fontuara, M., Pree, W. and Rumpe, B.: The UML Profile for Framework Architectures. (Addison-Wesley Ed., New York) Chap. 4, (2002), 68–112
8. van Gurp, J. and Bosch, J.: Design, implementation and evolution of object oriented frameworks: concepts and guidelines. Software–Practice and Experience, (2001), 277–300
9. Alur, D., Crupi, J. and Malks, D.: Core J2EE Patterns: Best Practices and Design Strategies. Prentice Hall / Sun Microsystems Press Ed. (2001), 152–407
10. Gamma E., Helm R., Johnson R and Vlissides J.: Design Patterns – Elements of Reusable Object Oriented Software. *Addison-Wesley* Ed., N.Y. (1995).
11. Constantinides, C. and Elrad T.: Composing Concern with A Framework Approach, IEEE Software. (2001), 133–138
12. Dragomiroiu, M.. "Enterprise Frameworks for Virtual Learning Environments" Master Thesis, University of Limerick, 2003

Multimedia Synchronization Model for Two Level Buffer Policy in Mobile Environment

Keun-Wang Lee[1], Jong-Hee Lee[2], and Kwang-Hyoung Lee[2]

[1] Dept.of Science Chungwoon University, Korea
kwlee@cwunet.ac.kr
[2] School of Computing, Soong-sil University, Korea

Abstract. We propose Mobile Multimedia Synchronization Model (MMSM) as a new specification model including a two level buffer policy for Base Station (BS) and Mobile Host (MH). The proposed model has higher the guarantee of QoS such as the playing time than it of the previous work.

1 Introduction

With the advancement in mobile communication systems and portable computing technologies, demand for mobile multimedia services is increasing in the area of wireless communications, such as data transmission, video transmission, WWW access, and so on [1][2][3]. Mobile multimedia service is complex concept of wireless extension of wired multimedia service and mobile specific multimedia service. That is, mobile multimedia service is to add user mobility to multimedia services in wired networks [4].

In mobile networks, a Mobile Host (MH) has small memory, and a Base Station (BS) supports the limited resources than the sites in wired networks. Moreover, the mobile communication system has low power, and must provide high-quality access with MHs. That is, the synchronization in wireless networks is complex than that in wired networks. In particular, because of the small memory and the limited resources, a MH may suffer from either the buffer underflow or the buffer overflow. Therefore, an adaptive synchronization method is needed for mobile multimedia networks.

The previous works have been done in describing the synchronization model for multimedia applications. Among those, Petri-net based specification models provide a good method to specify temporal relationships. The integration of various media and the definition of QoS requirements should be supported and easily described. However, previous extended Petri-net based models like as Object Composition Petri-Net (OCPN) and Real Time Synchronization Model (RTSM) have some constraints in modeling the QoS parameters of both intramedia and intermedia. Therefore, we propose a two level synchronization model which guarantees the QoS in Mobile Environment (ME).

A. Yazici and C. Şener (Eds.): ISCIS 2003, LNCS 2869, pp. 1060–1068, 2003.

2 Related Work

The OCPN model has been proved to have the ability to specify any arbitrary temporal relationship among media and it may be applied to both stored data applications and live applications[3][5]. The OCPN model weakly describes synchronous temporal relationships between media at an object level. A multimedia application that is comprised of video, audio and text object can be expressed by OCPN technique that is shown in Fig. 1. Generally, audio data is very jitter sensitive and cannot tolerate random delays between frame segments; hence, delay between audio frames may result in unrecognizable audio quality. In contrast, some extent of random delay between video frames may be acceptable in video data. Therefore a late transmission of video frames does not influence the QoS.

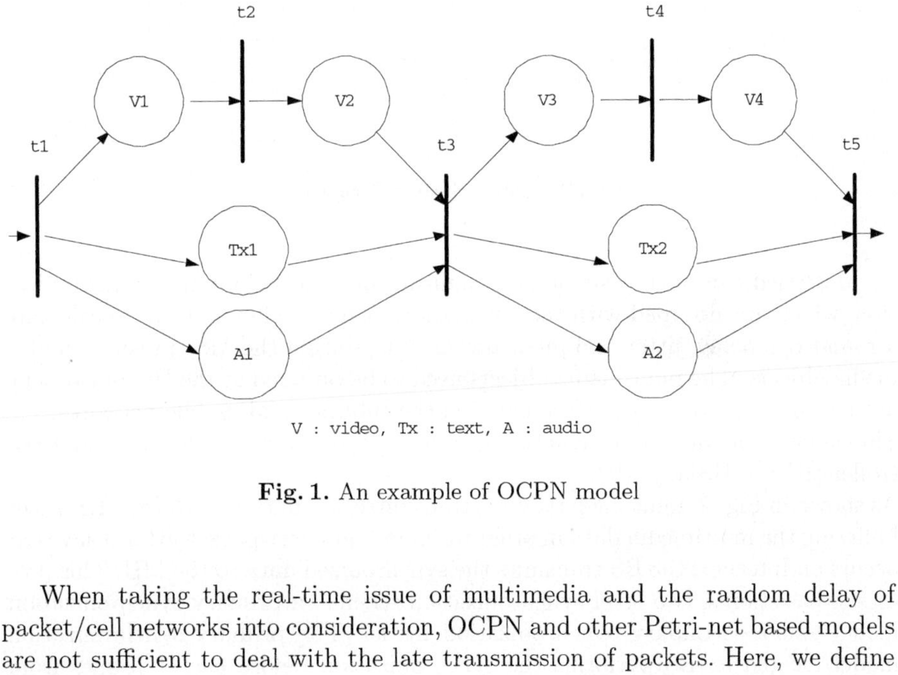

Fig. 1. An example of OCPN model

When taking the real-time issue of multimedia and the random delay of packet/cell networks into consideration, OCPN and other Petri-net based models are not sufficient to deal with the late transmission of packets. Here, we define late transmission of a packet to be that the packet fails to reach its destination in time and should be dropped. Also, the RTSM model is not sufficient in describing various synchronization relations. If the text object is one of the key medium, it is assigned as an enforced place just as an audio object. Once one of enforced place is unblocked, each transition of RTSM is fired. When an audio object is unblocked, the transition is fired, even if text object is still activated. Therefore the text object is not guaranteed to display its content.

3 MMSM

We assume that Multimedia Servers (MSs) on Internet act as repositories for multimedia applications orchestrated according to the synchronization model. A MS searches the requested data from its databases and transmits it to the BS. Fig. 2 shows the mobile system structure.

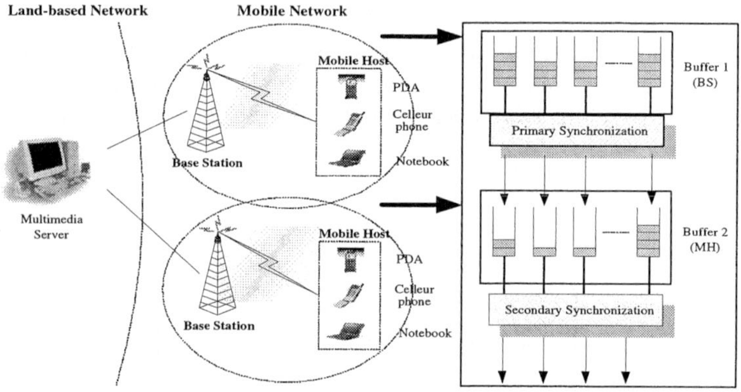

Fig. 2. Mobile System Structure.

Multimedia data consists of many multimedia objects, a unit of synchronization, which are stamped with the current local time to allow the BS to calculate a round trip delay, jitter and inter-arrival time, during the MS transmits multimedia objects. The multimedia objects need to be buffered at the BS for carrying out synchronization as interface between the Internet and mobile networks.
Mobile multimedia system structure consists of three parts: Radio Network Controller (RNC), BS and MH.
As shown in Fig. 2, multimedia data is transmitted from the BS to the MH. After buffering the multimedia data in order to smooth an inter-packet jitter delay that occurs on Internet, the BS transmits the synchronized data to the MH. This process is based on a two level synchronization scheme: a primary synchronization model and a secondary synchronization model. The primary synchronization model located at BS performs the synchronization before packet frames from the secondary synchronization model are transmitted to MH through RF channel. The secondary synchronization model located at MH is used for supporting smooth playback for multimedia packet frames.

3.1 Definition and Firing Rule of MMSM

The definition of MMSM to specify Petri-net in BS and MH is the following. The MMSM specified by the tuple $[P, T, K, A, DIFF, R, D, J, Re, M]$ where P is regular places(single circles), T is transitions, K is key places, X $((P \cup K))$

is all places, $A((X \times T) \cup (T \times X))$ is directed *arcs*, $DIFF$ is difference between maximum duration time and actual duration time, J is maximum delay jitter, and Re is type of media.
Also, Each place may be in one of the following states; 0 is no token, 1 is token is blocked Cross in the place, 2 is token is unblocked Dot in the place. Places are used to represent a medium unit and their corresponding actions. The Place can have tokens. A Place without token means that it is currently inactive. A place with token is active and could be in one of the two states: blocked or unblocked. When a transition is fired and then token is added into a place, the action of the place is executed, and the token is blocked before finishing the action. The token is unblocked after finishing. Each place has some parameter that determines its relative importance compared with other mediums. Firing rules of MMSM are described as follows: 1) The firing occurs immediately if the end of time medium is done. 2) Transition t_i fires immediately when the arrived key medium places contain an unblocked token. 3) Upon firing, a set of backtracking rules is exercised to remove tokens from their input places. 4) Transition t_i removes a token from each of its input places and adds a token to each of its output places. 5) After receiving a token, a place p_j remains in the active state for the interval specified by the duration j. During this interval, the token is blocked. If transition t_i is fired, the remained token should be removed also. This removal process is shown in Fig. 3.

Fig. 3. Backtracking of MMSM.

When the transition t_4 is fired, the input place with no token is backtracked. Dotted line represents the branch that needs to be backtracked. Before meeting a place with token, the gate value of the transition of that branch is set to zero. Since the gate values of t_2 and t_3 is set to zero, t_2 and t_3 is immediately fired. The backtracking stops respectively at p_4 and p_2. After backtracking and firing, only p_6 and p_7 may have a token.

3.2 Concept of Multiple Key Media and Time Medium

In MMSM, there are two kinds of places as regular places and key places. To differentiate a key place from a regular place, a double circle is drawn for key

place as shown in Fig. 5 where transition t_4 is fed by two regular places, V_3 and Tx_1 and one key place, Au_1.
The firing rule about key places is that once multiple key places get unblocked, the transition following it will be immediately fired regardless of the states of other places feeding this transition. Therefore, if Au_1 becomes unblocked in Fig. 6, transition t_4 will be immediately fired regardless of the states of V_3 and Tx_1. At the same time, tokens in the places before transition t_4, such as V_1, V_2, V_3 or Tx_1, must be cleared since these places are obsolete due to the firing of t_4. We call this action of clearing all obsolete tokens backtracking, since the action is backtracked from the fired transition in MMSM.
Time medium is a virtual medium and normally contains a deterministic duration of time which specifies the real-time constraint between two transitions.

4 Playing Algorithm Including the QoS Parameter

It is required that synchronization model can describe various multimedia objects flexibly in the view point of time relationship and also respond QoS requirement about jitter which is time difference between intra-media and skew which is time difference between inter-media. We suggest multimedia synchronization model that is based on the Petri-net and services desirable QoS requirement.

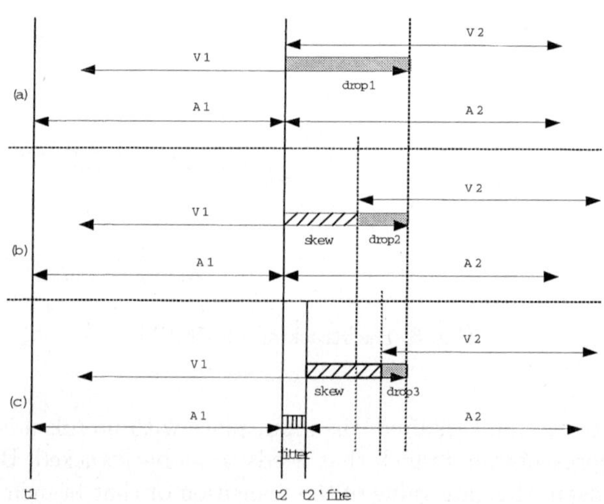

Fig. 4. Presentation of jitter and skew.

The proposed model applies maximum jitter and skew values which can be allowed, and then it presents high QoS and real time characteristics. In this paper we expend Petri-net and propose new synchronization specification model. We compared with other models and showed high QoS. Fig. 4 shows dropping status

of jitter and skew. In Fig. 4(a), drop1 apply not to skew and jitter. In Fig. 4(b), only apply to skew. In Fig. 4(c), drop3 apply to skew and jitter.
Each place p_i has time-related four parameters τ_{diff}, τ_r, τ_d, and τ_j as well as key medium in order to handle QoS parameters for intermedia synchronization. Fig. 5 presents the MMSM with QoS parameter.
Intermedia skew value 0 means that the two media streaming is completely synchronized. For instance, it can be considered as the synchronized state if it is within 80ms between audio and video streams. If skew value 80ms is applied to key medium of audio, the maximum delay jitter τ_j will be destroyed, which will result in degrading the audio quality. Because the maximum delay jitter of audio within media is 10ms, waiting longer than 10ms could be a factor that destroys the audio quality. Therefore, τ_j is compensated by means of applying the maximum delay jitter τ_j.
Maximum delay jitter τ_j represents maximum delay jitter of the place p_i. The delay is a interval between medium i and medium i+1, and it is used to obtain the better QoS by additionally playing out as much as the time of maximum delay jitter.

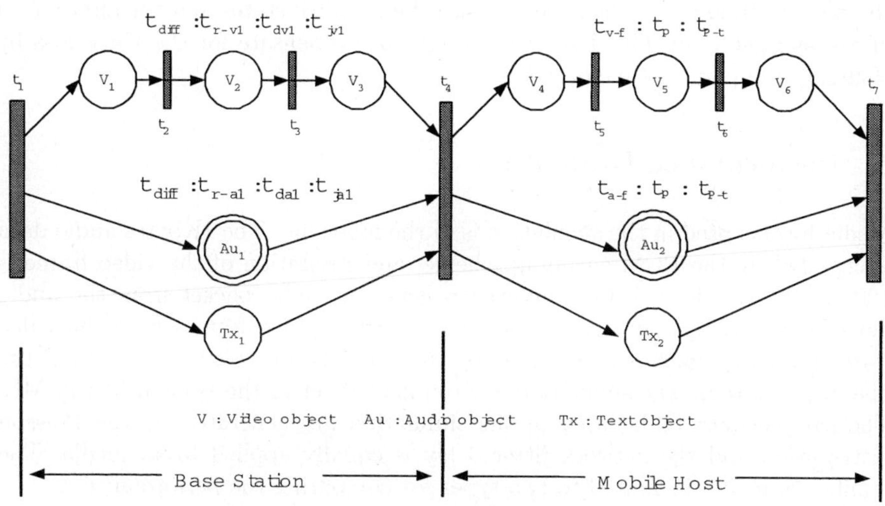

Fig. 5. MMSM with the QoS Parameter.

Audio medium τ_{diff} represents a time difference between duration time and relative duration time. Video medium τ_{diff} is a result of jitter-compensatory time algorithm and it is obtained from comparing τ_{diff} with τ_{ja1} of audio medium. Applying maximum jitter delay not only improves QoS but also has an effect on compensating a time of playing out a place except key medium. Playing time algorithm is the following.

Algorithm Playing Time
Procedure
Begin
While *media* then
$\tau_{m-f} := \tau_d / p_n$; / * P_n *is the number of media frames to be played out during the maximum duration time,* τ_{m-f} is the frame time to be played out from each media.
$M_c := \tau_{r-m} \ / \ \tau_{m-f}$; /*$M_c$ is the number of frame arrived in the current media.
$M_c := INT\ (M_c)$; $\tau_p := \tau_{r-mp} \ / \ M_c$; /*$\tau_p$ is the playing time of a video frame.
$\tau_{p-t} := \tau_p$ X M_c; /*τ_{p-t} is the smoothing playing time of a media.
End.

The display of the frames for duration time is defined as playing control. Note that a frame is not always playing out within the exact time interval whenever a frame buffer is available. The previous playing control skips simply the frames that do not arrive within the maximum delay time of a frame buffer. However, if the frames are skipped frequently, some scene is unnatural, so user will prefer to reduce the number of the omitted frames for a smooth movie rather than to increase the number of the omitted frame for the stick playing. In case that the playing time loss is incurred because the network states and the alternation of average delay for duration time, we try to compensate for the video loss by changing the playing time of video.

5 Performance Evaluation

Media format used in the simulation is in the following. The 1Kbytes audio data is encoded by the PCM encoding scheme, and resolution of the video frame is 120 X 120. At the BS, the application gets one audio packet from the audio device every 125ms, and it gets one, two or third video frames from the video frame grabber, which is determined by the run-time processing overhead of the operating system. The simulation environment is set to the BS and MH in ME. The sample data to be used in the simulation are generated by the Poisson distribution and the network jitter delay is equally applied to all media. The number of media is limited to two types for comparing the performance.
Notice that the delay value generated by the normal distribution is forced to be within the range [0.5*mean, 4*mean] in the program to make the delay values more realistic. The number of transitions is set to 200 and the maximum delay jitter is 10ms. On the purpose to verify the algorithm, OCPN and RTSM are also evaluated in the same simulation environment.
Fig. 6 shows the simulation results of the three models in terms of the video duration time. A measure of evaluation is, when the delay of an audio occurs, to measure how much the playing time of a video has improved. The duration time of OCPN model dramatically decreased. However, the proposed MMSM model shows the better performance than the RTSM model.
The result shows that MMSM model increases more and decreases more the loss

rate than previous OCPN model and RTSM model in terms of audio and video, and demonstrates that the playing rate for audio streams in MMSM model is increased to about 9.5% and 7.4% in case of without and with delay, respectively.

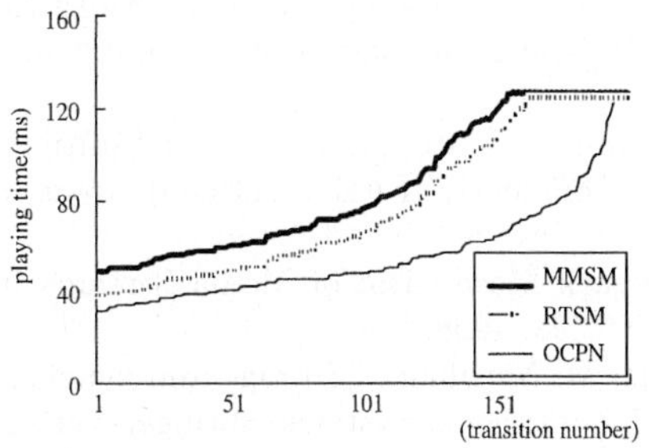

Fig. 6. Playing time with delay in BS.

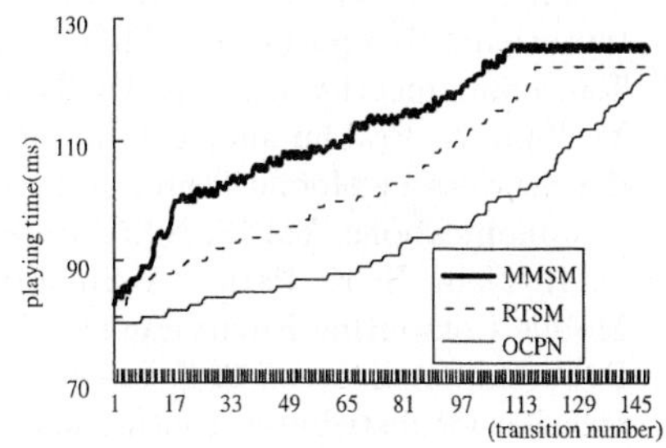

Fig. 7. Two abnormal media in MH.

In Fig. 7, the comparison of playing time of the three models is plotted against the transition number in case of the late arrival of two media. That is, when an audio and a video object are delayed, it represents the duration time of OCPN and RTSM model, and shows the duration time of MMSM model is improved than that of other models by adopting the relative duration time for two media.

6 Conclusions

In this paper we proposed the inter-media and intra-media synchronization based on a two level buffer policy. One decrease the delay time of packet frames from multimedia server to BS using the buffer policy in BS, and the other smoothes the playback of a media. The media unit with variable size can be also handled by use of a two level buffer policy. The proposed synchronization scheme is able to cope with the temporal increase of the mobile network load and unpredictable discontinuation. 1) The proposed method meets the requirements of synchronization between media data by handling dynamically the adaptive waiting time resulted from variations of delay time and the interval adjustment using maximum delay jitter time at BS in ME. 2) The playing time scheme using the frame buffer of MH supports the smooth and natural playback. This model can provide modeling specifications from the live applications to the pre-orchestrated applications in ME. MMSM model adaptively manages the waiting time of frame buffer, which leads to minimize the gap from the variation of delay time and it results in naturally playing to MH in ME.

References

1. D. H. Nam and S. K. Park, "Adaptive Multimedia Stream Presentation in Mobile Computing Environment," Proceedings of IEEE TENCON, 1999.
2. A. Boukerche, S. Hong and T. Jacob, "MoSync: A Synchronization Scheme for Cellular Wireless and Mobile Multimedia Systems," Proceedings of the Ninth International Symposium on Modeling, Analysis and Simulation of Computer and Telecommunication Systems IEEE, 2001.
3. M. Woo, N. Prabhu and A. Grafoor, "Dynamic Resource Allocation for Multimedia Services in Mobile Communication Environments,"IEEE J. selected Areas in Communications, Vol.13, No.5, June. 1995.
4. D. H. Nam, S. K. Park, "A Smooth Playback Mechanism of Media Streams in Mobile Computing Environment," ITC-CSCC'98, 1998.
5. P. W. Jardetzky, and C. J. Sreenan, and R. M. Needham, "Storage and synchronization for distributed continuous media," Multimedia Systems/Springer-Verlag, 1995.
6. C.-C. Yang and J.-H. Huang, "A Multimedia Synchronization Model and Its Implementation in Transport Protocols," IEEE J. selected Areas in Communications, Vol.14, No.1, Jan. 1996.

SSE-CMM BPs to Meet the Requirements of ALC_DVS.1 Component in CC

Sang-ho Kim[1], Eun-ser Kim[1], Choon-seong Leem[3], Ho-jun Shin[4], and Tai-hoon Kim[2]

[1] KISA, 78, Garak-Dong, Songpa-Gu, Seoul, Korea
{shkim,taihoon}@kisa.or.kr
[2] Chung-Ang University, 221, Huksuk-Dong, Dongjak-Gu, Seoul, Korea
eslee@object.cau.ac.kr
[3] Yonsei University, 134, Shinchon-Dong, Seodaemun-Gu, Seoul, Korea
leem@yonsei.ac.kr
[4] Catholic University of Daegu , 330, Hayangup, Kyungsan, Kyungbuk, Korea
jun7438@chollian.net

Abstract. Security assurance requirements about the security of development environment for IT product or system are described in ALC_DVS (Development Security) family in the part 3 of the Common Criteria (CC). But if the fact the site environment IT products or systems are being developed may meet the requirements of ALC_DVS family is assured by performing an authorized process evaluation criteria like as the SSE-CMM and evaluator recognize that fact, developer can reduce the burden for preparing the site-visiting and evaluator can save the time for site-visit evaluation. In this paper we analyze the compliance between ALC_DVS.1 of the CC and Base Practices (BPs) of the Systems Security Engineering Capability Maturity Model (SSE-CMM), and review the capability level of the SSE-CMM to meet the requirements of ALC_DVS.1

1 Introduction

The Common Criteria (CC) philosophy is to provide assurance based upon an evalua-tion of the IT product or system that is to be trusted [1][2][3].

Evaluation has been the traditional means of providing assurance. In fact, there are many evaluation criteria. The Trusted Computer System Evaluation Criteria (TCSEC), the European Information Technology Security Evaluation Criteria (ITSEC), and the Canadian Trusted Computer Product Evaluation Criteria (CTCPEC) existed, and they have evolved into a single evaluation entity, the CC. The CC is a standard for specifying and evaluating the security features of IT products and systems, and is intended to replace previous security criteria such as the TCSEC. The CC is presented as a set of distinct but related 3 parts. Part 3, Security assurance components, establishes a set of assurance components as a standard way of expressing the assurance requirements for Target of Evaluation (TOEs), catalogues the set of assurance components, families, and classes, and presents evaluation assurance levels that define the predefined CC scale for rating assurance for TOEs, which is called the Evaluation Assurance Levels (EALs). But about the evaluation with the CC, for example, the evaluation for EAL 3, whenever each product or system is evaluated, same evaluation process is required for all component included

A. Yazici and C. Şener (Eds.): ISCIS 2003, LNCS 2869, pp. 1069–1075, 2003.

in EAL 3. Especially, ALC_DVS.1 component which means development security and included in EAL 3, may be evaluated each time evaluation proceeded. Therefore, many kinds of methods are researched to solve this problem [4][5][6][7][8][9].

In this paper we propose that ALC_DVS.1 component doesn't have to be evaluated for every evaluation if the developer's company already acquires the capability level 2 of some Process Areas (PAs) in the SSE-CMM by reviewing the compliance between Base Practices (BPs) of PAs and the elements of ALC_DVS.1 component.

2 Overview of Development Security Family ALC_DVS

2.1 Objectives of ALC_DVS

Development security is concerned with physical, procedural, personnel, and other security measures that may be used in the development environment to protect the TOE. ALC_DVS family includes the physical security of the development location and any procedures to select development staff. It is important that this family deals with measures to remove and reduce threats existing at the developer's site. Threats to be countered at the TOE user's site are normally covered in the security environment subclause of a Protection Profile (PP) or Security Target (ST).

2.2 Evidence Elements of ALC_DVS.1 Component

ALC_DVS.1 component consists of one developer action element, two evidence elements, and two evaluator action elements. Evidence elements contains following contents:

- The evidence required,
- What the evidence shall demonstrate,
- What information the evidence shall convey.

Contents and presentation of evidence elements of ALC_DVS.1 component are described as like following (Requirements for content and presentation of evidence are identified by appending the letter 'C' to the element number):

ALC_DVS.1.1C: The development security documentation shall describe all the physical, procedural, personnel, and other security measures that are necessary to protect the confidentiality and integrity of the TOE design and implementation in its development environment.

ALC_DVS.1.2C: The development security documentation shall provide evidence that these security measures are followed during the development and maintenance of the TOE.

3 SSE-CMM

Modern statistical process control suggests that higher quality products can be produced more cost-effectively by emphasizing the quality of the processes that produce them, and the maturity of the organizational practices inherent in those processes. More efficient processes are warranted, given the increasing cost and time required for the development of secure systems and trusted products. The operation and maintenance of secure systems relies on the processes that link the people and technologies. These interdependencies can be managed more cost effectively by emphasizing the quality of the processes being used, and the maturity of the organizational practices inherent in the processes. The SSE-CMM model is a standard metric for security engineering practices cover-ing:

- The entire life cycle, including development, operation, maintenance, and decommissioning activities
- The whole organization, including management, organizational, and engineering activities
- Concurrent interactions with other disciplines, such as system, software, hardware, human factors, and test engineering; system management, operation, and maintenance
- Interactions with other organizations, including acquisition, system management, certification, accreditation, and evaluation

4 Performance Analyses

4.1 Comparison in Process Area

The SSE-CMM has two dimensions, "domain" and "capability." The domain dimension is perhaps the easier of the two dimensions to understand. This dimension simply consists of all the practices that collectively define security engineering. These practices are called Base Practices (BPs). The base practices have been organized into Process Areas (PAs) in a way that meets a broad spectrum of security engineering organizations. There are many ways to divide the security engineering domain into PAs. One might try to model the real world, creating process areas that match security engineering services. Other strategies attempt to identify conceptual areas that form fundamental security engineering building blocks. The SSE-CMM compromises between these competing goals in the cur-rent set of process areas. Each process area has a set of goals that represent the expected state of an organization that is successfully performing the PA. An organization that performs the BPs of the PA should also achieve its goals. There are eleven PAs related to security in the SSE-CMM, and we found next three PAs which have compliance with ALC_DVS.1 component:

- PA01 Administer Security Controls
- PA08 Monitor Security Posture
- PA09 Provide Security Input

4.2 Comparison in Base Practice

All of the BPs in each PA mentioned earlier need not have compliance with the evidence elements of ALC_DVS.1. But if any BP included in the PA is excluded or failed when the evaluation is preceded, the PA itself is concluded as fail. Evidence element ALC_DVS.1.1C requires that the development security documentation shall describe all the physical, procedural, personnel, and other security measures that are necessary to protect the confidentiality and integrity of the TOE design and implementation in its development environment. But ALC_DVS.1.1C dose not describe what are the physical, procedural, personnel, and other security measures. Evidence element ALC_DVS.1.2C requires that the development security documentation shall provide evidence that the security measures described in ALC_DVS.1.1C are followed during the development and maintenance of the TOE. Some BPs contains example work products, and work products are all the documents, reports, files, data, etc., generated in the course of performing any process. Rather than list individual work products for each process area, the SSE-CMM lists Example Work Products (EWPs) of a particular base practice, to elaborate further the intended scope of a BP. These lists are illustrative only and reflect a range of organizational and product contexts. As though they are not to be construed as mandatory work products, we can analysis the compliance between ALC_DVS.1 component and BPs by comparing evidence elements with these work products. We categorized these example work products as eight parts:

1. Physical measures related to the security of development site and system.
2. Procedural measures related to the access to development site and system.
3. Procedural measures related to the configuration management and maintenance of development site and system.
4. Procedural measures (contain personnel measures) related to the selection, control, assignment and replacement of developers.
5. Procedural measures (contain personnel measures) related to the qualification, consciousness, training of developers.
6. Procedural measures related to the configuration management of the development work products.
7. Procedural measures related to the product development and incident response in the development environment.
8. Other security measures considered as need for security of development environment.

Categorized eight parts above we suggested are based on the contents of evidence requirement ALC_DVS.1.1C, and contains all types' measures mentioned in ALC_DVS.1.1C. But the eight parts we suggested may contain the possibility to be divided to more parts. We can classify work products included in BPs according to eight parts category mentioned above. Next table 1 describes the result.

From the table above, we can verify that some BPs of SSE-CMM may meet the requirements of ALC_DVS.1.1C by comparing the contents of evidence element with work products. The requirements described in ALC_DVS.1.2C can be satisfied by records express the development processes, and some BPs can meet the requirements of evidence element ALC_DVS.1.2C. We researched all BPs and selected the BPs which can

Table 1. Categorization of work products

Number of category	Work Products	Related BP
1	control implementation	BP.01.02
1	sensitive media lists	BP.01.04
2	control implementation	BP.01.02
2	control disposal	BP.01.04
2	sensitive media lists	BP.01.04
2	sanitization, downgrading, disposal	BP.01.04
2	architecture recommendation	BP.09.05
2	implementation recommendation	BP.09.05
2	security architecture recommendation	BP.09.05
2	users manual	BP.09.06
3	records of all software updates	BP.01.02
3	system security configuration	BP.01.02
3	system security configuration changes	BP.01.02
3	records of all confirmed software updates	BP.01.02
3	security changes to requirements	BP.01.02
3	security changes to design documentation	BP.01.02
3	control implementation	BP.01.02
3	security reviews	BP.01.02
3	control disposal	BP.01.02
3	maintenance and administrative logs	BP.01.04
3	periodic maintenance and administrative reviews	BP.01.04
3	administration and maintenance failure	BP.01.04
3	administration and maintenance exception	BP.01.04
3	sensitive media lists	BP.01.04
3	sanitization, downgrading, and disposal	BP.01.04
3	architecture recommendations	BP.09.05
3	implementation recommendations	BP.09.05
3	security architecture recommendations	BP.09.05
3	administrators manual	BP.09.06
4	an organizational security structure chart	BP.01.01
4	documented security roles	BP.01.01
4	documented security accountabilities	BP.01.01
4	documented security authorizations	BP.01.01
4	sanitization, downgrading, and disposal	BP.01.04
5	user review of security training material	BP.01.03
5	logs of all awareness, training and education undertaken, and the results of that	BP.01.03
5	training periodic reassessments of the user community level of knowledge, awareness and training with regard to security	BP.01.03
5	records of training, awareness and educational material	BP.01.03
6	documented security responsibilities	BP.01.01
6	records of all distribution problems	BP.01.02
6	periodic summaries of trusted software distribution	BP.01.02
6	sensitive information lists	BP.01.04
6	sanitization, downgrading, and disposal	BP.01.04
7	periodic reassessments of the user community level of knowledge, awareness and training with regard to security	BP.01.03
7	design recommendations	BP.09.05
7	design standards, philosophies, principles	BP.09.05
7	coding standards	BP.09.05
8	philosophy of protection	BP.09.05
8	security profile	BP.09.06
8	system configuration instructions	BP.09.05

satisfy the requirements of evidence element ALC_DVS.1.2C. We list BPs related to ALC_DVS.1.2C as like:

- BP.08.01 Analyze event records to determine the cause of an event, how it proceeded, and likely future events.

- BP.08.02 Monitor changes in threats, vulnerabilities, impacts, risks, and the environment
- BP.08.03 Identify security relevant incidents
- BP.08.04 Monitor the performance and functional effectiveness of security safeguards
- BP.08.05 Review the security posture of the system to identify necessary changes
- BP.08.06 Manage the response to security relevant incidents
- And all BPs included in PA01

Therefore, if the PA01, PA08 and PA09 are performed exactly, it is possible ALC_DVS.1 component is satisfied. But one more consideration is needed to meet the requirements completely.

4.3 Capability Level

Process capability is defined as the quantifiable range of expected results that can be achieved by following a process. The capability side of the SSE-CMM reflects statistical process control concepts which define the use of process capability and provides guidance in improving the process capability of the security engineering practices that are referenced in the domain side of the SSE-CMM. The capability of an organization's process helps to predict the ability of a project to meet goals. SSE-CMM contains the generic practices, that is, the practices that apply to all processes. The generic practices are used in a process appraisal to determine the capability of any process. The generic practices are grouped according to common feature and capability level. In capability level 2, the performance of the base practices in the process area is planned and tracked. Performance according to specified procedures is verified. Work products conform to specified standards and requirements. Measurement is used to track process area performance, thus enabling the organization to manage its activities based on actual performance. The primary distinction from Level 1, Performed Informally, is that the performance of the process is planned and managed. Capability level 2 comprises the 4 common features. In capability level 3, base practices are performed according to a well-defined process using approved, tailored versions of standard, documented processes. This capability level comprises the 3 common features. The primary distinction between Level 2 and Level 3 is that the process of Level 3 is planned and managed using an organization-wide standard process. The critical distinction between generic practices 2.1.3 and 3.1.1, the Level 2 and Level 3 process descriptions, is the scope of application of the policies, standards, and procedures. In 2.1.3, the standards and procedures may be in use in only a specific instance of the process, e.g., on a particular project. In 3.1.1, policies, standards, and procedures are being established at an organizational level for common use, and are termed the "standard process definition". Therefore, for the evaluation of IT products or systems, we think the application of an organization-wide standard process is not proper, and capability level 2 is sufficient.

5 Conclusions

Security assurance requirements about the development environment of IT product or system are described in ALC_DVS (Development Security) family included in the part 3 of the Common Criteria (CC). And form the result of research we proceeded, we learned that if some PAs in the SSE-CMM is observed, the requirements of ALC_DVS family is assured. Therefore, if a authorized process evaluation criteria (in this paper, we used the SSE-CMM, but it is not only one, we thought) is observed and evaluator recognize that fact, developer can reduce the burden for preparing and evaluator can save the time for the evaluation. For example, in this paper, we analyze the compliance between the evidence elements of ALC_DVS.1 and example work products of BPs conformed to capability level 2.

References

1. ISO. ISO/IEC 15408–1:1999 Information technology – Security techniques – Evaluation criteria for IT security – Part 1: Introduction and general model
2. ISO. ISO/IEC 15408–2:1999 Information technology – Security techniques – Evaluation criteria for IT security – Part 2: Security functional requirements
3. ISO. ISO/IEC 15408–3:1999 Information technology – Security techniques – Evaluation criteria for IT security – Part 3: Security assurance requirements
4. Tai-hoon Kim, Tae-seung Lee, Kyu-min Cho, Koung-goo Lee: The Comparison Between The Level of Process Model and The Evaluation Assurance Level. The Journal of The Information Assurance, Vol.2, No.2, KIAS (2002)
5. Tai-hoon Kim, Yune-gie Sung, Kyu-min Cho, Sang-ho Kim, Byung-gyu No: A Study on The Efficiency Elevation Method of IT Security System Evaluation via Process Improve-ment, The Journal of The Information Assurance, Vol.3, No.1, KIAS (2003)
6. Tai-hoon Kim, Tae-seung Lee, Min-chul Kim, Sun-mi Kim: Relationship Between Assurance Class of CC and Product Development Process, The 6th Conference on Software Engi-neering Technology, SETC (2003).
7. Ho-Jun Shin, Haeng-Kon Kim, Tai-Hoon Kim, Sang-Ho Kim: A study on the Requirement Analysis for Lifecycle based on Common Criteria, Proceedings of The 30th KISS Spring Conference, KISS (2003)
8. Tai-Hoon Kim, Byung-Gyu No, Dong-chun Lee: Threat Description for the PP by Using the Concept of the Assets Protected by TOE, ICCS 2003, LNCS 2660, Part 4, pp. 605–613
9. Haeng-Kon Kim, Tai-Hoon Kim, Jae-sung Kim: Reliability Assurance in Development Process for TOE on the Common Criteria, 1st ACIS International Conference on SERA

Improved Structure Management of Gateway Firewall Systems for Effective Networks Security

Si Choon Noh[1], Dong Chun Lee[2], and Kuinam J. Kim[1]

[1] Dept. of of Information Security Kyonggi Univ., Korea
nsc1@kt.co.kr
[2] Dept. of Computer Science Howon Univ., Korea

Abstract. In this paper we propose an improved structure management of gateway firewall systems. This management have effective network security comparing to the general structure management which consist of network configurations, topology management, topology and role management of bastion hosts, control management of network equipment and multiple firewalls.

1 Introduction

The firewall is one of the most well-known solutions in the network security. Moreover, they certainly are outstanding security tools that offer multiple security service functions [2,3]. However, firewall is merely an auxiliary support tool needed to enhance the level of security. Accordingly, more firewall installation cannot be equated to the completion of security measures. It is necessary to conduct sufficient technological review and analysis of structure, performance, and usage of networks where firewalls are placed from the point of view of users who utilize respective networks.
Additionally, comprehensive management measures that ensure continuous maintenance and improvement are needed to address questions such as whether network configuration is at fault, and to solve other problems related to network lay-out or topology [5,6]. Regretfully, not much research is conducted on the management of firewall structure improvement at the utilization stage. Firewall technology development and research sources related to utilization can be summarized into three themes: source technology development, system design & build-up, and system configuration management of utilization processes [8,9]. Firewall structure management is the method used to yield optimal efficiency by combining technology, resources and components already completed. Continual reengineering needs to be performed going forth according to the changes on Internet environment and in hacking infiltration patterns. In this paper we propose a system management model to increase the efficiency of firewall utilization by leveraging structure management.

A. Yazici and C. Şener (Eds.): ISCIS 2003, LNCS 2869, pp. 1076–1083, 2003.

2 General Structure of Gateway Firewall

The basic components of the gateway firewall system are external router, application switch, bastion host, and internal router [2,3]. Other components used selectively are DMZ server, Proxy server, Network Address Translation (NAT), and Caching server. General structure entails configuring one topology by combining each configuration element. However, there are some similarities both in the structural and functional levels. Such common similarities are host role, location of host lay-out,and load balancing among hosts, firewall utilization rule management and comprehensive firewall control function aspects among network structures. General structure of the network is as shown on Figure 1.

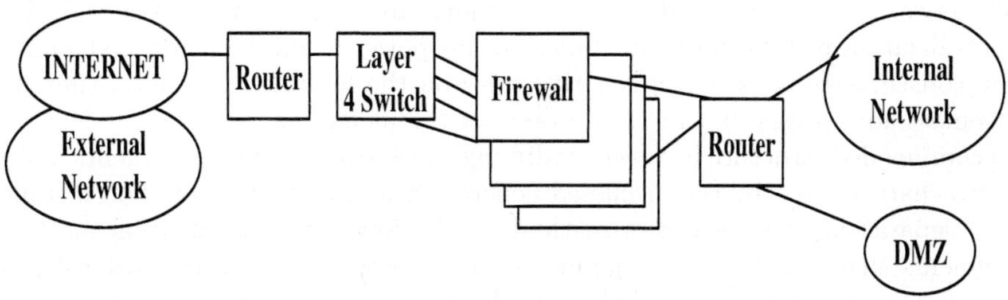

Fig. 1. General Structure.

The exit point that connects all forms of topology to the external network through the firewall is unified into one. In other words, the boundary point on the Internet or other network group is one. Location of the firewall layout is the concept of a parallel layout. In the case of multiple firewall layout, firewall is the method that is laid out on the same level instead of leveraging a hierarchy structure on the network structure, which entails top and bottom. Firewall utilization rule management has only the rule-dedicated bastion host that performs a utilization rule during the packet filtering process. Accordingly, loads on all rule management is concentrated into one host. Multiple firewall of operations and function control management are separated per firewall. As a result, monitor and operation consoles are laid out on each firewall. If the number of instaling firewalls increase, monitors and consoles for management increase, which in turn increases management load. By realizing system monitoring and control based on the use of multiple equipment, it is possible to delay the time needed for understanding comprehensive situations for required levels and additional operators needed. The following elements of inefficiency and latent risks exist at the time of operating the general structure of gateway firewalls.

1. Firewall changes into a bottleneck problem of the entire network at the time of gateway interval traffic overloading.

2. Spreads as the fault of the entire network at the time of a gateway firewall system fault.
3. Potential risk due to the concentration of all types of firewall utilization rules into one host.
4. Accompanied modification of the sole path gateway's structure at the time of modifying the lower hierarchical system of a gateway.

3 Improved Structure of Gateway Firewall

3.1 System Structure

Potential risks and trouble elements of the discussed general structure of gateway firewalls lay in the fact that the trafficking path and firewall functions within all network exit points and gateway sections are unified and centralized. The centralization of this path and function are powerful mechanisms that enable the consistent application of security rules on the firewall. Therefore, they are foremost advantages, but are also potential threat factors.
Recommended structure involves modifying the above mentioned elements of five areas characterized by the discussed general structure into the method of function separation and dispersion method on the function concentration method. Elements that are subject to modification are network structure, host role, location of host lay-out, load balancing between hosts, firewall utilization rule management, and overall firewall control.
In the system structure, paths are decided depending on the type of packet such as DMZ, TCP/IP, VPN, Extranet, and on destination IP instead of volume balancing. Each host performs a filtering function by the areas designated in advance. Extranet sections process non-Internet work data. Efficiency of multiple firewall management is increased by the integrated management of entire hosts by leveraging Enterprise Management Security (ESM).

3.2 Traffic Path

This is the change in the trafficking path on the gateway, and this is the pluralization of paths. All traffic that flows into the gateway separates into Internet traffic and non-Internet traffic and connects to the in-house network. Among these, Internet traffic distributes to the DMZ,TCP/IP,VPN section according to the destination address. Packet for DMZ reaches up to DMZ after going through the external router (♯1) → L4(♯1) → DMZ host. General TCP/IP packet connects up to the internal network after going through the external router (♯1) → L4(♯1) → main host internal network. Packet for VPN connects to the internal network after going through the external router (♯1) → L4(♯1) → VPN host → internal router.
Connection of non-Internet traffic is realized into external router (♯2) → L4(♯2) → Extranet host → internal router → internal network. In the improved structure, the path of the traffic distribution is pluralized as shown Fig. 2. The risk is dispersed more compared to the case in which single path is applied.

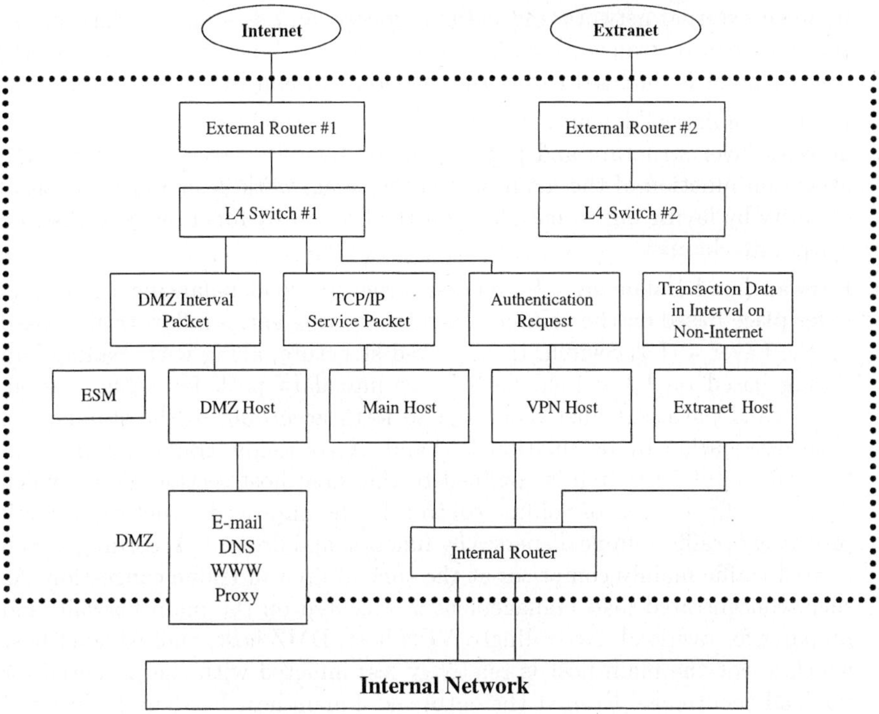

Fig. 2. Improved System Structure.

Table 1. Traffic Path

Type	Destination	Path Routing
Internet Interval Traffic	**DMZ**	External Router(#1) - L4(#1) - DMZ host
	Internal Network (TCP/IP packet)	External Router(#1) - L4(#1) - Main host - Internal Router - Internal Network
	Internal Network (VPN packet)	External Router(#1) - L4(#1) - VPN host - Internal Router - Internal Network
Non-Internet Interval Traffic	**Internal Network**	External Router(#2) - L4(#2) - Extranet host - Internal Router - Internal Network

3.3 Functional Mechanism

From the aspect of external contact point function, location of firewall lay-out, firewall load balancing, host function, firewall utilization rule management and overall control of the multiple firewalls, the firewall is changed into a mechanism that is different from the general structure.

1. Exit point function : Connection path with Internet or external network separates Internet section and non-Internet section. In other words, external connection path that is not the Internet section configures the dedicated line

between external network and exterior router, and sets up the Extranet so that data can be transmitted. Accordingly to the above mentioned, external contact point is dualized to Internet section and non-Internet section.

2. Location of firewall layout : Pluralization into parallel layout on the gateway network layer structure and path layout by function takes place. Since the execution function of the main host is the same, work is shared in terms of quantity by laying out in parallel, and the firewall by function is laid out on a separate channel.
3. Firewall Load Balancing : In general structure, load balancing by firewall takes place based on the volume control, targeting entire inflow traffic based on the Layer 4 (L4) Switch. In improved structure, along with loading balancing based on L4 switch, path is set into data path for authorization, DMZ band path, extranet band and so forth according to the standard of path designation by destination IP band. Accordingly, traffic volume control volume of L4 switch is confined to the main host section alone, which decreases the amount of volume control. In the improved structure, firewall processing traffic volume disperses by function and firewall. Accordingly, web related traffic mainly comprises at the time of firewall traffic congestion. As such, concentrated load management is executed on the main firewall, and prepares for overload. Accordingly, VPN host, DMZ host, and extranet host which is not the main host is relatively less inflicted with the potential for the load occurrence. Even at the outbreak of main host bottleneck, overload is limited to the main host. As a result, the possibility of entire network function stoppage decreases.
4. Host Function : Role is different according to host. In other words, host by function that is assigned dedicated role by function performs each role. Role sharing by function shares by the type of TCP/IP service or by the characteristics of packet. The method is one that entails specializing the role of host by main, VPN, DMZ, and Extranet host function.
   Extranet host and DMZ dedicated host process authorization request IP on the VPN host or if the destination IP is Extranet and DMZ.
   Other services are accommodated by the main host. Each firewall assumes clear purpose due to the above mentioned configuration of host by function. Problem that breaks out in one host does not spill over to other hosts. Thus, they are managed independently. Moreover, it is possible to resolve the issue of load concentration pertaining to specific firewall since balance is maintained among the centralization and distribution of services.
5. Firewall Utilization Rule Management : Packet filtering rule has functions for source IP control, destination address control, control by TCP/IP service, packet size control, virus check and so forth. All types of firewall rules on the general structure have centralization risk and performance delay elements because they are concentrated into one main firewall. All types of rules in the improved structure are dispersed to four types of firewalls. Therefore, they can reduce risk of centralization and delay in performance. Each rule is separated by four types of firewalls. All firewalls do not perform all rules.

Instead, each firewall needs to merely process the rules that apply to the functions that are dedicated to each firewall.

6. Overall Control of the Multiple Firewalls : Dedicated equipment ESM is used to ensure overall control and management of firewalls characterized by diverse multiple roles. ESM is the integrated management technology that is used between different types of equipment such as IDS and VPN including the firewall, but firewall dedicated or multi-purpose ESM is used for lay-out. If and when the ESM is used, system monitoring, logging, alarm and system control are executed with consistent view.

4 Performance Analysis

4.1 Analysis Environment

System utilization test was conducted to analyze the performance of the improved system structure that is recommended on this research paper. As for the categories of analysis, they pertained to the four areas that were pointed out into the elements of inefficiency and potential risks of general structure of gateway firewall.

Pre-improvement structure that was used in this test comprises single path up to the Application switch through the external router, which is one of the exit points. Application multiple paths were configured between switch and firewall up to the number of firewall. Section of the firewall after the internal router configures single path up to the internal network, and is the phase of the single path in overall. Improved structure has dualized exit point. At this time, external network configures into dedicated line method, targeting data for work that does not require the use of Internet, and is dedicated to the communication of data.

Application Switch → Firewall section configures into multiple channels up to the number of firewalls. The path from the firewall to the internal network divides into DMZ section and internal network.

The firewall type used in this test is the hybrid method, and the firewall topology is the screen subnet gateway method.

4.2 Numerical Results

1. **Possibility of Application Switch Overloading:** Application switch is the section where the first round of overloading results due to the packet that passed through the traffic routing processing of the exterior router. Application switch performs path setting of the packet that is routing processed, session maintenance, and firewall load balancing. The following table 2 is the traffic volume that results from the application switch before and after the structure improvement. In the structure improvement, the possibility of application switch bottleneck caused by the congestion of balancing volume decreases 28%. Even if congestion results, it does not affect other firewalls since it is limited to the main firewall interval.

Table 2. Packet Distributed Job Rate

Unit : mill. Packets/day

General Structure					Improved Structure				
Processing Equipment	Path	Partition Index	Throughput	Part Rate	Processing Equipment	Path	Partition Index	Throughput	Part Rate
L4	Main	Auto Balancing	18	100%	L4	Main	Auto Balancing	23	72%
					Auto Point	VPN	Client Request	3.8	12%
					Auto Point	DMZ	IP band	3.8	12%
					Auto Point	Extranet	Other Path	1.6	5%

2. **Possibility of Main Firewall Bottleneck:** This is the measurement result that demonstrates how the traffic, processed with load balancing by the application switch, is shared by each firewall. The firewall that is the element of gateway section bottleneck before the structure improvement is the main firewall, and the point of the measurement is whether the load of the main firewall decreases. The traffic load decreased from the main firewall shows the results of dispersing into firewalls by each function. Total traffic volume of 100% that is processed by the main firewall in the general structure decreased from 72% to 28% in the case of modified structure. The possibility of bottleneck on the firewall can be said to yield decrease.

Table 3. Each Firewall Traffic Processing Rate

Unit : mill. Packets/day

Type	General Structure	Improved Structure				
Firewall	Main	Main	VPN	DMZ	Extranet	Total
Number of Firewall	7	4	1	1	1	7
Part Rate	100%	72%	12%	12%	5%	100%
Processing number	18	23	3.8	3.8	1.6	32

3. **Data Loss Rate:** When the traffic volume exceeds the limit of the firewall CPU processing during the process in which the volume of transmission packet increases increasingly, the state of network delay increases suddenly, and packet loss begins to break out. Increase in the capacity of firewall processing after the conversion of the firewall structure into improved structure, reduces data loss rate by decreasing system overload. This research conducted ping test on the specific site of the transmission section that passes through the firewall in the lower part of the internal network pertaining to firewall, and the results were gathered.

Table 4. Data Loss Rate

Unit : mill. Packets/day

Type	General Structure			Improved Structure		
	Transporting Rate	Receiving Rate	Loss Rate	Transporting Rate	Receiving Rate	Loss Rate
Daum	1.768	1.296	26.7%	1296	1214	6.4%
Yahoo	1.721	1519	11.8%	12532	1195	4.7%
Average	1.745	1408	19.2%	1274	1204	5.5%

5 Conclusion

Gateway firewall system is the method that can reduce potential threat elements that result in the general structure where improved structure is needed.
As for the substance of improvement, this entails improving parts of network structure, the role and function of bastion host, bastion load balancing between hosts, firewall utilization rule management, multiple firewall equipment management and control function, and it entails reducing risk of centralization by separating and dispersing centralization function to the possible level. These measures maintain the strengths of the previous general structure while reducing the inherent threat elements. Gateway firewall bottleneck, fault spreading risks at the time of gateway firewall fault, risk according to firewall utilization rule centralization, and burden according to multiple firewall management, which are the problems that resulted before the improved structure can be reduced.

References

1. Dr.ThomasW.Shinder,Debra Littlejohn Shinder,ISA Server 2000,Syngress Media,Inc., 2001
2. SimonCupper, Brantchapman, Building Internet Firewalls, O'Reilly & Associates,Inc., 2000
3. David Baer, Towards Compatibility with Firewall and Keyword search, Distributed Computing Group, 2002
4. Gregory Yerxg, Firewall and Load Balancer, Infrastructure Work Shop, 2000
5. Edward J. Rhode, An Introduction to Load Balancing with planet Application Server, Soun Developer Network, 2000
6. A Link Load Balancing Solution for multi-home Networks, F5 Network, 2002
7. Emily Gladstone, Sans GCFW practical Assignment(V1.6), Glac Enterprise, 2002
8. Red Hat Linux 7.3, Firewall Configuration, 2002
9. Windows Net meeting, Firewall Configuration, 2002
10. Linux Network Administrators Guide (Chapter 9), Testing a Firewall configuration
11. SANS GIAC SEC Practical, How do we define Responsible Disclosure, 2003
12. http ://www.data.com/Lab-Tests/index.html
13. http ://www.oullim.co.kr

Supplement of Security-Related Parts of ISO/IEC TR 15504

Sang-ho Kim[1], Choon-seong Leem[2], Tai-hoon Kim[1], and Jae-sung Kim[1]

[1] KISA, 78, Garak-Dong, Songpa-Gu, Seoul, Korea
{shkim,taihoon,jskim}@kisa.or.kr
[2] Yonsei University, 134, Shinchon-Dong, Seodaemun-Gu, Seoul, Korea
leem@yonsei.ac.kr

Abstract. ISO/IEC TR 15504, the Software Process Improvement Capability Determination (SPICE), provides a framework for the assessment of software processes. This framework can be used by organizations involved in planning, monitoring, controlling, and improving the acquisition, supply, development, operation, evolution and support of software. But, in the ISO/IEC TR 15504, considerations for security are relatively poor to others. For example, the considerations for security related to software development and developer are lacked. In this paper we propose a process related to security by comparing ISO/IEC TR 15504 to ISO/IEC 21827 and ISO/IEC 15408. The proposed scheme may be contributed to the improvement of security for IT product or system.

1 Introduction

The IT products like as firewall, IDS (Intrusion Detection System) and VPN (Virtual Private Network) are made to perform special functions related to security, so the developers of these products or systems should consider many kinds of things related to security not only design itself but also development environment to protect integrity of products. When we are making these kinds of software products, ISO/IEC TR 15504 may provide a framework for the assessment of software processes, and this frame-work can be used by organizations involved in planning, monitoring, controlling, and improving the acquisition, supply, development, operation, evolution and support of software. [1][2][3][4][5][6][7][8][9]. But, in the ISO/IEC TR 15504, considerations for security are relatively poor to other security-related criteria such as ISO/IEC 21827 or ISO/IEC 15408 [10][11][12]. In fact, security related to software development is concerned with many kinds of measures that may be applied to the development environment or developer to protect the confidentiality and integrity of the IT product or system developed. In this paper we propose some measures related to development process security by analyzing the ISO/IEC 21827, the Systems Security Engineering Capability Maturity Model (SSE-CMM) and ISO/IEC 15408, Common Criteria (CC). And we present a Process for Security for ISO/IEC TR 15504.

A. Yazici and C. Şener (Eds.): ISCIS 2003, LNCS 2869, pp. 1084–1089, 2003.

2 ISO/IEC TR 15504

2.1 Framework of ISO/IEC TR 15504

ISO/IEC 15504 provides a framework for the assessment of software processes. This framework can be used by organizations involved in planning, managing, monitoring, controlling, and improving the acquisition, supply, development, operation, evolution and support of software. ISO/IEC 15504 provides a structured approach for the assessment of software processes for the following purposes:

- by or on behalf of an organization with the objective of understanding the state of its own processes for process improvement,
- by or on behalf of an organization with the objective of determining the suitability of its own processes for a particular requirement or class of requirements,
- by or on behalf of one organization with the objective of determining the suitability of another organization's processes for a particular contract or class of contracts.

The framework for process assessment:

- encourages self-assessment,
- takes into account the context in which the assessed processes operate,
- produces a set of process ratings (a process profile) rather than a pass/fail result
- through the generic practices, addresses the adequacy of the management of the assessed processes,
- is appropriate across all application domains and sizes of organization.

The process assessment framework is based on assessing a specific process instance. A process instance is a singular instantiation of a process that is uniquely identifiable and about which information can be gathered in a manner that provides repeatable ratings. Each process instance is characterized by a set of five process capability level ratings, each of which is an aggregation of the practice adequacy ratings that belong to that level. Hence the practice adequacy ratings are the foundation for the rating system.

2.2 Process Dimension of ISO/IEC TR 15504

ISO/IEC TR 15504-5 defines the process dimension of the assess model. The process dimension is directly mapped to that of the reference model in ISO/IEC TR 15504-2, and adopts the same process definitions and structure given by the reference model. The three life cycle process groupings are:

- The primary life cycle processes consisting of the process categories Engineering and Customer-Supplier,

- The Supporting life cycle processes consisting of the process category Support,
- The Organizational life cycle processes consisting of the process categories Management and Organization.

The process dimension contains five process categories which are:

- CUS, Customer-Supplier,
- MAN, Management,
- ENG, Engineering,
- ORG, Organization,
- SUP, Support.

The description of each process category includes a characterization of the processes it contains, followed by a list of the process names.

2.3 Assessment Model and Indicators of Process Performance

ISO/IEC TR 15504-5 describes the assessment model, and the assessment model expands the reference model depicted in the ISO/IEC TR 15504-2 by adding the definition and the use of assessment indicators which are defined to support an assessor's judgment of the performance and capability of an implemented process. Base practice, input and output work products and their associated characteristics relate to the processes defined in the process dimension of the reference model, and are chosen to explicitly address the achievement of the defined process purpose. The base practices and work products are indicators of a level 1 process performance. The presence of the work products with the existence of the characteristics of the work products, and evidence of performance of the base practices, provide objective evidence of the achievement of the purpose of the process.

3 New Security Related Process

3.1 Work Products of ISO/IEC TR 15504 Related to Development Security

As mentioned earlier, ISO/IEC TR 15504 provides a framework for the assessment of software processes, and this framework can be used by organizations involved in planning, managing, monitoring, controlling, and improving the acquisition, supply, development, operation, evolution and support of software. ISO/IEC TR 15504 does not define any Process related to security, but the security-related parts are expressed in some Work Products (WP) as like;

ISO/IEC TR 15504 may use these work products as input materials, and these may be the evidence that security-related considerations are being considered. But this implicit method is not good for the 'security' and more complete or concrete counter-measures are needed. Therefore, we propose some new processes which deal with the security.

Table 1. Security-related parts expressed in some WPs

ID	WP Class	WP Type	WP Characteristics
10	1.3	Coding standard	- Security considerations
51	3.2	Contract	- References to any special customer needs (i.e., confidentiality requirements, security, hardware, etc.)
52	2.2	Requirement specification	- Identify any security considerations/constraints
53	2.3	System design/architecture	- Security/data protection characteristics
54	2.3	High level software design	- Any required security characteristics required
74	1.4/2.1	Installation strategy plan	- Identification of any safety and security requirements
80	2.5	Handling and storage guide	- Addressing appropriate critical safety and security issues
101	2.3	Database design	- Security considerations
104	2.5	Development environment	- Security considerations

3.2 Development Security Process

For example, we want to deal the security for the site where the software is developed. In the ISO/IEC TR 15504-5, there is the Engineering process category (ENG) which consists of processes that directly specify, implement or maintain the software product, its relation to the system and its customer documentation. In circumstances where the system is composed totally of software, the Engineering processes deal only with the construction and maintenance of such software. The processes belonging to the Engineering process category are ENG.1 (Development process), ENG.1.1 (System requirements analysis and design process), ENG.1.2 (Software requirements analysis process), ENG.1.3 (Software design proc-ess), ENG.1.4 (Software construction process), ENG.1.5 (Software integration proc-ess), ENG.1.6 (Software testing process), ENG.1.7 (System integration and testing process), and ENG.2 (Development process). These processes commonly contain the 52nd work product (Requirement specification), and some of them have 51st, 53rd, 54th work products separately. Therefore, each process included in the ENG category may contain the condition, 'Identify any security considerations/constraints'. But the phrase 'Identify any security considerations/constraints' may apply to the 'software or hardware (may contain firmware) development process' and not to the 'development site' itself. In this paper we will present a new process applicable to the software development site. In fact, the process we propose can be included in the MAN or ORG categories, but this is not the major fact in this paper, and that will be a future work. We can find the requirements for Development security in the ISO/IEC 15408 as like;

Development security covers the physical, procedural, personnel, and other security measures used in the development environment. It includes physical security of the development location(s) and controls on the selection and hiring of development staff.

Development security is concerned with physical, procedural, personnel, and other security measures that may be used in the development environment to protect the integrity of products. It is important that this requirement deals with measures to re-move and reduce threats existing in the developing site (not in the operation site). These contents in the phrase above are not the perfect, but will suggest a guide for development site security at least. Next is the Development Security process we propose.

Process Identifier : ENG.3
Process Name : Development Security process
Process Type : New Process
Process Purpose : The purpose of the Development Security process is to protect the confidentiality and integrity of the system components (such as hardware, software, firmware, manual, operations and network, etc) design and implementation in its development environment.
Process Outcomes :

- access control strategy will be developed and released to manage records for en-trance and exit to site, logon and logout of system component according to the re-leased strategy,
- roles, responsibilities, and accountabilities related to security are defined and re-leased,
- training and education programs related to security are defined and followed,
- security review strategy will be developed and documented to manage each change steps.

Base Practices:

- ENG.3.BP.1: Develop physical measures. Develop and release the physical measures for protecting the access to the development site and product.
- ENG.3.BP.2: Develop personnel measures. Develop and release the personnel measures for selecting and training of staffs.
- ENG.3.BP.3: Develop procedural measures. Develop the strategy for processing the change of requirements considering security.

ENG.3 Development Security process may have more base practices (BP), but we think these BPs will be the base for future work.

4 Conclusions

In this paper we presented a new Process applicable to the software development site. In fact, the Process we proposed is not perfect not yet. But this is the base of the consideration for security in ISO/IEC TR 15504. As mentioned earlier, ISO/IEC TR 15504 provides a framework for the assessment of software processes, and this framework can be used by organizations involved in planning, monitoring, controlling, and improving the acquisition, supply, development, operation, evolution and support of software. Therefore, it is important to include considerations for security in the Process dimension. In this paper we did not contain or explain any component for Capability dimension, so the ENG.3 Process we suggest may conform to capability level 2. Therefore, more research efforts will be needed. Because the assessment cases using the ISO/IEC TR 15504 are increased, some processes concerns to security are needed and should be included in the ISO/IEC TR 15504.

References

1. ISO. ISO/IEC TR 15504–1:1998 Information technology – Software process assessment – Part 1: Concepts and introductory guide
2. ISO. ISO/IEC TR 15504–2:1998 Information technology – Software process assessment – Part 2: A reference model for processes and process capability
3. ISO. ISO/IEC TR 15504–3:1998 Information technology – Software process assessment – Part 3: Performing an assessment
4. ISO. ISO/IEC TR 15504–4:1998 Information technology – Software process assessment – Part 4: Guide to performing assessments
5. ISO. ISO/IEC TR 15504–5:1998 Information technology – Software process assessment – Part 5: An assessment model and indicator guidance
6. ISO. ISO/IEC TR 15504–6:1998 Information technology – Software process assessment – Part 6: Guide to competency of assessors
7. ISO. ISO/IEC TR 15504–7:1998 Information technology – Software process assessment – Part 7: Guide for use in process improvement
8. ISO. ISO/IEC TR 15504–8:1998 Information technology – Software process assessment – Part 8: Guide for use in determining supplier process capability
9. ISO. ISO/IEC TR 15504–9:1998 Information technology – Software process assessment – Part 9: Vocabulary
10. ISO. ISO/IEC 15408–1:1999 Information technology – Security techniques – Evaluation criteria for IT security – Part 1: Introduction and general model
11. ISO. ISO/IEC 15408–2:1999 Information technology – Security techniques – Evaluation criteria for IT security – Part 2: Security functional requirements
12. ISO. ISO/IEC 15408–3:1999 Information technology – Security techniques – Evaluation criteria for IT security – Part 3: Security assurance requirements
13. Tai-hoon Kim, Yune-gie Sung, Kyu-min Cho, Sang-ho Kim, Byung-gyu No: A Study on The Efficiency Elevation Method of IT Security System Evaluation via Process Improve-ment, The Journal of The Information Assurance, Vol.3, No.1, KIAS (2003)
14. Tai-hoon Kim, Tae-seung Lee, Min-chul Kim, Sun-mi Kim: Relationship Between Assur-ance Class of CC and Product Development Process, The 6th Conference on Software En-gineering Technology, SETC (2003)
15. Tai-Hoon Kim, Byung-Gyu No, Dong-chun Lee: Threat Description for the PP by Using the Concept of the Assets Protected by TOE, ICCS 2003, LNCS 2660, Part 4, pp. 605–613

New CX Searching Algorithm for Handoff Control in Wireless ATM Networks

Dong Chun Lee[1], Gi-sung Lee[1], Chiwon Kang[2], and Joong Kyu Park[3]

[1] Dept. of Computer Science Howon Univ., Korea
{ldch,gslee}@sunny.howon.ac.kr
[2] Senior Researcher, KDM, Korea
[3] President, Saerom Computer & Communication CO., Ltd., Korea

Abstract. The Crossover Switch (CX) plays an important role in ensuring fast and seamless handoff in Wireless ATM Networks(WANs). Networks are managed via one of the following two methods; the centralized connection management where a connection server performs network connection management, and the distributed connection management where each node performs network connection management. The two methods have their own drawbacks. Where connection management is performed in a centralized manner, propagation delay occurs. Distributed connection management leads to increased overall system overhead. For reducing those problems, we propose a Distributed Anchor CX Searching algorithm. Within networks that are grouped together, connection management is done for each group by anchor switches, and Permanent Virtual Circuit (PVC) with a narrow bandwidth is assigned between anchors for exchange of information. The proposed algorithm enables quick searching of a targeted CX, makes management of the overall network easier, and reduces system overhead.

1 Introduction

The development of both MAC protocols and effective and seamless handoff approaches is currently of critical concern to the WANs. In efforts to provide an effective handoff for wired and wireless networks, various schemes have been presented and a lot of research is underway. The handoff algorithm [5]in wireless networks must meet the general requirements for the previous cellular networks as well as ATM's unique requirements. Since WANs focus on providing data application services, they should not only prevent the cells from being lost and duplicated but also ensure sequences during handoff. The method for virtual connection during handoff is divided into path extension and path re-routing. Additionally, it is broken down into backward/forward handoff, depending on whether either the existing base station or a new one calls for handoff [6]. In order to ensure an optimal path during path re-routing, a CX needs to be dynamically selected for each connection to a mobile terminal. This dynamic process of selecting crossover switches has to be initiated by an interrupt of the originating side that has called for connection. Until an optimal CX is searched, an algorithm for selecting CX should be implemented for every switch on the path for

A. Yazici and C. Şener (Eds.): ISCIS 2003, LNCS 2869, pp. 1090–1097, 2003.

virtual connection. Therefore, all switches within the network should support this CX selection algorithm. The remote the crossover switches selected by the algorithm become from the existing base station, the more the cells must be transferred between the existing base station and the crossover switches. This means longer delay time in switching a virtual path connection or much cell loss during handoff.

CX searching is mainly intended to analogize the minimum hop number path to the CX for VC, which is configured by BSnew and currently in use. The selected CX will affect the shorter resultant path as well as circuit reuse. Among currently available CX searching algorithms, the Prior Path Knowledge CX Searching algorithm [3]adopts a centralized approach to network connection management where complete topology information is required during routing. The Distributed Hunt CX Searching algorithm[4] adopts a distributed approach to network connection management where Link-State or Distance-Vector routing is used [1]. The Prior Path Knowledge CX Searching algorithm has the advantage of reducing overall system overhead where a connection server performs overall network connection management. However, it causes longer propagation delays in the process of updating the connection information for each node. The Distributed Hunt CX Searching algorithm that uses a distributed approach in network connection management has the advantage of causing no propagation delay where each node has connection management databases. However, it increases costs to maintain connection management databases for each node as well as overall system overhead resulting from the fact that connection configuration is made by each node. In this paper we propose a Distributed Anchor CX Searching Algorithm to reduce these problems.

2 Related Work

For the Prior Path CX Searching algorithm that uses a centralized approach to network connection management, the role of a connection server is important. Bsnew calls on the connection server to search for every possible convergence node, finding the minimum hop path among every possible crossover switch from BSnew to the convergence node. If multiple CXs are searched, a node closest to CLSold should be selected as CX. Once a targeted CX is selected, BSnew requests the connection server to create a partial path for the CX. The Distributed Hunt CX Searching Algorithm is used to find the minimum hop by allowing each node to voluntarily search for every possible convergence without any connection server. By maintaining the Local Connectivity Table (LCT), each node continues to update the information about connection setup and release for itself and its neighboring nodes. BSnew identifies the LCT to make sure whether CLSnew is a CX or not. If CLSnew isn't a CX, it broadcasts CX search packets via CLSnew to all switches within the network before waiting for responses. After a limited period of time awaiting responses, BSnew performs a mapping of every possible CX, selecting among them a node with a minimum hop as CX. If multiple nodes are selected that have the same min. hop count, a random node is selected as CX. Finally, if a CX is configured and BSnew receives a control packet to get ACK, a partial path is created. For the Backward Tracking CX Searching algorithm, BSold sends backtrack search packet to the predecessor (i.e., CLSold). The predecessor makes inquires of BSnew about the routing table to find the next hop node. As a result of making inquires of the connection server, if both the predecessor and the next hop node are included in the CLSold and CLSdest, the backtrack packet is forwarded to the next predecessor. Otherwise, the node is selected as CX.

3 Distributed Anchor CX Searching Algorithm

All nodes in an ATM network are grouped together by a specific number of nodes. The anchor switch refers to the node with the largest degree among nodes in each group. That's because the node with the largest degree in each group has higher probability of being selected as CX. The network model is designed in such a way that an anchor switch in each group is interconnected with anchors in other groups. To ensure information exchange between anchors, resources with a narrow bandwidth are assigned using the PVC, which allows you to search for CXs quickly. Anchor switches continue to update new information while maintaining the Group Connectivity Table (GCT) that includes their present connection IDs, connection IDs for all nodes in the group, and the information about the adjacent groups connected with this group via PVCs. Each node does not maintain the LCT. The anchor in each group continues to monitor and update the connection status of every node in each group and of every anchor node that is connected by PVC. The process of searching algorithm for CXs is as follows:

1. The anchor in each group makes inquiries about the GCT. If the position to which the anchor has moved is searched for the switch just adjacent to the present BSold within the group, the anchor directs path extension. Otherwise, BSnew performs the next step to reset paths.
2. If BSnew 's cluster is the anchor of a group, BSnew sends a search packet to an adjacent anchor reset by a PVC to request it to reset the VC. If BSnew 's cluster isn't the anchor of a group, BSnew sends a search packet to the anchor of the group and the anchor sends a search packet to an adjacent anchor reset by a PVC.
3. The anchor of each group knows the connection information about all nodes of the group. Upon receipt of a search packet, the anchor of a group makes inquiries about the GCT of the sending anchor. If a corresponding node exists, the anchor stops sending a packet while sending an ACK signal to BSnew. It repeats this process to allow all nodes of the already set VC to perform this algorithm.
4. In comparison with the hop number sent by multiple anchors for a limited period of time, the node with a minimum hop number is selected as CX.

5. If multiple CXs are searched, a random CX is selected.
6. If a CX is selected, a VC from the CX to BSnew is set, and a VC from BSold to the CX is released.

The Distributed Anchor CX Discovery algorithm also describes the following thing.

Algorithm Distributed Anchor CX Discovery

1. G=(V,E)represents the ATM backbone network, and H=(V, E)represents the anchor switch in ATM network (i.e., subset G).
2. 'O' is the currently path: CLS$_{old}$ $\rightarrow$ CLS$_{dest}$, and 'A' is the path connected by an anchor.
3. 'O' is 'G's subgraph, where 'A' is 'O's subgraph.
   V(A) $= O_1 or A_1 = CLS_{old}, A_2, \cdots, O_y, or A_z = CLS_{dest}$,where z<y. Begin
4. Obtain the node information for the discovered path: $CLS_{old} \rightarrow CLS_{dest}$.
   If(($CLS_{new} \rightarrow \in A_i) \bigcap (CLS_{old} \in A_i$)),
   then CX $= CLS_{old}$ / $*$ Anchor A_i leading to path extension. $*$ /
   goto Done:
   else Begin
5. Respective A_i in V(A), where i= 1, 2, $\cdots$, z,
6. Compute the minimum hop number for $CLS_{new} \rightarrow A_i$.
7. This path is referred to as 'M_i'.
   If ($M_i \neq 0$),
   Begin / $*$ Anchor A_i leading to path rerouting $*$
   Compute A_x. where $M_x =$ shortest $\{M_i\}$.
   CX $= A_x$. / $*$ anchor becomes a CX.$*$ /

   Or
   if path of $CLS_{new} \rightarrow$ CX have many paths, Begin where ($i.e., |M_x| = |M_y| = \cdots = |M_z|$)
   If shortest $\{M_i\} = \{M_x, M_y, \cdots, M_z\}$,
   Select any CX.(i. e., CX $= O_y$)
   end
   end
   else
   Begin
   G is partitioned(i.e., CLS_{new} cannot have access to CX.)
   end
   end
   Done:
   End

Using the notion of anchor, a PVC with a narrow bandwidth is set for exchange of information between anchors, which allows for faster and more efficient CX searching, lowers system overhead and additional costs caused by the

Distributed Hunt CX Searching Algorithm, and significantly reduces propagation delay time between connection servers and nodes caused by the Prior Path Knowledge CX Searching Algorithm. Since the anchor determines path extension or path rerouting, it can reduce problems arising during path rerouting by leading to path extension between the just adjacent clusters. In addition, the anchor can resolve one of the drawbacks occurring during path extension, so-called the routing Loop problem, through control of each node and faster alternative routing. In term of PVC assignment, the proposed scheme based on the PVC assigned only between anchor nodes can reduce a waste of bandwidth characterized by the VCT scheme as well as eliminate an additional procedure scheme for setting a PVC, when moving to another region.

4 Performance Analysis

A simulation is conducted to analyze the performance of the proposed algorithm. Firstly, a network model is designed to evaluate the proposed algorithm. The proposed algorithm is evaluated in comparison with the previous algorithms in terms of convergence characteristics and resultant path characteristics. The cluster concept has been used in the network-level handoff, while the model has been designed using a higher-level network concept. In order to ensure quick CX searching, a network model that adopts the concept 'Anchor' was used in grouped networks. An anchor was defined as the node with the largest degree among nodes in each group. Using PVCs, some bandwidth was assigned between anchors and their adjacent anchors. The anchor in a group was linked to every node of its group with whatever paths it may choose. One hundred numbers of the node (i.e., ATM switch) were created for use in the performance test. One hundred numbers of the node were used to compare convergence characteristics. In comparing resultant path characteristics and reuse rate, a network model was designed for performance analysis with the number of the node assigned 30, 50, and 100, respectively. The network model used for simulation has set one group by 5 to 6 nodes, with the average degree set by 6 to 7 anchor nodes and 3 to 4 normal nodes. Assuming that an inter-cluster handoff occurred, mobile terminal's handoff regions were taken into account to ensure path rerouting, not path extension. In order to find the minimum hop, the well-known Dijkstra's Algorithm was used, which can be simply expressed as follows: Where the path from the vertex'V0' to the intermediate vertex 'u' is decided as distance [u], and a path from 'u' to 'w' is to be selected, if distance [u], it can be expressed as follows: distance is [w] where distance [u] is the minimum distance value selected from the yet-to-be searched vertex 'V0'. The same weights were assigned to links to ensure fairness. Differentiated simulations were made to the node groups that were not connected. The connectivity between nodes is determined by the following probability:

$$P_e(x,y) = \frac{ke}{n}\beta exp\frac{-d(x,y)}{\alpha L}$$

where e is link degree, d (x, y) is Euclidean distance between the nodes 'x' and 'y', α (α >0) is parameter that controls the number of connection for remote nodes, $\beta(\beta \leq 1)$ is parameter that controls the edge number of each node, n is number of two nodes, L is largest distance between the two nodes, and ke/n is scaling factor.

5 Numerical Result

In order to the performance of the proposed algorithm, a comparative analysis was performed according to the following items;
Convergence Characteristics: Focus was put on how to quickly search for a target CX. A factor that needs consideration is the number of implementation required when searching for a target CX. Ultimately, this characteristics can be broken down to reduced handoff latency time by way of performing new path routing in search of a CX with the minimum hop number and the smaller number of implementation. Where the number of the node is 100, the following are the convergence characteristics obtained from a comparative analysis of respective algorithms.

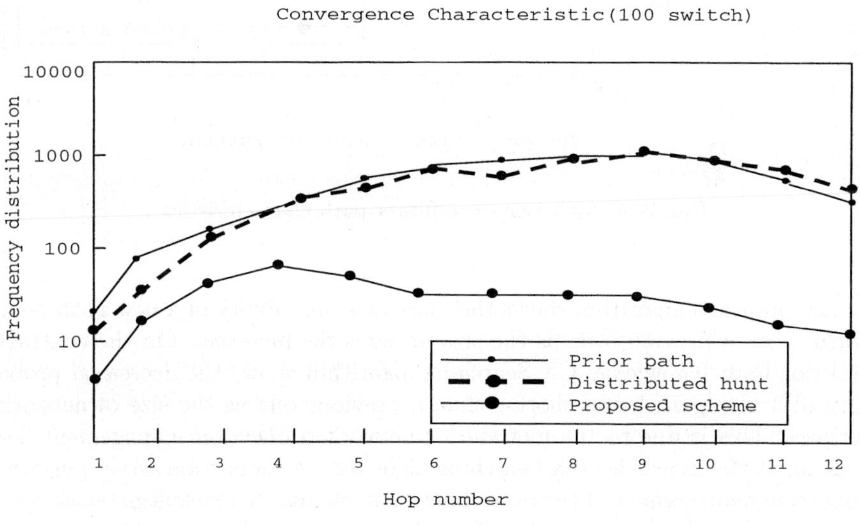

Fig. 1. Convergence characteristics

Fig. 1 shows a comparison of hop number and the execution number when searching for CXs in a network. The proposed algorithm enables a more simplified network because connections between anchors are made via PVCs and the nodes between anchors substantially serve only as repeaters. The proposed algorithm achieves improved performance 2.2 and 2.4 times higher than the Prior

Path Knowledge CX Searching and the Distributed Anchor CX Searching. This algorithm allows faster CX searching and more significantly reduced execution number than the previous algorithms. Fig. 2 shows a comparison of the algorithm proposing resultant path characteristics.It also shows a comparison of varying network sizes, indicating the probability of paths newly connected from all nodes having smaller numbers of nodes than the previous paths (i.e., probability of the previous paths being longer).

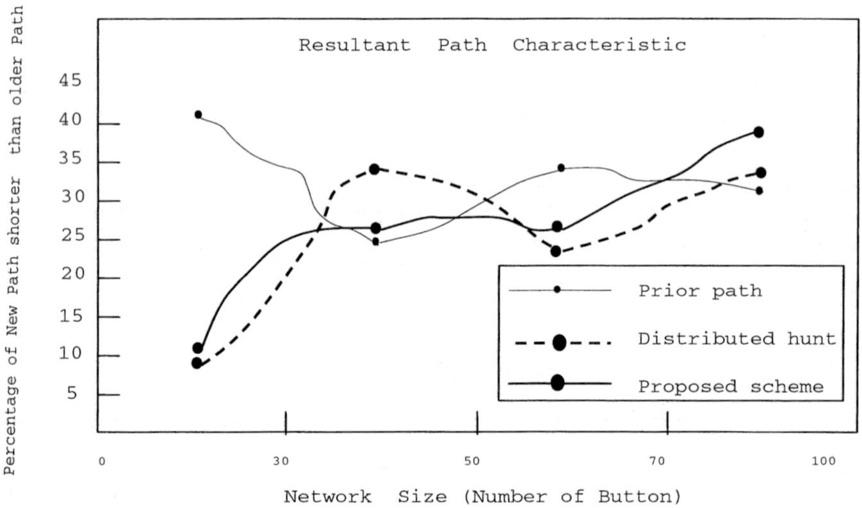

Fig. 2. Comparison of resultant path characteristics

The proposed algorithm shows the increased probability of a new path being shorter than a previous one as the size of networks increases. On the contrary, the Prior Path Knowledge CX Searching algorithm shows the decreased probability of a new path being shorter than a previous one as the size of networks increases. This is due to the method for network connection management. For the Prior Path Knowledge CX Searching algorithm, a connection server performs connection management of the overall network, leading to efficient network management in small-scale networks. However, it achieves lower performance due to propagation delays as the size of networks becomes larger. The algorithm proposed here continues to achieve improved resultant path characteristics as the size of networks increases, showing better performance than other existing algorithms starting from 80 numbers of nodes. This shows that the proposed algorithm achieves better point-to-point delay characteristics or overall link utilization with the increased size of a network.

6 Conclusion

In this paper we propose the Distributed Anchor CX Search algorithm in WANs. The proposed algorithm uses the concept 'Grouping' to define an anchor of a group where the anchor performs connection management of the group. In addition, PVCs are connected between anchors, allowing more reduced waste of bandwidth and easier prediction of mobility than the existing PVC assignment schemes. The proposed algorithm is expected to enable faster CX searching, easier management of the entire network, and reduced system overhead or propagation delay time, thus providing faster and seamless handoff in WANs.

References

1. Chai-Keong Toh, "Performance Evaluation of Cross Switch Discovery Algorithms for Wireless ATM LANs," Prof. of IEEE INFOCOM'96, 1996
2. OIiver T.W.YU, Victor C.M.Leung," Connection Architecture and Protocols to Support Efficient Handoffs over an ATM/B-ISDN Personal Communication Network," Mobil Network and Application 1, Vol. 1, no. 2, 1996.
3. Anthony S. Acampora, Mahmoud Naghshineh, "An Architecture and Methodology for Mobile-Executed Handoff in Cellular ATM Networks," IEEE Trans. on SAC. Vol. 12, no. 8. Oct., 1994.
4. Chai-Keong Toh, "The Design & Implementation of a Hybrid Handover Protocol for Multi Media Wireless LANs," ACM First International Conference on Mobile Computing & Networking, 1995.
5. Bora A. Akyol, Donald C.COX "Rerouting for Handoff in a Wireless ATM network," IEEE Personal Comm. Magazine, 1996
6. Duk Kyung Kim, Dan Keun Sung, "Handoff/Resource Managements Based on PVCs and SVCs in Broadband Personal Communication Networks," Prof. of IEEE VT'96. 1996.

Performance Improvement Scheme of NIDS through Optimizing Intrusion Pattern Database

Jae-Myung Kim[1], Kyu-Ho Lee[1], Jong-Seob Kim[2], and Kuinam J. Kim[3]

[1] CTO & Senior Researcher Secuve Co., Ltd., Korea
{cosmos,perry}@secuve.com
[2] Superintendent, National Institute of Scientific Investigation, Korea
[3] Prof., Dept. of Information Security Kyonggi Univ., Korea

Abstract. This paper aims to present a separated, optimized pattern database classification model, which may be subsequently applied to improve Network-based Intrusion Detection System (NIDS) efficiency. Using the model that classification basis is determined by examining the validity of a specific intrusion on a given specific target, NIDS is able to search only valid patterns in each captured packet of pattern database. In terms of performance and results, the NIDS resource requirement for pattern database searches is reduced and the NIDS is able to analyze more valid packets.

1 Introduction

As the use of the Internet and its applications increases; as do the prevalence of and the negative potential of invasive network and computer security breaching activities. The need for Intrusion Detection System (IDS) has amplified and thus accordingly, various solutions based on detecting misuse and anomalies have been developed [1]. The first method, the 'anomaly detection' method, scores favorably in terms of detecting network intrusions and attacks; however the method fails to adequately deliver its application in reality, where the false-alarm rate is too high to detect intrusions only with the extracted normal action models [2]. The second method, 'misuse detection', is highly able to extract intrusion detection patterns, but in the reality of network usage, intrusions patterns are greatly diversified and as the network bandwidth is increased, the amount of data requiring instant analyze will also increase. The drawbacks of both methods just mentioned are considered to negatively affect the performance ability of the intrusion detection system process [3-4]. This paper focuses on presenting the concept that the performance of NIDS can be improved by determining whether a specific attack is valid in accordance with the specific OS. Given that NIDS is able to identify the specific host information such as OS in a particular network, the system will only match the intrusion patterns that are valid in the host, thus reducing the amount of space that the intrusion detection system is required to search. Therefore, by reducing the search space, the actual performance of the system is improved. With the idea of improving system performance, we will present an efficient mechanism to classify intrusion pattern database by the

A. Yazici and C. Şener (Eds.): ISCIS 2003, LNCS 2869, pp. 1098–1105, 2003.

host information. Through the collection of actual intrusion detection patterns and by establishing databases, we aim to inspect the functions of the presented models through trial examinations.

2 IDS

2.1 Classification of IDS

There are various types of IDS's and they are generally classified by Kumar classification or COAST classification. Note: this paper will mainly focus upon the 'misuse detection method' in relation to network-based intrusion detection classification.

Kumar Classification: By categorizing the results of intrusive actions, S Kumar classifies intrusions into two groups: 'anomalous intrusions' and 'misuse intrusions' [5]. The anomalous intrusion is based on an anomalous action of a computer environment, and misuse intrusion means a well-developed attack pattern.

COAST Classification:COAST classifies intrusion detection systems by two methods [6]. The first method uses data source based classification, which categorizes the detection as being single-hosted based, multi-host based and network-host based. The second method uses an intrusion detection model that classifies detections as being anomaly or misuse.

2.2 Technical Elements of IDS

The IDS that is shown in Fig.1 has mainly four stages: raw data collection, data reduction and filtering, intrusion analysis and detection, and reporting and response.

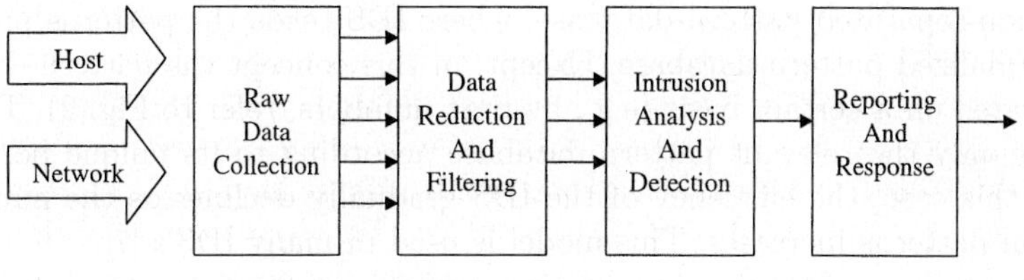

Fig. 1. Technical Elements of IDS

The 'raw data collection' stage is where IDS collects the audit datum- formed by the object being detected such as a network packets or system log files. The collected audit datum is then converted into meaningful information- that may be used for intrusion determination in the 'data reduction and filtering' stage. During the 'analysis and detection' stage, IDS analyzes the outcome information from the previous stage and determines whether or not the system has been intruded. The 'intrusion analysis and detection' stage is the core stage of IDS, and it is divided into anomaly detection method and misuse detection method, based upon whether the objective of the system is to detect anomalous use of the system, or to detect vulnerability of the system, or to detect an application program bug. As for the 'reporting and response' stage, if the intrusion detection system has determined that the system has been intruded, it automatically responds to the intrusion or it notifies the security administrator to the nature of intrusion.

3 Models of Separated Intrusion Pattern Database

3.1 Intrusion Pattern Database of General IDS

Intrusion pattern database of IDS is classified by the following concepts. The first concept is that there is no actual intrusion pattern database. In this instance, rather then having formalized intrusion database, the IDS itself has its own hard coded intrusion pattern. As a strong point, it can detect intrusions with greater speed due to optimized detecting routines. However, IDS using this concept will have to deal with possibilities of encountering new patterns and for each time new patterns are supplemented, the program should also be modified. The second concept related to the classification of intrusion pattern databases, is that there is an actual non-separated pattern database. It consists of formalized intrusion patterns that can be read by the IDS. Once the IDS is implemented, new intrusion patterns can be added or updated, allowing greater speed in detecting new attacks. But as the number of patterns grows, the amount of search space also increases and this lowers the efficiency of the IDS. In regard to this point of lower efficiency, the non-separated pattern database model is not widely used. The third concept considered, is that the pattern database is separated according to certain information. Basically, it works in a similar manner to that of the non-separated pattern database, where IDS reads the patterns produced by a formalized pattern database. Except, in this concept the pattern database is separated on a certain basis (e.g., by port numbers; refer to Fig. 2). The IDS searches only the relevant pattern database according to its unique port number. In this case, the efficiency of the IDS gradually declines as the number of intrusion patterns increases. This model is used in many IDS's [7].

3.2 Separated Pattern Database Using Host Information

Amongst highly recognized Web sites that deal with issues related to information security vulnerability, two categories standout as being most discussed and identified in regard to intrusion patterns [7-8]. The first intrusion pattern category can be presented directly in a formalized format called an 'Attack Signature'. However, the second intrusion pattern category cannot be presented in such a format as if it has various forms of intrusion patterns and it must be directly

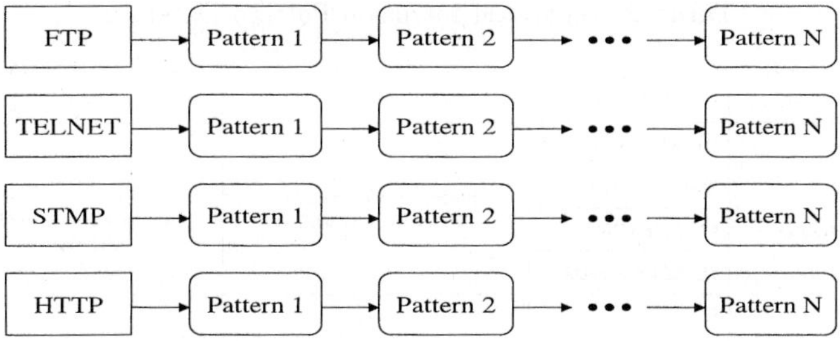

Fig. 2. Common Intrusion Pattern Database

Table 1. Pattern Classification

Classification	Content
Service Ports	- HTTP / SMTP - FTP / TELNET - Etc
Operating Systems	- SunOS / HP-UX / AIX - DG-UX / LINUX / Windows - Etc

implemented as a program. For this reason, the only first intrusion pattern category will be dealt with in this paper. Intrusion patterns can be classified as below:

The legacy NIDS uses intrusion pattern database per service in general. However, we suggest that the performance of NIDS would be more efficient through using separated intrusion pattern database depending on the particular OS. Separated intrusion pattern database becomes most efficient when the patterns are evenly divided and allocated to the database. Therefore, this paper separates intrusion pattern database by the introducing a new form of classification that is able to allocate the patterns evenly in the database.

Our implanted NIDS has two components. The first component, 'front-end' is a module that collects packet and host information, and reduces raw data. And the other, 'engine module' is a module that analyzes and determines intrusion, and does intrusion detection alerting. The pattern composition of intrusion pattern database is shown in Table 2 and LEX & YACC is used in order to interpret syntax and token of intrusion pattern which is shown Fig. 3.

Fig. 4 shows the effects of intrusion pattern database that are classified by OS. The intrusion pattern database classified by OS is compared with that classified by services.

The least favorable search scenario is to search 1+2+3+4+5+6+7 using the existing pattern database of IDS. However, if the Database mode 1(based on OS type), previously suggested in this section, uses the destination host packet, we only need to search 1+2+[SunOS pattern of other services]. [SunOS pattern of other services] is marked with a hyphenated arrow in Fig. 3.

Table 2. Separated Intrusion Pattern Database

Class	Pattern DB	Explanation	Remarks
Service Prots	HTTP Pattern DB	Patterns of attack related to each service port contained	Containing patterns valid to all OS
	SMTP Pattern DB		
	FTP Pattern DB		
	TELNET Pattern DB		
	Etc	Others	
Operating Systems	SunOS Pattern DB	Patterns of attack related to each OS	Containing patterns valid to specific OS
	HP-UX Pattern DB		
	AIX Pattern DB		
	DG/UX Pattern DB		
	Linux Pattern DB		
	Windows Pattern DB		
	Etc	Others	

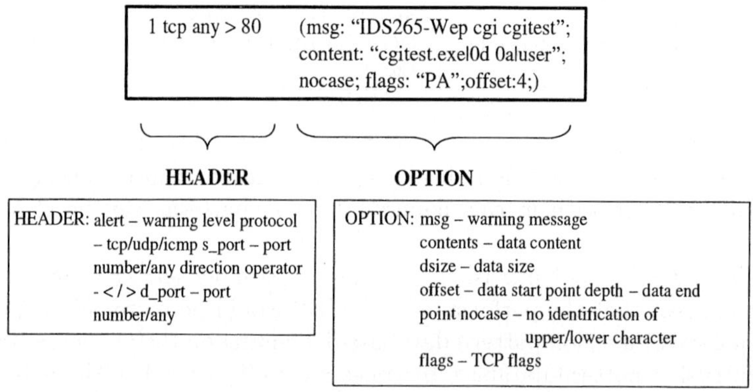

Fig. 3. Syntax of Intrusion Pattern

In general, the process sequence of intrusion analysis and detection is as the following: receiving packet, comparison of protocol, comparison of port, comparison of flag and other minor options, and the comparison of packet contents [7]. In this process, the most time-exacting phase (spending over 90% of the total) is the 'packet contents comparison' process. In our implemented system, NIDS compares service port information from the onset. This means that the sequence of intrusion analysis is reduced by omitting the flag and packet data(data/payload) comparison sequences, thus requiring less computer resources when compared to a search of all 3+4+5+6+7 services classes. Therefore, when intrusion pattern database is used with patterns that are efficient to a specific OS, efficiency in detecting intrusions will increase. This is due to a decrease in computer operations required for matching the patterns. NIDS through this reduction is able to efficiently monitor and analyze more packets

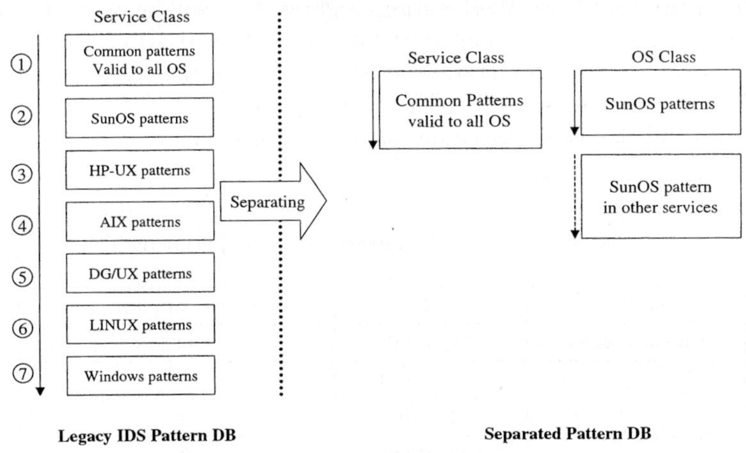

Fig. 4. Benefits of Separated Pattern Database

4 Experimental Results

A series of test scenarios were set in place to accurately test the efficiency of the intrusion sequence process for searching the exact pattern within the intrusion pattern database. All patterns used in this experiment were collected from actual system and network vulnerability located in various public Web sites [5-8].

4.1 Objects of Test

Three pattern databases were loaded in memory to proceed in the test. All the conditions concerning objects are identical except for the pattern databases loaded in the memory. The following thing are the pattern databases that were loaded in the computer memory.

- Linear Model: linear shaped pattern database without separating pattern database
- Service Model: Pattern database divided by service
- OS Model: Pattern database classified by service and OS

4.2 Attack Sequence Processing Efficiency Test

Purpose: Measure each object's efficiency concerning attack sequence amongst pattern database

Methods: Produce the packet containing attack signature with implemented attack program. Let the packet flow in the network for one minute. Measure the number of transferred packets and the number of packets that each object detected as an intrusion. 112 patterns used in the test are equally divided as pattern DB 1 Repeat the test 10 times, calculate average number.

Test Environment: Two Workstations and two PCs will be connected via the Intranet, which is a component of Internet. IDS and attack programs will be located in each Workstation at the time that the packet generator is loaded into located in the PC. The packet generator will be used for the first scenario and the attack program for the second scenario.

Table 3. Pattern Database used in experiment

Model	DB	Number of patterns
Linear Model	Single DB	112
Service Model	HTTP DB	30
	FTP DB	27
	SMTP DB	26
	Etc	29
OS Model	HTTP	15
	FTP	15
	SMTP	16
	Service Etc	19
	UNIX	12
	Linux	12
	Windows	11
	OS Etc	12

4.3 Results and Analysis

Test results are shown in Fig. 5.

In the 'attack sequence' process efficiency test, the OS model detected the highest number of packets. The OS model is 3.7 times more efficient than the linear model and 30.8% more efficient than the service model. This proves the efficiency of the model. However, the number didn't reach the estimate of 35%, that was calculated using the separated pattern database model effect. This is due to the insufficient number of intrusion patterns, expanding overhead of using message queue. Accurate analysis in attack patterns and separating pattern database effectively will bring out more satisfactory results.

5 Conclusion

In this paper we has presented an improved method to detect intrusion among specific hardware platforms. While this paper used patterns classified using only the OS information of the target host; other important factors such as variety /

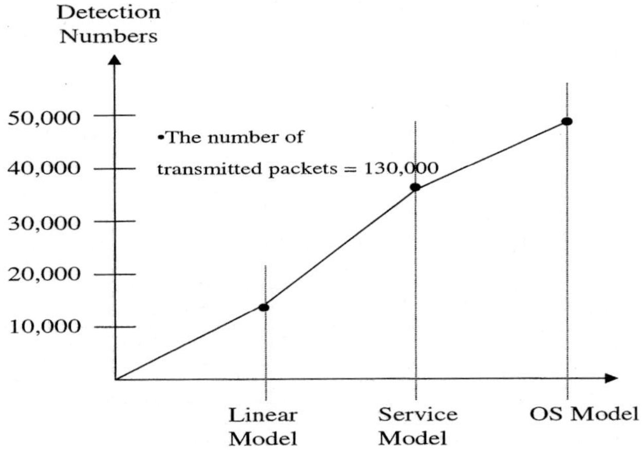

Fig. 5. Experimental Results

different versions of OS, application versions, and patches, should be considered relevant. Obtaining further information about monitoring hosts and classifying intrusion pattern database's accurately would be highly constructive. It may be stated that by arranging intrusion patterns differently in consideration of network traffic and by hacking trends, there will be an increase in the efficiency of IDS. With the goal of efficiency and security, this area will continue to be tackled in research initiatives, throughout the world.

References

1. H. Debar, M. Dacier, and Andreas Wespi, Towards a Taxonomy of Intrusion Detection Systems, IBM Research Division, Zurich Research Lab., Research Report RZ 3030, June 1998.
2. T.F. Lunt, "Automated Audit Trail Analysis and Intrusion Detection: A Survey", Proc. of 11th National Computer Security Conf., 1998.
3. B.Mukherjee, T.L. Heberlein, and K.N.Kevitt, "Network Intrusion Detection", IEEE Network, 8(3):26-41, May/June 1994 2001
4. R. Heady, G.Luger, A.Maccabe, and M.Servilla, "The Architecture of a Network Level Intrusion Detection System", Technical Report, Computer Science Department, University of New Mexico, August 1990.
5. S. Kumar, Classification and Detection of Computer Intrusions, Purdue University, Aug, 1995
6. COAST, "Intrusion Detection", http://www.cs.purdue.edu/coast/intrusion-detection/welcome.html
7. SNORT, "The Open Source Network Intrusion Detection System" http://www.snort.org/
8. WHITEHATS, "Whitehats Network Security Resource", http://www.whitehats.com/

Author Index

Lecture Notes in Computer Science

For information about Vols. 1–2791
please contact your bookseller or Springer-Verlag

Vol. 2717: J.C. Gee, J.B.A. Maintz, M.W. Vannier (Eds.), Biomedical Image Registration. Proceedings, 2003. XIV, 410 pages. 2003.

Vol. 2792: T. Rist, R. Aylett, D. Ballin, J. Rickel (Eds.), Intelligent Virtual Agents. Proceedings, 2003. XV, 364 pages. 2003. (Subseries LNAI).

Vol. 2793: R. Backhouse, J. Gibbons (Eds.), Generic Programming. IX, 223 pages. 2003.

Vol. 2794: P. Kemper, W. H. Sanders (Eds.), Computer Performance Evaluation. Proceedings, 2003. X, 309 pages. 2003.

Vol. 2795: L. Chittaro (Ed.), Human-Computer Interaction with Mobile Devices and Services. Proceedings, 2003. XV, 494 pages. 2003.

Vol. 2796: M. Cialdea Mayer, F. Pirri (Eds.), Automated Reasoning with Analytic Tableaux and Related Methods. Proceedings, 2003. X, 271 pages. 2003. (Subseries LNAI).

Vol. 2797: O.R. Zaïane, S.J. Simoff, C. Djeraba (Eds.), Mining Multimedia and Complex Data. Proceedings, 2002. XII, 281 pages. 2003. (Subseries LNAI).

Vol. 2798: L. Kalinichenko, R. Manthey, B. Thalheim, U. Wloka (Eds.), Advances in Databases and Information Systems. Proceedings, 2003. XIII, 431 pages. 2003.

Vol. 2799: J.J. Chico, E. Macii (Eds.), Integrated Circuit and System Design. Proceedings, 2003. XVII, 631 pages. 2003.

Vol. 2800: S. Spaccapietra, S. March, K. Aberer (Eds.), Journal on Data Semantics I. XV, 233 pages. 2003.

Vol. 2801: W. Banzhaf, T. Christaller, P. Dittrich, J.T. Kim, J. Ziegler (Eds.), Advances in Artificial Life. Proceedings, 2003. XVI, 905 pages. 2003. (Subseries LNAI).

Vol. 2803: M. Baaz, J.A. Makowsky (Eds.), Computer Science Logic. Proceedings, 2003. XII, 589 pages. 2003.

Vol. 2804: M. Bernardo, P. Inverardi (Eds.), Formal Methods for Software Architectures. Proceedings, 2003. VII, 287 pages. 2003.

Vol. 2805: K. Araki, S. Gnesi, D. Mandrioli (Eds.), FME 2003: Formal Methods. Proceedings, 2003. XVII, 942 pages. 2003.

Vol. 2806: J. Favela, D. Decouchant (Eds.), Groupware: Design, Implementation, and Use. Proceedings, 2003. XII, 382 pages. 2003.

Vol. 2807: V. Matoušek, P. Mautner (Eds.), Text, Speech and Dialogue. Proceedings, 2003. XIII, 426 pages. 2003. (Subseries LNAI).

Vol. 2808: E. Snekkenes, D. Gollmann (Eds.), Computer Security – ESORICS 2003. Proceedings, 2003. X, 345 pages. 2003.

Vol. 2810: M.R. Berthold, H.-J. Lenz, E. Bradley, R. Kruse, C. Borgelt (Eds.), Advances in Intelligent Data Analysis V. Proceedings, 2003. XV, 624 pages. 2003.

Vol. 2811: G. Karlsson, M.I. Smirnov (Eds.), Quality for All. Proceedings, 2003. XII, 295 pages. 2003.

Vol. 2812: G. Benson, R. Page (Eds.), Algorithms in Bioinformatics. Proceedings, 2003. X, 528 pages. 2003. (Subseries LNBI).

Vol. 2813: I.-Y. Song, S.W. Liddle, T.W. Ling, P. Scheuermann (Eds.), Conceptual Modeling – ER 2003. Proceedings, 2003. XIX, 584 pages. 2003.

Vol. 2814: M.A. Jeusfeld, Ó. Pastor (Eds.), Conceptual Modeling for Novel Application Domains. Proceedings, 2003. XVI, 410 pages. 2003.

Vol. 2815: Y. Lindell, Composition of Secure Multi-Party Protocols. XVI, 192 pages. 2003.

Vol. 2816: B. Stiller, G. Carle, M. Karsten, P. Reichl (Eds.), Group Communications and Charges. Proceedings, 2003. XIII, 354 pages. 2003.

Vol. 2817: D. Konstantas, M. Leonard, Y. Pigneur, S. Patel (Eds.), Object-Oriented Information Systems. Proceedings, 2003. XII, 426 pages. 2003.

Vol. 2818: H. Blanken, T. Grabs, H.-J. Schek, R. Schenkel, G. Weikum (Eds.), Intelligent Search on XML Data. XVII, 319 pages. 2003.

Vol. 2819: B. Benatallah, M.-C. Shan (Eds.), Technologies for E-Services. Proceedings, 2003. X, 203 pages. 2003.

Vol. 2820: G. Vigna, E. Jonsson, C. Kruegel (Eds.), Recent Advances in Intrusion Detection. Proceedings, 2003. X, 239 pages. 2003.

Vol. 2821: A. Günter, R. Kruse, B. Neumann (Eds.), KI 2003: Advances in Artificial Intelligence. Proceedings, 2003. XII, 662 pages. 2003. (Subseries LNAI).

Vol. 2822: N. Bianchi-Berthouze (Ed.), Databases in Networked Information Systems. Proceedings, 2003. X, 271 pages. 2003.

Vol. 2823: A. Omondi, S. Sedukhin (Eds.), Advances in Computer Systems Architecture. Proceedings, 2003. XIII, 409 pages. 2003.

Vol. 2824: Z. Bellahsène, A.B. Chaudhri, E. Rahm, M. Rys, R. Unland (Eds.), Database and XML Technologies. Proceedings, 2003. X, 283 pages. 2003.

Vol. 2825: W. Kuhn, M. Worboys, S. Timpf (Eds.), Spatial Information Theory. Proceedings, 2003. XI, 399 pages. 2003.

Vol. 2826: A. Krall (Ed.), Software and Compilers for Embedded Systems. Proceedings, 2003. XI, 403 pages. 2003.

Vol. 2827: A. Albrecht, K. Steinhöfel (Eds.), Stochastic Algorithms: Foundations and Applications. Proceedings, 2003. VIII, 167 pages. 2003.

Vol. 2828: A. Lioy, D. Mazzocchi (Eds.), Communications and Multimedia Security. Proceedings, 2003. VIII, 265 pages. 2003.

Vol. 2829: A. Cappelli, F. Turini (Eds.), AI*IA 2003: Advances in Artificial Intelligence. Proceedings, 2003. XIV, 552 pages. 2003. (Subseries LNAI).

Vol. 2830: F. Pfenning, Y. Smaragdakis (Eds.), Generative Programming and Component Engineering. Proceedings, 2003. IX, 397 pages. 2003.

Vol. 2831: M. Schillo, M. Klusch, J. Müller, H. Tianfield (Eds.), Multiagent System Technologies. Proceedings, 2003. X, 229 pages. 2003. (Subseries LNAI).

Vol. 2832: G. Di Battista, U. Zwick (Eds.), Algorithms – ESA 2003. Proceedings, 2003. XIV, 790 pages. 2003.

Vol. 2833: F. Rossi (Ed.), Principles and Practice of Constraint Programming – CP 2003. Proceedings, 2003. XIX, 1005 pages. 2003.

Vol. 2834: X. Zhou, S. Jähnichen, M. Xu, J. Cao (Eds.), Advanced Parallel Processing Technologies. Proceedings, 2003. XIV, 679 pages. 2003.

Vol. 2835: T. Horváth, A. Yamamoto (Eds.), Inductive Logic Programming. Proceedings, 2003. X, 401 pages. 2003. (Subseries LNAI).

Vol. 2836: S. Qing, D. Gollmann, J. Zhou (Eds.), Information and Communications Security. Proceedings, 2003. XI, 416 pages. 2003.

Vol. 2837: N. Lavrač, D. Gamberger, H. Blockeel, L. Todorovski (Eds.), Machine Learning: ECML 2003. Proceedings, 2003. XVI, 504 pages. 2003. (Subseries LNAI).

Vol. 2838: N. Lavrač, D. Gamberger, L. Todorovski, H. Blockeel (Eds.), Knowledge Discovery in Databases: PKDD 2003. Proceedings, 2003. XVI, 508 pages. 2003. (Subseries LNAI).

Vol. 2839: A. Marshall, N. Agoulmine (Eds.), Management of Multimedia Networks and Services. Proceedings, 2003. XIV, 532 pages. 2003.

Vol. 2840: J. Dongarra, D. Laforenza, S. Orlando (Eds.), Recent Advances in Parallel Virtual Machine and Message Passing Interface. Proceedings, 2003. XVIII, 693 pages. 2003.

Vol. 2841: C. Blundo, C. Laneve (Eds.), Theoretical Computer Science. Proceedings, 2003. XI, 397 pages. 2003.

Vol. 2842: R. Gavaldà, K.P. Jantke, E. Takimoto (Eds.), Algorithmic Learning Theory. Proceedings, 2003. XI, 313 pages. 2003. (Subseries LNAI).

Vol. 2843: G. Grieser, Y. Tanaka, A. Yamamoto (Eds.), Discovery Science. Proceedings, 2003. XII, 504 pages. 2003. (Subseries LNAI).

Vol. 2844: J.A. Jorge, N.J. Nunes, J.F. e Cunha (Eds.), Interactive Systems. Proceedings, 2003. XIII, 429 pages. 2003.

Vol. 2846: J. Zhou, M. Yung, Y. Han (Eds.), Applied Cryptography and Network Security. Proceedings, 2003. XI, 436 pages. 2003.

Vol. 2847: R. de Lemos, T.S. Weber, J.B. Camargo Jr. (Eds.), Dependable Computing. Proceedings, 2003. XIV, 371 pages. 2003.

Vol. 2848: F.E. Fich (Ed.), Distributed Computing. Proceedings, 2003. X, 367 pages. 2003.

Vol. 2849: N. García, J.M. Martínez, L. Salgado (Eds.), Visual Content Processing and Representation. Proceedings, 2003. XII, 352 pages. 2003.

Vol. 2850: M.Y. Vardi, A. Voronkov (Eds.), Logic for Programming, Artificial Intelligence, and Reasoning. Proceedings, 2003. XIII, 437 pages. 2003. (Subseries LNAI)

Vol. 2851: C. Boyd, W. Mao (Eds.), Information Security. Proceedings, 2003. XI, 443 pages. 2003.

Vol. 2852: F.S. de Boer, M.M. Bonsangue, S. Graf, W.-P. de Roever (Eds.), Formal Methods for Components and Objects. Proceedings, 2003. VIII, 509 pages. 2003.

Vol. 2853: M. Jeckle, L.-J. Zhang (Eds.), Web Services – ICWS-Europe 2003. Proceedings, 2003. VIII, 227 pages. 2003.

Vol. 2854: J. Hoffmann, Utilizing Problem Structure in Planning. XIII, 251 pages. 2003. (Subseries LNAI)

Vol. 2855: R. Alur, I. Lee (Eds.), Embedded Software. Proceedings, 2003. X, 373 pages. 2003.

Vol. 2856: M. Smirnov, E. Biersack, C. Blondia, O. Bonaventure, O. Casals, G. Karlsson, George Pavlou, B. Quoitin, J. Roberts, I. Stavrakakis, B. Stiller, P. Trimintzios, P. Van Mieghem (Eds.), Quality of Future Internet Services. IX, 293 pages. 2003.

Vol. 2857: M.A. Nascimento, E.S. de Moura, A.L. Oliveira (Eds.), String Processing and Information Retrieval. Proceedings, 2003. XI, 379 pages. 2003.

Vol. 2858: A. Veidenbaum, K. Joe, H. Amano, H. Aiso (Eds.), High Performance Computing. Proceedings, 2003. XV, 566 pages. 2003.

Vol. 2859: B. Apolloni, M. Marinaro, R. Tagliaferri (Eds.), Neural Nets. Proceedings, 2003. X, 376 pages. 2003.

Vol. 2860: D. Geist, E. Tronci (Eds.), Correct Hardware Design and Verification Methods. Proceedings, 2003. XII, 426 pages. 2003.

Vol. 2862: D. Feitelson, L. Rudolph, U. Schwiegelshohn (Eds.), Job Scheduling Strategies for Parallel Processing. Proceedings, 2003. VII, 269 pages. 2003.

Vol. 2863: P. Stevens, J. Whittle, G. Booch (Eds.), «UML» 2003 – The Unified Modeling Language. Proceedings, 2003. XIV, 415 pages. 2003.

Vol. 2864: A.K. Dey, A. Schmidt, J.F. McCarthy (Eds.), UbiComp 2003: Ubiquitous Computing. Proceedings, 2003. XVII, 368 pages. 2003.

Vol. 2865: S. Pierre, M. Barbeau, E. Kranakis (Eds.), Ad-Hoc, Mobile, and Wireless Networks. Proceedings, 2003. X, 293 pages. 2003.

Vol. 2867: M. Brunner, A. Keller (Eds.), Self-Managing Distributed Systems. Proceedings, 2003. XIII, 274 pages. 2003.

Vol. 2868: P. Perner, R. Brause, H.-G. Holzhütter (Eds.), Medical Data Analysis. Proceedings, 2003. VIII, 127 pages. 2003.

Vol. 2869: A. Yazici, C. Şener (Eds.), Computer and Information Sciences – ISCIS 2003. Proceedings, 2003. XIX, 1110 pages. 2003.

Vol. 2870: D. Fensel, K. Sycara, J. Mylopoulos (Eds.), The Semantic Web - ISWC 2003. Proceedings, 2003. XV, 931 pages. 2003.

Vol. 2871: N. Zhong, Z.W. Raś, S. Tsumoto, E. Suzuki (Eds.), Foundations of Intelligent Systems. Proceedings, 2003. XV, 697 pages. 2003. (Subseries LNAI)

Vol. 2876: M. Schroeder, G. Wagner (Eds.), Rules and Rule Markup Languages for the Semantic Web. Proceedings, 2003. VII, 173 pages. 2003.

Vol. 2881: E. Horlait, T. Magedanz, R.H. Glitho (Eds.), Mobile Agents for Telecommunication Applications. Proceedings, 2003. IX, 297 pages. 2003.